NEW

ANNUAL 2003–04

Published by Invincible Press, an imprint of HarperCollins*Publishers*,
77–85 Fulham Palace Road, Hammersmith, London W6 8JB

First published 1887

A CIP catalogue record for this book is available from the British Library

The HarperCollins website address is: www.harpercollins.co.uk

Editorial compilation by Hayters-Teamwork, Image House, Station Road, London, N17 9LR

Typesetting by Letterpart Limited, Reigate, Surrey

Printed and bound in Great Britain by Clays Ltd, St Ives plc

Distributed by The Magazine Marketing Company, Octagon House, White Hart Meadows, Ripley, Woking, Surrey GU23 6HR. Telephone (01483) 211222

ISBN 0-00-716964-7

CONTENTS

WILL FERGUSON'S BIGGEST GAMBLE PAY OFF?

BY ROB BEASLEY, CHIEF FOOTBALL REPORTER, NEWS OF THE WORLD

Sir Alex Ferguson has presided over plenty of departures in his sixteen years at the helm of Manchester United. Remember the controversy when Eric Cantona quit overnight and the demise of the self-proclaimed 'Guv'nor' Paul Ince? Andy Cole, Mark Hughes, Jaap Stam and Peter Schmeichel have all gone through the Old Trafford exit door too. But United continued to thrive regardless.

Now, arguably the biggest star of them all has been jettisoned. David Beckham has gone from rain in Manchester to reign in Spain. And Ferguson's decision to sell the golden boy has been described as his biggest-ever gamble. There have been accusations that the manager has acted out of spite and jealousy; that he couldn't handle Beckham's megastar status and showbiz lifestyle. There have also been suspicions that Beckham's book would reveal all about the boot-in-the-head controversy and strain relations between them to breaking point.

Remember how long Stam stayed after his book gave away dressing room secrets and tales of Ferguson's infamous furies. But could it just be that he has again spotted that the time was right to move a player on for professional reasons – even an icon like Beckham?

Much has been made of the £25m. fee, especially as £8m. is said to be made up of bonuses based on Real Madrid's future success. They have also reportedly put only £5m. down with the rest spread over the course of Beckham's contract. Real may be the most glamorous club in the world, but United are by far the richest.

So why give away a player like Beckham for next to nothing? This was certainly not an offer that was impossible to refuse for a club of United's wealth and ambition. But there was a strong feeling among some seriously influential figures at Old Trafford that Beckham was not playing up to the grade last season. Remember, he was left out for the two most important matches of their season – against Arsenal at Highbury and the return with Real Madrid in the Champions League.

There were mumblings that his best displays came when he was wearing the Three Lions of England on his chest – not the red of United. Now that could be perceived as a plaudit for Sven Goran Eriksson and a sleight on Sir Alex; the Swede's calm, measured approach, and not Sir Alex's fiery ways, reaping the world-class performances.

But that wasn't the view at Old Trafford, and certainly not of Ferguson himself. He decided it was time to freshen up his squad, bring in new talent and he'd been told that to do that he had to sell before he could buy. In a dramatically depressed transfer market, he quickly realised that what had been viewed as an embarrassment of riches was actually just something of an embarrassment.

His £30m. outlay on Rio Ferdinand and £28m. for Juan Sebastian Veron now looked expensive extravagances. In the new transfer market, they were worth a fraction of what United had paid out. On top of that, skipper Roy Keane was the wrong side of 30 and admitting that a hip problem had severely restricted his all-action capabilities.

So where were the saleable assets who could command the sort of fee that would allow Ferguson into the market to compete for a Ronaldinho or a Patrick Vieira? Ruud van Nistelrooy, Ryan Giggs, Paul Scholes and finally Beckham. After that you are struggling. There was absolutely no chance of Ferguson selling his Dutch striker, whose goals had carried United forward at home and abroad. Everyone knows that Paul Scholes will never leave Old Trafford. So you are then left with Giggs or Beckham.

Now Inter Milan had been going on about Giggs for ages, but never actually got round to doing something about it. That left Beckham. Barcelona wanted him and were ready to pay £30m. Ferguson could have had some fun with that. But while he had decided Beckham's Old Trafford career was over, it was the player himself who would decide his destination. Not surprisingly it was the Real deal that he preferred – swapping Keane & Co for Ronaldo, Zidane, Raul, Roberto Carlos and Figo.

So Beckham has gone. United will surely remain a force and the England skipper will surely reach new heights in Spain. His departure from will again prove the saying that no one is bigger than the club. But just speculate for a moment what happens if it all goes pear-shaped for United now? Will the same adage then apply to Ferguson? The canny Scot has probably not lost a wink of sleep over it all.

THE GREATEST GAME – AND THE CRUELLEST

BY STUART BARNES

It's the greatest game in the world, but it can also be the cruellest. Ask Martin O'Neill, his Celtic players and their marvellous supporters who, in the space of 72 hours, saw the UEFA Cup go to FC Porto in extra-time and the Scottish Premier League title to Rangers by a single goal.

Ask Sheffield United, who reached the semi-finals of the F.A. Cup and Worthington Cup and the First Division Play-off Final and finished with nothing but memories. Or those fans of Shrewsbury Town, who were top of the world after Everton were knocked out of the F.A. Cup and bottom of the Third Division four short months later.

Abroad, even more so than in the domestic game, we have become almost immune to managerial sackings, whatever the circumstances. Yet the dismissal by Real Madrid of Vicente del Bosque after another Spanish title win to make way for the Manchester United No 2 Carlos Queiroz was enough to leave an impression on the hardest of hearts.

For the neutrals, however, those highs and lows provided compelling watching – or listening. If there has been a more dramatic two hours of commentary than that which chartered the fortunes of Celtic and Rangers on the final day of the SPL season, I would love to hear it. While Michael Thomas's last-minute championship-winning goal for Arsenal at Anfield in 1989 remains arguably the biggest single moment of drama, the events at Ibrox, where Rangers were swamping Dunfermline 6-1, and Rugby Park, Kilmarnock, where their Glasgow rivals were sweeping to a 4-0 victory, provided an ever-changing canvas from the moment that Michael Mols opened the scoring for Rangers in the third minute.

For all the impact television has made on the game, radio can deliver a unique insight into situations like this with its capacity to switch matches as soon as another goal goes in and the balance of power shifts for the umpteenth time. It was thrilling stuff for the listener. Quite what it was like at the two grounds for supporters clutching radios to their ears while at the same time following events on the pitch can only be imagined.

After that sort of finale – and it wasn't a bad race for the Premiership title in England either – the chance for player and supporter alike to unwind during a summer break from the game seemed particularly inviting. Except there is no such thing any more, even in those years without World Cup or European Championship Finals.

Granted, this summer has been peculiar because of the soap opera-like events in Manchester, Madrid and many other locations surrounding the transfer of David Beckham from Old Trafford to the Bernabeu, not to mention events like the tragic death of Marc-Vivien Foe at the Confederations Cup and the takeover of Chelsea by the Russian oil magnate Roman Abramovich. But long gone are the days when football went into cold storage for three months and cricket, tennis and golf took over the spotlight.

With the old season still fresh in the mind, the new campaign is upon us and it certainly looks an inviting one. Abramovich's arrival at Stamford Bridge has not met with all-round approval, but the question of whether his millions will finally transform Chelsea into genuine championship contenders rather than interested onlookers is one of the big talking points.

Will Manchester United make light of the loss of Beckham, invest the cash in the right areas and extend their domestic dominance? Can Arsene Wenger, with considerably less to spend, persuade his Arsenal side to forget last season's failure to stay to stay the course and convince them they are every bit the equals of United?

Does the signing of Harry Kewell represent the last piece in the jigsaw needed for Liverpool to become contenders again? Can Newcastle, fourth in 2001-02 and third last season, continue to climb under Sir Bobby Robson?

Then, there is the return to the top flight after a long absence of two of the most famous old clubs in the country. Few will have begrudged Dave Jones the chance to savour success by taking Wolves up after all the personal problems he has had to face.

But Jones, along with Harry Redknapp, knows how hard it will now be to consolidate. Against the odds – and he was the first to admit it – Redknapp led Portsmouth to the First Division title, a triumph also rich in irony with West Ham United, the club he left in acrimonious circumstances, going in the opposite direction.

EUROPEAN CHAMPIONSHIP 2004

Wales, for so long the poor relations of British football, are leading the way in qualifying for the 2004 European Championship in Portugal. Under the astute guidance of Mark Hughes, who made 72 appearances for his country in a 15-year international career, they have taken maximum points from four matches, including a 2-1 victory over Italy, who started as strong favourites to win Group Nine.

Another 70,000 crowd at the Millennium Stadium saw them beat Azerbaijan 4-0, an indication of the upsurge in interest in a side who have proved equally resolute away from home. Although the September 6 return match with Italy will be crucial, there is genuine optimism that Wales can reach the finals of a major championship for the first time in a generation, particularly as Italy also dropped points in a 1-1 draw against Serbia-Montenegro.

They did qualify at the 1976 European Championship – losing to Yugoslavia in the quarter-finals – but in those days the tournament ran on a two-leg, knock-out basis after the group stage. The last time Wales appeared on the big stage was at the 1958 World Cup in Sweden, where they reached the quarter-finals before losing 1-0 to the eventual winners Brazil, who had introduced a 17-year-old Pele to the world.

England need something out of the Group Seven game with Turkey on October 11 to avoid being forced into the play-offs. When the teams met at the Stadium of Light, England gave one of their best performances under Sven Goran Eriksson to win 2-0. But a previous 2-2 draw against Macedonia at Southampton may prove costly. They have still to play in Macedonia – while Turkey's one other fixture is against Liechtenstein.

Scotland are back in the reckoning for at least a play-off place after an embarrassing 2-2 draw with the Faroe Islands in their opening match in Group Five, a 1-1 draw against Germany confirming the improvement shown by Bertie Vogts's team. The Republic of Ireland, pointless from two games in Group Ten when Mick McCarthy resigned, also have grounds for optimism under McCarthy's replacement Brian Kerr, although difficult matches against Russia and Switzerland are ahead.

Northern Ireland are playing only for pride after failing to score in five games in Group Six. Including friendlies, they go into the new season without a goal in 972 minutes of football, but there were glimpses of better times ahead during a goalless draw with Spain.

The draw for next summer's tournament will be made on November 30, 2003, with the opening match involving hosts Portugal on June 12, 2004 at the Dragao Stadium, Porto. The Final is at the new Stadium of Light in Lisbon on July 4. Venues and capacities are: Aveiro (30,000); Braga (30,000); Coimbra (30,000); Faro – Louie (30,000); Guimaeres (30,000); Leiria (30,000); Lisbon – Jose Alvalade (50,000); Lisbon – Luz (65,000); Porto – Dragao (50,000); Porto – Bessa (30,000).

SCHEDULE OF MATCHES

(All kick-off times BST-7.45pm unless stated)

GROUP GAMES

June 12: Portugal v (Group) A2, Porto – Dragao (5pm); A3 v A4, Faro – Louie.
June 13: B3 v B4, Leiria (5pm); B1 v B2, Lisbon – Luz.
June 14: C3 v C4, Guimaeres (5pm); C1 v C2, Lisbon – Jose Alvalade.
June 15: D3 v D4, Aveiro (5pm); D1 v D2, Porto – Dragao.
June 16: A2 v A3, Porto – Bessa (5pm); A4 v Portugal, Lisbon – Luz.
June 17: B2 v B3, Coimbra (5pm); B4 v B1, Leiria.
June 18: C2 v C3, Braga (5pm); C4 v C1, Porto – Dragao.
June 19: D2 v D3, Porto – Bessa (5pm); D4 v D1, Aveiro.
June 20: A4 v A2, Faro – Louie; A3 v Portugal, Lisbon – Jose Alvalade.
June 21: B4 v B2, Coimbra; B3 v B1, Lisbon – Luz.
June 22: C4 v C2, Guimaeres; C3 v C1, Porto – Bessa.

June 23: D4 v D2, Braga; D3 v D1, Lisbon – Jose Alvalade.

QUARTER-FINALS

June 24: Q-F 1, winner A v second B, Lisbon – Luz.
June 25: Q-F 2, winner B v second A, Lisbon – Jose Alvalade.
June 26: Q-F 3, winner C v second D, Faro – Louie.
June 27: Q-F 4 winner D v second C, Porto – Dragao.

SEMI-FINALS

June 30: Winner of 1 v winner of 3, Lisbon – Jose Alvalade.
July 1: Winner of 2 v winner of 4, Porto – Dragao.

FINAL

July 4: Lisbon – Luz.

QUALIFYING POSITIONS END OF 2002-03 SEASON

GROUP 1

	P	*W*	*D*	*L*	*F*	*A*	*Pts*
France	5	5	0	0	19	2	15
Slovenia	5	3	1	1	10	7	10
Israel	5	2	2	1	6	3	8
Cyprus	6	2	1	3	7	11	7
Malta	7	0	0	7	3	22	0

Results: Cyprus 1, France 2; Slovenia 3, Malta 0; France 5, Slovenia 0; Malta 0, Israel 2; Malta 0, France 4; Cyprus 2, Malta 1; Cyprus 1, Israel 1; France 6, Malta 0; Slovenia 4, Cyprus 1; Israel 1, France 2; Malta 1, Slovenia 3; Israel 2, Cyprus 0; Malta 1, Cyprus 2; Israel 0, Slovenia 0.

To play – Sept. 6: France v Cyprus, Slovenia v Israel; Sept. 10: Israel v Malta, Slovenia v France; Oct. 11: Cyprus v Slovenia, France v Israel.

GROUP 2

	P	*W*	*D*	*L*	*F*	*A*	*Pts*
Denmark	6	4	1	1	12	6	13
Norway	6	3	2	1	8	4	11
Romania	6	3	1	2	15	7	10
Bosnia-Herzegovina	5	2	0	3	4	7	6
Luxembourg	5	0	0	5	0	15	0

Results: Bosnia-Herzegovina 0, Romania 3; Norway 2, Denmark 2; Denmark 2, Luxembourg 0; Romania 0, Norway 1; Luxembourg 0, Romania 7; Norway 2, Bosnia-Herzegovina 0; Romania 2, Denmark 5; Bosnia-Herzegovina 2, Luxembourg 0; Denmark 0, Bosnia-Herzegovina 2; Luxembourg 0, Norway 2; Denmark 1, Norway 0; Romania 2, Bosnia-Herzegovena 0; Luxembourg 0, Denmark 2; Norway 1, Romania 1.

To play – Sept. 6: Bosnia-Herzegovena v Norway, Romania v Luxembourg; Sept. 10: Denmark v Romania, Luxemboug v Bosnia-Herzegovena; Oct. 11: Norway v Luxembourg, Bosnia-Herzegovena v Denmark.

GROUP 3

	P	W	D	L	F	A	Pts
Czech Republic	5	4	1	0	14	1	13
Holland	5	4	1	0	11	2	13
Austria	6	3	0	3	9	8	9
Moldova	6	1	0	5	3	13	3
Belarus	6	1	0	5	2	15	3

Results: Austria 2, Moldova 0; Holland 3, Belarus 0; Belarus 0, Austria 2; Moldova 0, Czech Republic 2; Austria 0, Holland 3; Czech Republic 2, Belarus 0; Belarus 2, Moldova 1; Holland 1, Czech Republic 1; Czech Republic 4, Austria 0; Moldova 1, Holland 2; Moldova 1, Austria 0; Belarus 0, Holland 2; Czech Republic 5, Moldova 0; Austria 5, Belarus 0.

To play – Sept. 6: Belarus v Czech Republic, Holland v Austria; Sept. 10: Czech Republic v Holland, Moldova v Belarus; Oct. 11: Austria v Czech Republic, Holland v Moldova.

GROUP 4

	P	W	D	L	F	A	Pts
Sweden	5	3	2	0	12	2	11
Hungary	6	3	2	1	13	4	11
Latvia	5	3	1	1	6	3	10
Poland	5	2	1	2	7	4	7
San Marino	7	0	0	7	0	25	0

Results: Latvia 0, Sweden 0; San Marino 0, Poland 2; Poland 0, Latvia 1; Sweden 1, Hungary 1; Hungary 3, San Marino 0; San Marino 0, Latvia 1; Poland 0, Hungary 0; Poland 5, San Marino 0; Hungary 1, Sweden 2; Latvia 3, San Marino 0; San Marino 0, Sweden 6; Hungary 3, Latvia 1; San Marino 0, Hungary 5; Sweden 3, Poland 0.

To play – Sept. 6: Latvia v Poland, Sweden v San Marino; Sept. 10: Latvia v Hungary, Poland v Sweden; Oct. 11: Hungary v Poland, Sweden v Latvia.

GROUP 5

	P	W	D	L	F	A	Pts
Germany	5	3	2	0	8	3	11
Iceland	5	3	0	2	9	5	9
Scotland	5	2	2	1	7	5	8
Lithuania	6	2	1	3	4	9	7
Faroe Islands	5	0	1	4	4	10	1

Results: Faroe Islands 2, **Scotland** 2; Lithuania 0, Germany 2 Iceland 0, **Scotland** 2; Lithuania 2, Faroe Islands 0; Germany 2, Faroe Islands 1; Iceland 3, Lithuania 0; **Scotland** 2, Iceland 1; Germany 1, Lithuania 1; Lithuania 1, **Scotland** 0; **Scotland** 1, Germany 1; Iceland 2, Faroe Islands 1; Faroe Islands 0, Germany 2; Lithuania 0, Iceland 3.

To play – Aug. 20: Faroe Islands v Iceland; Sept. 6: Iceland v Germany, **Scotland** v Faroe Islands; Sept. 10: Faroe Islands v Lithuania, Germany v **Scotland**; Oct. 11: Germany v Iceland, **Scotland** v Lithuania.

GROUP 6

	P	W	D	L	F	A	Pts
Greece	6	4	0	2	6	4	12
Spain	6	3	2	1	10	3	11
Ukraine	6	2	3	1	10	8	9
Armenia	5	1	1	3	6	11	4
Northern Ireland	5	0	2	3	0	6	2

Results: Armenia 2, Ukraine 2; Greece 0, Spain 2; Spain 3, **Northern Ireland** 0; Ukraine 2, Greece 0; Greece 2, Armenia 0; **Northern Ireland** 0, Ukraine 0; Armenia 1, **Northern Ireland** 0; Ukraine 2, Spain 2; **Northern Ireland** 0, Greece 2; Spain 3, Armenia 0; Ukraine 4, Armenia 3; Spain 0, Greece 1; **Northern Ireland** 0, Spain 0; Greece 1, Ukraine 0.

To play – Sept. 6: Armenia v Greece, Ukraine v **Northern Ireland**; Sept. 10: **Northern Ireland** v Armenia, Spain v Ukraine; Oct. 11: Armenia v Spain, Greece v **Northern Ireland**.

GROUP 7

	P	W	D	L	F	A	Pts
Turkey	6	5	0	1	14	5	15
England	5	4	1	0	10	4	13
Slovakia	6	2	0	4	8	8	6
Macedonia	6	1	2	3	9	11	5
Liechtenstein	5	0	1	4	2	15	1

Results: Turkey 3, Slovakia 0; Liechtenstein 1, Macedonia 1; Macedonia 1, Turkey 2; Slovakia 1, **England** 2; **England** 2, Macedonia 2; Turkey 5, Liechtenstein 0; Liechtenstein 0, **England** 2; Macedonia 0, Slovakia 2; Slovakia 4, Liechtenstein 0; **England** 2, Turkey 0; Macedonia 3, Liechtenstein 1; Slovakia 0, Turkey 1; **England** 2, Slovakia 1; Turkey 3, Macedonia 2.

To play – Sept. 6: Liechtenstein v Turkey, Macedonia v **England**; Sept. 10: **England** v Liechtenstein, Slovakia v Macedonia; Oct. 11: Liechtenstein v Slovakia, Turkey v **England**.

GROUP 8

	P	W	D	L	F	A	Pts
Bulgaria	5	3	2	0	8	3	11
Croatia	5	3	1	1	7	2	10
Belgium	6	3	1	2	7	8	10
Estonia	6	2	2	2	4	2	8
Andorra	6	0	0	6	1	12	0

Results: Belgium 0, Bulgaria 2; Croatia 0, Estonia 0; Andorra 0, Belgium 1; Bulgaria 2, Croatia 0; Bulgaria 2, Andorra 1; Estonia 0, Belgium 1; Croatia 4, Belgium 0; Estonia 0, Bulgaria 0; Croatia 2, Andorra 0; Andorra 0, Estonia 2; Estonia 2, Andorra 0; Bulgaria 2, Belgium 2; Estonia 0, Croatia 1; Belgium 3, Andorra 0.

To play – Sept. 6: Andorra v Croatia, Bulgaria v Estonia; Sept. 10: Andorra v Bulgaria, Belgium v Croatia; Oct. 11: Belgium v Estonia, Croatia v Bulgaria.

GROUP 9

	P	W	D	L	F	A	Pt
Wales	4	4	0	0	10	1	12
Italy	5	3	1	1	8	3	10
Finland	6	2	0	4	6	8	6
Serbia-Montenegro	5	1	2	2	6	8	5
Azerbaijan	6	1	1	4	4	14	4

Results: Azerbaijan 0, Italy 2; Finland 0, **Wales** 2; Finland 3, Azerbaijan 0; Italy 1, Serbia-Montenegro 1; **Wales** 2, Italy 1; Serbia-Montenegro 2, Finland 0; Azerbaijan 0, **Wales** 2; Serbia-Montenegro 2, Azerbaijan 2; **Wales** 4, Azerbaijan 0; Italy 2, Finland 0; Finland 3, Serbia-Montenegro 0; Azerbaijan 2, Serbia-Montenegro 1; Finland 0, Italy 2.

To play – Aug. 20: Serbia-Montenegro v **Wales**; Sept. 6: Azerbaijan v Finland, Italy v **Wales**; Sept. 10: Serbia-Montenegro v Italy, **Wales** v Finland; Oct. 11: Italy v Azerbaijan, **Wales** v Serbia-Montenegro.

GROUP 10

	P	W	D	L	F	A	Pts
Switzerland	6	3	3	0	12	7	12
Republic of Ireland	6	3	1	2	9	8	10
Russia	5	2	1	2	11	9	7
Albania	6	1	2	3	8	11	5
Georgia	5	1	1	3	3	8	4

Results: Russia 4, **Republic of Ireland** 2; Switzerland 4, Georgia 1; Albania 1, Switzerland 1; Georgia 0, Russia 0 (abandoned half-time floodlight failure); **Republic of Ireland** 1, Switzerland 2; Russia 4, Albania 1; Albania 3, Russia 1; Georgia 1, **Republic of Ireland** 2; Albania 0, **Republic of Ireland** 0; Georgia 0, Switzerland 0; Georgia 1, Russia 0; **Republic of Ireland** 2, Albania 1; Switzerland 2, Russia 2; **Republic of Ireland** 2, Georgia 0; Switzerland 3, Albania 2.

To play – Sept. 6: Georgia v Albania, **Republic of Ireland** v Russia; Sept. 10: Albania v Georgia, Russia v Switzerland; Oct. 11: Russia v Georgia, Switzerland v **Republic of Ireland**.

PREVIOUS FINALS

1960	*USSR	2	Yugoslavia	1	(Paris)
1964	Spain	2	USSR	1	(Madrid)
1968	***Italy	2	Yugoslavia	0	(Rome)
1972	West Germany	3	USSR	0	(Brussels)
1976	**Czechoslovakia	2	West Germany	2	(Belgrade)
1980	West Germany	2	Belgium	1	(Rome)
1984	France	2	Spain	0	(Paris)
1988	Holland	2	USSR	0	(Munich)
1992	Denmark	2	Germany	0	(Gothenburg)
1996	+Germany	2	Czech Republic	1	(Wembley)
2000	+France	2	Italy	1	(Rotterdam)

(***Replay after 1-1; **Czechoslovakia won 5-3 on pens; *After extra-time; +Golden goal winner)

Austria and Switzerland will be joint hosts for the 2008 Finals.

SOCCER DIARY 2002-03

JULY 2002

4 League newcomers **Boston Utd.** suspend manager **Steve Evans** pending an F.A. hearing into financial irregularities at the club. **Wimbledon** announce they will continue to ground-share with **Crystal Palace** while the move to Milton Keynes is finalised, **5** Following the collapse of ITV Digital, the Football League sign a £95m., four-year contract with Sky for showing live matches. **Middlesbrough** agree a multi-million pound sponsorship with Dial-a-Phone. **8 Terry Venables** swops his ITV pundit's job for the manager's chair at **Leeds Utd. 9 Arsenal** pay £2.1m. for **Lille** defender **Pascal Cygan**. **10** A crowd of 4,657 watch breakaway club **AFC Wimbledon** play their first match. **11 Watford** appoint coach **Ray Lewington** as their new manager. **15** Youth director **Martin Hinshelwood** is appointed **Brighton & H.A.** manager. **16** Referees are told to respond to verbal abuse with immediate red cards. **17 David Seaman**, 39, signs a one-year extension to his contract at **Arsenal**. **19 Boston Utd.** are fined £100,000 and have four points deducted by the F.A. for contract irregularities. **20 Liverpool** pull out of talks to buy **Lee Bowyer** from **Leeds Utd. 22 Rio Ferdinand** moves from **Leeds Utd.** to **Manchester Utd.** for a British record fee of £30m. **Graeme Souness, Blackburn Rov.** manager, agrees a new four-year contract. **24 Richard Wright** joins **Everton** from **Arsenal** for £3.5m. **26 Dwight Yorke** is re-united with his old strike partner **Andy Cole** in a £2.6m. transfer from **Manchester Utd.** to **Blackburn Rov. Michael Knighton** sells **Carlisle Utd.** to Irish businessman **John Courtenay**, who brings back manager **Roddy Collins**, sacked in April. **28 Middlesbrough** sign **George Boateng** from **Aston Villa** for £5m. **29 Arsenal** pay £4.5m. for **Brazil** World Cup winner **Gilberto Silva** from **Atletico Mineiro**. **30 Birmingham City** sign **Clinton Morrison** from **Crystal Palace** for a club-record £4.25m.

AUGUST 2002

1 Fears for the future of several clubs are voiced after the Football League lose a £131.9m. claim in the High Court against Carlton and Granada, parent companies of ITV Digital. **Tranmere Rov.** sack manager **Dave Watson** after losing 7-0 to **Birmingham City** in a pre-season friendly. **2 Dennis Wise**, sent home from a tour of Finland after an incident which left team-mate **Callum Davidson** with a fractured cheekbone, is sacked by **Leicester City**. **3 Celtic** open their defence of the Scottish Premier League title by beating **Dunfermline** 2-1. **Motherwell** manager **Terry Butcher** is sent to the stands for dissent during the 3-2 defeat by **Livingston**. New boys **Gretna** open their Third Division programme with a 1-1 draw against **Morton**. **5 Arsenal** receive a suspended £50,000 fine from the F.A. for a poor disciplinary record last season. **Portsmouth** are given a suspended £30,000 fine. **Lincoln City** come out of administration. **6** Football League chairman **Keith Harris** and chief executive **David Burns** resign in the wake of the ITV Digital affair. **Geoffrey Richmond** steps down as chairman of **Bradford City**, a club with debts of £36m. The Brazilian **Juninho** joins **Middlesbrough** for the third time in a £3.7m transfer from **Atletico Madrid. Terry Venables** makes his first signing for **Leeds Utd.,** paying **Liverpool** £2.75m for **Nick Barmby. 8 Liverpool** announce a new £15m., three-year sponsorship with Carlsberg. **9 Bradford City** are given Football League permission to start the season, despite missing the deadline for a rescue package. **10 Rotherham Utd.** take pride of place as the Nationwide League season kicks off, winning 6-0 at **Millwall.** Newcomes **Boston Utd.** open with a 2-2 draw against **Bournemouth**. **11 Arsenal** beat **Liverpool** in the Community Shield – formerly the Charity Shield. Highbury stalwart **Tony Adams** confirms his retirement. **13** The F.A. fine **Birmingham City**'s **Geoff Horsfield** £3,000 and **George Boateng,** of **Middlesbrough**, £2,500 for incidents last season. **13** Ten players are sent off in three Bell's Scottish League Cup second round ties – four in the **Forfar Athletic–Queen's Park** tie, three in the **Queen of the South–Morton** match and three from **Dumbarton–Ayr Utd. 15 Stephen Wright** leaves **Liverpool** for **Sunderland** for £3m. **16 Robbie Savage** is fined £10,000 by the F.A. for using the toilet in the referee's room before a **Leicester City** match last season. **17-18** Fifteen players are sent off over the weekend in the English League. Four are dismissed in a Third Division game, three **Carlisle Utd.** players and one from **Lincoln City**. **Kilmarnock** finish with eight men against **Motherwell**. **21 Northern Ireland** captain **Neil Lennon** withdraws from the friendly against **Cyprus** after a death threat. The game is goalless. **Colin Healy** and new cap **Graham Barrett** score for the first time in the **Republic of Ireland**'s 3-0 win over **Finland**. **Wales** draw 1-1 with **Croatia** and **Scotland** lose 1-0 to **Denmark**. **Sunderland** sign **Matthew Piper** from **Leicester City** for £3.5m. Less than three months after joining **Fulham** as director of football, **Franco Baresi** leaves the club. **22 Neil Lennon** announces his retirement from international football. **Chelsea** players **John Terry** and **Jody Morris**, together with **Des Byrne**, of **Wimbledon**, are cleared of affray outside a night-club. **Byrne** is fined £2,000 for possessing an offensive weapon. **23** The Football League order **Leicester City** to reinstate **Dennis Wise**. **26** Four players, two from each side, are sent off in the **Wycombe Wand.–Q.P.R.** game. **27 Manchester Utd.**, facing a 1-0 deficit from the first leg, beat **Zalaegerszegi** 5-0 in the Champions League qualifying round. **28 Newcastle Utd.** defeat Zeljeznicar 5-0 on aggregate. **Celtic** go out on the away goals rule after a 3-3 scoreline with **Basle**. **Damien Duff** ends speculation about his future by agreeing a new four-year contract with **Blackburn Rov. 29 Arsenal** announce a pre-tax loss for the year of £22.3m. **30 Sunderland** pay £8.2m. for **Tore Andre Flo** from **Rangers** and £1.8m for **Marcus Stewart** from **Ipswich Town**. **W.B.A.** break their transfer record twice in a day, paying **Tranmere Rov.** £2.25m for **Jason Koumas** and bringing back **Lee Hughes** to the Hawthorns for £2.5m., half the figure **Coventy City** paid for him 12 months earlier. **Bradford City** players are paid for the first time in four months in a deal struck between the club and the P.F.A. Colombian **Faustino Asprilla** turns his back on a planned move to Darlington worth a reported £17,000 a week. As the new transfer window closes, **Tottenham** sign Robbie Keane from **Leeds Utd.** for £7m.

SEPTEMBER 2002

2 Lee Bowyer and **Jonathan Woodgate**, left out of **England** squads during court proceedings, are named for the friendly against **Portugal**. **Roy Keane** is ruled out for four months by a hip injury. **Charlton Athletic** captain **Graham Stuart** faces more than six months out with cruciate ligament damage. **3 Paul Scholes**, omitted from the **England** squad because of an ankle injury, plays for **Manchester Utd.** against **Middlesbrough**. **4 Danny Higginbotham** threatens to leave **Derby Co.** after the club fail to pay players for August. **6** The **Derby Co.** players are paid after club bankers release funds. Former **Tranmere Rov.** stalwart **Ray Mathias** is appointed manager. **7 Scotland** are held 2-2 by the **Faroe Islands**, one of the worst results in their history. In other European Championship qualifiers, **Wales** win 2-0 in **Finland** and the **Republic of Ireland** lose 4-2 in **Russia. Alan Smith** scores his first **England** goal in a 1-1 friendly international draw against **Portugal**. **10** Seven First Division sides lose to lower opposition in round one of the Worthington Cup, **Cheltenham Town** taking pride of place with a 3-0 away win over **Norwich City. 13 James Beattie** is fined two weeks' wages by **Southampton** after a drink-driving ban. **17 Burnley** manager **Stan Ternent** receives a two-match touchline ban and is fined £2,500 by the F.A. for abusive language towards referee **Barry Knight**. **18 Leicester City** win the right, on appeal, to dismiss **Dennis Wise** over the incident with **Callum Davidson**. **Wise** later joins **Millwall**. **19 Swansea City** player-manager **Nick Cusack** is the first managerial casualty of the season. **Brian Flynn**, former long-serving **Wrexham** manager, takes over. **20 Steve Evans**, suspended during the F.A. hearing into contract irregularities at **Boston Utd.**, resigns as manager. Acting manager **Neil Thompson** withdraws his own resignation. **24** ITV and Sky win the rights to screen Champions League matches from 2003-6 for £240m. **25 Craig Bellamy** is banned for three matches by UEFA and fined two weeks' wages by **Newcastle Utd.** for butting a **Dynamo Kiev** player. **26** The green light is finally given for the £750m. rebuilding of Wembley Stadium, three times the projected cost in 1996. **Leeds Utd.** announce pre-tax losses of nearly £34m. **Watford** players agree to defer 12 percent of their wages to help save the club from administration. **30** Demolition work begins at Wembley Stadium. **Manchester Utd.** post record pre-tax profits of £32.3m. **Rangers** announce record losses of £19.1m.

OCTOBER 2002

1 Everton's **David Weir** says he no longer wants to play for **Scotland. Wayne Rooney**, 16, becomes **Everton**'s youngest-ever scorer, in a Worthington Cup second round tie against **Wrexham. Charlton Athletic** lose on penalties at home to **Oxford Utd. Sunderland** win 7-0 away to **Cambridge Utd. Aberdeen** go out in the first round of the UEFA Cup to **Hertha Berlin. 2** More surprises and high scoring in the Worthington Cup: **Bolton Wand.** 0, **Bury** 1; **Wigan Athletic** 3, **W.B.A.** 1; **Coventry City** 8, **Rushden & Diamonds** 0; **Crystal Palace** 7, **Cheltenham Town** 0; **Chris Coleman** joins the **Fulham** coaching staff, admitting defeat at the end of a 21-month struggle to regain fitness after being seriously hurt in a car crash. **3** For the third successive season, **Chelsea** make an early exit from the UEFA Cup against unfancied opposition, this time **Viking FC**. **Rangers** and **Livingston** also bow out in the first round, but **Blackburn Rov., Celtic, Fulham, Ipswich Town** and **Leeds Utd.** all go through. **Barnsley** go into administration. **5 Exeter City** sack manager **John Cornforth**. **7 Dundee Utd.** dismiss manager **Alex Smith**. **8 Peter Reid**, the Premiership's third longest-serving manager, is sacked after seven-and-a-half years at **Sunderland**. **Jan Molby**'s offer to resign as **Hull City** manager is rejected. **9 Steve Coppell**, who quit **Brentford** at the end of last season, is appointed manager of **Brighton & H.A.**, replacing **Martin Hinshelwood**, who becomes director of football after three months in charge. **10 Howard Wilkinson**, the F.A.'s technical director, is named **Sunderland** manager. **Steve Cotterill** resigns at **Stoke City** after five months to become his assistant. **Jan Molby** is dismissed after six months at **Hull City** and replaced by **Peter Taylor**, who resigned in May after leading **Brighton & H.A.** to promotion. **11 George Burley**, the First Division's longest-serving manager, is sacked after nearly eight years at **Ipswich Town**. UEFA fine **PSV Eindhoven** £13,000 and **FK Sartid** £10,000 for racist abuse by fans in Champions League and UEFA Cup games against **Arsenal** and **Ipswich Town**. The fine on **PSV** is later increased to £22,400. **12 England** come from behind to win their European Championship qualifier 2-1 in **Slovakia**, but the win is accompanied by crowd violence and racist abuse directed at **Emile Heskey** and **Ashley Cole**. **Scotland** beat **Iceland** 2-0 to give coach **Bertie Vogts** his first win after seven games. **Northern Ireland** lose 3-0 in **Spain**. **15 Roy Keane** is fined a record £150,000 and banned for five games for a 'revenge' tackle on **Manchester City**'s **Alf Inge Haaland** and for cashing in on it in his autobiography. **Barnsley** sack manager **Steve Parkin**. **Carlisle Utd.** come out of administration. **Scotland** beat **Canada** 3-1 in a friendly. **Francis Jeffers** scores a hat-trick for **England U-21** against **Macedonia. 16 David Seaman** is beaten direct from a corner as **England** are held 2-2 by **Macedonia**, but **Wales** continue their revival with a 2-1 win over **Italy**. Other European Championship qualifiers: **Northern Ireland** 0, **Ukraine** 0; **Republic of Ireland** 1, **Switzerland** 2; **17 Leicester City** players agree to defer part of their wages to help club finances. **Crystal Palace** players offer to go without bonuses. Former **Portsmouth** and **Manchester City** coach **Neil McNab** is appointed manager of **Exeter City**. **21 Leicester City** go into administration as a takeover bid headed by **Gary Lineker** is put forward. **22 Michael Owen** scores a hat-trick for **Liverpool** in their Champions League win over **Spartak Moscow**. Caretaker **Neil Thompson** is confirmed as **Boston Utd.** manager. **23 Manchester Utd.** reach the second phase of the Champions League with two matches to spare. **Blackburn Rov.** manager **Graeme Souness** is banned from the touchline and fined £15,000 by the F.A. after being sent off against **Liverpool**. **Darlington** sack manager **Tommy Taylor**. **24 Patrick Vieira** is fined £25,000 – taking his total fines with **Arsenal** to £100,000 – and banned for two games by the F.A. for insulting referee **Andy D'Urso**. **Derby Co.** players agree to defer 25 percent of their wages. **25 Emile Heskey** pledges around £150,000 to the **Gary Lineker**-led consortium trying to take over his former club **Leicester City**. **28 Joe Royle** returns to management at **Ipswich Town**. **Team Bath** become the first student side in 122 years to reach the first round proper of the F.A. Cup. **29** There are two Division One records on the same night. **Grimsby Town**'s 6-5 win over **Burnley** produces the biggest aggregate scoreline since League restructuring. The attendance of 849 for **Wimbledon–Rotherham Utd.** is a new low. The Football League announce a two-year deal for match highlights to be shown on ITV. **30 Arsenal** reach the second phase of the Champions League. **Sunderland's Claudio Reyna** is ruled out for the season with a cruciate ligament injury. **31 Adam Crozier** resigns as F.A. chief executive after pressure from Premier

League clubs for greater control over the game. **Terry Yorath** quits as **Sheffield Wed.** manager. **George Burley**, sacked by **Ipswich Town**, turns down the chance to manage **Stoke City**.

NOVEMBER 2002

1 Steve McClaren resigns as **England** assistant coach to concentrate on managing **Middlesbrough**. **Tony Pulis**, former **Gillingham, Bristol City** and **Portsmouth** manager, takes the **Stoke City** job. **2 David Beckham** plays for **Manchester Utd.** against **Southampton** unaware than an alleged plot to kidnap his wife Victoria has been foiled. **Peterborough Utd.** defender **Simon Rea** is sent off for pulling back **Robert Earnshaw** after 15 seconds of the game against **Cardiff City**. **5 Mick McCarthy** resigns as **Republic of Ireland** manager in the wake of the **Roy Keane** affair. **Manchester City** are knocked out of the **Worthington Cup** by **Wigan Athletic Athletic**. **Wimbledon** are watched by a new low crowd of 664 in the tie against **Rotherham Utd.** Caretaker **Paul Hegarty** is confirmed as **Dundee Utd.** manager. **6** More Worthington Cup third round surprises, with **West Ham Utd.** losing at home to **Oldham Athletic**, **Tottenham** beaten at **Burnley** and **Leeds Utd.** falling to two **Sheffield Utd.** goals in the last minute. **7** Former **Sheffield Wed.** goalkeeper **Chris Turner** returns to Hillsborough as manager after leaving **Hartlepool Utd. 10 Niall Quinn** announces his retirement, because of a back injury, to **Sunderland** fans. **11** An inquest into the death of former **W.B.A.** and **England** striker **Jeff Astle** decides that repeated heading of the old leather ball contributed significantly to a brain disease. **12 Liverpool** go out of the Champions League, despite retrieving a 3-0 deficit in **Basle**. The **Roy Keane** affair claims another victim, **Brendan Menton** resigning as general secretary of the F.A.I. **13** A last-minute **Craig Bellamy** goal enables **Newcastle Utd.** to become the first side to reach the second stage of the Champions League after losing their first three group games. **14 Alan Smith** scores all four goals for **Leeds Utd.,** who reach round three of the UEFA Cup against **Hapoel Tel Aviv. Celtic** knock out **Blackburn Rov., Fulham** overcome **Dinamo Zagreb** and **Ipswich Town** lose on penalties to **Slovan Liberec**. **16** The worst-ever day in English football for sendings-off – 12 in the F.A. Cup first round and six in League matches. **18** Referee **Mike Riley** rescinds one of the two yellow cards shown to **Tottenham**'s **Simon Davies** against **Arsenal**. **Manchester City**'s **Nicolas Anelka** rejects a late call-up to play for **France** against **Yugoslavia**. **20 Wales** maintain an impressive start to their European Championship qualifying campaign by winning 2-0 in **Azerbaijan**. Friendly match results: **Portugal** 2, **Scotland** 0; **Greece** 0, **Republic of Ireland** 0. **Roger Mitchell** resigns as chief executive of the Scottish Premier League. **21** Football League clubs back proposals for a squad-based salary cap. **Mike Newell**, former **Blackburn Rov., Everton** and **Leicester City** striker, is appointed manager of **Hartlepool Utd. 23** Three **Exeter City** players and one from **Cambridge Utd.,** are sent off in a stoppage-time fracas. **24 Leeds Utd.** trigger a £25,000 fine for seven bookings against **Tottenham**. **25 Peter Doyle**, the town's Mayor, heads a consortium to take over **Barnsley**. **27 Thierry Henry** scores all three goals for **Arsenal** in a Champions League away win over **Roma**. The F.A. fine **Rotherham Utd.** £4,000 and **Sheffield Utd.** £2,000 for a players' brawl. **28 Aberdeen** manager **Ebbe Skovdahl** announces his intention to resign. **29 Tottenham** announce funding of £75m. to develop White Hart Lane and build a football academy. UEFA ban **Alan Shearer** for two games for elbowing **Fabio Cannavaro** in the **Newcastle Utd.–Inter Milan** game. **Martin Edwards** resigns from the board of **Manchester Utd.** plc and will step down as chairman of the football club at the end of the season. **Leeds Utd.** chairman **Peter Ridsdale** resigns from posts within the F.A. to concentrate on club commitments.

DECEMBER 2002

2 Stuart Watkiss leaves **Mansfield Town** by mutal consent after 11 months as manager. **3 Aston Villa** confirm that the F.A. are investigating the transfer dealings of former manager **John Gregory**. **Crystal Palace** manager **Trevor Francis** is fined £1,000 by the F.A. for cuffing substitute goalkeeper **Alex Kolinko** for his 'lighthearted' reaction to a goal by **Bradford City**. **Norwich City** manager **Nigel Worthington** receives a £500 fine and a one-match touchline ban over an incident with referee **Phil Dowd. 4 Wigan Athletic** beat

Fulham to reach the last eight of the Worthington Cup. Former **Manchester City** defender **Keith Curle** becomes player-manager of **Mansfield Town. Turkey** striker **Hakan Sukur** joins **Blackburn Rov.** after being released by **Parma. 5 Bradford City** players agree to defer a 'significant' part of their wages to help the club. **6 Fulham**'s **Barry Hayles** is ruled out for four months with a neck injury. **10** Football League clubs are boosted by a £20m. package of assistance from the F.A., Premier League and Football Stadia Improvement Fund. **11 Olivier Dacourt** is fined a week's wages by **Leeds Utd.** for criticising the club in an interview. **Steve Paterson** leaves **Inverness Caledonian Thistle** to become **Aberdeen** manager. **12 Scotland** and **Ireland** fail to win the vote to host the 2008 European Championship, which goes to Austria and Switzerland. **Liverpool** overcome **Vitesse Arnhem** and **Celtic** beat **Celta Vigo** in round three of the UEFA Cup. **Leeds Utd.** lose to **Malaga** and **Fulham** go out against **Hertha Berlin. 14** A crowd of more than 14,000 see **Hull City** play their last game at Boothferry Park. **15** Seven bookings for **Birminghan City** against **Fulham** mean a £25,000 fine. **16 Michael Owen** is succeeded as European Footballer of the Year by **Ronaldo. Port Vale** go into administration. **17** The F.A. are fined £9,000 by UEFA over crowd trouble at **England**'s European Championship qualifier against **Slovakia**. The Slovakian F.A. are fined £27,000 – a figure later reduced to £10,000. **Ronaldo** is named FIFA World Player of the Year. **Reading** defender **John Mackie** apologises for racially abusing **Sheffield Utd.**'s **Carl Asaba. 18** Ticket collection chaos delays the **Aston Villa–Liverpool** Worthington Cup quarter-final by 80 minutes. **York City** go into administration. **Sir Bert Millichip**, F.A. chairman from 1981-1996, dies aged 88. **Craig Bellamy** receives his second three-match UEFA ban of the season after being sent off for **Newcastle Utd.** against **Inter Milan.19** Former Cabinet minister **Sir Brian Mawhinney** is named the Football League's new chairman. **Dennis Bergkamp** is fined £5,000 by the F.A., but escapes suspension for pushing his boot into the chest of **Nils-Eric Johannson** in the **Arsenal–Blackburn Rov.** game. **Birmingham City** are fined £25,000 for misbehaviour by supporters during the game against **Aston Villa. 23 Fulham** scrap plans for a £100m. redevelopment of Craven Cottage. A crowd of more than 22,000 watch **Hull City** play their first game in the new Kingston Communications Stadium against **Hartlepool Utd. Walsall** draw a record crowd of 10,459 for a club match at Bescot, against **Sheffield Utd. 27 Tottenham**'s **Christian Ziege** has emergency surgery on his left leg for a rare disorder which could have finished his career. **30** In the New Year's Honours List, there are MBEs for **Derek Dooley, Sheffield Wed.** scoring legend and **Sheffield Utd.** chairman, and **Scotland**'s World Cup referee **Hugh Dallas**. A CBE goes to **Sunderland** chairman **Bob Murray**.

JANUARY 2003

2 World Cup winner **Christophe Dugarry** joins **Birmingham City** on loan from **Bordeaux.** The F.A. decide to stage all F.A. Cup semi-finals at Wembley when the new stadium is ready. **4 Shrewsbury Town** pull off the biggest F.A. Cup shock for ten years when beating **Everton** 2-1. **6 Northampton Town** sack manager **Kevan Broadhurst**. An F.A. Cup tradition is restored with the fourth round draw held on Monday lunchtime. **7 Chelsea** sack **Mark Bosnich** following a positive drugs test for cocaine. Former **Portsmouth** manager **Terry Fenwick** takes over at **Northampton Town. 8 Lee Bowyer's** turbulent career at **Leeds Utd.** ends with an initial short-term move to **West Ham Utd.** – and a six-match UEFA ban for stamping on the head of **Malaga** player **Gerardo. 10 Birmingham City** pay **Ipswich Town** £1.3m. for **Jamie Clapham** and **Tottenham** £250,000 for **Stephen Clemence. 11 Walsall**'s crowd of 11,037 for the match against **Wolves** is a record for any match at Bescot. **12 Chelsea** striker **Eidur Gudjohnsen** admits to losing £400,000 in five months at a casino. **13 Graham Allner** is sacked after nine months as **Cheltenham Town** manager. **14** The F.A. rule that **Chelsea** goalkeeper **Carlo Cudicini** should not be banned for his sending-off against **Middlesbrough. Ashley Cole** is fined £2,000 and banned for two games for abusive comments to referee **Paul Durkin** after **Arsenal**'s game at **Southampton. 16 Robbie Fowler** rejects a move from **Leeds Utd.** to **Manchester City**. **17 Wayne Rooney** signs his first professional contract with **Everton. 19 Michael Owen** admits losing up to £40,000 on the horses, but denies dropping £30,000 in an England squad card school at the World Cup. **21** An extra-time goal by **Michael Owen** against **Sheffield Utd.** puts **Liverpool** into the

Worthington Cup. **22** They meet **Manchester Utd.**, for whom two goals by **Paul** ...gainst **Blackburn Rov.** prove decisive. **Celtic** manager **Martin O'Neill** ends ...n about his immediate future by signing a 12-month rolling contract. ...**m City** pay an initial £1m. for **Matthew Upson** from **Arsenal**. **23** A record run of ...cessive Premiership appearances for **Southampton**'s **Wayne Bridge** ends because ...f injury. **24 Manchester City** pay £3m. for **Bordeaux** defender **David Sommeil**. **26** ...cal director and youth coach **Brian Kerr** is named the new **Republic of Ireland** manager. **27 Paul Gascoigne** travels to a remote corner of China to continue his career, signing a one-year contract with second division club **Gansu Tianma**. **Liverpool** goalkeeper **Chris Kirkland** is ruled out for the rest of the season with a knee injury. **28** Three days after taking **Farnborough Town** into an F.A. Cup tie at Highbury, **Graham Westley** resigns as manager and chairman to become manager of **Stevenage Borough**. **Gudjon Thordarson**, sacked five days after leading **Stoke City** to promotion, accepts an out-of-court settlement for unfair dismissal. **29 Robbie Fowler** changes his mind and joins **Manchester City** from **Leeds Utd.** for £6m. Manager **Steve Whitton** leaves **Colchester Utd.** by mutual consent. Former **Boston Utd.** manager **Steve Evans** is banned from management for 20 months and fined £8,000 by the F.A. for impeding an investigation into contract irregularities at the club. Former chairman **Pat Malkinson** is banned for 13 months and fined £5,250. **30 Paul Hegarty** is sacked as **Dundee Utd.** manager after less than three months in the job and replaced by the **Falkirk** manager **Ian McCall**. **31** With the transfer window closing, **Jonathan Woodgate** joins the exodus of players from **Leeds Utd.** and moves to **Newcastle Utd.** for £9m. **Middlesbrough** pay **Bolton Wand.** £4m. for **Michael Ricketts** and an initial £3m. for the **Derby Co.** pair **Malcolm Christie** and **Chris Riggott. Southampton** also make a double signing, **David Prutton** from **Nott'm. Forest** for £2.5m. and **Danny Higginbotham** from **Derby Co.** for £1.5m. **Bradford City** come out of administration.

FEBRUARY 2003

2 Manager **Terry Venables**, who considered his future after the sale of **Jonathan Woodgate**, decides to stay at **Leeds Utd. Alen Boksic** announces his retirement, five months before his contract expires with **Middlesbrough**. **3 Steven Gerrard** is banned for three games, on video evidence, for violent conduct which went unpunished in the Merseyside derby. **David O'Leary** reaches a settlement with **Leeds Utd.** over his sacking as manager. **4** Top scorer **James Beattie** agrees a new contract which will keep him at **Southampton** until 2006. A Premier League tribunal turns down the appeal by **Mark Bosnich** against his sacking by Chelsea for a positive test for cocaine. **5 Liverpool** sign a £100m., six-year-extension to their sponsorship deal with Reebok. **6 Dominic Matteo** ends his **Scotland** career to concentrate on club football at **Leeds Utd. 7 Celtic** manager **Martin O'Neill** has a two-match touchline ban, imposed after the game against **Celta Vigo**, halved by UEFA, who also impose a £4,200 fine. **8 Ecuador** striker **Agustin Delgado** walks out on **Southampton**, but later returns to the club. **10 Ipswich Town** become the latest club to file for administration. The Premier League reject an appeal by **Charlton Athletic** for a replay of last month's game on a heavily-sanded Stamford Bridge pitch, but fine **Chelsea** £5,000. **11 Roy Keane** retires from international football with the **Republic of Ireland. Crystal Palace** fine goalkeeper **Alex Kolinko** two weeks' wages for refusing to play against **Leicester City**. **12 Wayne Rooney**, 17, becomes the youngest player to win an **England** cap. **James Beattie**, **Paul Robinson**, **Paul Konchesky**, **Jermaine Jenas** and **Francis Jeffers** also play for the first time, but **England** lose 3-1 to **Australia** after fielding completely different teams in each half. The **Republic of Ireland** give new manager **Brian Kerr** a winning start, 2-0 against **Scotland, Wales** stretch their unbeaten run to a record nine games in a 2-2 draw with **Bosnia,** while **Northern Ireland** lose 1-0 to **Finland**. **Martin Keown** is fined £5,000 by the F.A. for an off-the-ball push on **Ruud van Nistelrooy** during the **Manchester Utd.–Arsenal** game. **13** After months of speculation, **Manchester City** decide not to sue **Roy Keane** for his 'revenge' tackle on **Alf-Inge Haaland** in the 2001 Manchester derby. **14 Leicester City** come out of administration. **15 David Beckham** is struck above his left eye by a football boot kicked in anger by manager **Sir Alex Ferguson** after **Manchester Utd.**'s F.A. Cup defeat by **Arsenal**. **Paul Groves**, **Grimsby Town**, player-manager makes the 700th appearance of his career. **18 Newcastle Utd.** tre **Bobby Robson** to a 70th birthday present by beating **Bayer Leverkusen** 3-1 in t Champions League. **19 Turkey** defender **Ozalan Alpay**, on the transfer list since returning from the World Cup, makes his peace with **Aston Villa** manager **Graham Taylor**. **21 Sir Alex Ferguson** is at the centre of more controversy when claiming that **England** coach **Sven Goran Eriksson** had informally agreed to take over at **Manchester Utd.** last year. **22 Leicester City** fans vote against changing the club's name back to Leicester Fosse. **Marlon Harewood** scores four times in the first half in **Nott'm. Forest**'s 6-0 win over **Stoke City**. **24 Terry Fenwick** is sacked after seven weeks as **Northampton Town** manager. **25 Manchester Utd.** qualify for the quarter-finals of the Champions League with two games to spare. **Exeter City** sack manager **Neil McNab** after four months in the job and replace him with former **Preston N.E.** manager **Gary Peters**. Former **Reading** midfielder **Phil Parkinson** lands his first managerial job, with **Colchester Utd.** A crowd of nearly 20,000 watch **Juninho** make his comeback, after eight months out with a knee injury, for **Middlesbrough** reserves. **26 Alan Shearer** scores a hat-trick in the first 36 minutes for **Newcastle Utd.** in a 3-1 Champions League win over **Bayer Leverkusen**. **27 Liverpool** and **Celtic** set up an all-British UEFA Cup quarter-final by beating **Auxerre** and **Stuttgart** respectively. **Reading** defender **John Mackie** receives a three-match ban, plus a five-game suspended ban, for racist comments to **Sheffield Utd.**'s **Carl Asaba**.

MARCH 2003

2 Liverpool beat **Manchester Utd.** 2-0 in the Worthington Cup Final. **3 Sir Bobby Robson** appeals for the return of a dozen England caps stolen from his Ipswich home. **4 Dion Dublin** apologises for butting **Robbie Savage** in the **Aston Villa–Birmingham City** derby. The League's only unbeaten record, **Oldham Athletic**'s away run, is ended by **Bristol City**. **5 Manchester City** chairman **David Bernstein** resigns amid unrest at the club. **6** Police investigate death threats against **Robbie Savage** over the incident with **Dion Dublin**. **7** FIFA announce that the 2014 World Cup Finals will be held in South America, with **Brazil** the only candidate. **10 Sunderland** sack manager **Howard Wilkinson** and assistant **Steve Cotterill** after five months in charge. **12 Mick McCarthy**, former **Republic of Ireland** manager, takes over at the Stadium of Light. **13** A fans' consortium is given the go-ahead to take over **Port Vale**. **14 El Hadji Diouf** apologises and is fined two weeks' wages by **Liverpool** for spitting at **Celtic** fans during the UEFA Cup tie. **15 Aberdeen** manager **Steve Paterson** misses the game against Dundee after a heavy drinking session the night before, but keeps his job. **16 Alan Shearer** decides against an **England** comeback after maintaining that he could still do a job for the team. **17 Derby Co.** manager **John Gregory** receives a five-match touchline ban and is fined £7,500 by the F.A. for abusive language towards fourth official **Steve Tomlinson** at **Portsmouth**. **18 El Hadji Diouf** is banned for two matches by UEFA for spitting at **Celtic** fans. **Celtic** are fined £2,300 for the behaviour of their supporters. **Lorenzo Amoruso** receives a two-match ban and 12 penalty points, incurring a further two-game ban, from the Scottish F.A. for spitting at **Ayr Utd.**'s **James Grady**. **19 Arsenal** and **Newcastle Utd.** fail to reach the quarter-finals of the Champions League. **20 Celtic** beat **Liverpool** 2-0 at Anfield to reach the semi-finals of the UEFA Cup 3-1 on aggregate. **Dennis Bergkamp** is fined £7,500 by the F.A. over an incident with **Lee Bowyer** in the **Arsenal–West Ham Utd.** game. Scottish Premier League clubs vote to scrap their January winter break. **21 Leeds Utd.** sack **Terry Venables** after nine months as manager and bring in former **Sunderland** manager **Peter Reid** as caretaker until the end of the season. **Derby Co.** suspend manager **John Gregory**. **23** For the second time in four seasons, **Celtic** are knocked out of the Scottish Cup by **Inverness Caledonian Thistle**. **25 Southend Utd.** sack manager **Rob Newman. 26 Fulham** announce that manager **Jean Tigana** will not have his contract renewed at the end of the season. **Huddersfield Town** sack their manager **Mick Wadsworth**. **Wales**'s European Championship qualifier against **Serbia & Montenegro**, scheduled for April 2 in Belgrade, is postponed until August over security fears. **27** Two days after **Darren Ambrose** moved to **Newcastle Utd.** for £1m., **Ipswich Town** sell **Hermann Hreidarsson** to **Charlton Athletic** for £900,000. **Nott'm. Forest** manager **Paul Hart** is fined £500 by the F.A. for improper conduct to match officials after the win over **Reading**. **29** A mixed bag of European

Championship qualifiers. **David Beckham** scores with a trademark free-kick, but **England** labour to a 2-0 win in **Liechtenstein**. **Craig Bellamy** scores **Wales**'s quickest-ever goal, after 13 seconds, to set up a 4-0 victory over **Azerbaijan**. The **Republic of Ireland** win 2-1 in **Georgia,** where their players are pelted with missiles, including an open penknife. **Kenny Miller** and **Lee Wilkie** scores for the first time for **Scotland,** who beat **Iceland** 2-1. **Northern Ireland** are goalless for a record seventh game when going down to an 87th minute winner by **Armenia. 30 Peter Ridsdale** bows to pressure and resigns as **Leeds Utd.** chairman. **31 George Burley**, sacked by **Ipswich Town,** takes over as interim manager at **Derby Co. Huddersfield Town** go into administration. Abuse from fans forces **Ron Noades** to quit as **Brentford** chairman.

APRIL 2003

1 Watford announce plans to buy back the freehold of their Vicarage Road ground. **Liverpool**'s **El Hadji Diouf** is named African Footballer of the Year. **2 Wayne Rooney** makes an impressive first international start as **England** beat **Turkey** 2-0 in a European Championship qualifier, marred by hooliganism. **Northern Ireland** have **James Quinn** and **Keith Gillespie** sent off in a 2-0 defeat by **Greece**. Other results: **Lithuania** 1, **Scotland** 0; **Albania** 0, **Republic of Ireland** 0. **5** The Division One record aggregate scoreline is equalled by **Burnley** 4, **Watford** 7. **6** A 50,000 crowd watch **Bristol City** beat **Carlisle Utd.** 2-0 in the LDV Vans Trophy Final. **7 Hamilton Acad.** midfielder **John Walker** is banned for three months after a positive drugs test. **9 Sunderland**, preparing for Nationwide League football, announce substantial staff cuts. **10** The need to cut costs also forces redundancies at the F.A. **11 Manchester City** goalkeeper **Peter Schmeichel** decides to retire at the end of the season. **12 Sunderland**'s Premiership fate is sealed. **Yeovil Town** are promoted to the Football League as Conference champions. **13 Arsenal** and **Southampton** reach the F.A. Cup Final. **14 Leeds Utd.** defender **Lucas Radebe** retires from international football after winning 69 caps for **South Africa**. **15 Portsmouth** win promotion to the Premiership and **Wigan Athletic** go up to Division One. **17 Jean Tigana**, previously told his contract would not be renewed at the end of the season, is dismissed early by **Fulham**. Former chairman **Peter Ridsdale** severs all ties with **Leeds Utd. 18** Manager **Trevor Francis** is sacked by **Crystal Palace. Steve Wignall**, former **Colchester Utd.** manager, takes over at **Southend Utd. 19 W.B.A.** are relegated from the Premiership. **Leicester City** regain their place at the first attempt. **Rushden & Diamonds** and **Hartlepool Utd.** win promotion from Division Three. **Wigan Athletic** are Second Division champions. **21 Grimsby Town** and **Sheffield Wed.** go down from the First Division, **Northampton Town** from Division Two. **22 Chesterfield** manager **Dave Rushbury** resigns. **23 Manchester Utd.** overcome a hat-trick by **Ronaldo** to beat **Real Madrid** 4-3, but lose their Champions League quarter-final 6-5 on aggregate. **24 Trevor Brooking** swops his commentator's seat for the caretaker manager's job at his old club **West Ham Utd.** after **Glenn Roeder** collapses with a brain tumour. **Celtic** reach their first European final for 33 years by beating **Boavista** 2-1 on aggregate in the UEFA Cup. **25 Republic of Ireland** goalkeeper **Dean Kiely** retires from international football to concentrate on extending his club career with **Charlton Athletic. 26 Mansfield Town** are relegated from Division Two on the day their game against **Tranmere Rov.** is abandoned at half-time for safety reasons after a man climbs onto the roof of a Prenton Park stand. **Huddersfield Town** also go down, while **Crewe Alexandra** are promoted. **Wrexham** go up from the Third Division. **27 Arsenal**'s **Thierry Henry** is named P.F.A. Player of the Year. **Portsmouth** are crowned First Division champions. **29 Shrewsbury Town** are relegated from the Football League after 53 years' membership and manager **Kevin Ratcliffe** resigns. **Mark Bosnich**, sacked by **Chelsea** after testing positive for cocaine, is banned for nine months – backdated to December 2002 – by the F.A. **Fulham** announce a record annual loss of £33.6m. **Real Madrid** deny any interest in signing **David Beckham** from **Manchester Utd. 30 Chelsea**'s **Marcel Desailly** wins a record 104th cap for **France** against **Egypt.** The **Republic of Ireland** beat **Norway** 1-0 and **Scotland** lose 2-0 at home to **Austria** in other friendly internationals.

MAY 2003

1 The F.A. are fined £70,000 for two pitch invasions and racist chanting during the **England–Turkey** game at the Stadium of Light. The fine is a record for a racist-related incident and UEFA warn that **England** will be thrown out of Euro 2004 if there is more trouble. **Sir Alex Ferguson** is fined £5,000 for suggesting UEFA rigged the Champions League quarter-final draw so **Manchester Utd.** were paired with **Real Madrid. 2 Stockport Co.** and **Sale Sharks** merge, with the rugby club moving to Edgeley Park. **Thierry Henry** completes a Player of the Year double by winning the Football Writers' Association award. **Birmingham City**'s **Christophe Dugarry** is fined £12,500 by the F.A. for spitting in the direction of **Joey Gudjonsson** during the match with **Aston Villa**. UEFA fine **Patrick Vieira** £2,300 for improper comments to the media over claims of racial abuse during the **Valencia–Arsenal** Champions League game. **Valencia** are fined £9,250. **3 Exeter City** are relegated from the Football League after 83 years. **Cheltenham Town** go down from Division Two. **Rushden & Diamonds** are Third Division champions after a last-day title decider against **Hartlepool Utd. 4 Manchester Utd.** win the Premiership for the eighth time in 11 seasons. **Brighton & H.A.** are relegated after one season in the First Division. **6 David Beckham** insists he wants to stay at **Manchester Utd. 8 Rochdale** manager **Paul Simpson** resigns. **9 John Gregory**, suspended by **Derby Co.** in March over 'serious allegations' is sacked as manager. **10 Doncaster Rov.** return to the Football League after five years by beating **Dagenham & Redbridge** 3-2 in the Conference Play-Off Final. **12 David Seaman** is left out of the squad for **England**'s next three matches, signalling the end of his international career. **Roy McFarland** returns to management with **Chesterfield. 13 Manchester Utd.**'s **Wes Brown** is ruled out until Christmas by a knee injury. **Dion Dublin** is fined £6,000 by the F.A. for butting **Robbie Savage** in the **Aston Villa–Birmingham City** game. **14 Aston Villa** manager **Graham Taylor** resigns. **15** Caretaker **Chris Coleman,** 32, is named **Fulham** manager, the youngest in the Premiership. Accountant **Mark Palios**, a former **Tranmere Rov.** player, is appointed chief executive of the F.A. More departures from **Leeds Utd.** – assistant manager **Eddie Gray** and coach **Brian Kidd. 16 Thierry Henry** signs a three-year extension to his contract with **Arsenal**, keeping him at Highbury until 2007. **17 Arsenal** beat **Southampton** 1-0 to retain the F.A. Cup. **20 David O'Leary**, sacked by **Leeds Utd.**, is named **Aston Villa** manager. After a trouble-free season, **Millwall** lift the ban imposed on supporters of some away clubs. **21 Celtic** lose 3-2 in extra-time to **FC Porto** in the UEFA Cup Final. **22 Gareth Southgate** scores after 36 seconds as **England** beat **South Africa** 2-1 in a friendly international. **23** Caretaker **Steve Kember** is appointed **Crystal Palace** manager. The new owners of **Luton Town** sack manager **Joe Kinnear**. First Division champions **Falkirk** are refused a place in the Scottish Premier League because of plans to share the ground of **Airdrie Utd. 24 Bournemouth** become the first side to score five goals in a Play-off Final, beating **Lincoln City** 5-2 to return to Division Two. **Gary Peters** resigns as manager of relegated **Exeter City**. **25 Rangers** win the Scottish championship for the 50th time by a single goal from **Celtic. Cardiff City** beat **Q.P.R.** 1-0 after extra-time in the Second Division Play-off Final. **26 Wolves** reach the Premiership with a 3-0 victory over **Sheffield Utd. 27 Wales** lose 2-0 to the **United States** in a friendly international, ending their record run of 10 games without defeat. **Scotland** draw 1-1 with **New Zealand. 28 AC Milan** beat **Juventus** on penalties after a goalless Champions League Final at Old Trafford. **30** Promoted **Hartlepool Utd.** sack manager **Mike Newell** after six months in the job. **Terry Dolan** is dismissed by **York City**. **Ipswich Town** come out of administration. **31 Rangers** complete a hat-trick of trophies by beating **Dundee** 1-0 to retain the Tennents Scottish Cup.

JUNE 2003

1 Former **Walsall, Grimsby Town, W.B.A.** and **Lincoln City** manager **Alan Buckley** takes over at **Rochdale. 2 Manchester City** win a UEFA Cup place through the Fair Play League. **3 Joe Cole** scores his first goal for **England**, who beat **Serbia-Montenegro** 2-1 in a friendly international. **Northern Ireland** lose 2-0 to Italy. **David Seaman** leaves **Arsenal** after 13 years to join **Manchester City. Bradford City** promise to assist the F.A. in an investigation into allegations of financial irregularities involving manager **Nicky Law. 4 York City**

captain **Chris Brass**, 27, becomes the League's youngest manager. **Steve Claridge** turns down a new contract with **Millwall** to become player-manager of **Weymouth**. **Rangers' Alex McLeish** is named Scottish Manager of the Year. **5** Interim manager **George Burley** is given the **Derby Co.** job on a permanent basis. The Scottish Premier League gets a Brazilian manager, with **Livingston**'s appointment of **Marcio Maximo Barcellos**. Proposals to expand the play-offs and impose sanctions on clubs going into administration were deferred by the Football League until an extraordinary general meeting in September. **6 Wimbledon** go into administration. **7 Manchester Utd.** admit they are ready to sell **David Beckham.** An injury-time own goal gives the **Republic of Ireland** a 2-1 win **over Albania**. In another Euro 2004 qualifier, **Scotland** draw 1-1 with **Germany**. **8 Liverpool** agree to pay £3.5m. for **Fulham**'s **Steve Finnan. 10 Manchester Utd.** announce they have accepted an offer from **Barcelona** for **David Beckham. 11 Michael Owen** becomes the youngest **England** player to win 50 caps and scores both goals in a 2-1 win over **Slovakia**. In other Euro 2004 qualifiers, **Northern Ireland** fail to score for the tenth successive international but hold Spain 0-0, while the **Republic of Ireland** beat **Georgia** 2-0. **12 Arsenal** manager **Arsene Wenger** and **Liverpool**'s **Gerard Houllier** are awarded hononary OBEs in the Queen's Birthday Honours list. **13** Amid increasing speculation about his future, **David Beckham** gets an OBE. **Manchester City** stalwart **Shaun Goater** receives an MBE. **17 David Beckham** ends all the speculation by agreeing to join **Real Madrid**. The fee is £18m. rising to a possible £25m. **19** Promoted **Portsmouth** pay a club-record fee of £1.9m. for **Vitesse Arnhem** defender **Dejan Stefanovic**. **20** Caretaker **Mick Tait** is confirmed as **Darlington** manager. **23 Mike Newell**, sacked by **Hartlepool Utd.** after leading them to promotion, is named **Luton Town** manager following a telephone poll among supporters. **24** The League Cup gets a new sponsor, Carling taking over from Worthington. **25 Carlos Queiroz**, the **Manchester Utd.** No 2, follows **David Beckham** to the Bernabeu by becoming **Real Madrid** coach. **26 Marc-Vivien Foe**, who was on loan at **Manchester City** last season, collapses and dies during **Cameroon**'s Confederations Cup semi-final against **Colombia**. **Tottenham** sign striker **Helder Postiga** from UEFA Cup winners **FC Porto** for an initial £6.25m., rising to a possible £8.25m. Former **Ross Co.** manager **Neale Cooper**, who won the European Cup Winners' Cup with **Aberdeen**, is appointed manager of **Hartlepool Utd.** Adams Park, home of **Wycombe Wand.**, becomes the Causeway Stadium in a £100,000 sponsorship deal with a software manufacturer. **27 Wimbledon**'s temporary move to the National Hockey Stadium at Milton Keynes falls through. **Peter Jackson**, sacked by **Huddersfield Town** in 1999, returns as manager, along with his old No 2 **Terry Yorath**.

QUOTE-UNQUOTE

'Slack, slovenly, supine' – House of Commons Select Committee's verdict on Sport England's monitoring of progress on the development of Wembley Stadium.

'We're a billion pound industry and it can't be run like a kebab house' – **Theo Paphitis**, Millwall chairman, after the Football League lost a £131.9m. claim against ITV Digital parent companies Carlton and Granada.

'Reluctantly, I'm giving the asylum back to the lunatics' – **Keith Harris** on his resignation as chairman of the Football League.

'What I will not tolerate is people sulking and chipping away. I can be extremely ruthless and nasty. If there is a cancer, it has to be eradicated immediately' – **Gerard Houllier** on unrest among some of his Liverpool fringe players.

'This problem stems not from football but from our own sick society' – **Dave Bowen**, Irish F.A. general secretary, on Neil Lennon's withdrawal from Northern Ireland's match against Cyprus following a death threat.

'There was only one decision to make. I cannot keep putting the people I love most through it every time' – **Neil Lennon** after announcing his retirement from international football, rather than risk subjecting his family to more sectarian abuse and intimidation.

NOT ALL AGREE TO HAIL KING HENRY

BY GERRY COX, FOOTBALL WRITERS' ASSOCIATION CHAIRMAN

Football, they say, is a game of opinions, and nothing divides fans, players and the media quite as much as the thorny question: 'Who is the best?' Whether it is player of the month, save of the season or the greatest player of all time, no-one can ever claim to have unanimous support.

So why should it be any different when football writers cast their votes for the Footballer of the Year, the oldest and still the most prestigious individual award in the game? Ever since the FWA was formed in 1947, the showpiece event and highlight of the season has been the dinner to honour the player who, in the opinion of the membership, has done most by precept and example to represent all that is best about the game.

This year was no exception. There was no shortage of candidates, as one would expect from a League that boasts some of the best football on show every week. Gianfranco Zola made much of the early season running, Alan Shearer showed that he was back to his lethal best as Newcastle United challenged at home and in Europe, and Ruud Van Nistelrooy claimed his place among the world's greatest strikers with a run of goals at the end of the season that helped Manchester United claim the title from Arsenal.

But while Arsenal missed out, their top Gunner won the main individual prize as Thierry Henry succeeded Robert Pires, his team-mate for club and country, to become Footballer of the Year. It was a close call, not least because Van Nistelrooy scored marginally more goals than Henry but also because the Dutchman claimed the championship medal that the Frenchman had taken a year earlier.

The question I was asked most when announcing the result at the beginning of May was: Why did Van Nistelrooy not win?' The answer is that throughout the history of the award, it has been about more than simply goals and medals. The first winner was Stanley Matthews, arguably the finest English player of all, and the great man went on to win again in 1963.

Yet he was a provider rather than scorer of goals, and it was more to do with the style of his play, the elegance and élan that won him accolades. So it has been ever since. David Ginola was another controversial choice in 1999, but the Tottenham winger showed touches of genius that were unsurpassed that season, and caught the imagination of football writers as well as supporters. So it is with Henry, who seems able to supply and score goals with equal ease. Van Nistelrooy may have scored more, but no one delivered more spectacular goals than the Frenchman.

Looking though the list of previous winners brings one anomaly to mind – defenders rarely win individual awards in the modern game. Perhaps it is the premium we all place on goals, or perhaps the quality of forward play is simply better than the defending in the English game, a reversal of the situation in Italy. The only two defenders to win the award in the past 25 years have been Steve Perryman in 1982 and Steve Nicol in 1989. But it was not always so. Billy Wright, Bobby Moore, Dave Mackay and Frank McLintock were all outstanding defenders and winners of the award in its first 25 years. Goalkeepers such as Bert Trautmann, Gordon Banks, Pat Jennings and Neville Southall were also winners in previous generations, but few keepers win votes today.

Yet when club supporters are asked to nominate their club's player of the season, it is often the unsung heroes in defence who get their votes. There are plenty of defenders in the Premiership who would grace the roll of honour. Who is to say Marcel Desailly or Sami Hyypia, for example, would not be worthy winners? But once again it is a goalscorer who takes the plaudits, and deservedly so in Henry's case. C'est la vie!

FOOTBALLER OF THE YEAR

(Original award by the Football Writers' Association to the 'player who, by precept and example, on the field and off, shall be considered to have done most for football').

1948 Stanley Matthews (Blackpool); **1949** Johnny Carey (Manchester Utd.); **1950** Joe Mercer (Arsenal); **1951** Harry Johnston (Blackpool); **1952** Billy Wright (Wolves); **1953** Nat Lofthouse (Bolton Wand.); **1954** Tom Finney (Preston N.E.); **1955** Don Revie (Manchester City); **1956** Bert Trautmann (Manchester City); **1957** Tom Finney (Preston N.E.); **1958** Danny Blanchflower (Tottenham); **1959** Syd Owen (Luton Town); **1960** Bill Slater (Wolves); **1961** Danny Blanchflower (Tottenham); **1962** Jimmy Adamson (Burnley); **1963** Stanley Matthews (Stoke City); **1964** Bobby Moore (West Ham Utd.); **1965** Bobby Collins (Leeds Utd.); **1966** Bobby Charlton (Manchester Utd.); **1967** Jack Charlton (Leeds Utd.); **1968** George Best (Manchester Utd.); **1969** Tony Book (Manchester City) & Dave Mackay (Derby Co.) – shared; **1970** Billy Bremner (Leeds Utd.); **1971** Frank McLintock (Arsenal); **1972** Gordon Banks (Stoke City); **1973** Pat Jennings (Tottenham); **1974** Ian Callaghan (Liverpool); **1975** Alan Mullery (Fulham); **1976** Kevin Keegan (Liverpool); **1977** Emlyn Hughes (Liverpool); **1978** Kenny Burns (Nott'm Forest); **1979** Kenny Dalglish (Liverpool); **1980** Terry McDermott (Liverpool); **1981** Frans Thijssen (Ipswich Town); **1982** Steve Perryman (Tottenham); **1983** Kenny Dalglish (Liverpool); **1984** Ian Rush (Liverpool); **1985** Neville Southall (Everton); **1986** Gary Lineker (Everton); **1987** Clive Allen (Tottenham); **1988** John Barnes (Liverpool); **1989** Steve Nicol (Liverpool); Special award to the Liverpool players for the compassion shown to bereaved families after the Hillsborough Disaster; **1990** John Barnes (Liverpool); **1991** Gordon Strachan (Leeds Utd.); **1992** Gary Lineker (Tottenham); **1993** Chris Waddle (Sheffield Wed.); **1994** Alan Shearer (Blackburn Rov.); **1995** Jurgen Klinsmann (Tottenham); **1996** Eric Cantona (Manchester Utd.); **1997** Gianfranco Zola (Chelsea); **1998** Dennis Bergkamp (Arsenal); **1999** David Ginola (Tottenham); **2000** Roy Keane (Manchester Utd.); **2001** Teddy Sheringham (Manchester Utd.); **2002** Robert Pires (Arsenal); **2003** Thierry Henry (Arsenal).

P.F.A. AWARDS

Player of the Year: **1974** Norman Hunter (Leeds Utd.); **1975** Colin Todd (Derby Co.); **1976** Pat Jennings (Tottenham); **1977** Andy Gray (Aston Villa); **1978** Peter Shilton (Nott'm Forest); **1979** Liam Brady (Arsenal); **1980** Terry McDermott (Liverpool); **1981** John Wark (Ipswich Town); **1982** Kevin Keegan (Southampton); **1983** Kenny Dalglish (Liverpool); **1984** Ian Rush (Liverpool); **1985** Peter Reid (Everton); **1986** Gary Lineker (Everton); **1987** Clive Allen (Tottenham); **1988** John Barnes (Liverpool); **1989** Mark Hughes (Manchester Utd.); **1990** David Platt (Aston Villa); **1991** Mark Hughes (Manchester Utd.); **1992** Gary Pallister (Manchester Utd.); **1993** Paul McGrath (Aston Villa); **1994** Eric Cantona (Manchester Utd.); **1995** Alan Shearer (Blackburn Rov.); **1996** Les Ferdinand (Newcastle Utd.); **1997** Alan Shearer (Newcastle Utd.); **1998** Dennis Bergkamp (Arsenal); **1999** David Ginola (Tottenham); **2000** Roy Keane (Manchester Utd.); **2001** Teddy Sheringham (Manchester Utd.); **2002** Ruud van Nistelrooy (Manchester Utd.); **2003** Thierry Henry (Arsenal).

Young Player of the Year: **1974** Kevin Beattie (Ipswich Town); **1975** Mervyn Day (West Ham Utd.); **1976** Peter Barnes (Manchester City); **1977** Andy Gray (Aston Villa); **1978** Tony Woodcock (Nott'm Forest); **1979** Cyrille Regis (W.B.A.); **1980** Glenn Hoddle (Tottenham); **1981** Gary Shaw (Aston Villa); **1982** Steve Moran (Southampton); **1983** Ian Rush (Liverpool); **1984** Paul Walsh (Luton Town); **1985** Mark Hughes (Manchester Utd.); **1986** Tony Cottee (West Ham Utd.); **1987** Tony Adams (Arsenal); **1988** Paul Gascoigne (Newcastle Utd.); **1989** Paul Merson (Arsenal); **1990** Matthew Le Tissier (Southampton); **1991** Lee Sharpe (Manchester Utd.); **1992** Ryan Giggs (Manchester Utd.); **1993** Ryan Giggs (Manchester Utd.); **1994** Andy Cole (Newcastle Utd.); **1995** Robbie Fowler (Liverpool); **1996** Robbie Fowler (Liverpool); **1997** David Beckham (Manchester Utd.);

1998 Michael Owen (Liverpool); **1999** Nicolas Anelka (Arsenal); **2000** Harry Kewell (Leeds Utd.); **2001** Steven Gerrard (Liverpool); **2002** Craig Ballamy (Newcastle Utd.); **2003** Jermaine Jenas (Newcastle Utd.).

Merit Awards: **1974** Bobby Charlton & Cliff Lloyd; **1975** Denis Law; **1976** George Eastham; **1977** Jack Taylor; **1978** Bill Shankly; **1979** Tom Finney; **1980** Sir Matt Busby; **1981** John Trollope; **1982** Joe Mercer; **1983** Bob Paisley; **1984** Bill Nicholson; **1985** Ron Greenwood; **1986** England 1966 World Cup-winning team; **1987** Sir Stanley Matthews; **1988** Billy Bonds; **1989** Nat Lofthouse; **1990** Peter Shilton; **1991** Tommy Hutchison; **1992** Brian Clough; **1993** Manchester Utd., 1968 European Champions; Eusebio (Benfica & Portugal); **1994** Billy Bingham; **1995** Gordon Strachan; **1996** Pele; **1997** Peter Beardsley; **1998** Steve Ogrizovic; **1999** Tony Ford; **2000** Gary Mabbutt; **2001** Jimmy Hill; **2002** Niall Quinn; **2003** Sir Bobby Robson.

MANAGER OF THE YEAR (1)

(Chosen by a panel including managers, players, media, fan representatives, referees, the England coach and representatives of the Premier League and Football Association.)

1966 Jock Stein (Celtic); **1967** Jock Stein (Celtic); **1968** Matt Busby (Manchester Utd.); **1969** Don Revie (Leeds Utd.); **1970** Don Revie (Leeds Utd.); **1971** Bertie Mee (Arsenal); **1972** Don Revie (Leeds Utd.); **1973** Bill Shankly (Liverpool); **1974** Jack Charlton (Middlesbrough); **1975** Ron Saunders (Aston Villa); **1976** Bob Paisley (Liverpool); **1977** Bob Paisley (Liverpool); **1978** Brian Clough (Nott'm Forest); **1979** Bob Paisley (Liverpool); **1980** Bob Paisley (Liverpool); **1981** Ron Saunders (Aston Villa); **1982** Bob Paisley (Liverpool); **1983** Bob Paisley (Liverpool); **1984** Joe Fagan (Liverpool); **1985** Howard Kendall (Everton); **1986** Kenny Dalglish (Liverpool); **1987** Howard Kendall (Everton); **1988** Kenny Dalglish (Liverpool); **1989** George Graham (Arsenal); **1990** Kenny Dalglish (Liverpool); **1991** George Graham (Arsenal); **1992** Howard Wilkinson (Leeds Utd.); **1993** Alex Ferguson (Manchester Utd.); **1994** Alex Ferguson (Manchester Utd.); **1995** Kenny Dalglish (Blackburn Rov.); **1996** Alex Ferguson (Manchester Utd.); **1997** Alex Ferguson (Manchester Utd.); **1998** Arsene Wenger (Arsenal); **1999** Alex Ferguson (Manchester Utd.); **2000** Sir Alex Ferguson (Manchester Utd.); **2001** George Burley (Ipswich Town); **2002** Arsene Wenger (Arsenal); **2003** Sir Alex Ferguson (Manchester Utd.).

MANAGER OF THE YEAR (2)

(As chosen by the League Managers' Association and awarded to 'the manager who has made best use of the resources available to him'.)

1993 Dave Bassett (Sheffield Utd.); **1994** Joe Kinnear (Wimbledon); **1995** Frank Clark (Nott'm Forest); **1996** Peter Reid (Sunderland); **1997** Danny Wilson (Barnsley); **1998** David Jones (Southampton); **1999** Alex Ferguson (Manchester Utd.); **2000** Alan Curbishley (Charlton Athletic); **2001** George Burley (Ipswich Town); **2002** Arsene Wenger (Arsenal); **2003** David Moyes (Everton).

SCOTTISH FOOTBALL WRITERS' ASSOCIATION

Player of the Year: **1965** Billy McNeill (Celtic); **1966** John Greig (Rangers); **1967** Ronnie Simpson (Celtic); **1968** Gordon Wallace (Raith); **1969** Bobby Murdoch (Celtic); **1970** Pat Stanton (Hibernian); **1971** Martin Buchan (Aberdeen); **1972** David Smith (Rangers); **1973** George Connelly (Celtic); **1974** World Cup Squad; **1975** Sandy Jardine (Rangers); **1976** John Greig (Rangers); **1977** Danny McGrain (Celtic); **1978** Derek Johnstone (Rangers); **1979** Andy Ritchie (Morton); **1980** Gordon Strachan (Aberdeen); **1981** Alan Rough (Partick Thistle); **1982** Paul Sturrock (Dundee Utd.); **1983** Charlie Nicholas (Celtic); **1984** Willie Miller (Aberdeen); **1985** Hamish McAlpine (Dundee Utd.); **1986**

Sandy Jardine (Hearts); **1987** Brian McClair (Celtic); **1988** Paul McStay (Celtic); **1989** Richard Gough (Rangers); **1990** Alex McLeish (Aberdeen); **1991** Maurice Malpas (Dundee Utd.); **1992** Ally McCoist (Rangers); **1993** Andy Goram (Rangers); **1994** Mark Hateley (Rangers); **1995** Brian Laudrup (Rangers); **1996** Paul Gascoigne (Rangers); **1997** Brian Laudrup (Rangers); **1998** Craig Burley (Celtic); **1999** Henrik Larsson (Celtic); **2000** Barry Ferguson (Rangers); **2001** Henrik Larsson (Celtic); **2002** Paul Lambert (Celtic); **2003** Barry Ferguson (Rangers).

SCOTTISH P.F.A. AWARDS

Player of the Year: 1978 Derek Johnstone (Rangers); **1979** Paul Hegarty (Dundee Utd.); **1980** Davie Provan (Celtic); **1981** Mark McGhee (Aberdeen); **1982** Sandy Clarke (Airdrieonians); **1983** Charlie Nicholas (Celtic); **1984** Willie Miller (Aberdeen); **1985** Jim Duffy (Morton); **1986** Richard Gough (Dundee Utd.); **1987** Brian McClair (Celtic); **1988** Paul McStay (Celtic); **1989** Theo Snelders (Aberdeen); **1990** Jim Bett (Aberdeen); **1991** Paul Elliott (Celtic); **1992** Ally McCoist (Rangers); **1993** Andy Goram (Rangers); **1994** Mark Hateley (Rangers); **1995** Brian Laudrup (Rangers); **1996** Paul Gascoigne (Rangers); **1997** Paolo Di Canio (Celtic) **1998** Jackie McNamara (Celtic); **1999** Henrik Larsson (Celtic); **2000** Mark Viduka (Celtic); **2001** Henrik Larsson (Celtic); **2002** Lorenzo Amoruso (Rangers); **2003** Barry Ferguson (Rangers).

Young Player of Year: 1978 Graeme Payne (Dundee Utd.); **1979** Ray Stewart (Dundee Utd.); **1980** John McDonald (Rangers); **1981** Charlie Nicholas (Celtic); **1982** Frank McAvennie (St. Mirren); **1983** Paul McStay (Celtic); **1984** John Robertson (Hearts); **1985** Craig Levein (Hearts); **1986** Craig Levein (Hearts); **1987** Robert Fleck (Rangers); **1988** John Collins (Hibernian); **1989** Billy McKinlay (Dundee Utd.); **1990** Scott Crabbe (Hearts); **1991** Eoin Jess (Aberdeen); **1992** Phil O'Donnell (Motherwell); **1993** Eoin Jess (Aberdeen); **1994** Phil O'Donnell (Motherwell); **1995** Charlie Miller (Rangers); **1996** Jackie McNamara (Celtic); **1997** Robbie Winters (Dundee Utd.); **1998** Gary Naysmith (Hearts); **1999** Barry Ferguson (Rangers) ; **2000** Kenny Miller (Hibernian); **2001** Stilian Petrov (Celtic); **2002** Kevin McNaughton (Aberdeen); **2003** James McFadden (Motherwell).

SCOTTISH MANAGER OF THE YEAR

1987 Jim McLean (Dundee Utd.); **1988** Billy McNeill (Celtic); **1989** Graeme Souness (Rangers); **1990** Andy Roxburgh (Scotland); **1991** Alex Totten (St. Johnstone); **1992** Walter Smith (Rangers); **1993** Walter Smith (Rangers); **1994** Walter Smith (Rangers); **1995** Jimmy Nicholl (Raith); **1996** Walter Smith (Rangers); **1997** Walter Smith (Rangers); **1998** Wim Jansen (Celtic); **1999** Dick Advocaat (Rangers); **2000** Dick Advocaat (Rangers); **2001** Martin O'Neill (Celtic); **2002** John Lambie (Partick Thistle); **2003** Alex McLeish (Rangers).

EUROPEAN FOOTBALLER OF THE YEAR

(Poll conducted by *France Football*) 1956 Stanley Matthews (Blackpool); **1957** Alfredo di Stefano (Real Madrid); **1958** Raymond Kopa (Real Madrid); **1959** Alfredo di Stefano (Real Madrid); **1960** Luis Suarez (Barcelona); **1961** Omar Sivori (Juventus); **1962** Josef Masopust (Dukla Prague); **1963** Lev Yashin (Moscow Dynamo); **1964** Denis Law (Manchester Utd.); **1965** Eusebio (Benfica); **1966** Bobby Charlton (Manchester Utd.); **1967** Florian Albert (Ferencvaros); **1968** George Best (Manchester Utd.); **1969** Gianni Rivera (AC Milan); **1970** Gerd Muller (Bayern Munich); **1971** Johan Cruyff (Ajax); **1972** Franz Beckenbauer (Bayern Munich); **1973** Johan Cruyff (Barcelona); **1974** Johan Cruyff (Barcelona); **1975** Oleg Blokhin (Dynamo Kiev); **1976** Franz Beckenbauer (Bayern Munich); **1977** Allan Simonsen (Borussia Moenchengladbach); **1978** Kevin Keegan (SV Hamburg); **1979** Kevin Keegan (SV Hamburg); **1980** Karl-Heinz Rummenigge (Bayern Munich); **1981** Karl-Heinz Rummenigge (Bayern Munich); **1982** Paolo Rossi (Juventus);

1983 Michel Platini (Juventus); **1984** Michel Platini (Juventus); **1985** Michel Platini (Juventus); **1986** Igor Belanov (Dynamo Kiev); **1987** Ruud Gullit (AC Milan); **1988** Marco van Basten (AC Milan); **1989** Marco van Basten (AC Milan); **1990** Lothar Matthaus (Inter Milan); **1991** Jean-Pierre Papin (Marseille); **1992** Marco van Basten (AC Milan); **1993** Roberto Baggio (Juventus); **1994** Hristo Stoichkov (Barcelona); **1995** George Weah (AC Milan); **1996** Matthias Sammer (Borussia Dortmund); **1997** Ronaldo (Inter Milan); **1998** Zinedine Zidane (Juventus); **1999** Rivaldo (Barcelona); **2000** Luis Figo (Real Madrid); **2001** Michael Owen (Liverpool); **2002** Ronaldo (Real Madrid).

FIFA WORLD FOOTBALLER OF YEAR

(Voted by national coaches): 1991 Lothar Matthaus (Inter Milan and Germany); **1992** Marco van Basten (AC Milan and Holland); **1993** Roberto Baggio (Juventus and Italy); **1994** Romario (Barcelona and Brazil); **1995** George Weah (AC Milan and Liberia); **1996** Ronaldo (Barcelona and Brazil); **1997** Ronaldo (Inter Milan and Brazil); **1998** Zinedine Zidane (Juventus and France); **1999** Rivaldo (Barcelona and Brazil); **2000** Zinedine Zidane (Juventus and France); **2001** Luis Figo (Real Madrid and Portugal); **2002** Ronaldo (Real Madrid and Brazil).

QUOTE-UNQUOTE

'My feelings for Manchester United the club, the players, the fans and the backroom staff are as strong as ever. I want to stay' – **David Beckham**.

'We accept that he (Beckham) is the most recognised footballer in the world, perhaps the most recognised person. So, yes, he is important to us and that's the reason we're going to keep him' – **Peter Kenyon**, Manchester United chief executive.

'I'm contracted to Manchester United for another two or three years, I think. As long as they want me, then I'll stay' – **David Beckham**.

'There are many better ways of spending money that has been hard earned with many sacrifices, other than hiring Mr Beckham' – **Silvio Berlusconi**, AC Milan president.

'No, no, no, no, never, no, no' – **Florentino Perez**, Real Madrid president, denying interest in signing Beckham.

'Manchester United confirm that in the event that all of the conditions are fulfilled, then the offer would be acceptable' – Old Trafford announcement that they had acceped a bid for Beckham from Barcelona presidential candidate Joan Laporta.

'David is very disappointed and surprised to learn of this statement by United and feel he has been used as a pawn in the Barcelona presidential elections' – Beckham's advisers.

'You wouldn't want to sell your second-hand car in such a way, never mind one of your finest assets' – **Gordon Taylor**, chief executive of the PFA

'He's been at that club since he was a nipper and it seems such a shame' – **Ted Beckham** on his son's imminent departure.

'Of course I would have been happier if the transfer had been done differently. But if I was going to leave Manchester United it would have been to this club. It is massive' – **David Beckham** after ending all the speculation by joining Real Madrid.

THE STORY OF THE PREMIERSHIP SEASON — 2002-03

AUGUST

17: On the opening day of the season, Chelsea come from two goals down to beat Charlton Athletic 3-2. Two newly-promoted sides lose, Manchester City 3-0 to Leeds Utd. and W.B.A. 1-0 to Manchester Utd.
18: The third new team, Birmingham City, have Senegal World Cup defender Aliou Cisse sent off in a 2-0 defeat by defending champions Arsenal. His red card is later rescinded by referee Mike Riley.
19: Two goals by Lomano LuaLua help Newcastle Utd. off to a flying start. They beat West Ham Utd. 4-0.
23: In the first 'heavyweight' match of the season, William Gallas gives Chelsea a third minute lead, but Manchester Utd. have the final say with a Ryan Giggs goal for a 2-2 result.
24: Arsenal's bid to better the record of 14 successive English League wins is frustrated by West Ham Utd. in a 2-2 draw. Middlesbrough's record signing Massimo Maccarone scores twice on his home debut, but Fulham reply twice in the last minute for a point. El Hadji Diouf, Senegal World Cup striker, gets two on his home debut for Liverpool who beat Southampton 3-0.
28: Jason McAteer's goal gives Sunderland a surprise away win over Leeds Utd. Manager Graeme Souness is sent from the dug-out as Blackburn Rov. hold Liverpool to 2-2 with a late equaliser by Corrado Grabbi.
31: Roy Keane is sent off for the 10th time in Manchester Utd. colours against Sunderland. Tottenham end the month on top of the table, thanks to a 90th minute Teddy Sheringham penalty against Southampton. Nicolas Anelka celebrates a hat-trick for Manchester City, but his first in the 3-1 win over Everton is later ruled a Tomasz Radzinksi own goal by the Dubious Goals Panel.

SEPTEMBER

1: Patrick Vieira is dismissed for the eighth time in his Arsenal career during the 1-1 draw with Chelsea.
2: Gary Speed and Alan Shearer reply twice in the final 10 minutes for Newcastle Utd. after Liverpool establish a two-goal lead.
10: Nicolas Anelka is on the mark against his old club, but Arsenal prevail 2-1 against Manchester City. Middlesbrough win the north-east derby 3-0 against Sunderland.
11: Liverpool surrender another two-goal advantage at Anfield, this time to Clinton Morrison's first goals for Birmingham City. A last-minute Sylvain Legwinski strike completes a 3-2 comeback win for Fulham after Tottenham lead 2-0 at half-time. Kevin Nolan's goal enables Bolton Wand. to win at Old Trafford for the second successive season. Southampton manager Gordon Strachan is ordered from the dug-out during the 1-0 win at Everton.
14: Arsenal set a top division record of scoring in 45 successive matches and a club record of 27 games without defeat when beating Charlton Athletic 3-0. Harry Kewell's header gives Leeds Utd. victory over Manchester Utd. on Rio Ferdinand's return to Elland Road. Milan Baros scores twice on his Premiership debut as Liverpool beat Bolton Wand. 3-2.
16: The most bizarre goal of the season, touched into his own net by Aston Villa goalkeeper Peter Enckelman from team-mate Olof Mellberg's throw-in, helps Birmingham City to a 3-0 win.
21: A tale of two goalkeepers at Anfield, where Russell Hoult is sent off for fouling Michael Owen. Substitute Joe Murphy saves Owen's penalty – his first touch in the Premiership – but Liverpool still beat W.B.A. 2-0. David Seaman is grateful for Kanu's

last-minute Arsenal winner after Gareth Farrelly's cross sails over his head for a Bolton Wand. equaliser. So too is Thierry Henry following his penalty miss. Peter Reid breaks one of his own rules by publicly criticising his Sunderland team after the 2-0 defeat by Newcastle Utd.
22: Alan Smith also fails from the penalty spot, but this miss proves costly as Leeds Utd. lose by the only goal against Blackburn Rov.
28: Arsenal look every inch a top-of-the-table side when brushing aside Leeds Utd. 4-1, scoring for a League record 47th successive game and setting a top division best of 23 matches unbeaten away from home. Michael Owen ends a lean spell with all three goals for Liverpool against Manchester City. Paolo Di Canio stakes an early claim for goal-of-the-season with a spectacular volley for West Ham Utd. in the 3-2 success at Chelsea.

OCTOBER

5: Alan Shearer scores both Newcastle Utd. goals in the 2-1 win over W.B.A., two by Stern John sets up the same scoreline for Birmingham City against West Ham Utd., and a Brett Ormerod double gives Southampton a 2-0 victory over Manchester City.
6: Two in the first nine minutes by Kanu point Arsenal to a 3-1 win over Sunderland and another record – 30 Premiership games without defeat. A last-minute Michael Owen winner against Chelsea keeps Liverpool in pursuit.
7: England coach Sven Goran Eriksson leaves early and misses a remarkable finish by Manchester Utd., who score three times to end 87 minutes of resistance by Everton.
19: Arsenal's record unbeaten run is ended by 16-year-old Wayne Rooney, who comes off the bench to hit a spectacular winner for Everton and become the youngest-ever Premiership scorer. Fabien Barthez comes under fire for delaying, and eventually saving, a Steed Malbranque penalty to give Manchester Utd. a point at Fulham.
20: Robbie Keane scores his first goals at White Hart Lane for Tottenham, who beat Bolton Wand. 3-1.
21: More Monday night blues for goalkeeper Peter Enckelman, who is sent off as Aston Villa go down 1-0 to Southampton.
23: A last-minute penalty by Paolo Di Canio, after Zat Knight brings down Jermain Defoe and is sent off, gives West Ham Utd. their third successive away win at Fulham.
26: Arsenal lose again, 2-1 to Blackburn Rov. So Michael Owen's 86th penalty winner against Tottenham enables Liverpool to end the month four points clear at the top. Franck Queudrue and Alan Smith are sent off in separate incidents as Middlesbrough and Leeds Utd. draw 2-2.
27: James Beattie scores a hat-trick, including a penalty, for Southampton, who come from 2-0 down to beat Fulham 4-2.

NOVEMBER

2: Diego Forlan's delight at scoring Manchester Utd.'s 85th minute winner against Southampton turns to embarrassment when he struggles to put his shirt back on. No such problems for Michael Owen, whose hot streak continues with both goals in Liverpool's victory over West Ham Utd.
3: Wayne Rooney underlines his immense potential with another brilliant strike to give Everton the points against Leeds Utd. Arsenal are back on track, courtesy of an own goal by Steve Marlet, Fulham's £11m striker, in another 1-0 scoreline.
4: Franck Queudrue is sent off for the second successive match as Middlesbrough lose 2-0 to Newcastle Utd.
9: Sir Alex Ferguson tears into his United side as City dominate the Manchester derby 3-1, Shaun Goater scoring twice. Gianfranco Zola celebrates his player-of-the-month award for October by scoring one goal and setting up two more for Eidur Gudjohnsen in Chelsea's 3-0 win over Birmingham City. Liverpool's fall from grace starts at Middlesbrough, where a mistake by Jerzy Dudek, punished by Gareth Southgate, costs them the Premiership's only unbeaten record.

16: Arsenal regain top spot with a 3-0 win over Tottenham. In the day's other derby, W.B.A. and Aston Villa finish goallesss.
17: Pressure builds on Terry Venables as Leeds Utd. concede two goals in the last two minutes to go down 4-2 at home to Bolton Wand. Fulham have Rufus Brevett and Steve Marlet sent off, but hold Birmingham City 0-0.
23: Ruud van Nistelrooy takes pride of place on a day of heavy scoring with a hat-trick in Manchester Utd.'s 5-3 win over Newcastle Utd. James Beattie's double helps Southampton beat Arsenal 3-2 and Facundo Sava gets two for ten-man Fulham who see off Liverpool 3-2.
30: Arsenal go four points clear of Liverpool, a Thierry Henry double setting up a 3-1 win over Aston Villa. Central defenders William Gallas and Marcel Desailly are both on the mark as Chelsea beat Sunderland 3-0 to move to one point behind Liverpool

DECEMBER

1: Diego Forlan's double, his first gifted by Jerzy Dudek, gives Manchester Utd. a 2-1 victory at Anfield. Alan Shearer rates a spectacular volley in the 2-1 win over Everton as one of the best goals of his career.
7: Arsenal's record run of scoring in 55 successive League matches comes to an end in a 2-0 defeat by Manchester Utd. Charlton Athletic celebrate the tenth anniversary of their return to The Valley by beating Liverpoool 2-0. Chelsea go second behind Arsenal with a 3-1 victory at Everton.
14: Marc-Vivien Foe scores twice as Manchester City retrieve a 2-0 deficit to earn a point against Charlton Athletic. A last-minute deflected strike by Thomas Hitzlsperger for Aston Villa defeats luckless W.B.A.
15: Tottenham, beaten 3-0 at Highbury a month earlier, stretch Arsenal in the return and are good value for a 1-1 result. Fading Liverpool go down 2-1 at Sunderland.
21: David Seaman makes his 700th League appearances in Arsenal's 2-0 win over Middlesbrough. Kevin Phillips, one goal all season, gets two as Sunderland come from 2-0 down to claim a point against W.B.A. In another game between struggling teams, Michael Ricketts scores in open play for the first time since January for Bolton Wand., who share the points with West Ham Utd.
22: Steven Gerrard apologises to Gary Naysmith for a two-footed tackle in a goalless Merseyside derby. A goal by Garry Flitcroft for Blackburn Rov. puts the brake on Manchester Utd.'s winning run.
26: James Milner, 16, takes over from Wayne Rooney as the youngest Premiership scorer in Leeds Utd.'s 2-1 win at Sunderland. Rooney is sent off for the first time as Everton and Birmingham City finish 1-1. Wayne Bridge makes a record 109th successive Premiership appearance in Southampton's goalless draw at Chelsea. Christian Ziege is sent off for the second successive game, but Tottenham gain a point after being two down to Charlton Athletic.
28: James Milner scores again for Leeds Utd., who end Chelsea's 11-match unbeaten run 2-0. Manchester Utd. beat Birmingham City by the same scoreline, with David Beckham scoring his first League goal since August. A last-minute winner by Jo Tessem for Southampton pushes Sunderland further into trouble.
29: Liverpool accuse Francis Jeffers of diving for the penalty, converted by Thierry Henry, which earns a draw for Arsenal, who end the year five points clear of Chelsea and Manchester Utd. at the top. Newcastle Utd. and Everton are a further three points adrift.

JANUARY

1: Plenty of late drama as 2003 kicks off. Arsenal survive a two-goal Chelsea comeback to win 3-2. Manchester Utd. score twice in the last few minutes after a Juan Veron own goal gives Sunderland an early lead. Tomasz Radzinski earns Everton a 2-2 draw with Manchester City in the last minute.

11: Lee Bowyer is denied a victory on his West Ham Utd. debut by a late equaliser by Jermaine Jenas which gives Newcastle Utd. a 2-2 draw. James Beattie enhances his England credentials with two more goals for Southampton, but Middlesbrough come from 2-0 down for a point.
12: Thierry Henry scores his 99th and 100th goals for Arsenal; who overwhelm Birmingham City 4-0 in a match delayed for half-an-hour by a partial failure of the St Andrews floodlights. Robbie Keane gets a hat-trick in Tottenham's 4-3 win over Everton.
18: Alan Shearer scores after 10secs – the second fastest-ever Premiership goal – for Newcastle Utd., who beat Manchester City 2-0. Diego Forlan's injury-time strike gives Manchester Utd. a 2-1 victory over Chelsea. Liverpool end their worst League run for nearly 50 years, 11 games without a win, thanks to an Emile Heskey header at Southampton. American Brian McBride makes it three goals in his first two games for Everton with two in the 2-1 win over Sunderland.
19: Thierry Henry's hat-trick accounts for ten-man West Ham Utd. and restores Arsenal's five-point advantage at the top.
22: Own goals by Richard Rufus and Mark Fish are not enough for troubled West Ham Utd., who go down 4-2 to Charlton Athletic, for whom Radostin Kishishev scores his first goal for the club.
28: Joey Gudjonsson scores on his debut for Aston Villa, who win away for the first time – and end the only unbeaten home record – with a 5-2 success against Middlesbrough. Chelsea twice come from behind to beat Leeds Utd. 3-2 with two goals in the last 10 minutes.
29: Three last-minute goals have an impact at both ends of the table. Emile Heskey's equaliser for Liverpool against Arsenal prevents the defending champions from moving seven points clear. Newcastle Utd. climb to second place, thanks to Jermaine Jenas's winner at Tottenham. Jermain Defoe's goal gives West Ham Utd. their first home win of the season, against Blackburn Rov., and lifts them off the bottom.

FEBRUARY

1: Three own goals – two by Michael Proctor and one from Stephen Wright – cost struggling Sunderland a 3-1 home defeat by Charlton Athletic. Ten-man W.B.A. spoil Robbie Fowler's debut for Manchester City with a 2-1 away win. At the top, a last-minute goal by Robert Pires, his second of the game, gives Arsenal a hard-earned victory over Fulham, but Manchester Utd. are comfortable 2-0 winners at Southampton.
2: Steven Gerrard scores his first League goal for five months as Liverpool put the damper on West Ham Utd.'s revival with a 3-0 success. Dion Dublin's brace in Aston Villa's 3-0 win over Blackburn Rov. takes his tally to seven in seven games.
8: Teddy Sheringham scores the 300th goal of his club career in Tottenham's 4-1 win over Sunderland. Seth Johnson's first for Leeds Utd. accounts for West Ham Utd. Middlesbrough end a run of eight away games without a win, or a goal, with Geremi's spectacular free-kick which earns a point at Liverpool.
9: Laurent Robert puts Newcastle Utd. ahead against Arsenal and is then sent off in a 1-1 draw. The Manchester derby delivers the same scoreline as a result of substitute Shaun Goater's late equaliser for City.
22: A day of important early and late goals. Arsenal score four times in the first 19 minutes to overwhelm Manchester City 5-1 and establish a five-point lead at the top. Manchester Utd. need a last-minute Ole Solskjaer goal for a point against Bolton Wand. Gianfranco Zola's 300th appearance for Chelsea is spoiled by Dwight Yorke and David Dunn giving Blackburn Rov. victory with strikes in the last four minutes. Two in the last seven minutes by Tomasz Radzinksi enable Everton to come from behind and beat Southampton, while Chris Riggott (2) and Malcolm Christie score for the first time for Middlesbrough, who win 3-1 at Sunderland.
23: Trevor Sinclair's double gives West Ham Utd. a 2-1 victory in a relegation battle against W.B.A. Birmingham City's victory over Liverpool by the same scoreline is their first in ten games.
24: Tottenham's Darren Anderton is sent off for the first time in his career in the 1-1 draw with Fulham, who have goalkeeper Maik Taylor dismissed.

MARCH

1: Juninho, out for eight months with a knee injury, makes his first appearance since the World Cup Final and earns Middlesbrough a point with an equaliser against Everton. Jimmy Floyd Hasselbaink scores a spectacular headed own goal as Chelsea lose 2-1 to Newcastle Utd. Les Ferdinand defies a bruised eye socket to score against former club Tottenham in West Ham Utd.'s 2-0 win.
2: Charlton Athletic's club-record run of five successive Premiership wins is ended by Arsenal, who beat them 2-0.
3: Aston Villa's Dion Dublin and Joey Gudjonsson are sent off in a 2-0 defeat by Birmingham City in an ugly local derby also marred by fighting fans.
5: Mikael Silvestre's first goal of the season gives Manchester Utd. a 2-1 win over Leeds Utd. A record Riverside crowd of 34,814 see a goal by Middlesbrough's Geremi inflict Newcastle Utd.'s first League defeat of 2003.
8: In the only Premiership match this Saturday, Liverpool take maximum points at home for the first time in four months by beating Bolton Wand. 2-0.
15: Arsenal lose for the first time in 2003 – 2-0 to Blackburn Rov., who complete the double over the leaders. David Beckham's winner at Villa Park enables Manchester Utd. to close the gap to two points. Mick McCarthy's first game in charge of Sunderland is a 2-0 home defeat by Bolton Wand. Southampton goalkeeper Antti Niemi makes some great saves against Fulham, then joins the attack for an injury-time corner and volleys against the crossbar to set up an equaliser for Michael Svensson.
16: Robbie Fowler's first goal for Manchester City earns a 1-0 victory over Birmingham City.
22: Manchester Utd. go top for the first time this season with a Ruud van Nistelrooy hat-trick against Fulham. Newcastle Utd. score three times in the last five minutes for a 5-1 win over Blackburn Rov. to stay on their heels. Chelsea also hit five against Manchester City, while Freddie Kanoute, out for most of the season, scores for the first time since September as West Ham Utd. beat Sunderland 2-0 to move out of the bottom three at the expense of Bolton Wand.
23: Arsenal regain pole position with a two-point advantage after a 2-1 victory over Everton, Pascal Cygan heading his first goal for the club. Peter Reid starts a caretaker role at Leeds Utd. with a 3-1 defeat at Liverpool.
24: A last-minute penalty by Jay-Jay Okocha gives Bolton Wand. victory over Tottenham and lifts them back above West Ham Utd.

APRIL

5: Manchester Utd.'s biggest win over Liverpool for 40 years – 4-0 after Sami Hyypia is sent off in the fourth minute – and Arsenal's 1-1 draw at Aston Villa means the big two are locked on 67 points. Mark Viduka scores a hat-trick as Leeds Utd. sweep away relegation worries with a 6-1 away win over Charlton Athletic. Sunderland suffer a record ninth successive defeat – 2-1 against Chelsea.
6: Wayne Rooney follows up his impressive performance for England against Turkey with a goal for Everton, who undermine Newcastle Utd.'s title hopes in a 2-1 win.
12: Paul Scholes scores a hat-trick as Manchester Utd. come from behind to overwhelm Newcastle Utd. 6-2 at St James' Park. Sunderland are relegated after a 2-0 defeat by Birmingham City, for whom Christophe Dugarry scores his first goal. Two by Mark Viduka, bringing his tally to nine in five games, earns Leeds Utd. a point against Tottenham.
16: The big game of the season ends 2-2. But it's advantage Manchester Utd. – three points ahead from an extra fixture played – after Arsenal have Sol Campbell sent off and lose Patrick Vieira with a knee injury. Vieira is ruled out for the rest of the season, while Campbell misses the last three League games, plus the F.A. Cup Final.
19: Paul Scholes reaches 100 goals for Manchester Utd., scoring twice in a 3-1 victory over Blackburn Rov. Arsenal win 2-0 at Middlesbrough. W.B.A. are relegated, despite a 2-1 success at Sunderland. A spectacular strike by Jay-Jay Okocha gives Bolton Wand. the verdict over West Ham Utd. in a relegation six-pointer marred by a players' brawl at

the end. Everton have David Weir and Gary Naysmith sent off in a 2-1 home defeat by Liverpool. Alan Smith's dismissal in Leeds Utd.'s 3-2 defeat at Southampton is the ninth of his career. Chris Coleman's first game in temporary charge of Fulham following Jean Tigana's departure brings a 2-1 win over Newcastle Utd.

21: Manager Glenn Roeder collapses with a brain tumour after West Ham Utd.'s 1-0 win over Middlesbrough. Chelsea do their Champions League chances a power of good, while ending Everton's hopes of a top four place, with a 4-1 success. Liverpool stay in the hunt with two goals in the final five minutes to beat Charlton Athletic 2-1. Christophe Dugarry scores twice as Birmingham City win for the sixth time in eight matches, 3-2 against Southampton, to effectively end relegation fears.

26: Arsenal are held 2-2 by Bolton Wand. after leading 2-0 and lose ground in the title race. Michael Owen scores four times – and passes 100 League goals for Liverpool – in a 6-0 away victory over W.B.A.

27: Manchester Utd. open up a five-point lead at the top, from an extra match played, by winning 2-0 at Tottenham. Freddie Kanoute's 81st minute goal gives West Ham Utd. victory over Manchester City in their first game under caretaker-manager Trevor Brooking.

MAY

3: On his 100th appearance for the club, Ruud van Nistelrooy scores his third hat-trick of the season in a 4-1 victory over Charlton Athletic which takes Manchester Utd. to the brink of the title. In his last home game for West Ham Utd., Paolo Di Canio scores the only goal against Chelsea to keep their survival hopes alive. Wins for Fulham and Aston Villa make them safe. Newcastle Utd. clinch a Champions League place, but Liverpool are left sweating after Nicolas Anelka, the player they did not want to keep, scores a last-minute winner for Manchester City at Anfield.

4: Arsenal lose 3-2 at home to Leeds Utd., so Manchester Utd. are crowned champions for the eighth time in 11 seasons.

7: The Premiership's first-ever hat-trick double is registered by Jermaine Pennant, on his full League debut, and Robert Pires as Arsenal wallop Southampton 6-1.

11: On a dramatic last day of the season, Bolton Wand. stay up by beating Middlesbrough 2-1. West Ham Utd. go down, their 2-2 draw with Birmingham City proving irrelevant. Chelsea defeat Liverpool 2-1 in a game deciding the fourth Champions League place. Blackburn Rov. win 4-0 at Tottenham to edge out Everton for a UEFA Cup spot. Everton lose 2-1 to Manchester Utd., for whom Ruud van Nistelrooy wins the Golden Boot award with his 25th goal of the season. Sunderland suffer a 15th successive defeat as Freddie Ljungberg scores a hat-trick in Arsenal's 4-0 win. Michael Svensson spoils Manchester City's farewell-to-Maine-Road party with the only goal of the game for Southampton.

PREMIER LEAGUE TEAMS OF THE DECADE

Manchester United and Arsenal players dominated the Premier League's top domestic and overseas teams of the decade in a vote by supporters via the League's website. The domestic team was: Seaman, Gary Neville, Adams, Bruce, Stuart Pearce, Beckham, Ince, Scholes, Giggs, Shearer, Owen. The overseas line-up was: Schmeichel, Petrescu, Desailly, Stam, Irwin, Ljungberg, Vieira, Keane, Pires, Cantona, Henry. Alan Shearer and Eric Cantona were chosen as the best players and Sir Alex Ferguson the top manager. Other winners: best goal – David Beckham against Wimbledon (1996); best save – Peter Schmeichel for Manchester United against Newcastle (1997); best game – Liverpool 4, Newcastle 3 (1996).

F.A. BARCLAYCARD PREMIERSHIP RESULTS 2002-03

	Arsenal	Aston Villa	Birmingham City	Blackburn Rov.	Bolton Wand.	Charlton Athletic	Chelsea	Everton	Fulham	Leeds Utd.	Liverpool	Manchester City	Manchester Utd.	Middlesbrough	Newcastle Utd.	Southampton	Sunderland	Tottenham	W.B.A.	West Ham Utd.
Arsenal	–	3–1	2–0	1–2	2–1	2–0	3–2	2–1	2–1	2–3	1–1	2–1	2–2	2–0	1–0	6–1	3–1	3–0	5–2	3–1
Aston Villa	1–1	–	0–2	3–0	2–0	2–0	2–0	3–2	3–1	0–0	0–1	1–0	0–1	1–0	0–1	0–1	1–0	0–1	2–1	4–1
Birmingham City	0–4	3–0	–	0–1	3–1	1–1	1–3	1–1	0–0	2–1	2–1	0–2	0–1	3–0	0–2	3–2	2–0	1–1	1–0	2–2
Blackburn Rov.	2–0	0–0	1–1	–	0–0	1–0	2–3	0–1	2–1	1–0	2–2	1–0	1–0	1–0	5–2	1–0	0–0	1–2	1–1	2–2
Bolton Wand.	2–2	1–0	4–2	1–1	–	1–2	1–1	1–0	0–0	0–3	2–3	2–0	1–1	2–1	4–3	1–1	1–1	1–0	1–1	1–0
Charlton Athletic	0–3	3–0	0–2	3–1	1–1	–	2–3	2–1	0–1	1–6	2–0	2–2	1–3	1–0	0–2	2–1	1–1	0–1	2–2	4–2
Chelsea	1–1	2–0	3–0	1–2	1–0	4–1	–	4–1	1–1	3–2	2–1	5–0	2–2	1–0	3–0	0–0	3–0	1–1	2–0	2–3
Everton	2–1	2–1	1–1	2–1	0–0	1–0	1–3	–	2–0	2–0	1–2	2–2	1–2	2–1	2–1	2–1	2–1	2–2	1–1	0–0
Fulham	0–1	2–1	0–1	0–4	4–1	1–0	0–0	2–0	–	1–0	3–2	0–1	1–1	1–0	2–1	2–2	1–0	3–2	3–0	0–1
Leeds Utd.	1–4	3–1	2–0	2–3	2–4	1–2	2–0	0–1	2–0	–	0–1	3–0	1–0	2–3	0–3	1–1	0–1	2–2	0–0	1–0
Liverpool	2–2	1–1	2–2	1–1	2–0	2–1	1–0	0–0	2–0	3–1	–	1–2	1–2	1–1	2–2	3–0	0–0	2–1	2–0	2–0
Manchester City	1–5	3–1	1–0	2–2	2–0	0–1	0–3	3–1	4–1	2–1	0–3	–	3–1	0–0	1–0	0–1	3–0	2–3	1–2	0–1
Manchester Utd.	2–0	1–1	2–0	3–1	0–1	4–1	2–1	3–0	3–0	2–1	4–0	1–1	–	1–0	5–3	2–1	2–1	1–0	1–0	3–0
Middlesbrough	0–2	2–5	1–0	1–0	2–0	1–1	1–1	1–1	2–2	2–2	1–0	3–1	3–1	–	1–0	2–2	3–0	5–1	3–0	2–2
Newcastle Utd.	1–1	1–1	1–0	5–1	1–0	2–1	2–1	2–1	2–0	0–2	1–0	2–0	2–6	2–0	–	2–1	2–0	2–1	2–1	4–0
Southampton	3–2	2–2	2–0	1–1	0–0	0–0	1–1	1–0	4–2	3–2	0–1	2–0	0–2	0–0	1–1	–	2–1	1–0	1–0	1–1
Sunderland	0–4	1–0	0–1	0–0	0–2	1–3	1–2	0–1	0–3	1–2	2–1	0–3	1–1	1–3	0–1	0–1	–	2–0	1–2	0–1
Tottenham	1–1	1–0	2–1	0–4	3–1	2–2	0–0	4–3	1–1	2–0	2–3	0–2	0–2	0–3	0–1	2–1	4–1	–	3–1	3–2
W.B.A.	1–2	0–0	1–1	0–2	1–1	0–1	0–2	1–2	1–0	1–3	0–6	1–2	1–3	1–0	2–2	1–0	2–2	2–3	–	1–2
West Ham Utd.	2–2	2–2	1–2	2–1	1–1	0–2	1–0	0–1	1–1	3–4	0–3	0–0	1–1	1–0	2–2	0–1	2–0	2–0	0–1	–

Read across for home results, down for away

NATIONWIDE LEAGUE RESULTS 2002-03 – FIRST DIVISION

	Bradford City	Brighton & H.A.	Burnley	Coventry City	Crystal Palace	Derby Co.	Gillingham	Grimsby Town	Ipswch Town	Leicester City	Millwall	Norwich City	Nott'm. Forest	Portsmouth	Preston N.E.	Reading	Rotherham Utd.	Sheffield Utd.	Sheffield Wed.	Stoke City	Walsall	Watford	Wimbledon	Wolves
Bradford City	–	0–1	2–2	1–1	2–1	0–0	1–3	0–0	2–0	0–0	0–1	2–1	1–0	0–5	1–1	0–1	4–2	0–5	1–1	4–2	1–2	2–1	3–5	0–0
Brighton & H.A.	3–2	–	2–2	0–0	0–0	1–0	2–4	1–2	1–1	0–1	1–0	0–2	1–0	1–1	0–2	0–1	2–0	2–4	1–1	1–2	0–2	4–0	2–3	4–1
Burnley	0–2	1–3	–	3–1	0–0	2–0	2–0	1–1	1–1	1–2	2–2	2–0	1–0	0–3	2–0	2–5	2–6	0–1	2–7	2–1	2–1	4–7	1–0	2–1
Coventry City	0–2	0–0	0–1	–	1–0	3–0	0–0	3–2	2–4	1–2	2–3	1–1	0–1	0–4	1–2	2–0	2–1	2–1	1–1	0–1	0–0	0–1	2–2	0–2
Crystal Palace	1–1	5–0	1–1	1–1	–	0–1	2–2	2–0	1–1	0–0	1–0	2–0	0–0	2–3	2–0	0–1	0–0	2–2	0–0	1–0	2–0	0–1	0–1	4–2
Derby Co.	1–2	1–0	1–2	1–0	0–1	–	1–1	1–3	1–4	1–1	1–2	2–1	0–0	1–2	0–2	3–0	3–0	2–1	2–2	2–0	2–2	3–0	3–2	1–4
Gillingham	1–0	3–0	4–2	0–2	2–1	1–0	–	3–0	1–3	3–2	1–0	1–0	1–4	1–3	1–1	0–1	1–1	1–1	1–1	1–1	0–1	3–0	3–3	0–4
Grimsby Town	1–2	2–2	6–5	0–2	1–4	1–2	1–1	–	3–0	1–2	0–2	1–1	0–3	0–1	3–3	0–3	0–0	1–4	2–0	2–0	0–1	1–0	0–0	0–1
Ipswich Town	1–2	2–2	2–2	2–1	1–2	0–1	0–1	2–2	–	6–1	4–1	1–1	3–4	3–0	3–0	3–1	1–2	3–2	2–1	0–0	3–2	4–2	1–5	2–4
Leicester City	4–0	2–0	0–1	2–1	1–0	3–1	2–0	2–0	1–2	–	4–1	1–1	1–0	1–1	2–1	2–1	2–1	0–0	1–1	0–0	2–0	2–0	4–0	1–0
Millwall	1–0	1–0	1–1	2–0	3–2	3–0	2–2	2–0	1–1	2–2	–	0–2	1–2	0–5	2–1	0–2	0–6	1–0	3–0	3–1	0–3	4–0	1–1	1–1
Norwich City	3–2	0–1	2–0	2–0	2–0	1–0	1–0	4–0	0–2	0–0	3–1	–	0–0	1–0	2–0	0–1	1–1	2–3	3–0	2–2	2–1	4–0	1–0	0–3
Nott'm. Forest	3–0	3–2	2–0	1–1	2–1	3–0	4–1	2–2	2–1	2–2	3–3	4–0	–	1–2	2–2	2–0	3–2	3–0	4–0	6–0	1–1	0–1	2–0	2–2
Portsmouth	3–0	4–2	1–0	1–1	1–1	6–2	1–0	3–0	1–1	0–2	1–0	3–2	2–0	–	3–2	3–0	3–2	1–2	1–2	3–0	3–2	3–0	4–1	1–0
Preston N.E.	1–0	2–2	3–1	2–2	1–2	4–2	3–0	3–0	0–0	2–0	2–1	1–2	1–1	1–1	–	1–0	0–2	2–0	2–2	4–3	5–0	1–1	3–5	0–2
Reading	1–0	1–2	3–0	1–2	2–1	2–1	2–1	2–1	3–1	1–3	2–0	0–2	1–0	0–0	5–1	–	3–0	0–2	2–1	1–1	0–0	1–0	0–1	0–1
Rotherham Utd.	3–2	1–0	0–0	1–0	1–3	2–1	1–1	0–1	2–1	1–1	1–3	1–1	2–2	2–3	0–0	0–0	–	1–2	0–2	4–0	0–0	2–1	2–1	0–0
Sheffield Utd.	3–0	2–1	4–2	0–0	2–1	2–0	2–2	2–1	0–0	2–1	3–1	0–1	1–0	1–1	1–0	1–3	1–0	–	3–1	2–1	1–1	1–2	1–1	3–3
Sheffield Wed.	2–1	1–1	1–3	5–1	0–0	1–3	0–2	0–0	0–1	0–0	0–1	2–2	2–0	1–3	0–1	3–2	1–2	2–0	–	0–0	2–1	2–2	4–2	0–4
Stoke City	2–1	1–0	0–1	1–2	1–1	1–3	0–0	1–2	2–1	0–1	0–1	1–1	2–2	1–1	2–1	1–0	2–0	0–0	3–2	–	1–0	1–2	2–1	0–2
Walsall	0–1	1–0	3–2	0–0	3–4	3–2	1–0	3–1	0–2	1–4	1–2	0–0	2–1	1–2	3–3	0–2	3–4	0–1	1–0	4–2	–	2–0	2–0	0–1
Watford	1–0	1–0	2–1	5–2	3–3	2–0	0–1	2–0	0–2	1–2	0–0	2–1	1–1	2–2	0–1	0–3	1–2	2–0	1–0	1–2	2–0	–	3–2	1–1
Wimbledon	2–2	1–0	2–1	0–1	2–2	0–2	0–1	3–3	0–1	2–3	2–0	4–2	2–3	2–1	2–0	3–0	2–1	1–0	3–0	1–1	3–2	0–0	–	3–2
Wolves	1–2	1–1	3–0	0–2	4–0	1–1	6–0	4–1	1–1	1–1	3–0	1–0	2–1	1–1	4–0	0–1	0–0	1–3	2–2	0–0	3–1	0–0	1–1	–

Read across for home results, down for away

NATIONWIDE LEAGUE RESULTS 2002-03 – SECOND DIVISION

	Barnsley	Blackpool	Brentford	Bristol City	Cardiff City	Cheltenham Town	Chesterfield	Colchester Utd.	Crewe Alexandra	Huddersfield Town	Luton Town	Mansfield Town	Northampton Town	Notts Co.	Oldham Athletic	Peterborough Utd.	Plymouth Argyle	Port Vale	Q.P.R.	Stockport Co.	Swindon Town	Tranmere Rov.	Wigan Athletic	Wycombe Wand.
Barnsley	–	2–1	1–0	1–4	3–2	1–1	2–1	1–1	1–2	0–1	2–3	0–1	1–2	0–0	2–2	1–2	1–1	2–1	1–0	1–0	1–1	1–1	1–3	1–1
Blackpool	1–2	–	1–0	0–0	1–0	3–1	1–1	3–1	0–1	1–1	5–2	3–3	2–1	1–1	0–0	3–0	1–1	3–2	1–3	1–3	0–0	3–0	0–2	1–0
Brentford	1–2	5–0	–	1–0	0–2	2–2	2–1	1–1	1–2	1–0	0–0	1–1	3–0	1–1	0–0	1–1	0–0	1–1	1–2	1–2	3–1	1–2	0–1	1–0
Bristol City	2–0	2–0	0–0	–	2–0	3–1	4–0	1–2	2–2	1–0	1–1	5–2	3–0	3–2	2–0	1–0	0–0	2–0	1–3	1–1	2–0	2–0	0–1	3–0
Cardiff City	1–1	2–1	2–0	0–2	–	2–1	1–0	0–3	2–1	4–0	0–0	1–0	1–2	0–2	1–1	3–0	1–1	3–1	1–2	2–1	1–1	4–0	0–0	1–0
Cheltenham Town	1–3	3–0	1–0	2–3	1–1	–	0–0	1–1	0–4	1–0	2–2	3–1	1–1	1–4	1–1	1–1	1–2	0–1	1–1	0–2	2–0	3–1	0–2	0–0
Chesterfield	1–0	1–0	0–2	2–0	0–3	2–2	–	0–4	0–2	1–0	2–1	1–2	4–0	0–0	0–1	0–0	3–2	2–1	2–4	1–0	2–4	1–0	0–0	4–0
Colchester Utd.	1–1	0–2	0–1	2–2	1–2	1–1	2–0	–	1–2	2–0	0–5	1–0	2–0	1–1	0–1	1–1	0–0	4–1	0–1	1–0	1–0	2–2	1–0	0–1
Crewe Alexandra	2–0	3–0	2–1	1–1	1–1	1–0	0–0	2–0	–	1–0	0–1	2–0	3–3	0–3	1–2	0–1	0–1	1–1	2–0	1–0	0–1	2–0	0–1	4–2
Huddersfield Town	1–0	0–0	0–2	1–2	1–0	3–3	4–0	1–1	1–1	–	0–1	1–1	2–0	3–0	1–1	0–1	1–0	2–2	0–3	2–1	2–3	1–2	0–0	0–0
Luton Town	2–3	1–3	0–1	2–2	2–0	2–1	3–0	1–2	0–4	3–0	–	2–3	3–2	2–2	0–0	2–3	1–0	0–0	0–0	1–1	3–0	0–0	1–1	1–0
Mansfield Town	0–1	4–0	0–0	4–5	0–1	0–2	0–2	4–2	0–5	0–2	3–2	–	2–1	3–2	0–1	1–5	4–3	0–1	0–4	4–2	2–1	6–1	1–2	0–0
Northampton Town	1–0	0–1	1–2	1–2	0–1	1–2	0–1	4–1	1–1	0–0	3–0	2–0	–	2–0	0–2	0–1	2–2	3–0	1–1	0–3	1–0	0–4	0–2	0–5
Notts Co.	3–2	3–1	2–2	2–0	0–1	1–0	1–1	2–3	2–2	3–2	2–1	2–2	2–1	–	1–3	2–2	0–2	1–0	3–0	3–2	1–1	0–1	0–2	1–1
Oldham Athletic	2–1	1–1	2–1	1–0	1–2	0–0	4–0	2–0	1–3	4–0	1–2	6–1	4–0	1–1	–	0–0	0–1	1–1	0–0	2–0	4–0	2–0	0–2	0–2
Peterborough Utd.	1–3	1–0	5–1	1–3	2–0	4–1	1–0	0–1	0–0	0–1	1–1	0–0	0–0	1–0	0–1	–	2–0	1–2	0–2	2–0	1–1	0–0	1–1	1–2
Plymouth Argyle	1–1	1–3	3–0	2–0	2–2	3–1	0–1	0–0	1–3	2–1	2–1	3–1	0–0	1–0	2–2	6–1	–	3–0	0–1	4–1	1–1	0–1	1–3	1–0
Port Vale	0–0	1–0	1–0	2–3	0–2	1–2	5–2	1–0	1–2	5–1	1–2	4–2	3–2	3–2	1–1	1–0	1–2	–	0–0	0–1	1–1	1–4	0–1	1–1
Q.P.R.	1–0	2–1	1–1	1–0	0–4	4–1	3–1	2–0	0–0	3–0	2–0	2–2	0–1	2–0	1–2	2–0	2–2	4–0	–	1–0	2–0	1–2	0–1	2–1
Stockport Co.	4–1	2–2	2–3	1–4	1–1	1–1	2–1	1–1	1–4	2–1	2–3	2–0	4–0	0–0	1–2	2–1	2–1	1–1	1–1	–	2–5	2–3	1–1	2–1
Swindon Town	3–1	1–1	2–1	1–1	0–1	0–3	3–0	2–2	1–3	0–1	2–1	2–1	2–0	5–0	0–1	1–1	2–0	1–2	3–1	0–1	–	1–1	2–1	0–3
Tranmere Rov.	1–0	2–1	3–1	1–1	3–3	1–0	2–1	1–1	2–1	2–1	1–3	3–1	4–0	2–2	1–2	1–1	2–1	1–0	3–0	1–0	0–1	–	0–2	1–0
Wigan Athletic	1–0	1–1	2–0	2–0	2–2	0–0	3–1	2–1	2–0	1–0	1–1	3–2	1–0	3–1	3–1	2–2	0–1	0–1	1–1	2–1	2–0	0–0	–	3–0
Wycombe Wand.	2–2	1–2	4–0	2–1	0–4	1–1	2–0	0–0	1–2	0–0	1–2	3–3	1–1	3–1	2–2	3–2	2–1	3–1	4–1	1–4	2–3	1–3	0–2	–

Read across for home results, down for away

NATIONWIDE LEAGUE RESULTS 2002-03 – THIRD DIVISION

	Boston Utd.	Bournemouth	Bristol Rov.	Bury	Cambridge Utd.	Carlisle Utd.	Darlington	Exeter City	Hartlepool Utd.	Hull City	Kidderminster H.	Leyton Orient	Lincoln City	Macclesfield Town	Oxford Utd.	Rochdale	Rushden & D's	Scunthorpe Utd.	Shrewsbury Town	Southend Utd.	Swansea City	Torquay Utd.	Wrexham	York City
Boston Utd.	–	2–2	0–0	1–1	1–3	0–0	1–0	0–3	0–1	0–1	3–0	0–1	2–0	2–1	1–3	3–1	1–1	1–0	6–0	1–0	1–0	2–1	3–3	3–0
Bournemouth	2–1	–	1–0	1–2	1–1	3–1	2–0	2–0	2–1	0–0	0–0	3–1	0–1	2–2	1–1	3–3	3–1	2–1	2–1	1–0	3–0	1–1	2–0	1–0
Bristol Rov.	1–1	0–0	–	2–1	3–1	1–2	2–1	1–1	1–0	1–1	1–2	1–2	2–0	1–1	0–2	1–2	1–2	2–1	0–0	0–1	3–1	1–1	0–3	0–1
Bury	0–0	2–1	0–1	–	0–1	1–1	2–2	1–0	1–1	1–0	1–1	0–1	2–0	2–1	1–1	1–1	0–1	0–0	4–3	1–3	3–2	0–1	0–3	2–1
Cambridge Utd.	1–2	2–1	3–1	1–2	–	2–1	1–2	2–1	0–0	1–2	0–2	2–1	0–0	3–1	1–1	2–2	4–1	1–1	5–0	1–1	1–0	0–1	2–2	3–0
Carlisle Utd.	4–2	0–2	0–0	1–2	0–1	–	2–2	0–2	1–3	1–5	2–2	3–0	1–4	1–0	1–0	0–2	1–2	1–2	1–2	1–0	2–2	1–2	1–2	1–1
Darlington	2–3	2–2	1–0	3–1	1–2	2–0	–	2–2	2–2	2–0	2–1	2–2	0–0	0–0	0–1	0–1	2–2	1–1	5–1	2–1	2–2	1–1	0–1	2–1
Exeter City	0–2	1–3	0–0	1–2	1–2	1–0	0–4	–	1–2	3–1	2–5	1–0	2–0	1–1	2–2	1–1	1–1	1–1	1–1	1–0	1–0	1–2	1–0	0–1
Hartlepool Utd.	2–0	0–0	2–0	0–0	3–0	2–1	4–1	2–1	–	2–0	2–1	4–1	2–1	0–2	3–1	2–2	1–2	2–2	3–0	2–1	4–0	3–2	4–3	0–0
Hull City	1–0	3–1	1–0	1–1	1–1	4–0	0–1	2–2	2–0	–	4–1	1–1	0–1	1–3	0–0	3–0	1–1	2–0	2–0	2–2	1–1	1–1	1–2	0–0
Kidderminster H.	0–0	1–0	1–1	3–2	2–1	1–2	1–1	4–3	2–2	1–0	–	3–2	1–1	0–2	1–3	0–0	0–2	1–3	2–2	1–0	2–2	2–0	0–2	1–2
Leyton Orient	3–2	0–0	1–2	1–2	1–1	2–1	2–1	1–1	1–2	2–0	0–0	–	1–1	3–2	1–2	0–1	0–0	2–0	0–2	2–1	3–1	2–0	0–1	0–1
Lincoln City	1–1	1–2	2–1	1–1	2–2	0–1	1–1	1–0	3–0	1–1	1–0	1–1	–	3–0	0–1	2–0	1–2	1–0	1–1	2–1	1–0	1–1	1–1	1–0
Macclesfield Town	2–0	0–1	2–1	0–0	1–1	2–2	1–0	1–1	0–1	0–1	2–0	3–1	0–1	–	2–1	3–2	0–1	2–3	1–2	2–1	1–3	3–3	0–1	1–1
Oxford Utd.	2–1	3–0	0–1	2–1	1–1	0–0	1–1	2–2	0–1	0–0	2–1	0–2	1–0	0–1	–	2–0	3–0	0–1	2–2	0–1	1–0	2–2	0–2	2–0
Rochdale	1–0	1–1	1–1	1–2	4–3	0–1	1–1	3–3	4–0	2–1	0–1	1–0	0–1	3–1	2–1	–	0–1	1–2	1–1	1–2	1–2	0–2	2–2	0–1
Rushden & D's	1–0	2–1	2–1	0–1	4–1	1–1	2–0	1–0	1–1	4–2	3–1	2–0	1–0	3–0	0–2	3–3	–	2–0	5–1	3–0	1–1	3–0	2–2	2–1
Scunthorpe Utd.	2–0	0–2	2–2	0–1	1–2	3–1	0–1	1–1	4–0	3–1	1–1	2–1	0–0	1–1	2–0	3–1	0–0	–	1–1	4–1	2–0	5–1	1–1	2–1
Shrewsbury Town	1–2	0–0	2–5	4–1	3–1	2–3	2–2	1–0	0–1	1–1	2–3	2–1	1–2	2–3	1–2	3–1	1–1	1–2	–	0–1	0–0	2–3	1–2	2–2
Southend Utd.	4–2	0–1	2–2	1–2	2–1	0–1	2–0	1–0	0–1	3–0	0–2	1–0	0–1	1–0	2–1	1–0	2–1	1–2	2–3	–	0–2	3–0	0–1	1–0
Swansea City	0–0	2–0	0–1	2–3	2–0	1–2	1–0	0–1	2–2	4–2	0–4	0–1	2–0	1–0	3–2	1–1	2–2	1–1	2–0	1–0	–	0–1	0–0	1–2
Torquay Utd.	1–1	4–0	2–1	1–1	3–2	2–3	3–1	1–0	1–1	1–4	2–2	2–2	0–0	2–2	2–3	2–2	1–1	1–1	2–1	3–1	0–0	–	2–1	3–1
Wrexham	1–1	3–2	3–2	2–2	5–0	6–1	0–0	4–0	2–0	0–0	0–2	0–0	0–2	1–3	1–0	2–5	3–0	2–1	3–3	3–0	4–0	2–1	–	1–1
York City	2–0	1–0	2–2	1–1	3–1	2–1	1–0	0–2	0–0	1–1	0–0	3–2	1–1	2–1	0–1	2–2	0–0	1–3	2–1	2–0	3–1	4–3	1–1	–

Read across for home results, down for away

FINAL TABLES 2002-03

F.A. BARCLAYCARD PREMIERSHIP

			HOME					AWAY						
		P	W	D	L	F	A	W	D	L	F	A	Pts	GD
1	Manchester Utd.	38	16	2	1	42	12	9	6	4	32	22	83	+40
2	Arsenal	38	15	2	2	47	20	8	7	4	38	22	78	+43
3	Newcastle Utd.	38	15	2	2	36	17	6	4	9	27	31	69	+15
4	Chelsea	38	12	5	2	41	15	7	5	7	27	23	67	+30
5	Liverpool	38	9	8	2	30	16	9	2	8	31	25	64	+20
6	Blackburn Rov.	38	9	7	3	24	15	7	5	7	28	28	60	+9
7	Everton	38	11	5	3	28	19	6	3	10	20	30	59	–1
8	Southampton	38	9	8	2	25	16	4	5	10	18	30	52	–3
9	Manchester City	38	9	2	8	28	26	6	4	9	19	28	51	–7
10	Tottenham	38	9	4	6	30	29	5	4	10	21	33	50	–11
11	Middlesbrough	38	10	7	2	36	21	3	3	13	12	23	49	+4
12	Charlton Athletic	38	8	3	8	26	30	6	4	9	19	26	49	–11
13	Birmingham City	38	8	5	6	25	23	5	4	10	16	26	48	–8
14	Fulham	38	11	3	5	26	18	2	6	11	15	32	48	–9
15	Leeds Utd.	38	7	3	9	25	26	7	2	10	33	31	47	+1
16	Aston Villa	38	11	2	6	25	14	1	7	11	17	33	45	–5
17	Bolton Wand.	38	7	8	4	27	24	3	6	10	14	27	44	–10
18	West Ham Utd.	38	5	7	7	21	24	5	5	9	21	35	42	–17
19	W.B.A.	38	3	5	11	17	34	3	3	13	12	31	26	–36
20	Sunderland	38	3	2	14	11	31	1	5	13	10	34	19	–44

(Manchester Utd. and Arsenal go straight into the Champions League group stage; Newcastle Utd. and Chelsea into the third qualifying round. Liverpool, Blackburn Rov., Manchester City and Southampton go into the UEFA Cup.)

Prize-money: 1 £10.06m, 2 £9.55m, 3 £9.05m, 4 £8.55m, 5 £8.04m, 6 £7.54m, 7 £7.04m, 8 £6.53m, 9 £6.03m, 10 £5.53m, 11 £5.03m, 12 £4.52m, 13 £4.02m, 14 £3.52, 15 £3.01, 16 £2.51m, 17 £2.01m, 18 £1.50m, 19 £1.00m, 20 £503,000.
Biggest win: W.B.A. 0, Liverpool 6.
Highest attendance: 67,721 (Manchester Utd. v Charlton Athletic).
Lowest attendance: 14,017 (Fulham v Blackburn Rov.).
Manager of Year: Sir Alex Ferguson (Manchester Utd.).
Player of Year: Ruud van Nistelrooy (Manchester Utd.).
Golden Boot: 25 Ruud van Nistelrooy (Manchester Utd.).
Golden Glove: Carlo Cudicini (Chelsea).
Football Writers' Association Player of Year: Thierry Henry (Arsenal).
PFA Player of Year: Thierry Henry (Arsenal).
PFA Young Player of Year: Jermaine Jenas (Newcastle Utd.).
PFA divisional team: Friedel (Blackburn Rov.), Carr (Tottenham), Campbell (Arsenal), Gallas (Chelsea), Cole (Arsenal), Vieira (Arsenal), Scholes (Manchester Utd.), Pires (Arsenal), Dyer (Newcastle Utd.), Shearer (Newcastle Utd.), Henry (Arsenal).
Fair Play award: Manchester Utd.
Best Behaved Supporters' award: Manchester City.
Groundsman of Year: Roy Rigby (Manchester City).
Leading scorers (all club competitions): 44 Van Nistelrooy (Manchester Utd.); 32 Henry (Arsenal); 28 Owen (Liverpool); 25 Shearer (Newcastle Utd.); 24 Beattie (Southampton); 22 Viduka (Leeds Utd.); 20 Scholes (Manchester Utd.); 16 Kewell (Leeds Utd.), Pires (Arsenal), Zola (Chelsea); 15 Giggs (Manchester Utd.), Hasselbaink (Chelsea), Solskjaer (Manchester Utd.); 14 Anelka (Manchester City), Dublin (Aston Villa); 13 Cole (Blackburn Rov.), Keane (Tottenham), Malbranque (Fulham), Sheringham (Tottenham), Wiltord (Arsenal), Yorke (Blackburn Rov.).

NATIONWIDE LEAGUE

FIRST DIVISION

			HOME					AWAY						
		P	W	D	L	F	A	W	D	L	F	A	Pts	GD
1	Portsmouth	46	17	3	3	52	22	12	8	3	45	23	98	+52
2	Leicester City	46	16	5	2	40	12	10	9	4	33	28	92	+33
3	Sheffield Utd.	46	13	7	3	38	23	10	4	9	34	29	80	+20
4	Reading	46	13	3	7	33	21	12	1	10	28	25	79	+15
5	Wolves*	46	9	10	4	40	19	11	6	6	41	25	76	+37
6	Nott'm Forest	46	14	7	2	57	23	6	7	10	25	27	74	+32
7	Ipswich Town	46	10	5	8	49	39	9	8	6	31	25	70	+16
8	Norwich City	46	14	4	5	36	17	5	8	10	24	32	69	+11
9	Millwall	46	11	6	6	34	32	8	3	12	25	37	66	–10
10	Wimbledon	46	12	5	6	39	28	6	6	11	37	45	65	+3
11	Gillingham	46	10	6	7	33	31	6	8	9	23	34	62	–9
12	Preston N.E.	46	11	7	5	44	29	5	6	12	24	41	61	–2
13	Watford	46	11	5	7	33	26	6	4	13	21	44	60	–16
14	Crystal Palace	46	8	10	5	29	17	6	7	10	30	35	59	+7
15	Rotherham Utd.	46	8	9	6	27	25	7	5	11	35	37	59	0
16	Burnley	46	10	4	9	35	44	5	6	12	30	45	55	–24
17	Walsall	46	10	3	10	34	34	5	6	12	23	35	54	–12
18	Derby Co.	46	9	5	9	33	32	6	2	15	22	42	52	–19
19	Bradford City	46	7	8	8	27	35	7	2	14	24	38	52	–22
20	Coventry City	46	6	6	11	23	31	6	8	9	23	31	50	–16
21	Stoke City	46	9	6	8	25	25	3	8	12	20	44	50	–24
22	Sheffield Wed.	46	7	7	9	29	32	3	9	11	27	41	46	–17
23	Brighton & H.A.	46	7	6	10	29	31	4	6	13	20	36	45	–18
24	Grimsby Town	46	5	6	12	26	39	4	6	13	22	46	39	–37

(* Also promoted via play-offs)

Biggest win: Millwall 0, Rotherham Utd. 6; Nott'm Forest 6, Stoke City 0; Wolves 6, Gillingham 0.
Highest attendance: 33,016 (Derby Co. v Reading).
Lowest attendance: 849 (Wimbledon v Rotherham Utd.).
Top League scorer: 26 Svetoslav Todorov (Portsmouth).
Manager of Year: Harry Redknapp (Portsmouth).
PFA divisional team: Hislop (Portsmouth), Irwin (Wolves), Dawson (Nott'm Forest), Lescott (Wolves), Taylor (Portsmouth), Brown (Sheffield Utd.), Izzet (Leicester City), Merson (Portsmouth), Tonge (Sheffield Utd.), Johnson (Nott'm Forest), Dickov (Leicester City).
Fair Play award: Reading.
Groundsman of Year: Jonathan Calderwood (Wolves).
Leading scorers (all club competitions): 29 Johnson (Nott'm Forest); 26 Todorov (Portsmouth); 24 Connolly (Wimbledon), Miller (Wolves), Shipperley (Wimbledon); 22 Brown (Sheffield Utd.); 21 Counago (Ipswich Town), Harewood (Nott'm Forest); 20 Dickov (Leicester City); 18 Bent, D (Ipswich Town), Kabba (Sheffield Utd.) – 1 for Crystal Palace, 6 for Grimsby Town; 17 Forster (Reading), Taylor (Burnley); 16 Cresswell (Preston N.E.), Junior (Walsall), Lee (Rotherham Utd.); 15 Gray (Bradford City), McVeigh (Norwich City); 14 Johnson (Crystal Palace), Zamora (Brighton & H.A.).

SECOND DIVISION

			HOME					AWAY						
		P	W	D	L	F	A	W	D	L	F	A	Pts	GD
1	Wigan Athletic	46	14	7	2	37	16	15	6	2	31	9	100	+43
2	Crewe Alexandra	46	11	5	7	29	19	14	6	3	47	21	86	+36
3	Bristol City	46	15	5	3	43	15	9	6	8	36	33	83	+31
4	Q.P.R.	46	14	4	5	38	19	10	7	6	31	26	83	+24
5	Oldham Athletic	46	11	6	6	39	18	11	10	2	29	20	82	+30
6	Cardiff City*	46	12	6	5	33	20	11	6	6	35	23	81	+25
7	Tranmere Rov.	46	14	5	4	38	23	9	6	8	28	34	80	+9
8	Plymouth Argyle	46	11	6	6	39	24	6	8	9	24	28	65	+11
9	Luton Town	46	8	8	7	32	28	9	6	8	35	34	65	+5
10	Swindon Town	46	10	5	8	34	27	6	7	10	25	36	60	–4
11	Peterborough Utd.	46	8	7	8	25	20	6	9	8	26	34	58	–3
12	Colchester Utd.	46	8	7	8	24	24	6	9	8	28	32	58	–4
13	Blackpool	46	10	8	5	35	25	5	5	13	21	39	58	–8
14	Stockport Co.	46	8	8	7	39	38	7	2	14	26	32	55	–5
15	Notts Co.	46	10	7	6	37	32	3	9	11	25	38	55	–8
16	Brentford	46	8	8	7	28	21	6	4	13	19	35	54	–9
17	Port Vale	46	9	5	9	34	31	5	6	12	20	39	53	–16
18	Wycombe Wand.	46	8	7	8	39	38	5	6	12	20	28	52	–7
19	Barnsley	46	7	8	8	27	31	6	5	12	24	33	52	–13
20	Chesterfield	46	11	4	8	29	28	3	4	16	14	45	50	–30
21	Cheltenham Town	46	6	9	8	26	31	4	9	10	27	37	48	–15
22	Huddersfield Town	46	7	9	7	27	24	4	3	16	12	37	45	–22
23	Mansfield Town	46	9	2	12	38	45	3	6	14	28	52	44	–31
24	Northampton Town	46	7	4	12	23	31	3	5	15	17	48	39	–39

(* Also promoted via play-offs)

Biggest win: Brentford 5, Blackpool 0; Colchester Utd. 0, Luton Town 5; Mansfield Town 6, Tranmere Rov. 1; Mansfield Town 0, Crewe Alexandra 5; Northampton Town 0, Wycombe Wand. 5; Oldham Athletic 6, Mansfield Town 1; Plymouth Argyle 6, Peterborough Utd. 1; Swindon Town 5, Notts Co. 0.
Highest attendance: 18,085 (Bristol City v Plymouth Argyle).
Lowest attendance: 2,721 (Colchester Utd. v Wigan Athletic).
Top League scorer: 31 Robert Earnshaw (Cardiff City).
Manager of Year: Paul Jewell (Wigan Athletic).
PFA divisional team: Filan (Wigan Athletic), Eaden (Wigan Athletic), De Vos (Wigan Athletic), Hall (Oldham Athletic), Bell (Bristol City), Murray (Bristol City), Bullard (Wigan Athletic), Kavanagh (Cardiff City), Bullock (Blackpool), Earnshaw (Cardiff City), Hulse (Crewe Alexandra).
Fair Play award: Crewe Alexandra.
Groundsman of Year: Mike Heather (Cheltenham Town).
Leading scorers (all club competitions): 35 Earnshaw (Cardiff City); 29 Beckett (Stockport Co.); 27 Hulse (Crewe Alexandra), Murray (Bristol City); 26 Parkin (Swindon Town); 25 Stallard (Notts. Co.); 23 Howard (Luton Town); 22 Ellington (Wigan Athletic), Haworth (Tranmere Rov.); 19 Clarke (Peterborough Utd.), Christie (Mansfield Town); Murphy (Blackpool); 18 Dyer (Barnsley); 17 Roberts (Bristol City), Smith (Huddersfield Town); 16 Ashton (Crewe Alexandra), Eyres (Oldham Athletic), Liddell (Wigan Athletic), Taylor (Blackpool), Thorne (Cardiff City), Thorpe (Luton Town).

THIRD DIVISION

			HOME					AWAY						
		P	W	D	L	F	A	W	D	L	F	A	Pts	GD
1	Rushden & Diamonds	46	16	5	2	48	19	8	10	5	25	28	87	+26
2	Hartlepool Utd.	46	16	5	2	49	21	8	8	7	22	30	85	+20
3	Wrexham	46	12	7	4	48	26	11	8	4	36	24	84	+34
4	Bournemouth*	46	14	7	2	38	18	6	7	10	22	30	74	+12
5	Scunthorpe Utd.	46	11	8	4	40	20	8	7	8	28	29	72	+19
6	Lincoln City	46	10	9	4	29	18	8	7	8	17	19	70	+9
7	Bury	46	8	8	7	25	26	10	8	5	32	30	70	+1
8	Oxford Utd.	46	9	7	7	26	20	10	5	8	31	27	69	+10
9	Torquay Utd.	46	9	11	3	41	31	7	7	9	30	40	66	0
10	York City	46	11	9	3	34	24	6	6	11	18	29	66	–1
11	Kidderminster Harr.	46	8	8	7	30	33	8	7	8	32	30	63	–1
12	Cambridge Utd.	46	10	7	6	38	25	6	6	11	29	45	61	–3
13	Hull City	46	9	10	4	34	19	5	7	11	24	34	59	+5
14	Darlington	46	8	10	5	36	27	4	8	11	22	32	54	–1
15	Boston Utd.	46	11	6	6	34	22	4	7	12	21	34	54	–1
16	Macclesfield Town	46	8	6	9	29	28	6	6	11	28	35	54	–6
17	Southend Utd.	46	12	1	10	29	23	5	2	16	18	36	54	–12
18	Leyton Orient	46	9	6	8	28	24	5	5	13	23	37	53	–10
19	Rochdale	46	7	6	10	30	30	5	10	8	33	40	52	–7
20	Bristol Rov.	46	7	7	9	25	27	5	8	10	25	30	51	–7
21	Swansea City	46	9	6	8	28	25	3	7	13	20	40	49	–17
22	Carlisle	46	5	5	13	26	40	8	5	10	26	38	49	–26
23	Exeter City	46	7	7	9	24	31	4	8	11	26	33	48	–14
24	Shrewsbury Town	46	5	6	12	34	39	4	8	11	28	53	41	–30

(* Also promoted via play-offs)

Biggest win: Boston Utd. 6, Shrewsbury Town 0;
Highest attendance: 22,319 (Hull City v Hartlepool Utd.).
Lowest attendance: 1,576 (Macclesfield Town v Hartlepool Utd.).
Top League scorer: 34 Andy Morrell (Wrexham).
Manager of Year: Denis Smith (Wrexham).
PFA divisional team: Fettis (Hull City), Edwards (Wrexham), Lee (Hartlepool Utd.), Westwood (Hartlepool Utd.), Underwood (Rushden & Diamonds), Humphreys (Hartlepool Utd.), Tinkler (Hartlepool Utd.), Hall (Rushden & Diamonds), Russell (Torquay Utd.), Morrell (Wrexham), Kitson (Cambridge Utd.).
Fair Play Award: Hartlepool Utd.
Groundsman of Year: Dave Brown (Hartlepool Utd.)
Leading scorers (all club competitions): 35 Morrell (Wrexham); 25 Kitson (Cambridge Utd.); 21 Carruthers (Scunthorpe Utd.); 20 Henriksen (Kidderminster Harr.), Rodgers (Shrewsbury Town); 19 Duffield (Boston Utd.) – 15 for York City; 17 Conlon (Darlington), Jemson (Shrewsbury Town), Riza (Cambridge Utd.); 16 Devine (Exeter City) – 8 for Wycombe Wand., Gritton (Torquay Utd.), Hall (Rushden & Diamonds), Lowe (Rushden & Diamonds), Torpey (Scunthorpe Utd.), Williams (Hartlepool Utd.); 15 Graham (Torquay Utd.), McEvilly (Rochdale), Thomas (Swansea City).

NATIONWIDE LEAGUE PLAY-OFFS 2003

Wolves benefactor Sir Jack Hayward finally saw his £60m. investment pay dividends when the club he first supported as a boy returned to the top flight of English football after an absence of 19 years by beating Sheffield United 3-0 in the First Division Play-off Final. It was also a moment to savour for manager Dave Jones, who was forced to leave his previous club Southampton because of child abuse allegations – which were later found to be groundless – and who took on the task of trying to bring back the good times to Molineux.

Driven on from midfield by veteran Paul Ince, Wolves had a game many thought would be a tight, tense affair all tied up by half-time. Mark Kennedy's low drive from 20 yards came after six minutes; Ince flicked on Kennedy's corner for Nathan Blake to glance in after 22; Kenny Miller touched home Shaun Newton's cross on the stroke of half time.

United, whose manager Neil Warnock was sent from the dug-out for the second half for remonstrating too forcibly with referee Steve Bennett, had come back from two goals down to beat Nottingham Forest 4-3 in the second leg of the semi-finals. But this deficit was beyond them, Michael Brown wasting their one chance of a comeback with a penalty saved by Matt Murray after Paul Butler handled.

Cardiff City, away from the game's second tier for 18 years, also stepped back when substitute Andy Campbell settled a dour Division Two Final with the extra-time winner against Q.P.R. after a goalless 90 minutes. Campbell, who replaced leading scorer Robert Earnshaw, took a long pass from Gareth Whalley in his stride to finish with great aplomb as the clock showed 114 minutes.

Bournemouth, relegated 12 months earlier, became the first side to score five times in a play-off final when beating Lincoln City 5-2 in the Third Division decider. Lincoln boasted the season's best defensive record, but were twice caught out by headers by midfielder-turned-defender Carl Fletcher, who doubled his tally for the campaign, and were always chasing the game. Steve Fletcher, no relation, Steve Purches and Garreth O'Connor were also on the mark for Bournemouth, with 6ft 7in Ben Futcher and Mark Bailey replying.

In the first Conference Final to decide the newly-won second promotion place, an extra-time goal by Francis Tierney enabled Doncaster Rovers to return to the Football League after an absence of five seasons with a 3-2 victory over Dagenham & Redbridge at the Britannia Stadium.

SEMI-FINALS, FIRST LEGS

DIVISION 1

Nott'm. Forest 1 (Johnson 55), **Sheffield Utd.** 1 (Brown 58 pen). Att: 29,064. **Wolves** 2 (Murty 75 og, Naylor 84), **Reading** 1 (Forster 25). Att: 27,678.

DIVISION 2

Cardiff City 1 (Thorne 74), **Bristol City** 0. Att: 19,146. **Oldham Athletic** 1 (Eyres 28), **Q.P.R.** 1 (Langley 47). Att: 12,152.

DIVISION 3

Bury 0, **Bournemouth** 0. Att: 5,782. **Lincoln City** 5 (Weaver 15, Mayo 18, Smith 55, Yeo 82, 90), **Scunthorpe Utd.** 3 (Calvo-Garcia 26, 69, Stanton 70). Att: 8,902.

CONFERENCE

Dagenham & Redbridge 2 (Stein 7, 66 pen), **Morecambe** 1 (Shipp 29 og). Att: 3,447. **Doncaster Rov.** 1 (Whitman 90), **Chester City** 1 (McIntyre 37). Att: 6,857.

SEMI-FINALS, SECOND LEGS

DIVISION 1

Reading 0, **Wolves** 1 (Rae 81). Att: 24,060 (**Wolves** won 3-1 on agg). **Sheffield Utd.** 4 (Brown 60, Kabba 68, Peschisolido 112, Walker 117 og), **Nott'm. Forest** 3 (Johnson 30, Reid 58, Page 119 og). Att: 30,212 (aet, **Sheffield Utd.** won 5-4 on agg).

DIVISION 2

Bristol City 0, **Cardiff City** 0. Att: 16,307 (**Cardiff City** won 1-0 on agg). **Q.P.R.** 1 (Furlong 82), **Oldham Athletic** 0. Att: 17,201 (**Q.P.R.** won 2-1 on agg).

DIVISION 3

Bournemouth 3 (O'Connor 21, Hayter 38, 60), **Bury** 1 (Preece 67). Att: 7,945 (**Bournemouth** won 3-1 on agg). **Scunthorpe Utd.** 0, **Lincoln City** 1 (Yeo 88). Att: 8,295 (**Lincoln City** won 6-3 on agg).

CONFERENCE

Chester City 1 (Hatswell 31), **Doncaster Rov.** 1 (Barnes 57). Att: 5,702 (aet, **Doncaster Rov.** won 4-3 on pens). **Morecambe** 2 (West 50 og, Rigoglioso 86), **Dagenham & Redbridge** 1 (Terry 89). Att: 5,405 (aet, **Dagenham & Redbridge** won 3-2 on pens).

FINALS – MILLENNIUM STADIUM

DIVISION 1 – MAY 26, 2003

Sheffield Utd. 0, **Wolves** 3 (Kennedy 6, Blake 22, Miller 45). Att: 69,473.
Sheffield Utd. (4-4-2): Kenny, Curtis, Jagielka, Page, Kozluk, Ndlovu (Peschisolido 63), Rankine (McCall 46), Brown, Tonge, Asaba (Allison 73), Kabba. **Subs not used:** Kelly, Montgomery. **Booked:** Tonge, Brown. **Manager:** Neil Warnock.
Wolves (4-4-2): Murray, Irwin, Butler, Lescott, Naylor, Newton, Ince, Cameron, Kennedy, Blake (Proudlock 87), Miller (Sturridge 75). **Subs not used:** Oakes, Rae, Edworthy. **Booked:** Irwin. **Manager:** Dave Jones.
Referee: S.Bennett (Kent). **Half-time:** 0-3.

DIVISION 2 – MAY 25, 2003

Cardiff City 1 (Campbell 114), **Q.P.R.** 0. Att: 66,096 (aet).
Cardiff City (4-4-2): Alexander, Weston (Croft 70), Prior, Gabbidon, Barker, Boland, Kavanagh, Whalley, Legg (Bonner 115), Thorne, Earnshaw (Campbell 79). **Subs not used:** Margetson, Bowen. **Booked:** Kavanagh. **Manager:** Lennie Lawrence.
Q.P.R. (4-4-2): Day, Kelly, Carlisle, Shittu, Padula (Williams 80), Gallen, Bircham, Palmer, McLeod, Pacquette (Thomson 61), Furlong. **Subs not used:** Culkin, Forbes, Angell. **Booked:** Furlong, Palmer, Bircham. **Manager:** Ian Holloway.
Referee: H. Webb (South Yorks). **Half-time:** 0-0.

DIVISION 3 – MAY 24, 2003

Bournemouth 5 (S. Fletcher 29, C. Fletcher 45, 77, S. Purches 56, O'Connor 60), **Lincon City** 2 (Futcher 35, Bailey 75). Att: 32,148.
Bournemouth (4-4-2): Moss, Young, C. Fletcher, Gulliver, Cummings, Elliott (Thomas 90), Browning, S. Purches, O'Connor (Stock 80), Hayter, S. Fletcher (Holmes 85). **Subs not used:** Stewart, McDonald. **Manager:** Sean O'Driscoll.
Lincoln City (3-4-3): Marriott, Weaver, Morgan, Futcher, Bailey, Gain, Butcher, Bimson (Connelly 57), Smith (Yeo 50), Cropper (Willis 73), Mayo. **Subs not used:** Sedgemore, Bloomer. **Booked:** Weaver, Morgan. **Manager:** Keith Alexander.
Referee: A. Kaye (West Yorks). **Half-time:** 2-1.

FINAL – BRITANNIA STADIUM

CONFERENCE – MAY 10, 2003

Dagenham & Redbridge 2 (Stein 63, Mustafa 78), **Doncaster Rov.** 3 (Green 39, Morley 55, Tierney 110). Att: 13,092 (aet).
Dagenham & Redbridge (4-4-2): Roberts, Mustafa, Cole, Matthews, Goodwin (Smith 69), Janney, Shipp, Terry (Heffer 93), McGrath (Vickers 69), Stein, West. **Subs not used:** Gothard, Hill. **Booked:** McGrath, Matthews, Smith. **Manager:** Garry Hill.
Doncaster Rov. (4-4-2): Warrington, Marples, Morley, Foster, Ryan, Paterson (Blunt 81), Green, Ravenhill, Tierney, Barnes, Whitman (Blundell 81). **Subs not used:** Nelson, Doolan, Albrighton. **Booked:** Ryan, Ravenhill. **Manager:** Dave Penney.
Referee: A Marriner (Birmingham). **Half-time:** 0-1

PLAY-OFF FINALS – HOME & AWAY

1987 Divs. 1/2: **Charlton Athletic** beat Leeds Utd. 2-1 in replay (Birmingham City) after 1-1 agg (1-0h, 0-1a). Charlton Athletic remained in Div. 1. Losing semi-finalists: Ipswich Town and Oldham Athletic. **Divs. 2/3**: **Swindon Town** beat Gillingham 2-0 in replay (Crystal Palace) after 2-2 agg (0-1a, 2-1h). Swindon Town promoted to Div. 2. Losing semi-finalists: Sunderland and Wigan Athletic; Sunderland relegated to Div. 3. **Divs. 3/4**: **Aldershot** beat Wolves 3-0 on agg (2-0h, 1-0a) and promoted to Div. 3. Losing semi-finalists: Bolton Wand. and Colchester Utd.; Bolton Wand. relegated to Div.4.

1988 Divs. 1/2: **Middlesbrough** beat Chelsea 2-1 on agg (2-0h, 0-1a) and promoted to Div. 1; Chelsea relegated to Div. 2. Losing semi-finalists: Blackburn Rov. and Bradford City. **Divs. 2/3**: **Walsall** beat Bristol City 4-0 in replay (h) after 3-3 agg (3-1a, 0-2h) and promoted to Div. 2. Losing semi-finalists: Sheffield Utd. and Notts Co; Sheffield Utd. relegated to Div. 3. **Divs. 3/4**: **Swansea City** beat Torquay Utd. 5-4 on agg (2-1h, 3-3a) and promoted to Div. 3. Losing semi-finalists: Rotherham Utd. and Scunthorpe Utd.; Rotherham Utd. relegated to Div.4.

1989 Div. 2: **Crystal Palace** beat Blackburn Rov. 4-3 on agg (1-3a, 3-0h). Losing semi-finalists: Watford and Swindon Town. **Div. 3**: **Port Vale** beat Bristol Rov. 2-1 on agg (1-1a, 1-0h). Losing semi-finalists: Fulham and Preston N.E. **Div.4**: **Leyton Orient** beat Wrexham 2-1 on agg (0-0a, 2-1h). Losing semi-finalists: Scarborough and Scunthorpe Utd.

PLAY-OFF FINALS AT WEMBLEY

1990 Div. 2: **Swindon Town** 1, Sunderland 0 (att: 72,873). Swindon Town promoted, then demoted for financial irregularities; Sunderland promoted. Losing semi-finalists: Blackburn Rov. and Newcastle Utd. **Div. 3**: **Notts Co.** 2, Tranmere Rov. 0 (att: 29,252). Losing semi-finalists: Bolton Wand. and Bury. **Div.4**: **Cambridge Utd.** 1, Chesterfield 0 (att: 26,404). Losing semi-finalists: Maidstone and Stockport Co.

1991 Div. 2: **Notts Co.** 3, Brighton & H.A. 1 (att: 59,940). Losing semi-finalists: Middlesbrough and Millwall. **Div. 3**: **Tranmere Rov.** 1, Bolton Wand. 0 (att: 30,217). Losing semi-finalists: Brentford and Bury. **Div.4**: **Torquay Utd.** 2, Blackpool 2 – Torquay Utd. won 5-4 on pens (att: 21,615). Losing semi-finalists: Burnley and Scunthorpe Utd.

1992 Div. 2: **Blackburn Rov.** 1, Leicester City 0 (att: 68,147). Losing semi-finalists: Derby Co. and Cambridge Utd. **Div. 3**: **Peterborough Utd.** 2, Stockport Co. 1 (att: 35,087). Losing semi-finalists: Huddersfield Town and Stoke City. **Div.4**: **Blackpool** 1, Scunthorpe Utd. 1 – Blackpool won 4-3 on pens (att: 22,741). Losing semi-finalists: Barnet and Crewe Alexandra.

1993 Div. 1; **Swindon Town** 4, Leicester City 3 (att: 73,802). Losing semi-finalists: Portsmouth and Tranmere Rov. **Div. 2**: **W.B.A.** 3, Port Vale 0 (att: 53,471). Losing semi-finalists: Stockport Co. and Swansea City. **Div. 3**: **York City** 1, Crewe Alexandra 1 – York City won 5-3 on pens (att: 22,416). Losing semi-finalists: Bury and Walsall.

1994 Div. 1: **Leicester City** 2, Derby Co. 1 (att: 73,671). Losing semi-finalists: Millwall and Tranmere Rov. **Div. 2**: **Burnley** 2, Stockport Co. 1 (att: 44,806). Losing semi-finalists: Plymouth Argyle and York City. **Div. 3**: **Wycombe Wand.** 4, Preston N.E. 2 (att: 40,109). Losing semi-finalists: Carlisle Utd. and Torquay Utd.

1995 Div. 1: **Bolton Wand.** 4, Reading 3 (att: 64,107). Losing semi-finalists: Tranmere Rov. and Wolves. **Div. 2**: **Huddersfield Town** 2, Bristol Rov. 1 (att: 59,175). Losing semi-finalists: Brentford and Crewe Alexandra. **Div. 3**: **Chesterfield** 2, Bury 0 (att: 22,814). Losing semi-finalists: Mansfield Town and Preston N.E.

1996 Div. 1: **Leicester City** 2, Crystal Palace 1, aet (att: 73,573). Losing semi-finalists: Charlton Athletic and Stoke City. **Div. 2**: **Bradford City** 2, Notts Co. 0 (att: 39,972). Losing semi-finalists: Blackpool and Crewe Alexandra. **Div. 3**: **Plymouth Argyle** 1, Darlington 0 (att: 43,431). Losing semi-finalists: Colchester Utd. and Hereford.

1997 Div. 1: **Crystal Palace** 1, Sheffield Utd. 0, (att: 64,383). Losing semi-finalists: Ipswich Town and Wolves. **Div. 2**: **Crewe Alexandra** 1, Brentford 0 (att: 34,149). Losing semi-finalists: Bristol City and Luton Town. **Div. 3**: **Northampton Town** 1, Swansea City 0 (att: 46,804). Losing semi-finalists: Cardiff City and Chester City.

1998 Div. 1: Charlton Athletic 4, Sunderland 4, aet Charlton Athletic won 7-6 on pens. (att: 77, 739). Losing semi-finalists: Ipswich Town and Sheffield United. **Div. 2: Grimsby Town** 1, Northampton Town 0 (att: 62,988). Losing semi-finalists: Bristol Rov. and Fulham. **Div. 3: Colchester Utd.** 1, Torquay Utd. 0 (att: 19,486). Losing semi-finalists: Barnet and Scarborough.

1999 Div. 1: Watford 2, Bolton Wand. 0, (att. 70,343). Losing semi-finalists: Ipswich Town and Birmingham City. **Div. 2: Manchester City** 2, Gillingham 2, aet Manchester City won 3-1 on pens. (att. 76,935). Losing semi-finalists: Preston N.E. and Wigan Athletic. **Div. 3: Scunthorpe Utd.** 1, Leyton Orient 0, (att. 36,985). Losing semi-finalists: Rotherham Utd. and Swansea City.

2000 Div. 1: Ipswich Town 4, Barnsley 2 (att: 73,427). Losing semi-finalists: Birmingham City and Bolton Wand. **Div. 2: Gillingham** 3, Wigan Athletic 2, aet (att: 53,764). Losing semi-finalists: Millwall and Stoke City. **Div. 3: Peterborough Utd.** 1, Darlington 0 (att: 33,383). Losing semi-finalists: Barnet and Hartlepool Utd.

PLAY-OFF FINALS AT MILLENNIUM STADIUM

2001 Div. 1: Bolton Wand. 3, Preston N.E. 0 (att: 54,328). Losing semi-finalists: Birmingham City and W.B.A. **Div. 2: Walsall** 3, Reading 2, aet (att: 50,496). Losing semi-finalists: Stoke City and Wigan Athletic. **Div. 3: Blackpool** 4, Leyton Orient 2 (att: 23,600). Losing semi-finalists: Hartlepool Utd. and Hull City.

2002 Div 1: Birmingham City 1, Norwich City 1, aet Birmingham City won 4-2 on pens. (att: 71,597). Losing semi-finalists: Millwall and Wolves. **Div 2: Stoke City** 2, Brentford 0 (att: 42,523). Losing semi-finalists: Cardiff City and Huddersfield Town. **Div 3: Cheltenham Town** 3, Rushden & Diamonds 1 (att: 24,368). Losing semi-finalists: Hartlepool Utd. and Rochdale.

HISTORY OF THE PLAY-OFFS

Play-off matches were introduced by the Football League to decide final promotion and relegation issues at the end of season 1986-87.

A similar series styled "Test Matches" had operated between Divisions One and Two for six seasons from 1893-98, and was abolished when both divisions were increased from 16 to 18 clubs.

Eighty-eight years later, the play-offs were back in vogue. In the first three seasons (1987-88-89), the Finals were played home-and-away, and since they were made one-off matches in 1990, they have featured regularly in Wembley's spring calendar, until the old stadium closed its doors and the action switched to the Millennium Stadium in Cardiff in 2001.

Through the years, these have been the ups and downs of the play-offs:

1987 Initially, the 12 clubs involved comprised the one that finished directly above those relegated in Divisions One, Two and Three and the three who followed the sides automatically promoted in each section. Two of the home-and-away Finals went to neutral-ground replays, in which **Charlton Athletic** clung to First Division status by denying Leeds Utd. promotion while **Swindon Town** beat Gillingham to complete their climb from Fourth Division to Second in successive seasons, via the play-offs, Sunderland fell into the Third and Bolton Wand. into Division Four, both for the first time. **Aldershot** went up after finishing only sixth in Division Four; in their Final, they beat Wolves, who had finished nine points higher and missed automatic promotion by one point.

1988 Chelsea were relegated from the First Division after losing on aggregate to **Middlesbrough**, who had finished third in Division Two. So Middlesbrough, managed by Bruce Rioch, completed the rise from Third Division to First in successive seasons, only two years after their very existence had been threatened by the bailiffs. Also promoted via the play-offs: **Walsall** from Division Three and **Swansea City** from the Fourth. Relegated, besides Chelsea: Sheffield Utd. (to Division Three) and Rotherham Utd. (to Division Four).

1989 After two seasons of promotion-relegation play-offs, the system was changed to involve the four clubs who had just missed automatic promotion. That format has remained. Steve Coppell's **Crystal Palace**, third in Division Two, returned to the top flight after eight years, beating Blackburn Rov. 4-3 on aggregate after extra time. Similarly, **Port Vale** confirmed third place in Division Three with promotion via the play-offs. For **Leyton Orient**, promotion seemed out of the question in Division Four when they stood 15th. on March 1. But eight wins and a draw in the last nine home games swept them to sixth in the final table, and two more home victories in the play-offs completed their season in triumph.

1990 The play-off Finals now moved to Wembley over three days of the Spring Holiday week-end. On successive afternoons, **Cambridge Utd.** won promotion from Division Four and **Notts County** from the Third. Then, on Bank Holiday Monday, the biggest crowd for years at a Football League fixture (72,873) saw Ossie Ardiles' **Swindon Town** beat Sunderland 1-0 to reach the First Division for the first time. A few weeks later, however, Wembley losers **Sunderland** were promoted instead, by default; Swindon were found guilty of "financial irregularities" and stayed in Division Two.

1991 Again, the season's biggest League crowd (59,940) gathered at Wembley for the First Division Final in which **Notts Co.** (having missed promotion by one point) still fulfilled their ambition, beating Brighton & H.A. 3-1. In successive years, County had climbed from Third Division to First via the play-offs – the first club to achieve double promotion by this route. Bolton Wand. were denied automatic promotion in Division Three on goal difference, and lost at Wembley to an extra-time goal by **Tranmere Rov.** The Fourth Division Final made history, with Blackpool beaten 5-4 on penalties by

Torquay Utd. – first instance of promotion being decided by a shoot-out. In the table, Blackpool had finished seven points ahead of Torquay.

1992 Wembley that Spring Bank Holiday was the turning point in the history of **Blackburn Rov**. Bolstered by Kenny Dalglish's return to management and owner Jack Walker's millions, they beat Leicester City 1-0 by Mike Newell's 45th-minute penalty to achieve their objective – a place in the new Premier League. Newell, who also missed a second-half penalty, had recovered from a broken leg just in time for the play-offs. In the Fourth Division Final **Blackpool** (denied by penalties the previous year) this time won a shoot-out 4-3 against Scunthorpe Utd., who were unlucky in the play-offs for the fourth time in five years. **Peterborough Utd.** climbed out of the Third Division for the first time, beating Stockport Co. 2-1 at Wembley.

1993 The crowd of 73,802 at Wembley to see **Swindon Town** beat Leicester City 4-3 in the First Division Final was 11,000 bigger than that for the F.A. Cup Final replay between Arsenal and Sheffield Wed. Leicester rallied from three down to 3-3 before Paul Bodin's late penalty wiped away Swindon Town's bitter memories of three years earlier, when they were denied promotion after winning at Wembley. In the Third Division Final, **York City** beat Crewe Alexandra 5-3 in a shoot-out after a 1-1 draw, and in the Second Division decider, **W.B.A.** beat Port Vale 3-0. That was tough on Vale, who had finished third in the table with 89 points – the highest total never to earn promotion in any division. They had beaten Albion twice in the League, too.

1994 Wembley's record turn-out of 158,586 spectators at the three Finals started with a crowd of 40,109 to see Martin O'Neill's **Wycombe Wand.** beat Preston N.E. 4-2. They thus climbed from Conference to Second Division with successive promotions. **Burnley**'s 2-1 victory in the Second Division Final was marred by the sending-off of two Stockport Co. players, and in the First Division decider **Leicester City** came from behind to beat Derby Co. and end the worst Wembley record of any club. They had lost on all six previous appearances there – four times in the F.A. Cup Final and in the play-offs of 1992 and 1993.

1995 Two months after losing the Coca-Cola Cup Final to Liverpool, Bruce Rioch's **Bolton Wand.** were back at Wembley for the First Division play-off Final. From two goals down to Reading in front of a crowd of 64,107, they returned to the top company after 15 years, winning 4-3 with two extra-time goals. **Huddersfield Town** ended the first season at their new £15m. home with promotion to the First Division via a 2-1 victory against Bristol Rov. – manager Neil Warnock's third play-off success (after two with Notts Co.). Of the three clubs who missed automatic promotion by one place, only **Chesterfield** achieved it in the play-offs, comfortably beating Bury 2-0.

1996 Under new manager **Martin O'Neill** (a Wembley play-off winner with Wycombe Wand. in 1994), **Leicester City** returned to the Premiership a year after leaving it. They had finished fifth in the table, but in the Final came from behind to beat third-placed Crystal Palace by Steve Claridge's shot in the last seconds of extra time. In the Second Division **Bradford City** came sixth, nine points behind Blackpool (3rd), but beat them (from two down in the semi-final first leg) and then clinched promotion by 2-0 v Notts Co. at Wembley. It was City's greatest day since they won the Cup in 1911. **Plymouth Argyle** beat Darlington in the Third Division Final to earn promotion a year after being relegated. It was manager Neil Warnock's fourth play-off triumph in seven seasons after two with Notts Co. (1990 and 1991) and a third with Huddersfield Town in 1995.

1997 High drama at Wembley as **Crystal Palace** left it late against Sheffield Utd. in the First Division play-off final. The match was scoreless until the last 10 seconds when David Hopkin lobbed Blades' keeper Simon Tracey from 25 yards to send the Eagles back to the Premiership after two seasons of Nationwide action. In the Second Division play-off final, **Crewe Alexandra** beat Brentford 1-0 courtesy of a Shaun Smith goal.

Northampton Town celebrated their first Wembley appearance with a 1-0 victory over Swansea City thanks to John Frain's injury-time free-kick in the Third Division play-off final.

1998 In one of the finest games ever seen at Wembley, **Charlton Athletic** eventually triumphed 7-6 on penalties over Sunderland. For Charlton Athletic, Wearside-born Clive Mendonca scored a hat-trick and Richard Rufus his first career goal in a match that lurched between joy and despair for both sides as it ended 4-4. Sunderland defender Michael Gray's superb performance ill deserved to end with his weakly struck spot kick being saved by Sasa Ilic. In the Third Division, the penalty spot also had a role to play, as **Colchester Utd.**'s David Gregory scored the only goal to defeat Torquay Utd., while in the Second Division a Kevin Donovan goal gave **Grimsby Town** victory over Northampton Town.

1999: Elton John, watching via a personal satellite link in Seattle, saw his **Watford** side overcome Bolton Wand. 2-0 to reach the Premiership. Against technically superior opponents, Watford prevailed with application and teamwork. They also gave Bolton a lesson in finishing through match-winners by Nick Wright and Allan Smart. **Manchester City** staged a remakarble comeback to win the Second Division Final after trailing to goals by Carl Asaba and Robert Taylor for Gillingham. Kevin Horlock and Paul Dickov scored in stoppage time and City went on to win on penalties. A goal by Spaniard Alex Calvo-Garcia earned **Scunthorpe Utd.** a 1-0 success against Leyton Orient in the Third Division Final.

2000: After three successive play-off failures, **Ipswich Town** finally secured a place in the Premiership. They overcame the injury loss of leading scorer David Johnson to beat Barnsley 4-2 with goals by 36-year-old Tony Mowbray, Marcus Stewart and substitutes Richard Naylor and Martijn Reuser. With six minutes left of extra-time in the Second Division Final, **Gillingham** trailed Wigan Athletic 2-1. But headers by 38-year-old player-coach Steve Butler and fellow substitute Andy Thomson gave them a 3-2 victory. Andy Clarke, approaching his 33rd birthday, scored the only goal of the Third Division decider for **Peterborough Utd.** against Darlington.

2001: Bolton Wand., unsuccessful play-off contenders in the two previous seasons, made no mistake at the third attempt. They flourished in the new surroundings of the Millennium Stadium to beat Preston N.E. 3-0 with goals by Gareth Farrelly, Michael Ricketts – his 24th of the season – and Ricardo Gardner to reach the Premiership. **Walsall**, relegated 12 months earlier, scored twice in a three-minute spell of extra time to win 3-2 against Reading in the Second Division Final, while **Blackpool** capped a marked improvement in the second half of the season by overcoming Leyton Orient 4-2 in the Third Division Final.

2002: Holding their nerve to win a penalty shoot-out 4-2, **Birmingham City** wiped away the memory of three successive defeats in the semi-finals of the play-offs to return to the top division after an absence of 16 years. Substitue Darren Carter completed a fairy-tale first season as a professional by scoring the fourth spot-kick against Norwich City. **Stoke City** became the first successful team to come from the south dressing room in 12 finals since football was adopted by the home of Welsh rugby, beating Brentford 2-0 in the Second Division Final with Deon Burton's strike and a Ben Burgess own goal. Julian Alsop's 26th goal of the season helped **Cheltenham Town** defeat League newcomers Rushden & Diamonds 3-1 in the Third Division decider.

PLAY-OFF CROWDS YEAR BY YEAR

YEAR	MATCHES	AGG. ATT.
1987	20	310,000
1988	19	305,817
1989	18	234,393
1990	15	291,428
1991	15	266,442
1992	15	277,684
1993	15	319,907
1994	15	314,817
1995	15	295,317
1996	15	308,515
1997	15	309,085
1998	15	320,795
1999	15	372,969
2000	15	333,999
2001	15	317,745
2002	15	327,894
2003	15	374,461
	267	5,281,268

QUOTE-UNQUOTE

'He's like a speedboat with no driver' – **Andy Townsend**, ITV pundit, on Manchester City's Darren Huckerby.

'I'd rather buy a Bob the Builder CD for my two-year-old son' – **Jason McAteer**, Republic of Ireland player, on Roy Keane's controversial autobiography.

'It's my belief that the football bubble has burst . . . . . . for greedy, short-term agents and greedy short-term players and I, for one, am pleased about that. There are people out there with bloody noses and there are one or two old scores being settled in the game' – **Steve Gibson**, Middlesbrough chairman, on the game's financial crisis.

'It's the young players I feel sorry for, like Jobi McAnuff. He'd be bringing the house down, if there was a house to bring down' – **Neil Shipperley**, Wimbledon captain, on dwindling gates at Selhurst Park.

'I said to him: "You have had a drop of rain on you. Now you must make sure you are not caught in a big shower" ' – **Claudio Ranieri**, Chelsea manager, after defender John Terry was acquitted of affray.

'Some of them don't know a ball from a banana' – **John Lambie**, Partick Thistle manager, on players' agents.

'That's a word you don't hear around training grounds any more . . . mortgage' – **Niall Quinn**, Sunderland stalwart, on today's high earners.

'At least we have made the country happy. When you are dominating a competition like Michael Schumacher dominates F1, everybody wants to see someone else win' – **Arsene Wenger** after his Arsenal team suffered four successive defeats.

'Thursday nights are for taking the wife out to dinner' – **Graeme Souness**, Blackburn Rovers manager, calling for UEFA Cup ties to be moved to Wednesday.

LEAGUE CLUB MANAGERS

Figure in brackets = number of managerial changes at club since the War.
Date present manager took over shown on right.
Dario Gradi, appointed by Crewe Alexandra in June, 1983, currently has the longest service with one club.

F.A. BARCLAYCARD PREMIERSHIP

Arsenal (11)	Arsene Wenger	October 1996
Aston Villa (18)	David O'Leary	May 2003
Birmingham City (21)	Steve Bruce	December 2001
Blackburn Rov. (21)	Graeme Souness	March 2000
Bolton Wand. (17)	Sam Allardyce	October 1999
Charlton Athletic (12)	Alan Curbishley	July 1991
Chelsea (18)	Claudio Ranieri	September 2000
Everton (16)	David Moyes	March 2002
Fulham (23)	Chris Coleman	May 2003
Leeds Utd. (19)	Peter Reid	May 2003
Leicester City (18)	Micky Adams	April 2002
Liverpool (9)	Gerard Houllier †	July 1998
Manchester City (24)	Kevin Keegan	May 2001
Manchester Utd. (8)	Sir Alex Ferguson	November 1986
Middlesbrough (16)	Steve McClaren	June 2001
Newcastle Utd. (17)	Sir Bobby Robson	September 1999
Portsmouth (21)	Harry Redknapp	March 2002
Southampton (14)	Gordon Strachan	October 2001
Tottenham (16)	Glenn Hoddle	March 2001
Wolves (18)	Dave Jones	January 2001

(† Joint manager until Roy Evans resigned in November 1998).

NATIONWIDE LEAGUE – FIRST DIVISION

Bradford City (26)	Nicky Law	December 2001
Burnley (19)	Stan Ternent	June 1998
Cardiff City (25)	Lennie Lawrence	February 2002
Coventry City (23)	Gary McAllister	April 2002
Crystal Palace (30)	Steve Kember	May 2003
Crewe Alexandra (17)	Dario Gradi	June 1983
Derby Co. (17)	George Burley	June 2003
Gillingham (16)	Andy Hessenthaler	June 2000
Ipswich Town (9)	Joe Royle	October 2002
Millwall (21)	Mark McGhee	September 2000
Norwich City (21)	Nigel Worthington	January 2001
Nott'm. Forest (12)	Paul Hart	July 2001
Preston N.E. (21)	Craig Brown	April 2002
Reading (15)	Alan Pardew	October 1999
Rotherham Utd. (18)	Ronnie Moore	May 1997
Sheffield Utd. (29)	Neil Warnock	December 1999
Stoke City (20)	Tony Pulis	November 2002
Sunderland (19)	Mick McCarthy	March 2003
Walsall (27)	Colin Lee	January 2002
Watford (23)	Ray Lewington	July 2002
W.B.A. (24)	Gary Megson	March 2000
West Ham Utd. (8)	Glenn Roeder	June 2001
Wigan Athletic (15)	Paul Jewell	June 2001
Wimbledon (10)	Stuart Murdoch	June 2002

(Number of changes since elected to Football League: Wimbledon 1977; Wigan Athletic 1978).

SECOND DIVISION

Barnsley (15)	Glyn Hodges	October 2002
Blackpool (21)	Steve McMahon	January 2000
Bournemouth (18)	Sean O'Driscoll	August 2000
Brentford (24)	Wally Downes	June 2002
Brighton & H.A. (25)	Steve Coppell	October 2002
Bristol City (18)	Danny Wilson	June 2000
Chesterfield (16)	Roy McFarland	May 2003
Colchester Utd. (20)	Phil Parkinson	February 2003
Grimsby Town (25)	Paul Groves	December 2001
Hartlepool Utd. (27)	Neale Cooper	June 2003
Luton Town (19)	Mike Newell	June 2003
Notts Co. (25)	Bill Dearden	January 2002
Oldham Athletic (19)	Iain Dowie	May 2002
Peterborough Utd. (20)	Barry Fry	May 1996
Plymouth Argyle (25)	Paul Sturrock	October 2000
Port Vale (17)	Brian Horton	January 1999
Q.P.R. (21)	Ian Holloway	February 2001
Rushden & Diamonds (–)	Brian Talbot	April 1997
Sheffield Wed. (22)	Chris Turner	November 2002
Stockport Co. (29)	Carlton Palmer	November 2001
Swindon Town (20)	Andy King	December 2001
Tranmere Rov. (15)	Ray Mathias	September 2002
Wrexham (17)	Denis Smith	October 2001
Wycombe Wand. (4)	Lawrie Sanchez	February 1999

(Number of changes since elected to Football League: Peterborough Utd. 1960; Wycombe Wand. 1993; Rushden & Diamonds 2001).

THIRD DIVISION

Boston Utd. (1)	Neil Thompson	October 2002
Bristol Rov. (20)	Ray Graydon	April 2002
Bury (19)	Andy Preece	December 2000
Cambridge Utd. (13)	John Taylor	January 2002
Carlisle Utd. Utd (27)	Roddy Collins†	July 2002
Cheltenham Town (2)	Bobby Gould	January 2003
Darlington (29)	Mick Tait	June 2003
Doncaster Rov. (–)	Dave Penney	January 2002
Huddersfield Town (21)	Peter Jackson	June 2003
Hull City (21)	Peter Taylor	October 2002
Kidderminster Harr. (1)	Ian Britton	April 2002
Leyton Orient (19)	Paul Brush	October 2001
Lincoln City (23)	Keith Alexander	May 2002
Macclesfield Town (3)	David Moss	November 2001
Mansfield Town (22)	Keith Curle	December 2002
Northampton Town (24)	Martin Wilkinson	February 2003
Oxford Utd. (17)	Ian Atkins	November 2001
Rochdale (27)	Alan Buckley	June 2003
Scunthorpe Utd. (21)	Brian Laws	February 1997
Southend Utd. (25)	Steve Wignall	April 2003
Swansea City (26)	Brian Flynn	October 2002
Torquay Utd. (28)	Leroy Rosenior	May 2002
Yeovil Town (–)	Gary Johnson	June 2001
York City (19)	Chris Brass	June 2003

† Second spell at the club. (Number of changes since elected to Football League: Oxford Utd. 1962; Macclesfield Town 1997; Kidderminster Harr. 2000; Cheltenham Town 1999; Boston Utd. 2002; Yeovil Town 2003; since Doncaster Rov. returned to League 2003).

OTHER COMPETITIONS 2002-03

LDV VANS TROPHY

FIRST ROUND

Northern: Chesterfield 2, Halifax Town 0; Lincoln City 4, York City 3; Mansfield Town 0, Crewe Alexandra 4; Notts Co. 2, Wigan Athletic 3; Oldham Athletic 3, Carlisle Utd. 4 (aet, golden goal); Port Vale 3, Hull City 1; Rochdale 0, Bury 1; Scarborough 1, Doncaster Rov. 2 (aet, golden goal); Scunthorpe Utd. 2, Blackpool 3; Shrewsbury Town 3, Morecambe 0; Southport 3, Leigh RMI 4; Stockport Co. 1, Darlington 0; Tranmere Rov. 5, Hartlepool Utd. 0; Wrexham 2, Huddersfield Town 1.
Southern: Boston Utd. 4, Yeovil Town 2; Cambridge Utd. 4, Rushden & Diamonds 0; Cheltenham Town 4, Colchester Utd. 1; Chester City 1, Plymouth Argyle 2; Dagenham & Redbridge 1, Kidderminster Harr. 3; Exeter City 1, Bristol Rov. 0; Hereford Utd. 3, Northampton Town 4 (aet, golden goal); Leyton Orient 3, Peterborough Utd. 2; Oxford Utd. 2, Bournemouth 3; Q.P.R. 0, Bristol City 0 (aet, Bristol City won 5-4 on pens); Stevenage Borough 2, Swansea City 1; Swindon Town 6, Southend Utd. 1; Torquay Utd. 0, Wycombe Wand. 4; Woking 0, Luton Town 2.

SECOND ROUND

Northern: Bury 1, Barnsley 0; Carlisle Utd. 1, Stockport Co. 0 (aet, golden goal); Crewe Alexandra 2, Blackpool 0; Leigh RMI 3, Wrexham 4 (aet, golden goal); Lincoln City 1, Shrewsbury Town 2 (aet, golden goal); Macclesfield Town 1, Tranmere Rov. 2 (aet, golden goal); Port Vale 1, Chesterfield 1 (aet, Port Vale won 4-3 on pens); Wigan Athletic 0, Doncaster Rov. 1.
Southern: Boston Utd. 1, Bristol City 2 (aet, golden goal); Bournemouth 1, Leyton Orient 0; Cheltenham Town 1, Wycombe Wand. 2 (aet, golden goal); Exeter City 0, Cardiff City 3; Kidderminster Harr. 3, Swindon Town 2 (aet, golden goal); Northampton Town 2, Cambridge Utd. 4; Plymouth Argyle 0, Brentford 1; Stevenage Borough 3, Luton Town 4.

QUARTER-FINALS

Northern: Bury 2, Tranmere Rov. 0; Carlisle Utd. 2, Wrexham 0; Crewe Alexandra 8, Doncaster Rov. 0; Shrewsbury Town 2, Port Vale 1 (aet, golden goal).
Southern: Bournemouth 2, Cardiff City 1 (aet, golden goal); Brentford 2, Kidderminster Harr. 1; Bristol City 3, Wycombe Wand. 0; Luton Town 1, Cambridge Utd. 2 (aet, golden goal).

SEMI-FINALS

Northern: Carlisle Utd. 3, Bury 2; Shrewsbury Town 4, Crewe Alexandra 2.
Southern: Bournemouth 1, Bristol City 3; Brentford 1, Cambridge Utd. 2

AREA FINALS

Northern first leg: Carlisle Utd. 1 (Rundle 23), Shrewsbury Town 0. Att: 5,163. **Second leg:** Shrewsbury Town 0, Carlisle Utd. 0. Att: 6,273 (Carlisle Utd. won 1-0 on agg).
Southern first leg: Bristol City 4 (Doherty 21, Burnell 64, Murray 67, Robins 77), Cambridge Utd. 2 (Kitson 34, 54). Att: 7,173. **Second leg:** Cambridge Utd. 0, Bristol City 3 (Carey 11, Murray 45, Roberts 80). Att: 3,956 (Bristol City won 7-2 on agg).

FINAL

BRISTOL CITY 2, CARLISLE UNITED 0

Millennium Stadium, (50,913), Sunday, April 6, 2003

Bristol City (4-4-2): Phillips, Carey, Butler, Coles, Bell (Hill 85), Murray, Burnell, Doherty, Tinnion (Brown 80), Peacock, Roberts (Rosenior 62). **Subs not used:** Stowell, Beadle. **Scorers:** Peacock (78), Rosenior (89). **Booked:** Burnell, Tinnion. **Manager:** Danny Wilson.

Carlisle Utd. (4-4-2): Glennon, Shelley, Kelly (Maddison 80), Raven, Murphy, McCarthy, Green, Summerbell (McDonagh 85), Rundle, Farrell (Wake 75), Foran. **Subs not used:** Russell, McGill. **Booked:** Kelly, Foran. **Manager:** Roddy Collins.

Referee: P. Walton (Northamptonshire). **Half-time:** 0-0.

FINALS – RESULTS

Associated Members' Cup
1984 (Hull City) Bournemouth 2, Hull City 1
Freight Rover Trophy
1985 (Wembley) Wigan Athletic 3, Brentford 1
1986 (Wembley) Bristol City 3, Bolton Wand. 0
1987 (Wembley) Mansfield Town 1, Bristol City 1 (aet; Mansfield Town won 5-4 on pens.)
Sherpa Van Trophy
1988 (Wembley) Wolves 2, Burnley 0
1989 (Wembley) Bolton Wand. 4, Torquay Utd. 1
Leyland Daf Cup
1990 (Wembley) Tranmere Rov. 2, Bristol Rov. 1
1991 (Wembley) Birmingham City 3, Tranmere Rov. 2
Autoglass Trophy
1992 (Wembley) Stoke City 1, Stockport Co. 0
1993 (Wembley) Port Vale 2, Stockport Co. 1
1994 (Wembley) Huddersfield Town 1, Swansea City 1 (aet; Swansea City won 3-1 on pens.)
Auto Windscreens Shield
1995 (Wembley) Birmingham City 1, Carlisle Utd. 0 (Birmingham City won in sudden-death overtime)
1996 (Wembley) Rotherham Utd. 2, Shrewsbury Town 1
1997 (Wembley) Carlisle Utd. 0, Colchester Utd. 0 (aet; Carlisle Utd. won 4-3 on pens.)
1998 (Wembley) Grimsby Town 2, Bournemouth 1 (Grimsby Town won with golden goal in extra time)
1999 (Wembley) Wigan Athletic 1, Millwall 0
2000 (Wembley) Stoke City 2, Bristol City 1
LDV Vans Trophy
2001 (Millennium Stadium) Port Vale 2, Brentford 1
2002 (Millennium Stadium) Blackpool 4, Cambridge Utd. 1
2003 (Millennium Stadium) Bristol City 2, Carlisle Utd. 0

OTHER LEAGUE CLUBS' CUP COMPETITIONS

FINALS – AT WEMBLEY

Full Members' Cup (Discontinued after 1992)
1985-86 Chelsea 5, Manchester City 4
1986-87 Blackburn Rov. 1, Charlton Athletic 0

Simod Cup
1987-88 Reading 4, Luton Town 1
1988-89 Nott'm. Forest 4, Everton 3

Zenith Data Systems Cup
1989-90 Chelsea 1, Middlesbrough 0
1990-91 Crystal Palace 4, Everton 1
1991-92 Nott'm Forest 3, Southampton 2

ANGLO-ITALIAN CUP (Discontinued after 1996: * Home club)

1970 *Napoli 0, Swindon Town 3
1971 *Bologna 1, Blackpool 2 (aet)
1972 *AS Roma 3, Blackpool 1
1973 *Fiorentina 1, Newcastle Utd. 2
1993 Derby Co. 1, Cremonese 3 (at Wembley)
1994 Notts Co. 0, Brescia 1 (at Wembley)
1995 Ascoli 1, Notts Co. 2 (at Wembley)
1996 Port Vale 2, Genoa 5 (at Wembley)

F.A. CHALLENGE VASE FINALS

At Wembley
1975 Hoddesdon Town 2, Epsom & Ewell 1
1976 Billericay Town 1, Stamford 0*
1977 Billericay Town 2, Sheffield 1 (replay Nottingham, after a 1-1 draw at Wembley)
1978 Blue Star 2, Barton Rov. 1
1979 Billericay Town 4, Almondsbury Greenway 1
1980 Stamford 2, Guisborough Town 0
1981 Whickham 3, Willenhall Town 2*
1982 Forest Green Rov. 3, Rainworth Miners' Welfare 0
1983 V.S. Rugby 1, Halesowen Town 0
1984 Stansted 3, Stamford 2
1985 Halesowen Town 3, Fleetwood Town 1
1986 Halesowen Town 3, Southall 0
1987 St. Helens Town 3, Warrington Town 2
1988 Colne Dynamoes 1, Emley 0*
1989 Tamworth 3, Sudbury Town 0 (replay Peterborough Utd., after a 1-1 draw at Wembley)
1990 Yeading 1, Bridlington 0 (replay Leeds Utd., after 0-0 draw at Wembley)
1991 Guiseley 3, Gresley Rov. 1 (replay Bramall Lane, Sheffield, after a 4-4 draw at Wembley)
1992 Wimborne Town 5, Guiseley 3
1993 Bridlington Town 1, Tiverton Town 0
1994 Diss Town 2, Taunton Town 1*
1995 Arlesey Town 2, Oxford City 1
1996 Brigg Town 3, Clitheroe 0
1997 Whitby Town 3, North Ferriby Utd. 0
1998 Tiverton Town 1, Tow Law Town 0
1999 Tiverton Town 1, Bedlington Terriers 0
2000 Deal Town 1, Chippenham Town 0

At Villa Park
2001 Taunton Town 2, Berkhamsted 1
2002 Whitley Bay 1, Tiptree Utd. 0*

At Upton Park
2003 Brigg Town 2, AFC Sudbury 1

(Sponsors: Carlsberg since 1995; * After extra time)

F.A. TROPHY

THIRD ROUND

Alfreton Town 2, Halesowen Town 1; Aylesbury Utd. 1 Kingstonian 0; Canvey Island 5, Cirencester Town 1; Chester City 1, Worksop Town 2; Colwyn Bay 1, Blyth Spartans 0; Dagenham & Redbridge 5, Marlow 2; Dover Athletic 1, Gravesend & Northfleet 0; Dulwich Hamlet 0, Margate 2; Eastbourne Borough 0, Farnborough Town 1; Farsley Celtic 1, Gainsborough Trinity 1; Forest Green Rov. 4, Barnet 2; Gloucester City 3, Lewes 2; Halifax Town 4, Doncaster Rov. 1; Hayes 2, Crawley Town 1; Hereford Utd. 1, Yeovil Town 2; Heybridge Swifts 0, Hendon 0; Ilkeston Town 0, Burscough 3; Kettering Town 1, Altrincham 1; Lancaster City 0, Morecambe 1; Leek Town 1, Southport 2; Leigh RMI 1, Vauxhall Motors 2; Northwich Victoria 3, Barrow 1; Purfleet 1, Grays Athletic 2; Rugby Utd. 0, Telford Utd. 2; Stalybridge Celtic 0, Scarborough 3; Stevenage Borough 2, Oxford Utd. City 1; Sutton Utd. 1, Havant & Waterlooville 3; Tamworth 3, Nuneaton Borough 0; Wakefield & Emley 1, Burton Albion 0; Windsor & Eton 3, Thame Utd. 2; Woking 3, Chesham Utd. 0; Worcester City 3, Newport Co. 2. **REPLAYS:** Altrincham 3, Kettering Town 3 (Altrincham won 5-3 on pens); Gainsborough Trinity 2, Farsley Celtic 1; Hendon 2, Heybridge Swifts 1.

FOURTH ROUND

Alfreton Town 1, Burscough 1; Altrincham 0, Aylesbury Utd. 1; Colwyn Bay 0, Havant & Waterlooville 2; Dagenham & Redbridge 0, Southport 0; Gainsborough Trinity 0, Forest Green Rov. 2; Gloucester City 0, Woking 0; Halifax Town 3, Grays Athletic 2; Northwich Victoria 2, Canvey Island 1; Scarborough 1, Dover Athletic 1; Tamworth 3, Stevenage Borough 0; Telford Utd. 2, Farnborough Town 3; Windsor & Eton 1, Vauxhall Motors 1; Wakefield & Emley 0, Hendon 0; Worcester City 0, Margate 2; Worksop Town 2, Hayes 3; Yeovil Town 2, Morecambe 1. **REPLAYS:** Burscough 2, Alfreton Town 0; Dover Athletic 2, Scarborough 1; Hendon 0, Wakefield & Emley 1; Southport 2, Dagenham & Redbridge 2 (aet, Southport won 4-3 on pens); Vauxhall Motors 0, Windsor & Eton 3; Woking 0, Gloucester City 2.

FIFTH ROUND

Aylesbury Utd. 2, Windsor & Eton 2; Burscough 5, Wakefield & Emley 0; Dover Athletic 0, Forest Green Rov. 3; Farnborough Town 2, Halifax Town 0; Gloucester City 1, Southport 1; Havant & Waterlooville 3, Hayes 0; Margate 0, Tamworth 2; Yeovil Town 2, Northwich Victoria 1. **REPLAYS:** Windsor & Eton 1, Aylesbury Utd. 1 (aet, Aylesbury Utd. won 5-4 on pens); Southport 1, Gloucester City 3.

SIXTH ROUND

Aylesbury Utd. 2, Gloucester City 1; Farnborough Town 1, Tamworth 2; Forest Green Rov. 1, Havant & Waterlooville 2; Yeovil Town 0, Burscough 2.

SEMI-FINALS

First leg: Aylesbury Utd. 1, Burscough 1; Tamworth 1, Havant & Waterlooville 0.
Second leg: Burscough 1, Aylesbury Utd. 0 (Burscough won 2-1 on agg); Havant & Waterlooville 1, Tamworth 1 (aet, Tamworth won 2-1 on agg).

FINAL

BURSCOUGH 2, TAMWORTH 1

Villa Park, (14,265), Sunday, May 18, 2003

Burscough (3-5-2): M. Taylor, Macauley (White 77), J. Taylor, Teale, Byrne (Bluck 84), Norman, Burns, Lawless, Bowen, Martindale (McHale 80), Wright: **Subs not used:** McGuire, Molyneux. **Scorer:** Martindale (26, 55). **Booked:** Lawless. **Manager:** Shaun Teale.

Tamworth (4-4-2): Acton, Warner, Robinson, Walsh, Follett, Colley, McGorry, Cooper, Evans (Turner 65), Rickards (Hatton 88), Sale (Hallam 55). **Subs not used:** Barnes, Grocutt. **Scorer:** Cooper (79). **Booked:** Robinson, Walsh. **Manager:** Darron Gee.

Referee: U. Rennie (South Yorkshire). **Half-time:** 1-0.

F.A. CHALLENGE TROPHY FINALS

At Wembley

1970 Macclesfield Town 2, Telford Utd. 0
1971 Telford Utd. 3, Hillingdon Borough 2
1972 Stafford Rangers 3, Barnet 0
1973 Scarborough 2, Wigan Athletic 1*
1974 Morecambe 2, Dartford 1
1975 Matlock Town 4, Scarborough 0
1976 Scarborough 3, Stafford Rangers 2*
1977 Scarborough 2, Dagenham 1
1978 Altrincham 3, Leatherhead 1
1979 Stafford Rangers 2, Kettering Town 0
1980 Dagenham 2, Mossley 1
1981 Bishop's Stortford 1, Sutton Utd. 0
1982 Enfield 1, Altrincham 0*
1983 Telford Utd. 2, Northwich Victoria 1
1984 Northwich Victoria 2, Bangor City 1 (replay Stoke City, after a 1-1 draw at Wembley)
1985 Wealdstone 2, Boston Utd. 1
1986 Altrincham 1, Runcorn 0
1987 Kidderminster Harriers 2, Burton Albion 1 (replay W.B.A., after a 0-0 draw at Wembley)
1988 Enfield 3, Telford Utd. 2 (replay W.B.A., after a 0-0 draw at Wembley)
1989 Telford Utd. 1, Macclesfield Town 0*
1990 Barrow 3, Leek Town 0
1991 Wycombe Wand. 2, Kidderminster Harriers 1
1992 Colchester Utd. 3, Witton Albion 1
1993 Wycombe Wand. 4, Runcorn 1
1994 Woking 2, Runcorn 1
1995 Woking 2, Kidderminster 1
1996 Macclesfield Town 3, Northwich Victoria 1
1997 Woking 1, Dagenham & Redbridge 0*
1998 Cheltenham Town 1, Southport 0
1999 Kingstonian 1, Forest Green Rov. 0
2000 Kingstonian 3, Kettering Town 2

At Villa Park

2001 Canvey Island 1, Forest Green Rov. 0
2002 Yeovil Town 2, Stevenage Borough 0
2003 Burscough 2, Tamworth 1

(Sponsors: Umbro since 1995; * After extra time)

F.A. YOUTH CUP WINNERS

Year	Winners	Runners-up	Aggregate
1953	Manchester Utd.	Wolves	9-3
1954	Manchester Utd.	Wolves	5-4
1955	Manchester Utd.	W.B.A.	7-1
1956	Manchester Utd.	Chesterfield	4-3
1957	Manchester Utd.	West Ham Utd.	8-2
1958	Wolves	Chelsea	7-6
1959	Blackburn Rov.	West Ham Utd.	2-1
1960	Chelsea	Preston N.E.	5-2
1961	Chelsea	Everton	5-3
1962	Newcastle Utd.	Wolves	2-1
1963	West Ham Utd.	Liverpool	6-5

1964	Manchester Utd.	Swindon Town	5-2
1965	Everton	Arsenal	3-2
1966	Arsenal	Sunderland	5-3
1967	Sunderland	Birmingham City	2-0
1968	Burnley	Coventry City	3-2
1969	Sunderland	W.B.A.	6-3
1970	Tottenham	Coventry City	4-3
1971	Arsenal	Cardiff City	2-0
1972	Aston Villa	Liverpool	5-2
1973	Ipswich Town	Bristol City	4-1
1974	Tottenham	Huddersfield Town	2-1
1975	Ipswich Town	West Ham Utd.	5-1
1976	W.B.A.	Wolves	5-0
1977	Crystal Palace	Everton	1-0
1978	Crystal Palace	Aston Villa	*1-0
1979	Millwall	Manchester City	2-0
1980	Aston Villa	Manchester City	3-2
1981	West Ham Utd.	Tottenham	2-1
1982	Watford	Manchester Utd.	7-6
1983	Norwich City	Everton	6-5
1984	Everton	Stoke City	4-2
1985	Newcastle Utd.	Watford	4-1
1986	Manchester City	Manchester Utd.	3-1
1987	Coventry City	Charlton Athletic	2-1
1988	Arsenal	Doncaster Rov.	6-1
1989	Watford	Manchester City	2-1
1990	Tottenham	Middlesbrough	3-2
1991	Millwall	Sheffield Wed.	3-0
1992	Manchester Utd.	Crystal Palace	6-3
1993	Leeds Utd.	Manchester Utd.	4-1
1994	Arsenal	Millwall	5-3
1995	Manchester Utd.	Tottenham	†2-2
1996	Liverpool	West Ham Utd.	4-1
1997	Leeds Utd.	Crystal Palace	3-1
1998	Everton	Blackburn Rov.	5-3
1999	West Ham Utd.	Coventry City	9-0
2000	Arsenal	Coventry City	5-1
2001	Arsenal	Blackburn Rov.	6-3
2002	Aston Villa	Everton	4-2
2003	Manchester Utd.	Middlesbrough	3-1

(* One match only; † Manchester Utd. won 4-3 on pens.)

WELSH CUP FINAL

Barry Town 2, Cwmbran Town 2 – aet, Barry Town won 4-3 on pens (at Llanelli).

WOMEN'S F.A. CUP FINAL

Fulham 3, Charlton Athletic 0 (at Selhurst Park).

WOMEN'S PREMIER LEAGUE CUP FINAL

Fulham 1, Arsenal 1 – aet, Fulham won 3-2 on pens (at County Ground, Swindon).

F.A. SUNDAY CUP FINAL

Duke of York (Northamptonshire) 3, Allerton (Liverpool) 1 (at Anfield).

F.A. COMMUNITY SHIELD

ARSENAL 1, LIVERPOOL 0

Millennium Stadium, (67,337), Sunday August 11, 2002

Arsenal (4-4-2): Seaman, Lauren, Keown, Campbell, Cole, Wiltord, Parlour, Vieira (capt), Edu (Gilberto Silva 46), Bergkamp (Toure 86), Henry. **Subs not used:** Taylor, Cygan, Upson, Luzhny, Aliadiere. **Scorer:** Gilberto Silva (68). **Booked:** Vieira, Wiltord, Henry, Gilberto Silva.

Liverpool (4-4-2): Dudek, Xavier (Babbel 78), Henchoz, Hyypia (capt), Traore (Cheyrou 88), Gerrard, Hamann (Murphy 68), Riise, Diouf, Owen (Smicer 86), Heskey (Baros 74). **Subs not used:** Kirkland, Carragher. **Booked:** Gerrard, Murphy.

Referee: A. Wiley (Staffs). **Half-time:** 0-0.

CHARITY SHIELD RESULTS

Year	Winners	Runners-up	Score
1908	Manchester Utd.	Q.P.R.	4-0 (after 1-1 draw)
1909	Newcastle Utd.	Northampton Town	2-0
1910	Brighton & H.A.	Aston Villa	1-0
1911	Manchester Utd.	Swindon Town	8-4
1912	Blackburn Rov.	Q.P.R.	2-1
1913	Professionals	Amateurs	7-2
1920	W.B.A.	Tottenham	2-0
1921	Tottenham	Burnley	2-0
1922	Huddersfield Town	Liverpool	1-0
1923	Professionals	Amateurs	2-0
1924	Professionals	Amateurs	3-1
1925	Amateurs	Professionals	6-1
1926	Amateurs	Professionals	6-3
1927	Cardiff City	Corinthians	2-1
1928	Everton	Blackburn Rov.	2-1
1929	Professionals	Amateurs	3-0
1930	Arsenal	Sheffield Wed.	2-1
1931	Arsenal	W.B.A.	1-0
1932	Everton	Newcastle Utd.	5-3
1933	Arsenal	Everton	3-0
1934	Arsenal	Manchester City	4-0
1935	Sheffield Wed.	Arsenal	1-0
1936	Sunderland	Arsenal	2-1
1937	Manchester City	Sunderland	2-0
1938	Arsenal	Preston N.E.	2-1
1948	Arsenal	Manchester Utd.	4-3
1949	Portsmouth	Wolves	*1-1
1950	England World Cup XI	F.A. Canadian Tour Team	4-2
1951	Tottenham	Newcastle Utd.	2-1
1952	Manchester Utd.	Newcastle Utd.	4-2
1953	Arsenal	Blackpool	3-1
1954	Wolves	W.B.A.	*4-4
1955	Chelsea	Newcastle Utd.	3-0
1956	Manchester Utd.	Manchester City	1-0
1957	Manchester Utd.	Aston Villa	4-0
1958	Bolton Wand.	Wolves	4-1
1959	Wolves	Nott'm. Forest	3-1

1960	Burnley	Wolves	*2-2
1961	Tottenham	F.A. XI	3-2
1962	Tottenham	Ipswich Town	5-1
1963	Everton	Manchester Utd.	4-0
1964	Liverpool	West Ham Utd.	*2-2
1965	Manchester Utd.	Liverpool	*2-2
1966	Liverpool	Everton	1-0
1967	Manchester Utd.	Tottenham	*3-3
1968	Manchester City	W.B.A.	6-1
1969	Leeds Utd.	Manchester City	2-1
1970	Everton	Chelsea	2-1
1971	Leicester City	Liverpool	1-0
1972	Manchester City	Aston Villa	1-0
1973	Burnley	Manchester City	1-0
1974	Liverpool	Leeds Utd.	1-1
	(Liverpool won 6-5 on penalties)		
1975	Derby Co.	West Ham Utd.	2-0
1976	Liverpool	Southampton	1-0
1977	Liverpool	Manchester Utd.	*0-0
1978	Nott'm. Forest	Ipswich Town	5-0
1979	Liverpool	Arsenal	3-1
1980	Liverpool	West Ham Utd.	1-0
1981	Aston Villa	Tottenham	*2-2
1982	Liverpool	Tottenham	1-0
1983	Manchester Utd.	Liverpool	2-0
1984	Everton	Liverpool	1-0
1985	Everton	Manchester Utd.	2-0
1986	Everton	Liverpool	*1-1
1987	Everton	Coventry City	1-0
1988	Liverpool	Wimbledon	2-1
1989	Liverpool	Arsenal	1-0
1990	Liverpool	Manchester Utd.	*1-1
1991	Arsenal	Tottenham	*0-0
1992	Leeds Utd.	Liverpool	4-3
1993	Manchester Utd.	Arsenal	1-1
	(Manchester Utd. won 5-4 on penalties)		
1994	Manchester Utd.	Blackburn Rov.	2-0
1995	Everton	Blackburn Rov.	1-0
1996	Manchester Utd.	Newcastle Utd.	4-0
1997	Manchester Utd.	Chelsea	1-1
	(Manchester Utd. won 4-2 on penalties)		
1998	Arsenal	Manchester Utd.	3-0
1999	Arsenal	Manchester Utd.	2-1
2000	Chelsea	Manchester Utd.	2-0
2001	Liverpool	Manchester Utd.	2-1

COMMUNITY SHIELD RESULTS

Year	Winners	Runners-up	Score
2002	Arsenal	Liverpool	1-0

(Fixture played at Wembley since 1974. Millennium Stadium since 2001.
*Trophy shared)

ATTENDANCES 2002-03

League attendances continued to climb in 2002-03. The Premiership reported a record high of 13.4million. The average crowd of 35,445 was also the biggest in top-flight football since 1950-51. Chief executive Richard Scudamore said: 'This is testament to the quality and excitement of the competition, not only for this season, but year in year out. We have now seen attendances increase by 68% over the first eleven seasons of the Premier League – a tremendous achievement by any standards. The fans are central to the continued success and appeal. Their passion and commitment helps keep us the world's most successful domestic league competition.'

The Division One aggregate total of 8.5million was the biggest at this level since 1959. Officials say crowds are double those in Spain and France and 50% more than Italy and Germany. Division Two showed a small drop from the previous season; Division Three the best aggregate for 30 years. These figures follow a rise of more than 15% for Worthington Cup ties. 'They are a tribute to the clubs and the exciting football being played,' said Football League chairman Sir Brian Mawhinney. 'Fans are responding positively.'

LEAGUE CROWDS SINCE 1980

	Total	**Div. One**	**Div. Two**	**Div. Three**	**Div. Four**
1979-80	24,623,975	12,163,002	6,112,025	3,999,328	2,349,620
1980-81	21,907,569	11,392,894	5,175,442	3,637,854	1,701,379
1981-82	20,006,961	10,420,793	4,750,463	2,836,915	1,998,790
1982-83	18,766,158	9,295,613	4,974,937	2,943,568	1,552,040
1983-84	18,358,631	8,711,448	5,359,757	2,729,942	1,557,484
1984-85	17,849,835	9,761,404	4,030,823	2,667,008	1,390,600
1985-86	16,498,868	9,037,854	3,555,343	2,495,991	1,409,680
1986-87	17,383,032	9,144,676	4,168,131	2,354,784	1,715,441
1987-88	17,968,887	8,094,571	5,350,754	2,751,275	1,772,287
1988-89	18,477,565	7,809,993	5,827,805	3,048,700	1,791,067
1989-90	19,466,826	7,887,658	6,884,439	2,803,551	1,891,178
1990-91	19,541,341	8,618,709	6,297,733	2,847,813	1,777,086
1991-92	20,487,273	9,989,160	5,809,787	2,993,352	1,694,974
New format	**Total**	**Premier**	**Div. One**	**Div. Two**	**Div. Three**
1992-93	20,657,327	9,759,809	5,874,017	3,483,073	1,540,428
1993-94	21,693,889	10,655,059	6,487,104	2,972,702	1,579,024
1994-95	21,856,223	11,213,371	6,044,293	3,037,752	1,560,807
1995-96	21,844,416	10,469,107	6,566,349	2,843,652	1,965,308
1996-97	22,791,527	10,804,762	6,804,606	3,332,451	1,849,708
1997-98	24,679,527	11,091,773	8,330,018	3,503,264	1,767,220
1998-99	25,435,981	11,620,765	7,543,369	4,169,697	2,102,150
1999-2000	25,342,478	11,668,222	7,811,420	3,700,433	2,162,403
2000-01	26,067,729	12,503,732	7,912,046	3,490,250	2,161,701
2001-02	27,835,107	13,043,118	8,402,142	3,981,252	2,408,595
2002-03	28,340,946	13,468,965	8,519,866	3,892,400	2,459,715

Note: All-time record Football League attendance aggregate: 41,271,414 in season 1948-49 (88 clubs). The average was 22,333.

HONOURS LIST

F.A. PREMIER LEAGUE

	First	Pts.	Second	Pts.	Third	Pts.
1992-3*a*	Manchester Utd.	84	Aston Villa	74	Norwich City	72
1993-4*a*	Manchester Utd.	92	Blackburn Rov.	84	Newcastle Utd.	77
1994-5*a*	Blackburn Rov.	89	Manchester Utd.	88	Nott'm Forest	77
1995-6*b*	Manchester Utd.	82	Newcastle Utd.	78	Liverpool	71
1996-7*b*	Manchester Utd.	75	Newcastle Utd.	68	Arsenal	68
1997-8*b*	Arsenal	78	Manchester Utd.	77	Liverpool	65
1998-9*b*	Manchester Utd.	79	Arsenal	78	Chelsea	75
1999-00*b*	Manchester Utd.	91	Arsenal	73	Leeds Utd.	69
2000-01*b*	Manchester Utd.	80	Arsenal	70	Liverpool	69
2001-02*b*	Arsenal	87	Liverpool	80	Manchester Utd.	77
2002-03*b*	Manchester Utd.	83	Arsenal	78	Newcastle Utd.	69

Maximum points: *a*, 126; *b*, 114.

FOOTBALL LEAGUE

FIRST DIVISION

1992-3	Newcastle Utd.	96	West Ham Utd.	88	††Portsmouth	88
1993-4	Crystal Palace	90	Nott'm Forest	83	††Millwall	74
1994-5	Middlesbrough	82	††Reading	79	Bolton Wand.	77
1995-6	Sunderland	83	Derby Co.	79	††Crystal Palace	75
1996-7	Bolton Wand.	98	Barnsley	80	††Wolves	76
1997-8	Nott'm Forest	94	Middlesbrough	91	††Sunderland	90
1998-9	Sunderland	105	Bradford City	87	††Ipswich Town	86
1999-00	Charlton Athletic	91	Manchester City	89	Ipswich Town	87
2000-01	Fulham	101	Blackburn Rov.	91	Bolton Wand.	87
2001-02	Manchester City	99	W.B.A.	89	††Wolves	86
2002-03	Portsmouth	98	Leicester City	92	††Sheffield Utd.	80

Maximum points: 138. ††Not promoted after play-offs.

SECOND DIVISION

1992-3	Stoke City	93	Bolton Wand.	90	††Port Vale	89
1993-4	Reading	89	Port Vale	88	††Plymouth Argyle	85
1994-5	Birmingham City	89	††Brentford	85	††Crewe Alexandra	83
1995-6	Swindon Town	92	Oxford Utd.	83	††Blackpool	82
1996-7	Bury	84	Stockport Co.	82	††Luton Town	78
1997-8	Watford	88	Bristol City	85	Grimsby Town	72
1998-9	Fulham	101	Walsall	87	Manchester City	82
1999-00	Preston N.E.	95	Burnley	88	Gillingham	85
2000-01	Milwall	93	Rotherham Utd.	91	††Reading	86
2001-02	Brighton & H.A.	90	Reading	84	††Brentford	83
2002-03	Wigan Athletic	100	Crewe Alexandra	86	††Bristol City	83

Maximum points: 138. †† Not promoted after play-offs.

THIRD DIVISION

1992-3*a*	Cardiff City	83	Wrexham	80	Barnet	79
1993-4*a*	Shrewsbury Town	79	Chester City	74	Crewe Alexandra	73
1994-5*a*	Carlisle Utd.	91	Walsall	83	Chesterfield	81
1995-6*b*	Preston N.E.	86	Gillingham	83	Bury	79
1996-7*b*	Wigan Athletic	87	Fulham	87	Carlisle Utd.	84

1997-8*b*	Notts County	99	Macclesfield Town	82	Lincoln City	75
1998-9*b*	Brentford	85	Cambridge Utd.	81	Cardiff City	80
1999-00*b*	Swansea City	85	Rotherham Utd.	84	Northampton Town	82
2000-01*b*	Brighton & H.A.	92	Cardiff City	82	*Chesterfield	80
2001-02*b*	Plymouth Argyle	102	Luton Town	97	Mansfield Town	79
2002-03*b*	Rushden & Diamonds	87	Hartlepool Utd.	85	Wrexham	84

Maximum points: *a*, 126; *b*, 138; * Deducted 9 points for financial irregularities.

FOOTBALL LEAGUE 1888-1992

	First	Pts.	Second	Pts.	Third	Pts.
1888-89*a*	Preston N.E.	40	Aston Villa	29	Wolves	28
1889-90*a*	Preston N.E.	33	Everton	31	Blackburn Rov.	27
1890-1*a*	Everton	29	Preston N.E.	27	Notts Co.	26
1891-2*b*	Sunderland	42	Preston N.E.	37	Bolton Wand.	36

OLD FIRST DIVISION

	First	Pts.	Second	Pts.	Third	Pts.
1892-3*c*	Sunderland	48	Preston N.E.	37	Everton	36
1893-4*c*	Aston Villa	44	Sunderland	38	Derby Co.	36
1894-5*c*	Sunderland	47	Everton	42	Aston Villa	39
1895-6*c*	Aston Villa	45	Derby Co.	41	Everton	39
1896-7*c*	Aston Villa	47	Sheffield Utd.	36	Derby Co.	36
1897-8*c*	Sheffield Utd.	42	Sunderland	39	Wolves	35
1898-9*d*	Aston Villa	45	Liverpool	43	Burnley	39
1899-1900*d*	Aston Villa	50	Sheffield Utd.	48	Sunderland	41
1900-1*d*	Liverpool	45	Sunderland	43	Notts Co.	40
1901-2*d*	Sunderland	44	Everton	41	Newcastle Utd.	37
1902-3*d*	The Wednesday	42	Aston Villa	41	Sunderland	41
1903-4*d*	The Wednesday	47	Manchester City	44	Everton	43
1904-5*d*	Newcastle Utd.	48	Everton	47	Manchester City	46
1905-6*e*	Liverpool	51	Preston N.E.	47	The Wednesday	44
1906-7*e*	Newcastle Utd.	51	Bristol City	48	Everton	45
1907-8*e*	Manchester Utd.	52	Aston Villa	43	Manchester City	43
1908-9*e*	Newcastle Utd.	53	Everton	46	Sunderland	44
1909-10*e*	Aston Villa	53	Liverpool	48	Blackburn Rov.	45
1910-11*e*	Manchester Utd.	52	Aston Villa	51	Sunderland	45
1911-12*e*	Blackburn Rov.	49	Everton	46	Newcastle Utd.	44
1912-13*e*	Sunderland	54	Aston Villa	50	Sheffield Wed.	49
1913-14*e*	Blackburn Rov.	51	Aston Villa	44	Middlesbrough	43
1914-15*e*	Everton	46	Oldham Athletic	45	Blackburn Rov.	43
1919-20*f*	W.B.A.	60	Burnley	51	Chelsea	49
1920-1*f*	Burnley	59	Manchester City	54	Bolton Wand.	52
1921-2*f*	Liverpool	57	Tottenham	51	Burnley	49
1922-3*f*	Liverpool	60	Sunderland	54	Huddersfield Town	53
1923-4*f*	*Huddersfield Town	57	Cardiff City	57	Sunderland	53
1924-5*f*	Huddersfield Town	58	W.B.A.	56	Bolton Wand.	55
1925-6*f*	Huddersfield Town	57	Arsenal	52	Sunderland	48
1926-7*f*	Newcastle Utd.	56	Huddersfield Town	51	Sunderland	49
1927-8*f*	Everton	53	Huddersfield Town	51	Leicester City	48
1928-9*f*	Sheffield Wed.	52	Leicester City	51	Aston Villa	50
1929-30*f*	Sheffield Wed.	60	Derby Co.	50	Manchester City	47
1930-1*f*	Arsenal	66	Aston Villa	59	Sheffield Wed.	52
1931-2*f*	Everton	56	Arsenal	54	Sheffield Wed.	50
1932-3*f*	Arsenal	58	Aston Villa	54	Sheffield Wed.	51
1933-4*f*	Arsenal	59	Huddersfield Town	56	Tottenham	49
1934-5*f*	Arsenal	58	Sunderland	54	Sheffield Wed.	49
1935-6*f*	Sunderland	56	Derby Co.	48	Huddersfield Town	48

1936-7*f*	Manchester City	57	Charlton Athletic	54	Arsenal	52
1937-8*f*	Arsenal	52	Wolves	51	Preston N.E.	49
1938-9*f*	Everton	59	Wolves	55	Charlton Athletic	50
1946-7*f*	Liverpool	57	Manchester Utd.	56	Wolves	56
1947-8*f*	Arsenal	59	Manchester Utd.	52	Burnley	52
1948-9*f*	Portsmouth	58	Manchester Utd.	53	Derby Co.	53
1949-50*f*	*Portsmouth	53	Wolves	53	Sunderland	52
1950-1*f*	Tottenham	60	Manchester Utd.	56	Blackpool	50
1951-2*f*	Manchester Utd.	57	Tottenham	53	Arsenal	53
1952-3*f*	*Arsenal	54	Preston N.E.	54	Wolves	51
1953-4*f*	Wolves	57	W.B.A.	53	Huddersfield Town	51
1954-5*f*	Chelsea	52	Wolves	48	Portsmouth	48
1955-6*f*	Manchester Utd.	60	Blackpool	49	Wolves	49
1956-7*f*	Manchester Utd.	64	Tottenham	56	Preston N.E.	56
1957-8*f*	Wolves	64	Preston N.E.	59	Tottenham	51
1958-9*f*	Wolves	61	Manchester Utd.	55	Arsenal	50
1959-60*f*	Burnley	55	Wolves	54	Tottenham	53
1960-1*f*	Tottenham	66	Sheffield Wed.	58	Wolves	57
1961-2*f*	Ipswich Town	56	Burnley	53	Tottenham	52
1962-3*f*	Everton	61	Tottenham	55	Burnley	54
1963-4*f*	Liverpool	57	Manchester Utd.	53	Everton	52
1964-5*f*	*Manchester Utd.	61	Leeds Utd.	61	Chelsea	56
1965-6*f*	Liverpool	61	Leeds Utd.	55	Burnley	55
1966-7*f*	Manchester Utd.	60	Nott'm Forest	56	Tottenham	56
1967-8*f*	Manchester City	58	Manchester Utd.	56	Liverpool	55
1968-9*f*	Leeds Utd.	67	Liverpool	61	Everton	57
1969-70*f*	Everton	66	Leeds Utd.	57	Chelsea	55
1970-1*f*	Arsenal	65	Leeds Utd.	64	Tottenham	52
1971-2*f*	Derby Co.	58	Leeds Utd.	57	Liverpool	57
1972-3*f*	Liverpool	60	Arsenal	57	Leeds Utd.	53
1973-4*f*	Leeds Utd.	62	Liverpool	57	Derby Co.	48
1974-5*f*	Derby Co.	53	Liverpool	51	Ipswich Town	51
1975-6*f*	Liverpool	60	Q.P.R.	59	Manchester Utd.	56
1976-7*f*	Liverpool	57	Manchester City	56	Ipswich Town	52
1977-8*f*	Nott'm Forest	64	Liverpool	57	Everton	55
1978-9*f*	Liverpool	68	Nott'm Forest	60	W.B.A.	59
1979-80*f*	Liverpool	60	Manchester Utd.	58	Ipswich Town	53
1980-1*f*	Aston Villa	60	Ipswich Town	56	Arsenal	53
1981-2*g*	Liverpool	87	Ipswich Town	83	Manchester Utd.	78
1982-3*g*	Liverpool	82	Watford	71	Manchester Utd.	70
1983-4*g*	Liverpool	80	Southampton	77	Nott'm Forest	74
1984-5*g*	Everton	90	Liverpool	77	Tottenham	77
1985-6*g*	Liverpool	88	Everton	86	West Ham Utd.	84
1986-7*g*	Everton	86	Liverpool	77	Tottenham	71
1987-8*h*	Liverpool	90	Manchester Utd.	81	Nott'm Forest	73
1988-9*j*	†Arsenal	76	Liverpool	76	Nott'm Forest	64
1989-90*j*	Liverpool	79	Aston Villa	70	Tottenham	63
1990-1*j*	Arsenal	83	Liverpool	76	Crystal Palace	69
1991-2*g*	Leeds Utd.	82	Manchester Utd.	78	Sheffield Wed.	75

Maximum points: *a*, 44; *b*, 52; *c*, 60; *d*, 68; *e*, 76; *f*, 84; *g*, 126; *h*, 120; *j*, 114.
*Won on goal average. †Won on goal diff. No comp. 1915-19 – 1939-46

OLD SECOND DIVISION 1892-1992

	First	Pts.	Second	Pts.	Third	Pts.
1892-3*a*	Small Heath	36	Sheffield Utd.	35	Darwen	30
1893-4*b*	Liverpool	50	Small Heath	42	Notts Co.	39
1894-5*c*	Bury	48	Notts County	39	Newton Heath	38
1895-6*c*	*Liverpool	46	Manchester City	46	Grimsby Town	42

1896-7*c*	Notts Co. 42	Newton Heath 39	Grimsby Town 38
1897-8*c*	Burnley 48	Newcastle Utd. 45	Manchester City 39
1898-9*d*	Manchester City 52	Glossop 46	Leicester Fosse 45
1899-1900*d*	The Wednesday 54	Bolton Wand. 52	Small Heath 46
1900-1*d*	Grimsby Town 49	Small Heath 48	Burnley 44
1901-2*d*	W.B.A. 55	Middlesbrough 51	Preston N.E. 42
1902-3*d*	Manchester City 54	Small Heath 51	Woolwich Arsenal 48
1903-4*d*	Preston N.E. 50	Woolwich Arsenal 49	Manchester Utd. 48
1904-5*d*	Liverpool 58	Bolton Wand. 56	Manchester Utd. 53
1905-6*e*	Bristol City 66	Manchester Utd. 62	Chelsea 53
1906-7*e*	Nott'm Forest 60	Chelsea 57	Leicester Fosse 48
1907-8*e*	Bradford City 54	Leicester Fosse 52	Oldham Athletic 50
1908-9*e*	Bolton Wand. 52	Tottenham 51	W.B.A. 51
1909-10*e*	Manchester City 54	Oldham Athletic 53	Hull City 53
1910-11*e*	W.B.A. 53	Bolton Wand. 51	Chelsea 49
1911-12*e*	*Derby Co. 54	Chelsea 54	Burnley 52
1912-13*e*	Preston N.E. 53	Burnley 50	Birmingham City 46
1913-14*e*	Notts County 53	Bradford City P.A. .. 49	Woolwich Arsenal 49
1914-15*e*	Derby Co. 53	Preston N.E. 50	Barnsley 47
1919-20*f*	Tottenham 70	Huddersfield Town .. 64	Birmingham City 56
1920-1*f*	*Birmingham City 58	Cardiff City 58	Bristol City 51
1921-2*f*	Nott'm Forest 56	Stoke City 52	Barnsley 52
1922-3*f*	Notts County 53	West Ham Utd. 51	Leicester City 51
1923-4*f*	Leeds Utd. 54	Bury 51	Derby Co. 51
1924-5*f*	Leicester City 59	Manchester Utd. 57	Derby Co. 55
1925-6*f*	Sheffield Wed. 60	Derby Co. 57	Chelsea 52
1926-7*f*	Middlesbrough 62	Portsmouth 54	Manchester City 54
1927-8*f*	Manchester City 59	Leeds Utd. 57	Chelsea 54
1928-9*f*	Middlesbrough 55	Grimsby Town 53	Bradford City 48
1929-30*f*	Blackpool 58	Chelsea 55	Oldham Athletic 53
1930-1*f*	Everton 61	W.B.A. 54	Tottenham 51
1931-2*f*	Wolves 56	Leeds Utd. 54	Stoke City 52
1932-3*f*	Stoke City 56	Tottenham 55	Fulham 50
1933-4*f*	Grimsby Town 59	Preston N.E. 52	Bolton Wand. 51
1934-5*f*	Brentford 61	Bolton Wand. 56	West Ham Utd. 56
1935-6*f*	Manchester Utd. 56	Charlton Athletic 55	Sheffield Utd. 52
1936-7*f*	Leicester City 56	Blackpool 55	Bury 52
1937-8*f*	Aston Villa 57	Manchester Utd. 53	Sheffield Utd. 53
1938-9*f*	Blackburn Rov. 55	Sheffield Utd. 54	Sheffield Wed. 53
1946-7*f*	Manchester City 62	Burnley 58	Birmingham City 55
1947-8*f*	Birmingham City 59	Newcastle Utd. 56	Southampton 52
1948-9*f*	Fulham 57	W.B.A. 56	Southampton 55
1949-50*f*	Tottenham 61	Sheffield Wed. 52	Sheffield Utd. 52
1950-1*f*	Preston N.E. 57	Manchester City 52	Cardiff City 50
1951-2*f*	Sheffield Wed. 53	Cardiff City 51	Birmingham City 51
1952-3*f*	Sheffield Utd. 60	Huddersfield Town .. 58	Luton Town 52
1953-4*f*	*Leicester City 56	Everton 56	Blackburn Rov. 55
1954-5*f*	*Birmingham City 54	Luton Town 54	Rotherham Utd. 54
1955-6*f*	Sheffield Wed. 55	Leeds Utd. 52	Liverpool 48
1956-7*f*	Leicester City 61	Nott'm Forest 54	Liverpool 53
1957-8*f*	West Ham Utd. 57	Blackburn Rov. 56	Charlton Athletic 55
1958-9*f*	Sheffield Wed. 62	Fulham 60	Sheffield Utd. 53
1959-60*f*	Aston Villa 59	Cardiff City 58	Liverpool 50
1960-1*f*	Ipswich Town 59	Sheffield Utd. 58	Liverpool 52
1961-2*f*	Liverpool 62	Leyton Orient 54	Sunderland 53
1962-3*f*	Stoke City 53	Chelsea 52	Sunderland 52
1963-4*f*	Leeds Utd. 63	Sunderland 61	Preston N.E. 56
1964-5*f*	Newcastle Utd. 57	Northampton Town . 56	Bolton Wand. 50

	First	Pts.	Second	Pts.	Third	Pts.
1965-6*f*	Manchester City	59	Southampton	54	Coventry City	53
1966-7*f*	Coventry City	59	Wolves	58	Carlisle Utd.	52
1967-8*f*	Ipswich Town	59	Q.P.R.	58	Blackpool	58
1968-9*f*	Derby Co.	63	Crystal Palace	56	Charlton Athletic	50
1969-70*f*	Huddersfield Town	60	Blackpool	53	Leicester City	51
1970-1*f*	Leicester City	59	Sheffield Utd.	56	Cardiff City	53
1971-2*f*	Norwich City	57	Birmingham City	56	Millwall	55
1972-3*f*	Burnley	62	Q.P.R.	61	Aston Villa	60
1973-4*f*	Middlesbrough	65	Luton Town	50	Carlisle Utd.	49
1974-5*f*	Manchester Utd.	61	Aston Villa	58	Norwich City	53
1975-6*f*	Sunderland	56	Bristol City	53	W.B.A.	53
1976-7*f*	Wolves	57	Chelsea	55	Nott'm Forest	52
1977-8*f*	Bolton Wand.	58	Southampton	57	Tottenham	56
1978-9*f*	Crystal Palace	57	Brighton & H.A.	56	Stoke City	56
1979-80*f*	Leicester City	55	Sunderland	54	Birmingham City	53
1980-1*f*	West Ham Utd.	66	Notts Co.	53	Swansea City	50
1981-2*g*	Luton Town	88	Watford	80	Norwich City	71
1982-3*g*	Q.P.R.	85	Wolves	75	Leicester City	70
1983-4*g*	†Chelsea	88	Sheffield Wed.	88	Newcastle Utd.	80
1984-5*g*	Oxford Utd.	84	Birmingham City	82	Manchester City	74
1985-6*g*	Norwich City	84	Charlton Athletic	77	Wimbledon	76
1986-7*g*	Derby Co.	84	Portsmouth	78	††Oldham Athletic	75
1987-8*h*	Millwall	82	Aston Villa	78	Middlesbrough	78
1988-9*j*	Chelsea	99	Manchester City	82	Crystal Palace	81
1989-90*j*	†Leeds Utd.	85	Sheffield Utd.	85	†† Newcastle Utd.	80
1990-1*j*	Oldham Athletic	88	West Ham Utd.	87	Sheffield Wed.	82
1991-2*j*	Ipswich Town	84	Middlesbrough	80	†† Derby Co.	78

Maximum points: *a*, 44; *b*, 56; *c*, 60; *d*, 68; *e*, 76; *f*, 84; *g*, 126; *h*, 132; *j*, 138. * Won on goal average. † Won on goal difference. †† Not promoted after play-offs.

THIRD DIVISION 1958-92

	First	Pts.	Second	Pts.	Third	Pts.
1958-9	Plymouth Argyle	62	Hull City	61	Brentford	57
1959-60	Southampton	61	Norwich City	59	Shrewsbury Town	52
1960-1	Bury	68	Walsall	62	Q.P.R.	60
1961-2	Portsmouth	65	Grimsby Town	62	Bournemouth	59
1962-3	Northampton Town	62	Swindon Town	58	Port Vale	54
1963-4	*Coventry City	60	Crystal Palace	60	Watford	58
1964-5	Carlisle Utd.	60	Bristol City	59	Mansfield Town	59
1965-6	Hull City	69	Millwall	65	Q.P.R.	57
1966-7	Q.P.R.	67	Middlesbrough	55	Watford	54
1967-8	Oxford Utd.	57	Bury	56	Shrewsbury Town	55
1968-9	*Watford	64	Swindon Town	64	Luton Town	61
1969-70	Orient	62	Luton Town	60	Bristol Rov.	56
1970-1	Preston N.E.	61	Fulham	60	Halifax Town	56
1971-2	Aston Villa	70	Brighton & H.A.	65	Bournemouth	62
1972-3	Bolton Wand.	61	Notts Co.	57	Blackburn Rov.	55
1973-4	Oldham Athletic	62	Bristol Rov.	61	York City	61
1974-5	Blackburn Rov.	60	Plymouth Argyle	59	Charlton Athletic	55
1975-6	Hereford	63	Cardiff City	57	Millwall	56
1976-7	Mansfield Town	64	Brighton & H.A.	61	Crystal Palace	59
1977-8	Wrexham	61	Cambridge Utd.	58	Preston N.E.	56
1978-9	Shrewsbury Town	61	Watford	60	Swansea City	60
1979-80	Grimsby Town	62	Blackburn Rov.	59	Sheffield Wed.	58
1980-1	Rotherham Utd.	61	Barnsley	59	Charlton Athletic	59
†1981-2	*Burnley	80	Carlisle Utd.	80	Fulham	78
†1982-3	Portsmouth	91	Cardiff City	86	Huddersfield Town	82
†1983-4	Oxford Utd.	95	Wimbledon	87	Sheffield Utd.	83

†1984-5	Bradford City 94	Millwall 90	Hull City 87
†1985-6	Reading 94	Plymouth Argyle 87	Derby Co. 84
†1986-7	Bournemouth 97	Middlesbrough 94	Swindon Town 87
†1987-8	Sunderland 93	Brighton & H.A. 84	Walsall 82
†1988-9	Wolves 92	Sheffield Utd. 84	Port Vale 84
†1989-90	Bristol Rov. 93	Bristol City 91	Notts Co. 87
†1990-1	Cambridge Utd. 86	Southend Utd. 85	Grimsby Town 83
†1991-2	Brentford 82	Birmingham City 81	††Huddersfield T 78

* Won on goal average. † Maximum points 138 (previously 92). †† Not promoted after play-offs.

FOURTH DIVISION 1958-92

	First	Pts.	Second	Pts.	Third	Pts.	Fourth	Pts.
1958-9	Port Vale	64	Coventry City	60	York City	60	Shrewsbury Town	58
1959-60	Walsall	65	Notts Co.	60	Torquay Utd.	60	Watford	57
1960-1	Peterborough Utd.	66	Crystal Palace	64	Northampton Town	60	Bradford City P.A.	60
1961-2	Millwall	56	Colchester Utd.	55	Wrexham	53	Carlisle Utd.	52
1962-3	Brentford	62	Oldham Athletic	59	Crewe Alexandra	59	Mansfield Town	57
1963-4	*Gillingham	60	Carlisle Utd.	60	Workington	59	Exeter City	58
1964-5	Brighton & H.A.	63	Millwall	62	York City	62	Oxford Utd.	61
1965-6	*Doncaster Rov.	59	Darlington	59	Torquay Utd.	58	Colchester Utd.	56
1966-7	Stockport Co.	64	Southport	59	Barrow	59	Tranmere Rov.	58
1967-8	Luton Town	66	Barnsley	61	Hartlepool Utd.	60	Crewe Alexandra	58
1968-9	Doncaster Rov.	59	Halifax Town	57	Rochdale	56	Bradford City	56
1969-70	Chesterfield	64	Wrexham	61	Swansea City	60	Port Vale	59
1970-1	Notts Co.	69	Bournemouth	60	Oldham Athletic	59	York City	56
1971-2	Grimsby Town	63	Southend Utd.	60	Brentford	59	Scunthorpe Utd.	57
1972-3	Southport	62	Hereford	58	Cambridge Utd.	57	Aldershot	56
1973-4	Peterborough Utd.	65	Gillingham	62	Colchester Utd.	60	Bury	59
1974-5	Mansfield Town	68	Shrewsbury Town	62	Rotherham Utd.	58	Chester City	57
1975-6	Lincoln City	74	Northampton Town	68	Reading	60	Tranmere Rov.	58
1976-7	Cambridge Utd.	65	Exeter City	62	Colchester Utd.	59	Bradford City	59
1977-8	Watford	71	Southend Utd.	60	Swansea City	56	Brentford	59
1978-9	Reading	65	Grimsby Town	61	Wimbledon	61	Barnsley	61
1979-80	Huddersfield Town	66	Walsall	64	Newport	61	Portsmouth	60
1980-1	Southend Utd.	67	Lincoln City	65	Doncaster Rov.	56	Wimbledon	55
†1981-2	Sheffield Utd.	96	Bradford City	91	Wigan Athletic	91	Bournemouth	88
†1982-3	Wimbledon	98	Hull City	90	Port Vale	88	Scunthorpe Utd.	83
†1983-4	York City	101	Doncaster Rov.	85	Reading	82	Bristol City	82
†1984-5	Chesterfield	91	Blackpool	86	Darlington	85	Bury	84
†1985-6	Swindon Town	102	Chester City	84	Mansfield Town	81	Port Vale	79
†1986-7	Northampton Town	99	Preston N.E.	90	Southend Utd.	80	††Wolves	79
†1987-8	Wolves	90	Cardiff City	85	Bolton Wand.	78	††Scunthorpe Utd.	77
†1988-9	Rotherham Utd.	82	Tranmere Rov.	80	Crewe Alexandra	78	††Scunthorpe Utd.	77
†1989-90	Exeter City	89	Grimsby Town	79	Southend Utd.	75	††Stockport Co.	74
†1990-1	Darlington	83	Stockport Co.	82	Hartlepool Utd.	82	Peterborough Utd.	80
1991-2*a*	Burnley	83	Rotherham Utd.	77	Mansfield Town	77	Blackpool	76

* Won on goal average. Maximum points: †, 138; *a*, 126; previously 92. †† Not promoted after play-offs.

THIRD DIVISION – SOUTH 1920-58

	First	Pts.	Second	Pts.	Third	Pts.
1920-1*a*	Crystal Palace	59	Southampton	54	Q.P.R.	53
1921-2*a*	*Southampton	61	Plymouth Argyle	61	Portsmouth	53
1922-3*a*	Bristol City	59	Plymouth Argyle	53	Swansea City	53
1923-4*a*	Portsmouth	59	Plymouth Argyle	55	Millwall	54
1924-5*a*	Swansea City	57	Plymouth Argyle	56	Bristol City	53
1925-6*a*	Reading	57	Plymouth Argyle	56	Millwall	53

1926-7*a*	Bristol City	62	Plymouth Argyle	60	Millwall	56
1927-8*a*	Millwall	65	Northampton Town	55	Plymouth Argyle	53
1928-9*a*	*Charlton Athletic	54	Crystal Palace	54	Northampton Town	52
1929-30*a*	Plymouth Argyle	68	Brentford	61	Q.P.R.	51
1930-31*a*	Notts Co.	59	Crystal Palace	51	Brentford	50
1931-2*a*	Fulham	57	Reading	55	Southend Utd.	53
1932-3*a*	Brentford	62	Exeter City	58	Norwich City	57
1933-4*a*	Norwich City	61	Coventry City	54	Reading	54
1934-5*a*	Charlton Athletic	61	Reading	53	Coventry City	51
1935-6*a*	Coventry City	57	Luton Town	56	Reading	54
1936-7*a*	Luton Town	58	Notts Co.	56	Brighton & H.A.	53
1937-8*a*	Millwall	56	Bristol City	55	Q.P.R.	53
1938-9*a*	Newport	55	Crystal Palace	52	Brighton & H.A.	49
1946-7*a*	Cardiff City	66	Q.P.R.	57	Bristol City	51
1947-8*a*	Q.P.R.	61	Bournemouth	57	Walsall	51
1948-9*a*	Swansea City	62	Reading	55	Bournemouth	52
1949-50*a*	Notts Co.	58	Northampton Town	51	Southend Utd.	51
1950-1*d*	Nott'm Forest	70	Norwich City	64	Reading	57
1951-2*d*	Plymouth Argyle	66	Reading	61	Norwich City	61
1952-3*d*	Bristol Rov.	64	Millwall	62	Northampton Town	62
1953-4*d*	Ipswich Town	64	Brighton & H.A.	61	Bristol City	56
1954-5*d*	Bristol City	70	Leyton Orient	61	Southampton	59
1955-6*d*	Leyton Orient	66	Brighton & H.A.	65	Ipswich Town	64
1956-7*d*	*Ipswich Town	59	Torquay Utd.	59	Colchester Utd.	58
1957-8*d*	Brighton & H.A.	60	Brentford	58	Plymouth Argyle	58

THIRD DIVISION – NORTH 1921-58

	First	Pts.	Second	Pts.	Third	Pts.
1921-2*b*	Stockport Co.	56	Darlington	50	Grimsby Town	50
1922-3*b*	Nelson	51	Bradford P.A.	47	Walsall	46
1923-4*a*	Wolves	63	Rochdale	62	Chesterfield	54
1924-5*a*	Darlington	58	Nelson	53	New Brighton	53
1925-6*a*	Grimsby Town	61	Bradford P.A.	60	Rochdale	59
1926-7*a*	Stoke City	63	Rochdale	58	Bradford P.A.	57
1927-8*a*	Bradford P.A.	63	Lincoln City	55	Stockport Co.	54
1928-9*a*	Bradford City	63	Stockport Co.	62	Wrexham	52
1929-30*a*	Port Vale	67	Stockport Co.	63	Darlington	50
1930-1*a*	Chesterfield	58	Lincoln City	57	Wrexham	54
1931-2*c*	*Lincoln City	57	Gateshead	57	Chester City	50
1932-3*a*	Hull City	59	Wrexham	57	Stockport Co.	54
1933-4*a*	Barnsley	62	Chesterfield	61	Stockport Co.	59
1934-5*a*	Doncaster Rov.	57	Halifax Town	55	Chester City	54
1935-6*a*	Chesterfield	60	Chester City	55	Tranmere Rov.	54
1936-7*a*	Stockport Co.	60	Lincoln City	57	Chester City	53
1937-8*a*	Tranmere Rov.	56	Doncaster Rov.	54	Hull City	53
1938-9*a*	Barnsley	67	Doncaster Rov.	56	Bradford City	52
1946-7*a*	Doncaster Rov.	72	Rotherham Utd.	64	Chester City	56
1947-8*a*	Lincoln City	60	Rotherham Utd.	59	Wrexham	50
1948-9*a*	Hull City	65	Rotherham Utd.	62	Doncaster Rov.	50
1949-50*a*	Doncaster Rov.	55	Gateshead	53	Rochdale	51
1950-1*d*	Rotherham Utd.	71	Mansfield Town	64	Carlisle Utd.	62
1951-2*d*	Lincoln City	69	Grimsby Town	66	Stockport Co.	59
1952-3*d*	Oldham Athletic	59	Port Vale	58	Wrexham	56
1953-4*d*	Port Vale	69	Barnsley	58	Scunthorpe Utd.	57
1954-5*d*	Barnsley	65	Accrington	61	Scunthorpe Utd.	58
1955-6*d*	Grimsby Town	68	Derby Co.	63	Accrington	59
1956-7*d*	Derby Co.	63	Hartlepool Utd.	59	Accrington	58
1957-8*d*	Scunthorpe Utd.	66	Accrington	59	Bradford City	57

Maximum points: *a*, 84; *b*, 76; *c*, 80; *d*, 92. * Won on goal average.

CHAMPIONSHIP WINNERS

F.A. PREMIER LEAGUE
Manchester Utd. 8
Arsenal 2
Blackburn Rov. 1

FOOTBALL LEAGUE
DIV.1 (NEW)
Sunderland 2
Bolton Wand. 1
Charlton Athletic 1
Crystal Palace 1
Fulham 1
Manchester City 1
Middlesbrough 1
Newcastle Utd. 1
Nott'm Forest 1
Portsmouth 1

DIV.1 (ORIGINAL)
Liverpool 18
Arsenal 10
Everton 9
Aston Villa 7
Manchester Utd. 7
Sunderland 6
Newcastle Utd. 4
Sheffield Wed. 4
Huddersfield Town 3
Leeds Utd. 3
Wolves 3
Blackburn Rov. 2
Burnley 2
Derby Co. 2
Manchester City 2
Portsmouth 2
Preston N.E. 2
Tottenham 2
Chelsea 1
Ipswich Town 1
Nott'm Forest 1
Sheffield Utd. 1
W.B.A. 1

DIV.2 (NEW)
Birmingham City 1
Brighton & H.A. 1
Bury 1
Fulham 1
Millwall 1
Preston N.E. 1
Reading 1
Stoke City 1
Swindon Town 1
Watford 1
Wigan Athletic 1

DIV.2 (ORIGINAL)
Leicester City 6
Manchester City 6
Sheffield Wed. 5
Birmingham City 4
Derby Co. 4
Liverpool 4
Ipswich Town 3
Leeds Utd. 3
Middlesbrough 3
Notts County 3
Preston N.E. 3
Aston Villa 2
Bolton Wand. 2
Burnley 2
Chelsea 2
Grimsby Town 2
Manchester Utd. 2
Norwich City 2
Nott'm Forest 2
Stoke City 2
Tottenham 2
W.B.A. 2
West Ham Utd. 2
Wolves 2
Blackburn Rov. 1
Blackpool 1
Bradford City 1
Brentford 1
Bristol City 1
Bury 1
Coventry City 1
Crystal Palace 1
Everton 1
Fulham 1
Huddersfield Town 1
Luton Town 1
Millwall 1
Newcastle Utd. 1
Oldham Athletic 1
Oxford Utd. 1
Q.P.R. 1
Sheffield Utd. 1
Sunderland 1

APPLICATIONS FOR RE-ELECTION
(System discontinued 1987)

14 Hartlepool Utd.
12 Halifax Town
11 Barrow
11 Southport
10 Crewe Alexandra
10 Newport
10 Rochdale
8 Darlington
8 Exeter City
7 Chester City
7 Walsall
7 Workington
7 York City
6 Stockport Co.
5 Accrington
5 Gillingham
5 Lincoln City
5 New Brighton
4 Bradford P.A.
4 Northampton Town
4 Norwich City
3 Aldershot
3 Bradford City
3 Crystal Palace
3 Doncaster Rov.
3 Hereford
3 Merthyr Tyd.
3 Swindon Town
3 Torquay Utd.
3 Tranmere Rov.
2 Aberdare
2 Ashington
2 Bournemouth
2 Brentford
2 Colchester Utd.
2 Durham C.
2 Gateshead
2 Grimsby Town
2 Millwall
2 Nelson
2 Oldham Athletic
2 Q.P.R.
2 Rotherham Utd.
2 Scunthorpe Utd.
2 Southend Utd.
2 Watford
1 Blackpool
1 Brighton & H.A.
1 Bristol Rov.
1 Cambridge Utd.
1 Cardiff City
1 Carlisle Utd.
1 Charlton Athletic
1 Mansfield Town

1	Port Vale	1	Shrewsbury Town	1	Thames
1	Preston N.E.	1	Swansea City	1	Wrexham

RELEGATED CLUBS (TO 1992)

1892-3 In Test matches, Darwen and Sheffield Utd. won promotion in place of Accrington and Notts Co.
1893-4 Tests, Liverpool and Small Heath won promotion. Darwen and Newton Heath relegated.
1894-5 After Tests, Bury promoted, Liverpool relegated.
1895-6 After Tests, Liverpool promoted, Small Heath relegated.
1896-7 After Tests, Notts Co. promoted, Burnley relegated.
1897-8 Test system abolished after success of Burnley and Stoke City, League extended. Blackburn Rov. and Newcastle Utd. elected to First Division. Automatic promotion and relegation introduced.

FIRST DIVISION TO SECOND DIVISION

1898-9 Bolton Wand., Sheffield Wed.
1899-00 Burnley, Glossop
1900-1 Preston N.E., W.B.A.
1901-2 Small Heath, Manchester City
1902-3 Grimsby Town, Bolton Wand.
1903-4 Liverpool, W.B.A.
1904-5 League extended. Bury and Notts Co., two bottom clubs in First Division, re-elected.
1905-6 Nott'm Forest, Wolves
1906-7 Derby Co., Stoke City
1907-8 Bolton Wand., Birmingham City
1908-9 Manchester City, Leicester Fosse
1909-10 Bolton Wand., Chelsea
1910-11 Bristol City, Nott'm Forest
1911-12 Preston N.E., Bury
1912-13 Notts Co., Woolwich Arsenal
1913-14 Preston N.E., Derby Co.
1914-15 Tottenham, *Chelsea
1919-20 Notts Co., Sheffield Wed.
1920-1 Derby Co., Bradford P.A.
1921-2 Bradford City, Manchester Utd.
1922-3 Stoke City, Oldham Athletic
1923-4 Chelsea, Middlesbrough
1924-5 Preston N.E., Nott'm Forest
1925-6 Manchester City, Notts Co.
1926-7 Leeds Utd., W.B.A.
1927-8 Tottenham, Middlesbrough
1928-9 Bury, Cardiff City
1929-30 Burnley, Everton
1930-1 Leeds Utd., Manchester Utd.
1931-2 Grimsby Town, West Ham Utd.
1932-3 Bolton Wand., Blackpool
1933-4 Newcastle Utd., Sheffield Utd.
1934-5 Leicester City, Tottenham
1935-6 Aston Villa, Blackburn Rov.
1936-7 Manchester Utd., Sheffield Wed.
1937-8 Manchester City, W.B.A.
1938-9 Birmingham City, Leicester City
1946-7 Brentford, Leeds Utd.
1947-8 Blackburn Rov., Grimsby Town
1948-9 Preston N.E., Sheffield Utd.

1949-50	Manchester City, Birmingham City
1950-1	Sheffield Wed., Everton
1951-2	Huddersfield Town, Fulham
1952-3	Stoke City, Derby Co.
1953-4	Middlesbrough, Liverpool
1954-5	Leicester City, Sheffield Wed.
1955-6	Huddersfield Town, Sheffield Utd.
1956-7	Charlton Athletic, Cardiff City
1957-8	Sheffield Wed., Sunderland
1958-9	Portsmouth, Aston Villa
1959-60	Luton Town, Leeds Utd.
1960-61	Preston N.E., Newcastle Utd.
1961-2	Chelsea, Cardiff City
1962-3	Manchester City, Leyton Orient
1963-4	Bolton Wand., Ipswich Town
1964-5	Wolves, Birmingham City
1965-6	Northampton Town, Blackburn Rov.
1966-7	Aston Villa, Blackpool
1967-8	Fulham, Sheffield Utd.
1968-9	Leicester City, Q.P.R.
1969-70	Sheffield Wed., Sunderland
1970-1	Burnley, Blackpool
1971-2	Nott'm Forest, Huddersfield Town
1972-3	W.B.A., Crystal Palace
1973-4	Norwich City, Manchester Utd., Southampton
1974-5	Chelsea, Luton Town, Carlisle Utd.
1975-6	Sheffield Utd., Burnley, Wolves
1976-7	Tottenham, Stoke City, Sunderland
1977-8	Leicester City, West Ham Utd., Newcastle Utd.
1978-9	Q.P.R., Birmingham City, Chelsea
1979-80	Bristol City, Derby Co., Bolton Wand.
1980-1	Norwich City, Leicester City, Crystal Palace
1981-2	Leeds Utd., Wolves, Middlesbrough
1982-3	Manchester City, Swansea City, Brighton & H.A.
1983-4	Birmingham City, Notts Co., Wolves
1984-5	Norwich City, Sunderland, Stoke City
1985-6	Ipswich Town, Birmingham City, W.B.A.
1986-7	Leicester City, Manchester City, Aston Villa
1987-8	Chelsea**, Portsmouth, Watford, Oxford Utd.
1988-9	Middlesbrough, West Ham Utd., Newcastle Utd.
1989-90	Sheffield Wed., Charlton Athletic, Millwall
1990-1	Sunderland, Derby Co.
1991-2	Luton Town, Notts Co., West Ham Utd.

* Subsequently re-elected to First Division when League extended after the war.
** Relegated after play-offs.

SECOND DIVISION TO THIRD DIVISION

1920-1	Stockport Co.
1921-2	Bradford City, Bristol City
1922-3	Rotherham Utd., Wolves
1923-4	Nelson, Bristol City
1924-5	Crystal Palace, Coventry City
1925-6	Stoke City, Stockport Co.
1926-7	Darlington, Bradford City
1927-8	Fulham, South Shields
1928-9	Port Vale, Clapton Orient
1929-30	Hull City, Notts County

1930-1	Reading, Cardiff City
1931-2	Barnsley, Bristol City
1932-3	Chesterfield, Charlton Athletic
1933-4	Millwall, Lincoln City
1934-5	Oldham Athletic, Notts Co.
1935-6	Port Vale, Hull City
1936-7	Doncaster Rov., Bradford City
1937-8	Barnsley, Stockport Co.
1938-9	Norwich City, Tranmere Rov.
1946-7	Swansea City, Newport
1947-8	Doncaster Rov., Millwall
1948-9	Nott'm Forest, Lincoln City
1949-50	Plymouth Argyle, Bradford P.A.
1950-1	Grimsby Town, Chesterfield
1951-2	Coventry City, Q.P.R.
1952-3	Southampton, Barnsley
1953-4	Brentford, Oldham Athletic
1954-5	Ipswich Town, Derby Co.
1955-6	Plymouth Argyle, Hull City
1956-7	Port Vale, Bury
1957-8	Doncaster Rov., Notts Co.
1958-9	Barnsley, Grimsby Town
1959-60	Bristol City, Hull City
1960-1	Lincoln City, Portsmouth
1961-2	Brighton & H.A., Bristol Rov.
1962-3	Walsall, Luton Town
1963-4	Grimsby Town, Scunthorpe Utd.
1964-5	Swindon Town, Swansea City
1965-6	Middlesbrough, Leyton Orient
1966-7	Northampton Town, Bury
1967-8	Plymouth Argyle, Rotherham Utd.
1968-9	Fulham, Bury
1969-70	Preston N.E., Aston Villa
1970-1	Blackburn Rov., Bolton Wand.
1971-2	Charlton Athletic, Watford
1972-3	Huddersfield Town, Brighton & H.A.
1973-4	Crystal Palace, Preston N.E., Swindon Town
1974-5	Millwall, Cardiff City, Sheffield Wed.
1975-6	Portsmouth, Oxford Utd., York City
1976-7	Carlisle Utd., Plymouth Argyle, Hereford Utd.
1977-8	Hull City, Mansfield Town, Blackpool
1978-9	Sheffield Utd., Millwall, Blackburn Rov.
1979-80	Fulham, Burnley, Charlton Athletic
1980-1	Preston N.E., Bristol City, Bristol Rov.
1981-2	Cardiff City, Wrexham, Orient
1982-3	Rotherham Utd., Burnley, Bolton Wand.
1983-4	Derby Co., Swansea City, Cambridge Utd.
1984-5	Notts Co., Cardiff City, Wolves
1985-6	Carlisle Utd., Middlesbrough, Fulham
1986-7	Sunderland**, Grimsby Town, Brighton & H.A.
1987-8	Sheffield Utd.**, Reading, Huddersfield Town
1988-9	Shrewsbury Town, Birmingham City, Walsall
1989-90	Bournemouth, Bradford City, Stoke City
1990-1	W.B.A., Hull City
1991-2	Plymouth Argyle, Brighton & H.A., Port Vale

** Relegated after play-offs.

THIRD DIVISION TO FOURTH DIVISION

1958-9	Rochdale, Notts Co., Doncaster Rov., Stockport Co.
1959-60	Accrington, Wrexham, Mansfield Town, York City
1960-1	Chesterfield, Colchester Utd., Bradford City, Tranmere Rov.
1961-2	Newport, Brentford, Lincoln City, Torquay Utd.
1962-3	Bradford City P.A., Brighton & H.A., Carlisle Utd., Halifax Town
1963-4	Millwall, Crewe Alexandra, Wrexham, Notts Co.
1964-5	Luton Town, Port Vale, Colchester Utd., Barnsley
1965-6	Southend Utd., Exeter City, Brentford, York City
1966-7	Doncaster Rov., Workington, Darlington, Swansea City
1967-8	Scunthorpe Utd., Colchester Utd., Grimsby Town, Peterborough Utd. (demoted)
1968-9	Oldham Athletic, Crewe Alexandra, Hartlepool Utd., Northampton Town
1969-70	Bournemouth, Southport, Barrow, Stockport Co.
1970-1	Gillingham, Doncaster Rov., Bury, Reading
1971-2	Mansfield Town, Barnsley, Torquay Utd., Bradford City
1972-3	Scunthorpe Utd., Swansea City, Brentford, Rotherham Utd.
1973-4	Cambridge Utd., Shrewsbury Town, Rochdale, Southport
1974-5	Bournemouth, Watford, Tranmere Rov., Huddersfield Town
1975-6	Aldershot, Colchester Utd., Southend Utd., Halifax Town
1976-7	Reading, Northampton Town, Grimsby Town, York City
1977-8	Port Vale, Bradford City, Hereford, Portsmouth
1978-9	Peterborough Utd., Walsall, Tranmere Rov., Lincoln City
1979-80	Bury, Southend Utd., Mansfield Town, Wimbledon
1980-1	Sheffield Utd., Colchester Utd., Blackpool, Hull City
1981-2	Wimbledon, Swindon Town, Bristol City, Chester City
1982-3	Reading, Wrexham, Doncaster Rov., Chesterfield
1983-4	Scunthorpe Utd., Southend Utd., Port Vale, Exeter City
1984-5	Burnley, Orient, Preston N.E., Cambridge Utd.
1985-6	Lincoln City, Cardiff City, Wolves, Swansea City
1986-7	Bolton Wand.**, Carlisle Utd., Darlington, Newport
1987-8	Doncaster Rov., York City, Grimsby Town, Rotherham Utd.**
1988-9	Southend Utd., Chesterfield, Gillingham, Aldershot
1989-90	Cardiff City, Northampton Town, Blackpool, Walsall
1990-1	Crewe Alexandra, Rotherham Utd., Mansfield Town
1991-2	Bury, Shrewsbury Town, Torquay Utd., Darlington

** Relegated after plays-offs.

DEMOTED FROM FOURTH DIVISION TO CONFERENCE

1987	Lincoln City
1988	Newport
1989	Darlington
1990	Colchester Utd.
1991	No demotion
1992	No demotion

DEMOTED FROM THIRD DIVISION TO CONFERENCE

1993	Halifax Town
1994-6	No demotion
1997	Hereford
1998	Doncaster Rov.
1999	Scarborough
2000	Chester City
2001	Barnet
2002	Halifax Town
2003	Exeter City, Shrewsbury Town

RELEGATED CLUBS (SINCE 1993)

1993

Premier League to Div. 1: Crystal Palace, Middlesbrough, Nott'm Forest
Div. 1 to Div. 2: Brentford, Cambridge Utd., Bristol Rov.
Div. 2 to Div. 3: Preston N.E., Mansfield Town, Wigan Athletic, Chester City

1994

Premier League to Div. 1: Sheffield Utd., Oldham Athletic, Swindon Town
Div. 1 to Div. 2: Birmingham City, Oxford Utd., Peterborough Utd.
Div. 2 to Div. 3: Fulham, Exeter City, Hartlepool Utd., Barnet

1995

Premier League to Div. 1: Crystal Palace, Norwich City, Leicester City, Ipswich Town
Div. 1 to Div. 2: Swindon Town, Burnley, Bristol City, Notts Co.
Div. 2 to Div. 3: Cambridge Utd., Plymouth Argyle, Cardiff City, Chester City, Leyton Orient

1996

Premier League to Div. 1: Manchester City, Q.P.R., Bolton Wand.
Div. 1 to Div. 2: Millwall, Watford, Luton Town
Div. 2 to Div. 3: Carlisle Utd., Swansea City, Brighton & H.A., Hull City

1997

Premier League to Div. 1: Sunderland, Middlesbrough, Nott'm Forest
Div. 1 to Div. 2: Grimsby Town, Oldham Athletic, Southend Utd.
Div. 2 to Div. 3: Peterborough Utd., Shrewsbury Town, Rotherham Utd., Notts Co.

1998

Premier League to Div. 1: Bolton Wand., Barnsley, Crystal Palace
Div. 1 to Div. 2: Manchester City, Stoke City, Reading
Div. 2 to Div. 3: Brentford, Plymouth Argyle, Carlisle Utd., Southend Utd.

1999

Premier League to Div. 1: Charlton Athletic, Blackburn Rov., Nott'm Forest
Div. 1 to Div. 2: Bury, Oxford Utd., Bristol City
Div. 2 to Div. 3: York City, Northampton Town, Lincoln City, Macclesfield Town

2000

Premier League to Div. 1: Wimbledon, Sheffield Wed., Watford
Div. 1 to Div. 2: Walsall, Port Vale, Swindon Town
Div. 2 to Div. 3: Cardiff City, Blackpool, Scunthorpe Utd., Chesterfield

2001

Premier League to Div. 1: Manchester City, Coventry City, Bradford City
Div. 1 to Div. 2: Huddersfield Town, Q.P.R., Tranmere Rov.
Div. 2 to Div. 3: Bristol Rov., Luton Town, Swansea City, Oxford Utd.

2002

Premier League to Div. 1: Ipswich Town, Derby Co., Leicester City
Div. 1 to Div. 2: Crewe Alexandra, Barnsley, Stockport Co.
Div. 2 to Div. 3: Bournemouth, Bury, Wrexham, Cambridge Utd.

2003

Premier League to Div. 1: West Ham Utd., W.B.A., Sunderland
Div. 1 to Div. 2: Sheffield Wed., Brighton & H.A., Grimsby Town
Div. 2 to Div. 3: Cheltenham Town, Huddersfield Town, Mansfield Town, Northampton Town

BBC TO SHOW ENGLAND GAMES IN NEW TV DEAL

All England home internationals will be shown live on the BBC under a new four-year television agreement with the F.A. running from the start of the 2004-05 season. Delayed broadcasts and highlights will be on Sky in the deal, reported to be worth £300m. It replaces the current £345m. package spread over three years and reflects the current depressed climate for sports TV rights.

The BBC also have first pick of F.A. Cup ties, showing three live games over a weekend from the third round onwards. Sky will show one live tie. Both broadcasters have the Final live.

The announcement came shortly before the deadline for bids for a new package to replace the £1.1bn. Sky paid for live Premiership football. This time, the BBC may also be involved to avoid EU monopoly rules. Sky's coverage this season kicks off with promoted Portsmouth against Aston Villa.

LIVE ON SKY

AUGUST: Sat 9: Preston N.E. v West Ham Utd. Ut., Nott'm. Forest v Sunderland. **Sat 16:** Portsmouth v Aston Villa, W.B.A. v Burnley. **Sun 17:** Liverpool v Chelsea. **Mon 18:** Brighton & H.A. v Q.P.R. **Sat 23:** Newcastle Utd. v Manchester Utd., Preston N.E. v Sunderland. **Sun 24:** Middlesbrough v Arsenal. **Mon 25:** Blackburn Rov. v Manchester City, Reading v Rotherham Utd., Cardiff City v Derby Co. **Wed 27:** Manchester Utd. v Wolves. **Sat 30:** Everton v Liverpool. **Sun 31:** Manchester City v Arsenal.
SEPTEMBER: Mon 1: Wycombe Wand. v Sheffield Wed. **Sat 6:** Bournemouth v Bristol City. **Mon 8:** Doncaster Rov. v Hull City. **Sat 13:** Watford v Millwall, Rotherham Utd. v Crewe Alexandra. **Sun 14:** Birmingham City v Fulham. **Mon 15:** Leicester City v Leeds Utd. **Sat 20:** Wolves v Chelsea, Stoke City v Norwich City. **Sun 21:** Manchester Utd. v Arsenal. **Fri 26:** Arsenal v Newcastle Utd. **Sat 27:** Bradford City v Sheffield Utd., Sunderland v Reading. **Sun 28:** Manchester City v Tottenham. **Mon 29:** Walsall v Gillingham.
OCTOBER: Sat 4: Liverpool v Arsenal, Derby Co. v West Ham Utd. **Sun 5:** Aston Villa v Bolton Wand. **Sun 19:** Everton v Southampton. **Mon 20:** Blackburn Rov. v Charlton Athletic. **Sat 25:** Bolton Wand. v Birmingham City. **Sun 26:** Tottenham v Middlesbrough.
NOVEMBER: Sun 2: Leicester City v Blackburn Rov. **Mon 3:** Birmingham City v Charlton Athletic. **Sun 9:** Liverpool v Manchester Utd., Chelsea v Newcastle Utd. **Mon 10:** Blackburn Rov.v Everton. **Sun 23:** Tottenham v Aston Villa. **Mon 24:** Fulham v Portsmouth. **Sat 29:** Wolves v Newcastle Utd.
DECEMBER: Sat 6: Newcastle Utd. v Liverpool. **Sun 7:** Southampton v Charlton Athletic; **Sat 13:** Manchester Utd. v Manchester City. **Sun 14:** Leeds Utd. v Fulham.

PAY PER VIEW

AUGUST: Sun 17: Leeds Utd. v Newcastle Utd. **Sun 24:** Aston Villa v Liverpool. **Sun 31:** Southampton v Manchester Utd.
SEPTEMBER: Sun 14: Manchester City v Aston Villa. **Sun 21:** Middlesbrough v Everton. **Sun 28:** Charlton Athletic v Liverpool.
OCTOBER: Sun 5: Middlesbrough v Chelsea. **Sun 19:** Leicester City v Tottenham. **Sun 26:** Charlton Athletic v Arsenal.
NOVEMBER: Sun 2: Fulham v Liverpool. **Sat 8:** Wolves v Birmingham City.

THE CHANGING FACE OF FOOTBALL

Football League chairmen will have further discussions in September on whether to introduce major changes in the game, including a new-look play-off system, parachute payments to relegated clubs and penalties for those going into administration.

Support for expanding the play-offs from four to six teams, the idea of Crystal Palace chief executive Phil Alexander was voiced at the AGM. But concern expressed by the F.A. and the Premier League meant that it will not be implemented, as planned, for the 2003-04 season. Parachute payments already exist for clubs relegated from the Premiership and from Division Three to the Conference. Now it is intended to have them for those going down from Divisions One and Two. To prevent clubs going into administration gaining any unfair advantages, the League is considering the deduction of points, denial of promotion and automatic relegation.

September's EGM will be asked to ratify a shake-up in the way the League is run. Chairman Sir Brian Mawhinney has already won approval for an overhaul of the management structure and to raise the profile of the League with Division One as the flagship, in an effort to recreate the success of the Premiership. Sir Brian, a former Conservative Cabinet Minister who was elected chairman in December 2002, said: 'The current value of the Football League is not fully appreciated. We have the best second-tier division in the world and want to enhance our standing.We are taking professional advice on how to go about a re-branding of the product.' The collapse of ITV Digital, with severe financial implications for clubs, and threats by some in Division One to break away have resulted in a difficult 18 months for the League. Now with the planned appointment of new executives with responsibilities for the three divisions, Sir Brian is hoping to turn the tide.

Conference clubs have already voted for a 12-point deduction for clubs going into administration. 'We've done this to set the standard for the good of football,' said chief executive John Moules. 'This will produce a level playing field.'

Player loans between **Premiership** clubs are now permitted, within the transfer window (June 1-August 31 and January 1-31). Clubs will be allowed two such signings at any one time, with a maxium of four through the season. The rule relating to Premiership signings has been changed so that payment of transfer fees can be spread over the length of contract. Previously, clubs had to pay 50% up front and the balance within 12 months.

The **Scottish Premier League** winter break, introduced for the 1998-99 season with the aim of minimising the number of matches lost to the weather, has been scrapped. Chairmen voted to do away with the January shut-down because of the effect of losing gate money for almost a month.

The **Scottish F.A.** will now be run by a board of directors, comprising 10 or 11 members, following a decision of the AGM. The Council, which used to hold power, will continue in an advisory role only. Officials believe they will be able to run affairs more quickly and efficiently. Delegates were told that turnover was at a record £15.4m. and that Hampden Park was now on a sound financial footing.

FIFA have banned players from removing their shirts to celebrate goals 'to restore order and discipline to the game'. President Sepp Blatter said 'too much flesh' had been on display at the Confederations Cup held in France in June. A ban was first introduced in 1996. It was later relaxed. Then players were ordered not to display slogans or personal messages on their vests.

Rule-makers at the **International Board** decided against introducing rugby-style sin-bins, but agreed to teams winning the toss in penalty shoot-outs to be able to choose whether to go first or second. Previously they were obliged to go first.

There will be a slimmed-down Champions League this season in an attempt to reduce fixture congestion. The second group stage will be replaced by a two-leg knock-out system for the last 16 teams. **UEFA** is keen to boost the profile of the UEFA Cup and will change the format of the tournament from the 2004-05 season. After the preliminary knock-out round, 40 teams will be split into eight groups, with each playing two home and two away games, based on seeding. The top three in each group will be joined by eight clubs from the Champions League for the start of the knock-out schedule.

F.A. CUP 2002-03

FIRST ROUND

Barnsley 1, Blackpool 4
Barrow 2, Moor Green 0
Bournemouth 2, Doncaster Rov. 1
Bristol Rov. 0, Runcorn 0
Bury 0, Plymouth Argyle 3
Carlisle Utd. 2, Lincoln City 1
Chesterfield 1, Morecambe 2
Colchester Utd. 0, Chester City 1
Dagenham & Redbridge 3, Havant & Waterlooville 2
Dover Athletic 0, Oxford Utd. 1
Farnborough Town 5, Harrogate Town 1
Forest Green Rov. 0, Exeter City 0
Hereford Utd. 0, Wigan Athletic 1
Heybridge Swifts 0, Bristol City 7
Hull City 0, Macclesfield Town 3
Kidderminster Harr. 2, Rushden & Diamonds 2
Leyton Orient 1, Margate 1
Luton Town 4, Guiseley 0
Northampton Town 3, Boston Utd. 2
Northwich Victoria 0, Scunthorpe Utd. 3
Oldham Athletic 2, Burton Albion 2
Port Vale 0, Crewe Alexandra 1
Rochdale 3, Peterborough Utd. 2
Scarborough 0, Cambridge Utd.0
Shrewsbury Town 4, Stafford Rangers 0
Slough 1, Harrogate Railway 2
Southend Utd. 1, Hartlepool Utd. 1
Southport 4, Notts Co. 2
Stevenage Borough 1, Hastings 0
Stockport Co. 4, St Albans 1
Swindon Town 1, Huddersfield Town 0
Team Bath 2, Mansfield Town 4
Tiverton Town 1, Crawley Town 1
Torquay Utd. 5, Boreham Wood 0
Tranmere Rov. 2, Cardiff City 2
Vauxhall Motors 0, Q.P.R. 0
Wrexham 0, Darlington 2
Wycombe Wand. Wand 2, Brentford 4
Yeovil Town 0, Cheltenham Town 2
York City 2, Swansea City 1.

FIRST ROUND REPLAYS

Burton Albion 2, Oldham Athletic 2†
(Oldham Athletic won 5-4 on pens)
Cambridge Utd. 2, Scarborough 1†
Cardiff City 2, Tranmere Rov. 1
Crawley Town 3, Tiverton Town 1
Exeter City 2, Forest Green Rov. 1
Hartlepool Utd. 1, Southend Utd. 2
Margate 1, Leyton Orient 0
Q.P.R. 1, Vauxhall Motors 1†
(Vauxhall Motors won 4-3 on pens)
Runcorn 1, Bristol Rov. 3†
Rushden & Diamonds 2, Kidderminster Harr. 1

SECOND ROUND

Blackpool 3, Torquay Utd. 1
Bristol Rov. 1, Rochdale 1
Cambridge Utd. 2, Northampton Town 2
Crawley Town 1, Dagenham & Redbridge 2
Crewe Alexandra 3, Mansfield Town 0
Darlington 4, Stevenage Borough 1
Exeter City 3, Rushden & Diamonds 1
Harrogate Railway 1, Bristol City 3
Macclesfield Town 2, Vauxhall Motors 0
Margate 0, Cardiff City 3
Morecambe 3, Chester City 2
Oldham Athletic 1, Cheltenham Town 2
Oxford Utd. 1, Swindon Town 0
Scunthorpe Utd. 0, Carlisle Utd. 0
Shrewsbury Town 3, Barrow 1
Southend Utd. 1, Bournemouth 1
Southport 0, Farnborough Town 3
Stockport Co. 0, Plymouth Argyle 3
Wigan Athletic 3, Luton Town 0
York City 1, Brentford 2

SECOND ROUND REPLAYS

Bournemouth 3, Southend Utd. 2
Carlisle Utd. 0, Scunthorpe Utd. 1
Northampton Town 0, Cambridge Utd. 1
Rochdale 3, Bristol Rov. 2

† After extra-time

ROUND-BY-ROUND HIGHLIGHTS

ROUND ONE

Little Vauxhall Motors pull off the major surprise, knocking out Q.P.R. on penalties in a replay. There are wins for four Conference sides over League opposition – Chesterfield 1, Morecambe 2; Colchester Utd. 0, Chester City 1; Margate 1, Leyton Orient 0 in a replay; Southport 4, Notts Co. 2. Team Bath, the first student side in 122 years to reach the first round proper, lose 4-2 to Mansfield Town. Steve Torpey scores all Scunthorpe Utd. goals in the 3-0 win over Northwich Victoria.

ROUND TWO

Vauxhall Motors bow out to two Macclesfield Town goals in the final ten minutes and, for once, there are no upsets in the round. Biggest crowd – more than 11,000 – see a goal by Jefferson Louis for Oxford Utd. account for Swindon Town and earn his team a third round draw against Arsenal.

ROUND THREE

Two goals by Nigel Jemson, the second in the 89th minute, give Shrewsbury Town a 2-1 victory over Everton in the competition's biggest upset for ten years. Teacher Danny Carroll gets two for Farnborough Town who win 3-2 at Darlington and draw Arsenal in the next round. Matt Jansen, who almost lost his life in a holiday moped accident, makes a scoring comeback with two for Blackburn Rov. in their 4-1 success at Villa Park. Transfer-listed Danny Dichio goes one better with all three in 19 minutes for W.B.A. who beat Bradford City 3-1. Dennis Bergkamp scores his 100th goal for Arsenal who put out Oxford Utd. 2-0. Goalkeeper Carlo Cudicini is sent off for violent conduct, but Chelsea hold on to knock out Middlesbrough 1-0. Manchester City are beaten by a Danny Murphy penalty for Liverpool in the last-ever tie at Maine Road. Alan Shearer criticises Newcastle Utd.'s commitment after the 3-2 defeat by Wolves. Lee Holmes, 15, became the youngest-ever player in the competition proper when coming off the bench for Derby Co. in their single goal defeat by Brentford. Dagenham & Redbridge, in the third round for the third successive year, defeat Plymouth Argyle 2-0 in a replay.

ROUND FOUR

Ten-man Farnborough Town, who conceded home advantage, have their run ended 5-1 at Highbury, Shrewsbury Town's hopes of another upset are crushed in a 4-0 home defeat by Chelsea and Dagenham & Redbridge lose to a last-minute Norwich City goal. But Rochdale surprise Coventry City 2-0, while W.B.A. fall to a late Heidar Helguson goal for Watford. Paul Peschisolido's 89th minute strike for Sheffield Utd. puts the damper on a spirited comeback by Ipswich Town who retrieve a 3-0 deficit. Manchester Utd. hit West Ham Utd. for six. Steed Malbranque scores all three Fulham goals to knock out Charlton Athletic. The big surprise is delivered by Crystal Palace, who beat Liverpool 2-0 in a replay at Anfield (Julian Gray and a Stephane Henchoz own goal). Matthew Oakley's first two goals of the season for Southampton, the second in extra-time, knock out Millwall in a replay.

ROUND FIVE

Arsenal win the heavyweight tie of the round, goals by Edu – a free-kick which deflects off David Beckham – and Sylvain Wiltord accounting for Manchester Utd. at Old Trafford. Crystal Palace, beaten 2-1 by Leeds Utd., protest when Tommy Black's shot, clearly over the line, is not spotted by Dermot Gallagher or his assistant. A twice-taken Tommy Smith penalty gives Watford victory at the Stadium of Light and deepens Sunderland's woe, while Burnley beat Fulham 3-0 in a replay.

ROUND SIX

Frank Lampard's 84th minute goal earns Chelsea a 2-2 draw at Highbury, but Arsenal prevail 3-1 in the replay, despite having Pascal Cygan sent off. Sheffield Utd. repeat their Worthington Cup win over Leeds Utd. with a Steve Kabba goal. Tommy Smith, back after escaping serious injury in a car crash, and Stephen Glass, told he will not be offered a new contract in the summer, score the goals in Watford's win over Burnley. Southampton beat Wolves with a Chris Marsden strike and an own goal by Paul Butler.

SEMI-FINALS

A goal by Freddie Ljungberg and a marvellous late save in his 1,000th senior game by David Seaman from subsitute Paul Peschisolido earn Arsenal a controversial 1-0 win over Sheffield Utd. and a place in the Final for a record 16th time. Sheffield manager Neil Warnock calls for the suspension of referee Graham Poll for failing to give a foul for Sol Campbell's tackle on Wayne Allison and, seconds later, running in front of Michael Tonge during the build up to Ljungberg's 34th minute goal. Southampton reach the Final for the first time since 1976 by overcoming Watford's spirited challenge. Brett Ormerod (43) and a Paul Robinson own goal (80) give them control before Marcus Gayle pulls one back two minutes from the end of normal time.

FINAL

It produced the most unlikely of starts and most unpredictable of finishes. But, for the most part, the Final went the way many expected, with Arsenal's superior individual ability and greater collective experience of the big occasion proving too much for Southampton's strong running and all-round commitment.

Overcoming the absence of the suspended Sol Campbell and injured Patrick Vieira, Arsenal retained the trophy with a 38th minute goal from Robert Pires, who converted the easiest of the many chances which came the way of his team, particularly in the first half when they could, and really should, have built up a handsome lead.

It was a goal to savour for the Frenchman, who missed the previous season's success against Chelsea with a knee ligament injury and whose below-par form in the latter stages of this campaign had been a contributory factor to Arsenal's failure to make a real mark on first the Champions League and then Manchester Utd.'s decisive surge in the title race.

Not far behind in terms of personal satisfaction was Oleg Luzhny, supposedly the weak link in the defence but rising to the challenge of subduing 24-goal James Beattie with a performance which could arguably have earned him, and not Thierry Henry, the man-of-the-match award. Beattie, admittedly, did not receive the best of service, manager Gordon Strachan having left out winger Fabrice Fernandes to accommodate 21-year-old Chris Baird in an attempt to stifle the threat of Pires and Ashley Cole going forward.

The game had a startling opening, Freddie Ljungberg releasing Henry, who stayed on his feet with Claus Lundekvam tugging at his shirt and risking a sending-off with 20 seconds on the clock. Henry placed his shot too near Antti Niemi, and before a quarter-of-an hour had elapsed, Baird cleared off the line from Dennis Bergkamp and Henry shot straight at Niemi from Bergkamp's pass.

When the goal came, Ray Parlour began the move by finding Henry, who cleverly played in Bergkamp for a cross met by Ljungberg. His shot came off Lundekvam and broke invitingly for Pires to score from eight yards. Pires and Ljungberg wasted further chances and Niemi saved well from Henry before going off with a calf injury. Southampton, for all their hard work, had just one miss by Michael Svensson to reflect on – until replacement goalkeeper Paul Jones launched a long clearance, substitute Joe Tessem flicked it on and Brett Ormerod's volley produced an instinctive save by captain-for-the-day David Seaman.

Their attempt to sustain the momentum was frustrated as Arsenal ran down the clock so effectively that there was a spell of almost seven minutes when they dictated possession. Then, five minutes into injury time Beattie made his one telling contribution by connecting with Matthew Oakley's corner, only to see Cole scramble the ball off the line.

ARSENAL 1, SOUTHAMPTON 0

Millennium Stadium, (73,726), Saturday, May 17, 2003

Arsenal (4-4-2): Seaman, Lauren, Keown, Luzhny, Cole, Ljungberg, Parlour, Gilberto Silva, Pires, Bergkamp (Wiltord 77), Henry. **Subs not used:** Taylor, Van Bronckhorst, Kanu, Toure. **Scorer:** Pires (38). **Booked:** Keown, Henry. **Manager:** Arsene Wenger.

Southampton (4-4-2): Niemi (Jones 65); Baird (Fernandes 87), Lundekvam, Svensson, M, Bridge, Telfer, Oakley, Svensson, A (Tessem 75), Marsden, Beattie, Ormerod. **Subs not used:** Higginbotham, Williams. **Booked:** Beattie, Telfer, Marsden, Svensson, M. **Manager:** Gordon Strachan.

Referee: G. Barber (Herts). **Half-time:** 1-0. **Man-of-the-match:** Thierry Henry. **Presentation:** Sir Bobby Robson.

FINAL FACTS AND FIGURES

• With the Millennium Stadium roof closed to the elements, this was the first F.A. Cup Final to be played indoors.

• Arsenal were appearing in a record 16th Final, one more than Manchester Utd. It was their ninth victory, one fewer than the Old Trafford club.

• Arsenal became the first team to retain the trophy since Tottenham defeated Q.P.R 1-0 in a replay in 1982 to follow up their 3-2 replay victory over Manchester City.

• David Seaman was the first goalkeeper to lift the trophy since Dave Beasant captained Wimbledon to their surprise 1-0 win over Liverpool in 1988.

• David Seaman and his Arsenal team-mate Ray Parlour were each playing in a record-equalling fifth Final.

• Only Gilberto Silva and Oleg Luzhny of the Arsenal had not played in an F.A. Cup Final before. No Southampton player had been that far.

• Paul Jones became the first goalkeeper to come on as a substitute in an F.A. Cup Final when he replaced the injured Antti Niemi.

• Chris Baird was such an unexpected choice for Southampton that he did not appear in the match programme profiles.

• The BBC's John Motson was commentating on his 24th F.A. Cup Final, one more than Kenneth Wolstenholme.

HOW THEY REACHED THE FINAL

ARSENAL

Round 3: 2-0 home to Oxford Utd. (Bergkamp, McNiven og)
Round 4: 5-1 'away' to Farnborough Town (Jeffers 2, Campbell, Bergkamp, Lauren) – tie played at Highbury.
Round 5: 2-0 away to Manchester Utd. (Edu, Wiltord)
Round 6: 2-2 home to Chelsea (Jeffers, Henry); 3-1 away to Chelsea (Terry og, Wiltord, Lauren).

Semi-final (Old Trafford): 1-0 v Sheffield Utd. (Ljungberg).

SOUTHAMPTON

Round 3: 4-0 home to Tottenham (Svensson, M, Tessem, Svensson, A, Beattie).
Round 4: 1-1 home to Millwall (Davies); 2-1 away to Millwall (Oakley 2).
Round 5: 2-0 home to Norwich City (Svensson, A, Tessem).
Round 6: 2-0 home to Wolves (Marsden, Butler og).
Semi-final (Aston Villa Park): 2-1 v Watford (Ormerod, Robinson og).

LEADING SCORERS (FROM FIRST ROUND PROPER)

5 Jemson (Shrewsbury Town).
4 Baptiste (Farnborough Town), Malbranque (Fulham), McDonnell (Crawley Town), McDougald (Dagenham & Redbridge), Ndah (Wolves), Van Nistelrooy (Manchester Utd.).
3 Bent, D (Ipswich Town), Carroll (Farnborough Town), Claridge (Millwall), Connor (Rochdale), Dichio (W.B.A.), Duffy (Rushden & Diamonds), Gritton (Torquay Utd.), Jeffers (Arsenal), Iwelumo (Stoke City), Kabba (Sheffield Utd.), Moore, I (Burnley), Murray (Bristol City), Pears (Tiverton Town), Phillips (Sunderland), Platt (Rochdale), Roberts (Bristol City), Torpey (Scunthorpe Utd.), Wotton (Plymouth Argyle), Yorke (Blackburn Rov.).

QUOTE-UNQUOTE

'He's the biggest English talent I've seen since I took over at Highbury' – **Arsene Wenger**, Arsenal manager, on Everton's Wayne Rooney.

'The passion I had for the club when I was a kid is still there' – **Gary Lineker** on fronting a consortium to take over Leicester City.

'I'll probably get done for a sexist comment, but it's becoming a game for girls. We might as well play netball' – **Steve Bruce**, Birmingham City manager, complaining about the dismissal of Olivier Tebily against W.B.A.

'As far as I'm concerned it's already a game for girls. We're watching a non-contact sport' – **Sam Allardyce**, Bolton Wanderers manager, after the red card for Ricardo Gardner against Birmingham City.

'It will be difficult for me to leave a job I have enjoyed so much and which has given me so much satisfaction' – **Adam Crozier** on his resignation as F.A. chief executive after a power struggle with Premier League chairmen.

'He leaves the F.A. in a very strong position, financially, structurally and in a football sense' – **Geoff Thompson**, chairman of the F.A., which later suffered a cash crisis forcing major job cuts.

'I always said I would leave with my head held high, my chin up and my chest out. That's what I'm doing' – **Mick McCarthy** after stepping down as Republic of Ireland manager in the wake of the Roy Keane affair.

'Some people had totally unrealistic ambitions. Two defeats and Mick is gone. It's a disgrace' – **Jason McAteer**, Republic of Ireland midfielder.

'A football team is like a beautiful woman. When you do not tell her, she forgets she is beautiful' – **Arsene Wenger**, Arsenal manager.

'At times like this I wonder if I should open the dressing room door and let the fans tell the players exactly how I feel' – **Sir Alex Ferguson** after Manchester United's 3-1 defeat by Manchester City.

ARSENAL RETAIN CUP

THIRD ROUND	FOURTH ROUND	FIFTH ROUND	SIXTH ROUND	SEMI-FINALS	FINAL
***Arsenal** 2	**Arsenal** 5	**Arsenal** 2	***Arsenal** 2:3	**Arsenal** 1	**Arsenal** 1
Oxford Utd. 0					
*Darlington 2	**Farnborough Town . 1				
Farnborough Town 3					
*Manchester Utd. 4	*Manchester Utd. 6	*Manchester Utd. 0			
Portsmouth 1					
*West Ham Utd. 3	West Ham Utd. 0				
Nott'm. Forest 2					
*Stoke City 3	*Stoke City 3	*Stoke City 0	Chelsea 2:1		
Wigan Athletic 0					
*Bournemouth ... 0:†A2	Bournemouth 0				
Crewe Alexandra 0:2					
*Shrewsbury Town 2	*Shrewsbury Town 0	Chelsea 2			
Everton 1					
*Chelsea 1	Chelsea 4				
Middlesbrough 0					
*Sheffield Utd. 4	*Sheffield Utd. 4	*Sheffield Utd. 2	*Sheffield Utd. 1	Sheffield Utd. 0	
Cheltenham Town 0					
*Ipswich Town 4	Ipswich Town 3				
Morecambe 0					
*Walsall .... 0:†B1	*Walsall 1	Walsall 0			
Reading 0:1					
*Rotherham Utd. 0	Wimbledon 0				
Wimbledon 3					
*Blackpool 1	*Crystal Palace 0:2	*Crystal Palace 1	Leeds Utd. 0		
Crystal Palace 2					
*Manchester City 0	Liverpool 0:0				
Liverpool 1					
*Gillingham 4	*Gillingham 1:1	Leeds Utd. 2			
Sheffield Wed. 1					
*Scunthorpe Utd. 0	Leeds Utd. 1:2				
Leeds Utd. 2					

*Aston Villa 1
Blackburn Rov. 4
*Bolton Wand. 1:0
Sunderland .... 1:†2
*Macclesfield Town ... 0
Watford 2
*W.B.A. 3
Bradford City 1
*Fulham 3
Birmingham City 1
*Charlton Athletic 3
Exeter City 1
*Brentford 1
Derby Co. 0
*Grimsby Town 2:0
Burnley 2:4
*Wolves 3
Newcastle Utd. 2
*Leicester City 2
Bristol City 0
*Preston N.E. 1
Rochdale 2
*Cardiff City 2:0
Coventry City 2:3
*Norwich City 3
Brighton & H.A. 1
*Plymouth Argyle ... 2:0
Dag. & Redbridge .. 2:2
*Cambridge Utd. ... 1:2
Millwall 1:3
Tottenham 0
***Southampton** 4

*Blackburn Rov. 3:2
Sunderland .... 3:†C2
*Watford 1
W.B.A. 0
*Fulham 3
Charlton Athletic 0
*Brentford 0
Burnley 3
*Wolves 4
Leicester City 1
*Rochdale 2
Coventry City 0
*Norwich City 1
Dag. & Redbridge 0
Millwall 1:1
***Southampton** .... 1:†2

*Sunderland 0
Watford 1
*Fulham 1:0
Burnley 1:3
*Wolves 3
Rochdale 1
Norwich City 0
***Southampton** 2

*Watford 2
Burnley 0
Wolves 0
***Southampton** 2

Watford 1
Southampton 2

Southampton 0

* Drawn at home. ** Farnborough Town drawn at home – tie played at Highbury. † After extra-time. A – Bournemouth won 3-1 on pens. B – Walsall won 4-1 on pens. C – Sunderland won 3-0 on pens. Semi-finals: Arsenal v Sheffield Utd. (Old Trafford); Southampton v Watford (Aston Villa Park).

F.A. CUP FINAL TEAMS 1900-2003

1900 BURY – Thompson; Darrock, Davidson, Pray, Leeming, Ross, Richards, Wood, McLuckie, Sagar, Plant. **SOUTHAMPTON** – Robinson; Meehan, Durber, Meston, Chadwick, Petrie, Turner, Yates, Farrell, Wood, Milward. **Scorers:** Bury – McLuckie 2, Wood, Plant.

1901 TOTTENHAM – Clawley; Erentz, Tait, Norris, Hughes, Jones, Smith, Cameron, Brown, Copeland, Kirwan. **SHEFFIELD UTD.** – Foulke; Thickett, Boyle, Johnson, Morren, Needham, Bennett, Field, Hedley, Priest, Lipsham. **Scorers:** (first match) Tottenham – Brown 2, Sheff. Utd. – Bennett, Priest. **Scorers:** (second match) Tottenham – Cameron, Smith, Brown, Sheff. Utd. – Priest.

1902 SHEFFIELD UTD. – Foulke; Thickett, Boyle, Needham, Wilkinson, Johnson, Barnes, Common, Hedley, Priest, Lipsham. (Bennett injured in first match and Barnes took his place in the replay). **SOUTHAMPTON** – Robinson; C. B. Fry, Molyneux, Bowman, Lee, A. Turner, Wood, Brown, Chadwick, J. Turner, Metson. **Scorers:** (first match) Sheff. Utd. – Common, Southampton – Wood. **Scorers:** (second match) Sheff. Utd. – Hedley, Barnes, Southampton – Brown.

1903 BURY – Monteith; Lindsey, McEwan, Johnson, Thorpe, Ross, Richards, Wood, Sagar, Leeming, Plant. **DERBY CO.** – Fryer; Methven, Morris, Warren, Goodall (A.), May, Warrington, York, Boag, Richards, Davis. **Scorers:** Bury – Ross, Sagar, Leeming 2, Wood, Plant.

1904 MANCHESTER CITY – Hillman; McMahon, Burgess, Frost, Hynde, S. B. Ashworth, Meredith, Livingstone, Gillespie, Turnbull (A.), Booth. **BOLTON WAND.** – D. Davies; Brown, Struthers, Clifford, Greenhalgh, Freebairn, Stokes, Marsh, Yenson, White, Taylor. **Scorer:** Manchester City – Meredith.

1905 ASTON VILLA – George; Spencer, Miles, Pearson, Leake, Windmill, Brawn, Garratty, Hampton, Bache, Hall. **NEWCASTLE UTD.** – Lawrence; McCombie, Carr, Gardner, Aitken, McWilliam, Rutherford, Howie, Appleyard, Veitch, Gosnell. **Scorer:** Aston Villa – Hampton 2.

1906 EVERTON – Scott; Balmer (W.), Crelly, Makepeace, Taylor, Abbott, Sharp, Bolton, Young, Settle, H. P. Hardman. **NEWCASTLE UTD.** – Lawrence; McCombie, Carr, Gardner, Aitken, McWilliam, Rutherford, Howie, Veitch, Orr, Gosnell. **Scorer:** Everton – Young.

1907 SHEFFIELD WED. – Lyall; Layton, Burton, Brittleton, Crawshaw, Bartlett, Chapman, Bradshaw, Wilson, Stewart, Simpson. **EVERTON** – Scott; Balmer (W.), Balmer (R.), Makepeace, Taylor, Abbott, Sharp, Bolton, Young, Settle, H. P. Hardman. **Scorers:** Sheff. Wed. – Stewart, Simpson, Everton – Sharp.

1908 WOLVES – Lunn; Jones, Collins, Rev. K. R. G. Hunt, Wooldridge, Bishop, Harrison, Shelton, Hedley, Radford, Pedley. **NEWCASTLE UTD.** – Lawrence; McCracken, Pudan, Gardner, Veitch, McWilliam, Rutherford, Howie, Appleyard, Speedle, Wilson. **Scorers:** Wolves – Hunt, Hedley, Harrison, Newcastle Utd. – Howie.

1909 MANCHESTER UTD. – Moger; Stacey, Hayes, Duckworth, Roberts, Bell, Meredith, Halse, Turnbull (J.), Turnbull (A.), Wall. **BRISTOL CITY** – Clay; Annan, Cottle, Hanlin, Wedlock, Spear, Staniforth, Hardy, Gilligan, Burton, Hilton. **Scorer:** Manchester Utd. – Turnbull (A.).

1910 NEWCASTLE UTD. – Lawrence; McCracken, Carr, Veitch, Low, McWilliam, Rutherford, Howie, Shepherd, Higgins, Wilson. (Whitson was injured in first match and Carr took his place in the replay). **BARNSLEY** – Mearns; Downs, Ness, Glendinning, Boyle, Utley, Bartrop, Gadsby, Lillycrop, Tufnell, Forman. **Scorers:** (first match) Newcastle Utd. – Rutherford, Barnsley – Tufnell. **Scorer:** (second match) Newcastle Utd. – Shepherd 2 (1 pen.).

1911 BRADFORD CITY – Mellors; Campbell, Taylor, Robinson, Torrance, McDonald, Logan, Spiers, O'Rourke, Devine, Thompson. (Gildea played centre half in the first match). **NEWCASTLE UTD.** – Lawrence; McCracken, Whitson, Veitch, Low, Willis, Rutherford, Jobey, Stewart, Higgins, Wilson. **Scorer:** Bradford City – Spiers.

1912 BARNSLEY – Cooper; Downs, Taylor, Glendinning, Bratley, Utley, Bartrop, Tufnell, Lillycrop, Travers, Moore. **W.B.A.** – Pearson; Cook, Pennington, Baddeley, Buck, McNeal, Jephcott, Wright, Pailor, Bower, Shearman. **Scorer:** Barnsley – Tufnell.

1913 ASTON VILLA – Hardy; Lyons, Weston, Barber, Harrop, Leach, Wallace, Halse, Hampton, Stephenson (C.), Bache. **SUNDERLAND** – Butler; Gladwin, Ness, Cuggy, Thompson, Low, Mordue, Buchan, Richardson, Holley, Martin. **Scorer:** Aston Villa – Barber.

1914 BURNLEY – Sewell; Bamford, Taylor, Halley, Boyle, Watson, Nesbit, Lindley, Freeman, Hodgson, Mosscrop. **LIVERPOOL** – Campbell; Longworth, Pursell, Fairfoul, Ferguson, McKinlay, Sheldon, Metcalfe, Miller, Lacey, Nicholl. **Scorer:** Burnley – Freeman.

1915 SHEFFIELD UTD. – Gough; Cook, English, Sturgess, Brelsford, Utley, Simmons, Fazackerley, Kitchen, Masterman, Evans. **CHELSEA** – Molyneux; Bettridge, Harrow, Taylor, Logan, Walker, Ford, Halse, Thompson, Croal, McNeil. **Scorers:** Sheff. Utd. – Simmons, Fazackerley, Kitchen.

1920 ASTON VILLA – Hardy; Smart, Weston, Ducat, Barson, Moss, Wallace, Kirton, Walker, Stephenson (C.), Dorrell. **HUDDERSFIELD TOWN** – Mutch; Wood, Bullock, Slade, Wilson, Watson, Richardson, Mann, Taylor, Swan, Islip. **Scorer:** Aston VIlla – Kirton.

1921 TOTTENHAM – Hunter; Clay, McDonald, Smith, Walters, Grimsdell; Banks, Seed, Cantrell, Bliss, Dimmock. **WOLVES** – George; Woodward, Marshall, Gregory, Hodnett, Riley, Lea, Burrill, Edmonds, Potts, Brooks. **Scorer:** Tottenham – Dimmock.

1922 HUDDERSFIELD TOWN – Mutch; Wood, Wadsworth, Slade, Wilson, Watson, Richardson, Mann, Islip, Stephenson, Smith (W.H.). **PRESTON N.E.** – J. F. Mitchell; Hamilton, Doolan, Duxbury, McCall, Williamson, Rawlings, Jefferis, Roberts, Woodhouse, Quinn. **Scorer:** Huddersfield Town – Smith (pen.).

1923 BOLTON WAND. – Pym; Haworth, Finney, Nuttall, Seddon, Jennings, Butler, Jack, Smith (J. R.), Smith (J.), Vizard. **WEST HAM UTD.** – Hufton; Henderson, Young, Bishop, Kay, Tresadern, Richards, Brown, Watson (V.), Moore, Ruffell. **Scorers:** Bolton Wand. – Jack, Smith (J. R.).

1924 NEWCASTLE UTD. – Bradley; Hampson, Hudspeth, Mooney, Spencer, Gibson, Low, Cowan, Harris, McDonald, Seymour. **ASTON VILLA** – Jackson; Smart, Mort, Moss, Dr. V. E. Milne, Blackburn, York, Kirton, Capewell, Walker, Dorrell. **Scorers:** Newcastle Utd. – Harris, Seymour.

1925 SHEFFIELD UTD. – Sutcliffe; Cook, Milton, Pantling, King, Green, Mercer, Boyle, Johnson, Gillespie, Tunstall. **CARDIFF CITY** – Farquharson; Nelson, Blair, Wake, Keenor, Hardy, Davies (W.), Gill, Nicholson, Beadles, Evans (J.). **Scorer:** Sheff. Utd. – Tunstall.

1926 BOLTON WAND. – Pym; Haworth, Greenhalgh, Nuttall, Seddon, Jennings, Butler, Jack, Smith (J. R.), Smith (J.), Vizard. **MANCHESTER CITY** – Goodchild; Cookson, McCloy, Pringle, Cowan, McMullan, Austin, Browell, Roberts, Johnson, Hicks. **Scorer:** Bolton Wand. – Jack.

1927 CARDIFF CITY – Farquharson; Nelson, Watson, Keenor, Sloan, Hardy, Curtis, Irving, Ferguson, Davies (L.), McLachlan. **ARSENAL** – Lewis; Parker, Kennedy, Baker, Butler, John, Hulme, Buchan, Brain, Blyth, Hoar. **Scorer:** Cardiff City – Ferguson.

1928 BLACKBURN ROV. – Crawford; Hutton, Jones, Healless, Rankin, Campbell, Thornewell, Puddefoot, Roscamp, McLean, Rigby. **HUDDERSFIELD TOWN** – Mercer; Goodall, Barkas, Redfern, Wilson, Steele, Jackson (A.), Kelly, Brown, Stephenson, Smith (W.H.). **Scorers:** Blackburn Rov. – Roscamp 2, McLean, Huddersfield Town – Jackson.

1929 BOLTON WAND. – Pym; Haworth, Finney, Kean, Seddon, Nuttall, Butler, McClelland, Blackmore, Gibson, Cook (W.). **PORTSMOUTH** – Gilfillan; Mackie, Bell, Nichol, McIlwaine, Thackeray, Forward, Smith (J.), Weddle, Watson, Cook (F.). **Scorers:** Bolton Wand. – Butler, Blackmore.

1930 ARSENAL – Preedy; Parker, Hapgood, Baker, Seddon, John, Hulme, Jack, Lambert, James, Bastin. **HUDDERSFIELD TOWN** – Turner; Goodall, Spence, Naylor, Wilson, Campbell, Jackson (A.), Kelly, Davies, Raw, Smith (W. H.). **Scorers:** Arsenal – James, Lambert.

1931 W.B.A. – Pearson; Shaw, Trentham, Magee, Richardson (W.), Edwards, Glidden, Carter, Richardson (W. G.), Sandford, Wood. **BIRMINGHAM CITY** – Hibbs; Liddell, Barkas, Cringan, Morrall, Leslie, Briggs, Crosbie, Bradford, Gregg, Curtis. **Scorers:** W.B.A. – Richardson (W. G.) 2, Birmingham City – Bradford.

1932 NEWCASTLE UTD. – McInroy; Nelson, Fairhurst, McKenzie, Davidson, Weaver, Boyd, Richardson, Allen, McMenemy, Lang. **ARSENAL** – Moss; Parker, Hapgood, Jones (C.), Roberts, Male, Hulme, Jack, Lambert, Bastin, John. **Scorers:** Newcastle Utd. – Allen 2, Arsenal – John.

1933 EVERTON – Sagar; Cook, Cresswell, Britton, White, Thomson, Geldard, Dunn, Dean, Johnson, Stein. **MANCHESTER CITY** – Langford; Cann, Dale, Busby, Cowan, Bray, Toseland, Marshall, Herd, McMullan, Brook. **Scorers:** Everton – Stein, Dean, Dunn.

1934 MANCHESTER CITY – Swift; Barnett, Dale, Busby, Cowan, Bray, Toseland, Marshall, Tilson, Herd, Brook. **PORTSMOUTH** – Gilfillan; Mackie, Smith (W.), Nichol, Allen, Thackeray, Worrall, Smith (J.), Weddle, Easson, Rutherford. **Scorers:** Manchester City – Tilson 2, Portsmouth – Rutherford.

1935 SHEFFIELD WED. – Brown; Nibloe, Catlin, Sharp, Millership, Burrows, Hooper, Surtees, Palethorpe, Starling, Rimmer. **W.B.A.** – Pearson; Shaw, Trentham, Murphy, Richardson (W.), Edwards, Glidden, Carter, Richardson (W. G.), Sandford, Boyes. **Scorers:** Sheff. Wed. – Rimmer 2, Palethorpe, Hooper, W.B.A. – Boyes, Sandford.

1936 ARSENAL – Wilson; Male, Hapgood, Crayston, Roberts, Copping, Hulme, Bowden, Drake, James, Bastin. **SHEFFIELD UTD.** – Smith; Hooper, Wilkinson, Jackson, Johnson, McPherson, Barton, Barclay, Dodds, Pickering, Williams. **Scorer:** Arsenal – Drake.

1937 SUNDERLAND – Mapson; Gorman, Hall, Thomson, Johnston, McNab, Duns, Carter, Gurney, Gallacher, Burbanks. **PRESTON N.E.** – Burns; Gallimore, Beattie (A.), Shankly, Tremelling, Milne, Dougal, Beresford, O'Donnell (F.), Fagan, O'Donnell (H). **Scorers:** Sunderland – Gurney, Carter, Burbanks, Preston N.E. – O'Donnell (F.).

1938 PRESTON N.E. – Holdcroft; Gallimore, Beattie (A.), Shankly, Smith, Batey, Watmough, Mutch, Maxwell, Beattie (R.), O'Donnell (H.). **HUDDERSFIELD TOWN** – Hesford; Craig, Mountford, Willingham, Young, Boot, Hulme, Isaac, McFadyen, Barclay, Beasley. **Scorer:** Preston N.E. – Mutch (pen.).

1939 PORTSMOUTH – Walker; Morgan, Rochford, Guthrie, Rowe, Wharton, Worrall, McAlinden, Anderson, Barlow, Parker. **WOLVES** – Scott; Morris, Taylor, Galley, Cullis, Gardiner, Burton, McIntosh, Westcott, Dorsett, Maguire. **Scorers:** Portsmouth – Barlow, Anderson, Parker 2, Wolves – Dorsett.

1946 DERBY CO. – Woodley; Nicholas, Howe, Bullions, Leuty, Musson, Harrison, Carter, Stamps, Doherty, Duncan. **CHARLTON ATHLETIC** – Bartram; Phipps, Shreeve, Turner (H.), Oakes, Johnson, Fell, Brown, A. A. Turner, Welsh, Duffy. **Scorers:** Derby Co. – Turner (H.) (o.g.), Doherty, Stamps 2, Charlton Athletic – Turner (H.).

1947 CHARLTON ATHLETIC – Bartram; Croker (P.), Shreeve, Johnson, Phipps, Whittaker, Hurst, Dawson, Robinson (W.), Welsh, Duffy. **BURNLEY** – Strong; Woodruff, Mather, Attwell, Brown, Bray, Chew, Morris, Harrison, Potts, F. P. Kippax. **Scorer:** Charlton Athletic – Duffy.

1948 MANCHESTER UTD. – Crompton; Carey, Aston, Anderson, Chilton, Cockburn, Delaney, Morris, Rowley, Pearson, Mitten. **BLACKPOOL** – Robinson; Shimwell, Crosland, Johnston, Hayward, Kelly, Matthews, Munro, Mortensen, Dick, Rickett. **Scorers:** Manchester Utd. – Rowley 2, Pearson, Anderson, Blackpool – Shimwell (pen.), Mortensen.

1949 WOLVES – Williams; Pritchard, Springthorpe, Crook (W.), Shorthouse, Wright, Hancocks, Smyth, Pye, Dunn, Mullen. **LEICESTER CITY** – Bradley; Jelly, Scott, Harrison (W.), Plummer, King, Griffiths, Lee, Harrison (J.), Chisholm, Adam. **Scorers:** Wolves – Pye 2, Smyth, Leicester City – Griffiths.

1950 ARSENAL – Swindin; Scott, Barnes, Forbes, Compton (L.), Mercer, Cox, Logie, Goring, Lewis, Compton (D.). **LIVERPOOL** – Sidlow; Lambert, Spicer, Taylor, Hughes, Jones, Payne, Baron, Stubbins, Fagan, Liddell. **Scorer:** Arsenal – Lewis 2.

1951 NEWCASTLE UTD. – Fairbrother; Cowell, Corbett, Harvey, Brennan, Crowe, Walker, Taylor, Milburn, Robledo (G.), Mitchell. **BLACKPOOL** – Farm; Shimwell, Garrett, Johnston, Hayward, Kelly, Matthews, Mudie, Mortensen, W. J. Slater, Perry. **Scorer:** Newcastle Utd. – Milburn 2.

1952 NEWCASTLE UTD. – Simpson; Cowell, McMichael, Harvey, Brennan, Robledo (E.), Walker, Foulkes, Milburn, Robledo (G.), Mitchell. **ARSENAL** – Swindin; Barnes, Smith (L.), Forbes, Daniel, Mercer, Cox, Logie, Holton, Lishman, Roper. **Scorer:** Newcastle Utd. – Robledo (G.).

1953 BLACKPOOL – Farm; Shimwell, Garrett, Fenton, Johnston, Robinson, Matthews, Taylor, Mortensen, Mudie, Perry. **BOLTON WAND.** – Hanson; Ball, Banks (R.), Wheeler, Barrass, Bell, Holden, Moir, Lofthouse, Hassall, Langton. **Scorers:** Blackpool – Mortensen 3, Perry, Bolton Wand. – Lofthouse, Moir, Bell.

1954 W.B.A. – Sanders; Kennedy, Millard, Dudley, Dugdale, Barlow, Griffin, Ryan, Allen, Nicholls, Lee. **PRESTON N.E.** – Thompson; Cunningham, Walton, Docherty, Marston, Forbes, Finney, Foster, Wayman, Baxter, Morrison. **Scorers:** W.B.A. – Allen 2 (1 pen.), Griffin, Preston N.E. – Morrison, Wayman.

1955 NEWCASTLE UTD. – Simpson; Cowell, Batty, Scoular, Stokoe, Casey, White, Milburn, Keeble, Hannah, Mitchell. **MANCHESTER CITY** – Trautmann; Meadows, Little, Barnes, Ewing, Paul, Spurdle, Hayes, Revie, Johnstone, Fagan. **Scorers:** Newcastle Utd. – Milburn, Mitchell, Hannah, Manchester City – Johnstone.

1956 MANCHESTER CITY – Trautmann; Leivers, Little, Barnes, Ewing, Paul, Johnstone, Hayes, Revie, Dyson, Clarke. **BIRMINGHAM CITY** – Merrick; Hall, Green, Newman, Smith, Boyd, Astall, Kinsey, Brown, Murphy, Govan. **Scorers:** Manchester City – Hayes, Dyson, Johnstone, Birmingham City – Kinsey.

1957 ASTON VILLA – Sims; Lynn, Aldis, Crowther, Dugdale, Saward, Smith, Sewell, Myerscough, Dixon, McParland. **MANCHESTER UTD.** – Wood; Foulkes, Byrne, Colman, Blanchflower, Edwards, Berry, Whelan, Taylor (T.), Charlton, Pegg. **Scorers:** Aston Villa – McParland 2, Manchester Utd. – Taylor.

1958 BOLTON WANDERERS – Hopkinson; Hartle, Banks (T.), Hennin, Higgins, Edwards, Birch, Stevens, Lofthouse, Parry, Holden. **MANCHESTER UTD.** – Gregg; Foulkes, Greaves, Goodwin, Cope, Crowther, Dawson, Taylor (E.), Charlton, Viollet, Webster. **Scorer:** Bolton Wand. – Lofthouse 2.

1959 NOTT'M FOREST – Thomson; Whare, McDonald, Whitefoot, McKinlay, Burkitt, Dwight, Quigley, Wilson, Gray, Imlach. **LUTON TOWN** – Baynham; McNally, Hawkes, Groves, Owen, Pacey, Bingham, Brown, Morton, Cummins, Gregory. **Scorers:** Nott'm. Forest – Dwight, Wilson, Luton Town – Pacey.

1960 WOLVES – Finlayson; Showell, Harris, Clamp, Slater, Flowers, Deeley, Stobart, Murray, Broadbent, Horne. **BLACKBURN ROV.** – Leyland; Bray, Whelan, Clayton, Woods, McGrath, Bimpson, Dobing, Dougan, Douglas, MacLeod. **Scorers:** Wolves – McGrath (o.g.), Deeley 2.

1961 TOTTENHAM – Brown; Baker, Henry, Blanchflower, Norman, Mackay, Jones, White, Smith, Allen, Dyson. **LEICESTER CITY** – Banks; Chalmers, Norman, McLintock, King, Appleton, Riley, Walsh, McIlmoyle, Keyworth, Cheesebrough. **Scorers:** Tottenham – Smith, Dyson.

1962 TOTTENHAM – Brown; Baker, Henry, Blanchflower, Norman, Mackay, Medwin, White, Smith, Greaves, Jones. **BURNLEY** – Blacklaw; Angus, Elder, Adamson, Cummings, Miller, Connelly, McIlroy, Pointer, Robson, Harris. **Scorers:** Tottenham – Greaves, Smith, Blanchflower (pen.), Burnley – Robson.

1963 MANCHESTER UTD. – Gaskell; Dunne, Cantwell, Crerand, Foulkes, Setters, Giles, Quixall, Herd, Law, Charlton. **LEICESTER CITY** – Banks; Sjoberg, Norman, McLintock, King, Appleton, Riley, Cross, Keyworth, Gibson, Stringfellow. **Scorers:** Manchester Utd. – Law, Herd 2, Leicester City – Keyworth.

1964 WEST HAM UTD. – Standen; Bond, Burkett, Bovington, Brown, Moore, Brabrook, Boyce, Byrne, Hurst, Sissons. **PRESTON N.E.** – Kelly; Ross, Smith, Lawton, Singleton, Kendall, Wilson, Ashworth, Dawson, Spavin, Holden. **Scorers:** West Ham Utd. – Sissons, Hurst, Boyce, Preston N.E. – Holden, Dawson.

1965 LIVERPOOL – Lawrence; Lawler, Byrne, Strong, Yeats, Stevenson, Callaghan, Hunt, St. John, Smith, Thompson. **LEEDS UTD.** – Sprake; Reaney, Bell, Bremner, Charlton, Hunter, Giles, Storrie, Peacock, Collins, Johanneson. **Scorers:** Liverpool – Hunt, St. John, Leeds Utd. – Bremner.

1966 EVERTON – West; Wright, Wilson, Gabriel, Labone, Harris, Scott, Trebilcock, Young, Harvey, Temple. **SHEFFIELD WED.** – Springett; Smith, Megson, Eustace, Ellis, Young, Pugh, Fantham, McCalliog, Ford, Quinn. **Scorers:** Everton – Trebilcock 2, Temple, Sheff. Wed. – McCalliog, Ford.

1967 TOTTENHAM – Jennings; Kinnear, Knowles, Mullery, England, Mackay, Robertson, Greaves, Gilzean, Venables, Saul. **CHELSEA** – Bonetti; Harris (A.), McCreadie, Hollins, Hinton, Harris (R.), Cooke, Baldwin, Hateley, Tambling, Boyle. **Scorers:** Tottenham – Robertson, Saul, Chelsea – Tambling.

1968 W.B.A. – Osborne; Fraser, Williams, Brown, Talbut, Kaye (Clarke), Lovett, Collard, Astle, Hope, Clark. **EVERTON** – West; Wright, Wilson, Kendall, Labone, Harvey, Husband, Ball, Royle, Hurst, Morrissey. **Scorer:** W.B.A. – Astle.

1969 MANCHESTER CITY – Dowd; Book, Pardoe, Doyle, Booth, Oakes, Summerbee, Bell, Lee, Young, Coleman. **LEICESTER CITY** – Shilton; Rodrigues, Nish, Roberts, Woollett, Cross, Fern, Gibson, Lochhead, Clarke, Glover (Manley). **Scorer:** Manchester City – Young.

1970 CHELSEA – Bonetti; Webb, McCreadie, Hollins, Dempsey, Harris (R.) (Hinton), Baldwin, Houseman, Osgood, Hutchinson, Cooke. **LEEDS UTD.** – Sprake; Madeley, Cooper, Bremner, Charlton, Hunter, Lorimer, Clarke, Jones, Giles, Gray. **Scorers:** Chelsea – Houseman, Hutchinson, Leeds Utd. – Charlton, Jones. **Replay: CHELSEA** – Bonetti; Harris (R.), McCreadie, Hollins, Dempsey, Webb, Baldwin, Cooke, Osgood (Hinton), Hutchinson, Houseman. **LEEDS UTD.** – Harvey; Madeley, Cooper, Bremner, Charlton, Hunter, Lorimer, Clarke, Jones, Giles, Gray. **Scorers:** Chelsea – Osgood, Webb, Leeds Utd. – Jones.

1971 ARSENAL – Wilson; Rice, McNab, Storey (Kelly), McLintock, Simpson, Armstrong, Graham, Radford, Kennedy, George. **LIVERPOOL** – Clemence; Lawler, Lindsay, Smith, Lloyd, Hughes, Callaghan, Evans (Thompson), Heighway, Toshack, Hall. **Scorers:** Arsenal – Kelly, George, Liverpool – Heighway.

1972 LEEDS UTD. – Harvey; Reaney, Madeley, Bremner, Charlton, Hunter, Lorimer, Clarke, Jones, Giles, Gray. **ARSENAL** – Barnett; Rice, McNab, Storey, McLintock, Simpson, Armstrong, Ball, Radford (Kennedy), George, Graham. **Scorer:** Leeds Utd. – Clarke.

1973 SUNDERLAND – Montgomery; Malone, Guthrie, Horswill, Watson, Pitt, Kerr, Hughes, Halom, Porterfield, Tueart. **LEEDS UTD.** – Harvey; Reaney, Cherry, Bremner, Madeley, Hunter, Lorimer, Clarke, Jones, Giles, Gray (Yorath). **Scorer:** Sunderland – Porterfield.

1974 LIVERPOOL – Clemence; Smith, Lindsay, Thompson, Cormack, Hughes, Keegan, Hall, Heighway, Toshack, Callaghan. **NEWCASTLE UTD.** – McFaul; Clark, Kennedy, McDermott, Howard, Moncur, Smith (Gibb), Cassidy, Macdonald, Tudor, Hibbitt. **Scorers:** Liverpool – Keegan (2), Heighway.

1975 WEST HAM UTD. – Day; McDowell, Lampard, Bonds, Taylor (T.), Lock, Jennings, Paddon, Taylor (A.), Brooking, Holland. **FULHAM** – Mellor; Cutbush, Fraser, Mullery, Lacy, Moore, Mitchell, Conway, Busby, Slough, Barrett. **Scorer:** West Ham Utd. – Taylor (A.) 2.

1976 SOUTHAMPTON – Turner; Rodrigues, Peach, Holmes, Blyth, Steele, Gilchrist, Channon, Osgood, McCalliog, Stokes. **MANCHESTER UTD.** – Stepney; Forsyth, Houston, Daly, Greenhoff (B.), Buchan, Coppell, McIlroy, Pearson, Macari, Hill (McCreery). **Scorer:** Southampton – Stokes.

1977 MANCHESTER UTD. – Stepney; Nicholl, Albiston, McIlroy, Greenhoff (B.), Buchan, Coppell, Greenhoff (J.), Pearson, Macari, Hill (McCreery). **LIVERPOOL** – Clemence; Neal, Jones, Smith, Kennedy, Hughes, Keegan, Case, Heighway, McDermott, Johnson (Callaghan). **Scorers:** Manchester Utd. – Pearson, Greenhoff (J.), Liverpool – Case.

1978 IPSWICH TOWN – Cooper; Burley, Mills, Talbot, Hunter, Beattie, Osborne (Lambert), Wark, Mariner, Geddis, Woods. **ARSENAL** – Jennings; Rice, Nelson, Price, O'Leary, Young, Brady (Rix), Sunderland, Macdonald, Stapleton, Hudson. **Scorer:** Ipswich Town – Osborne.

1979 ARSENAL – Jennings; Rice, Nelson, Talbot, O'Leary, Young, Brady, Sunderland, Stapleton, Price (Walford), Rix. **MANCHESTER UTD.** – Bailey; Nicholl, Albiston, McIlroy, McQueen, Buchan, Coppell, Greenhoff (J.), Jordan, Macari, Thomas. **Scorers:** Arsenal – Talbot, Stapleton, Sunderland, Manchester Utd. – McQueen, McIlroy.

1980 WEST HAM UTD. – Parkes; Stewart, Lampard, Bonds, Martin, Devonshire, Allen, Pearson, Cross, Brooking, Pike. **ARSENAL** – Jennings; Rice, Devine (Nelson), Talbot, O'Leary, Young, Brady, Sunderland, Stapleton, Price, Rix. **Scorer:** West Ham Utd. – Brooking.

1981 TOTTENHAM – Aleksic; Hughton, Miller, Roberts, Perryman, Villa (Brooke), Ardiles, Archibald, Galvin, Hoddle, Crooks. **MANCHESTER CITY** – Corrigan; Ranson, McDonald, Reid, Power, Caton, Bennett, Gow, Mackenzie, Hutchison (Henry), Reeves. **Scorer:** Tottenham – Hutchison (o.g.), Manchester City – Hutchison. **Replay: TOTTENHAM** – Aleksic; Hughton, Miller, Roberts, Perryman, Villa, Ardiles, Archibald, Galvin, Hoddle, Crooks. **MANCHESTER CITY** – Corrigan; Ranson, McDonald (Tueart), Reid, Power, Caton, Bennett, Gow, Mackenzie, Hutchison, Reeves. **Scorers:** Tottenham – Villa 2, Crooks, Manchester City – Mackenzie, Reeves (pen.).

1982 TOTTENHAM – Clemence; Hughton, Miller, Price, Hazard (Brooke), Perryman, Roberts, Archibald, Galvin, Hoddle, Crooks. **Q.P.R.** – Hucker; Fenwick, Gillard, Waddock, Hazell, Roeder, Currie, Flanagan, Allen (Micklewhite), Stainrod, Gregory. **Scorers:** Tottenham – Hoddle, Q.P.R. – Fenwick. **Replay: TOTTENHAM** – Clemence; Hughton, Miller, Price, Hazard (Brooke), Perryman, Roberts, Archibald, Galvin, Hoddle, Crooks. **Q.P.R.** – Hucker; Fenwick, Gillard, Waddock, Hazell, Neill, Currie, Flanagan, Micklewhite (Burke), Stainrod, Gregory. **Scorer:** Tottenham – Hoddle (pen.).

1983 MANCHESTER UTD. – Bailey; Duxbury, Albiston, Wilkins, Moran, McQueen, Robson, Muhren, Stapleton, Whiteside, Davies. **BRIGHTON & H.A.** – Moseley; Ramsey (Ryan), Pearce, Grealish, Gatting, Stevens, Case, Howlett, Robinson, Smith, Smillie. **Scorers:** Manchester Utd. – Stapleton, Wilkins, Brighton & H.A. – Smith, Stevens. **Replay: MANCHESTER UTD.** – Bailey; Duxbury, Albiston, Wilkins, Moran, McQueen, Robson, Muhren, Stapleton, Whiteside, Davies. **BRIGHTON & H.A.** – Moseley; Gatting, Pearce, Grealish, Foster, Stevens, Case, Howlett (Ryan), Robinson, Smith, Smillie. **Scorers:** Manchester Utd. – Robson 2, Whiteside, Muhren (pen.).

1984 EVERTON – Southall; Stevens, Bailey, Ratcliffe, Mountfield, Reid, Steven, Heath, Sharp, Gray, Richardson. **WATFORD** – Sherwood; Bardsley, Price (Atkinson), Taylor, Terry, Sinnott, Callaghan, Johnston, Reilly, Jackett, Barnes. **Scorers:** Everton – Sharp, Gray.

1985 MANCHESTER UTD. – Bailey; Gidman, Albiston (Duxbury), Whiteside, McGrath, Moran, Robson, Strachan, Hughes, Stapleton, Olsen. **EVERTON** – Southall; Stevens, Van den Hauwe, Ratcliffe, Mountfield, Reid, Steven, Sharp, Gray, Bracewell, Sheedy. **Scorer:** Manchester Utd. – Whiteside. **Sent-off:** Moran.

1986 LIVERPOOL – Grobbelaar; Lawrenson, Beglin, Nicol, Whelan, Hansen, Dalglish, Johnston, Rush, Molby, MacDonald. **EVERTON** – Mimms; Stevens (Heath), Van den Hauwe, Ratcliffe, Mountfield, Reid, Steven, Lineker, Sharp, Bracewell, Sheedy. **Scorers:** Liverpool – Rush 2, Johnston, Everton – Lineker.

1987 COVENTRY CITY – Ogrizovic; Phillips, Downs, McGrath, Kilcline (Rodger), Peake, Bennett, Gynn, Regis, Houchen, Pickering. **TOTTENHAM** – Clemence; Hughton (Claesen), Thomas (M.), Hodge, Gough, Mabbutt, Allen (C.), Allen (P.), Waddle, Hoddle, Ardiles (Stevens). **Scorers:** Coventry City – Bennett, Houchen, Mabbutt (o.g.), Tottenham – Allen (C.), Mabbutt.

1988 WIMBLEDON – Beasant; Goodyear, Phelan, Jones, Young, Thorn, Gibson (Scales), Cork (Cunningham), Fashanu, Sanchez, Wise. **LIVERPOOL** – Grobbelaar; Gillespie, Ablett, Nicol, Spackman (Molby), Hansen, Beardsley, Aldridge (Johnston), Houghton, Barnes, McMahon. **Scorer:** Wimbledon – Sanchez.

1989 LIVERPOOL – Grobbelaar; Ablett, Staunton (Venison), Nicol, Whelan, Hansen, Beardsley, Aldridge (Rush), Houghton, Barnes, McMahon. **EVERTON** – Southall; McDonald, Van den Hauwe, Ratcliffe, Watson, Bracewell (McCall), Nevin, Steven, Sharp, Cottee, Sheedy (Wilson). **Scorers:** Liverpool – Aldridge, Rush 2, Everton – McCall 2.

1990 MANCHESTER UTD. – Leighton; Ince, Martin (Blackmore), Bruce, Phelan, Pallister (Robins), Robson, Webb, McClair, Hughes, Wallace. **CRYSTAL PALACE** – Martyn; Pemberton, Shaw, Gray (Madden), O'Reilly, Thorn, Barber (Wright), Thomas, Bright, Salako, Pardew. **Scorers:** Manchester Utd. – Robson, Hughes 2, Crystal Palace – O'Reilly, Wright 2. **Replay: MANCHESTER UTD.** – Sealey; Ince, Martin, Bruce, Phelan, Pallister, Robson, Webb, McClair, Hughes, Wallace. **CRYSTAL PALACE** – Martyn; Pemberton, Shaw, Gray, O'Reilly, Thorn, Barber (Wright), Thomas, Bright, Salako (Madden), Pardew. **Scorer:** Manchester Utd. – Martin.

1991 TOTTENHAM – Thorstvedt; Edinburgh, Van den Hauwe, Sedgley, Howells, Mabbutt, Stewart, Gascoigne (Nayim), Samways (Walsh), Lineker, Allen. **NOTT'M FOREST** –

Crossley; Charles, Pearce, Walker, Chettle, Keane, Crosby, Parker, Clough, Glover (Laws), Woan (Hodge). **Scorers:** Tottenham – Stewart, Walker (o.g.), Nott'm. Forest – Pearce.

1992 LIVERPOOL – Grobbelaar; Jones (R.), Burrows, Nicol, Molby, Wright, Saunders, Houghton, Rush (I.), McManaman, Thomas. **SUNDERLAND** – Norman; Owers, Ball, Bennett, Rogan, Rush (D.) (Hardyman), Bracewell, Davenport, Armstrong (Hawke), Byrne, Atkinson. **Scorers:** Liverpool – Thomas, Rush (I.).

1993 ARSENAL – Seaman; Dixon, Winterburn, Linighan, Adams, Parlour (Smith), Davis, Merson, Jensen, Wright (O'Leary), Campbell. **SHEFFIELD WED.** – Woods; Nilsson, Worthington, Palmer, Hirst, Anderson (Hyde), Waddle (Bart-Williams), Warhurst, Bright, Sheridan, Harkes. **Scorers:** Arsenal – Wright, Sheff. Wed. – Hirst. **Replay: ARSENAL** – Seaman; Dixon, Winterburn, Linighan, Adams, Davis, Jensen, Merson, Smith, Wright (O'Leary), Campbell. **SHEFFIELD WED.** – Woods; Nilsson (Bart-Williams), Worthington, Palmer, Hirst, Wilson (Hyde), Waddle, Warhurst, Bright, Sheridan, Harkes. **Scorers:** Arsenal – Wright, Linighan, Sheff. Wed. – Waddle.

1994 MANCHESTER UTD. – Schmeichel; Parker, Bruce, Pallister, Irwin (Sharpe), Kanchelskis (McClair), Keane, Ince, Giggs, Cantona, Hughes. **CHELSEA** – Kharine; Clarke, Johnsen, Kjeldbjerg, Sinclair, Burley (Hoddle), Newton, Wise, Peacock, Stein (Cascarino), Spencer. **Scorers:** Manchester Utd. – Cantona 2 (2 pens.), Hughes, McClair.

1995 EVERTON – Southall; Jackson, Watson, Unsworth, Ablett, Horne, Parkinson, Hinchcliffe, Stuart, Limpar (Amokachi), Rideout (Ferguson). **MANCHESTER UTD.** – Schmeichel; Neville (G.), Bruce (Giggs), Pallister, Irwin, Butt, Keane, Ince, Sharpe (Scholes), McClair, Hughes. **Scorer:** Everton – Rideout.

1996 MANCHESTER UTD. – Schmeichel; Irwin, May, Pallister, Neville (P.), Beckham (Neville, G.), Keane, Butt, Giggs, Cantona, Cole (Scholes). **LIVERPOOL** – James; McAteer, Scales, Wright, Babb, Jones (Thomas), McManaman, Redknapp, Barnes, Collymore (Rush), Fowler. **Scorer:** Manchester Utd. – Cantona.

1997 CHELSEA – Grodas; Sinclair, Lebouef, Clarke, Minto, Petrescu, Di Matteo, Newton, Wise, Zola (Vialli), Hughes (M.). **MIDDLESBROUGH** – Roberts; Blackmore, Pearson, Festa, Fleming, Stamp, Emerson, Mustoe (Vickers), Hignett (Kinder), Juninho, Ravanelli, (Beck). **Scorers:** Chelsea – Di Matteo, Newton.

1998 ARSENAL – Seaman; Dixon, Adams, Keown, Winterburn, Parlour, Petit, Vieira, Overmars, Wreh (Platt), Anelka. **NEWCASTLE** – Given; Barton (Watson), Dabizas, Howey, Pearce (Andersson), Pistone, Batty, Lee, Speed, Shearer, Ketsbaia (Barnes). **Scorers:** Arsenal – Overmars, Anelka.

1999 MANCHESTER UTD. – Schmeichel; Neville (G.), Johnsen, May, Neville (P.); Beckham, Scholes (Stam), Keane (Sheringham), Giggs; Cole (Yorke), Solskjaer. **NEWCASTLE UTD.** – Harper; Griffin, Charvet, Dabizas, Domi; Lee, Hamann (Ferguson), Speed, Solano (Maric); Ketsbaia (Glass), Shearer. **Scorers:** Manchester Utd. – Sheringham, Scholes.

2000 CHELSEA – De Goey; Melchiot, Desailly, Leboeuf, Babayaro, Di Matteo, Wise, Deschamps, Poyet, Weah (Flo), Zola (Morris). **ASTON VILLA** – James; Ehiogu, Southgate, Barry, Delaney. Taylor (Stone), Boateng, Merson, Wright (Hendrie), Dublin, Carbone (Joachim). **Scorer:** Chelsea – Di Matteo.

2001 LIVERPOOL – Westerveld; Babbel, Henchoz, Hyypia, Carragher, Murphy (Berger), Hamann (McAllister), Gerrard, Smicer (Fowler), Heskey, Owen. **ARSENAL** – Seaman; Dixon (Bergkamp), Keown, Adams, Cole, Ljungberg (Kanu), Grimandi, Vieira, Pires, Henry, Wiltord (Parlour). **Scorers:** Liverpool – Owen 2, Arsenal – Ljungberg.

2002 ARSENAL – Seaman; Lauren, Campbell, Adams, Cole, Wiltord (Keown), Parlour, Vieira, Ljungberg, Bergkamp (Edu), Henry (Kanu). **CHELSEA** – Cudicini; Melchiot, Desailly, Gallas, Babayaro (Terry), Gronkjaer, Lampard, Petit, Le Saux, Hasselbaink (Zola), Gudjohnsen. **Scorers:** Arsenal – Parlour, Ljungberg.

2003 ARSENAL – Seaman; Lauren, Keown, Luzhny, Cole, Ljungberg, Parlour, Gilberto Silva, Pires, Bergkamp (Wiltord), Henry. **SOUTHAMPTON** – Niemi (Jones); Baird (Fernandes), Lundekvam, Svensson (M.), Bridge, Telfer, Oakley, Svensson (A.) (Tessem), Marsden, Beattie, Ormerod. **Scorer:** Arsenal – Pires.

F.A. CUP FINALS – COMPLETE RESULTS

AT KENNINGTON OVAL

1872 The Wanderers beat Royal Engineers (1-0)

AT LILLIE BRIDGE, LONDON

1873 The Wanderers beat Oxford University (2-1)

AT KENNINGTON OVAL

1874 Oxford University beat Royal Engineers (2-0)
1875 Royal Engineers beat Old Etonians (2-0 after a 1-1 draw)
1876 The Wanderers beat Old Etonians (3-0 after a 0-0 draw)
1877†† The Wanderers beat Oxford University (2-1)
1878* The Wanderers beat Royal Engineers (3-1)
1879 Old Etonians beat Clapham Rov. (1-0)
1880 Clapham Rov. beat Oxford University (1-0)
1881 Old Carthusians beat Old Etonians (3-0)
1882 Old Etonians beat Blackburn Rov. (1-0)
1883†† Blackburn Olympic beat Old Etonians (2-1)
1884 Blackburn Rov. beat Queen's Park (Glasgow) (2-1)
1885 Blackburn Rov. beat Queen's Park (Glasgow) (2-0)
1886†*a* Blackburn Rov. beat W.B.A. (2-0 after a 0-0 draw)
1887 Aston Villa beat W.B.A. (2-0)
1888 W.B.A. beat Preston N.E. (2-1)
1889 Preston N.E. beat Wolves (3-0)
1890 Blackburn Rov. beat Sheffield Wed. (6-1)
1891 Blackburn Rov. beat Notts Co. (3-1)
1892 W.B.A. beat Aston Villa (3-0)

AT FALLOWFIELD, MANCHESTER

1893 Wolves beat Everton (1-0)

AT GOODISON PARK

1894 Notts Co. beat Bolton Wand. (4-1)

AT CRYSTAL PALACE

1895 Aston Villa beat W.B.A. (1-0)
1896 Sheffield Wed. beat Wolves (2-1)
1897 Aston Villa beat Everton (3-2)
1898 Nott'm. Forest beat Derby Co. (3-1)
1899 Sheffield Utd. beat Derby Co. (4-1)
1900 Bury beat Southampton (4-0)
1901††† Tottenham beat Sheffield Utd. (3-1 after a 2-2 draw)
1902 Sheffield Utd. beat Southampton (2-1 after a 1-1 draw)
1903 Bury beat Derby Co. (6-0)
1904 Manchester City beat Bolton Wand. (1-0)
1905 Aston Villa beat Newcastle Utd. (2-0)
1906 Everton beat Newcastle Utd. (1-0)
1907 Sheffield Wed. beat Everton (2-1)
1908 Wolves beat Newcastle Utd. (3-1)
1909 Manchester Utd. beat Bristol City (1-0)
1910** Newcastle Utd. beat Barnsley (2-0 after a 1-1 draw)
1911*b* Bradford City beat Newcastle Utd. (1-0 after a 0-0 draw)
1912*c* Barnsley beat W.B.A. (1-0 after a 0-0 draw)
1913 Aston Villa beat Sunderland (1-0)
1914 Burnley beat Liverpool (1-0)

AT OLD TRAFFORD

1915 Sheffield Utd. beat Chelsea (3-0)

AT STAMFORD BRIDGE

1920†† Aston Villa beat Huddersfield Town (1-0)
1921 Tottenham beat Wolves (1-0)
1922 Huddersfield Town beat Preston N.E. (1-0)

AT WEMBLEY

1923 Bolton Wand. beat West Ham Utd. (2-0)
1924 Newcastle Utd. beat Aston Villa (2-0)
1925 Sheffield Utd. beat Cardiff City (1-0)
1926 Bolton Wand. beat Manchester City (1-0)
1927 Cardiff City beat Arsenal (1-0)
1928 Blackburn Rov. beat Huddersfield Town (3-1)
1929 Bolton Wand. beat Portsmouth (2-0)
1930 Arsenal beat Huddersfield Town (2-0)
1931 W.B.A. beat Birmingham City (2-1)
1932 Newcastle Utd. beat Arsenal (2-1)
1933 Everton beat Manchester City (3-0)
1934 Manchester City beat Portsmouth (2-1)
1935 Sheffield Wed. beat W.B.A. (4-2)
1936 Arsenal beat Sheffield Utd. (1-0)
1937 Sunderland beat Preston N.E. (3-1)
1938†† Preston N.E. beat Huddersfield Town (1-0)
1939 Portsmouth beat Wolves (4-1)
1946†† Derby Co. beat Charlton Athletic (4-1)
1947†† Charlton Athletic beat Burnley (1-0)
1948 Manchester Utd. beat Blackpool (4-2)
1949 Wolves beat Leicester City (3-1)
1950 Arsenal beat Liverpool (2-0)
1951 Newcastle Utd. beat Blackpool (2-0)
1952 Newcastle Utd. beat Arsenal (1-0)
1953 Blackpool beat Bolton Wand. (4-3)
1954 W.B.A. beat Preston N.E. (3-2)
1955 Newcastle Utd. beat Manchester City (3-1)
1956 Manchester City beat Birmingham City (3-1)
1957 Aston Villa beat Manchester Utd. (2-1)
1958 Bolton Wand. beat Manchester Utd. (2-0)
1959 Nott'm. Forest beat Luton Town (2-1)
1960 Wolves beat Blackburn Rov. (3-0)
1961 Tottenham beat Leicester City (2-0)
1962 Tottenham beat Burnley (3-1)
1963 Manchester Utd. beat Leicester City (3-1)
1964 West Ham Utd. beat Preston N.E. (3-2)
1965†† Liverpool beat Leeds Utd. (2-1)
1966 Everton beat Sheffield Wed. (3-2)
1967 Tottenham beat Chelsea (2-1)
1968†† W.B.A. beat Everton (1-0)
1969 Manchester City beat Leicester City (1-0)
1970††• Chelsea beat Leeds Utd. (2-1 after a 2-2 draw)
1971†† Arsenal beat Liverpool (2-1)
1972 Leeds Utd. beat Arsenal (1-0)
1973 Sunderland beat Leeds Utd. (1-0)
1974 Liverpool beat Newcastle Utd. (3-0)
1975 West Ham Utd. beat Fulham (2-0)

1976	Southampton beat Manchester Utd. (1-0)
1977	Manchester Utd. beat Liverpool (2-1)
1978	Ipswich Town beat Arsenal (1-0)
1979	Arsenal beat Manchester Utd. (3-2)
1980	West Ham Utd. beat Arsenal (1-0)
1981	Tottenham beat Manchester City (3-2 after a 1-1 draw)
1982	Tottenham beat Q.P.R. (1-0 after a 1-1 draw)
1983	Manchester Utd. beat Brighton & H.A. (4-0 after a 2-2 draw)
1984	Everton beat Watford (2-0)
1985††	Manchester Utd. beat Everton (1-0)
1986	Liverpool beat Everton (3-1)
1987††	Coventry City beat Tottenham (3-2)
1988	Wimbledon beat Liverpool (1-0)
1989††	Liverpool beat Everton (3-2)
1990	Manchester Utd. beat Crystal Palace (1-0 after a 3-3 draw)
1991††	Tottenham beat Nott'm. Forest (2-1)
1992	Liverpool beat Sunderland (2-0)
1993††	Arsenal beat Sheffield Wed. (2-1 after a 1-1 draw)
1994	Manchester Utd. beat Chelsea (4-0)
1995	Everton beat Manchester Utd. (1-0)
1996	Manchester Utd. beat Liverpool (1-0)
1997	Chelsea beat Middlesbrough (2-0)
1998	Arsenal beat Newcastle Utd. (2-0)
1999	Manchester Utd. beat Newcastle Utd. (2-0)
2000	Chelsea beat Aston Villa (1-0)

AT MILLENNIUM STADIUM

2001	Liverpool beat Arsenal (2-1)
2002	Arsenal beat Chelsea (2-0)
2003	Arsenal beat Southampton (1-0)

†† After extra time. * Won outright but restored to the Association. *a* Replayed at Baseball Ground, Derby Co. † A special trophy was awarded for the third consecutive win. ††† Replayed at Burnden Park, Bolton Wand. ** Replayed at Goodison Park, Liverpool. *b* Replayed at Old Trafford, Manchester, new trophy provided. *c* Replayed at Bramall Lane, Sheffield. • Replayed at Old Trafford.
(All replays since 1981 played at Wembley.)

SUMMARY OF F.A. CUP WINS

Manchester Utd.	10	Chelsea	3	Charlton Athletic	1
Arsenal	9	Sheffield Wed.	3	Clapham Rov.	1
Tottenham	8	West Ham Utd.	3	Coventry City	1
Aston Villa	7	Bury	2	Derby Co.	1
Blackburn Rov.	6	Nott'm Forest	2	Huddersfield Town	1
Liverpool	6	Old Etonians	2	Ipswich Town	1
Newcastle Utd.	6	Preston N.E.	2	Leeds Utd.	1
Everton	5	Sunderland	2	Notts Co.	1
The Wanderers	5	Barnsley	1	Old Carthusians	1
W.B.A.	5	Blackburn Olympic	1	Oxford University	1
Bolton Wand.	4	Blackpool	1	Portsmouth	1
Manchester City	4	Bradford City	1	Royal Engineers	1
Sheffield Utd.	4	Burnley	1	Southampton	1
Wolves	4	Cardiff City	1	Wimbledon	1

APPEARANCES IN FINALS

(Figures do not include replays)

Arsenal 16
Manchester Utd. 15
Newcastle Utd. 13
Everton 12
Liverpool 12
Aston Villa 10
W.B.A. 10
Tottenham 9
Blackburn Rov. 8
Manchester City 8
Wolves 8
Bolton Wand. 7
Chelsea 7
Preston N.E. 7
Old Etonians 6
Sheffield Utd. 6
Sheffield Wed. 6
Huddersfield Town 5
The Wanderers* 5
Derby Co. 4
Leeds Utd. 4
Leicester City 4
Oxford University 4
Royal Engineers 4
Southampton 4
Sunderland 4
West Ham Utd. 4
Blackpool 3
Burnley 3
Nott'm Forest 3
Portsmouth 3
Barnsley 2
Birmingham City 2
Bury* 2
Cardiff City 2
Charlton Athletic 2
Clapham Rov. 2
Notts Co. 2
Queen's Park (Glas.) 2
Blackburn Olympic* 1
Bradford City* 1
Brighton & H.A. 1
Bristol City 1
Coventry City* 1
Crystal Palace 1
Fulham 1
Ipswich Town* 1
Luton Town 1
Middlesbrough 1
Old Carthusians* 1
Q.P.R. 1
Watford 1
Wimbledon* 1

(* Denotes undefeated)

APPEARANCES IN SEMI-FINALS

(Figures do not include replays)

Arsenal 23, Everton 23, Manchester Utd. 22, Liverpool 21, Aston Villa 19, W.B.A. 19, Tottenham 17, Blackburn Rov. 16, Newcastle Utd. 16, Sheffield Wed. 16, Chelsea 15, Wolves 14, Bolton Wand. 13, Derby Co. Co. 13, Sheffield Utd. 13, Nott'm Forest 12, Southampton 11, Sunderland 11, Manchester City 10, Preston N.E. 10, Birmingham City 9, Burnley 8, Leeds Utd. 8, Huddersfield Town 7, Leicester City 7, Fulham 6, Old Etonians 6, Oxford University 6, West Ham Utd. 6, Notts Co. 5, Portsmouth 5, The Wanderers 5, Luton Town 4, Queen's Park (Glasgow) 4, Royal Engineers 4, Watford 4, Blackpool 3, Cardiff City 3, Clapham Rov. 3, *Crystal Palace 3, Ipswich Town 3, Millwall 3, Norwich City 3, Old Carthusians 3, Oldham Athletic 3, Stoke City 3, The Swifts 3, Barnsley 2, Blackburn Olympic 2, Bristol City 2, Bury 2, Charlton Athletic 2, Grimsby Town 2, Middlesbrough 2, Swansea City Town 2, Swindon Town 2, Wimbledon 2, Bradford City 1, Brighton & H.A. 1, Cambridge University 1, Chesterfield 1, Coventry City 1, Crewe Alexandra 1, Darwen 1, Derby Co. Junction 1, Hull City 1, Marlow 1, Old Harrovians 1, Orient 1, Plymouth Argyle 1, Port Vale 1, Q.P.R. 1, Rangers (Glasgow) 1, Reading 1, Shropshire Wand. 1, Wycombe Wand. 1, York City 1.

*(*A previous and different Crystal Palace club also reached the semi-final in season 1871-72)*

TEN FOR JACKSON IN F.A. CUP TIE

Paul Jackson claimed a share of F.A. Cup history when he scored ten goals – five in each half – in Stocksbridge Park Steels' 17-1 win over Oldham Town in a preliminary round tie. He equalled the record of Chris Marron, who got ten for South Shields against Radcliffe in 1947.

GOALKEEPERS SHARE MAN-OF-THE-MATCH AWARD

Huddersfield Town's two goalkeepers shared the man-of-the-match award after a 1-0 defeat by Crewe Alexandra. Scott Bevan had a magnificent game before he was sent off after 61 minutes for a foul. Then substitute Phil Senior made some fine saves on his League debut for the club. Another unusual presentation on the same day was made to referee Neale Barry, named sponsors' man-of-the-match for his handling of the Aston Villa-Tottenham game.

FOOTBALL'S CHANGING HOMES

Manchester City and **Darlington** may be clubs far apart on the football ladder, but they will share a sense of pride at the start of the new season when kicking off in impressive new stadiums.

After 80 years at Maine Road, Manchester City have moved from Maine Road in Moss Side across the city to the 48,000-seater City of Manchester Stadium, built for £77m. for the Commonwealth Games in 2002 when it staged the opening and closing ceremonies, athletics and rugby sevens. After the Games, a new permanent north stand replaced the temporary seating to create a complete 'bowl' and the running track was removed. What was ground level for the Games was then dug out and an extra tier of seating added to bring spectators closer to the action.

Darlington have left Feethams for the 25,000-seater Reynolds Arena, named after owner-chairman George Reynolds whose £20m. has built it on the outskirts of the town. Despite average attendances of 3,300, Reynolds believes it will transform the fortunes of the club which he aims to take into the First Division.

Division Three rivals **Hull City** showed last season what a difference a new ground can make. They left Boothferry Park for the £27m. Kingston Communications Stadium and had two club-record attendances in a week. A crowd of 22,467 saw them play Sunderland in a friendly-match 'opener' and the gate of 22,319 for the Boxing Day League fixture against Hartlepool Utd. was a record for the Division.

Arsenal, who first hoped to move to a new £250m. stadium holding 60,000 at Ashburton Grove in 2004, then had to put the date back to 2005, face a further hold-up. Costs have risen to £400m. and because of the delay in securing funding for the project half-a-mile from Highbury, the club now expect the move to take place for the start of the 2006-07 season. Meanwhile, Arsenal continue with a 38,500 limit, putting them around £1m. behind Manchester United in gate receipts for every home match. While **Liverpool** continue to work towards a new 55,000-capacity stadium, **Everton** have abandoned plans to move to an all-events arena in the city's King's Dock for financial reasons. The club say they will continue to look for an alternative site.

Portsmouth are planning a £26m. redevelopment of Fratton Park with an initial capacity of 28,000 and the pitch rotated 90 degrees. **Fulham** will continue to share Loftus Road with Q.P.R. while considering a more modest scheme to develop Craven Cottage after a proposed new stadium on the site proved too expensive.

Swansea City could be moving to a new 20,000 all-seater stadium in 2005 after the Council raised £24m. for the project by selling land for a retail park. The stadium, at Morfa, would be shared with the new Swansea and Neath rugby club. **Cardiff City** want to sell Ninian Park for housing and have submitted plans to build a new ground opposite on a site currently occupied by an athletics stadium. Initial capacity would be 30,000. Plans by **Colchester United** for a 10,000-capacity new stadium have been on show to the public. A poll of **Chesterfield** fans was 58% in favour of a move from Saltergate to a new ground at Wheeldon Mill.

At the time of going to press, the future for **Wimbledon** was uncertain after a proposed temporary move to the National Hockey Stadium at Milton Keynes fell through. Elsewhere, **Brighton & H.A.** were awaiting the outcome of a public inquiry into plans for a new 22,000-seater ground at Falmer, needed to replace the 7,000-capacity Withdean Stadium. **Brentford** will remain at Griffin Park while planning for a new home at nearby Lionel Road. **York City** have been given permission to stay at Bootham Crescent for at least another season while looking for a move, possibly to Huntington.

Norwich City are spending £6.5m. on a new 8,000-seater south stand at Carrow Road after selling three acres of river-fronting land for new homes. It will incease capacity to 24,000 and could be further expanded to accommodate 12,000 fans. Owner-chairman Barry Hearn is planning to ensure the long-term future of **Leyton Orient** with a £10m. scheme to redevelop the Matchroom Stadium into a modern 10,500-capacity arena.

In Scotland, **Hearts** and **Hibs** have had discussions about the possibility of building and sharing a new ground in the Straiton area of Edinburgh.

WORTHINGTON CUP 2002-03

PRELIMINARY ROUND

Bristol Rov. 0, Boston Utd. 2.

FIRST ROUND

Boston Utd. 1, Cardiff City 5; Bournemouth 3, Brentford 3 (aet, Brentford won 4-2 on pens); Brighton & H.A. 2, Exeter City 1 (aet); Bristol City 0, Oxford Utd. 1; Burnley 3, Blackpool 0; Bury 1, Stoke City 0; Cambridge Utd. 3, Reading 1; Coventry City 3, Colchester Utd. 0; Crystal Palace 2, Plymouth Argyle 1; Grimsby Town 0, Chesterfield 1; Hartlepool Utd. 1, Tranmere Rov. 2; Huddersfield Town 2, Darlington 0; Hull City 2, Leicester City 4 (aet); Leyton Orient 3, Q.P.R. 2; Lincoln City 1, Stockport Co. 3; Macclesfield Town 4, Barnsley 1 (aet); Mansfield Town 1, Derby Co. 3; Northampton Town 0, Wigan Athletic 1; Norwich City 0, Cheltenham Town 3; Nott'm. Forest 4, Kidderminster Harr. 0; Oldham Athletic 3, Notts Co. 2; Port Vale 0, Crewe Alexandra 2; Portsmouth 2, Peterborough Utd. 0; Preston N.E. 2, Scunthorpe Utd. 1 (aet); Rotherham Utd. 3, Carlisle Utd. 1; Rushden & Diamonds 0, Millwall 0 (aet, Rushden & Diamonds won 5-3 on pens); Sheffield Utd. 1, York City 0; Sheffield Wed. 1, Rochdale 0; Southend Utd. 1, Wimbledon 4; Swansea City 2, Wolves 3; Swindon Town 1, Wycombe Wand. 2 (aet); Torquay Utd. 0, Gillingham 1; Walsall 1, Shrewsbury Town 0; Watford 1, Luton Town 2; Wrexham 2, Bradford City 1.

FINAL

LIVERPOOL 2, MANCHESTER UNITED 0

Millennium Stadium, (72,500), Sunday, March 2, 2003

Liverpool (4-4-2): Dudek, Carragher, Henchoz, Hyypia (capt), Riise, Diouf (Biscan 90), Gerrard, Hamann, Murphy, Heskey (Baros 61, Smicer 86), Owen. **Scorers:** Gerrard (39), Owen (86). **Booked:** Henchoz. **Manager:** Gerard Houllier.

Manchester Utd. (4-4-1-1): Barthez, G. Neville, Ferdinand, Brown (Solskjaer 73), Silvestre, Beckham, Keane (capt), Veron, Giggs, Scholes, Van Nistelrooy. **Manager:** Sir Alex Ferguson.

Referee: P. Durkin (Portland). **Half-time:** 1-0. **Man-of-the-match:** Jerzy Dudek.

The goals were claimed by Steven Gerrard and Michael Owen, but the honours went to Jerzy Dudek, who completed his goalkeeping rehabilitation with a top-drawer performance which highlighted Liverpool's seventh League Cup success and a sixth trophy for their manager Gerard Houllier.

Just as American Brad Friedel had claimed the man-of-the-match award when Blackburn Rovers overcame Tottenham 12 months earlier, so Dudek earned the accolade for frustrating all Manchester United's efforts to justify their position as favourites for the trophy.

The difference was that while Friedel merely extended a season-long run of excellence, Dudek had committed a series of costly mistakes approaching the mid-way point in the campaign and lost his place to Chris Kirkland as a result. That the Pole regained it nearly two months later was due entirely to a serious knee injury sustained by 21-year-old England prospect Kirkland in an FA Cup fourth round tie against Crystal Palace.

But if United were hoping to capitalise on any weakness in that department, Dudek denied them with two fine saves from Ruud van Nistelrooy and equally effective blocks which kept out efforts from Juan Veron and Paul Scholes. When he was beaten, Stephane Henchoz was there near the line to clear from Veron.

Liverpool were also splendidly served at the back by their captain Sami Hyypia, while Gerrard's mastery of Roy Keane in the middle of the field was highlighted by his 39th minute goal for which Owen and John Arne Riise did the spadework and David Beckham was an unwilling ally.

When United lost to Arsenal in the FA Cup a fortnight earlier, the first goal by Edu deflected in off Beckham's shoulder. The England captain was later struck above the eye by a football boot flung across the dressing room by an angry Sir Alex Ferguson. This time, Beckham was hit on the leg by Gerrard's drive which looped beyond Fabien Barthez to put Liverpool in front.

Their second, after 86 minutes, was created by Dietmar Hamann after Mikael Silvestre's lay-off had put Rio Ferdinand under pressure. Hamann won the ball and sent Owen racing through to beat Barthez at the end where his two goals in the final eight minutes won the 2001 F.A. Cup Final against Arsenal. There was no way back after that for a disappointing United side, whose afternoon went from bad to worse when Arsenal defeated Charlton Athletic to go eight points clear at the top of the Premiership.

HOW THEY REACHED THE FINAL

LIVERPOOL

Round 3: 3-1 home to Southampton (Berger, Baros, Diouf)
Round 4: 1-1 home to Ipswich Town (Diouf pen) aet, won 5-4 on pens
Round 5: 4-3 away to Aston Villa (Murphy 2, Baros, Gerrard)
Semi-finals: v Sheffield Utd. – first leg, 1-2 away (Mellor); second leg, 2-0, aet, home (Diouf, Owen).

MANCHESTER UNITED

Round 3: 2-0 home to Leicester City (Beckham pen, Richardson)
Round 4: 2-0 away to Burnley (Forlan, Solskjaer)
Round 5: 1-0 home to Chelsea (Forlan)
Semi-finals: v Blackburn Rov. – first leg, 1-1 home (Scholes); second leg, 3-1 away (Scholes 2, Van Nistelrooy pen).

LEADING SCORERS

5 – Ellington (Wigan Athletic)
4 – Cole (Blackburn Rov.), Dublin (Aston Villa), McSheffrey (Coventry City)
3 – Diouf (Liverpool), Earnshaw (Cardiff City), Jack (Crewe Alexandra), John (Birmingham City), Johnson (Crystal Palace), Mills (Coventry City), Scholes (Manchester Utd.), Shipperley (Wimbledon), Stewart (Sunderland), Vassell (Aston Villa), Whitaker (Macclesfield Town).

HAT-TRICK IN 11 MINUTES FOR SUBSTITUTE

Substitute Carl Asaba scored a hat-trick between the 77th and 88th minutes in Sheffield United's 4-2 victory at Brighton. Two of the goals were penalties. Iyseden Christie netted three in 11 minutes and added a fourth in the second half of Mansfield Town's 4-2 win over Colchester.

SEVENTH LEAGUE CUP WIN FOR LIVERPOOL

SECOND ROUND

- **Bye**
- *Southampton 6
- Tranmere Rov. 1
- *Ipswich Town 3
- Brighton & H.A. 1
- *Brentford 1
- Middlesbrough 4
- *Aston Villa 3
- Luton Town 0
- *Charlton Athletic 0
- Oxford Utd. .... †A0
- *Macclesfield Town ... 1
- Preston N.E. 2
- *Leyton Orient 2
- Birmingham City 3
- *Sheffield Utd. 4
- Wycombe Wand. 1
- Bye
- Bye
- *Cambridge Utd. 0
- Sunderland 7
- *Crystal Palace 7
- Cheltenham Town 0
- *Coventry City 8
- Rushden & Diamonds . 0
- *Derby Co. 1
- Oldham Athletic ...... †2
- *Chesterfield 1
- West Ham Utd. ..... †B1

THIRD ROUND

- ***Liverpool** 3
- Southampton 1
- *Ipswich Town 3
- Middlesbrough 1
- Aston Villa 3
- *Oxford Utd. 0
- Preston N.E. 2
- *Birmingham City 0
- *Sheffield Utd. 2
- Leeds Utd. 1
- *Arsenal 2
- Sunderland 3
- *Crystal Palace 3
- Coventry City 0
- Oldham Athletic 1
- *West Ham Utd. 0

FOURTH ROUND

- ***Liverpool** .... †F1
- Ipswich Town 1
- *Aston Villa 5
- Preston N.E. 0
- *Sheffield Utd. 2
- Sunderland 0
- *Crystal Palace 2
- Oldham Athletic 0

FIFTH ROUND

- **Liverpool** 4
- *Aston Villa 3
- *Sheffield Utd. 3
- Crystal Palace 1

SEMI-FINALS

- **Liverpool** .... 1:†2
- *Sheffield Utd. 2:0

FINAL

- **Liverpool** 2

*Wigan Athletic .... 3 W.B.A. 1	*Wigan Athletic 1	*Wigan Athletic 2	*Wigan Athletic 0	
*Manchester City ...... 3 Crewe Alexandra 2	Manchester City 0			
• Bye	*Fulham 3	Fulham 1		
*Bolton Wand. .... 0 Bury 1	Bury 1			Blackburn Rov. 1:1
• Bye	*Blackburn Rov. ... †D2	*Blackburn Rov. 4		
*Nott'm. Forest .... 1 Walsall 2	Walsall 2		Blackburn Rov. 2	
*Portsmouth .... 1 Wimbledon 3	*Wimbledon 1	Rotherham Utd. 0		
*Rotherham Utd. .. †C4 Wolves 4	Rotherham Utd. 3			**Manchester Utd.** 0
• Bye	*Newcastle Utd. 3	Everton 1		
*Wrexham .... 0 Everton 3	Everton .... †E3		Chelsea 0	
• Bye	*Chelsea 2	*Chelsea 4		
*Stockport Co. .... 1 Gillingham .... †2	Gillingham 1			***Manchester Utd.** ... 1:3
*Huddersfield Town .. 0 Burnley 1	*Burnley 2	*Burnley 0		
*Tottenham .... 1 Cardiff City 0	Tottenham 1		***Manchester Utd.** 1	
*Sheffield Wed. .... 1 Leicester City .... †2	Leicester City 0	**Manchester Utd.** 2		
• Bye	***Manchester Utd.** 2			

* Drawn at home; in semi-finals drawn at home in first leg. † After extra-time. A – Oxford Utd. won 6-5 on pens. B – West Ham Utd. won 5-4 on pens. C – Rotherham Utd. won 4-2 on pens. D – Blackburn Rov. won 5-4 on pens. E – Everton won 3-2 on pens. F – Liverpool won 5-4 on pens.

LEAGUE CUP – COMPLETE RESULTS

LEAGUE CUP FINALS

1961* Aston Villa beat Rotherham Utd. 3-2 on agg. (0-2a, 3-0h)
1962 Norwich City beat Rochdale 4-0 on agg. (3-0a, 1-0h)
1963 Birmingham City beat Aston Villa 3-1 on agg. (3-1h, 0-0a)
1964 Leicester City beat Stoke City 4-3 on agg. (1-1a, 3-2h)
1965 Chelsea beat Leicester City 3-2 on agg. (3-2h, 0-0a)
1966 W.B.A. beat West Ham Utd. 5-3 on agg. (1-2a, 4-1h)

AT WEMBLEY

1967 Q.P.R. beat W.B.A. (3-2)
1968 Leeds Utd. beat Arsenal (1-0)
1969* Swindon Town beat Arsenal (3-1)
1970* Manchester City beat W.B.A. (2-1)
1971 Tottenham beat Aston Villa (2-0)
1972 Stoke City beat Chelsea (2-1)
1973 Tottenham beat Norwich City (1-0)
1974 Wolves beat Manchester City (2-1)
1975 Aston Villa beat Norwich City (1-0)
1976 Manchester City beat Newcastle Utd. (2-1)
1977†* Aston Villa beat Everton (3-2 after 0-0 and 1-1 draws)
1978†† Nott'm. Forest beat Liverpool (1-0 after 0-0 draw)
1979 Nott'm. Forest beat Southampton (3-2)
1980 Wolves beat Nott'm. Forest (1-0)
1981††† Liverpool beat West Ham Utd. (2-1 after 1-1 draw)

MILK CUP

1982* Liverpool beat Tottenham (3-1)
1983* Liverpool beat Manchester Utd. (2-1)
1984** Liverpool beat Everton (1-0 after *0-0 draw)
1985 Norwich City beat Sunderland (1-0)
1986 Oxford Utd. beat Q.P.R. (3-0)

LITTLEWOODS CUP

1987 Arsenal beat Liverpool (2-1)
1988 Luton Town beat Arsenal (3-2)
1989 Nott'm. Forest beat Luton Town (3-1)
1990 Nott'm. Forest beat Oldham Athletic (1-0)

RUMBELOWS CUP

1991 Sheffield Wed. beat Manchester Utd. (1-0)
1992 Manchester Utd. beat Nott'm. Forest (1-0)

COCA-COLA CUP

1993 Arsenal beat Sheffield Wed. (2-1)
1994 Aston Villa beat Manchester Utd. (3-1)
1995 Liverpool beat Bolton Wand. (2-1)
1996 Aston Villa beat Leeds Utd. (3-0)
1997 Leicester City beat Middlesbrough (*1-0 after *1-1 draw) ★
1998 Chelsea beat Middlesbrough (2-0)

WORTHINGTON CUP (AT MILLENNIUM STADIUM FROM 2001)

1999	Tottenham beat Leicester City (1-0)
2000	Leicester City beat Tranmere Rov. (2-1)
2001	Liverpool beat Birmingham City (5-4 on pens after *1-1 draw)
2002	Blackburn Rov. beat Tottenham (2-1)
2003	Liverpool beat Manchester Utd. (2-0)

* After extra time. † First replay at Hillsborough, second replay at Old Trafford. †† Replayed at Old Trafford. ††† Replayed at Aston Villa Park. ** Replayed at Maine Road. ★ Replayed at Hillsborough

SUMMARY OF LEAGUE CUP WINNERS

Liverpool	7	Manchester City	2	Manchester Utd.	1
Aston Villa	5	Norwich City	2	Oxford Utd.	1
Nott'm. Forest	4	Wolves	2	Q.P.R.	1
Leicester City	3	Blackburn Rov.	1	Sheffield Wed.	1
Tottenham	3	Birmingham City	1	Stoke City	1
Arsenal	2	Leeds Utd.	1	Swindon Town	1
Chelsea	2	Luton Town	1	W.B.A.	1

LEAGUE CUP FINAL APPEARANCES

9 Liverpool; **7** Aston Villa; **6** Nott'm. Forest; **5** Arsenal, Leicester City, Tottenham Manchester Utd.; **4** Norwich City; **3** Chelsea, Manchester City, W.B.A.; **2** Birmingham City, Everton, Leeds Utd., Luton Town, Middlesbrough, Q.P.R., Sheffield Wed., Stoke City, West Ham Utd., Wolves; **1** Blackburn Rov., Bolton Wand., Newcastle Utd., Oldham Athletic, Oxford Utd., Rochdale, Rotherham Utd., Southampton, Sunderland, Swindon Town, Tranmere Rov. **(Figures do not include replays).**

LEAGUE CUP SEMI-FINAL APPEARANCES

12 Liverpool; **11** Aston Villa; **10** Tottenham; **9** Arsenal; **8** Manchester Utd.; **7** Chelsea, West Ham Utd.; **6** Nott'm. Forest; **5** Leeds Utd., Leicester City, Manchester City, Norwich City; **4** Birmingham City, Blackburn Rov., Middlesbrough, Sheffield Wed., W.B.A.; **3** Bolton Wand., Burnley, Crystal Palace, Everton, Ipswich Town, Q.P.R., Sunderland, Swindon Town, Wolves; **2** Bristol City, Coventry City, Luton Town, Oxford Utd., Plymouth Argyle, Southampton, Stoke City, Tranmere Rov., Wimbledon; **1** Blackpool, Bury, Cardiff City, Carlisle Utd., Chester City, Derby Co., Huddersfield Town, Newcastle Utd., Oldham Athletic, Peterborough, Rochdale, Rotherham Utd., Sheffield Utd., Shrewsbury Town, Stockport Co., Walsall, Watford. **(Figures do not include replays).**

DUFF AND HENRY IN TEAM OF THE YEAR

Damien Duff and Thierry Henry were named in a Team of the Year 2002 chosen by voters on the UEFA website. The side, in 4-4-2 formation, was: Rustu (Turkey), Puyol (Spain), Nesta (Italy), Chivu (Romania), Roberto Carlos (Brazil), Seedorf (Holland), Ballack (Germany), Zidane (France), Duff (Republic of Ireland), Henry (France), Ronaldo (Brazil). Coach: Senol Gunes (Turkey).

SOLO SCORERS BEAT TEAM EFFORT

Manchester United's Ruud van Nistelrooy (25), Arsenal's Thierry Henry (24) and Southampton's James Beattie (23) scored more League goals themselves than relegated Sunderland's total of 21 for the season – a new Premiership low.

SCOTTISH FINAL TABLES 2002-03

BANK OF SCOTLAND PREMIER LEAGUE

			HOME					AWAY						
		P	W	D	L	F	A	W	D	L	F	A	Pts	GD
1	Rangers	38	18	0	1	55	12	13	4	2	46	16	97	+73
2	Celtic	38	18	1	0	56	12	13	3	3	42	14	97	+72
3	Hearts	38	12	3	4	36	24	6	6	7	21	27	63	+6
4	Kilmarnock	38	9	5	5	26	21	7	4	8	21	35	57	–9
5	Dunfermline	38	9	3	7	32	30	4	4	11	22	41	46	–17
6	Dundee	38	6	7	6	29	27	4	7	8	21	33	44	–10
7	Hibernian	38	8	3	8	28	29	7	3	9	28	35	51	–8
8	Aberdeen	38	5	7	7	19	21	8	3	8	22	33	49	–13
9	Livingston	38	5	4	10	23	28	4	4	11	25	34	35	–14
10	Partick Thistle	38	5	6	8	23	23	3	5	11	14	35	35	–21
11	Dundee Utd.	38	2	7	10	18	32	5	4	10	17	36	32	–33
12	Motherwell	38	6	4	9	31	34	1	3	15	14	37	28	–26

(League split after 33 matches. Teams stay within top six or bottom six regardless of points won. No relegation – Falkirk denied promotion from First Division).

Leading scorers (all club competitions): 44 Larsson (Celtic); 25 Hartson (Celtic); 22 Crawford (Dunfermline); 20 De Boer (Rangers); 19 McFadden (Motherwell), Sutton (Celtic); 18 Ferguson (Rangers); 17 Burns (Partick Thistle); 16 Arveladze (Rangers); 15 De Vries (Hearts); 14 Brewster (Dunfermline), Lovell (Dundee), Mols (Rangers), Petrov (Celtic). **Manager of Year:** Alex McLeish.

BELL'S FIRST DIVISION

			HOME					AWAY						
		P	W	D	L	F	A	W	D	L	F	A	Pts	GD
1	Falkirk*	36	15	2	1	46	10	10	4	4	34	22	81	+48
2	Clyde	36	12	4	2	37	17	9	5	4	29	20	72	+29
3	St Johnstone	36	9	3	6	22	13	11	4	3	27	16	67	+20
4	Inverness CT	36	10	2	6	35	23	10	3	5	39	22	65	+29
5	Queen of South	36	6	7	5	22	18	6	5	7	23	30	48	–3
6	Ayr Utd.	36	6	6	6	19	18	6	3	9	15	26	45	–10
7	St Mirren	36	6	5	7	24	32	3	5	10	18	39	37	–29
8	Ross Co.	36	7	4	7	26	19	2	4	12	16	27	35	–4
9	Alloa Athletic	36	3	2	13	24	49	6	6	6	15	23	35	–33
10	Arbroath	36	2	5	11	17	30	1	1	16	13	47	15	–47

(*Falkirk denied promotion by SPL).

Leading scorers (all club competitions): 27 Wyness (Inverness CT); 24 Coyle (Falkirk); 21 Ritchie (Inverness CT); 19 Cameron (St Mirren), Miller (Falkirk); 16 Samuel (Falkirk); 14 O'Neill (Queen of the South); 13 Robson (Inverness CT); 12 Keogh (Clyde), Gillies (St Mirren); 11 Hay (St Johnstone). **Manager of Year:** Alan Kernaghan (Clyde).

BELL'S SECOND DIVISION

			HOME					AWAY						
		P	W	D	L	F	A	W	D	L	F	A	Pts	GD
1	Raith Rov.	36	10	4	4	28	14	6	7	5	25	22	59	+17
2	Brechin City	36	8	4	6	32	31	8	3	7	31	28	55	+4
3	Airdrie Utd.	36	8	8	2	24	15	6	4	8	27	29	54	+7
4	Forfar Athletic	36	8	5	5	32	25	6	4	8	23	28	51	+2
5	Berwick Rangers	36	6	6	6	21	24	7	4	7	22	24	49	–5
6	Dumbarton	36	8	5	5	31	23	5	4	9	17	24	48	+1
7	Stenhousemuir	36	8	6	4	32	27	4	5	9	17	24	47	–2
8	Hamilton Acad.	36	7	3	8	23	26	5	8	5	20	22	47	–5
9	Stranraer	36	8	4	6	28	23	4	4	10	21	34	44	–8
10	Cowdenbeath	36	5	5	8	20	21	3	7	8	26	36	36	–11

Leading scorers (all club competitions): 24 Templeman (Brechin City); 19 Bavidge (Forfar Athletic), Harty (Stranraer), Vareille (Airdrie Utd.); 18 Tosh (Forfar Athletic); 15 Burke (Berwick Rangers), McPhee (Hamilton Acad.); 14 Wood (Berwick Rangers); 12 Brown (Cowdenbeath), Gordon (Cowdenbeath), Moore (Stranraer). **Manager of Year:** Dick Campbell (Brechin City) and Antonio Calderon (Raith Rov).

BELL'S THIRD DIVISION

			HOME					AWAY						
		P	W	D	L	F	A	W	D	L	F	A	Pts	GD
1	Morton	36	13	4	1	42	14	8	5	5	25	19	72	+34
2	East Fife	36	10	4	4	35	22	10	7	1	38	15	71	+36
3	Albion Rov.	36	9	6	3	31	20	11	4	3	31	16	70	+26
4	Peterhead	36	13	4	1	49	15	7	4	7	27	22	68	+39
5	Stirling Albion	36	9	4	5	24	16	6	7	5	26	28	56	+6
6	Gretna	36	4	8	6	26	27	7	4	7	24	23	45	0
7	Montrose	36	4	5	9	17	31	3	7	8	18	30	33	–26
8	Queen's Park	36	3	5	10	21	29	4	6	8	18	22	32	–12
9	Elgin City	36	3	7	8	17	24	2	6	10	16	39	28	–30
10	East Stirling	36	0	5	13	11	46	2	2	14	21	59	13	–73

Leading scorers (all club competitions): 28 Williams (Morton); 23 Deuchar (East Fife); 21 Stewart (Peterhead); 16 Johnston (Peterhead); 14 Nicholas (Stirling Albion); 13 Dobie (Gretna), Gemmill (Queen's Park); 12 Bone (Peterhead) –3 for Ross Co., Graham, J (East Fife), Herkes (East Fife); 11 Roddie (Peterhead). **Manager of Year:** Ian Wilson (Peterhead).

AGE IS NO BARRIER

Two 16-year-olds scored against goalkeepers twice their age in the Premiership last season. Everton's Wayne Rooney beat David Seaman (39) in the 2-1 win over Arsenal and James Milner scored against Ed de Goey (36) in Leeds United's 2-0 victory over Chelsea.

SMITH TWICE A SINNER AT ST MARY'S

Alan Smith was sent off twice at St Mary's Stadium last season – for Leeds United against Southampton in the Premiership and while playing for England in a European Championship qualifier against Macedonia.

SCOTTISH HONOURS LIST

PREMIER DIVISION

	First	Pts.	Second	Pts.	Third	Pts.
1975-6	Rangers	54	Celtic	48	Hibernian	43
1976-7	Celtic	55	Rangers	46	Aberdeen	43
1977-8	Rangers	55	Aberdeen	53	Dundee Utd.	40
1978-9	Celtic	48	Rangers	45	Dundee Utd.	44
1979-80	Aberdeen	48	Celtic	47	St Mirren	42
1980-81	Celtic	56	Aberdeen	49	Rangers	44
1981-2	Celtic	55	Aberdeen	53	Rangers	43
1982-3	Dundee Utd.	56	Celtic	55	Aberdeen	55
1983-4	Aberdeen	57	Celtic	50	Dundee Utd.	47
1984-5	Aberdeen	59	Celtic	52	Dundee Utd.	47
1985-6	*Celtic	50	Hearts	50	Dundee Utd.	47
1986-7	Rangers	69	Celtic	63	Dundee Utd.	60
1987-8	Celtic	72	Hearts	62	Rangers	60
1988-9	Rangers	56	Aberdeen	50	Celtic	46
1989-90	Rangers	51	Aberdeen	44	Hearts	44
1990-1	Rangers	55	Aberdeen	53	Celtic	41
1991-2	Rangers	72	Hearts	63	Celtic	62
1992-3	Rangers	73	Aberdeen	64	Celtic	60
1993-4	Rangers	58	Aberdeen	55	Motherwell	54
1994-5	Rangers	69	Motherwell	54	Hibernian	53
1995-6	Rangers	87	Celtic	83	Aberdeen	55
1996-7	Rangers	80	Celtic	75	Dundee Utd.	60
1997-8	Celtic	74	Rangers	72	Hearts	67

PREMIER LEAGUE

	First	Pts.	Second	Pts.	Third	Pts.
1998-99	Rangers	77	Celtic	71	St Johnstone	57
1999-2000	Rangers	90	Celtic	69	Hearts	54
2000-01	Celtic	97	Rangers	82	Hibernian	66
2001-02	Celtic	103	Rangers	85	Livingston	58
2002-03	*Rangers	97	Celtic	97	Hearts	63

Maximum points: 72 except 1986-8, 1991-4 (88), 1994-2000 (108), 2001-02 (114).
* Won on goal difference.

FIRST DIVISION (Scottish Championship until 1975-76)

	First	Pts.	Second	Pts.	Third	Pts.
1890-1*a*	††Dumbarton	29	Rangers	29	Celtic	24
1891-2*b*	Dumbarton	37	Celtic	35	Hearts	30
1892-3*a*	Celtic	29	Rangers	28	St Mirren	23
1893-4*a*	Celtic	29	Hearts	26	St Bernard's	22
1894-5*a*	Hearts	31	Celtic	26	Rangers	21
1895-6*a*	Celtic	30	Rangers	26	Hibernian	24
1896-7*a*	Hearts	28	Hibernian	26	Rangers	25
1897-8*a*	Celtic	33	Rangers	29	Hibernian	22
1898-9*a*	Rangers	36	Hearts	26	Celtic	24
1899-1900*a*	Rangers	32	Celtic	25	Hibernian	24
1900-1*c*	Rangers	35	Celtic	29	Hibernian	25
1901-2*a*	Rangers	28	Celtic	26	Hearts	22
1902-3*b*	Hibernian	37	Dundee	31	Rangers	29
1903-4*d*	Third Lanark	43	Hearts	39	Rangers	38

1904-5*a*	†Celtic	41	Rangers	41	Third Lanark	35
1905-6*a*	Celtic	46	Hearts	39	Rangers	38
1906-7*f*	Celtic	55	Dundee	48	Rangers	45
1907-8*f*	Celtic	55	Falkirk	51	Rangers	50
1908-9*f*	Celtic	51	Dundee	50	Clyde	48
1909-10*f*	Celtic	54	Falkirk	52	Rangers	49
1910-11*f*	Rangers	52	Aberdeen	48	Falkirk	44
1911-12*f*	Rangers	51	Celtic	45	Clyde	42
1912-13*f*	Rangers	53	Celtic	49	Hearts	41
1913-14*g*	Celtic	65	Rangers	59	Hearts	54
1914-15*g*	Celtic	65	Hearts	61	Rangers	50
1915-16*g*	Celtic	67	Rangers	56	Morton	51
1916-17*g*	Celtic	64	Morton	54	Rangers	53
1917-18*f*	Rangers	56	Celtic	55	Kilmarnock	43
1918-19*f*	Celtic	58	Rangers	57	Morton	47
1919-20*h*	Rangers	71	Celtic	68	Motherwell	57
1920-1*h*	Rangers	76	Celtic	66	Hearts	56
1921-2*h*	Celtic	67	Rangers	66	Raith	56
1922-3*g*	Rangers	55	Airdrieonians	50	Celtic	40
1923-4*g*	Rangers	59	Airdrieonians	50	Celtic	41
1924-5*g*	Rangers	60	Airdrieonians	57	Hibernian	52
1925-6*g*	Celtic	58	Airdrieonians	50	Hearts	50
1926-7*g*	Rangers	56	Motherwell	51	Celtic	49
1927-8*g*	Rangers	60	Celtic	55	Motherwell	55
1928-9*g*	Rangers	67	Celtic	51	Motherwell	50
1929-30*g*	Rangers	60	Motherwell	55	Aberdeen	53
1930-1*g*	Rangers	60	Celtic	58	Motherwell	56
1931-2*g*	Motherwell	66	Rangers	61	Celtic	48
1932-3*g*	Rangers	62	Motherwell	59	Hearts	50
1933-4*g*	Rangers	66	Motherwell	62	Celtic	47
1934-5*g*	Rangers	55	Celtic	52	Hearts	50
1935-6*g*	Celtic	68	Rangers	61	Aberdeen	61
1936-7*g*	Rangers	61	Aberdeen	54	Celtic	52
1937-8*g*	Celtic	61	Hearts	58	Rangers	49
1938-9*f*	Rangers	59	Celtic	48	Aberdeen	46
1946-7*f*	Rangers	46	Hibernian	44	Aberdeen	39
1947-8*g*	Hibernian	48	Rangers	46	Partick	46
1948-9*i*	Rangers	46	Dundee	45	Hibernian	39
1949-50*i*	Rangers	50	Hibernian	49	Hearts	43
1950-1*i*	Hibernian	48	Rangers	38	Dundee	38
1951-2*i*	Hibernian	45	Rangers	41	East Fife	37
1952-3*i*	*Rangers	43	Hibernian	43	East Fife	39
1953-4*i*	Celtic	43	Hearts	38	Partick	35
1954-5*f*	Aberdeen	49	Celtic	46	Rangers	41
1955-6*f*	Rangers	52	Aberdeen	46	Hearts	45
1956-7*f*	Rangers	55	Hearts	53	Kilmarnock	42
1957-8*f*	Hearts	62	Rangers	49	Celtic	46
1958-9*f*	Rangers	50	Hearts	48	Motherwell	44
1959-60*f*	Hearts	54	Kilmarnock	50	Rangers	42
1960-1*f*	Rangers	51	Kilmarnock	50	Third Lanark	42
1961-2*f*	Dundee	54	Rangers	51	Celtic	46
1962-3*f*	Rangers	57	Kilmarnock	48	Partick	46
1963-4*f*	Rangers	55	Kilmarnock	49	Celtic	47
1964-5*f*	*Kilmarnock	50	Hearts	50	Dunfermline	49
1965-6*f*	Celtic	57	Rangers	55	Kilmarnock	45
1966-7*f*	Celtic	58	Rangers	55	Clyde	46
1967-8*f*	Celtic	63	Rangers	61	Hibernian	45
1968-9*f*	Celtic	54	Rangers	49	Dunfermline	45

1969-70*f*	Celtic	57	Rangers	45	Hibernian	44
1970-1*f*	Celtic	56	Aberdeen	54	St Johnstone	44
1971-2*f*	Celtic	60	Aberdeen	50	Rangers	44
1972-3*f*	Celtic	57	Rangers	56	Hibernian	45
1973-4*f*	Celtic	53	Hibernian	49	Rangers	48
1974-5*f*	Rangers	56	Hibernian	49	Celtic	45

* Won on goal average. †Won on deciding match. ††Title shared.
Competition suspended 1940-46 (Second World War).

SCOTTISH CHAMPIONSHIP WINS

Rangers	*50	Hibernian	4	Kilmarnock	1
Celtic	38	Dumbarton	*2	Motherwell	1
Aberdeen	4	Dundee	1	Third Lanark	1
Hearts	4	Dundee Utd.	1	(* Incl. 1 shared)	

FIRST DIVISION

(Since formation of Premier Division)

	First	Pts.	Second	Pts.	Third	Pts.
1975-6*d*	Partick	41	Kilmarnock	35	Montrose	30
1976-7*j*	St Mirren	62	Clydebank	58	Dundee	51
1977-8*j*	*Morton	58	Hearts	58	Dundee	57
1978-9*j*	Dundee	55	Kilmarnock	54	Clydebank	54
1979-80*j*	Hearts	53	Airdrieonians	51	Ayr	44
1980-1*j*	Hibernian	57	Dundee	52	St Johnstone	51
1981-2*j*	Motherwell	61	Kilmarnock	51	Hearts	50
1982-3*j*	St Johnstone	55	Hearts	54	Clydebank	50
1983-4*j*	Morton	54	Dumbarton	51	Partick	46
1984-5*j*	Motherwell	50	Clydebank	48	Falkirk	45
1985-6*j*	Hamilton	56	Falkirk	45	Kilmarnock	44
1986-7*k*	Morton	57	Dunfermline	56	Dumbarton	53
1987-8*k*	Hamilton	56	Meadowbank	52	Clydebank	49
1988-9*j*	Dunfermline	54	Falkirk	52	Clydebank	48
1989-90*j*	St Johnstone	58	Airdrieonians	54	Clydebank	44
1990-1*j*	Falkirk	54	Airdrieonians	53	Dundee	52
1991-2*k*	Dundee	58	Partick	57	Hamilton	57
1992-3k	Raith	65	Kilmarnock	54	Dunfermline	52
1993-4*k*	Falkirk	66	Dunfermline	65	Airdrieonians	54
1994-5*l*	Raith	69	Dunfermline	68	Dundee	68
1995-6*l*	Dunfermline	71	Dundee Utd.	67	Greenock Morton	67
1996-7*l*	St Johnstone	80	Airdrieonians	60	Dundee	58
1997-8*l*	Dundee	70	Falkirk	65	Raith	60
1998-9*l*	Hibernian	89	Falkirk	66	Ayr	62
1999-2000*l*	St Mirren	76	Dunfermline	71	Falkirk	68
2000-01*l*	Livingston	76	Ayr Utd.	69	Falkirk	56
2001-02*l*	Partick Thistle	66	Airdie	56	Ayr Utd.	52
2002-03*l*	Falkirk	81	Clyde	72	St Johnstone	67

Maximum points: a, 36; *b*, 44; *c*, 40; *d*, 52; *e*, 60; *f*, 68; *g*, 76; *h*, 84; *i*, 60; *j*, 78; *k*, 88; *l*, 108. * Won on goal difference.

SECOND DIVISION

	First	Pts.	Second	Pts.	Third	Pts.
1921-2*a*	Alloa	60	Cowdenbeath	47	Armadale	45
1922-3*a*	Queen's Park	57	Clydebank	52	St Johnstone	50
1923-4*a*	St Johnstone	56	Cowdenbeath	55	Bathgate	44

1924-5*a*	Dundee Utd. 50	Clydebank 48	Clyde 47
1925-6*a*	Dunfermline 59	Clyde 53	Ayr 52
1926-7*a*	Bo'ness 56	Raith 49	Clydebank 45
1927-8*a*	Ayr 54	Third Lanark 45	King's Park 44
1928-9*b*	Dundee Utd. 51	Morton 50	Arbroath 47
1929-30*a*	*Leith Athletic 57	East Fife 57	Albion 54
1930-1*a*	Third Lanark 61	Dundee Utd. 50	Dunfermline 47
1931-2*a*	*East Stirling 55	St Johnstone 55	Stenhousemuir 46
1932-3*c*	Hibernian 55	Queen of South 49	Dunfermline 47
1933-4*c*	Albion 45	Dunfermline 44	Arbroath 44
1934-5*c*	Third Lanark 52	Arbroath 50	St Bernard's 47
1935-6*c*	Falkirk 59	St Mirren 52	Morton 48
1936-7*c*	Ayr 54	Morton 51	St Bernard's 48
1937-8*c*	Raith 59	Albion 48	Airdrieonians 47
1938-9*c*	Cowdenbeath 60	Alloa 48	East Fife 48
1946-7*d*	Dundee Utd. 45	Airdrieonians 42	East Fife 31
1947-8*e*	East Fife 53	Albion 42	Hamilton 40
1948-9*e*	*Raith 42	Stirling 42	Airdrieonians 41
1949-50*e*	Morton 47	Airdrieonians 44	St Johnstone 36
1950-1*e*	*Queen of South 45	Stirling 45	Ayr 36
1951-2*e*	Clyde 44	Falkirk 43	Ayr 39
1952-3*e*	Stirling 44	Hamilton 43	Queen's Park 37
1953-4*e*	Motherwell 45	Kilmarnock 42	Third Lanark 36
1954-5*e*	Airdrieonians 46	Dunfermline 42	Hamilton 39
1955-6*b*	Queen's Park 54	Ayr 51	St Johnstone 49
1956-7*b*	Clyde 64	Third Lanark 51	Cowdenbeath 45
1957-8*b*	Stirling 55	Dunfermline 53	Arbroath 47
1958-9*b*	Ayr 60	Arbroath 51	Stenhousemuir 46
1959-60*b*	St Johnstone 53	Dundee Utd. 50	Queen of South 49
1960-1*b*	Stirling 55	Falkirk 54	Stenhousemuir 50
1961-2*b*	Clyde 54	Queen of South 53	Morton 44
1962-3*b*	St Johnstone 55	East Stirling 49	Morton 48
1963-4*b*	Morton 67	Clyde 53	Arbroath 46
1964-5*b*	Stirling 59	Hamilton 50	Queen of South 45
1965-6*b*	Ayr 53	Airdrieonians 50	Queen of South 47
1966-7*b*	Morton 69	Raith 58	Arbroath 57
1967-8*b*	St Mirren 62	Arbroath 53	East Fife 49
1968-9*b*	Motherwell 64	Ayr 53	East Fife 48
1969-70*b*	Falkirk 56	Cowdenbeath 55	Queen of South 50
1970-1*b*	Partick 56	East Fife 51	Arbroath 46
1971-2*b*	*Dumbarton 52	Arbroath 52	Stirling 50
1972-3*b*	Clyde 56	Dunfermline 52	Raith 47
1973-4*b*	Airdrieonians 60	Kilmarnock 58	Hamilton 55
1974-5*b*	Falkirk 54	Queen of South 53	Montrose 53

SECOND DIVISION (MODERN)

	First .... Pts.	Second .... Pts.	Third .... Pts.
1975-6*d*	*Clydebank 40	Raith 40	Alloa 35
1976-7*f*	Stirling 55	Alloa 51	Dunfermline 50
1977-8*f*	*Clyde 53	Raith 53	Dunfermline 48
1978-9*f*	Berwick Rangers 54	Dunfermline 52	Falkirk 50
1979-80*f*	Falkirk 50	East Stirling 49	Forfar 46
1980-1*f*	Queen's Park 50	Queen of South 46	Cowdenbeath 45
1981-2*f*	Clyde 59	Alloa 50	Arbroath 50
1982-3*f*	Brechin 55	Meadowbank 54	Arbroath 49
1983-4*f*	Forfar 63	East Fife 47	Berwick Rangers 43
1984-5*f*	Montrose 53	Alloa 50	Dunfermline 49
1985-6*f*	Dunfermline 57	Queen of South 55	Meadowbank 49

1986-7*f*	Meadowbank 55	Raith 52	Stirling 52
1987-8*f*	Ayr 61	St Johnstone 59	Queen's Park 51
1988-9*f*	Albion 50	Alloa 45	Brechin 43
1989-90*f*	Brechin 49	Kilmarnock 48	Stirling 47
1990-1*f*	Stirling 54	Montrose 46	Cowdenbeath 45
1991-2*f*	Dumbarton 52	Cowdenbeath 51	Alloa 50
1992-3*f*	Clyde 54	Brechin 53	Stranraer 53
1993-4*f*	Stranraer 56	Berwick Rangers 48	Stenhousemuir 47
1994-5*g*	Greenock Morton ... 64	Dumbarton 60	Stirling 58
1995-6*g*	Stirling 81	East Fife 67	Berwick Rangers 60
1996-7*g*	Ayr 77	Hamilton 74	Livingston 64
1997-8*g*	Stranraer 61	Clydebank 60	Livingston 59
1998-9*g*	Livingston 77	Inverness Cal. 72	Clyde 53
1999-2000*g*	Clyde 65	Alloa 64	Ross County 62
2000-01*g*	Partick Thistle 75	Arbroath 58	Berwick Rangers 54
2001-02*g*	Queen of South 67	Alloa Athletic 59	Forfar Athletic 53
2002-03*g*	Raith Rov. 59	Brechin City 55	Airdrie Utd. 54

Maximum points: *a*, 76; *b*, 72; *c*, 68; *d*, 52; *e*, 60; *f*, 78; *g*, 108. * Won on goal average.

THIRD DIVISION (MODERN)

	First .... Pts.	**Second .... Pts.**	**Third .... Pts.**
1994-5	Forfar 80	Montrose 67	Ross County 60
1995-6	Livingston 72	Brechin 63	Caledonian Th. 57
1996-7	Inverness Cal.T. 76	Forfar 67	Ross County 77
1997-8	Alloa 76	Arbroath 68	Ross County 67
1998-9	Ross County 77	Stenhousemuir 64	Brechin 59
1999-2000	Queen's Park 69	Berwick Rangers 66	Forfar 61
2000-01	*Hamilton 76	Cowdenbeath 76	Brechin 72
2001-02	Brechin City 73	Dumbarton 61	Albion Rov. 59
2002-03	Morton 72	East Fife 71	Albion Rov. 70

Maximum points: 108. * Won on goal difference.

RELEGATED FROM PREMIER DIVISION

1975-6	Dundee, St Johnstone	1989-90	Dundee
1976-7	Kilmarnock, Hearts	1990-1	No relegation
1977-8	Ayr, Clydebank	1991-2	St Mirren, Dunfermline
1978-9	Hearts, Motherwell	1992-3	Falkirk, Airdrieonians
1979-80	Dundee, Hibernian	1993-4	St J'stone, Raith, Dundee
1980-1	Kilmarnock, Hearts	1994-5	Dundee Utd.
1981-2	Partick, Airdrieonians	1995-6	Falkirk, Partick Thistle
1982-3	Morton, Kilmarnock	1996-7	Raith
1983-4	St Johnstone, Motherwell	1997-8	Hibernian
1984-5	Dumbarton, Morton	1998-9	Dunfermline
1985-6	No relegation	1999-2000	No relegation
1986-7	Clydebank, Hamilton	2000-01	St Mirren
1987-8	Falkirk, Dunfermline, Morton	2001-02	St Johnstone
1988-9	Hamilton	2002-03	No relegation

RELEGATED FROM FIRST DIVISION

1975-6	Dunfermline, Clyde	1978-9	Montrose, Queen of South
1976-7	Raith, Falkirk	1979-80	Arbroath, Clyde
1977-8	Alloa, East Fife	1980-1	Stirling, Berwick Rangers

1981-2	East Stirling, Queen of South	1993-4	Dumbarton, Stirling Alb., Clyde, Morton, Brechin
1982-3	Dunfermline, Queen's Park	1994-5	Ayr, Stranraer
1983-4	Raith, Alloa	1995-6	Hamilton, Dumbarton
1984-5	Meadowbank, St Johnstone	1996-7	Clydebank, East Fife
1985-6	Ayr, Alloa	1997-8	Partick, Stirling Alb.
1986-7	Brechin, Montrose	1998-9	Hamilton, Stranraer
1987-8	East Fife, Dumbarton	1999-2000	Clydebank
1988-9	Kilmarnock, Queen of South	2000-01	Morton, Alloa
1989-90	Albion, Alloa	2001-02	Raith Rov.
1990-1	Clyde, Brechin	2002-03	Alloa Athletic, Arbroath
1991-2	Montrose, Forfar		
1992-3	Meadowbank, Cowdenbeath		

RELEGATED FROM SECOND DIVISION

1993-4	Alloa, Forfar, E. Stirling, Montrose, Queen's Park, Arbroath, Albion, Cowdenbeath	1997-8	Stenhousemuir, Brechin
1994-5	Meadowbank, Brechin	1998-9	East Fife, Forfar
1995-6	Forfar, Montrose	1999-2000	Hamilton
1996-7	Dumbarton, Berwick Rangers	2000-01	Queen's Park, Stirling Alb.
		2001-02	Morton
		2002-03	Stranraer, Cowdenbeath

QUOTE-UNQUOTE

'Friedel must have got changed in a telephone box' – **Gordon Strachan** after his Southampton side were denied by the Blackburn Rovers goalkeeper.

'It was a traumatic evening because it went from safety to scary to blinking dangerous and heart throbbing' – **Sir Bobby Robson** after the rollercoaster victory over Feyenoord which put Newcastle United into the second phase of the Champions League.

'I feel mortally ill because we were so damned close' – **Bert van Marwijk**, Feyenoord coach, after Newcastle United's last-minute winner.

'Playing for Wales is more fun than playing for Manchester United at the moment, but then that is not hard' – **Ryan Giggs** during a patchy spell for his club and a revival in his country's fortunes.

'He acted like my 15-year-old daughter, so maybe I'll treat him like her and give him a hundred lines' – **Steve Bruce**, Birmingham City manager, after Robbie Savage's public show of disapproval when substituted against Sunderland.

'I don't think you can have four divisions of professional football any longer' – **Peter Kenyon**, Manchester United chief executive, insisting there should be no more than 44 full-time clubs.

'Makes my Saturday night does Claudio' – **Des Lynam**, ITV's Premiership presenter, after another entertaining interview by the Chelsea manager.

'It was just an escape for me which turned out to be a bad one' – **Eidur Gudjohnsen**, Chelsea striker, on losing £400,000 in five months at casinos.

'I just wish I had bought him a Game Boy' – **Claudio Ranieri**, Gudjohnsen's manager.

'I would never encourage anyone to gamble' – **Michael Owen**, Liverpool striker, on losing £40,000 on the horses.

'If it's true, it means he is not very good at gambling' – **Gerard Houllier**, Liverpool manager.

'For me to take the Manager of the Month award, I would have to win nine games out of eight' – **Neil Warnock**, Sheffield United manager, measuring his own lack of popularity.

SCOTTISH LEAGUE RESULTS 2002-03

BANK OF SCOTLAND PREMIER LEAGUE

	Aberdeen	Celtic	Dundee	Dundee Utd.	Dunfermline	Hearts	Hibernian	Kilmarnock	Livingston	Motherwell	Partick Thistle	Rangers
Aberdeen	–	0–4	0–0	1–2	3–1	1–1	0–1	0–1	0–0	1–1	0–1	2–2
	–	1–1	3–3	3–0	1–0	0–1	–	–	1–0	–	0–1	–
	–	–	–	–	–	–	–	–	–	–	2–1	–
Celtic	7–0	–	2–0	5–0	2–1	4–2	1–0	5–0	2–0	3–1	4–0	3–3
	–	–	6–2	2–0	1–0	1–0	3–2	2–0	2–1	–	–	1–0
Dundee	1–2	0–1	–	3–2	2–3	1–1	2–1	2–1	2–1	1–1	4–1	0–3
	–	1–1	–	–	2–2	1–2	3–0	2–2	0–0	–	–	2–2
	–	–	–	–	–	–	–	0–1	–	–	–	–
Dundee Utd.	1–1	0–2	0–0	–	1–2	0–3	1–1	1–2	2–3	1–1	1–1	0–3
	0–2	–	1–1	–	3–0	–	1–2	2–2	0–1	2–1	–	1–4
Dunfermline	3–0	1–4	4–2	4–1	–	3–1	1–1	0–2	2–1	1–0	4–1	0–6
	–	1–4	0–1	–	–	0–1	–	2–2	2–0	3–0	0–0	1–3
Hearts	0–0	1–4	1–2	2–0	2–0	–	5–1	1–1	2–1	4–2	1–0	0–4
	–	2–1	1–0	2–1	3–0	–	4–4	3–0	–	2–1	–	0–2
Hibernian	1–2	0–1	2–1	2–1	1–4	1–2	–	2–0	1–0	3–1	1–1	2–4
	2–0	–	–	1–1	1–3	–	–	–	2–2	1–0	2–3	0–2
	3–1	–	–	–	–	–	–	–	–	–	–	–
Kilmarnock	2–2	1–1	2–0	1–2	2–2	0–1	2–1	–	2–0	0–3	1–0	1–1
	2–0	0–4	–	–	1–1	1–0	6–2	–	–	1–0	1–0	0–1
Livingston	1–2	0–2	1–1	3–0	1–1	1–1	1–2	0–1	–	3–2	3–0	0–2
	1–2	–	–	1–2	–	1–1	1–2	0–4	–	1–0	3–1	1–2
Motherwell	1–2	2–1	1–1	1–2	2–1	6–1	0–2	0–1	1–5	–	1–1	1–0
	0–1	0–4	1–2	2–2	–	–	2–1	–	6–2	–	2–2	–
	2–3	–	–	–	–	–	–	–	–	–	–	–
Partick Thistle	2–1	0–1	1–1	0–0	4–0	2–2	0–3	3–0	2–2	2–0	–	1–2
	–	0–2	1–3	0–0	–	1–1	0–1	–	1–3	3–0	–	–
	–	–	–	0–1	–	–	–	–	–	–	–	–
Rangers	2–0	3–2	3–0	3–0	3–0	2–0	2–1	6–1	4–3	3–0	3–0	–
	2–1	1–2	3–1	–	6–1	1–0	–	4–0	–	2–0	2–0	–

Read across for home results, down for away. After 33 matches, League split into top six and bottom six teams, each playing five further games.

BELL'S FIRST DIVISION

	Alloa Athletic	Arbroath	Ayr Utd.	Clyde	Falkirk	Inverness CT	Queen of South	Ross Co.	St Johnstone	St Mirren
Alloa Athletic	–	0–3	0–1	1–4	1–6	0–6	0–1	1–1	1–3	2–3
	–	3–2	2–3	1–2	1–3	1–5	3–3	2–1	1–2	4–0
Arbroath	0–1	–	1–1	1–1	2–0	1–2	1–2	0–3	0–1	2–2
	0–1	–	1–2	1–2	1–4	1–3	0–0	2–1	2–3	1–1
Ayr Utd.	3–1	1–0	–	1–1	1–3	3–3	0–1	2–1	0–0	1–1
	0–1	4–0	–	0–3	1–0	1–0	0–1	1–1	0–1	0–0
Clyde	0–0	3–0	1–0	–	2–0	3–0	2–1	2–1	1–2	2–3
	2–2	4–2	3–0	–	0–0	4–1	2–2	1–0	2–1	3–2
Falkirk	3–0	2–1	3–0	2–1	–	1–1	3–0	2–0	1–0	2–0
	3–1	4–1	3–0	3–0	–	2–3	5–0	3–0	1–1	3–1
Inverness CT	0–0	5–0	2–0	1–0	1–2	–	5–3	2–0	2–1	4–1
	1–1	2–0	0–1	1–2	3–4	–	1–0	1–5	1–2	3–1
Queen of South	1–1	2–2	1–2	2–1	1–1	1–3	–	2–0	0–0	3–0
	0–1	3–0	1–1	1–1	2–1	0–0	–	1–0	1–2	0–2
Ross Co.	0–1	4–0	1–0	1–1	1–1	0–2	2–0	–	0–0	4–0
	1–2	3–1	4–1	1–1	0–1	0–2	0–3	–	2–3	2–0
St Johnstone	2–0	2–0	0–2	0–1	0–1	1–0	2–2	1–1	–	2–0
	3–0	2–1	1–0	1–2	0–1	2–0	0–1	2–0	–	1–1
St Mirren	3–1	2–0	1–0	1–4	4–4	0–4	2–1	1–1	0–2	–
	1–1	1–1	1–1	1–2	1–2	1–4	2–2	1–0	1–3	–

Read across for home results, down for away.

BELL'S SECOND DIVISION

	Airdrie Utd.	Berwick Rangers	Brechin City	Cowdenbeath	Dumbarton	Forfar Athletic	Hamilton Acad.	Raith Rov.	Stenhousemuir	Stranraer
Airdrie Utd.	–	2–1	2–4	0–0	0–1	1–0	0–0	0–0	2–0	2–1
	–	2–0	3–0	1–1	2–1	0–0	2–2	1–1	1–0	3–3
Berwick Rangers	2–2	–	0–3	2–1	1–2	2–1	2–1	1–1	2–2	3–4
	0–3	–	2–0	1–2	0–1	0–0	1–0	1–1	0–0	1–0
Brechin City	1–5	2–4	–	0–0	1–1	1–0	1–0	1–2	1–0	3–1
	0–1	2–2	–	5–7	1–1	3–4	4–1	1–0	2–1	3–1
Cowdenbeath	0–1	1–2	0–1	–	3–1	1–1	1–3	3–1	1–0	0–1
	1–2	0–1	1–0	–	2–0	2–2	0–1	1–1	3–3	0–0
Dumbarton	3–1	1–2	1–0	1–1	–	1–2	1–1	0–3	0–0	3–0
	2–1	2–2	1–3	3–1	–	1–2	3–1	4–1	3–1	1–1
Forfar Athletic	5–1	0–2	2–1	2–1	2–0	–	1–1	1–2	1–0	2–1
	1–1	2–2	1–5	1–1	0–1	–	0–1	4–2	3–3	4–0
Hamilton Acad.	1–0	1–2	1–2	1–0	1–0	1–2	–	0–4	2–3	1–5
	2–1	3–0	2–2	2–0	2–2	2–0	–	0–0	0–1	1–2
Raith Rov.	0–0	1–2	3–1	4–1	1–0	5–1	1–1	–	1–0	1–1
	1–0	1–0	1–2	2–1	2–1	0–1	1–1	–	0–1	3–0
Stenhousemuir	4–3	2–0	1–1	4–1	2–2	2–1	1–2	0–1	–	2–0
	3–3	1–0	2–2	1–1	2–1	1–4	2–2	1–3	–	1–0
Stranraer	2–0	1–0	3–1	2–3	1–0	2–0	1–2	2–2	2–1	–
	1–2	0–0	2–3	4–4	1–2	3–2	0–0	1–0	0–1	–

Read across for home results, down for away.

BELL'S THIRD DIVISION

	Albion Rov.	East Fife	East Stirling	Elgin City	Gretna	Montrose	Morton	Peterhead	Queen's Park	Stirling Albion
Albion Rov.	–	1–5	6–0	1–1	2–1	1–1	2–1	3–0	0–2	1–3
	–	0–0	3–1	1–1	1–1	3–0	2–1	0–0	2–1	2–1
East Fife	0–4	–	4–1	4–0	3–2	2–0	1–4	3–3	1–1	1–1
	1–1	–	3–0	5–0	2–1	2–0	0–1	0–2	1–0	2–1
East Stirling	0–3	1–4	–	1–2	0–4	1–1	1–1	1–4	0–4	1–1
	0–4	0–4	–	2–2	1–2	0–3	0–1	1–1	0–2	1–3
Elgin City	1–2	1–1	3–1	–	0–2	0–0	0–1	3–0	2–2	0–3
	0–1	0–1	3–0	–	2–2	0–2	0–0	0–4	0–0	2–2
Gretna	2–0	2–3	2–2	0–0	–	4–1	1–1	1–4	2–2	0–2
	1–2	3–3	3–1	2–1	–	2–2	0–1	1–1	0–1	0–0
Montrose	0–1	0–5	2–2	1–0	0–2	–	2–5	0–3	1–0	1–1
	1–1	0–2	5–4	2–0	0–1	–	0–0	1–2	1–1	0–1
Morton	0–1	2–1	4–1	4–0	2–2	4–2	–	1–0	3–0	5–1
	2–1	1–1	2–1	2–0	5–0	1–0	–	1–0	1–1	2–2
Peterhead	2–0	0–2	5–0	2–2	1–1	4–2	4–2	–	3–0	1–0
	0–0	2–2	6–0	3–2	1–1	3–0	3–1	–	3–1	6–0
Queen's Park	2–4	0–0	0–2	1–2	1–0	0–1	1–1	2–0	–	0–1
	1–1	1–2	3–4	3–2	1–2	1–1	0–1	1–2	–	3–3
Stirling Albion	0–1	0–0	3–0	1–1	0–1	1–1	2–0	1–0	1–0	–
	3–4	1–2	2–1	4–0	1–0	1–1	0–3	2–1	1–0	–

Read across for home results, down for away.

SCOTTISH LEAGUE CUP FINALS

1946 Aberdeen beat Rangers (3-2)
1947 Rangers beat Aberdeen (4-0)
1948 East Fife beat Falkirk (4-1 after 0-0 draw)
1949 Rangers beat Raith Rov. (2-0)
1950 East Fife beat Dunfermline Athletic (3-0)
1951 Motherwell beat Hibernian (3-0)
1952 Dundee beat Rangers (3-2)
1953 Dundee beat Kilmarnock (2-0)
1954 East Fife beat Partick Thistle (3-2)
1955 Hearts beat Motherwell (4-2)
1956 Aberdeen beat St Mirren (2-1)
1957 Celtic beat Partick Thistle (3-0 after 0-0 draw)
1958 Celtic beat Rangers (7-1)
1959 Hearts beat Partick Thistle (5-1)
1960 Hearts beat Third Lanark (2-1)
1961 Rangers beat Kilmarnock (2-0)
1962 Rangers beat Hearts (3-1 after 1-1 draw)
1963 Hearts beat Kilmarnock (1-0)
1964 Rangers beat Morton (5-0)
1965 Rangers beat Celtic (2-1)
1966 Celtic beat Rangers (2-1)
1967 Celtic beat Rangers (1-0)
1968 Celtic beat Dundee (5-3)
1969 Celtic beat Hibernian (6-2)
1970 Celtic beat St Johnstone (1-0)
1971 Rangers beat Celtic (1-0)
1972 Partick Thistle beat Celtic (4-1)
1973 Hibernian beat Celtic (2-1)
1974 Dundee beat Celtic (1-0)
1975 Celtic beat Hibernian (6-3)
1976 Rangers beat Celtic (1-0)
1977† Aberdeen beat Celtic (2-1)
1978† Rangers beat Celtic (2-1)
1979 Rangers beat Aberdeen (2-1)
1980 Dundee Utd. beat Aberdeen (3-0 after 0-0 draw)
1981 Dundee Utd. beat Dundee (3-0)
1982 Rangers beat Dundee Utd. (2-1)
1983 Celtic beat Rangers (2-1)
1984† Rangers beat Celtic (3-2)
1985 Rangers beat Dundee Utd. (1-0)
1986 Aberdeen beat Hibernian (3-0)
1987 Rangers beat Celtic (2-1)
1988† Rangers beat Aberdeen (5-3 on pens. after 3-3 draw)
1989 Rangers beat Aberdeen (3-2)
1990† Aberdeen beat Rangers (2-1)
1991† Rangers beat Celtic (2-1)
1992 Hibernian beat Dunfermline Athletic (2-0)
1993† Rangers beat Aberdeen (2-1)
1994 Rangers beat Hibernian (2-1)
1995 Raith Rov. beat Celtic (6-5 on pens. after 2-2 draw)
1996 Aberdeen beat Dundee (2-0)
1997 Rangers beat Hearts (4-3)
1998 Celtic beat Dundee Utd. (3-0)
1999 Rangers beat St Johnstone (2-1)

2000	Celtic beat Aberdeen (2-0)
2001	Celtic beat Kilmarnock (3-0)
2002	Rangers beat Ayr Utd. (4-0)
2003	Rangers beat Celtic (2-1)

(† After extra time; Skol Cup 1985-93, Coca-Cola Cup 1995-97, CIS Insurance 1999)

SUMMARY OF SCOTTISH LEAGUE CUP WINNERS

Rangers	23	Dundee	3	Motherwell	1
Celtic	12	East Fife	3	Partick Thistle	1
Aberdeen	6	Dundee Utd.	2	Raith Rov.	1
Hearts	4	Hibernian	2		

BELL'S SCOTTISH CHALLENGE CUP 2002-03

First round: Airdrie Utd. 3, Raith Rov. 0; Arbroath 0, Forfar Athletic 2; Berwick Rangers 1, Inverness CT 0; Cowdenbeath 0, Ross Co. 2 (aet); Dumbarton 1, East Fife 0; Elgin City 1, Brechin City 4; Montrose 1, Albion Rov. 0; Morton 3, Stirling Albion 2; Peterhead 0, Queen of the South 2; Queen's Park 2, Gretna 1; St Johnstone 3, Hamilton Acad. 0; St Mirren 7, East Stirling 0; Stenhousemuir 1, Falkirk 1 (aet, Falkirk won 3-2 on pens); Stranraer 1, Ayr Utd. 2.

Second round: Clyde 1, St Mirren 2; Berwick Rangers 2, Airdrie Utd. 0; Montrose 0, Falkirk 2; Queen of the South 1, Morton 0; Forfar Athletic 2, Queen's Park 2 (aet, Queen's Park won 6-5 on pens); Dumbarton 3, Ayr Utd. 0; Alloa Athletic 0, Ross Co. 1; Brechin City 3, St Johnstone 2.

Third round: Ross Co. 1, St Mirren 1 (aet, St Mirren won 6-5 on pens); Queen of the South 2, Dumbarton 0; Brechin City 1, Falkirk 1 (aet, Brechin City won 5-3 on pens); Berwick Rangers 1, Queen's Park 2.

Semi-finals: Queen's Park 3, Brechin City 4; St Mirren 3, Queen of the South 5.

FINAL

BRECHIN CITY 0, QUEEN OF THE SOUTH 2

Broadwood Stadium, (6,428), Sunday, October 20, 2002

Brechin City: Hay, McCulloch, Black, Smith, Cairney, Fotheringham, King, Riley (Millar 62), Grant, Jackson, Gibson (Templeman 50). **Subs not used:** Clark, Donnachie, Cairns. **Booked:** Jackson, Grant.

Queen of the South: Goram, Neilson, Anderson, McColligan, Aitken, Thomson, O'Neill, Bowey, Weatherson (O'Connor 75), Lyle (McLaughlin 84), McAlpine. **Subs not used:** Atkinson, Paton, Scott. **Scorers:** O'Neill (33), Lyle (47).

Referee: J. Underhill. **Half-time:** 0-1.

RANGERS RETAIN SCOTTISH LEAGUE CUP

SECOND ROUND	THIRD ROUND	FOURTH ROUND	SEMI-FINALS	FINAL
• Bye	***Celtic** 4			
		***Celtic** .... †C1		
*Inverness CT 3				
	Inverness CT 2			
St Mirren 1				
			Celtic 3	
*Berwick Rangers 0				
	*Partick Thistle 1			
Partick Thistle 3				
		Partick Thistle 1		
*Dundee 3				
	Dundee 0			
Queen of the South 1				
				Celtic 1
*Stranraer 1				
	*St Johnstone 0			
St Johnstone .... †3				
		*Livingston 0		
• Bye	Livingston 1			
			Dundee Utd. 0	
*Kilmarnock 0				
	*Airdrie Utd. 1			
Airdrie Utd. .... †B0				
		Dundee Utd. 2		
*Dundee Utd. 4				
	Dundee Utd. 2			
Queen's Park 1				
• Bye	*Aberdeen 3			
		*Aberdeen 0		
*East Fife 0				
	Motherwell 1			
Motherwell 2				
			Hearts 0	
*Stirling Albion 2				
	*Hearts 3	Hearts 1		
Hearts 3				
*Ross Co. 3				
	Ross Co. 0			
Hamilton Acad. 0				

Second Round	Third Round	Quarter-finals	Semi-finals	Final
*Cowdenbeath .... 1 Dunfermline Athletic .. †2	*Dunfermline Athletic .. 2			**Rangers** 2
		*Dunfermline Athletic .. 0		
*Ayr Utd. .... 0 Falkirk 2	Falkirk 0			
			Rangers 1	
*Alloa Athletic .... 0 Hibernian 2	*Hibernian 2			
		Rangers 1		
● Bye	**Rangers** 3			

FIRST ROUND: Airdrie Utd. 1, Elgin City 0; Albion Rov. 0, Hamilton Acad. 1; Berwick Rangers 4, Arbroath 2; Clyde 0, Ross Co. 1; Cowdenbeath 3, Montrose 2; Falkirk 2, Peterhead 0; Gretna 1, East Fife 2; Inverness CT 2, Dumbarton 0; †Morton 2, St Mirren 3; Queen of the South 2, Forfar Athletic 0; Queen's Park 1, East Stirling 0; †Raith Rov. 2, Alloa Athletic 3; Stranraer 6, Brechin City 1; †A Stirling Albion 3, Stenhousemuir 3.
* Drawn at home. † After extra-time. A – Stirling Albion won 4-2 on pens. B – Airdrie Utd. won 4-3 on pens. C – Celtic won 5-4 on pens. Both semi-finals at Hampden Park.

CIS INSURANCE CUP FINAL

CELTIC 1, RANGERS 2

Hampden Park, (52,000), Sunday, March 16, 2003

Celtic ((3-5-2): Douglas, Mjallby (Petrov 88), Balde, Valgaeren, Smith (Sylla 66), Lambert, Lennon, Sutton (Maloney 80), Thompson, Larsson, Hartson. **Subs not used:** Marshall, McNamara. **Scorer:** Larsson (57). **Booked:** Thompson, Lennon. **Sent off:** Lennon. **Manager:** Martin O'Neill.

Rangers (4-3-3): Klos, Ricksen, Moore, Amoruso, Bonnissel (Ross 64), Arteta (Konterman 78), De Boer (Arveladze 86), Ferguson, Caniggia, Mols, Lovenkrands. **Subs not used:** McCann, McGregor. **Scorers:** Caniggia (23), Lovenkrands (35). **Booked:** Amoruso. **Manager:** Alex McLeish.

Referee: K. Clark. **Half-time:** 0-2.

RANGERS COMPLETE HAT-TRICK OF HONOURS

THIRD ROUND

Dundee 2
*Partick Thistle 0

*Queen of the South . 0:1
Aberdeen 0:4

*Cowdenbeath 2
Alloa Athletic 3

*Falkirk 4
Hearts 0

*Inverness CT 2
Raith Rov. 0

*Queen's Park 2:2
Hamilton Acad. 2:3

*Celtic 3
St Mirren 0

*Airdrie Utd. 1:1
St Johnstone .... 1:+A1

*Ross Co. 1
Morton 2

*Forfar Athletic 2:0
Stranraer 2:1

*Gretna 1
Clyde 2

*Kilmarnock 0
Motherwell 1

FOURTH ROUND

***Dundee** 2
Aberdeen 0

*Alloa Athletic 0
Falkirk 2

*Inverness CT 6
Hamilton Acad. 1

*Celtic 3
St Johnstone 0

*Morton 0
Stranraer 2

*Clyde 0
Motherwell 2

FIFTH ROUND

Dundee 1:4
*Falkirk 1:1

*Inverness CT 1
Celtic 0

*Stranraer 0
Motherwell 4

SEMI-FINALS

Dundee 1
Inverness CT 0

Motherwell 3

FINAL

Dundee 0

Quarter-finals	Semi-finals	Final	Winner	
*Livingston 1:0 Dunfermline 1:2	*Dunfermline 1:2	*Dunfermline 1:0		**Rangers** 1
*Dundee Utd. 2 Hibernian 3	Hibernian 1:0		**Rangers** 4	
*Ayr Utd. 2 Peterhead 0	*Ayr Utd. 0	**Rangers** 1:3		
*Arbroath 0 **Rangers** 3	**Rangers** 1			

FIRST ROUND: East Stirling 1, Threave Rov. 1; Forfar Athletic 3, Huntly 1; Montrose 2, Berwick Rangers 1; Preston N.E. Athletic 0, Hamilton Acad. 1; Raith Rov. 1, Dumbarton 0; Selkirk 1, Cowdenbeath 4; Stenhousemuir 4, Brechin City 1; Stranraer 1, Whitehill 1.

REPLAYS: Threave Rov. 2, East Stirling 1; Whitehill 2, Stranraer 3.

SECOND ROUND: Airdrie Utd. 1, Threave Rov. 0; Forfar Athletic 3, Stenhousemuir 1; Gretna 3, Cove 0; Hamilton Acad. 1, East Fife 1; Keith 1, Cowdenbeath 3; Morton 4, Deronvale 3; Peterhead 1, Elgin City 0; Queen's Park 1, Albion Rov. 1; Raith Rov. 3, Montrose 1; Stranraer 4, Stirling Albion 1.

REPLAYS: Albion Rov. 0, Queen's Park 2; East Fife 2, Hamilton Acad. 2 (aet Hamilton Acad. won 5-3 on pens).
* Drawn at home. Both semi-finals at Hampden Park. + After extra-time. A St Johnstone won 4-2 on pens.

TENNENTS SCOTTISH CUP FINAL

DUNDEE 0, RANGERS 1

Hampden Park, (47,136), Saturday, May 31, 2003

Dundee (4-3-3): Speroni, Mackay (Milne 78), Mair, Khizanishvili, Hernandez Santos, Rae (Brady 85), Nemsadze, Smith (capt), Burchill (Novo 71), Caballero, Lovell. **Subs not used:** Langfield, Carranza. **Booked:** Novo. **Manager:** Jim Duffy.

Rangers (4-1-3-2): Klos, Ricksen, Moore, Amoruso, Numan (Muscat 69), Malcolm, Arveladze (Thompson 56), Ferguson (capt), McCann, Mols (Ross 45), De Boer. **Subs not used:** McGregor, McLean. **Scorer:** Amoruso (66). **Booked:** Arveladze, McCann. **Manager:** Alex McLeish.

Referee: K. Clark. **Half-time:** 0-0.

SCOTTISH CUP FINALS

1874	Queen's Park beat Clydesdale (2-0)
1875	Queen's Park beat Renton (3-0)
1876	Queen's Park beat Third Lanark (2-0 after 1-1 draw)
1877	Vale of Leven beat Rangers (3-2 after 0-0, 1-1 draws)
1878	Vale of Leven beat Third Lanark (1-0)
1879	Vale of Leven awarded Cup (Rangers withdrew after 1-1 draw)
1880	Queen's Park beat Thornlibank (3-0)
1881	Queen's Park beat Dumbarton (3-1)
1882	Queen's Park beat Dumbarton (4-1 after 2-2 draw)
1883	Dumbarton beat Vale of Leven (2-1 after 2-2 draw)
1884	Queen's Park awarded Cup (Vale of Leven withdrew from Final)
1885	Renton beat Vale of Leven (3-1 after 0-0 draw)
1886	Queen's Park beat Renton (3-1)
1887	Hibernian beat Dumbarton (2-1)
1888	Renton beat Cambuslang (6-1)
1889	Third Lanark beat Celtic (2-1)
1890	Queen's Park beat Vale of Leven (2-1 after 1-1 draw)
1891	Hearts beat Dumbarton (1-0)
1892	Celtic beat Queen's Park (5-1)
1893	Queen's Park beat Celtic (2-1)
1894	Rangers beat Celtic (3-1)
1895	St. Bernard's beat Renton (2-1)
1896	Hearts beat Hibernian (3-1)
1897	Rangers beat Dumbarton (5-1)
1898	Rangers beat Kilmarnock (2-0)
1899	Celtic beat Rangers (2-0)
1900	Celtic beat Queen's Park (4-3)
1901	Hearts beat Celtic (4-3)
1902	Hibernian beat Celtic (1-0)
1903	Rangers beat Hearts (2-0 after 0-0, 1-1 draws)
1904	Celtic beat Rangers (3-2)
1905	Third Lanark beat Rangers (3-1 after 0-0 draw)
1906	Hearts beat Third Lanark (1-0)
1907	Celtic beat Hearts (3-0)
1908	Celtic beat St. Mirren (5-1)
1909	Cup withheld because of riot after two drawn games in Final between Celtic and Rangers (2-2, 1-1)
1910	Dundee beat Clyde (2-1 after 2-2, 0-0 draws)
1911	Celtic beat Hamilton Academical (2-0 after 0-0 draw)
1912	Celtic beat Clyde (2-0)
1913	Falkirk beat Raith Rov. (2-0)
1914	Celtic beat Hibernian (4-1 after 0-0 draw)
1915-19	No competition (World War 1)
1920	Kilmarnock beat Albion Rov. (3-2)
1921	Partick Thistle beat Rangers (1-0)
1922	Morton beat Rangers (1-0)
1923	Celtic beat Hibernian (1-0)
1924	Airdrieonians beat Hibernian (2-0)
1925	Celtic beat Dundee (2-1)
1926	St. Mirren beat Celtic (2-0)
1927	Celtic beat East Fife (3-1)
1928	Rangers beat Celtic (4-0)
1929	Kilmarnock beat Rangers (2-0)
1930	Rangers beat Partick Thistle (2-1 after 0-0 draw)
1931	Celtic beat Motherwell (4-2 after 2-2 draw)
1932	Rangers beat Kilmarnock (3-0 after 1-1 draw)

1933	Celtic beat Motherwell (1-0)
1934	Rangers beat St. Mirren (5-0)
1935	Rangers beat Hamilton Academical (2-1)
1936	Rangers beat Third Lanark (1-0)
1937	Celtic beat Aberdeen (2-1)
1938	East Fife beat Kilmarnock (4-2 after 1-1 draw)
1939	Clyde beat Motherwell (4-0)
1940-6	No competition (World War 2)
1947	Aberdeen beat Hibernian (2-1)
1948†	Rangers beat Morton (1-0 after 1-1 draw)
1949	Rangers beat Clyde (4-1)
1950	Rangers beat East Fife (3-0)
1951	Celtic beat Motherwell (1-0)
1952	Motherwell beat Dundee (4-0)
1953	Rangers beat Aberdeen (1-0 after 1-1 draw)
1954	Celtic beat Aberdeen (2-1)
1955	Clyde beat Celtic (1-0 after 1-1 draw)
1956	Hearts beat Celtic (3-1)
1957†	Falkirk beat Kilmarnock (2-1 after 1-1 draw)
1958	Clyde beat Hibernian (1-0)
1959	St. Mirren beat Aberdeen (3-1)
1960	Rangers beat Kilmarnock (2-0)
1961	Dunfermline Athletic beat Celtic (2-0 after 0-0 draw)
1962	Rangers beat St. Mirren (2-0)
1963	Rangers beat Celtic (3-0 after 1-1 draw)
1964	Rangers beat Dundee (3-1)
1965	Celtic beat Dunfermline Athletic (3-2)
1966	Rangers beat Celtic (1-0 after 0-0 draw)
1967	Celtic beat Aberdeen (2-0)
1968	Dunfermline Athletic beat Hearts (3-1)
1969	Celtic beat Rangers (4-0)
1970	Aberdeen beat Celtic (3-1)
1971	Celtic beat Rangers (2-1 after 1-1 draw)
1972	Celtic beat Hibernian (6-1)
1973	Rangers beat Celtic (3-2)
1974	Celtic beat Dundee Utd. (3-0)
1975	Celtic beat Airdrieonians (3-1)
1976	Rangers beat Hearts (3-1)
1977	Celtic beat Rangers (1-0)
1978	Rangers beat Aberdeen (2-1)
1979†	Rangers beat Hibernian (3-2 after two 0-0 draws)
1980†	Celtic beat Rangers (1-0)
1981	Rangers beat Dundee Utd. (4-1 after 0-0 draw)
1982†	Aberdeen beat Rangers (4-1)
1983†	Aberdeen beat Rangers (1-0)
1984†	Aberdeen beat Celtic (2-1)
1985	Celtic beat Dundee Utd. (2-1)
1986	Aberdeen beat Hearts (3-0)
1987†	St. Mirren beat Dundee Utd. (1-0)
1988	Celtic beat Dundee Utd. (2-1)
1989	Celtic beat Rangers (1-0)
1990†	Aberdeen beat Celtic (9-8 on pens. after 0-0 draw)
1991†	Motherwell beat Dundee Utd. (4-3)
1992	Rangers beat Airdrieonians (2-1)
1993	Rangers beat Aberdeen (2-1)
1994	Dundee Utd. beat Rangers (1-0)
1995	Celtic beat Airdrieonians (1-0)
1996	Rangers beat Hearts (5-1)

1997	Kilmarnock beat Falkirk (1-0)
1998	Hearts beat Rangers (2-1)
1999	Rangers beat Celtic (1-0)
2000	Rangers beat Aberdeen (4-0)
2001	Celtic beat Hibernian (3-0)
2002	Rangers beat Celtic (3-2)
2003	Rangers beat Dundee (1-0)

(† After extra time; Cup sponsored by Tennents since season 1989-90)

SUMMARY OF SCOTTISH CUP WINNERS

Celtic 31, Rangers 31, Queen's Park 10, Aberdeen 7, Hearts 6, Clyde 3, Kilmarnock 3, St. Mirren 3, Vale of Leven 3, Dunfermline Ath. 2, Falkirk 2, Hibernian 2, Motherwell 2, Renton 2, Third Lanark 2, Airdrieonians 1, Dumbarton 1, Dundee 1, Dundee Utd. 1, East Fife 1, Morton 1, Partick Thistle 1, St. Bernard's 1.

QUOTE-UNQUOTE

'I've been missing football and this is a great opportunity for me' – **Paul Gascoigne** after joining the Chinese second division club Gansu Tianma.

'I risked getting my tyres nicked and my wheels gone to talk to Robbie and his wife' – **Kevin Keegan** after driving to Merseyside and persuading Robbie Fowler to join Manchester City

'I'm not a racist player. I am black and white' – **Jonathan Woodgate**, convicted of affray while at Leeds United, after joining Newcastle United.

'Should we have spent so heavily in the past? Perhaps not. But we lived the dream. Only by making the right decisions now can we rekindle the dream in the future' – **Peter Ridsdale**, chairman of debt-ridden Leeds United, after Jonathan Woodgate became the latest player to leave Elland Road.

'I'm not saying people's minds were elsewhere, but it could be possible couldn't it?' – **David James**, England goalkeeper after the 3-1 defeat by Australia.

'If I did it a hundred times, a million times, it could not happen again. If it did, I'd have carried on playing' – **Sir Alex Ferguson** on the dressing room incident in which David Beckham was struck above the left eye by a flying football boot kicked in anger by his Manchester United manager after the F.A. Cup defeat against Arsenal.

'Mr Wenger has lost his voice, as opposed to Mr Ferguson who has lost his head' – **Paul Burrell**, Arsenal's match-day announcer before the Champions League game against Ajax.

'What do you lot know anyway? How many caps have *you* won?' – **Howard Wilkinson**, Sunderland manager, at a post-match press conference

'Fifty seven actually, Howard' – **Jimmy Armfield**, commentator and former England captain.

'The idea was to have a go at them for the first 20 minutes. You could say it didn't work' – **Kevin Keegan** after watching his Manchester City side concede four goals in the first 20 minutes to Arsenal.

'I simply lost it' – **Dion Dublin** apologises for butting Robbie Savage in the Aston Villa-Birmingham City derby.

'I've put my backside in the bacon slicer' – **Mick McCarthy** after his appointment as Sunderland manager.

IRISH FOOTBALL 2002-03

EIRCOM LEAGUE

PREMIER DIVISION

		P	W	D	L	F	A	Pts
1	Bohemians	27	15	9	3	47	28	54
2	Shelbourne	27	15	4	8	44	26	49
3	Shamrock Rov.	27	12	7	8	42	29	43
4	Cork City	27	11	6	10	37	33	39
5	Longford Town	27	8	11	8	25	29	35
6	U.C.D.	27	8	9	10	23	25	33
7	St Patrick's Ath.	27	8	9	10	27	33	33
8	Derry City	27	8	7	12	31	37	31
9	Drogheda Utd.	27	8	6	13	26	40	30
10	Bray Wand.	27	4	8	15	31	53	20

Leading scorer: 18 Glen Crowe (Bohemians). **Player of Year:** Glen Crowe (Bohemians). **Young Player of Year:** Wes Hoolahan (Shelbourne). **Personality of Year:** Glen Crowe (Bohemians). **Goalkeeper of Year:** Barry Ryan (UCD).

FIRST DIVISION

		P	W	D	L	F	A	Pts
1	Waterford Utd.	22	13	7	2	37	25	46
2	Finn Harps	22	12	5	5	41	22	41
3	Galway Utd.	22	10	6	6	34	21	36
4	Cobh Ramblers	22	10	5	7	39	38	35
5	Kildare Co.	22	9	6	7	32	31	33
6	Sligo Rov.	22	8	6	8	28	27	30
7	Dublin City	22	8	4	10	36	35	28
8	Monaghan Utd.	22	5	11	6	26	27	26
9	Dundalk	22	5	8	9	28	36	23
10	Limerick F.C.	22	6	5	11	26	36	23
11	Athlone Town	22	5	6	11	26	40	21
12	Kilkenny City	22	3	7	12	23	38	16

Leading scorer: 16 Willie Bruton (Cobh Ramblers). **Player of Year:** Wayne Russell (Waterford Utd.).

FAI CARLSBERG CUP FINAL

Derry City 1 (Coyle), **Shamrock Rov.** 0 – Tolka Park, October 27, 2002

Derry City: Gough, Harkin, E. McCallion, McLaughlin, Hargan, Hutton, Martyn, Doherty, Friars (McCready), Coyle (T. McCallion), Kelly.

Shamrock Rov.: O'Dowd, Costello, Scully, Palmer, Byrne (Robinson), Colwell (Tracey), S.Grant (Francis), Dimich, Hunt, T. Grant, Keddy.

Referee: J. O'Neill (Waterford).

SMIRNOFF IRISH LEAGUE

PREMIER DIVISION

Top Six

		P	W	D	L	F	A	Pts
1	Glentoran	38	28	6	4	78	22	90
2	Portadown	38	24	8	6	89	36	80
3	Coleraine	38	21	10	7	66	38	73
4	Linfield	38	17	12	9	70	41	63
5	Omagh	38	15	6	17	47	57	51
6	Institute	38	12	6	20	44	75	42
Bottom Six								
1	Ards	38	12	10	16	27	39	46
2	Distillery	38	12	6	20	39	49	42
3	Cliftonville	38	9	14	15	37	43	41
4	Glenavon	38	8	12	18	41	67	36
5	Crusaders	38	9	9	20	26	61	36
6	Newry	38	8	7	23	33	69	31

Leading scorer: 29 Vinny Arkins (Portadown). **Player of Year:** Gary Smyth (Glentoran). **Young Player of Year:** Michael Gault (Linfield). **Manager of Year:** Roy Coyle (Glentoran).

FIRST DIVISION

		P	W	D	L	F	A	Pts
1	Dungannon Swifts	28	18	6	4	61	32	60
2	Ballymena Utd.	28	16	6	6	71	40	54
3	Limavady	28	15	5	8	53	37	50
4	Larne	28	13	4	11	35	30	43
5	Bangor	28	12	5	11	40	39	41
6	Carrick Rangers	28	8	4	16	44	76	28
7	Ballyclare Comrades	28	6	4	18	36	65	22
8	Armagh City	28	4	6	18	37	58	18

(Four clubs promoted from first division)

Leading scorer: 22 Shea Campbell (Ballymena Utd). **Player of Year:** Shea Campbell (Ballymena Utd). **Manager of Year:** Joe McAree (Dungannon).

NATIONWIDE IRISH CUP-FINAL

Coleraine 1 (Tallon), **Glentoran** 0, Windsor Park – May 3, 2003.

Coleraine: O'Hare, Clanachan, Flynn, Gaston, McAuley, Beatty, Gorman, Hamill, Tolan, McAllister (Armstrong), McCoosh.

Glentoran: Morris, Nixon, Glendenning, Leeman, Young, Smyth, Tim McCann, Lockhart (O'Neill), Smith, Armour (Halliday), Timothy McCann (Walker).

Referee: L. Irvine (Limavady).

CIS LEAGUE CUP FINAL

Glentoran 2 (Halliday, Smyth), **Linfield** 0 – Windsor Park, December 4, 2002.

COUNTY ANTRIM SHIELD FINAL

Glentoran 3 (Armour, Smith, Young), **Ballymena Utd.** 0 – The Oval, March 4, 2003.

OTHER LEAGUES 2002–03

NATIONWIDE CONFERENCE

		P	W	D	L	F	A	W	D	L	F	A	Pts	GD
1	Yeovil Town	42	16	5	0	54	13	12	6	3	46	24	95	+63
2	Morecambe	42	17	3	1	52	13	6	6	9	34	29	78	+44
3	Doncaster Rov.*	42	11	6	4	28	17	11	6	4	45	30	78	+26
4	Chester City	42	10	6	5	36	21	11	6	4	23	10	75	+28
5	Dag & Redbridge	42	12	5	4	38	23	9	4	8	33	36	72	+12
6	Hereford Utd.	42	9	5	7	36	22	10	2	9	28	29	64	+13
7	Scarborough	42	12	3	6	41	28	6	7	8	22	26	64	+9
8	Halifax Town	42	11	5	5	34	28	7	5	9	16	23	64	–1
9	Forest Green Rov.	42	12	3	6	41	29	5	5	11	20	33	59	–1
10	Margate	42	8	9	4	32	24	7	2	12	28	42	56	–6
11	Barnet	42	9	4	8	32	28	4	10	7	33	40	53	–3
12	Stevenage Borough	42	7	6	8	31	25	7	4	10	30	30	52	+6
13	Farnborough Town	42	8	6	7	37	29	5	6	10	20	27	51	+1
14	Northwich Victoria	42	6	5	10	26	34	7	7	7	40	38	51	–6
15	Telford Utd.	42	7	2	12	20	33	7	5	9	34	36	49	–15
16	Burton Albion	42	6	6	9	25	31	7	4	10	27	46	49	–25
17	Gravesend	42	8	5	8	37	35	4	7	10	25	38	48	–11
18	Leigh RMI	42	8	5	8	26	34	6	1	14	18	37	48	–27
19	Woking	42	8	7	6	30	35	3	7	11	22	46	47	–29
20	Nuneaton Borough	42	9	4	8	27	32	4	3	14	24	46	46	–27
21	Southport	42	6	8	7	31	32	5	4	12	23	37	45	–15
22	Kettering Town	42	4	3	14	23	39	4	4	13	14	34	31	–36

* Also promoted via play-offs

Manager of Year: Gary Johnson (Yeovil Town). **Player of Year:** Michael McIndoe (Yeovil Town). **Goalscorer of Year:** 25 Paul Barnes (Doncaster Rov.). **Highest attendance:** 8,111 (Yeovil Town v Chester City). **Relegated:** Nuneaton Borough (Dr Martens League); Southport (Unibond League); Kettering Town (Ryman League). **Promoted to Conference:** Accrington Stanley (Unibond League); Tamworth (Dr Martens League); Aldershot (Ryman League). **Leading scorers (all competitions):** 28 Barnes (Doncaster Rov.); 27 Jackson (Yeovil Town) – 5 for Stevenage Borough; 22 Blundell (Doncaster Rov.) – 21 for Northwich Victoria; 21 Stein (Dagenham & Redbridge); 20 Agogo (Barnet), Baptiste (Farnborough Town), Grayson (Forest Green Rov.); 19 Clare (Chester City) – 1 for Boston Utd.; 18 Curtis (Morecambe), Moore, C (Burton Albion); 17 West (Dagenham & Redbridge).

CONFERENCE CHAMPIONS

1979-80	Altrincham	1991-92*	Colchester Utd.
1980-81	Altrincham	1992-93*	Wycombe Wand.
1981-82	Runcorn	1993-94	Kidderminster H.
1982-83	Enfield	1994-95	Macclesfield Town
1983-84	Maidstone Utd.	1995-96	Stevenage Borough
1984-85	Wealdstone	1996-97*	Macclesfield Town
1985-86	Enfield	1997-98*	Halifax Town
1986-87*	Scarborough	1998-99*	Cheltenham Town
1987-88*	Lincoln City	1999-2000*	Kidderminster Harriers
1988-89*	Maidstone Utd.	2000-01*	Rushden & Diamonds
1989-90*	Darlington	2001-02*	Boston Utd.
1990-91*	Barnet	2002-03*	Yeovil Town

(* Promoted to Football League)

Conference – Record Attendance: 9,432, Lincoln City v Wycombe Wand., May 2, 1988.

NATIONWIDE CONFERENCE RESULTS 2002–03

	Barnet	Burton Albion	Chester City	Dag & Redbridge	Doncaster Rov.	Farnborough Town	Forest Green Rov.	Gravesend	Halifax Town	Hereford Utd.	Kettering Town	Leigh RMI	Margate	Morecambe	Northwich Victoria	Nuneaton Borough	Scarborough	Southport	Stevenage Borough	Telford Utd.	Woking	Yeovil Town
Barnet	–	2–2	0–3	2–1	1–2	1–2	2–0	1–4	0–0	2–1	0–2	4–0	0–1	1–1	3–4	2–1	3–0	3–1	0–2	3–0	0–0	2–1
Burton Albion	0–3	–	2–0	0–0	1–2	2–0	2–3	1–1	2–2	2–0	2–0	0–1	0–1	1–4	1–1	1–0	1–1	1–0	1–2	4–7	0–2	1–1
Chester City	1–1	2–1	–	5–2	1–0	0–2	0–1	1–1	2–0	0–1	0–0	2–1	5–0	2–1	2–3	1–2	0–0	2–0	2–0	4–1	2–2	2–2
Dag & Redbridge	5–1	1–2	1–0	–	3–3	1–0	3–1	4–0	0–0	1–0	3–1	3–1	3–0	1–1	2–0	1–2	1–0	0–3	3–2	1–1	1–1	0–4
Doncaster Rov.	2–1	1–0	0–0	5–1	–	1–0	1–0	4–1	0–0	2–0	1–0	1–0	3–1	1–1	1–2	1–1	0–1	0–0	0–0	1–3	3–1	0–4
Farnborough Town	2–2	5–1	1–2	1–0	0–0	–	0–3	1–1	3–0	2–2	0–1	1–0	4–1	2–3	3–2	0–2	1–1	2–1	0–1	2–2	5–0	2–4
Forest Green Rov.	4–4	2–0	0–2	5–2	1–2	3–1	–	2–1	0–2	1–3	1–0	4–1	4–1	1–0	1–0	6–1	0–0	0–2	0–3	1–1	3–2	2–1
Gravesend	2–2	3–2	0–1	1–2	2–2	0–0	1–1	–	1–0	3–0	0–2	1–3	1–2	3–2	1–1	4–1	5–2	1–3	2–1	0–2	4–2	2–4
Halifax Town	2–4	0–1	0–0	3–3	2–1	1–0	1–1	2–1	–	1–0	4–0	1–0	2–2	1–0	0–5	3–1	2–1	3–4	1–0	2–0	1–1	2–3
Hereford Utd.	4–0	4–0	0–0	2–1	2–4	2–1	1–1	3–0	1–1	–	2–0	0–1	2–3	1–2	1–2	2–1	0–1	0–2	2–2	2–0	5–0	0–0
Kettering Town	1–2	1–2	0–1	1–3	0–2	1–4	2–3	1–1	0–1	2–3	–	0–1	1–1	3–2	2–2	3–0	1–3	1–0	1–0	2–4	0–3	0–1
Leigh RMI	4–2	4–2	0–4	1–3	0–2	3–2	1–0	0–0	0–2	0–2	2–2	–	2–0	1–0	1–1	1–1	0–2	1–1	2–1	0–3	1–0	2–4
Margate	2–2	0–0	0–1	0–1	2–1	0–0	3–0	4–2	2–1	0–2	2–2	2–0	–	1–1	4–4	1–1	3–1	1–0	1–1	1–1	2–1	1–2
Morecambe	1–1	5–0	1–1	2–1	3–0	1–1	4–0	2–0	2–0	3–1	1–0	2–1	3–0	–	3–1	3–2	3–1	3–0	3–1	1–0	5–0	1–2
Northwich Victoria	1–1	1–3	1–1	0–2	1–2	2–2	2–1	1–2	0–2	2–2	1–2	0–1	1–0	3–2	–	3–1	0–2	2–1	1–1	2–1	1–3	1–2
Nuneaton Borough	3–2	1–2	1–0	1–3	0–3	0–2	3–2	0–1	2–0	0–3	1–0	0–2	3–2	1–1	1–4	–	1–1	3–2	3–0	1–0	1–1	1–1
Scarborough	1–1	4–1	0–1	0–1	2–5	1–0	3–0	3–2	0–1	2–1	4–1	2–0	3–2	1–0	4–1	4–1	–	2–2	1–2	1–4	1–1	2–1
Southport	2–1	2–2	1–3	2–3	0–4	0–0	2–2	1–1	2–0	1–2	0–0	4–2	0–2	2–3	1–1	1–0	1–1	–	3–2	1–1	5–1	0–1
Stevenage Borough	1–2	0–1	0–1	2–0	2–3	5–0	0–0	1–0	0–1	0–2	2–0	3–1	1–3	1–1	2–2	3–1	1–1	3–0	–	1–3	1–1	2–2
Telford Utd.	2–1	0–2	0–1	1–2	4–4	0–2	0–1	2–1	1–2	0–1	2–0	1–1	1–0	0–3	1–0	1–2	0–2	2–0	1–3	–	1–0	0–5
Woking	0–0	2–2	1–0	0–0	2–2	1–1	1–0	2–3	2–1	1–2	2–1	3–0	1–5	0–6	2–3	2–1	2–1	1–1	1–5	3–0	–	1–1
Yeovil Town	0–0	6–1	1–1	2–2	1–1	2–0	1–0	2–2	3–0	4–0	4–0	3–1	2–1	2–0	2–1	3–2	1–0	6–0	2–1	3–0	4–0	–

RYMAN LEAGUE

PREMIER DIVISION

		P	W	D	L	F	A	Pts	GD
1	Aldershot Town	46	33	6	7	81	36	105	+45
2	Canvey Island	46	28	8	10	112	56	92	+56
3	Hendon	46	22	13	11	70	56	79	+14
4	St Albans City	46	23	8	15	73	65	77	+8
5	Basingstoke Town	46	23	7	16	80	60	76	+20
6	Sutton Utd.	46	22	9	15	77	62	75	+15
7	Hayes	46	20	13	13	67	54	73	+13
8	Purfleet	46	19	15	12	68	48	72	+20
9	Bedford Town	46	21	9	16	66	58	72	+8
10	Maidenhead Utd.	46	16	17	13	75	63	65	+12
11	Kingstonian	46	16	17	13	71	64	65	+7
12	Billericay Town	46	17	11	18	46	44	62	+2
13	Bishop's Stortford	46	16	11	19	74	72	59	+2
14	Hitchin Town	46	15	13	18	69	67	58	+2
15	Ford Utd.	46	15	12	19	78	84	57	–6
16	Braintree Town	46	14	12	20	59	71	54	–12
17	Aylesbury Utd.	46	13	15	18	62	75	54	–13
18	Harrow Borough	46	15	9	22	54	75	54	–21
19	Grays Athletic	46	14	11	21	53	59	53	–6
20	Heybridge Swifts	46	13	14	19	52	80	53	–28
21	Chesham Utd.	46	14	10	22	56	81	52	–25
22	Boreham Wood	46	11	15	20	50	58	48	–8
23	Enfield	46	9	11	26	47	101	38	–54
24	Hampton & Richmond	46	3	14	29	35	86	23	–51

DR MARTENS LEAGUE

PREMIER DIVISION

		P	W	D	L	F	A	Pts	GD
1	Tamworth	42	26	10	6	73	32	88	+41
2	Stafford Rangers	42	21	12	9	76	40	75	+36
3	Dover	42	19	14	9	42	35	71	+7
4	Tiverton Town	42	19	12	11	60	43	69	+17
5	Chippenham Town	42	17	17	8	59	37	68	+22
6	Worcester City	42	18	13	11	60	39	67	+21
7	Crawley Town	42	17	13	12	64	51	64	+13
8	Havant and W	42	15	15	12	67	64	60	+3
9	Chelmsford	42	15	12	15	65	63	57	+2
10	Newport Co.	42	15	11	16	53	52	56	+1
11	Hednesford	42	14	13	15	59	60	55	–1
12	Moor Green	42	13	14	15	49	58	53	–9
13	Hinckley Utd.	42	12	16	14	61	64	52	–3
14	Bath City	42	13	13	16	50	61	52	–11
15	Welling	42	13	12	17	55	58	51	–3
16	Grantham Town	42	14	9	19	59	65	51	–6
17	Weymouth	42	12	15	15	44	62	51	–18
18	Cambridge City	42	13	10	19	54	56	49	–2
19	Halesowen	42	12	13	17	52	63	49	–11
20	Hastings Utd.	42	10	13	19	44	57	43	–13
21	Ilkeston Town	42	10	10	22	54	92	40	–38
22	Folkestone Invicta	42	7	7	28	57	105	28	–48

UNIBOND LEAGUE

PREMIER DIVISION

		P	W	D	L	F	A	Pts	GD
1	Accrington Stanley	44	30	10	4	97	44	100	+53
2	Barrow	44	24	12	8	84	52	84	+32
3	Vauxhall Motors	44	22	10	12	81	46	76	+35
4	Stalybridge	44	21	13	10	77	51	76	+26
5	Worksop	44	21	9	14	82	67	72	+15
6	Harrogate Town	44	21	8	15	75	63	71	+12
7	Bradford City P.A.	44	20	10	14	73	70	70	+3
8	Hucknall Town	44	17	15	12	72	62	66	+10
9	Droylsden	44	18	10	16	62	52	64	+10
10	Whitby	44	17	12	15	80	69	63	+11
11	Marine	44	17	10	17	63	60	61	+3
12	Wakefield & Emley	44	14	18	12	46	49	60	–3
13	Runcorn	44	15	15	14	69	74	60	–5
14	Altrincham	44	17	9	18	58	63	60	–5
15	Gainsborough	44	16	11	17	67	66	59	+1
16	Ashton Utd.	44	15	13	16	71	79	58	–8
17	Lancaster	44	16	9	19	71	75	57	–4
18	Burscough	44	14	9	21	44	51	51	–7
19	Blyth Spartans	44	14	9	21	67	87	51	–20
20	Frickley	44	13	8	23	45	78	47	–33
21	Gateshead	44	10	11	23	60	81	41	–21
22	Colwyn Bay	44	5	9	30	52	99	24	–47
23	Hyde	44	5	8	31	40	98	23	–58

WELSH PREMIER LEAGUE

		P	W	D	L	F	A	Pts	GD
1	Barry Town	34	26	5	3	84	26	83	+58
2	T.N.S.	34	24	8	2	68	21	80	+47
3	Bangor City	34	22	5	7	75	34	71	+41
4	Aberystwyth	34	17	9	8	54	38	60	+16
5	Connah's Quay	34	18	5	11	55	46	59	+9
6	Rhyl	34	17	7	10	52	33	58	+19
7	Afan Lido	34	14	10	10	44	34	52	+10
8	Caersws	34	15	6	13	57	52	51	+5
9	Cwmbran	34	14	8	12	51	40	50	+11
10	Newtown	34	12	6	16	48	54	42	–6
11	Port Talbot	34	11	6	17	36	51	39	–15
12	Flexsys Druids	34	11	5	18	37	51	38	–14
13	Haverfordwest	34	10	5	19	40	68	35	–28
14	Caernarfon	34	8	10	16	43	53	34	–10
15	Carmarthen	34	9	5	20	33	66	32	–33
16	Oswestry Town	34	6	10	18	36	67	28	–31
17	Welshpool Town	34	7	7	20	30	62	28	–32
18	Llanelli	34	4	5	25	42	89	17	–47

SCOT-ADS HIGHLAND LEAGUE

		P	W	D	L	F	A	Pts	GD
1	Deveronvale	28	21	6	1	90	24	69	+66
2	Keith	28	17	1	10	66	35	52	+31
3	Buckie Thistle	28	15	6	7	63	36	51	+27
4	Cove Rangers	28	14	7	7	70	46	49	+24
5	Nairn Co.	28	13	7	8	67	47	46	+20
6	Fraserburgh	28	14	4	10	61	45	46	+16
7	Clachnacuddin	28	13	4	11	46	50	43	–4
8	Huntly	28	12	5	11	53	42	41	+11
9	Inverurie Locos	28	11	7	10	50	50	40	0
10	Lossiemouth	28	12	4	12	41	53	40	–12
11	Forres Mech	28	12	2	14	59	62	38	–3
12	Rothes	28	8	5	15	26	50	29	–24
13	Wick Acad.	28	8	2	18	33	68	26	–35
14	Brora Rangers	28	3	6	19	30	77	15	–47
15	Fort William	28	2	4	22	20	90	10	–70

F.A. BARCLAYCARD PREMIERSHIP RESERVE LEAGUE

NORTH

		P	W	D	L	F	A	Pts	GD
1	Sunderland	28	17	4	7	51	26	55	+25
2	Middlesbrough	28	16	7	5	47	26	55	+21
3	Manchester City	28	17	3	8	55	27	54	+28
4	Aston Villa	28	16	4	8	59	44	52	+15
5	Liverpool	28	13	5	10	48	34	44	+14
6	Everton	28	12	7	9	44	36	43	+8
7	Leeds Utd.	28	10	11	7	45	37	41	+8
8	Manchester Utd.	28	12	5	11	45	37	41	+8
9	Bolton Wand.	28	11	5	12	45	48	38	–3
10	Birmingham City	28	11	4	13	33	39	37	–6
11	W.B.A.	28	8	11	9	27	31	35	–4
12	Newcastle Utd.	28	8	9	11	44	43	33	+1
13	Blackburn Rov.	28	10	3	15	34	51	33	–17
14	Sheffield Wed.	28	3	5	20	21	55	14	–34
15	Bradford City	28	3	3	22	20	84	12	–64

SOUTH

		P	W	D	L	F	A	Pts	GD
1	Watford	26	15	5	6	34	27	50	+7
2	Fulham	26	14	6	6	58	34	48	+24
3	Derby Co.	26	13	7	6	46	30	46	+16
4	Arsenal	26	13	6	7	56	38	45	+18
5	West Ham Utd.	26	10	11	5	29	26	41	+3
6	Tottenham	26	10	5	11	32	33	35	–1
7	Charlton Athletic	26	10	4	12	40	37	34	+3
8	Nott'm. Forest	26	10	4	12	39	42	34	–3
9	Leicester City	26	10	3	13	31	43	33	–12
10	Chelsea	26	8	8	10	31	33	32	–2
11	Ipswich Town	26	9	5	12	34	39	32	–5
12	Southampton	26	9	5	12	27	38	32	–11
13	Wimbledon	26	5	6	15	27	44	21	–17
14	Coventry City	26	4	9	13	18	38	21	–20

AVON INSURANCE LEAGUE

PREMIER DIVISION

		P	W	D	L	F	A	Pts	GD
1	Sheffield Utd.	20	11	4	5	36	19	37	+17
2	Walsall	20	9	6	5	40	31	33	+9
3	Huddersfield Town	20	9	5	6	30	22	32	+8
4	Barnsley	20	10	2	8	42	40	32	+2
5	Preston N.E.	20	10	2	8	30	30	32	0
6	Wolves	20	9	3	8	31	28	30	+3
7	Tranmere Rov.	20	8	5	7	37	40	29	–3
8	Rotherham Utd.	20	8	3	9	36	34	27	+2
9	Burnley	20	8	1	11	35	37	25	–2
10	Oldham Athletic	20	6	4	10	27	35	22	–8
11	Bury	20	3	3	14	24	52	12	–28

DIVISION ONE WEST

		P	W	D	L	F	A	Pts	GD
1	Stoke City	18	12	2	4	42	22	38	+20
2	Doncaster Rov.	18	10	2	6	40	29	32	+11
3	Shrewsbury Town	18	9	3	6	32	23	30	+9
4	Stockport Co.	18	8	5	5	40	27	29	+13
5	Macclesfield Town	18	9	1	8	33	26	28	+7
6	Rochdale	18	8	2	8	25	23	26	+2
7	Wigan Athletic	18	7	3	8	25	31	24	–6
8	Wrexham	18	6	1	11	27	40	19	–13
9	Blackpool	18	5	2	11	30	42	17	–12
10	Chesterfield	18	5	1	12	24	55	16	–31

DIVISION ONE EAST

		P	W	D	L	F	A	Pts	GD
1	Hull City	20	13	4	3	31	13	43	+18
2	Hartlepool Utd.	20	11	4	5	42	21	37	+21
3	Darlington	20	12	1	7	50	39	37	+11
4	Grimsby Town	20	10	3	7	27	33	33	–6
5	Boston Utd.	20	10	1	9	33	30	31	+3
6	Notts Co.	20	8	3	9	29	17	27	+12
7	Scunthorpe Utd.	20	9	0	11	42	35	27	+7
8	York City	20	8	2	10	26	37	26	–11
9	Mansfield Town	20	7	3	10	30	53	24	–23
10	Lincoln City	20	7	2	11	32	42	23	–10
11	Scarborough	20	3	1	16	17	39	10	–22

ARSENAL ARE TOP SCORERS FOR ONCE

Arsenal took some consolation from their attacking record when losing the championship to Manchester United last season. For the first time in 11 years of Premiership football, they scored more goals (85-74) than United.

TURNER PRIZE FOR WEDNESDAY

Chris Turner, a former Hillsborough goalkeeper, became Sheffield Wednesday's ninth manager in seven years when he left Hartlepool to take took over from Terry Yorath. The others were Trevor Francis, David Pleat, Ron Atkinson, Danny Wilson, Paul Jewell and Peter Shreeves (twice).

COMBINATION

		P	W	D	L	F	A	Pts	GD
1	Crystal Palace	25	16	5	4	60	23	53	+37
2	Norwich City	25	14	8	3	44	18	50	+26
3	Portsmouth	25	14	6	5	47	23	48	+24
4	Plymouth Argyle	25	15	3	7	48	36	48	+12
5	Reading	25	14	4	7	53	32	46	+21
6	Colchester Utd.	25	13	5	7	37	24	44	+13
7	Bristol City	25	13	5	7	47	40	44	+7
8	Brighton & H.A.	25	11	8	6	41	24	41	+17
9	Millwall	25	12	4	9	37	30	40	+7
10	Cardiff City	25	11	7	7	31	24	40	+7
11	Brentford	25	11	5	9	44	43	38	+1
12	Southend Utd.	25	11	5	9	37	38	38	–1
13	Oxford Utd.	25	11	3	11	37	36	36	+1
14	Q.P.R.	25	9	7	9	36	34	34	+2
15	Swindon Town	25	10	4	11	33	54	34	–21
16	Luton Town	25	8	8	9	34	31	32	+3
17	Leyton Orient	25	8	8	9	46	44	32	+2
18	Cheltenham Town	25	9	4	12	47	44	31	+3
19	Cambridge Utd.	25	8	5	12	40	45	29	–5
20	Peterborough Utd.	25	8	4	13	44	48	28	–4
21	Wycombe Wand.	25	7	4	14	27	48	25	–21
22	Bournemouth	25	5	6	14	40	57	21	–17
23	Bristol Rov.	25	5	6	14	27	47	21	–20
24	Gillingham	25	4	9	12	24	45	21	–21
25	Northampton Town	25	5	5	15	31	55	20	–24
26	Barnet	25	2	4	19	20	69	10	–49

QUOTE-UNQUOTE

'I'd be lying if I said I didn't miss England. I still feel I could do a good job' – **Alan Shearer** hinting at an international comeback.

'I believe my remaining football ambitions can be fulfilled at club level in the Premiership and in the Champions League' – **Alan Shearer** dismissing the idea after further consideration.

'It was incredible that no-one seemed to notice a man with big gloves, blonde hair and a bright orange shirt' – **Gordon Strachan** after his Southampton goalkeeper Antti Niemi came forward to volley against the crossbar and set up a last-minute equaliser for Michael Svensson against Fulham.

'There's too much fantasy in this lad's story for one of my shows' – **Bill Kenwright**, Everton's impresario deputy-chairman, on the emergence of Wayne Rooney.

'He's waited all his career to play in the Premier League and then this happens' – **Steve Bruce**, Birmingham City manager, sympathising with Andy Marriott after his new goalkeeper put the ball in front of him ready to clear, unaware that Tottenham's Robbie Keane was lurking behind him.

'They were keeping the ball like the Harlem Globetrotters' – **Gary Neville**, Manchester United defender, after the Champions League defeat by Real Madrid.

'It's lunchtime on Saturday, so it must be Manchester United in the Premiership' – **Ian Brown**, BBC Radio Five commentator, watching another early kick-off at Old Trafford.

'He will die on the bench at Manchester United' – **Eric Cantona** on his former Old Trafford manager Sir Alex Ferguson.

NEW BOYS IN GOOD SHAPE FOR THE STEP UP

Yeovil Town and Doncaster Rovers may have reached their goal in contrasting fashion, but both fully deserved the reward of a place in the Football League. Gary Johnson's Yeovil enjoyed an impressive march to the Conference title, which was never seriously threatened, while Rovers needed to survive the emotional roller-coaster of the play-offs to earn promotion.

It is heartening to see both clubs arrive in good shape as they aim to follow the likes of Rushden and Diamonds, Cheltenham Town and Wycombe Wanderers, who all made an impact in the Third Division after making the step up. Yeovil had already established themselves as the FA Cup's most feared giant-killers, knocking out 20 League clubs over the years, but for the club to really progress they had to play League football.

Johnson, previously manager of Cambridge United and the Latvia national team, proved he had what it took to bridge the gap and end the Somerset club's 108-year wait to join the professionals. After narrowly missing out on promotion in the two previous campaigns, when they had finished second and third, Yeovil took the final step by winning the title at a canter.

They should have little trouble adapting to the higher level, as all their players are already full-time and Johnson has recently signed a new three-year contract. The statistics give some indication of the ease with which Yeovil established their credentials. They finished 17 points clear, lost just three times, totalled 95 points and boasted a goal difference of plus 63.

Yeovil went through the second half of the season unbeaten and in the prolific Kirk Jackson had one of the Conference's most dangerous strikers. Jackson scored 24 goals in the League, the second highest total of the season. They also had the Conference's Player of the Year in Michael McIndoe and four players in the Team of the Year – Darren Way, Chris Weale, Terry Skiverton and McIndoe.

For Doncaster, success came in the first season of the Conference's promotion play-offs. They held their nerve in a penalty shoot-out against Chester City in the semi-finals. Then, Francis Tierney was the hero with an extra-time goal which brought a 3-2 victory over Dagenham and Redbridge at the Britannia Stadium. It enabled the South Yorkshire club to finally shake off the painful memories of relegation five years previously.

Rovers had lost their League status in acrimonious fashion. The team, in disarray, won just four matches all season. Then, chairman Ken Richardson was jailed for attempting to set fire to the stadium so he could sell the land.

Owner John Ryan invested £4m. to put Doncaster back on an even keel and the contrast between the club's last spell as a League club and the 2003-04 vintage could not be greater. Under the management of former Oxford United and Derby County player David Penney, they have the foundations in place to build on that achievement.

Work is set to begin in March on a new £12m., 15,000-capacity stadium to replace crumbling Belle Vue. After thousands followed their team to the play-off final, the club have the potential to pack it. Rovers' return was made even more remarkable as Penney, who had been at Doncaster throughout the whole of their stay in the Conference, was in his first full season as a manager.

Multi-millionaire Ryan has done so much that he could be forgiven for indulging himself a little when he took the field for the club he has supported since childhood late last season. He became the oldest player ever to appear for a British professional club when, aged 52 years and 11 months, he came on as a substitute in stoppage time of his side's match against Hereford United.

No-one will be more proud than Ryan when Doncaster kick off the new season at Leyton Orient.Yeovil also start with an away game – at Rochdale. First home League fixtures for the clubs are against Southend United and Carlisle United respectively.

NATIONAL REFEREES 2003-04

SELECT GROUP

Barber, Graham (Herts)
Barry, Neale (North Lincs)
Bennett, Steve (Kent)
Dean, Mike (Wirral)
Dowd, Phil (Staffs)
Dunn, Steve (Gloucs)
Durkin, Paul (Dorset)
D'Urso, Andy (Essex)
Foy, Chris (Merseyside)
Gallagher, Dermot (Oxon)
Halsey, Mark (Lancs)
Knight, Barry (Kent)
Messias, Matt (South Yorks)
Poll, Graham (Herts)
Rennie, Uriah (South Yorks)
Riley, Mike (West Yorks)
Styles, Rob (Hants)
*Walton, Peter (Northants)
*Webb, Howard (South Yorks)
Wiley, Alan (Staffs)
Winter, Jeff (Cleveland)

*New appointment to Select Group

NATIONAL GROUP

*Atkinson, Martin (West Yorks)
Armstrong, Paul (Berks)
Bates, Tony (Staffs)
Beeby, Richard (Northants)
Boyeson, Carl (East Yorks)
Butler, Alan (Notts)
Cable, Lee (Surrey)
Cain, George (Merseyside)
Clattenburg, Mark (Co Durham)
Cooper, Mark (West Midlands)
Cowburn, Mark (Lancs)
Crick, David (Surrey)
Crossley, Phil (Kent)
Curson, Brian (Leics)
Danson, Paul (Leics)
Evans, Eddie (Gtr Manchester)
Fletcher, Mick (Worcs)
*Friend, Kevin (Leics)
Hall, Andy (West Midlands)
Hegley, Grant (Herts)
Hill, Keith (Herts)
Ilderton, Eddie (Tyne & Wear)
Jones, Michael (Cheshire)
Joslin, Phil (Notts)
Kaye, Alan (West Yorks)
*Kettle, Trevor (Berks)
Laws, Graham (Tyne & Wear)
Leake, Tony (Lancs)
Mason, Lee (Lancs)
*Marriner, Andre (Warwicks)
Mathieson, Scott (Cheshire)
*Miller, Nigel (Co Durham)
Olivier, Ray (West Midlands)
Parkes, Trevor (West Midlands)
Pearson, Roy (Co Durham)
Penn, Andy (West Midlands)
Penton, Clive (Sussex)
Pike, Mike (Cumbria)
*Probert, Lee (Avon)
Prosser, Phil (West Yorks)
Pugh, David (Merseyside)
Robinson, Paul (East Yorks)
Ross, Joe (London)
Ryan, Michael (Lancs)
Salisbury, Graham (Lancs)
Stretton, Frazer (Notts)
*Tanner, Steve (Avon)
Taylor, Paul (Herts)
Thorpe,Mike (Suffolk)
Tomlin, Steve (East Sussex)
Warren, Mark (West Midlands)
Webster, Colin (Tyne & Wear)
Williamson, Iain (Berks)
*Wright, Kevin (Cambs)

* New appointment to National Group

UEFA CHAMPIONS LEAGUE 2002-03

FIRST QUALIFYING ROUND, FIRST LEG

Hibernians 2 (Chukinyere 7, Pulis 37), **Shelbourne** 2 (Byrne 6, Gannon 67). Att: 2,000. **Portadown** 0, Belshina Bobruisk 0. Att: 750. Skonto Riga 5 (Kolesnicenko 13, Zemlinskis 62, Korgalidze 65, Ksanavicius 87, Jelisejevs 89), **Barry Town** 0. Att: 3,500.

FIRST QUALIFYING ROUND, SECOND LEG

Barry Town 0, Skonto Riga 1 (Kolesnicenko 52). Att: 1,157 (Skonto Riga won 6-0 on agg). Belshina Bobruisk 3 (Strypeikis 5, Karolik 22, 59), **Portadown** 2 (Hamilton 39, Arkins 74). Att: 2,000 (Belshina Bobruisk won 3-2 on agg). **Shelbourne** 0, Hibernians 1 (Chukinyere 90). Att: 4,500 (Hibernians won 3-2 on agg).

FIRST QUALIFYING ROUND (ON AGGREGATE)

Apoel Nicosia 1, Flora 0; Dinamo Tirana 3, Kaunas 2; Pyunik 6, Tampere 0; Sheriff Tiraspol 4, Zhenis Astana 4 (Sheriff Tiraspol won on away goals); Torpedo Kutaisi 6, Torshavn 2; Vardar 4, Dudelange 1; Zeljeznicar 4, Akranes 0.

SECOND QUALIFYING ROUND (ON AGGREGATE)

Apoel Nicosia 5, Maribor 4; Basle 4, Zilina 1; Boavista 7, Hibernians 3; Brondby 5, Dinamo Tirana 0; Bruges 4, Dinamo Bucharest 1; Dynamo Kiev 6, Pyunik 2; Grazer 6, Sheriff Tiraspol 1; Legia Warsaw 4, Vardar 2; Levski Sofia 2, Skonto Riga 0; Maccabi Haifa 5, Belshina Bobruisk 0; Partizan Belgrade 5, Hammarby 1; Sparta Prague 5, Torpedo Kutaisi 1; Zalaegerszeg 2 Zagreb 2 (Zalaegerszeg won on away goal); Zeljeznicar 2, Lillestrom 0.

THIRD QUALIFYING ROUND, FIRST LEG

Celtic 3 (Larsson 4 pen, Sutton 52, Sylla 88), Basle 1 (Gimenez 2). Att: 58,520. Zalaegerszeg 1 (Koplarovic 90), **Manchester Utd.** 0. Att: 28,000. Zeljeznicar 0, **Newcastle Utd.** 1 (Dyer 56). Att: 35,000.

THIRD QUALIFYING ROUND, SECOND LEG

Basle 2 (Gimenez 18, Hakan Yakin 22), **Celtic** 0. Att: 32,000 (Agg 3-3, Basle won on away goal). **Manchester Utd.** 5 (Van Nistelrooy 6, 76 pen, Beckham 15, Scholes 21, Solskjaer 84), Zalaegerszeg 0. Att: 66,814 (**Manchester Utd.** won 5-1 on agg). **Newcastle Utd.** 4 (Dyer 23, LuaLua 37, Viana 74, Shearer 80), Zeljeznicar 0. Att: 34,064 (**Newcastle Utd.** won 5-0 on agg).

THIRD QUALIFYING ROUND (ON AGGREGATE)

AC Milan 2, Liberec 2 (AC Milan won on away goal); AEK Athens 4, Apoel Nicosia 2; Auxerre 1, Boavista 0; Barcelona 4, Legia Warsaw 0; Bayern Munich 6, Partizan Belgrade 1; Bruges 2, Shakhtar Donetsk 2 (aet, Bruges won 4-1 on pens); Dynamo Kiev 2, Levski Sofia 0; Feyenoord 3, Fenerbahce 0; Inter Milan 2, Sporting Lisbon 0; Lokomotiv Moscow 5, Graz AK 3; Maccabi Haifa 5, Sturm Graz 3; Rosenborg 4, Brondby 2; Sparta Prague 4, Genk 4 (Genk won on away goals).

FIRST GROUP STAGE

GROUP A

September 17, 2002
Arsenal 2 (Bergkamp 62, Ljungberg 77), Borussia Dortmund 0. Att: 34,907.
Arsenal (4-4-2): Seaman, Luzhny (Lauren 73), Keown, Campbell, Cole, Wiltord (Toure 88), Vieira, Gilberto Silva, Ljungberg (Cygan 84), Bergkamp, Henry.
Auxerre 0, **PSV Eindhoven** 0. Att: 21,000.

September 25, 2002
Borussia Dortmund 2 (Koller 6, Amoroso 78), **Auxerre** 1 (Mwaruwari 83). Att: 46,500.
PSV Eindhoven 0, **Arsenal** 4 (Gilberto Silva 1, Ljungberg 66, Henry 81, 90). Att: 24,000.
Arsenal (4-4-2): Seaman, Lauren, Keown (Cygan 10), Campbell, Cole, Wiltord, Gilberto Silva, Vieira, Ljungberg (Toure 86), Bergkamp (Kanu 80), Henry.

October 2, 2002
Auxerre 0, **Arsenal** 1 (Gilberto Silva 47). Att: 23,000.
Arsenal (4-4-2): Seaman, Lauren, Campbell, Cygan, Cole, Wiltord (Luzhny 83), Gilberto Silva, Vieira, Toure (Edu 60), Kanu, Henry (Pennant 58).
PSV Eindhoven 1 (Van der Schaaf 73), **Borussia Dortmund** 3 (Koller 21, Rosicky 69, Amoroso 90). Att: 29,000.

October 22, 2002
Arsenal 1 (Kanu 53), **Auxerre** 2 (Kapo 8, Fadiga 27). Att: 35,206.
Arsenal (4-4-2): Seaman, Lauren (Toure 76), Campbell, Cygan, Cole, Wiltord, Ljungberg, Vieira, Gilberto Silva (Pires 71), Kanu, Henry.
Borussia Dortmund 1 (Koller 10), **PSV Eindhoven** 1 (Bruggink 47). Att: 47,000.

October 30, 2002
Borussia Dortmund 2 (Gilberto Silva 38 og, Rosicky 63 pen), **Arsenal** 1 (Henry 18). Att: 52,000.
Arsenal (4-4-2): Seaman, Lauren, Campbell, Cygan, Cole, Wiltord (Kanu 79), Gilberto Silva (Edu 80), Vieira, Pires (Toure 67), Ljungberg, Henry.
PSV Eindhoven 3 (Bruggink 34, Rommedahl 48, Robben 64), **Auxerre** 0. Att: 30,000.

November 12, 2002
Arsenal 0, **PSV Eindhoven** 0. Att: 35,274.
Arsenal (4-4-2): Shaaban, Luzhny, Stepanovs, Cygan, Toure, Pires, Vieira (Gilberto Silva 76), Edu, Van Bronckhorst, Jeffers (Wiltord 68), Henry (Bergkamp 63). Sent-off: Toure.
Auxerre 1 (Mwaruwari 75), **Borussia Dortmund** 0. Att: 19,000.

FINAL TABLE

	P	*W*	*D*	*L*	*F*	*A*	*Pts*
ARSENAL	6	3	1	2	9	4	10
BOR. DORTMUND	6	3	1	2	8	7	10
Auxerre	6	2	1	3	4	7	7
PSV Eindhoven	6	1	3	2	5	8	6

GROUP B

September 17, 2002
Basle 2 (Hakan Yakin 50, Rossi 55), **Spartak Moscow** 0. Att: 29,500.
Valencia 2 (Aimar 20, Baraja 39), **Liverpool** 0. Att: 38,000.

Liverpool (4-4-2): Dudek, Carragher, Diao (Cheyrou 46), Hyypia, Traore, Murphy (Baros 76), Gerrard, Hamann, Riise, Diouf (Owen 46), Heskey. Sent-off: Hamann.

September 25, 2002
Liverpool 1 (Baros 34), **Basle** 1 (Rossi 43). Att: 37,634.
Liverpool (4-4-2): Dudek, Carragher, Henchoz, Hyypia, Riise, Murphy, Gerrard, Cheyrou, Heskey (Diouf 71), Owen (Berger 79), Baros.
Spartak Moscow 0, **Valencia** 3 (Angulo 6, Mista 70, Sanchez 85). Att: 15,000.

October 2, 2002
Liverpool 5 (Heskey 7, 89, Cheyrou 14, Hyypia 28, Diao 81), **Spartak Moscow** 0. Att: 40,812.
Liverpool (4-4-2): Dudek, Carragher, Henchoz (Traore 67), Hyypia, Riise, Gerrard (Diao 76), Hamann, Cheyrou (Diouf 82), Murphy, Owen, Heskey.
Valencia 6 (Carew 10, 12, Aurelio 17, Baraja 27, Aimar 58, Mista 60), **Basle** 2 (Rossi 46, Hakan Yakin 89). Att: 30,000.

October 22, 2002
Basle 2 (Ergic 32, 90), **Valencia** 2 (Baraja 35, Torres 72). Att: 29,503.
Spartak Moscow 1 (Danishevsky 23), **Liverpool** 3 (Owen 29, 70, 90). Att: 15,000.
Liverpool (4-4-2): Dudek, Carragher, Traore, Hyypia, Riise, Murphy, Diao, Hamann, Heskey (Vignal 55, Biscan 77), Owen, Baros (Diouf 71).

October 30, 2002
Liverpool 0, **Valencia** 1 (Rufete 34). Att: 41,831.
Liverpool (4-1-3-2): Dudek, Carragher (Cheyrou 82), Traore, Hyypia, Riise, Hamann, Gerrard, Diao, Murphy (Smicer 61), Owen, Heskey (Baros 61).

November 5, 2002
Spartak Moscow 0, **Basle** 2 (Rossi 18, Gimenez 89). Att: 3,000.

November 12, 2002
Basle 3 (Rossi 2, Gimenez 22, Atouba 29), **Liverpool** 3 (Murphy 61, Smicer 64, Owen 85). Att: 35,000.
Liverpool (4-4-1-1): Dudek, Carragher (Diouf 79), Traore, Hyypia, Riise, Murphy, Gerrard (Diao 46), Hamann, Heskey (Baros 61), Smicer, Owen.
Valencia 3 (Sanchez 37, 46, Aurelio 76), **Spartak Moscow** 0. Att: 25,000.

FINAL TABLE

	P	*W*	*D*	*L*	*F*	*A*	*Pts*
VALENCIA	6	5	1	0	17	4	16
BASLE	6	2	3	1	12	12	9
Liverpool	6	2	2	2	12	8	8
Spartak Moscow	6	0	0	6	1	18	0

GROUP C

September 17, 2002
Genk 0, **AEK Athens** 0. Att: 22,500.
Roma 0, **Real Madrid** 3 (Guti 41, 74, Raul 56). Att: 75,000.

September 25, 2002
AEK Athens 0, **Roma** 0. Att: 10,000.
Real Madrid 6 (Zokora 44 og, Salgado 45, Figo 54 pen, Guti 64, Celades 73, Raul 76), **Genk** 0. Att: 65,000.

October 2, 2002
AEK Athens 3 (Tsartas 6, Maladenis 25, Nikolaidis 28), **Real Madrid** 3 (Zidane 15, 39, Guti 60). Att: 15,000.
Genk 0, **Roma** 1 (Cassano 81). Att: 22,000.

October 22, 2002
Real Madrid 2 (McManaman 23, 43), **AEK Athens** 2 (Katsouranis 74, Centeno 86). Att: 61,040.
Roma 0, **Genk** 0. Att: 26,000.

October 30, 2002
AEK Athens 1 (Lakis 30), **Genk** 1 (Sonck 22). Att: 24,000.
Real Madrid 0, **Roma** 1 (Totti 26). Att: 70,000.

November 12, 2002
Genk 1 (Sonck 85), **Real Madrid** 1 (Tote 21). Att: 22,500.
Roma 1 (Delvecchio 40), **AEK Athens** 1 (Centeno 90). Att: 32,734.

FINAL TABLE

	P	*W*	*D*	*L*	*F*	*A*	*Pts*
REAL MADRID	6	2	3	1	15	7	9
ROMA	6	2	3	1	3	4	9
AEK Athens	6	0	6	0	7	7	6
Genk	6	0	4	2	2	9	4

GROUP D

September 17, 2002
Ajax 2 (Ibrahimovic 11, 34), **Lyon** 1 (Anderson 84). Att: 37,455.
Rosenborg 2 (Karadas 52, 64), **Inter Milan** 2 (Crespo 33, 79). Att: 21.040.

September 25, 2002
Inter Milan 1 (Crespo 74), **Ajax** 0. Att: 45,784.
Lyon 5 (Carriere 5, Vairelles 25, 45, Anderson 34, Luyindula 75), **Rosenborg** 0. Att: 36,000.

October 2, 2002
Inter Milan 1 (Cannavaro 72), **Lyon** 2 (Govou 21, Anderson 59). Att: 31,448.
Rosenborg 0, **Ajax** 0. Att: 20,948.

October 22, 2002
Ajax 1 (Ibrahimovic 41), **Rosenborg** 1 (Enerly 85 pen). Att: 42,026.
Lyon 3 (Anderson 21, 74, Carriere 43), **Inter Milan** 3 (Cacapa 31 og, Crespo 56, 65). Att: 38,632.

October 30, 2002
Inter Milan 3 (Recoba 30, Saarinen 52 og, Crespo 72), **Rosenborg** 0. Att: 33,686.
Lyon 0, **Ajax** 2 (Pienaar 7, Van der Vaart 90). Att: 38,584.

November 12, 2002
Ajax 1 (Van der Vaart 90), **Inter Milan** 2 (Crespo 50, 52). Att: 51,000.
Rosenborg 1 (Brattbakk 68), **Lyon** 1 (Govou 83). Att: 22,000.

FINAL TABLE

	P	W	D	L	F	A	Pts
INTER MILAN	6	3	2	1	12	8	11
AJAX	6	2	2	2	6	5	8
Lyon	6	2	2	2	12	9	8
Rosenborg	6	0	4	2	4	12	4

GROUP E

September 18, 2002
Dynamo Kiev 2 (Shatskikh 17, Khatskevitch 62), **Newcastle Utd.** 0. Att: 42,500.
Newcastle Utd. (4-1-3-2): Given, Griffin, O'Brien, Dabizas, Bernard (Robert 68), Hughes (Solano 68), Dyer, Speed, Viana, Bellamy, Shearer (Ameobi 79).
Feyenoord 1 (Van Hooijdonk 74), **Juventus** 1 (Camoranesi 32). Att: 40,000.

September 24, 2002
Juventus 5 (Di Vaio 14, 52, Del Piero 22, Davids 67, Nedved 79), **Dynamo Kiev** 0. Att: 40,000.
Newcastle Utd. 0, **Feyenoord** 1 (Pardo 4). Att: 40,540.
Newcastle Utd. (4-4-2): Given, Griffin, Dabizas, O'Brien, Hughes, Solano, Dyer, Speed, Robert, Bellamy (LuaLua 76), Shearer.

October 1, 2002
Feyenoord 0, **Dynamo Kiev** 0. Att: 48,000.
Juventus 2 (Del Piero 66, 81), **Newcastle Utd.** 0. Att: 41,424.
Newcastle Utd. (4-4-1-1): Given, Griffin (Ameobi 79), Dabizas, O'Brien, Hughes, Solano (Viana 70), Jenas (LuaLua 79), Speed, Robert, Dyer, Shearer.

October 23, 2002
Dynamo Kiev 2 (Khatskevitch 16, Belkevich 47), **Feyenoord** 0. Att: 50,000.
Newcastle Utd. 1 (Griffin 62), **Juventus** 0. Att: 48,370.
Newcastle Utd. (4-4-2): Harper, Griffin, O'Brien, Bramble, Hughes, Solano, Speed, Jenas, Robert (Viana 85), LuaLua (Ameobi 85), Shearer.

October 29, 2002
Juventus 2 (Di Vaio 4, 69), **Feyenoord** 0. Att: 35,789.
Newcastle Utd. 2 (Speed 58, Shearer 69 pen), **Dynamo Kiev** 1 (Shatskikh 47). Att: 40,185.
Newcastle Utd. (4-4-2): Harper, Griffin, O'Brien (Bernard 46), Bramble (Dabizas 27), Hughes, Solano (Dyer 82), Jenas, Speed, Robert, Ameobi, Shearer.

November 13, 2002
Dynamo Kiev 1 (Shatskikh 50), **Juventus** 2 (Salas 53, Zalayeta 60). Att: 78,000.
Feyenoord 2 (Bombarda 65, Lurling 71), **Newcastle Utd.** 3 (Bellamy 45, 90, Viana 49). Att: 45,000.
Newcastle Utd. (4-4-2); Given, Griffin, Dabizas, O'Brien, Hughes, Jenas, Dyer, Speed, Viana (Bernard 83), Bellamy, Shearer.

FINAL TABLE

	P	W	D	L	F	A	Pts
JUVENTUS	6	4	1	1	12	3	13
NEWCASTLE UTD.	6	3	0	3	6	8	9
Dynamo Kiev	6	2	1	3	6	9	7
Feyenoord	6	1	2	3	4	8	5

GROUP F

September 18, 2002
Manchester Utd. 5 (Giggs 10, Solksjaer 35, Veron 46, Van Nistelrooy 54, Forlan 89 pen), **Maccabi Haifa** 2 (Katan 8, Cohen 85). Att: 63,439.
Manchester Utd. (4-4-2): Barthez (Ricardo 67), O'Shea, Ferdinand, Blanc, Silvestre, Beckham, Veron, P. Neville, Giggs (Forlan 55), Van Nistelrooy (Pugh) 75), Solskjaer.
Olympiakos 6 (Kleine 27 og, Giannakopoulos 38, Djordjevic 44 pen, 63, 73, Zetterberg 86), **Bayer Leverkusen** 2 (Eleftheropoulos 22 og, Schneider 78 pen). Att: 14,000.

September 24, 2002
Bayer Leverkusen 1 (Berbatov 52), **Manchester Utd.** 2 (Van Nistelrooy 31, 44). Att: 22,500.
Manchester Utd. (4-4-1-1): Barthez, O'Shea (G. Neville 46), Blanc, Ferdinand, Silvestre, Beckham, P. Neville, Veron (Solskjaer 87), Butt, Giggs, Van Nistelrooy (Forlan 46).
Maccabi Haifa 3 (Ayegbini 27 pen, 60, 85), **Olympiakos** 0. Att: 20,000 (Played in Nicosia).

October 1, 2002
Maccabi Haifa 0, **Bayer Leverkusen** 2 (Babic 31, 63). Att: 6,000 (Played in Nicosia).
Manchester Utd. 4 (Giggs 19, 67, Veron 26, Solskjaer 77), **Olympiakos** 0. Att: 66,902.
Manchester Utd. (4-4-1-1): Barthez, G. Neville, Blanc (O'Shea 68), Ferdinand, Silvestre, Beckham, Veron, Butt, Giggs (Fortune 68), Scholes (Forlan 76), Solskjaer.

October 23, 2002
Bayer Leverkusen 2 (Babic 45, Santos 67), **Maccabi Haifa** 1 (Pralija 53). Att: 22,500.
Olympiakos 2 (Choutos 70, Djordjevic 74), **Manchester Utd.** 3 (Blanc 21, Veron 59, Scholes 84). Att: 15,000.
Manchester Utd. (4-4-1-1): Barthez, G. Neville, Blanc, O'Shea, Silvestre, Beckham (Chadwick 62), Veron (Richardson 87), P. Neville, Giggs (Fortune 62), Scholes, Forlan.

October 29, 2002
Bayer Leverkusen 2 (Santos 15, Schneider 89 pen), **Olympiakos** 0. Att: 23,500.
Maccabi Haifa 3 (Katan 40, Zautatas 56, Ayegbini 77 pen), **Manchester Utd.** 0. Att: 22,000 (Played in Nicosia).
Manchester Utd. (4-4-1-1): Ricardo, G. Neville, Ferdinand, O'Shea, Silvestre, Richardson (Nardiello 61), P. Neville, Scholes, Fortune, Forlan (Timm 78), Solskjaer.

November 13, 2002
Manchester Utd. 2 (Veron 42, Van Nistelrooy 69), **Bayer Leverkusen** 0. Att: 66,185.
Manchester Utd. (4-4-1-1): Ricardo, O'Shea, Ferdinand, Blanc (G. Neville 77), Silvestre, Beckham (Solskjaer 77), Veron, Fortune, Giggs (Chadwick 81), Scholes, Van Nistelrooy.
Olympiakos 3 (Alexandris 36, Niniadis 50, Antzas 79), **Maccabi Haifa** 3 (Badir 9, Ayegbini 10, Katan 41). Att: 12,500.

FINAL TABLE

	P	*W*	*D*	*L*	*F*	*A*	*Pts*
MANCHESTER UTD.	6	5	0	1	16	8	15
B. LEVERKUSEN	6	3	0	3	9	11	9
Maccabi Haifa	6	2	1	3	12	12	7
Olympiakos	6	1	1	4	11	17	4

GROUP G

September 18, 2002
AC Milan 2 (Inzaghi 57, 62), **Lens** 1 (Moreira 75). Att: 70,259.

Bayern Munich 2 (Salihamidzic 57, Elber 64), **Deportivo La Coruna** 3 (Makaay 12, 45, 77). Att: 40,000.

September 24, 2002
Deportivo La Coruna 0, AC Milan 4 (Seedorf 17, Inzaghi 33, 56, 62). Att: 32,000.
Lens 1 (Utaka 76), **Bayern Munich** 1 (Linke 23). Att: 38,000.

October 1, 2002
Bayern Munich 1 (Pizarro 54), **AC Milan** 2 (Inzaghi 52, 84). Att: 59,000.
Deportivo La Coruna 3 (Makaay 49, Capdevila 78, Cesar 83), **Lens** 1 (Moreira 10). Att: 28,000.

October 23, 2002
AC Milan 2 (Serginho 11, Inzaghi 64), **Bayern Munich** 1 (Tarnat 23). Att: 75,611.
Lens 3 (Coulibaly 60, Moreira 79, Thomert 85), **Deportivo La Coruna** 1 (Makaay 14). Att: 30,500.

October 29, 2002
Deportivo La Coruna 2 (Victor 54, Makaay 89), **Bayern Munich** 1 (Santa Cruz 76). Att: 33,000.
Lens 2 (Moreira 41, Utaka 49), **AC Milan** 1 (Shevchenko 32). Att: 40,000.

November 13, 2002
AC Milan 1 (Tomasson 34), **Deportivo La Coruna** 2 (Tristan 58, Makaay 71). Att: 56,294.
Bayern Munich 3 (Kovac 6, Salihamidzic 18, Feulner 86), **Lens** 3 (Fink 20 og, Bakari 54, Blanchard 90). Att: 22,000.

FINAL TABLE

	P	*W*	*D*	*L*	*F*	*A*	*Pts*
AC MILAN	6	4	0	2	12	7	12
DEP. LA CORUNA	6	4	0	2	11	12	12
Lens	6	2	2	2	11	11	8
Bayern Munich	6	0	2	4	9	13	2

GROUP H

September 17, 2002
Barcelona 3 (Luis Enrique 5, Mendieta 40, Saviola 43), **Bruges** 2 (Simons 22 pen, Englebert 85). Att: 83,300.
Lokomotiv Moscow 0, **Galatasaray** 2 (Sarr 72, Arif Erdem 81). Att: 20,000.

September 24, 2002
Bruges 0, **Lokomotiv Moscow** 0. Att: 25,000.
Galatasaray 0, **Barcelona** 2 (Kluivert 27, Luis Enrique 59). Att: 24,250.

October 1, 2002
Galatasaray 0, **Bruges** 0. Att: 23,000.
Lokomotiv Moscow 1 (Obiorah 56), **Barcelona** 3 (Kluivert 29, Saviola 31, 48). Att: 24,550.

October 23, 2002
Barcelona 1 (De Boer 75), **Lokomotiv Moscow** 0. Att: 62,000.
Bruges 3 (Martens 45, Verheyen 71, Saeternes 90), **Galatasaray** 1 (Pinto 55). Att: 22,500.

October 29, 2002
Bruges 0, **Barcelona** 1 (Riquelme 63). Att: 30,000.

Galatasaray 1 (Hasan Sas 72), **Lokomotiv Moscow** 2 (Loskov 70, Evseev 75). Att: 23,000.

November 13, 2002
Barcelona 3 (Dani 10, Gerard 44, Geovanni 56), **Galatasaray** 1 (Haspolatli 20). Att: 42,928.
Lokomotiv Moscow 2 (Julio Cesar 44, Loskov 90), **Bruges** 0.Att: 19,700.

FINAL TABLE

	P	*W*	*D*	*L*	*F*	*A*	*Pts*
BARCELONA	6	6	0	0	13	4	18
LOKOMOTIV MOSCOW	6	2	1	3	5	7	7
Bruges	6	1	2	3	5	7	5
Galatasaray	6	1	1	4	5	10	4

SECOND GROUP STAGE

GROUP A

November 27, 2002
Bayer Leverkusen 1 (Berbatov 39), **Barcelona** 2 (Saviola 48, Overmars 87). Att: 25,500.
Newcastle Utd. 1 (Solano 72), **Inter Milan** 4 (Morfeo 2, Almeyda 35, Crespo 45, Recoba 81). Att: 50,108.
Newcastle Utd. (4-4-2): Given, Griffin, O'Brien, Dabizas, Hughes (Caldwell 86), Solano, Dyer, Speed, Viana (Robert 46), Bellamy, Shearer. Sent-off: Bellamy.

December 10, 2002
Inter Milan 3 (Di Biagio 14, 27, Butt og), **Bayer Leverkusen** 2 (Zivkovic 62, Franca 90). Att: 36,342.

December 11, 2002
Barcelona 3 (Dani 7, Kluivert 35, Motta 58), **Newcastle Utd.** 1 (Ameobi 24). Att: 45,100.
Newcastle Utd. (4-4-2): Given, Griffin, O'Brien, Hughes, Bernard, Solano, Dyer, Speed, Robert, Ameobi, LuaLua (Chopra 84).

February 18, 2003
Barcelona 3 (Saviola 7, Cocu 29, Kluivert 66), **Inter Milan** 0. Att: 87,000.
Bayer Leverkusen 1 (Franca 25), **Newcastle Utd.** 3 (Ameobi 5, 15, LuaLua 32). Att: 22,500.
Newcastle Utd. (4-4-2): Given, Hughes, O'Brien, Bramble, Bernard, Jenas, Dyer, Speed, Robert, Ameobi (Cort 88), LuaLua (Chopra 83).

February 26, 2003
Inter Milan 0, **Barcelona** 0. Att: 71,740.
Newcastle Utd. 3 (Shearer 5, 11, 36 pen), **Bayer Leverkusen** 1 (Babic 73). Att: 40,508.
Newcastle Utd. (4-4-2): Given, Griffin, Bramble, Caldwell, Bernard, Kerr (Viana 82), Dyer (Solano 69), Speed, Robert, Ameobi, Shearer (LuaLua 81).

March 11, 2003
Barcelona 2 (Saviola 16, Kleine 49 og), **Bayer Leverkusen** 0. Att: 62,228.
Inter Milan 2 (Vieri 46, Cordoba 60), **Newcastle Utd.** 2 (Shearer 42, 49). Att: 53,459.
Newcastle Utd. (4-4-2): Given, Griffin, O'Brien (Hughes 59), Bramble, Bernard, Solano (LuaLua 83), Jenas, Speed, Robert (Viana 83), Bellamy, Shearer.

March 19, 2003
Bayer Leverkusen 0, **Inter Milan** 2 (Martins 36, Emre 9). Att: 43,000.
Newcastle Utd. 0, **Barcelona** 2 (Kluivert 60, Motta 74). Att: 51,883.
Newcastle Utd. (4-4-2): Given, Griffin, O'Brien, Bramble, Bernard, Solano (Ameobi 66), Jenas, Dyer, Robert (Viana 66), Bellamy, Shearer.

FINAL TABLE

	P	*W*	*D*	*L*	*F*	*A*	*Pts*
BARCELONA	6	5	1	0	12	2	16
INTER MILAN	6	3	2	1	11	8	11
Newcastle Utd.	6	2	1	3	10	13	7
Bayer Leverkusen	6	0	0	6	5	15	0

GROUP B

November 27, 2002
Roma 1 (Cassano 4), **Arsenal** 3 (Henry 6, 70, 75). Att: 70,000.
Arsenal (4-4-2): Shaaban, Luzhny, Campbell, Cygan, Cole, Ljungberg (Edu 90), Gilberto Silva, Vieira, Pires (Van Bronckhorst 78), Wiltord (Keown 84), Henry.
Valencia 1 (Angulo 90), **Ajax** (Ibrahimovic 88). Att: 48,000.

December 10, 2002
Ajax 2 (Ibrahimovic 11, Litmanen 66), **Roma** 1 (Batistuta 89). Att: 50,148.
Arsenal 0, **Valencia** 0. Att: 34,793.
Arsenal (4-4-2): Seaman, Lauren, Campbell, Cygan, Cole, Ljungberg (Wiltord 78), Vieira (Parlour 38), Gilberto Silva, Pires (Kanu 82), Bergkamp, Henry.

February 18, 2003
Arsenal 1 (Wiltord 5), **Ajax** 1 (De Jong 17). Att: 35,427.
Arsenal (4-4-2): Seaman (Taylor 46), Lauren, Campbell, Cygan, Cole, Wiltord, Vieira, Gilberto Silva (Jeffers 72), Pires, Bergkamp (Kanu 84), Henry.
Roma 0, **Valancia** 1 (Carew 78). Att: 31,000.

February 26, 2003
Ajax 0, **Arsenal** 0. Att: 51,500.
Arsenal (4-4-2): Seaman, Lauren, Campbell, Keown, Cole, Wiltord (Parlour 78), Gilberto Silva, Vieira, Pires (Van Bronckhorst 86), Bergkamp (Jeffers 78), Henry.
Valencia 0, **Roma** 3 (Totti 24, 30, Emerson 36). Att: 35,000.

March 11, 2003
Ajax 1 (Pasanen 56), **Valencia** 1 (Gonzalez 28 pen). Att: 48,633.
Arsenal 1 (Vieira 12), **Roma** 1 (Cassano 45). Att: 35,472.
Arsenal (4-4-2): Seaman, Lauren (Kanu 87), Keown, Cygan, Van Bronckhorst, Wiltord (Ljungberg 73), Gilberto Silva, Vieira, Pires, Bergkamp (Jeffers 73), Henry.

March 19, 2003
Roma 1 (Cassano 23), **Ajax** 1 (Van der Meyde 1). Att: 62,000.
Valencia 2 (Carew 34, 57), **Arsenal** 1 (Henry 49). Att: 50,000.
Arsenal (4-4-2): Taylor, Lauren, Campbell, Cygan, Toure (Kanu 86), Ljungberg, Gilberto Silva, Vieira, Wiltord (Jeffers 76), Pires, Henry.

FINAL TABLE

	P	W	D	L	F	A	Pts
VALENCIA	6	2	3	1	5	6	9
AJAX	6	1	5	0	6	5	8
Arsenal	6	1	4	1	6	5	7
Roma	6	1	2	3	7	8	5

GROUP C

November 26, 2002
AC Milan 1 (Shevchenko 39), **Real Madrid** 0. Att: 75,777.
Lokomotiv Moscow 1 (Ignashhevitch 31), **Borussia Dortmund** 2 (Frings 33, Koller 43), Att: 18,000.

December 11, 2002
Borussia Dortmund 0, **AC Milan** 1 (Inzaghi 49). Att: 49,000.
Real Madrid 2 (Raul 21, 75), **Lokomotov Moscow** 2 (Obiorah 47, Mnguni 74). Att: 55,000.

February 19, 2003
AC Milan 1 (Tomasson 62), **Lokomotiv Moscow** 0. Att: 72,028.
Real Madrid 2 (Raul 43, Ronaldo 55), **Borussia Dortmund** 1 (Koller 30). Att: 50,000.

February 25, 2003
Borussia Dortmund 1 (Koller 21), **Real Madrid** 0. Att: 52,000.
Lokomotiv Moscow 0, **AC Milan** 1 (Rivaldo 33 pen). Att: 30,000.

March 12, 2003
Borussia Dortmund 3 (Frings 39, Koller 58, Amoroso 66), **Lokomotiv Moscow** 0. Att: 48,000.
Real Madrid 3 (Raul 12, 56, Guti 85), **AC Milan** 1 (Rivaldo 81). Att: 78,000

March 18, 2003
AC Milan 0, **Borussia Dortmund** 1 (Koller 80). Att: 60,000.
Lokomotiv Moscow 0, **Real Madrid** 1 (Ronaldo 35).

FINAL TABLE

	P	W	D	L	F	A	Pts
AC MILAN	6	4	0	2	5	4	12
REAL MADRID	6	3	2	1	9	6	11
Borussia Dortmund	6	3	1	2	8	5	10
Lokomotiv Moscow	6	0	1	5	3	10	1

GROUP D

November 26, 2002
Basle 1 (Gimenez 1), **Manchester Utd.** 3 (Van Nistelrooy 62, 63, Solskjaer 68). Att: 35,000.
Manchester Utd. (4-5-1): Barthez, P. Neville, Brown (May 90), O'Shea, Silvestre, Solskjaer (Chadwick 88), Veron, Scholes, Fortune, Giggs, Van Nistelrooy (Forlan 73).
Deportivo La Coruna 2 (Tristan 9, Makaay 11), **Juventus** 2 (Birindelli 37, Nedved 56). Att: 30,000.

December 11, 2002
Juventus 4 (Trezeguet 3, Montero 34, Tacchinardi 43, Del Piero 51 pen), **Basle** 0. Att: 22,639.
Manchester Utd. 2 (Van Nistelrooy 7, 55), **Deportivo La Coruna** 0. Att: 67,014.
Manchester Utd. (4-4-2): Barthez, G. Neville, Brown, Silvestre, O'Shea (Beckham 81), Solskjaer, P. Neville (Forlan 81), Veron, Giggs, Scholes, Van Nistelrooy (Richardson 89).

February 19, 2003
Basle 1 (Hakan Yakin 30), **Deportivo La Coruna** 0. Att: 29,031.
Manchester Utd. 2 (Brown 3, Van Nistelrooy 85), **Juventus** 1 (Nedved 90). Att: 66,703.
Manchester Utd. (4-4-1-1): Barthez, G. Neville, Ferdinand, Brown, Silvestre (O'Shea 52), Beckham, Keane, Butt, Giggs (Forlan 89), Scholes, Van Nistelrooy (Solskjaer 79).

February 25, 2003
Deportivo La Coruna 1 (Tristan 5), **Basle** 0. Att: 27,000.
Juventus 0, **Manchester Utd.** 3 (Giggs 15, 41, Van Nistelrooy 67). Att: 59,111.
Manchester Utd. (4-1-4-1): Barthez, G. Neville, Keane, Ferdinand, O'Shea (Pugh 58), P. Neville, Beckham, Butt, Veron, Forlan (Giggs 8, Van Nistelrooy 46), Solskjaer.

March 12, 2003
Juventus 3 (Ferrara 12, Trezeguet 63, Tudor 90), **Deportivo La Coruna** 2 (Tristan 34, Makaay 51). Att: 25,070.
Manchester Utd. 1 (G. Neville 53), **Basle** 1 (Gimenez 14). Att: 66,870.
Manchester Utd. (4-5-1): Carroll, G. Neville, Ferdinand, Blanc (Scholes 73), O'Shea, Solskjaer, Fletcher (Beckham 73), Butt, P. Neville, Richardson (Giggs 46), Forlan.

March 18, 2003
Basle 2 (Cantaluppi 38, Gimenez 90), **Juventus** 1 (Tacchinardi 10). Att: 30,501.
Deportivo La Coruna 2 (Victor 32, Lynch 47 og), **Manchester Utd.** 0. Att: 25,000.
Manchester Utd. (3-5-2): Ricardo, Roche (Stewart 46), Blanc, O'Shea, Lynch, Fletcher, P. Neville, Butt, Pugh, Forlan (Webber 72), Giggs (Richardson 72).

FINAL TABLE

	P	*W*	*D*	*L*	*F*	*A*	*Pts*
MANCHESTER UTD.	6	4	1	1	11	5	13
JUVENTUS	6	2	1	3	11	11	7
Deportivo La Coruna	6	2	1	3	7	8	7
Basle	6	2	1	3	5	10	7

QUARTER-FINALS

FIRST LEGS

April 8, 2003
Ajax 0, **AC Milan** 0. Att: 51,000.
Real Madrid 3 (Figo 12, Raul 28, 49), **Manchester Utd.** 1 (Van Nistelrooy 52). Att: 75,000.
Manchester Utd. (4-4-1-1): Barthez, G. Neville (Solskjaer 86), Ferdinand, Brown, Silvestre (O'Shea 59), Beckham, Keane, Butt, Giggs, Scholes, Van Nistelrooy.

April 9, 2003
Inter Milan 1 (Vieri 14), **Valencia** 0. Att: 52,623.
Juventus 1 (Montero 16), **Barcelona** 1 (Saviola 77). Att: 48,500.

SECOND LEGS

April 22, 2003
Barcelona 1 (Xavi 66), **Juventus** 2 (Nedved 53, Zalayeta 114). Att: 98,000 (aet, **Juventus** won 3-2 on agg).
Valencia 2 (Aimar 6, Baraja 51), **Inter Milan** 1 (Vieri 4). Att: 48,000 (agg 2-2, **Inter Milan** won on away goal).

April 23, 2003
AC Milan 3 (Inzaghi 30, Shevchenko 64, Tomasson 90), **Ajax** 2 (Litmanen 63, Pienaar 78). Att: 76,079 (**AC Milan** won 3-2 on agg).
Manchester Utd. 4 (Van Nistelrooy 43, Helguera 52 og, Beckham 71, 84), **Real Madrid** 3 (Ronaldo 12, 50, 59). Att: 66,708 (**Real Madrid** won 6-5 on agg).
Manchester Utd. (4-3-2-1): Barthez, Brown, Ferdinand, Silvestre (P. Neville 78), O'Shea, Keane (Fortune 82), Butt, Veron (Beckham 62), Solskjaer, Giggs, Van Nistelrooy.

SEMI-FINALS

FIRST LEGS

May 6, 2003
Real Madrid 2 (Ronaldo 23, Roberto Carlos 73), **Juventus** 1 (Trezeguet 45). Att: 78,000.

May 7, 2003
AC Milan 0, **Inter Milan** 0. Att: 78,175.

SECOND LEGS

May 13, 2003
Inter Milan 1 (Martins 83), **AC Milan** 1 (Shevchenko 45). Att: 76,854 (agg 1-1, **AC Milan** won on away goal).

May 14, 2003
Juventus 3 (Trezeguet 12, Del Piero 42, Nedved 73), **Real Madrid** 1 (Zidane 89). Att: 60,253 (**Juventus** won 4-3 on agg).

EUROPEAN CUP FINAL

AC MILAN 0, JUVENTUS 0 (AET, AC MILAN WON 3-2 ON PENS)

Old Trafford, (63,215), Wednesday, May 28, 2003

AC Milan (4-4-2): Dida, Costacurta (Roque Junior 70), Nesta, Maldini (capt), Kaladze, Rui Costa (Ambrosini 87), Gattuso, Pirlo (Serginho 76), Seedorf, Inzaghi, Shevchenko. **Subs not used:** Abbiati, Rivaldo, Laursen, Brocchi. **Booked:** Costacurta. **Coach:** Carlo Ancelotti.

Juventus (4-4-2): Buffon, Thuram, Tudor (Birindelli 42), Ferrara, Montero, Camoranesi (Conte 46), Tacchinardi, Davids (Zalayeta 70), Zambrotta, Del Piero (capt), Trezeguet. **Subs not used:** Chimenti, Pessotto, Iuliano, Di Vaio. **Booked:** Tacchinardi, Conte. **Coach:** Marcello Lippi.

Referee: M. Merk (Germany). **Half-time:** 0-0.

Leading scorers (from first group stage): **12** Van Nistelrooy (Manchester Utd.); **10** Inzaghi (AC Milan); **9** Crespo (Inter Milan), Makaay (Deportivo La Coruna), Raul (Real Madrid); **8** Koller (Borussia Dortmund); **7** Henry (Arsenal), Saviola (Barcelona); **6** Ronaldo (Real Madrid), Shearer (Newcastle Utd.); **5** Anderson (Lyon), Ayegbini (Maccabi Haifa), Carew (Valencia), Del Piero (Juventus), Gimenez (Basle), Guti (Real Madrid), Ibrahimovic (Ajax), Kluivert (Barcelona), Rossi (Basle).

EUROPEAN CUP FINALS

1956	Real Madrid 4, Rheims 3 (Paris)
1957	Real Madrid 2, Fiorentina 0 (Madrid)
1958†	Real Madrid 3, AC Milan 2 (Brussels)
1959	Real Madrid 2, Rheims 0 (Stuttgart)
1960	Real Madrid 7, Eintracht Frankfurt 3 (Glasgow)
1961	Benfica 3, Barcelona 2 (Berne)
1962	Benfica 5, Real Madrid 3 (Amsterdam)
1963	AC Milan 2, Benfica 1 (Wembley)
1964	Inter Milan 3, Real Madrid 1 (Vienna)
1965	Inter Milan 1, Benfica 0 (Milan)
1966	Real Madrid 2, Partizan Belgrade 1 (Brussels)
1967	Celtic 2, Inter Milan 1 (Lisbon)
1968†	Manchester Utd. 4, Benfica 1 (Wembley)
1969	AC Milan 4, Ajax 1 (Madrid)
1970†	Feyenoord 2, Celtic 1 (Milan)
1971	Ajax 2, Panathinaikos 0 (Wembley)
1972	Ajax 2, Inter Milan 0 (Rotterdam)
1973	Ajax 1, Juventus 0 (Belgrade)
1974	Bayern Munich 4, Atletico Madrid 0 (replay Brussels, after a 1-1 draw, Brussels)
1975	Bayern Munich 2, Leeds Utd. 0 (Paris)
1976	Bayern Munich 1, St. Etienne 0 (Glasgow)
1977	Liverpool 3, Borussia Moenchengladbach 1 (Rome)
1978	Liverpool 1, Brugge 0 (Wembley)
1979	Nott'm. Forest 1, Malmo 0 (Munich)
1980	Nott'm. Forest 1, Hamburg 0 (Madrid)
1981	Liverpool 1, Real Madrid 0 (Paris)
1982	Aston Villa 1, Bayern Munich 0 (Rotterdam)
1983	SV Hamburg 1, Juventus 0 (Athens)
1984†	Liverpool 1, AS Roma 1 (Liverpool won 4-2 on penalties) (Rome)
1985	Juventus 1, Liverpool 0 (Brussels)
1986†	Steaua Bucharest 0, Barcelona 0 (Steaua won 2-0 on penalties) (Seville)
1987	Porto 2, Bayern Munich 1 (Vienna)
1988†	PSV Eindhoven 0, Benfica 0 (PSV won 6-5 on penalties) (Stuttgart)
1989	AC Milan 4, Steaua Bucharest 0 (Barcelona)
1990	AC Milan 1, Benfica 0 (Vienna)
1991†	Red Star Belgrade 0, Marseille 0 (Red Star won 5-3 on penalties) (Bari)
1992	Barcelona 1, Sampdoria 0 (Wembley)
1993	Marseille 1, AC Milan 0 (Munich)
1994	AC Milan 4, Barcelona 0 (Athens)
1995	Ajax 1, AC Milan 0 (Vienna)
1996†	Juventus 1, Ajax 1 (Juventus won 4-2 on penalties) (Rome)
1997	Borussia Dortmund 3, Juventus 1 (Munich)
1998	Real Madrid 1, Juventus 0 (Amsterdam)
1999	Manchester Utd. 2, Bayern Munich 1 (Barcelona)
2000	Real Madrid 3, Valencia 0 (Paris)
2001	Bayern Munich 1, Valencia 1 (Bayern Munich won 5-4 on penalties) (Milan)
2002	Real Madrid 2, Bayer Leverkusen 1, (Glasgow)
2003†	AC Milan 0, Juventus 0 (AC Milan won 3-2 on penalties) (Manchester)

(† After extra time)

UEFA CUP 2002-03

PRE-TOURNAMENT INTERTOTO CUP (SELECTED RESULTS)

FIRST ROUND

Coleraine 7, St Julia 2 (5-0h, 2-2a); FC Marek 3, **Caersws** 1 (2-0h, 1-1a); **St Patrick's Athletic** 3, Rijeka 3 (1-0h, 2-3a), **St Patrick's Athletic** won on away goals.

SECOND ROUND

Fulham 1, Haka 1 (0-0h, 1-1a), **Fulham** won on away goal; Gent 3, **St Patrick's Athletic** 3 (2-0h, 1-3a), Gent won on away goal; Troyes 4, **Coleraine** 2 (2-1h, 2-1a).

THIRD ROUND

Aston Villa 3, FC Zurich 2 (3-0h, 0-2a); **Fulham** 2, Egaleo 1 (1-0h, 1-1a).

SEMI-FINALS

Fulham 3, Sochaux 0 (1-0h, 2-0a); Lille 3, **Aston Villa** 1 (1-1h, 2-0a).

FINALS

First leg: Bologna 2, **Fulham** 2 (Inamoto, Legwinski). Att: 23,000. **Second leg: Fulham** 3 (Inamoto 3), Bologna 1. Att: 13,756. (**Fulham** won 5-3 on agg). **On aggregate:** Malaga 2, Villareal 1; Stuttgart 2, Lille 1.

QUALIFYING ROUND, FIRST LEG

Aberdeen 1 (Mackie 59), Nistru Otaci 0. Att: 9,894. Amica Wronki 5 (Bieniuk 35, Dembinski 57, Krol 64, Dawidowski 81, 85), **TNS** 0. Att: 1,200. Avenir Beggen 0, **Ipswich Town** 1 (Stewart 90). Att: 2,971. **Bangor City** 1 (Roberts 69), Sartid 0. Att: 967. **Glentoran** 0, Wisla Krakow 2 (Zurawski 73 pen, Dubicki 88). Att: 2,500. **Shamrock Rov.** 1 (McGuinness 49), Djurgarden 3 (Wowaoah 24, 52, Kallstrom 70). Att: 4,850. Stabaek 4 (Finstad 12, Gudmundsson 18, 90, Baldvinsson 75), **Linfield** 0. Att: 1,145. Varteks 5 (Huljev 28, Hrman 32, Mumlek 55 pen, Karic 70, Sklepic 90), **Dundalk** 0. Att: 4,500. Vaduz 1 (Burgmeier 61), **Livingston** 1 (Rubio 51). Att: 1,322.

QUALIFYING ROUND, SECOND LEG

Dundalk 0, Varteks 4 (Kristic 21, Halilovic 50, Huljev 50, Fumic 79). Att: 2,000 (Varteks won 9-0 on agg). Djurgarden 2 (Wowaoah 19, Chanko 21), **Shamrock Rov.** 0. Att: 7,273 (Djurgarden won 5-1 on agg). **Ipswich Town** 8 (Miller 3, 19, Counago 18, 21, 74, Brown 42, McGreal 61, Ambrose 79), Avenir Beggen 1 (Molitor 56). Att: 17,462 (**Ipswich Town** won 9-1 on agg). **Linfield** 1 (Ferguson 44), Stabaek 1 (Gudmundsson 82). Att: 1,200 (Stabaek won 5-1 on agg). **Livingston** 0, Vaduz 0. Att: 7,219 (agg 1-1, **Livingston** won on away goal). Nistru Otaci 0, **Aberdeen** 0. Att: 6,000 (**Aberdeen** won 1-0 on agg). Sartid 2 (Zecevic 14, Mirosavljevic 58), **Bangor City** 0. Att: 9,000 (Sartid won 2-1 on agg). **TNS** 2 (Anthrobus 20, Toner 28), Amica Wronki 7 (Krol 26, 72, 86, Burkhardt 34, 75, Sobocinski 66, Ludzinski 88). Att: 2,000. (Amica Wronki won 12-2 on agg). Wisla Krakow 4 (Kuzba 19, 59, Uche 74, 81), **Glentoran** 0. Att: 5,000 (Wisla Krakow won 6-0 on agg).

QUALIFYING ROUND (ON AGGREGATE)

AIK Solna 5, Vestmannyaer 1; Anorthosis 3, Grevenmacher 2; CSKA Sofia 5, Dinamo Minsk 1; Dynamo Tbilisi 5, TVMK Tallinn 1; Excelsior Mouscron 4, Fylkir 2; FC Copenhagen 7, Lokomotiv Tbilisi 2; Ferencvaros 5, Limassol 2; Gomel 5, HJK Helsinki 0; Hajduk Split 11, Gotu 0; Hapoel Tel Aviv 5, Partizan Tirana 1; Karnten 6, Metalurg Liepaja 2; Leixoes 4, Belasica 3; Litex Lovech 8, Atlantas Klaipeda 1; Maccabi Tel Aviv 4, Levadia Tallinnn 0; Metalurg Zaporizhya 3, Birkirkara 0; Midtjylland 3, Pobeda Prelip 2; National Bucharest 3, SK Tirana 2; Odense 2, MyPa 1; Polonia Warsaw 5, Sliema Wanderers 1; Puchov 2, Atyrau 0; Rapid Bucharest 5, Nova Gorica 1; Red Star Belgrade 5, Kairat Almaty 0; Sarajevo 3, Sigma Olomouc 3 (aet, Sarajevo won 5-3 on pens); Servette 5, Spartak Terevan 0; Siroki Brijeg 5, Senec 1; Suduva 6, Brann 4; Ujpest Dozsa 3, Klakksvik 2; Ventspils 3, Lugano 1; Zenit St Petersburg 13, Encamp 0; Zizkov 5, Domagnano 0; Zimbru Chisinau 5, Gothenburg 3; Primorje 6 Zvartnots 3.

FIRST ROUND, FIRST LEG

Aberdeen 0, Hertha Berlin 0. Att: 10,180. **Blackburn Rov.** 1 (Grabbi 27), CSKA Sofia 1 (Dimitrov 23). Att: 18,300. **Celtic** 8 (Larsson 16, 24, 29, Petrov 27, Sutton 35, Lambert 50, Hartson 72, Valgaeren 83), Suduva 1 (Radzinevicius 90). Att: 36,824. **Chelsea** 2 (Hasselbaink 43, De Lucas 69), Viking Stavanger 1 (Wright 90). Att: 15,772. Hajduk Split 0, **Fulham** 1 (Malbranque 50). Att: 25,000. **Ipswich Town** 1 (Armstrong 56), Sartid 1 (Mirosavljevic 32). Att: 16,933. **Leeds Utd.** 1 (Smith 80), Metalurg Zaporizhya 0. Att: 30,000. Sturm Graz 5 (Wetl 37, Szabics 50, Dag 51, Mujiri 57, 58), **Livingston** 2 (Zarate 89, Lovell 90). Att: 2,785. Zizkov 2 (Pikl 7, Straceny 60), **Rangers** 0. Att: 3,427.

FIRST ROUND, SECOND LEG

CSKA Sofia 3 (Gargarov 66, 88 pen, Agnaldo 69), **Blackburn Rov.** 3 (Thompson 30, Ostenstad 56, Duff 58). Att: 21,000 (agg 4-4, **Blackburn Rov.** won on away goals). **Fulham** 2 (Marlet 20, Malbranque 44 pen), Hajduk Split 2 (Djolonga 6, Vejic 41). Att: 18,500 (**Fulham** won 3-2 on agg). Hertha Berlin 1 (Preetz 89), **Aberdeen** 0. Att: 30,770 (Hertha Berlin won 1-0 on agg). **Livingston** 4 (Wilson 32 pen, 90, Xausa 56, Andrews 77), Sturm Graz 3 (Szabics 45, 54, Mujiri 48). Att: 5,208 (Sturm Graz won 8-6 on agg). Metalurg Zaporizhya 1 (Modebadze 24), **Leeds Utd.** 1 (Barmby 77). Att: 7,000 (**Leeds Utd.** won 2-1 on agg). **Rangers** 3 (De Boer 43, 59, McCann 97), Zizkov 1 (Licka 100). Att: 47,646 (aet, agg 3-3, Zizkov won on away goal). Sartid 0, **Ipswich Town** 1 (M. Bent 9 pen). Att: 16,000 (**Ipswich Town** won 2-1 on agg). Suduva 0, **Celtic** 2 (Fernandez 12, Thompson 24). Att: 1,200 (**Celtic** won 10-1 on agg). Viking Stavanger 4 (Berre 9, Kopteff 34, Nevland 60, 87), **Chelsea** 2 (Lampard 45, Terry 62), Att: 5,500 (Viking Stavanger won 5-4 on agg).

FIRST ROUND (ON AGGREGATE)

Alaves 5, Ankaragucu 1; Amica Wronki 4, Servette 4 (aet, Amica Wronki won on away goals); Anderlecht 2, Stabaek 2 (Anderlecht won on away goal); Anorthosis Famagusta 5, Iraklis 5 (Anorthosis Famagusta won on away goals); Apoel Nicosia 3, Grazer 1; Austria Vienna 5, Shakhtar Donetsk 2; Besiktas 7, Sarajevo 2; Boavista 4, Maccabi Tel Aviv 2; Bordeaux 10, Matador Puchov 1; Celta Vigo 2, Odense 1; Denizlispor 3 Lorient 3 (Denizlispor won on away goals); Dinamo Zagreb 9, Zalaegerszeg 1; Djurgarden 3, FC Copenhagen 1; FC Porto 6, Polonia Warsaw 2; Fenerbahce 6, AIK Stockholm 4; Ferencvaros 5, Kocaelispor 0; Grasshoppers 4, Zenit St Petersburg 3; Hapoel Tel Aviv 4, Karnten 1; Lazio 4, Xanthi 0; Legia Warsaw 7, Utrecht 2; Levski Sofia 5, Brondby 2; Malaga 1, Zeljeznicar 0; Midtjylland 2, Varteks 1; National Bucharest 3, Heerenveen 2; PAOK Salonika 5, Leixoes 3; Panathinaikos 3, Liteks Lovech 1; Paris St-Germain 4, Ujpest Dozsa 0; Parma 4, CSKA Moscow 3; Partizan Belgrade 6, Sporting Lisbon 4 (aet); Real Betis 4, Zimbru Chisinau 1; Red Star Belgrade 2, Chievo 0; Schalke 8, Gomel 1; Slavia Prague 7, Excelsior Mouscron 3; Slovan Liberec 4, Dinamo Tbilisi 2;

Sparta Prague 4, Siroki Brijeg 0; Stuttgart 8, Ventspils 2; Vitesse Arnhem 2, Rapid Bucharest 1; Werder Bremen 10, Metalurh Donetsk 2; Wisla Krakow 8 Primorje 1;

SECOND ROUND, FIRST LEG

Celtic 1 (Larsson 85), **Blackburn Rov.** 0. Att: 59,553. Dinamo Zagreb 0, **Fulham** 3 (Boa Morte 35, Marlet 59, Hayles 77). Att: 25,000. **Ipswich Town** 1 (D. Bent 69), Slovan Liberec 0. Att: 16,138. **Leeds Utd.** 1 (Kewell 82), Hapoel Tel Aviv 0. Att: 31,867.

SECOND ROUND, SECOND LEG

Blackburn Rov. 0, **Celtic** 2 (Larsson 15, Sutton 68). Att: 29,698 (**Celtic** won 3-0 on agg). **Fulham** 2 (Malbranque 89, Boa Morte 90), Dinamo Zagreb 1 (Olic 52). Att: 7,700 (**Fulham** won 5-1 on agg). Hapoel Tel Aviv 1 (Abukasis 2), **Leeds Utd.** 4 (Smith 30, 54, 62, 83). Att: 3,000 (Played in Florence, **Leeds Utd.** won 5-1 on agg). Slovan Liberec 1 (Baffour 88), **Ipswich Town** 0. Att: 6,509 (aet, agg 1-1, Slovan Liberec won 4-2 on pens).

SECOND ROUND (ON AGGREGATE)

Anderlecht 6, Midtjylland 1; Besiktas 2, Alaves 1; Boavista 3, Anorthosis Famagusta 1; Bordeaux 3, Djurgarden 1; Celta Vigo 4, Viking Stavanger 1; Denizlispor 2, Sparta Prague 1; FC Porto 3, Austria Vienna 0; Lazio 2, Red Star Belgrade 1; Malaga 4, Amica Wronki 2; PAOK Salonika 3, Grasshoppers 2; Panathinaikos 5, Fenerbahce 2; Paris St-Germain 3, National Bucharest 0; Real Betis 4, Zizkov 0; Schalke 3, Legia Warsaw 2; Slavia Prague 6, Partizan Belgrade 4; Stuttgart 2, Ferencvaros 0; Sturm Graz 1, Levski Sofia 1 (aet, Sturm Graz won 8-7 on pens); Vitesse Arnhem 5, Werder Bremen 4; Wisla Krakow 5, Parma 3.

THIRD ROUND, FIRST LEG

Hertha Berlin 2 (Beinlich 26, Sava og 68), **Fulham** 1 (Marlet 53). Att:14,477. **Celtic** 1 (Larsson 52), Celta Vigo 0. Att: 53,726. Malaga 0, **Leeds Utd.** 0. Att: 35,000. Vitesse Arnhem 0, **Liverpool** 1 (Owen 26). Att: 28,000.

THIRD ROUND, SECOND LEG

Celta Vigo 2 (Jesuli 24, McCarthy 54), **Celtic** 1 (Hartson 37). Att: 25,000 (Agg 2-2, **Celtic** won on away goal). **Fulham** 0, Hertha Berlin 0. Att: 15,161 (Hertha Berlin won 2-1 on agg). **Leeds Utd.** 1 (Bakke 23), Malaga 2 (Dely Valdes 14, 80). Att: 34,123 (Malaga won 2-1 on agg). **Liverpool** 1 (Owen 21), Vitesse Arnhem 0. Att: 23,576 (**Liverpool** won 2-0 on agg).

THIRD ROUND (ON AGGREGATE)

AEK Athens 8, Maccabi Haifa 1; Anderlecht 4, Bordeaux 2; Auxerre 2, Real Betis 1; Besiktas 3, Dynamo Kiev 1; Boavista 2, Paris St-Germain 2 (Boavista won on away goals); Denizlispor 1, Lyon 0; FC Porto 3, Lens 1; Lazio 3, Sturm Graz 2; Panathinaikos 3, Liberec 2; Slavia Prague 4, PAOK Salonika 1; Stuttgart 3, Bruges 1; Wisla Krakow 5, Schalke 2.

FOURTH ROUND, FIRST LEG

Auxerre 0, **Liverpool** 1 (Hyypia 73). Att: 20,452. **Celtic** 3 (Lambert 36, Maloney 45, Petrov 68), Stuttgart 1 (Kuranyi 27). Att: 59,000.

FOURTH ROUND, SECOND LEG

Liverpool 2 (Owen 67, Murphy 73), Auxerre 0. Att: 34,252 (**Liverpool** won 3-0 on agg). Stuttgart 3 (Tiffert 37, Hleb 75, Mutzel 87), **Celtic** 2 (Thompson 12, Sutton 14). Att: 45,000 (**Celtic** won 5-4 on agg).

FOURTH ROUND (ON AGGREGATE)

Besiktas 4, Slavia Prague 3; Boavista 3, Hertha Berlin 3 (Boavista won on away goals); FC Porto 8, Denizlispor 3; Lazio 5, Wisla Krakow 4; Malaga 1, AEK Athens 0; Panathinaikos 3, Anderlecht 2.

QUARTER-FINALS, FIRST LEG

Celtic 1 (Larsson 2), **Liverpool** 1 (Heskey 17). Att: 59,759. FC Porto 0, Panathinaikos 1 (Olisadebe 72). Att: 44,310. Lazio 1 (Inzaghi 55), Besiktas 0. Att: 25,000. Malaga 1 (Dely Valdes 17), Boavista 0. Att: 13,000.

QUARTER-FINALS, SECOND LEG

Besiktas 1 (Sergen 83), Lazio 2 (Fiore 5, Castroman 9). Att: 28,000 (Lazio won 3-1 on agg). Boavista 1 (Claudio 83), Malaga 0. Att: 8,500 (aet, agg 1-1, Boavista won 4-1 on pens). **Liverpool** 0, **Celtic** 2 (Thompson 45, Hartson 81). Att: 44,238 (**Celtic** won 3-1 on agg). Panathinaikos 0, FC Porto 2 (Derlei 16, 103). 15,000 (aet, FC Porto won 2-1 on agg).

SEMI-FINALS, FIRST LEG

Celtic 1 (Larsson 50), Boavista 1 (Valgaeren 49 og). Att: 60,000. FC Porto 4 (Maniche 10, Derlei 27, 50, Helder Postiga 56), Lazio 1 (Lopez (5). Att: 45,518.

SEMI-FINALS, SECOND LEG

Boavista 0, **Celtic** 1 (Larsson 80). Att: 11,000 (**Celtic** won 2-1 on agg). Lazio 0, FC Porto 0. Att: 65,000 (FC Porto won 4-1 on agg).

UEFA CUP FINAL

CELTIC 2, FC PORTO 3 (AET)

Seville, (52,972), Wednesday, May 21, 2003

Celtic (3-5-2): Douglas, Mjallby, Balde, Valgaeren (Laursen 65), Agathe, Petrov (Maloney 104), Lambert (capt) (McNamara 76), Lennon, Thompson, Sutton, Larsson. **Scorer:** Larsson (47, 57). **Subs not used:** Hedman, Sylla, Fernandez, Smith. **Booked:** Valgareen, Lennon, Balde, Petrov. **Sent-off:** Balde (95). **Manager:** Martin O'Neill.

FC Porto (4-1-3-2: Vitor Baia, Paulo Ferreira, Jorge Costa (capt) (Emanuel 71), Carvalho, Nuno Valente, Costinha (Ricardo Costa 9), Deco, Capucho (Marco Ferreira 98), Maniche, Derlei, Alenichev. **Scorers:** Derlei (45, 115), Alenichev (54). **Subs not used:** Nuno, Peixoto, Clayton, Tiago. **Booked:** Nuno Valente, Maniche, Paulo Ferreira. **Sent-off:** Nuno Valente (120). **Coach:** Jose Mourinho.

Referee: L. Michel (Slovakia). **Half-time:** 0-1.

Celtic lost their first European final for 33 years, but won plenty of respect for an enterprising performance and for the unswerving support of an estimated 40,000 fans inside and outside the Olympic Stadium.They were beaten in extra-time – just as the 1970 team had been by Feyenoord in the European Cup – after twice coming from behind with towering headers by Henrik Larsson.

It was scored in the 115th minute by Derlei with the aid of a deflection by Ulrik Laursen after Marco Ferreira's shot was half saved by Rab Douglas. Celtic were unable to find a third equaliser, enabling FC Porto to become the first Portuguese winners of the competition.

Although Celtic had overcome some tricky hurdles along the way – Blackburn Rovers, Celta Vigo, Stuttgart and Liverpool among them – this was the best side they had faced. Porto displayed great skill and technique, suggesting that the national side might prove a force when hosting the European Championship Finals in 2004. At the same time, the diving and play-acting of some players took the shine off their performance and rightly drew a rebuke afterwards from the Celtic manager Martin O'Neill.

The game's key figure, midfielder Deco, helped set up the first goal for Derlei on the stroke of half time, a lead which lasted barely two minutes of playing time before Larsson rose, hung and headed in Didier Agathe's cross from beyond the far post for his 200th goal for the club. Dmitiri Alenichev restored Porto's advantage after more good work by Deco, but again Larsson levelled quickly, heading in Alan Thompson's corner.

Both teams had a player sent off in the extra-time, with Bobo Balde's second yellow the more significant, coming as it did five minutes in and leaving Celtic the more vulnerable. Nuno Valente's dismissal came in the last minute.

UEFA CUP FINALS

1972 Tottenham beat Wolves 3-2 on agg. (2-1a, 1-1h)
1973 Liverpool beat Borussia Moenchengladbach 3-2 on agg. (3-0h, 0-2a)
1974 Feyenoord beat Tottenham 4-2 on agg. (2-2a, 2-0h)
1975 Borussia Moenchengladbach beat Twente Enschede 5-1 on agg. (0-0h, 5-1a)
1976 Liverpool beat Brugge 4-3 on agg. (3-2h, 1-1a)
1977 Juventus beat Atletico Bilbao on away goals after 2-2 agg. (1-0h, 1-2a)
1978 PSV Eindhoven beat Bastia 3-0 on agg. (0-0a, 3-0h)
1979 Borussia Moenchengladbach beat Red Star Belgrade 2-1 on agg. (1-1a, 1-0h)
1980 Eintracht Frankfurt beat Borussia Moenchengladbach on away goals after 3-3 agg. (2-3a, 1-0h)
1981 Ipswich Town beat AZ 67 Alkmaar 5-4 on agg. (3-0h, 2-4a)
1982 IFK Gothenburg beat SV Hamburg 4-0 on agg. (1-0h, 3-0a)
1983 Anderlecht beat Benfica 2-1 on agg. (1-0h, 1-1a)
1984 Tottenham beat Anderlecht 4-3 on penalties after 2-2 agg. (1-1a, 1-1h)
1985 Real Madrid beat Videoton 3-1 on agg. (3-0a, 0-1h)
1986 Real Madrid beat Cologne 5-3 on agg. (5-1h, 0-2a)
1987 IFK Gothenburg beat Dundee Utd. 2-1 on agg. (1-0h, 1-1a)
1988 Bayer Leverkusen beat Espanol 3-2 on penalties after 3-3 agg. (0-3a, 3-0h)
1989 Napoli beat VfB Stuttgart 5-4 on agg. (2-1h, 3-3a)
1990 Juventus beat Fiorentina 3-1 on agg. (3-1h, 0-0a)
1991 Inter Milan beat AS Roma 2-1 on agg. (2-0h, 0-1a)
1992 Ajax beat Torino on away goals after 2-2 agg. (2-2a, 0-0h)
1993 Juventus beat Borussia Dortmund 6-1 on agg. (3-1a, 3-0h)
1994 Inter Milan beat Salzburg 2-0 on agg. (1-0a, 1-0h)
1995 Parma beat Juventus 2-1 on agg. (1-0h, 1-1a)
1996 Bayern Munich beat Bordeaux 5-1 on agg. (2-0h, 3-1a)
1997 FC Schalke beat Inter Milan 4-1 on penalties after 1-1 agg. (1-0h, 0-1a)
1998 Inter Milan beat Lazio 3-0 (one match) – Paris
1999 Parma beat Marseille 3-0 (one match) – Moscow
2000 Galatasaray beat Arsenal 4-1 on penalties after 0-0 (one match) – Copenhagen
2001 Liverpool beat Alvaves 5-4 on golden goal (one match) – Dortmund
2002 Feyenoord beat Borussia Dortmund 3-2 (one match) – Rotterdam
2003 FC Porto beat Celtic 3-2 on silver goal (one match) – Seville

FAIRS CUP FINALS

(As UEFA Cup previously known)

1958 Barcelona beat London 8-2 on agg. (2-2a, 6-0h)
1960 Barcelona beat Birmingham 4-1 on agg. (0-0a, 4-1h)
1961 AS Roma beat Birmingham City 4-2 on agg. (2-2a, 2-0h)
1962 Valencia beat Barcelona 7-3 on agg. (6-2h, 1-1a)
1963 Valencia beat Dynamo Zagreb 4-1 on agg. (2-1a, 2-0h)
1964 Real Zaragoza beat Valencia 2-1 (Barcelona)
1965 Ferencvaros beat Juventus 1-0 (Turin)
1966 Barcelona beat Real Zaragoza 4-3 on agg. (0-1h, 4-2a)
1967 Dynamo Zagreb beat Leeds Utd. 2-0 on agg. (2-0h, 0-0a)
1968 Leeds Utd. beat Ferencvaros 1-0 on agg. (1-0h, 0-0a)
1969 Newcastle Utd. beat Ujpest Dozsa 6-2 on agg. (3-0h, 3-2a)
1970 Arsenal beat Anderlecht 4-3 on agg. (1-3a, 3-0h)
1971 Leeds Utd. beat Juventus on away goals after 3-3 agg. (2-2a, 1-1h)

CUP-WINNERS' CUP FINALS

1961 Fiorentina beat Rangers 4-1 on agg. (2-0 Glasgow first leg, 2-1 Florence second leg)
1962 Atletico Madrid beat Fiorentina 3-0 (replay Stuttgart, after a 1-1 draw, Glasgow)
1963 Tottenham beat Atletico Madrid 5-1 (Rotterdam)
1964 Sporting Lisbon beat MTK Budapest 1-0 (replay Antwerp, after a 3-3 draw, Brussels)
1965 West Ham Utd. beat Munich 1860 2-0 (Wembley)
1966† Borussia Dortmund beat Liverpool 2-1 (Glasgow)
1967† Bayern Munich beat Rangers 1-0 (Nuremberg)
1968 AC Milan beat SV Hamburg 2-0 (Rotterdam)
1969 Slovan Bratislava beat Barcelona 3-2 (Basle)
1970 Manchester City beat Gornik Zabrze 2-1 (Vienna)
1971† Chelsea beat Real Madrid 2-1 (replay Athens, after a 1-1 draw, Athens)
1972 Rangers beat Moscow Dynamo 3-2 (Barcelona)
1973 AC Milan beat Leeds Utd. 1-0 (Salonika)
1974 Magdeburg beat AC Milan 2-0 (Rotterdam)
1975 Dynamo Kiev beat Ferencvaros 3-0 (Basle)
1976 Anderlecht beat West Ham Utd. 4-2 (Brussels)
1977 SV Hamburg beat Anderlecht 2-0 (Amsterdam)
1978 Anderlecht beat Austria WAC 4-0 (Paris)
1979† Barcelona beat Fortuna Dusseldorf 4-3 (Basle)
1980† Valencia beat Arsenal 5-4 on penalties after a 0-0 draw (Brussels)
1981 Dynamo Tbilisi beat Carl Zeiss Jena 2-1 (Dusseldorf)
1982 Barcelona beat Standard Liege 2-1 (Barcelona)
1983† Aberdeen beat Real Madrid 2-1 (Gothenburg)
1984 Juventus beat Porto 2-1 (Basle)
1985 Everton beat Rapid Vienna 3-1 (Rotterdam)
1986 Dynamo Kiev beat Atletico Madrid 3-0 (Lyon)
1987 Ajax beat Lokomotiv Leipzig 1-0 (Athens)
1988 Mechelen beat Ajax 1-0 (Strasbourg)
1989 Barcelona beat Sampdoria 2-0 (Berne)
1990 Sampdoria beat Anderlecht 2-0 (Gothenburg)
1991 Manchester Utd. beat Barcelona 2-1 (Rotterdam)
1992 Werder Bremen beat Monaco 2-0 (Lisbon)
1993 Parma beat Royal Antwerp 3-1 (Wembley)

1994	Arsenal beat Parma 1-0 (Copenhagen)
1995†	Real Zaragoza beat Arsenal 2-1 (Paris)
1996	Paris St. Germain beat Rapid Vienna 1-0 (Brussels)
1997	Barcelona beat Paris St. Germain 1-0 (Rotterdam)
1998	Chelsea beat VfB Stuttgart 1-0 (Stockholm)
1999	Lazio beat Real Mallorca 2-1 (Villa Park, Birmingham)

(† After extra time)

INTER-CONTINENTAL CUP

OLIMPIA ASUNCION 0, REAL MADRID 2

Yokohama, (69,000), Tuesday, December 3, 2002

Olimpia Asuncion (4-4-2): Tavarelli, Isasi, Caceres, Zelaya, Jara, Orteman, Encisco, P. Benitez (Caballero 80), Cordoba (Baez 65), M. Benitez, Lopez.

Real Madrid (4-2-3-1): Iker Casillas, Salgado, Hierro, Ivan Helguera, Roberto Carlos, Cambiasso (Pavon 90), Makelele, Figo, Raul, Zidane (Solari 86), Ronaldo (Guti 82). **Scorers:** Ronaldo (14), Guti (84).

Referee: C. Simon (Brazil). **Half-time:** 0-1

COMPLETE RESULTS

Year	Winners	Runners-up	Score
1960	Real Madrid (Spa.)	Penarol (Uru.)	0-0 5-1
1961	Penarol (Uru.)	Benfica (Por.)	0-1 2-1 5-0
1962	Santos (Bra.)	Benfica (Por.)	3-2 5-2
1963	Santos (Bra.)	AC Milan (Ita.)	2-4 4-2 1-0
1964	Inter Milan (Ita.)	Independiente (Arg.)	0-1 2-0 1-0
1965	Inter Milan (Ita.)	Independiente (Arg.)	3-0 0-0
1966	Penarol (Uru.)	Real Madrid (Spa.)	2-0 2-0
1967	Racing (Arg.)	Celtic (Sco.)	0-1 2-1 1-0
1968	Estudiantes (Arg.)	Manchester Utd. (Eng.)	1-0 1-1
1969	AC Milan (Ita.)	Estudiantes (Arg.)	3-0 1-2
1970	Feyenoord (Hol.)	Estudiantes (Arg.)	2-2 1-0
1971	Nacional (Uru.)	Panathanaikos (Gre.)*	1-1 2-1
1972	Ajax (Hol.)	Independiente (Arg.)	1-1 3-0
1973	Independiente (Arg.)	Juventus (Ita.)*	1-0 #
1974	Atletico Madrid (Spa.)*	Independiente (Arg.)	0-1 2-0
1975	Not played		
1976	Bayern Munich (W.Ger.)	Cruzeiro (Bra.)	2-0 0-0
1977	Boca Juniors (Arg.)	Borussia Mönchengladbach (W.Ger.)*	2-2 3-0
1978	Not played		
1979	Olimpia Asuncion (Par.)	Malmö (Swe.)*	1-0 2-1
1980	Nacional (Arg.)	Nott'm. Forest (Eng.)	1-0
1981	Flamengo (Bra.)	Liverpool (Eng.)	3-0
1982	Penarol (Uru.)	Aston Villa (Eng.)	2-0
1983	Porto Alegre (Bra.)	SV Hamburg (W.Ger.)	2-1
1984	Independiente (Arg.)	Liverpool (Eng.)	1-0
1985	Juventus (Ita.)	Argentinos Juniors (Arg.)	2-2 (aet)

(Juventus won 4-2 on penalties)

1986	River Plate (Arg.)	Steaua Bucharest (Rum.)	1-0
1987	Porto (Por.)	Penarol (Uru.)	2-1 (aet)
1988	Nacional (Uru.)	PSV Eindhoven (Hol.)	1-1 (aet)
	(Nacional won 7-6 on penalties)		
1989	AC Milan (Ita.)	Nacional (Col.)	1-0 (aet)
1990	AC Milan (Ita.)	Olimpia Asuncion (Par.)	3-0
1991	Red Star (Yug.)	Colo Colo (Chi.)	3-0
1992	Sao Paulo (Bra.)	Barcelona (Spa.)	2-1
1993	Sao Paulo (Bra.)	AC Milan (Ita.)	3-2
1994	Velez Sarsfield (Arg.)	AC Milan (Ita.)	2-0
1995	Ajax (Hol.)	Gremio (Bra.)	0-0 (aet)
	(Ajax won 4-3 on penalties)		
1996	Juventus (Ita.)	River Plate (Arg.)	1-0
1997	Borussia Dortmund (Ger.)	Cruzeiro (Arg.)	2-0
1998	Real Madrid (Spa.)	Vasco da Gama (Bra.)	2-1
1999	Manchester Utd. (Eng.)	Palmeiras (Bra.)	1-0
2000	Boca Juniors (Arg.)	Real Madrid (Spa.)	2-1
2001	Bayern Munich (Ger.)	Boca Juniours (Arg.)	1-0
2002	Real Madrid (Spa.)	Olimpia Ascuncion (Par.)	2-0

Played as a single match in Japan since 1980
* European Cup runners-up. # One match only.
Summary: 41 contests; South America 21 wins, Europe 20 wins.

EUROPEAN SUPER CUP

FEYENOORD 1, REAL MADRID 3

Monaco, (10,000), Friday, August 3, 2002

Feyenoord (4-4-2): Zoetebier, Gyan (Buffel 72), Van Wonderen, Paauwe, Rzasa, Emerton, Bosvelt, Ono, Lurling, Kalou, Van Hooijdonk, **Scorer:** Van Hooijdonk (56).

Real Madrid (4-2-3-1): Iker Casillas, Salgado, Hierro, Ivan Helguera, Roberto Carlos, Cambiasso, Makalele, Figo, Raul, Zidane, Guti. **Scorers:** Paauwe (15 og), Roberto Carlos (21), Guti (60).

Referee: H. Dallas (Scotland). **Half-time:** 0-2.

QUOTE-UNQUOTE

'The buck stops with me. I am responsible for the team and 90 percent of the players here are my players' – **Kevin Ratcliffe** resigning as manager after Shrewsbury Town were relegated from the Football League.

'He has got to ask himself is Chelsea a serious community club, or is Ken Bates just looking for a fast buck? I say Ken Bates is a disgrace and Chelsea is a disgrace' – **Charles Clarke**, Education Secretary, criticising the only Premiership club not to be involved with a scheme to improve literacy levels among young people.

'He is responsible for an education system that is in a state of collapse. If he did his job properly, he wouldn't need gimmicks or personal abuse to hide the fact that he is a total failure' – **Ken Bates**, Chelsea chairman.

EUROPEAN TABLES

FRANCE

		P	W	D	L	F	A	Pts
1	Lyon	38	19	11	8	63	41	68
2	Monaco	38	19	10	9	66	33	67
3	Marseille	38	19	8	11	41	36	65
4	Bordeaux	38	18	10	10	57	36	64
5	Sochaux	38	17	13	8	46	31	64
6	Auxerre	38	18	10	10	38	29	64
7	Guingamp	38	19	5	14	59	46	62
8	Lens	38	14	15	9	43	31	57
9	Nantes	38	16	8	14	37	39	56
10	Nice	38	13	16	9	39	31	55
11	Paris SG	38	14	12	12	47	36	54
12	Bastia	38	12	11	15	40	48	47
13	Strasbourg	38	11	12	15	40	54	45
14	Lille	38	10	12	16	29	44	42
15	Rennes	38	10	10	18	35	45	40
16	Montpellier	38	10	10	18	37	54	40
17	Ajaccio	38	9	12	17	29	49	39
18	Le Havre	38	10	8	20	27	47	38
19	Sedan	38	9	9	20	41	59	36
20	Troyes	38	7	10	21	23	48	31

Leading Scorers: 26 Nonda (Monaco); 23 Pauleta (Bordeaux); 17 Drogba (Guingamp); 14 Camara (Sedan), Cisse (Auxerre); 13 Juninho (Lyon); 12 Anderson (Lyon), Diawara (Nice), Prso (Monaco), Sibierski (Lens); 11 Darcheville (Bordeaux), Giuly (Monaco), Luyindula (Lyon).
Cup Final: Auxerre 2, Paris SG 1.

GERMANY

		P	W	D	L	F	A	Pts
1	Bayern Munich	34	23	6	5	70	25	75
2	Stuttgart	34	17	8	9	53	39	59
3	Borussia Dortmund	34	15	13	6	51	27	58
4	Hamburg	34	15	11	8	46	36	56
5	Hertha Berlin	34	16	6	12	52	43	54
6	Werder Bremen	34	16	4	14	51	50	52
7	Schalke	34	12	13	9	46	40	49
8	Wolfsburg	34	13	7	14	39	42	46
9	VFL Bochum	34	12	9	13	55	56	45
10	1860 Munich	34	12	9	13	44	52	45
11	Hannover	34	12	7	15	47	57	43
12	Borussia M'gladbach	34	11	9	14	43	45	42
13	Hansa Rostock	34	11	8	15	35	41	41
14	Kaiserslautern	34	10	10	14	40	42	40
15	Bayer Leverkusen	34	11	7	16	47	56	40
16	Arminia Bielefeld	34	8	12	14	35	46	36
17	Nuremberg	34	8	6	20	33	60	30
18	Cottbus	34	7	9	18	34	64	30

Leading Scorers: 21 Christiansen (Bochum), Elber (Bayern); 16 Ailton (Werder Bremen), Kuranyi (Stuttgart); 15 Pizarro (Bayern); 14 Bobic (Hannover), Marcelinho (Hertha), Romeo (Hamburg), Schroth (1860 Munich); 13 Lauth (1860 Munich); 12 Ciric (Nuremberg), Maric (Wolfsburg).
Cup Final: Bayern Munich 3, Kaiserslautern 1.

HOLLAND

		P	W	D	L	F	A	Pts
1	PSV Eindhoven	34	26	6	2	87	20	84
2	Ajax	34	26	5	3	96	32	83
3	Feyenoord	34	25	5	4	89	39	80
4	Breda	34	13	13	8	42	31	52
5	NEC	34	14	9	11	41	40	51
6	Roda	34	14	8	12	58	54	50
7	Heerenveen	34	13	8	13	61	55	47
8	Utrecht	34	12	11	11	49	49	47
9	Waalwijk	34	14	4	16	44	51	46
10	Alkmaar	34	12	8	14	50	69	44
11	Willem II	34	11	9	14	48	51	42
12	FC Twente	34	10	11	13	36	45	41
13	Roosendaal	34	10	6	18	33	54	36
14	Vitesse	34	8	9	17	37	51	33
15	Groningen	34	7	11	16	28	44	32
16	Zwolle	34	8	8	18	31	62	32
17	Excelsior	34	5	8	21	38	72	23
18	De Graafschap	34	6	5	23	35	84	23

Leading Scorers: 35 Kezman (PSV Eindhoven); 28 Van Hooijdonk (Feyenoord); 20 Kuijt (Utrecht); 18 Buffel (Feyenoord), Van der Vaart (Ajax); 16 Hoogendorp (Waalwijk); 15 Amoah (Vitesse); 13 Ibrahimovic (Ajax); 12 Engelaar (Breda), Robben (PSV Eindhoven).
Cup Final: Utrecht 4, Feyenoord 1.

ITALY

		P	W	D	L	F	A	Pts
1	Juventus	34	21	9	4	64	29	72
2	Inter Milan	34	19	8	7	64	38	65
3	AC Milan	34	18	7	9	55	30	61
4	Lazio	34	15	15	4	57	32	60
5	Parma	34	15	11	8	55	36	56
6	Udinese	34	16	8	10	38	35	56
7	Chieve	34	16	7	11	51	39	55
8	Roma	34	13	10	11	55	46	49
9	Brescia	34	9	15	10	36	38	42
10	Perugia	34	10	12	12	40	48	42
11	Bologna	34	10	11	13	39	47	41
12	Modena	34	9	11	14	30	48	38
13	Empoli	34	9	11	14	36	46	38
14	Reggina	34	10	8	16	38	53	38
15	Atalanta	34	8	14	12	35	47	38
16	Piacenza	34	8	6	20	44	62	30
17	Como	34	4	12	18	29	57	24
18	Torino	34	4	9	21	23	58	21

Leading Scorers: 24 Vieri (Inter Milan); 17 Inzaghi (AC Milan), Mutu (Parma); 16 Del Piero (Juventus); 15 Adriano (Parma), Claudio Lopez (Lazio); 14 Hubner (Piacenza), Totti (Roma); 13 Di Natale (Empoli); 12 Baggio (Brescia), Signori (Bologna).
Cup Final: AC Milan 6, Roma 3 (on agg).

PORTUGAL

		P	W	D	L	F	A	Pts
1	FC Porto	34	27	5	2	73	26	86
2	Benfica	34	23	6	5	74	27	75
3	Sporting Lisbon	34	17	8	9	52	38	59
4	Vitória Guimarães	34	14	8	12	47	46	50
5	Uniño Leira	34	13	10	11	49	47	49
6	Paços de Ferreira	34	12	9	13	40	47	45
7	Maritimo	34	13	5	16	36	48	44
8	Gil Vicente	34	13	5	16	42	53	44
9	Belenenses	34	11	10	13	47	48	43
10	Boavista	34	10	13	11	32	31	43
11	Nacional	34	9	13	12	40	46	40
12	Moreirense	34	9	12	13	42	46	39
13	Beira Mar	34	10	9	15	43	50	39
14	Sporting Braga	34	8	14	12	34	47	38
15	Coimbra	34	8	13	13	38	48	37
16	Varzim	34	10	6	18	38	51	36
17	Santa Clara	34	8	11	15	39	54	35
18	Vitória Setúbal	34	6	13	15	40	53	31

Leading Scorers: 18 Faye Fary (Beira Mar), Simao (Benfica); 16 Adriano (Nacional); 15 Gaucho (Maritimo); 13 Helder Postiga (FC Porto), Tiago (Benfica); 12 Barroso (Sporting Braga), Maciel (Uniao Leiria); 11 Dario (Coimbra), Jardel (Sporting Lisbon), Paulo Alves (Gil Vincente), Sousa (Beira Mar).
Cup Final: FC Porto 1, Uniao Leiria 0.

SPAIN

		P	W	D	L	F	A	Pts
1	Real Madrid	38	22	12	4	86	42	78
2	Real Sociedad	38	22	10	6	71	45	76
3	Dep. La Coruña	38	22	6	10	67	47	72
4	Celta Vigo	38	18	10	10	45	36	61
5	Valencia	38	17	9	12	56	35	60
6	Barcelona	38	15	11	12	63	47	56
7	Athletic Bilbao	38	15	10	13	63	61	55
8	Mallorca	38	14	10	14	49	56	52
9	Real Betis	38	14	12	12	56	53	54
10	Sevilla	38	13	11	14	38	39	50
11	Osasuna	38	12	11	15	40	48	47
12	Atletico Madrid	38	12	11	15	51	56	47
13	Malaga	38	11	13	14	44	49	46
14	Real Valladolid	38	12	10	16	37	40	46
15	Villarreal	38	11	12	15	44	53	45
16	Racing Santander	38	13	5	20	54	64	44
17	Espanyol	38	10	13	15	48	54	43
18	Recreativo Huelva	38	8	12	18	35	61	36
19	Alaves	38	8	11	19	38	68	35
20	Rayo Vallecano	38	7	11	20	31	62	32

Leading Scorers: 29 Makaay (Dep. La Coruna); 23 Kahveci (Real Sociedad), Ronaldo (Real Madrid); 20 Kovacevic (Real Sociedad); 16 Kluivert (Barcelona), Raul (Real Madrid); 15 Fernando (Real Betis), Guerrero (Racing Santander); 14 Eto'o (Mallorca), Etxebarria (Athletic Bilbao), Pandiani (Mallorca), Urzaiz (Athletic Bilbao).
Cup Final: Mallorca 3, Recreativo Huelva 0.

CONFEDERATIONS CUP – FRANCE 2003

(Matches at Stade de France, Lyon, St Etienne)

GROUP A

June 18: France 1 (Henry 39 pen), Colombia 0. Att: 38,541. New Zealand 0, Japan 3 (Nakamura 11, 75, Nakata 65). Att: 36,038.
June 20: Colombia 3 (Lopez 59, Yepes 75, Hernandez 84), New Zealand 1 (De Gregorio 27). Att: 22,811. France 2 (Pires 43 pen, Govou 66), Japan 1 (Nakamura 60). Att: 33,070.
June 22: France 5 (Kapo 17, Henry 21, Cisse 70, Giuly 89, Pires 90), New Zealand 0. Att: 36,842. Japan 0, Colombia 1 (Hernandez 69). Att: 24,541.

GROUP B

June 19: Brazil 0, Cameroon 1 (Eto'o 83). Att: 46,719. Turkey 2 (Yilmaz 39 pen, Sanli 70), USA 1 (Beasley 36). Att: 16,944.
June 21: Brazil 1 (Adriano 22), USA 0. Att: 20,306. Cameroon 1 (Geremi 90), Turkey 0. Att: 43,743.
June 23: Brazil 2 (Adriano 23, Alex 90), Turkey 2 (Karadeniz 53, Yilmaz 80). Att: 29,170. USA 0, Cameroon 0. Att: 19,206.

GROUP PLACINGS

GROUP A	*P*	*W*	*D*	*L*	*F*	*A*	*Pts*
FRANCE	3	3	0	0	8	1	9
COLOMBIA	3	2	0	1	4	2	6
Japan	3	1	0	2	4	3	3
New Zealand	3	0	0	3	1	11	0

GROUP B	*P*	*W*	*D*	*L*	*F*	*A*	*Pts*
CAMEROON	3	2	1	0	2	0	7
TURKEY	3	1	1	1	4	4	4
Brazil	3	1	1	1	3	3	4
USA	3	0	1	2	1	3	1

SEMI-FINALS

June 26: Cameroon 1 (N'Diefi 9), Colombia 0. Att: 12,352. France 3 (Henry 10, Pires 25, Wiltord 43), Turkey 2 (Karadeniz 41, Sanli 48). Att: 41,195.

THIRD/FOURTH PLACE PLAY-OFF

June 28: Colombia 1 (Hernandez 63), Turkey 2 (Sanli 2, Yilmaz 87). Att: 18,237.

FINAL

CAMEROON 0, FRANCE 1 (golden goal)

Stade de France, (51,985), Sunday, June 29, 2003

Cameroon (4-4-2): Kameni, Perrier Doumbe, Song, Atouba, Mettomo, Geremi, Ndiefi (Eto'o 67), Mbami, Mezague (Emana 91), Idrissou, Djemba Djemba. **Booked:** Mbami.

France (4-4-2): Barthez, Lizarazu, Gallas, Desailly, Sagnol, Dacourt, Giuly, Wiltord, Pedretti, Henry, Cisse. **Scorer:** Henry (97). **Booked:** Dacourt.

Referee: V. Ivanov (Russia). Half-time: 0-0:

WORLD CUP SUMMARIES 1930-2002

1930 IN URUGUAY

WINNERS: Uruguay. RUNNERS-UP: Argentina. THIRD: U.S.A. FOURTH: Yugoslavia.
Other countries taking part: Belgium, Bolivia, Brazil, Chile, France, Mexico, Paraguay, Peru, Rumania, Yugoslavia. **Total entries**: 13.
Venue: All matches played in Montevideo.
Top scorer: Stabile (Argentina) 8 goals.
Final (30.7.30): **Uruguay 4** (Dorado 12, Cea 55, Iriarte 64, Castro 89), **Argentina 2** (Peucelle 29, Stabile 35). **Att**: 90,000.
Uruguay: Ballesteros; Nasazzi (Capt.), Mascheroni, Andrade, Fernandez, Gestido, Dorado, Scarone, Castro, Cea, Iriarte.
Argentina: Botasso; Della Torre, Paternoster, Evaristo (J.), Monti, Suarez, Peucelle, Varallo, Stabile, Ferreira (Capt.), Evaristo (M.).
Referee: Langenus (Belgium). **Half-time**: 1-2.

1934 IN ITALY

WINNERS: Italy. RUNNERS-UP: Czechoslovakia. THIRD: Germany. FOURTH: Austria.
Other countries in finals: Argentina, Austria, Belgium, Brazil, Egypt, France, Holland, Hungary, Romania, Spain, Sweden, Switzerland, U.S.A. **Total entries**: 29 (16 qualifiers).
Venues: Bologna, Florence, Genoa, Milan, Naples, Rome, Trieste, Turin.
Top scorers: Conen (Germany), Nejedly (Czechoslovakia), Schiavio (Italy), each 4 goals.
Final (Rome, 10.6.34): **Italy 2** (Orsi 82, Schiavio 97), **Czechoslovakia 1** (Puc 70), **after extra time. Att**: 50,000.
Italy: Combi (Capt.); Monzeglio, Allemandi, Ferraris, Monti, Bertolini, Guaita, Meazza, Schiavio, Ferrari, Orsi.
Czechoslovakia: Planicka (Capt.); Zenisek, Ctyroky, Kostalek, Cambal, Krcil, Junek, Svoboda, Sobotka, Nejedly, Puc.
Referee: Eklind (Sweden). **Half-time**: 0-0. **90 mins**: 1-1.

1938 IN FRANCE

WINNERS: Italy. RUNNERS-UP: Hungary. THIRD: Brazil. FOURTH: Sweden.
Other countries in finals: Belgium, Cuba, Czechoslovakia, Dutch East Indies, France, Germany, Holland, Norway, Poland, Rumania, Sweden, Switzerland. **Total entries**: 25 (15 qualifiers).
Venues: Antibes, Bordeaux, Le Havre, Lille, Marseilles, Paris, Reims, Strasbourg, Toulouse.
Top scorer: Leonidas (Brazil) 8 goals.
Final (Paris, 19.6.38): **Italy 4** (Colaussi 6, 36, Piola 15, 81), **Hungary 2** (Titkos 7, Sarosi 65). **Att**: 45,000.
Italy: Olivieri; Foni, Rava, Serantoni, Andreolo, Locatelli, Biavati, Meazza (Capt.), Piola, Ferrari, Colaussi.
Hungary: Szabo; Polgar, Biro, Szalay, Szucs, Lazar, Sas, Vincze, Sarosi (Capt.), Szengeller, Titkos.
Referee: Capdeville (France). **Half-time**: 3-1.

1950 IN BRAZIL

WINNERS: Uruguay. RUNNERS-UP: Brazil. THIRD: Sweden. FOURTH: Spain.
Other countries in finals: Bolivia, Chile, England, Italy, Mexico, Paraguay, Spain, Switzerland, U.S.A., Yugoslavia. **Total entries**: 29 (13 qualifiers).
Venues: Belo Horizonte, Curitiba, Porto Alegre, Recife, Rio de Janeiro, Sao Paulo.
Top scorer: Ademir (Brazil) 9 goals.
Deciding Match (Rio de Janeiro, 16.7.50): **Uruguay 2** (Schiaffino 64, Ghiggia 79), **Brazil 1** (Friaca 47). **Att**: 199,850.

(For the only time, the World Cup was decided on a final pool system, in which the winners of the four qualifying groups met in a six-match series. So, unlike previous and subsequent tournaments, there was no official Final as such, but Uruguay v Brazil was the deciding final match in the final pool).
Uruguay: Maspoli; Gonzales, Tejera, Gambetta, Varela (Capt.), Andrade, Ghiggia, Perez, Miguez, Schiaffino, Moran.
Brazil: Barbosa; Augusto (Capt.), Juvenal, Bauer, Danilo, Bigode, Friaca, Zizinho, Ademir, Jair, Chico.
Referee: Reader (England). **Half-time**: 0-0.

1954 IN SWITZERLAND

WINNERS: West Germany. RUNNERS-UP: Hungary. THIRD: Austria. FOURTH: Uruguay.
Other countries in finals: Belgium, Brazil, Czechoslovakia, England, France, Italy, Korea, Mexico, Scotland, Switzerland, Turkey, Uruguay, Yugoslavia. **Total entries**: 35 (16 qualifiers).
Venues: Basle, Berne, Geneva, Lausanne, Lugano, Zurich.
Top scorer: Kocsis (Hungary) 11 goals.
Final (Berne, 4.7.54): **West Germany 3** (Morlock 12, Rahn 17, 84), **Hungary 2** (Puskas 4, Czibor 9). **Att**: 60,000.
West Germany: Turek; Posipal, Kohlmeyer, Eckel, Liebrich, Mai, Rahn, Morlock, Walter (O.), Walter (F.) (Capt.), Schaefer.
Hungary: Grosics; Buzansky, Lantos, Bozsik, Lorant, Zakarias, Czibor, Kocsis, Hidegkuti, Puskas (Capt.), Toth (J.).
Referee: Ling (England). **Half-time**: 2-2.

1958 IN SWEDEN

WINNERS: Brazil. RUNNERS-UP: Sweden. THIRD: France. FOURTH: West Germany.
Other countries in finals: Argentina, Austria, Czechoslovakia, England, Hungary, Mexico, Northern Ireland, Paraguay, Scotland, Soviet Union, Wales, West Germany, Yugoslavia. **Total entries**: 47 (16 qualifiers).
Venues: Boras, Eskilstuna, Gothenburg, Halmstad, Helsingborg, Malmo, Norrkoping, Orebro, Sandviken, Stockholm, Vasteras.
Top scorer: Fontaine (France) 13 goals.
Final (Stockholm, 29.6.58): **Brazil 5** (Vava 10, 32, Pele 55, 88, Zagalo 76), **Sweden 2** (Liedholm 4, Simonsson 83). **Att**: 49,737.
Brazil: Gilmar; Santos (D.), Santos (N.), Zito, Bellini (Capt.), Orlando, Garrincha, Didi, Vava, Pele, Zagalo.
Sweden: Svensson; Bergmark, Axbom, Boerjesson, Gustavsson, Parling, Hamrin, Gren, Simonsson, Liedholm (Capt.), Skoglund.
Referee: Guigue (France). **Half-time**: 2-1.

1962 IN CHILE

WINNERS: Brazil. RUNNERS-UP: Czechoslovakia. THIRD: Chile. FOURTH: Yugoslavia.
Other countries in finals: Argentina, Bulgaria, Colombia, England, Hungary, Italy, Mexico, Soviet Union, Spain, Switzerland, Uruguay, West Germany, Yugoslavia. **Total entries**: 53 (16 qualifiers).
Venues: Arica, Rancagua, Santiago, Vina del Mar.
Top scorer: Jerkovic (Yugoslavia), 5 goals.
Final (Santiago, 17.6.62): **Brazil 3** (Amarildo 17, Zito 69, Vava 77), **Czechoslovakia 1** (Masopust 16). **Att**: 68,679.
Brazil: Gilmar; Santos (D.), Mauro (Capt.), Zozimo, Santos (N.), Zito, Didi, Garrincha, Vava, Amarildo, Zagalo.
Czechoslovakia: Schroiff; Tichy, Novak, Pluskal, Popluhar, Masopust (Capt.), Pospichal, Scherer, Kvasnak, Kadraba, Jelinek.
Referee: Latychev (Soviet Union). **Half-time**: 1-1.

1966 IN ENGLAND

WINNERS: England. RUNNERS-UP: West Germany. THIRD: Portugal. FOURTH: USSR.
Other countries in finals: Argentina, Brazil, Bulgaria, Chile, France, Hungary, Italy, Mexico, North Korea, Soviet Union, Spain, Switzerland, Uruguay. **Total entries**: 53 (16 qualifiers).
Venues: Birmingham (Villa Park), Liverpool (Goodison Park), London (Wembley and White City), Manchester (Old Trafford), Middlesbrough, Sheffield (Hillsborough), Sunderland.
Top scorer: Eusebio (Portugal) 9 goals.
Final (Wembley, 30.7.66): **England 4** (Hurst 19, 100, 120, Peters 78), **West Germany 2** (Haller 13, Weber 89), **after extra time. Att:** 93,802.
England: Banks; Cohen, Wilson, Stiles, Charlton (J.), Moore (Capt.), Ball, Hurst, Hunt, Charlton (R.), Peters.
West Germany: Tilkowski; Hottges, Schnellinger, Beckenbauer, Schulz, Weber, Haller, Held, Seeler (Capt.), Overath, Emmerich.
Referee: Dienst (Switzerland). **Half-time**: 1-1. **90 mins**: 2-2.

1970 IN MEXICO

WINNERS: Brazil. RUNNERS-UP: Italy. THIRD: West Germany. FOURTH: Uruguay.
Other countries in finals: Belgium, Bulgaria, Czechoslovakia, El Salvador, England, Israel, Mexico, Morocco, Peru, Romania, Soviet Union, Sweden, Uruguay. **Total entries**: 68 (16 qualifiers).
Venues: Guadalajara, Leon, Mexico City, Puebla, Toluca.
Top scorer: Muller (West Germany) 10 goals.
Final (Mexico City, 21.6.70): **Brazil 4** (Pele 18, Gerson 66, Jairzinho 71, Carlos Alberto 87), **Italy 1** (Boninsegna 38). **Att**: 107,412.
Brazil: Felix; Carlos Alberto (Capt.), Brito, Piazza, Everaldo, Clodoaldo, Gerson, Jairzinho, Tostao, Pele, Rivelino.
Italy: Albertosi; Burgnich, Facchetti (Capt.), Cera, Rosato, Bertini (Juliano 72), Domenghini, De Sisti, Mazzola, Boninsegna (Rivera 84), Riva.
Referee: Glockner (East Germany). **Half-time**: 1-1.

1974 IN WEST GERMANY

WINNERS: West Germany. RUNNERS-UP: Holland. THIRD: Poland. FOURTH: Brazil.
Other countries in finals: Argentina, Australia, Brazil, Bulgaria, Chile, East Germany, Haiti, Italy, Scotland, Sweden, Uruguay, Yugoslavia, Zaire. **Total entries**: 98 (16 qualifiers).
Venues: Berlin, Dortmund, Dusseldorf, Frankfurt, Gelsenkirchen, Hamburg, Hanover, Munich, Stuttgart.
Top scorer: Lato (Poland) 7 goals
Final (Munich, 7.7.74): **West Germany 2** (Breitner 25 pen., Muller 43), **Holland 1** (Neeskens 2 pen.). **Att**: 77,833.
West Germany: Maier; Vogts, Schwarzenbeck, Beckenbauer (Capt.), Breitner, Bonhof, Hoeness, Overath, Grabowski, Muller, Holzenbein.
Holland: Jongbloed; Suurbier, Rijsbergen (De Jong 69), Haan, Krol, Jansen, Van Hanegem, Neeskens, Rep, Cruyff (Capt.), Rensenbrink (Van der Kerkhof (R.) 46).
Referee: Taylor (England). **Half-time**: 2-1.

1978 IN ARGENTINA

WINNERS: Argentina. RUNNERS-UP: Holland. THIRD: Brazil. FOURTH: Italy.
Other countries in finals: Austria, France, Hungary, Iran, Italy, Mexico, Peru, Poland, Scotland, Spain, Sweden, Tunisia, West Germany. **Total entries**: 102 (16 qualifiers).
Venues: Buenos Aires, Cordoba, Mar del Plata, Mendoza, Rosario.
Top scorer: Kempes (Argentina) 6 goals.

Final (Buenos Aires, 25.6.78): **Argentina 3** (Kempes 38, 104, Bertoni 115), **Holland 1** (Nanninga 82), **after extra time. Att**: 77,000.
Argentina: Fillol; Passarella (Capt.), Olguin, Galvan, Tarantini, Ardiles (Larrosa 66), Gallego, Ortiz (Houseman 74), Bertoni, Luque, Kempes.
Holland: Jongbloed; Krol (Capt.), Poortvliet, Brandts, Jansen (Suurbier 73), Haan, Neeskens, Van der Kerkhof (W.), Rep (Nanninga 58), Van der Kerkhof (R.), Rensenbrink.
Referee: Gonella (Italy). **Half-time**: 1-0. **90 mins**: 1-1.

1982 IN SPAIN

WINNERS: Italy. RUNNERS-UP: West Germany. THIRD: Poland. FOURTH: France.
Other countries in finals: Algeria, Argentina, Austria, Belgium, Brazil, Cameroon, Chile, Czechoslovakia, El Salvador, England, France, Honduras, Hungary, Kuwait, New Zealand, Northern Ireland, Peru, Scotland, Soviet Union, Spain, Yugoslavia. **Total entries**: 109 (24 qualifiers).
Venues: Alicante, Barcelona, Bilbao, Coruna, Elche, Gijon, Madrid, Malaga, Oviedo, Seville, Valencia, Valladolid, Vigo, Zaragoza.
Top scorer: Rossi (Italy) 6 goals.
Final (Madrid, 11.7.82): **Italy 3** (Rossi 57, Tardelli 69, Altobelli 81), **West Germany 1** (Breitner 84). **Att**: 90,089.
Italy: Zoff (Capt.); Bergomi, Scirea, Collovati, Cabrini, Oriali, Gentile, Tardelli, Conti, Rossi, Graziani (Altobelli 18 – Causio 88).
West Germany: Schumacher; Kaltz, Stielike, Forster (K-H.), Forster (B.), Dremmler (Hrubesch 63), Breitner, Briegel, Rummenigge (Capt.) (Muller 70), Fischer, Littbarski.
Referee: Coelho (Brazil). **Half-time**: 0-0.

1986 IN MEXICO

WINNERS: Argentina. RUNNERS-UP: West Germany. THIRD: France. FOURTH: Belgium.
Other countries in finals: Algeria, Belgium, Brazil, Bulgaria, Canada, Denmark, England, Hungary, Iraq, Italy, Mexico, Morocco, Northern Ireland, Paraguay, Poland, Portugal, Scotland, South Korea, Soviet Union, Spain, Uruguay. **Total entries**: 118 (24 qualifiers).
Venues: Guadalajara, Irapuato, Leon, Mexico City, Monterrey, Nezahualcoyotl, Puebla, Queretaro, Toluca.
Top scorer: Lineker (England) 6 goals.
Final (Mexico City, 29.6.86): **Argentina 3** (Brown 23, Valdano 56, Burruchaga 85), **West Germany 2** (Rummenigge 74, Voller 82). **Att**: 115,026.
Argentina: Pumpido; Cuciuffo, Brown, Ruggeri, Olarticoechea, Batista, Giusti, Maradona (Capt.), Burruchaga (Trobbiani 89), Enrique, Valdano.
West Germany: Schumacher; Berthold, K-H.Forster, Jakobs, Brehme, Briegel, Eder, Matthaus, Magath (Hoeness 62), Allofs (Voller 45), Rummenigge (Capt.).
Referee: Filho (Brazil). **Half-time**: 1-0.

1990 IN ITALY

WINNERS: West Germany. RUNNERS-UP: Argentina. THIRD: Italy. FOURTH: England.
Other countries in finals: Austria, Belgium, Brazil, Cameroon, Colombia, Costa Rica, Czechoslovakia, Egypt, England, Holland, Rep. of Ireland, Romania, Scotland, Spain, South Korea, Soviet Union, Sweden, United Arab Emirates, U.S.A., Uruguay, Yugoslavia. **Total entries**: 103 (24 qualifiers).
Venues: Bari, Bologna, Cagliari, Florence, Genoa, Milan, Naples, Palermo, Rome, Turin, Udine, Verona.
Top scorer: Schillaci (Italy) 6 goals.
Final (Rome, 8.7.90): **Argentina 0, West Germany 1** (Brehme 85 pen.). **Att**: 73,603.
Argentina: Goycochea; Ruggeri (Monzon 45), Simon, Serrizuela, Lorenzo, Basualdo, Troglio, Burruchaga (Calderon 53), Sensini, Maradona (Capt.), Dezotti. **Sent-off**: Monzon (65), Dezotti (86) – first players ever to be sent off in World Cup Final.

West Germany: Illgner; Berthold (Reuter 75), Buchwald, Augenthaler, Kohler, Brehme, Matthaus (Capt.), Littbarski, Hassler, Klinsmann, Voller.
Referee: Codesal (Mexico). **Half-time**: 0-0.

1994 IN U.S.A.

WINNERS: Brazil. RUNNERS-UP: Italy. THIRD: Sweden. FOURTH: Bulgaria.
Other countries in finals: Argentina, Belgium, Bolivia, Bulgaria, Cameroon, Colombia, Germany, Greece, Holland, Mexico, Morocco, Nigeria, Norway, Rep. of Ireland, Romania, Russia, Saudi Arabia, South Korea, Spain, Switzerland, U.S.A. **Total entries**: 144 (24 qualifiers).
Venues: Boston, Chicago, Dallas, Detroit, Los Angeles, New York City, Orlando, San Francisco, Washington.
Top scorers: Salenko (Russia), Stoichkov (Bulgaria), each 6 goals.
Final (Los Angeles, 17.7.94): **Brazil 0, Italy 0**, after extra time; **Brazil** won 3-2 on pens. **Att**: 94,194.
Brazil: Taffarel; Jorginho (Cafu 21), Aldair, Marcio Santos, Branco, Mazinho, Mauro Silva, Dunga (Capt.), Zinho (Viola 105), Romario, Bebeto.
Italy: Pagliuca; Mussi (Apolloni 35), Baresi (Capt.), Maldini, Benarrivo, Berti, Albertini, D. Baggio (Evani 95), Donadoni, R. Baggio, Massaro.
Referee: Puhl (Hungary).
Shoot-out: Baresi over, Marco Santos saved, Albertini 1-0, Romario 1-1, Evani 2-1, Branco 2-2, Massaro saved, Dunga 2-3, R Baggio over.

1998 IN FRANCE

WINNERS: France. RUNNERS-UP: Brazil. THIRD: Croatia. FOURTH: Holland.
Other countries in finals: Argentina, Austria, Belgium, Bulgaria, Cameroon, Chile, Colombia, Denmark, England, Germany, Holland, Iran, Italy, Jamaica, Japan, Mexico, Morocco, Nigeria, Norway, Paraguay, Romania, Saudi Arabia, Scotland, South Africa, South Korea, Spain, Tunisia, U.S.A., Yugoslavia. **Total entries**: 172 (32 qualifiers).
Venues: Bordeaux, Lens, Lyon, Marseille, Montpellier, Nantes, Paris (St Denis, Parc des Princes), Saint-Etienne, Toulouse.
Top scorer: Davor Suker (Croatia) 6 goals.
Final (Paris St Denis, 12.7.98): **Brazil 0, France 3** (Zidane 27, 45, Petit 90). **Att**: 75,000.
Brazil: Traffarel; Cafu, Junior Baiano, Aldair, Roberto Carlos; Dunga (Capt.), Leonardo (Denilson 46), Cesar Sampaio (Edmundo 74), Rivaldo; Bebeto, Ronaldo.
France: Barthez; Thuram, Leboeuf, Desailly, Lizarazu; Karembeu (Boghossian 56), Deschamps (Capt.), Petit, Zidane, Djorkaeff (Viera 75); Guivarc'h (Dugarry 66). **Sent-off**: Desailly (68).
Referee: S Belqola (Morocco). **Half-time**: 0-2.

2002 IN JAPAN/SOUTH KOREA

WINNERS: Brazil. RUNNERS-UP: Germany. THIRD: Turkey. FOURTH: South Korea.
Other countries in finals: Argentina, Belgium, Cameroon, China, Costa Rica, Croatia, Denmark, Ecuador, England, France, Italy, Japan, Mexico, Nigeria, Paraguay, Poland, Portugal, Republic of Ireland, Russia, Saudi Arabia, Senegal, Slovenia, South Africa, Spain, Sweden, Tunisia, United States, Uruguay.
Venues: Japan – Ibaraki, Kobe, Miyagi, Niigata, Oita, Osaka, Saitama, Sapporo, Shizuoka, Yokohama. **South Korea** – Daegu, Daejeon, Gwangju, Incheon, Jeonju, Busan, Seogwipo, Seoul, Suwon. Ulsan.
Top scorer: Ronaldo (Brazil) 8 goals.
Final (Yokohama, 30.6.02): **Germany** 0, **Brazil** 2 (Ronaldo 67, 79). **Att:** 69,029.
Germany: Kahn (Capt.), Linke, Ramelow, Metzelder, Frings, Jeremies (Asamoah 77), Hamann, Schneider, Bode (Zeige 84), Klose (Bierhoff 74), Neuville.
Brazil: Marcos, Lucio, Edmilson, Roque Junior, Cafu (Capt.) Kleberson, Gilberto Silva, Roberto Carlos, Ronaldinho (Juninho 85), Rivaldo, Ronaldo (Denilson 90).
Referee: Collina (Italy). **Half-time:** 0-0.

BRITISH AND IRISH INTERNATIONALS 2002-03

(* Denotes new cap)

EUROPEAN CHAMPIONSHIP 2004 – QUALIFYING

FAROE ISLANDS 2, SCOTLAND 2

Toftir, (4,000), Saturday, September 7, 2002

Faroe Islands (4-4-2): Knudsen, Thorsteinsson, Johannesen, J. Jacobsen, Hansen, Borg, Johnsson, Benjaminsen, Ellttor (Lakjunl 89), C. Jacobsen (R. Jacobsen 75), Petersen (Flotum 78). **Scorers:** Petersen (6, 12). **Booked:** Borg, Knudsen.

Scotland (4-4-2): Douglas (Celtic), Ross (Rangers) (Alexander, Preston N.E., 75), Weir (Everton), Dailly (West Ham Utd.), Crainey (Celtic), Dickov (Leicester City) (Crawford, Dunfermline Athletic, 46), Ferguson (Rangers), Lambert (Celtic), Johnston (Middlesbrough), Kyle (Sunderland), Dobie (W.B.A.) (Thompson, Dundee Utd., 83). **Scorers:** Lambert (61), Ferguson (83). **Booked:** Ross, Weir, Thompson.

Referee: J. Granat (Poland). **Half-time:** 2-0.

FINLAND 0, WALES 2

Helsinki, (35,833), Saturday, September 7, 2002

Finland (4-2-3-1): Niemi, Nylund (Johannson 69), Tihinen, Hyypia, Saarinen (Kopteff 78), Riihilahti, Tainio, Nurmela (Kottila 86), Litmanen, Kolkka, Kuqi. **Booked:** Tihinen, Hyypia, Tainio.

Wales (4-3-2-1): Jones (Southampton), Delaney (Aston Villa), Melville (Fulham), Gabbidon (Cardiff City), Speed (Newcastle Utd.), Johnson (W.B.A.) (Bellamy, Newcastle Utd., 76), Pembridge (Everton), Savage (Birmingham City), Davies (Tottenham), Giggs (Manchester Utd.), Hartson (Celtic). **Scorers:** Hartson (30), Davies (72). **Booked:** Pembridge, Johnson.

Referee: K. Plautz (Austria). **Half-time:** 0-1.

RUSSIA 4, REPUBLIC OF IRELAND 2

Moscow, (22,000), Saturday, September 7, 2002

Russia (3-3-2-2): Ovchinnikov, Ignashevich, Onopko, Nizhegorodov, Loskov, Aldonin, Yanovsky, Karyaka, Gusev (Solomatin 28), Beschastnykh (Kerzhakov 46), Semak (Khokhlov 75). **Scorers:** Karyaka (21), Beschastnykh (26), Kerzhakov 69), Bobb (85 og). **Booked:** Ovchinnikov.

Rep. of Ireland (4-4-2): Given (Newcastle Utd.), Finnan (Fulham), Breen (West Ham Utd.), Cunningham (Birmingham City), Harte (Leeds Utd.), McAteer (Sunderland) (Doherty, Tottenham, 65), Kinsella (Aston Villa), Holland (Ipswich Town), Kilbane (Sunderland) (Babb, Sunderland, 85), Duff (Blackburn Rov.) (Morrison, Birmingham City, 18), Keane (Tottenham). **Scorers:** Doherty (68), Morrison (74).

Referee: C. Colombo (France). **Half-time:** 2-0.

SLOVAKIA 1, ENGLAND 2

Bratislava, (30,000), Saturday, October 12, 2002

Slovakia (3-5-2): Konig, Zeman, Dzurik, Hlinka, Pinte (Kozlej 88), Janocko (Mintal 88), Karhan, Petras, Leitner, Vittek (Reiter 80), Nemeth. **Scorer:** Nemeth (24). **Booked:** Zeman, Leitner, Vittek.

England (4-4-2): Seaman (Arsenal), G. Neville (Manchester Utd.), Woodgate (Leeds Utd.), Southgate (Middlesbrough), Cole (Arsenal), Beckham (Manchester Utd.), Gerrard (Liverpool) (Dyer, Newcastle Utd., 76), Butt (Manchester Utd.), Scholes (Manchester Utd.), Owen (Liverpool) (Hargreaves, Bayern Munich, 86), Heskey (Liverpool) (Smith, Leeds Utd., 90). **Scorers:** Beckham (64), Owen (82). **Booked:** Gerrard, Scholes.

Referee: D. Messina (Italy). **Half-time:** 1-0.

ICELAND 0, SCOTLAND 2

Reykjavik, (6,611), Saturday, October 12, 2002

Iceland (4-4-2): Arason, Thorsteinsson, L. Sigurdsson, Hreidarsson, Vidarsson (Baldvinsson 68), Gudnason (B. Gudjohnsen 77), Ingimarsson, Kristinsson, Gunnarsson, H. Sigurdsson (Helguson 46), E. Gudjohnsen. **Booked:** Kristinsson.

Scotland (3-5-2): Douglas (Celtic), Dailly (West Ham Utd.), Pressley (Hearts), Wilkie (Dundee), Ross (Rangers), Lambert (Celtic), Ferguson (Rangers), McNamara (Celtic) (Davidson, Leicester City, 35), Naysmith (Everton) (*Anderson, Aberdeen, 90), Crawford (Dunfermline Athletic) (Severin, Hearts, 90), Thompson (Dundee Utd.). **Scorers:** Dailly (7), Naysmith (62). **Booked:** Ross, Thompson, Davidson.

Referee: A. Sars (France). **Half-time:** 0-1.

SPAIN 3, NORTHERN IRELAND 0

Albacete, (16,000), Saturday, October 12, 2002

Spain (4-4-1-1): Iker Casillas, Michel Salgado, Puyol, Helguera, Bravo, Xavi, Baraja, Vicente, Joaquin (Mendieta 75), Raul (Morientes 66), Guti (Capi 88). **Scorers:** Baraja (19,89), Guti (59). **Booked:** Helguera.

Northern Ireland (4-5-1): Taylor (Fulham), A. Hughes (Newcastle Utd.), Taggart (Leicester City) (McCann, West Ham Utd., 70), Murdock (Preston N.E.), McCartney (Sunderland), Johnson (Birmingham City), Mulryne (Norwich City), Lomas (West Ham Utd.), Horlock (Manchester City) (M. Hughes, Wimbledon, 65), McVeigh (Norwich City) (Healy, Preston N.E., 65), Gillespie (Blackburn Rov.). **Booked:** Gillespie.

Referee: I. Dobrinov (Bulgaria). **Half-time:** 1-0.

ENGLAND 2, MACEDONIA 2

St Mary's Stadium, (32,095), Wednesday, October 16, 2002

England (4-4-2): Seaman (Arsenal), G. Neville (Manchester), Campbell (Arsenal), Woodgate (Leeds Utd.), Cole (Arsenal), Beckham (Manchester Utd.), Gerrard (Liverpool) (Butt, Manchester Utd., 55), Scholes (Manchester Utd.), Bridge (Southampton) (Vassell, Aston Villa, 58), Owen (Liverpool), Smith (Leeds Utd.). **Scorers:** Beckham (14), Gerrard (36). **Booked:** Beckham, Smith. **Sent-off:** Smith.

Macedonia (4-5-1): Milosevski. Popov, Sedlovski, Vasoski, Petrov, Grozdanovski, Trajanov (Stojanoski 90), Sumolikoski, Mitrevski, Sakiri, Tolevski (Pandev 62). **Scorers:** Sakiri (11), Trajanov (25). **Booked:** Vasoski.

Referee: A. Ibanez (Spain). **Half-time:** 2-2.

WALES 2, ITALY 1

Millennium Stadium, (70,000), Wednesday, October 16, 2002

Wales (4-4-2): Jones (Southampton), Delaney (Aston Villa), Melville (Fulham), Gabbidon (Cardiff City), Speed (Newcastle Utd.), Davies (Tottenham), Pembridge (Everton), Savage (Birmingham City), Giggs (Manchester Utd.), Bellamy (Newcastle Utd.) (Blake, Wolves, 90), Hartson (Celtic). **Scorers:** Davies (12), Bellamy (71). **Booked:** Savage, Bellamy.

Italy (4-3-1-2): Buffon, Panucci, Nesta, Cannavaro, Zauri, Tomassi, Di Biagio (Gattuso 64) (Marazzina 85), Ambrosini, Pirlo, Montella (Maccarone 70), Del Piero.

Scorer: Del Piero (32). **Booked:** Zauri, Di Biagio.

Referee: G. Veissiere (France). **Half-time:** 1-1.

NORTHERN IRELAND 0, UKRAINE 0

Windsor Park, (9,288), Wednesday, October 16, 2002

Northern Ireland (4-4-2): Taylor (Fulham), Lomas (West Ham Utd.), McCartney (Sunderland), A. Hughes (Newcastle Utd.), Horlock (Manchester City), Johnson (Birmingham City) (Murdock, Preston N.E., 83), Gillespie (Blackburn Rov.), Mulryne (Norwich City), M. Hughes (Wimbledon), McVeigh (Norwich City) (Kirk, Hearts, 65), Healy (Preston N.E.).

Ukraine (4-4-2): Reva, Luzhny, Starostyak, Tymoschuk, Radchenko, Kormiltsev, Husin, Kalinichenko (Rebrov 53), Zubov, Vorobei (Melashchenko 76), Voronin. **Booked:** Husin.

Referee: C. Bolognino (Italy). **Half-time:** 0-0.

REPUBLIC OF IRELAND 1, SWITZERLAND 2

Lansdowne Road, (40,000), Wednesday, October 16, 2002

Rep. of Ireland (4-4-2): Given (Newcastle Utd.), Kelly (Leeds Utd.), Breen (West Ham Utd.), Cunningham (Birmingham City), Harte (Leeds Utd.) (Doherty, Tottenham, 88), Kinsella (Aston Villa), Holland (Ipswich Town), Healy (Celtic), Kilbane (Sunderland) (Morrison, Birmingham City, 62), Keane (Tottenham), Duff (Blackburn Rov.) (Butler, Sunderland, 82). **Scorer:** Magnin (77 og). **Booked:** Cunningham.

Switzerland (4-3-1-2): Stiel, Haas, Murat Yakin, Muller, Magnin, Cabanas, Wicky (Cantaluppi 85), Vogel, Hakan Yakin (Celestini 85), Chapuisat, Frei (Thurre 71). **Scorers:** Hakan Yakin (45), Celestini (87). **Booked:** Stiel.

Referee: R.Pedersen (Norway). **Half-time:** 0-1.

AZERBAIJAN 0, WALES 2

Baku, (15,000), Wednesday, November 20, 2002

Azerbaijan (4-2-3-1): Hassanzade, Kerimov (Mammadov 46), Akhmedov (Asadov 74), Yadullayev, Niftaliyev, Imamaliyev, Sadygov, Vasilyev, M. Gurbanov (Ismaylov 61), Aliyev, G.Gurbanov. **Booked:** Sadygov, Ismaylov.

Wales (4-3-2-1): Jones (Southampton), Delaney (Aston Villa) (Weston, Cardiff City, 71), Meville (Fulham), Page (Sheffield Utd.), Barnard (Grimsby Town), Davies (Tottenham), Speed (Newcastle Utd.), Robinson (Portsmouth) (Trollope, Northampton Town, 90), Earnshaw (Cardiff City) (Roberts, Wigan Athletic, 89), Giggs (Manchester Utd.), Hartson (Celtic). **Scorers:** Speed (9), Hartson (68). **Booked:** Page, Barnard.

Referee: L. Huyghe (Belgium). **Half-time:** 0-1.

LIECHTENSTEIN 0, ENGLAND 2

Vaduz, (3,548), Saturday, March 29, 2003

Liechtenstein (4-3-2-1): Jehle, Telser, Hasler, Michael Stocklasa, D'Elia, Martin Stocklasa, Zech (Burgmeier 62), Gerster, Buchel (M. Beck 86), T. Beck, Frick (Nigg 82). **Booked:** Zech.

England (4-4-2): James (West Ham Utd.), G. Neville (Manchester Utd.), Ferdinand (Manchester Utd.), Southgate (Middlesbrough), Bridge (Southampton), Beckham (Manchester Utd.) (Murphy, Liverpool, 70), Gerrard (Liverpool) (Butt, Manchester Utd., 65), Scholes (Manchester Utd.), Dyer (Newcastle Utd.), Owen (Liverpool), Heskey (Liverpool) (Rooney, Everton, 80). **Scorers:** Owen (28), Beckham (53).

Referee: G. Kaspaferis (Greece). **Half-time:** 0-1.

SCOTLAND 2, ICELAND 1

Hampden Park, (37,548), Saturday, March 29, 2003

Scotland (3-4-1-2): Douglas (Celtic), Dailly (West Ham Utd.), Pressley (Hearts), Wilkie (Dundee), Alexander (Preston N.E.), Lambert (Celtic), Ferguson (Rangers), Naysmith (Everton), Hutchison (West Ham Utd.) (Devlin, Birmingham City, 65), Miller (Wolves) (McNamara, Celtic, 81), Crawford (Dunfermline Athletic). **Scorers:** Miller (12), Wilkie (70). **Booked:** Pressley, Crawford, Lambert.

Iceland (3-5-2): Arason, L. Sigurdsson, Bergsson, Ingimarsson, Gunnarsson (Gudjohnson 73), Thorsteinsson, Gretarsson, Gudjonsson, Vidarsson (I. Sigurdsson 82), Kristinsson, Gudjohnsen (Gudmundsson 88). **Scorer:** Gudjohnsen (48). **Booked:** I. Sigurdsson.

Referee: R. Tremmink (Holland). **Half-time:** 1-0

WALES 4, AZERBAIJAN 0

Millennium Stadium, (72,500), Saturday, March 29, 2003

Wales (4-3-2-1): Jones (Southampton), Davies (Tottenham), Melville (Fulham), Page (Sheffield Utd.), Speed (Newcastle Utd.) (Trollope, Northampton Town, 46), Oster (Sunderland), Pembridge (Everton), Savage (Birmingham City) (Robinson, Portsmouth, 19), Bellamy (Newcastle Utd.) (*Edwards, Aston Villa, 71), Giggs (Manchester Utd.), Hartson (Celtic). **Scorers:** Bellamy (1), Speed (40), Hartson (44), Giggs (52).

Azerbaijan (4-4-1-1): Hassanzade, K. Guliyev, E. Guliyev (Yadullayev 46), Akhmedov, Imamaliyev, Musayev, R. Mammadov, Hajlyev (F. Mammadov 46), M. Gurbanov, Aliyev (Taglzada 74), G. Gurbanov.

Referee: P. Leuba (Switzerland). **Half-time:** 3-0.

ARMENIA 1, NORTHERN IRELAND 0

Yerevan, (10,321), Saturday, March 29, 2003

Armenia (3-5-1-1): Berezovskj, Vardanyan, Hovsepyan, Billblo, Sarkislan (Artur Mkrtchyan 90), Voskanyan, Dokhoyan, Melikyan, Artravad Karamyan (Agvan Mkrtchyen 89), Petrosyan (Mkhitaryan 90), Arman Karamyan. **Scorer:** Petrosyan (86). **Booked:** Melikyan, Hovsepyan.

Northern Ireland (4-4-2): Taylor (Fulham), Hughes (Newcastle Utd.), Craigan (Partick Thistle), Williams (Stoke City), McCann (Cheltenham Town), Gillespie (Blackburn Rov.), Lomas (West Ham Utd.), Johnson (Birmingham City), McVeigh (Norwich City), Healy (Norwich City), Quinn (Willem 11) (Elliott, Hull City, 71).

Referee: R. Bezk (Liechtenstein). **Half-time:** 0-0.

GEORGIA 1, REPUBLIC OF IRELAND 2

Tbilisi, (15,000), Saturday, March 29, 2003

Georgia (3-4-1-2): Lomala, Khizaneishvili, Shashlashvili, Amisulashvili, Tskitishvili, Nemsadze, Jamarauli, Koblashvili, Kinkladze (Didava 71), Lashvili, Ketsbaia (Demetradze 46). **Scorer:** Koblashvili (61). **Booked:** Khizaneishvili.

Rep. of Ireland (4-4-2): Given (Newcastle Utd.), Carr (Tottenham), Breen (West Ham Utd.), Cunningham (Birmingham City), O'Shea (Manchester Utd.), Carsley (Everton), Holland (Ipswich Town), Kinsella (Aston Villa), Kilbane (Sunderland), Doherty (Tottenham), Duff (Blackburn Rov.). **Scorers:** Duff (18), Doherty (84). **Booked:** Doherty.

Referee: K. Vassaros (Greece). **Half-time:** 0-1.

ENGLAND 2, TURKEY 0

Stadium of Light, (47,667), Wednesday, April 2, 2003

England (4-4-2): James (West Ham Utd.), G. Neville (Manchester Utd.), Ferdinand (Manchester Utd.), Campbell (Arsenal), Bridge (Southampton), Beckham (Manchester Utd.), Butt (Manchester Utd.), Scholes (Manchester Utd.), Gerrard (Liverpool), Rooney (Everton) (Dyer, Newcastle Utd., 89), Owen (Liverpool) (Vassell, Aston Villa, 58). **Scorers:** Vassell (76), Beckham (90 pen). **Booked:** Beckham.

Turkey (4-4-2): Rustu, Fatih (Hakan Sukur 79), Alpay, Bulent, Ergun, Okan (Umit Davala 59), Tugay, Basturk (Hasan Sas 71), Emre, Nihat, Ilhan. **Booked:** Okan, Fatih.

Referee: U. Meier (Switzerland). **Half-time:** 0-0.

LITHUANIA 1, SCOTLAND 0

Kaunus, (6,400), Wednesday, April 2, 2003

Lithuania (4-4-2): Stauce, Gleveckas, Zvirgzdasukas, Dedura, Barasa, Morinas, Petrenko (Maciulevicius 72), Semberas, Mikalajunas (Dziaukstas 89), Jankauaskas (Fomenko 65), Razanauskas. **Scorer:** Razanauskas (73 pen).

Scotland (3-5-2): Gallacher (Dundee Utd.), Dailly (West Ham Utd.), Pressley (Hearts), Wilkie (Dundee), Alexander (Preston N.E.), McNamara (Celtic) (Gemmill, Everton, 81), Lambert (Celtic), Hutchison (West Ham Utd.), Naysmith (Everton), Crawford (Dunfermline Athletic) (Devlin, Birmingham City, 57), Miller (Wolves).

Referee: F. Stuchlik (Austria). **Half-time:** 0-0.

NORTHERN IRELAND 0, GREECE 2

Windsor Park, (7,196), Wednesday, April 2, 2003

Northern Ireland (4-4-2): Taylor (Fulham), Hughes (Newcastle Utd.), Craigan (Partick Thistle), Williams (Stoke City), McCartney (Sunderland), Gillespie (Blackburn Rov.), Lomas (West Ham Utd.), Johnson (Birmingham City), McCann (Cheltenham Town) (McVeigh, Norwich City, 68), Quinn (Willem 11), Healy (Norwich City) (Kirk, Hearts, 68). **Booked:** Gillespie, Williams, Lomas. **Sent-off:** Quinn, Gillespie.

Greece (3-5-2): Nikopolidis, Dabizas, Krygiakos, Konstantinidis, Giannakopoulos, Zagorakis, Tsartas (Kafes 75), Karagounis, Venetidis (Fissas 71), Charisteas, Nikolaidis (Vrizas 41). **Scorer:** Charisteas (3, 56). **Booked:** Venetidis, Karagounis, Krygiakos.

Referee: G. Gilewski (Poland). **Half-time:** 0-1.

ALBANIA 0, REPUBLIC OF IRELAND 0

Tirana, (20,000), Wednesday, April 2, 2003

Albania (3-4-1-2): Strakosha, Beqiri, Cipi, Aliaj, Duro, Lala, Hasi, Murati (Bellaj 67), Skela (Bushi 86), Rakili (Myrtaj 69), Tare. **Booked:** Bushi.

Rep. of Ireland (4-4-2): Given (Newcastle Utd.), Carr (Tottenham), Breen (West Ham Utd.), Cunningham (Birmingham City), O'Shea (Manchester Utd.), Carsley (Everton), Holland (Ipswich Town), Kinsella (Aston Villa), Kilbane (Sunderland), Keane (Tottenham) (Doherty, Tottenham, 67), Duff (Blackburn Rov.).

Referee: S. Farina (Italy). **Half-time:** 0-0.

SCOTLAND 1, GERMANY 1

Hampden Park, (48,037), Saturday, June 7, 2003

Scotland (4-4-2): Douglas (Celtic), Ross (Rangers) (McNamara, Celtic, 74), Pressley (Hearts), Webster (Hearts), Naysmith (Everton), Devlin (Birmingham City) (Rae, Dundee 59), Cameron (Wolves), Dailly (West Ham Utd.), Lambert (Celtic), Miller (Wolves) (Thompson, Rangers, 89), Crawford (Dunfermline Athletic). **Scorer:** Miller (69). **Booked:** Devlin, Dailly, Pressley, Thompson.

Germany (3-5-2): Kahn, Freidrich, Ramelow, Worns, Frings, Schneider (Kehl 84), Jeremies, Ballack, Rau (Freier 56), Bobic, Klose (Neuville 74). **Scorer:** Bobic (23). **Booked:** Frings, Freier, Ballack.

Referee: D. Messina (Italy). **Half-time:** 0-1.

REPUBLIC OF IRELAND 2, ALBANIA 1

Lansdowne Road, (33,000), Saturday, June 7, 2003

Rep. of Ireland (4-3-1-2): Given (Newcastle Utd.), Carr (Tottenham), Breen (West Ham Utd.), Cunningham (Birmingham City), O'Shea (Manchester Utd.), Holland (Ipswich Town), Kinsella (Aston Villa) (Carsley, Everton, 55), Kilbane (Sunderland) (Reid, Millwall, 75), Duff (Blackburn Rov.), Connolly (Wimbledon) (Doherty, Tottenham, 65), Keane (Tottenham). **Scorers:** Keane (6), Aliaj (90 og). **Booked:** Carr, Kinsella.

Albania (3-1-4-2): Strakosha (Beqaj 75), Beqiri, Cipi, Aliaj, Hasi, Duro, Lala, Skela, Murati (Bellaj 57), Tare, Rakili (Myrtaj 85). **Scorer:** Skela (8). **Booked:** Lala, Beqiri, Cipi.

Referee: T. Mikulski (Poland). **Half-time:** 1-1.

ENGLAND 2, SLOVAKIA 1

Riverside Stadium, (35,000), Wednesday, June 11, 2003

England (4-1-3-2): James (West Ham Utd.), Mills (Leeds Utd.) (Hargreaves, Bayern Munich, 43), Southgate (Middlesbrough), Upson (Birmingham City), Cole (Arsenal), P. Neville (Manchester Utd.), Gerrard (Liverpool), Scholes (Manchester Utd.), Lampard (Chelsea), Rooney (Everton) (Vassell, Aston Villa, 58), Owen (Liverpool). **Scorer:** Owen (62 pen, 73).

Slovakia (4-4-2): Konig, Hanek, Zeman, Petras, Labant (Debnar 38), Janocko, Demo (Mintal 55), Zabavnik, Michalik, Vittek, Nemeth (Reiter 75). **Scorer:** Janocko (31). **Booked:** Hanek, Vittek, Debnar.

Referee: W. Stark (Germany). **Half-time:** 0-1.

NORTHERN IRELAND 0, SPAIN 0

Windsor Park, (11,365), Wednesday, June 11, 2003

Northern Ireland (4-5-1): Taylor (Fulham), Baird (Southampton), Hughes (Newcastle Utd.), McCartney (Sunderland), Kennedy (Wigan Athletic), Healy (Preston N.E.), Johnson (Birmingham City), Griffin (Dundee Utd.), Doherty (Bristol City) (Toner, Leyton Orient, 80), Jones (Crewe Alexandra) (McVeigh, Norwich City, 73), Smith (Glentoran) (Williams, Stoke City, 90). **Booked:** Johnson.

Spain (4-4-1-1): Iker Casillas, Puyol, Marchena, Helguera, Juanfran, Etxeberria (De Pedro 78), Baraja, Sergio (Joaquin 66), Vicente (Morientes 66), Valeron, Raul. **Booked:** De Pedro.

Referee: C. Larsen (Denmark). **Half-time:** 0-0.

REPUBLIC OF IRELAND 2, GEORGIA 0

Lansdowne Road, (36,000), Wednesday, June 11, 2003

Rep. of Ireland (4-4-2): Given (Newcastle Utd.), Carr (Tottenham), Breen (West Ham Utd.), Cunningham (Birmingham City), O'Shea (Manchester Utd.), Carsley (Everton), Holland (Ipswich Town), Healy (Celtic) (Kinsella, Aston Villa, 86), Kilbane (Sunderland), Keane (Tottenham), Doherty (Tottenham) (Lee, Rotherham Utd., 88). **Scorers:** Doherty (43), Keane (59).

Georgia (3-1-4-2): Lomaia, Z. Khizanishvili, O. Khizanishvili, Kaladze, Rekhviashvili, Burduli, Didava (Aleksidze 76), Asatiani, Amisulashvili, Demetradze (Daraselia 62), Arveladze. **Booked:** O. Khizanishvili.

Referee: E. Gonzalez (Spain). **Half-time:** 1-0.

FRIENDLY INTERNATIONALS

SCOTLAND 0, DENMARK 1

Hampden Park, (28,766), Wednesday, August 21, 2002

Scotland (3-5-2): Douglas (Celtic), Weir (Everton) (Severin, Hearts, 77), Dailly (West Ham Utd.), Ross (Rangers), Stockdale (Middlesbrough) (Alexander, Preston N.E., 71), McNaughton (Aberdeen) (Crainey, Celtic, 46), Lambert (Celtic) (*McInnes, W.B.A., 81), Ferguson (Rangers), Naysmith (Everton) (Johnston, Middlesbrough, 71), Kyle (Sunderland), Thompson (Dundee Utd.) (Dobie, W.B.A., 55).

Denmark (4-4-2): Sorensen, Bogelund (Michaelson 46), Laursen (Wieghorst 66), Henriksen (Lustu 83), N. Jensen, Rommedahl (Gronkjaer 46), Gravesen (C. Jensen 46), Poulsen, Lovenkrands (Silberbauer 77), Tomasson, Sand. **Scorer:** Sand (8).

Referee: L.Irvine (Northern Ireland). **Half-time:** 0-1.

CROATIA 1, WALES 1

Varazdin, (6,000), Wednesday, August 21, 2002

Croatia (4-4-2): Pletikosa, Zivkovic (Tomas 59), Tapalovic (Butina 46), Simunic (Babic 75), R. Kovac (Vranjes 59), N. Kovac (S. Maric 46), Saric, Vugrinec (Petric 46), Vlaovic (Leko 46), Rapaic (Bazina 59), T. Maric (M. Maric 46). **Scorer:** Petric (79).

Wales (4-4-2): Jones (Southampton), Delaney (Aston Villa), Gabbidon (Cardiff City), Melville (Fulham), Barnard (Grimsby Town) (Weston, Cardiff City, 59), Pembridge (Everton), Robinson (Portsmouth) (Evans, Bradford City, 70), Johnson (W.B.A.), Davies (Tottenham), Hartson (Celtic) (Taylor, Burnley, 59), Earnshaw (Cardiff City) (Trollope, Fulham, 79). **Scorer:** Davies (11). **Booked:** Hartson, Delaney.

Referee: L-M Frohlich (Germany). **Half-time:** 0-1.

NORTHERN IRELAND 0, CYPRUS 0

Windsor Park, (6,922), Wednesday, August 21, 2002

Northern Ireland (4-4-2): Taylor (Fulham), Griffin (Dundee Utd.) (Duff, Cheltenham Town, 46), Williams (Wimbledon), Murdock (Preston N.E.), McCartney (Sunderland), Gillespie (Blackburn Rov.) (Feeney, Bournemouth, 68), Johnson (Birmingham City), Horlock (Manchester City), Kennedy (Wigan Athletic), Healy (Preston N.E.), Quinn (Willem 11).

Cyprus (3-5-2): Panayiotou, Okkarides, Konnafis, Daskalakis (M. Nikalaou 46), Theodotou, Satsias, Eleftheriou, N. Nikolaou (Michail 43), Spyrou, Okkas, Yiasoumi (Agathokleous 60). **Booked:** Eleftheriou.

Referee: S. Jones (Wales). **Half-time:** 0-0.

FINLAND 0, REPUBLIC OF IRELAND 3

Helsinki, (12,225), Wednesday, August 21, 2002

Finland (4-4-1-1): Jaaskelainen, Pasanen, Tihinen, Hyypia (Kuivasto 46), Saarinen, Nurmela (Kopteff 69), Ilola (Riihilahti 59), Tainio (Hietanen 80), Kolkka (Kottila 78), Litmanen, Johansson (Kuqi 59).

Rep. of Ireland (4-4-2): Kiely (Charlton Athletic) (Given, Newcastle Utd., 75), Kelly (Leeds Utd.), Breen (West Ham Utd.), Cunningham (Birmingham City) (Doherty, (Tottenham, 46), Harte (Leeds Utd.) (*Barrett, Arsenal, 75), *Butler (Sunderland) (Kilbane, Sunderland, 46), Carsley (Everton) (Holland, Ipswich Town, 87), Kinsella (Charlton Athletic) (McPhail, Leeds Utd., 46), McAteer (Sunderland) (Healy, Celtic, 46), Duff (Blackburn Rov.) (Delap, Southampton, 46), Keane (Leeds Utd.) (*Goodwin (Stockport Co. Co, 83). **Scorers:** Keane (12), Healy (74), Barrett (83).

Referee: R.Pedersen (Norway). **Half-time:** 0-1.

ENGLAND 1, PORTUGAL 1

Villa Park, (40,058), Saturday, September 7, 2002

England (4-4-2): James (West Ham Utd.), Mills (Leeds Utd.) (Hargreaves, Bayern Munich, 46), Ferdinand (Manchester Utd.) (Woodgate, Leeds Utd., 46), Southgate (Middlesbrough), A. Cole (Arsenal) (Bridge, Southampton, 46), *Bowyer (Leeds Utd.) (Sinclair, West Ham Utd., 62), Gerrard (Liverpool) (*Dunn, Blackburn Rov., 46), Butt (Manchester Utd.) (Murphy, Liverpool, 62), Heskey (Liverpool), Smith (Leeds Utd.), Owen (Liverpool) (J. Cole, West Ham Utd., 62). **Scorer:** Smith (40).

Portugal (3-4-2-1): Vitor Baia (Ricardo 46), Fernando Meira (Jorge Silva 75), Fernando Couto (Joao Pinto 46), Beto (Paulo Ferreira 46), Sergio Conceicao (Capucho 46), Rui Costa (Costinha 46), Petit (Vidigal 64), Rui Jorge (Boa Morte 46), Figo (Viana 46), Simao (Nuno Valente 46), Pauleta (Nuno Gomes 46). **Scorer:** Costinha (79).

Referee: T. Ovrebo (Norway). **Half-time:** 1-0.

SCOTLAND 3, CANADA 1

Easter Road, (16,207), Tuesday, October 15, 2002

Scotland (3-5-2): *Gallacher (Dundee Utd.), Anderson (Aberdeen), Pressley (Hearts), Wilkie (Dundee) (*Murray, Hibernian, 75), Alexander (Preston N.E.), *Devlin (Birmingham City), Dailly (West Ham Utd.), Gemmill (Everton) (Severin, Hearts, 65), Ross (Rangers) (Davidson, Leicester City, 46), Thompson (Dundee Utd.) (McFadden, Motherwell, 81), Crawford (Dunfermline) (Kyle, Sunderland, 87). **Scorers:** Crawford (11, 73), Thompson (50).

Canada (3-5-2): Hirschfeld, Fenwick, McKenna, Hastings, Pozniak, Nsaliwa, Imhof, (Xausa 82), Stalteri, De Guzman, Radzinski, De Rosario. **Scorer:** De Rosario (9 pen). **Booked:** Fenwick.

Referee: L. Huyghe (Belgium). **Half-time:** 1-1.

PORTUGAL 2, SCOTLAND 0

Braga, (8,000), Wednesday, November 20, 2002

Portugal (3-4-1-2): Quim (Nelson 88), Fernando Couto, Fernando Meira, Rocha, Sergio Conceicao, Figo (Ferreira 46), Rui Costa (Mendes 58), Rui Jorge (Riberro 58), Tiago (Assis 84), Pauleta (Nuno Gomes 46), Sabrosa (Neca 77). **Scorer:** Pauleta (8, 17). **Booked:** Fernando Couto.

Scotland (3-5-2): Douglas (Celtic), Anderson (Aberdeen) (McInnes, W.B.A., 23), Pressley (Hearts), Wilkie (Dundee) (Severin, Hearts, 84), Alexander (Preston N.E.), Dailly (West Ham Utd.), Lambert (Celtic) (Williams, Nott'm. Forest, 68), Naysmith (Everton), Ross (Rangers) (Devlin, Birmingham City, 46), Crawford (Dunfermline Athletic), Dobie (W.B.A.) (Kyle (Sunderland, 77).

Referee: V. Angehelinei (Romania). **Half-time:** 2-0.

GREECE 0, REPUBLIC OF IRELAND 0

Athens, (5,500), Wednesday, November 20, 2002

Greece (4-4-2): Nikopolidis (Chiotis 46), Seitaridis (Patsatzoglou 46), Dabizas (Goumas 46), Kyrgiakos, Fyssas (Venetidis 46), Giannakopoulos (Georgiadis 46), Basinas (Zagorakis 60), Karagounis (Kafes 60), Tsartas (Amanatidis 46), Nikolaidis (Papadopoulos 46), Charisteas.

Rep. of Ireland (4-4-2): Given (Newcastle Utd.), Finnan (Fulham), Cunningham (Birmingham City), O'Shea (Manchester Utd.), Dunne (Manchester City), Healy (Celtic), Carsley (Everton), Holland (Ipswich Town), McPhail (Leeds Utd.), *Crowe (Bohemians) (Delap, Southampton, 85), Doherty (Tottenham). **Booked:** McPhail.

Referee: A. Trentalange (Italy). **Half-time:** 0-0.

ENGLAND 1, AUSTRALIA 3

Upton Park, (34,590), Wednesday, February 12, 2003

England (first half 4-4-2): James (West Ham Utd.), G. Neville (Manchester Utd.), Ferdinand (Manchester Utd.), Campbell (Arsenal), A. Cole (Arsenal), Beckham (Manchester Utd.), Lampard (Chelsea), Scholes (Manchester Utd.), Dyer (Newcastle Utd.), Owen (Liverpool), *Beattie (Southampton).

England (second half 4-3-3): *Robinson (Leeds Utd.), Mills (Leeds Utd.), Brown (Manchester Utd.), King (Tottenham), *Konchesky (Charlton Athletic), Hargreaves (Bayern Munich), Murphy (Liverpool), *Jenas (Newcastle Utd.), Vassell (Aston Villa), *Jeffers (Arsenal), *Rooney (Everton). **Scorer:** Jeffers (70).

Australia (4-4-2): Schwarzer, Neill, Popovic, Moore, Lazaridis, Emerton, Okon, Skoko (Bresciano 46), Chipperfield (Grella 76), Kewell (Aloisi 56), Viduka (Sterjovski 84). **Scorers:** Popovic (17), Kewell (42), Emerton (84). **Booked:** Lazaridis.

Referee: M. Mejuto Gonzalez (Spain). **Half-time:** 0-2.

SCOTLAND 0, REPUBLIC OF IRELAND 2

Hampden Park, (33,337), Wednesday, February 12, 2003

Scotland (3-4-1-2): Sullivan (Tottenham) (Gallacher Dundee Utd., 46), Anderson (Aberdeen), Caldwell (Newcastle Utd.), Dailly (West Ham Utd.), Alexander (Preston N.E.), Ferguson (Rangers) (Cameron, Wolves, 64), Lambert (Celtic) (Gemmill, Everton, 46), Naysmith (Everton), McCann (Rangers) (*Smith, Celtic, 64), Hutchison (West Ham Utd.) (Devlin, Birmingham City, 46), Crawford (Dunfermline) (Thompson, Rangers, 64).

Rep. of Ireland (4-4-2): Kiely (Charlton Athletic) (Colgan, Hibernian, 80), Carr (Tottenham), Breen (West Ham Utd.) (O'Brien, Newcastle Utd., 90), O'Shea (Manchester Utd.) (Dunne, Manchester City, 80), Harte (Leeds Utd.), Reid (Millwall) (Carsley, Everton, 77), Holland (Ipswich Town), Kinsella (Aston Villa) (Healy, Celtic, 77), Kilbane (Sunderland), Morrison (Birmingham City), Doherty (Tottenham) (Connolly, Wimbledon, 73). **Scorers:** Kilbane (9), Morrison (17).

Referee: E. Braamhaar (Holland). **Half-time:** 0-2.

WALES 2, BOSNIA-HERZEGOVINA 2

Millennium Stadium, (25,000), Wednesday, February 12, 2003

Wales (4-3-2-1): Ward (Nott'm. Forest) (Crossley, Middlesbrough, 46), Weston (Cardiff City) (Jones, Leicester City, 61), Melville (Fulham), Page (Sheffield Utd.), Speed (Newcastle Utd.), Davies (Tottenham), Savage (Birmingham City) (Oster, Sunderland, 88), Pembridge (Everton), Earnshaw (Cardiff City) (Koumas, W.B.A., 76), Bellamy (Newcastle Utd.), Hartson (Celtic) (Taylor, Burnley, 82). **Scorers:** Earnshaw (8), Hartson (74).

Bosnia-Herzegovina (4-5-1): Hasagic, Berberovic, Konjic, Hibic, Music, Beslija, Biscevic (Velagic 90), Grujic (Mulina 77), Barbarez (Moskovic 78), Baljic (Hrgovic 78), Bolic (Halilovic 90). **Scorers:** Baljic (5), Barbarez (64).

Referee: D. Malcolm (Northern Ireland). **Half-time:** 1-1.

NORTHERN IRELAND 0, FINLAND 1

Windsor Park, (6,137), Wednesday, February 12, 2003

Northern Ireland (4-4-2): Taylor (Fulham) (Carroll, Manchester Utd., 46), Hughes (Newcastle Utd.), Williams (Wimbledon), McCartney (Sunderland) (*Craigan, Partick Thistle, 66), Kennedy (Wigan Athletic), Gillespie (Blackburn Rov.), Lomas (West Ham Utd.), Johnson (Birmingham City), McVeigh (Norwich City) (Elliott, Hull City, 76), Quinn (Willem 11) (Kirk, Hearts, 60), Healy (Preston N.E.).

Finland (4-5-1): Jaaskelainen, Kuivasto, Hyypia (Heikkinen 69), Tihinen, Hietanen, Nurmela, Riihilahti, Vayrynan (Johansson 62), Valakari, Kolkka (Kopteff 76), Forssell (Kuqi 46). **Scorer:** Hyypia (49). **Booked:** Hietanen.

Referee: D. McDonald (Scotland). **Half-time:** 0-0.

SCOTLAND 0, AUSTRIA 2

Hampden Park, (12,189), Wednesday, April 30, 2003

Scotland (3-4-1-2): Gallacher (Dundee Utd.), Wilkie (Dundee), *Webster (Hearts), Pressley (Hearts), Devlin (Birmingham City) (Smith, Celtic, 84), Burley (Derby Co.) (Cameron, Wolves, 63), Naysmith (Everton), Dailly (West Ham Utd.) (Gemmill, Everton, 46), Hutchison (West Ham Utd.) (Miller, Wolves, 61), Thompson (Rangers) (Crawford, Dunfermline Athletic, 46), McFadden (Motherwell). **Booked:** Wilkie.

Austria (4-5-1): Mandl, Scharner, Ehmann, Stranzl, Dospel, Aufhauser, Schopp, Flogel, Wagner, Kirchler (Herzog 84), Haas (Brunmayr 63). **Scorers:** Kirchler (27), Haas (33). **Booked:** Scharner, Schopp.

Referee: N. Vollquartz (Denmark). **Half-time:** 0-2.

REPUBLIC OF IRELAND 1, NORWAY 0

Lansdowne Road, (32,643), Wednesday, April 30, 2003

Rep. of Ireland (4-3-1-2): Given (Newcastle Utd.) (Colgan, Hibernian, 60), Carr (Tottenham), Breen (West Ham Utd.), Dunne (Manchester City), Harte (Leeds Utd.) (Finnan, Fulham, 60), Holland (Ipswich Town), Kinsella (Aston Villa) (Carsley, Everton, 65), Kilbane (Sunderland) (*Quinn, Sheffield Wed., 85), Duff (Blackburn Rov.) (*Lee, Rotherham Utd., 74), Keane (Tottenham) (Crowe, Bohemians, 90), Connolly (Wimbledon) (Healy, Celtic, 74). **Scorer:** Duff (17).

Norway (4-1-4-1): Olsen (Holtan 46), Basma (Aas 56), Hangeland, R. Johnsen (Hansen 46), Bergdolmo, Andersen (F. Johnsen 90), Carew, Svindal, Leonhardsen, Iversen (Rudi 65), Rushfeld (Flo 46).

Referee: M. McCurry (Scotland). **Half-time:** 1-0.

SOUTH AFRICA 1, ENGLAND 2

Durban, (48,000), Thursday, May 22, 2003

South Africa (4-4-2): Baloyi, Mabizela, Radebe, A. Mokoena, Molefe, Fredericks, (Mazibuko 77), Sibaya, T. Mokoena (Mendu 69), Buckley, Bartlett, McCarthy (Manyathela 68). **Scorer:** McCarthy (18 pen). **Booked:** Mabizela, Molefe.

England (4-4-2): James (West Ham Utd.) (Robinson, Leeds Utd., 46), Mills (Leeds Utd.), Ferdinand (Manchester Utd.) (*Upson (Birmingham City, 46), Southgate (Middlesbrough), P. Neville (Manchester Utd.), Beckham (Manchester Utd.) (Jenas, Newcastle Utd., 51), Gerrard (Liverpool) (Barry, Aston Villa, 82), Scholes (Manchester Utd.) (Cole, West Ham Utd., 75), Sinclair (West Ham Utd.) (Lampard, Chelsea, 58); Owen (Liverpool), Heskey (Liverpool) (Vassell, Aston Villa, 65). **Scorers:** Southgate (1), Heskey (64). **Booked:** Mills.

Referee: L. K. Chong (Mauritius). **Half-time:** 1-1.

UNITED STATES 2, WALES 0

San Jose, (12,262), Monday, May 26, 2003

United States (4-4-2): Rimando, Suarez (Petke 78), Brown, Agoos, Vanney, Stewart (Lagos 83), Convey (Ching 75), Mulrooney, Lewis, Donovan, Kirovski (Eskandarian 89). **Scorers:** Donovan (41 pen), Lewis (60). **Booked:** Suarez.

Wales (4-5-1): P. Jones (Southampton) (Ward, Nott'm. Forest, 46), M. Jones (Leicester City), Melville (Fulham), Williams (Reading), *Vaughan (Crewe Alexandra), Davies (Tottenham), Oster (Sunderland) (*Pipe, Coventry City, 70), Pembridge (Everton) (Robinson, Portsmouth, 78), Johnson (W.B.A.), Koumas (W.B.A.), Taylor (Burnley) (Roberts, Wigan Athletic, 57). **Booked:** M. Jones, Pembridge, Oster. **Sent-off:** M. Jones.

Referee: B. Tellez (Mexico). **Half-time:** 1-0.

SCOTLAND 1, NEW ZEALAND 1

Tynecastle, (10,016), Tuesday, May 27, 2003

Scotland (4-4-2): Douglas (Celtic), Ross (Rangers) (Alexander (Preston N.E., 46), Pressley (Hearts), Webster (Hearts), Naysmith (Everton), Devlin (Birmingham City), Dailly (West Ham Utd.), McNamara (Celtic) (*Kerr, Newcastle Utd., 82), McFadden (Motherwell), Kyle (Sunderland) (Gray, Bradford City, 59), Crawford (Dunfermline Athletic). **Scorer:** Crawford (11). **Booked:** Dailly, Webster, Alexander, Devlin.

New Zealand (4-4-2): Utting (Batty 46), Mulligan (Oughton 46), Zoricich (Smith 69), Nelsen, Davis, Jackson (De Gregorio 54), Elliott, Burton, Coveny, Lines (Bouckenrooghe 80), Hickey. **Scorer:** Nelsen (47). **Booked:** Mulligan.

Referee: M. Ingvarsson (Sweden). **Half-time:** 1-0.

ENGLAND 2, SERBIA-MONTENEGRO 1

Walkers Stadium, (30,900), Tuesday, June 3, 2003

England (4-3-1-2): James (West Ham Utd.); Mills (Leeds Utd.) (Carragher, Liverpool, 61), Southgate (Middlesbrough) (*Terry, Chelsea, 46), Upson (Birmingham City) (Barry, Aston Villa, 84), A. Cole (Arsenal) (Bridge, Southampton, 46), Gerrard (Liverpool) (Hargreaves, Bayern Munich, 46), P. Neville (Manchester Utd.) (Beattie, Southampton, 87), Lampard (Chelsea) (J. Cole, West Ham Utd., 61), Scholes (Manchester Utd.) (Jenas, Newcastle Utd., 46), Owen (Liverpool) (Rooney, Everton, 46), Heskey (Liverpool) (Vassell, Aston Villa, 61). **Scorers:** Gerrard (35), J. Cole (82).

Serbia-Montenegro (3-4-2-1): Jevric (Zilic 67), Mirkovic (Brnovic 46), Vidic (D. Kovacevic 82), Stefanovic (Krstajic 50), Markovic (Njegus 67), Duljaj (Boskovic 46), N. Kovacevic (Malbasa 46), Dmitrovic (Trobok 46), Vukic (Djordjevic 46), Ilic (Mijatovic 67), Jestrovic (Milosevic 75). **Scorer:** Jestrovic (45). **Booked:** Vidic.

Referee: P. Allaerts (Belgium). **Half-time:** 1-1.

ITALY 2, NORTHERN IRELAND 0

Campobasso, (18,270), Tuesday, June 3, 2003

Italy (4-4-2): Toldo, Oddo, Legrottaglie (Bonera 57), Cannavaro (Ferrari 46), Grosso (Birindelli 69), Fiore, Perrotta (Tomassi 57), Ambrosini, Di Vaio (Nervo 69), Corradi (Delvecchio 46), Miccoli (Di Natale 57). **Scorers:** Corradi (31), Delvecchio (67).

Northern Ireland (4-4-2): Taylor (Fulham) (Carroll, Manchester Utd., 55), *Baird (Southampton), Hughes (Newcastle Utd.), McCartney (Sunderland), Kennedy (Wigan Athletic) (Williams, Wimbledon, 55), Johnson (Birmingham City) (*Toner, Leyton Orient, 69), Griffin (Dundee Utd.), *Doherty (Bristol City) (Elliott, Hull City), McVeigh (Norwich City) (*Jones, Crewe Alexandra, 55), Healy (Preston N.E.) (*Hamilton, Portadown, 76), *Smith (Glentoran). **Booked:** Johnson.

Referee: L. Baptista (Portugal). **Half-time:** 1-0.

BRITISH AND IRISH UNDER-21 INTERNATIONALS

EUROPEAN U-21 CHAMPIONSHIP – QUALIFYING ROUND

FINLAND 2, WALES 1

Valkeakoski, (2,500), Friday, September 6, 2002

Wales: Brown (Gillingham), Moss (Shrewsbury Town), Price (Hull City), Pejic (Wrexham), Day (Manchester City) (Rees, Millwall, 85), Tolley (Shrewsbury Town), Valentine (Darlington), Mumford (Swansea City) (Gall, Bristol Rov., 75), Birchall (Arsenal) (Stock, Bournemouth, 83), Williams (Manchester Utd.), Vaughan (Crewe Alexandra).

Scorers – Finland: Lagerblom (65), Sjolund (89). **Wales:** Birchall (38). **Half-time:** 0-1.

RUSSIA 2, REPUBLIC OF IRELAND 0

Moscow, (3,000), Saturday, September 7, 2002

Rep. of Ireland: Murphy (W.B.A), Thompson (Nott'm. Forest), Goodwin (Stockport Co.), Byrne (Sunderland), Tierney (Manchester Utd.), Butler (Sunderland), Miller (Celtic), Keane (Preston N.E.) (Daly, Stockport Co., 72), Hoolihan (Shelbourne), Burgess (Stockport Co.) (Reid, Nott'm. Forest, 57), Barrett (Arsenal).

Scorers – Russia: Pavlioutchenko (28), Kussov (29). **Half-time:** 2-0.

SLOVAKIA 0, ENGLAND 4

Trnava, (3,800), Friday, October 11, 2002

England: Murray (Wolves), Samuel (Aston Villa), Bramble (Newcastle Utd.) (Dawson, Nott'm. Forest, 69), Barry (Aston Villa), Konchesky (Charlton Athletic) (Clarke, Everton, 81), Prutton (Nott'm. Forest), Carrick (West Ham Utd.), Jenas (Newcastle Utd.), Cole (West Ham Utd.), Jeffers (Arsenal), Ameobi (Newcastle Utd.) (Taylor, Portsmouth, 81).

Scorers – England: Ameobi (34), Jeffers (63, 76), Cole (87). **Sent-off:** Poncak (Slovakia). **Half-time:** 0-1.

ICELAND 0, SCOTLAND 2

Hafnarfjordur, (1,000), Friday, October 11, 2002

Scotland: Soutar (Dundee), Caldwell (Newcastle Utd.), Murray (Hibernian), Kennedy (Celtic), Doig (Nott'm. Forest), Kerr (Newcastle Utd.), Duff (Dundee Utd.), Williams (Nott'm. Forest), Kyle (Sunderland), Hughes (Rangers) (Fletcher, Manchester Utd., 69), McManus (Hibernian) (Lynch, Celtic, 85).

Scorers – Scotland: Kyle (17), Lynch (88). **Sent-off:** Skulason (Iceland). **Half-time:** 0-1.

SPAIN 1, NORTHERN IRELAND 0

Almansa,(2,000), Friday, October 11, 2002

Northern Ireland: Morris (Glentoran), Baird (Southampton), Capaldi (Birmingham City), Clyde (Wolves), Simms (Hartlepool Utd.), Melaugh (Aston Villa), Close (Middlesbrough) (Hughes, Tottenham), Toner (Leyton Orient), McEvilly (Rochdale) (Braniff, Millwall), Browne (Manchester City) (McFlynn, Margate), McCourt (Rochdale).

Scorer – Spain: Capaldi (90 og). **Half-time:** 0-0.

ENGLAND 3, MACEDONIA 1

Madejski Stadium, Reading, (15,500), Tuesday, October 15, 2002

England: Kirkland (Liverpool) (Murray, Wolves 5), Konchesky (Charlton Athletic), Bramble (Newcastle Utd.), Barry (Aston Villa), Samuel (Aston Villa), Carrick (West Ham Utd.), Cole (West Ham Utd.) (Crouch, Aston Villa, 70), Jenas (Newcastle Utd.), Prutton (Nott'm. Forest) Ameobi (Newcastle Utd.) (Wright-Phillips, Manchester City, 55), Jeffers (Arsenal).

Scorers – England: Jeffers (32, 53, 73). **Macedonia:** Baldovaliev (70). **Half-time:** 1-0.

WALES 1, ITALY 2

Ninian Park, Cardiff, (2,202), Tuesday, October 15, 2002

Wales: Brown (Gillingham), Moss (Shrewsbury Town), Price (Hull City) (Collins, Cardiff City, 84), Pejic (Wrexham), Day (Manchester City), Tolley (Shrewsbury Town), Valentine (Darlington), Mumford (Swansea City), Birchall (Arsenal) (G. Williams, Crystal Palace, 80), M. Williams (Manchester Utd.), Fowler (Coventry City) (Stock, Bournemouth, 65).

Scorers – Wales: Tolley (4). **Italy:** Sculli (52), D'Agostino (80 pen). **Half-time:** 1-0.

NORTHERN IRELAND 1, UKRAINE 1

Showgrounds, Ballymena, (2,000), Tuesday, October 15, 2002

Northern Ireland: Morris (Glentoran), Baird (Southampton) (Buchanan, Bolton Wand.), Capaldi (Birmingham City), Clyde (Wolves), Simms (Hartlepool Utd.), Melaugh (Aston Villa), Close (Middlesbrough), Toner (Leyton Orient) (Hughes, Tottenham), McEvilly (Rochdale), Browne (Manchester City) (Black, Morecambe), McCourt (Rochdale).

Scorers – Northern Ireland: Baird (39). Ukraine 1 (Kabanov 83). **Half-time:** 1-0.

REPUBLIC OF IRELAND 2, SWITZERLAND 3

Buckley Park, Kilkenny, (1,500), Tuesday, October 15, 2002

Rep. of Ireland: Murphy (W.B.A.), Thompson (Nott'm. Forest) (Hunt, Shamrock Rov., 88), Goodwin (Stockport Co.), Byrne (Sunderland), Tierney (Manchester Utd.), Butler (Sunderland) (Doyle, Celtic, 46), Miller (Celtic), Barrett (Arsenal), Hoolihan (Shelbourne), Reid (Nott'm. Forest) (O'Flynn, Cork City, 77), Daly (Stockport Co.).

Scorers – Rep. of Ireland: Reid (1), Miller (8). **Switzerland:** Cerrone (43), Rochat (74), Vonlanthen (87). **Half-time:** 2-1.

AZERBAIJAN 0, WALES 1

Baku, (1,200), Tuesday, November 19, 2002

Wales: Brown (Gillingham), Moss (Shrewsbury Town), Price (Hull City), Pejic (Wrexham), Day (Manchester City), Tolley (Shrewsbury Town), Pipe (Coventry City), Mumford (Swansea City) Birchall (Arsenal) (Collins, Cardiff City, 82), Gall (Bristol Rov.), Valentine (Darlington) (Brough, Notts Co., 58).

Scorer – Wales: Gall (73). **Half-time:** 0-0.

PORTUGAL 4, ENGLAND 2

Rio Maior, (3,000), Friday, March 28, 2003

England: Bywater (West Ham Utd.), Samuel (Aston Villa), Dawson (Nott'm. Forest), Bramble (Newcastle Utd.) (Crouch, Aston Villa, 86), Konchesky (Charlton Athletic), Prutton (Southampton) (Pennant, Arsenal, 68), Cole (West Ham Utd.), Carrick (West Ham Utd.) (Stewart, Leicester City, 46), Barry (Aston Villa), Defoe (West Ham Utd.), Ameobi (Newcastle Utd.). **Sent-off:** Ameobi (83).

Scorers – Portugal: Postiga (7), Barry (11 og), Martins (61), Ronaldo (71). **England:** Ameobi (9, 33). **Half-time:** 2-2.

SCOTLAND 1, ICELAND 0

Broadwood Stadium, Cumbernauld, (3,192), Friday, March 28, 2003

Scotland: Souter (Dundee), Caldwell (Newcastle Utd.), Murray (Hibernian), Kennedy (Celtic), Webster (Hearts), Kerr (Newcastle Utd.), Canero (Kilmarnock), Williams (Nott'm. Forest), Kyle (Sunderland), Stewart (Manchester Utd.) (Hughes, Rangers, 80), McFadden (Motherwell) (Maloney, Celtic, 62).

Scorer – Scotland: Maloney (69). **Half-time:** 0-0.

WALES 1, AZERBAIJAN 0

Barry, (1,834), Friday, March 28, 2003

Wales: Whitefield (Wrexham), Moss (Shrewsbury Town), Price (Hull City), Rees (Millwall), Day (Mansfield Town), Mumford (Swansea City), Pipe (Coventry City) (Brough, Notts Co., 80), Tolley (Shrewsbury Town), Collins (Cardiff City), G. Williams (Crystal Palace) (M. Williams, Manchester Utd. 65), Vaughan (Crewe Alexandra).

Scorer – Wales: Pipe (7). **Half-time:** 1-0.

ARMENIA 2, NORTHERN IRELAND 0

Abovyan, (300), Friday, March 28, 2003

Northern Ireland: Morris (Glentoran), Close (Middlesbrough), Herron (Q.P.R.), McFlynn (Margate), Simms (Hartlepool Utd.), Capaldi (Birmingham City), Hughes (Tottenham), Melaugh (Rochdale), McEvilly (Rochdale), Feeney (Bournemouth), Morrison (Sheffield Utd.).

Scorers – Armenia: Meloyan (25), Davtvan (65). **Half-time:** 1-0.

GEORGIA 1, REPUBLIC OF IRELAND 1

Tbilisi, (3,500), Friday, March 28, 2003

Rep. of Ireland: Stack (Arsenal), Brennan (Newcastle Utd.), Goodwin (Stockport Co.), Thompson (Nott'm. Forest) (O'Connor, Brentford, 80), Paisley (Manchester City), Tierney (Manchester Utd.) (Byrne, Sunderland, 45), Miller (Celtic), Thornton (Sunderland), Daly (Stockport Co.), Reid (Nott'm. Forest), Hoolihan (Shelbourne) (Hunt, Dunfermline, 82). **Sent-off:** Reid.

Scorers – Georgia: Akhalaia (20). **Rep. of Ireland:** Hunt (84). **Half-time:** 1-0

ENGLAND 1, TURKEY 1

St James' Park, Newcastle, (21,085), Tuesday, April 1, 2003

England: Murray (Wolves), Samuel (Aston Villa) (Johnson, West Ham Utd., 70), Dawson (Nott'm. Forest), Clarke (Everton), Konchesky (Charlton Athletic), Prutton (Southampton), J. Cole (West Ham Utd.), Jenas (Newcastle Utd.), Barry (Aston Villa), Defoe (West Ham Utd.) (C. Cole, Chelsea, 65), Jeffers (Arsenal).

Scorers – England: Jeffers (25). **Turkey:** Sanli (13). **Half-time:** 1-1.

LITHUANIA 2, SCOTLAND 1

Vilnius, (2,000), Tuesday, April 1, 2003

Scotland: Soutar (Dundee), Caldwell (Newcastle Utd.), Murray (Hibernian), Kennedy (Celtic), Webster (Hearts), Kerr (Newcastle Utd.), Canero (Kilmarnock) (Lynch, Preston N.E., 84), Williams (Nott'm. Forest), Kyle (Sunderland), Stewart (Manchester Utd.), McFadden (Motherwell) (Maloney, Celtic, 46).

Scorers – Lithuania: Kucys (34), Cesnauskis (82). **Scotland:** Kyle (2). **Half-time:** 1-1.

NORTHERN IRELAND 2, GREECE 6

The Oval, Belfast, (611), Tuesday, April 1, 2003

Northern Ireland: Morris (Glentoran), Baird (Southampton) (McCourt, Rochdale), Herron (Q.P.R.), Toner (Leyton Orient) ((McFlynn, Margate)), Simms (Hartlepool Utd.), Capaldi (Birmingham City), Hughes (Tottenham), Melaugh (Rochdale), Braniff (Millwall), Feeney (Bournemouth) (McEvilly, Rochdale), Morrison (Sheffield Utd.) **Sent-off:** McCourt (84).

Scorers – Northern Ireland: Toner (35), McEvilly (57 pen). **Greece:** Lagos (3), Fotakis (37), Papadopoulos (41, 61, 82 pen), Salpigidis (47). **Half-time:** 1-3.

ALBANIA 1, REPUBLIC OF IRELAND 0

Tirana, (1,500), Tuesday, April 1, 2003

Rep. of Ireland: Stack (Arsenal), Brennan (Newcastle Utd.), Goodwin (Stockport Co.), Byrne (Sunderland), Thompson, (Nott'm. Forest), Paisley (Manchester City) (Rossiter, Kidderminster Harr., 46), Miller (Celtic), Thornton (Sunderland), Daly (Stockport Co.), O'Connor (Brentford) (Hunt, Dunfermline, 76), Barrett (Arsenal).

Scorer – Albania: Rizvanolli (71). **Half-time:** 0-0.

SCOTLAND 2 GERMANY 2

Rugby Park, Kilmarnock, (5,052), Friday, June 6, 2003

Scotland: Soutar (Dundee), Caldwell (Newcastle Utd.), Murray (Hibernian), Kennedy (Celtic), Crainey (Celtic), Kerr (Newcastle Utd.), Canero (Kilmarnock), Pearson (Motherwell), Kyle (Sunderland), Fletcher (Manchester Utd.) (Gallagher, Blackburn Rov., 85), Lynch (Preston N.E.) (McManus, Hibernian, 59).

Scorers – Scotland: Lynch (15), Caldwell (25). **Germany:** Lauth (9), Balitsch (28). **Half-time:** 2-2.

REPUBLIC OF IRELAND 2, ALBANIA 1

Dalymount Park, Dublin, (3,000), Friday June 6, 2003

Rep. of Ireland: Stack (Arsenal), Kelly (Tottenham), Cryan (Sheffield Utd.), Thompson (Nott'm. Forest), Capper (Sunderland), Butler (Sunderland) (Gilroy, Scarborough, 69), Miller (Celtic), Thornton (Sunderland), Reid (Nott'm. Forest), Barrett (Arsenal), O'Flynn (Cork City) (Elliott, Manchester City, 75).

Scorers – Rep. of Ireland: Barrett (43), O'Flynn (53). **Albania:** Mansaku (85). **Half-time:** 2-0.

(Albania awarded the match 3-0 because the Republic of Ireland's Liam Miller was ineligible, having previously received two yellow cards)

ENGLAND 2, SLOVAKIA 0

Stadium of Light, Sunderland, (11,223), Tuesday, June 10, 2003

England: Evans (Chelsea), Parnaby (Middlesbrough), Jagielka (Sheffield Utd.), Clarke (Everton), Konchesky (Charlton Athletic), Pennant (Arsenal), Sidwell (Reading), Prutton (Southampton), Barry (Aston Villa), Ameobi (Newcastle Utd.) (Zamora, Brighton & H.A.,71), Defoe (West Ham Utd.) (Cole, Chelsea, 58).

Scorers – England: Dolezaj (40 og), Jagielka (83). **Half-time:** 1-0.

NORTHERN IRELAND 1, SPAIN 4

Mourneview Park, Lurgan, (1,500),Tuesday, June 10, 2003

Northern Ireland: Morris (Glentoran), Hughes (Tottenham), Capaldi (Plymouth Argyle), Duff (Cheltenham Town), Simms (Hartlepool Utd.), Melaugh (Rochdale), McCann (Portadown) (McFlynn, Margate), Close (Middlesbrough), Braniff (Millwall), Browne (Manchester City) (Clarke, Peterborough Utd.), Morrison (Sheffield Utd.) (Campbell, Ballymena Utd.).

Scorers – Northern Ireland: Braniff (49). **Spain:** Torres (1, 26), Lopes (66), Larena (68). **Half-time:** 0-2.

REPUBLIC OF IRELAND 1, GEORGIA 1

Buckley Park, Kilkenny, (1,500), Tuesday, June 10, 2003

Rep. of Ireland: Connor (Waterford), Capper (Sunderland), Kelly (Tottenham), Cryan (Sheffield Utd.), Thompson (Nott'm. Forest), Gilroy (Scarborough), Butler (Sunderland), Barrett (Arsenal), O'Flynn (Cork City) (Elliott, Manchester City, 68), Thornton (Sunderland) (O'Connor, Brentford, 75), Reid (Nott'm. Forest) (Hoolihan, Shelbourne, 89). **Sent-off:** Gilroy (63).

Scorers – Rep. of Ireland: Cryan (53). **Georgia:** Akhalaia (25). **Half-time:** 0-1

FRIENDLIES

SCOTLAND 1, DENMARK 1

East End Park, Dunfermline, (2,914), Tuesday, August 20, 2002

Scotland: Soutar (Dundee) (McGregor, Rangers, 46), McCunnie (Dundee Utd.), Murray (Hibernian), Dowie (Rangers), Doig (Nott'm. Forest), Kerr (Newcastle Utd.), Canero (Kilmarnock), Hughes (Rangers) (McLean, Rangers, 85), O'Connor Hibernian, Stewart (Manchester Utd.) (McManus, Hibernian, 61), Maloney (Cewltic) (McFadden, Motherwell, 46).

Scorers – Scotland: Canero (30). **Denmark:** Bechmann (12). **Half-time:** 1-1.

FINLAND 0, REPUBLIC OF IRELAND 1

Helsinki, (1,500), Tuesday, August 20, 2002

Rep. of Ireland: Murphy (W.B.A.), S. Byrne (West Ham Utd.) (Shelley, Carlisle Utd., 62), C. Byrne (Sunderland), Goodwin (Stockport Co.) (McGuinness, Bohemians, 46), Tierney (Manchester Utd.), Miller (Celtic), Mattis (Huddersfield Town) (M. Doyle, Celtic, 75), Keane (Preston N.E. N. E.) (Gamble, Reading, 62), Barrett (Arsenal) (R. Doyle, U.C.D, 46), Burgess (Blackburn Rov.) (Daly, Stockport Co., 69), Hoolihan (Shelbourne).

Scorer – Rep. of Ireland: Daly (90). **Half-time:** 0-0.

SCOTLAND 2, ISRAEL 1

New Douglas Park, Hamilton, (3,021), Wednesday, September 4, 2002

Scotland: McGregor (Rangers) (Gordon, Hearts, 46), McCunnie (Dundee Utd.) (Kennedy, Celtic, 46), Hammell (Motherwell), Dowie (Rangers) (Caldwell, Newcastle Utd., 46), Doig (Nott'm. Forest), Kerr (Newcastle Utd.), Duff (Dundee Utd.), Pearson (Motherwell) (O'Brien, Livingston, 78), McFadden (Motherwell) (Lynch, Celtic, 65), Stewart (Manchester Utd.), Maloney (Celtic).

Scorers – Scotland: Maloney (3), Kennedy (86). **Israel:** Barda (15). **Half-time:** 1-1.

ENGLAND 1, YUGOSLAVIA 1

Reebok Stadium, Bolton, (10,531), Friday, September 6, 2002

England: Kirkland (Liverpool), Samuel (Aston Villa) (Parnaby, Middlesbrough, 78), Bramble (Newcastle Utd.), Barry (Aston Villa), Konchesky (Charlton Athletic) (Lescott, Wolves, 89), Pennant (Arsenal) (Wright-Phillips, Manchester City, 61), Jenas (Newcastle Utd.), Carrick (West Ham Utd.), Prutton (Nott'm. Forest) (Etherington, Tottenham, 74), Defoe (West Ham Utd.) (Ameobi, Newcastle Utd., 61), Jeffers (Arsenal).

Scorers – England: Wright-Phillips (80).**Yugoslavia:** Lazovic (41): **Half-time:** 0-1.

SCOTLAND 1, NORTHERN IRELAND 1

St Mirren Park, (2,351), Friday, September 6, 2002

Scotland: Soutar (Dundee) (McEwan, Livingston, 46), McCunnie(Dundee Utd.), Hammell (Motherwell), Kennedy (Celtic), Doig (Nott'm. Forest), Kerr (Newcastle Utd.), Canero (Kilmarnock) (Duff, Dundee Utd., 46), Pearson (Motherwell) (Lynch, Celtic, 68), McFadden (Motherwell) (McLean, Rangers, 46), Stewart (Manchester Utd.), Maloney (Celtic) (McManus, Hibernian, 61). **Sent-off:** Stewart (80).

Northern Ireland: Morris (Glentoran), Baird (Southampton), Capaldi (Birmingham City), Clyde (Wolves), Simms (Hartlepool Utd.), Melaugh (Aston Villa), Close (Middlesbrough) (McCann, Linfield, 78), Toner (Leyton Orient), McEvilly (Rochdale) (McFlynn, Margate, 65), Browne (Manchester City) (Braniff, Millwall, 46), Morrison (Sheffield Wed.) (McCourt, Rochdale, 10)

Scorers – Scotland: Clyde (73 og). **Northern Ireland:** McEvilly (30). **Half-time:** 0-1.

SCOTLAND 2, GHANA 0

Palmerston Park, Dumfries, (3,119), Monday, October 14, 2002

Scotland: Gordon (Hearts) (McEwan, Livingston, 46), Caldwell (Newcastle Utd.), Hammell (Motherwell), Kennedy (Celtic), Doig (Nott'm. Forest), Kerr (Newcastle Utd.), Duff (Dundee Utd.) (McParland, Celtic, 76), Murray (Hibernian) (Simmons, Hearts, 51), McFadden (Motherwell) (McLean, Rangers, 48), Hughes (Rangers) (O'Brien, Livingston, 76), McManus (Hibernian) (Lynch, Celtic, 48).

Scorers – Scotland: Caldwell (9), Kerr (15). **Half-time:** 2-0.

BELGIUM 2, SCOTLAND 0

Molenbeek, (643), Tuesday, November 19, 2002

Scotland: Soutar (Dundee) (McGregor, Rangers, 46), Doig (Nott'm. Forest) (Hammell, Motherwell, 46), Caldwell (Newcastle Utd.), Kennedy (Celtic), Crainey (Celtic), Hughes (Rangers) (Pearson, Motherwell, 69), Murray (Hibernian), Kerr (Newcastle Utd.), Duff (Dundee Utd.) (Canero, Kilmarnock, 67), Maloney (Celtic) (McLean, Rangers, 81), Lynch (Celtic) (Boyd, Kilmarnock, 46).

Scorers – Belgium: Chatelle (25), Snelders (87). **Half-time:** 1-0.

ITALY 1, ENGLAND 0

Carrara, (3,966), Tuesday, February 11, 2002

England: Murray (Wolves) (Grant, Derby Co., 46), Samuel (Aston Villa) (Lescott, Wolves, 55), Dawson (Nott'm. Forest), Clarke (Everton), Taylor (Portsmouth) (McEveley, Blackburn Rov., 71), Wright-Phillips (Manchester City) (Nolan, Bolton Wand. 61), Prutton (Southampton) (Ambrose, Ipswich Town, 79), Carrick (West Ham Utd.), Barry (Aston Villa), Ameobi (Newcastle Utd.), Zamora (Brighton & H.A.) (Bent, Ipswich Town, 71).

Scorer – Italy: Borriello (75). **Half-time:** 0-0.

SCOTLAND 2, REPUBLIC OF IRELAND 0

Rugby Park, Kilmarnock, (2,987), Tuesday, February 11, 2003

Scotland: Soutar (Dundee) (McGregor, Rangers, 46), Caldwell (Newcastle Utd.), Hammell (Motherwell), Kennedy (Celtic), Doig (Nott'm. Forest) (Crainey, Celtic, 46), Kerr (Newcastle Utd.), Canero (Kilmarnock) (Duff, Dundee Utd., 80), Pearson (Motherwell) (Hughes, Rangers, 46), Kyle (Sunderland) (Lynch, Preston N.E., 67), Williams (Nott'm. Forest) (Stewart, Manchester Utd., 46), Maloney (Celtic) (McFadden, Motherwell, 46)

Rep. of Ireland: Stack (Arsenal), Brennan (Newcastle Utd.), Tierney (Manchester Utd.) (Byrne, Shamrock Rov., 85), Byrne (Sunderland), Goodwin (Stockport Co.), Thompson (Nott'm Forest) (Hunt, Dunfermline, 56), Butler (Sunderland), Reid (Nott'm Forest), (Thornton, Sunderland, 45), Barrett (Arsenal) (Daly, Stockport Co., 45), Dempsey (Dunfermline) (Lester, Bohemians, 85), Hoolihan (Shelbourne) (Nelligan, Kidderminster Harr., 45).

Scorers – Scotland: Maloney (41), Lynch (69). **Half-time:** 1-0.

NORTHERN IRELAND 3, FINLAND 1

Glenavon, (800), Tuesday, February 11, 2003

Northern Ireland: Morris (Glentoran) (Blayney, Southampton), Capaldi (Birmingham City), Simms (Hartlepool Utd.), Clyde (Wolves), Melaugh (Rochdale) (McFlynn, Margate), Hughes (Tottenham), Toner (Leyton Orient), Feeney (Bournemouth) (McEvilly, Rochdale), Braniff (Millwall) (Browne, Manchester City), Morrison (Sheffield Wed.) (McCourt, Rochdale).

Scorers – Northern Ireland: Melaugh (45), McEvilly (88), McFlynn (89). **Finland:** Oravainen (87).

SCOTLAND 1, AUSTRIA 0

Dens Park, Dundee, (2,085), Tuesday, April 29, 2003

Scotland: Soutar (Dundee) (McGregor, Rangers, 46), Caldwell (Newcastle Utd.), Pearson (Motherwell), Kennedy (Celtic), Crainey (Celtic), Kerr (Newcastle Utd.), Canero (Kilmarnock) (Duff, Dundee Utd.), Hughes (Rangers) (Noble, West Ham Utd., 72), McManus (Hibernian) (Lynch, Preston N.E., 46), Stewart (Manchester Utd.) (Montgomery, Sheffield Utd., 52), Maloney (Celtic).

Scorer – Scotland: Lynch (65). **Half-time:** 0-0.

ENGLAND 3. SERBIA-MONTENEGRO 2

Kingston Communications Stadium, Hull, (24,004), Monday, June 2, 2003

England: Evans (Chelsea) (Bywater, West Ham Utd., 51), Parnaby (Middlesbrough) (Johnson, West Ham Utd., 58), Jagielka (Sheffield Utd.), Clarke (Everton), Konchesky (Charlton Athletic), Pennant (Arsenal) (Bent, Ipswich Town, 81), Prutton (Southampton), Sidwell (Reading), Zamora (Brighton & H.A.) (Ambrose, Newcastle Utd., 58), Ameobi (Newcastle Utd.) (Cole, Chelsea, 51), Defoe (West Ham Utd.).

Scorers – England: Ameobi (15), Defoe (66), Bent (87). **Serbia-Montenegro:** Petrovic (49), Stanic (85).

REPUBLIC OF IRELAND 2, GERMANY 2

Turner's Cross, Cork, (4,000), Monday, June 2, 2003

Rep. of Ireland: Stack (Arsenal), Kelly (Tottenham), Cryan (Sheffield Utd.), Thompson (Nott'm. Forest), Capper (Sunderland), Butler (Sunderland) (Elliott, Manchester City, 68), Miller (Celtic), Thornton (Sunderland), (Hoolihan, Shelbourne, 84), Reid (Nott'm. Forest), (Ward, Wolves, 90), O'Flynn (Cork City), Barrett (Arsenal).

Scorers – Rep. of Ireland: O'Flynn (20), Miller (87). **Germany:** Auer (30), Hitzlsperger (33). **Half-time**: 1-2.

EUROPEAN U-21 CHAMPIONSHIP QUALIFYING TABLES

The eight teams to compete in the Finals in May/June 2004 will be decided by a group stage and subsequent play-offs. The host country will be chosen from the eight qualifiers.

GROUP 1

	P	W	D	L	F	A	Pts
France	5	5	0	0	10	0	15
Cyprus	6	4	0	2	8	3	12
Slovenia	5	2	2	1	3	1	8
Israel	5	1	1	3	1	8	4
Malta	7	0	1	6	0	10	0

GROUP 2

	P	W	D	L	F	A	Pts
Denmark	6	5	0	1	21	3	15
Norway	6	4	1	1	11	3	13
Bosnia-Herzegovina	5	3	1	1	4	4	10
Romania	6	1	0	5	4	7	3
Luxembourg	5	0	0	5	0	23	0

GROUP 3

	P	W	D	L	F	A	Pts
Czech Republic	5	5	0	0	14	1	15
Belarus	6	4	0	2	8	6	12
Austria	6	3	1	2	5	6	10
Holland	5	0	2	3	4	9	2
Moldova	6	0	1	5	3	12	1

GROUP 4

	P	W	D	L	F	A	Pts
Poland	5	4	1	0	19	4	13
Hungary	6	4	0	2	16	9	12
Sweden	5	3	1	1	13	7	10
Latvia	5	2	0	3	7	11	6
San Marino	7	0	0	7	5	29	0

GROUP 5

	P	W	D	L	F	A	Pts
Lithuania	5	3	0	2	8	7	9
Germany	3	2	1	0	7	3	7
Scotland	4	2	1	1	6	4	7
Iceland	4	0	0	4	1	8	0

GROUP 6

	P	W	D	L	F	A	Pts
Spain	6	4	1	1	12	2	13
Greece	6	3	2	1	10	6	11
Ukraine	6	1	5	0	7	3	8
Armenia	5	1	1	3	4	12	4
Northern Ireland	5	0	1	4	4	14	1

GROUP 7

	P	W	D	L	F	A	Pts
Turkey	6	5	1	0	15	4	16
Portugal	5	4	0	1	13	7	12
England	5	3	1	1	12	6	10
Slovakia	6	1	0	5	3	11	3
Macedonia	6	0	0	6	2	17	0

GROUP 8

	P	W	D	L	F	A	Pts
Croatia	4	2	2	0	7	3	8
Belgium	4	2	1	1	6	4	7
Bulgaria	4	1	1	2	5	8	4
Estonia	4	0	2	2	2	5	2

GROUP 9

	P	W	D	L	F	A	Pts
Italy	5	5	0	0	12	3	15
Serbia-Montenegro	5	3	1	1	11	8	10
Finland	6	2	1	3	10	9	7
Wales	4	2	0	2	6	4	6
Azerbaijan	6	0	0	6	0	15	0

GROUP 10

	P	W	D	L	F	A	Pts
Switzerland	6	5	1	0	10	3	16
Russia	5	4	0	1	10	2	12
Albania	6	2	1	3	6	7	7
Republic of Ireland	6	0	2	4	4	11	2
Georgia	5	0	2	3	2	9	2

TEALE SPOT-ON FOR RETURN TO VILLA PARK

Former Aston Villa defender Shaun Teale booked himself a return to Villa Park by scoring the stoppage-time penalty that enabled Burscough to beat Aylesbury United 2-1 on aggregate and reach the F.A. Trophy Final. Player-manager Teale then led his team to a 2-1 victory over Tamworth. The competition proved a triumph for the smaller clubs, with not a single Conference side reaching the last four.

FIRST IN, LAST OUT FOR SHREWSBURY

On their Football League debut in 1950, Shrewsbury Town met Scunthorpe United in a Third Division North game which ended 0-0. In the club's final match of last season before dropping into the Nationwide Conference, Scunthorpe were again the opponents and were 2-1 winners.

OTHER BRITISH INTERNATIONAL RESULTS

ENGLAND

v. ALBANIA

		E	A
1989	Tirana (W.C.)	2	0
1989	Wembley (W.C.)	5	0
2001	Tirana (W.C.)	3	1
2001	Newcastle (W.C.)	2	0

v. ARGENTINA

		E	A
1951	Wembley	2	1
1953*	Buenos Aires	0	0
1962	Rancagua (W.C.)	3	1
1964	Rio de Janeiro	0	1
1966	Wembley (W.C.)	1	0
1974	Wembley	2	2
1977	Buenos Aires	1	1
1980	Wembley	3	1
1986	Mexico City (W.C.)	1	2
1991	Wembley	2	2
1998†	St Etienne (W.C.)	2	2
2000	Wembley	0	0
2002	Sapporo (W.C.)	1	0

(* Abandoned after 21 mins. – rain)
(† England lost 3-4 on pens.)

v. AUSTRALIA

		E	A
1980	Sydney	2	1
1983	Sydney	0	0
1983	Brisbane	1	0
1983	Melbourne	1	1
1991	Sydney	1	0
2003	West Ham	1	3

v. AUSTRIA

		E	A
1908	Vienna	6	1
1908	Vienna	11	1
1909	Vienna	8	1
1930	Vienna	0	0
1932	Chelsea	4	3
1936	Vienna	1	2
1951	Wembley	2	2
1952	Vienna	3	2
1958	Boras (W.C.)	2	2
1961	Vienna	1	3
1962	Wembley	3	1
1965	Wembley	2	3
1967	Vienna	1	0
1973	Wembley	7	0
1979	Vienna	3	4

v. BELGIUM

		E	B
1921	Brussels	2	0
1923	Highbury	6	1
1923	Antwerp	2	2
1924	West Bromwich	4	0
1926	Antwerp	5	3
1927	Brussels	9	1
1928	Antwerp	3	1
1929	Brussels	5	1
1931	Brussels	4	1
1936	Brussels	2	3
1947	Brussels	5	2
1950	Brussels	4	1
1952	Wembley	5	0
1954	Basle (W.C.)	4	4
1964	Wembley	2	2
1970	Brussels	3	1
1980	Turin (E.C.)	1	1
1990	Bologna (W.C.)	1	0
1998*	Casablanca	0	0
1999	Sunderland	2	1

(* England lost 3-4 on pens.)

v. BOHEMIA

		E	B
1908	Prague	4	0

v. BRAZIL

		E	B
1956	Wembley	4	2
1958	Gothenburg (W.C.)	0	0
1959	Rio de Janeiro	0	2
1962	Vina del Mar (W.C.)	1	3
1963	Wembley	1	1
1964	Rio de Janeiro	1	5
1969	Rio de Janeiro	1	2
1970	Guadalajara (W.C.)	0	1
1976	Los Angeles	0	1
1977	Rio de Janeiro	0	0
1978	Wembley	1	1
1981	Wembley	0	1
1984	Rio de Janeiro	2	0
1987	Wembley	1	1
1990	Wembley	1	0
1992	Wembley	1	1
1993	Washington	1	1
1995	Wembley	1	3
1997	Paris (T.F.)	0	1
2000	Wembley	1	1
2002	Shizuoka (W.C.)	1	2

v. BULGARIA

		E	B
1962	Rancagua (W.C.)	0	0
1968	Wembley	1	1
1974	Sofia	1	0
1979	Sofia (E.C.)	3	0
1979	Wembley (E.C.)	2	0

		E	B
1996	Wembley	1	0
1998	Wembley (E.C.)	0	0
1999	Sofia (E.C.)	1	1

v. CAMEROON

		E	C
1990	Naples (W.C.)	3	2
1991	Wembley	2	0
1997	Wembley	2	0
2002	Kobe (Japan)	2	2

v. CANADA

		E	C
1986	Vancouver	1	0

v. CHILE

		E	C
1950	Rio de Janeiro (W.C.)	2	0
1953	Santiago	2	1
1984	Santiago	0	0
1989	Wembley	0	0
1998	Wembley	0	2

v. CHINA

		E	C
1996	Beijing	3	0

v. C.I.S.
(formerly Soviet Union)

		E	C
1992	Moscow	2	2

v. COLOMBIA

		E	C
1970	Bogota	4	0
1988	Wembley	1	1
1995	Wembley	0	0
1998	Lens (W.C.)	2	0

v. CROATIA

		E	C
1995	Wembley	0	0

v. CYPRUS

		E	C
1975	Wembley (E.C.)	5	0
1975	Limassol (E.C.)	1	0

v. CZECH REPUBLIC

		E	C
1998	Wembley	2	0

v. CZECHOSLOVAKIA

		E	C
1934	Prague	1	2
1937	Tottenham	5	4
1963	Bratislava	4	2
1966	Wembley	0	0
1970	Guadalajara (W.C.)	1	0
1973	Prague	1	1
1974	Wembley (E.C.)	3	0
1975*	Bratislava (E.C.)	1	2
1978	Wembley (E.C.)	1	0
1982	Bilbao (W.C.)	2	0
1990	Wembley	4	2
1992	Prague	2	2

(* Aband. 0-0, 17 mins. prev. day – fog)

v. DENMARK

		E	D
1948	Copenhagen	0	0
1955	Copenhagen	5	1
1956	W'hampton (W.C.)	5	2
1957	Copenhagen (W.C.)	4	1
1966	Copenhagen	2	0
1978	Copenhagen (E.C.)	4	3
1979	Wembley (E.C.)	1	0
1982	Copenhagen (E.C.)	2	2
1983	Wembley (E.C.)	0	1
1988	Wembley	1	0
1989	Copenhagen	1	1
1990	Wembley	1	0
1992	Malmo (E.C.)	0	0
1994	Wembley	1	0
2002	Niigata (W.C.)	3	0

v. EAST GERMANY

		E	EG
1963	Leipzig	2	1
1970	Wembley	3	1
1974	Leipzig	1	1
1984	Wembley	1	0

v. ECUADOR

		E	Ec
1970	Quito	2	0

v. EGYPT

		E	Eg
1986	Cairo	4	0
1990	Cagliari (W.C.)	1	0

v. F.I.F.A.

		E	F
1938	Arsenal	3	0
1953	Wembley	4	4
1963	Wembley	2	1

v. FINLAND

		E	F
1937	Helsinki	8	0
1956	Helsinki	5	1
1966	Helsinki	3	0
1976	Helsinki (W.C.)	4	1
1976	Wembley (W.C.)	2	1
1982	Helsinki	4	1
1984	Wembley (W.C.)	5	0
1985	Helsinki (W.C.)	1	1
1992	Helsinki	2	1
2000	Helsinki (W.C.)	0	0
2001	Liverpool (W.C.)	2	1

v. FRANCE

		E	F
1923	Paris	4	1
1924	Paris	3	1
1925	Paris	3	2
1927	Paris	6	0
1928	Paris	5	1
1929	Paris	4	1
1931	Paris	2	5
1933	Tottenham	4	1
1938	Paris	4	2
1947	Arsenal	3	0
1949	Paris	3	1
1951	Arsenal	2	2
1955	Paris	0	1
1957	Wembley	4	0
1962	Sheffield Wed. (E.C.)	1	1
1963	Paris (E.C.)	2	5
1966	Wembley (W.C.)	2	0
1969	Wembley	5	0
1982	Bilbao (W.C.)	3	1
1984	Paris	0	2
1992	Wembley	2	0
1992	Malmo (E.C.)	0	0
1997	Montpellier (T.F.)	1	0
1999	Wembley	0	2
2000	Paris	1	1

v. GEORGIA

		E	G
1996	Tbilisi (W.C.)	2	0
1997	Wembley (W.C.)	2	0

v. GERMANY/WEST GERMANY

		E	G
1930	Berlin	3	3
1935	Tottenham	3	0
1938	Berlin	6	3
1954	Wembley	3	1
1956	Berlin	3	1
1965	Nuremberg	1	0
1966	Wembley	1	0
1966	Wembley (W.C.F.)	4	2
1968	Hanover	0	1
1970	Leon (W.C.)	2	3
1972	Wembley (E.C.)	1	3
1972	Berlin (E.C.)	0	0
1975	Wembley	2	0
1978	Munich	1	2
1982	Madrid (W.C.)	0	0
1982	Wembley	1	2
1985	Mexico City	3	0
1987	Dusseldorf	1	3
1990*	Turin (W.C.)	1	1
1991	Wembley	0	1
1993	Detroit	1	2
1996†	Wembley (E.C.)	1	1
2000	Charleroi (E.C.)	1	0
2000	Wembley (W.C.)	0	1
2001	Munich (W.C.)	5	1

(* England lost 3-4 on pens.)
(† England lost 5-6 on pens.)

v. GREECE

		E	G
1971	Wembley (E.C.)	3	0
1971	Athens (E.C.)	2	0
1982	Salonika (E.C.)	3	0
1983	Wembley (E.C.)	0	0
1989	Athens	2	1
1994	Wembley	5	0
2001	Athens (W.C.)	2	0
2001	Manchester Utd. (W.C.)	2	2

v. HOLLAND

		E	H
1935	Amsterdam	1	0
1946	Huddersfield	8	2
1964	Amsterdam	1	1
1969	Amsterdam	1	0
1970	Wembley	0	0
1977	Wembley	0	2
1982	Wembley	2	0
1988	Wembley	2	2
1988	Dusseldorf (E.C.)	1	3
1990	Cagliari (W.C.)	0	0
1993	Wembley (W.C.)	2	2
1993	Rotterdam (W.C.)	0	2
1996	Wembley (E.C.)	4	1
2001	Tottenham	0	2
2002	Amsterdam	1	1

v. HUNGARY

		E	H
1908	Budapest	7	0
1909	Budapest	4	2
1909	Budapest	8	2
1934	Budapest	1	2
1936	Highbury	6	2
1953	Wembley	3	6
1954	Budapest	1	7
1960	Budapest	0	2
1962	Rancagua (W.C.)	1	2
1965	Wembley	1	0
1978	Wembley	4	1
1981	Budapest (W.C.)	3	1
1981	Wembley (W.C.)	1	0
1983	Wembley (E.C.)	2	0
1983	Budapest (E.C.)	3	0
1988	Budapest	0	0
1990	Wembley	1	0
1992	Budapest	1	0
1996	Wembley	3	0
1999	Budapest	1	1

v. ICELAND

		E	I
1982	Reykjavik	1	1

v. REPUBLIC OF IRELAND

		E	RI
1946	Dublin	1	0
1950	Everton	0	2
1957	Wembley (W.C.)	5	1
1957	Dublin (W.C.)	1	1
1964	Dublin	3	1
1977	Wembley	1	1
1978	Dublin (E.C.)	1	1
1980	Wembley (E.C.)	2	0
1985	Wembley	2	1
1988	Stuttgart (E.C.)	0	1
1990	Cagliari (W.C.)	1	1
1990	Dublin (E.C.)	1	1
1991	Wembley (E.C.)	1	1
1995*	Dublin	0	1

(* Abandoned 27 mins. – crowd riot)

v. ISRAEL

		E	I
1986	Tel Aviv	2	1
1988	Tel Aviv	0	0

v. ITALY

		E	I
1933	Rome	1	1
1934	Arsenal	3	2
1939	Milan	2	2
1948	Turin	4	0
1949	Tottenham	2	0
1952	Florence	1	1
1959	Wembley	2	2
1961	Rome	3	2
1973	Turin	0	2
1973	Wembley	0	1
1976	New York	3	2
1976	Rome (W.C.)	0	2
1977	Wembley (W.C.)	2	0
1980	Turin (E.C.)	0	1
1985	Mexico City	1	2
1989	Wembley	0	0
1990	Bari (W.C.)	1	2
1996	Wembley (W.C.)	0	1
1997	Nantes (T.F.)	2	0
1997	Rome (W.C.)	0	0
2000	Turin	0	1
2002	Leeds	1	2

v. JAPAN

		E	J
1995	Wembley	2	1

v. KUWAIT

		E	K
1982	Bilbao (W.C.)	1	0

v. LIECHTENSTEIN

		E	L
2003	Vaduz (E.C.)	2	0

v. LUXEMBOURG

		E	L
1927	Luxembourg	5	2
1960	Luxembourg (W.C.)	9	0
1961	Arsenal (W.C.)	4	1
1977	Wembley (W.C.)	5	0
1977	Luxembourg (W.C.)	2	0
1982	Wembley (E.C.)	9	0
1983	Luxembourg (E.C.)	4	0
1998	Luxembourg (E.C.)	3	0
1999	Wembley (E.C.)	6	0

v. MACEDONIA

		E	M
2002	Southamton (E.C.)	2	2

v. MALAYSIA

		E	M
1991	Kuala Lumpur	4	2

v. MALTA

		E	M
1971	Valletta (E.C.)	1	0
1971	Wembley (E.C.)	5	0
2000	Valletta	2	1

v. MEXICO

		E	M
1959	Mexico City	1	2
1961	Wembley	8	0
1966	Wembley (W.C.)	2	0
1969	Mexico City	0	0
1985	Mexico City	0	1
1986	Los Angeles	3	0
1997	Wembley	2	0
2001	Derby	4	0

v. MOLDOVA

		E	M
1996	Kishinev	3	0
1997	Wembley (W.C.)	4	0

v. MOROCCO

		E	M
1986	Monterrey (W.C.)	0	0
1998	Casablanca	1	0

v. NEW ZEALAND

		E	NZ
1991	Auckland	1	0
1991	Wellington	2	0

v. NIGERIA

		E	N
1994	Wembley	1	0
2002	Osaka (W.C.)	0	0

v. NORWAY

		E	N
1937	Oslo	6	0
1938	Newcastle	4	0
1949	Oslo	4	1
1966	Oslo	6	1

		E	N
1980	Wembley (W.C.)	4	0
1981	Oslo (W.C.)	1	2
1992	Wembley (W.C.)	1	1
1993	Oslo (W.C.)	0	2
1994	Wembley	0	0
1995	Oslo	0	0

v. PARAGUAY

		E	P
1986	Mexico City (W.C.)	3	0
2002	Liverpool	4	0

v. PERU

		E	P
1959	Lima	1	4
1961	Lima	4	0

v. POLAND

		E	P
1966	Everton	1	1
1966	Chorzow	1	0
1973	Chorzow (W.C.)	0	2
1973	Wembley (W.C.)	1	1
1986	Monterrey (W.C.)	3	0
1989	Wembley (W.C.)	3	0
1989	Katowice (W.C.)	0	0
1990	Wembley (E.C.)	2	0
1991	Poznan (E.C.)	1	1
1993	Chorzow (W.C.)	1	1
1993	Wembley (W.C.)	3	0
1996	Wembley (W.C.)	2	1
1997	Katowice (W.C.)	2	0
1999	Wembley (E.C.)	3	1
1999	Warsaw (E.C.)	0	0

v. PORTUGAL

		E	P
1947	Lisbon	10	0
1950	Lisbon	5	3
1951	Everton	5	2
1955	Oporto	1	3
1958	Wembley	2	1
1961	Lisbon (W.C.)	1	1
1961	Wembley (W.C.)	2	0
1964	Lisbon	4	3
1964	Sao Paulo	1	1
1966	Wembley (W.C.)	2	1
1969	Wembley	1	0
1974	Lisbon	0	0
1974	Wembley (E.C.)	0	0
1975	Lisbon (E.C.)	1	1
1986	Monterrey (W.C.)	0	1
1995	Wembley	1	1
1998	Wembley	3	0
2000	Eindhoven (E.C.)	2	3
2002	Aston Villa	1	1

v. ROMANIA

		E	R
1939	Bucharest	2	0
1968	Bucharest	0	0
1969	Wembley	1	1
1970	Guadalajara (W.C.)	1	0
1980	Bucharest (W.C.)	1	2
1981	Wembley (W.C.)	0	0
1985	Bucharest (W.C.)	0	0
1985	Wembley (W.C.)	1	1
1994	Wembley	1	1
1998	Toulouse (W.C.)	1	2
2000	Charleroi (E.C.)	2	3

v. SAN MARINO

		E	SM
1992	Wembley (W.C.)	6	0
1993	Bologna (W.C.)	7	1

v. SAUDI ARABIA

		E	SA
1988	Riyadh	1	1
1998	Wembley	0	0

v. SERBIA-MONTENEGRO

		E	S-M
2003	Leicester	2	1

v. SLOVAKIA

		E	S
2002	Bratislava (E.C.)	2	1
2003	Middlesbrough (E.C.)	2	1

v. SOUTH AFRICA

		E	SA
1997	Manchester Utd.	2	1
2003	Durban	2	1

v. SOUTH KOREA

		E	SK
2002	Seoguipo	1	1

v. SOVIET UNION (see also C.I.S.)

		E	SU
1958	Moscow	1	1
1958	Gothenburg (W.C.)	2	2
1958	Gothenburg (W.C.)	0	1
1958	Wembley	5	0
1967	Wembley	2	2
1968	Rome (E.C.)	2	0
1973	Moscow	2	1
1984	Wembley	0	2
1986	Tbilisi	1	0
1988	Frankfurt (E.C.)	1	3
1991	Wembley	3	1

v. SPAIN

		E	S
1929	Madrid	3	4
1931	Arsenal	7	1
1950	Rio de Janeiro (W.C.)	0	1
1955	Madrid	1	1

		E	S
1955	Wembley	4	1
1960	Madrid	0	3
1960	Wembley	4	2
1965	Madrid	2	0
1967	Wembley	2	0
1968	Wembley (E.C.)	1	0
1968	Madrid (E.C.)	2	1
1980	Barcelona	2	0
1980	Naples (E.C.)	2	1
1981	Wembley	1	2
1982	Madrid (W.C.)	0	0
1987	Madrid	4	2
1992	Santander	0	1
1996*	Wembley (E.C.)	0	0
2001	Aston Villa	3	0

(* England won 4-2 on pens.)

v. SWEDEN

		E	S
1923	Stockholm	4	2
1923	Stockholm	3	1
1937	Stockholm	4	0
1948	Arsenal	4	2
1949	Stockholm	1	3
1956	Stockholm	0	0
1959	Wembley	2	3
1965	Gothenburg	2	1
1968	Wembley	3	1
1979	Stockholm	0	0
1986	Stockholm	0	1
1988	Wembley (W.C.)	0	0
1989	Stockholm (W.C.)	0	0
1992	Stockholm (E.C.)	1	2
1995	Leeds	3	3
1998	Stockholm (E.C.)	1	2
1999	Wembley (E.C.)	0	0
2001	Manchester Utd.	1	1
2002	Saitama (W.C.)	1	1

v. SWITZERLAND

		E	S
1933	Berne	4	0
1938	Zurich	1	2
1947	Zurich	0	1
1949	Arsenal	6	0
1952	Zurich	3	0
1954	Berne (W.C.)	2	0
1962	Wembley	3	1
1963	Basle	8	1
1971	Basle (E.C.)	3	2
1971	Wembley (E.C.)	1	1
1975	Basle	2	1
1977	Wembley	0	0
1980	Wembley (W.C.)	2	1
1981	Basle (W.C.)	1	2
1988	Lausanne	1	0
1995	Wembley	3	1
1996	Wembley (E.C.)	1	1
1998	Berne	1	1

v. TUNISIA

		E	T
1990	Tunis	1	1
1998	Marseille (W.C.)	2	0

v. TURKEY

		E	T
1984	Istanbul (W.C.)	8	0
1985	Wembley (W.C.)	5	0
1987	Izmir (E.C.)	0	0
1987	Wembley (E.C.)	8	0
1991	Izmir (E.C.)	1	0
1991	Wembley (E.C.)	1	0
1992	Wembley (W.C.)	4	0
1993	Izmir (W.C.)	2	0
2003	Sunderland (E.C.)	2	0

v UKRAINE

		E	U
2000	Wembley	2	0

v. URUGUAY

		E	U
1953	Montevideo	1	2
1954	Basle (W.C.)	2	4
1964	Wembley	2	1
1966	Wembley (W.C.)	0	0
1969	Montevideo	2	1
1977	Montevideo	0	0
1984	Montevideo	0	2
1990	Wembley	1	2
1995	Wembley	0	0

v. U.S.A.

		E	USA
1950	Belo Horizonte (W.C.)	0	1
1953	New York	6	3
1959	Los Angeles	8	1
1964	New York	10	0
1985	Los Angeles	5	0
1993	Boston	0	2
1994	Wembley	2	0

v. YUGOSLAVIA

		E	Y
1939	Belgrade	1	2
1950	Arsenal	2	2
1954	Belgrade	0	1
1956	Wembley	3	0
1958	Belgrade	0	5
1960	Wembley	3	3
1965	Belgrade	1	1
1966	Wembley	2	0
1968	Florence (E.C.)	0	1
1972	Wembley	1	1
1974	Belgrade	2	2
1986	Wembley (E.C.)	2	0
1987	Belgrade (E.C.)	4	1
1989	Wembley	2	1

ENGLAND'S RECORD

England's first international was a 0-0 draw against Scotland in Glasgow, on the West of Scotland cricket ground, Partick, on November 30, 1872. Now, 130 years on, their complete International record, at the start of 2003-04, is:

P	W	D	L	F	A
803	451	197	155	1806	822

ENGLAND "B" TEAM RESULTS

(England score shown first)

1949	Finland (A)	4	0
1949	Holland (A)	4	0
1950	Italy (A)	0	5
1950	Holland (H)	1	0
1950	Holland (A)	0	3
1950	Luxembourg (A)	2	1
1950	Switzerland (H)	5	0
1952	Holland (A)	1	0
1952	France (A)	1	7
1953	Scotland (A)	2	2
1954	Scotland (H)	1	1
1954	Germany (A)	4	0
1954	Yugoslavia (A)	1	2
1954	Switzerland (A)	0	2
1955	Germany (H)	1	1
1955	Yugoslavia (H)	5	1
1956	Switzerland (H)	4	1
1956	Scotland (A)	2	2
1957	Scotland (H)	4	1
1978	W. Germany (A)	2	1
1978	Czechoslovakia (A)	1	0
1978	Singapore (A)	8	0
1978	Malaysia (A)	1	1
1978	N. Zealand (A)	4	0
1978	N. Zealand (A)	3	1
1978	N. Zealand (A)	4	0
1979	Austria (A)	1	0
1979	N. Zealand (H)	4	1
1980	U.S.A. (H)	1	0
1980	Spain (H)	1	0
1980	Australia (H)	1	0
1981	Spain (A)	2	3
1984	N. Zealand (H)	2	0
1987	Malta (A)	2	0
1989	Switzerland (A)	2	0
1989	Iceland (A)	2	0
1989	Norway (A)	1	0
1989	Italy (H)	1	1
1989	Yugoslavia (H)	2	1
1990	Rep. of Ireland (A)	1	4
1990	Czechoslovakia (H)	2	0
1990	Algeria (A)	0	0
1991	Wales (A)	1	0
1991	Iceland (H)	1	0
1991	Switzerland (H)	2	1
1991	Spanish XI (A)	1	0
1992	France (H)	3	0
1992	Czechoslovakia (A)	1	0
1992	C.I.S. (A)	1	1
1994	N. Ireland (H)	4	2
1995	Rep. of Ireland (H)	2	0
1998	Chile (H)	1	2
1998	Russia (H)	4	1

GREAT BRITAIN V. REST OF EUROPE (F.I.F.A.)

		GB	*RofE*
1947	Glasgow	6	1
1955	Belfast	1	4

SCOTLAND

v. ARGENTINA

		S	*A*
1977	Buenos Aires	1	1
1979	Glasgow	1	3
1990	Glasgow	1	0

v. AUSTRALIA

		S	*A*
1985*	Glasgow (W.C.)	2	0
1985*	Melbourne (W.C.)	0	0
1996	Glasgow	1	0
2000	Glasgow	0	2

(* World Cup play-off)

v. AUSTRIA

		S	*A*
1931	Vienna	0	5

		S	A
1933	Glasgow	2	2
1937	Vienna	1	1
1950	Glasgow	0	1
1951	Vienna	0	4
1954	Zurich (W.C.)	0	1
1955	Vienna	4	1
1956	Glasgow	1	1
1960	Vienna	1	4
1963*	Glasgow	4	1
1968	Glasgow (W.C.)	2	1
1969	Vienna (W.C.)	0	2
1978	Vienna (E.C.)	2	3
1979	Glasgow (E.C.)	1	1
1994	Vienna	2	1
1996	Vienna (W.C.)	0	0
1997	Glasgow (W.C.)	2	0
(* Abandoned after 79 minutes)			
2003	Glasgow	0	2

v. BELARUS

		S	B
1997	Minsk (W.C.)	1	0
1997	Aberdeen (W.C.)	4	1

v. BELGIUM

		S	B
1947	Brussels	1	2
1948	Glasgow	2	0
1951	Brussels	5	0
1971	Liege (E.C.)	0	3
1971	Aberdeen (E.C.)	1	0
1974	Brugge	1	2
1979	Brussels (E.C.)	0	2
1979	Glasgow (E.C.)	1	3
1982	Brussels (E.C.)	2	3
1983	Glasgow (E.C.)	1	1
1987	Brussels (E.C.)	1	4
1987	Glasgow (E.C.)	2	0
2001	Glasgow (W.C.)	2	2
2001	Brussels (W.C.)	0	2

v. BOSNIA

		S	B
1999	Sarajevo (E.C.)	2	1
1999	Glasgow (E.C.)	1	0

v. BRAZIL

		S	B
1966	Glasgow	1	1
1972	Rio de Janeiro	0	1
1973	Glasgow	0	1
1974	Frankfurt (W.C.)	0	0
1977	Rio de Janeiro	0	2
1982	Seville (W.C.)	1	4
1987	Glasgow	0	2
1990	Turin (W.C.)	0	1
1998	St. Denis (W.C.)	1	2

v. BULGARIA

		S	B
1978	Glasgow	2	1
1986	Glasgow (E.C.)	0	0
1987	Sofia (E.C.)	1	0
1990	Sofia (E.C.)	1	1
1991	Glasgow (E.C.)	1	1

v. CANADA

		S	C
1983	Vancouver	2	0
1983	Edmonton	3	0
1983	Toronto	2	0
1992	Toronto	3	1
2002	Edinburgh	3	1

v. CHILE

		S	C
1977	Santiago	4	2
1989	Glasgow	2	0

v. C.I.S. (formerly Soviet Union)

		S	C
1992	Norrkoping (E.C.)	3	0

v. COLOMBIA

		S	C
1988	Glasgow	0	0
1996	Miami	0	1
1998	New York	2	2

v. COSTA RICA

		S	C
1990	Genoa (W.C.)	0	1

v. CROATIA

		S	C
2000	Zagreb (W.C.)	1	1
2001	Glasgow (W.C.)	0	0

v. CYPRUS

		S	C
1968	Nicosia (W.C.)	5	0
1969	Glasgow (W.C.)	8	0
1989	Limassol (W.C.)	3	2
1989	Glasgow (W.C.)	2	1

v. CZECH REPUBLIC

		S	C
1999	Glasgow (E.C.)	1	2
1999	Prague (E.C.)	2	3

v. CZECHOSLOVAKIA

		S	C
1937	Prague	3	1
1937	Glasgow	5	0
1961	Bratislava (W.C.)	0	4
1961	Glasgow (W.C.)	3	2
1961*	Brussels (W.C.)	2	4
1972	Porto Alegre	0	0
1973	Glasgow (W.C.)	2	1
1973	Bratislava (W.C.)	0	1
1976	Prague (W.C.)	0	2

		S	C
1977	Glasgow (W.C.)	3	1

(* World Cup play-off)

v. DENMARK

		S	D
1951	Glasgow	3	1
1952	Copenhagen	2	1
1968	Copenhagen	1	0
1970	Glasgow (E.C.)	1	0
1971	Copenhagen (E.C.)	0	1
1972	Copenhagen (W.C.)	4	1
1972	Glasgow (W.C.)	2	0
1975	Copenhagen (E.C.)	1	0
1975	Glasgow (E.C.)	3	1
1986	Neza (W.C.)	0	1
1996	Copenhagen	0	2
1998	Glasgow	0	1
2002	Glasgow	0	1

v. EAST GERMANY

		S	EG
1974	Glasgow	3	0
1977	East Berlin	0	1
1982	Glasgow (E.C.)	2	0
1983	Halle (E.C.)	1	2
1986	Glasgow	0	0
1990	Glasgow	0	1

v. ECUADOR

		S	E
1995	Toyama, Japan	2	1

v. EGYPT

		S	E
1990	Aberdeen	1	3

v. ESTONIA

		S	E
1993	Tallinn (W.C.)	3	0
1993	Aberdeen	3	1
1996	Tallinn (W.C.)	* No result	
1997	Monaco (W.C.)	0	0
1997	Kilmarnock (W.C.)	2	0
1998	Edinburgh (E.C.)	3	2
1999	Tallinn (E.C.)	0	0

(* Estonia absent)

v. FAROE ISLANDS

		S	F
1994	Glasgow (E.C.)	5	1
1995	Toftir (E.C.)	2	0
1998	Aberdeen (E.C.)	2	1
1999	Toftir (E.C.)	1	1
2002	Toftir (E.C.)	2	2

v. FINLAND

		S	F
1954	Helsinki	2	1
1964	Glasgow (W.C.)	3	1
1965	Helsinki (W.C.)	2	1
1976	Glasgow	6	0
1992	Glasgow	1	1
1994	Helsinki (E.C.)	2	0
1995	Glasgow (E.C.)	1	0
1998	Edinburgh	1	1

v. FRANCE

		S	F
1930	Paris	2	0
1932	Paris	3	1
1948	Paris	0	3
1949	Glasgow	2	0
1950	Paris	1	0
1951	Glasgow	1	0
1958	Orebro (W.C.)	1	2
1984	Marseilles	0	2
1989	Glasgow (W.C.)	2	0
1990	Paris (W.C.)	0	3
1997	St. Etienne	1	2
2000	Glasgow	0	2
2002	Paris	0	5

v. GERMANY/WEST GERMANY

		S	G
1929	Berlin	1	1
1936	Glasgow	2	0
1957	Stuttgart	3	1
1959	Glasgow	3	2
1964	Hanover	2	2
1969	Glasgow (W.C.)	1	1
1969	Hamburg (W.C.)	2	3
1973	Glasgow	1	1
1974	Frankfurt	1	2
1986	Queretaro (W.C.)	1	2
1992	Norrkoping (E.C.)	0	2
1993	Glasgow	0	1
1999	Bremen	1	0
2003	Glasgow (E.C.)	1	1

v. GREECE

		S	G
1994	Athens (E.C.)	0	1
1995	Glasgow	1	0

v. HOLLAND

		S	H
1929	Amsterdam	2	0
1938	Amsterdam	3	1
1959	Amsterdam	2	1
1966	Glasgow	0	3
1968	Amsterdam	0	0
1971	Amsterdam	1	2
1978	Mendoza (W.C.)	3	2
1982	Glasgow	2	1
1986	Eindhoven	0	0
1992	Gothenburg (E.C.)	0	1
1994	Glasgow	0	1
1994	Utrecht	1	3
1996	Birmingham (E.C.)	0	0

		S	H
2000	Arnhem	0	0

v. HUNGARY

		S	H
1938	Glasgow	3	1
1955	Glasgow	2	4
1955	Budapest	1	3
1958	Glasgow	1	1
1960	Budapest	3	3
1980	Budapest	1	3
1987	Glasgow	2	0

v. ICELAND

		S	I
1984	Glasgow (W.C.)	3	0
1985	Reykjavik (W.C)	1	0
2002	Reykjavik (E.C)	2	0
2003	Glasgow (E.C)	2	1

v. IRAN

		S	I
1978	Cordoba (W.C.)	1	1

v. REPUBLIC OF IRELAND

		S	RI
1961	Glasgow (W.C.)	4	1
1961	Dublin (W.C.)	3	0
1963	Dublin	0	1
1969	Dublin	1	1
1986	Dublin (E.C.)	0	0
1987	Glasgow (E.C.)	0	1
2000	Dublin	2	1
2003	Glasgow (E.C.)	0	2

v. ISRAEL

		S	I
1981	Tel Aviv (W.C.)	1	0
1981	Glasgow (W.C.)	3	1
1986	Tel Aviv	1	0

v. ITALY

		S	I
1931	Rome	0	3
1965	Glasgow (W.C.)	1	0
1965	Naples (W.C.)	0	3
1988	Perugia	0	2
1992	Glasgow (W.C.)	0	0
1993	Rome (W.C.)	1	3

v. JAPAN

		S	J
1995	Hiroshima	0	0

v. LATVIA

		S	L
1996	Riga (W.C.)	2	0
1997	Glasgow (W.C.)	2	0
2000	Riga (W.C.)	1	0
2001	Glasgow (W.C.)	2	1

v. LITHUANIA

		S	L
1998	Vilnius (E.C.)	0	0
1999	Glasgow (E.C.)	3	0
2003	Kaunus (E.C.)	0	1

v. LUXEMBOURG

		S	L
1947	Luxembourg	6	0
1986	Glasgow (E.C.)	3	0
1987	Esch (E.C.)	0	0

v. MALTA

		S	M
1988	Valletta	1	1
1990	Valletta	2	1
1993	Glasgow (W.C.)	3	0
1993	Valletta (W.C.)	2	0
1997	Valletta	3	2

v. MOROCCO

		S	M
1998	St. Etienne (W.C.)	0	3

v. NEW ZEALAND

		S	NZ
1982	Malaga (W.C.)	5	2
2003	Edinburgh	1	1

v. NIGERIA

		S	N
2002	Aberdeen	1	2

v. NORWAY

		S	N
1929	Bergen	7	3
1954	Glasgow	1	0
1954	Oslo	1	1
1963	Bergen	3	4
1963	Glasgow	6	1
1974	Oslo	2	1
1978	Glasgow (E.C.)	3	2
1979	Oslo (E.C.)	4	0
1988	Oslo (W.C.)	2	1
1989	Glasgow (W.C.)	1	1
1992	Oslo	0	0
1998	Bordeaux (W.C.)	1	1

v. PARAGUAY

		S	P
1958	Norrkoping (W.C.)	2	3

v. PERU

		S	P
1972	Glasgow	2	0
1978	Cordoba (W.C.)	1	3
1979	Glasgow	1	1

v. POLAND

		S	P
1958	Warsaw	2	1
1960	Glasgow	2	3
1965	Chorzow (W.C.)	1	1

		S	P
1965	Glasgow (W.C.)	1	2
1980	Poznan	0	1
1990	Glasgow	1	1
2001	Bydgoszcz	1	1

v. PORTUGAL

		S	P
1950	Lisbon	2	2
1955	Glasgow	3	0
1959	Lisbon	0	1
1966	Glasgow	0	1
1971	Lisbon (E.C.)	0	2
1971	Glasgow (E.C.)	2	1
1975	Glasgow	1	0
1978	Lisbon (E.C.)	0	1
1980	Glasgow (E.C.)	4	1
1980	Glasgow (W.C.)	0	0
1981	Lisbon (W.C.)	1	2
1992	Glasgow (W.C.)	0	0
1993	Lisbon (W.C.)	0	5
2002	Braga	0	2

v. ROMANIA

		S	R
1975	Bucharest (E.C.)	1	1
1975	Glasgow (E.C.)	1	1
1986	Glasgow	3	0
1990	Glasgow (E.C.)	2	1
1991	Bucharest (E.C.)	0	1

v. RUSSIA

		S	R
1994	Glasgow (E.C.)	1	1
1995	Moscow (E.C.)	0	0

v. SAN MARINO

		S	SM
1991	Serravalle (E.C.)	2	0
1991	Glasgow (E.C.)	4	0
1995	Serravalle (E.C.)	2	0
1995	Glasgow (E.C.)	5	0
2000	Serravalle (W.C.)	2	0
2001	Glasgow (W.C.)	4	0

v. SAUDI ARABIA

		S	SA
1988	Riyadh	2	2

v. SOUTH AFRICA

		S	SA
2002	Hong Kong	0	2

v. SOUTH KOREA

		S	SK
2002	Busan	1	4

v. SOVIET UNION
(see also C.I.S. and RUSSIA)

		S	SU
1967	Glasgow	0	2
1971	Moscow	0	1
1982	Malaga (W.C.)	2	2
1991	Glasgow	0	1

v. SPAIN

		S	Sp
1957	Glasgow (W.C.)	4	2
1957	Madrid (W.C.)	1	4
1963	Madrid	6	2
1965	Glasgow	0	0
1975	Glasgow (E.C.)	1	2
1975	Valencia (E.C.)	1	1
1982	Valencia	0	3
1985	Glasgow (W.C.)	3	1
1985	Seville (W.C.)	0	1
1988	Madrid	0	0

v. SWEDEN

		S	Swe
1952	Stockholm	1	3
1953	Glasgow	1	2
1975	Gothenburg	1	1
1977	Glasgow	3	1
1980	Stockholm (W.C.)	1	0
1981	Glasgow (W.C.)	2	0
1990	Genoa (W.C.)	2	1
1995	Solna	0	2
1996	Glasgow (W.C.)	1	0
1997	Gothenburg (W.C.)	1	2

v. SWITZERLAND

		S	Sw
1931	Geneva	3	2
1948	Berne	1	2
1950	Glasgow	3	1
1957	Basle (W.C.)	2	1
1957	Glasgow (W.C.)	3	2
1973	Berne	0	1
1976	Glasgow	1	0
1982	Berne (E.C.)	0	2
1983	Glasgow (E.C.)	2	2
1990	Glasgow (E.C.)	2	1
1991	Berne (E.C.)	2	2
1992	Berne (W.C.)	1	3
1993	Aberdeen (W.C.)	1	1
1996	Birmingham (E.C.)	1	0

v. TURKEY

		S	T
1960	Ankara	2	4

v. U.S.A.

		S	USA
1952	Glasgow	6	0
1992	Denver	1	0
1996	New Britain, Conn	1	2
1998	Washington	0	0

v. URUGUAY

		S	U
1954	Basle (W.C.)	0	7

		S	U
1962	Glasgow	2	3
1983	Glasgow	2	0
1986	Neza (W.C.)	0	0

v. YUGOSLAVIA

		S	Y
1955	Belgrade	2	2
1956	Glasgow	2	0
1958	Vaasteras (W.C.)	1	1
1972	Belo Horizonte	2	2
1974	Frankfurt (W.C.)	1	1
1984	Glasgow	6	1
1988	Glasgow (W.C.)	1	1
1989	Zagreb (W.C.)	1	3

v. ZAIRE

		S	Z
1974	Dortmund (W.C.)	2	0

WALES

v. ALBANIA

		W	A
1994	Cardiff (E.C.)	2	0
1995	Tirana (E.C.)	1	1

v. ARGENTINA

		W	A
1992	Gifu (Japan)	0	1
2002	Cardiff	1	1

v. ARMENIA

		W	A
2001	Yerevan (W.C.)	2	2
2001	Cardiff (W.C.)	0	0

v. AUSTRIA

		W	A
1954	Vienna	0	2
1955	Wrexham	1	2
1975	Vienna (E.C.)	1	2
1975	Wrexham (E.C.)	1	0
1992	Vienna	1	1

v. AZERBAIJAN

		W	A
2002	Baku (E.C.)	2	0
2003	Cardiff (E.C.)	4	0

v. BELARUS

		W	B
1998	Cardiff (E.C.)	3	2
1999	Minsk (E.C.)	2	1
2000	Minsk (W.C.)	1	2
2001	Cardiff (W.C.)	1	0

v. BELGIUM

		W	B
1949	Liege	1	3
1949	Cardiff	5	1
1990	Cardiff (E.C.)	3	1
1991	Brussels (E.C.)	1	1
1992	Brussels (W.C.)	0	2
1993	Cardiff (W.C.)	2	0
1997	Cardiff (W.C.)	1	2
1997	Brussels (W.C.)	2	3

v. BOSNIA-HERZEGOVINA

		W	B-H
2003	Cardiff	2	2

v. BRAZIL

		W	B
1958	Gothenburg (W.C.)	0	1
1962	Rio de Janeiro	1	3
1962	Sao Paulo	1	3
1966	Rio de Janeiro	1	3
1966	Belo Horizonte	0	1
1983	Cardiff	1	1
1991	Cardiff	1	0
1997	Brasilia	0	3
2000	Cardiff	0	3

v. BULGARIA

		W	B
1983	Wrexham (E.C.)	1	0
1983	Sofia (E.C.)	0	1
1994	Cardiff (E.C.)	0	3
1995	Sofia (E.C.)	1	3

v. CANADA

		W	C
1986	Toronto	0	2
1986	Vancouver	3	0

v. CHILE

		W	C
1966	Santiago	0	2

v. COSTA RICA

		W	C
1990	Cardiff	1	0

v. CROATIA

		W	C
2002	Varazdin	1	1

v. CYPRUS

		W	C
1992	Limassol (W.C.)	1	0
1993	Cardiff (W.C.)	2	0

v. CZECHOSLOVAKIA (see also R.C.S.)

		W	C
1957	Cardiff (W.C.)	1	0
1957	Prague (W.C.)	0	2
1971	Swansea (E.C.)	1	3
1971	Prague (E.C.)	0	1
1977	Wrexham (W.C.)	3	0
1977	Prague (W.C.)	0	1

		W	C
1980	Cardiff (W.C.)	1	0
1981	Prague (W.C.)	0	2
1987	Wrexham (E.C.)	1	1
1987	Prague (E.C.)	0	2

v. CZECH REPUBLIC

		S	CR
2002	Cardiff	0	0

v. DENMARK

		W	D
1964	Copenhagen (W.C.)	0	1
1965	Wrexham (W.C.)	4	2
1987	Cardiff (E.C.)	1	0
1987	Copenhagen (E.C.)	0	1
1990	Copenhagen	0	1
1998	Copenhagen (E.C.)	2	1
1999	Anfield (E.C.)	0	2

v. EAST GERMANY

		W	EG
1957	Leipzig (W.C.)	1	2
1957	Cardiff (W.C.)	4	1
1969	Dresden (W.C.)	1	2
1969	Cardiff (W.C.)	1	3

v. ESTONIA

		W	E
1994	Tallinn	2	1

v. FAROE ISLANDS

		W	FI
1992	Cardiff (W.C.)	6	0
1993	Toftir (W.C.)	3	0

v. FINLAND

		W	F
1971	Helsinki (E.C.)	1	0
1971	Swansea (E.C.)	3	0
1986	Helsinki (E.C.)	1	1
1987	Wrexham (E.C.)	4	0
1988	Swansea (W.C.)	2	2
1989	Helsinki (W.C.)	0	1
2000	Cardiff	1	2
2002	Helsinki (E.C.)	2	0

v. FRANCE

		W	F
1933	Paris	1	1
1939	Paris	1	2
1953	Paris	1	6
1982	Toulouse	1	0

v. GEORGIA

		W	G
1994	Tbilisi (E.C.)	0	5
1995	Cardiff (E.C.)	0	1

v. GERMANY/WEST GERMANY

		W	G
1968	Cardiff	1	1
1969	Frankfurt	1	1
1977	Cardiff	0	2
1977	Dortmund	1	1
1979	Wrexham (E.C.)	0	2
1979	Cologne (E.C.)	1	5
1989	Cardiff (W.C.)	0	0
1989	Cologne (W.C.)	1	2
1991	Cardiff (E.C.)	1	0
1991	Nuremberg (E.C.)	1	4
1995	Dusseldorf (E.C.)	1	1
1995	Cardiff (E.C.)	1	2
2002	Cardiff	1	0

v. GREECE

		W	G
1964	Athens (W.C.)	0	2
1965	Cardiff (W.C.)	4	1

v. HOLLAND

		W	H
1988	Amsterdam (W.C.)	0	1
1989	Wrexham (W.C.)	1	2
1992	Utrecht	0	4
1996	Cardiff (W.C.)	1	3
1996	Eindhoven (W.C.)	1	7

v. HUNGARY

		W	H
1958	Sanviken (W.C.)	1	1
1958	Stockholm (W.C.)	2	1
1961	Budapest	2	3
1963	Budapest (E.C.)	1	3
1963	Cardiff (E.C.)	1	1
1974	Cardiff (E.C.)	2	0
1975	Budapest (E.C.)	2	1
1986	Cardiff	0	3

v. ICELAND

		W	I
1980	Reykjavik (W.C.)	4	0
1981	Swansea (W.C.)	2	2
1984	Reykjavik (W.C.)	0	1
1984	Cardiff (W.C.)	2	1
1991	Cardiff	1	0

v. IRAN

		W	I
1978	Tehran	1	0

v. REPUBLIC OF IRELAND

		W	RI
1960	Dublin	3	2
1979	Swansea	2	1
1981	Dublin	3	1
1986	Dublin	1	0
1990	Dublin	0	1
1991	Wrexham	0	3
1992	Dublin	1	0
1993	Dublin	1	2
1997	Cardiff	0	0

v. ISRAEL

		W	I
1958	Tel Aviv (W.C.)	2	0
1958	Cardiff (W.C.)	2	0
1984	Tel Aviv	0	0
1989	Tel Aviv	3	3

v. ITALY

		W	I
1965	Florence	1	4
1968	Cardiff (W.C.)	0	1
1969	Rome (W.C.)	1	4
1988	Brescia	1	0
1996	Terni	0	3
1998	Anfield (E.C.)	0	2
1999	Bologna (E.C.)	0	4
2002	Cardiff (E.C.)	2	1

v. JAMAICA

		W	J
1998	Cardiff	0	0

v. JAPAN

		W	J
1992	Matsuyama	1	0

v. KUWAIT

		W	K
1977	Wrexham	0	0
1977	Kuwait City	0	0

v. LUXEMBOURG

		W	L
1974	Swansea (E.C.)	5	0
1975	Luxembourg (E.C.)	3	1
1990	Luxembourg (E.C.)	1	0
1991	Luxembourg (E.C.)	1	0

v. MALTA

		W	M
1978	Wrexham (E.C.)	7	0
1979	Valletta (E.C.)	2	0
1988	Valletta	3	2
1998	Valletta	3	0

v. MEXICO

		W	M
1958	Stockholm (W.C.)	1	1
1962	Mexico City	1	2

v. MOLDOVA

		W	M
1994	Kishinev (E.C.)	2	3
1995	Cardiff (E.C.)	1	0

v. NORWAY

		W	N
1982	Swansea (E.C.)	1	0
1983	Oslo (E.C.)	0	0
1984	Trondheim	0	1
1985	Wrexham	1	1
1985	Bergen	2	4
1994	Cardiff	1	3
2000	Cardiff (W.C.)	1	1
2001	Oslo (W.C.)	2	3

v. POLAND

		W	P
1973	Cardiff (W.C.)	2	0
1973	Katowice (W.C.)	0	3
1991	Radom	0	0
2000	Warsaw (W.C.)	0	0
2001	Cardiff (W.C.)	1	2

v. PORTUGAL

		W	P
1949	Lisbon	2	3
1951	Cardiff	2	1
2000	Chaves	0	3

v. QATAR

		W	Q
2000	Doha	1	0

v. R.C.S. (formerly Czechoslovakia)

		W	RCS
1993	Ostrava (W.C.)	1	1
1993	Cardiff (W.C.)	2	2

v. REST OF UNITED KINGDOM

		W	UK
1951	Cardiff	3	2
1969	Cardiff	0	1

v. ROMANIA

		W	R
1970	Cardiff (E.C.)	0	0
1971	Bucharest (E.C.)	0	2
1983	Wrexham	5	0
1992	Bucharest (W.C.)	1	5
1993	Cardiff (W.C.)	1	2

v. SAN MARINO

		W	SM
1996	Serravalle (W.C.)	5	0
1996	Cardiff (W.C.)	6	0

v. SAUDI ARABIA

		W	SA
1986	Dahran	2	1

v. SOVIET UNION

		W	SU
1965	Moscow (W.C.)	1	2
1965	Cardiff (W.C.)	2	1
1981	Wrexham (W.C.)	0	0
1981	Tbilisi (W.C.)	0	3
1987	Swansea	0	0

v. SPAIN

		W	S
1961	Cardiff (W.C.)	1	2
1961	Madrid (W.C.)	1	1
1982	Valencia	1	1

		W	S
1984	Seville (W.C.)	0	3
1985	Wrexham (W.C.)	3	0

v. SWEDEN

		W	S
1958	Stockholm (W.C.)	0	0
1988	Stockholm	1	4
1989	Wrexham	0	2
1990	Stockholm	2	4
1994	Wrexham	0	2

v. SWITZERLAND

		W	S
1949	Berne	0	4
1951	Wrexham	3	2
1996	Lugano	0	2
1999	Zurich (E.C.)	0	2
1999	Wrexham (E.C.)	0	2

v. TUNISIA

		W	T
1998	Tunis	0	4

v. TURKEY

		W	T
1978	Wrexham (E.C.)	1	0
1979	Izmir (E.C.)	0	1
1980	Cardiff (W.C.)	4	0
1981	Ankara (W.C.)	1	0
1996	Cardiff (W.C.)	0	0
1997	Istanbul (W.C.)	4	6

v. UKRAINE

		W	U
2001	Cardiff (W.C.)	1	1
2001	Kiev (W.C.)	1	1

v. URUGUAY

		W	U
1986	Wrexham	0	0

v. U.S.A.

		W	USA
2003	San Jose	0	2

v. YUGOSLAVIA

		W	Y
1953	Belgrade	2	5
1954	Cardiff	1	3
1976	Zagreb (E.C.)	0	2
1976	Cardiff (E.C.)	1	1
1982	Titograd (E.C.)	4	4
1983	Cardiff (E.C.)	1	1
1988	Swansea	1	2

NORTHERN IRELAND

v. ALBANIA

		NI	A
1965	Belfast (W.C.)	4	1
1965	Tirana (W.C.)	1	1
1983	Tirana (E.C.)	0	0
1983	Belfast (E.C.)	1	0
1992	Belfast (W.C.)	3	0
1993	Tirana (W.C.)	2	1
1996	Belfast (W.C.)	2	0
1997	Zurich (W.C.)	0	1

v. ALGERIA

		NI	A
1986	Guadalajara (W.C.)	1	1

v. ARGENTINA

		NI	A
1958	Halmstad (W.C.)	1	3

v. ARMENIA

		NI	A
1996	Belfast (W.C.)	1	1
1997	Yerevan (W.C.)	0	0
2003	Yerevan (E.C.)	0	1

v. AUSTRALIA

		NI	A
1980	Sydney	2	1
1980	Melbourne	1	1
1980	Adelaide	2	1

v. AUSTRIA

		NI	A
1982	Madrid (W.C.)	2	2
1982	Vienna (E.C.)	0	2
1983	Belfast (E.C.)	3	1
1990	Vienna (E.C.)	0	0
1991	Belfast (E.C.)	2	1
1994	Vienna (E.C.)	2	1
1995	Belfast (E.C.)	5	3

v. BELGIUM

		NI	B
1976	Liege (W.C.)	0	2
1977	Belfast (W.C.)	3	0
1997	Belfast	3	0

v. BRAZIL

		NI	B
1986	Guadalajara (W.C.)	0	3

v. BULGARIA

		NI	B
1972	Sofia (W.C.)	0	3
1973	Sheffield (W.C.)	0	0
1978	Sofia (E.C.)	2	0
1979	Belfast (E.C.)	2	0
2001	Sofia (W.C.)	3	4
2001	Belfast (W.C.)	0	1

v. CANADA

		NI	C
1995	Edmonton	0	2
1999	Belfast	1	1

v. CHILE

		NI	C
1989	Belfast	0	1
1995	Edmonton, Canada	0	2

v. COLOMBIA

		NI	C
1994	Boston, USA	0	2

v. CYPRUS

		NI	C
1971	Nicosia (E.C.)	3	0
1971	Belfast (E.C.)	5	0
1973	Nicosia (W.C.)	0	1
1973	Fulham (W.C.)	3	0
2002	Belfast	0	0

v. CZECHOSLOVAKIA/CZECH REPUBLIC

		NI	C
1958	Halmstad (W.C.)	1	0
1958	Malmo (W.C.)	2	1
2001	Belfast (W.C.)	0	1
2001	Teplice (W.C.)	1	3

v. DENMARK

		NI	D
1978	Belfast (E.C.)	2	1
1979	Copenhagen (E.C.)	0	4
1986	Belfast	1	1
1990	Belfast (E.C.)	1	1
1991	Odense (E.C.)	1	2
1992	Belfast (W.C.)	0	1
1993	Copenhagen (W.C.)	0	1
2000	Belfast (W.C.)	1	1
2001	Copenhagen (W.C.)	1	1

v. FAROE ISLANDS

		NI	FI
1991	Belfast (E.C.)	1	1
1991	Landskrona, Sw. (E.C.)	5	0

v. FINLAND

		NI	F
1984	Pori (W.C.)	0	1
1984	Belfast (W.C.)	2	1
1998	Belfast (E.C.)	1	0
1999	Helsinki (E.C.)	1	4
2003	Belfast	0	1

v. FRANCE

		NI	F
1951	Belfast	2	2
1952	Paris	1	3
1958	Norrkoping (W.C.)	0	4
1982	Paris	0	4
1982	Madrid (W.C.)	1	4
1986	Paris	0	0
1988	Belfast	0	0
1999	Belfast	0	1

v. GERMANY/WEST GERMANY

		NI	G
1958	Malmo (W.C.)	2	2
1960	Belfast (W.C.)	3	4
1961	Berlin (W.C.)	1	2
1966	Belfast	0	2
1977	Cologne	0	5
1982	Belfast (E.C.)	1	0
1983	Hamburg (E.C.)	1	0
1992	Bremen	1	1
1996	Belfast	1	1
1997	Nuremberg (W.C.)	1	1
1997	Belfast (W.C.)	1	3
1999	Belfast (E.C.)	0	3
1999	Dortmund (E.C.)	0	4

v. GREECE

		NI	G
1961	Athens (W.C.)	1	2
1961	Belfast (W.C.)	2	0
1988	Athens	2	3
2003	Belfast (E.C.)	0	2

v. HOLLAND

		NI	H
1962	Rotterdam	0	4
1965	Belfast (W.C.)	2	1
1965	Rotterdam (W.C.)	0	0
1976	Rotterdam (W.C.)	2	2
1977	Belfast (W.C.)	0	1

v. HONDURAS

		NI	H
1982	Zaragoza (W.C.)	1	1

v. HUNGARY

		NI	H
1988	Budapest (W.C.)	0	1
1989	Belfast (W.C.)	1	2
2000	Belfast	0	1

v. ICELAND

		NI	I
1977	Reykjavik (W.C.)	0	1
1977	Belfast (W.C.)	2	0
2000	Reykjavik (W.C.)	0	1
2001	Belfast (W.C.)	3	0

v. REPUBLIC OF IRELAND

		NI	RI
1978	Dublin (E.C.)	0	0
1979	Belfast (E.C.)	1	0
1988	Belfast (W.C.)	0	0
1989	Dublin (W.C.)	0	3
1993	Dublin (W.C.)	0	3
1993	Belfast (W.C.)	1	1
1994	Belfast (E.C.)	0	4

		NI	RI
1995	Dublin (E.C.)	1	1
1999	Dublin	1	0

v. ISRAEL

		NI	I
1968	Jaffa	3	2
1976	Tel Aviv	1	1
1980	Tel Aviv (W.C.)	0	0
1981	Belfast (W.C.)	1	0
1984	Belfast	3	0
1987	Tel Aviv	1	1

v. ITALY

		NI	I
1957	Rome (W.C.)	0	1
1957	Belfast	2	2
1958	Belfast (W.C.)	2	1
1961	Bologna	2	3
1997	Palermo	0	2
2003	Campobasso	0	2

v. LATVIA

		NI	L
1993	Riga (W.C.)	2	1
1993	Belfast (W.C.)	2	0
1995	Riga (E.C.)	1	0
1995	Belfast (E.C.)	1	2

v. LIECHTENSTEIN

		NI	L
1994	Belfast (E.C.)	4	1
1995	Eschen (E.C.)	4	0
2002	Vaduz	0	0

v. LITHUANIA

		NI	L
1992	Belfast (W.C.)	2	2
1993	Vilnius (W.C.)	1	0

v. LUXEMBOURG

		NI	L
2000	Luxembourg	3	1

v. MALTA

		NI	M
1988	Belfast (W.C.)	3	0
1989	Valletta (W.C.)	2	0
2000	Ta'Qali	3	0
2000	Belfast (W.C.)	1	0
2001	Valletta (W.C.)	1	0

v. MEXICO

		NI	M
1966	Belfast	4	1
1994	Miami	0	3

v. MOLDOVA

		NI	M
1998	Belfast (E.C.)	2	2
1999	Kishinev (E.C.)	0	0

v. MOROCCO

		NI	M
1986	Belfast	2	1

v. NORWAY

		NI	N
1974	Oslo (E.C.)	1	2
1975	Belfast (E.C.)	3	0
1990	Belfast	2	3
1996	Belfast	0	2
2001	Belfast	0	4

v. POLAND

		NI	P
1962	Katowice (E.C.)	2	0
1962	Belfast (E.C.)	2	0
1988	Belfast	1	1
1991	Belfast	3	1
2002	Limassol (Cyprus)	1	4

v. PORTUGAL

		NI	P
1957	Lisbon (W.C.)	1	1
1957	Belfast (W.C.)	3	0
1973	Coventry (W.C.)	1	1
1973	Lisbon (W.C.)	1	1
1980	Lisbon (W.C.)	0	1
1981	Belfast (W.C.)	1	0
1994	Belfast (E.C.)	1	2
1995	Oporto (E.C.)	1	1
1997	Belfast (W.C.)	0	0
1997	Lisbon (W.C.)	0	1

v. ROMANIA

		NI	R
1984	Belfast (W.C.)	3	2
1985	Bucharest (W.C.)	1	0
1994	Belfast	2	0

v. SLOVAKIA

		NI	S
1998	Belfast	1	0

v. SOVIET UNION

		NI	SU
1969	Belfast (W.C.)	0	0
1969	Moscow (W.C.)	0	2
1971	Moscow (E.C.)	0	1
1971	Belfast (E.C.)	1	1

v. SPAIN

		NI	S
1958	Madrid	2	6
1963	Bilbao	1	1
1963	Belfast	0	1
1970	Seville (E.C.)	0	3
1972	Hull (E.C.)	1	1
1982	Valencia (W.C.)	1	0
1985	Palma, Majorca	0	0
1986	Guadalajara (W.C.)	1	2
1988	Seville (W.C.)	0	4
1989	Belfast (W.C.)	0	2

		NI	S
1992	Belfast (W.C.)	0	0
1993	Seville (W.C.)	1	3
1998	Santander	1	4
2002	Belfast	0	5
2002	Albacete (E.C.)	0	3
2003	Belfast (E.C.)	0	0

v. SWEDEN

		NI	S
1974	Solna (E.C.)	2	0
1975	Belfast (E.C.)	1	2
1980	Belfast (W.C.)	3	0
1981	Stockholm (W.C.)	0	1
1996	Belfast	1	2

v. SWITZERLAND

		NI	S
1964	Belfast (W.C.)	1	0
1964	Lausanne (W.C.)	1	2
1998	Belfast	1	0

v. THAILAND

		NI	T
1997	Bangkok	0	0

v. TURKEY

		NI	T
1968	Belfast (W.C.)	4	1
1968	Istanbul (W.C.)	3	0
1983	Belfast (E.C.)	2	1
1983	Ankara (E.C.)	0	1
1985	Belfast (W.C.)	2	0
1985	Izmir (W.C.)	0	0
1986	Izmir (E.C.)	0	0
1987	Belfast (E.C.)	1	0
1998	Istanbul (E.C.)	0	3
1999	Belfast (E.C.)	0	3

v. UKRAINE

		NI	U
1996	Belfast (W.C.)	0	1
1997	Kiev (W.C.)	1	2
2002	Belfast (E.C.)	0	0

v. URUGUAY

		NI	U
1964	Belfast	3	0
1990	Belfast	1	0

v.YUGOSLAVIA

		NI	Y
1975	Belfast (E.C.)	1	0
1975	Belgrade (E.C.)	0	1
1982	Zaragoza (W.C.)	0	0
1987	Belfast (E.C.)	1	2
1987	Sarajevo (E.C.)	0	3
1990	Belfast (E.C.)	0	2
1991	Belgrade (E.C.)	1	4
2000	Belfast	1	2

REPUBLIC OF IRELAND

v. ALBANIA

		RI	A
1992	Dublin (W.C.)	2	0
1993	Tirana (W.C.)	2	1
2003	Tirana (E.C.)	0	0
2003	Dublin (E.C.)	2	1

v. ALGERIA

		RI	A
1982	Algiers	0	2

v. ANDORRA

		RI	A
2001	Barcelona (W.C.)	3	0
2001	Dublin (W.C.)	3	1

v. ARGENTINA

		RI	A
1951	Dublin	0	1
1979*	Dublin	0	0
1980	Dublin	0	1
1998	Dublin	0	2

(* Not regarded as full Int.)

v. AUSTRIA

		RI	A
1952	Vienna	0	6
1953	Dublin	4	0
1958	Vienna	1	3
1962	Dublin	2	3
1963	Vienna (E.C.)	0	0
1963	Dublin (E.C.)	3	2
1966	Vienna	0	1
1968	Dublin	2	2
1971	Dublin (E.C.)	1	4
1971	Linz (E.C.)	0	6
1995	Dublin (E.C.)	1	3
1995	Vienna (E.C.)	1	3

v. BELGIUM

		RI	B
1928	Liege	4	2
1929	Dublin	4	0
1930	Brussels	3	1
1934	Dublin (W.C.)	4	4
1949	Dublin	0	2
1950	Brussels	1	5
1965	Dublin	0	2
1966	Liege	3	2
1980	Dublin (W.C.)	1	1
1981	Brussels (W.C.)	0	1
1986	Brussels (E.C.)	2	2
1987	Dublin (E.C.)	0	0
1997*	Dublin (W.C.)	1	1

		RI	B
1997*	Brussels (W.C.)	1	2

(* World Cup play-off)

v. BOLIVIA

		RI	B
1994	Dublin	1	0
1996	East Rutherford, N.J. ...	3	0

v. BRAZIL

		RI	B
1974	Rio de Janeiro	1	2
1982	Uberlandia	0	7
1987	Dublin	1	0

v. BULGARIA

		RI	B
1977	Sofia (W.C.)	1	2
1977	Dublin (W.C.)	0	0
1979	Sofia (E.C.)	0	1
1979	Dublin (E.C.)	3	0
1987	Sofia (E.C.)	1	2
1987	Dublin (E.C.)	2	0

v. CAMEROON

		RI	C
2002	Niigata (W.C.)	1	1

v. CHILE

		RI	C
1960	Dublin	2	0
1972	Recife	1	2
1974	Santiago	2	1
1982	Santiago	0	1
1991	Dublin	1	1

v. CHINA

		RI	C
1984	Sapporo	1	0

v. CROATIA

		RI	C
1996	Dublin	2	2
1998	Dublin (E.C.)	2	0
1999	Zagreb (E.C.)	0	1
2001	Dublin	2	2

v. CYPRUS

		RI	C
1980	Nicosia (W.C.)	3	2
1980	Dublin (W.C.)	6	0
2001	Nicosia (W.C.)	4	0
2001	Dublin (W.C.)	4	0

v. CZECHOSLOVAKIA/CZECH REPUBLIC

		RI	C
1938	Prague	2	2
1959	Dublin (E.C.)	2	0
1959	Bratislava (E.C.)	0	4
1961	Dublin (W.C.)	1	3
1961	Prague (W.C.)	1	7
1967	Dublin (E.C.)	0	2
1967	Prague (E.C.)	2	1
1969	Dublin (W.C.)	1	2
1969	Prague (W.C.)	0	3
1979	Prague	1	4
1981	Dublin	3	1
1986	Reykjavik	1	0
1994	Dublin	1	3
1996	Prague	0	2
1998	Olomouc	1	2
2000	Dublin	3	2

v. DENMARK

		RI	D
1956	Dublin (W.C.)	2	1
1957	Copenhagen (W.C.)	2	0
1968*	Dublin (W.C.)	1	1
1969	Copenhagen (W.C.)	0	2
1969	Dublin (W.C.)	1	1
1978	Copenhagen (E.C.)	3	3
1979	Dublin (E.C.)	2	0
1984	Copenhagen (W.C.)	0	3
1985	Dublin (W.C.)	1	4
1992	Copenhagen (W.C.)	0	0
1993	Dublin (W.C.)	1	1
2002	Dublin	3	0

(* Abandoned after 51 mins. – fog)

v. ECUADOR

		RI	E
1972	Natal	3	2

v. EGYPT

		RI	E
1990	Palermo (W.C.)	0	0

v. ESTONIA

		RI	E
2000	Dublin (W.C.)	2	0
2001	Tallinn (W.C.)	2	0

v. FINLAND

		RI	F
1949	Dublin (W.C.)	3	0
1949	Helsinki (W.C.)	1	1
1990	Dublin	1	1
2000	Dublin	3	0
2002	Helsinki	3	0

v. FRANCE

		RI	F
1937	Paris	2	0
1952	Dublin	1	1
1953	Dublin (W.C.)	3	5
1953	Paris (W.C.)	0	1
1972	Dublin (W.C.)	2	1
1973	Paris (W.C.)	1	1
1976	Paris (W.C.)	0	2
1977	Dublin (W.C.)	1	0
1980	Paris (W.C.)	0	2
1981	Dublin (W.C.)	3	2

		RI	F
1989	Dublin	0	0

v. GEORGIA

		RI	G
2002	Tbilisi (E.C.)	2	1
2003	Dublin (E.C.)	2	0

v. GERMANY/WEST GERMANY

		RI	G
1935	Dortmund	1	3
1936	Dublin	5	2
1939	Bremen	1	1
1951	Dublin	3	2
1952	Cologne	0	3
1955	Hamburg	1	2
1956	Dublin	3	0
1960	Dusseldorf	1	0
1966	Dublin	0	4
1970	Berlin	1	2
1979	Dublin	1	3
1981	Bremen	0	3
1989	Dublin	1	1
1994	Hanover	2	0
1995*	Dublin	1	0
2002	Ibaraki (W.C.)	1	1

(*v. W. Germany 'B')

v. GREECE

		RI	G
2000	Dublin	0	1
2002	Athens	0	0

v. HOLLAND

		RI	H
1932	Amsterdam	2	0
1934	Amsterdam	2	5
1935	Dublin	3	5
1955	Dublin	1	0
1956	Rotterdam	4	1
1980	Dublin (W.C.)	2	1
1981	Rotterdam (W.C.)	2	2
1982	Rotterdam (E.C.)	1	2
1983	Dublin (E.C.)	2	3
1988	Gelsenkirchen (E.C.)	0	1
1990	Palermo (W.C.)	1	1
1994	Tilburg	1	0
1994	Orlando (W.C.)	0	2
1995*	Liverpool (E.C.)	0	2
1996	Rotterdam	1	3

(* Qual. Round play-off)

		RI	H
2000	Amsterdam (W.C.)	2	2
2001	Dublin (W.C.)	1	0

v. HUNGARY

		RI	H
1934	Dublin	2	4
1936	Budapest	3	3
1936	Dublin	2	3
1939	Cork	2	2
1939	Budapest	2	2
1969	Dublin (W.C.)	1	2
1969	Budapest (W.C.)	0	4
1989	Budapest (W.C.)	0	0
1989	Dublin (W.C.)	2	0
1992	Gyor	2	1

v. ICELAND

		RI	I
1962	Dublin (E.C.)	4	2
1962	Reykjavik (E.C.)	1	1
1982	Dublin (E.C.)	2	0
1983	Reykjavik (E.C.)	3	0
1986	Reykjavik	2	1
1996	Dublin (W.C.)	0	0
1997	Reykjavik (W.C.)	4	2

v. IRAN

		RI	I
1972	Recife	2	1
2001*	Dublin (W.C.)	2	0
2001*	Tehran (W.C.)	0	1

(*Qual. Round play-off)

v. ISRAEL

		RI	I
1984	Tel Aviv	0	3
1985	Tel Aviv	0	0
1987	Dublin	5	0

v. ITALY

		RI	I
1926	Turin	0	3
1927	Dublin	1	2
1970	Florence (E.C.)	0	3
1971	Dublin (E.C.)	1	2
1985	Dublin	1	2
1990	Rome (W.C.)	0	1
1992	Boston, USA	0	2
1994	New York (W.C.)	1	0

v. LATVIA

		RI	L
1992	Dublin (W.C.)	4	0
1993	Riga (W.C.)	2	0
1994	Riga (E.C.)	3	0
1995	Dublin (E.C.)	2	1

v. LIECHTENSTEIN

		RI	L
1994	Dublin (E.C.)	4	0
1995	Eschen (E.C.)	0	0
1996	Eschen (W.C.)	5	0
1997	Dublin (W.C.)	5	0

v. LITHUANIA

		RI	L
1993	Vilnius (W.C.)	1	0
1993	Dublin (W.C.)	2	0
1997	Dublin (W.C.)	0	0

		RI	L
1997	Zalgiris (W.C.)	2	1

v. LUXEMBOURG

		RI	L
1936	Luxembourg	5	1
1953	Dublin (W.C.)	4	0
1954	Luxembourg (W.C.)	1	0
1987	Luxembourg (E.C.)	2	0
1987	Luxembourg (E.C.)	2	1

v. MACEDONIA

		RI	M
1996	Dublin (W.C.)	3	0
1997	Skopje (W.C.)	2	3
1999	Dublin (E.C.)	1	0
1999	Skopje (E.C.)	1	1

v. MALTA

		RI	M
1983	Valletta (E.C.)	1	0
1983	Dublin (E.C.)	8	0
1989	Dublin (W.C.)	2	0
1989	Valletta (W.C.)	2	0
1990	Valletta	3	0
1998	Dublin (E.C.)	1	0
1999	Valletta (E.C.)	3	2

v. MEXICO

		RI	M
1984	Dublin	0	0
1994	Orlando (W.C.)	1	2
1996	New Jersey	2	2
1998	Dublin	0	0
2000	Chicago	2	2

v. MOROCCO

		RI	M
1990	Dublin	1	0

v. NIGERIA

		RI	N
2002	Dublin	1	2

v. NORWAY

		RI	N
1937	Oslo (W.C.)	2	3
1937	Dublin (W.C.)	3	3
1950	Dublin	2	2
1951	Oslo	3	2
1954	Dublin	2	1
1955	Oslo	3	1
1960	Dublin	3	1
1964	Oslo	4	1
1973	Oslo	1	1
1976	Dublin	3	0
1978	Oslo	0	0
1984	Oslo (W.C.)	0	1
1985	Dublin (W.C.)	0	0
1988	Oslo	0	0
1994	New York (W.C.)	0	0

		RI	N
2003	Dublin	1	0

v. PARAGUAY

		RI	P
1999	Dublin	2	0

v. POLAND

		RI	P
1938	Warsaw	0	6
1938	Dublin	3	2
1958	Katowice	2	2
1958	Dublin	2	2
1964	Cracow	1	3
1964	Dublin	3	2
1968	Dublin	2	2
1968	Katowice	0	1
1970	Dublin	1	2
1970	Poznan	0	2
1973	Wroclaw	0	2
1973	Dublin	1	0
1976	Poznan	2	0
1977	Dublin	0	0
1978	Lodz	0	3
1981	Bydgoscz	0	3
1984	Dublin	0	0
1986	Warsaw	0	1
1988	Dublin	3	1
1991	Dublin (E.C.)	0	0
1991	Poznan (E.C.)	3	3

v. PORTUGAL

		RI	P
1946	Lisbon	1	3
1947	Dublin	0	2
1948	Lisbon	0	2
1949	Dublin	1	0
1972	Recife	1	2
1992	Boston, USA	2	0
1995	Dublin (E.C.)	1	0
1995	Lisbon (E.C.)	0	3
1996	Dublin	0	1
2000	Lisbon (W.C.)	1	1
2001	Dublin (W.C.)	1	1

v. ROMANIA

		RI	R
1988	Dublin	2	0
1990*	Genoa	0	0
1997	Bucharest (W.C.)	0	1
1997	Dublin (W.C.)	1	1

(* Rep. won 5-4 on pens.)

v. RUSSIA (See also Soviet Union)

		RI	R
1994	Dublin	0	0
1996	Dublin	0	2
2002	Dublin	2	0
2002	Moscow (E.C.)	2	4

v. SAUDI ARABIA

		RI	SA
2002	Yokohama (W.C.)	3	0

v. SOUTH AFRICA

		RI	SA
2000	New Jersey	2	1

v. SOVIET UNION
(See also Russia)

		RI	SU
1972	Dublin (W.C.)	1	2
1973	Moscow (W.C.)	0	1
1974	Dublin (E.C.)	3	0
1975	Kiev (E.C.)	1	2
1984	Dublin (W.C.)	1	0
1985	Moscow (W.C.)	0	2
1988	Hanover (E.C.)	1	1
1990	Dublin	1	0

v. SPAIN

		RI	S
1931	Barcelona	1	1
1931	Dublin	0	5
1946	Madrid	1	0
1947	Dublin	3	2
1948	Barcelona	1	2
1949	Dublin	1	4
1952	Madrid	0	6
1955	Dublin	2	2
1964	Seville (E.C.)	1	5
1964	Dublin (E.C.)	0	2
1965	Dublin (W.C.)	1	0
1965	Seville (W.C.)	1	4
1965	Paris (W.C.)	0	1
1966	Dublin (E.C.)	0	0
1966	Valencia (E.C.)	0	2
1977	Dublin	0	1
1982	Dublin (E.C.)	3	3
1983	Zaragoza (E.C.)	0	2
1985	Cork	0	0
1988	Seville (W.C.)	0	2
1989	Dublin (W.C.)	1	0
1992	Seville (W.C.)	0	0
1993	Dublin (W.C.)	1	3
2002*	Suwon (W.C.)	1	1

(*Rep. lost 3-2 on pens.)

v. SWEDEN

		RI	S
1949	Stockholm (W.C.)	1	3
1949	Dublin (W.C.)	1	3
1959	Dublin	3	2
1960	Malmo	1	4
1970	Dublin (E.C.)	1	1
1970	Malmo (E.C.)	0	1
1999	Dublin	2	0

v. SWITZERLAND

		RI	S
1935	Basle	0	1
1936	Dublin	1	0
1937	Berne	1	0
1938	Dublin	4	0
1948	Dublin	0	1
1975	Dublin (E.C.)	2	1
1975	Berne (E.C.)	0	1
1980	Dublin	2	0
1985	Dublin (W.C.)	3	0
1985	Berne (W.C.)	0	0
1992	Dublin	2	1
2002	Dublin (E.C.)	1	2

v. TRINIDAD & TOBAGO

		RI	T&T
1982	Port of Spain	1	2

v. TUNISIA

		RI	T
1988	Dublin	4	0

v. TURKEY

		RI	T
1966	Dublin (E.C.)	2	1
1967	Ankara (E.C.)	1	2
1974	Izmir (E.C.)	1	1
1975	Dublin (E.C.)	4	0
1976	Ankara	3	3
1978	Dublin	4	2
1990	Izmir	0	0
1990	Dublin (E.C.)	5	0
1991	Istanbul (E.C.)	3	1
1999	Dublin (E.C.)	1	1
1999	Bursa (E.C.)	0	0

v. URUGUAY

		RI	U
1974	Montevideo	0	2
1986	Dublin	1	1

v. U.S.A.

		RI	USA
1979	Dublin	3	2
1991	Boston	1	1
1992	Dublin	4	1
1992	Washington	1	3
1996	Boston	1	2
2000	Foxboro	1	1
2002	Dublin	2	1

v. YUGOSLAVIA

		RI	Y
1955	Dublin	1	4
1988	Dublin	2	0
1998	Belgrade (E.C.)	0	1
1999	Dublin (E.C.)	2	1

INTERNATIONAL APPEARANCES SINCE THE WAR (1946-2003)

(As at start of season 2003-04. In year shown, 2003 = season 2002-03 etc. *Also a pre-war International player. Totals include appearances as substitute).

ENGLAND

A'Court, A. (Liverpool, 1958-9) 5
Adams, T. (Arsenal, 1987-2001) 66
Allen, A. (Stoke City, 1960) 3
Allen, C. (Q.P.R., Tottenham, 1984-8) 5
Allen, R. (W.B.A., 1952-5) 5
Anderson, S. (Sunderland, 1962) 2
Anderson, V. (Nott'm Forest, Arsenal, Manchester Utd., 1979-88) 30
Anderton, D. (Tottenham, 1994-2002) 30
Angus, J. (Burnley, 1961) 1
Armfield, J. (Blackpool, 1959-66) 43
Armstrong, D. (Middlesbrough, Southampton, 1980-4) 3
Armstrong, K. (Chelsea, 1955) 1
Astall, G. (Birmingham City, 1956) 2
Astle, J. (W.B.A., 1969-70) 5
Aston, J. (Manchester Utd., 1949-51) 17
Atyeo, J. (Bristol City, 1956-7) 6

Bailey, G. (Manchester Utd., 1985) 2
Bailey, M. (Charlton Athletic, 1964-5) 2
Baily, E. (Tottenham, 1950-3) 9
Baker, J. (Hibernian, Arsenal, 1960-6) 8
Ball, A. (Blackpool, Everton, Arsenal, 1965-75) 72
Ball, M. (Everton, 2001) 1
Banks, G. (Leicester City, Stoke City, 1963-72) 73
Banks, T. (Bolton Wand., 1958-9) 6
Bardsley, D. (Q.P.R., 1993) 2
Barham, M. (Norwich City, 1983) 2
Barlow, R. (W.B.A., 1955) 1
Barmby, N. (Tottenham, Middlesbrough, Everton, Liverpool, 1995-2002) 23
Barnes, J. (Watford, Liverpool, 1983-96) 79
Barnes, P. (Manchester City, W.B.A., Leeds Utd., 1978-82) 22
Barrass, M. (Bolton Wand., 1952-3) ... 3
Barrett, E. (Oldham Athletic, Aston Villa, 1991-3) 3
Barton, W. (Wimbledon, Newcastle Utd., 1995) 3
Barry, G. (Aston Villia, 2000-03) 8
Batty, D. (Leeds Utd., Blackburn Rov., Newcastle Utd., Leeds Utd., 1991-2000) 42
Baynham, R. (Luton Town, 1956) 3
Beardsley, P. (Newcastle Utd., Liverpool, Newcastle Utd., 1986-96) 59
Beasant, D. (Chelsea, 1990) 2
Beattie, J. (Southampton, 2003) 2
Beattie, K. (Ipswich Town, 1975-8) 9
Beckham, D. (Manchester Utd., 1997-2003) 60
Bell, C. (Manchester City, 1968-76) . 48
Bentley, R. (Chelsea, 1949-55) 12
Berry, J. (Manchester Utd., 1953-6) ... 4
Birtles, G. (Nott'm Forest, 1980-1) 3
Blissett, L. (Watford, AC Milan, 1983-4) 14
Blockley, J. (Arsenal, 1973) 1
Blunstone, F. (Chelsea, 1955-7) 5
Bonetti, P. (Chelsea, 1966-70) 7
Bould, S. (Arsenal, 1994) 2
Bowles, S. (Q.P.R., 1974-7) 5
Bowyer, L. (Leeds Utd., 2003) 1
Boyer, P. (Norwich City, 1976) 1
Brabrook, P. (Chelsea, 1958-60) 3
Bracewell, P. (Everton, 1985-6) 3
Bradford, G. (Bristol Rov., 1956) 1
Bradley, W. (Manchester Utd., 1959) .. 3
Bridge, W. (Southampton, 2002-3) ... 12
Bridges, B. (Chelsea, 1965-6) 4
Broadbent, P. (Wolves, 1958-60) 7
Broadis, I. (Manchester City, Newcastle Utd., 1952-4) 14
Brooking, T. (West Ham Utd., 1974-82) 47
Brooks, J. (Tottenham, 1957) 3
Brown, A. (W.B.A., 1971) 1
Brown, K. (West Ham Utd., 1960) 1
Brown, W. (Manchester Utd., 1999-2003) 7
Bull, S. (Wolves, 1989-91) 13
Butcher, T. (Ipswich Town, Rangers, 1980-90) 77
Butt, N. (Manchester Utd., 1997-2003) 27
Byrne, G. (Liverpool, 1963-6) 2
Byrne, J. (Crystal Palace, West Ham Utd., 1962-5) 11
Byrne, R. (Manchester Utd., 1954-8) 33

Callaghan, I. (Liverpool, 1966-78) 4
Campbell, S. (Tottenham, Arsenal, 1996-2003) 54
Carragher, J. (Liverpool, 1999-2003) .. 9
Carrick, M. (West Ham Utd., 2001-2) 2
*Carter, H. (Derby Co., 1947) 7
Chamberlain, M. (Stoke City, 1983-5) 8
Channon, M. (Southampton, Manchester City, 1973-8) 46
Charles, G. (Nott'm Forest, 1991) 2
Charlton, J. (Leeds Utd., 1965-70) .. 35
Charlton, R. (Manchester Utd., 1958-70) 106
Charnley, R. (Blackpool, 1963) 1
Cherry, T. (Leeds Utd., 1976-80) 27
Chilton, A. (Manchester Utd., 1951-2) 2
Chivers, M. (Tottenham, 1971-4) 24
Clamp, E. (Wolves, 1958) 4
Clapton, D. (Arsenal, 1959) 1
Clarke, A. (Leeds Utd., 1970-6) 19
Clarke, H. (Tottenham, 1954) 1
Clayton, R. (Blackburn Rov., 1956-60) 35
Clemence, R. (Liverpool, Tottenham, 1973-84) 61
Clement, D. (Q.P.R., 1976-7) 5
Clough, B. (Middlesbrough, 1960) 2
Clough, N. (Nott'm. Forest, Liverpool, 1989-93) 14
Coates, R. (Burnley, Tottenham, 1970-1) 4
Cockburn, H. (Manchester Utd., 1947-52) 13
Cohen, G. (Fulham, 1964-8) 37
Cole, Andy (Manchester Utd., 1995-2002) 15
Cole, Ashley (Arsenal, 2001-3) 19
Cole, J. (West Ham Utd., 2001-3) 10
Collymore, S. (Nott'm Forest, Aston Villa, 1995-7) 3
Compton, L. (Arsenal, 1951) 2
Connelly, J. (Burnley, Manchester Utd., 1960-6) 20
Cooper, C. (Nott'm Forest, 1995) 2
Cooper, T. (Leeds Utd., 1969-75) 20
Coppell, S. (Manchester Utd., 1978-83) 42
Corrigan, J. (Manchester City, 1976-82) 9
Cottee, T. (West Ham Utd., Everton, 1987-9) 7
Cowans, G. (Aston Villa, Bari, Aston Villa 1983-91) 10
Crawford, R. (Ipswich Town, 1962) 2
Crowe, C. (Wolves, 1963) 1
Cunningham, L. (W.B.A., Real Madrid, 1979-81) 6
Curle, K. (Manchester City, 1992) 3
Currie, A. (Sheffield Utd., Leeds Utd., 1972-9) 17

Daley, T. (Aston Villa, 1992) 7
Davenport, P. (Nott'm Forest, 1985) ... 1
Deane, B. (Sheffield Utd., 1991-3) 3
Deeley, N. (Wolves, 1959) 2
Devonshire, A. (West Ham Utd., 1980-4) 8
Dickinson, J. (Portsmouth, 1949-57) 48
Ditchburn, E. (Tottenham, 1949-57) .. 6
Dixon, K. (Chelsea, 1985-7) 8
Dixon, L. (Arsenal, 1990-9) 22
Dobson, M. (Burnley, Everton, 1974-5) 5
Dorigo, T. (Chelsea, Leeds Utd., 1990-4) 15
Douglas, B. (Blackburn Rov., 1959-63) 36
Doyle, M. (Manchester City, 1976-7) .. 5
Dublin, D. (Coventry City, Aston Villa, 1998-9) 4
Dunn, D. (Blackburn Rov., 2003) 1
Duxbury, M. (Manchester Utd., 1984-5) 10
Dyer, K. (Newcastle, 2000-03) 16

Eastham, G. (Arsenal, 1963-6) 19
Eckersley, W. (Blackburn Rov., 1950-4) 17
Edwards, D. (Manchester Utd., 1955-8) 18
Ehiogu, U. (Aston Villa, Middlesbrough, 1996-2002) 4
Ellerington, W. (Southampton, 1949) .. 2
Elliott, W. (Burnley, 1952-3) 5

Fantham, J. (Sheffield Wed., 1962) ... 1
Fashanu, J. (Wimbledon, 1989) 2
Fenwick, T. (Q.P.R., 1984-8) 20
Ferdinand, L. (Q.P.R., Newcastle Utd., Tottenham 1993-8) 18
Ferdinand, R. (West Ham Utd., Leeds Utd., Manchester Utd., 1997-2003) 32
Finney, T. (Preston N.E., 1947-59) ... 76
Flowers, R. (Wolves, 1955-66) 49
Flowers, T. (Southampton, Blackburn Rov., 1993-8) 11
Foster, S. (Brighton & H.A., 1982) 3
Foulkes, W. (Manchester Utd., 1955) . 1
Fowler, R. (Liverpool, Leeds Utd., 1996-2002) 26
Francis, G. (Q.P.R., 1975-6) 12
Francis, T. (Birmingham City, Nott'm Forest, Manchester City, Sampdoria, 1977-86) 52
Franklin, N. (Stoke City, 1947-50) ... 27
Froggatt, J. (Portsmouth, 1950-3) 13

Froggatt, R. (Sheffield Wed., 1953) 4

Garrett, T. (Blackpool, 1952-4) 3
Gascoigne, P. (Tottenham, Lazio, Rangers, Middlesbrough 1989-98) 57
Gates, E. (Ipswich Town, 1981) 2
George, C. (Derby Co., 1977) 1
Gerrard, S. (Liverpool, 2000-03) 18
Gidman, J. (Aston Villa, 1977) 1
Gillard, I. (Q.P.R., 1975-6) 3
Goddard, P. (West Ham Utd., 1982) ... 1
Grainger, C. (Sheffield Utd., Sunderland, 1956-7) 7
Gray, A. (Crystal Palace, 1992) 1
Gray, M. (Sunderland, 1999) 3
Greaves, J. (Chelsea, Tottenham, 1959-67) 57
Greenhoff, B. (Manchester Utd., Leeds Utd., 1976-80) 18
Gregory, J. (Q.P.R., 1983-4) 6
Guppy, S. (Leicester City, 2000) 1

Hagan, J. (Sheffield Utd., 1949) 1
Haines, J. (W.B.A., 1949) 1
Hall, J. (Birmingham City, 1956-7) .. 17
Hancocks, J. (Wolves, 1949-50) 3
Hardwick, G. (Middlesbrough, 1947-8) 13
Harford, M. (Luton Town, 1988-9) 2
Hargreaves, O. (Bayern Munich, 2002-3) 13
Harris, G. (Burnley, 1966) 1
Harris, P. (Portsmouth, 1950-4) 2
Harvey, C. (Everton, 1971) 1
Hassall, H. (Huddersfield Town, Bolton Wand., 1951-4) 5
Hateley, M. (Portsmouth, AC Milan, Monaco, Rangers, 1984-92) 32
Haynes, J. (Fulham, 1955-62) 56
Hector, K. (Derby Co., 1974) 2
Hellawell, M. (Birmingham City, 1963) 2
Hendrie, L. (Aston Villa, 1999) 1
Henry, R. (Tottenham, 1963) 1
Heskey, E. (Leicester City, Liverpool, 1999-2003) 34
Hill, F. (Bolton Wand., 1963) 2
Hill, G. (Manchester Utd., 1976-8) 6
Hill, R. (Luton Town, 1983-6) 3
Hinchcliffe, A. (Everton, Sheffield Wed., 1997-9) 7
Hinton, A. (Wolves, Nott'm Forest, 1963-5) 3
Hirst, D. (Sheffield Wed., 1991-2) 3
Hitchens, G. (Aston Villa, Inter Milan, 1961-2) 7
Hoddle, G. (Tottenham, Monaco, 1980-8) 53
Hodge, S. (Aston Villa, Tottenham, Nott'm Forest, 1986-91) 24
Hodgkinson, A. (Sheffield Utd., 1957-61) 5
Holden, D. (Bolton Wand., 1959) 5
Holliday, E. (Middlesbrough, 1960) 3
Hollins, J. (Chelsea, 1967) 1
Hopkinson, E. (Bolton Wand., 1958-60) 14
Howe, D. (W.B.A., 1958-60) 23
Howe, J. (Derby Co., 1948-9) 3
Howey, S. (Newcastle Utd., 1995-6) .. 4
Hudson, A. (Stoke City, 1975) 2
Hughes, E. (Liverpool, Wolves, 1970-80) 62
Hughes, L. (Liverpool, 1950) 3
Hunt, R. (Liverpool, 1962-9) 34
Hunt, S. (W.B.A., 1984) 2
Hunter, N. (Leeds Utd., 1966-75) 28
Hurst, G. (West Ham Utd., 1966-72) 49

Ince, P. (Manchester Utd., Inter Milan, Liverpool, Middlesbrough, 1993-2000) 53

James, D. (Liverpool, Aston Villa, West Ham Utd. 1997-2003) 16
Jeffers, F. (Arsenal, 2003) 1
Jenas, J. (Newcastle Utd., 2003) 3
Jezzard, B. (Fulham, 1954-6) 2
Johnson, D. (Ipswich Town, Liverpool, 1975-80) 8
Johnson, S. (Derby Co., 2001) 1
Johnston, H. (Blackpool, 1947-54) .. 10
Jones, M. (Leeds Utd., Sheffield Utd., 1965-70) 3
Jones, R. (Liverpool, 1992-5) 8
Jones, W.H. (Liverpool, 1950) 2

Kay, A. (Everton, 1963) 1
Keegan, K. (Liverpool, Hamburg, Southampton, 1973-82) 63
Kennedy, A. (Liverpool, 1984) 2
Kennedy, R. (Liverpool, 1976-80) 17
Keown, M. (Everton, Arsenal, 1992-2002) 43
Kevan, D. (W.B.A., 1957-61) 14
Kidd, B. (Manchester Utd., 1970) 2
King, L. (Tottenham, 2002-3) 2
Knowles, C. (Tottenham, 1968) 4
Konchesky, P. (Charlton Athletic, 2003) 1

Labone, B. (Everton, 1963-70) 26
Lampard, F., Snr. (West Ham Utd., 1973-80) 2
Lampard, F., Jnr. (West Ham Utd., Chelsea, 2000-03) 11
Langley, J. (Fulham, 1958) 3

Langton, R. (Blackburn Rov., Preston N.E., Bolton Wand., 1947-51) 11
Latchford, R. (Everton, 1978-9) 12
Lawler, C. (Liverpool, 1971-2) 4
*Lawton, T. (Chelsea, Notts Co., 1947-9) 15
Lee, F. (Manchester City, 1969-72) .. 27
Lee, J. (Derby Co., 1951) 1
Lee, R. (Newcastle Utd., 1995-9) 21
Lee, S. (Liverpool, 1983-4) 14
Le Saux, G. (Blackburn Rov., Chelsea, 1994-2001) 36
Le Tissier, M. (Southampton, 1994-7) 8
Lindsay, A. (Liverpool, 1974) 4
Lineker, G. (Leicester City, Everton, Barcelona, Tottenham, 1985-92) .. 80
Little, B. (Aston Villa, 1975) 1
Lloyd, L. (Liverpool, Nott'm Forest, 1971-80) 4
Lofthouse, N. (Bolton Wand., 1951-9) 33
Lowe, E. (Aston Villa, 1947) 3

Mabbutt, G. (Tottenham, 1983-92) .. 16
Macdonald, M. (Newcastle Utd., 1972-6) 14
Madeley, P. (Leeds Utd., 1971-7) 24
Mannion, W. (Middlesbrough, 1947-52) 26
Mariner, P. (Ipswich Town, Arsenal, 1977-85) 35
Marsh, R. (Q.P.R., Manchester City, 1972-3) 9
Martin, A. (West Ham Utd., 1981-7) 17
Martyn, N. (Crystal Palace, Leeds Utd., 1992-2002) 23
Marwood, B. (Arsenal, 1989) 1
Matthews, R. (Coventry City, 1956-7) . 5
*Matthews, S. (Stoke City, Blackpool, 1947-57) 37
McCann, G. (Sunderland, 2001) 1
McDermott, T. (Liverpool, 1978-82) . 25
McDonald, C. (Burnley, 1958-9) 8
McFarland, R. (Derby Co., 1971-7) .. 28
McGarry, W. (Huddersfield Town, 1954-6) 4
McGuinness, W. (Manchester Utd., 1959) 2
McMahon, S. (Liverpool, 1988-91) ... 17
McManaman, S. (Liverpool, Real Madrid, 1995-2002) 37
McNab, R. (Arsenal, 1969) 4
McNeil, M. (Middlesbrough, 1961-2) .. 9
Meadows, J. (Manchester City, 1955) . 1
Medley, L. (Tottenham, 1951-2) 6
Melia, J. (Liverpool, 1963) 2
Merrick, G. (Birmingham City, 1952-4) 23
Merson, P. (Arsenal, Middlesbrough, Aston Villa, 1992-9) 21
Metcalfe, V. (Huddersfield Town, 1951) 2
Milburn, J. (Newcastle Utd., 1949-56) 13
Miller, B. (Burnley, 1961) 1
Mills, D. (Leeds Utd., 2001-3) 17
Mills, M. (Ipswich Town, 1973-82) ... 42
Milne, G. (Liverpool, 1963-5) 14
Milton, A. (Arsenal, 1952) 1
Moore, R. (West Ham Utd., 1962-74) 108
Morley, A. (Aston Villa, 1982-3) 6
Morris, J. (Derby Co., 1949-50) 3
Mortensen, S. (Blackpool, 1947-54) . 25
Mozley, B. (Derby Co., 1950) 3
Mullen, J. (Wolves, 1947-54) 12
Mullery, A. (Tottenham, 1965-72) 35
Murphy, D. (Liverpool, 2002-3) 7

Neal, P. (Liverpool, 1976-84) 50
Neville, G. (Manchester Utd., 1995-2003) 57
Neville, P. (Manchester Utd., 1996-2003) 40
Newton, K. (Blackburn Rov., Everton, 1966-70) 27
Nicholls, J. (W.B.A., 1954) 2
Nicholson, W. (Tottenham, 1951) 1
Nish, D. (Derby Co., 1973-4) 5
Norman, M. (Tottenham, 1962-5) 23

O'Grady, M. (Huddersfield Town, Leeds Utd., 1963-9) 2
Osgood, P. (Chelsea, 1970-4) 4
Osman, R. (Ipswich Town, 1980-4) .. 11
Owen, M. (Liverpool, 1998-2003) 50
Owen, S. (Luton Town, 1954) 3

Paine, T. (Southampton, 1963-6) 19
Pallister, G. (Middlesbrough, Manchester Utd., 1988-97) 22
Palmer, C. (Sheffield Wed., 1992-4) . 18
Parker, P. (Q.P.R., Manchester Utd., 1989-94) 19
Parkes, P. (Q.P.R., 1974) 1
Parlour, R. (Arsenal, 1999-2001) 10
Parry, R. (Bolton, 1960) 2
Peacock, A. (Middlesbrough, Leeds Utd., 1962-6) 6
Pearce, S. (Nott'm Forest, West Ham Utd., 1987-2000) 78
Pearson, Stan (Manchester Utd., 1948-52) 8
Pearson, Stuart (Manchester Utd., 1976-8) 15
Pegg, D. (Manchester Utd., 1957) 1
Pejic, M. (Stoke City, 1974) 4
Perry, W. (Blackpool, 1956) 3

Perryman, S. (Tottenham, 1982) 1
Peters, M. (West Ham Utd., Tottenham, 1966-74) 67
Phelan, M. (Manchester Utd., 1990) .. 1
Phillips, K. (Sunderland, 1999-2002) 8
Phillips, L. (Portsmouth, 1952-5) 3
Pickering, F. (Everton, 1964-5) 3
Pickering, N. (Sunderland, 1983) 1
Pilkington, B. (Burnley, 1955) 1
Platt, D. (Aston Villa, Bari, Juventus, Sampdoria, Arsenal, 1990-6) 62
Pointer, R. (Burnley, 1962) 3
Powell, C. (Charlton Athletic, 2001-2) 5
Pye, J. (Wolves, 1950) 1

Quixall, A. (Sheffield Wed., 1954-5) ... 5

Radford, J. (Arsenal, 1969-72) 2
Ramsey, A. (Southampton, Tottenham, 1949-54) 32
Reaney, P. (Leeds Utd., 1969-71) 3
Redknapp, J. (Liverpool, 1996-2000) 17
Reeves, K. (Norwich City, Manchester City, 1980) 2
Regis, C. (W.B.A., Coventry City, 1982-8) 5
Reid, P. (Everton, 1985-8) 13
Revie, D. (Manchester City, 1955-7) ... 6
Richards, J. (Wolves, 1973) 1
Richardson, K. (Aston Villa, 1994) 1
Rickaby, S. (W.B.A., 1954) 1
Ricketts, M. (Bolton Wand., 2002) 1
Rimmer, J. (Arsenal, 1976) 1
Ripley, S. (Blackburn Rov., 1994-7) ... 2
Rix, G. (Arsenal, 1981-4) 17
Robb, G. (Tottenham, 1954) 1
Roberts, G. (Tottenham, 1983-4) 6
Robinson, P. (Leeds Utd., 2003) 2
Robson, B. (W.B.A., Manchester Utd., 1980-92) 90
Robson, R. (W.B.A., 1958-62) 20
Rocastle, D. (Arsenal, 1989-92) 14
Rooney, W. (Everton, 2003) 5
Rowley, J. (Manchester Utd., 1949-52) 6
Royle, J. (Everton, Manchester City, 1971-7) 6
Ruddock, N. (Liverpool, 1995) 1

Sadler, D. (Manchester Utd., 1968-71) 4
Salako, J. (Crystal Palace, 1991-2) 5
Sansom, K. (Crystal Palace, Arsenal, 1979-88) 86
Scales, J. (Liverpool, 1995) 3
Scholes, P. (Manchester Utd., 1997-2003) 57
Scott, L. (Arsenal, 1947-9) 17
Seaman, D. (Q.P.R., Arsenal, 1989-2003) 75
Sewell, J. (Sheffield Wed., 1952-4) 6
Shackleton, L. (Sunderland, 1949-55) 5
Sharpe, L. (Manchester Utd., 1991-4) 8
Shaw, G. (Sheffield Utd., 1959-63) 5
Shearer, A. (Southampton, Blackburn Rov., Newcastle Utd., 1992-2000) 63
Shellito, K. (Chelsea, 1963) 1
Sheringham, E. (Tottenham, Manchester Utd., Tottenham, 1993-2002) 51
Sherwood, T. (Tottenham, 1999) 3
Shilton, P (Leicester City, Stoke City, Nott'm. Forest, Southampton, Derby Co., 1971-90) 125
Shimwell, E. (Blackpool, 1949) 1
Sillett, P. (Chelsea, 1955) 3
Sinclair, T. (West Ham Utd., 2002-3) 11
Sinton, A. (Q.P.R., Sheffield Wed, 1992-4) 12
Slater, W. (Wolves, 1955-60) 12
Smith, A. (Arsenal, 1989-92) 13
Smith, A. (Leeds Utd., 2001-3) 6
Smith, L. (Arsenal, 1951-3) 6
Smith, R. (Tottenham, 1961-4) 15
Smith, T. (Birmingham City, 1960) 2
Smith, T. (Liverpool, 1971) 1
Southgate, G. (Aston Villa, Middlesbrough, 1996-2003) 55
Spink, N. (Aston Villa, 1983) 1
Springett, R. (Sheffield Wed., 1960-6) 33
Staniforth, R. (Huddersfield Town, 1954-5) 8
Statham, D. (W.B.A., 1983) 3
Stein, B. (Luton Town, 1984) 1
Stepney, A. (Manchester Utd., 1968) . 1
Sterland, M. (Sheffield Wed., 1989) ... 1
Steven, T. (Everton, Rangers, Marseille, 1985-92) 36
Stevens, G. (Everton, Rangers, 1985-92) 46
Stevens, G. (Tottenham, 1985-6) 7
Stewart, P. (Tottenham, 1992) 3
Stiles, N. (Manchester Utd., 1965-70) 28
Stone, S. (Nott'm. Forest, 1996) 8
Storey, P. (Arsenal, 1971-3) 19
Storey-Moore, I. (Nott'm Forest, 1970) 1
Streten, B. (Luton Town, 1950) 1
Summerbee, M. (Manchester City, 1968-73) 8
Sunderland, A. (Arsenal, 1980) 1
Sutton, C. (Blackburn Rov., 1997) 1
Swan, P. (Sheffield Wed., 1960-2) ... 19

Swift, W. (Manchester City, 1947-9) . 19

Talbot, B. (Ipswich Town, Arsenal, 1977-80) 6
Tambling, R. (Chelsea, 1963-6) 3
Taylor, E. (Blackpool, 1954) 1
Taylor, J. (Fulham, 1951) 2
Taylor, P. (Liverpool, 1948) 3
Taylor, P. (Crystal Palace, 1976) 4
Taylor, T. (Manchester Utd., 1953-8) 19
Temple, D. (Everton, 1965) 1
Terry, J. (Chelsea, 2003) 1
Thomas, D. (Coventry City, 1983) 2
Thomas, G. (Crystal Palace, 1991-2) .. 9
Thomas, D. (Q.P.R., 1975-6) 8
Thomas, M. (Arsenal, 1989-90) 2
Thompson, Peter (Liverpool, 1964-70) 16
Thompson, Phil (Liverpool, 1976-83) 42
Thompson, T. (Aston Villa, Preston N.E., 1952-7) 2
Thomson, R. (Wolves, 1964-5) 8
Todd, C. (Derby Co., 1972-7) 27
Towers, A. (Sunderland, 1978) 3
Tueart, D. (Manchester City, 1975-7) .. 6

Ufton, D. (Charlton Athletic, 1954) 1
Unsworth, D. (Everton, 1995) 1
Upson, M. (Birmingham City, 2003) ... 3

Vassell, D. (Aston Villa, 2002-3) 14
Venables, T. (Chelsea, 1965) 2
Venison, B. (Newcastle Utd., 1995) ... 2
Viljoen, C. (Ipswich Town, 1975) 2
Viollet, D. (Manchester Utd., 1960) 2

Waddle, C. (Newcastle Utd., Tottenham, Marseille, 1985-92) 62
Waiters, A. (Blackpool, 1964-5) 5
Walker, D. (Nott'm Forest, Sampdoria, 1989-94) 59
Walker, I. (Tottenham, 1996-7) 3
Wallace, D. (Southampton, 1986) 1
Walsh, P. (Luton Town, 1983-4) 5
Walters, M. (Rangers, 1991) 1
Ward, P. (Brighton & H.A., 1980) 1
Ward, T. (Derby Co., 1948) 2
Watson, D. (Sunderland, Manchester City, Werder Bremen, Southampton, Stoke City, 1974-82) 65
Watson, D. (Norwich City, Everton, 1984-8) 12
Watson, W. (Sunderland, 1950-1) 4
Webb, N. (Nott'm Forest, Manchester Utd., 1988-92) 26
Weller, K. (Leicester City, 1974) 4
West, G. (Everton, 1969) 3
Wheeler, J. (Bolton Wand., 1955) 1
White, D. (Manchester City, 1993) 1
Whitworth, S. (Leicester City, 1975-6) 7
Whymark, T. (Ipswich Town, 1978) 1
Wignall, F. (Nott'm Forest, 1965) 2
Wilcox, J. (Blackburn Rov., Leeds Utd., 1996-2000) 3
Wilkins, R. (Chelsea, Manchester Utd., AC Milan, 1976-87) 84
Williams, B. (Wolves, 1949-56) 24
Williams, S. (Southampton, Arsenal, 1983-5) 6
Willis, A. (Tottenham, 1952) 1
Wilshaw, D. (Wolves, 1954-7) 12
Wilson, R. (Huddersfield Town, Everton, 1960-8) 63
Winterburn, N. (Arsenal, 1990-3) 2
Wise, D. (Chelsea, 1991-2001) 21
Withe, P. (Aston Villa, 1981-5) 11
Wood, R. (Manchester Utd., 1955-6) .. 3
Woodcock, A. (Nott'm Forest, Cologne, Arsenal, 1977-86) 42
Woodgate, J. (Leeds Utd., 1999-2003) 4
Woods, C. (Norwich City, Rangers, Sheffield Wed., 1984-93) 43
Worthington, F. (Leicester City, 1974-5) 8
Wright, I. (Crystal Palace, Arsenal, West Ham Utd., 1991-9) 33
Wright, M. (Southampton, Derby Co., Liverpool, 1984-96) 45
Wright, R. (Ipswich Town, Arsenal, 2000-02) 2
Wright, T. (Everton, 1968-70) 11
Wright, W. (Wolves, 1947-59) 105

Young, G. (Sheffield Wed., 1965) 1

NORTHERN IRELAND

Aherne, T. (Belfast Celtic, Luton Town, 1947-50) 4
Anderson, T. (Manchester Utd., Swindon Town, Peterborough Utd., 1973-9) 22
Armstrong, G. (Tottenham, Watford, Real Mallorca, W.B.A., 1977-86) 63

Baird, C. (Southampton, 2003) 2
Barr, H. (Linfield, Coventry City, 1962-3) 3
Best, G. (Manchester Utd., Fulham, 1964-77) 37
Bingham, W. (Sunderland, Luton Town, Everton, Port Vale, 1951-64) 56
Black, K. (Luton Town, Nott'm Forest, 1988-94) 30
Blair, R. (Oldham Athletic, 1975-6) ... 5
Blanchflower, R.D. (Barnsley, Aston Villa, Tottenham, 1950-63) 56
Blanchflower, J. (Manchester Utd., 1954-8) 12
Bowler, G. (Hull City, 1950) 3
Braithwaite, R. (Linfield, Middlesbrough, 1962-5) 10
Brennan, R. (Luton Town, Birmingham City, Fulham, 1949-51) 5
Briggs, W. (Manchester Utd., Swansea City, 1962-5) 2
Brotherston, N. (Blackburn Rov., 1980-5) 27
Bruce, W. (Glentoran, 1961-7) 2

Campbell, D. (Nott'm Forest, Charlton Athletic, 1987-8) 10
Campbell, J. (Fulham, 1951) 2
Campbell, R. (Crusaders, 1963-5) 2
Campbell, R. (Bradford City, 1982) 2
Campbell, W. (Dundee, 1968-70) 6
Carey, J. (Manchester Utd., 1947-9) .. 7
Carroll, R. (Wigan Athletic, Manchester Utd., 1997-2003) 13
Casey, T. (Newcastle Utd., Portsmouth, 1955-9) 12
Caskey, W. (Derby Co., Tulsa Roughnecks, 1979-82) 7
Cassidy, T. (Newcastle Utd., Burnley, 1971-82) 24
Caughey, M. (Linfield, 1986) 2
Clarke, C. (Bournemouth, Southampton, Q.P.R., Portsmouth, 1986-93) 38
Cleary, J. (Glentoran, 1982-5) 5
Clements, D. (Coventry City, Sheffield Wed., Everton, New York City Cosmos, 1965-76) 48
Cochrane, A. (Coleraine, Burnley, Middlesbrough, Gillingham, 1976-84) 26
Cochrane, D. (Leeds Utd., 1947-50) 10
Connell, T. (Coleraine, 1978) 1
Coote, A. (Norwich City, 1999-2000) . 6
Cowan, J. (Newcastle Utd., 1970) 1
Coyle, F. (Coleraine, Nott'm Forest, 1956-8) 4
Coyle, L. (Derry C., 1989) 1
Coyle, R. (Sheffield Wed., 1973-4) 5
Craig, D. (Newcastle Utd., 1967-75) 25
Craigan, S. (Partick Thistle, 2003) 3
Crossan, E. (Blackburn Rov., 1950-5) . 3
Crossan, J. (Sparta Rotterdam, Sunderland, Manchester City, Middlesbrough, 1960-8) 24
Cunningham, W. (St Mirren, Leicester City, Dunfermline, 1951-62) 30
Cush, W. (Glenavon, Leeds Utd., Portadown, 1951-62) 26

D'Arcy, S. (Chelsea, Brentford, 1952-3) 5
Davison, A. (Bolton Wand., Bradford City C., Grimsby Town, 1996-7) 3
Dennison, R. (Wolves, 1988-97) 18
Devine, J. (Glentoran, 1990) 1
Dickson, D. (Coleraine, 1970-3) 4
Dickson, T. (Linfield, 1957) 1
Dickson, W. (Chelsea, Arsenal, 1951-5) 12
Doherty, L. (Linfield, 1985-8) 2
*Doherty, P. (Derby Co., Huddersfield Town, Doncaster Rov., 1946-50) 6
Doherty, T. (Bristol City, 2003) 2
Donaghy, M. (Luton Town, Manchester Utd., Chelsea, 1980-94) 91
Dougan, D. (Portsmouth, Blackburn Rov., Aston Villa, Leicester City, Wolves, 1958-73) 43
Douglas, J. (Belfast Celtic, 1947) 1
Dowd, H. (Glenavon, 1974) 3
Dowie, I. (Luton Town, Southampton, Crystal Palace, West Ham Utd., Q.P.R., 1990-2000) 59
Duff, M. (Cheltenham Town, 2002-3) . 2
Dunlop, G. (Linfield, 1985-90) 4

Eglington, T. (Everton, 1947-9) 6
Elder, A. (Burnley, Stoke City, 1960-70) 40
Elliott, S. (Motherwell, Hull City, 2001-3) 15

Farrell, P. (Everton, 1947-9) 7
Feeney, J. (Linfield, Swansea City, 1947-50) 2
Feeney, W. (Glentoran, 1976) 1

Feeney, W. (Bournemouth, 2002-3) 3
Ferguson, G. (Linfield, 1999-2001) 5
Ferguson, W. (Linfield, 1966-7) 2
Ferris, R. (Birmingham City, 1950-2) . 3
Fettis, A. (Hull City, Nott'm. Forest, Blackburn Rov., 1992-9) 25
Finney, T. (Sunderland, Cambridge Utd., 1975-80) 14
Fleming, G. (Nott'm Forest, Manchester City, Barnsley, 1987-95) 31
Forde, J. (Ards, 1959-61) 4

Gallogly, C. (Huddersfield Town, 1951) 2
Gaston, R. (Coleraine, 1969) 1
Gillespie, K. (Manchester Utd., Newcastle Utd., Blackburn Rov., 1995-2003) 47
Gorman, W. (Brentford, 1947-8) 4
Graham, W. (Doncaster Rov., 1951-9) 14
Gray, P. (Luton Town, Sunderland, Nancy, Burnley, Oxford Utd., 1993-2001) 25
Gregg, H. (Doncaster Rov., Manchester Utd., 1954-64) 25
Griffin, D. (St Johnstone, Dundee Utd., 1996-2003) 25

Hamill, R. (Glentoran, 1999) 1
Hamilton, B. (Linfield, Ipswich Town, Everton, Millwall, Swindon Town, 1969-80) 50
Hamilton, G. (Glentoran, 2003) 1
Hamilton, W. (Q.P.R., Burnley, Oxford Utd., 1978-86) 41
Harkin, J. (Southport, Shrewsbury Town, 1968-70) 5
Harvey, M. (Sunderland, 1961-71) ... 34
Hatton, S. (Linfield, 1963) 2
Healy, D. (Manchester Utd., Preston N.E., 2000-03) 26
Healy, F. (Coleraine, Glentoran, 1982-3) 4
Hegan, D. (W.B.A., Wolves, 1970-3) ... 7
Hill, C. (Sheffield Utd., Leicester City, Trelleborg, Northampton Town, 1990-9) 27
Hill, J. (Norwich City, Everton, 1959-64) 7
Hinton, E. (Fulham, Millwall, 1947-51) 7
Holmes, S. (Wrexham, 2002) 1
Horlock, K. (Swindon Town, Manchester City, 1995-2003) 32
Hughes, A. (Newcastle Utd., 1997-2003) 31
Hughes, M. (Manchester City, Strasbourg, West Ham Utd., Wimbledon, 1992-2003) 65

Hughes, P. (Bury, 1987) 3
Hughes, W. (Bolton Wand., 1951) 1
Humphries, W. (Ards, Coventry City, Swansea City, 1962-5) 14
Hunter, A. (Blackburn Rov., Ipswich Town, 1970-80) 53
Hunter, B. (Wrexham, Reading, 1995-2000) 15
Hunter, V. (Coleraine, 1962) 2

Irvine, R. (Linfield, Stoke City, 1962-5) 8
Irvine, W. (Burnley, Preston N.E., Brighton & H.A., 1963-72) 23

Jackson, T. (Everton, Nott'm Forest, Manchester Utd., 1969-77) 35
Jamison, J. (Glentoran, 1976) 1
Jenkins, I. (Chester City, Dundee Utd., 1997-2000) 6
Jennings, P. (Watford, Tottenham, Arsenal, Tottenham, 1964-86) 119
Johnson, D. (Blackburn Rov., Birmingham City, 1999-2003) 24
Johnston, W. (Glenavon, Oldham Athletic, 1962-6) 2
Jones, J. (Glenavon, 1956-7) 3
Jones, S. (Crewe Alexandra, 2003) 2

Keane, T. (Swansea City, 1949) 1
Kee, P. (Oxford Utd., Ards, 1990-5) ... 9
Keith, R. (Newcastle Utd., 1958-62) 23
Kelly, H. (Fulham, Southampton, 1950-1) 4
Kelly, P. (Barnsley, 1950) 1
Kennedy, P. (Watford, Wigan Athletic, 1999-2003) 17
Kirk, A. (Hearts, 2000-03) 5

Lawther, W. (Sunderland, Blackburn Rov., 1960-2) 4
Lennon, N. (Crewe Alexandra, Leicester City, Celtic, 1994-2002) 40
Lockhart, N. (Linfield, Coventry City, Aston Villa, 1947-56) 8
Lomas, S. (Manchester City, West Ham Utd., 1994-2003) 45
Lutton, B. (Wolves, West Ham Utd., 1970-4) 6

Magill, E. (Arsenal, Brighton & H.A., 1962-6) 26
Magilton, J. (Oxford Utd., Southampton, Sheffield Wed., Ipswich Town, 1991-2002) 52
Martin, C. (Glentoran, Leeds Utd., Aston Villa, 1947-50) 6

McAdams, W. (Manchester City, Bolton Wand., Leeds Utd., 1954-62) 15
*McAlinden, J. (Portsmouth, Southend Utd., 1947-9) 2
McBride, S. (Glenavon, 1991-2) 4
McCabe, J. (Leeds Utd., 1949-54) 6
McCann, G. (West Ham Utd., Cheltenham Town, 2002-3) 6
McCarthy, J. (Port Vale, Birmingham City, 1996-2001) 18
McCartney, G. (Sunderland, 2002-3) 12
McCavana, T. (Coleraine, 1954-5) 3
McCleary, J. (Cliftonville, 1955) 1
McClelland, J. (Arsenal, Fulham, 1961-7) 6
McClelland, J. (Mansfield Town, Rangers, Watford, Leeds Utd., 1980-90) 53
McCourt, F. (Manchester City, 1952-3) 6
McCourt, P. (Rochdale, 2002) 1
McCoy, R. (Coleraine, 1987) 1
McCreery, D. (Manchester Utd., Q.P.R., Tulsa Roughnecks, Newcastle Utd., 1976-90) 67
McCrory, S. (Southend Utd., 1958) 1
McCullough, W. (Arsenal, Millwall, 1961-7) 10
McCurdy, C. (Linfield, 1980) 1
McDonald, A. (Q.P.R., 1986-96) 52
McElhinney, G. (Bolton Wand., 1984-5) 6
McEvilly, L. (Rochdale, 2002) 1
McFaul, W. (Linfield, Newcastle Utd., 1967-74) 6
McGarry, J. (Cliftonville, 1951) 3
McGaughey, M. (Linfield, 1985) 1
McGibbon, P. (Manchester Utd., Wigan Athletic, 1995-2000) 7
McGrath, C. (Tottenham, Manchester Utd., 1974-9) 21
McIlroy, J. (Burnley, Stoke City, 1952-66) 55
McIlroy, S. (Manchester Utd., Stoke City, Manchester City, 1972-87) 88
McKeag, W. (Glentoran, 1968) 2
McKenna, J. (Huddersfield Town, 1950-2) 7
McKenzie, R. (Airdrie, 1967) 1
McKinney, W. (Falkirk, 1966) 1
McKnight, A. (Celtic, West Ham Utd., 1988-9) 10
McLaughlin, J. (Shrewsbury Town, Swansea City, 1962-6) 12
McMahon, G. (Tottenham, Stoke City, 1995-8) 17
McMichael, A. (Newcastle Utd., 1950-60) 40
McMillan, S. (Manchester Utd., 1963) 2
McMordie, A. (Middlesbrough, 1969-73) 21
McMorran, E. (Belfast Celtic, Barnsley, Doncaster Rov., 1947-57) 15
McNally, B. (Shrewsbury Town, 1987-8) 5
McParland, P. (Aston Villa, Wolves, 1954-62) 34
McVeigh, P. (Tottenham, Norwich City, 1999-2003) 10
Montgomery, F. (Coleraine, 1955) 1
Moore, C. (Glentoran, 1949) 1
Moreland, V. (Derby Co., 1979-80) 6
Morgan, S. (Port Vale, Aston Villa, Brighton & H.A., Sparta Rotterdam, 1972-9) 18
Morrow, S. (Arsenal, Q.P.R., 1990-2000) 39
Mullan, G. (Glentoran, 1983) 5
Mulryne, P. (Manchester Utd., Norwich City, 1997-2003) 18
Murdock, C. (Preston N.E., 2000-03) 17

Napier, R. (Bolton Wand., 1966) 1
Neill, T. (Arsenal, Hull City, 1961-73) 59
Nelson, S. (Arsenal, Brighton & H.A., 1970-82) 51
Nicholl, C. (Aston Villa, Southampton, Grimsby Town, 1975-83) 51
Nicholl, J. (Manchester Utd., Toronto Blizzard, Sunderland, Rangers, W.B.A., 1976-86) 73
Nicholson, J. (Manchester Utd., Huddersfield Town, 1961-72) 41
Nolan, I. (Sheffield Wed., Bradford City, Wigan Athletic, 1997-2002) 18

O'Boyle, G. (Dunfermline, St Johnstone, 1994-9) 13
O'Doherty, A. (Coleraine, 1970) 2
O'Driscoll, J. (Swansea City, 1949) 3
O'Kane, W. (Nott'm Forest, 1970-5) . 20
O'Neill, C. (Motherwell, 1989-91) 3
O'Neill, J. (Sunderland, 1962) 1
O'Neill, J. (Leicester City, 1980-6) ... 39
O'Neill, M. (Distillery, Nott'm Forest, Norwich City, Manchester City, Notts Co., 1972-85) 64
O'Neill, M. (Newcastle Utd., Dundee Utd., Hibernian, Coventry City, 1989-97) 31

Parke, J. (Linfield, Hibernian, Sunderland, 1964-8) 14
Patterson, D. (Crystal Palace, Luton Town, Dundee Utd., 1994-9) 17
Peacock, R. (Glasgow Celtic, Coleraine, 1952-62) 31

Penney, S. (Brighton & H.A., 1985-9) 17
Platt, J. (Middlesbrough, Ballymena, Coleraine, 1976-86) 23

Quinn, J. (Blackburn Rov., Swindon Town, Leicester City, Bradford City, West Ham Utd., Bournemouth, Reading, 1985-96) 46
Quinn, S.J. (Blackpool, W.B.A., Willem 11, 1996-2003) 29

Rafferty, W. (Wolves, 1980) 1
Ramsey, P. (Leicester City, 1984-9) .. 14
Rice, P. (Arsenal, 1969-80) 49
Robinson, S. (Bournemouth, 1997-2000) 5
Rogan, A. (Celtic, Sunderland, Millwall, 1988-97) 17
Ross, W. (Newcastle Utd., 1969) 1
Rowland, K. (West Ham Utd., Q.P.R., 1994-9) 19
Russell, A. (Linfield, 1947) 1
Ryan, R. (W.B.A., 1950) 1

Sanchez, L. (Wimbledon, 1987-9) 3
Scott, J. (Grimsby Town, 1958) 2
Scott, P. (Everton, York City, Aldershot, 1976-9) 10
Sharkey, P. (Ipswich Town, 1976) 1
Shields, J. (Southampton, 1957) 1
Simpson, W. (Rangers, 1951-9) 12
Sloan, D. (Oxford Utd., 1969-71) 2
Sloan, J. (Arsenal, 1947) 1
Sloan, T. (Manchester Utd., 1979) 3
Smith, A. (Glentoran, 2003) 2
Smyth, S. (Wolves, Stoke City, 1948-52) 9
Smyth, W. (Distillery, 1949-54) 4
Sonner, D. (Ipswich Town, Sheffield Wed., Birmingham City, 1997-2001) 7
Spence, D. (Bury, Blackpool, Southend Utd., 1975-82) 27
*Stevenson, A. (Everton, 1947-8) 3
Stewart, A. (Glentoran, Derby Co., 1967-9) 7
Stewart, D. (Hull City, 1978) 1
Stewart, I. (Q.P.R., Newcastle Utd., 1982-7) 31
Stewart, T. (Linfield, 1961) 1

Taggart, G. (Barnsley, Bolton Wand., Leicester City, 1990-2003) 51
Taylor, M. (Fulham, 1999-2003) 29
Todd, S. (Burnley, Sheffield Wed., 1966-71) 11
Toner, C. (Leyton Orient, 2003) 2
Trainor, D. (Crusaders, 1967) 1
Tully, C. (Glasgow Celtic, 1949-59) .. 10

Uprichard, W. (Swindon Town, Portsmouth, 1952-9) 18

Vernon, J. (Belfast Celtic, W.B.A., 1947-52) 17

Walker, J. (Doncaster Rov., 1955) 1
Walsh, D. (W.B.A., 1947-50) 9
Walsh, W. (Manchester City, 1948-9) .. 5
Watson, P. (Distillery, 1971) 1
Welsh, E. (Carlisle Utd., 1966-7) 4
Whiteside, N. (Manchester Utd., Everton, 1982-90) 38
Whitley, Jeff (Manchester City, 1997-2001) 7
Whitley, Jim (Manchester City, 1998-2000) 3
Williams, M. (Chesterfield, Wimbledon, Watford, Wimbledon, Stoke City, 1999-2003) 25
Williams, P. (W.B.A., 1991) 1
Wilson, D. (Brighton & H.A., Luton Town, Sheffield Wed., 1987-92) ... 24
Wilson, K. (Ipswich Town, Chelsea, Notts Co., Walsall, 1987-95) 42
Wilson, S. (Glenavon, Falkirk, Dundee, 1962-8) 12
Wood, T. (Walsall, 1996) 1
Worthington, N. (Sheffield Wed., Leeds Utd., Stoke City, 1984-97) 66
Wright, T. (Newcastle Utd., Nott'm Forest, Reading, Manchester City, 1989-2000) 31

SCOTLAND

Aird, J. (Burnley, 1954) 4
Aitken, G. (East Fife, 1949-54) 8
Aitken, R. (Celtic, Newcastle Utd., St Mirren, 1980-92) 57
Albiston, A. (Manchester Utd., 1982-6) 14
Alexander, G. (Preston N.E., 2002-3) 12
Allan, T. (Dundee, 1974) 2
Anderson, J. (Leicester City, 1954) 1
Anderson, R. (Aberdeen, 2003) 4
Archibald, S. (Aberdeen, Tottenham, Barcelona, 1980-6) 27
Auld, B. (Celtic, 1959-60) 3

Baird, H. (Airdrie, 1956) 1
Baird, S. (Rangers, 1957-8) 7
Bannon, E. (Dundee Utd., 1980-6) .. 11

Bauld, W. (Hearts, 1950) ... 3
Baxter, J. (Rangers, Sunderland, 1961-8) ... 34
Bell, W. (Leeds Utd., 1966) ... 2
Bernard, P. (Oldham Athletic, 1995) .. 2
Bett, J. (Rangers, Lokeren, Aberdeen, 1982-90) ... 26
Black, E. (Metz, 1988) ... 2
Black, I. (Southampton, 1948) ... 1
Blacklaw, A. (Burnley, 1963-6) ... 3
Blackley, J. (Hibernian, 1974-7) ... 7
Blair, J. (Blackpool, 1947) ... 1
Blyth, J. (Coventry City, 1978) ... 2
Bone, J. (Norwich City, 1972-3) ... 2
Booth, S. (Aberdeen, Borussia Dortmund, Twente Enschede, 1993-2002) ... 20
Bowman, D. (Dundee Utd., 1992-4) ... 6
Boyd, T. (Motherwell, Chelsea, Celtic, 1991-2002) ... 72
Brand, R. (Rangers, 1961-2) ... 8
Brazil, A. (Ipswich Town, Tottenham, 1980-3) ... 13
Bremner, D. (Hibernian, 1976) ... 1
Bremner, W. (Leeds Utd., 1965-76) . 54
Brennan, F. (Newcastle Utd., 1947-54) ... 7
Brogan, J. (Celtic, 1971) ... 4
Brown, A. (East Fife, Blackpool, 1950-4) ... 14
Brown, H. (Partick, 1947) ... 3
Brown, J. (Sheffield Utd., 1975) ... 1
Brown, R. (Rangers, 1947-52) ... 3
Brown, W. (Dundee, Tottenham, 1958-66) ... 28
Brownlie, J. (Hibernian, 1971-6) ... 7
Buchan, M. (Aberdeen, Manchester Utd., 1972-8) ... 34
Buckley, P. (Aberdeen, 1954-5) ... 3
Burchill, M. (Celtic, 2000) ... 6
Burley, C. (Chelsea, Celtic, Derby Co., 1995-2003) ... 46
Burley, G. (Ipswich Town, 1979-82) . 11
Burns, F. (Manchester Utd.. 1970) ... 1
Burns, K. (Birmingham City, Nott'm Forest, 1974-81) ... 20
Burns, T. (Celtic, 1981-8) ... 8

Calderwood, C. (Tottenham, Aston Villa, 1995-2000) ... 36
Caldow, E. (Rangers, 1957-63) ... 40
Caldwell, G. (Neecastle Utd., 2002) ... 4
Caldwell, S. (Newcastle Utd., 2001) ... 2
Callaghan, T. (Dunfermline, 1970) ... 2
Cameron, C. (Hearts, Wolves, 1999-2003) ... 19
Campbell, R. (Falkirk, Chelsea, 1947-50) ... 5
Campbell, W. (Morton, 1947-8) ... 5
Carr, W. (Coventry City, 1970-3) ... 6
Chalmers, S. (Celtic, 1965-7) ... 5
Clark, J. (Celtic, 1966-7) ... 4
Clark, R. (Aberdeen, 1968-73) ... 17
Clarke, S. (Chelsea, 1988-94) ... 6
Collins, J. (Hibernian, Celtic, Monaco, Everton, 1988-2000) ... 58
Collins, R. (Celtic, Everton, Leeds Utd., 1951-65) ... 31
Colquhoun, E. (Sheffield Utd, 1972-3) ... 9
Colquhoun, J. (Hearts, 1988) ... 1
Combe, J. (Hibernian, 1948) ... 3
Conn, A. (Hearts, 1956) ... 1
Conn, A. (Tottenham, 1975) ... 2
Connachan, E. (Dunfermline, 1962) ... 2
Connelly, G. (Celtic, 1974) ... 2
Connolly, J. (Everton, 1973) ... 1
Connor, R. (Dundee, Aberdeen, 1986-91) ... 4
Cooke, C. (Dundee, Chelsea, 1966-75) ... 16
Cooper, D. (Rangers, Motherwell, 1980-90) ... 22
Cormack, P. (Hibernian, 1966-72) ... 9
Cowan, J. (Morton, 1948-52) ... 25
Cowie, D. (Dundee, 1953-8) ... 20
Cox, C. (Hearts, 1948) ... 1
Cox, S. (Rangers, 1948-54) ... 25
Craig, J.P. (Celtic, 1968) ... 1
Craig, J. (Celtic, 1977) ... 1
Craig, T. (Newcastle Utd., 1976) ... 1
Crainey, S. (Celtic, 2002-3) ... 4
Crawford, S. (Raith, Dunfermline, 1995-2003) ... 13
Crerand, P. (Celtic, Manchester Utd., 1961-6) ... 16
Cropley, A. (Hibernian, 1972) ... 2
Cruickshank, J. (Hearts, 1964-76) ... 6
Cullen, M. (Luton Town, 1956) ... 1
Cumming, J. (Hearts, 1955-60) ... 9
Cunningham, W. (Preston N.E., 1954-5) ... 8
Curran, H. (Wolves, 1970-1) ... 5

Dailly, C. (Derby Co., Blackburn Rov., West Ham Utd., 1997-2003) ... 46
Dalglish, K. (Celtic, Liverpool, 1972-87) ... 102
Davidson, C. (Blackburn Rov., Leicester City, 1999-2003) ... 17
Davidson, J. (Partick, 1954-5) ... 8
Dawson, A. (Rangers, 1980-3) ... 5
Deans, D. (Celtic, 1975) ... 2
*Delaney, J. (Manchester Utd., 1947-8) ... 4
Devlin, P. (Birmingham, 2003) ... 8
Dick, J. (West Ham Utd., 1959) ... 1
Dickov, P. (Manchester City, 2001-3) .. 4
Dickson, W. (Kilmarnock, 1970-1) ... 5
Dobie, S. (W.B.A., 2002-3) ... 6
Docherty, T. (Preston N.E., Arsenal, 1952-9) ... 25

Dodds, D. (Dundee Utd., 1984) 2
Dodds, W. (Aberdeen, Dundee Utd., Rangers, 1997-2002) 25
Donachie, W. (Manchester City, 1972-9) 35
Donnelly, S. (Celtic, 1997-9) 10
Dougall, C. (Birmingham City, 1947) .. 1
Dougan, R. (Hearts, 1950) 1
Douglas, R. (Celtic, 2002-3) 9
Doyle, J. (Ayr, 1976) 1
Duncan, A. (Hibernian, 1975-6) 6
Duncan, D. (East Fife, 1948) 3
Duncanson, J. (Rangers, 1947) 1
Durie, G. (Chelsea, Tottenham, Rangers, 1988-98) 43
Durrant, I. (Rangers, Kilmarnock, 1988-2000) 21

Elliott, M. (Leicester City, 1997-2002) 18
Evans, A. (Aston Villa, 1982) 4
Evans, R. (Celtic, Chelsea, 1949-60) 48
Ewing, T. (Partick, 1958) 2

Farm, G. (Blackpool, 1953-9) 10
Ferguson, B. (Rangers, 1999-2003) . 15
Ferguson, D. (Dundee Utd., Everton, 1992-7) 7
Ferguson, D. (Rangers, 1988) 2
Ferguson, I. (Rangers, 1989-97) 9
Ferguson, R. (Kilmarnock, 1966-7) 7
Fernie, W. (Celtic, 1954-8) 12
Flavell, R. (Airdrie, 1947) 2
Fleck, R. (Norwich City, 1990-1) 4
Fleming, C. (East Fife, 1954) 1
Forbes, A. (Sheffield Utd., Arsenal, 1947-52) 14
Ford, D. (Hearts, 1974) 3
Forrest, J. (Motherwell, 1958) 1
Forrest, J. (Rangers, Aberdeen, 1966-71) 5
Forsyth, A. (Partick, Manchester Utd., 1972-6) 10
Forsyth, C. (Kilmarnock, 1964) 4
Forsyth, T. (Motherwell, Rangers, 1971-8) 22
Fraser, D. (W.B.A., 1968-9) 2
Fraser, W. (Sunderland, 1955) 2
Freedman, D. (Crystal Palace, 2002) .. 2

Gabriel, J. (Everton, 1961-4) 2
Gallacher, K. (Dundee Utd., Coventry City, Blackburn Rov., Newcastle Utd., 1988-2001) 53
Gallacher, P. (Dundee Utd., 2003) 5
Galloway, M. (Celtic, 1992) 1
Gardiner, I. (Motherwell, 1958) 1
Gemmell, T. (St Mirren, 1955) 2
Gemmell, T. (Celtic, 1966-71) 18
Gemmill, A. (Derby Co., Nott'm Forest, Birmingham City, 1971-81) 43
Gemmill, S. (Nott'm Forest, Everton 1995-2003) 27
Gibson, D. (Leicester City, 1963-5) 7
Gillespie, G. (Liverpool, 1988-91) 13
Gilzean, A. (Dundee, Tottenham, 1964-71) 22
Glass, S. (Necastle Utd., 1999) 1
Glavin, R. (Celtic, 1977) 1
Glen, A. (Aberdeen, 1956) 2
Goram, A. (Oldham Athletic, Hibernian, Rangers, 1986-98) 44
Gough, R. (Dundee Utd., Tottenham, Rangers, 1983-93) 61
Gould, J. (Celtic, 2000-01) 2
Govan, J. (Hibernian, 1948-9) 6
Graham, A. (Leeds Utd., 1978-81) ... 10
Graham, G. (Arsenal, Manchester Utd., 1972-3) 12
Gray, A. (Aston Villa, Wolves, Everton, 1976-85) 20
Gray, A. (Bradford City, 2003) 2
Gray, E. (Leeds Utd., 1969-77) 12
Gray, F. (Leeds Utd., Nott'm Forest, 1976-83) 32
Grant, J. (Hibernian, 1958) 2
Grant, P. (Celtic, 1989) 2
Green, A. (Blackpool, Newcastle Utd., 1971-2) 6
Greig, J. (Rangers, 1964-76) 44
Gunn, B. (Norwich City, 1990-4) 6

Haddock, H. (Clyde, 1955-8) 6
Haffey, F. (Celtic, 1960-1) 2
Hamilton, A. (Dundee, 1962-6) 24
Hamilton, G. (Aberdeen, 1947-54) 5
Hamilton, W. (Hibernian, 1965) 1
Hansen, A. (Liverpool, 1979-87) 26
Hansen, J. (Partick, 1972) 2
Harper, J. (Aberdeen, Hibernian, 1973-8) 4
Hartford, A. (W.B.A., Manchester City, Everton, 1972-82) 50
Harvey, D. (Leeds Utd., 1973-7) 16
Haughney, M. (Celtic, 1954) 1
Hay, D. (Celtic, 1970-4) 27
Hegarty, P. (Dundee Utd., 1979-83) ... 8
Henderson, J. (Portsmouth, Arsenal, 1953-9) 7
Henderson, W. (Rangers, 1963-71) .. 29
Hendry, C. (Blackburn Rov., Rangers, Coventry City, Bolton Wand., 1994-2001) 51
Herd, D. (Arsenal, 1959-61) 5
Herd, G. (Clyde, 1958-61) 5
Herriot, J. (Birmingham City, 1969-70) 8
Hewie, J. (Charlton Athletic, 1956-60) 19
Holt, D. (Hearts, 1963-4) 5

Holt, G. (Kilmarnock, Norwich City, 2001-2) 3
Holton, J. (Manchester Utd., 1973-5) 15
Hope, R. (W.B.A., 1968-9) 2
Hopkin, D. (Crystal Palace, Leeds Utd., 1997-2000) 7
Houliston, W. (Queen of the South, 1949) 3
Houston, S. (Manchester Utd., 1976) . 1
Howie, H. (Hibernian, 1949) 1
Hughes, J. (Celtic, 1965-70) 8
Hughes, W. (Sunderland, 1975) 1
Humphries, W. (Motherwell, 1952) 1
Hunter, A. (Kilmarnock, Celtic, 1972-4) 4
Hunter, W. (Motherwell, 1960-1) 3
Husband, J. (Partick, 1947) 1
Hutchison, D. (Everton, Sunderland, West Ham Utd., 1999-2003) 23
Hutchison, T. (Coventry City, 1974-6) 17

Imlach, S. (Nott'm Forest, 1958) 4
Irvine, B. (Aberdeen, 1991-4) 9

Jackson, C. (Rangers, 1975-7) 21
Jackson, D. (Hibernian, Celtic, 1995-9) 29
Jardine, A. (Rangers, 1971-80) 38
Jarvie, A. (Airdrie, 1971) 3
Jess, E. (Aberdeen, Coventry City, Aberdeen, 1993-9) 17
Johnston, A. (Sunderland, Rangers, Middlesbrough, 1999-2003) 17
Johnston, M. (Watford, Celtic, Nantes, Rangers, 1984-92) 38
Johnston, W. (Rangers, WBA, 1966-78) 22
Johnstone, D. (Rangers, 1973-80) 14
Johnstone, J. (Celtic, 1965-75) 23
Johnstone, L. (Clyde, 1948) 2
Johnstone, R. (Hibernian, Manchester City, 1951-6) 17
Jordan, J. (Leeds Utd., Manchester Utd., AC Milan, 1973-82) 52

Kelly, H. (Blackpool, 1952) 1
Kelly, J. (Barnsley, 1949) 2
Kennedy, J. (Celtic, 1964-5) 6
Kennedy, S. (Rangers, 1975) 5
Kennedy, S. (Aberdeen, 1978-82) 8
Kerr, A. (Partick, 1955) 2
Kerr, B. (Newcastle Utd, 2003) 1
Kyle, K. (Sunderland, 2002-3) 8

Lambert P. (Motherwell, Borussia Dortmund, Celtic, 1995-2003) 38
Law, D. (Huddersfield Town, Manchester City, Torino, Manchester Utd., 1959-74) 55
Lawrence T. (Liverpool, 1963-9) 3
Leggat, G. (Aberdeen, Fulham, 1956-60) 18
Leighton, J. (Aberdeen, Manchester Utd., Hibernian, Aberdeen, 1983-99) 91
Lennox, R. (Celtic, 1967-70) 10
Leslie, L. (Airdrie, 1961) 5
Levein, C. (Hearts, 1990-5) 16
Liddell, W. (Liverpool, 1947-55) 28
Linwood, A. (Clyde, 1950) 1
Little, R. (Rangers, 1953) 1
Logie, J. (Arsenal, 1953) 1
Long, H. (Clyde, 1947) 1
Lorimer, P. (Leeds Utd., 1970-6) 21

Macari, L. (Celtic, Manchester Utd., 1972-8) 24
Macaulay, A. (Brentford, Arsenal, 1947-8) 7
MacDonald, A. (Rangers, 1976) 1
MacDougall, E. (Norwich City, 1975-6) 7
Mackay, D. (Hearts, Tottenham, 1957-66) 22
Mackay, G. (Hearts, 1988) 4
MacLeod, J. (Hibernian, 1961) 4
MacLeod, M. (Celtic, Borussia Dort., Hibernian, 1985-91) 20
Malpas, M. (Dundee Utd., 1984-93) 55
Marshall, G. (Celtic, 1992) 1
Martin, B. (Motherwell, 1995) 2
Martin, F. (Aberdeen, 1954-5) 6
Martin, N. (Hibernian, Sunderland, 1965-6) 3
Martis, J. (Motherwell, 1961) 1
Mason, J. (Third Lanark, 1949-51) 7
Masson, D. (Q.P.R., Derby Co., 1976-8) 17
Mathers, D. (Partick, 1954) 1
Matteo, D. (Leeds Utd., 2001-2) 6
McAllister, B. (Wimbledon, 1997) 3
McAllister, G. (Leicester City, Leeds Utd., Coventry City, 1990-9) 57
McAvennie, F. (West Ham Utd., Celtic, 1986-8) 5
McBride, J. (Celtic, 1967) 2
McCall, S. (Everton, Rangers, 1990-8) 40
McCalliog, J. (Sheffield Wed., Wolves, 1967-71) 5
McCann, N. (Hearts, Rangers, 1999-2003) 16
McCann, R. (Motherwell, 1959-61) 5
McClair, B. (Celtic, Manchester Utd., 1987-93) 30
McCloy, P. (Rangers, 1973) 4

McCoist, A. (Rangers, Kilmarnock, 1986-99) 61
McColl, I. (Rangers, 1950-8) 14
McCreadie, E. (Chelsea, 1965-9) 23
McDonald, J. (Sunderland, 1956) 2
McFadden, J. (Motherwell, 2002-3) 4
McFarlane, W. (Hearts, 1947) 1
McGarr, E. (Aberdeen, 1970) 2
McGarvey, F. (Liverpool, Celtic, 1979-84) 7
McGhee, M. (Aberdeen, 1983-4) 4
McGinlay, J. (Bolton Wand., 1995-7) 14
McGrain, D. (Celtic, 1973-82) 62
McGrory, J. (Kilmarnock, 1965-6) 3
McInally, A. (Aston Villa, Bayern Munich, 1989-90) 8
McInally, J. (Dundee Utd., 1987-93) 10
McInnes, D. (W.B.A., 2003) 2
McKay, D. (Celtic, 1959-62) 14
McKean, R. (Rangers, 1976) 1
McKenzie, J. (Partick, 1954-6) 9
McKimmie, S. (Aberdeen, 1989-96) . 40
McKinlay, T. (Celtic, 1996-8) 22
McKinlay, W. (Dundee Utd., Blackburn Rov., 1994-9) 29
McKinnon, R. (Rangers, 1966-71) ... 28
McKinnon, R. (Motherwell, 1994-5) ... 3
McLaren, A. (Preston N.E., 1947-8) ... 4
McLaren, A. (Hearts, Rangers, 1992-6) 24
McLaren, A. (Kilmarnock, 2001) 1
McLean, G. (Dundee, 1968) 1
McLean, T. (Kilmarnock, Rangers, 1969-71) 6
McLeish, A. (Aberdeen, 1980-93) 77
McLintock, F. (Leicester City, Arsenal, 1963-71) 9
McMillan, I. (Airdrie, 1952-61) 6
McNamara, J. (Celtic, 1997-2003) .. 18
McNaught, W. (Raith, 1951-5) 5
McNaughton, K. (Aberdeen, 2002-3) .. 2
McNeill, W. (Celtic, 1961-72) 29
McPhail, J. (Celtic, 1950-4) 5
McPherson, D. (Hearts, Rangers, 1989-93) 27
McQueen, G. (Leeds Utd., Manchester Utd., 1974-81) 30
McStay, P. (Celtic, 1984-97) 76
McSwegan, G. (Hearts, 2000) 2
Millar, J. (Rangers, 1963) 2
Miller, C. (Dundee Utd., 2001) 1
Miller, K. (Rangers, Wolves, 2001-3) .. 5
Miller, W. (Celtic, 1946-7) 6
Miller, W. (Aberdeen, 1975-90) 65
Mitchell, R. (Newcastle Utd., 1951) ... 2
Mochan, N. (Celtic, 1954) 3
Moir, W. (Bolton Wand., 1950) 1
Moncur, R. (Newcastle Utd., 1968-72) 16
Morgan, W. (Burnley, Manchester Utd., 1968-74) 21
Morris, H. (East Fife, 1950) 1
Mudie, J. (Blackpool, 1957-8) 17
Mulhall, G. (Aberdeen, Sunderland, 1960-4) 3
Munro, F. (Wolves, 1971-5) 9
Munro, I. (St Mirren, 1979-80) 7
Murdoch, R. (Celtic, 1966-70) 12
Murray, I. (Hibernian, 2003) 1
Murray, J. (Hearts, 1958) 5
Murray, S. (Aberdeen, 1972) 1

Narey, D. (Dundee Utd., 1977-89) ... 35
Naysmith, G. (Hearts, Everton, 2000-03) 15
Nevin, P. (Chelsea, Everton, Tranmere Rov., 1987-96) 26
Nicholas, C. (Celtic, Arsenal, Aberdeen, 1983-9) 20
Nicholson, B. (Dunfermline, 2001-2) .. 2
Nicol, S. (Liverpool, 1985-92) 27

O'Connor, G. (Hibernian, 2002) 2
O'Donnell, P. (Motherwell, 1994) 1
O'Hare, J. (Derby Co., 1970-2) 13
O'Neil, B. (Celtic, VfL Wolfsburg, Derby Co., 1996-2001) 6
O'Neil, J. (Hibernian, 2001) 1
Ormond, W. (Hibernian, 1954-9) 6
Orr, T. (Morton, 1952) 2

Parker, A. (Falkirk, Everton, 1955-6) 15
Parlane, D. (Rangers, 1973-7) 12
Paton, A. (Motherwell, 1952) 2
Pearson, T. (Newcastle Utd., 1947) 2
Penman, A. (Dundee, 1966) 1
Pettigrew, W. (Motherwell, 1976-7) 5
Plenderleith, J. (Manchester City, 1961) 1
Pressley, S. (Hearts, 2000-03) 10
Provan, D. (Rangers, 1964-6) 5
Provan, D. (Celtic, 1980-2) 10

Quinn, P. (Motherwell, 1961-2) 9

Rae, A. (Wolves, 2002) 1
Rae, G. (Dundee, 2001-3) 3
Redpath, W. (Motherwell, 1949-52) ... 9
Reilly, L. (Hibernian, 1949-57) 38
Ring, T. (Clyde, 1953-8) 12
Rioch, B. (Derby Co., Everton, 1975-8) 24
Ritchie, P. (Hearts, Bolton Wand., 1999-2000) 6
Ritchie, W. (Rangers, 1962) 1
Robb, D. (Aberdeen, 1971) 5
Robertson, A. (Clyde, 1955) 5

Robertson, D. (Rangers, 1992-4) 3
Robertson, H. (Dundee, 1962) 1
Robertson, J. (Tottenham, 1964) 1
Robertson, J. (Nott'm Forest, Derby Co., 1978-84) 28
Robertson, J. (Hearts, 1991-6) 14
Robinson, R. (Dundee, 1974-5) 4
Ross, M. (Rangers, 2002-3) 10
Rough, A. (Partick, Hibernian, 1976-86) 53
Rougvie, D. (Aberdeen, 1984) 1
Rutherford, E. (Rangers, 1948) 1

Schaedler, E. (Hibernian, 1974) 1
Scott, A. (Rangers, Everton, 1957-66) 16
Scott, J. (Hibernian, 1966) 1
Scott, J. (Dundee, 1971) 2
Scoular, J. (Portsmouth, 1951-3) 9
Severin, S. (Hearts, 2002-3) 8
Sharp, G. (Everton, 1985-8) 12
Shaw, D. (Hibernian, 1947-9) 8
Shaw, J. (Rangers, 1947) 4
Shearer, D. (Aberdeen, 1994-6) 7
Shearer, R. (Rangers, 1961) 4
Simpson, N. (Aberdeen, 1983-8) 4
Simpson, R. (Celtic, 1967-9) 5
Sinclair, J. (Leicester City, 1966) 1
Smith, D. (Aberdeen, Rangers, 1966-8) 2
Smith, G. (Hibernian, 1947-57) 18
Smith, H. (Hearts, 1988-92) 3
Smith, J.E. (Celtic, 1959) 2
Smith, J. (Aberdeen, Newcastle Utd., 1968-74) 4
Smith, J. (Celtic, 2003) 2
Souness, G. (Middlesbrough, Liverpool, Sampdoria, Rangers, 1975-86) 54
Speedie, D. (Chelsea, Coventry City, 1985-9) 10
Spencer, J. (Chelsea, Q.P.R., 1995-7) 14
Stanton, P. (Hibernian, 1966-74) 16
Steel, W. (Morton, Derby Co., Dundee, 1947-53) 30
Stein, C. (Rangers, Coventry City, 1969-73) 21
Stephen, J. (Bradford City, 1947-8) ... 2
Stewart, D. (Leeds Utd., 1978) 1
Stewart, J. (Kilmarnock, Middlesbrough, 1977-9) 2
Stewart, M. (Manchester Utd., 2002) . 3
Stewart, R. (West Ham Utd., 1981-7) 10
St John, I. (Motherwell, Liverpool, 1959-65) 21
Stockdale, R. (Middlesbrough, 2002-3) 5
Strachan, G. (Aberdeen, Manchester Utd., Leeds Utd., 1980-92) 50
Sturrock, P. (Dundee Utd., 1981-7) .. 20
Sullivan, N. (Wimbledon, Tottenham, 1997-2003) 28

Telfer, P. (Coventry City, 2000) 1
Telfer, W. (St Mirren, 1954) 1
Thompson, S. (Dundee Utd., Rangers, 2002-3) 10
Thomson, W. (St Mirren, 1980-4) 7
Thornton, W. (Rangers, 1947-52) 7
Toner, W. (Kilmarnock, 1959) 2
Turnbull, E. (Hibernian, 1948-58) 8

Ure, I. (Dundee, Arsenal, 1962-8) 11

Waddell, W. (Rangers, 1947-55) 17
Walker, A. (Celtic, 1988-95) 3
Walker, N. (Hearts, 1993-6) 2
Wallace, I. (Coventry City, 1978-9) 3
Wallace, W. (Hearts, Celtic, 1965-9) .. 7
Wardhaugh, J. (Hearts, 1955-7) 2
Wark, J. (Ipswich Town, Liverpool, 1979-85) 29
Watson, J. (Motherwell, Huddersfield Town, 1948-54) 2
Watson, R. (Motherwell, 1971) 1
Webster, A. (Hearts, 2003) 3
Weir, A. (Motherwell, 1959-60) 6
Weir, D. (Hearts, Everton, 1997-2003) 37
Weir, P. (St Mirren, Aberdeen, 1980-4) 6
White, J. (Falkirk, Tottenham, 1959-64) 22
Whyte, D. (Celtic, Middlesbrough, Aberdeen, 1988-99) 12
Wilkie, L. (Dundee, 2002-3) 8
Williams, G. (Nott'm Forest, 2002-3) . 5
Wilson, A. (Portsmouth, 1954) 1
Wilson, D. (Rangers, 1961-5) 22
Wilson, I. (Leicester City, Everton, 1987-8) 5
Wilson, P. (Celtic, 1975) 1
Wilson, R. (Arsenal, 1972) 2
Wood, G. (Everton, Arsenal, 1978-82) 4
Woodburn, W. (Rangers, 1947-52) ... 24
Wright, K. (Hibernian, 1992) 1
Wright, S. (Aberdeen, 1993) 2
Wright, T. (Sunderland, 1953) 3

Yeats, R. (Liverpool, 1965-6) 2
Yorston, H. (Aberdeen, 1955) 1
Young, A. (Hearts, Everton, 1960-6) ... 8
Young, G. (Rangers, 1947-57) 53
Younger, T. (Hibernian, Liverpool, 1955-8) 24

WALES

Aizlewood, M. (Charlton Athletic, Leeds Utd., Bradford City, Bristol C., Cardiff City, 1986-95) 39
Allchurch, I. (Swansea City, Newcastle Utd., Cardiff City, 1951-66) 68
Allchurch, L. (Swansea City, Sheffield Utd., 1955-64) 11
Allen, B. (Coventry City, 1951) 2
Allen, M. (Watford, Norwich City, Millwall, Newcastle Utd., 1986-94) 14

Baker, C. (Cardiff City, 1958-62) 7
Baker, W. (Cardiff City, 1948) 1
Barnard, D. (Barnsley, Bradford City, Barnsley, Grimsby Town, 1998-2003) 18
Barnes, W. (Arsenal, 1948-55) 22
Bellamy, C. (Norwich City, Coventry City, Newcastle Utd., 1998-2003) 20
Berry, G. (Wolves, Stoke City, 1979-83) 5
Blackmore, C. (Manchester Utd., Middlesbrough, 1985-97) 39
Blake, N. (Sheffield Utd., Bolton Wand., Blackburn Rov., Wolves, 1994-2003) 23
Bodin, P. (Swindon Town, Crystal Palace, Swindon Town, 1990-5) 23
Bowen, D. (Arsenal, 1955-9) 19
Bowen, J. (Swansea City, Birmingham City, 1994-7) 2
Bowen, M. (Tottenham, Norwich City, West Ham Utd., 1986-97) 41
Boyle, T. (Crystal Palace, 1981) 2
Browning, M. (Bristol R., Huddersfield Town, 1996-7) 5
Burgess, R. (Tottenham, 1947-54) ... 32
Burton, A. (Norwich City, Newcastle Utd., 1963-72) 9

Cartwright, L. (Coventry City, Wrexham, 1974-9) 7
Charles, Jeremy (Swansea City, Q.P.R., Oxford Utd., 1981-7) 19
Charles, John (Leeds Utd., Juventus, Cardiff City, 1950-65) 38
Charles, M. (Swansea City, Arsenal, Cardiff City, 1955-63) 31
Clarke, R. (Manchester City, 1949-56) 22
Coleman, C. (Crystal Palace, Blackburn Rov., Fulham, 1992-2002) 32
Cornforth, J. (Swansea City, 1995) 2
Coyne, D. (Tranmere Rov., Grimsby Town, 1996-2002) 2
Crossley, M. (Nott'm Forest, Middlesbrough, 1997-2003) 6
Crowe, V. (Aston Villa, 1959-63) 16
Curtis, A. (Swansea City, Leeds Utd., Southampton, Cardiff City, 1976-87) 35

Daniel, R. (Arsenal, Sunderland, 1951-7) 21
Davies, A. (Manchester Utd., Newcastle Utd., Swansea City, Bradford City, 1983-90) 13
Davies, C. (Charlton Athletic, 1972) ... 1
Davies, D. (Everton, Wrexham, Swansea City, 1975-83) 52
Davies, E.R. (Newcastle Utd., 1953-8) 6
Davies, G. (Fulham, Chelsea, Manchester City, 1980-6) 16
Davies, R.T. (Norwich City, Southampton, Portsmouth, 1964-74) 29
Davies, R.W. (Bolton Wand., Newcastle Utd., Manchester Utd., Manchester City, Blackpool, 1964-74) 34
Davies, S. (Manchester Utd., 1996) ... 1
Davies, S. (Tottenham, 2001-3) 15
Davis, G. (Wrexham, 1978) 3
Deacy, N. (PSV Eindhoven, Beringen, 1977-9) 12
Delaney, M. (Aston Villa, 2000-03) .. 19
Derrett, S. (Cardiff City, 1969-71) 4
Dibble, A. (Luton Town, Manchester City, 1986-9) 3
Durban, A. (Derby Co., 1966-72) 27
Dwyer, P. (Cardiff City, 1978-80) 10

Earnshaw, R. (Cardiff City, 2002-3) 4
Edwards, C. (Swansea City, 1996) 1
Edwards, G. (Birmingham City, Cardiff City, 1947-50) 12
Edwards, I. (Chester City, Wrexham, 1978-80) 4
Edwards, L. (Charlton Athletic, 1957) 2
Edwards, R. (Bristol City, 1997-8) 4
Edwards, R. (Aston Villa, 2003) 1
Emmanuel, W. (Bristol City, 1973) 2
England, M. (Blackburn Rov., Tottenham, 1962-75) 44
Evans, B. (Swansea City, Hereford, 1972-4) 7
Evans, I. (Crystal Palace, 1976-8) 13
Evans, P. (Brentford, Bradford City, 2002-3) 2
Evans, R. (Swansea City, 1964) 1

Felgate, D. (Lincoln City, 1984) 1
Flynn, B. (Burnley, Leeds Utd., 1975-84) 66

Ford, T. (Swansea City, Sunderland, Aston Villa, Cardiff City, 1947-57) 38
Foulkes, W. (Newcastle Utd., 1952-4) 11
Freestone, R. (Swansea City, 2000-03) 1

Gabbidon, D. (Cardiff City, 2002-3) 4
Giggs, R. (Manchester Utd., 1992-2003) 40
Giles, D. (Swansea City, Crystal Palace, 1980-3) 12
Godfrey, B. (Preston N.E., 1964-5) 3
Goss, J. (Norwich City, 1991-6) 9
Green, C. (Birmingham City, 1965-9) 15
Green, R. (Wolves, 1998) 2
Griffiths, A. (Wrexham, 1971-7) 17
Griffiths, H. (Swansea City, 1953) 1
Griffiths, M. (Leicester City, 1947-54) 11

Hall, G. (Chelsea, 1988-92) 9
Harrington, A. (Cardiff City, 1956-62) 11
Harris, C. (Leeds Utd., 1976-82) 23
Harris, W. (Middlesbrough, 1954-8) ... 6
Hartson, J. (Arsenal, West Ham Utd., Wimbledon, Coventry City, Celtic, 1995-2003) 35
Haworth, S. (Cardiff City, Coventry City, 1997-8) 5
Hennessey, T. (Birmingham City, Nott'm Forest, Derby Co., 1962-73) 39
Hewitt, R. (Cardiff City, 1958) 5
Hill, M. (Ipswich Town, 1972) 2
Hockey, T. (Sheffield Utd., Norwich City, Aston Villa, 1972-4) 9
Hodges, G. (Wimbledon, Newcastle Utd., Watford, Sheffield Utd., 1984-96) 18
Holden, A. (Chester City, 1984) 1
Hole, B. (Cardiff City, Blackburn Rov., Aston Villa, Swansea City, 1963-71) 30
Hollins, D. (Newcastle Utd., 1962-6) 11
Hopkins, J. (Fulham, Crystal Palace, 1983-90) 16
Hopkins, M. (Tottenham, 1956-63) .. 34
Horne, B. (Portsmouth, Southampton, Everton, Birmingham City, 1988-97) 59
Howells, R. (Cardiff City, 1954) 2
Hughes, C. (Luton Town, Wimbledon, 1992-7) 8
Hughes, I. (Luton Town, 1951) 4
Hughes, M. (Manchester Utd., Barcelona, Bayern Munich, Manchester Utd., Chelsea, Southampton, 1984-99) 72
*Hughes, W. (Birmingham City, 1947) 3
Hughes, W.A. (Blackburn Rov., 1949) . 5
Humphreys, J. (Everton, 1947) 1

Jackett, K. (Watford, 1983-8) 31
James, E.G. (Blackpool, 1966-71) 9
James, L. (Burnley, Derby Co., Q.P.R., Swansea City, Sunderland, 1972-83) 54
James, R. (Swansea City, Stoke City, Q.P.R., Leicester City, Swansea City, 1979-88) 47
Jarvis, A. (Hull City, 1967) 3
Jenkins, S. (Swansea City, Huddersfield Town, 1996-2002) 16
Johnson, A. (Nott'm Forest, W.B.A., 1999-2003) 10
Johnson, M. (Swansea City, 1964) 1
Jones, A. (Port Vale, Charlton Athletic, 1987-90) 6
Jones, Barrie (Swansea City, Plymouth Argyle, Cardiff City, 1963-9) 15
*Jones, Bryn (Arsenal, 1947-9) 4
Jones, C. (Swansea City, Tottenham, Fulham, 1954-69) 59
Jones, D. (Norwich City, 1976-80) 8
Jones, E. (Swansea City, Tottenham, 1947-9) 4
Jones, J. (Liverpool, Wrexham, Chelsea, Huddersfield Town, 1976-86) 72
Jones, K. (Aston Villa, 1950) 1
Jones, L. (Liverpool, Tranmere Rov., 1997) 2
Jones, M. (Leeds Utd., Leicester City, 2000-03) 13
Jones, P. (Stockport Co., Southampton, 1997-2003) 31
Jones, R. (Sheffield Wed., 1994) 1
*Jones, T.G. (Everton, 1946-9) 13
Jones, V. (Wimbledon, 1995-7) 9
Jones, W. (Bristol Rov., 1971) 1

Kelsey, J. (Arsenal, 1954-62) 41
King, J. (Swansea City, 1955) 1
Kinsey, N. (Norwich City, Birmingham City, 1951-6) 7
Knill, A. (Swansea City, 1989) 1
Koumas, J. (Tranmere Rov., W.B.A., 2001-3) 4
Krzywicki, R. (W.B.A., Huddersfield Town, 1970-2) 8

Lambert, R. (Liverpool, 1947-9) 5
Law, B. (Q.P.R., 1990) 1
Lee, C. (Ipswich Town, 1965) 2

Leek, K. (Leicester City, Newcastle Utd., Birmingham City, Northampton Town, 1961-5) 13
Legg, A. (Birmingham City, Cardiff City, 1996-2001) 6
Lever, A. (Leicester City, 1953) 1
Lewis, D. (Swansea City, 1983) 1
Llewellyn, C. (Norwich City, 1998) 2
Lloyd, B. (Wrexham, 1976) 3
Lovell, S. (Crystal Palace, Millwall, 1982-6) 6
Lowndes, S. (Newport, Millwall, Brighton & H.A., Barnsley, 1983-8) 10
Lowrie, G. (Coventry City, Newcastle Utd., 1948-9) 4
Lucas, M. (Leyton Orient, 1962-3) 4
Lucas, W. (Swansea City, 1949-51) 7

Maguire, G. (Portsmouth, 1990-2) 7
Mahoney, J. (Stoke City, Middlesbrough, Swansea City, 1968-83) 50
Mardon, P. (W.B.A., 1996) 1
Marriott, A. (Wrexham, 1996-8) 5
Marustik, C. (Swansea City, 1982-3) .. 6
Medwin, T. (Swansea City, Tottenham, 1953-63) 29
Melville, A. (Swansea City, Oxford Utd., Sunderland, Fulham, 1990-2003) 58
Mielczarek, R. (Rotherham Utd., 1971) 1
Millington, A. (W.B.A., Peterborough Utd., Swansea City, 1963-72) 21
Moore, G. (Cardiff City, Chelsea, Manchester Utd., Northampton Town, Charlton Athletic, 1960-71) 21
Morris, W. (Burnley, 1947-52) 5

Nardiello, D. (Coventry City, 1978) 2
Neilson, A. (Newcastle Utd., Southampton, 1992-7) 5
Nicholas, P. (Crystal Palace, Arsenal, Crystal Palace, Luton Town, Aberdeen, Chelsea, Watford, 1979-92) 73
Niedzwiecki, E. (Chelsea, 1985-8) 2
Nogan, L. (Watford, Reading, 1991-6) 2
Norman, T. (Hull City, 1986-8) 5
Nurse, M. (Swansea City, Middlesbrough, 1960-3) 12

O'Sullivan, P. (Brighton & H.A., 1973-8) 3
Oster, J. (Everton, Sunderland, 1997-2003) 7

Page, M. (Birmingham City, 1971-9) 28
Page, R. (Watford, Sheffield Utd., 1997-2003) 28
Palmer, D. (Swansea City, 1957) 3
Parry, J. (Swansea City, 1951) 1
Pascoe, C. (Swansea City, Sunderland, 1984-92) 10
Paul, R. (Swansea City, Manchester City, 1949-56) 33
Pembridge, M. (Luton Town, Derby Co., Sheffield Wed., Benfica, Everton, 1992-2003) 48
Perry, J. (Cardiff City, 1994) 1
Phillips, D. (Plymouth Argyle, Manchester City, Coventry City, Norwich City, Nott'm. Forest, 1984-96) 62
Phillips, J. (Chelsea, 1973-8) 4
Phillips, L. (Cardiff City, Aston Villa, Swansea City, Charlton Athletic, 1971-82) 58
Pipe, D. (Coventry City, 2003) 1
Pontin, K. (Cardiff City, 1980) 2
Powell, A. (Leeds Utd., Everton, Birmingham City, 1947-51) 8
Powell, D. (Wrexham, Sheffield Utd. 1968-71) 11
Powell, I. (Q.P.R., Aston Villa, 1947-51) 8
Price, P. (Luton Town, Tottenham, 1980-4) 25
Pring, K. (Rotherham Utd., 1966-7) ... 3
Pritchard, H. (Bristol City, 1985) 1

Rankmore, F. (Peterborough Utd., 1966) 1
Ratcliffe, K. (Everton, Cardiff City, 1981-93) 59
Ready, K. (Q.P.R., 1997-8) 5
Reece, G. (Sheffield Utd., Cardiff City, 1966-75) 29
Reed, W. (Ipswich Town, 1955) 2
Rees, A. (Birmingham City, 1984) 1
Rees, J. (Luton Town, 1992) 1
Rees, R. (Coventry City, W.B.A., Nott'm Forest, 1965-72) 39
Rees, W. (Cardiff City, Tottenham, 1949-50) 4
Richards, S. (Cardiff City, 1947) 1
Roberts, A. (Q.P.R., 1993) 1
Roberts, D. (Oxford Utd., Hull City, 1973-8) 17
Roberts, G. (Tranmere Rov., 2000-01) 4
Roberts, I. (Watford, Huddersfield Town, Leicester City, Norwich City, 1990-2002) 15
Roberts, J. (Arsenal, Birmingham City, 1971-6) 21
Roberts, J. (Bolton Wand., 1949) 1
Roberts, M. (Q.P.R., 1997) 1
Roberts, N. (Wrexham, Wigan Athletic, 2000-03) 3
Roberts, P. (Portsmouth, 1974) 4

Robinson, C. (Wolves, Portsmouth, 2000-03) 12
Robinson, J. (Charlton Athletic, 1996-2002) 30
Rodrigues, P. (Cardiff City, Leicester City, Sheffield Wed. 1965-74) 40
Rouse, V. (Crystal Palace, 1959) 1
Rowley, T. (Tranmere Rov., 1959) 1
Rush, I. (Liverpool, Juventus, Liverpool, 1980-96) 73

Saunders, D. (Brighton & H.A., Oxford Utd., Derby Co., Liverpool, Aston Villa, Galatasaray, Nott'm Forest, Sheffield Utd., Benfica, Bradford City, 1986-2001) 75
Savage, R. (Crewe Alexandra, Leicester City, Birmingham City, 1996-2003) 29
Sayer, P. (Cardiff City, 1977-8) 7
Scrine, F. (Swansea City, 1950) 2
Sear, C. (Manchester City, 1963) 1
Sherwood, A. (Cardiff City, Newport, 1947-57) 41
Shortt, W. (Plymouth Argyle, 1947-53) 12
Showers, D. (Cardiff City, 1975) 2
Sidlow, C. (Liverpool, 1947-50) 7
Slatter, N. (Bristol Rov., Oxford Utd., 1983-9) 22
Smallman, D. (Wrexham, Everton, 1974-6) 7
Southall, N. (Everton, 1982-97) 92
Speed, G. (Leeds Utd., Everton, Newcastle Utd., 1990-2003) 73
Sprake, G. (Leeds Utd., Birmingham City, 1964-75) 37
Stansfield, F. (Cardiff City, 1949) 1
Stevenson, B. (Leeds Utd., Birmingham City, 1978-82) 15
Stevenson, N. (Swansea City, 1982-3) 4
Stitfall, R. (Cardiff City, 1953-7) 2
Sullivan, D. (Cardiff City, 1953-60) .. 17
Symons, K. (Portsmouth, Manchester City, Fulham, 1992-2002) 36

Tapscott, D. (Arsenal, Cardiff City, 1954-9) 14
Taylor, G. (Crystal Palace, Sheffield Utd., Burnley, 1996-2003) 12
Thomas, D. (Swansea City, 1957-8) ... 2
Thomas, M. (Wrexham, Manchester Utd., Everton, Brighton & H.A., Stoke City, Chelsea, W.B.A., 1977-86) ... 51
Thomas, M. (Newcastle Utd., 1987) ... 1
Thomas, R. (Swindon Town, Derby Co., Cardiff City, 1967-78) 50
Thomas, S. (Fulham, 1948-9) 4
Toshack, J. (Cardiff City, Liverpool, Swansea City, 1969-80) 40
Trollope, P. (Derby Co., Fulham, Northampton Town, 1997-2003) 9

Van den Hauwe, P. (Everton, 1985-9) 13
Vaughan, D. (Crewe Alexandra, 2003) . 1
Vaughan, N. (Newport, Cardiff City, 1983-5) 10
Vearncombe, G. (Cardiff City, 1958-61) 2
Vernon, R. (Blackburn Rov., Everton, Stoke City, 1957-68) 32
Villars, A. (Cardiff City, 1974) 3

Walley, T. (Watford, 1971) 1
Walsh, I. (Crystal Palace, 1980-2) 18
Ward, D. (Bristol Rov., Cardiff City, 1959-62) 2
Ward, D. (Notts Co., Nott'm Forest, 2000-03) 4
Webster, C. (Manchester Utd., 1957-8) 4
Weston, R. (Arsenal, Cardiff City, 2000-03) 4
Williams, A. (Reading, Wolves, Reading, 1994-2003) 13
Williams, Andy (Southampton, 1997-8) 2
Williams, D. (Norwich City, 1986-7) ... 5
Williams, G. (Cardiff City, 1951) 1
Williams, G. (Derby Co., Ipswich Town, 1988-96) 13
Williams, G.E. (W.B.A., 1960-9) 26
Williams, G.G. (Swansea City, 1961-2) 5
Williams, H.J. (Swansea City, 1965-72) 3
Williams, H.T. (Newport, Leeds Utd., 1949-50) 4
Williams, S. (W.B.A., Southampton, 1954-66) 43
Witcomb, D. (W.B.A., Sheffield Wed., 1947) 3
Woosnam, P. (Leyton Orient, West Ham Utd., Aston Villa, 1959-63) 17

Yorath, T. (Leeds Utd., Coventry City, Tottenham, Vancouver Whitecaps, 1970-81) 59
Young, E. (Wimbledon, Crystal Palace, Wolves, 1990-6) 21

REPUBLIC OF IRELAND

Aherne, T. (Belfast Celtic, Luton Town, 1946-54) 16
Aldridge, J. (Oxford Utd., Liverpool, Real Sociedad, Tranmere Rov., 1986-97) 69
Ambrose, P. (Shamrock R., 1955-64) . 5
Anderson, J. (Preston N.E., Newcastle Utd., 1980-9) 16

Babb, P. (Coventry City, Liverpool, Sunderland, 1994-2003) 35
Bailham, E. (Shamrock R., 1964) 1
Barber, E. (Bohemians, Birmingham City, 1966) 2
Barrett, G. (Arsenal, 2003) 1
Beglin, J. (Liverpool, 1984-7) 15
Braddish, S. (Dundalk, 1978) 2
Branagan, K. (Bolton Wand., 1997) 1
Bonner, P. (Celtic, 1981-96) 80
Brady, L. (Arsenal, Juventus, Sampdoria, Inter-Milan, Ascoli, West Ham Utd., 1975-90) 72
Brady, R. (Q.P.R., 1964) 6
Breen, G. (Birmingham City, Coventry City, West Ham Utd., 1996-2003) 56
*Breen, T. (Shamrock R., 1947) 3
Brennan, F. (Drumcondra, 1965) 1
Brennan, S. (Manchester Utd., Waterford, 1965-71) 19
Browne, W. (Bohemians, 1964) 3
Buckley, L. (Shamrock R., Waregem, 1984-5) 2
Burke, F. (Cork Ath., 1952) 1
Butler, P. (Sunderland, 2000) 1
Butler, T. (Sunderland, 2003) 2
Byrne, A. (Southampton, 1970-4) 14
Byrne, J. (Q.P.R., Le Havre, Brighton & H.A., Sunderland, Millwall, 1985-93) 23
Byrne, P. (Shamrock R., 1984-6) 8

Campbell, A. (Santander, 1985) 3
Campbell, N. (St Patrick's Ath., Fortuna Cologne, 1971-7) 11
Cantwell, N. (West Ham Utd., Manchester Utd., 1954-67) 36
Carey, B. (Manchester Utd., Leicester City, 1992-4) 3
*Carey, J. (Manchester Utd., 1946-53) 21
Carolan, J. (Manchester Utd., 1960) .. 2
Carr, S. (Tottenham, 1999-2003) 24
Carroll, B. (Shelbourne, 1949-50) 2
Carroll, T. (Ipswich Town, 1968-73) . 17
Carsley, L. (Derby Co., Blackburn Rov., Coventry City, Everton, 1997-2003) 28

Cascarino, A. (Gillingham, Millwall, Aston Villa, Chelsea, Marseille, Nancy, 1986-2000) 88
Chandler, J. (Leeds Utd., 1980) 2
Clarke, J. (Drogheda, 1978) 1
Clarke, K. (Drumcondra, 1948) 2
Clarke, M. (Shamrock R., 1950) 1
Clinton, T. (Everton, 1951-4) 3
Coad, P. (Shamrock R., 1947-52) 11
Coffey, T. (Drumcondra, 1950) 1
Colfer, M. (Shelbourne, 1950-1) 2
Colgan, N. (Hibernian, 2002-3) 3
Conmy, O. (Peterborough Utd., 1965-70) 5
Connolly, D. (Watford, Feyenoord, Excelsior, Feyenoord, Wimbledon, 1996-2003) 37
Conroy, G. (Stoke City, 1970-7) 27
Conway, J. (Fulham, Manchester City, 1967-77) 20
Corr, P. (Everton, 1949-50) 4
Courtney, E. (Cork Utd., 1946) 1
Coyle, O. (Bolton Wand., 1994) 1
Coyne, T. (Celtic, Tranmere Rov., Motherwell, 1992-8) 22
Crowe, G. (Bohemians, 2003) 2
Cummins, G. (Luton Town, 1954-61) 19
Cuneen, T. (Limerick, 1951) 1
Cunningham, K. (Wimbledon, Birmingham City, 1996-2003) 48
Curtis, D. (Shelbourne, Bristol City, Ipswich Town, Exeter City) 17
Cusack, S. (Limerick, 1953) 1

Daish, L. (Cambridge Utd., Coventry City, 1992-6) 5
Daly, G. (Manchester Utd., Derby Co., Coventry City, Birmingham City, Shrewsbury Town, 1973-87) 48
Daly, M. (Wolves, 1978) 2
Daly, P. (Shamrock R., 1950) 1
Deacy, E. (Aston Villa, 1982) 4
Delap, R. (Derby Co., Southampton, 1998-2003) 9
De Mange, K. (Liverpool, Hull City, 1987-9) 2
Dempsey, J. (Fulham, Chelsea, 1967-72) 19
Dennehy, J. (Cork Hibs., Nott'm Forest, Walsall, 1972-7) 11
Desmond, P. (Middlesbrough, 1950) ... 4
Devine, J. (Arsenal, 1980-5) 13
Doherty, G. (Tottenham, 2000-03) 18
Donovan, D. (Everton, 1955-7) 5
Donovan, T. (Aston Villa, 1980) 2
Doyle, C. (Shelbourne, 1959) 1
Duff, D. (Blackburn Rov., 1998-2003) 36

Duffy, B. (Shamrock R., 1950) 1
Dunne, A. (Manchester Utd., Bolton Wand., 1962-76) 33
Dunne, J. (Fulham, 1971) 1
Dunne, P. (Manchester Utd., 1965-7) . 5
Dunne, R. (Everton, Manchester City, 2000-03) 17
Dunne, S. (Luton Town, 1953-60) 15
Dunne, T. (Bolton Wand., 1975) 1
Dunning, P. (Shelbourne, 1971) 2
Dunphy, E. (York City, Millwall, 1966-71) 23
Dwyer, N. (West Ham Utd., Swansea City, 1960-5) 14

Eccles, P. (Shamrock R., 1986) 1
Eglington, T. (Shamrock R., Everton, 1946-56) 24
Evans, M. (Southampton, 1997) 1

Fagan, E. (Shamrock R., 1973) 1
Fagan, F. (Manchester City, Derby Co., 1955-61) 8
Fairclough, M. (Dundalk, 1982) 2
Fallon, S. (Celtic, 1951-5) 8
Farrell, P. (Shamrock R., Everton, 1946-57) 28
Farrelly, G. (Aston Villa, Everton, Bolton Wand., 1996-2000) 6
Finnan, S. (Fulham, 2000-03) 22
Finucane, A. (Limerick, 1967-72) 11
Fitzgerald, F. (Waterford, 1955-6) 2
Fitzgerald, P. (Leeds Utd., 1961-2) 5
Fitzpatrick, K. (Limerick, 1970) 1
Fitzsimons, A. (Middlesbrough, Lincoln City, 1950-9) 26
Fleming, C. (Middlesbrough, 1996-8) 10
Fogarty, A. (Sunderland, Hartlepool Utd., 1960-4) 11
Foley, D. (Watford, 2000-01) 6
Foley, T. (Northampton Town, 1964-7) 9
Fullam, J. (Preston N.E., Shamrock R., 1961-70) 11

Gallagher, C. (Celtic, 1967) 2
Gallagher, M. (Hibernian, 1954) 1
Galvin, A. (Tottenham, Sheffield Wed., Swindon Town, 1983-90) 29
Gannon, E. (Notts. Co., Sheffield Wed., Shelbourne, 1949-55) 14
Gannon, M. (Shelbourne, 1972) 1
Gavin, J. (Norwich City, Tottenham, Norwich City, 1950-7) 7
Gibbons, A. (St Patrick's Ath., 1952-6) 4
Gilbert, R. (Shamrock R., 1966) 1
Giles, C. (Doncaster Rov., 1951) 1
Giles, J. (Manchester Utd., Leeds Utd., W.B.A., Shamrock R., 1960-79) ... 59
Given, S. (Blackburn Rov., Newcastle Utd., 1996-2003) 52
Givens, D. (Manchester Utd., Luton Town, Q.P.R., Birmingham City, Neuchatel, Switz., 1969-82) 56
Glynn, D. (Drumcondra, 1952-5) 2
Godwin, T. (Shamrock R., Leicester City, Bournemouth, 1949-58) 13
Goodman, J. (Wimbledon, 1997) 4
Goodwin, J. (Stockport Co., 2003) 1
*Gorman, W. (Brentford, 1947) 2
Grealish, A. (Orient, Luton Town, Brighton & H.A., W.B.A., 1976-86) 45
Gregg, E. (Bohemians, 1978-80) 8
Grimes, A. (Manchester Utd., Coventry City, Luton Town, 1978-88) 18

Hale, A. (Aston Villa, Doncaster Rov., Waterford, 1962-72) 13
Hamilton, T. (Shamrock R., 1959) 2
Hand, E. (Portsmouth, 1969-76) 20
Harte, I. (Leeds Utd., 1996-2003) ... 49
Hartnett, J. (Middlesbrough, 1949-54) 2
Haverty, J. (Arsenal, Blackburn Rov., Millwall, Celtic, Bristol R., Shelbourne, 1956-67) 32
Hayes, A. (Southampton, 1979) 1
*Hayes, W. (Huddersfield Town, 1947) 2
Hayes, W. (Limerick, 1949) 1
Healey, R. (Cardiff City, 1977-80) 2
Healy, C. (Celtic, 2002-3) 9
Heighway, S. (Liverpool, Minnesota, 1971-82) 34
Henderson, B. (Drumcondra, 1948) 2
Hennessy, J. (Shelbourne, St Patrick's Ath., 1956-69) 5
Herrick, J. (Cork Hibs., Shamrock R., 1972-3) 3
Higgins, J. (Birmingham City, 1951) ... 1
Holland, M. (Ipswich Town, 2000-03) 33
Holmes, J. (Coventry City, Tottenham, Vancouver W'caps, 1971-81) 30
Houghton, R. (Oxford Utd., Liverpool, Aston Villa, Crystal Palace, Reading, 1986-97) 73
Howlett, G. (Brighton & H.A., 1984) .. 1
Hughton, C. (Tottenham, West Ham Utd., 1980-92) 53
Hurley, C. (Millwall, Sunderland, Bolton Wand., 1957-69) 40

Irwin, D. (Manchester Utd., 1991-2000) 56

Kavanagh, G. (Stoke City, 1998-9) 4
Keane, Robbie (Wolves, Coventry City, Inter Milan, Leeds Utd., Tottenham, 1998-2003) 43
Keane, Roy (Nott'm. Forest, Manchester Utd., 1991-2002) 58
Keane, T. (Swansea City, 1949) 4
Kearin, M. (Shamrock R., 1972) 1
Kearns, F. (West Ham Utd., 1954) 1
Kearns, M. (Oxford Utd., Walsall, Wolves, 1970-80) 18
Kelly, A. (Sheffield Utd., Blackburn Rov., 1993-2002) 34
Kelly, D. (Walsall, West Ham Utd., Leicester City, Newcastle Utd., Wolves, Sunderland, Tranmere Rov., 1988-98) 26
Kelly, G. (Leeds Utd., 1994-2003) ... 52
Kelly, J.A. (Drumcondra, Preston N.E., 1957-73) 47
Kelly, J. (Wolves, 1961-2) 5
Kelly, M. (Portsmouth, 1988-91) 4
Kelly, N. (Nott'm Forest, 1954) 1
Kenna, J. (Blackburn Rov., 1995-2000) 27
Kennedy, M. (Portsmouth, 1986) 2
Kennedy, M. (Liverpool, Wimbledon, Manchester City, Wolves, 1996-2002) 33
Keogh, J. (Shamrock R., 1966) 1
Keogh, S. (Shamrock R., 1959) 1
Kernaghan, A. (Middlesbrough, Man. C., 1993-6) 22
Kiely, D. (Charlton Athletic, 2000-03) 8
Kiernan, F. (Shamrock R., Southampton, 1951-2) 5
Kilbane, K. (W.B.A., Sunderland, 1997-2003) 46
Kinnear, J. (Tottenham, Brighton & H.A., 1967-76) 26
Kinsella, M. (Charlton Athletic, Aston Villa 1998-2003) 41

Langan, D. (Derby Co., Birmingham City, Oxford Utd., 1978-88) 26
Lawler, R. (Fulham, 1953-6) 8
Lawlor, J. (Drumcondra, Doncaster Rov., 1949-51) 3
Lawlor, M. (Shamrock R., 1971-3) 5
Lawrenson, M. (Preston N.E., Brighton & H.A., Liverpool, 1977-88) 39
Lee, A. (Rotherham Utd., 2003) 2
Leech, M. (Shamrock R., 1969-73) 8
Lowry, D. (St Patrick's Ath., 1962) 1

McAlinden, J. (Portsmouth, 1946) 2
McAteer, J. (Bolton Wand., Liverpool, Blackburn Rov., Sunderland, 1994-2003) 51
McCann, J. (Shamrock R., 1957) 1
McCarthy, M. (Manchester City, Celtic, Lyon, Millwall, 1984-92) 57
McConville, T. (Dundalk, Waterford, 1972-3) 6
McDonagh, J. (Everton, Bolton Wand., Sunderland, Notts. Co., 1981-6) ... 25
McDonagh, J. (Shamrock R., 1984-5) 3
McEvoy, A. (Blackburn Rov., 1961-7) 17
McGee, P. (Q.P.R., Preston N.E., 1978-81) 15
McGoldrick, E. (Crystal Palace, Arsenal, 1992-5) 15
McGowan, D. (West Ham Utd., 1949) 3
McGowan, J. (Cork Utd., 1947) 1
McGrath, M. (Blackburn Rov., Bradford City, 1958-66) 22
McGrath, P. (Manchester Utd., Aston Villa, Derby Co., 1985-97) 83
Mackey, G. (Shamrock R., 1957) 3
McLoughlin, A. (Swindon Town, Southampton, Portsmouth, 1990-2000) 42
McMillan, W. (Belfast Celtic, 1946) 2
McNally, B. (Luton Town, 1959-63) ... 3
McPhail, S. (Leeds Utd., 2000-03) 7
Macken, A. (Derby Co., 1977) 1
Mahon, A. (Tranmere Rov., 2000) 3
Malone, G. (Shelbourne, 1949) 1
Mancini, T. (Q.P.R., Arsenal, 1974-5) . 5
Martin, C. (Glentoran, Leeds Utd., Aston Villa, 1946-56) 30
Martin, M. (Bohemians, Manchester Utd., 1972-83) 52
Maybury, A. (Leeds Utd., 1998-9) 2
Meagan, M. (Everton, Huddersfield Town, Drogheda, 1961-70) 17
Milligan, M. (Oldham Athletic, 1992) . 1
Mooney, J. (Shamrock R., 1965) 2
Moore, A. (Middlesbrough, 1996-7) 8
Moran, K. (Manchester Utd., Sporting Gijon, Blackburn Rov., 1980-94) .. 71
Moroney, T. (West Ham Utd., 1948-54) 12
Morris, C. (Celtic, Middlesbrough, 1988-93) 35
Morrison, C. (Crystal Palace, Birmingham City, 2002-3) 10
Moulson, G. (Lincoln City, 1948-9) 3
Mucklan, C. (Drogheda, 1978) 1
Mulligan, P. (Shamrock R., Chelsea, Crystal Palace, W.B.A., Shamrock R., 1969-80) 50
Munroe, L. (Shamrock R., 1954) 1
Murphy, A. (Clyde, 1956) 1
Murphy, B. (Bohemians, 1986) 1
Murphy, J. (Crystal Palace, 1980) 3
Murray, T. (Dundalk, 1950) 1

Newman, W. (Shelbourne, 1969) 1
Nolan, R. (Shamrock R., 1957-63) .. 10

O'Brien, A. (Newcastle Utd., 2001-3) . 6
O'Brien, F. (Philadelphia Forest, 1980) 3
O'Brien, L. (Shamrock R., Manchester Utd., Newcastle Utd., Tranmere Rov., 1986-97) 16
O'Brien, R. (Notts Co., 1976-7) 5
O'Byrne, L. (Shamrock R., 1949) 1
O'Callaghan, B. (Stoke City, 1979-82) 6
O'Callaghan, K. (Ipswich Town, Portsmouth, 1981-7) 21
O'Connell, A. (Dundalk, Bohemians, 1967-71) 2
O'Connor, T. (Shamrock R., 1950) 4
O'Connor, T. (Fulham, Dundalk, Bohemians, 1968-73) 7
O'Driscoll, J. (Swansea City, 1949) 3
O'Driscoll, S. (Fulham, 1982) 3
O'Farrell, F. (West Ham Utd., Preston N.E., 1952-9) 9
*O'Flanagan, Dr. K. (Arsenal, 1947) ... 3
O'Flanagan, M. (Bohemians, 1947) 1
O'Hanlon, K (Rotherham Utd., 1988) . 1
O'Keefe, E. (Everton, Port Vale, 1981-5) 5
O'Leary, D. (Arsenal, 1977-93) 68
O'Leary, P. (Shamrock R., 1980-1) 7
O'Neill, F. (Shamrock R., 1962-72) .. 20
O'Neill, J. (Everton, 1952-9) 17
O'Neill, J. (Preston N.E., 1961) 1
O'Neill, K. (Norwich City, Middlesbrough, 1996-2000) 13
O'Regan, K. (Brighton & H.A., 1984-5) 4
O'Reilly, J. (Cork Utd., 1946) 3
O'Shea, J. (Manchester Utd., 2002-3) 7

Peyton, G. (Fulham, Bournemouth, Everton, 1977-92) 33
Peyton, N. (Shamrock R., Leeds Utd., 1957-61) 6
Phelan, T. (Wimbledon, Manchester City, Chelsea, Everton, Fulham, 1992-2000) 42

Quinn, A. (Sheffield Wed., 2003) 1
Quinn, B. (Coventry City, 2000) 4
Quinn, N. (Arsenal, Manchester City, Sunderland, 1986-2002) 91

Reid, S. (Millwall, 2002-3) 9
Richardson, D. (Shamrock R., Gillingham, 1972-80) 3
Ringstead, A. (Sheffield Utd., 1951-9) 20
Robinson, M. (Brighton & H.A., Liverpool, Q.P.R., 1981-6) 24
Roche, P. (Shelbourne, Manchester Utd., 1972-6) 8
Rogers, E. (Blackburn Rov., Charlton Athletic, 1968-73) 19
Ryan, G. (Derby Co., Brighton & H.A., 1978-85) 18
Ryan, R. (W.B.A., Derby Co., 1950-56) 16

Sadlier, R. (Millwall, 2002) 1
Savage, D. (Millwall, 1996) 5
Saward, P. (Millwall, Aston Villa, Huddersfield Town, 1954-63) 18
Scannell, T. (Southend Utd., 1954) 1
Scully, P. (Arsenal, 1989) 1
Sheedy, K. (Everton, Newcastle Utd., 1984-93) 46
Sheridan, J. (Leeds Utd., Sheffield Wed., 1988-96) 34
Slaven, B. (Middlesbrough, 1990-3) ... 7
Sloan, P. (Arsenal, 1946) 2
Smyth, M. (Shamrock R., 1969) 1
Stapleton, F. (Arsenal, Manchester Utd., Ajax, Derby Co., Le Havre, Blackburn Rov., 1977-90) 71
Staunton, S. (Liverpool, Aston Villa, Liverpool, Crystal Palace, Aston Villa, 1989-2002) 102
*Stevenson, A. (Everton, 1947-9) 6
Strahan, F. (Shelbourne, 1964-5) 5
Swan, M. (Drumcondra, 1960) 1
Synnott, N. (Shamrock R., 1978-9) 3

Thomas, P. (Waterford, 1974) 2
Townsend, A. (Norwich City, Chelsea, Aston Villa, Middlesbrough, 1989-97) 70
Traynor, T. (Southampton, 1954-64) ... 8
Treacy, R. (W.B.A., Charlton Athletic, Swindon Town, Preston N.E., Shamrock R., 1966-80) 42
Tuohy, L. (Shamrock R., Newcastle Utd., Shamrock R., 1956-65) 8
Turner, A. (Celtic, 1963) 2

Vernon, J. (Belfast Celtic, 1946) 2

Waddock, G. (Q.P.R., Millwall, 1980-90) 21
Walsh, D. (W.B.A., Aston Villa, 1946-54) 20
Walsh, J. (Limerick, 1982) 1
Walsh, M. (Blackpool, Everton, Q.P.R., Porto, 1976-85) 21
Walsh, M. (Everton, Norwich City, 1982-3) 4
Walsh, W. (Manchester City, 1947-50) 9

Waters, J. (Grimsby Town, 1977-80) ... 2
Whelan, R. (St Patrick's Ath., 1964) .. 2
Whelan, R. (Liverpool, Southend Utd., 1981-95) ... 53
Whelan, L. (Manchester Utd., 1956-7) ... 4
Whittaker, R. (Chelsea, 1959) ... 1

INTERNATIONAL GOALSCORERS 1946-2003

(As at start of season 2003-04)

ENGLAND

Charlton, R ... 49
Lineker ... 48
Greaves ... 44
Finney ... 30
Lofthouse ... 30
Shearer ... 30
Platt ... 27
Robson, B ... 26
Hurst ... 24
Mortensen ... 23
Owen ... 22
Channon ... 21
Keegan ... 21
Peters ... 20
Haynes ... 18
Hunt, R ... 18
Lawton ... 16
Taylor, T ... 16
Woodcock ... 16
Chivers ... 13
Mariner ... 13
Scholes ... 13
Smith, R ... 13
Francis, T ... 12
Barnes, J ... 11
Beckham ... 11
Douglas ... 11
Mannion ... 11
Sheringham ... 11
Clarke, A ... 10
Flowers, R ... 10
Gascoigne ... 10
Lee, F ... 10
Milburn ... 10
Wilshaw ... 10
Beardsley ... 9
Bell ... 9
Bentley ... 9
Hateley ... 9
Wright, I ... 9
Ball ... 8
Broadis ... 8
Byrne, J ... 8
Hoddle ... 8
Kevan ... 8
Anderton ... 7
Connelly ... 7
Coppell ... 7
Fowler ... 7
Paine ... 7
Charlton, J ... 6
Johnson ... 6
Macdonald ... 6
Mullen ... 6
Rowley ... 6
Waddle ... 6
Adams ... 5
Atyeo ... 5
Baily ... 5
Brooking ... 5
Carter ... 5
Edwards ... 5
Ferdinand, L ... 5
Heskey ... 5
Hitchens ... 5
Latchford ... 5
Neal ... 5
Pearce ... 5
Pearson, Stan ... 5
Pearson, Stuart ... 5
Pickering, F ... 5
Barmby ... 4
Barnes, P ... 4
Bull ... 4
Dixon, K ... 4
Hassall ... 4
Revie ... 4
Robson, R ... 4
Steven ... 4
Vassell ... 4
Watson, Dave (Sunderland) ... 4
Webb ... 4
Baker ... 3
Blissett ... 3
Butcher ... 3
Currie ... 3
Elliott ... 3
Francis, G ... 3
Gerrard ... 3
Grainger ... 3
Kennedy, R ... 3
McDermott ... 3
McManaman ... 3
Matthews, S ... 3
Merson ... 3
Morris ... 3
O'Grady ... 3
Peacock ... 3
Ramsey ... 3
Sewell ... 3
Wilkins ... 3
Wright, W ... 3
Allen, R ... 2
Anderson ... 2
Bradley ... 2
Broadbent ... 2
Brooks ... 2
Cowans ... 2
Eastham ... 2
Froggatt, J ... 2
Froggatt, R ... 2
Haines ... 2
Hancocks ... 2
Hunter ... 2
Ince ... 2
Keown ... 2
Lee, R ... 2
Lee, S ... 2
Moore ... 2
Perry ... 2
Pointer ... 2
Royle ... 2
Smith, A ... 2
Southgate ... 2
Stone ... 2
Taylor, P ... 2
Tueart ... 2
Wignall ... 2
Worthington ... 2
A'Court ... 1
Astall ... 1
Beattie ... 1
Bowles ... 1
Bradford ... 1
Bridges ... 1
Campbell ... 1
Chamberlain ... 1
Cole, Andy ... 1
Cole, J ... 1
Crawford ... 1
Dixon, L ... 1
Ehiogu ... 1
Ferdinand, R ... 1
Goddard ... 1
Hirst ... 1
Hughes, E ... 1
Kay ... 1
Kidd ... 1

Langton 1
Lawler 1
Lee, J 1
Le Saux 1
Mabbutt 1
Marsh 1
Medley 1
Melia 1
Mullery 1
Murphy 1
Nicholls 1
Nicholson 1
Palmer 1
Parry 1
Redknapp 1
Sansom 1
Shackleton 1
Stiles 1
Summerbee 1
Tambling 1
Thompson, Phil 1
Viollet 1
Wallace 1
Walsh 1
Weller 1
Wise 1
Withe 1
Wright, M 1

N. IRELAND

Clarke 13
Armstrong 12
Quinn, J.M. 12
Dowie 11
Bingham 10
Crossan, J 10
McIlroy, J 10
McParland 10
Best 9
Whiteside 9
Dougan 8
Healy 8
Irvine, W 8
O'Neill, M (1972-85) .. 8
McAdams 7
Taggart, G 7
Wilson, S 7
Gray 6
McLaughlin 6
Nicholson, J 6
Wilson, K 6
Cush 5
Hamilton, W 5
Hughes, M 5
Magilton 5
McIlroy, S 5
Simpson 5
Smyth, S 5
Walsh, D 5
Anderson, T 4
Hamilton, B 4
McGrath 4
McMorran 4
O'Neill, M. (1989-96) . 4
Brotherston 3
Harvey, M 3
Lockhart 3
Lomas 3
McDonald 3
McMordie 3
Morgan, S 3
Mulryne 3
Nicholl, C 3
Quinn, S.J. 3
Spence, D 3
Tully 3
Blanchflower, D 2
Casey 2
Clements 2
Doherty, P 2
Harkin 2
Finney 2
Lennon 2
McMahon 2
Neill, W 2
O'Neill, J 2
Peacock 2
Penney 2
Stewart, I 2
Barr 1
Black 1
Blanchflower, J 1
Brennan 1
Campbell, W 1
Caskey 1
Cassidy 1
Cochrane, T 1
Crossan, E 1
D'Arcy 1
Doherty, L 1
Elder 1
Elliott 1
Ferguson 1
Ferris 1
Gillespie 1
Griffin 1
Hill, C 1
Humphries 1
Hunter, A 1
Hunter, B 1
Johnston 1
Jones, J 1
McCartney 1
McClelland (1961) 1
McCrory 1
McCurdy 1
McGarry 1
McVeigh 1
Moreland 1
Morrow 1
Nelson 1
Nicholl, J 1
O'Boyle 1
O'Kane 1
Patterson, D 1
Rowland 1
Stevenson 1
Walker 1
Welsh 1
Whitley, Jeff 1
Williams 1
Wilson, D 1

SCOTLAND

Dalglish 30
Law 30
Reilly 22
McCoist 19
Johnston, M 14
Collins, J 12
Gilzean 12
Steel 12
Jordan 11
Collins, R 10
Johnstone, R 10
Stein 10
Gallacher 9
McStay 9
Mudie 9
St John 9
Brand 8
Gemmill, A 8
Leggat 8
Robertson, J (1978-84) . 8
Wilson, D 8
Dodds 7
Durie 7
Gray, A 7
Wark 7
Booth 6
Brown, A 6
Cooper 6
Gough 6
Liddell 6
Rioch 6
Waddell 6
Henderson, W 5
Hutchison 5
Macari 5
Masson 5
McAllister G. 5
McQueen 5
Murdoch 5
Nevin 5
Nicholas 5

O'Hare 5
Scott, A 5
Strachan 5
Young, A 5
Archibald 4
Caldow 4
Crawford 4
Dailly 4
Hamilton 4
Hartford 4
Herd, D. 4
Jackson, D 4
Johnstone, J 4
Lorimer 4
Mackay, D 4
Mason 4
McGinlay 4
McKinlay, W. 4
McLaren 4
Smith, G 4
Souness 4
Baxter 3
Bremner, W 3
Burley, C 3
Chalmers 3
Gibson 3
Graham, G 3
Gray, E 3
Greig 3
Hendry 3
Lennox 3
MacDougall 3
McInally, A 3
McNeill 3
McPhail 3
Morris 3
Robertson, J (1991-5) .. 3
Sturrock 3
White 3
Baird, S 2
Bauld 2
Cameron 2
Ferguson, B 2
Flavell 2
Fleming 2
Graham, A 2
Harper 2
Hewie 2
Holton 2
Hopkin 2
Houliston 2
Jess 2
Johnstone, A 2
Johnstone, D 2
McClair 2
McGhee 2
McMillan 2
Miller, K 2
Pettigrew 2

Ring 2
Robertson, A 2
Shearer, D 2
Thompson, ... 2
Aitken, R 1
Bannon 1
Bett 1
Bone 1
Boyd 1
Brazil 1
Buckley 1
Burns 1
Calderwood 1
Campbell, R 1
Combe 1
Conn 1
Craig 1
Curran 1
Davidson 1
Dobie 1
Docherty 1
Duncan, M 1
Elliott 1
Fernie 1
Freedman 1
Gray, F 1
Gemmell, T 1
Henderson, J 1
Howie 1
Hughes, J 1
Hunter, W 1
Hutchison, T 1
Jackson, C 1
Jardine 1
Johnstone, L 1
Lambert 1
Linwood 1
Mackay, G 1
MacLeod 1
McAvennie 1
McCall 1
McCalliog 1
McCann 1
McKenzie 1
McKimmie 1
McKinnon 1
McLean 1
McLintock 1
McSwegan 1
Miller, W 1
Mitchell 1
Morgan 1
Mulhall 1
Murray, J 1
Narey 1
Naysmith 1
Ormond 1
Orr 1
Parlane 1

Provan, D 1
Quinn 1
Ritchie, P 1
Sharp 1
Stewart, R 1
Thornton 1
Wallace, I 1
Weir, A 1
Weir, D 1
Wilkie 1

WALES

Rush 28
Allchurch, I 23
Ford 23
Saunders 22
Hughes, M 16
Charles, John 15
Jones, C 15
Toshack 13
Hartson 10
James, L 10
Davies, R.T 8
Giggs 8
James, R 8
Vernon 8
Davies, R.W 7
Flynn 7
Walsh, I 7
Bellamy 6
Charles, M 6
Curtis, A 6
Griffiths, A 6
Medwin 6
Pembridge 6
Speed 6
Clarke, R 5
Leek 5
Blake 4
Coleman 4
Deacy 4
Edwards, I 4
Tapscott 4
Thomas, M 4
Woosnam 4
Allen, M 3
Bodin 3
Bowen, M 3
Davies, S 3
England 3
Melville 3
Palmer, D 3
Rees, R 3
Robinson, J 3
Davies, G 2
Durban, A 2
Dwyer 2
Earnshaw 2

Edwards, G 2
Giles, D 2
Godfrey 2
Griffiths, M 2
Hodges 2
Horne 2
Jones, Barrie 2
Jones, Bryn 2
Lowrie 2
Nicholas 2
Phillips, D 2
Reece, G 2
Robinson 2
Savage 2
Slatter 2
Symons 2
Yorath 2
Barnes 1
Blackmore 1
Bowen, D 1
Boyle, T 1
Burgess, R 1
Charles, Jeremy 1
Evans, I 1
Foulkes 1
Harris, C 1
Hewitt, R 1
Hockey 1
Jones, A 1
Jones, D 1
Jones, J 1
Krzywicki 1
Lovell 1
Mahoney 1
Moore, G. 1
O'Sullivan 1
Paul 1
Powell, A 1
Powell, D 1
Price, P 1
Roberts, P 1
Smallman 1
Williams, A 1
Williams, G.E 1
Williams, G.G 1
Young 1

REP. OF IRELAND

Quinn, N 21
Stapleton 20
Aldridge 19
Cascarino 19
Givens 19
Keane, Robbie 16
Cantwell 14
Daly 13
Brady 9
Keane, Roy 9
Kelly, D 9
Sheedy 9
Connolly 8
Curtis 8
Grealish 8
Harte 8
McGrath, P 8
Fitzsimons 7
Ringstead 7
Staunton 7
Townsend 7
Breen G 6
Coyne 6
Houghton 6
McEvoy 6
Martin, C 6
Moran 6
Cummins 5
Fagan, F 5
Giles 5
Lawrenson 5
Rogers 5
Sheridan 5
Treacy 5
Walsh, D 5
Byrne, J 4
Doherty 4
Duff 4
Holland 4
Irwin 4
Kilbane 4
McGee 4
Martin, M 4
Morrison 4
O'Neill, K 4
Robinson 4
Tuohy 4
Carey, J 3
Coad 3
Conway 3
Dunne, R 3
Farrell 3
Fogarty 3
Haverty 3
Kennedy, Mark 3
Kinsella 3
McAteer 3
Ryan, R 3
Waddock 3
Walsh, M 3
Whelan 3
Conroy 2
Dennehy 2
Eglington 2
Fallon 2
Fitzgerald, P 2
Foley 2
Gavin 2
Hale 2
Hand 2
Hurley 2
Kelly, G 2
Leech 2
McCarthy 2
McLoughlin 2
O'Connor 2
O'Farrell 2
O'Reilly, J 2
Reid 2
Ambrose 1
Anderson 1
Barrett 1
Carroll 1
Dempsey 1
Duffy 1
Finnan 1
Fitzgerald, J 1
Fullam, J 1
Galvin 1
Glynn 1
Grimes 1
Healy 1
Holmes 1
Hughton 1
Kavanagh 1
Kernaghan 1
Mancini 1
McCann 1
McPhail 1
Mooney 1
Moroney 1
Mulligan 1
O'Callaghan, K 1
O'Keefe 1
O'Leary 1
O'Neill, F 1
Ryan, G 1
Slaven 1
Sloan 1
Strahan 1
Waters 1

HOME INTERNATIONAL RESULTS

Note: In the results that follow, W.C. = World Cup, E.C. = European Championship. TF = Tournoi de France. For Northern Ireland read Ireland before 1921.

ENGLAND V. SCOTLAND

Played 110; England 45; Scotland 41; drawn 24. Goals: England 192, Scotland 169.

		E	S			E	S
1872	Glasgow	0	0	1932	Wembley	3	0
1873	The Oval	4	2	1933	Glasgow	1	2
1874	Glasgow	1	2	1934	Wembley	3	0
1875	The Oval	2	2	1935	Glasgow	0	2
1876	Glasgow	0	3	1936	Wembley	1	1
1877	The Oval	1	3	1937	Glasgow	1	3
1878	Glasgow	2	7	1938	Wembley	0	1
1879	The Oval	5	4	1939	Glasgow	2	1
1880	Glasgow	4	5	1947	Wembley	1	1
1881	The Oval	1	6	1948	Glasgow	2	0
1882	Glasgow	1	5	1949	Wembley	1	3
1883	Sheffield	2	3	1950	Glasgow (W.C.)	1	0
1884	Glasgow	0	1	1951	Wembley	2	3
1885	The Oval	1	1	1952	Glasgow	2	1
1886	Glasgow	1	1	1953	Wembley	2	2
1887	Blackburn	2	3	1954	Glasgow (W.C.)	4	2
1888	Glasgow	5	0	1955	Wembley	7	2
1889	The Oval	2	3	1956	Glasgow	1	1
1890	Glasgow	1	1	1957	Wembley	2	1
1891	Blackburn	2	1	1958	Glasgow	4	0
1892	Glasgow	4	1	1959	Wembley	1	0
1893	Richmond	5	2	1960	Glasgow	1	1
1894	Glasgow	2	2	1961	Wembley	9	3
1895	Goodison Park	3	0	1962	Glasgow	0	2
1896	Glasgow	1	2	1963	Wembley	1	2
1897	Crystal Palace	1	2	1964	Glasgow	0	1
1898	Glasgow	3	1	1965	Wembley	2	2
1899	Birmingham	2	1	1966	Glasgow	4	3
1900	Glasgow	1	4	1967	Wembley (E.C.)	2	3
1901	Crystal Palace	2	2	1968	Glasgow (E.C.)	1	1
1902	Birmingham	2	2	1969	Wembley	4	1
1903	Sheffield	1	2	1970	Glasgow	0	0
1904	Glasgow	1	0	1971	Wembley	3	1
1905	Crystal Palace	1	0	1972	Glasgow	1	0
1906	Glasgow	1	2	1973	Glasgow	5	0
1907	Newcastle	1	1	1973	Wembley	1	0
1908	Glasgow	1	1	1974	Glasgow	0	2
1909	Crystal Palace	2	0	1975	Wembley	5	1
1910	Glasgow	0	2	1976	Glasgow	1	2
1911	Goodison Park	1	1	1977	Wembley	1	2
1912	Glasgow	1	1	1978	Glasgow	1	0
1913	Stamford Bridge	1	0	1979	Wembley	3	1
1914	Glasgow	1	3	1980	Glasgow	2	0
1920	Sheffield	5	4	1981	Wembley	0	1
1921	Glasgow	0	3	1982	Glasgow	1	0
1922	Birmingham	0	1	1983	Wembley	2	0
1923	Glasgow	2	2	1984	Glasgow	1	1
1924	Wembley	1	1	1985	Glasgow	0	1
1925	Glasgow	0	2	1986	Wembley	2	1
1926	Manchester	0	1	1987	Glasgow	0	0
1927	Glasgow	2	1	1988	Wembley	1	0
1928	Wembley	1	5	1989	Glasgow	2	0
1929	Glasgow	0	1	1996	Wembley (E.C.)	2	0
1930	Wembley	5	2	1999	Glasgow (E.C.)	2	0
1931	Glasgow	0	2	1999	Wembley (E.C.)	0	1

ENGLAND V. WALES

Played 97; England won 62; Wales 14; drawn 21. Goals: England 239, Wales 90.

		E	W
1879	The Oval	2	1
1880	Wrexham	3	2
1881	Blackburn	0	1
1882	Wrexham	3	5
1883	The Oval	5	0
1884	Wrexham	4	0
1885	Blackburn	1	1
1886	Wrexham	3	1
1887	The Oval	4	0
1888	Crewe	5	1
1889	Stoke	4	1
1890	Wrexham	3	1
1891	Sunderland	4	1
1892	Wrexham	2	0
1893	Stoke	6	0
1894	Wrexham	5	1
1895	London	1	1
1896	Cardiff	9	1
1897	Sheffield	4	0
1898	Wrexham	3	0
1899	Bristol	4	0
1900	Cardiff	1	1
1901	Newcastle	6	0
1902	Wrexham	0	0
1903	Portsmouth	2	1
1904	Wrexham	2	2
1905	Anfield	3	1
1906	Cardiff	1	0
1907	Fulham	1	1
1908	Wrexham	7	1
1909	Nottingham	2	0
1910	Cardiff	1	0
1911	Millwall	3	0
1912	Wrexham	2	0
1913	Bristol	4	3
1914	Cardiff	2	0
1920	Highbury	1	2
1921	Cardiff	0	0
1922	Anfield	1	0
1923	Cardiff	2	2
1924	Blackburn	1	2
1925	Swansea	2	1
1926	Selhurst Park	1	3
1927	Wrexham	3	3
1927	Burnley	1	2
1928	Swansea	3	2
1929	Stamford Bridge	6	0
1930	Wrexham	4	0
1931	Anfield	3	1
1932	Wrexham	0	0
1933	Newcastle	1	2
1934	Cardiff	4	0
1935	Wolverhampton	1	2
1936	Cardiff	1	2
1937	Middlesbrough	2	1
1938	Cardiff	2	4
1946	Manchester	3	0
1947	Cardiff	3	0
1948	Villa Park	1	0
1949	Cardiff (W.C.)	4	1
1950	Sunderland	4	2
1951	Cardiff	1	1
1952	Wembley	5	2
1953	Cardiff (W.C.)	4	1
1954	Wembley	3	2
1955	Cardiff	1	2
1956	Wembley	3	1
1957	Cardiff	4	0
1958	Birmingham	2	2
1959	Cardiff	1	1
1960	Wembley	5	1
1961	Cardiff	1	1
1962	Wembley	4	0
1963	Cardiff	4	0
1964	Wembley	2	1
1965	Cardiff	0	0
1966	Wembley (E.C.)	5	1
1967	Cardiff (E.C.)	3	0
1969	Wembley	2	1
1970	Cardiff	1	1
1971	Wembley	0	0
1972	Cardiff	3	0
1972	Cardiff (W.C.)	1	0
1973	Wembley (W.C.)	1	1
1973	Wembley	3	0
1974	Cardiff	2	0
1975	Wembley	2	2
1976	Wrexham	2	1
1976	Cardiff	1	0
1977	Wembley	0	1
1978	Cardiff	3	1
1979	Wembley	0	0
1980	Wrexham	1	4
1981	Wembley	0	0
1982	Cardiff	1	0
1983	Wembley	2	1
1984	Wrexham	0	1

ENGLAND V. N. IRELAND

Played 96; England won 74; Ireland 6; drawn 16. Goals: England 319, Ireland 80.

		E	I
1882	Belfast	13	0
1883	Aigburth, Liverpool	7	0
1884	Belfast	8	1
1885	Manchester	4	0
1886	Belfast	6	1
1887	Sheffield	7	0
1888	Belfast	5	1
1889	Goodison Park	6	1
1890	Belfast	9	1
1891	Wolverhampton	6	1
1892	Belfast	2	0
1893	Birmingham	6	1
1894	Belfast	2	2
1895	Derby	9	0
1896	Belfast	2	0
1897	Nottingham	6	0
1898	Belfast	3	2
1899	Sunderland	13	2
1900	Dublin	2	0
1901	Southampton	3	0
1902	Belfast	1	0
1903	Wolverhampton	4	0
1904	Belfast	3	1
1905	Middlesbrough	1	1
1906	Belfast	5	0
1907	Goodison Park	1	0
1908	Belfast	3	1
1909	Bradford (Park Ave)	4	0
1910	Belfast	1	1
1911	Derby	2	1
1912	Dublin	6	1
1913	Belfast	1	2
1914	Middlesbrough	0	3
1919	Belfast	1	1
1920	Sunderland	2	0
1921	Belfast	1	1
1922	West Bromwich	2	0
1923	Belfast	1	2
1924	Goodison Park	3	1
1925	Belfast	0	0
1926	Anfield	3	3
1927	Belfast	0	2
1928	Goodison Park	2	1
1929	Belfast	3	0
1930	Sheffield	5	1
1931	Belfast	6	2
1932	Blackpool	1	0
1933	Belfast	3	0
1935	Goodison Park	2	1
1935	Belfast	3	1
1936	Stoke	3	1
1937	Belfast	5	1
1938	Manchester	7	0
1946	Belfast	7	2
1947	Goodison Park	2	2
1948	Belfast	6	2
1949	Manchester (W.C.)	9	2
1950	Belfast	4	1
1951	Birmingham	2	0
1952	Belfast	2	2
1953	Goodison Park (W.C.)	3	1
1954	Belfast	2	0
1955	Wembley	3	0
1956	Belfast	1	1
1957	Wembley	2	3
1958	Belfast	3	3
1959	Wembley	2	1
1960	Belfast	5	2
1961	Wembley	1	1
1962	Belfast	3	1
1963	Wembley	8	3
1964	Belfast	4	3
1965	Wembley	2	1
1966	Belfast (E.C.)	2	0
1967	Wembley (E.C.)	2	0
1969	Belfast	3	1
1970	Wembley	3	1
1971	Belfast	1	0
1972	Wembley	0	1
1973	*Goodison Park	2	1
1974	Wembley	1	0
1975	Belfast	0	0
1976	Wembley	4	0
1977	Belfast	2	1
1978	Wembley	1	0
1979	Wembley (E.C.)	4	0
1979	Belfast	2	0
1979	Belfast (E.C.)	5	1
1980	Wembley	1	1
1982	Wembley	4	0
1983	Belfast	0	0
1984	Wembley	1	0
1985	Belfast (W.C.)	1	0
1985	Wembley (W.C.)	0	0
1986	Wembley (E.C.)	3	0
1987	Belfast (E.C.)	2	0

(* Switched from Belfast because of political situation in N. Ireland)

SCOTLAND V. WALES

Played 102; Scotland won 60; Wales 19; drawn 23. Goals: Scotland 237, Wales 112.

		S	W
1876	Glasgow	4	0
1877	Wrexham	2	0
1878	Glasgow	9	0
1879	Wrexham	3	0
1880	Glasgow	5	1
1881	Wrexham	5	1
1882	Glasgow	5	0
1883	Wrexham	3	0
1884	Glasgow	4	1
1885	Wrexham	8	1
1886	Glasgow	4	1
1887	Wrexham	2	0
1888	Edinburgh	5	1
1889	Wrexham	0	0
1890	Paisley	5	0
1891	Wrexham	4	3
1892	Edinburgh	6	1
1893	Wrexham	8	0
1894	Kilmarnock	5	2
1895	Wrexham	2	2
1896	Dundee	4	0
1897	Wrexham	2	2
1898	Motherwell	5	2
1899	Wrexham	6	0
1900	Aberdeen	5	2
1901	Wrexham	1	1
1902	Greenock	5	1
1903	Cardiff	1	0
1904	Dundee	1	1
1905	Wrexham	1	3
1906	Edinburgh	0	2
1907	Wrexham	0	1
1908	Dundee	2	1
1909	Wrexham	2	3
1910	Kilmarnock	1	0
1911	Cardiff	2	2
1912	Tynecastle	1	0
1913	Wrexham	0	0
1914	Glasgow	0	0
1920	Cardiff	1	1
1921	Aberdeen	2	1
1922	Wrexham	1	2
1923	Paisley	2	0
1924	Cardiff	0	2
1925	Tynecastle	3	1
1926	Cardiff	3	0
1927	Glasgow	3	0
1928	Wrexham	2	2
1929	Glasgow	4	2
1930	Cardiff	4	2
1931	Glasgow	1	1
1932	Wrexham	3	2
1933	Edinburgh	2	5
1934	Cardiff	2	3
1935	Aberdeen	3	2
1936	Cardiff	1	1
1937	Dundee	1	2
1938	Cardiff	1	2
1939	Edinburgh	3	2
1946	Wrexham	1	3
1947	Glasgow	1	2
1948	Cardiff (W.C.)	3	1
1949	Glasgow	2	0
1950	Cardiff	3	1
1951	Glasgow	0	1
1952	Cardiff (W.C.)	2	1
1953	Glasgow	3	3
1954	Cardiff	1	0
1955	Glasgow	2	0
1956	Cardiff	2	2
1957	Glasgow	1	1
1958	Cardiff	3	0
1959	Glasgow	1	1
1960	Cardiff	0	2
1961	Glasgow	2	0
1962	Cardiff	3	2
1963	Glasgow	2	1
1964	Cardiff	2	3
1965	Glasgow (E.C.)	4	1
1966	Cardiff (E.C.)	1	1
1967	Glasgow	3	2
1969	Wrexham	5	3
1970	Glasgow	0	0
1971	Cardiff	0	0
1972	Glasgow	1	0
1973	Wrexham	2	0
1974	Glasgow	2	0
1975	Cardiff	2	2
1976	Glasgow	3	1
1977	Glasgow (W.C.)	1	0
1977	Wrexham	0	0
1977	Anfield (W.C.)	2	0
1978	Glasgow	1	1
1979	Cardiff	0	3
1980	Glasgow	1	0
1981	Swansea	0	2
1982	Glasgow	1	0
1983	Cardiff	2	0
1984	Glasgow	2	1
1985	Glasgow (W.C.)	0	1
1985	Cardiff (W.C.)	1	1
1997	Kilmarnock	0	1

SCOTLAND V. N. IRELAND

Played 92; Scotland won 61; Ireland 15; drawn 16. Goals: Scotland 254, Ireland 81.

		S	I
1884	Belfast	5	0
1885	Glasgow	8	2
1886	Belfast	7	2
1887	Belfast	4	1
1888	Belfast	10	2
1889	Glasgow	7	0
1890	Belfast	4	1
1891	Glasgow	2	1
1892	Belfast	3	2
1893	Glasgow	6	1
1894	Belfast	2	1
1895	Glasgow	3	1
1896	Belfast	3	3
1897	Glasgow	5	1
1898	Belfast	3	0
1899	Glasgow	9	1
1900	Belfast	3	0
1901	Glasgow	11	0
1902	Belfast	5	1
1903	Glasgow	0	2
1904	Dublin	1	1
1905	Glasgow	4	0
1906	Dublin	1	0
1907	Glasgow	3	0
1908	Dublin	5	0
1909	Glasgow	5	0
1910	Belfast	0	1
1911	Glasgow	2	0
1912	Belfast	4	1
1913	Dublin	2	1
1914	Belfast	1	1
1920	Glasgow	3	0
1921	Belfast	2	0
1922	Glasgow	2	1
1923	Belfast	1	0
1924	Glasgow	2	0
1925	Belfast	3	0
1926	Glasgow	4	0
1927	Belfast	2	0
1928	Glasgow	0	1
1929	Belfast	7	3
1930	Glasgow	3	1
1931	Belfast	0	0
1932	Glasgow	3	1
1933	Belfast	4	0
1934	Glasgow	1	2
1935	Belfast	1	2
1936	Edinburgh	2	1
1937	Belfast	3	1

		S	I
1938	Aberdeen	1	1
1939	Belfast	2	0
1946	Glasgow	0	0
1947	Belfast	0	2
1948	Glasgow	3	2
1949	Belfast	8	2
1950	Glasgow	6	1
1951	Belfast	3	0
1952	Glasgow	1	1
1953	Belfast	3	1
1954	Glasgow	2	2
1955	Belfast	1	2
1956	Glasgow	1	0
1957	Belfast	1	1
1958	Glasgow	2	2
1959	Belfast	4	0
1960	Glasgow	5	1
1961	Belfast	6	1
1962	Glasgow	5	1
1963	Belfast	1	2
1964	Glasgow	3	2
1965	Belfast	2	3
1966	Glasgow	2	1
1967	Belfast	0	1
1969	Glasgow	1	1
1970	Belfast	1	0
1971	Glasgow	0	1
1972	Glasgow	2	0
1973	Glasgow	1	2
1974	Glasgow	0	1
1975	Glasgow	3	0
1976	Glasgow	3	0
1977	Glasgow	3	0
1978	Glasgow	1	1
1979	Glasgow	1	0
1980	Belfast	0	1
1981	Glasgow (W.C.)	1	1
1981	Glasgow	2	0
1981	Belfast (W.C.)	0	0
1982	Belfast	1	1
1983	Glasgow	0	0
1984	Belfast	0	2
1992	Glasgow	1	0

WALES V. N. IRELAND

Played 90; Wales won 42; Ireland 27; drawn 21. Goals: Wales 182, Ireland 127.

		W	I			W	I
1882	Wrexham	7	1	1933	Wrexham	4	1
1883	Belfast	1	1	1934	Belfast	1	1
1884	Wrexham	6	0	1935	Wrexham	3	1
1885	Belfast	8	2	1936	Belfast	2	3
1886	Wrexham	5	0	1937	Wrexham	4	1
1887	Belfast	1	4	1938	Belfast	0	1
1888	Wrexham	11	0	1939	Wrexham	3	1
1889	Belfast	3	1	1947	Belfast	1	2
1890	Shrewsbury	5	2	1948	Wrexham	2	0
1891	Belfast	2	7	1949	Belfast	2	0
1892	Bangor	1	1	1950	Wrexham (W.C.)	0	0
1893	Belfast	3	4	1951	Belfast	2	1
1894	Swansea	4	1	1952	Swansea	3	0
1895	Belfast	2	2	1953	Belfast	3	2
1896	Wrexham	6	1	1954	Wrexham (W.C.)	1	2
1897	Belfast	3	4	1955	Belfast	3	2
1898	Llandudno	0	1	1956	Cardiff	1	1
1899	Belfast	0	1	1957	Belfast	0	0
1900	Llandudno	2	0	1958	Cardiff	1	1
1901	Belfast	1	0	1959	Belfast	1	4
1902	Cardiff	0	3	1960	Wrexham	3	2
1903	Belfast	0	2	1961	Belfast	5	1
1904	Bangor	0	1	1962	Cardiff	4	0
1905	Belfast	2	2	1963	Belfast	4	1
1906	Wrexham	4	4	1964	Swansea	2	3
1907	Belfast	3	2	1965	Belfast	5	0
1908	Aberdare	0	1	1966	Cardiff	1	4
1909	Belfast	3	2	1967	Belfast (E.C.)	0	0
1910	Wrexham	4	1	1968	Wrexham (E.C.)	2	0
1911	Belfast	2	1	1969	Belfast	0	0
1912	Cardiff	2	3	1970	Swansea	1	0
1913	Belfast	1	0	1971	Belfast	0	1
1914	Wrexham	1	2	1972	Wrexham	0	0
1920	Belfast	2	2	1973	*Goodison Park	0	1
1921	Swansea	2	1	1974	Wrexham	1	0
1922	Belfast	1	1	1975	Belfast	0	1
1923	Wrexham	0	3	1976	Swansea	1	0
1924	Belfast	1	0	1977	Belfast	1	1
1925	Wrexham	0	0	1978	Wrexham	1	0
1926	Belfast	0	3	1979	Belfast	1	1
1927	Cardiff	2	2	1980	Cardiff	0	1
1928	Belfast	2	1	1982	Wrexham	3	0
1929	Wrexham	2	2	1983	Belfast	1	0
1930	Belfast	0	7	1984	Swansea	1	1
1931	Wrexham	3	2				
1932	Belfast	0	4				

(* Switched from Belfast because of political situation in N. Ireland)

RECORDS SECTION

Compiled by Albert Sewell

INDEX

GOALSCORING

(† Football League pre 1992-3. * Home team)

Highest: *Arbroath 36, Bon Accord (Aberdeen) 0, in **Scottish Cup** 1st Round, Sept. 12, 1885. On same day, also in Scottish Cup 1st Round, Dundee Harp beat Aberdeen Rov. 35-0.

Internationals: England 15, *France 0, in Paris, 1906 (Amateur); England 13 *Ireland 0, in Belfast, Feb. 18, 1882 (record in U.K.); *England 9, Scotland 3, at Wembley, Apr. 15, 1961; Biggest England win at Wembley: 9-0 v Luxembourg (E.Champ), Dec. 15, 1982.

Other record wins: Scotland: 11-0 v Ireland (Glasgow, Feb. 23, 1901); **Northern Ireland:** 7-0 v Wales (Belfast, Feb. 1, 1930); **Wales:** 11-0 v Ireland (Wrexham, Mar. 3, 1888); **Rep. of Ireland:** 8-0 v Malta (E. Champ., Dublin, Nov. 16, 1983).

Record International defeats: England: 1-7 v Hungary (Budapest, May 23, 1954); **Scotland:** 3-9 v England (Wembley, April 15, 1961); **Ireland:** 0-13 v England (Belfast, Feb. 18, 1882); **Wales:** 0-9 v Scotland (Glasgow, March 23, 1878); **Rep. of Ireland:** 0-7 v Brazil (Uberlandia, May 27, 1982).

World Cup: Qualifying round – Australia 31, American Samoa 0, world record Int. score (April 11, 2001); Australia 22, Tonga 0 (April 9, 2001); Iran 19, Guam 0 (Nov. 25, 2000); Maldives 0, Iran 17 (June 2, 1997). **Finals – highest scores:** Hungary 10, El Salvador 1 (Spain, June 15, 1982); Hungary 9, S. Korea 0 (Switzerland, June 17, 1954); Yugoslavia 9, Zaire 0 (W. Germany, June 18, 1974).

European Championship: Qualifying round – highest scorers: Spain 12, Malta 1 (Seville, Dec. 21, 1983); – France 10, Azerbaijan 0 (Auxerre, Sept. 6, 1995). **Finals – highest score:** Holland 6, Yugoslavia 1 (Quarter-final, Rotterdam, June 25, 2000).

F.A. Cup: *Preston N.E. 26, Hyde 0, 1st Round, Oct. 15, 1887.

League Cup: *West Ham Utd. 10, Bury 0 (2nd Round, 2nd Leg, Oct 25, 1983); *Liverpool 10, Fulham 0 (2nd Round, 1st Leg, Sept. 23, 1986). **Record Aggregates:** Liverpool 13, Fulham 2 (10-0h, 3-2a), Sept. 23-Oct. 7, 1986; West Ham Utd. 12, Bury 1 (2-1a, 10-0h), Oct. 4-25, 1983; Liverpool 11, Exeter City 0 (5-0h, 6-0a), Oct 7-28, 1981.

F.A. Premier League (beginning 1992-3): *Manchester Utd. 9, Ipswich Town 0, Mar. 4, 1995. **Record away win:** Manchester Utd. 8, *Nott'm. Forest 1, Feb. 6, 1999.

Highest aggregate scores in Premier League – 9: Manchester Utd. 9, Ipswich Town 0, Mar. 4, 1995; Nott'm. Forest 1, Manchester Utd. 8, Feb. 6, 1999; Blackburn Rov. 7, Sheff. Wed. 2, Aug. 25, 1997; Southampton 6, Manchester Utd. 3, Oct. 26, 1996; Tottenham 7, Southampton 2, Mar. 11, 2000.

†Football League (First Division): *Aston Villa 12, Accrington 2, Mar. 12, 1892; *Tottenham 10, Everton 4, Oct. 11, 1958 (highest 1st. Div. aggregate that century); *W.B.A. 12, Darwen 0, Apr. 4, 1892; *Nott'm. Forest 12, Leicester Fosse 0, Apr. 21, 1909. **Record away wins:** Sunderland 9, *Newcastle Utd. 1, Dec. 5, 1908; Wolves 9, *Cardiff City 1, Sept. 3, 1955.

New First Division (beginning 1992-3): *Bolton Wand. 7, Swindon Town 0, Mar. 8, 1997; Sunderland 7, Oxford Utd. 0, Sept. 19, 1998. **Record away win:** Birmingham City 7, *Stoke City 0, Jan. 10, 1998; Birmingham City 7, *Oxford Utd. 0, Dec. 12, 1998.

Record aggregates (11 goals): *Grimsby Town 6, Burnley 5, Oct. 29, 2002; *Burnley 4, Watford 7, Apr. 5, 2003.

†**Second Division:** *Manchester City 11, Lincoln City 3, Mar. 23, 1895; *Newcastle Utd. 13, Newport County 0, Oct. 5, 1946; *Small Heath 12, Walsall Town Swifts 0, Dec. 17, 1892; *Darwen 12, Walsall 0, Dec. 26, 1896; *Small Heath 12, Doncaster Rov. 0, Apr. 11, 1903. **Record away win:** Sheffield Utd. 10, *Burslem Port Vale 0, Dec. 10, 1892.

New Second Division (beginning 1992-3): *Hartlepool Utd. 1, Plymouth Argyle 8, May 7, 1994.

†**Third Division:** *Gillingham 10, Chesterfield 0, Sept. 5, 1987; *Tranmere Rov. 9, Accrington Stanley 0, Apr. 18, 1959; *Brighton & H.A. 9, Southend Utd. 1, Nov. 22, 1965; *Brentford 9, Wrexham 0, Oct. 15, 1963. **Record away win:** Fulham 8, *Halifax Town 0, Sept. 16, 1969.

New Third Division (beginning 1992-3): *Barnet 1, Peterborough Utd. 9, Sept. 5, 1998.

†**Third Division (North):** *Stockport Co. 13, Halifax Town 0 (still joint biggest win in F. League – see Div. 2) Jan. 6, 1934; *Tranmere Rov. 13, Oldham Athletic 4, Dec. 26, 1935. *(17 is highest Football League aggregate score).* **Record away win:** Barnsley 9, *Accrington Stanley 0, Feb. 3, 1934.

†**Third Division (South):** *Luton Town 12, Bristol Rov. 0, Apr. 13, 1936; *Gillingham 9, Exeter City 4, Jan. 7, 1951. **Record away win:** Walsall 8, *Northampton Town 0, Apr. 8, 1947.

†**Fourth Division:** *Oldham Athletic 11, Southport 0, Dec. 26, 1962; *Hartlepool Utd. 10, Barrow 1, Apr. 4, 1959; *Wrexham 10, Hartlepool Utd. 1, Mar. 3, 1962. **Record away win:** Rotherham Utd. 8, *Crewe Alexandra 1, Sept. 8, 1973.

Scottish Premier Division – Highest aggregate: 11 goals – Celtic 8, Hamilton 3, Jan. 3, 1987; Motherwell 5, Aberdeen 6, Oct. 20, 1999. **Other highest team scores:** Aberdeen 8, Motherwell 0 (Mar. 26, 1979); Kilmarnock 1, Rangers 8 (Sept. 6, 1980); Hamilton 0, Celtic 8 (Nov. 5, 1988).

Scottish League Div. 1: *Celtic 11, Dundee 0, Oct. 26, 1895. **Record away win:** Hibs 11, *Airdrie 1, Oct. 24, 1959.

Scottish League Div. 2: *Airdrieonians 15, Dundee Wanderers 1, Dec. 1, 1894. (biggest win in history of League football in Britain).

Record modern Scottish League aggregate (12 goals): Brechin City 5, Cowdenbeath 7, Div. 2, Jan. 18, 2003.

Record British score since 1900: Stirling Albion 20, Selkirk 0 (Scottish Cup 1st. Round, Dec. 8, 1984). Winger Davie Thompson (7 goals) was one of 9 Stirling players to score.

FOOTBALL LEAGUE – BEST IN SEASON (Before restructure in 1992)

Div.		*Goals*	*Games*
1	W.R. (Dixie) Dean, Everton, 1927-8	60	39
2	George Camsell, Middlesbrough, 1926-7	59	37
3(S)	Joe Payne, Luton Town, 1936-7	55	39
3(N)	Ted Harston, Mansfield Town, 1936-7	55	41
3	Derek Reeves, Southampton, 1959-60	39	46
4	Terry Bly, Peterborough Utd., 1960-1	52	46

(Since restructure in 1992)

Div.		*Goals*	*Games*
1	Guy Whittingham, Portsmouth, 1992-3	42	46
2	Jimmy Quinn, Reading, 1993-4	35	46
3	Andy Morrell, Wrexham, 2002-03	34	45

F.A. PREMIER LEAGUE – BEST IN SEASON

Andy Cole **34 goals** (Newcastle Utd. – 40 games, 1993-4); Alan Shearer **34 goals** (Blackburn Rov. – 42 games, 1994-5).

FOOTBALL LEAGUE – BEST MATCH HAULS
(Before restructure in 1992)

Div.		*Goals*
1	Ted Drake (Arsenal), away to Aston Villa, Dec. 14, 1935	7
	James Ross (Preston N.E.) v Stoke City, Oct 6, 1888	7
2	*Neville (Tim) Coleman (Stoke City) v Lincoln City, Feb. 23, 1957 .	7
	Tommy Briggs (Blackburn Rov.) v Bristol Rov., Feb. 5, 1955	7
3(S)	Joe Payne (Luton Town) v Bristol Rov., April 13, 1936	**10**
3(N)	Robert ('Bunny') Bell (Tranmere Rov.) v Oldham Athletic, Dec. 26, 1935 – he also missed a penalty	**9**
3	Barrie Thomas (Scunthorpe Utd.) v Luton Town, April 24, 1965	5
	Keith East (Swindon Town) v Mansfield Town, Nov. 20, 1965	5
	Steve Earle (Fulham) v Halifax Town, Sept. 16, 1969	5
	Alf Wood (Shrewsbury Town) v Blackburn Rov., Oct. 2, 1971	5
	Tony Caldwell (Bolton Wand.) v Walsall, Sept 10, 1983	5
	Andy Jones (Port Vale) v Newport Co., May 4, 1987	5
4	Bert Lister (Oldham Athletic) v Southport, Dec. 26, 1962	6

* Scored from the wing

(SINCE RESTRUCTURE IN 1992)

Div.	*Goals*
1	**4** in match – John Durnin (Oxford Utd. v Luton Town, 1992-3); Guy Whittingham (Portsmouth v Bristol Rov. 1992-3); Craig Russell (Sunderland v Millwall, 1995-6): Darren Byfield (Rotherham Utd. at Millwall, 2002–03); David Connolly (Wimbledon at Bradford City, 2002–03); Marlon Harewood (Nott'm. F. v Stoke City, 2002–03); Michael Chopra (Watford at Burnley, 2002–03).
2	**5** in match – Paul Barnes (Burnley v Stockport Co., 1996-7); Robert Taylor (all 5, Gillingham at Burnley, 1998-9); Lee Jones (all 5, Wrexham v Cambridge Utd., 2001-02).
3	**5** in match – Tony Naylor (Crewe Alexandra v Colchester Utd., 1992-3); Steve Butler (Cambridge Utd. v Exeter City, 1993-4); Guiliano Grazioli (Peterborough Utd. at Barnet, 1998-9).

F.A. PREMIER LEAGUE – BEST MATCH HAUL

5 goals in match: Andy Cole (Manchester Utd. v Ipswich Town, 1994-5); Alan Shearer (Newcastle Utd. v Sheffield Wed., 1999-2000).

SCOTTISH LEAGUE

Div.		*Goals*
Prem.	Kenny Miller (Rangers) v St. Mirren, Nov. 4, 2000	**5**
	Paul Sturrock (Dundee Utd.) v Morton, Nov. 20, 1984	**5**
1	Jimmy McGrory (Celtic) v Dunfermline Athletic, Jan. 14, 1928	**8**
1	Owen McNally (Arthurlie) v Armadale, Oct. 1, 1927	**8**
2	Jim Dyet (King's Park) v Forfar Athletic, Jan. 2, 1930, on his debut for the club	**8**
2	John Calder (Morton) v Raith Rov., April 18, 1936	**8**
2	Norman Haywood (Raith Rov.) v Brechin, Aug. 20, 1937	**8**

SCOTTISH LEAGUE – BEST IN SEASON

Prem.	Brian McClair (Celtic, 1986-7)	**35**
1	William McFadyen (Motherwell, 1931-2)	**53**
2	*Jimmy Smith (Ayr, 1927-8 – 38 appearances)	**66**

(*British record)

CUP FOOTBALL

Scottish Cup: John Petrie (Arbroath) v Bon Accord, at Arbroath, 1st Round, Sept. 12, 1885 .... **13**

F.A. Cup: Ted MacDougall (Bournemouth) v Margate, 1st Round, Nov. 20, 1971 .... **9**

F.A. Cup Final: Billy Townley (Blackburn Rov.) v Sheffield Wed., at Kennington Oval, 1890; Jimmy Logan (Notts Co.) v Bolton Wand., at Everton, 1894; Stan Mortensen (Blackpool) v Bolton Wand., at Wembley, 1953 .... **3**

League Cup: Frank Bunn (Oldham Athletic) v Scarborough (3rd Round), Oct. 25, 1989 .... **6**

Scottish League Cup: Jim Fraser (Ayr) v Dumbarton, Aug. 13, 1952 .... **5**

Jim Forrest (Rangers) v Stirling Albion, Aug. 17, 1966 .... **5**

Scottish Cup: Most goals in match since war: **10** by **Gerry Baker** (St. Mirren) in 15-0 win (1st. Round) v Glasgow Univ., Jan 30, 1960; **9** by his brother **Joe Baker** (Hibernian) in 15-1 win (2nd. Round) v Peebles Rov., Feb. 11, 1961.

AGGREGATE LEAGUE SCORING RECORDS

Goals

* Arthur Rowley (1947-65, WBA, Fulham, Leicester City, Shrewsbury Town) **434**

† Jimmy McGrory (1922-38, Celtic, Clydebank) **410**

Hughie Gallacher (1921-39, Airdrieonians, Newcastle Utd., Chelsea, Derby Co., Notts Co., Grimsby Town, Gateshead) **387**

William ('Dixie') Dean (1923-37, Tranmere Rov., Everton, Notts County) **379**

Hugh Ferguson (1916-30, Motherwell, Cardiff City, Dundee) **362**

▪ Jimmy Greaves (1957-71, Chelsea, Tottenham, West Ham Utd.) **357**

Steve Bloomer (1892-1914, Derby Co., Middlesbrough, Derby Co.) **352**

George Camsell (1923-39, Durham City, Middlesbrough) **348**

Dave Halliday (1920-35, St. Mirren, Dundee, Sunderland, Arsenal, Manchester City, Clapton Orient) **338**

John Aldridge (1979-98, Newport, Oxford Utd., Liverpool, Tranmere Rov.) **329**

John Atyeo (1951-66, Bristol City) **315**

Joe Smith (1908-29, Bolton Wand., Stockport Co.) **315**

Victor Watson (1920-36, West Ham Utd., Southampton) **312**

Harry Johnson (1919-36, Sheffield Utd., Mansfield Town) **309**

Bob McPhail (1923–1939, Airdrie, Rangers) **306**

(* **Rowley** scored 4 for WBA, 27 for Fulham, 251 for Leicester City, 152 for Shrewsbury Town. ▪ **Greaves's** 357 is record top-division total (he also scored 9 League goals for AC Milan). **Aldridge** also scored 33 League goals for Real Sociedad. † **McGrory** scored 397 for Celtic, 13 for Clydebank.)

Most League goals for one club: 349 – Dixie Dean (Everton 1925-37); **326 – George Camsell** (Middlesbrough 1925-39); **315 – John Atyeo** (Bristol City 1951-66); **306 – Vic Watson** (West Ham Utd. 1920-35); **291 – Steve Bloomer** (Derby Co. 1892-1906, 1910-14); **259 – Arthur Chandler** (Leicester City 1923-35); **255 – Nat Lofthouse** (Bolton Wand. 1946-61); **251 – Arthur Rowley** (Leicester City 1950-58).

Over 500 Goals: Jimmy McGrory (Celtic, Clydebank and Scotland) scored a total of 550 goals in his first-class career (1922-38).

Over 1,000 goals: Brazil's **Pele** is reputedly the game's all-time highest scorer with 1,282 goals in 1,365 matches (1956-77), but many of them were scored in friendlies for his club, Santos. He scored his 1,000th goal, a penalty, against Vasco da Gama in the Maracana Stadium, Rio, on November 19, 1969. Pele (born Oct. 23, 1940) played regularly for Santos from the age of 16. During his career, he was sent off only once. He played 95 'A' Internationals for Brazil and in their World Cup-winning teams in 1958 and 1970. • Pele (Edson Arantes do Nascimento) was subsequently Brazil's Minister for Sport. He never played at Wembley, apart from being filmed there scoring a goal for a commercial. Aged 57, Pele received an 'honorary knighthood' (Knight Commander of the British Empire) from the Queen at Buckingham Palace on December 3, 1997.

MOST LEAGUE GOALS IN SEASON: DEAN'S 60

W.R. ('Dixie') Dean, Everton centre-forward, created a League scoring record in 1927-8 with an aggregate of 60 in 39 First Division matches. He also scored three goals in F.A. Cup-ties, and 19 in representative games (total for the season 82).

George Camsell, of Middlesbrough, previously held the record with 59 goals in 37 Second Division matches in 1926-7, his total for the season being 75.

SHEARER'S RECORD 'FIRST'

Alan Shearer (Blackburn Rov.) is the only player to score more than 30 top-division goals in 3 successive seasons since the war: 31 in 1993-4, 34 in 1994-5, 31 in 1995-6. **David Halliday** (Sunderland) topped 30 First Div. goals in 4 consecutive seasons with totals of 38, 36, 36 and 49 from 1925-26 to 1928-29.

MOST GOALS IN A MATCH

TOP SCORE by a player in a first-class club match is **13** in the Scottish Cup and **10** in the Football League.

September 12, 1885: John Petrie set the all-time British individual record for a first-class match when, in Arbroath's 36-0 win against Bon Accord (Scottish Cup first round), he scored **13**

April 13, 1936: Joe Payne set the still-existing individual record on his debut as a centre-forward, for Luton Town v Bristol Rov. (Div. III South). In a 12-0 win he scored **10**

December 26, 1935: Robert ('Bunny') Bell for Tranmere Rov. v Oldham Athletic (Div. III North) beat Drake's 12-day-old record in a 13-4 win by scoring **9**

October 6, 1888: James Ross for Preston N.E. (7-0 v Stoke City) set a League record in its first season by scoring all **7**

December 14, 1935: Ted Drake for Arsenal in 7-1 win away to Aston Villa (Div. 1). Scored six goals with his first six shots and in all equalled Ross's top-division record by scoring **7**

February 5, 1955: Tommy Briggs for Blackburn Rov. v Bristol Rov. set Second Division record during 8-3 win by scoring **7**

February 23, 1957: Neville ('Tim') Coleman for Stoke City v Lincoln City (8-0) in Second Division set a record as a winger by scoring **7**

OTHER BIG HAULS

Eric Gemmell for Oldham Athletic v Chester City in Third Division North (11-2), January 19, 1952, and **Albert Whitehurst** for Bradford City v Tranmere Rov. (Third Division North) (8-0), March 6, 1929; both scored **seven**.

W.H. (Billy) Minter scored **seven** goals for St. Albans City in replayed F.A. Cup 4th Qualifying Round against Dulwich Hamlet, November 22, 1922. Dulwich won 8-7, and Minter's seven is still the most goals scored in one match by a player in a losing side.

Denis Law scored **seven** but only one counted and he finished a loser in Manchester City's F.A. Cup 4th Round tie at Luton Town in 1961. The original match on January 28 was washed out (69 mins.) when City led 6-2 (Law 6). He scored a seventh when the game was played again, but Luton won 3-1.

Louis Page, England outside-left, when tried for the first time as centre-forward, accomplished the **double hat-trick** for Burnley in a First Division match against Birmingham City, at St. Andrews, April 10, 1926. Burnley won 7-1.

Davie Wilson, Rangers outside-left, scored **six** goals from centre-forward at Falkirk in Scottish League, March 17, 1962. Result: 7-1.

Geoff Hurst was the last player to score **six** in a League match, in West Ham Utd.'s 8-0 win v Sunderland (Div. 1) on October 19, 1968.

ROWLEY'S ALL-TIME RECORD

Arthur Rowley is English football's **top club scorer** with a total of 464 goals for WBA, Fulham, Leicester City and Shrewsbury Town (1947-65). They comprised 434 in the League, 26 F.A. Cup, 4 League Cup.

Jimmy Greaves is second with a total of 420 goals for Chelsea, AC Milan, Tottenham and West Ham Utd., made up of 366 League, 35 F.A. Cup, 10 League Cup and 9 in Europe. He also scored nine goals for Italian club AC Milan.

John Aldridge, Tranmere Rovers manager, retired as a player at the end of the season 1997-98 with a career total of 329 Football League goals for Newport, Oxford Utd., Liverpool and Tranmere Rov. (1997-98). In all competitions for those clubs he scored 410 goals in 737 apps. He also scored 45 goals in 63 games for Spanish club Real Sociedad.

MOST GOALS IN INTERNATIONAL MATCHES

THIRTEEN BY

Archie Thompson for Australia v American Samoa in World Cup (Oceania Group qualifier) at Coff's Harbour, New South Wales, April 11, 2001. Result: 31-0.

SEVEN BY

Stanley Harris for England v France in Amateur International in Paris, November 1, 1906. Result: 15-0.

SIX BY

Nat Lofthouse for Football League v Irish League, at Wolves, September 24, 1952. Result: 7-1.
Joe Bambrick for Ireland against Wales, in Belfast, February 1, 1930. Result: 7-0.
W.C. Jordan in Amateur International for England v France, at Park Royal, March 23, 1908. Result: 12-0.
Vivian Woodward for England v Holland in Amateur International, at Chelsea, December 11, 1909. Result: 9-1.

FIVE BY

Steve Bloomer for England v Wales (Cardiff City) March 16, 1896. Result: 9-1.
Hughie Gallacher for Scotland against Ireland (Belfast), February 23, 1929. Result: 7-3.
Willie Hall for England v Ireland, at Old Trafford, Manchester, November 16, 1938. Five in succession (first three in 3½ mins. – fastest International hat-trick). Result: 7-0.
Malcolm Macdonald for England v Cyprus (Wembley) April 16, 1975. Result: 5-0.
Hughie Gallacher for Scottish League against Irish League (Belfast) November 11, 1925. Result: 7-3.
Barney Battles for Scottish League against Irish League (Firhill Park, Glasgow) October 31, 1928. Result: 8-2.
Bobby Flavell for Scottish League against Irish League (Belfast) April 30, 1947. Result: 7-4.
Joe Bradford for Football League v Irish League (Everton) September 25, 1929. Result: 7-2.
Albert Stubbins for Football League v Irish League (Blackpool) October 18, 1950. Result: 6-3.
Brian Clough for Football League v Irish League (Belfast) September 23, 1959. Result: 5-0.

LAST ENGLAND PLAYER TO SCORE . . .

3 goals: Michael Owen v Germany (5-1), World Cup qual., Munich, Sept. 1, 2001.
4 goals: Ian Wright v San Marino (7-1), World Cup qual., Bologna, Nov. 17, 1993.
5 goals: Malcolm Macdonald v Cyprus (5-0), Eur. Champ. qual., Wembley, Apr. 16, 1975.

INTERNATIONAL TOP SHOTS

		Goals	*Games*
England	– Bobby Charlton (1958-70)	49	106
N. Ireland	– Colin Clarke (1986-92)	13	38
Scotland	– Denis Law (1958-74)	30	55
	– Kenny Dalglish (1971-86)	30	102

Wales	– Ian Rush (1980-96)	28	73
Rep. of I.	– Niall Quinn (1986-2002)	21	91

ENGLAND'S TOP MARKSMEN

(As at start of season 2003-04)

	Goals	*Games*
Bobby Charlton (1958-70)	49	106
Gary Lineker (1984-92)	48	80
Jimmy Greaves (1959-67)	44	57
Tom Finney (1946-58)	30	76
Nat Lofthouse (1950-58)	30	33
Alan Shearer (1992-2000)	30	63
Vivian Woodward (1903-11)	29	23
Steve Bloomer (1895-1907)	28	23
David Platt (1989-96)	27	62
Bryan Robson (1979-91)	26	90
Geoff Hurst (1966-72)	24	49
Stan Mortensen (1947-53)	23	25
Tommy Lawton (1938-48)	22	23
Michael Owen (1998-2003)	22	50
Mike Channon (1972-77)	21	46
Kevin Keegan (1972-82)	21	63
Martin Peters (1966-74)	20	67
George Camsell (1929-36)	18	9
'Dixie' Dean (1927-32)	18	16
Johnny Haynes (1954-62)	18	56
Roger Hunt (1962-69)	18	34
Tommy Taylor (1953-57)	16	19
Tony Woodcock (1978-86)	16	42

CONSECUTIVE GOALS FOR ENGLAND

Steve Bloomer scored in **TEN** consecutive appearances (19 goals) for **England** between March 1895 and March 1899.

In modern times, **Paul Mariner** (Ipswich Town) scored in five consecutive **England** appearances (7 goals) between November 1981 and June 1982.

MOST GOALS FOR ENGLAND U-21S

13 – Alan Shearer (11 apps.)
Francis Jeffers (13 apps.)

'GOLDEN GOAL' DECIDERS

The Football League, in an experiment to avoid penalty shoot-outs, introduced a new 'golden goal' system in the 1994-95 **Auto Windscreens Shield** to decide matches in the knock-out stages of the competition in which scores were level after 90 minutes. The first goal scored in overtime ended play.

Iain Dunn (Huddersfield Town) became the first player in British football to settle a match by this sudden-death method. His 107th-minute goal beat Lincoln City 3-2 on Nov. 30, 1994, and to mark his 'moment in history' he was presented with a golden football trophy.

The AWS Final of 1995 was decided when **Paul Tait** headed the only goal for Birmingham City against Carlisle Utd. 13 minutes into overtime – the first time a match at Wembley had been decided by the 'golden goal' formula.

First major International tournament match to be decided by sudden death was the Final of the **1996 European Championship** at Wembley in which Germany beat Czech Rep. 2-1 by **Oliver Bierhoff's** goal in the 95th minute.

In the **1998 World Cup Finals** (2nd Round), host country France beat Paraguay 1-0 on **Laurent Blanc's** Golden Goal (114 mins.).

France won the **2000 European Championship** with Golden Goals in the semi-final, 2-1 v Portugal (Zinedine Zidane pen, 117 mins), and in the Final, 2-1 v Italy (David Trezeguet, 103 mins).

Galatasaray (Turkey) won the **European Super Cup** 2-1 against Real Madrid (Monaco, August 25, 2000) with a 103rd min Golden Goal, a penalty.

Liverpool won the **UEFA Cup** 5-4 against Alaves with a 117th min Golden Goal, an own goal, in the Final in Dortmund (May 19, 2001).

In the **2002 World Cup Finals**, 3 matches were decided by Golden Goals: in the 2nd Round Senegal beat Sweden 2-1 (Henri Camara, 104 mins) and South Korea beat Italy 2-1 (Ahn Jung – hwan, 117 mins); in the Quarter-final, Turkey beat Senegal 1-0 (Ilhan Mansiz, 94 mins).

France won the 2003 FIFA Confederations Cup Final against Cameroon (Paris, June 29) with a 97th-minute Golden Goal by Thierry Henry.

Doncaster Rov. won promotion to Football League with a 110th-minute Golden Goal winner (3–2) in the Conference Play-off Final against Dagenham & Redbridge at Stoke City (May 10, 2003).

GOLD TURNS TO SILVER

Starting with the 2003 Finals of the UEFA Cup and Champions' League/European Cup, UEFA introduced a new rule by which a Silver Goal could decide the winners if the scores were 'level' after 90 minutes.

Team leading after 15 minutes' extra time win match. If sides level, a second period of 15 minutes to be played. If still no winner, result to be decided by penalty shoot-out.

UEFA said the change was made because the Golden Goal put too much pressure on referees and prompted teams to play negative football.

Although both 2003 Euro Finals went to extra time, neither was decided by a Silver Goal. The new rule will apply in the 2004 European Championship Finals.

PREMIERSHIP TOP SHOTS (1992-2003)

Alan Shearer	221	Ian Wright	113
Andy Cole	153	Dion Dublin	108
Les Ferdinand	137	Michael Owen	102
Robbie Fowler	134	Matthew Le Tissier	101
Teddy Sheringham	130	(As at start of season 2003-04)	
Dwight Yorke	116		

LEAGUE GOAL RECORDS

The highest goal-scoring aggregates in the Football League, Premier and Scottish League are as follows:

FOR

	Goals	*Games*	*Club*	*Season*
Prem.	97	38	Manchester Utd.	1999-2000
Div. 1	128	42	Aston Villa	1930-1
New Div. 1	108	46	Manchester City	2001-02
Div. 2	122	42	Middlesbrough	1926-7
New Div. 2	89	46	Millwall	2000-01
Div. 3(S)	127	42	Millwall	1927-8
Div. 3(N)	128	42	Bradford City	1928-9
Div. 3	111	46	Q.P.R.	1961-2
New Div. 3	96	46	Luton Town	2001-02
Div. 4	134	46	Peterborough Utd.	1960-1
Scot. Prem.	101	44	Rangers	1991-2
Scot. L. 1	132	34	Hearts	1957-8
Scot. L. 2	142	34	Raith Rov.	1937-8
Scot. L. 3 (Modern)	87	36	Ross County	1998-9

AGAINST

	Goals	Games	Club	Season
Prem.	100	42	Swindon Town	1993-4
Div. 1	125	42	Blackpool	1930-1
New Div. 1	102	46	Stockport Co.	2001-02
Div. 2	141	34	Darwen	1898-9
New Div. 2	102	46	Chester City	1992-3
Div. 3(S)	135	42	Merthyr T.	1929-30
Div. 3(N)	136	42	Nelson	1927-8
Div. 3	123	46	Accrington S.	1959-60
New Div. 3	113	46	Doncaster Rov.	1997-8
Div. 4	109	46	Hartlepool Utd.	1959-60
Scot. Prem.	100	36	Morton	1984-5
Scot. Prem.	100	44	Morton	1987-8
Scot. L. 1	137	38	Leith A.	1931-2
Scot. L. 2	146	38	Edinburgh City	1931-2
Scot. L. 3 (Modern)	105	36	East Strling	2002-03

BEST DEFENSIVE RECORDS – *Denotes under old offside law

Div.	Goals Agst.	Games	Club	Season
Prem.	17	38	Arsenal	1998-9
1	16	42	Liverpool	1978-9
1	*15	22	Preston N.E.	1888-9
New Div. 1	28	46	Sunderland	1998-9
2	18	28	Liverpool	1893-4
2	*22	34	Sheffield Wed.	1899-1900
2	24	42	Birmingham City	1947-8
2	24	42	Crystal Palace	1978-9
New Div. 2	25	46	Wigan Athletic	2002-03
3(S)	*21	42	Southampton	1921-2
3(S)	30	42	Cardiff City	1946-7
3(N)	*21	38	Stockport Co.	1921-2
3(N)	21	46	Port Vale	1953-4
3	30	46	Middlesbrough	1986-7
New Div. 3	20	46	Gillingham	1995-6
4	25	46	Lincoln City	1980-1

SCOTTISH LEAGUE

Div.	Goals Agst.	Games	Club	Season
Prem.	18	38	Celtic	2001-02
1	*12	22	Dundee	1902-3
1	*14	38	Celtic	1913-14
2	20	38	Morton	1966-7
2	*29	38	Clydebank	1922-3
2	29	36	East Fife	1995-6
New Div. 3	21	36	Brechin	1995-6

TOP SCORERS (LEAGUE ONLY)

		Goals	Div.
2002-03	Andy Morrell (Wrexham)	34	3
2001-02	Shaun Goater (Manchester City)	28	1
	Bobby Zamora (Brighton & H.A.)	28	2
2000-01	Bobby Zamora (Brighton & H.A.)	28	3

1999-2000	Kevin Phillips (Sunderland)	30	Prem.
1998-9	Lee Hughes (W.B.A.)	31	1
1997-8	Pierre van Hooijdonk (Nott'm Forest)	29	1
	Kevin Phillips (Sunderland)	29	1
1996-7	Graeme Jones (Wigan Athletic)	31	3
1995-6	Alan Shearer (Blackburn Rov.)	31	Prem.
1994-5	Alan Shearer (Blackburn Rov.)	34	Prem.
1993-4	Jimmy Quinn (Reading)	35	2
1992-3	Guy Whittingham (Portsmouth)	42	1
1991-2	Ian Wright (Crystal Palace 5, Arsenal 24)	29	1
1990-1	Teddy Sheringham (Millwall)	33	2
1989-90	Mick Quinn (Newcastle Utd.)	32	2
1988-9	Steve Bull (Wolves)	37	3
1987-8	Steve Bull (Wolves)	34	4
1986-7	Clive Allen (Tottenham)	33	1
1985-6	Gary Lineker (Everton)	30	1
1984-5	Tommy Tynan (Plymouth Argyle)	31	3
	John Clayton (Tranmere Rov.)	31	4
1983-4	Trevor Senior (Reading)	36	4
1982-3	Luther Blissett (Watford)	27	1
1981-2	Keith Edwards (Hull City 1, Sheffield Utd. 35)	36	4
1980-1	Tony Kellow (Exeter City)	25	3
1979-80	Clive Allen (Queens Park Rangers)	28	2
1978-9	Ross Jenkins (Watford)	29	3
1977-8	Steve Phillips (Brentford)	32	4
	Alan Curtis (Swansea City)	32	4
1976-7	Peter Ward (Brighton & H.A.)	32	3
1975-6	Dixie McNeil (Hereford)	35	3
1974-5	Dixie McNeil (Hereford)	31	3
1973-4	Brian Yeo (Gillingham)	31	4
1972-3	Bryan (Pop) Robson (West Ham Utd.)	28	1
1971-2	Ted MacDougall (Bournemouth)	35	3
1970-1	Ted MacDougall (Bournemouth)	42	4
1969-70	Albert Kinsey (Wrexham)	27	4
1968-9	Jimmy Greaves (Tottenham)	27	1
1967-8	George Best (Manchester Utd.)	28	1
	Ron Davies (Southampton)	28	1
1966-7	Ron Davies (Southampton)	37	1
1965-6	Kevin Hector (Bradford P.A.)	44	4
1964-5	Alick Jeffrey (Doncaster Rov.)	36	4
1963-4	Hugh McIlmoyle (Carlisle Utd.)	39	4
1962-3	Jimmy Greaves (Tottenham)	37	1
1961-2	Roger Hunt (Liverpool)	41	2
1960-1	Terry Bly (Peterborough Utd.)	52	4

100 LEAGUE GOALS

Manchester City, First Div. champions in 2001-02, scored 108 goals.

Bolton Wanderers, First Div. Champions in 1996-7, reached exactly 100 goals, the first side to complete a century in League football since 103 by Northampton Town (Div. 4 Champions) in 1986-7.

Last League Champions to reach **100** League goals: **Tottenham** (115 in 1960-1). Last century of goals in the top division: **111** by runners-up **Tottenham** in 1962-3.

In **1930-1**, the Championship top three all scored a century of League goals: 1 Arsenal (127), 2 Aston Villa (128), 3 Sheffield Wed. (102).

100 GOALS AGAINST

Swindon Town, relegated with 100 goals against in 1993-4, were the first top-division club to concede a century of League goals since **Ipswich Town** (121) went down in 1964. Most goals conceded in the top division: 125 by **Blackpool** in 1930-31, but they avoided relegation.

MOST LEAGUE GOALS ON ONE DAY

A record of 209 goals in the four divisions of the Football League (43 matches) was set on **January 2, 1932**: 56 in Div. 1, 53 in Div. 2, 57 in Div. 3 South and 43 in Div. 3 North. There were two 10-goal aggregates: Bradford City 9, Barnsley 1 in Div. 2 and Coventry City 5, Fulham 5 in Div. 3 South.

That total of 209 League goals on one day was equalled on **February 1, 1936** (44 matches): 46 in Div. 1, 46 in Div. 2, 49 in Div. 3 South and 69 in Div. 3 North. Two matches in the Northern Section produced 23 of the goals: Chester 12, York City 0 and Crewe Alexandra 5, Chesterfield 6.

MOST GOALS IN TOP DIV. ON ONE DAY

This record has stood since December 26, 1963, when **66 goals** were scored in the ten First Division matches played.

MOST F.A. PREMIER LEAGUE GOALS ON ONE DAY

47, in nine matches on May 8, 1993 (last day of season).

FEWEST PREMIERSHIP GOALS IN ONE WEEK-END

10, in 10 matches on November 24/25, 2001

FEWEST FIRST DIV. GOALS ON ONE DAY

For full/near full programme: **Ten goals,** all by home clubs, in ten matches on April 28, 1923 (day of Wembley's first F.A. Cup Final).

SCORER IN 8 CONSECUTIVE PREMIERSHIP MATCHES

Ruud van Nistelrooy (Manchester Utd., in seasons 2001-02 and 2002-03).

SCORER IN 13 CONSECUTIVE LEAGUE MATCHES

Tom Phillipson for Wolves (Div. 2, season 1926-7).

SCORER FOR 5 PREMIERSHIP CLUBS

Stan Collymore is the only player to do this – for Nott'm. Forest, Liverpool, Aston Villa, Leicester City and Bradford City.

SCORERS IN MOST CONSECUTIVE LEAGUE MATCHES

Arsenal broke the record by scoring in 55 successive Premiership fixtures: the last match in season 2000-01, then all 38 games in winning the Championship in 2001–02, and the first 16 in season 2002–03. The sequence ended with a 2–0 defeat away to Man. Utd. on December 7, 2002.

Chesterfield previously held the record, having scored in 46 consecutive matches in Div. 3 (North), starting on Christmas Day 1929 and ending on December 27, 1930.

SIX-OUT-OF-SIX HEADERS

When **Oxford Utd.** beat Shrewsbury Town 6-0 (Div. 2) on April 23, 1996, all six goals were headers.

FIVE IN A MATCH

Latest players to score 5 goals in a top-division match: **Tony Woodcock** (for Arsenal in 6-2 win away to Aston Villa) and **Ian Rush** (Liverpool 6, Luton Town 0), both on October

29, 1983; **Andy Cole** (Manchester Utd. 9, Ipswich Town 0) on March 4, 1995; **Alan Shearer** (Newcastle Utd. 8, Sheffield Wed. 0) on September 19, 1999.

ALL–ROUND MARKSMAN

Alan Cork scored in four divisions of the Football League and in the F.A. Premier League in his 18-season career with Wimbledon, Sheffield Utd., and Fulham (1977-95).

MOST CUP GOALS

F.A. Cup – most goals in one season: 20 by Jimmy Ross (Preston N.E., runners-up 1887-8); 15 by Albert (Sandy) Brown (Tottenham, winners 1900-1).

Most F.A. Cup goals in individual careers: 48 by Harry Cursham (Notts Co. 1880-87); this century: 44 by Ian Rush (39 for Liverpool, 4 for Chester City, 1 for Newcastle Utd. 1979-98). Denis Law was the previous highest F.A. Cup scorer this century with 41 goals for Huddersfield Town, Manchester City and Manchester Utd. (1957-74).

Most F.A. Cup Final goals by individual: 5 by Ian Rush for Liverpool (2 in 1986, 2 in 1989, 1 in 1992).

HOTTEST CUP HOT-SHOT

Geoff Hurst scored 21 cup goals in season 1965-66: 11 League Cup, 4 F.A. Cup and 2 Cup-Winners' Cup for West Ham Utd., and 4 in the World Cup for England.

SCORERS IN EVERY ROUND

Twelve players have scored in **every round** of the F.A. Cup in one season, from opening to Final inclusive: **Archie Hunter** (Aston Villa, winners 1887); **Sandy Brown** (Tottenham, winners 1901); **Harry Hampton** (Aston Villa, winners 1905); **Harold Blackmore** (Bolton Wand., winners 1929); **Ellis Rimmer** (Sheffield Wed., winners 1935); **Frank O'Donnell** (Preston N.E., beaten 1937); **Stan Mortensen** (Blackpool, beaten 1948); **Jack Milburn** (Newcastle Utd., winners 1951); **Nat Lofthouse** (Bolton Wand., beaten 1953); **Charlie Wayman** (Preston N.E., beaten 1954); **Jeff Astle** (W.B.A., winners 1968); **Peter Osgood** (Chelsea, winners 1970).

Blackmore and the next seven completed their 'set' in the Final at Wembley; Osgood did so in the Final replay at Old Trafford.

Only player to score in every **Football League Cup** round possible in one season: **Tony Brown** for W.B.A., winners 1965-6, with 9 goals in 10 games (after bye in Round 1).

TEN IN A ROW

Dixie McNeill scored for Wrexham in **ten successive** F.A. Cup rounds (18 goals): 11 in Rounds 1-6, 1977-8; 3 in Rounds 3-4, 1978-9; 4 in Rounds 3-4, 1979-80.

Stan Mortensen (Blackpool) scored 25 goals in 16 F.A. Cup rounds out of 17 (1946-51).

TOP MATCH HAULS IN F.A. CUP

Ted MacDougall scored nine goals, a record for the competition proper, in the F.A. Cup first round on November 20, 1971, when Bournemouth beat Margate 11-0. On November 23, 1970 he had scored six in an 8-1 first round replay against Oxford City.

Other six-goal F.A. Cup scorers include **George Hilsdon** (Chelsea v Worksop, 9-1, 1907-8), **Ronnie Rooke** (Fulham v Bury, 6-0, 1938-9), **Harold Atkinson** (Tranmere Rov. v Ashington, 8-1, 1952-3), **George Best** (Manchester Utd. v Northampton Town 1969-70, 8-2 away), and **Duane Darby** (Hull City v Whitby, 8-4, 1996-7).

Denis Law scored all **six** for Manchester City at Luton Town (6-2) in an F.A. Cup 4th Round tie on January 28, 1961, but none of them counted – the match was abandoned (69 mins.) because of a waterlogged pitch. He also scored City's goal when the match was played again, but they lost 3-1.

Tony Philliskirk scored **five** when Peterborough Utd. beat Kingstonian 9-1 in an F.A. Cup 1st Round replay on November 25, 1992, but had them wiped from the records. With the score at 3-0, the Kingstonian goalkeeper was concussed by a coin thrown from the crowd and unable to play on. The F.A. ordered the match to be replayed at Peterborough Utd. behind closed doors, and Kingstonian lost 1-0.

• Two players have scored **ten goals** in F.A. Cup preliminary round matches: **Chris Marron** for South Shields against Radcliffe in September 1947; **Paul Jackson**, aged 21, when Sheffield-based club Stocksbridge Park Steels beat Oldham Town 17–1 on August 31, 2002. He scored 5 in each half and all ten with his feet – goal times 6, 10, 22, 30, 34, 68, 73, 75, 79, 84 mins.

QUICKEST GOALS AND RAPID SCORING

Six seconds after kick-off by **Albert Mundy** for Aldershot v Hartlepool Utd., October 25, 1958; **Barrie Jones** for Notts County v Torquay Utd., March 31, 1962; **Keith Smith** for Crystal Palace v Derby Co., December 12, 1964.

9.6 seconds by **John Hewitt** for Aberdeen at Motherwell, 3rd Round, January 23, 1982 (fastest goal in Scottish Cup history).

A goal in **4 seconds** was claimed by **Jim Fryatt,** for Bradford P.A. v Tranmere Rov. (Div. 4, April 25, 1965), and by **Gerry Allen** for Whitstable Town v Danson (Kent League, March 3,1989). Backed by filmed evidence, **Damian Mori** scored in 4 seconds for Adelaide City v Sydney Utd. (Australian National League, December 6, 1995).

Colin Cowperthwaite reputedly scored in **3½ seconds** for Barrow v Kettering (Alliance Premier League) on December 8, 1979, but the timing was unofficial.

Phil Starbuck scored for Huddersfield Town only **3 seconds** after entering the field as 54th min. substitute at home to Wigan Athletic (Div. 2) on Easter Monday, April 12, 1993. A corner-kick was delayed, awaiting his arrival, and he scored with a header.

Malcolm Macdonald scored after **5 seconds** (officially timed) in Newcastle Utd.'s 7-3 win in a pre-season friendly at St. Johnstone on July 29, 1972. From the kick-off, the ball was passed to him, and Macdonald, spotting the goalkeeper off his line, smashed a shot over him and into the net.

Scored first kick: Billy Foulkes (Newcastle Utd.) for Wales v England at Cardiff City, October 20, 1951, in his first International match.

Six goals in seven minutes in Preston N.E.'s record 26-0 F.A. Cup 1st Round win v Hyde, October 15, 1887.

Five in 20 minutes: Frank Keetley in Lincoln City's 9-1 win over Halifax Town in Div. III (North), January 16, 1932; **Brian Dear** for West Ham Utd. v W.B.A. (6-1, Div.1) April 16, 1965.

Four in five minutes: by **John McIntyre** for Blackburn Rov. v Everton (Div. 1), September 16, 1922; **W.G. (Billy) Richardson** for W.B.A. v West Ham Utd. (Div. 1), November 7, 1931.

Three in three minutes: Billy Lane for Watford v Clapton Orient (Div.3S), December 20, 1933; **Johnny Hartburn** for Leyton Orient v Shrewsbury Town (Div. 3S), January 22, 1955; **Gary Roberts** for Brentford v Newport, (Freight Rover Trophy, South Final), May 17, 1985; **Gary Shaw** for Shrewsbury Town v Bradford City (Div. 3), December 22, 1990.

Three in 2½ minutes: Jimmy Scarth for Gillingham v Leyton Orient (Div. 3S), November 1, 1952.

Two in nine seconds: Jamie Bates with last kick of first half, **Jermaine McSporran** 9 seconds into second half when Wycombe Wand. beat Peterborough Utd. 2-0 at home (Div. 2) on September 23, 2000.

Arsenal scored six goals in 18 minutes (71-89 mins.) in 7-1 home win v Sheffield Wed., February 15, 1992.

Sunderland scored eight goals in 28 minutes at Newcastle Utd. (9-1 Div 1), December 5, 1908. Newcastle went on to win the Championship.

Southend Utd. scored all seven goals in 29 minutes in 7-0 win at home to Torquay Utd. (Leyland Daf Cup, Southern quarter-final), February 26, 1991. Score was 0-0 until 55th. minute.

Six goals in first 19 minutes by Tranmere Rov. when they beat Oldham Athletic 13-4 (Div. 3 North) on December 26, 1935.

Notts Co. scored six second-half goals in 12 minutes (Tommy Lawton 3, Jackie Sewell 3) when they beat Exeter City 9-0 (Div. 3 South) at Meadow Lane on October 16, 1948.

World's fastest goal: 2.8 seconds, direct from kick-off, by Argentinian **Ricardo Olivera** for Rio Negro v Soriano (Uruguayan League), December 26, 1998.

Fastest International goal: 8.3 secs. by **Davide Gualtieri** for San Marino v England (World Cup qual., Bologna, November 17, 1993).

Fastest International Hat-trick: 3 minutes 15 seconds by **Masashi Nakayami** for Japan in 9-0 win v Brunei in Macao (Asian Cup), February 16, 2000.

Fastest International hat-trick in British matches: 3½ minutes by **Willie Hall** for England v N. Ireland at Old Trafford, Manchester, November 16, 1938. (Hall scored 5 in 7-0 win); 4½ minutes by **Arif Erdem** for Turkey v N. Ireland, European Championship, at Windsor Park, Belfast, on September 4, 1999.

Fastest International goal by substitute: 5 seconds by **John Jensen** for Denmark v Belgium (Eur. Champ.), October 12, 1994.

Fastest England goals: 17 seconds by **Tommy Lawton** v Portugal in Lisbon, May 25, 1947. 27 seconds by **Bryan Robson** v. France in World Cup at Bilbao, Spain on June 16, 1982; 37 seconds by **Gareth Southgate** v South Africa in Durban, May 22, 2003; 30 seconds by **Jack Cock** v Ireland, Belfast, October 25, 1919; 30 seconds by **Bill Nicholson** v Portugal at Goodison Park, May 19, 1951. 38 seconds by **Bryan Robson** v Yugoslavia at Wembley, December 13, 1989; 42 seconds by **Gary Lineker** v Malaysia in Kuala Lumpur, June 12, 1991.

Fastest goal by England substitute: 10 seconds by **Teddy Sheringham** v Greece (World Cup qualifying match) at Old Trafford, October 6, 2001.

Fastest F.A. Cup Final goals: 30 seconds by **John Devey**, for Aston Villa v W.B.A., 1895; at Wembley: 42 seconds by **Roberto di Matteo**, for Chelsea v Middlesbrough, 1997.

Fastest goal by substitute in F.A. Cup Final: 96 seconds by **Teddy Sheringham** for Manchester Utd. V Newcastle Utd. at Wembley, May 22, 1999.

Fastest League Cup Final goal: 3 minutes by **Derek Lythgoe** for Norwich City v Rochdale, 1962.

Fastest goal in cup final: 4.07 seconds by 14-year-old **Owen Price** for Ernest Bevin College, Tooting, beaten 3-1 by Barking Abbey in Heinz Ketchup Cup Final at Arsenal Stadium on May 18, 2000. Owen, on Tottenham's books, scored from inside his own half when the ball was played back to him from kick-off.

Fastest F.A. Cup hat-tricks: In 3 minutes by **Billy Best** for Southend Utd. v Brentford (2nd. Round, December 7, 1968); 2 minutes 20 seconds by **Andy Locke** for Nantwich v Droylesden (1st. Qual. Round, September 9, 1995).

F.A. Premier League – fastest scoring: Four goals in 4 minutes, 44 seconds by Tottenham at home to Southampton on Sunday, February 7, 1993.

Fastest First Division hat-tricks since war: Graham Leggat, 3 goals in 3 minutes (first half) when Fulham beat Ipswich Town 10-1 on Boxing Day, 1963; **Nigel Clough,** 3 goals in 4 minutes (81, 82, 85 pen) when Nott'm Forest beat Q.P.R. 4-0 on Sunday, December 13, 1987.

Fastest goal in Champions League: 20.07 seconds by **Gilbert Silva** for Arsenal away to PSV Eindhoven (Group A), September 26, 2002.

F.A. Premier League – fastest hat-trick: 4½ minutes (26, 29, 31) by **Robbie Fowler** in Liverpool 3, Arsenal 0 on Sunday, August 28, 1994.

Fastest hat-trick of headers: Dixie Dean's 5 goals in Everton's 7–2 win at home to Chelsea (Div. 1) on November 14, 1931 included 3 headers between 5th and 15th-minutes.

Fastest Premier League goals: 10 seconds by **Ledley King** for Tottenham away to Bradford City, December 9, 2000; 10.4 seconds by **Alan Shearer** for Newcastle Utd. V Manchester City, January 18, 2003: 11 seconds by **Mark Viduka** for Leeds Utd. V Charlton Athletic Ath., March 17, 2001; 13 seconds by **Chris Sutton** for Blackburn Rov. at Everton, April 1, 1995; 13 seconds by **Dwight Yorke** for Aston Villa at Coventry City, September 30, 1995.

Fastest top-division goal: 7 seconds by **Bobby Langton** for Preston N.E. v Manchester City (Div. 1), August 25, 1948.

Fastest Premier League goal by substitute: 9 seconds by **Shaun Goater**, Manchester City's equaliser away to Manchester Utd. (1–1), Feb. 9, 2003.

Four in 13 minutes by Premier League substitute: Ole Gunnar Solskjaer for Manchester Utd. away to Nott'm. Forest, Feb. 6, 1999.

Fastest new-First Division goal: 10 seconds by **Keith O'Neill** for Norwich City v Stoke City, April 12, 1997.

Fastest Scottish hat-trick: 2½ mins. by **Ian St. John** for Motherwell away to Hibernian (Scottish League Cup), August 15, 1959.

Fastest all-time hat-trick: Reported at 1 min. 50 secs. by **Eduardo Maglioni** for Independiente against Gimnasia de la Plata in Argentina, March 18, 1973.

Fastest goal in Women's Football: 7 seconds by **Angie Harriott** for Launton Ladies v Thame Utd. (Southern League, Prem. Div.), season 1998-9.

FASTEST GOALS IN WORLD CUP FINAL SERIES

10.8 secs. by **Hakan Sukur** for Turkey against South Korea in 3rd/4th-place match at Taegu, June 29, 2002.

15 secs. by **Vaclav Masek** for Czechoslovakia v Mexico (in Vina, Chile, 1962).
27 secs. by **Bryan Robson** for England v France (in Bilbao, Spain, 1982).

TOP MATCH SCORES SINCE WAR

By English clubs: **13-0** by Newcastle Utd. v Newport (Div. 2, Oct. 1946); **13-2** by Tottenham v Crewe Alexandra (F.A. Cup 4th. Rd. replay, Feb. 1960); **13-0** by Chelsea v Jeunesse Hautcharage, Lux. (Cup-Winners' Cup 1st. Rd., 2nd. Leg, Sept. 1971).

By Scottish club: **20-0** by Stirling Albion v Selkirk (E. of Scotland League) in Scottish Cup 1st. Rd. (Dec. 1984). That is the highest score in British first-class football since Preston N.E. beat Hyde 26-0 in F.A. Cup, Oct. 1887.

GOALS BY WINGERS

	Season	Matches	Goals
Football League	(Div. I)		
Cliff Bastin (Arsenal)	1932-3	42	33
Scottish League	(Div. I)		
Bob Ferrier (Motherwell)	1929-30	27	32
Scottish League	(Div. II)		
Ken Dawson (Falkirk)	1935-6	34	39

GOALS BY GOALKEEPERS

Goalkeepers who have scored with long clearances include:

Pat Jennings for Tottenham away to Manchester Utd. (goalkeeper Alex Stepney) in the F.A. Charity Shield on August 12, 1967.

Peter Shilton for Leicester City at Southampton (goalkeeper Campbell Forsyth) on October 14, 1967 (Div. 1).

Ray Cashley for Bristol City at home to Hull City (goalkeeper Jeff Wealands) on September 18, 1973 (Div. 2).

Steve Sherwood for Watford away to Coventry City (goalkeeper Raddy Avramovic) on January 14, 1984 (Div. 1).

Steve Ogrizovic for Coventry City away to Sheffield Wed. (goalkeeper Martin Hodge) on October 25, 1986 (Div. 1).

Andy Goram for Hibernian at home to Morton (goalkeeper David Wylie) on May 7, 1988 (Scottish Premier Div.).

Andy McLean, on Irish League debut, for Cliftonville v Linfield (goalkeeper George Dunlop) on August 20, 1988.

Alan Paterson for Glentoran against Linfield (goalkeeper George Dunlop) on November 30, 1988 (Irish League Cup Final at The Oval, Belfast). His long punt (87 mins) gave Glentoran a 2-1 victory – the only instance of a goalkeeper scoring the winning goal in a senior cup final in the UK.

Ray Charles for East Fife at Stranraer (goalkeeper Bernard Duffy) on February 28, 1990 (Scottish Div. 2).

Iain Hesford scored Maidstone's winner (3-2 v Hereford, Div. 4, November 2, 1991) with long kick-out that went first bounce past Tony Elliott in opposite goal.

Chris Mackenzie for Hereford at home to Barnet (goalkeeper Mark Taylor) in Div. 3, August 12, 1995.

Aston Villa's **Mark Bosnich** scored the last goal (a penalty) when Australia beat Solomon Islands 13-0 in World Cup Oceania Zone qualifier in Sydney on June 11, 1997.

With a free-kick from his own half, Notts Co. goalkeeper **Steve Mildenhall** scored past Mansfield Town 'keeper Kevin Pilkington for the winning goal (4-3,away) in the Worthington Cup 1st Round on August 21, 2001.

Most goals by a goalkeeper in a League season: 5 (all penalties) by **Arthur Birch** for Chesterfield (Div. 3 North), 1923-4.

Arthur Wilkie, Reading's goalkeeper at home to Halifax Town (Div. 3) on August 31, 1962, injured a hand, then played as a forward and scored twice in a 4-2 win.

Alex Stepney was Manchester Utd.'s joint top scorer for two months in season 1973-4 with two penalties.

Alan Fettis, N. Ireland goalkeeper, scored twice for Hull City in Div. 2 in season 1994-5: as a substitute in 3-1 home win v Oxford Utd. (Dec. 17) and, when selected outfield, with last-minute winner (2-1) at Blackpool on May 6.

Peter Schmeichel, Manchester Utd.'s goalkeeper, headed an 89th minute equaliser (2-2) from Ryan Giggs' corner in the UEFA Cup 1st. Round, 2nd leg against Rotor Volgograd (Russia) on September 26, 1995, but United lost the tie on away goals.

On October 20, 2001, **Schmeichel** became the first goalkeeper to score in the Premiership when, following a corner, he volleyed Aston Villa's second goal in their 3-2 defeat at Everton.

In League matches for Swansea City, **Roger Freestone** scored with a penalty at Oxford Utd. (Div. 2, April 30, 1995) and, in 1995-6 (Div. 2) with penalties at home to Shrewsbury Town (August 12) and Chesterfield (August 26).

Goalkeeper **Jimmy Glass**, on loan from Swindon Town, scored the winner that kept Carlisle Utd. in the Football League on May 8, 1999. With only ten seconds of injury time left, he went upfield for a corner and shot the goal that beat Plymouth Argyle 2-1 at Brunton Park. It preserved Carlisle Utd.'s League existence since 1928 and sent Scarborough down to the Conference.

Tony Roberts (Dagenham & Redbridge), only known goalkeeper to score from open play in the F.A. Cup, away to Basingstoke in 4th Qual. Round on October 27, 2001. His last-minute equaliser (2-2) forced a replay, which Dagenham won 3-0 and went on to the 3rd Round proper.

Jose Luis Chilavert, Paraguay's Int. goalkeeper, scored a hat-trick of penalties when his club Velez Sarsfield beat Ferro Carril Oeste 6-1 in the Argentine League on November 28, 1999.

OWN GOALS

Most by player in one season: 5 by **Robert Stuart** (Middlesbrough) in 1934-35.

Three in match by one team: Sheffield Wed.'s Vince Kenny, Norman Curtis and Eddie Gannon in 5–4 defeat at home to W.B.A. (Div. 1) on December 26, 1952; **Rochdale's** George Underwood, Kenny Boyle and Danny Murphy in 7–2 defeat at Carlisle (Div. 3 North), December 25, 1954; **Sunderland's** Stephen Wright and Michael Proctor (2) in 24, 29, 32 minutes at home to Charlton Athletic (1–3, Premiership), February 1, 2003.

Two in match by one player: Chris Nicholl (Aston Villa) scored all 4 goals in 2-2 draw away to Leicester City (Div. 1), March 20, 1976; **Jamie Carragher** (Liverpool) in first half at home to Manchester Utd. (2-3) in Premiership, September 11, 1999; **Jim Goodwin** (Stockport Co.) in 1–4 defeat away to Plymouth Argyle (Div. 2), September 23, 2002; **Michael Proctor** (Sunderland) in 1–3 defeat at home to Charlton Athletic Ath. (Premiership), February 1, 2003.

Fastest own goals: 8 seconds by **Pat Kruse** of Torquay Utd., for Cambridge Utd. (Div. 4), January 3, 1977; in **First Division**, 16 seconds by **Steve Bould** (Arsenal) away to Sheffield Wed., February 17, 1990.

Late own-goal man: Frank Sinclair (Leicester City) put through his own goal in the 90th minute of Premiership matches away to Arsenal (L1-2) and at home to Chelsea (D2-2) in August 1999.

Half an own goal each: Chelsea's second goal in a 3-1 home win against Leicester City on December 18, 1954 was uniquely recorded as 'shared own goal'. Leicester City defenders **Stan Milburn** and **Jack Froggatt**, both lunging at the ball in an attempt to clear, connected simultaneously and sent it rocketing into the net.

Match of 149 own goals: When Adama, Champions of Malagasy (formerly Madagascar) won a League match 149–0 on October 31, 2002, all 149 were **own goals** scored by opponents Stade Olympique De L'Emryne. They repeatedly put the ball in their own net in protest at a refereeing decision.

MOST SCORERS IN MATCH

Liverpool set a Football League record with **EIGHT** scorers when they beat Crystal Palace 9-0 (Div.1) on September 12, 1989. Their marksmen were: Steve Nicol (7 and 88 mins), Steve McMahon (16), Ian Rush (45), Gary Gillespie (56), Peter Beardsley (61), John Aldridge pen. (67), John Barnes (79) and Glenn Hysen (82).

Fifteen years earlier, **Liverpool** had gone one better with **NINE** different scorers when they achieved their record win, 11-0 at home to Stromsgodset (Norway) in the Cup-Winners' Cup 1st. round, 1st leg on September 17, 1974.

Eight players scored for **Swansea City** when they beat Sliema, Malta, 12-0 in the Cup-Winners' Cup 1st round, 1st leg on September 15, 1982.

Nine **Stirling Albion** players scored in the 20-0 win against Selkirk in the Scottish Cup 1st. Round on December 8, 1984.

LONG SCORING RUNS

The record in England is held by **Bill Prendergast**, who scored in 13 consecutive League and Cup appearances for Chester (Div. 3 North, Sept-Dec., 1938).

Dixie Dean scored in 12 consecutive games (23 goals) for Everton in Div. 2 in 1930-1.

Danish striker **Finn Dossing** scored in 15 consecutive matches (Scottish record) for Dundee Utd. (Div. 1) in 1964-5.

Marco Negri (Rangers) scored in all the first 10 Premier games of 1997-8, a total of 12 goals.

Jermain Defoe, 18, on loan from West Ham Utd., equalled a single-season post-war record by scoring for Bournemouth in 10 consecutive matches (Div. 2), October-January 2000-01. **Billy McAdams** did likewise for Manchester City (1957-8), as did **Ron Davies** for Southampton (1966-7).

John Aldridge (Liverpool) scored in 10 successive First Division matches – the last game of season 1986-7 and the first nine in 1987-8.

Kevin Russell (Wrexham) scored in nine consecutive matches in Div. 4, March-May, 1988.

Ruud van Nistelrooy (Manchester Utd.) set a new record for scoring in most consecutive Premiership matches – 8 (11 goals) in December-January, 2001-02. He repeated the feat in the last 8 Premiership games (13 goals, including 5 penalties and 2 hat-tricks) of season 2002–03.

Ian Wright scored on 12 successive first-team appearances, including 7 Premiership, for Arsenal (Sept. 15-Nov. 23, 1994).

50-GOAL PLAYERS

With **52** goals for **Wolves** in 1987-8 (34 League, 12 Sherpa Van Trophy, 3 Littlewoods Cup, 3 F.A. Cup), **Steve Bull** became the first player to score 50 in a season for a League club since **Terry Bly** for 4th Division newcomers Peterborough Utd. in 1960-1. Bly's 54 comprised 52 League goals and 2 in the F.A. Cup, and included 7 hat-tricks, still a post-war League record.

Bull was again the country's top scorer with 50 goals in season 1988-9: 37 League, 2 Littlewoods Cup and 11 Sherpa Van Trophy.

Between Bly and Bull, the highest individual scoring total for a season was 49 by two players: Ted MacDougall (Bournemouth 1970-1, 42 League, 7 F.A. Cup) and Clive Allen (Tottenham 1986-7, 33 League, 12 Littlewoods Cup, 4 F.A. Cup).

HOT SHOTS

Jimmy Greaves was First Division top scorer (League goals) six times in 11 seasons: 32 for Chelsea (1958-9), 41 for Chelsea (1960-1) and, for Tottenham, 37 in 1962-3, 35 in 1963-4, 29 in 1964-5 (joint top) and 27 in 1968-9.

Brian Clough (Middlesbrough) was the Second Division's leading scorer in three successive seasons: 40 goals in 1957-8, 42 in 1958-9 and 39 in 1959-60.

John Hickton (Middlesbrough) was top Div. 2 scorer three times in four seasons: 24 goals in 1967-8, 24 in 1969-70 and 25 in 1970-1.

MOST HAT-TRICKS

Nine by **George Camsell** (Middlesbrough) in Div. 2, 1926-7, is the record for one season. Most League hat-tricks in career: 37 by **Dixie Dean** for Tranmere Rov. and Everton (1924-38).

Most **top division** hat-tricks in a season since last war: six by **Jimmy Greaves** for Chelsea (1960-1). **Alan Shearer** scored five hat-tricks for Blackburn Rov. in the Premier League, season 1995-96.

Frank Osborne (Tottenham) scored three consecutive hat-tricks in Div. 1 in October-November 1925, against Liverpool, Leicester City (away) and West Ham Utd.

Tom Jennings (Leeds Utd.) scored hat-tricks in three successive First Div. matches (Sept-Oct, 1926): 3 goals v Arsenal, 4 at Liverpool, 4 v Blackburn Rov. Leeds Utd. were relegated at the end of the season.

Jack Balmer (Liverpool) scored only three hat-tricks in a 17-year career - in successive First Div. matches (Nov. 1946): 3 v Portsmouth, 4 at Derby Co., 3 v Arsenal. No other Liverpool player scored during that 10-goal sequence by Balmer.

Gilbert Alsop scored hat-tricks in three successive matches for Walsall in Div. 3 South in April 1939: 3 at Swindon Town, 3 v Bristol City and 4 v Swindon Town.

Alf Lythgoe scored hat-tricks in three successive games for Stockport Co. (Div. 3 North) in March 1934: 3 v Darlington, 3 at Southport and 4 v Wrexham.

TRIPLE HAT-TRICKS

There have been at least three instances of **3 hat-tricks being scored** for **one team** in a Football League match:-

April 21, 1909: Enoch West, Billy Hooper and Alfred Spouncer scored 3 apiece for Nott'm. Forest (12-0 v Leicester Fosse, Div. 1).

March 3, 1962: Ron Barnes, Wyn Davies and Roy Ambler registered hat-tricks in Wrexham's 10-1 win against Hartlepool Utd. (Div. 4).

November 7, 1987: Tony Adcock, Paul Stewart and David White each scored 3 goals for Manchester City in 10-1 win at home to Huddersfield Town (Div. 2).

For the first time in the Premiership, **three hat-tricks** were completed **on one day** (September 23, 1995): Tony Yeboah for Leeds Utd. at Wimbledon; Alan Shearer for Blackburn Rov. v Coventry City; and Robbie Fowler with 4 goals for Liverpool v Bolton Wand.

In the F.A. Cup, **Jack Carr**, **George Elliott** and **Walter Tinsley** each scored 3 in Middlesbrough's 9-3 first round win against Goole in Jan. 1915. **Les Allen** scored 5, **Bobby Smith** 4 and **Cliff Jones** 3 when Tottenham beat Crewe Alexandra 13-2 in a fourth-round replay in February 1960.

HAT-TRICKS v THREE 'KEEPERS

When West Ham Utd. beat Newcastle Utd. 8-1 (Div.1) at home on April 21, 1986 **Alvin Martin** scored 3 goals against different 'keepers: Martin Thomas injured a shoulder and was replaced, in turn, by outfield players Chris Hedworth and Peter Beardsley.

Jock Dodds of Lincoln City had done the same **against** West Ham Utd. on December 18, 1948, scoring past **Ernie Gregory**, **Tommy Moroney** and **George Dick**. The Hammers lost 3-4.

David Herd (Manchester Utd.) scored against three Sunderland goalkeepers (Jim Montgomery, Charlie Hurley and Johnny Parke) in 5-0 First Division home win on Nov. 26, 1966.

Brian Clark, of Bournemouth, scored against three Rotherham Utd. goalkeepers (Jim McDonagh,, Conal Gilbert and Michael Leng twice) in 7-2 win at Rotherham Utd. (Div. 3) on Oct. 10, 1972.

On Oct. 16, 1993 (Div.3) **Chris Pike** (Hereford) scored a hat-trick against different goalkeepers. Opponents Colchester Utd., beaten 5-0, became the first team in League history to have two 'keepers sent off in the same game.

Joe Bradford of Birmingham City scored three hat-tricks in eight days in September 1929-30 v Newcastle Utd. (won 5-1) on the 21st, 5 for the Football League v Irish League (7-2) on the 25th, and 3 in his club's 5-7 defeat away to Blackburn Rov. on the 28th.

PREMIERSHIP DOUBLE HAT-TRICK

Robert Pires and **Jermaine Pennant** each scored 3 goals in Arsenal's 6–1 win at home to Southampton (May 7, 2003).

TON UP – BOTH ENDS

Manchester City are the only club to **score and concede** a century of League goals in the same season. When fifth in the 1957-8 Championship, they scored 104 goals and gave away 100.

TOURNAMENT TOP SHOTS

Most individual goals in a World Cup Final series: 13 by **Just Fontaine** for France, in Sweden 1958.

Most in European Championship Finals: 9 by **Michel Platini** for France, in France 1984.

MOST GOALS ON CLUB DEBUT

Jim Dyet scored **eight** in King's Park's 12-2 win against Forfar Athletic (Scottish Div. 2, Jan. 2, 1930).

Len Shackleton scored **six** times in Newcastle Utd.'s 13-0 win v Newport County (Div. 2, Oct. 5, 1946) in the week he joined them from Bradford Park Avenue.

MOST GOALS ON LEAGUE DEBUT

Five by **George Hilsdon**, for Chelsea (9-2) v Glossop, Div. 2 Sept. 1, 1906.

Alan Shearer, with three goals for Southampton (4-2) v Arsenal, April 9, 1988, became, at 17, the youngest player to score a First Division hat-trick on his full debut.

CLEAN-SHEET RECORDS

On the way to promotion from Div. 3 in season 1995-6, **Gillingham's** ever-present goalkeeper **Jim Stannard** set a clean-sheet record. In 46 matches, he achieved 29 shut-outs (17 at home, 12 away), beating the 28 by Ray Clemence for Liverpool (42 matches in Div. 1, 1978-9) and the previous best in a 46-match programme of 28 by Port Vale (Div. 3 North, 1953-4). In conceding only 20 League goals in 1995-6, Gillingham created a defensive record for the lower divisions.

Chris Woods, Rangers' England goalkeeper, set a British record in season 1986-7 by going 1,196 minutes without conceding a goal. The sequence began in the UEFA Cup match against Borussia Moenchengladbach on Nov. 26, 1986 and ended when Rangers were sensationally beaten 1-0 at home by Hamilton in the Scottish Cup 3rd. Round on Jan. 31, 1987 with a 70th.-minute goal by Adrian Sprott.

The previous British record of 1,156 minutes without a goal conceded was held by Aberdeen goalkeeper **Bobby Clark** (season 1970-1).

There have been three instances of clubs keeping 11 consecutive clean sheets in the Football League: Millwall (Div. 3 South, 1925-6), York City (Div. 3, 1973-4) and Reading (Div. 4, 1978-9). In his sequence, Reading goalkeeper **Steve Death** set the existing League shut-out record of 1,103 minutes.

Mark Leonard (Chesterfield) kept a clean sheet in 8 consecutive Div.3 away games (Jan-April 1994). Believed an away-match record in British football.

Sasa Ilic remained unbeaten for over 14 hours with 9 successive shut-outs (7 in FL Div. 1, 2 in play-offs) to equal a Charlton Athletic club record in Apr./May 1998. He had 12 clean sheets in 17 first team games after winning promotion from the reserves with 6 successive clean sheets.

Sebastiano Rossi kept a clean sheet in 8 successive away matches for AC Milan (Nov. 1993-Apr. 1994).

A world record of 1,275 minutes without conceding a goal was set in 1990-1 by **Abel Resino**, the Atletico Madrid goalkeeper. He was finally beaten by Sporting Gijon's Enrique in Atletico's 3-1 win on March 19, 1991.

In International football, the record is held by **Dino Zoff** with a shut-out for Italy (Sept. 1972 to June 1974) lasting 1,142 minutes.

LOW SCORING

Fewest goals by any club in season in Football League: **24** by **Stoke City** (Div. 1, 42 matches, 1984-5); **24** by **Watford** (Div. 2, 42 matches, 1971-2). In 46-match programme, **27** by **Stockport Co.** (Div. 3, 1969-70).

Arsenal were the lowest Premier League scorers in its opening season (1992-3) with 40 goals in 42 matches, but won both domestic cup competitions. In subsequent seasons the lowest Premier League scorers were **Ipswich Town** (35) in 1993-4, **Crystal Palace** (34) in 1994-5, **Manchester City** (33) in 1995-6 and **Leeds Utd.** (28) in 1996–7 until **Sunderland** set the Premiership's new fewest-goals record with only 21 in 2002–03.

LONG TIME NO SCORE

Longest non-scoring sequences in Football League: 11 matches by **Coventry City** in 1919-20 (Div. 2); 11 matches by **Hartlepool Utd.** in 1992-3 (Div. 2). After beating Crystal Palace 1-0 in the F.A. Cup 3rd round on Jan. 2, they went 13 games and 2 months without scoring (11 League, 1 F.A. Cup, 1 Autoglass Trophy). The sequence ended after 1,227 blank minutes with a 1-1 draw at Blackpool (League) on March 6.

In the **Premier League** (Oct.-Jan. season 1994-5) Crystal Palace failed to score in nine consecutive matches.

The British non-scoring record is held by Scottish club **Stirling Albion**: 14 consecutive matches (13 League, 1 Scottish Cup) and 1,292 minutes play, from Jan. 31, 1981 until Aug. 8, 1981 (when they lost 4-1 to Falkirk in the League Cup).

In season 1971-2, **Mansfield Town** did not score in any of their first nine home games in Div. 3. They were relegated on goal difference of minus two.

F.A. CUP CLEAN SHEETS

Most consecutive F.A. Cup matches without conceding a goal: 11 by **Bradford City**. The sequence spanned 8 rounds, from 3rd. in 1910-11 to 4th. Round replay in 1911-12, and included winning the Cup in 1911.

ATTENDANCES

GREATEST WORLD CROWDS

World Cup, Maracana Stadium, Rio de Janeiro, July 16, 1950. Final match (Brazil v Uruguay) attendance 199,850; receipts £125,000.

Total attendance in three matches (including play-off) between Santos (Brazil) and AC Milan for the Inter-Continental Cup (World Club Championship) 1963, exceeded 375,000.

BRITISH RECORD CROWDS

Most to pay: 149,547, Scotland v England, at Hampden Park, Glasgow, April 17, 1937. This was the first all-ticket match in Scotland (receipts £24,000).

At Scottish F.A. Cup Final: 146,433, Celtic v Aberdeen, at Hampden Park, April 24, 1937. Estimated another 20,000 shut out.

For British club match (apart from a Cup Final): 143,470, Rangers v Hibernian, at Hampden Park, March 27, 1948 (Scottish Cup semi-final).

F.A. Cup Final: 126,047, Bolton Wand. v West Ham Utd., at Wembley, April 28, 1923. Estimated 150,000 in stadium.

World Cup Qualifying Ties: 120,000, Cameroon v Morocco, Yaounde, November 29, 1981; 107,580, Scotland v Poland, Hampden Park, October 13, 1965.

European Cup: 135,826, Celtic v Leeds Utd. (semi-final, 2nd. leg) at Hampden Park, Glasgow, April 15, 1970.

European Cup Final: 127,621, Real Madrid v Eintracht Frankfurt, at Hampden Park, Glasgow, May 18, 1960.

European Cup-Winners' Cup Final: 100,000, West Ham Utd. v TSV Munich, at Wembley, May 19, 1965.
Scottish League: 118,567, Rangers v Celtic, January 2, 1939.
Scottish League Cup Final: 107,609, Celtic v Rangers, at Hampden Park, October 23, 1965.
Football League old format: First Div.: 83,260, Manchester Utd. v Arsenal, January 17, 1948 (at Maine Road); **Second Div.:** 70,302 Tottenham v Southampton, February 25, 1950; **Third Div. South:** 51,621, Cardiff City v Bristol City, April 7, 1947; **Third Div. North:** 49,655, Hull City v Rotherham Utd., December 25, 1948; **Third Div.:** 49,309, Sheffield Wed. v Sheffield Utd., December 26, 1979; **Fourth Div.:** 37,774, Crystal Palace v Millwall, March 31, 1961.
F.A. Premier League: 67,721, Manchester Utd. V Charlton Athletic Ath., May 3, 2003.
Football League – New Div. 1: 41,214, Sunderland v Stoke City, April 25, 1998; **New Div. 2:** 32,471, Manchester City v York City, May 8, 1999; **New Div. 3:** 22,319 Hull City v Hartlepool Utd., December 26, 2002.
In English Provinces: 84,569, Manchester City v Stoke City (F.A. Cup 6th Round), March 3, 1934.
Record for Under-21 International: 32,865 England v France at Derby Co., February 9, 1999.
Record for friendly match: 104,679, Rangers v Eintracht Frankfurt, at Hampden Park, Glasgow, October 17, 1961.
Record Football League aggregate (season): 41,271,414 (1948-9) – 88 clubs.
Record Football League aggregate (single day): 1,269,934, December 27, 1949.
Record average home League attendance for season: 67,543 by Manchester Utd. in 2000-01.
Long-ago League attendance aggregates: 10,929,000 in 1906-07 (40 clubs); 28,132,933 in 1937-8 (88 clubs).
Last 1m. crowd aggregate, League: 1,007,200, December 27, 1971.
Record Amateur match attendance: 100,000 for F.A. Amateur Cup Final, Pegasus v Harwich & Parkeston at Wembley, April 11, 1953.
Record Cup-tie aggregate: 265,199, at two matches between Rangers and Morton, in the Scottish Cup Final, 1947-8.
Abandoned match attendance records: In **England** – 63,480 at Newcastle Utd. v Swansea City F.A. Cup 3rd round, Jan. 10, 1953, abandoned 8 mins (0-0), fog.
In Scotland: 94,596 at Scotland v Austria (4-1), Hampden Park, May 8, 1963. Referee Jim Finney ended play (79 minutes) after Austria had two players sent off and one carried off.
What is still **Colchester Utd.'s** record crowd (19,072) was for the F.A. Cup 1st round tie v Reading on Nov. 27, 1948, abandoned 35 minutes (0-0), fog.

SMALLEST CROWDS

Smallest League attendances: 13, Stockport Co. v Leicester City (Div. 2, May 7, 1921; played at Old Trafford – Stockport ground closed); 469, Thames v Luton Town (Div. 3 South, December 6, 1930).
Lowest post-war League attendance: 450 Rochdale v Cambridge Utd. (Div. 3, February 5, 1974).
Lowest F.A. Premier League crowd: 3,039 for Wimbledon v Everton, Jan. 26, 1993 (smallest top-division attendance since war).
Lowest Saturday post-war top-division crowd: 3,231 for Wimbledon v Luton Town, Sept. 7, 1991 (Div. 1).
Lowest Football League crowds, new format – Div. 1: 849 for Wimbledon v Rotherham Utd., (Div. 1) October 29, 2002 (smallest att. in top two divisions since war); **Div. 2:** 1,077, Hartlepool Utd. v Cardiff City, March 22, 1994; **Div. 3:** 739, Doncaster Rov. v Barnet, March 3, 1998.
Other low First Division crowds since the war: 3,121 for Wimbledon v Sheffield W., Oct. 2, 1991; 3,231 for Wimbledon v Luton Town, Sept. 7, 1991; 3,270 for Wimbledon v Coventry City, Dec. 28, 1991; 3,496 for Wimbledon v Luton Town, Feb. 14, 1990.
Lowest top-division crowd at a major ground since the war: 4,554 for Arsenal v Leeds Utd. (May 5, 1966) – fixture clashed with live TV coverage of Cup-Winners' Cup Final (Liverpool v Borussia Dortmund).

Smallest League Cup attendances: 612, Halifax Town v Tranmere Rov. (1st Round, 2nd Leg) September 6, 2000; 664, Wimbledon v Rotherham Utd. (3rd Round), November 5, 2002.

Smallest League Cup attendance at top-division ground: 1,987 for Wimbledon v Bolton Wand. (2nd Round, 2nd Leg) Oct. 6, 1992.

Smallest Wembley crowds for England matches: 15,628 v Chile (Rous Cup, May 23, 1989 – affected by Tube strike); 20,038 v Colombia (Friendly, Sept. 6, 1995); 21,432 v Czech. (Friendly, Apr. 25, 1990); 21,142 v Japan (Umbro Cup, June 3, 1995); 23,600 v Wales (British Championship, Feb. 23, 1983); 23,659 v Greece (Friendly, May 17, 1994); 23,951 v East Germany (Friendly, Sept. 12, 1984); 24,000 v N. Ireland (British Championship, Apr. 4, 1984); 25,756 v Colombia (Rous Cup, May 24, 1988); 25,837 v Denmark (Friendly, Sept. 14, 1988).

Smallest Int. modern crowd: 221 for Poland v N. Ireland (4-1, friendly) at Limassol, Cyprus, on February 13, 2002. Played at neutral venue at Poland's World Cup training base.

Smallest Int. modern crowds at home: N.Ireland: 2,500 v Chile (Belfast, May 26, 1989 – clashed with ITV live screening of Liverpool v Arsenal Championship decider); **Scotland:** 7,843 v N.Ireland (Hampden Park, May 6, 1969); **Wales:** 2,315 v N.Ireland (Wrexham, May 27, 1982).

Smallest attendance for post-war England match: 2,378 v San Marino (World Cup) at Bologna (Nov. 17, 1993). Tie clashed with Italy v Portugal (World Cup) shown live on Italian TV.

Smallest paid attendance for British first-class match: 29 for Clydebank v East Stirling, CIS Scottish League Cup 1st Round, July 31, 1999. Played at Morton's Cappielow Park ground, shared by Clydebank, the match clashed with the Tall Ships Race which attracted 200,000 to the area.

NO SPECTATORS

F.A. Cup 3rd. Round, 2nd. Replay, March 3, 1915: Norwich City 0, Bradford City 2, at Lincoln. Played behind closed doors, so that vital war work was not disrupted.

Cup-Winners' Cup, 1st. Round, 2nd. Leg, October 1, 1980: West Ham Utd. 5, Castilla (Spain) 1. UEFA ordered match to be played behind closed doors after misconduct by West Ham Utd. fans in 1st. Leg in Madrid (Castilla 3, West Ham 1).

European Championship, Qualifying Round, April 2, 2003: Slovakia 4, Liechtenstein 0 at Spartak Stadium, Trnava. UEFA ordered match to be played behind closed doors following racial abuse of England players by Slovakia crowd in Bratislava, October 12.

F.A. CUP CROWD RECORD (OUTSIDE FINAL)

The first F.A. Cup-tie shown on closed-circuit TV (5th. Round, Saturday, March 11, 1967, kick-off 7pm) drew a total of 105,000 spectators to Goodison Park and Anfield. This is the biggest attendance for a single F.A. Cup match other than the Final. At Goodison, 64,851 watched the match 'for real', while 40,149 saw the TV version on eight giant screens at Anfield. Everton beat Liverpool 1-0.

LOWEST SEMI-FINAL CROWD

The smallest F.A. Cup semi-final attendance since the war was 17,987 for Manchester Utd. v Crystal Palace replay, at Villa Park on April 12, 1995. Crystal Palace supporters largely boycotted tie after a fan died in car-park clash outside pub in Walsall before first match. Previous lowest: 25,963 for Wimbledon v Luton Town, at Tottenham on April 9, 1988.

Lowest quarter-final crowd since the war: 8,735 for Chesterfield v Wrexham on March 9, 1997.

Smallest F.A. Cup 3rd. Round attendances for matches between League clubs: 1,833 for Chester City v Bournemouth (at Macclesfield Town) Jan. 5, 1991; 1,966 for Aldershot v Oxford Utd., Jan. 10, 1987.

PRE-WEMBLEY CUP FINAL CROWDS

AT CRYSTAL PALACE

1895	42,560	1897	65,891	1899	73,833
1896	48,036	1898	62,017	1900	68,945

1901	110,802	1905	101,117	1910	76,980
1902	48,036	1906	75,609	1911	69,098
Replay	33,050	1907	84,584	1912	54,434
1903	64,000	1908	74,967	1913	120,028
1904	61,734	1909	67,651	1914	72,778

AT OLD TRAFFORD

1915 50,000

AT STAMFORD BRIDGE

1920 .... 50,018 1921 .... 72,805 1922 53,000

RECEIPTS RECORDS

Wembley Stadium underwent its first considerable alteration during 1962-3 in preparation for the World Cup in 1966. Higher admission fees at the 1963 F.A. Cup Final resulted in 100,000 spectators paying a record £89,000.

This is how Wembley's receipts records subsequently rose:

1968 F.A. Cup Final (Everton v W.B.A.) £110,000
1968 European Cup Final (Manchester Utd. v Benfica) £120,000
1976 F.A. Cup Final (Southampton v Manchester Utd.) £420,000
1978 F.A. Cup Final (Ipswich Town v Arsenal) £500,000
1981 England v Hungary (World Cup) £671,000
1982 F.A. Cup Final (Tottenham v Q.P.R.) £886,000
(plus £605,000 for replay)
1984 F.A. Cup Final (Everton v Watford) £919,000
*1985 F.A. Cup Final (Manchester Utd. v Everton) £1,100,000
1986 F.A. Cup Final (Liverpool v Everton) £1,100,000
†1987 League Cup Final (Arsenal v Liverpool) £1,000,000
1987 F.A. Cup Final (Coventry City v Tottenham) £1,286,737
1988 F.A. Cup Final (Wimbledon v Liverpool) £1,422,814
1989 F.A. Cup Final (Liverpool v Everton) £1,600,000
1990 League Cup Final (Nott'm Forest v Oldham Athletic) £1,650,000
1990 F.A. Cup Final (Manchester Utd. v Crystal Palace – first match) .. £2,000,000
1991 League Cup Final (Manchester Utd. v Sheffield Wed.) £2,000,000
1991 F.A. Cup Final (Nott'm F. v Tottenham) £2,016,000
1992 F.A. Cup Final (Liverpool v Sunderland) £2,548,174
1993 F.A. Cup Final (Arsenal v Sheffield W. – first match) £2,818,000
(Replay took receipts for both matches to £4,695,200)
1994 F.A. Cup Final record (Manchester Utd. v Chelsea) £2,962,167
1997 League Cup Final record (Leicester City v Middlesbrough) £2,750,000
1998 League Cup Final record (Chelsea v Middlesbrough) £2,983,000
•2000 F.A. Cup Final record (Chelsea v Aston Villa) £3,100,000

(* Britain's first £1m. gate; †First £1m. gate for League Cup Final; • British club match receipts record)

Record England match receipts: £4,100,000 (v. Germany, Wembley, European Championship semi-final, June 26, 1992 – att: 75,862)

EARLY CUP FINAL RECEIPTS

1885 Blackburn Rov. v Queens Park £442
1913 Aston Villa v Sunderland £9,406
1923 Bolton Wand. v West Ham Utd., first Wembley Final £27,776
1939 Portsmouth v Wolves £29,000
1946 Derby Co. v Charlton Athletic £45,000

WORLD RECORD MATCH RECEIPTS

£4,300,000 for **World Cup Final**, Argentina v West Germany (Rome, July 8, 1990).

INTERNATIONAL RECORDS

MOST APPEARANCES

Peter Shilton, England goalkeeper, then aged 40, retired from International football after the 1990 World Cup Finals with the European record number of caps – 125. Previous record (119) was set by **Pat Jennings**, Northern Ireland's goalkeeper from 1964-86, who retired on his 41st birthday during the 1986 World Cup in Mexico. Shilton's England career spanned 20 seasons from his debut against East Germany at Wembley on Nov. 25, 1970.

Four players have completed a century of appearances in full International matches for England. **Billy Wright** of Wolves, was the first, retiring in 1959 with a total of 105 caps.

Bobby Charlton, of Manchester Utd., beat Wright's record in the World Cup match against West Germany in Leon, Mexico, in June 1970 and **Bobby Moore,** of West Ham Utd., overtook Charlton's 106 caps against Italy in Turin, in June 1973. Moore played 108 times for England, a record that stood until **Shilton** reached 109 against Denmark in Copenhagen (June 7, 1989).

Kenny Dalglish became Scotland's first 100-cap International v Romania (Hampden Park, March 26, 1986).

World's most-capped player: Mohamed Al-Deayea (Saudi Arabia goalkeeper), made his 165th International appearance, v Republic of Ireland (World Cup) at Yokohama, Japan, on June 11, 2002.

Most-capped European goalkeeper: Thomas Ravelli, 143 Internationals for Sweden (1981-97).

Gillian Coultard, (Doncaster Belles), England Women's captain, received a special presentation from Geoff Hurst to mark 100 caps when England beat Holland 1-0 at Upton Park on October 30, 1997. She made her Int. debut at 18 in May 1981, and retired at the end of season 1999-2000 with a record 119 caps (30 goals).

BRITAIN'S MOST-CAPPED PLAYERS

(As at start of season 2003-04)

England

Peter Shilton 125
Bobby Moore 108
Bobby Charlton 106
Billy Wright 105
Bryan Robson 90

Scotland

Kenny Dalglish 102
Jim Leighton 91
Alex McLeish 77
Paul McStay 76
Tommy Boyd 71

Wales

Neville Southall 92
Dean Saunders 75
Peter Nicholas 73
Ian Rush 73
Mark Hughes 72
Joey Jones 72

Northern Ireland

Pat Jennings 119
Mal Donaghy 91

Sammy McIlroy 88

Republic of Ireland

Steve Staunton 102
Niall Quinn 91
Tony Cascarino 88
Paul McGrath 83
Pat Bonner 80
Ray Houghton 73
Liam Brady 72
Frank Stapleton 71
Kevin Moran 71
Andy Townsend 70

MOST ENGLAND CAPS IN ROW

Most consecutive International appearances: 70 by **Billy Wright**, for England from October 1951 to May 1959. He played 105 of England's first 108 post-war matches.

England captains most times: Billy Wright and **Bobby Moore**, 90 each.

England captains – 4 in match (v Serbia & Montenegro at Leicester June 3, 2003): **Michael Owen** was captain for the first half and after the interval the armband passed to **Emile Heskey** (for 15 minutes), **Philip Neville** (26 minutes) and substitute **Jamie Carragher** (9 minutes, including time added).

MOST PLAYERS FROM ONE CLUB IN ENGLAND SIDES

Arsenal supplied seven men (a record) to the England team v Italy at Highbury on November 14, 1934. They were: Frank Moss, George Male, Eddie Hapgood, Wilf Copping, Ray Bowden, Ted Drake and Cliff Bastin. In addition, Arsenal's Tom Whittaker was England's trainer.

Since then until 2001, the most players from one club in an England team was six from **Liverpool** against Switzerland at Wembley in September 1977. The side also included a Liverpool old boy, Kevin Keegan (Hamburg).

Seven **Arsenal** men took part in the England – France (0-2) match at Wembley on February 10, 1999. Goalkeeper David Seaman and defenders Lee Dixon, Tony Adams and Martin Keown lined up for England. Nicolas Anelka (2 goals) and Emmanuel Petit started the match for France and Patrick Vieira replaced Anelka.

Manchester Utd. equalled Arsenal's 1934 record by providing England with seven players in the World Cup qualifier away to Albania on March 28, 2001. Five started the match – David Beckham (captain), Gary Neville, Paul Scholes, Nicky Butt and Andy Cole – and two went on as substitutes: Wes Brown and Teddy Sheringham.

INTERNATIONAL SUBS RECORDS

Malta substituted all 11 players in their 1-2 home defeat against England on June 3, 2000. Six substitutes by England took the total replacements in the match to 17, then an International record.

Most substitutions in match by **England**: 11 in second half by Sven Goran Eriksson against Holland at Tottenham on August 15, 2001; 11 against Italy at Leeds on March 27, 2002; Italy sent on 8 players from the bench – the total of 19 substitutions was then a record for an England match: 11 against Australia at Upton Park on February 12, 2003 (entire England team changed at half-time).

Forty-three players, a record for an England match, were used in the International against Serbia & Montenegro at Leicester on June 3, 2003. England sent on 10 substitutes in the second half and their opponents changed all 11 players.

The **Republic of Ireland** sent on 12 second-half substitutes, using 23 players in all, when they beat Russia 2-0 in a friendly International in Dublin on February 13, 2002.

ENGLAND'S WORLD CUP-WINNERS

At Wembley, July 30, 1966, 4-2 v West Germany (2-2 after 90 mins), scorers Hurst 3, Peters. Team: Banks; Cohen, Wilson, Stiles, Charlton (J.), Moore (Captain), Ball, Hurst,

Charlton (R.), Hunt, Peters. Manager **Alf Ramsey** fielded that same eleven in six successive matches (an England record): the World Cup quarter-final, semi-final and Final, and the first three games of the following season. England wore red shirts in the Final and Her Majesty the Queen presented the Cup to Bobby Moore. The players each received a £1,000 bonus, plus £60 World Cup Final appearance money, all less tax, and Ramsey a £6,000 bonus from the F.A. The match was shown live on TV (in black and white).

BRAZIL'S RECORD RUN

Brazil hold the record for the longest unbeaten sequence in International football: 45 matches from 1993-7. The previous record of 31 matches undefeated was held by Hungary between June 1950 and July 1954.

ENGLAND MATCHES ABANDONED

May 17, 1953 v **Argentina** (Friendly, Buenos Aires) after 23 mins. (0–0) – rain.

Oct. 29, 1975 v **Czechoslovakia** (Eur. Champ. Qual., Bratislava) after 17 mins. (0–0) – fog. Played next day.

Feb. 15, 1995 v **Rep. of Ireland** (Friendly, Dublin) after 27 mins. (1–0) – crowd disturbance.

ENGLAND POSTPONEMENT

Nov 21, 1979 v **Bulgaria** (Eur. Champ. qual., Wembley postponed for 24 hours – fog.

ENGLAND UNDER COVER

England played indoors for the first time when they beat Argentina 1-0 in the World Cup at the Sapporo Dome, Japan, on June 7, 2002.

ALL-SEATED INTERNATIONALS

The first **all-seated crowd** (30,000) for a full International in Britain saw **Wales** and **West Germany** draw 0-0 at Cardiff City Arms Park on May 31, 1989. The terraces were closed.

England's first all-seated International at Wembley was against Yugoslavia (2-1) on December 13, 1989 (attendance 34,796). The terracing behind the goals was closed for conversion to seating.

The first **full-house all-seated** International at Wembley was for England v Brazil (1-0) on March 28, 1990, when a capacity 80,000 crowd paid record British receipts of £1,200,000.

Cardiff's new **Millennium Stadium** set attendance records for **Wales** in consecutive friendly Internationals: 66,500 v Finland, March 28, 2000, then 72,500 v Brazil, May 23, 2000 – Britain's first indoor International.

ENGLAND 'ON THE ROAD'

Since Wembley Stadium closed in October 2000, England have played home fixtures at twelve club grounds (to end of season 2002-03): Aston Villa (2), Liverpool (2), Manchester Utd. (2), Derby, Tottenham, Newcastle, Leeds, Southampton, Upton Park, Sunderland, Leicester and Middlesbrough.

FIRST BLACK CAPS

First black player for **England** in a senior International was Nott'm. Forest full-back **Viv Anderson** against Czechoslovakia at Wembley on November 29, 1978.

Aston Villa's **Ugo Ehiogu** was **England's** first black captain (U-21 v Holland at Portsmouth, April 27, 1993).

Paul Ince (Manchester Utd.) became the first black player to captain **England** in a **full International** (v U.S.A., Boston, June 9, 1993).

First black British International was **Eddie Parris** (Bradford Park Avenue) for Wales against N. Ireland in Belfast on December 5, 1931.

MOST NEW CAPS IN ENGLAND TEAM

6, by Sir Alf Ramsey (v Portugal, April 3, 1974).

6, by Sven-Goran Eriksson (v Australia, February 12, 2003; 5 at half-time when 11 changes made).

PLAYED FOR MORE THAN ONE COUNTRY

Multi-nationals in senior International football include: **Johnny Carey** (1938-53) – caps Rep. of Ireland 29, N. Ireland 7; **Ferenc Puskas** (1945-62) – caps Hungary 84, Spain 4; **Alfredo di Stefano** (1950-6) – caps Argentina 7, Spain 31; **Ladislav Kubala** (1948-58) – caps, Hungary 3, Czechoslovakia 11, Spain 19, only player to win full Int. honours with 3 countries. Kubala also played in a fourth Int. team, scoring twice for FIFA v England at Wembley in 1953.

Eleven players, including Carey, appeared for both N. Ireland and the Republic of Ireland in seasons directly after the last war.

Cecil Moore, capped by N. Ireland in 1949 when with Glentoran, played for USA v England in 1953.

Hawley Edwards played for England v Scotland in 1874 and for Wales v Scotland in 1876.

Jack Reynolds (Distillery and W.B.A.) played for both Ireland (5 times) and England (8) in the 1890s.

Bobby Evans (Sheffield Utd.) had played 10 times for Wales when capped for England, in 1910-11. He was born in Chester of Welsh parents.

In recent years several players have represented USSR and one or other of the breakaway republics. The same applies to Yugoslavia and its component states. **Josip Weber** played for Croatia in 1992 and made a 5-goal debut for Belgium in 1994.

3-GENERATION INTERNATIONAL FAMILY

When Bournemouth striker **Warren Feeney** was capped away to Liechtenstein on March 27, 2002, he became the third generation of his family to play for N. Ireland. He followed in the footsteps of his grandfather James (capped twice in 1950) and father Warren Snr. (1 in 1976).

FATHERS & SONS CAPPED BY ENGLAND

George Eastham senior (pre-war) and **George Eastham junior**; **Brian Clough** and **Nigel Clough**; **Frank Lampard** senior and **Frank Lampard** junior.

FATHER & SON SAME-DAY CAPS

Iceland made father-and-son Int. history when they beat Estonia 3-0 in Tallin on April 24, 1996. Arnor Gudjohnsen (35) started the match and was replaced (62 mins.) by his 17-year-old son Eidur.

LONGEST UNBEATEN START TO ENGLAND CAREER

By **Steven Gerrard**, 18 matches (W14, D4) to end of season 2002–3.

SUCCESSIVE ENGLAND HAT-TRICKS

The last player to score a hat-trick in consecutive England matches was **Dixie Dean** on the summer tour in May 1927, against Belgium (9-1) and Luxembourg (5-2).

POSTWAR HAT-TRICKS v ENGLAND

November 25, 1953, scorer **Nandor Hidegkuti** (England 3, Hungary 6, Wembley); May 11, 1958, scorer **Aleksandar Petakovic** (Yugoslavia 5, England 0, Belgrade); May 17, 1959, scorer **Juan Seminario** (Peru 4, England 1, Lima); June 15, 1988, scorer **Marco Van Basten** (Holland 3, England 1, European Championship, Dusseldorf).

NO-SAVE GOALKEEPERS

Chris Woods did not have one save to make when England beat San Marino 6-0 (World Cup) at Wembley on February 17, 1993. He touched the ball only six times throughout the match.

Gordon Banks had a similar no-save experience when England beat Malta 5-0 (European Championship) at Wembley on May 12, 1971. Malta did not force a goal-kick or corner, and the four times Banks touched the ball were all from back passes.

FOOTBALL'S GOVERNING BODIES

As at June 2003: A total of 204 National Associations were members of the Federation Internationale de Football Association (**F.I.F.A.**, founded May, 1904), and the Union of European Football Associations (**U.E.F.A.**, founded June, 1954) embraced 52 countries.

The seven original members of the F.I.F.A. were Belgium, Denmark, France, Holland, Spain, Sweden and Switzerland.

FIFA WORLD YOUTH CHAMPIONSHIP (UNDER-20)

Finals: 1977 (Tunis) Soviet Union 2, Mexico 2 (Soviet won 9-8 on pens.); **1979** (Tokyo) Argentina 3, Soviet Union 1; **1981** (Sydney) W. Germany 4, Qatar 0; **1983** (Mexico City) Brazil 1, Argentina 0; **1985** (Moscow) Brazil 1, Spain 0; **1987** (Santiago) Yugoslavia 1, W. Germany 1 (Yugoslavia won 5-4 on pens.); **1989** (Riyadh) Portugal 2, Nigeria 0; **1991** (Lisbon) Portugal 0, Brazil 0 (Portugal won 4-2 on pens.); **1993** (Sydney) Brazil 2, Ghana 1; **1995** (Qatar) Argentina 2, Brazil 0; **1997** (Kuala Lumpur) Argentina 2, Uruguay 1; **1999** (Lagos) Spain 4, Japan 0; **2001** (Buenos Aires) Argentina 3, Ghana 0; **2002**, tournament not played.

FAMOUS CLUB FEATS

The Double: There have been ten instances of a club winning the Football League/ Premiership title and the F.A. Cup in the same season. **Manchester Utd.** and **Arsenal** have each done so three times:-

Preston N.E. 1888-89; **Aston Villa** 1896-97; **Tottenham** 1960-61; **Arsenal** 1970-71, 1997-98, 2001-02; **Liverpool** 1985-86; **Manchester Utd.** 1993-94, 1995-96, 1998-99.

The Treble: Liverpool were the first English club to win three major competitions in one season when in 1983-84, Joe Fagan's first season as manager, they were League Champions, League Cup winners and European Cup winners.

Alex Ferguson's **Manchester Utd.** achieved an even more prestigious treble in 1998-99, completing the domestic double of Premiership and F.A. Cup and then winning the European Cup.

Liverpool completed a unique treble by an English club with three cup successes under Gerard Houllier in season 2000-01: the League Cup, F.A. Cup and UEFA Cup.

Liverpool the first English club to win five major trophies in one calendar year (February-August 2001): League Cup, F.A. Cup, UEFA Cup, Charity Shield, UEFA Super Cup.

As Champions in season 2001-02, **Arsenal** set a Premiership record by winning the last 13 matches. They were the first top-division club since Preston N.E. in the League's inaugural season (1888-9) to maintain an unbeaten away record.

(See Scottish section for treble feats by Rangers and Celtic.)

Home Runs: Sunderland lost only one home Div. 1 game out of 73 in five seasons, 1891 to 1896. **Brentford** won all 21 home games in 1929-30 in the Third Division (South). Others have won all home games in a smaller programme.

Record Home Run: Liverpool went 85 competitive first-team games unbeaten at home between losing 2-3 to Birmingham City on January 21, 1978 and 1-2 to Leicester City on January 31, 1981. They comprised 63 in the League, 9 League Cup, 7 in European competition and 6 F.A. Cup. Leicester were relegated that season.

Millwall were unbeaten at home in the League for 59 consecutive matches from 1964-67.

Third to First: Charlton Athletic, in 1936, became the first club to advance from the Third to First Division in successive seasons. **Queen's Park Rangers** were the second club to achieve the feat in 1968, and **Oxford Utd.** did it in 1984 and 1985 as Champions of each division. Subsequently, **Derby Co.** (1987), **Middlesbrough** (1988), **Sheffield Utd.** (1990) and **Notts Co.** (1991) climbed from Third Division to First in consecutive seasons.

Watford won successive promotions from the modern Second Division to the Premier League in 1997-8, 1998-9. **Manchester City** equalled the feat in 1998-9, 1999-2000.

Fourth to First: Northampton Town, in 1965 became the first club to rise from the Fourth to the First Division. **Swansea City** climbed from the Fourth Division to the First (three promotions in four seasons), 1977-8 to 1980-1. **Wimbledon** repeated the feat, 1982-3 to 1985-6 **Watford** did it in five seasons, 1977-8 to 1981-2. **Carlisle Utd.** climbed from Fourth Division to First, 1964-74.

Non-League to First: When **Wimbledon** finished third in the Second Division in 1986, they completed the phenomenal rise from non-League football (Southern League) to the First Division in nine years. Two years later they won the F.A. Cup.

Tottenham, in 1960-1, not only carried off the First Division Championship and the F.A. Cup for the first time this century but set up other records by opening with 11 successive wins, registering most First Division wins (31), most away wins in the League's history (16), and equalling Arsenal's First Division records of 66 points and 33 away points. They already held the Second Division record of 70 points (1919-20).

Arsenal, in 1993, became the first club to win both English domestic cup competitions (F.A. Cup and League Cup) in the same season. **Liverpool** repeated the feat in 2000-01.

Preston N.E., in season 1888-9, won the first League Championship without losing a match and the F.A. Cup without having a goal scored against them. Only other English club to remain unbeaten through a League season were **Liverpool** (Div. 2 Champions in 1893-4).

Bury, in 1903, also won the F.A. Cup without conceding a goal.

Everton won Div. 2, Div. 1 and the F.A. Cup in successive seasons, 1930-1, 1931-2, 1932-3.

Liverpool won the League Championship in 1964, the F.A. Cup in 1965 and the Championship again in 1966. In 1978 they became the first British club to win the European Cup in successive seasons. **Nott'm. Forest** repeated the feat in 1979 and 1980.

Liverpool won the League Championship six times in eight seasons (1976-83) under **Bob Paisley's** management.

Sir Alex Ferguson's **Manchester Utd.** have won the F.A. Premier League in eight of its eleven seasons (1993-2003). They were runners-up on two other occasions, each time within a point of the Champions.

Most Premiership wins in season: 28 by Manchester Utd. (1999-2000).

Biggest points-winning margin by League Champions: 18 by Manchester Utd. (1999-2000).

COVENTRY UNIQUE

Coventry City are the only club to have played in the Premier League, all four previous divisions of the Football League and in both sections (North and South) of the old Third Division.

Grimsby Town were the other club to play in the four divisions of the Football League and its two Third Division sections.

FAMOUS UPS & DOWNS

Sunderland: Relegated in 1958 after maintaining First Division status since their election to the Football League in 1890. They dropped into Division 3 for the first time in 1987.

Aston Villa: Relegated with **Preston N.E.** to the Third Division in 1970.

Arsenal up: When the League was extended in 1919, Woolwich Arsenal (sixth in Division Two in 1914-15, last season before the war) were elected to Division One. Arsenal have been in the top division ever since.

Tottenham down: At that same meeting in 1919 Chelsea (due for relegation) retained their place in Division One but the bottom club (Tottenham) had to go down to Division Two.

Preston N.E. and Burnley down: Preston N.E., the first League Champions in season 1888-9, dropped into the Fourth Division in 1985. So did Burnley, also among the League's original members in 1888. In 1986, Preston N.E. had to apply for re-election.

Wolves' fall: Wolves, another of the Football League's original members, completed the fall from First Division to Fourth in successive seasons (1984-5-6).

Lincoln City out: Lincoln City became the first club to suffer automatic demotion from the Football League when they finished bottom of Div. 4, on goal difference, in season 1986-7. They were replaced by Scarborough, champions of the GM Vauxhall Conference. Lincoln City regained their place a year later.

Swindon Town up and down: In the 1990 play-offs, Swindon Town won promotion to the First Division for the first time, but remained in the Second Division because of financial irregularities.

MOST CHAMPIONSHIP WINS

Liverpool, by winning the First Division in 1976-7, established a record of 10 Championship victories. They later increased the total to 18. **Manchester Utd.** are second with 15 League titles (7 Football League, 8 Premier League) and **Arsenal** third with 12 (10 Football League, 2 Premier Leagal).

LONGEST CURRENT MEMBERS OF TOP DIVISION

Arsenal (since 1919), **Everton** (1954), **Liverpool** (1962), **Manchester Utd.** (1975), **Southampton** (1978).

CHAMPIONS: FEWEST PLAYERS

Liverpool used only 14 players (five ever-present) when they won the League Championship in season 1965-6. **Aston Villa** also called on no more than 14 players to win the title in 1980-81, with seven ever-present.

CHAMPIONS WITH FEWEST DEFEATS

Arsenal (season 1990-01, 38 matches) are the only League Champions to lose only once since **Preston N.E.** were undefeated as the first title winners in 1888-9 (22 matches).

LEAGUE HAT-TRICKS

Huddersfield Town created a record in 1925-6 by winning the League Championship for the third year in succession.

Arsenal equalled this League hat-trick in 1933-4-5, **Liverpool** in 1982-3-4 and **Manchester United** in 1999-2000-01.

'SUPER DOUBLE' WINNERS

Since the war, there have been three instances of players appearing in and then managing F.A. Cup and Championship-winning teams:

Joe Mercer: Player in Arsenal Championship teams 1948, 1953 and in their 1950 F.A. Cup side; manager of Manchester City when they won Championship 1968, F.A. Cup 1969.

Kenny Dalglish: Player in Liverpool Championship-winning teams 1979, 1980, 1982, 1983, 1984, player-manager 1986, 1988, 1990: player-manager when Liverpool won F.A. Cup (to complete Double) 1986; manager of Blackburn Rov., Champions 1995.

George Graham: Played in Arsenal's Double-winning team in 1971, and as manager took them to Championship success in 1989 and 1991 and the F.A. Cup – League Cup double in 1993.

BACK FIRST TIME

The following clubs won promotion the season after losing their position in the First Division of the League (*as Champions):

Sheffield Wed. *1899-1900, *1951-2, *1955-6, *1958-9, 1990-1; **Bolton Wand.** 1899-1900, *1908-9, 1910-11; **W.B.A.** *1901-2; **Manchester City** *1902-3, *1909-10, 1950-1; **Burnley** *1897-8.

Small Heath 1902-3; **Liverpool** *1904-5; **Nott'm. Forest** *1906-7; **Preston N.E.** *1912-13, 1914-15; **Notts Co.** *1913-14; **Derby Co.** *1914-15.

Tottenham *1919-20, 1977-8; **Leeds Utd.** 1927-8, 1931-2; **Middlesbrough** *1928-9; **Everton** *1930-1; **Manchester Utd.** 1937-8, *1974-5; **Huddersfield Town** 1952-3.

Aston Villa *1959-60, 1987-8; **Chelsea** 1962-3; *1988-9; **Norwich City** 1974-5, 1981-2, *1985-6; **Wolves** 1976-7, 1982-3; **Birmingham City** 1979-80, 1984-5.

West Ham Utd., relegated in 1992, won promotion to the **Premier League** in 1993; ***Crystal Palace** and **Nott'm. Forest** both returned to the **Premiership** in 1994, a year after relegation; so did **Leicester City** in 1996, ***Bolton Wand.** in 1997, ***Nott'm Forest** and **Middlesbrough** in 1998, ***Charlton Athletic** in 2000 ***Manchester City** in 2002 and **Leicester City** in 2003.

ORIGINAL TWELVE

The original 12 members of the Football League (formed in 1888) were: **Accrington, Aston Villa, Blackburn Rov., Bolton Wand., Burnley, Derby Co., Everton, Notts Co., Preston N.E., Stoke City, W.B.A.** and **Wolves**.

Results on the opening day (September 8, 1888): Bolton Wand. 3, Derby Co. 6; Everton 2, Accrington 1; Preston N.E. 5, Burnley 2; Stoke City 0, W.B.A. 2; Wolves 1, Aston Villa 1. Preston N.E. had the biggest first-day crowd: 6,000. Blackburn Rov. and Notts Co. did not play that day. They kicked off a week later (September 15) – Blackburn Rov. 5, Accrington 5; Everton 2, Notts Co. 1.

FASTEST CLIMBS

Three promotions in four seasons by two clubs – **Swansea City:** 1978 third in Div.4; 1979 third in Div.3; 1981 third in Div.2; **Wimbledon:** 1983 Champions of Div.4; 1984 second in Div.3; 1986 third in Div.2.

MERSEYSIDE RECORD

Liverpool is the only city to have staged top-division football – through Everton and/or Liverpool – in **every season** since League football began in 1888.

EARLIEST RELEGATONS POST-WAR

From top division: **Q.P.R.** went down from the old First Division on March 29, 1969. From modern First Division: **Stockport Co.** on March 16, 2002, with 7 matches still to play.

LEAGUE RECORDS

MOST POINTS IN A SEASON

The following records applied before the introduction of three points for a win in the Football League in 1981-2.

Lincoln City set a **Football League** record in season 1975-6 with 74 points from 46 games (including 32 victories) in **Division 4**.

First Division: Liverpool (1978-9), 68 points from 42 matches.

Second Division: Tottenham (1919-20), 70 points from 42 matches.

Third Division: Aston Villa (1971-2) 70 points from 46 matches.

Since 3 points for win (pre-Premier League):

First Division: Everton (1984-5) and Liverpool (1987-8) 90 points: **Second Division:** Chelsea (1988-9) 99 points; **Third Division:** Bournemouth (1986-7) 97 points; **Fourth Division:** Swindon Town (1985-6) 102 points.

Since change of League format:
Premier League: Manchester Utd. (1993-4) 92 points; **First Division**: Sunderland (1998-9) 105 points (record for any division); **Second Division**: Fulham (1998-9) 101 points; **Third Division**: Plymouth Argyle (2001-02) 102 points.

Fewest Points: Doncaster Rov. 8 points (of possible 68) in Second Division, 1904-5. Stirling Albion 6 points (of possible 60) in Scottish League Division A, 1954-5.

DOUBLE CHAMPIONS

Nine men have played in and managed League Championship-winning teams:

Ted Drake Player – Arsenal 1934, 1935, 1938. Manager – Chelsea 1955.
Bill Nicholson Player – Tottenham 1951. Manager – Tottenham 1961.
Alf Ramsey Player – Tottenham 1951. Manager – Ipswich Town 1962.
Joe Mercer Player – Everton 1939, Arsenal 1948, 1953. Manager – Manchester City 1968.
Dave Mackay Player – Tottenham 1961. Manager – Derby Co. 1975.
Bob Paisley Player – Liverpool 1947. Manager – Liverpool 1976, 1977, 1979, 1980, 1982, 1983.
Howard Kendall Player – Everton 1970. Manager – Everton 1985, 1987.
Kenny Dalglish Player – Liverpool 1979, 1980, 1982, 1983, 1984. Player-manager – Liverpool 1986, 1988, 1990. Manager – Blackburn Rov. 1995.
George Graham Player – Arsenal 1971. Manager – Arsenal 1989, 1991.

MOST LEAGUE CHAMPIONSHIP MEDALS

Kenny Dalglish: 9 – 8 for Liverpool (5 as player, 1979-80-82-83-84; 3 as player-manager, 1986-88-90); 1 for Blackburn Rov. (as manager, 1995). As a player he also won 4 Scottish Championship medals with Celtic (1972-73-74-77). **Phil Neal**: 8 for Liverpool (1976-77-79-80-82-83-84-86); **Alan Hansen**: 8 for Liverpool (1979-80-82-83-84-86-88-90) : **Ryan Giggs**: 8 for Manchester Utd. (1993–94–96–97–99–2000–01–03).

CANTONA'S FOUR-TIMER

Eric Cantona played in four successive Championship-winning teams: Marseille 1990-1, Leeds Utd. 1991-2, Manchester Utd. 1992-3 and 1993-4.

ARRIVALS AND DEPARTURES

The following are the Football League arrivals and departures since 1923:

Year	*In*	*Out*
1923	Doncaster Rov.	Stalybridge Celtic
	New Brighton	
1927	Torquay Athletic	Aberdare Athletic
1928	Carlisle Utd.	Durham City
1929	York City	Ashington
1930	Thames	Merthyr Tydfil
1931	Mansfield Town	Newport County
	Chester City	Nelson
1932	Aldershot	Thames
	Newport County	Wigan Borough
1938	Ipswich Town	Gillingham
1950	Colchester Utd.	
	Gillingham	
	Scunthorpe Utd.	
	Shrewsbury Town	
1951	Workington	New Brighton
1960	Peterborough Utd.	Gateshead
1962	Oxford Utd.	Accrington Stanley (resigned)

1970	Cambridge Utd.	Bradford P.A.
1972	Hereford Utd.	Barrow
1977	Wimbledon	Workington
1978	Wigan Athletic	Southport
1987	Scarborough	Lincoln City
1988	Lincoln City	Newport County
1989	Maidstone Utd.	Darlington
1990	Darlington	Colchester Utd.
1991	Barnet	
1992	Colchester Utd.	Aldershot, Maidstone (resigned)
1993	Wycombe Wand.	Halifax Town
1997	Macclesfield Town	Hereford Utd.
1998	Halifax Town	Doncaster Rov.
1999	Cheltenham Town	Scarborough
2000	Kidderminster Harriers	Chester City
2001	Rushden & Diamonds	Barnet
2002	Boston Utd.	Halifax Town
2003	Yeovil Town, Doncaster Rov.	Exeter City, Shrewsbury Town

Leeds City were expelled from Div. 2 in October, 1919; Port Vale took over their fixtures.

EXTENSIONS TO FOOTBALL LEAGUE

Clubs	*Season*	*Clubs*	*Season*
12 to 14	1891-2	44 to 66+	1920-1
14 to 28*	1892-3	66 to 86†	1921-2
28 to 31	1893-4	86 to 88	1923-4
31 to 32	1894-5	88 to 92	1950-1
32 to 36	1898-9	92 to 93	1991-2
36 to 40	1905-6	(Reverted to 92 when Aldershot closed, March 1992)	
40 to 44	1919-20		

* Second Division formed. + Third Division (South) formed from Southern League clubs. † Third Division (North) formed.

Football League reduced to 70 clubs and three divisions on the formation of the F.A. Premier League in 1992; increased to 72 season 1994-5, when Premier League reduced to 20 clubs.

RECORD RUNS

Nott'm. Forest hold the record unbeaten sequence in the English League – 42 matches spanning the last 26 of season 1977-8 and the first 16 of 1978-9. The run began on 19, November 1977 and ended on December 9, 1978 when Forest lost 0-2 at Liverpool. Their sequence comprised 21 wins and 21 draws.

Best debuts: Ipswich Town won the First Division at their first attempt in 1961-2. **Peterborough Utd.** in their first season in the Football League (1960-1) not only won the Fourth Division but set the all-time scoring record for the League of 134 goals. **Hereford Utd.** were promoted from the Fourth Division in their first League season, 1972-3. **Wycombe Wand.** were promoted from the Third Division (via the play-offs) in their first League season, 1993-4.

Record winning sequence in a season: 14 consecutive League victories (all in Second Division): **Manchester Utd.** 1904-5, **Bristol City** 1905-6 and **Preston N.E.** 1950-1.

Best winning start to League season: 13 successive victories in Div. 3 by **Reading**, season 1985-6.

Best starts in 'old' First Division: 11 consecutive victories by **Tottenham** in 1960-1; 10 by **Manchester Utd.** in 1985-6. **Newcastle Utd.** won their first 11 matches in the **'new' First Division** in 1992-3.

Longest unbeaten sequence (all competitions): 40 by **Nott'm. Forest**, March-December 1978. It comprised 21 wins, 19 draws (in 29 League matches, 6 League Cup, 4 European Cup, 1 Charity Shield).

Longest unbeaten start to League season: 29 matches – **Leeds Utd.,** Div. 1 1973-4 (19 wins, 10 draws, goals 51-16); **Liverpool,** Div. 1 1987-8 (22 wins, 7 draws, goals 67-13).

Most consecutive League matches unbeaten in a season: 30 **Burnley** (21 wins, 9 draws, goals 68-17), September 6, 1920 – March 25, 1921, Div. 1.

Longest winning sequence in Div. 1: 13 matches by **Tottenham** – last two of season 1959-60, first 11 of 1960-1.

Longest winning one-season sequences in Championship: 13 matches by **Preston N.E.** in 1891-2 (September 12–January 2); 13 by **Sunderland,** also in 1891-2 (November 14–April 2).

Premier League – best starts to season: 12 games unbeaten – **Nott'm. Forest** in 1995-6, **Arsenal** in 1997-8, **Aston Villa** in 1998-9, **Liverpool** 2002-03.

Premier League – most consecutive wins (two seasons): 14 by **Arsenal,** February-August, 2002.

Premier League's record unbeaten runs: 30 matches (W25, D5) by **Arsenal** (Dec. 23, 2001–Oct. 6, 2002), ending with 2–1 defeat away to Everton. **In one season**, 25 matches (15W, 10D) by Nott'm. Forest (Feb.-Nov. 1995). It ended with a 7-0 defeat at Blackburn.

Premier League – longest unbeaten away run: 23 matches (W16, D7) by **Arsenal** (Aug. 18, 2001–Sept. 28, 2002).

Record home-win sequences: Bradford Park Avenue won 25 successive home games in Div. 3 North – the last 18 in 1926-7 and the first 7 the following season. Longest run of home wins in the top division is 21 by **Liverpool** – the last 9 of 1971-2 and the first 12 of 1972-3.

WORST SEQUENCES

Cambridge Utd. experienced the longest run without a win in Football League history in season 1983-4: 31 matches (21 lost, 10 drawn) between October 8 and April 23. They finished bottom of the Second Division.

Previous worst no-win League sequence was 30 by **Crewe Alexandra** (Div. 3 North) in season 1956-7.

Worst losing start to a League season: 12 consecutive defeats by **Manchester Utd.** (Div. 1) in 1930-1.

Worst Premier League start: **Swindon Town** 15 matches without win (6 draws, 9 defeats), 1993-4.

Worst Premier League sequence: Sunderland 20 matches without win (2 draws, 18 defeats) 2002-03.

Premier League – most consecutive defeats: Sunderland last 15 matches, season 2002-03.

Longest non-winning start to League season: 25 matches (4 draws, 21 defeats) by **Newport County**, Div. 4 (Aug. 15, 1970 – Jan. 9, 1971). Worst no-win League starts since then: 16 matches by **Burnley** (9 draws, 7 defeats in Div. 2, 1979-80); 16 by **Hull City** (10 draws, 6 defeats in Div. 2, 1989-90); 16 by **Sheffield Utd.** (4 draws, 12 defeats in Div. 1, 1990-91).

Most consecutive League defeats: 18 by **Darwen** (Div. 1) 1898-9. **In modern times:** 15 by **Walsall** (Div. 2, 1988-9) and **Sunderland** (Premiership, 2002-03), longest such sequences since last War.

Most League defeats in season: 34 by **Doncaster Rov.** (Div. 3) 1997-8.

Fewest League wins in season: 1 by **Loughborough Town** (Div. 2, season 1899-1900). They lost 27, drew 6, goals 18-100 and dropped out of the League. (See also Scottish section).

Fewest home Leagues wins in season: 1 by **Loughborough Town** (Div. 2, 1899-1900), **Notts Co.** (Div. 1, 1904-5), **Woolwich Arsenal** (Div. 1, 1912-13), **Blackpool** (Div. 1, 1966-7), **Rochdale** (Div. 3, 1973-4).

Most home League defeats in season: 18 by **Cambridge Utd.** (Div. 3, 1984-5).

Away League defeats record: 24 in row by **Nelson** (Div. 3 North) – 3 in April 1930 followed by all 21 in season 1930-31. They then dropped out of the League.

Biggest defeat in Champions' season: During **Newcastle Utd.'s** Championship-winning season in 1908-9, they were beaten 9-1 at home by Sunderland on December 5.

WORST START BY EVENTUAL CHAMPIONS

Sunderland took only 2 points from their first 7 matches in season 1912-13 (2 draws, 5 defeats). They won 25 of the remaining 31 games to clinch their fifth League title.

SUNDERLAND'S FOUR-TIME WORST

Sunderland were relegated to the Nationwide League at the end of season 2002–03 as the worst-ever team in the Premiership: fewest wins (4), fewest points (19), fewest goals (21) and with the longest run of consecutive defeats (15).

UNBEATEN LEAGUE SEASON

Only two clubs have completed an English League season unbeaten: **Preston N.E.** (22 matches in 1888-9, the League's first season) and **Liverpool** (28 matches in Div. 2, 1893-4).

100 PER CENT HOME RECORDS

Five clubs have won every home League match in a season, four of them in the old Second Division: **Liverpool** (14) in 1893-4, **Bury** (15) in 1894-5, **Sheffield Wed.** (17) in 1899-1900 and **Small Heath**, subsequently Birmingham (17) in 1902-3. The last club to do it, **Brentford**, won all 21 home games in Div. 3 South in 1929-30.

Rotherham Utd. just failed to equal that record in 1946-7. They won their first 20 home matches in Div. 3 North, then drew the last 3-3 v Rochdale.

WORST HOME RUNS

Most consecutive home League defeats: 8 by **Rochdale,** who took only 11 points in Div. 3 North in season 1931-2; 8 by **Stockport Co.** (Div.1) in season 2001-02; 8 by Sunderland (Premiership), season 2002–03.

Between November 1958 and October 1959 **Portsmouth** drew 2 and lost 14 out of 16 consecutive home games.

West Ham Utd. did not win in the Premiership at Upton Park in season 2002–03 until the 13th. home match on January 29.

MOST AWAY WINS IN SEASON

Doncaster Rov. won 18 of their 21 away League fixtures when winning the Div. 3 North Championship in 1946-7.

AWAY WINS RECORD

Most **consecutive away League wins: 10 by Tottenham** (Div. 1) – 8 at start of 1960-1, after ending previous season with 2 away victories.

100 PER CENT HOME WINS ON ONE DAY

Div. 1 – All 11 home teams won on Feb. 13, 1926 and on Dec. 10, 1955. **Div. 2** – All 12 home teams won on Nov. 26, 1988. **Div. 3**, all 12 home teams won in the week-end programme of Oct. 18-19, 1968.

NO HOME WINS IN DIV. ON ONE DAY

Div. 1 – 8 away wins, 3 draws in 11 matches on Sept. 6, 1986. **Div. 2** – 7 away wins, 4 draws in 11 matches on Dec. 26, 1987. **Premier League** – 6 away wins, 5 draws in 11 matches on Dec. 26, 1994.

The week-end **Premiership** programme on Dec. 7-8-9, 1996 produced no home win in the ten games (4 aways, 6 draws). There was again no home victory (3 away wins, 7 draws) in the week-end **Premiership** fixtures on September 23-24, 2000.

MOST DRAWS IN A SEASON (FOOTBALL LEAGUE)

23 by **Norwich City** (Div. 1, 1978-9), **Exeter City** (Div. 4, 1986-7). **Cardiff City** and **Hartlepool Utd.** (both Div. 3, 1997-8). Norwich City played 42 matches, the others 46.

MOST DRAWS IN ONE DIV. ON ONE DAY

On September 18, 1948 **nine** out of 11 First Division matches were drawn.

MOST DRAWS IN PREMIER DIV. PROGRAMME

Over the week-ends of December 2-3-4, 1995, and September 23-24, 2000, seven out of the ten matches finished level.

FEWEST DRAWS IN SEASON (46 MATCHES)

3 by **Reading** (Div. 3 South, 1951–2); **Bradford City Park Avenue** (Div. 3 North, 1956–7); **Tranmere Rov.** (Div. 4, 1984–5); **Southend Utd.** (Div. 3, 2002–3).

HIGHEST-SCORING DRAWS IN LEAGUE

Leicester City 6, Arsenal 6 (Div. 1 April 21, 1930) and **Charlton Athletic 6, Middlesbrough 6** (Div 2. October 22, 1960)

Latest 6-6 draw in first-class football was between Tranmere Rov. and Newcastle Utd. in the Zenith Data Systems Cup 1st. Round on October 1, 1991. The score went from 3-3 at 90 minutes to 6-6 after extra time, and Tranmere Rov. won 3-2 on penalties.

Most recent 5-5 draws in top division: Southampton v Coventry City (Div. 1, May 4, 1982); Q.P.R. v Newcastle Utd. (Div. 1, Sept. 22, 1984).

DRAWS RECORDS

Most consecutive drawn matches in Football League: 8 by **Torquay Utd.** (Div. 3), Oct. 25 – Dec. 13, 1969.

Longest sequence of draws by the same score: six 1-1 results by **Q.P.R.** in season 1957-8.

Tranmere Rov. became the first club to play **five consecutive 0-0 League draws**, in season 1997-8.

IDENTICAL RECORDS

There is only **one instance** of two clubs in one division finishing a season with identical records. In 1907-8, **Blackburn Rov.** and **Woolwich Arsenal** were bracketed equal 14th. in the First Division with these figures: P38, W12, D12, L14, Goals 51-63, Pts. 36.

The total of **1195 goals** scored in the Premier League in season 1993-4 was **repeated** in 1994-5.

CHAMPIONS OF ALL DIVISIONS

Wolves and **Burnley** are the only clubs to have won the Championships of the old **Divisions 1, 2, 3 and 4**. Wolves were also **Champions** of the **Third Division North**.

UPS & DOWNS RECORD

Northampton Town went from **Fourth Division** to **First** and back again in nine seasons (1961-9). **Carlisle Utd.** did the same from 1974-87.

MAJOR POINTS DEDUCTIONS

Season 2000–01: Chesterfield (Div. 3) had 9 points deducted (plus £20,000 fine) for breach of transfer regulations and under-reporting gate receipts. They finished in third (promotion) place.

Season 2002–03: Boston Utd. entered the Football League under a double penalty. On charges of contractual irregularities, they were fined £100,000 by the F.A. and deducted 4 points.

NIGHTMARE STARTS

Most goals conceded by a goalkeeper on League debut: 13 by **Steve Milton** when Halifax Town lost 13-0 at Stockport Co. (Div. 3 North) on January 6, 1934.

Post-war: 11 by Crewe Alexandra's new goalkeeper **Dennis Murray** (Div. 3 North) on September 29, 1951, when Lincoln City won 11-1.

RELEGATION ODD SPOTS

In season 1937-8, **Manchester City** were the highest-scoring team in the First Division with 80 goals (3 more than Champions Arsenal), but they finished in 21st place and were relegated – a year after winning the Championship. They scored more goals than they conceded (77).

Twelve years earlier, in 1925-6, City went down to Division 2 despite totalling 89 goals – still the most scored in any division by a relegated team. Manchester City also scored 31 F.A. Cup goals that season, but lost the Final 1-0 to Bolton Wanderers.

Cardiff City were relegated from Div. 1 in season 1928-9, despite conceding fewest goals in the division (59). They also scored fewest (43).

On their way to relegation from the First Division in season 1984–85, **Stoke City** twice lost ten matches in a row.

RELEGATION TREBLES

Two Football League clubs have been relegated three seasons in succession. **Bristol City** fell from First Division to Fourth in 1980-1-2, and **Wolves** did the same in 1984-5-6.

CHRISTMAS 'CERTAINTY'

West Ham Utd.'s demotion in May 2003 maintained the pattern that no club bottom of the Premiership at Christmas has ever avoided relegation.

OLDEST CLUBS

Oldest Association Football Club is **Sheffield F.C.** (formed in 1857). The original minute book is still in existence.

The oldest Football League clubs are **Notts Co.**, 1862; **Nott'm. Forest**, 1865; and **Sheffield Wed.**, 1866.

FOUR DIVISIONS

In **May, 1957**, the Football League decided to re-group the two sections of the Third Division into Third and Fourth Divisions in **season 1958-9**.

The Football League was reduced to three divisions on the formation of the F.A. Premier League in **1992**.

THREE UP – THREE DOWN

The Football League Annual General Meeting of June 1973 agreed to adopt the promotion and relegation system of three up and three down.

The **new system** came into effect in **season 1973-4** and applied only to the first three divisions; four clubs were still relegated from the Third and four promoted from the Fourth.

It was the first change in the promotion and relegation system for the top two divisions in 81 years.

PLAY-OFF FINALS

HIGHEST SCORES

Div. 1	1993	(Wembley)	Swindon Town 4, Leicester City 3
	1995	(Wembley)	Bolton Wand. 4, Reading 3
	1998	(Wembley)	Charlton Athletic 4, Sunderland 4 (Charlton Athletic won 7–6 on pens.)
Div. 2	1993	(Wembley)	W.B.A. 3, Port Vale 0
	2000	(Wembley)	Gillingham 3, Wigan Athletic 2
	2001	(Cardiff)	Walsall 3, Reading 2
Div. 3	2003	(Cardiff)	Bournemouth 5, Lincoln City 2

BIGGEST ATTENDANCES

Div. 1	1998	(Wembley)	Charlton Athletic v Sunderland	77,739
Div. 2	1999	(Wembley)	Manchester City v Gillingham	76,935
Div. 3	1997	(Wembley)	Northampton Town v Swansea City	46,804

MOST LEAGUE APPEARANCES

Players with more than 700 Football League appearances (as at end of season 2002-03):

1005 **Peter Shilton** 1966-97 (286 Leicester City, 110 Stoke City, 202 Nott'm. Forest, 188 Southampton, 175 Derby Co., 34 Plymouth Argyle, 1 Bolton Wand., 9 Leyton Orient).

931 **Tony Ford** 1975-2002 (423 Grimsby Town, 9 Sunderland, 112 Stoke City, 114 W.B.A., 5 Bradford City, 76 Scunthorpe Utd., 103 Mansfield Town, 89 Rochdale).

824 **Terry Paine** 1956-77 (713 Southampton, 111 Hereford).

795 **Tommy Hutchison** 1968-91 (165 Blackpool, 314 Coventry City, 46 Manchester City, 92 Burnley, 178 Swansea City). In addition, 68 Scottish League apps. for Alloa 1965-68, giving career League app. total of 863.

782 **Robbie James** 1973-94 (484 Swansea City, 48 Stoke City, 87 Q.P.R., 23 Leicester City, 89 Bradford City, 51 Cardiff City).

777 **Alan Oakes** 1959-84 (565 Manchester City, 211 Chester City, 1 Port Vale).

773 **Dave Beasant** 1980-2003 (340 Wimbledon, 20 Newcastle Utd., 6 Grimsby Town, 4 Wolves, 133 Chelsea, 88 Southampton, 139 Nott'm. F., 27 Portsmouth, 16 Brighton).

770 **John Trollope** 1960-80 (all for Swindon Town, record total for one club).

764 **Jimmy Dickinson** 1946-65 (all for Portsmouth).

761 **Roy Sproson** 1950-72 (all for Port Vale).

760 **Mick Tait** 1974-97 (64 Oxford Utd., 106 Carlisle Utd., 33 Hull City, 240 Portsmouth, 99 Reading, 79 Darlington, 139 Hartlepool Utd.).

758 **Billy Bonds** 1964-88 (95 Charlton Athletic, 663 West Ham Utd.).

758 **Ray Clemence** 1966-88 (48 Scunthorpe Utd., 470 Liverpool, 240 Tottenham).

757 **Pat Jennings** 1963-86 (48 Watford, 472 Tottenham, 237 Arsenal).

757 **Frank Worthington** 1966-88 (171 Huddersfield Town, 210 Leicester City, 84 Bolton Wand., 75 Birmingham City, 32 Leeds Utd., 19 Sunderland, 34 Southampton, 31 Brighton & H.A., 59 Tranmere Rov., 23 Preston N.E., 19 Stockport Co.).

749 **Ernie Moss** 1968-88 (469 Chesterfield, 35 Peterborough Utd., 57 Mansfield Town, 74 Port Vale, 11 Lincoln City, 44 Doncaster Rov., 26 Stockport Co., 23 Scarborough, 10 Rochdale).

746 **Les Chapman** 1966-88 (263 Oldham Athletic, 133 Huddersfield Town, 70 Stockport Co., 139 Bradford City, 88 Rochdale, 53 Preston N.E.).

744 **Asa Hartford** 1967-90 (214 W.B.A., 260 Manchester City, 3 Nott'm. F., 81 Everton, 28 Norwich City, 81 Bolton Wand., 45 Stockport Co., 7 Oldham Athletic, 25 Shrewsbury Town).

743 **Alan Ball** 1963-84 (146 Blackpool, 208 Everton, 177 Arsenal, 195 Southampton, 17 Bristol Rov.).

743 **John Hollins** 1963-84 (465 Chelsea, 151 Q.P.R., 127 Arsenal).

743 **Phil Parkes** 1968-91 (52 Walsall, 344 Q.P.R., 344 West Ham Utd., 3 Ipswich Town).

737 **Steve Bruce** 1979-99 (205 Gillingham, 141 Norwich City, 309 Manchester Utd. 72 Birmingham City, 10 Sheffield Utd.).

732 **Mick Mills** 1966-88 (591 Ipswich Town, 103 Southampton, 38 Stoke City).

731 **Ian Callaghan** 1959-81 (640 Liverpool, 76 Swansea City, 15 Crewe Alexandra).

725 **Steve Perryman** 1969-90 (655 Tottenham, 17 Oxford Utd., 53 Brentford).

722 **Martin Peters** 1961-81 (302 West Ham Utd., 189 Tottenham, 207 Norwich City, 24 Sheffield Utd.).

718 **Mike Channon** 1966-86 (511 Southampton, 72 Manchester City, 4 Newcastle Utd., 9 Bristol Rov., 88 Norwich City, 34 Portsmouth).

718 **Phil Neal** 1968-89 (186 Northampton Town, 455 Liverpool, 77 Bolton Wand.).

716 **Ron Harris** 1961-83 (655 Chelsea, 61 Brentford).
716 **Mike Summerbee** 1959-79 (218 Swindon Town, 357 Manchester City, 51 Burnley, 3 Blackpool, 87 Stockport Co.).
714 **Glenn Cockerill** 1976-98 (186 Lincoln City, 26 Swindon Town, 62 Sheffield Utd., 387 Southampton, 90 Leyton Orient, 40 Fulham, 23 Brentford).
712 **David Seaman** 1982-2003 (91 Peterborough Utd, 75 Birmngham City, 141 Q.P.R., 405 Arsenal).
705 **John Wile** 1968-86 (205 Peterborough Utd., 500 W.B.A.).
701 **Neville Southall** 1980-2000 (39 Bury, 578 Everton, 9 Port Vale, 9 Southend, 12 Stoke, 53 Torquay, 1 Bradford City).

• **Stanley Matthews** made 701 League apps. 1932-65 (322 Stoke City, 379 Blackpool), incl. 3 for Stoke City at start of 1939-40 before season abandoned (war).
• Goalkeeper **John Burridge** made a total of 771 League appearances in a 28-season career in English and Scottish football (1968-96). He played 691 games for 15 English clubs (Workington, Blackpool, Aston Villa, Southend Utd., Crystal Palace, Q.P.R., Wolves, Derby Co., Sheffield Utd., Southampton, Newcastle Utd., Scarborough, Lincoln City, Manchester City and Darlington) and 80 for 5 Scottish clubs (Hibernian, Aberdeen, Dumbarton, Falkirk and Queen of the South).

LONGEST LEAGUE APPEARANCE SEQUENCE

Harold Bell, centre-half of Tranmere Rov., was ever-present for the first nine post-war seasons (1946-55), achieving a League record of 401 consecutive matches. Counting F.A. Cup and other games, his run of successive appearances totalled 459.

The longest League sequence since Bell's was 394 appearances by goalkeeper **Dave Beasant** for Wimbledon, Newcastle Utd. and Chelsea. His nine-year run began on August 29, 1981 and was ended by a broken finger sustained in Chelsea's League Cup-tie against Portsmouth on October 31, 1990. Beasant's 394 consecutive League games comprised 304 for Wimbledon (1981-8), 20 for Newcastle Utd. (1988-9) and 70 for Chelsea (1989-90).

Phil Neal made 366 consecutive First Division appearances for Liverpool between December 1974 and September 1983, a remarkable sequence for an outfield player in top-division football.

EVER-PRESENT DEFENCE

The **entire defence** of Huddersfield Town played in all 42 Second Division matches in season 1952-3, namely, Bill Wheeler (goal), Ron Staniforth and Laurie Kelly (full-backs), Bill McGarry, Don McEvoy and Len Quested (half-backs). In addition, Vic Metcalfe played in all 42 League matches at outside-left.

FIRST SUBSTITUTE USED IN LEAGUE

Keith Peacock (Charlton Athletic), away to Bolton Wand. (Div. 2) on August 21, 1965.

FROM PROMOTION TO CHAMPIONS

Clubs who have become Champions of England a year after winning promotion: **Liverpool** 1905, 1906; **Everton** 1931, 1932; **Tottenham** 1950, 1951; **Ipswich Town** 1961, 1962; **Nott'm. Forest** 1977, 1978. The first four were placed top in both seasons: Forest finished third and first.

PREMIERSHIP'S FIRST MULTI-NATIONAL LINE-UP

Chelsea made history on December 26, 1999 when they started their Premiership match at Southampton without a single British player in the side. They won 2–1.

Fulham's Unique XI: In the Worthington Cup 3rd. Round at home to Bury on November 6, 2002, **Fulham** fielded 11 players of 11 different nationalities. Ten were full Internationals, with Lee Clark an England U–21 cap.

THREE-NATION CHAMPION

Trevor Steven earned eight Championship medals, in three countries: two with Everton (1985, 1987); five with Rangers (1990, 1991, 1993, 1994, 1995) and one with Marseille in 1992.

LEEDS NO-WAY AWAY

Leeds Utd., in 1992-3, provided the first instance of a club failing to win an away League match as reigning Champions.

PIONEERS IN 1888 AND 1992

Three clubs among the twelve who formed the Football League in 1888 were also founder members of the F.A. Premier League: **Aston Villa**, **Blackburn Rov.** and **Everton**.

CHAMPIONS (MODERN) WITH TWO CLUBS – PLAYERS

Francis Lee (Manchester City 1968, Derby Co. 1975); **Ray Kennedy** (Arsenal 1971, Liverpool 1979, 1980, 1982); **Archie Gemmill** (Derby Co. 1972, 1975, Nott'm. F. 1978); **John McGovern** (Derby Co. 1972, Nott'm. F. 1978) **Larry Lloyd** (Liverpool 1973, Nott'm. F. 1978); **Peter Withe** (Nott'm. F. 1978, Aston Villa 1981); **John Lukic** (Arsenal 1989, Leeds Utd. 1992); **Kevin Richardson** (Everton 1985, Arsenal 1989); **Eric Cantona** (Leeds Utd. 1992, Manchester Utd. 1993, 1994, 1996, 1997); **David Batty** (Leeds Utd. 1992, Blackburn Rov. 1995), **Bobby Mimms** (Everton 1987, Blackburn Rov. 1995), **Henning Berg** (Blackburn Rov. 1995, Manchester United 1999, 2001).

TITLE TURNABOUTS

In January 1996, Kevin Keegan's **Newcastle Utd.** led the Premier League by 13 points. They finished runners-up to Manchester Utd.

At Christmas 1997, **Arsenal** were 13 points behind leaders Manchester Utd. and still 11 points behind at the beginning of March 1998. But a run of 10 wins took the title to Highbury.

On March 2, 2003, **Arsenal**, with 9 games left, went 8 points clear of Manchester Utd., who had a match in hand. United won the Championship by 5 points.

• In March 2002, **Wolves** were in second (automatic promotion) place in Nationwide Div. 1, 11 points ahead of W.B.A., who had 2 games in hand. They were overtaken by Albion on the run-in, finished third, then failed in the play-offs. A year later they won promotion to the Premiership via the play-offs.

CLUB CLOSURES

Four clubs have left the Football League in mid-season: **Leeds City** (expelled Oct. 1919); **Wigan Borough** (Oct. 1931, debts of £20,000); **Accrington Stanley** (March 1962, debts £62,000); **Aldershot** (March 1992, debts £1.2m.). **Maidstone Utd.**, with debts of £650,000, closed August 1992, on the eve of the season.

FOUR-DIVISION MEN

In season 1986-7, goalkeeper **Eric Nixon,** became the first player to appear in **all four divisions** of the Football League **in one season**. He served two clubs in Div. 1: Manchester City (5 League games) and Southampton (4); in Div. 2 Bradford City (3); in Div. 3 Carlisle Utd. (16); and in Div. 4 Wolves (16). Total appearances: 44.

Harvey McCreadie, a teenage forward, played in four divisions over two seasons inside a calendar year – from Accrington (Div. 3) to Luton Town (Div. 1) in January 1960, to Div. 2 with Luton Town later that season and to Wrexham (Div. 4) in November.

Tony Cottee played in all four divisions in season 2000-01, for Leicester City (Premiership), Norwich City (Div. 1), Barnet (Div. 3, player-manager) and Millwall (Div. 2).

FATHERS & SONS

When player-manager **Ian Bowyer** (39) and **Gary Bowyer** (18) appeared together in the **Hereford Utd.** side at Scunthorpe Utd. (Div.4, April 21, 1990), they provided the first instance of father and son playing in the same team in a Football League match for 39 years. Ian Bowyer played as substitute, and Gary scored Hereford's injury-time equaliser in a 3-3 draw.

Alec (39) and **David** (just 17) **Herd** were the previous father-and-son duo in League football – for **Stockport Co.**, 2-0 winners at Hartlepool Utd. (Div.3 North) on May 5, 1951.

When **Preston N.E.** won 2-1 at Bury in Div. 3 on January 13, 1990, the opposing goalkeepers were brothers: **Alan Kelly** (21) for Preston N.E. and **Gary** (23) for Bury. Their father, **Alan Kelly Senior** (who kept goal for Preston N.E. in the 1964 F.A. Cup Final and won 47 Rep. of Ireland caps) flew from America to watch the sons he taught to keep goal line up on opposite sides.

George Eastham Snr. (manager) and son **George Eastham Jnr.** were inside-forward partners for Ards in the Irish League in season 1954-5.

FATHER & SON BOTH CHAMPIONS

John Aston Snr. won a Championship medal with Manchester Utd. in 1952 and **John Aston Jnr.** did so with Utd. in 1967.

FATHER & SON RIVAL MANAGERS

When **Bill Dodgin senior** took Bristol Rov. to Fulham for an F.A. Cup 1st Round tie in Nov. 1970, the opposing manager was his son, **Bill junior**.

FATHER & SON ON OPPOSITE SIDES

It happened for the first time in F.A. Cup history (1st. Qual. Round on Sept. 14, 1996) when 21-year-old **Nick Scaife** (Bishop Auckland) faced his father **Bobby** (41), who played for Pickering. Both were in midfield. Home side Bishops won 3-1.

THREE BROTHERS IN SAME SIDE

Southampton provided the first instance for 65 years of three brothers appearing together in a First Division side when **Danny Wallace** (24) and his 19-year-old twin brothers **Rodney** and **Ray** played against Sheffield Wed.on October 22, 1988. In all, they made 25 appearances together for Southampton until September 1989.

A previous instance in Div. 1 was provided by the Middlesbrough trio, **William**, **John** and **George Carr** with 24 League appearances together from January 1920 to October 1923.

The **Tonner** brothers, **Sam, James** and **Jack**, played together in 13 Second Division matches for Clapton Orient in season 1919-20.

Brothers **David**, **Donald** and **Robert Jack** played together in Plymouth Argyle's League side in 1920.

TWIN TEAM-MATES (see also Wallace twins above)

Twin brothers **David** and **Peter Jackson** played together for three League clubs (Wrexham, Bradford City and Tranmere Rov.) from 1954-62.

The **Morgan** twins, **Ian** and **Roger**, played regularly in the Q.P.R. forward line from 1964-68.

W.B.A's **Adam** and **James Chambers**, 18, were the first twins to represent England (v Cameroon in World Youth Championship, April 1999). They first played together in Albion's senior team, aged 19, in the League Cup 2nd. Round against Derby Co. in September 2000.

SIR TOM DOES THE HONOURS

Sir Tom Finney, England and Preston N.E. legend, opened the Football League's new headquarters on their return to Preston on Feb. 23, 1999. Preston had been the League's original base for 70 years before they moved to Lytham St. Annes in 1959.

SHORTENED MATCHES

The 0-0 score in the **Bradford City v Lincoln City Third Division fixture** on May 11, 1985, abandoned through fire after 40 minutes, was subsequently confirmed as a result. It is the shortest officially completed League match on record, and was the fourth of only five instances in Football League history of the score of an unfinished match being allowed to stand.

The other occasions: **Middlesbrough 4, Oldham Athletic 1** (Div. 1, April 3, 1915), abandoned after 55 minutes when Oldham Athletic defender Billy Cook refused to leave the field after being sent off; **Barrow 7, Gillingham 0** (Div. 4, Oct. 9, 1961), abandoned after 75 minutes because of bad light, the match having started late because of Gillingham's delayed arrival.

A crucial **Manchester derby** (Div.1) was abandoned after 85 minutes, and the result stood, on April 27, 1974, when a pitch invasion at Old Trafford followed the only goal, scored for City by Denis Law, which relegated Manchester Utd., Law's former club.

Only instance of a first-class match in England being abandoned 'through shortage of players' occurred in the First Division at Bramall Lane on March 16, 2002. Referee Eddie Wolstenholme halted play after 82 minutes because Sheffield Utd. were reduced to 6 players against W.B.A. They had had 3 men sent off (goalkeeper and 2 substitutes), and with all 3 substitutes used and 2 players injured, were left with fewer than the required minimum of 7 on the field. Promotion contenders W.B.A. were leading 3-0, and the League ordered the result to stand.

The last 60 seconds of **Birmingham City v Stoke City** (Div. 3, 1-1, on Feb. 29, 1992) were played behind locked doors. The ground had been cleared after a pitch invasion.

A First Division fixture, **Sheffield Wed. v Aston Villa** (Nov. 26, 1898), was abandoned through bad light after 79½ mins. with Wed. leading 3-1. The Football League ruled that the match should be completed, and the remaining 10½ minutes were played **four months later** (Mar. 13, 1899), when Wed. added another goal to make the result 4-1.

F.A. CUP RECORDS

(See also Goalscoring section)

CHIEF WINNERS

Ten Times: Manchester Utd.
Nine Times: Arsenal.
Eight Times: Tottenham.
Seven Times: Aston Villa.
Three Times in Succession: The Wanderers (1876-7-8) and Blackburn Rov. (1884-5-6).
Trophy Handed Back: The F.A. Cup became the Wanderers' absolute property in 1878, but they handed it back to the Association on condition that it was not to be won outright by any club.
In Successive Years by Professional Clubs: Blackburn Rov. (in 1890 and 1891); Newcastle Utd. (in 1951 and 1952); Tottenham (in 1961 and 1962); Tottenham again (in 1981 and 1982) and Arsenal (in 2002 and 2003).
Record Final-tie score: Bury 6, Derby Co. 0 (1903).
Most F.A. Cup wins at Wembley: Manchester Utd. 9, Arsenal 7, Tottenham 6, Newcastle Utd. 5, Liverpool 5.

F.A. CUP: SECOND DIVISION WINNERS

Notts Co. (1894), Wolves (1908), Barnsley (1912), West Bromwich Albion (1931), Sunderland (1973), Southampton (1976), West Ham Utd. (1980). When Tottenham won the Cup in 1901 they were a Southern League club.

'OUTSIDE' SEMI-FINALISTS

Wycombe Wand., in 2001, became only the eighth team from outside the top two divisions to reach the semi-finals, following Millwall (1937), Port Vale (1954), York City

(1955), Norwich City (1959), Crystal Palace (1976), Plymouth Argyle (1984) and Chesterfield (1997). None reached the Final.

FOURTH DIVISION QUARTER-FINALISTS

Oxford Utd. (1964), Colchester Utd. (1971), Bradford City (1976), Cambridge Utd. (1990).

F.A. CUP – FOUR TROPHIES

The latest F.A. Cup, first presented at Wembley in 1992, is a replica of the one it replaced, which had been in existence since 1911. 'It was falling apart and was not going to last much longer,' said the FA.

The new trophy is the fourth F.A. Cup. These were its predecessors:

1895 First stolen from shop in Birmingham while held by Aston Villa. Never seen again.
1910 Second presented to Lord Kinnaird on completing 21 years as F.A. president.
1992 Third 'gracefully retired' after 80 years' service (1911-91).

There are three F.A. Cups currently in existence. The retired model is still used for promotional work. The present trophy stays with the winners until the following March. A third, identical Cup is secreted in the F.A. vaults as cover against loss of the existing trophy.

FINALISTS RELEGATED

Four clubs have reached the F.A. Cup Final in a season of relegation, and all lost at Wembley: Manchester City 1926, Leicester City 1969, Brighton & H.A. 1983, Middlesbrough 1997.

GIANT-KILLING IN F.A. CUP

(* Home team; R = Replay; Season 2003 = 2002-03)

2003	*Chesterfield	1	Morecambe	2
2003	*Colchester Utd.	0	Chester City	1
2003	*Southport	4	Notts Co.	2
2003	Margate	1	Leyton Orient	0R
	(at Dover)			
2003	*Q.P.R.	1	Vauxhall Mot	1 R
	(Vauxhall won on pens.)			
2003	*Shrewsbury T.	2	Everton	1
2003	*Dagenham & R.	2	Plymouth	0 R
2003	*Darlington	2	Farnborough	3
2003	*Rochdale	2	Coventry City	0
2003	*Liverpool	0	Crystal Palace	2
2003	*Sunderland	0	Watford	1
2002	*Wigan Athletic	0	Canvey Island	1
2002	*Canvey Island	1	Nothampton T.	0
2002	*Dagenham & R	3	Exeter City	0R
2002	*Cardiff City	2	Leeds Utd.	1
2002	*Derby Co.	1	Bristol Rov.	3
2001	*Wycombe Wand.	2	Wolves	1
2001	*Wimbledon	2	Wycombe Wand.	2R
	(Wycombe Wand. won on pens).			
2001	*Leicester City	1	Wycombe Wand.	2
2001	*Brentford	1	Kingstonian	3
2001	*Yeovil	5	Colchester Utd.	1
2001	*Southend Utd.	0	Kingstonian	1
2001	*Nuneaton	1	Stoke City	0R
2001	*Hull City	0	Kettering	1R
2001	*Northwich Vic.	1	Bury	0R
2001	*Port Vale	1	Canvey Island	2R
2001	*Lincoln City	0	Dagenham & R.	1
2001	*Morecambe	2	Cambridge Utd.	1
2001	*Blackpool	0	Yeovil	1
2001	*Everton	0	Tranmere Rov.	3
2001	*Tranmere Rov.	4	Southampton	3R
2000	*Rushden & D	2	Scunthorpe Utd.	0
2000	*Chesterfield	1	Enfield	2
2000	*Hereford	1	York City	0
2000	*Ilkeston Town	2	Carlisle Utd.	1
2000	*Hereford	1	Hartlepool Utd.	0
1999	*Bedlington T	4	Colchester Utd.	1
1999	*Hednesford	3	Barnet	1
1999	*Mansfield Town	1	Southport	2
1999	*Rushden & D	1	Shrewsbury Town	0
1999	*Southend Utd.	0	Doncaster Rov.	1
1999	*Yeovil Town	2	Northampton T	0
1999	*Aston Villa	0	Fulham	2
1998	*Hull City	0	Hednesford	2
1998	Lincoln City	3	Emley	3R
	(at Huddersfield; Emley won on pens).			
1998	*Leyton O	0	Hendon	1R
1998	*Swindon Town	1	Stevenage	2
1998	*Stevenage	2	C'bridge Utd.	1
1997	*Millwall	0	Woking	1R
1997	*Brighton & H.A.	1	Sudbury Town	1R
	(Sudbury won on pens).			
1997	*Blackpool	0	Hednesford	1
1997	*Cambridge Utd.	0	Woking	2
1997	*Leyton O.	1	Stevenage	2
1997	*Hednesford	1	York City	0
1997	*Chesterfield	1	Nott'm. Forest	0
1996	*Hitchin	2	Bristol Rov.	1
1996	*Woking	2	Barnet	1R

1996 *Bury .... 0 Blyth Spartans 2
1996 *Gravesend .... 2 Colchester Utd. ... 0
1995 *Kingstonian .... 2 Brighton & H.A. ... 1
1995 *Enfield .... 1 Cardiff City 0
1995 *Marlow .... 2 Oxford Utd. 0
1995 *Woking .... 1 Barnet 0R
1995 *Hitchin .... 4 Hereford 2R
1995 *Torquay Utd. ...... 0 Enfield 1R
1995 *Altrincham .... 1 Wigan Athletic 0
1995 *Wrexham .... 2 Ipswich Town 1
1995 *Scarboro' .... 1 Port Vale 0
1994 *Colchester Utd. .. 3 Sutton 4
1994 *Yeovil .... 1 Fulham 0
1994 *Torquay Utd. ...... 0 Sutton 1
1994 *Halifax Town ...... 2 W.B.A. 1
1994 *Birmingham C. .. 1 Kid'minster 2
1994 *Stockport Co. ..... 2 Q.P.R. 1
1994 *Liverpool .... 0 Bristol City 1R
1994 *Arsenal .... 1 Bolton Wand. 3R
1994 *Leeds Utd. .... 2 Oxford Utd. 3R
1994 *Luton Town .... 2 Newcastle Utd. . 0R
1994 *Kidderminster .... 1 Preston N.E. 0
1994 *Cardiff City .... 1 Manchester City .. 0
1993 *Hereford .... 1 Yeovil 2R
1993 *Torquay Utd. ...... 2 Yeovil 5
1993 *Altrincham .... 2 Chester City 0R
1993 *Cardiff City .... 2 Bath 3
1993 *Chesterfield .... 2 Macclesfield 2R
(Macclesfield Town won on pens).
1993 *Marine .... 4 Halifax Town 1
1993 *Stafford .... 2 Lincoln City 1R
1993 *Hartlepool Utd. .. 1 Crystal Palace 0
1993 *Liverpool .... 0 Bolton Wand. 2R
1992 *Fulham .... 0 Hayes 2
1992 *Crawley .... 4 Northampton 2
1992 *Telford .... 2 Stoke City 1R
1992 *Aldershot .... 0 Enfield 1
1992 *Halifax Town ...... 1 Witton A. 2R
1992 *Maidstone .... 1 Kettering 2
1992 *Walsall .... 0 Yeovil 1R
1992 *Farnborough ...... 4 Torquay Utd. 3
1992 *Wrexham .... 2 Arsenal 1
1991 *Scarboro' .... 0 Leek 2
1991 *Northampton ..... 0 Barnet 1R
1991 *Hayes .... 1 Cardiff City 0R
1991 *Chorley .... 2 Bury 1
1991 *Shrewsbury T ..... 1 Wimbledon 0
1991 *W.B.A. .... 2 Woking 4
1990 *Aylesbury .... 1 Southend Utd. 0
1990 *Scarborough ...... 0 Whitley Bay 1
1990 *Welling .... 1 Gillingham 0R
1990 *Whitley Bay .... 2 Preston N.E. 0
1990 *Northampton ..... 1 Coventry City 0
1990 *Cambridge Utd. . 1 Millwall 0R
1989 *Sutton .... 2 Coventry City 1
1989 *Halifax Town ...... 2 Kettering 3R
1989 *Kettering .... 2 Bristol Rov. 1
1989 *Bognor .... 2 Exeter City 1
1989 *Leyton Orient ..... 0 Enfield 1R
1989 *Altrincham .... 3 Lincoln City 2
1989 *Wrexham .... 2 Runcorn 3R
1988 *Sutton .... 3 Aldershot 0
1988 *Peterborough ..... 1 Sutton 3
1988 *Carlisle Utd. ...... 2 Maccesfield 4
1988 *Macc'field .... 4 Rotherham Utd. ... 0
1988 *Chester City .... 0 Runcorn 1
1988 *Cambridge Utd. . 0 Yeovil 1
1987 *Caernarfon .... 1 Stockport Co. 0
1987 Chorley .... 3 Wolves 0R
(at Bolton)
1987 *Telford .... 3 Burnley 0
1987 *York City .... 1 Caernarfon 2R
1987 *Aldershot .... 3 Oxford Utd. 0
1987 *Wigan Athletic ... 1 Norwich City 0
1987 *Charlton Ath. ..... 1 Walsall 2
1986 *Stockport Co. ..... 0 Telford 1
1986 *Wycombe W. ...... 2 Colchester Utd. ... 0
1986 *Dagenham .... 2 Cambridge Utd. 1
1986 *Blackpool .... 1 Altrincham 2
1986 *Birmingham C. .. 1 Altrincham 2
1986 *Peterboro' .... 1 Leeds Utd. 0
1985 *Telford .... 2 Lincoln City 1
1985 *Preston N.E. ...... 1 Telford 4
1985 *Telford .... 2 Bradford City 1
1985 *Telford .... 3 Darlington 0R
1985 *Blackpool .... 0 Altrincham 1
1985 *Wimbledon .... 1 Nott'm. Forest ... 0R
1985 *Orient .... 2 W.B.A. 1
1985 *Dagenham .... 1 Peterborough 0
1985 *Swindon Town ... 1 Dagenham 2R
1985 *York City .... 1 Arsenal 0
1984 *Halifax Town ...... 2 Whitby 3
1984 *Bournemouth ..... 2 Manchester Utd. .. 0
1984 *Telford .... 3 Stockport Co. 0
1984 *Telford .... 3 Northampton 2R
1984 Telford .... 4 *Rochdale 1
1983 *Cardiff City .... 2 Weymouth 3
1981 *Exeter City .... 3 Leicester City 1R
1981 *Exeter City .... 4 Newcastle Utd. . 0R
1980 *Halifax Town ...... 1 Manchester City .. 0
1980 *Harlow .... 1 Leicester City 0R
1980 *Chelsea .... 0 Wigan Athletic 1
1979 *Newport .... 2 West Ham Utd. ... 1
1978 *Wrexham .... 4 Newcastle 1R
1978 *Stoke City .... 2 Blyth S 3
1976 *Leeds Utd. .... 0 Crystal Palace 1
1975 *Brighton & H.A. . 0 Leatherhead 1
1975 *Burnley .... 0 Wimbledon 1
1972 *Hereford .... 2 Newcastle 1R
1971 *Colchester Utd. .. 3 Leeds Utd. 2
1969 *Mansfield Town .. 3 West Ham Utd. ... 0
1967 *Swindon Town ... 3 West Ham Utd. . 0R
1967 *Manchester U. ... 1 Norwich City 2
1966 *Ipswich Town ..... 2 Southport 3R
1965 *Peterboro' .... 2 Arsenal 1
1964 *Newcastle Utd. .. 1 Bedford Town 2
1964 *Aldershot .... 2 Aston Villa 1R
1961 *Coventry City ..... 1 Kings Lynn 2

1961	*Chelsea	1	Crewe Alex.	2
1960	*Manchester City	1	South'ton	5
1959	*Norwich City	3	Manchester U	0
1959	*Worcester	2	Liverpool	1
1959	*Tooting	3	Bournemouth	1
1959	*Tooting	2	Northampton	1
1958	*Newcastle Utd.	1	Scunthorpe Utd.	3
1957	*Wolves	0	Bournemouth	1
1957	*Bournemouth	3	Tottenham	1
1957	*Derby Co.	1	N. Brighton	3
1956	*Derby Co.	1	Boston United	6
1955	*York City	2	Tottenham	1
1955	*Blackpool	0	York City	2
1954	*Arsenal	1	Norwich City	2
1954	*Port Vale	2	Blackpool	0
1952	*Everton	1	Leyton Orient	3
1949	*Yeovil Town	2	Sunderland	1
1948	*Colchester Utd.	1	Huddersfield	0
1948	*Arsenal	0	Bradford City	1
1938	*Chelmsford	4	Southampton	1
1933	*Walsall	2	Arsenal	0
1922	*Everton	0	Crystal Palace	6

YEOVIL TOP GIANT-KILLERS

Yeovil's victories over Colchester Utd. and Blackpool in season 2000-01 gave them a total of 20 F.A. Cup wins against League opponents. They hold another non-League record by reaching the third round 13 times.

This is Yeovil's triumphant Cup record against League clubs: 1924-5 Bournemouth 3-2; 1934-5 Crystal Palace 3-0, Exeter City 4-1; 1938-9 Brighton & H.A. 2-1; 1948-9 Bury 3-1, Sunderland 2-1; 1958-9 Southend Utd. 1-0; 1960-1 Walsall 1-0; 1963-4 Southend Utd. 1-0, Crystal Palace 3-1; 1970-1 Bournemouth 1-0; 1972-3 Brentford 2-1; 1987-8 Cambridge Utd. 1-0; 1991-2 Walsall 1-0; 1992-3 Torquay Utd. 5-2, Hereford 2-1; 1993-4 Fulham 1-0; 1998-9 Northampton 2-0; 2000-01 Colchester Utd. 5-1, Blackpool 1-0.

NON-LEAGUE BEST IN F.A. CUP

Since League football began in 1888, three non-League clubs have reached the F.A. Cup Final. **Sheffield Wed.** (Football Alliance) were runners-up in 1890, as were **Southampton** (Southern League) in 1900 and 1902. **Tottenham** won the Cup as a Southern League team in 1901.

Otherwise, the **furthest progress** by non-League clubs has been to the **5th. Round** on 5 occasions: Colchester Utd. 1948, Yeovil 1949, Blyth Spartans 1978, Telford 1985 and Kidderminster 1994.

Greatest number of non-League sides to reach the **3rd. Round** is 6 in 1978: Blyth, Enfield, Scarborough, Tilbury, Wealdstone and Wigan Athletic. Since then, 5 in 1988: Bath City, Macclesfield Town, Maidstone, Sutton and Yeovil.

Most to reach **Round 4**: 3 in 1957 (Rhyl, New Brighton, Peterborough Utd.) and 1975 (Leatherhead, Stafford and Wimbledon).

Five non-League clubs reaching **Round 3** in 2001 was a Conference record. They were Chester City, Yeovil, Dagenham & Redbridge, Morecambe and Kingstonian.

In season 2002–3, **Team Bath** became the first University-based side to reach the F.A. Cup 1st. Round since Oxford University (Finalists in 1880).

NON-LEAGUE 'LAST TIMES' IN F.A. CUP

Last time no non-League club reached Round 3: 1951. Last time only one did so: 1969 (Kettering Town). Last time only two: 2000 (Hereford and Rushden & Diamonds) and 2002 (Canvey Island and Dagenham & Redbridge).

TOP-DIVISION SCALPS

Victories in F.A. Cup by non-League clubs over top-division teams since 1900 include:- 1900-1 (Final, replay); **Tottenham** 3, Sheffield Utd. 1 (Tottenham then in Southern League); 1919-20 **Cardiff City** 2, Oldham Athletic 0, and Sheffield Wed. 0, **Darlington** 2; 1923-4 **Corinthians** 1, Blackburn Rov. 0; 1947-8 **Colchester Utd.** 1, Huddersfield Town 0; 1948-9 **Yeovil Town** 2, Sunderland 1; 1971-2 **Hereford Utd.** 2, Newcastle Utd. 1; 1974-5 Burnley 0, **Wimbledon** 1; 1985-6 Birmingham City 1, **Altrincham** 2; 1988-9 **Sutton Utd.** 2, Coventry City 1.

MOST WEMBLEY FINALS

Eight players appeared in five F.A. Cup Finals at Wembley, replays excluded:-

- Joe Hulme (Arsenal: 1927, lost; 1930 won; 1932 lost; 1936 won; Huddersfield Town: 1938 lost).
- Johnny Giles (Manchester Utd.: 1963 won; Leeds Utd.: 1965 lost; 1970 drew at Wembley, lost replay at Old Trafford; 1972 won; 1973 lost).
- Pat Rice (all for Arsenal: 1971 won; 1972 lost; 1978 lost; 1979 won; 1980 lost).
- Frank Stapleton (Arsenal: 1978 lost; 1979 won; 1980 lost; Manchester Utd.: 1983 won; 1985 won).
- Ray Clemence (Liverpool: 1971 lost; 1974 won; 1977 lost; Tottenham: 1982 won; 1987 lost).
- Mark Hughes (Manchester Utd.: 1985 won; 1990 won; 1994 won; 1995 lost; Chelsea: 1997 won).
- John Barnes (Watford: 1984 lost; Liverpool: 1988 lost; 1989 won; 1996 lost; Newcastle Utd.: 1998, sub, lost): he was the first player to lose Wembley F.A. Cup Finals with three different clubs.
- Roy Keane (Nott'm Forest: 1991 lost; Manchester Utd.: 1994 won; 1995 lost; 1996 won; 1999 won).

Stapleton, Clemence and Hughes also played in a replay, making six actual F.A. Cup Final appearances for each of them.

Glenn Hoddle also made six F.A. Cup Final appearances at Wembley: 5 for Tottenham (incl. 2 replays), in 1981, 1982 and 1987, and 1 for Chelsea as sub in 1994.

▲Paul Bracewell played in four F.A. Cup Finals without being on the winning side – for Everton 1985, 1986, 1989, Sunderland 1992.

MOST WEMBLEY/CARDIFF FINAL APPEARANCES

5 by **David Seaman** and **Ray Parlour** (Arsenal): 1993 won; 1998 won; 2001 lost; 2002 won; 2003 won.

F.A. CUP-WINNING GOALKEEPER-CAPTAINS

1988 **Dave Beasant** (Wimbledon); 2003 **David Seaman** (Arsenal).

F.A. CUP DEBUTS IN FINAL

Alan Davies (Manchester Utd. V Brighton & H.A., 1983); **Chris Baird** (Southampton v Arsenal, 2003).

F.A. CUP SEMI-FINALS AT WEMBLEY

1991 Tottenham 3, Arsenal 1; **1993** Sheffield Wed. 2, Sheffield Utd. 1; Arsenal 1, Tottenham 0; **1994** Chelsea 2, Luton 0; Manchester Utd. 1, Oldham 1; **2000** Aston Villa beat Bolton 4-1 on pens. (after 0-0); Chelsea 2, Newcastle Utd 1.

FIRST F.A. CUP ENTRANTS (1871-2)

Barnes, Civil Service, Crystal Palace, Clapham Rov., Donnington School (Spalding), Hampstead Heathens, Harrow Chequers, Hitchin, Maidenhead, Marlow, Queen's Park (Glasgow), Reigate Priory, Royal Engineers, Upton Park and Wanderers. Total 15. Three scratched. **Record F.A. Cup entry 674 in 1921.**

CUP 'FIRSTS'

Out of country: Cardiff City, by defeating Arsenal 1-0 in the 1927 Final at Wembley, became the first and only club to take the F.A. Cup out of England.

All-English Winning XI: First club to win the F.A. Cup with all-English XI: Blackburn Olympic in 1883. Others since: W.B.A. in 1888 and 1931, Bolton Wand. (1958), Manchester City (1969), West Ham Utd. (1964 and 1975).

Non-English Winning XI: Liverpool in 1986 (Mark Lawrenson, born Preston N.E., was a Rep. of Ireland player).

Won both Cups: Old Carthusians won the F.A. Cup in 1881 and the F.A. Amateur Cup in 1894 and 1897. **Wimbledon** won Amateur Cup in 1963, F.A. Cup in 1988.

MOST GAMES NEEDED TO WIN F.A. CUP

Barnsley played a record 12 matches (20 hours' football) to win the F.A. Cup in season 1911-12. All six replays (one in Rd. 1, three in Rd. 4 and one in each of semi-final and Final) were brought about by goalless draws.

Arsenal played 11 F.A. Cup games when winning the trophy in 1979. Five of them were in the 3rd. Rd. against Sheffield Wed..

LONGEST F.A. CUP TIES

6 matches (11 hours): **Alvechurch v Oxford City** (4th. qual. round, 1971-2). Alvechurch won 1-0.

5 matches (9 hours, 22 mins – record for competition proper): **Stoke City v Bury** (3rd. round, 1954-5). Stoke City won 3-2.

5 matches: Chelsea v Burnley (4th. round, 1955-6). Chelsea won 2-0.

5 matches: Hull City v Darlington (2nd. round, 1960-1). Hull City won 3-0.

5 matches: Arsenal v Sheffield Wed. (3rd. round, 1978-9). Arsenal won 2-0.

Other marathons (qualifying comp., all 5 matches, 9 hours): **Barrow v Gillingham** (last qual. round, 1924-5) – winners Barrow; **Leyton v Ilford** (3rd. qual. round, 1924-5) – winners Leyton; **Falmouth Town v Bideford** (3rd. qual. round, 1973-4) – winners Bideford.

End of Cup Final replays: The F.A. decided that, with effect from 1999, there would be no Cup Final replays. In the event of a draw after extra time, the match would be decided on penalties.

F.A. Cup marathons ended in season 1991-2, when the penalty shoot-out was introduced to decide ties still level after one replay and extra time.

- In 1932-3 **Brighton & H.A.** (Div. 3 South) played 11 F.A. Cup games, including replays, and scored 43 goals, without getting past Rd 5. They forgot to claim exemption and had to play from 1st Qual. Round.

LONGEST ROUND

The longest round in F.A. Cup history was the **third round** in **season 1962-3**. It took 66 days to complete, lasting from January 5 to March 11, and included 261 postponements because of bad weather.

LONGEST UNBEATEN F.A. CUP RUN

23 matches by **Blackburn Rov.** In winning the Cup in three consecutive years (1884-5-6), they won 21 ties (one in a replay), and their first Cup defeat in four seasons was in a first round replay of the next competition.

RE-STAGED F.A. CUP TIES

Sixth round, March 9, 1974: Newcastle Utd. 4, Nott'm. Forest 3. Match declared void by F.A. and ordered to be replayed following a pitch invasion after Newcastle Utd. had a player sent off. Forest claimed the hold-up caused the game to change its pattern. The tie went to two further matches at Goodison Park (0-0, then 1-0 to Newcastle Utd.).

Third round, January 5, 1985: Burton Albion 1, Leicester City 6 (at Derby Co.). Burton goalkeeper Paul Evans was hit on the head by a missile thrown from the crowd, and continued in a daze. The F.A. ordered the tie to be played again, behind closed doors at Coventry City (Leicester City won 1- 0).

First round replay, November 25, 1992: Peterborough Utd. 9 (Tony Philliskirk 5), Kingstonian 1. Match expunged from records because, at 3-0 after 57 mins, Kingstonian were reduced to ten men when goalkeeper Adrian Blake was concussed by a 50 pence coin thrown from the crowd. The tie was re-staged on the same ground behind closed doors (Peterborough Utd. won 1-0).

Fifth round: Within an hour of Cup-holders Arsenal beating Sheffield Utd. 2-1 at Highbury on February 13, 1999, the Football Association took the unprecedented step of declaring the match void because an unwritten rule of sportsmanship had been broken. With United's Lee Morris lying injured, their goalkeeper Alan Kelly kicked the ball into touch. Play resumed with Arsenal's Ray Parlour throwing it in the direction of

Kelly, but Nwankwo Kanu took possession and centred for Marc Overmars to score the 'winning' goal. After four minutes of protests by manager Steve Bruce and his players, referee Peter Jones confirmed the goal. Both managers absolved Kanu of cheating but Arsenal's Arsene Wenger offered to replay the match. With the F.A. immediately approving, it was re-staged at Highbury ten days later (ticket prices halved) and Arsenal again won 2-1.

F.A. CUP PRIZE MONEY

The makeover of the F.A. Cup competition took off in 2001-02 with the introduction of prize money round by round (semi-finals excepted). Cup winners Arsenal received £2,675,000.

Payments were made to winning clubs as follows: Extra Prelim. Round £500; Prelim. Round £1,000; 1st Qual. Round £7,500; 2nd Qual. Round £7,500; 3rd Qual. Round £10,000; 4th Qual. Round £20,000; 1st Round proper £20,000; 2nd Round £30,000; 3rd Round £50,000; 4th Round £75,000; 5th Round £150,000; 6th Round £400,000; Runners-up £1m; Winners £2m.

The same scale of payments applied in season 2002-03.

F.A. CUP FOLLIES 1999-2000

The F.A. broke with tradition by deciding the 3rd. Round should be moved from its regular January date and staged before Christmas. Criticism was strong, gates poor and the 3rd. Round in 2001-01 reverted to the New Year.

By allowing the holders Manchester Utd. to withdraw from the 1999-2000 Cup competition in order to play in FIFA's inaugural World Club Championship in Brazil in January, the F.A. were left with an odd number of clubs in the 3rd. Round. Their solution was a **'lucky losers'** draw among clubs knocked out in Round 2. Darlington, beaten at Gillingham, won it to re-enter the competition, then lost 2-1 away to Aston Villa.

WAR-TIME MARATHON

Match of 203 minutes: Stockport Co.'s second-leg tie with Doncaster Rov. in the Third Division North Cup, March 30, 1946, lasted 203 minutes and a replay was still necessary. Both legs were drawn 2-2 and Doncaster Rov. won the replay 4-0.

F.A. CUP FINAL HAT-TRICKS

There have been only three in the history of the competition: **Billy Townley** (Blackburn Rov., 1890), **Jimmy Logan** (Notts Co., 1894) and **Stan Mortensen** (Blackpool, 1953).

FIVE WINNING MEDALS

The Hon. Arthur Kinnaird (The Wanderers and Old Etonians), **Charles Wollaston** (The Wanderers) and **Jimmy Forrest** (Blackburn Rov.) each earned five F.A. Cup winners' medals. Kinnaird, later president of the F.A., played in nine of the first 12 F.A. Cup Finals, and was on the winning side three times for The Wanderers, in 1873 (captain), 1877, 1878 (captain), and twice as captain of Old Etonians (1879, 1882).

MOST F.A. CUP WINNERS' MEDALS AT WEMBLEY

4 – **Mark Hughes** (3 for Manchester Utd., 1 for Chelsea).

3 – **18 players: Dick Pym** (3 clean sheets in Finals), **Bob Haworth, Jimmy Seddon, Harry Nuttall, Billy Butler** (all Bolton Wand.); **David Jack** (2 Bolton Wand., 1 Arsenal); **Bob Cowell, Jack Milburn, Bobby Mitchell** (all Newcastle Utd.); **Dave Mackay** (Tottenham); **Frank Stapleton** (1 Arsenal, 2 Manchester Utd.); **Bryan Robson** (3 times winning captain), **Arthur Albiston, Gary Pallister** (all Manchester Utd.); **Bruce Grobbelaar, Steve Nicol, Ian Rush** (all Liverpool); **Roy Keane, Peter Schmeichel; Dennis Wise** (1 Wimbledon, 2 Chelsea).

- Arsenal's **David Seaman** and **Ray Parlour** have each earned 4 winners' medals (2 at Wembley, 2 at Cardiff).

MOST F.A. CUP APPEARANCES

88 by **Ian Callaghan** (79 for Liverpool, 7 for Swansea City, 2 for Crewe Alexandra); 87 by **John Barnes** (31 for Watford, 51 for Liverpool, 5 for Newcastle Utd.); 86 by **Stanley Matthews** (37 for Stoke City, 49 for Blackpool); 86 by **Peter Shilton** for six clubs (Leicester City, Stoke City, Nott'm. Forest, Southampton, Derby Co. and Plymouth Argyle); 84 by **Bobby Charlton** (80 for Manchester Utd., 4 for Preston N.E.); 81 by **David Seaman** (5 for Peterborough Utd., 5 for Birmingham City, 17 for Q.P.R., 54 for Arsenal.

THREE-CLUB FINALISTS

Three players have appeared in the F.A. Final for three clubs: **Harold Halse** for Manchester Utd. (1909), Aston Villa (1913) and Chelsea (1915); **Ernie Taylor** for Newcastle Utd. (1951), Blackpool (1953) and Manchester Utd. (1958); **John Barnes** for Watford (1984), Liverpool (1998, 1989, 1996) and Newcastle Utd. (1998).

CUP MAN WITH TWO CLUBS IN SAME SEASON

Stan Crowther, who played for Aston Villa against Manchester Utd. in the 1957 F.A. Cup Final, appeared for both Aston Villa and United in the 1957-8 competition. United signed him directly after the Munich air crash and, in the circumstances, he was given special dispensation to play for them in the Cup, including the Final.

CAPTAIN'S CUP DOUBLE

Martin Buchan is the only player to have captained Scottish and English F.A. Cup-winning teams – Aberdeen in 1970 and Manchester Utd. in 1977.

MEDALS BEFORE AND AFTER

Two players appeared in F.A. Cup Final teams before and after the war: **Raich Carter** was twice a winner (Sunderland 1937, Derby Co. 1946) and **Willie Fagan** twice on the losing side (Preston N.E. 1937, Liverpool 1950).

DELANEY'S COLLECTION

Scotland winger **Jimmy Delaney** uniquely earned Scottish, English, N. Ireland and Rep. of Ireland cup medals. He was a winner with Celtic (1937), Manchester Utd. (1948) and Derry City (1954) and a runner-up with Cork City (1956).

STARS WHO MISSED OUT

Internationals who never won an F.A. Cup winner's medal include: **Tommy Lawton, Tom Finney, Johnny Haynes, Gordon Banks, George Best, Terry Butcher, Peter Shilton, Martin Peters, Nobby Stiles, Alan Ball** and **Malcolm Macdonald.**

CUP WINNERS AT NO COST

Not one member of **Bolton's** 1958 F.A. Cup-winning team cost the club a transfer fee. Five were Internationals and the eleven each joined the club for a £10 signing-on fee.

ALL-INTERNATIONAL CUP WINNERS

In **Manchester Utd.'s** 1985 Cup-winning team v Everton, all 11 players were full Internationals, as was the substitute who played. So were ten of Everton's team.

Arsenal's Cup-winning line-ups in the 2002 and 2003 Finals were all full Internationals.

NO-CAP CUP WINNERS

Sunderland, in 1973, were the last F.A. Cup-winning team not to include an International player, although some were capped later.

HIGH-SCORING SEMI-FINALS

The **record team score** in F.A. Cup semi-finals is 6: 1891-2 WBA 6, Nott'm. Forest 2; 1907-8 Newcastle Utd. 6, Fulham 0; 1933-4 Manchester City 6, Aston Villa 1.

Most goals in semi-finals (aggregate): 17 in 1892 (4 matches) and 1899 (5 matches). In modern times: 15 in 1958 (3 matches, including Manchester Utd. 5, Fulham 3 – highest-scoring semi-final since last war); 16 in 1989-90 (Crystal Palace 4, Liverpool 3; Manchester Utd. v Oldham Athletic 3-3, 2-1. **All 16 goals** in those three matches were scored by **different players**.

Last hat-trick in an F.A. Cup semi-final was scored by **Alex Dawson** for Manchester Utd. in 5-3 replay win against Fulham at Highbury in 1958.

FOUR SPECIAL AWAYS

For the only time in F.A. Cup history, **all four quarter-finals** in season 1986-7 were won by the away team.

F.A. CUP – DRAWS RECORD

In season 1985-6, **seven** of the eight F.A. Cup 5th. Round ties went to replays – a record for that stage of the competition.

LUCK OF THE DRAW

In the F.A. Cup on Jan. 11, 1947, eight of **London**'s ten Football League clubs involved in the 3rd. Round were drawn at home (including Chelsea v Arsenal). Only Crystal Palace played outside the capital (at Newcastle Utd.).

Contrast: In the 3rd. Round in Jan. 1992, Charlton Athletic were the only London club drawn at home (against Barnet), but the venue of the Farnborough v West Ham Utd. tie was reversed on police instruction. So Upton Park staged Cup-ties on successive days, with West Ham Utd. at home on the Saturday and Charlton Athletic (who shared the ground) on Sunday.

Arsenal were drawn away in every round on the way to reaching the F.A. Cup Finals of 1971 and 1972. **Manchester Utd.** won the Cup in 1990 without playing once at home.

The 1999 F.A. Cup finalists **Manchester Utd.** and **Newcastle Utd.** were both drawn at home every time in Rounds 3-6.

On their way to the semi-finals of both domestic Cup competitions in season 2002–03, **Sheffield Utd.** were drawn at home ten times out of ten and won all ten matches – six in the League's Worthington Cup and four in the F.A. Cup.

F.A. CUP: ALL TOP-DIVISION VICTIMS

Only instance of an F.A. Cup-winning club meeting top-division opponents in every round was provided by Manchester Utd. in 1947-8. They beat Aston Villa, Liverpool, Charlton Athletic, Preston N.E., then Derby Co. in the semi-final and Blackpool in the Final.

HOME ADVANTAGE

For the first time in F.A. Cup history, all eight ties in the 1992-3 5th. Round were won (no replays) by the **clubs drawn at home**. Only other instance of eight home wins at the 'last 16' stage of the F.A. Cup was in 1889-90, in what was then the 2nd. Round.

FEWEST TOP-DIVISION CLUBS IN LAST 16 (5TH. ROUND)

5 in 1958; **6** in 1927, 1970, 1982; **7** in 1994, 2003; **8** in 2002.

SIXTH-ROUND ELITE

For the first time in F.A. Cup 6th. Round history, dating from 1926, when the format of the competition changed, **all eight quarter-finalists** in 1995-6 were from the top division.

F.A. CUP SEMI-FINAL – DOUBLE DERBIES

There have been only two instances of both F.A. Cup semi-finals in the same year being local derbies: **1950** Liverpool beat Everton 2-0 (Maine Road), Arsenal beat Chelsea 1-0 after 2-2 draw (both at Tottenham); **1993** Arsenal beat Tottenham 1-0 (Wembley), Sheffield Wed. beat Sheffield Utd. 2-1 (Wembley).

TOP CLUB DISTINCTION

Since the Football League began in 1888, there has never been an F.A. Cup Final in which **neither club** represented the top division.

SPURS OUT – AND IN

Tottenham were banned, pre-season, from the 1994-5 F.A. Cup competition because of financial irregularities, but were readmitted on appeal and reached the semi-finals.

BROTHERS IN F.A. CUP FINAL TEAMS (Modern Times)

1950 Denis and Leslie Compton (Arsenal); **1952** George and Ted Robledo (Newcastle Utd.); **1967** Ron and Allan Harris (Chelsea); **1977** Jimmy and Brian Greenhoff (Manchester Utd.); **1996** and **1999** Gary and Phil Neville (Manchester Utd.)

F.A. CUP – FIRST SPONSORS

Littlewoods Pools became the first sponsors of the F.A. Cup in season 1994-5 in a £14m., 4-year deal.

French insurance giants **AXA** took over (season 1998-9) in a sponsorship worth £25m. over 4 years.

TRADITION RETURNS

With effect May, 2003, the F.A. Cup Final reverted to being played on the last Saturday of the season.

FIRST GOALKEEPER-SUBSTITUTE IN CUP FINAL

Paul Jones (Southampton), who replaced the injured Antti Niemi against Arsenal.

LEAGUE CUP RECORDS

(See also Goalscoring section)

Highest scores: West Ham Utd. 10-0 v Bury (2nd. Rd., 2nd. Leg 1983-4; agg. 12-1); Liverpool 10-0 v Fulham (2nd. Rd., 1st. Leg 1986-7; agg. 13-2).

Most League Cup goals (career): 49 Geoff Hurst (43 West Ham Utd., 6 Stoke City, 1960-75); 49 Ian Rush (48 Liverpool, 1 Newcastle Utd., 1981-98).

Highest scorer (season): 12 Clive Allen (Tottenham 1986-7 in 9 apps).

Most goals in match: 6 Frank Bunn (Oldham Athletic v Scarborough, 3rd. Rd., 1989-90).

Fewest goals conceded by winners: 3 by Leeds Utd. (1967-8), Tottenham (1970-1), Aston Villa (1995-6).

Most winner's medals: 5 Ian Rush (Liverpool).

Most appearances in Final: 6 Kenny Dalglish (Liverpool 1978-87), Ian Rush (Liverpool 1981-95).

Alan Hardaker Man of the Match Award was introduced in the 1990 Final, in recognition of the League's late secretary who proposed the competition in 1960.

League Cup sponsors: Milk Cup 1981-6, Littlewoods Cup 1987-90, Rumbelows Cup 1991-2, Coca-Cola Cup 1993-8. Bass Brewers took over from season 1998-9 with a 5-year sponsorship of the Worthington Cup worth £23m. It ended in 2003.

Norwich City unique: In 1985, Norwich City became (and they remain) the only club to win a major domestic cup and be relegated in the same season. They won the League's Milk Cup and went down from the old First Division.

Liverpool's League Cup records: Winners a record 7 times. **Ian Rush** only player to win 5 times. Rush also first to play in 8 winning teams in Cup Finals **at Wembley**, all with Liverpool (F.A. Cup 1986-89-92; League Cup 1981-82-83-84-95).

Britain's first under-cover Cup Final: Worthington (League) Cup Final between Blackburn Rov. and Tottenham at Cardiff's Millennium Stadium on Sunday, February 24, 2002. With rain forecast, the retractable roof was closed on the morning of the match.

DISCIPLINE

SENDINGS-OFF

The record total of sendings-off for a season in **English domestic football competitions** is 437 in 2001–02 (excluding non-League dismissals in F.A. Cup). They comprised 78 red cards for Premiership club players (66 League, 6 F.A. Cup, 6 Worthington Cup) and 359 Nationwide club players (329 League, 11 F.A. Cup, 16 Worthington Cup, 2 LDV Vaux Trophy, 1 in play-offs).

The sendings-off total for **season 2002–03** was only 1 short of the record at 436, comprising 71 in the Premier League, 319 Nationwide League, 19 (League club players) in the F.A. Cup, 11 in the Worthington Cup, 11 in the LDV Vaux Trophy and 5 in the play-offs. In addition, Liverpool, Arsenal and Newcastle Utd. each had a player sent off in the Champions League.

Everton (7) had most red cards in the Premiership, 2002–03. Clubs with most dismissals in all competitions were Oldham Athletic, Q.P.R. and Cambridge Utd. (10 each).

Most sendings-off in season in **English top division:** 71 in Premiership, 2002-03.

November 16, 2002 was the **worst day** for dismissals in **English football history** with 18 players sent off (1 Premier League, 5 Nationwide League, 12 in F.A. Cup 1st. Round – 7 of them non-League).

That equalled the blackest day for disciplinary action in the F.A. Cup (12 in 1st. Round on November 20, 1982).

Most players sent off in **English League football on one day**: 16 on March 16, 2002 (2 Prem. League, 14 Nationwide League); on November 23, 2002 (4 Premier League, 12 Nationwide League).

Most players sent off in one **Football League programme**: 15 in week-end of Sat., Dec. 22 (11) and Sun., Dec. 23 (4), 1990.

Most players ordered off in **Anglo-Scottish football on one day**: 25, all League, on Oct. 16, 1999 (14 in England, 11 in Scotland).

• In the entire first season of post-war League football (1946-7) only 12 players were sent off, followed by 14 in 1949-50, and the total League dismissals for the first nine seasons after the war was 104.

The worst pre-war total was 28 in each of seasons 1921-2 and 1922-3.

ENGLAND SENDINGS-OFF

Alan Smith became the ninth player England have had sent off in their International history (1872) to date) when he was shown the red card in the last minute of the European Championship qualifier against Macedonia at Southampton on October 16, 2002.

June 5, 1968 **Alan Mullery** v Yugoslavia (Florence, Eur. Champ.)
June 6, 1973 **Alan Ball** v Poland (Chorzow, World Cup qual.)
June 15, 1977 **Trevor Cherry** v Argentina (Buenos Aires, friendly)
June 6, 1986 **Ray Wilkins** v Morocco (Monterrey, World Cup Finals)
June 30, 1998 **David Beckham** v Argentina (St. Etienne, World Cup Finals)
Sept. 5, 1998 **Paul Ince** v Sweden (Stockholm, Eur. Champ. qual.)
June 5, 1999 **Paul Scholes** v Sweden (Wembley, Eur. Champ. qual.)
Sept. 8, 1999 **David Batty** v Poland (Warsaw, Eur. Champ. qual.)
Oct. 16, 2002 **Alan Smith** v Macedonia (Southampton, Eur. Champ. qual.)

Other countries: Most recent sendings-off of players representing the other Home Countries: **N. Ireland James Quinn** and **Keith Gillespie** v Greece (European Champ., Belfast, April 2003). – **Scotland – Matt Elliott** v Faroe Islands (European Champ., Toftir, June, 1999); **Wales – Matthew Jones** v U.S.A. (Friendly, San Jose, May 2003). **Rep. of Ireland – Gary Kelly** (v Holland World Cup qual., Dublin, September 2001).

England dismissals at other levels:-

U-23 (4): **Stan Anderson** (v Bulgaria, Sofia, May 19, 1957); **Alan Ball** (v Austria, Vienna, June 2, 1965); **Kevin Keegan** (v E. Germany, Magdeburg, June 1, 1972); **Steve Perryman** (v Portugal, Lisbon, Nov. 19, 1974).

U-21 (12): **Sammy Lee** (v Hungary, Keszthely, June 5, 1981); **Mark Hateley** (v Scotland, Hampden Park, April 19, 1982); **Paul Elliott** (v Denmark, Maine Road, Manchester, March 26, 1986); **Tony Cottee** (v W. Germany, Ludenscheid, September 8, 1987); **Julian Dicks** (v Mexico, Toulon, France, June 12, 1988); **Jason Dodd** (v Mexico, Toulon, May 29, 1991; 3 Mexico players also sent off in that match); **Matthew Jackson** (v France, Toulon, May 28, 1992); **Robbie Fowler** (v Austria, Kafkenberg, October 11, 1994); **Alan Thompson** (v Portugal, Oporto, September 2, 1995); **Terry Cooke** (v Portugal, Toulon, May 30, 1996); **Ben Thatcher** (v Italy, Rieti, October 10, 1997); **John Curtis** (v Greece, Heraklion, November 13, 1997); **Jody Morris** (v Luxembourg, Grevenmacher, October 13, 1998); **Stephen Wright** (v Germany, Derby Co., October 6, 2000); **Alan Smith** (v Finland, Valkeakoski, October 10, 2000); **Luke Young** and **John Terry** (v Greece, Athens, June 5, 2001); **Shola Ameobi** (v Portugal, Rio Maior, March 28, 2003).
England 'B' (1): **Neil Webb** (v Algeria, Algiers, December 11, 1990).

MOST DISMISSALS IN INTERNATIONAL MATCHES

19 (10 Chile, 9 Uruguay), June 25, 1975; **6** (2 Mexico, 4 Argentina), 1956; **6** (5 Ecuador, 1 Uruguay), Jan. 4, 1977 (4 Ecuadorians sent off in 78th min., match abandoned, 1-1); **5** (Holland 3, Brazil 2), June 6, 1999 in Goianio, Brazil.

INTERNATIONAL STOPPED THROUGH DEPLETED SIDE

Portugal v Angola (5-1), friendly International in Lisbon on November 14, 2001, abandoned (68 mins) because Angola were down to 6 players (4 sent off, 1 carried off, no substitutes left).

MOST 'CARDS' IN WORLD CUP FINALS MATCH

18 (16 yellow, 2 red, both colours equally shared) in Germany v Cameroon group qualifier, Shizuoka, Japan, June 11, 2002.

FIVE OFF IN ONE MATCH

For the first time since League football began in 1888, **five** players were sent off in one match (two Chesterfield, three Plymouth Argyle) in Div. 2 at Saltergate on **Feb. 22, 1997**. Four were dismissed (two from each side) in a goalmouth brawl in the last minute.

Second instance of **five** sent off in a League match was on **Dec. 2, 1997**: 4 Bristol Rov. players, 1 Wigan Athletic in Div. 2 match at Wigan. Four of those dismissals came in the 45th minute.

Only the third instance of **five** players sent off in an English League match occurred on **Nov. 23, 2002**: Exeter City 3, Cambridge Utd. 2 – all in the last minute.

There have been eleven instances of **four** Football League club players being sent off in one match:

Jan. 8, 1955 Crewe Alexandra v Bradford City (Div. 3 North), two players from each side.

Dec. 13, 1986 Sheffield Utd. (1 player) v Portsmouth (3) in Div. 2.

Aug. 18, 1987 Port Vale v Northampton Town (Littlewoods Cup 1st. Round, 1st. Leg), two players from each side.

Dec. 12, 1987 Brentford v Mansfield Town (Div. 3), two players from each side.

Sept. 6, 1992 First instance in British first-class football of **four players from one side** being sent off in one match. Hereford Utd.'s seven survivors, away to Northampton Town (Div. 3), held out for a 1-1 draw.

Mar. 1, 1977 Norwich City v Huddersfield Town (Div. 1), two from each side.

Oct. 4, 1977 Shrewsbury Town (1 player), Rotherham Utd. (3) in Div. 3.

Aug. 22, 1998 Gillingham v Bristol Rov. (Div. 2), two from each side, all after injury-time brawl.

Mar. 16, 2001 Bristol City v Millwall (Div. 2), two from each side.

Aug. 17, 2002 Lincoln City (1 player), Carlisle Utd. (3) in Div. 3; **Aug. 26, 2002** (Wycombe Wand. v Q.P.R. (Div. 2), two from each side.

Four Stranraer players were sent off away to Airdrie (Scottish Div. 1) on Dec. 3, 1994, and that Scottish record was equalled when **four Hearts men** were ordered off away to Rangers (Prem. Div.) on **Sept. 14, 1996**. **Albion Rov.** had **four players** sent off (3 in last 8 mins) away to Queen's Park (Scottish Div. 3) on **August 23, 1997**.

Modern instances of **three players from one side** being sent off:

Dec. 13, 1986 Portsmouth (away to Sheffield Utd., Div. 2); **Aug. 23, 1989** Falkirk (home to Hearts, Scottish Skol Cup 3rd. Round); **Apr. 20, 1992** Newcastle Utd. (away to Derby Co., Div. 2); **May 2, 1992** Bristol City (away to Watford, Div. 2); **Nov. 23, 1996** Wycombe Wand. (home to Preston N.E., Div. 2); **Feb. 8, 1997** Darlington (away to Scarborough, Div. 3); **Oct. 4, 1997** Rotherham Utd. (away to Shrewsbury Town, Div. 3); **Mar. 28, 1998** Barnsley (home to Liverpool, Premiership); **Sept. 26, 1998** Southend Utd. (away to Swansea City, Div. 3); **May 1, 1999** West Ham Utd. (home to Leeds Utd., Premiership); **Oct. 9, 1999** Torquay Utd. away to Northampton Town (Div. 3); **Dec. 28, 1999** Cardiff City away to Cambridge Utd. (Div. 2); **Apr. 29, 2000** Halifax Town away to York City (Div. 3); **Apr. 16, 2001** Carlisle Utd. away to Scunthorpe Utd. (Div. 3); **Apr. 1, 2002** Kidderminster away to Bristol Rov. (Div. 3); **Mar. 16, 2002** Sheffield Utd. home to W.B.A. (Div.1).

Aug. 24, 1994: Three Sheffield Utd. players, and one from Udinese, were sent off in the Anglo-Italian Cup at Bramall Lane on Aug. 24, 1994. In addition, Utd. manager Dave Bassett was ordered from the bench.

Most dismissals one team, one match: Five players of America Tres Rios in first ten minutes after disputed goal by opponents Itaperuna in Brazilian cup match in Rio de Janeiro on Nov. 23, 1991. Tie then abandoned and awarded to Itaperuna.

Eight dismissals in one match: Four on each side in S. American Super Cup quarter-final (Gremio, Brazil v Penarol, Uruguay) in Oct. 1993.

Five dismissals in one season – **Dave Caldwell** (2 with Chesterfield, 3 with Torquay Utd.) in 1987-88.

First instance of **four dismissals in Scottish match**: three **Rangers** players (all English – Terry Hurlock, Mark Walters, Mark Hateley) and **Celtic's** Peter Grant in Scottish Cup quarter-final at Parkhead on Mar. 17, 1991 (Celtic won 2-0).

Four players (3 Hamilton, 1 Airdrie) were sent off in Scottish Div. 1 match on Oct. 30, 1993.

Four players (3 Ayr, 1 Stranraer) were sent off in Scottish Div. 1 match on Aug. 27, 1994.

In Scottish Cup first round replays on Dec. 16, 1996, there were two instances of **three players of one side sent off**: Albion Rov. (away to Forfar) and Huntly (away to Clyde).

FASTEST SENDINGS-OFF

World record – 10 secs: Giuseppe Lorenzo (Bologna) for striking opponent in Italian League match v Parma, December 9, 1990.

Domestic – 13 secs: Kevin Pressman (Sheffield Wed. goalkeeper at Wolves, Div. 1, Sunday, Aug. 14, 2000); **15 secs: Simon Rea** (Peterborough Utd. at Cardiff, Div. 2, Nov. 2, 2002). **19 secs: Mark Smith** (Crewe Alexandra goalkeeper at Darlington, Div. 3, Mar. 12, 1994). **In Div. 1 – 85 secs: Liam O'Brien** (Manchester Utd. at Southampton, Jan. 3, 1987). **Premier League – 72 secs: Tim Flowers** (Blackburn Rov. goalkeeper v Leeds Utd., Feb. 1, 1995).

In World Cup – 55 secs: Jose Batista (Uruguay v Scotland at Neza, Mexico, June 13, 1986).

In European competition – 90 secs: Sergei Dirkach (Dynamo Moscow v Ghent UEFA Cup 3rd round, 2nd leg, December 11, 1991).

Fastest F.A. Cup dismissal – 52 secs: Ian Culverhouse (Swindon Town defender, deliberate hand-ball on goal-line, away to Everton, 3rd. Round, Sunday Jan. 5, 1997).

Fastest League Cup dismissal – 33 secs: Jason Crowe (Arsenal substitute v Birmingham City, 3rd Round, Oct. 14, 1997).

Fastest Sending-off on debut: See **Jason Crowe** (above).

Fastest Sending-off of substitute – 0 secs: Walter Boyd (Swansea City) for striking opponent before ball in play after he went on (83 mins) at home to Darlington, Div. 3, Nov. 23, 1999.

MOST SENDINGS-OFF IN CAREER

21 – Willie Johnston (Rangers 7, WBA 6, Vancouver Whitecaps 4, Hearts 3, Scotland 1)
21 – Roy McDonough (13 in Football League – Birmingham City, Walsall, Chelsea, Colchester Utd., Southend Utd., Exeter City, Cambridge Utd. – 8 non-league).

13 – Steve Walsh (Wigan Athletic, Leicester City, Norwich City, Coventry City).

12 – **Vinnie Jones** (Wimbledon, Leeds Utd., Sheffield Utd., Chelsea, Q.P.R.).
12 – **Mark Dennis** (Birmingham City, Southampton, Q.P.R.).
11 – **Roy Keane** (Manchester Utd., Rep. of Ireland).
11 – **Dennis Wise** (Wimbledon, Chelsea, Leicester City).
11 – **Alan Smith** (Leeds Utd., England U–21, England).
8 – **Patrick Vieira** (Arsenal).
Most Premiership Sendings-off: Patrick Vieira 8, Vinnie Jones 7, Roy Keane 7.

- **Carlton Palmer** holds the unique record of having been sent off with each of his five Premiership clubs: Sheffield Wed., Leeds Utd., Southampton, Nott'm. Forest and Coventry City.

WEMBLEY SENDINGS-OFF

Manchester Utd.'s **Kevin Moran** is the only player to be sent off in the F.A. Cup Final (v Everton, 1985). His dismissal was one of 22 in major matches at Wembley:
Aug. 1948 **Branko Stankovic** (Yugoslavia) v Sweden, Olympic Games.
July 1966 **Antonio Rattin** (Argentina captain) v England, World cup q-final.
Aug. 1974 **Billy Bremner** (Leeds Utd.) and **Kevin Keegan** (Liverpool), Charity Shield.
Mar. 1977 **Gilbert Dresch** (Luxembourg) v England, World Cup.
May 1985 **Kevin Moran** (Manchester Utd.) v Everton, F.A. Cup Final.
Apr. 1993 **Lee Dixon** (Arsenal) v Tottenham, F.A. Cup semi-final.
May 1993 **Peter Swan** (Port Vale) v W.B.A., Div. 2 Play-off Final.
Mar. 1994 **Andrei Kanchelskis** (Manchester Utd.) v Aston Villa, League Cup Final.
May 1994 **Mike Wallace** and **Chris Beaumont** (Stockport Co.) v Burnley, Div. 2 Play-off Final.
June 1995 **Tetsuji Hashiratani** (Japan) v England, Umbro Cup.
May 1997 **Brian Statham** (Brentford) v Crewe Alexandra, Div. 2 Play-off Final.
Apr. 1998 **Capucho** (Portugal) v England, friendly.
Nov. 1998 **Ray Parlour** (Arsenal) and Tony Vareilles (Lens), Champions League.
Mar. 1999 **Justin Edinburgh** (Tottenham) v Leicester City, League Cup Final.
June 1999 **Paul Scholes** (England) v Sweden, European Championship qual.
Feb. 2000 **Clint Hill** (Tranmere) v Leicester City, League Cup Final.
Apr. 2000 **Mark Delaney** (Aston Villa) v Bolton Wand., F.A. Cup semi-final.
May 2000 **Kevin Sharp** (Wigan Athletic) v Gillingham, Div. 2 Play-off Final.
Aug. 2000 **Roy Keane** (Manchester Utd. captain) v Chelsea, Charity Shield.

WEMBLEY'S SUSPENDED CAPTAINS

Suspension prevented four **club captains** playing at Wembley in modern finals, in successive years.

Three were in F.A. Cup Finals – **Glenn Roeder** (Q.P.R., 1982), **Steve Foster** (Brighton & H.A., 1983) and **Wilf Rostron** (Watford, 1984) – and Sunderland's **Shaun Elliott** was barred from the 1985 Milk Cup Final.

Roeder was banned from Q.P.R.'s 1982 Cup Final replay against Tottenham, and Foster was ruled out of the first match in Brighton & H.A.'s 1983 Final against Manchester Utd.

BOOKINGS RECORDS

Most players of one Football League club booked in one match is **TEN** – members of the Mansfield Town team away to Crystal Palace in F.A. Cup third round, January 1963.

Fastest bookings – 3 seconds after kick-off, **Vinnie Jones** (Chelsea, home to Sheffield Utd., F.A. Cup fifth round, February 15, 1992); 5 seconds after kick-off: **Vinnie Jones** (Sheffield Utd., away to Manchester City, Div. 1, January 19, 1991). He was sent-off (54 mins) for second bookable offence.

FIGHTING TEAM-MATES

Charlton Athletic's **Mike Flanagan** and **Derek Hales** were sent off for fighting each other five minutes from end of F.A. Cup 3rd Round tie at home to Southern League Maidstone on Jan. 9, 1979.

Bradford City's **Andy Myers** and **Stuart McCall** had a fight during the 1-6 Premiership defeat at Leeds on Sunday, May 13, 2001.

On Sept. 28, 1994 the Scottish F.A. suspended Hearts players **Graeme Hogg** and **Craig Levein** for ten matches for fighting each other in a pre-season 'friendly' v Raith.

FOOTBALL'S FIRST BETTING SCANDAL

A Football League investigation into the First Division match which ended Manchester Utd 2, Liverpool 0 at Old Trafford on Good Friday, April 2, 1915 proved that the result had been 'squared' by certain players betting on the outcome. Four members of each team were suspended for life, but some of the bans were lifted when League football resumed in 1919 in recognition of the players' war service.

PLAYERS JAILED

Ten professional footballers found guilty of conspiracy to fraud by 'fixing' matches for betting purposes were given prison sentences at Nottingham Assizes on Jan. 26, 1965.

Jimmy Gauld (Mansfield Town), described as the central figure, was given four years. Among the others sentenced, Tony Kay (Sheffield Wed., Everton & England), Peter Swan (Sheffield Wed. & England) and David 'Bronco' Layne (Sheffield Wed.) were suspended from football for life by the F.A.

LONG SUSPENSIONS

The longest suspension in modern times for a player in British football was imposed on Manchester Utd.'s French international captain **Eric Cantona**, following his attack on a spectator as he left the pitch after being sent off at Crystal Palace (Prem. League) on Jan. 25, 1995. He was banned from football for 8 months.

The club immediately suspended him to the end of the season and fined him 2 weeks' wages (est. £20,000). Then, on a disrepute charge, the F.A. fined him £10,000 (February 1995) and extended the ban to September 30 (which FIFA confirmed as world wide).

A subsequent 2-weeks' jail sentence on Cantona for assault was altered, on appeal, to 120 hours' community service, which took the form of coaching schoolboys in the Manchester area.

Mark Dennis, the Q.P.R. defender, was sent off for the 11th time in his career away to Tottenham (Div. 1) on November 14, 1987. (Two of those dismissals were for after-match tunnel offences; in addition, Dennis had then been cautioned 64 times in ten seasons and answered two disrepute charges concerning newspaper articles).

On December 10, the F.A. imposed on him a 53-day suspension, which was amended on appeal (January 25) to an 8-match ban. This was the longest suspension of a Football League player since **Kevin Keegan** (Liverpool) and **Billy Bremner** (Leeds Utd.) were each banned for 5 weeks (10 matches) after being sent off in the F.A. Charity Shield at Wembley in August 1974.

On December 6, 1988 Dennis was sent off for **12th. time** (Q.P.R. v Fulham reserves) and fined £1,000.

Steve Walsh (Leicester City) has been sent off 13 times in his 18-season career (4 times with Wigan Athletic, 9 with Leicester City; 11 times in League, twice in F.A. Cup; 12 times away, once at home).

Before the disciplinary points system was introduced in season 1972-73, offenders were suspended for a specific number of weeks. Other lengthy suspensions imposed by the F.A. for on-field offences:

November 1969: Derek Dougan (Wolves) 8 weeks; **John Fitzpatrick** (Manchester Utd.) 8 weeks.

January 1970: Ronnie Rees (Nott'm Forest) 6 weeks; **George Best** (Manchester Utd.) 6 weeks.

January 1971: Peter Osgood (Chelsea) 8 weeks, following second trio of cautions in a year.

December 1971: Kevin Lewis (Manchester Utd.) 5 months; **Denis Hollywood** and **Brian O'Neil** (both Southampton) 9 weeks.

October 1987: Steve Walsh (Leicester City) 9 matches – original ban of 6 games (following the sixth sending-off of his career) increased to 9 when he reached 21 disciplinary points.

April 1988: Chris Kamara (Swindon Town) suspended to end of season (6 matches).

October 1988: Paul Davis (Arsenal) suspended for 9 matches, and fined a record £3,000, for breaking jaw of Glen Cockerill (Southampton) – off-ball incident caught on video.

January 1992: Frank Sinclair (Chelsea) suspended for 9 matches (fined £600) after being found guilty of assault on referee Paul Alcock (clash of heads) while playing for W.B.A. on loan.

January 1993: Alan Gough, Fulham goalkeeper, suspended for 42 days for assaulting referee in Autoglass Trophy match at Gillingham on December 8.

November 1994: Andy Townsend (Aston Villa) suspended for 6 matches (3 for 21 discip. points, 3 for sending-off).

October 26, 1997: Emmanuel Petit (Arsenal) pushes referee Paul Durkin when sent off at home to Aston Villa (Prem.). F.A. impose 3-match ban and £1,000 fine.

August 1998: F.A. suspend **David Batty** (Newcastle Utd.) for first 6 Prem. matches of season 1998-9 and fine him £1,500 for pushing referee David Elleray when sent off at Blackburn Rov. in last game of previous season.

October 1998: Paolo Di Canio (Sheff. Wed.) banned for 11 matches and fined £10,000 for pushing referee Paul Alcock after being sent off at home to Arsenal (Prem.), Sept. 26.

October 2002: F.A. suspend **Roy Keane** (Manchester Utd.) for 5 matches and fine him a record £150,000 on disrepute charges following publication of his autobiography.

Seven-month ban: Frank Barson, 37-year-old Watford centre-half, sent off at home to Fulham (Div. 3 South) on September 29, 1928, was suspended by the F.A. for the remainder of the season.

Twelve-month ban: Oldham Athletic full-back **Billy Cook** was given a 12-month suspension for refusing to leave the field when sent off at Middlesbrough (Div. 1), on April 3, 1915. The referee abandoned the match with 35 minutes still to play, and the score (4-1 to Middlesbrough) was ordered to stand.

Long Scottish bans: September 1954: Willie Woodburn, Rangers and Scotland centre-half, suspended for rest of career after fifth sending-off in 6 years.

Billy McLafferty, Stenhousemuir striker, was banned (April 14) for 8½ months, to Jan. 1, 1993, and fined £250 for failing to appear at a disciplinary hearing after being sent off against Arbroath on Feb. 1.

Twelve-match ban: On May 12, 1994 Scottish F.A. suspended Rangers forward **Duncan Ferguson** for 12 matches for violent conduct v Raith on Apr. 16. On Oct. 11, 1995, Ferguson (then with Everton) sent to jail for 3 months for the assault (served 44 days); Feb. 1, 1996 Scottish judge quashed 7 matches that remained of SFA ban on Ferguson.

On September 29, 2001 the SFA imposed a **17-match suspension** on Forfar Athletic's former Scottish International **Dave Bowman** for persistent foul and abusive language when sent off against Stranraer on September 22. As his misconduct continued, he was shown **5 red cards** by the referee.

FINES ETC. – MODERN

2000 (January) F.A. fine Notts Co. manager **Gary Brazil** £250 and Bournemouth manager Mel Machin £100 for comments to referee Jeff Winter after F.A. Cup 1st Round replay, November 9. Football League fine **Barnet** £2,500 for late arrival at Hartlepool, November 2. F.A. ban **Ben Thatcher** (Wimbledon) for 2 matches for elbowing Sunderland's Nicky Summerbee, January 3 – on video evidence (player not sent off). F.A. fine West Ham Utd. captain **Steve Lomas** £6,000 for comments to officials after match at Chelsea, November 7. F.A. fine **Hull City** £2,500 for failing to assist with enquiries into running of club. F.A. suspend referee **Rob Harris** for month for 'not applying the rules' at Tranmere v Sunderland F.A. Cup (4), January 8, Tranmere having replaced a sent-off player with a substitute.

2000 (March) F.A. fine **Paul Gascoigne** (Middlesbrough) £5,000, with 3-match ban, for elbowing offence v Aston Villa (February 14) in which Gascoigne broke an arm (charged on video evidence – incident missed by match officials). F.A. fine **Paolo Di Canio** (West Ham Utd.) £5,000 for making gesture to opponent v Aston Villa (January 15). UEFA fine **Chelsea** £7,500 and **Marseille** £37,000 for spectator misconduct

(Champions League, February 29). F.A. fine **Leeds Utd.** and **Tottenham** £150,000 each for mass player-brawl at Elland Road (Premier League), February 12. F.A. fine Wolves striker **Ade Akinbiyi** £2,000 with 4-match suspension for head-butting Nott'm Forest player, February 26. Seven **Leicester City** men – players and officials, past or present – collectively fined £75,000 by F.A. for misconduct relating to distribution of tickets for 1999 Worthington Cup Final.

2000 (April) Football League fine **Bolton Wand.** £45,000 for poaching manager Sam Allardyce from Notts Co. F.A. fine **Emmanuel Petit** (Arsenal) £5,000 for obscene gesture to Aston Villa fans, March 5. F.A. fine **Steve Claridge** £900 for breach of rules when betting on his team to beat Barnsley, January 29 (they did by 3-0, Claridge hat-trick). F.A. fine **Chelsea** £50,000 for players' part in tunnel brawl at home to Wimbledon, February 12 (see also May). F.A. fine Chelsea captain **Dennis Wise** £7,500 for 'insulting behaviour' in same incident. F.A. fine Tranmere Rov. manager **John Aldridge** £750 for incident at Worthington Cup Final v Leicester and for comments to match officials after League matches v Birmingham and Portsmouth.

2000 (May) F.A. fine **Wimbledon** £50,000 and captain **Kenny Cunningham** £5,000 for their part in tunnel brawl at Chelsea, February 12 (see April).

2000 (July) UEFA **fine Portuguese F.A. £70,300** and ban 3 of their players from all **European** competitions, club and country, as sequel to fracas when France awarded penalty (handball by Everton's **Abel Xavier**) for Golden Goal decider in Euro 2000 semi-final. Suspensions: **Xavier** 9 months, **Nuno Gomes** 8 months, **Paulo Bento** 6 months. F.A. fine **Bryan Robson** (Middlesbrough manager) £7,500 for confrontation with referee after defeat at Coventry, April 15. F.A. Fine **John Hartson** (Wimbledon) £5,000 on charge of abusive language to referee away to Bradford City, April 30.

2000 (October) F.A. fine **Paul Ince** (Middlesbrough) £15,000 for misconduct (abusive language at home to Derby Co., Sept. 6. F.A. fine **Gilles Grimandi** (Arsenal) £3,000 (1-match ban) for stamping on Gary McAllister (Liverpool), August 21. F.A. fine Swindon Town manager **Colin Todd** £2,500 for verbal assault on referee at Exeter (Worthington Cup, Sept. 5). UEFA fine **David Beckham** £4,000 for spitting towards referee in Manchester Utd.'s Champions League defeat away to PSV Eindhoven, Sept. 26. F.A. give Arsenal manager **Arsene Wenger** 12-match touchline ban and fine him 4 weeks' wages after 'tunnel row' with fourth official at Sunderland, August 19 (Wenger to appeal – see Feb. 2001). F.A. fine **Ipswich Town** £2,500 for sub-standard floodlights v Manchester Utd., August 22. F.A. fine **Neil Lennon** (Leicester City) £4,000 for ticket-selling offences (1999 Worthington Cup Final). F.A. fine **Crystal Palace** £20,000. **Nott'm. Forest** £15,000 for players' mass confrontation at Selhurst Park, August 28. UEFA fine **Arsenal** £8,300 for offences at Champions League match away to Lazio. Oct. 17.

2000 (November) F.A. fine **Norwich City** £30,000 (reduced on appeal to £12,000 plus £12,000 suspended) and **Blackpool** £6,000 for players' mass brawl at Norwich (Worthington Cup, Sept. 19). F.A. fine Tranmere Rov. manager **John Aldridge** £2,500 with 14-day touchline ban for throwing water bottle away to Barnsley, Oct. 17. F.A. fine **Preston N.E.** and **Sheffield Utd.** £15,000 each after 19-player brawl at Preston, August 19 (Sheffield Utd. manager **Neil Warnock** fined £2,000). F.A. ban **Stan Collymore** (Bradford City) 3 matches for stamping on Paul Gascoigne when playing for Leicester City v Everton, Sept. 29 (incident investigated by F.A. video panel).

2000 (December) UEFA fine **Manchester Utd.** £2,000 for players' misconduct v PSV Eindhoven (Champions League), Oct. 18.

2001 (January) F.A. fine **Paul Jewell** (Sheffield Wed. manager) £1,000 for comments to referee at Birmingham (Worthington Cup), December 12.

2001 (February) Arsenal manager **Arsene Wenger's** appeal (see October) upheld – reprimanded and fine reduced to £10,000. **Patrick Vieira** fined £10,000 by F.A. (1-match ban) for kicking Olivier Dacourt, Leeds Utd., Nov. 26. **Matt Elliott** (Leicester City) fined £5,000 by F.A. and **Hassan Kachloul** (Southampton) £2,000 on 'improper conduct' charges F.A. fine **Colin Todd** (Derby Co. assistant-manager) £2,500, with 3-match touchline ban, for verbal abuse of match official when Swindon Town manager.

2001 (March) F.A. fine **Gary Neville** (Manchester Utd.) £30,000, with 2-match ban, for foul and abusive language to assistant-referee after F.A. Cup defeat v West Ham Utd., Jan. 28 (see April re appeal). F.A. fine **Jim Magilton** (Ipswich Town) £5,000, with 1-match ban, for comments to referee at Chelsea, Jan. 20. F.A. fine Wimbledon manager **Terry Burton** £2,000, with 2-match touchline ban, for comments to assistant-referee at F.A. Cup 4th Round replay v Wycombe Wand., Feb. 20.

2001 (April) F.A. fine Wycombe Wand. manager **Lawrie Sanchez** £2,000, with 3-match touchline ban, for comments to assistant-referee at F.A. Cup 6th Round win at Leicester, March 10. F.A. fine Ipswich Town defender **Hermann Hreidarsson** £1,500 for jumping into crowd to celebrate goal v Bradford City, March 4. F.A. fine **Gillingham** £15,000 and **Crystal Palace** £5,000 following 12-player brawl at Gillingham, Dec. 26. Football League tribunal docks **Chesterfield** (Div. 3 leaders) 9 points, plus £20,000 fine, for breach of transfer regulations and under-reporting gate receipts (subsequent appeal turned down). F.A. fine **Nott'm. Forest** and **Preston N.E.** £5,000 each after mass confrontation of players at Nottingham, November 4. F.A. Appeal Board reduce fine on **Gary Neville** (Manchester Utd.) – see March – to £7,000; 2-match ban stays. FIFA ban Scotland captain **Colin Hendry** from 6 Int. matches (reduced to 3 on appeal) for elbowing a San Marino player in World Cup qualifier at Hampden Park, March 28.

2001 (May) F.A. fine **Lee Hendrie** (Aston Villa) £5,000 for 'over-exuberant' celebration of winning goal at home to Leicester City, April 4.

2001 (August) F.A. impose fines (suspended to end of season) for poor disciplinary records in 2000-01: **Derby Co.** £100,000; **Everton** and **Sheffield Wed.** £50,000; **Millwall** and **Bury** £25,000; **Torquay Utd.** and **Exeter City** £12,500.

2001 (September) F.A. find **Martin Keown** (Arsenal) £10,000 with 1-match ban for striking Mark Viduka (Leeds Utd.) at Highbury, May 5. UEFA fine **English F.A.** £2,400 for 4 England U-21 players being booked v Germany, August 31, UEFA fine **Newcastle Utd.** £2,800 for 3 bookings v Troyes (InterToto Cup), August 21. F.A. fine Birmingham City manager **Trevor Francis** £1,500 for protests at play-off semi-final v Preston N.E. in May.

2001 (November) F.A. fine **Mark Wright**, Oxford Utd. manager, £1,750 with 4-match touchline ban for abusive language to referee v Scunthorpe Utd., October 20.

2001 (December) F.A. fine Watford £5,000 and W.B.A. £2,500 for 16-player brawl, September 15.

2002 (January) F.A. find **David Ginola** (Aston Villa) £22,000 with 2-match ban for confrontation with 4th official when sent off v Leicester City, December 1. Football League fines: **Carlisle Utd.** £25,000 for fielding ineligible player v Mansfield Town, November 10; **Luton Town** £20,000 for failing to fulfil fixture at Kidderminster, December 1 (claiming 20 players ill or injured).

2002 (February) F.A. fines: **Portsmouth** £10,000 after 15 bookings in less than a month; **Wolves** £2,500 for players' misconduct v W.B.A., December 2; managers **Mark McGhee** (Millwall) £7,500 and **Steve Bruce** (Birmingham City) £5,000 for confrontations with referee, January 10.

2002 (March) F.A. fines: **Everton** £25,000 for disorderly conduct at Fulham, December 8 (£30,000 Fulham fine subsequently rescinded); **Mauricio Taricco** (Tottenham) £5,000 for improper conduct v Chelsea (Worthington Cup semi-final, 2nd leg). F.A. ban **Thierry Henry** (Arsenal) 3 domestic matches for improper conduct towards referee v Newcastle Utd., December 18. Premier League fine **Liverpool** £20,000 for illegal approach when signing **Christian Ziege** from Middlesbrough, August 2000; Ziege fined £20,000 for breach of rules.

2002 (April) F.A. fine Blackburn Rov. manager **Graeme Souness** £10,000 (1-match touchline ban) for verbal abuse of referee at Middlesbrough (F.A. Cup 5th Round, February 16).

2002 (May) F.A. fines: Derby Co. manager **John Gregory** £5,000 for improper conduct at Premiership match v Newcastle Utd., April 13. **Sheffield Utd.** £10,000 for players' misconduct at abandoned match v W.B.A., March 16; manager **Neil Warnock** £2,000, with 2-match ban for misconduct; 3 players punished – **Patrick Suffo** £3,000, with 3-match ban, **Keith Curle** £500 (2-match ban), **George Santos** 2-match ban. Wales F.A. fine **Cardiff City** £20,000 for crowd trouble v Leeds Utd. (F.A. Cup 3rd Round, January 6). N. Ireland manager **Sammy McIlroy** and assistant **Jim Harvey** each banned for 1 match and fined £4,000 by FIFA for misconduct at World Cup qualifier away to Malta, October 6.

2002 (July) F.A. fine new League club **Boston Utd.** £100,000 (with 4 points deduction) for contractual irregularities.

2002 (August) **Robbie Savage** (Birmingham City) fined £10,000 by F.A. for 'improper conduct' (using referee's toilet before Leicester City's home match v Aston Villa, April 20).

2002 (August) F.A. fines for poor disciplinary records, season 2001–02: **Arsenal** £50,000, suspended for year, (9 domestic sendings-off); **Portsmouth** £30,000 (suspended for year) for 6 red, 95 yellow cards; **Derby Co.** £15,000, **Tranmere Rov.** £15,000, **Sheff. Wed.** £5,000, **Sheff. Utd.** £5,000. Other F.A. fines: **Geoff Horsfield** (Birmingham City) £3,000 for off-ball incident in play-off s-final v Millwall, April 18); **George Boateng** (Mid'bro') £2,500 for throwing boot into crowd with former club Aston Villa at Leicester City, April 20).

2002 (September) F.A. fine Burnley manager **Stan Ternent** £2,500 (with 2-match touchline ban) for abusive language to referee at home to Wolves, March 30.

2002 (October) F.A. fine **Roy Keane** (Manchester Utd.) record £150,000 (with 5-match suspension) on disrepute charges following publication of autobiography. **Graeme Souness** (Blackburn Rov. manager) fined £15,000 (with 3-match touchline ban) after being 'sent off' by referee v Liverpool, August 28. Arsenal captain **Patrick Vieira** fined £25,000 (with 2-match suspension) for 'insulting language' to referee when sent off at Chelsea (Premier, September 1).

2002 (November) F.A. fine **Rotherham Utd.** £4,000 and **Sheff. Utd.** £2,000 for player incidents at end of match at Bramall Lane, September 14.

2002 (December) F.A. fines: **Birmingham City** £25,000 for spectator misconduct v Aston Villa, September 16; **Dennis Bergkamp** (Arsenal) £5,000 for misconduct, home to Blackburn Rov., October 26; **Trevor Francis** (Crystal Palace manager) £1,000 for cuffing reserve 'keeper Alex Kolinko (on bench) for laughing when Bradford City scored at Selhurst Park, August 13; Norwich City manager **Nigel Worthington** £500 (with 1-match touchline ban) after being ordered from bench, home to Sheff. Utd., September 7. UEFA fine **English F.A.** £9,000 and **Slovakian F.A.** £27,000 (reduced to £9,000 on appeal) because of crowd trouble at Eur. Champ. Qual. Match, Bratislava, October 12.

2003 (January) F.A. fine **Ashley Cole** (Arsenal) £2,000 (with 2-match ban) for 'insulting words' to match official at Southampton, November 23. **Bristol City** fined £50,000 by Football League (£25,000 suspended for 2 years) and ordered to pay Gillingham £50,000 compensation for illegal approach to manager Tony Pulis, June 1999. F.A. fine former Boston Utd. Manager **Steve Evans** £8,000, ban him from management for 18 months following July inquiry into club's financial affairs; former Boston Utd. chairman **Pat Malkinson** fined £5,250 and banned for 13 months from involvement in football.

2003 (February) F.A. suspend **Steven Gerrard** (Liverpool) for 3 matches for violent conduct (two-footed tackle) at home to Everton, December 22 (conviction on TV evidence). F.A. fine **Martin Keown** (Arsenal) £5,000 for 'confrontation' with Ruud van Nistelrooy away to Manchester Utd., December 7.

2003 (March) F.A. fines: Derby Co. manager **John Gregory** £7,500 (with 5-match touchline ban) for 'abusive language' to fourth official at Portsmouth, February 8; **Dennis Bergkamp** (Arsenal) £7,500 for elbowing Lee Bowyer (West Ham Utd.) at Highbury, January 19; **Paul Hart** (Nott'm. Forest manager) £500 for 'improper conduct' to match officials, home to Reading, December 21.

2003 (April) F.A. fine **Craig Bellamy** (Newcastle Utd.) £5,000 (with 1-match ban) for 'insulting remarks' to referee at Mid'bro', March 5.

2003 (May) F.A. fines: **Christophe Dugarry** (Birmingham City) £12,500 for spitting incident away to Aston Villa, March 3; **Dion Dublin** (Aston Villa) £6,000 for 'improper behaviour' after being sent off v Birmingham City, March 3. UEFA fines: **English F.A.** £68,000 following pitch invasions and racist chanting at England–Turkey Eur. Champ. qual. match, Sunderland, April 2; **Sir Alex Ferguson** £4,800 for 'improper statements', alleging that Champion's League quarter-final draw was 'fixed' so that Man. Utd. met Real Madrid; Arsenal captain **Patrick Vieira** £2,300 for alleging UEFA not tough enough in dealing with racism after Champions League match away to Valencia, March 19.

TOP FINES

Clubs: £1,500,000 (increased from original £600,000) Tottenham, Dec. 1994; **£150,000** Leeds Utd., Mar. 2000; **£150,000** Tottenham, Mar. 2000; **£105,000** Chelsea, Jan. 1991; **£100,000** Boston Utd., July 2002; **£90,000** Tottenham, Jan. 1996; **£75,000** Chelsea, July 1988; **£75,000** Everton, Apr. 1994; **£60,000** Wimbledon, Jan. 1996; **£55,000** Birmingham City, Feb. 1994; **£50,000** Norwich City, June 1989; **£50,000** Arsenal, Nov. 1990; **£50,000** Barnet, Nov. 1992; **£50,000** Middlesbrough, Jan. 1997; **£50,000** Arsenal, Aug. 1997; **£50,000** Everton, July 1999; **£50,000** Chelsea, Apr. 2000; **£50,000** Wimbledon, May 2000; **£50,000** Arsenal, Aug. 2002; **£50,000** Bristol City, Jan. 2003.

Players: £150,000 Roy Keane (Manchester Utd.); Oct. 2002; **£45,000** Patrick Vieira (Arsenal), Oct. 1999; **£32,000** Robbie Fowler (Liverpool), Apr. 1999; **£25,000** Patrick Vieira (Arsenal); Oct. 2002; **£22,000** David Ginola (Aston Villa), Jan. 2002; **£20,000** Vinnie Jones (Wimbledon), Nov. 1992; **£20,000** Patrick Vieira (Arsenal), Dec. 1998; **£20,000** John Hartson (Wimbledon – offence when with West Ham Utd.), Jan. 1999; **£20,000** Christian Ziege (ex-Liverpool), Mar. 2002; **£17,500** Ian Wright (West Ham Utd.), May 1999; **£15,000** Ian Wright (Arsenal), July 1997; **£15,000** Paul Ince (Middlesbrough), Oct. 2000; **£12,500** Christophe Dugarry (Birmingham City), May 2003; **£10,000** Paolo Di Canio (Sheff. Wed.), Oct. 1998; **£10,000** Faustino Asprilla (Newcastle Utd.), Apr. 1996; **£10,000** Eric Cantona (Manchester Utd.), Feb. 1995; **£10,000** Patrick Vieira (Arsenal), Feb. 2001; **£10,000** Martin Keown (Arsenal), Sept. 2001; **£10,000** Robbie Savage (Birmingham City), Aug. 2002.

- In seven seasons with Arsenal (1996-2003) Patrick Vieira was fined a total of £102,000 by the F.A. for offences that included six sendings-off.

Managers: £15,000 Graeme Souness (Blackburn), Oct. 2002. **£10,000** Arsene Wenger (Arsenal), Feb. 2001; **£10,000** Graeme Souness (Blackburn) Apr. 2002; **£7,500** Bryan Robson (Middlesbrough), July 2000; **£7,500** Mark McGhee (Millwall), Feb. 2002; **£7,500** John Gregory (Derby). Mar. 2003; **£5,000** Brian Clough (Nott'm. Forest), Feb. 1989; **£5,000** Ruud Gullit (Newcastle Utd.), Sept. 1999; **£5,000** John Gregory (Aston Villa), Nov. 1999; **£5,000** Steve Bruce (Birmingham), Feb. 2002; **£4,800** Sir Alex Ferguson (Manchester Utd.) by UEFA, May 2003.

Football Association: £68,000 by UEFA, May 2003; **£9,000** by UEFA, Dec. 2002.

MANAGERS

INTERNATIONAL RECORDS

(As at start of season 2003-04)

	P	*W*	*D*	*L*	*F*	*A*
Sven-Goran Eriksson (England – appointed Coach Jan. 2001)	29	16	9	4	55	27
Sammy McIlroy (N. Ireland – appointed Jan. 2000)	26	5	6	15	19	38
Berti Vogts (Scotland – appointed Feb. 2002)	15	3	3	9	13	27
Mark Hughes (Wales – appointed Aug. 1999)	27	8	10	9	29	32
Brian Kerr (Rep. of Ireland – appointed Jan. 2003)	6	5	1	0	9	2
Mick McCarthy (Rep. of Ireland (Final Record) Feb. 1996 – Oct. 2002)	68	29	20	19	112	66

ENGLAND'S MANAGERS

		P	*W*	*D*	*L*
1946-62	**Walter Winterbottom**	139	78	33	28
1963-74	**Sir Alf Ramsey**	113	69	27	17
1974	**Joe Mercer**, caretaker	7	3	3	1
1974-77	**Don Revie**	29	14	8	7
1977-82	**Ron Greenwood**	55	33	12	10
1982-90	**Bobby Robson**	95	47	30	18
1990-93	**Graham Taylor**	38	18	13	7
1994-96	**Terry Venables**, coach	23	11	11	1
1996-99	**Glenn Hoddle**, coach	28	17	6	5

1999	**Howard Wilkinson**, caretaker	1	0	0	1
1999-2000	**Kevin Keegan**, coach	18	7	7	4
2000	**Howard Wilkinson**, caretaker	1	0	1	0
2000	**Peter Taylor**, caretaker	1	0	0	1
2001-2003	**Sven-Goran Eriksson**, coach	29	16	9	4

INTERNATIONAL MANAGER CHANGES

England: Walter Winterbottom 1946-62 (initially coach); **Alf Ramsey** (Feb. 1963-May 1974); **Joe Mercer** (caretaker May 1974); **Don Revie** (July 1974-July 1977); **Ron Greenwood** (Aug. 1977-July 1982); **Bobby Robson** (July 1982-July 1990); **Graham Taylor** (July 1990-Nov. 1993); **Terry Venables**, coach (Jan. 1994-June 1996); **Glenn Hoddle**, coach (June 1996-Feb. 1999); **Howard Wilkinson** (caretaker Feb. 1999); **Kevin Keegan** coach (Feb. 1999-Oct. 2000); **Howard Wilkinson** (caretaker Oct. 2000); **Peter Taylor** (caretaker Nov. 2000); **Sven Goran Eriksson** (from Jan. 2001).

N. Ireland (modern): **Billy Bingham** (1967-Aug. 1971); **Terry Neill** (Aug. 1971-Mar. 1975); **Dave Clements** (player-manager Mar. 1975-1976); **Danny Blanchflower** (June 1976-Nov. 1979); **Billy Bingham** (Feb. 1980-Nov. 1993); **Bryan Hamilton** Feb. 1994-Feb. 1998); **Lawrie McMenemy** (since Feb. 1998); **Sammy McIlroy** (since Jan. 2000).

Scotland (modern): **Bobby Brown** (Feb. 1967-July 1971); **Tommy Docherty** (Sept. 1971- Dec. 1972); **Willie Ormond** (Jan. 1973-May 1977); **Ally MacLeod** (May 1977-Sept.1978); **Jock Stein** (Oct. 1978-Sept. 1985); **Alex Ferguson** (caretaker Oct. 1985-June 1986); **Andy Roxburgh**, coach (July 1986-Sept. 1993); **Craig Brown** (Sept. 1993-Oct. 2001); **Berti Vogts** (since Feb. 2002).

Wales (modern): **Mike Smith** (July 1974-Dec. 1979); **Mike England** (Mar. 1980-Feb. 1988); **David Williams** (caretaker Mar. 1988); **Terry Yorath** (Apr. 1988-Nov. 1993); **John Toshack** (Mar. 1994, one match); **Mike Smith** (Mar. 1994-June 1995); **Bobby Gould** (Aug. 1995-June 1999); **Mark Hughes** (since Aug. 1999).

Rep. of Ireland (modern): **Liam Tuohy** (Sept. 1971-Nov. 1972); **Johnny Giles** (Oct. 1973-Apr. 1980, initially player-manager); **Eoin Hand** (June 1980-Nov. 1985); **Jack Charlton** (Feb. 1986-Dec. 1995); **Mick McCarthy** (Feb. 1996-Oct. 2002); **Brian Kerr** (since Jan. 2003).

FIRST BLACK ENGLAND MANAGER

Chris Ramsey, 36, in charge of England's U-20 squad for the World Youth Championship in Nigeria, April 1999. He was Brighton & H.A.'s right-back in the 1983 F.A. Cup Final v Manchester Utd.

YOUNGEST LEAGUE MANAGERS

Ivor Broadis, 23, appointed player-manager of Carlisle Utd., August 1946; **Chris Brass**, 27, appointed player-manager of York City, June 2003; **Terry Neill**, 28, appointed player manager of Hull City, June 1970;

Graham Taylor, 28, appointed manager of Lincoln City, December 1972.

LONGEST-SERVING LEAGUE MANAGERS – ONE CLUB

Fred Everiss, secretary-manager of W.B.A. for 46 years (1902-48); since last war, **Sir Matt Busby**, in charge of Manchester Utd. for 25 seasons (1945-69, 1970-71; **Jimmy Seed** at Charlton Athletic for 23 years (1933-56).

LAST ENGLISH MANAGER TO WIN CHAMPIONSHIP

Howard Wilkinson (Leeds Utd.), season 1991–92.

1,000-TIME MANAGERS

Only four have managed in more than 1,000 English League games: **Alec Stock**, **Brian Clough**, **Jim Smith** and **Graham Taylor**. **Sir Matt Busby**, **Dario Gradi**, **Dave Bassett** and **Lennie Lawrence** have each managed more than 1,000 matches in all competitions.

SHORT-TERM MANAGERS

		Departed
3 Days	Bill Lambton (Scunthorpe Utd.)	April 1959
7 Days	Tim Ward (Exeter City)	March 1953
7 Days	Kevin Cullis (Swansea City)	February 1996
10 Days	Dave Cowling (Doncaster Rov.)	October 1997
10 Days	Peter Cormack (Cowdenbeath)	December 2000
13 Days	Johnny Cochrane (Reading)	April 1939
13 Days	Micky Adams (Swansea City)	October 1997
16 Days	Jimmy McIlroy (Bolton Wand.)	November 1970
20 Days	Paul Went (Leyton Orient)	October 1981
27 Days	Malcolm Crosby (Oxford Utd.)	January 1998
28 Days	Tommy Docherty (Q.P.R.)	December 1968
32 Days	Steve Coppell (Manchester City)	November 1996
41 Days	Steve Wicks (Lincoln City)	October 1995
44 Days	Brian Clough (Leeds Utd.)	September 1974
44 Days	Jock Stein (Leeds Utd.)	October 1978
48 Days	John Toshack (Wales)	March 1994
48 Days	David Platt (Sampdoria coach)	February 1999
49 Days	Brian Little (Wolves)	October 1986
49 Days	Terry Fenwick (Northampton Town)	February 2003
61 Days	Bill McGarry (Wolves)	November 1985
63 Days	Dave Booth (Peterborough Utd.)	January 1991

• In May 1984, Crystal Palace named **Dave Bassett** as manager, but he changed his mind four days later, without signing the contract, and returned to Wimbledon.

• In an angry outburst after a play-off defeat in May 1992, Barnet chairman Stan Flashman sacked manager **Barry Fry** and re-instated him a day later.

EARLY-SEASON MANAGER SACKINGS

2000 Alan Buckley (Grimsby Town) 10 days; **1997** Kerry Dixon (Doncaster Rov.) 12 days; **1996** Sammy Chung (Doncaster Rov.) on morning of season's opening League match; **1996** Alan Ball (Manchester City) 12 days; **1994** Kenny Hibbitt (Walsall) and Kenny Swain (Wigan Athletic) 20 days; **1993** Peter Reid (Manchester City) 12 days; **1991** Don Mackay (Blackburn Rov.) 14 days; **1989** Mick Jones (Peterborough Utd.) 12 days; **1980** Bill McGarry (Newcastle Utd.) 13 days; **1979** Dennis Butler (Port Vale) 12 days; **1977** George Petchey (Leyton O.) 13 days; **1977** Willie Bell (Birmingham City) 16 days; **1971** Len Richley (Darlington) 12 days.

FEWEST MANAGERS

West Ham Utd. have had only nine managers in their 105-year history: Syd King, Charlie Paynter, Ted Fenton, Ron Greenwood, John Lyall, Lou Macari, Billy Bonds, Harry Redknapp and Glenn Roeder.

RECORD START FOR MANAGER

Arsenal were unbeaten in 17 League matches from the start of season 1947-8 under new manager Tom Whittaker.

MANAGER CHOSEN BY POLL

A month after being sacked by Third Division promotion winners Hartlepool Utd., **Mike Newell** became manager of Luton Town in unique circumstances. He was appointed via a telephone poll which the club, under a new board, conducted among fans, players, shareholders and season-ticket holders.

MANAGER DOUBLES

Four managers have won the League Championship with different clubs: **Tom Watson**, secy-manager with Sunderland (1892-3-5) and Liverpool (1901); **Herbert Chapman** with Huddersfield Town (1923-4, 1924-5) and Arsenal (1930-1, 1932-3); **Brian Clough** with

Derby Co. (1971-2) and Nott'm. Forest (1977-8); **Kenny Dalglish** with Liverpool (1985-6, 1987-8, 1989-90) and Blackburn Rov. (1994-5).

Managers to win the F.A. Cup with different clubs: **Billy Walker** (Sheffield Wed. 1935, Nott'm. Forest 1959); **Herbert Chapman** (Huddersfield Town 1922, Arsenal 1930).

Kenny Dalglish (Liverpool) and **George Graham** (Arsenal) completed the Championship/F.A. Cup double as both player and manager with a single club. **Joe Mercer** won the Championship as a player with Everton, the Championship twice and F.A. Cup as a player with Arsenal and both competitions as manager of Manchester City.

FIRST CHAIRMAN-MANAGER

On December 20, 1988, after two years on the board, Dundee Utd. manager **Jim McLean** was elected chairman, too. McLean, Scotland's longest-serving manager (appointed by Utd. on November 24, 1971), resigned at end of season 1992-3 (remained chairman).

Ron Noades was chairman-manager of Brentford from July 1998 – March 2001.

TOP DIVISION PLAYER–MANAGERS

Les Allen (Q.P.R. 1968-9); **Johnny Giles** (W.B.A. 1976-7); **Howard Kendall** (Everton 1981-2); **Kenny Dalglish** (Liverpool, 1985-90); **Trevor Francis** (Q.P.R., 1988-9); **Terry Butcher** (Coventry City, 1990-1), **Peter Reid** (Manchester City, 1990-93), **Trevor Francis** (Sheffield Wed., 1991-4), **Glenn Hoddle**, (Chelsea, 1993-5), **Bryan Robson** (Middlesbrough, 1994-7), **Ray Wilkins** (Q.P.R., 1994-6), **Ruud Gullit** (Chelsea, 1996-8), **Gianluca Vialli** (Chelsea, 1998-2000).

FOREIGN TRIUMPHS

Former Dutch Int. **Ruud Gullit** became the first foreign manager to win a major English competition when Chelsea took the F.A. Cup in 1997.

In season 1997-8 Chelsea won the Coca-Cola Cup and the Cup-Winners' Cup for Gullit's successor, the Italian **Gianluca Vialli**; Arsenal won the Premiership and F.A. Cup double under Frenchman **Arsene Wenger**; Dutchman **Wim Jansen** took Celtic to triumph in the Scottish Championship and Coca-Cola Cup.

Under Frenchman **Gerard Houllier**, Liverpool achieved a triple success in 2000-01, winning the Worthington Cup, F.A. Cup and UEFA Cup. They won the Worthington Cup again in 2003.

In 2001-02 **Arsene Wenger** took Arsenal to his second Premiership – F.A. Cup double in five seasons, and to his third F.A. Cup success in 2002–03.

Arsene Wenger and **Gerard Houllier** became the first foreign managers to receive such recognition when they were awarded honorary OBEs in the Queen's Birthday Honours in June 2003 'for their contribution to English football and Franco–British relations.'

In 1998-9 Rangers completed the Scottish treble under Dutchman **Dick Advocaat**.In 1999-2000 Chelsea won the F.A. Cup under **Vialli** and Rangers completed the Scottish Premier League and S.F.A. Cup double for **Advocaat**.

MANAGERS OF POST-WAR CHAMPIONS

1947 George Kay (Liverpool); **1948** Tom Whittaker (Arsenal); **1949** Bob Jackson (Portsmouth); **1950** Bob Jackson (Portsmouth); **1951** Arthur Rowe (Tottenham); **1952** Matt Busby (Manchester Utd.); **1953** Tom Whittaker (Arsenal).

1954 Stan Cullis (Wolves); **1955** Ted Drake (Chelsea); **1956** Matt Busby (Manchester Utd.); **1957** Matt Busby (Manchester Utd.); **1958** Stan Cullis (Wolves); **1959** Stan Cullis (Wolves); **1960** Harry Potts (Burnley).

1961 *Bill Nicholson (Tottenham); **1962** Alf Ramsey (Ipswich Town); **1963** Harry Catterick (Everton); **1964** Bill Shankly (Liverpool); **1965** Matt Busby (Manchester Utd.); **1966** Bill Shankly (Liverpool); **1967** Matt Busby (Man Utd.).

1968 Joe Mercer (Manchester City); **1969** Don Revie (Leeds Utd.); **1970** Harry Catterick (Everton); **1971** *Bertie Mee (Arsenal); **1972** Brian Clough (Derby Co.); **1973** Bill Shankly (Liverpool); **1974** Don Revie (Leeds Utd.).

1975 Dave Mackay (Derby Co.); **1976** Bob Paisley (Liverpool); **1977** Bob Paisley (Liverpool); **1978** Brian Clough (Nott'm. Forest); **1979** Bob Paisley (Liverpool); **1980** Bob Paisley (Liverpool); **1981** Ron Saunders (Aston Villa).

1982 Bob Paisley (Liverpool); **1983** Bob Paisley (Liverpool); **1984** Joe Fagan (Liverpool); **1985** Howard Kendall (Everton); **1986** *Kenny Dalglish (Liverpool – player/manager); **1987** Howard Kendall (Everton).

1988 Kenny Dalglish (Liverpool – player/manager); **1989** George Graham (Arsenal); **1990** Kenny Dalglish (Liverpool); **1991** George Graham (Arsenal); **1992** Howard Wilkinson (Leeds Utd.); **1993** Alex Ferguson (Manchester Utd.).

1994 *Alex Ferguson (Manchester Utd.); **1995** Kenny Dalglish (Blackburn Rov.); **1996** *Alex Ferguson (Manchester Utd.); **1997** Alex Ferguson (Manchester Utd.); **1998** *Arsene Wenger (Arsenal); **1999** *Alex Ferguson (Manchester Utd.); **2000** Sir Alex Ferguson (Manchester Utd.); **2001** Sir Alex Ferguson; **2002** *Arsene Wenger (Arsenal); **2003** Sir Alex Ferguson (Manchester Utd.).

(* Double winners)

SIR ALEX IS TOPS

With 25 major prizes **Sir Alex Ferguson** has the most successful managerial record with Scottish and English clubs combined. At **Aberdeen** (1978-86) he won ten top prizes: 3 Scottish Championships, 4 Scottish Cups, 1 Scottish League Cup, 1 Cup-Winners' Cup, 1 European Super Cup.

Manchester Utd. winning the Premiership in 2001 made Sir Alex the outright most successful manager in English football, the first to win seven League titles, the first to win three in a row. He achieved an eighth Premiership success in 2003.

It was their 15th major trophy in the last 14 seasons: 1990 F.A. Cup, 1991 Cup-Winners' Cup, 1992 League Cup, 1993 League Championship, 1994 League Championship and F.A. Cup, 1996 Championship and F.A. Cup; 1997 Championship; 1999 Championship, F.A. Cup and European Cup; 2000 Championship; 2001 Championship, 2003 Championship.

United are unbeaten in 9 domestic semi-finals (F.A. Cup 5, League Cup 4) under Sir Alex.

Aged 57, he signed a new 3-year contract with United (May 4, 1999), making him **Britain's highest-paid manager**, reputedly at £1.67m. a year. When that contract ended in 2002, he changed his mind about retiring and signed to stay in charge at Old Trafford for a future 3 years to June 2005, (reported at £3.5m. a year).

BOB PAISLEY'S HONOURS

Bob Paisley won 13 major competitions for Liverpool (1974-83): 6 League Championships, 3 European Cups, 3 League Cups, 1 UEFA Cup.

MANAGERS WITH MOST F.A. CUP SUCCESSES

4 Sir Alex Ferguson (Manchester Utd.); **3** Charles Foweraker (Bolton Wand.), John Nicholson (Sheffield Utd.), Bill Nicholson (Tottenham), Arsene Wenger (Arsenal).

RECORD FEE FOR MANAGER

Tottenham paid Leeds Utd. £3m. compensation when they appointed **George Graham** In October 1998.

RELEGATION 'DOUBLES'

Managers associated with two clubs relegated in same season: **John Bond** in 1985-6 (Swansea City and Birmingham City); **Ron Saunders** in 1985-6 (W.B.A. – and their reserve team – and Birmingham City); **Bob Stokoe** in 1986-7 (Carlisle Utd. and Sunderland); **Billy McNeill** in 1986-7 (Manchester City and Aston Villa); **Dave Bassett** in 1987-8 (Watford and Sheffield Utd.); **Mick Mills** in 1989-90 (Stoke City and Colchester Utd.).

WEMBLEY STADIUM

When Wembley Stadium closed after England's World Cup qualifying match against Germany in October 2000, demolition was due to begin within weeks and 'new

Wembley' scheduled to open in 2004. The reality was two years of frustration and embarrassment for the Football Association, the F.A.-owned Wembley National Stadium Ltd. and the Government after plans for a £430m. loan from City banks fell through.

The finances eventually agreed included a £426m. loan from West Deutsche Landesbank, the German finance house, a minimum £100m. from the Football Association and £120m. previously given by Sport England. Building is contracted to the Australian-based construction company Multiplex.

After the two-year delay, the bulldozers and giant excavator Goliath moved into Wembley in September 2002. By December, the crowns atop the symbolic concrete towers were removed and placed in storage, to be exhibited in the Wembley Experience Museum.

That will be among the attractions when, after a 39 months' building programme, the £757m., 90,000-seat stadium opens early in 2006, with a showpiece England match against, possibly, Brazil or Germany, preceding the return of the F.A. Cup Final to its traditional home.

A £70m.-a-year income is predicted for the stadium, and for 30 years from 2006 the Wembley schedule will include all England Internationals, F.A. Cup semi-finals and Final, the League Cup Final, Play-off Finals, F.A. Community Shield and the Rugby League Challenge Cup Final.

INVASION DAY

Memorable scenes were witnessed at the **first F.A. Cup Final at Wembley, April 28, 1923**, between **Bolton Wand.** and **West Ham Utd.**. An accurate return of the attendance could not be made owing to thousands breaking in, but there were probably more than 200,000 spectators present. The match was delayed for 40 minutes by the crowd invading the pitch. Official attendance was 126,047.

Gate receipts totalled £27,776. The two clubs and the Football Association each received £6,365 and the F.A. refunded £2,797 to ticket-holders who were unable to get to their seats. Cup Final admission has since been by ticket only.

REDUCED CAPACITY

Capacity of the all-seated **Wembley Stadium** was 78,000. The last 100,000 attendance was for the 1985 F.A. Cup Final between Manchester Utd. and Everton.

WEMBLEY'S FIRST UNDER LIGHTS

November 30, 1955 (England 4, Spain 1), when the floodlights were switched on after 73 minutes (afternoon match played in damp, foggy conditions).

First Wembley International played throughout under lights: England 8, N. Ireland 3 on evening of November 20, 1963 (att: 55,000).

MOST WEMBLEY APPEARANCES BY PLAYER

57 by Peter Shilton (52 England, 2 League Cup Finals, 1 F.A. Cup Final, 1 Charity Shield, 1 Football League XI).

WEMBLEY HAT-TRICKS

Three players have scored hat-tricks in major cup finals at Wembley: **Stan Mortensen** for Blackpool v Bolton Wand. (F.A. Cup Final, 1953), **Geoff Hurst** for England v West Germany (World Cup Final, 1966) and **David Speedie** for Chelsea v Manchester City (Full Members Cup, 1985).

ENGLAND'S WEMBLEY DEFEATS

England have lost 18 matches to foreign opponents at Wembley:

Nov.	1953	3-6 v Hungary	Feb.	1977	0-2 v Holland
Oct.	1959	2-3 v Sweden	Mar.	1981	1-2 v Spain
Oct.	1965	2-3 v Austria	May	1981	0-1 v Brazil
Apr.	1972	1-3 v W. Germany	Oct.	1982	1-2 v W. Germany
Nov.	1973	0-1 v Italy	Sept.	1983	0-1 v Denmark

June	1984	0-2 v Russia	Feb.	1997	0-1 v Italy
May	1990	1-2 v Uruguay	Feb.	1998	0-2 v Chile
Sept.	1991	0-1 v Germany	Feb.	1999	0-2 v France
June	1995	1-3 v Brazil	Oct.	2000	0-1 v Germany

A further defeat came in **Euro 96**. After drawing the semi-final with Germany 1-1, England went out 6-5 on penalties.

FASTEST GOALS AT WEMBLEY

In first-class matches: **38 seconds** by **Bryan Robson** in England's 2-1 win against Yugoslavia on December 13, 1989; **44 seconds** by **Bryan Robson** for England in 4-0 win v N. Ireland on February 23, 1982; **42 seconds** by **Roberto di Matteo** for Chelsea in the 1997 F.A. Cup Final v Middlesbrough.

Fastest goal in **any** match at Wembley: **20 seconds** by **Maurice Cox** for Cambridge University against Oxford on December 5, 1979.

FOUR WEMBLEY HEADERS

When **Wimbledon** beat Sutton Utd. 4-2 in the F.A. Amateur Cup Final at Wembley on May 4, 1963, Irish centre-forward **Eddie Reynolds** headed all four goals.

WEMBLEY ONE-SEASON DOUBLES

In 1989, **Nott'm. Forest** became the first club to win two Wembley Finals in the same season (Littlewoods Cup and Simod Cup).

In 1993, **Arsenal** made history there as the first club to win the League (Coca-Cola) Cup and the F.A. Cup in the same season. They beat Sheffield Wed. 2-1 in both finals.

SUDDEN DEATH DECIDERS

First Wembley Final decided on sudden death (first goal scored in overtime): April 23, 1995 – **Birmingham City** beat Carlisle Utd. (1-0, Paul Tait 103 mins.) to win Auto Windscreens Shield.

First instance of a 'golden goal' deciding a major International tournament was at Wembley on June 30, 1996, when **Germany** beat the Czech Republic 2-1 in the European Championship Final with Oliver Bierhoff's goal in the 95th. minute.

MILLENNIUM STADIUM, CARDIFF

Wales' new national stadium is the ground its chairman **Glanmor Griffiths** proudly built. On the site of Cardiff Arms Park, world-famous home of Welsh Rugby, it cost £130m. (£50m. from Lottery grants), took two years to build with retractable roof and a 73,434 all-seated capacity. Facilities include 126 hospitality boxes, 380 wheelchair spaces, 112 turnstiles, 38 food outlets and 17 public bars.

The stadium opened on June 26, 1999 with Wales beating the reigning World rugby champions South Africa. The first soccer international there was Wales v Finland on March 29, 2000.

The first 11 soccer matches played at the Millennium Stadium were won by the team using the North dressing-room. Stoke City ended the sequence when they beat Brentford 2-0 in the Div. 2 play-off Final on May 11, 2002.

The Millennium Stadium has solved English football's problem caused by the closure of Wembley, staging all the major domestic Finals in seasons 2000-01-02-03.

In the F.A. Charity Shield fixture on Sunday, August 12, 2001, Liverpool and Manchester Utd. became the first British clubs to meet under a closed-in roof.

The retractable roof has been closed for three major Finals: Worthington Cup, 2002 and 2003, F.A. Cup, 2003.

SHADOWS OVER SOCCER

DAYS OF TRAGEDY – CLUBS

Season 1988-9 brought the worst disaster in the history of British sport, with the death of *95 Liverpool supporters (200 injured) at the **F.A. Cup semi-final** against Nott'm. Forest at **Hillsborough, Sheffield**, on Saturday, April 15. The tragedy built up in the minutes preceding kick-off, when thousands surged into the ground at the Leppings Lane end. Many were crushed in the tunnel between entrance and terracing, but most of the victims were trapped inside the perimeter fencing behind the goal. The match was abandoned without score after six minutes' play. The dead included seven women and girls, two teenage sisters and two teenage brothers. The youngest victim was a boy of ten, the oldest 67-year-old Gerard Baron, whose brother Kevin played for Liverpool in the 1950 Cup Final. (*Total became 96 in March 1993, when Tony Bland died after being in a coma for nearly four years).

The two worst disasters in one season in British soccer history occurred at the end of 1984-5. On May 11, the last Saturday of the League season, 56 people (two of them visiting supporters) were burned to death – and more than 200 taken to hospital – when fire destroyed the main stand at the **Bradford City-Lincoln City** match at Valley Parade.

The wooden, 77-year-old stand was full for City's last fixture before which, amid scenes of celebration, the club had been presented with the Third Division Championship trophy. The fire broke out just before half-time and, within five minutes, the entire stand was engulfed.

Eighteen days later, on May 29, at the European Cup Final between **Liverpool** and **Juventus** at the Heysel Stadium, Brussels, 39 spectators (31 of them Italian) were crushed or trampled to death and 437 injured. The disaster occurred an hour before the scheduled kick-off when Liverpool supporters charged a Juventus section of the crowd at one end of the stadium, and a retaining wall collapsed.

The sequel was a 5-year ban by UEFA on English clubs generally in European competition, with a 6-year ban on Liverpool.

On May 26, 1985 ten people were trampled to death and 29 seriously injured in a crowd panic on the way into the **Olympic Stadium, Mexico City** for the Mexican Cup Final between local clubs National University and America.

More than 100 people died and 300 were injured in a football disaster at **Nepal's national stadium** in Katmandu in March 1988. There was a stampede when a violent hailstorm broke over the capital. Spectators rushed for cover, but the stadium exits were locked, and hundreds were trampled in the crush.

In South Africa, on January 13, 1991 40 black fans were trampled to death (50 injured) as they tried to escape from fighting that broke out at a match in the gold-mining town of Orkney, 80 miles from Johannesburg. The friendly, between top teams **Kaiser Chiefs** and **Orlando Pirates**, attracted a packed crowd of 20,000. Violence erupted after the referee allowed Kaiser Chiefs a disputed second-half goal to lead 1-0.

Disaster struck at the French Cup semi-final (May 5, 1992), with the death of 15 spectators and 1,300 injured when a temporary metal stand collapsed in the Corsican town of Bastia. The tie between Second Division **Bastia** and French Champions **Marseille** was cancelled. **Monaco**, who won the other semi-final, were allowed to compete in the next season's Cup-Winners' Cup.

A total of 318 died and 500 were seriously injured when the crowd rioted over a disallowed goal at the National Stadium in Lima, Peru, on May 24, 1964. **Peru** and **Argentina** were competing to play in the Olympic Games in Tokyo.

That remained sport's heaviest death toll until October 20, 1982, when (it was revealed only in July 1989) 340 Soviet fans were killed in Moscow's Lenin Stadium at the UEFA Cup second round first leg match between **Moscow Spartak** and **Haarlem (Holland)**. They were crushed on an open stairway when a last-minute Spartak goal sent departing spectators surging back into the ground.

Among other crowd disasters abroad: **June 1968** – 74 died in **Argentina**. Panic broke out at the end of a goalless match between River Plate and Boca Juniors at Nunez, Buenos Aires, when Boca supporters threw lighted newspaper torches on to fans in the tiers below.

February 1974 – 49 killed in **Egypt** in crush of fans clamouring to see Zamalek play Dukla Prague.

September 1971 – 44 died in **Turkey**, when fighting among spectators over a disallowed goal (Kayseri v Siwas) led to a platform collapsing.

The then worst disaster in the history of British football, in terms of loss of life, occurred at Glasgow Rangers' ground at **Ibrox Park**, January 2, 1971.

Sixty-six people were trampled to death (100 injured) as they tumbled down Stairway 13 just before the end of the **Rangers v Celtic** New Year's match. That disaster led to the 1975 Safety of Sports Grounds legislation.

The Ibrox tragedy eclipsed even the Bolton disaster in which 33 were killed and about 500 injured when a wall and crowd barriers collapsed near a corner-flag at the **Bolton Wand. v Stoke City** F.A. Cup sixth round tie on March 9, 1946. The match was completed after half an hour's stoppage.

In a previous crowd disaster at **Ibrox** on April 5, 1902, part of the terracing collapsed during the Scotland v England International and 25 people were killed. The match, held up for 20 minutes, ended 1-1, but was never counted as an official International.

Eight leading players and three officials of **Manchester Utd.** and eight newspaper representatives were among the 23 who perished in the air crash at Munich on February 6, 1958, during take-off following a European Cup-tie in Belgrade. The players were Roger Byrne, Geoffrey Bent, Eddie Colman, Duncan Edwards, Mark Jones, David Pegg, Tommy Taylor and Liam Whelan, and the officials were Walter Crickmer (secretary), Tom Curry (trainer) and Herbert Whalley (coach). The newspaper representatives were Alf Clarke, Don Davies, George Follows, Tom Jackson, Archie Ledbrooke, Henry Rose, Eric Thompson and Frank Swift (former England goalkeeper of Manchester City).

On May 14, 1949, the entire team of Italian Champions **Torino,** 8 of them Internationals, were killed when the aircraft taking them home from a match against Benfica in Lisbon crashed at Superga, near Turin. The total death toll of 28 included all the club's reserve players, the manager, trainer and coach.

On February 8, 1981, 24 spectators died and more than 100 were injured at a match **in Greece**. They were trampled as thousands of the 40,000 crowd tried to rush out of the stadium at Piraeus after Olympiakos beat AEK Athens 6-0.

On November 17, 1982, 24 people (12 of them children) were killed and 250 injured when fans stampeded at the end of a match at the Pascual Guerrero stadium in **Cali, Colombia**. Drunken spectators hurled fire crackers and broken bottles from the higher stands on to people below and started a rush to the exits.

On December 9, 1987, the 18-strong team squad of **Alianza Lima,** one of Peru's top clubs, were wiped out, together with 8 officials and several youth players, when a military aircraft taking them home from Puccalpa crashed into the sea off Ventillana, ten miles from Lima. The only survivor among 43 on board was a member of the crew.

On April 28, 1993, 18 members of **Zambia's International** squad and 5 ZFA officials died when the aircraft carrying them to a World Cup qualifying tie against Senegal crashed into the Atlantic soon after take-off from Libreville, Gabon.

On October 16, 1996, 81 fans were crushed to death and 147 seriously injured in the 'Guatemala Disaster' at the World Cup qualifier against Costa Rica in Mateo Flores stadium. The tragedy happened an hour before kick-off, allegedly caused by ticket forgery and overcrowding – 60,000 were reported in the 45,000-capacity ground – and safety problems related to perimeter fencing.

On July 9, 1996, 8 people died, 39 injured in riot after derby match between **Libya's two top clubs** in Tripoli. Al-Ahli had beaten Al-Ittihad 1-0 by a controversial goal.

On April 6, 1997, 5 spectators were crushed to death at **Nigeria's national stadium** in Lagos after the 2-1 World Cup qualifying victory over Guinea. Only two of five gates were reported open as the 40,000 crowd tried to leave the ground.

It was reported from the **Congo** (October 29, 1998) that a bolt of lightning struck a village match, killing all 11 members of the home team Benatshadi, but leaving the opposing players from Basangana unscathed. It was believed the surviving team wore better-insulated boots.

On January 10, 1999 eight fans died and 13 were injured in a stampede at **Egypt's Alexandria Stadium**. Some 25,000 spectators had pushed into the ground. Despite the tragedy, the cup-tie between Al-Ittihad and Al-Koroum was completed.

Three people suffocated and several were seriously injured when thousands of fans forced their way into **Liberia's national stadium** in Monrovia at a goalless World Cup qualifying match against Chad on April 23, 2000. The stadium (capacity 33,000) was reported 'heavily overcrowded'.

On Sunday, July 9, 2000 12 spectators died from crush injuries when police fired tear gas into the 50,000 crowd after South Africa scored their second goal in a World Cup group qualifier against Zimbabwe in **Harare**. A stampede broke out as fans scrambled to leave the national stadium. Players of both teams lay face down on the pitch as fumes swept over them. FIFA launched an investigation and decided that the result would stand, with South Africa leading 2-0 at the time of the 84th-minute abandonment.

On April 11, 2001, at one of the biggest matches of the South African season, 43 died and 155 were injured in a crush at **Ellis Park, Johannesburg**. After tearing down a fence, thousands of fans surged into a stadium already packed to its 60,000 capacity for the Premiership derby between top Soweto teams Kaizer Chiefs and Orlando Pirates. The match was abandoned at 1-1 after 33 minutes. In January 1991, 40 died in a crowd crush at a friendly between the same clubs at Orkney, 80 miles from Johannesburg.

On April 29, 2001, seven people were trampled to death and 51 injured when a riot broke out at a match between two of Congo's biggest clubs, Lupopo and Mazembe at **Lubumbashi**, southern Congo.

On May 6, 2001, two spectators were killed in Iran and hundreds were injured when a glass fibre roof collapsed at the over-crowded Mottaqi Stadium at **Sari** for the match between Pirouzi and Shemshak Noshahr.

On May 9, 2001, in Africa's worst football disaster, 123 died and 93 were injured in a stampede at the national stadium in **Accra, Ghana**. Home team Hearts of Oak were leading 2-1 against Asante Kotoko five minutes from time, when Asanti fans started hurling bottles on to the pitch. Police fired tear gas into the stands, and the crowd panicked in a rush for the exits, which were locked. It took the death toll at three big matches in Africa in April/May to 173.

On August 12, 2001, two players were killed by lightning and ten severely burned at a **Guatemala** Third Division match between Deportivo Culquimulilla and Pueblo Nuevo Vinas.

On November 1, 2002, two players died from injuries after lightning struck Deportivo Cali's training ground in **Colombia**.

DAYS OF TRAGEDY – PERSONAL

Sam Wynne, Bury right-back, collapsed five minutes before half-time in the First Division match away to Sheffield Utd. on April 30, 1927, and died in the dressing-room.

In the Rangers v Celtic League match on September 5, 1931, **John Thomson**, the 23-year-old Celtic and Scotland goalkeeper, sustained a fractured skull when diving at an opponent's feet just before half-time and died the same evening.

Sim Raleigh (Gillingham), injured in a clash of heads at home to Brighton & H.A. (Div. 3 South) on December 1, 1934, continued to play but collapsed in second half and died in hospital the same night.

James Thorpe, 23-year-old Sunderland goalkeeper, was injured during the First Division match at home to Chelsea on February 1, 1936 and died in a diabetic coma three days later.

Derek Dooley, Sheffield Wed. centre-forward and top scorer in 1951-52 in the Football League with 46 goals in 30 matches, broke a leg in the League match at Preston N.E. on February 14, 1953, and, after complications set in, had to lose the limb by amputation.

John White (27), Tottenham's Scottish International forward, was killed by lightning on a golf course at Enfield, North London in July, 1964.

Two players were killed by lightning during the **Army Cup Final** replay at Aldershot in April, 1948.

Tommy Allden (23), Highgate Utd. centre-half was struck by lightning during an Amateur Cup quarter-final with Enfield Town on February 25, 1967. He died the following day. Four other players were also struck but recovered.

Roy Harper died while refereeing the York City–Halifax Town (Div. 4) match on May 5, 1969.

Jim Finn collapsed and died from a heart attack while refereeing Exeter City v Stockport Co. (Div. 4) on September 16, 1972.

Scotland manager **Jock Stein**, 62, collapsed and died at the end of the Wales-Scotland World Cup qualifying match (1-1) at Ninian Park, Cardiff on September 10, 1985.

David Longhurst, 25-year-old York City forward, died after being carried off two minutes before half-time in the Fourth Division fixture at home to Lincoln City on September 8, 1990. The match was abandoned (0-0). The inquest revealed that Longhurst suffered from a rare heart condition.

Mike North collapsed while refereeing Southend Utd. v Mansfield Town (Div. 3) on April 16, 2001 and died shortly afterwards. The match was abandoned and re-staged on May 8, with the receipts donated to his family.

Marc-Vivien Foe, 28, on his 63rd appearance in Cameroon's midfield, collapsed unchallenged in the centre circle after 72 minutes of the FIFA Confederations Cup semi-final against Colombia in Lyon, France, on June 26, 2003, and despite the efforts of the stadium medical staff he could not be revived. He had been on loan to Manchester City from Olympique Lyonnais in season 2002–03, and poignantly scored the club's last goal at Maine Road.

GREAT SERVICE

'For services to Association Football', **Stanley Matthews** (Stoke City, Blackpool and England), already a C.B.E., became the first professional footballer to receive a knighthood. This was bestowed in 1965, his last season.

Before he retired and five days after his 50th birthday, he played for Stoke City to set a record as the oldest First Division footballer (v. Fulham, February 6, 1965).

Over a brilliant span of 33 years, he played in 886 first-class matches, including 54 full Internationals (plus 31 in war time), 701 League games (including 3 at start of season 1939-40, which was abandoned on the outbreak of war) and 86 F.A. Cup-ties, and scored 95 goals. He was never booked in his career.

Sir Stanley died on February 23 2000, three weeks after his 85th birthday. His ashes were buried under the centre circle of Stoke's Britannia Stadium. After spending a number of years in Toronto, he made his home back in the Potteries in 1989, having previously returned to his home town, Hanley, Stoke-on-Trent in October, 1987 to unveil a life-size bronze statue of himself.

The inscription reads: 'Sir Stanley Matthews, CBE. Born Hanley, 1 February 1915. His name is symbolic of the beauty of the game, his fame timeless and international, his sportsmanship and modesty universally acclaimed. A magical player, of the people, for the people.'

On his home-coming in 1989, Sir Stanley was made President of Stoke City, the club he joined as a boy of 15 and served as a player for 20 years between 1931 and 1965, on either side of his spell with Blackpool.

In July 1992 FIFA honoured him with their 'Gold merit award' for outstanding services to the game.

Former England goalkeeper **Peter Shilton** has made more first-class appearances (1,387) than any other footballer in British history. He played his 1,000th. League game in Leyton Orient's 2-0 home win against Brighton & H.A. on Dec. 22, 1996 and in all played 9 times for Orient in his final season. He retired from International football after the 1990 World Cup in Italy with 125 caps, then a world record.

Shilton's career spanned 32 seasons, 20 of them on the International stage. He made his League debut for Leicester City in May 1966, two months before England won the World Cup.

His 1,387 first-class appearances comprise a record 1,005 in the Football League, 125 Internationals, 102 League Cup, 86 F.A. Cup, 13 for England U-23s, 4 for the Football League and 52 other matches (European Cup, UEFA Cup, World Club

Championship, Charity Shield, European Super Cup, Full Members' Cup, Play-offs, Screen Sports Super Cup, Anglo-Italian Cup, Texaco Cup, Simod Cup, Zenith Data Systems Cup and Autoglass Trophy).

Shilton appeared more times at Wembley (57) than any other player: 52 for England, 2 League Cup Finals, 1 F.A. Cup Final, 1 Charity Shield match, and 1 for the Football League. He passed a century of League appearances with each of his first five clubs: Leicester City (286), Stoke City (110), Nott'm. Forest (202), Southampton (188) and Derby Co. (175) and subsequently played for Plymouth Argyle, Bolton Wand. and Leyton Orient.

His club honours, all gained with Nott'm. Forest: League Championship 1978, League Cup 1979, European Cup 1979 and 1980, PFA Player of Year 1978.

Five other British footballers have made more than 1,000 first-class appearances:

Ray Clemence, formerly with Tottenham, Liverpool and England, retired through injury in season 1987-8 after a goalkeeping career of 1,119 matches starting in 1965-6. Clemence played 50 times for his first club, Scunthorpe Utd.; 665 for Liverpool; 337 for Tottenham; his 67 representative games included 61 England caps.

A third great British goalkeeper, **Pat Jennings**, ended his career (1963-86) with a total of 1,098 first-class matches for Watford, Tottenham, Arsenal and N. Ireland. They were made up of 757 in the Football League, 119 full Internationals, 84 F.A. Cup appearances, 72 League/Milk Cup, 55 European club matches, 2 Charity Shield, 3 Other Internationals, 1 Under-23 cap, 2 Texaco Cup, 2 Anglo-Italian Cup and 1 Super Cup. Jennings played his 119th. and final International on his 41st birthday, June 12, 1986, against Brazil in Guadalajara in the Mexico World Cup.

Yet another outstanding 'keeper, **David Seaman**, passed the 1,000 appearances milestone for clubs and country in season 2002–03, reaching 1,004 when aged 39, he captained Arsenal to F.A. Cup triumph against Southampton. Spanning 21 seasons, his total comprised 929 club appearances: Peterborough Utd. 106, Birmingham City 84, Q.P.R. 175, Arsenal 564, plus 75 caps for England.

With Arsenal, Seaman won 3 Championship medals, the F.A. Cup 4 times, the Double twice, the League Cup and Cup-Winners' Cup once each. After 13 seasons at Highbury, he joined Manchester City (June 2003) on a free transfer.

Defender **Graeme Armstrong**, 42-year-old commercial manager for an Edinburgh whisky company and part-time assistant-manager and captain of Scottish Third Division club Stenhousemuir, made the 1000th first team appearance of his career in the Scottish Cup 3rd Round against Rangers at Ibrox on January 23, 1999. He was presented with the Man of the Match award before kick-off.

Against East Stirling on Boxing Day, he had played his 864th League game, breaking the British record for an outfield player set by another Scot, Tommy Hutchison, with Alloa, Blackpool, Coventry City, Manchester City, Burnley and Swansea City.

Armstrong's 24-year career, spent in the lower divisions of the Scottish League, began as a 1-match trialist with Meadowbank Thistle in 1975 and continued via Stirling Albion, Berwick Rangers, Meadowbank and, from 1992, Stenhousemuir.

Tony Ford became the first English outfield player to reach 1000 senior appearances in Rochdale's 1-0 win at Carlisle (Auto Windscreens Shield) on March 7, 2000. Grimsby-born, he began his 26-season midfield career with Grimsby Town and played for 7 other League clubs: Sunderland (loan), Stoke City, W.B.A., Bradford City (loan), Scunthorpe Utd., Mansfield Town and Rochdale. He retired, aged 42, in 2001 with a career record of 1072 appearances (121 goals) and his total of 931 League games is exceeded only by Peter Shilton's 1005.

EIGHT KNIGHTS OF SOCCER

In the Queen's Golden Jubilee Honours, on June 15, 2002, Newcastle Utd.'s 69-year-old manager **Bobby Robson** was awarded a knighthood for his services to football. He became the eighth player or manager to be so honoured.

The elite list reads: **Stanley Matthews** (1965), **Alf Ramsey** (1967), **Matt Busby** (1968), **Bobby Charlton** (1994), **Tom Finney** (1998), **Geoff Hurst** (1998), **Alex Ferguson** (1999) and **Bobby Robson** (2002).

PENALTIES

The **penalty-kick** was introduced to the game, following a proposal to the Irish F.A. in 1890 by William McCrum, son of the High Sheriff for Co. Omagh, and approved by the International Football Board on June 2, 1891.

First penalty scored in a first-class match in England was by John Heath, for Wolves v Accrington Stanley (5-0 in Div. 1, September 14, 1891).

The greatest influence of the penalty has come since the 1970s, with the introduction of the shoot-out to settle deadlocked ties in various competitions.

Manchester Utd. were the first club to win a competitive match in British football via a shoot-out (4-3 away to Hull City, Watney Cup semi-final, August 1, 1970); in that penalty contest, George Best was the first player to score, Denis Law the first to miss.

The shoot-out was adopted by FIFA and UEFA the same year (1970).

In season 1991-2, penalty shoot-outs were introduced to decide **F.A. Cup ties** still level after one replay and extra time.

Wembley saw its first penalty contest in the 1974 Charity Shield. Since then many major matches across the world have been settled in this way, including:

1974 **F.A. Charity Shield** (Wembley): Liverpool beat Leeds Utd. 6-5 (after 1-1).
1976 **Eur. Champ. Final** (Belgrade): Czech. beat W. Germany 5-3 (after 2-2).
1980 **Cup-Winners' Cup Final** (Brussels): Valencia beat Arsenal 5-4 (0-0).
1980 **Eur. Champ. 3rd/4th place play-off** (Naples): Czechoslovakia beat Italy 9-8 (after 1-1).
1982 **World Cup s-final** (Seville): West Germany beat France 5-4 (after 3-3).
1984 **European Cup Final** (Rome): Liverpool beat AS Roma 4-2 (after 1-1).
1984 **UEFA Cup Final**: Tottenham (home) beat Anderlecht 4-3 (2-2 agg.).
1984 **Eur. Champ. s-final** (Lyon, France): Spain beat Denmark 5-4 (after 1-1).
1986 **European Cup Final** (Seville): Steaua Bucharest beat Barcelona 2-0 (0-0). Barcelona's four penalties were all saved.
1986 **World Cup q-finals** (in Mexico): France beat Brazil 4-3 (after 1-1); West Germany beat Mexico 4-1 (after 0-0); Belgium beat Spain 5-4 (after 1-1).
1987 **Freight Rover Trophy Final** (Wembley): Mansfield Town Town beat Bristol City 5-4 (after 1-1).
1987 **Scottish League (Skol) Cup Final** (Hampden Park): Rangers beat Aberdeen 5-3 (after 3-3).
1988 **European Cup Final** (Stuttgart): PSV Eindhoven beat Benfica 6-5 (after 0-0).
1988 **UEFA Cup Final**: Bayer Leverkusen (home) beat Espanyol 3-2 after 3-3 (0-3a, 3-0h).
1990 **Scottish F.A. Cup Final** (Hampden Park): Aberdeen beat Celtic 9-8 (0-0).
1990 **World Cup** (in Italy): 2nd. Round: Rep. of Ireland beat Romania 5-4 (after 0-0); q-final: Argentina beat Yugoslavia 3-2 (after 0-0); s-finals: Argentina beat Italy 4-3 (after 1-1); West Germany beat England 4-3 (1-1).
1991 **European Cup Final** (Bari): Red Star Belgrade beat Marseille 5-3 (after 0-0).
1991 **Barclays League Play-off** (4th. Div. Final – Wembley): Torquay Utd. beat Blackpool 5-4 (after 2-2).
1992 **F.A. Cup s-final** replay (Villa Park): Liverpool beat Portsmouth 3-1 (after 0-0).
1992 **Barclays League Play-off** (4th. Div. Final – Wembley): Blackpool beat Scunthorpe Utd. 4-3 (after 1-1).
1992 **Eur. Champ. s-final** (Gothenburg): Denmark beat Holland 5-4 (after 2-2).
1993 **Barclays League Play-off**: (3rd Div. Final – Wembley): York City beat Crewe Alexandra 5-3 (after 1-1).
1993 **F.A. Charity Shield** (Wembley): Manchester Utd. beat Arsenal 5-4 (after 1-1).
1994 **League (Coca-Cola) Cup s-final**: Aston Villa beat Tranmere Rov. 5-4 (after 4-4, 1-3a, 3-1h).
1994 **Autoglass Trophy Final** (Wembley): Swansea City beat Huddersfield Town 3-1 (after 1-1).
1994 **World Cup** (in U.S.A.): **2nd. Round**: Bulgaria beat Mexico 3-1 (after 1-1); q-final: Sweden beat Romania 5-4 (after 2-2); **Final**: Brazil beat Italy 3-2 (after 0-0).

1994 **Scottish League (Coca-Cola) Cup Final** (Ibrox Park): Raith beat Celtic 6-5 (after 2-2).
1995 **Cup-Winners' Cup s-final**: Arsenal beat Sampdoria away 3-2 (5-5 agg.)
1995 **Copa America Final** (Montevideo): Uruguay beat Brazil 5-3 (after 1-1).
1996 **European Cup Final** (Rome): Juventus beat Ajax 4-2 (after 1-1).
1996 **European U-21 Champ. Final** (Barcelona): Italy beat Spain 4-2 (after 1-1).
1996 **Eur. Champ. q-finals**: England beat Spain (Wembley) 4-2 after 0-0; France beat Holland (Anfield) 5-4 after 0-0; **s-finals**: Germany beat England (Wembley) 6-5 after 1-1; Czech Republic beat France (Old Trafford) 6-5 after 0-0.
1997 **Auto Windscreens Shield Final** (Wembley): Carlisle Utd. beat Colchester Utd. 4-3 (after 0-0)
1997 **UEFA Cup Final**: FC Schalke beat Inter Milan 4-1 (after 1-1 agg.).
1998 **Nationwide League play-off** (1st Div. Final Wembley): Charlton Athletic beat Sunderland 7-6 (after 4-4).
1998 **World Cup Finals**: Argentina beat England (2nd Round) 4-3 (after 2-2); France beat Italy (Q-final) 4-3 (after 0-0; Brazil beat Holland (S-final) 4-2 (after 1-1).
1999 **Nationwide League play-offs Div. 1 s-final**: Watford beat Birmingham City 7-6 away (after 1-1); **Div. 2 Final (Wembley)**: Manchester City beat Gillingham 3-1 (after 2-2).
1999 **Women's World Cup Final** (Rose Bowl, Pasedena, California) U.S.A. beat China 5-4 (after 0-0). **Third/Fourth place play-off** (same venue): Brazil beat Norway 5-4 (after 0-0).
2000 **African Nations Cup Final** (Lagos): Cameroon beat Nigeria 4-3 (after 0-0).
2000 **F.A. Cup s-final** (Wembley): Aston Villa beat Bolton Wand. 4-1 (after 0-0).
2000 **UEFA Cup Final** (Copenhagen): Galatasaray beat Arsenal 4-1 (after 0-0).
2000 **Eur. Champ. s-final** (Amsterdam): Italy beat Holland 3-1 (after 0-0). Holland missed 5 penalties in match – 2 in normal play, 3 in shoot-out. Italy survived with ten men after 33rd minute sending-off.
2000 **Olympic Final** (Sydney): Cameroon beat Spain 5-3 (after 2-2). Spain led 2-0, then had 2 men sent off.
2001 **League (Worthington) Cup Final** (Millennium Stadium, Cardiff): Liverpool beat Birmingham City 5-4 (after 1-1).
2001 **Champions League Final** (Milan): Bayern Munich beat Valencia 5-4 (after 1-1).
2002 **Eur. U-21 Champ. Final** (Basle): Czech Republic beat France 3-1 (after 0-0).
2002 **Nationwide League** play-off (1st Div. Final, Millennium Stadium, Cardiff): Birmingham City beat Norwich City 4-2 (after 1-1).
2002 **World Cup Finals**: Spain beat Rep. of Ireland (2nd Round) 3-2 (after 1-1); South Korea beat Spain (Q-final) 5-3 (after 0-0).
2003 **Champions League Final** (Old Trafford): AC Milan beat Juventus 3–2 (after 0–0).

Footnote: Highest-recorded score in a penalty shoot-out between Football League clubs was **Aldershot's 11-10** victory at home to **Fulham** after their 1-1 draw in the Freight Rover Trophy Southern quarter-final on February 10, 1987. Seven spot-kicks were missed or saved in a record 28-penalty shoot-out at senior level.

In South America in 1992, in a 26-shot competition, **Newell's Old Boys** beat America 11-10 in the Copa Libertadores.

Longest-recorded penalty contest in first-class matches was in Argentina in 1988 – from 44 shots, **Argentinos Juniors** beat **Racing Club 20-19**. **Genclerbirligi** beat **Galatasaray** 17-16 in a Turkish Cup-tie in 1996. Only one penalty was missed.

Highest-scoring shoot-outs in **Int. football**: North Korea beat Hong Kong 11-10 (after 3-3 draw) in an Asian Cup match in 1975; and Ivory Coast beat Ghana 11-10 (after 0-0 draw) in African Nations Cup Final, 1992.

Most penalties needed to settle an adult game in Britain: 44 in Norfolk Primary Cup 4th Round replay, December 2000. Aston Village side **Freethorpe** beat Foulsham 20-19 (5 kicks missed). All 22 players took 2 penalties each, watched by a crowd of 20. The sides had drawn 2-2, 4-4 in a tie of 51 goals.

Penalty that took 24 days: That is how long elapsed between the award and the taking of a penalty in an Argentine Second Division match between **Atalanta** and **Defensores** in 2003. A riot ended the original match with 5 minutes left, and the game was resumed on 30 April behind closed doors with the penalty that caused the abandonment. Lucas Ferreiro scored it to give Atalanta a 1–0 win.

ENGLAND'S CRUCIAL PENALTY SHOOT-OUTS

1990 World Cup Semi-final: Beaten 4-3 by West Germany.
1996 European Champ. Q-final: Beat Spain 4-2
1996 European Champ. S-final: Beaten 6-5 by Germany
1998 World Cup (2nd Round): Beaten 4-3 by Argentina.

INTERNATIONAL PENALTIES, MISSED

Four penalties out of five were missed when **Colombia** beat **Argentina** 3-0 in a Copa America group tie in Paraguay in July 1999. Martin Palmeiro missed three for Argentina and Colombia's Hamilton Ricard had one spot-kick saved.

In the European Championship semi-final against Italy in Amsterdam on June 29, 2000, **Holland** missed five penalties – two in normal time, three in the penalty contest which Italy won 3-1 (after 0-0). Dutch captain Frank de Boer missed twice from the spot.

F.A. CUP SHOOT-OUTS

In **12 seasons** since the introduction of this method to settle F.A. Cup ties (from Round 1) that are level after two matches, a total of **57 ties** in the competition proper have been decided by such means (5 in 1991-2, 6 in 1992-3, 4 in 1993-4, 4 in 1994-5, 4 in 1995-6; 3 in 1996-7, 12 in 1997-8, 5 in 1998-9, 4 in 1999-2000, 2 in 2000-01, 3 in 2001-02, 5 in 2002-03).

The **first** penalty contest in the F.A. Cup took place in **1972**. In days of the play-off for third place, the match was delayed until the eve of the following season when losing semi-finalists **Birmingham City** and **Stoke City** met at St. Andrew's on Aug. 5. The score was 0-0 and Birmingham City won 4-3 on penalties.

Highest recorded F.A. Cup shoot-out went to 24 kicks, with Macclesfield Town beating Forest Green Rov. (away) 11-10 in 1st Round replay on November 28, 2001.

Shoot-out abandoned: The F.A. Cup 1st Round replay between Oxford City and Wycombe Wand. at Wycombe on November 9, 1999 was abandoned (1-1) after extra time because, as the penalty shoot-out was about to begin, a fire broke out under a stand. Wycombe won the second replay 1-0 at Oxford Utd.'s ground.

MISSED CUP FINAL PENALTIES

John Aldridge (Liverpool) became the first player to miss a penalty in the F.A. Cup Final at Wembley – and the second in the competition's history (previously Charlie Wallace, of Aston Villa, in the 1913 Final against Sunderland at Crystal Palace) – when Wimbledon's Dave Beasant saved his shot in May 1988. Seven previous penalties had been scored in this Final at Wembley.

Another crucial penalty miss at Wembley was by Arsenal's **Nigel Winterburn,** Luton Town's Andy Dibble saving his spot-kick in the 1988 Littlewoods Cup Final, when a goal would have put Arsenal 3-1 ahead. Instead, they lost 3-2.

Winterburn was the third player to fail with a League Cup Final penalty at Wembley, following **Ray Graydon** (Aston Villa) against Norwich City in 1975 and **Clive Walker** (Sunderland), who shot wide in the 1985 Milk Cup Final, also against Norwich City (won 1-0). Graydon had his penalty saved by Kevin Keelan, but scored from the rebound and won the cup for Aston Villa (1-0).

Tottenham's **Gary Lineker** saw his penalty saved by Nott'm. Forest goalkeeper Mark Crossley in the 1991 F.A. Cup Final.

Derby Co.'s Martin Taylor saved a penalty from **Eligio Nicolini** in the Anglo-Italian Cup Final at Wembley on March 27, 1993, but Cremonese won 3-1.

LEAGUE PENALTIES RECORD

Most penalties in Football League match: Five – 4 to Crystal Palace (3 missed), 1 to Brighton & H.A. (scored) in Div. 2 match at Selhurst Park on March 27 (Easter

Monday), 1989. Crystal Palace won 2-1. Three of the penalties were awarded in a 5-minute spell. The match also produced 5 bookings and a sending-off.

Other teams missing 3 penalties in a match: **Burnley** v Grimsby Town (Div. 2), February 13, 1909; **Manchester City** v Newcastle Utd. (Div. 1), January 17, 1912.

HOTTEST MODERN SPOT-SHOT

Matthew Le Tissier ended his career in season 2001-02 with the distinction of having netted 48 out of 49 first-team penalties for Southampton. He scored the last 27 after his only miss when Nott'm. Forest keeper Mark Crossley saved in a Premier League match at The Dell on March 24, 1993.

SPOT-KICK HAT-TRICKS

Right-back **Joe Willetts** scored three penalties when Hartlepool Utd. beat neighbours Darlington 6–1 (Div. 3N) on Good Friday 1951.

Danish International **Jan Molby**'s only hat-trick in English football, for Liverpool in a 3-1 win at home to Coventry City (Littlewoods Cup, 4th round replay, Nov. 26, 1986) comprised three goals from the penalty spot.

It was the first such hat-trick in a major match for two years – since **Andy Blair** scored three penalties for Sheffield Wed. against Luton Town (Milk Cup 4th. round, Nov. 20 1984).

Portsmouth's **Kevin Dillon** scored a penalty hat-trick in the Full Members Cup (2nd rd.) at home to Millwall (3-2) on Nov. 4, 1986.

Alan Slough scored a hat-trick of penalties in an away game and was on the losing side, when Peterborough Utd. were beaten 4-3 at Chester City (Div. 3, Apr. 29, 1978).

Penalty hat-tricks in **International football**: **Dimitris Saravakos** (in 9 mins.) for Greece v Egypt in 1990. He scored 5 goals in match; **Henrik Larsson**, among his 4 goals in Sweden's 6-0 home win v Moldova in World Cup qualifying match, June 6, 2001.

MOST PENALTY GOALS (LEAGUE) IN SEASON

Thirteen out of 13 by **Francis Lee** for Manchester City (Div. 1) in 1971-2. His goal total for the season was 33. In season 1988-9, **Graham Roberts** scored 12 League penalties for Second Division Champions Chelsea.

PENALTY-SAVE SEQUENCES

Ipswich Town goalkeeper **Paul Cooper** saved eight of the ten penalties he faced in 1979-80. **Roy Brown** (Notts Co.) saved six in a row in season 1972-3.

Andy Lomas, goalkeeper for Chesham Utd. (Diadora League) claimed a record eight **consecutive** penalty saves – three at the end of season 1991-2 and five in 1992-3.

Mark Bosnich (Aston Villa) saved five in two consecutive matches in 1993-4: three in Coca-Cola Cup semi-final penalty shoot-out v Tranmere Rov. (Feb. 26), then two in Premiership at Tottenham (Mar. 2).

MISSED PENALTIES SEQUENCE

Against Wolves in Div. 2 on Sept. 28, 1991, **Southend Utd.** missed their seventh successive penalty (five of them the previous season).

SCOTTISH RECORDS

(See also under 'Goals' & 'Discipline')

RANGERS' MANY RECORDS

Rangers' record-breaking feats include:-
League Champions: 50 times (once joint holders) – world record.
Winning every match in Scottish League (18 games, 1898-9 season).

Major hat-tricks: Rangers have completed the domestic treble (League Championship, League Cup and Scottish F.A. Cup) a record seven times (1948-9, 1963-4, 1975-6, 1977-8, 1992-3, 1998-9, 2002-3).
League & Cup double: 16 times.
Nine successive Championships (1989-97). Four men played in all nine sides: Richard Gough, Ally McCoist, Ian Ferguson and Ian Durrant.
105 major trophies: Championships 50, Scottish Cup 31, League Cup 23, Cup-Winners' Cup 1.

CELTIC'S GRAND SLAM

Celtic's record in 1966-7 was the most successful by a British club in one season. They won the **Scottish League**, the **Scottish Cup**, the **Scottish League Cup** and became the first British club to win the **European Cup**. They also won the **Glasgow Cup**.

Celtic have 3 times achieved the Scottish treble (League Championship, League Cup and F.A. Cup), in 1966-7, 1968-9 and 2000-01 (in Martin O'Neill's first season as their manager). They became Scottish Champions for 2000-01 with a 1-0 home win against St. Mirren on April 7 – the earliest the title had been clinched for 26 years, since Rangers' triumph on March 29, 1975.

They have won the Scottish Cup 31 times, sharing the record with Rangers, and have completed the League and Cup double 12 times.

Celtic won nine consecutive Scottish League titles (1966-74) under Jock Stein.

LARSSON SUPREME

After missing most of the previous campaign with a broken leg, Swedish International **Henrik Larsson**, with 53 goals in season 2000-01, set a post-war record for Celtic and equalled the Scottish Premier League record of 35 by Brian McClair (Celtic) in 1986-7. Larsson's 35 earned him Europe's Golden Shoe award.

SCOTTISH CUP HAT-TRICKS

Aberdeen's feat of winning the Scottish F.A. Cup in 1982-3-4 made them only the third club to achieve that particular hat-trick.

Queen's Park did it twice (1874-5-6 and 1880-1-2), and **Rangers** have won the Scottish Cup three years in succession on three occasions: 1934-5-6, 1948-9-50 and 1962-3-4.

SCOTTISH CUP FINAL DISMISSALS

Three players have been sent off in the Scottish F.A. Cup Final: **Jock Buchanan** (Rangers v. Kilmarnock, 1929), **Roy Aitken** (Celtic v Aberdeen, 1984) and **Walter Kidd** (Hearts captain v Aberdeen, 1986).

RECORD SEQUENCES

Celtic hold the Scottish League record run of success with 62 matches undefeated, from November 13, 1915 to April 21, 1917, when Kilmarnock won 2-0 at Parkhead.

Greenock Morton in 1963-4 were undefeated in home League matches, obtained a record 67 points out of 72 and scored 135 goals, clinching promotion from Div. 2 as early as February 29.

Queen's Park did not have a goal scored against them during the first seven seasons of their existence (1867-74, before the Scottish League was formed).

WORST HOME SEQUENCE

After gaining promotion to Div. 1 in 1992, **Cowdenbeath** went a record 38 consecutive home League matches without a win. They ended the sequence (drew 8, lost 30) when beating Arbroath 1-0 on April 2, 1994, watched by a crowd of 225.

ALLY'S RECORDS

Ally McCoist became the first player to complete 200 goals in the Premier Division when he scored Rangers' winner (2-1) at Falkirk on December 12, 1992. His first was against Celtic in September 1983, and he reached 100 against Dundee on Boxing Day 1987.

When McCoist scored twice at home to Hibernian (4-3) on December 7, 1996, he became Scotland's record post-war League marksman, beating Gordon Wallace's 264.

Originally with St. Johnstone (1978-81), he spent two seasons with Sunderland (1981-3), then joined Rangers for £200,000 in June 1983.

In 15 seasons at Ibrox, he scored 355 goals for Rangers (250 League), and helped them win 10 Championships (9 in succession), 3 Scottish Cups and earned a record 9 League Cup winner's medals. He won the European Golden Boot in consecutive seasons (1991-2, 1992-3).

His 9 Premier League goals in three seasons for Kilmarnock gave him a career total of 281 Scottish League goals when he retired at the end of 2000-01.

FIVE IN A MATCH

Paul Sturrock set an individual scoring record for the Scottish Premier Division with 5 goals in Dundee Utd.'s 7-0 win at home to Morton on November 17, 1984. **Marco Negri** equalled the feat with all 5 when Rangers beat Dundee Utd. 5-1 at Ibrox (Premier Division) on August 23, 1997, and **Kenny Miller** scored 5 in Rangers' 7-1 win at home to St. Mirren on November 4, 2000.

SEATS MILESTONE FOR CELTIC

In season 1998-9, **Celtic** became the first British club with an **all-seated** capacity of 60,000. That figure was exceeded by **Manchester Utd.** (61,629) in 1999-2000.

NEGRI'S TEN-TIMER

Marco Negri scored in Rangers' first ten League matches (23 goals) in season 1997-8 – a Premier Division record. The previous best sequence was 8 by Ally MacLeod for Hibernian in 1978.

DOUBLE SCOTTISH FINAL

Rangers v Celtic drew **129,643** and **120,073** people to the Scottish Cup Final and replay at Hampden Park, Glasgow, in 1963. Receipts for the two matches totalled £50,500.

MOST SCOTTISH CHAMPIONSHIP MEDALS

13 by **Sandy Archibald** (Rangers, 1918-34). Post-war record: **10** by **Bobby Lennox** (Celtic, 1966-79).

Alan Morton won **nine** Scottish Championship medals with Rangers in 1921-23-24-25-27-28-29-30-31. **Ally McCoist** played in the Rangers side that won nine successive League titles (1989-97).

Between 1927 and 1939 **Bob McPhail** helped Rangers win nine Championships, finish second twice and third once. He scored 236 League goals but was never top scorer in a single season.

SCOTTISH CUP – NO DECISION

The **Scottish F.A.** withheld their Cup and medals in 1908-9 after Rangers and Celtic played two drawn games in the Final. Spectators rioted.

FEWEST LEAGUE WINS IN SEASON

Clydebank won only one of 36 matches in Div. 1, season 1999-2000. That victory did not come until March 7 (2-1 at home to Raith).

HAMPDEN'S £63M. REDEVELOPMENT

On completion of redevelopment costing £63m. **Hampden Park**, home of Scottish football and the oldest first-class stadium in the world, was re-opened full scale for the Rangers-Celtic Cup Final on May 29, 1999.

Work on the 'new Hampden' (capacity 52,000) began in 1992. The North and East stands were restructured (£12m.); a new South stand and improved West stand cost £51m. The Millennium Commission contributed £23m. and the Lottery Sports Fund provided a grant of £3.75m.

DEMISE OF AIRDRIE AND CLYDEBANK

In May 2002, First Division **Airdrieonians**, formed in 1878, went out of business. They had debts of £3m. Their place in the Scottish League was taken by **Gretna**, from the English Unibond League, who were voted into Div. 3. Second Division **Clydebank** folded in July 2002 and were taken over by the new **Airdrie United** club.

GREAT SCOTS

In February 1988, the Scottish F.A. launched a national **Hall of Fame**, initially comprising the first 11 Scots to make 50 International appearances, to be joined by all future players to reach that number of caps. Each member receives a gold medal, invitation for life at all Scotland's home matches, and has his portrait hung at Scottish F.A. headquarters in Glasgow.

MORE CLUBS IN 2000

The **Scottish Premier League** increased from 10 to 12 clubs in season 2000-1.

The **Scottish Football League** admitted two new clubs – Peterhead and Elgin City from the Highland League – to provide three divisions of 10 in 2000-1.

NOTABLE SCOTTISH 'FIRSTS'

- The father of League football was a Scot, **William McGregor**, a draper in Birmingham City. The 12-club Football League kicked off in September 1888, and McGregor was its first president.
- **Hibernian** were the first British club to play in the European Cup, by invitation. They reached the semi-final when it began in 1955-6.
- **Celtic** were Britain's first winners of the European Cup, in 1967.
- Scotland's First Division became the **Premier Division** in season 1975-6.
- Football's **first International** was staged at the West of Scotland cricket ground, Partick, on November 30, 1872: Scotland 0, England 0.
- Scotland introduced its **League Cup** in 1945-6, the first season after the war. It was another 15 years before the Football League Cup was launched.
- The Scottish F.A. Cup has been **sponsored** by Tennents for the last 14 seasons.
- Scotland pioneered the use in British football of **two substitutes** per team in League and Cup matches.
- The world's **record football score** belongs to Scotland: Arbroath 36, Bon Accord 0 (Scottish Cup first round) on September 12, 1885.
- The Scottish F.A. introduced the **penalty shoot-out** to their Cup Final in 1990.
- On Jan. 22, 1994 all six matches in the **Scottish Premier Division** ended as draws.
- Scotland's new Premier League introduced a **3-week shut-down** in January 1999 – first instance of British football adopting the winter break system that operates in a number of European countries. The SPL ended its New Year closure after 2003.
- **Rangers** made history at home to St. Johnstone (Premier League, 0-0, March 4, 2000) when fielding a team entirely without Scottish players.

SCOTTISH CUP SHOCK RESULTS

1885-86 (1) Arbroath 36, Bon Accord 0
1921-22 (F) Morton 1, Rangers 0
1937-38 (F) East Fife 4, Kilmarnock 2 (replay, after 1-1)
1960-61 (F) Dunfermline 2, Celtic 0 (replay, after 0-0)
1966-67 (1) Berwick Rangers 1, Rangers 0
1979-80 (3) Hamilton 2, Keith 3
1984-85 (1) Stirling Albion 20, Selkirk 0
1984-85 (3) Inverness Thistle 3, Kilmarnock 0
1986-87 (3) Rangers 0, Hamilton 1
1994-95 (4) Stenhousemuir 2, Aberdeen 0
1998-99 (3) Aberdeen 0, Livingston 1
1999-2000 (3) Celtic 1, Inverness Caledonian Thistle 3
2002-03 (5) Inverness Caledonian Thistle 1, Celtic 0

Scottish League (Coca-Cola) Cup Final shock
1994-95 Raith 2, Celtic 2 (Raith won 6-5 on pens.)

SCOTTISH DISCIPLINE (MODERN) – MAJOR PUNISHMENTS

1989 (June) fine **Hearts** £93,000, following TV infringement at UEFA Cup q-final.
1994 (August) Scottish League fine **Celtic** record £100,000 for poaching manager Tommy Burns from Kilmarnock.
1996 (November) UEFA fine **Celtic** £42,000 and **Alan Stubbs** £28,000 for using unlicensed agents in summer transfer from Bolton Wanderers.
1999 (August) Scottish Premier League fine **Celtic** £45,000 for their part in disturbances at home match with Rangers, May 2.
2000 (April) Scottish League deduct a record 15 points from **Hamilton Academical**, following their players (in protest over unpaid wages) refusing to turn up for Div. 2 fixture at Stenhousemuir on April 1. As a result, Hamilton relegated at end of season.

MISCELLANEOUS

NATIONAL ASSOCIATIONS FORMED

F.A. on Oct. 26 .... **1863**
F.A. of Wales **1876**
Scottish F.A. **1873**
Irish F.A. **1904**
Federation of International Football Associations (FIFA) **1904**

NATIONAL & INTERNATIONAL COMPETITIONS LAUNCHED

F.A. Cup **1871**
Welsh Cup **1877**
Scottish Cup **1873**
Irish Cup **1880**
Football League **1888**
F.A. Premier League **1992**
Scottish League **1890**
Scottish Premier League **1998**
Scottish League Cup **1945**
Football League Cup **1960**
Home International Championship **1883-4**
World (Jules Rimet) Cup, at Montevideo **1930**
European Championship **1958**
European Cup **1955**
Fairs/UEFA Cup **1955**
Cup-Winners' Cup **1960**
Youth International (16-18 age-groups) **1946-7**
Olympic Games Tournament, at Shepherd's Bush **1908**

INNOVATIONS

Size of Ball: Fixed in **1872.**
Shinguards: Introduced and registered by Sam Weller Widdowson (Nott'm. Forest & England) in **1874.**
Referee's Whistle: First used on Nott'm. Forest's ground in **1878.**
Professionalism: Legalised in England in the summer of **1885** as a result of agitation by Lancashire clubs.
Goal-nets: Invented and patented in **1890** by Mr. J. A. Brodie of Liverpool. They were first used in the North v South match in January, **1891.**
Referees and Linesmen: Replaced umpires and referees in January, **1891.**

Penalty-kick: Introduced at Irish F.A.'s request in the season **1891-2.** The penalty law ordering the goalkeeper to remain on the goal-line came into force in September, **1905,** and the order to stand on his goal-line until the ball is kicked arrived in **1929-30.**

White ball: First came into official use in **1951.**

Floodlighting: First F.A. Cup-tie (replay), Kidderminster Harriers v Brierley Hill Alliance, **1955.**

Heated pitch to beat frost tried by Everton at Goodison Park in **1958.**

First Soccer Closed-circuit TV: At Coventry City ground in October **1965** (10,000 fans saw their team win at Cardiff City, 120 miles away).

Substitutes (one per team) were first allowed in Football League matches at the start of season **1965-6**. Three substitutes (one a goalkeeper) allowed, two of which could be used, in Premier League matches, **1992-93**. The Football League introduced three substitutes for **1993-94**.

Three points for a win: This was introduced by the Football League in **1981-2,** by FIFA in World Cup games in 1994, and by the Scottish League in the same year.

Offside law amended, player 'level' no longer offside, and 'professional foul' made sending-off offence, **1990**.

Penalty shoot-outs introduced to decide F.A. Cup ties level after one replay and extra time, **1991-2**.

New back-pass rule – goalkeeper must not handle ball kicked to him by team-mate, **1992**.

Linesmen became 'referees' assistants', **1998**.

Goalkeepers not to hold ball longer than 6 seconds, **2000**.

Free-kicks advanced by ten yards against opponents failing to retreat, **2000**.

CUP AND LEAGUE DOUBLES

League Championship and F.A. Cup: Preston N.E., 1889; Aston Villa, 1897; Tottenham, 1961; Arsenal, 1971; Liverpool 1986; Manchester Utd. 1994, 1996; Arsenal 1998; Manchester Utd. 1999; Arsenal 2002.

F.A. Cup and Promotion: W.B.A., 1931.

F.A. Cup and Football League Cup: Arsenal, 1993; Liverpool, 2001 (also won UEFA Cup).

League Championship and Football League Cup: Nott'm Forest, 1978; Liverpool, 1982; Liverpool, 1983; Liverpool, 1984 (also won European Cup).

Scottish League Championship and Cup Double: Rangers, (16): 1928-30-34-35-49-50-53-63-64-76-78-92-93-96-2000-2003. Celtic, (12): 1907-8-14-54-67-69-71-72-74-77-88-2001. Aberdeen, (1): 1984.

Scottish Treble (Championship, Cup, League Cup): Rangers 7 times (1949-64-76-78-93-99, 2003); Celtic 3 times (1967-69-2001) (also won European Cup in 1967).

DERBY DAYS: COMPLETE LEAGUE RESULTS

Arsenal v Tottenham: Played 132 (all top div.); Arsenal 53 wins, Tottenham 45, Drawn 34.

Aston Villa v Birmingham City: Played 98; Aston Villa 39, Birmingham City 34, Drawn 25.

Everton v Liverpool: Played 168 (all top div.); Liverpool 61, Everton 54, Drawn 53.

Ipswich Town v Norwich City: Played 70; Ipswich Town 34, Norwich City 24, Drawn 12.

Manchester City v Manchester Utd.: Played 128; United 49, City 33, Drawn 46.

Middlesbrough v Newcastle Utd.: Played 100; Newcastle Utd. 40, Middlesbrough 33, Drawn 27.

Newcastle Utd. v Sunderland: Played 126; Newcastle Utd. 46, Sunderland 41, Drawn 39 (incl. 1990 play-offs – Sunderland win and draw).

Middlesbrough v Sunderland: Played 122; Sunderland 53, Middlesbrough 38, Drawn 31.

Nott'm. Forest v Notts Co.: Played 86; Forest 35, County 28, Drawn 23.

Sheffield Utd. v Sheffield Wed.: Played 104; United 39, Wednesday 32, Drawn 33.

Port Vale v Stoke City: Played 44; Stoke City 16, Port Vale 13, Drawn 14.

Bristol City v Bristol Rovers: Played 86; City 33, Rovers 25, Drawn 28.

Celtic v Rangers: Played 268; Rangers 105, Celtic 83, Drawn 80.

Dundee v Dundee Utd.: Played 116; United 57, Dundee 35, Drawn 24.

Hearts v Hibernian: Played 228; Hearts 93, Hibernian 67, Drawn 68.

YOUNGEST AND OLDEST

Youngest Caps	*Age*
Norman Whiteside (N. Ireland v Yugoslavia, June 17, 1982)	**17** years **41** days
Ryan Green (Wales v Malta, June 3, 1998)	**17** years **226** days
Wayne Rooney (England v Australia, February 12, 2003)	**17** years **111** days
Johnny Lambie (Scotland v Ireland, March 20, 1886)	**17** years **92** days
Jimmy Holmes (Rep. of Ireland v Austria, May 30, 1971)	**17** years **200** days

England's youngest cap (pre-Rooney) since 1900: Michael Owen (v Chile, Wembley, February 11, 1998) 18 years 59 days.

Youngest England scorer: Michael Owen (18 years, 164 days) v Morocco, Casablanca, May 27, 1998.

Youngest England captains: Bobby Moore (v Czech., Bratislava, May 29, 1963), 22 years, 47 days; Michael Owen (v Paraguay, Anfield, April 17, 2002), 22 years, 117 days.

Youngest England players to reach 50 caps: Michael Owen (23 years, 6 months) v Slovakia at Middlesbrough, June 11, 2003; Bobby Moore (25 years, 7 months) v Wales at Wembley, November 16, 1966.

Youngest player in World Cup Final: Pele (Brazil) aged 17 years, 237 days v Sweden in Stockholm, June 12, 1958.

Youngest player to appear in World Cup Finals: Norman Whiteside (N. Ireland v Yugoslavia in Spain – June 17, 1982, age 17 years and 42 days.

Youngest First Division player: Derek Forster (Sunderland goalkeeper v Leicester City, August 22, 1964) aged 15 years, 185 days.

Youngest First Division scorer: At 16 years and 57 days, schoolboy Jason Dozzell (substitute after 30 minutes for Ipswich Town at home to Coventry City on February 4, 1984). Ipswich Town won 3-1 and Dozzell scored their third goal.

Youngest F.A. Premier League player: Gary McSheffrey (Coventry City v Aston Villa, February 27, 1999), 16 years, 198 days.

Youngest F.A. Premier League scorer: James Milner (Leeds Utd. away to Sunderland, December 26, 2002), 16 years, 357 days.

Youngest player sent off in Premier League: Wayne Rooney (Everton, away to Birmingham City, December 26, 2002) aged 17 years, 59 days.

Youngest First Division hat-trick scorer: Alan Shearer, aged 17 years, 240 days, in Southampton's 4-2 home win v Arsenal (April 9, 1988) on his full debut. Previously, Jimmy Greaves (17 years, 309 days) with 4 goals for Chelsea at home to Portsmouth (7-4), Christmas Day, 1957.

Youngest to complete 100 Football League goals: Jimmy Greaves (20 years, 261 days) when he did so for Chelsea v Manchester City, November 19, 1960.

Youngest Football League scorer: Ronnie Dix (for Bristol Rov. v Norwich City, Div. 3 South, March 3, 1928) aged 15 years, 180 days.

Youngest players in Football League: Albert Geldard (Bradford Park Avenue v Millwall, Div. 2, September 16, 1929) aged 15 years, 158 days; Ken Roberts (Wrexham v Bradford Park Avenue, Div. 3 North, September 1, 1951) also 15 years, 158 days.

Youngest player in Scottish League: Goalkeeper Ronnie Simpson (Queens Park) aged 15 in 1946.

Youngest player in F.A. Cup: Andy Awford, Worcester City's England Schoolboy defender, aged 15 years, 88 days when he substituted in second half away to Boreham Wood (3rd. qual. round) on October 10, 1987.

Youngest player in F.A. Cup proper: Schoolboy Lee Holmes (15 years, 277 days) for Derby Co. away to Brentford in 3rd. Round on January 4, 2003.

Youngest Wembley Cup Final captain: Barry Venison (Sunderland v Norwich City, Milk Cup Final, March 24, 1985 – replacing suspended captain Shaun Elliott) – aged 20 years, 220 days.

Youngest F.A. Cup-winning captain: Bobby Moore (West Ham Utd., 1964, v Preston N.E.), aged 23 years, 20 days.

Youngest F.A. Cup Final captain: David Nish aged 21 years and 212 days old when he captained Leicester City against Manchester City at Wembley on April 26, 1969.

Youngest F.A. Cup Final player: James Prinsep (Clapham Rov. v Old Etonians, 1879) aged 17 years, 245 days.

Youngest F.A. Cup Final player since 1900: Paul Allen (West Ham Utd. v Arsenal, 1980) aged 17 years, 256 days.

Youngest F.A. Cup Final scorer: Norman Whiteside (Manchester Utd. v Brighton & H.A. in 1983 replay at Wembley), aged 18 years, 19 days.

Youngest F.A. Cup Final managers: Stan Cullis, Wolves (33) v Leicester City, 1949; Steve Coppell, Crystal Palace (34) v Manchester Utd., 1990; Ruud Gullit, Chelsea (34) v Mid'bro', 1997.

Youngest player in Football League Cup: Kevin Davies (Chesterfield sub at West Ham Utd., 2nd Round, 2nd Leg on September 22, 1993) aged 16 years, 180 days.

Youngest Wembley scorer: Norman Whiteside (Manchester Utd. v Liverpool, Milk Cup Final, March 26, 1983) aged 17 years, 324 days.

Youngest Wembley Cup Final goalkeeper: Chris Woods (18 years, 125 days) for Nott'm Forest v Liverpool, League Cup Final on March 18, 1978.

Youngest Wembley F.A. Cup Final goalkeeper: Peter Shilton (19 years, 219 days) for Leicester City v Manchester City, April 26, 1969.

Youngest senior International at Wembley: Salomon Olembe (sub for Cameroon v England, November 15, 1997), aged 16 years, 342 days.

Youngest winning manager at Wembley: Roy McDonough, aged 33 years. 6 months, 24 days as player-manager of Colchester Utd., F.A. Trophy winners on May 10, 1992.

Youngest scorer in full International: Mohamed Kallon (Sierra Leone v Congo, African Nations Cup, April 22, 1995), reported as aged 15 years, 192 days.

Youngest player sent off in World Cup Final series: Rigobert Song (Cameroon v Brazil, in USA, June 1994) aged 17 years, 358 days.

Youngest F.A. Cup Final referee: Kevin Howley, of Middlesbrough, aged 35 when in charge of Wolves v Blackburn Rov., 1960.

Youngest player in England U-23 team: Duncan Edwards (v. Italy, Bologna, January 20, 1954), aged 17 years, 112 days.

Youngest player in England U-21 team: Lee Sharpe (v. Greece, away, February 7, 1989), aged 17 years, 254 days.

Youngest player in Scotland U-21 team: Christian Dailly (v Romania, Hampden Park, Sept. 11, 1990), aged 16 years, 330 days.

Youngest player in senior football: Cameron Campbell Buchanan, Scottish-born outside right, aged 14 years, 57 days when he played for Wolves v W.B.A. in War-time League match, September 26, 1942.

Youngest player in peace-time senior match: Eamon Collins (Blackpool v Kilmarnock, Anglo-Scottish Cup quarter-final 1st. leg, September 9, 1980) aged 14 years, 323 days.

World's youngest player in top-division match: Centre-forward Fernando Rafael Garcia, aged 13, played for 23 minutes for Peruvian club Juan Aurich in 3-1 win against Estudiantes on May 19, 2001.

Oldest player to appear in Football League: New Brighton manager Neil McBain (51 years, 120 days) as emergency goalkeeper away to Hartlepool Utd. (Div. 3 North, March 15, 1947).

Other oldest post-war League players: Sir Stanley Matthews (Stoke City, 1965, 50 years, 5 days); Peter Shilton (Leyton Orient 1997, 47 years, 126 days); Dave Beasant (Brighton & H.A. 2003, 44 years, 46 days); Alf Wood (Coventry City, 1958, 43 years, 199 days); Tommy Hutchison (Swansea City, 1991, 43 years, 172 days).

Oldest Football League debutant: Andy Cunningham, for Newcastle Utd. at Leicester City (Div. 1) on February 2, 1929, aged 38 years, 2 days.

Oldest player to appear in First Division: Sir Stanley Matthews (Stoke City v Fulham, February 6, 1965), aged 50 years, 5 days – on that his last League appearance, the only 50-year-old ever to play in the top division.

Oldest players in Premier League: Goalkeepers John Burridge (Manchester City v Q.P.R., May 14, 1995), aged 43 years, 5 months, 11 days; Steve Ogrizovic (Coventry City v Sheffield Wed., May 6, 2000), aged 42 years, 7 months, 24 days; Neville Southall (Bradford City v Leeds Utd., March 12, 2000), aged 41 years, 5 months, 26 days. Outfield: Gordon Strachan (Coventry City v Derby Co., May 3, 1997) aged 40 years, 2 months, 24 days.

Oldest player for British professional club: John Ryan (owner-chairman of Conference club Doncaster Rov., played as substitute for last minute in 4–2 win at Hereford on April 26, 2003), aged 52 years, 11 months, 3 weeks.

Oldest F.A. Cup Final player: Walter (Billy) Hampson (Newcastle Utd. v Aston Villa on April 26, 1924), aged 41 years, 257 days.

Oldest F.A. Cup-winning team: Arsenal 1950 (average age 31 years, 2 months). Eight of the players were over 30, with the three oldest centre-half Leslie Compton 37, and skipper Joe Mercer and goalkeeper George Swindin, both 35.

Oldest World Cup-winning captain: Dino Zoff, Italy's goalkeeper v W. Germany in 1982 Final, aged 40 years, 92 days.

Oldest player capped by England: Stanley Matthews (v. Denmark, Copenhagen, May 15, 1957), aged 42 years, 103 days.

Oldest England scorer: Stanley Matthews (v N. Ireland, Belfast, October 6, 1956), aged 41 years, 248 days.

Oldest British International player: Billy Meredith (Wales v England at Highbury, March 15, 1920), aged 45 years, 229 days.

Oldest 'new cap': Arsenal centre-half Leslie Compton, at 38 years, 64 days when he made his England debut in 4-2 win against Wales at Sunderland on November 15, 1950. **For Scotland:** Goalkeeper Ronnie Simpson (Celtic) at 36 years, 186 days v England at Wembley, April 15, 1967.

Longest Football League career: This spanned 32 years and 10 months, by Stanley Matthews (Stoke City, Blackpool, Stoke City) from March 19, 1932 until February 6, 1965.

Smallest F.A. Cup-winning captain: 5ft. 4in. – Bobby Kerr (Sunderland v Leeds Utd., 1973).

SHIRT NUMBERING

Numbering players in Football League matches was made compulsory in 1939. Players wore numbered shirts (1-22) in the F.A. Cup Final as an experiment in 1933 (Everton 1-11 v Manchester City 12-22).

Squad numbers for players were introduced by the F.A. Premier League at the start of season 1993-4. They were optional in the Football League until made compulsory in 1999-2000.

Names on shirts: For first time, players wore names as well as numbers on shirts in League Cup and F.A. Cup Finals, 1993.

SUBSTITUTES

In **1965**, the Football League, by 39 votes to 10, agreed that **one substitute** be allowed for an injured player at any time during a League match. First substitute used in Football League: Keith Peacock (Charlton Athletic), away to Bolton Wand. in Div. 2, August 21, 1965.

Two substitutes per team were approved for the League (Littlewoods) Cup and F.A. Cup in season 1986-7 and two were permitted in the Football League for the first time in 1987-8.

Three substitutes (one a goalkeeper), two of which could be used, introduced by the Premier League for 1992-3. The Football League followed suit for 1993-4.

Three substitutes (one a goalkeeper) were allowed at the World Cup Finals for the first time at US '94.

Three substitutes (any position) introduced by Premier League and Football League in 1995-6.

First substitute to score in F.A. Cup Final: Eddie Kelly (Arsenal v Liverpool, 1971).

The **first recorded use of a substitute was in 1889** (Wales v Scotland at Wrexham on April 15) when Sam Gillam arrived late – although he was a Wrexham player – and Allen Pugh (Rhostellyn) was allowed to keep goal until he turned up. The match ended 0-0.

When Dickie Roose, the Welsh goalkeeper, was injured against England at Wrexham, March 16, 1908, Dai Davies (Bolton Wand.) was allowed to take his place as substitute. Thus Wales used 12 players. England won 7-1.

END OF WAGE LIMIT

Freedom from the maximum wage system – in force since the formation of the Football League in 1888 – was secured by the Professional Footballers' Association in 1961. About this time Italian clubs renewed overtures for the transfer of British stars and Fulham's **Johnny Haynes** became the first British player to earn £100 a week.

THE BOSMAN RULING

On December 15, 1995 the **European Court of Justice** ruled that clubs had no right to transfer fees for out-of-contract players, and the outcome of the 'Bosman case' irrevocably changed football's player-club relationship. It began in 1990, when the contract of 26-year-old **Jean-Marc Bosman**, a midfield player with FC Liege, Belgium, expired. French club Dunkirk wanted him but were unwilling to pay the £500,000 transfer fee, so Bosman was compelled to remain with Liege. He responded with a lawsuit against his club and UEFA on the grounds of 'restriction of trade', and after five years at various court levels the European Court of Justice ruled not only in favour of Bosman but of all professional footballers.

The end of restrictive labour practices revolutionised the system. It led to a proliferation of transfers, rocketed the salaries of elite players who, backed by an increasing army of agents, found themselves in a vastly improved bargaining position as they moved from team to team, league to league, nation to nation. Removing the limit on the number of foreigners clubs could field brought an increasing ratio of such signings, not least in England and Scotland.

Bosman's one-man stand opened the way for footballers to become millionaires, but ended his own career. All he received for his legal conflict was 16 million Belgian francs (£312,000) in compensation, a testimonial of poor reward and martyrdom as the man who did most to change the face of football.

Celtic were the first British club to lose out, when Scottish International John Collins moved to Monaco in June 1996. Subsequent Bosman-free transfers involving British clubs include: Gianluca Vialli, Juventus to Chelsea (7/96); Michael Hughes, Strasbourg to West Ham Utd. (7/96); Gustavo Poyet, Real Zaragoza to Chelsea (5/97); David Connolly, Watford to Feyenoord (7/97); Jonathan Gould, Bradford City to Celtic (8/97); Brian Laudrup, Rangers to Chelsea (6/98); Shaka Hislop, Newcastle Utd. to West Ham Utd. (7/98); Gerry Taggart, Bolton Wand. to Leicester City (7/98); Mikael Forssell, HJK Helsinki to Chelsea (11/98); Steve McManaman, Liverpool to Real Madrid (7/99); Andy Melville, Sunderland to Fulham (5/99); Peter Schmeichel, Manchester Utd. to Sporting Lisbon (6/99); Markus Babbel, Bayern Munich to Liverpool (1/00); Pegguy Arphexad, Leicester City to Liverpool (7/00); Gary McAllister, Coventry City to Liverpool (7/00); Paul Okon, Fiorentina to Middlesbrough (7/00); Benito Carbone, Aston Villa to Bradford City (8/00); Winston Bogarde, Barcelona to Chelsea (8/00); Jari Litmanen, Barcelona to Liverpool (1/01); Teddy Sheringham, Manchester Utd. to Tottenham (6/01); Nelson Vivas, Arsenal to Inter Milan (6/01); Sol Campbell, Tottenham to Arsenal (6/01); Laurent Blanc, Inter Milan to Man. Utd. (8/01) ; Jamie Redknapp, Liverpool to Tottenham (4/02); Peter Schmeichel, Aston Villa to Manchester City (7/02); Enriqe de Lucas, Espanyol to Chelsea (7/02); Jay Jay Okocha, Paris SG. to Bolton Wand. (7/02); Shaka Hislop, West Ham Utd. to Portsmouth (7/02); Youri Djorkaeff, Kaiserslautern to Bolton Wand. (7/02); Denis Irwin, Manchester Utd. to Wolves (7/02); Paul Ince, Mid'bro' to Wolves (8/02); Ronny Johnsen, Manchester Utd. to Aston Villa (8/02); David Seaman, Arsenal to Manchester City (7/03); Teddy Sheringham, Tottenham to Portsmouth (7/03).

GREATEST SHOCKS

Excluding such tragedies as the Munich air crash (Feb. 1958), the Bradford City fire disaster (May 1985), Heysel (May 1985) and Hillsborough (April 1989), here in date order are, arguably, the greatest shocks in football history:

(1) Jan. 1933 F.A. Cup 3rd. Round: Walsall 2, Arsenal 0.
(2) Jan. 1949 F.A. Cup 4th. Round: Yeovil 2, Sunderland 1.
(3) June 1950 World Cup Finals: U.S.A. 1, England 0 (Belo Horizonte, Brazil).
(4) Nov. 1953 England 3, Hungary 6 (Wembley).
(5) Sept. 1962 Cup-Winners' Cup 1st. Round, 1st. Leg: Bangor 2, Napoli 0.
(6) Mar. 1966 World Cup stolen in London (found a week later).
(7) June 1966 World Cup Finals: N. Korea 1, Italy 0 (Middlesbrough).
(8) Jan. 1967 Scottish Cup 1st. Round: Berwick Rangers 1, Glasgow Rangers 0.
(9) Mar. 1969 League Cup Final: Swindon Town 3, Arsenal 1.
(10) Feb. 1971 F.A. Cup 5th. Round: Colchester Utd. 3, Leeds Utd. 2.

(11) Jan. 1972 F.A. Cup 3rd. Round: Hereford Utd. 2, Newcastle Utd. 1.
(12) May 1973 F.A. Cup Final: Sunderland 1, Leeds Utd. 0.
(13) July 1974 Bill Shankly retires as Liverpool manager.
(14) May 1976 F.A. Cup Final: Southampton 1, Manchester Utd. 0.
(15) July 1977 England manager Don Revie defects to coach Utd. Arab Emirates.
(16) June 1982 World Cup Finals: Algeria 2, West Germany 1 (Gijon, Spain).
(17) Jan. 1984 F.A. Cup 3rd. Round: Bournemouth 2, Manchester Utd. (holders) 0.
(18) May 1988 F.A. Cup Final: Wimbledon 1, Liverpool 0 .
(19) June 1990 World Cup Finals: Cameroon 1, Argentina (World Champions) 0 (Milan).
(20) Sept. 1990 European Championship (Qual. Round): Faroe Islands 1, Austria 0.
(21) Feb. 1991 Kenny Dalglish resigns as Liverpool manager.
(22) Jan. 1992 F.A. Cup 3rd. Round: Wrexham 2, Arsenal 1.
(23) June 1992 European Championship Final: Denmark 2, Germany (World Champions) 0.
(24) June 1993 U.S. Cup '93: U.S.A. 2, England 0 (Foxboro, Boston).
(25) July 1994 World Cup Finals: Bulgaria 2, Germany 1 (New York City).
(26) Feb. 1998 Concacaf Gold Cup: U.S.A. 1, Brazil 0 (Los Angeles).
(27) July 1998 World Cup Q-final: Croatia 3 Germany 0.
(28) July 1996 Olympic s-final (Athens, Georgia): Nigeria beat Brazil 4-3 with extra-time 'golden goal' (Brazil led 3-1 with 13 mins. left).
(29) Feb. 2000 Scottish Cup 3rd. Round: Celtic 1, Inverness Cal. Thistle 3.
(30) Nov. 2000 Scotland 0, Australia 2 (friendly, Hampden Park)
(31) June 2001 Confed. Cup 3rd place play-off: Australia 1, Brazil 0 (Ulsan, S. Korea).
(32) July 2001 Honduras 2, Brazil 0 (Copa America quarter-final).
(33) Oct. 2002 European Championship (Qual. Round): England 2, Macedonia 2.
(34) Feb. 2003 England 1, Australia 3 (friendly, Upton Park).
(35) Mar. 2003 Scottish Cup 5th. Round: Inverness Cal. Thistle 1, Celtic 0.

OTHER INTERNATIONAL SHOCKS

(Read in conjunction with Greatest Shocks above)

1982 Spain 0, N. Ireland 1 (World Cup Finals in Spain).
1990 Scotland 0, Costa Rica 1 (World Cup Finals in Italy).
1990 Sweden 1, Costa Rica 2 (World Cup Finals in Italy).
1993 Argentina 0, Colombia 5 (World Cup qual. round).
1993 France 2, Israel 3 (World Cup qual. round).
1993 San Marino score fastest goal in Int. records: 8.3 secs. v England (World Cup qual. round).
1994 Moldova 3, Wales 2; Georgia 5, Wales 0 (both Euro. Champ. qual. round).
1995 Belarus 1, Holland 0 (European Champ. qual. round).
2001 Australia 1, France 0 (Confed. Cup, S. Korea). France won tournament.
2001 German 1, England 5 (World Cup qual. round).
2002 France 0, Senegal 1 (World Cup Finals, opening match, in S. Korea).
2002 France, World Cup holders, out without scoring.
2002 World Cup joint hosts South Korea beat Italy with Golden Goal, then Spain on penalties.

GREAT RECOVERIES

On December 21, 1957, Charlton Athletic were losing 5-1 against Huddersfield Town (Div. 2) at The Valley with only 28 minutes left, and from the 15th minute, had been reduced to ten men by injury, but they won 7-6, with left-winger Johnny Summers scoring five goals. Huddersfield Town (managed by Bill Shankly) remain the only team to score six times in a League match and lose.

Among other notable comebacks: on November 12, 1904 (Div. 1), Sheffield Wed. were losing 0-5 at home to Everton, but drew 5-5. At Anfield on December 4, 1909 (Div.1), Liverpool trailed 2-5 to Newcastle Utd. at half-time, then won 6-5. On Boxing

Day, 1927, in Div. 3 South, Northampton Town won 6-5 at home to Luton Town after being 1-5 down at half-time. On September 22, 1984 (Div. 1), Q.P.R. drew 5-5 at home to Newcastle Utd. after trailing 0-4 at half-time. On April 12, 1993 (Div. 1) Swindon Town were 1-4 down at Birmingham City with 30 minutes left, but won 6-4.

Other astonishing turnabouts in Div.1 include: Grimsby Town (3-5 down) won 6-5 at W.B.A. on Apr. 30, 1932; and Derby Co. beat Manchester Utd. 5-4 (from 1-4) on Sept. 5, 1936.

With 5 minutes to play, Ipswich Town were losing 3-0 at Barnsley (Div. 1, March 9, 1996), but drew 3-3.

On Sunday, Jan. 19, 1997 (Div. 1), Q.P.R. were 0-4 down away to Port Vale at half-time and still trailing 1-4 with 5 minutes left. They drew 4-4.

Celtic trailed 0-2, 1-3 and 2-4 away to Dunfermline (Scottish First Div., Nov. 19,1966) but won 5-4 with a last-minute penalty.

Premier League comebacks: Jan. 4, 1994 – Liverpool were 3 down after 24 mins. at home to Manchester Utd., drew 3-3; Nov. 8, 1997 – Derby Co. led 3-0 after 33 mins. at Elland Road, but Leeds Utd. won 4-3 with last-minute goal; Sept. 29, 2001 – Manchester Utd. won 5-3 at Tottenham after trailing 3-0 at half-time.

Tranmere Rov. retrieved a 3-0 half-time deficit to beat Southampton 4-3 in an F.A. Cup fifth round replay at home on Feb. 20, 2001.

GOALS THAT WERE WRONGLY GIVEN

Tottenham's last-minute winner at home to Huddersfield (Div. 1) on April 2, 1952: Eddie Baily's corner-kick struck referee W.R. Barnes in the back, and the ball rebounded to Baily, who centred for Len Duquemin to head into the net. Baily had infringed the Laws by playing the ball twice, but the result (1-0) stood. Those two points helped Spurs to finish Championship runners-up; Huddersfield were relegated.

The second goal (66 mins) in **Chelsea's** 2-1 home win v Ipswich Town (Div. 1) on Sept. 26, 1970: Alan Hudson's low shot from just beyond the penalty-area hit the stanchion on the outside of goal and the ball rebounded on to the pitch. But instead of the goal-kick, referee Roy Capey gave a goal, on a linesman's confirmation. TV pictures proved otherwise. But the Football League quoted from the Laws of the Game: 'The referee's decision on all matters is final.' And though it was wrong, the goal stood and sent Chelsea on the way to victory.

MATCHES OFF

Worst day for postponements: Feb. 9, 1963, when 57 League fixtures in England and Scotland were frozen off. Only 7 Football League matches took place, and the entire Scottish programme was wiped out

Worst other weather-hit days:

Jan. 12, 1963 and Feb. 2, 1963 – on both those Saturdays, only 4 out of 44 Football League matches were played.

Jan. 1, 1979 – 43 out of 46 Football League fixtures postponed.

Jan. 17, 1987 – 37 of 45 scheduled Football League fixtures postponed; only 2 Scottish matches survived.

Feb. 8-9, 1991 – only 4 of the week-end's 44 Barclays League matches survived the freeze-up (4 of the postponements were on Friday night). In addition, 11 Scottish League matches were off.

Jan. 27, 1996 – 44 Cup and League matches in England and Scotland were frozen off. The ten fixtures played comprised 3 F.A. Cup (4th. Round), 1 in Div. 1, 5 in Scottish Cup (3rd. Round), 1 in Scottish Div. 2.

Fewest matches left on one day by postponements was during the Second World War – Feb. 3, 1940 when, because of snow, ice and fog only one out of 56 regional league fixtures took place. It resulted Plymouth Argyle 10, Bristol City 3.

The Scottish Cup second round tie between Inverness Thistle and Falkirk in season 1978-9 was **postponed 29 times** because of snow and ice. First put off on Jan. 6, it was eventually played on Feb. 22. Falkirk won 4-0.

Pools Panel's busiest days: Jan. 17, 1987 and Feb. 9, 1991 – on both dates they gave their verdict on 48 postponed coupon matches.

FEWEST 'GAMES OFF'

Season 1947-8 was the best since the war for Football League fixtures being played to schedule. Only **six** were postponed.

LONGEST SEASON

The latest that League football has been played in a season was **June 7, 1947** (six weeks after the F.A. Cup Final). The season was extended because of mass postponements caused by bad weather in mid-winter.

The latest the F.A. Cup competition has ever been completed was in season 1981-2, when Tottenham beat Q.P.R. 1-0 in a Final replay at Wembley on May 27.

Worst winter hold-up was in season 1962-3. The Big Freeze began on Boxing Day and lasted until March, with nearly 500 first-class matches postponed. The F.A. Cup 3rd. Round was the longest on record – it began with only three out of 32 ties playable on January 5 and ended 66 days and 261 postponements later on March 11. The Lincoln City-Coventry City tie was put off 15 times. The Pools Panel was launched that winter, on January 26, 1963.

Hottest day for a Football League programme is believed to have been Saturday, September 1, 1906, when temperatures across the country were over 90°.

FOOTBALL LEAGUE SECRETARIES

Harry Lockett (1888-1902), **Tom Charnley** (1902-33), **Fred Howarth** (1933-57), **Alan Hardaker** (1957-79), **Graham Kelly** (1979-88), **David Dent** (1989-2001). **Andy Williamson** succeeded David Dent in June 2001, with the title Head of Operations

Football League Chairman: Sir Brian Mawhinney (appointed December 2002). **Chief Executive:**

F.A. Premier League: Secretary: Mike Foster. Chairman: David Richards (Sheffield Wed.). Chief Executive: Richard Scudamore.

FOOTBALL ASSOCIATION SECRETARIES/ CHIEF EXECUTIVES

Ebenezer Morley (1863-66), **Robert Willis** (1866-68), **R.G. Graham** (1868-70), **Charles Alcock** (1870-95, paid from 1887), 1895-1934 **Sir Frederick Wall**, 1934-62 **Sir Stanley Rous**, 1962-73 **Denis Follows**, 1973-89 **Ted Croker** (latterly chief executive), 1989-99 **Graham Kelly** (chief executive), 2000-02 **Adam Crozier** (chief executive). Since May 2003 **Mark Palios** (chief executive).

F.A. Chairman: Geoffrey Thompson (appointed June, 1999).

FOOTBALL'S SPONSORS

Football League: Canon 1983-6; Today Newspaper 1986-7; Barclays 1987-93; Endsleigh Insurance 1993-6; Nationwide Building Society 1996-2001 then extended to 2004.
League Cup: Milk Cup 1982-6; Littlewoods 1987-90; Rumbelows 1991-2; Coca-Cola Cup 1993-8; Worthington Cup 1998-2003; Carling Cup 2003-6.
Premier League: Carling 1993-2001; Barclaycard 2001-04.
F.A. Cup: Littlewoods 1994-8; AXA 1998-2002.

SOCCER HEADQUARTERS

Football Association: 25 Soho Square, London W1D 4FA (moved from Lancaster Gate, London W2, September 2000). Chief Executive: Mark Palios.
F.A. Premier League: 11 Connaught Place, London W1 2ET. Chief Executive: Richard Scudamore. Secretary: Mike Foster.
Football Foundation: 25 Soho Square, London W1D 4FF. Chief Executive: Peter Lee.
Football League: Edward VII Quay, Navigation Way, Preston PR2 2YF. Head of Operations: Andy Williamson. **London Office:** 11 Connaught Place, London W2 2ET.
Professional Footballers' Association: 2 Oxford Utd. Court, Bishopsgate, Manchester M2 3WQ. Chief Executive: Gordon Taylor.
Scottish Football Association: 6 Park Gardens, Glasgow G3 7YF. Chief Executive: David Taylor.

Scottish Premier League: National Stadium, Hampden Park, Glasgow GU2 9BA. Chief Executive:
Scottish Football League: Hampden Park, Glasgow G42 9EB. Secretary: Peter Donald.
Irish Football Association: 20 Windsor Avenue, Belfast BT9 6EG. Secretary: David Bowen.
Irish Football League: 96 University Street, Belfast BT7 1HE. Secretary: Harry Wallace.
League of Ireland: 80 Merrion Square, Dublin 2. Secretary: Eamonn Morris.
Republic of Ireland F.A.: 80 Merrion Square, Dublin 2. Secretary:
Welsh Football Association: 3 Westgate Street, Cardiff CF1 1DD. Secretary: David Collins.
Football Conference: Collingwood House, Schooner Court, Crossways, Dartford, Kent DAZ 6QQ.
FIFA: P.O. Box 85, 8030 Zurich, Switzerland.
UEFA: Route de Geneve, CH-1260, Nyon, Geneva, Switzerland.

WORLD'S LARGEST STADIA

(Source: *FIFA NEWS*)

Capacity 165,000: Maracana, Rio de Janeiro, Brazil; **150,000** Rungnado Stadium, Pyongyang, North Korea; **125,000** Magalhaes Pinto Stadium, Belo Horizonte, Brazil; **120,000** Morumbi Stadium, Sao Paulo, Brazil; Stadium of Light, Lisbon, Portugal; Krirangan Stadium, Salt Lake, Calcutta; Senayan Stadium, Jakarta, Indonesia; **119,000** Castelao Stadium, Fortaleza, Brazil; **115,000** Arrudao Stadium, Recife, Brazil; Azteca Stadium, Mexico City; Nou Camp, Barcelona, Spain; **114,000** Bernabeu Stadium, Madrid; **100,000** Nasser Stadium, Cairo, Egypt; Azadi Stadium, Tehran, Iran; Red Star Stadium, Belgrade, Yugoslavia; Central Stadium, Kiev, USSR.

F.A. NATIONAL FOOTBALL CENTRE

This is provisionally due to open at Burton-upon-Trent in May 2004 (originally scheduled for August 2003). On a site of 350 acres and built at a cost of £50m., it will comprise 14 pitches, sports science clinic, swimming pools, indoor training facilities and luxury accommodation. England teams at all levels will train there.

NEW HOMES OF SOCCER

Newly-constructed League grounds in England since the war: 1946 Hull City (Boothferry Park); 1950 Port Vale (Vale Park); 1955 Southend Utd. (Roots Hall); 1988 Scunthorpe Utd. (Glanford Park); 1990 Walsall (Bescot Stadium); 1990 Wycombe Wand. (Adams Park); 1992 Chester City (Deva Stadium, Bumpers Lane); 1993 Millwall (New Den); 1994 Huddersfield Town (Alfred McAlpine Stadium, Kirklees); 1994 Northampton Town (Sixfields Stadium); 1995 Middlesbrough (Riverside Stadium); 1997 Bolton Wand. (Reebok Stadium); 1997 Derby Co. (Pride Park); 1997 Stoke City (Britannia Stadium); 1997 Sunderland (Stadium of Light); 1998 Reading (Madejski Stadium); 1999 Wigan Athletic (JJB Stadium); 2001 Southampton (St. Mary's Stadium); 2001 Oxford Utd. (Kassam Stadium); 2002 Leicester City (Walkers Stadium); 2002 Hull City (Kingston Communications Stadium); 2003 Manchester City (City of Manchester Stadium); 2003 Darlington (Reynolds Arena).

GROUND-SHARING

Crystal Palace and **Charlton Athletic** (Selhurst Park, 1985-91); **Bristol Rov.** and **Bath City** (Twerton Park, Bath, 1986-96); **Partick Thistle** and **Clyde** (Firhill Park, Glasgow, 1986-91; in seasons 1990-1, 1991-2 **Chester City** shared **Macclesfield Town's** ground (Moss Rose). **Crystal Palace** and **Wimbledon** have shared Selhurst Park, since season 1991-2, when **Charlton Athletic** (tenants) moved to rent Upton Park from **West Ham Utd. Clyde** moved to Douglas Park, **Hamilton Academicals'** home, in 1991-2. **Stirling Albion** shared **Stenhousemuir's** ground, Ochilview Park, in 1992-3. In 1993-4, **Clyde** shared **Partick's** home until moving to their new ground. In 1994-5, **Celtic** shared Hampden Park with **Queen's Park** (while Celtic Park was redeveloped); **Hamilton** shared **Partick's** ground. **Airdrie** shared **Clyde's** Broadwood Stadium. **Bristol Rov.** left Bath City's ground at the start of season 1996-7, sharing Bristol Rugby Club's Memorial Ground. **Clydebank** shared **Dumbarton's** Boghead Park from 1996-7 until renting **Greenock Morton's** Cappielow Park in season

1999-2000. **Brighton** shared **Gillingham's** ground in seasons 1997-8, 1998-9. With their future at Craven Cottage unresolved, **Fulham** shared Q.P.R.'s home at Loftus Road in seasons 2002–3, 2003–4.

ARTIFICIAL TURF

Q.P.R. were the first British club to install an artificial pitch, in 1981. They were followed by **Luton Town** in 1985, and **Oldham Athletic** and **Preston N.E. in 1986**. Q.P.R. reverted to grass in 1988, as did Luton Town and promoted Oldham Athletic in season 1991-2 (when artificial pitches were banned in Div. 1). **Preston N.E.** were the last Football League club playing 'on plastic' in 1993-4, and their Deepdale ground was restored to grass for the start of 1994-5.

Stirling Albion were the **first Scottish club** to play on plastic, in season 1987-8.

F.A. SOCCER SCHOOL

The Football Association's **national soccer school**, at Lilleshall, aimed at providing the backbone of England's World Cup challenge in the 1990s, was opened by the Duke of Kent (President) on September 4, 1984. It was sponsored by GM Motors, and the first intake comprised 25 boys aged fourteen.

The School of Excellence produced England Internationals Nick Barmby, Andy Cole, Sol Campbell, Ian Walker and Michael Owen. It closed in 1999, to be replaced nationwide by academies at leading clubs.

DOUBLE RUNNERS-UP

There have been nine instances of clubs finishing **runner-up in both the League Championship and F.A. Cup in the same season**: 1928 Huddersfield Town; 1932 Arsenal; 1939 Wolves; 1962 Burnley; 1965 and 1970 Leeds Utd.; 1986 Everton; 1995 Manchester Utd; 2001 Arsenal.

CORNER-KICK RECORDS

Not a single corner-kick was recorded when **Newcastle Utd.** drew 0-0 at home to **Portsmouth** (Div.1) on December 5, 1931.

The record for **most corners** in a match for one side is believed to be **Sheffield Utd.'s 28** to West Ham Utd.'s 1 in Div.2 at Bramall Lane on October 14, 1989. For all their pressure, Sheffield Utd. lost 2-0.

Nott'm. Forest led Southampton 22-2 on corners (Premier League, Nov. 28, 1992) but lost the match 1-2.

Tommy Higginson (Brentford, 1960s) once passed back to his own goalkeeper from a corner kick.

When **Wigan Athletic** won 4–0 at home to Cardiff City (Div. 2) on February 16, 2002, all four goals were headed in from corners taken by N. Ireland International **Peter Kennedy**.

Steve Staunton (Rep. of Ireland) is believed to be the only player to score direct from a corner in **two** Internationals.

OFFSIDES NIL

Not one offside decision was given in the **Brazil-Turkey** World Cup semi-final at Saitama, Japan, on June 26, 2002.

'PROFESSIONAL FOUL' DIRECTIVE

After the 1990 World Cup Finals, F.I.F.A. dealt with the '**professional foul**', incorporating this directive into the Laws of the Game: 'If, in the opinion of the referee, a player who is moving towards his opponents' goal, with an obvious opportunity to score, is intentionally impeded by an opponent through unlawful means – thus denying the attacking player's team the aforesaid goalscoring opportunity – the offender should be sent from the field of play.'

SACKED AT HALF-TIME

Leyton Orient sacked **Terry Howard** on his 397th. appearance for the club – at half-time in a Second Division home defeat against Blackpool (Feb. 7, 1995) for 'an unacceptable performance'. He was fined two weeks' wages, given a free transfer and moved to Wycombe Wanderers.

Harald Schumacher, former Germany goalkeeper, was sacked as Fortuna Koln coach when they were two down at half-time against Waldhof Mannheim (Dec. 15, 1999). They lost 5-1.

MOST GAMES BY 'KEEPER FOR ONE CLUB

Alan Knight made 683 League appearances for Portsmouth, over 23 seasons (1978-2000), a record for a goalkeeper at one club. The previous holder was Peter Bonetti with 600 League games for Chelsea (20 seasons, 1960-79).

PLAYED TWO GAMES ON SAME DAY

Jack Kelsey played full-length matches for both club and country on Wed., November 26, 1958. In the afternoon he kept goal for Wales in a 2-2 draw against England at Villa Park, and he then drove to Highbury to help Arsenal win 3-1 in a prestigious floodlit friendly against Juventus.

On the same day, winger **Danny Clapton** played for England (against Wales and Kelsey) and then in part of Arsenal's match against Juventus.

On November 11, 1987, **Mark Hughes** played for Wales against Czechoslovakia (European Championship) in Prague, then flew to Munich and went on as substitute that night in a winning Bayern Munich team, to whom he was on loan from Barcelona.

On February 16, 1993 goalkeeper **Scott Howie** played in Scotland's 3-0 U-21 win v Malta at Tannadice Park, Dundee (k.o. 1.30pm) and the same evening played in Clyde's 2-1 home win v Queen of South (Div. 2).

Ryman League **Hornchurch**, faced by end-of-season fixture congestion, played **two matches on the same night** (May 1, 2001). They lost 2-1 at home to Ware and drew 2-2 at Clapton.

GOING PUBLIC

Manchester Utd. became the fourth British club (after Tottenham, Hibernian and Millwall) to 'go public' with a share issue in June 1991. Many other clubs have since "floated" on the Stock Exchange.

MEDIA INVEST IN TOP CLUBS

In season 1999-2000, satellite broadcaster **BSkyB** bought 9.9% share stakes in Manchester Utd. (£84m), Chelsea (£40m), Leeds Utd. (£13.8m), Manchester City (£12m) and a 5% share in Sunderland (£6.5m). **Granada TV** bought a £22m. stake in Liverpool. Cable giants **NTL** acquired 9.9% shares/sponsorship investment in Newcastle Utd. (£35m) and Aston Villa (£26m) and Leicester City (£12.5m). They agreed a £31m. sponsorship with Rangers.

RECORD CLUB LOSSES

Fulham, brokered by Harrods owner Mohamed Al Fayed, made British football's then record loss of £23.3m. in the year to June 30, 2001 (in which they won promotion to the Premiership as Div. 1 Champions). The club's debts rose to £61.7m. Previous highest loss was £18.7m. by **Newcastle Utd.** in 2000. In September 2002, **Leeds Utd.** reported a new record British club loss of £33.9m for the year ending June 30. It took their debts to £77m.

FIRST 'MATCH OF THE DAY'

BBC TV (recorded highlights): Liverpool 3, Arsenal 2 on August 22, 1964. **First complete match to be televised:** Arsenal 3, Everton 2 on August 29, 1936. **First League match televised in colour:** Liverpool 2, West Ham Utd. 0 on November 15, 1969.

'MATCH OF THE DAY' – BIGGEST SCORES

Football League: Tottenham 9, Bristol Rov. 0 (Div. 2, 1977-8). **Premier League:** Nott'm Forest 1, Manchester Utd. 8 (1998-9).

FIRST COMMENTARY ON RADIO

Arsenal 1, **Sheffield Utd.** 1 (Div. 1) broadcast on BBC, January 22, 1927.

OLYMPIC SOCCER WINNERS

1908 Great Britain (in London); **1912** Great Britain (Stockholm); **1920** Belgium (Antwerp); **1924** Uruguay (Paris); **1928** Uruguay (Amsterdam); **1932** No soccer in Los Angeles Olympics.

1936 Italy (Berlin); **1948** Sweden (London); **1952** Hungary (Helsinki); **1956** USSR (Melbourne); **1960** Yugoslavia (Rome); **1964** Hungary (Tokyo); **1968** Hungary (Mexico); **1972** Poland (Munich); **1976** E. Germany (Montreal); **1980** Czechoslovakia (Moscow); **1984** France (Los Angeles); **1988** USSR (Seoul); **1992** Spain (Barcelona); **1996** Nigeria (Atlanta); **2000** Cameroon (Sydney).

Highest scorer in Final tournament: Ferenc Bene (Hungary) 12 goals, 1964.

Record crowd for Olympic Soccer Final: 108,800 (France v Brazil, Los Angeles 1984).

MOST AMATEUR CUP WINS

Bishop Auckland set the F.A. Amateur Cup record with 10 wins, and in 1957 became the only club to carry off the trophy in three successive seasons. Five wins: Clapton and Crook Town. The competition was discontinued after the Final on April 20, 1974. (Bishop's Stortford 4, Ilford 1, at Wembley).

FOOTBALL FOUNDATION

This was formed (May 2000) to replace the **Football Trust**, which had been in existence since 1975 as an initiative of the Pools companies to provide financial support at all levels, from schools football to safety and ground improvement work throughout the game. The Foundation, chaired by **Tom Pendry** and with representatives of the Government, F.A. and Premier League on board, was empowered to distribute 5% of the Premiership's TV money to football's grass-roots level.

TESTIMONIALS

The first £1m. testimonial was **Sir Alex Ferguson's** at Old Trafford on October 11, 1999, when a full-house crowd of 54,842 saw a Rest of the World team beat Manchester Utd. 4-2. United's manager pledged that a large percentage of the receipts would go to charity.

Two nights after Manchester Utd. completed the Double in May, 1994, 42,079 packed Old Trafford for **Mark Hughes'** testimonial (1-3 Celtic). The estimated proceeds of £500,000 equalled the then testimonial record of **Ally McCoist's** match (Rangers 1, Newcastle Utd. 2) on August 3, 1993.

The match for **Bryan Robson**, Manchester Utd. and England captain, against Celtic at Old Trafford on Tuesday, November 20, 1990 was watched by a crowd of 41,658, and receipts of £300,000 were a then record for a testimonial.

Kenny Dalglish's testimonial (Liverpool v Real Sociedad) at Anfield on August 14, 1990 attracted 30,461 spectators, with receipts estimated at £150,000.

On December 4, 1990, **Willie Miller**'s testimonial (Aberdeen v World XI) packed Pittodrie to its 22,500 capacity, and raised an estimated £150,000.

The match for 82-year-old **Sir Matt Busby**, between Manchester Utd. and a Rep. of Ireland XI at Old Trafford on Sunday, August 11, 1991 was watched by 35,410 (estimated benefit £250,000).

Ian Rush's testimonial brought an estimated £250,000 from a 25,856 crowd at Anfield on December 6, 1994 (Liverpool 6, Celtic 0).

Three lucrative testimonials were staged in May 1996. Arsenal's **Paul Merson** earned a reported £400,000 (a percentage to charity) from his match against an Int. XI at Highbury (May 9, att: 31,626); the Republic of Ireland's new manager **Mick McCarthy** received an estimated £300,000 from a 40,000 crowd who saw Celtic beaten 3-0 at Lansdowne

Road, Dublin on May 26; and **Stuart Pearce** benefited by some £200,000 from a turn-out of 23,815 when Nott'm. Forest beat Newcastle Utd. 6-5 at the City Ground on May 8.

Testimonial sums reported in season 1996-7 included: **Bryan Gunn**, Norwich City goalkeeper, £250,000 for 21,000 sell-out v Manchester Utd., Nov. 4; **Brian McClair**, Manchester Utd., £380,000 v Celtic, April 14.

Among testimonials in 1997-8: A full-house 50,000 at Ibrox paid an estimated £500,000 for retiring manager **Walter Smith** (Rangers 1, Liverpool 0) on March 3, 1998.

Paul McGrath's testimonial at Lansdowne Road, Dublin (May 17, 1998) produced record receipts of £600,000. A crowd of 39,000 saw Jack Charlton's XI beat a Rep. Of Ireland XI 3-2.

A crowd of 49,468 attended Ibrox (Rangers 4, Middlesbrough 4) on March 2, 1999 for former Rangers player **Alan McLaren's** testimonial. His fund benefited by an estimated £500,000.

A capacity crowd of 36,733 packed St. James' Park, paying an estimated £250,000, for **Peter Beardsley's** testimonial (Newcastle Utd. 1, Celtic 3) on Jan. 27, 1999.

Among testimonials in 2000-01: **Denis Irwin** (Manchester Utd.) estimated receipts £1m. from Manchester Utd. 2, Manchester City 0, Old Trafford, (att. 45,158) August 16; **David Seaman** (Arsenal 0, Barcelona 2, (att. 33,297), May 22. He donated part of the £600,000 estimated receipts to the Willow Foundation Charity, set up by Bob Wilson, his goalkeeping coach at Highbury. The testimonial for **Tom Boyd** (Celtic) against Manchester Utd. (May 15, 2001) attracted a 57,000 crowd with receipts estimated at £1m.

In season 2001-02: For **Ryan Giggs**, a full-house 66,967 (record Testimonial attendance) paid £1m. to see Manchester Utd. 3, Celtic 4 on August 1. Undisclosed sums were donated to charities.

Receipts estimated at £500,000 were produced by the 35,887 crowd at Tottenham v Fiorentina (August 8) for **Bill Nicholson**, who managed Tottenham from 1958-74.

Gary Kelly's Testimonial (Leeds Utd. 1, Celtic 4) drew 26,440 at Elland Road on May 7, 2002, and receipts of £600,000 were donated to cancer charities.

Tony Adams' second Testimonial (1-1 v Celtic on May 13, 2002) two nights after Arsenal completed the Double, was watched by 38,021 spectators. Of £1m. receipts, he donated a substantial percentage to Sporting Chance, the charity that helps sportsmen/women with drink, drug, gambling problems.

Another one-club player, **Matthew Le Tissier**, ended his playing career at Southampton with 31.904 spectators (receipts £500,000) watching a 9-9 draw with an England XI on May 14, 2002.

On the same night, Sunderland and a Republic of Ireland XI drew 0-0 in front of 35,702 at the Stadium of Light. The beneficiary, **Niall Quinn**, was donating his entire Testimonial proceeds, estimated at £1m., to children's hospitals in Sunderland and Dublin, and to homeless children in Africa and Asia.

WHAT IT USED TO COST

Minimum admission to League football was one shilling in 1939. After the war, it was increased to 1s. 3d. in 1946; 1s. 6d. in 1951; 1s. 9d. in 1952; 2s. in 1955; 2s. 6d. in 1960; 4s. in 1965; 5s. in 1968; 6s. in 1970; and 8s. (40p) in 1972. After that, the fixed minimum charge was dropped.

Wembley's first Cup Final programme in 1923 cost three pence (1¼p in today's money). The programme for the 'farewell' F.A. Cup Final in May, 2000 was priced £10.

WHAT THEY USED TO EARN

In the 1930s, First Division players were on £8 a week (£6 in close season) plus bonuses of £2 win, £1 draw. The maximum wage went up to £12 when football resumed post-war in 1946 and had reached £20 by the time the limit was abolished in 1961.

ENGLAND TOP EURO-PRIZE WINNERS

There have been **132 European club competitions** since what is now the Champions' League was launched in season 1955-6; 48 for the European Cup, 45 for the Fairs/UEFA Cup and 39 for the Cup-Winners' Cup, which ended in 1999.

Despite the five-year enforced absence that followed the Heysel disaster in 1985, **English clubs** jointly head the prize list, Liverpool's success in the 2001 UEFA Cup taking the total to 27 triumphs: 9 in the Champions' Cup, 8 in the Cup-Winners' Cup and 10 in the Fairs/UEFA Cup.

Italy joined England on 27 Euro successes in 2003, followed by Spain wth 25. The 132 winners represent 17 countries.

England's 27 prizes are shared among 13 clubs: Liverpool 7 (4 EC, 3 UEFA); Manchester Utd. 3 (2 EC, 1 CWC); Tottenham 3 (1 CWC, 2 UEFA); Chelsea 2 (2 CWC); Leeds Utd. 2 (2 UEFA); Nott'm. Forest 2 (2 EC); Arsenal 2 (1 UEFA, 1 CWC); Aston Villa 1 (EC); Everton 1 (CWC); Ipswich Town 1 (UEFA); Manchester City 1 (CWC); Newcastle Utd. 1 (UEFA); West Ham Utd. 1 (CWC).

Scotland's three successes have been achieved by Celtic (EC); Rangers and Aberdeen (both CWC).

EUROPEAN TRIUMPHS, COUNTRY BY COUNTRY

	European Cup/ Champions League	Cup-Winners' Cup	Fairs Cup/ UEFA Cup	Total
England	9	8	10	27
Italy	10	7	10	27
Spain	10	7	8	25
West Germany/Germany	6	4	6	16
Holland	6	1	4	11
Portugal	3	1	1	5
Belgium	–	3	1	4
Scotland	1	2	–	3
USSR	–	3	–	3
France	1	1	–	2
Sweden	–	–	2	2
Yugoslavia	1	–	1	2
Czechoslovakia	–	1	–	1
East Germany	–	1	–	1
Hungary	–	–	1	1
Romania	1	–	–	1
Turkey	–	–	1	1
Total:	48	39	45	132

EUROPEAN TROPHY WINNERS – SUMMARY

European Cup (48 competitions, 21 different winners): **9** Real Madrid; **6** AC Milan; **4** Ajax Amsterdam, Liverpool; Bayern Munich; **2** Benfica, Inter Milan, Juventus, Manchester Utd., Nott'm. Forest; **1** Aston Villa, Barcelona, Borussia Dortmund, Celtic, Feyenoord, Hamburg SV, Marseille, PSV Eindhoven, FC Porto, Red Star Belgrade, Steaua Bucharest.

Cup-Winners' Cup (39 competitions, 32 different winners): **4** Barcelona; **2** Anderlecht, Chelsea, Dynamo Kiev, AC Milan; **1** Aberdeen, Ajax Amsterdam, Arsenal, Atletico Madrid, Bayern Munich, Borussia Dortmund, Dynamo Tbilisi, Everton, Fiorentina, Hamburg SV, Juventus, Lazio, Magdeburg, Manchester City, Manchester Utd., Mechelen, Paris St. Germain, Parma, Rangers, Real Zaragoza, Sampdoria, Slovan Bratislava, Sporting Lisbon, Tottenham, Valencia, Werder Bremen, West Ham Utd.

UEFA Cup (orig. Fairs Cup) (45 competitions, 29 different winners): **3** Barcelona, Inter Milan, Juventus, Liverpool; **2** Borussia Moenchengladbach, Feyenoord, IFK Gothenburg, Leeds Utd., Parma, Real Madrid, Tottenham, Valencia; **1** Ajax Amsterdam, Anderlecht, Arsenal, Bayer Leverkusen, Bayern Munich, Dynamo Zagreb, Eintracht Frankfurt, PSV Eindhoven, Ferencvaros, Ipswich Town, Napoli, Newcastle Utd., Real Zaragoza, AS Roma, FC Schalke, Galatasaray, FC Porto.

- Four clubs have won all three trophies – Barcelona, Bayern Munich, Juventus and Ajax.
- The Champions League was introduced into the European Cup in 1992-3 to counter the threat of a European Super League.

BRITAIN'S 30 TROPHIES IN EUROPE

Liverpool's success in the 2001-01 UEFA Cup took the number of **British** club triumphs in European Football to 30:

European Cup (10)	**Cup-Winners' Cup (10)**	**Fairs/UEFA Cup (10)**
1967 Celtic	1963 Tottenham	1968 Leeds Utd.
1968 Manchester Utd.	1965 West Ham Utd.	1969 Newcastle Utd.
1977 Liverpool	1970 Manchester City	1970 Arsenal
1978 Liverpool	1971 Chelsea	1971 Leeds Utd.
1979 Nott'm Forest	1972 Rangers	1972 Tottenham
1980 Nott'm Forest	1983 Aberdeen	1973 Liverpool
1981 Liverpool	1985 Everton	1976 Liverpool
1982 Aston Villa	1991 Manchester Utd.	1981 Ipswich Town
1984 Liverpool	1994 Arsenal	1984 Tottenham
1999 Manchester Utd.	1998 Chelsea	2001 Liverpool

END OF CUP-WINNERS' CUP

The **European Cup-Winners' Cup**, inaugurated in 1960-61, terminated with the 1999 final. The competition merged into a revamped, 121-club **UEFA Cup**.

Also with effect from season 1999-2000, the **European Cup/Champions League** was increased by 8 clubs to 32.

From its inception in 1955, the **European Cup** comprised only championship-winning clubs until 1998-9, when selected runners-up were introduced. Further expansion came in 1999-2000 with the inclusion of clubs finishing third in certain leagues and fourth in 2002.

EUROPEAN CLUB COMPETITIONS – SCORING RECORDS

European Cup – Record aggregate: 18-0 by Benfica v Dudelange (Lux) (8-0a, 10-0h), prelim. round, 1965-6.
Record single-match score: 12-0 by Feyenoord v KR Reykjavik (Ice), 1st. round, 1st. leg, 1969-70 (aggregate was 16-0).

Cup-Winners' Cup – *Record aggregate: 21-0 by Chelsea v Jeunesse Hautcharage (Lux) (8-0a, 13-0h), 1st. round, 1971-2.
Record single-match score: 16-1 by Sporting Lisbon v Apoel Nicosia, 2nd. round, 1st. leg, 1963-4 (aggregate was 18-1).

UEFA Cup (prev. Fairs Cup) – *Record aggregate: 21-0 by Feyenoord v US Rumelange (Lux) (9-0h, 12-0a), 1st. round, 1972-3.
Record single-match score: 14-0 by Ajax Amsterdam v Red Boys (Lux) 1st. round, 2nd leg, 1984-5 (aggregate also 14-0).

Record British score in Europe: 13-0 by **Chelsea** at home to Jeunesse Hautcharage (Lux) in Cup-Winners' Cup 1st. round, 2nd. leg, 1971-2. Chelsea's overall 21-0 win in that tie is highest aggregate by British club in Europe.

Individual scoring record for European tie (over two legs): **10 goals** (6 home, 4 away) by **Kiril Milanov** for Levski Spartak in 19-3 agg. win CWC 1st round v Lahden Reipas, 1976-7. Next highest: **8 goals** by **Jose Altafini** for AC Milan v US Luxembourg (European Cup, prelim. round, 1962-3, agg. 14-0) and by **Peter Osgood** for Chelsea v Jeunesse Hautcharage (Cup-Winners' Cup, 1st. round 1971-2, agg. 21-0). Altafini and Osgood each scored 5 goals at home, 3 away.

Individual single-match scoring record in European competition: **6** goals by **Mascarenhas** for Sporting Lisbon in 16-1 Cup-Winner's Cup 2nd. round, 1st. leg win v Apoel, 1963-4; **6** by **Lothar Emmerich** for Borussia Dortmund in 8-0 CWC 1st. round, 2nd. leg win v Floriana 1965-6; **6** by **Kiril Milanov** for Levski Spartak in 12-2 CWC 1st. round, 1st. leg win v Lahden Reipas, 1976-7.

Most goals in single European campaign: **15** by **Jurgen Klinsmann** for Bayern Munich (UEFA Cup 1995-6).

Most goals (career total) **by British player in European competition**: **30** by **Peter Lorimer** (Leeds Utd., in 9 campaigns).

(*Joint record European aggregate)

First European 'Treble': Clarence Seedorf is the only player to win the European Cup with three clubs: Ajax in 1995, Real Madrid in 1998 and AC Milan in 2003.

EUROPEAN FOOTBALL – BIG RECOVERIES

In the 48-year history of European competition, only four clubs have survived a **4-goal** deficit after the first leg had been completed:

1961-2 (Cup-Winners' Cup 1st. Rd.): Leixoes (Portugal) beat Chaux de Fonds (Luxembourg) 7-6 on agg. (lost 2-6a, won 5-0h).

1962-3 (Fairs Cup 2nd. Rd.): Valencia (Spain) beat **Dunfermline** 1-0 in play-off in Lisbon after 6-6 agg. (Valencia won 4-0h, lost 2-6a).

1984-5 (UEFA Cup 2nd. Rd.): Partizan Belgrade beat **Q.P.R.** on away goals (lost 2-6 away, at Highbury, won 4-0 home).

1985-6 (UEFA Cup 3rd. Rd.): Real Madrid beat Borussia Moenchengladbach on away goals (lost 1-5a, won 4-0h) and went on to win competition.

In the **European Cup**, there are eight instances of clubs reaching the next round after **arrears of three goals** in the first leg:

1958-9 (Prel. Rd.) Schalke beat KB Copenhagen (0-3, 5-2, 3-1).
1965-6 (Q-final) Partizan Belgrade beat Sparta Prague (1-4, 5-0).
1970-1 (S-final) Panathinaikos beat Red Star Belgrade on away goal (1-4, 3-0).
1975-6 (2nd. Rd.) Real Madrid beat **Derby Co.** (1-4, 5-1).
1985-6 (S-final) Barcelona beat IFK Gothenburg on pens. (0-3, 3-0).
1988-9 (1st. Rd.) Werder Bremen beat Dynamo Berlin (0-3, 5-0).
1988-9 (2nd. Rd.) Galatasaray (Turkey) beat Neuchatel Xamax (Switz.) (0-3, 5-0).
1992-3 (1st. Rd.) **Leeds Utd.** beat VfB Stuttgart 2-1 in play-off in Barcelona. Over two legs, VfB won on away goal (3-0h, 1-4 away) but a third match was ordered because they broke 'foreigners' rule in team selection.

In the **Cup-Winners' Cup**, six clubs survived a **3-goal** deficit:

1963-4 (Q-final) Sporting Lisbon beat **Manchester Utd.** (1-4, 5-0).
1963-4 (S-final) MTK Budapest beat **Celtic** (0-3, 4-0).
1978-9 (2nd. Rd.) Barcelona beat Anderlecht on pens. (0-3, 3-0).
1980-1 (1st. Rd.) Carl Zeiss Jena beat AS Roma (0-3, 4-0).
1984-5 (Q-final) Rapid Vienna beat Dynamo Dresden (0-3, 5-0).
1989-90 (1st. Rd.) Grasshoppers (Switz.) beat Slovan Bratislava (0-3, 4-0).

In the **Fairs Cup/UEFA Cup**, there have been more than 20 occasions when clubs have survived a deficit of **3 goals**, the most notable example being the 1988 UEFA Cup Final, which Bayer Leverkusen won 3-2 on pens., having lost the first leg 0-3 away to Espanol and won the return 3-0 to level the aggregate.

Apart from Leeds Utd., two other British clubs have won a European tie from a 3-goal, first leg deficit: **Kilmarnock** 0-3, 5-1 v Eintracht Frankfurt (Fairs Cup 1st. Round, 1964-5); **Hibernian** 1-4, 5-0 v Napoli (Fairs Cup 2nd. Round, 1967-8).

English clubs have three times gone out of the **UEFA Cup** after leading 3-0 from the first leg: 1975-6 (2nd. Rd.) **Ipswich Town** lost 3-4 on agg. to Bruges; 1976-7 (Q-final) **Q.P.R.** lost on pens. to AEK Athens after 3-3 agg; 1977-8 (3rd. Rd.) **Ipswich Town** lost on pens. to Barcelona after 3-3 agg.

HEAVIEST ENGLISH-CLUB DEFEATS IN EUROPE

(Single-leg scores)

European Cup: Ajax 5, Liverpool 1 (2nd. Rd.), Dec. 1966 (agg. 7-3); Real Madrid 5, Derby Co. 1 (2nd. Rd.), Nov. 1975 (agg. 6-5).

Cup-Winners' Cup: Sporting Lisbon 5, Manchester Utd. 0 (Q-final), Mar. 1964 (agg. 6-4).

Fairs/UEFA Cup: Bayern Munich 6, Coventry City 1 (2nd. Rd.), Oct. 1970 (agg. 7-3). Combined London team lost 6-0 (agg. 8-2) in first Fairs Cup Final in 1958.

SHOCK ENGLISH-CLUB DEFEATS

1968-69 (E. Cup, 1st. Rd.): Manchester City beaten by Fenerbahce, 1-2 agg.
1971-72 (CWC, 2nd. Rd.): Chelsea beaten by Atvidaberg on away goals.
1993-94 (E. Cup, 2nd. Rd.): Manchester Utd. beaten by Galatasaray on away goals.
1994-95 (UEFA Cup, 1st. Rd.): Blackburn Rov. beaten by Trelleborgs, 2-3 agg.

2000-01 (UEFA Cup, 1st Rd.): Chelsea beaten by St. Gallen, Swit. 1-2 agg.

FIFA'S HALL OF CHAMPIONS

Ten retired players, honoured for 'sporting success that contributed to the positive image of the game' – Sir Stanley Matthews, Sir Bobby Charlton (England), Pele (Brazil), Franz Beckenbauer (W. Germany), Johan Cruyff (Holland), Alfredo di Stefano (Argentina), Eusebio (Portugal), Michel Platini (France), Ferenc Puskas (Hungary), Lev Yashin (Soviet Union). Managers: Sir Matt Busby (Manchester Utd.), Rinus Michels (Ajax Amsterdam).

The names were announced in January 1998.

P.F.A. FAIR PLAY AWARD (Bobby Moore Trophy from 1993)

1988	Liverpool	1996	Crewe Alexandra
1989	Liverpool	1997	Crewe Alexandra
1990	Liverpool	1998	Cambridge Utd.
1991	Nott'm. Forest	1999	Grimsby Town
1992	Portsmouth	2000	Crewe Alexandra
1993	Norwich City	2001	Crewe Alexandra
1994	Crewe Alexandra	2002	Crewe Alexandra
1995	Crewe Alexandra	2003	Crewe Alexandra

RECORD MEDALS SALE

West Ham Utd. bought (June 2000) the late **Bobby Moore's** collection of medals and trophies for £1.8m. at Christie's auction in London. It was put up for sale by his first wife Tina and included his World Cup winner's medal.

A No. 6 duplicate red shirt made for England captain **Bobby Moore** for the 1966 World Cup Final fetched £44,000 at an auction at Wolves' ground in Sept. 1999. Moore kept the shirt he wore in that Final and gave the replica to England physio Harold Shepherdson.

Sir Geoff Hurst's 1966 World Cup-winning shirt fetched a record £91,750 at Christie's on September 28, 2000. His World Cup Final cap fetched £37,600 and his Man of the Match trophy £18,800. Proceeds totalling £274,410 from the 129 lots went to Hurst's three daughters and charities of his choice, including the Bobby Moore Imperial Cancer Research Fund.

In August 2001, Sir Geoff sold his World Cup-winner's medal to his former club West Ham Utd. (for their museum) at a reported £150,000.

'The **Billy Wright Collection**' – caps, medals and other memorabilia from his illustrious career – fetched over £100,000 at Christie's in Glasgow on Nov. 21, 1996.

At the sale in Oct. 1993, trophies, caps and medals earned by **Ray Kennedy**, former England, Arsenal and Liverpool player, fetched a then record total of £88,407. Kennedy, suffering from Parkinson's Disease, received £73,000 after commission.

The P.F.A. paid £31,080 for a total of 60 lots – including a record £16,000 for his 1977 European Cup winner's medal – to be exhibited at their Manchester museum. An anonymous English collector paid £17,000 for the medal and plaque commemorating Kennedy's part in the Arsenal Double in 1971.

Previous record for one player's medals, shirts etc. collection: £30,000 (**Bill Foulkes**, Manchester Utd. in 1992). The sale of **Dixie Dean**'s medals etc. in 1991 realised £28,000.

In March 2001, **Gordon Banks**' 1966 World Cup-winner's medal fetched a new record £124,750, and at auctions in season 2001-02: In London on Sept. 21, TV's Nick Hancock, a Stoke City fan, paid £23,500 for **Sir Stanley Matthews**' 1953 F.A. Cup-winner's medal. He also bought one of Matthews' England caps for £3,525 and paid £2,350 for a Stoke Div. 2 Championship medal (1963).

Dave Mackay's 1961 League Championship and F.A. Cup winner's medals sold for £18,000 at Sotherby's. Tottenham bought them for their museum.

A selection of England World Cup-winning manager **Sir Alf Ramsey**'s memorabilia – England caps, championship medals with Ipswich Town etc. – fetched more than £80,000 at Christie's. They were offered for sale by his family, and his former clubs Tottenham and Ipswich Town were among the buyers.

Ray Wilson's 1966 England World Cup-winning shirt fetched £80,750. Also in March 2002, the No. 10 shirt worn by **Pele** in Brazil's World Cup triumph in 1970 was sold for a record £157,750 at Christies. It went to an anonymous telephone bidder.

VARSITY MATCH

Oxford and **Cambridge** have met 119 times, each winning 46 times with 27 draws. The fixture began in 1874. Latest result: Oxford 1, Cambridge 0 (at Q.P.R. ground, March 12, 2003).

LONGEST UNBEATEN CUP RUN

Liverpool established the longest unbeaten Cup sequence by a Football League club: 25 successive rounds in the League/Milk Cup between semi-final defeat by Nott'm. Forest (1-2 agg.) in 1980 and defeat at Tottenham (0-1) in the third round on October 31, 1984. During this period Liverpool won the tournament in four successive seasons, a feat no other Football League club has achieved in any competition.

NEAR £1M. RECORD DAMAGES

A High Court judge in Newcastle (May 7, 1999) awarded Bradford City's 28-year-old striker **Gordon Watson** record damages for a football injury: £909,143. He had had his right leg fractured in two places by Huddersfield Town's Kevin Gray on Feb. 1, 1997.

Huddersfield Town were 'proven negligent for allowing their player to make a rushed tackle'. The award was calculated at £202,643 for loss of earnings, £730,500 for 'potential career earnings' if he had joined a Premiership club, plus £26,000 to cover medical treatment and care.

Watson, awarded £50,000 in an earlier legal action, had a 6-inch plate inserted in the leg. He resumed playing for City in season 1998-9.

BIG HALF-TIME SCORES

Tottenham 10, Crewe Alexandra 1 (F.A. Cup 4th. Rd. replay, Feb. 3, 1960; result 13-2); Tranmere Rov. 8, Oldham Athletic 1 (Div. 3N., Dec. 26, 1935; result 13-4); Chester City 8, York City 0 (Div. 3N., Feb. 1, 1936; result 12-0; believed to be record half-time scores in League football).

Nine goals were scored in the first half – Burnley 4, Watford 5 in Div. 1 on April 5, 2003. Result: 4–7.

Stirling Albion led Selkirk 15-0 at half-time (result 20-0) in the Scottish Cup 1st. Rd., Dec. 8, 1984.

World record half-time score: 16-0 when Australia beat American Samoa 31-0 (another world record) in the World Cup Oceania qualifying group at Coff's Harbour, New South Wales, on April 11, 2001.

• On March 4, 1933 Coventry City beat Q.P.R. (Div. 3 South) 7-0, having led by that score at half-time. This repeated the half-time situation in Bristol City's 7-0 win over Grimsby Town on Dec. 26, 1914.

• Only instance of club failing to win League match after leading 5-0 at half-time: Sheffield Wed. 5, Everton 5 (Div. 1, Nov. 12, 1904; Wed. scored 5 in first half, Everton 5 in second).

TOP SECOND-HALF TEAM

Most goals scored by a team in one half of a League match is eleven. Stockport Co. led Halifax Town 2-0 at half-time in Div. 3 North on Jan. 6, 1934 and won 13-0.

FIVE NOT ENOUGH

Last team to score 5 in League match and lose: Reading, beaten 7-5 at Doncaster Rov. (Div. 3, Sept. 25, 1982).

LONG SERVICE WITH ONE CLUB

Bill Nicholson, OBE, has been associated with Tottenham for 65 years – as a wing-half (1938-55), then the club's most successful manager (1958-74) with 8 major prizes, subsequently chief advisor and scout. Now 84, he is club president, is an honorary freeman of the borough, still lives close to the ground, has an executive suite named after him at the club, and the stretch of roadway from Tottenham High Road to the main gates has the nameplate Bill Nicholson Way.

Ted Bates is the Grand Old Man of Southampton with 66 years of unbroken service to the club and awarded the Freedom of the City in April, 2001. He joined Saints as an inside-forward from Norwich City in 1937, made 260 peace-time appearances for the club, became reserve-team trainer in 1953 and manager at The Dell for 18 years (1955-73), taking Southampton into the top division in 1966. He was subsequently chief executive, director and now, at 85, is club president.

Dario Gradi, MBE, 61, is the longest-serving manager in British football, having completed 20 seasons and more than 1,000 matches in charge of Crewe Alexandra (appointed June 1983). Never a League player, he previously managed Wimbledon and Crystal Palace. At Crewe, where he is also a director, his policy of finding and grooming young talent has earned the club more than £14m. in transfer fees.

Bob Paisley was associated with Liverpool for 57 years from 1939, when he joined them from Bishop Auckland, until he died in February 1996. He served them as player, trainer, coach, assistant-manager, manager, director and vice-president.

Ronnie Moran, who joined Liverpool in as a player 1952, retired from the Anfield coaching staff in season 1998-9.

Ernie Gregory served West Ham Utd. for 52 years as goalkeeper and coach. He joined them as boy of 14 from school in 1935, retired in May 1987.

Ted Sagar, Everton goalkeeper, 23 years at Goodison Park (1929-52, but only 16 League seasons because of War).

Alan Knight, goalkeeper, played 23 seasons (1977-2000) for his only club, Portsmouth.

Roy Sproson, defender, played 21 League seasons for his only club, Port Vale (1950-71).

Allan Ball, goalkeeper, 20 seasons with Queen of the South (1963-83).

Pat Bonner, goalkeeper, 19 seasons with Celtic (1978-97).

Danny McGrain, defender, 17 years with Celtic (1970-87).

TIGHT AT HOME

Fewest home goals conceded in League season (modern times): 4 by **Liverpool** (Div. 1, 1978-9); 4 by **Manchester Utd.** (Premier League, 1994-5) – both in 21 matches.

FOOTBALL POOLS

Littlewoods launched them in 1923 with a capital of £100. Coupons were first issued (4,000 of them) outside Manchester Utd.'s ground, the original 35 investors staking a total of £4-7s.-6d (pay-out £2-12s).

Vernons joined Littlewoods as the leading promoters. The Treble Chance, leading to bonanza dividends, was introduced in 1946 and the Pools Panel began in January 1963, to counter mass fixture postponements caused by the Big Freeze winter.

But business was hard hit by the launch of the National Lottery in 1994. Dividends slumped, the work-force was drastically cut and in June 2000 the Liverpool-based Moores family sold Littlewoods Pools in a £161m. deal.

The record prize remains the £2,924,622 paid to a Worsley, Manchester, syndicate in November 1994.

Fixed odds football – record pay-out: £654,375 by Ladbrokes (May 1993) to Jim Wright, of Teignmouth, Devon. He placed a £1,000 each-way pre-season bet on the champions of the three Football League divisions – Newcastle Utd. (8–1), Stoke City (6–1) and Cardiff City (9–1).

Record for match accumulator: **£164,776** to £4 stake on 18 correct results, October 5, 6, 7, 2002. The bet, with Ladbrokes in Colchester Utd., was made by Army chef Mark Simmons.

TRANSFER DEADLINE

This was introduced by the Football League in 1911, to prevent clubs in contention for honours or fighting relegation gaining an unfair advantage in the closing weeks.

The original deadline was March 16. It is now 5 p.m. on the fourth Thursday in March, after which only in exceptional circumstances (e.g. if a side has no fit goalkeeper) can a transferred player appear for his new club that season.

After the last war, frantic spending was the norm on deadline day, but in recent years last-day business has dwindled to a comparative trickle.

TRANSFER WINDOW

This was introduced to Britain in September 2002 via FIFA regulations to bring uniformity across Europe (the rule previously applied in a number of other countries). The transfer of contracted players is restricted to two periods: June 1–August 31 and January 1–31).

On appeal, Football League (Nationwide) clubs continued to sign/sell players through season 2002–03 (excluding deals with Premiership clubs).

TEMPORARY TRANSFERS

These were introduced (originally limited to two per club) as 'permit loan transfers' by the Football League in 1967.

PROGRAMME PIONEERS

Chelsea pioneered football's magazine-style programme when they introduced a 16-page issue for their First Division match against Portsmouth on Christmas Day 1948. It cost sixpence (2½p).

TRIBUNAL-FEE RECORDS

Top tribunal fee: £2.5m for **Chris Bart-Williams** (Sheffield Wed. to Nott'm. Forest, June 1995).

Biggest discrepancy: Andy Walker, striker, Bolton Wand. to Celtic, June 1994: Bolton Wand. asked £2.2m, Celtic offered £250,000. Tribunal decided £550,000.

LONGEST THROW-IN?

That by Notts Co.'s **Andy Legg** was measured (season 1994-5) at 41 metres (45 yards) and claimed as the longest throw by any footballer in the world, until 1997-8, when **Dave Challinor** (Tranmere Rov.) reached 46.3 metres (50½ yards).

BALL JUGGLING: WORLD RECORD CLAIMS

Sam Ik (South Korea) juggled a ball non-stop for 18 hours, 11 minutes, 4 seconds in March 1995. Thai footballer **Sam-Ang Sowanski** juggled a ball for 15 hours without letting it touch the ground in Bangkok in April 2000.

Milene Domingues, wife of Brazilian star Ronaldo and a player for Italian women's team Fiammamonza, Milan, became the 'Queen of Keepy Uppy' when for 9 hours, 6 minutes she juggled a ball 55,187 times.

SUBS' SCORING RECORD

Barnet's 5-4 home win v Torquay Utd. (Div. 3, Dec. 28, 1993) provided the first instance of **all four substitutes** scoring in a major League match in England.

FOOTBALL'S OLDEST ANNUAL

Now in its 117th edition, this publication began as the 16-page ***Athletic News Football Supplement & Club Directory*** in 1887. From the long-established ***Athletic News***, it became the ***Sunday Chronicle Annual*** in 1946, the ***Empire News*** in 1956, the ***News of the World & Empire News*** in 1961 and, since 1965, the ***News of the World Annual***.

TRANSFER TRAIL

For space reasons, it is no longer possible to include every million-pound transfer involving British clubs since the first such deal: **Trevor Francis** from Birmingham City to Nott'm. Forest (£1,180,000) in Feb. 1979. For the same reason, deals below £5m are not included.

★ = British record fee at that time
A = Record all-British deal
B = Record for goalkeeper
C = Record for defender
D = Record deal between English and Scottish clubs
E = Record fee paid by Scottish club
F = Record fee to Scottish club
H = Record winger import
J = Record received for winger
K = Record for teenager
L = Most expensive foreign import
M = Record English-club signing
N = British record for striker
P = Record British export
(• Re dates, 1/00 = Jan 2000 etc)

	Player	From	To	Date	£
★CA	Rio Ferdinand	Leeds Utd.	Manchester Utd.	7/02	29,100,000
★LM	Juan Sebastian Veron	Lazio	Manchester Utd.	7/01	28,100,000
P	David Beckham	Manchester Utd.	Real Madrid	7/03	25,000,000
★	Nicolas Anelka	Arsenal	Real Madrid	8/99	22,500,000
J	Marc Overmars	Arsenal	Barcelona	7/00	22,000,000
N	Ruud van Nistelrooy	PSV Eindhoven	Manchester Utd.	4/01	19,000,000
AC	Rio Ferdinand	West Ham Utd.	Leeds Utd.	11/00	18,000,000
★	Alan Shearer	Blackburn Rov.	Newcastle Utd.	7/96	15,000,000
	Jimmy F. Hasselbaink	Atl. Madrid	Chelsea	6/00	15,000,000
	Jaap Stam	Manchester Utd.	Lazio	8/01	13,300,000
	Robbie Keane	Coventry City	Inter Milan	7/00	13,000,000
	Sylvain Wiltord	Bordeaux	Arsenal	8/00	13,000,000
	Nicolas Anelka	Paris St. Germain	Manchester City	5/02	13,000,000
	Dwight Yorke	Aston Villa	Manchester Utd.	8/98	12,600,000
	Juninho	Middlesbrough	Atl. Madrid	7/97	12,000,000
	Jimmy F. Hasselbaink	Leeds Utd.	Atl. Madrid	8/99	12,000,000
DE	Tore Andre Flo	Chelsea	Rangers	11/00	12,000,000
	Robbie Keane	Inter Milan	Leeds Utd.	12/00	12,000,000
	Steve Marlet	Lyon	Fulham	8/01	11,500,000
	Sergei Rebrov	Dynamo Kiev	Tottenham	5/00	11,000,000
	Frank Lampard	West Ham Utd.	Chelsea	6/01	11,000,000
	Robbie Fowler	Liverpool	Leeds Utd.	11/01	11,000,000
	Jaap Stam	PSV Eindhoven	Manchester Utd.	5/98	10,750,000
	Thierry Henry	Juventus	Arsenal	8/99	10,500,000
	Laurent Robert	Paris St. Germain	Newcastle Utd.	8/01	10,500,000
	Chris Sutton	Blackburn Rov.	Chelsea	7/99	10,000,000
	Emile Heskey	Leicester City	Liverpool	2/00	10,000,000
	El Hadji Diouf	Lens	Liverpool	6/02	10,000,000
	Juan Pablo Angel	River Plate (Arg.)	Aston Villa	1/01	9,500,000
	Jonathan Woodgate	Leeds Utd.	Newcastle Utd.	1/03	9,000,000
F	Giovanni van Bronckhorst	Rangers	Arsenal	6/01	8,500,000
★	Stan Collymore	Nott'm Forest	Liverpool	6/95	8,500,000
K	Hugo Viana	Sporting Lisbon	Newcastle Utd.	6/02	8,500,000
	Dean Richards	Southampton	Tottenham	9/01	8,100,000
	Massimo Maccarone	Empoli	Middlesbrough	7/02	8,100,000
	Andrei Kanchelskis	Everton	Fiorentina	1/97	8,000,000
	Dietmar Hamann	Newcastle Utd.	Liverpool	7/99	8,000,000
	Ugo Ehiogu	Aston Villa	Middlesbrough	10/00	8,000,000
	Francis Jeffers	Everton	Arsenal	6/01	8,000,000
	Andy Cole	Manchester Utd.	Blackburn Rov.	12/01	8,000,000
B	Fabien Barthez	Monaco	Manchester Utd.	5/00	7,800,000
	Jesper Gronkjaer	Ajax Amsterdam	Chelsea	10/00	7,800,000

	Player	From	To	Date	Fee
★	Dennis Bergkamp	Inter Milan	Arsenal	6/95	7,500,000
	Kevin Davies	Southampton	Blackburn Rov.	6/98	7,500,000
	John Hartson	West Ham Utd.	Wimbledon	1/99	7,500,000
	Emmanuel Petit	Barcelona	Chelsea	6/01	7,500,000
	Diego Forlan	Independiente (Arg.)	Manchester Utd.	1/02	7,500,000
	Olivier Dacourt	Lens	Leeds Utd.	5/00	7,200,000
★	Andy Cole	Newcastle Utd.	Manchester Utd.	1/95	7,000,000
	Fabrizio Ravanelli	Juventus	Middlesbrough	7/96	7,000,000
	Stan Collymore	Liverpool	Aston Villa	5/97	7,000,000
H	Marc Overmars	Ajax Amsterdam	Arsenal	6/97	7,000,000
	Duncan Ferguson	Everton	Newcastle Utd.	11/98	7,000,000
	Lauren	Real Mallorca	Arsenal	5/00	7,000,000
	Carl Cort	Wimbledon	Newcastle Utd.	7/00	7,000,000
	Edwin Van der Sar	Juventus	Fulham	8/01	7,000,000
	Boudewijn Zenden	Barcelona	Chelsea	8/01	7,000,000
	Seth Johnson	Derby Co.	Leeds Utd.	10/01	7,000,000
	Robbie Keane	Leeds Utd.	Tottenham	8/02	7,000,000
	Paul Merson	Middlesbrough	Aston Villa	8/98	6,750,000
	Corrado Grabbi	Ternana (It.)	Blackburn Rov.	6/01	6,750,000
	Tore Andre Flo	Rangers	Sunderland	8/02	6,750,000
	Faustino Asprilla	Parma	Newcastle Utd.	2/96	6,700,000
	David Platt	Bari	Juventus	6/92	6,500,000
	Olivier Dacourt	Everton	Lens	6/99	6,500,000
	Kieron Dyer	Ipswich Town	Newcastle Utd.	7/99	6,500,000
	Craig Bellamy	Coventry City	Newcastle Utd.	6/01	6,500,000
	Gareth Southgate	Aston Villa	Middlesbrough	7/01	6,500,000
	Michael Ball	Everton	Rangers	8/01	6,500,000
	John Hartson	Coventry City	Celtic	8/01	6,500,000
	Helder Postiga	FC Porto	Tottenham	6/03	6,250,000
	William Gallas	Marseille	Chelsea	5/01	6,200,000
	Paul Ince	Manchester Utd.	Inter Milan	6/95	6,000,000
	Les Ferdinand	Q.P.R.	Newcastle Utd.	6/95	6,000,000
	Les Ferdinand	Newcastle Utd.	Tottenham	7/97	6,000,000
	Faustino Asprilla	Newcastle Utd.	Parma	1/98	6,000,000
	Robbie Keane	Wolves	Coventry City	8/99	6,000,000
	Marc-Vivien Foe	West Ham Utd.	Lyon	5/00	6,000,000
	Chris Sutton	Chelsea	Celtic	7/00	6,000,000
	Mark Viduka	Celtic	Leeds Utd.	7/00	6,000,000
	Nick Barmby	Everton	Liverpool	7/00	6,000,000
	Emmanuel Petit	Arsenal	Barcelona	7/00	6,000,000
	Richard Wright	Ipswich Town	Arsenal	7/01	6,000,000
	Bosko Balaban	Dynamo Zagreb	Aston Villa	8/01	6,000,000
	Mikel Arteta	Barcelona	Rangers	7/02	5,800,000
	Nick Barmby	Middlesbrough	Everton	10/96	5,750,000
	Dion Dublin	Coventry City	Aston Villa	11/98	5,750,000
	Eyal Berkovic	West Ham Utd.	Celtic	7/99	5,750,000
	Neil Lennon	Leicester City	Celtic	12/00	5,700,000
	Mario Stanic	Parma	Chelsea	6/00	5,600,000
★	David Platt	Aston Villa	Bari	7/91	5,500,000
★	Paul Gascoigne	Tottenham	Lazio	6/92	5,500,000
	Fabrizio Ravanelli	Middlesbrough	Marseille	9/97	5,500,000
	Gary Speed	Everton	Newcastle Utd.	2/98	5,500,000
	Georgi Kinkladze	Manchester City	Ajax	5/98	5,500,000
	Andrei Kanchelskis	Fiorentina	Rangers	7/98	5,500,000
	Steve Stone	Nott'm Forest	Aston Villa	3/99	5,500,000
	Robert Pires	Marseille	Arsenal	7/00	5,500,000
	Christian Ziege	Middlesbrough	Liverpool	8/00	5,500,000
	Igor Biscan	Dynamo Zagreb	Liverpool	12/00	5,500,000
	Tomas Repka	Fiorentina	West Ham Utd.	9/01	5,500,000

David Dunn	Blackburn Rov.	Birmingham City	7/03	5,500,000
Pierluigi Casiraghi	Lazio	Chelsea	5/98	5,400,000
Christian Dailly	Derby Co.	Blackburn Rov.	8/98	5,300,000
Nick Barmby	Tottenham	Middlesbrough	8/95	5,250,000
Dietmar Hamann	Bayern Munich	Newcastle Utd.	7/98	5,250,000
David Platt	Juventus	Sampdoria	7/93	5,200,000
Lee Hughes	W.B.A.	Coventry City	8/01	5,000,001
Trevor Steven	Rangers	Marseille	8/91	5,000,000
Chris Sutton	Norwich City	Blackburn Rov.	7/94	5,000,000
Andrei Kanchelskis	Manchester Utd.	Everton	8/95	5,000,000
Paul Merson	Arsenal	Middlesbrough	7/97	5,000,000
Graeme Le Saux	Blackburn Rov.	Chelsea	8/97	5,000,000
Henning Berg	Blackburn Rov.	Manchester Utd.	8/97	5,000,000
Arthur Numan	PSV Eindhoven	Rangers	7/98	5,000,000
Elena Marcelino	Real Mallorca	Newcastle Utd.	6/99	5,000,000
Giovanni V. Bronckhorst	Feyenoord	Rangers	7/98	5,000,000
Michael Bridges	Sunderland	Leeds Utd.	7/99	5,000,000
Ben Thatcher	Wimbledon	Tottenham	7/00	5,000,000
Ade Akinbiyi	Wolves	Leicester City	7/00	5,000,000
Edu	Corinthians (Braz.)	Arsenal	1/01	5,000,000
Olof Mellberg	Racing Santander	Aston Villa	7/01	5,000,000
Don Hutchison	Sunderland	West Ham Utd.	8/01	5,000,000
Chris Kirkland	Coventry City	Liverpool	8/01	5,000,000
Jermaine Jenas	Nott'm. Forest	Newcastle Utd.	2/02	5,000,000
Peter Crouch	Portsmouth	Aston Villa	3/02	5,000,000
Salif Diao	Sedan (Fr.)	Liverpool	5/02	5,000,000
Titus Bramble	Ipswich Town	Newcastle Utd.	7/02	5,000,000
Harry Kewell	Leeds Utd.	Liverpool	7/03	5,000,000

BRITISH RECORD TRANSFERS FROM FIRST £1,000 DEAL

Player	From	To	Date	£
Alf Common	Sunderland	Middlesbrough	2/1905	1,000
Syd Puddefoot	West Ham Utd.	Falkirk	2/22	5,000
Warney Cresswell	S. Shields	Sunderland	3/22	5,500
Bob Kelly	Burnley	Sunderland	12/25	6,500
David Jack	Bolton Wand.	Arsenal	10/28	10,890
Bryn Jones	Wolves	Arsenal	8/38	14,500
Billy Steel	Morton	Derby Co.	9/47	15,000
Tommy Lawton	Chelsea	Notts Co.	11/47	20,000
Len Shackleton	Newcastle Utd.	Sunderland	2/48	20,500
Johnny Morris	Manchester Utd.	Derby Co.	2/49	24,000
Eddie Quigley	Sheffield Wed.	Preston N.E.	12/49	26,500
Trevor Ford	Aston Villa	Sunderland	10/50	30,000
Jackie Sewell	Notts Co.	Sheffield Wed.	3/51	34,500
Eddie Firmani	Charlton Athletic	Sampdoria	7/55	35,000
John Charles	Leeds Utd.	Juventus	4/57	65,000
Denis Law	Manchester City	Torino	6/61	100,000
Denis Law	Torino	Manchester Utd.	7/62	115,000
Allan Clarke	Fulham	Leicester City	6/68	150,000
Allan Clarke	Leicester City	Leeds Utd.	6/69	165,000
Martin Peters	West Ham Utd.	Tottenham	3/70	200,000
Alan Ball	Everton	Arsenal	12/71	220,000
David Nish	Leicester City	Derby Co.	8/72	250,000
Bob Latchford	Birmingham City	Everton	2/74	350,000
Graeme Souness	Middlesbrough	Liverpool	1/78	352,000
Kevin Keegan	Liverpool	Hamburg	6/77	500,000
David Mills	Middlesbrough	W.B.A.	1/79	516,000
Trevor Francis	Birmingham City	Nott'm. Forest	2/79	1,180,000

Steve Daley	Wolves	Manchester City	9/79	1,450,000
Andy Gray	Aston Villa	Wolves	9/79	1,469,000
Bryan Robson	W.B.A.	Manchester Utd.	10/81	1,500,000
Ray Wilkins	Manchester Utd.	AC Milan	5/84	1,500,000
Mark Hughes	Manchester Utd.	Barcelona	5/86	2,300,000
Ian Rush	Liverpool	Juventus	6/87	3,200,000
Chris Waddle	Tottenham	Marseille	7/89	4,250,000
David Platt	Aston Villa	Bari	7/91	5,500,000
Paul Gascoigne	Tottenham	Lazio	6/92	5,500,000
Andy Cole	Newcastle Utd.	Manchester Utd.	1/95	7,000,000
Dennis Bergkamp	Inter Milan	Arsenal	6/95	7,500,000
Stan Collymore	Nott'm. Forest	Liverpool	6/95	8,500,000
Alan Shearer	Blackburn Rov.	Newcastle Utd.	7/96	15,000,000
Nicolas Anelka	Arsenal	Real Madrid	8/99	22,500,000
Juan Sebastian Veron	Lazio	Manchester Utd.	7/01	28,100,000
Rio Ferdinand	Leeds Utd.	Manchester Utd.	7/02	29,100,000

- **World's first £1m. transfer:** Guiseppe Savoldi, Bologna to Napoli, July 1975.

TOP FOREIGN SIGNINGS

Player	From	To	Date	£
Zinedine Zidane	Juventus	Real Madrid	7/01	47,200,000
Luis Figo	Barcelona	Real Madrid	7/00	37,200,000
Hernan Crespo	Parma	Lazio	7/00	35,000,000
Ronaldo	Inter Milan	Real Madrid	8/02	33,000,000
Gianluigi Buffon	Parma	Juventus	7/01	32,600,000
Christian Vieri	Lazio	Inter Milan	6/99	31,000,000
Alessandro Nesta	Lazio	AC Milan	8/02	30,200,000
Hernan Crespo	Lazio	Inter Milan	8/02	29,000,000
Gaizka Mendieta	Valencia	Lazio	7/01	28,500,000
Pavel Nedved	Lazio	Juventus	7/01	25,000,000
Rui Costa	Fiorentina	AC Milan	7/01	24,500,000
Gabriel Batistuta	Fiorentina	Roma	5/00	22,000,000
Lilian Thuram	Parma	Juventus	6/01	22,000,000
Nicolas Anelka	Real Madrid	Paris St. Germain	7/00	21,700,000
Filippo Inzaghi	Juventus	AC Milan	7/01	21,700,000
Denilson	Sao Paulo	Real Betis	7/97	21,400,000
Marcio Amoroso	Udinese	Parma	6/99	21,000,000
Antonio Cassano	Bari	Roma	3/01	20,000,000
Javier Saviola	River Plate	Barcelona	7/01	20,000,000
Juan Sebastian Veron	Parma	Lazio	6/99	19,800,000
Hidetoshi Nakata	Roma	Parma	7/01	19,100,000
Ronaldo	Barcelona	Inter Milan	6/97	18,000,000
Francesco Toldo	Fiorentina	Inter Milan	7/01	18,000,000
Christian Vieri	Atletico Madrid	Lazio	8/98	17,500,000
David Trezeguet	Monaco	Juventus	6/00	17,500,000
Savo Milosevic	Real Zaragoza	Parma	7/00	17,000,000
Andrei Shevchenko	Dynamo Kiev	AC Milan	6/99	15,700,000
Vincenzo Montella	Sampdoria	Roma	6/99	15,300,000
Clarence Seedorf	Real Madrid	Inter Milan	12/99	15,000,000
Mathias Almeyda	Lazio	Parma	7/00	14,800,000
Ronald de Boer	Ajax	Barcelona	1/99	14,000,000
Frank de Boer	Ajax	Barcelona	1/99	
Claudio Lopez	Valencia	Lazio	7/00	14,000,000
Shabani Nonda	Rennes	Monaco	6/00	13,500,000
Gianluigi Lentini	Torino	AC Milan	7/92	13,000,000
Walter Samuel	Boca Juniors	Roma	6/00	13,000,000
Geovanni	Cruzeiro	Barcelona	6/01	12,700,000
Jose Mari Romero	Atletico Madrid	AC Milan	12/99	12,700,000

Gianluca Vialli	Sampdoria	Juventus	6/92	12,500,000
Ronaldo	PSV Eindhoven	Barcelona	7/96	12,500,000
Rivaldo	Dep. La Coruna	Barcelona	8/97	12,500,000

WORLD RECORD GOALKEEPER FEE

£32.6m for **Gianluigi Buffon** (Parma to Juventus, July 2001).

RECORD CONFERENCE FEE

£250,000: **Andy Clarke**, Barnet to Wimbledon, Feb 1991; **Barry Hayles**, Stevenage Borough to Bristol Rov., Aug. 1997; **Jason Roberts**, Hayes to Wolves, Sept. 1997.

RECORD FEE BETWEEN NON-LEAGUE CLUBS

£180,000 for **Justin Jackson**, Morecambe to Rushden & Diamonds (Conference), June 2000.

WORLD RECORD FEE FOR TEENAGER

£19m. for **Antonio Cassano**, 18, Bari to Roma, March 2001.

BRITISH RECORD FEES FOR TEENAGERS

£8.5. for **Hugo Viana,** aged 19, Sporting Lisbon to Newcastle Utd., June 2002.
£6m. for **Robbie Keane**, aged 19, Wolves to Coventry City, Aug. 1999.

QUOTE-UNQUOTE

'When I saw him on the pitch I thought "hmmm, he is a dangerous man" ' – **Claudio Ranieri**, Chelsea manager, after Paolo Di Canio came off the bench to score the winner for West Ham United.

'You have just seen the best goalkeeper the Premiership has ever had' – **Kevin Keegan**, Manchester City manager, after a marvellous display by Peter Schmeichel against Liverpool.

'It's our greatest achievement' – **Sir Alex Ferguson** after Manchester United overhauled Arsenal to win the title.

'He's the best. Matt himself would say the same' – **Sir Bobby Charlton** putting Sir Alex Ferguson ahead of Sir Matt Busby in the Manchester United Hall of Fame.

'Over the whole season, if you look at the F.A. Cup and the Premier League, then we were certainly the best team in England' – **Arsene Wenger**, Arsenal manager.

'I am completely drained, emotionally unstable. The world has finally come off my shoulders' – **Sam Allardyce**, Bolton Wanderers manager, after escaping relegation on the last day of the season

'I'm embarrassed to be their gaffer. The players are not playing to their capabilities. A blind man on a galloping horse can see that' – **Stan Ternent**, manager, after Burnley started season 2002–03 with four defeats.

FINAL WHISTLE – OBITUARIES 2002-03

JULY

RAY WOOD, 71, who won Championship medals as Manchester Utd.'s goalkeeper in 1956 and 1957, then went to the F.A. Cup Final with the Busby Babes among Wembley's hottest favourites to complete the first Double of the 20th century. But in those pre-substitute days, they were effectively reduced to 10 men after only 6 minutes when Aston Villa's Irish Int. winger Peter McParland violently charged into Wood, who was knocked unconscious and carried off with a broken cheekbone. He returned of no more than nuisance value on the wing, and after United had pulled back a goal in reply to two by McParland, he resumed in goal for the last 8 minutes. The following February Wood, by then a reserve 'keeper at Old Trafford after the signing of Harry Gregg, survived the Munich air crash. His career began at Third Division Darlington, and a £5,000 transfer took him to Old Trafford in December 1949. Capped 3 times by England, he left United (205 apps.) in December 1958 for 8 seasons with Huddersfield Town, then played for Bradford City (1965-66) and Barnsley (1966-68). Coaching appointments took him to Canada, Zambia, Cyprus, Greece, Kuwait, Kenya and United Arab Emirates before he retired from football and went into business in Sussex.

FRANK TAYLOR, 81, was the only journalist to survive the Manchester United air disaster at Munich in February 1958. Dragged from the wreckage with 12 broken ribs and severe injuries to arm and leg, he spent 21 weeks in hospital, then returned home – and to the *New Chronicle* – to read his own obituary, having originally been listed among the dead through a passport mix-up. He wrote a wide-ranging column in the *Daily Mirror* sports pages until retiring in 1985. His moving account of Munich was published on its 25th anniversary and repeated in paperback in 1998.

AUGUST

BOB MCKINLAY, 69, was Nott'm. Forest's centre-half in 614 League matches over 18 years (1951-69), including an unbroken run of 265 appearances from 1959-65. He was captain from 1962-66, and his career highlight was an F.A. Cup winner's medal against Luton Town in 1959. A Scot from Lochgelly, he joined Forest in 1949, stayed with them until he was 37, then went home to play for Albion Rov. On retirement, he returned to Nottingham to work as a prison officer.

HARRY SHARRATT, 71, kept goal for the greatest amateur team of all, Bishop Auckland. He won 3 Amateur Cup medals with them (1955-56-57) and 6 England caps at that level. He entertained the spectators with more than his magnificent goalkeeping. With play at the other end, as it mostly was in Bishops' matches, he would go into the crowd to cadge sweets and cigarettes and once watched the proceedings while perched on top of his crossbar. One Boxing Day, in need of company, he built a snowman on his goal-line.

SEPTEMBER

IAN HUTCHINSON, 54, who died after a long illness, was a thrustful Chelsea forward whose bravery on the field and in the treatment room endeared him to Stamford Bridge supporters, as did an immense throw-in (measured at 112ft.). Originally with Burton Albion, he joined Chelsea from Cambridge Utd. for a bargain £5,000 in July 1968 and formed a formidable strike partnership with Peter Osgood. He played a big part in Chelsea's first F.A. Cup success in 1970, scoring the second equaliser against Leeds Utd. at Wembley, and in the replay at Old Trafford delivered his trademark long throw for David Webb to score the winning goal. He scored 58 goals in 144 apps. for Chelsea before being forced to retire at 28 in 1976.

MAURO, 72, was centre-back and captain of the Brazil team that won the 1962 World Cup in Chile and a member of the renowned Santos side of the early Sixties. He had been a reserve for Brazil at both the 1954 and 1958 World Cups.

OCTOBER

RON GRAY, 82, played pre-war at left-half for Sheffield Utd., and held managerial posts at Watford (1950-51), Millwall (1956-58), Millwall again (1961-63, taking them to the 4th Div. Championship in 1962) and Lincoln City (1966-70). Then, as chief scout for Ipswich Town from 1970 into the Eighties, he discovered a number of Internationals for the club, including George Burley and Terry Butcher.

BILLY McADAMS, 67, was a well-travelled centre-forward who started his career in the Irish League with Distillery. He came into English football in 1953 with Manchester City (127 League apps., 62 goals) and moved on to Bolton Wand., Leeds Utd., Brentford, Q.P.R. and finally Barrow. In his 15-year career in England, he made 343 League apps. (149 goals) for 6 clubs. He was capped 15 times by Northern Ireland, and his 7 Int. goals included a hat-trick in the – 3-4 World Cup qualifying defeat against West Germany in his native Belfast in October 1960.

NOVEMBER

ROB HINDMARSH, 41, began as a centre-back with Sunderland (1978-83), then helped Derby Co. win successive promotions to return to the old First Division in 1987. He later coached Wolves and in America. He died from motor neurone disease only a few months after being diagnosed.

JUAN SCHIAFFINO, 77, was Uruguay's play-maker when Brazil, hot favourites for the 1950 World Cup, were beaten 2-1 in Rio in the last game of that tournament (played on a round-robin basis). He scored the equaliser and set up the winner. Having helped Penarol win 6 Uruguayan titles between 1944 and 1954, he moved to Europe with AC Milan at a world record £72,000 and won two Serie A medals. On retirement, he returned to Montevideo for spells in charge of his old club Penarol and the national team.

DECEMBER

ALAN ASHMAN, 74, reached the heights in management with W.B.A., taking them to F.A. Cup triumph against Everton in 1968, and six years later guiding unfashionable Carlisle Utd. to the old First Division. As a dashing centre-forward he scored 98 goals in 207 League apps. for Carlisle., then managed them from 1963-67 on his way to W.B.A. (1967-71). He returned to manage Carlisle (1972-75) and subsequently managed Workington and Walsall for short spells.

BILLY DRENNAN, MBE, 84, was the dynamic secretary of the Irish Football Association from 1950-83, and UEFA recognised his service to the game with their Ruby Award. His administrative partnership with Harry Cavan (president), provided invaluable backing to team manager Peter Doherty, who took Northern Ireland to the World Cup Finals for the first time (Sweden 1958), in which they defied all the odds in reaching the quarter-finals.

SIR BERT MILLICHIP, 88, was chairman of the Football Association for 15 years (1981-96) and during the darkest days in English football – the Bradford City fire disaster and the tragedies of Heysel and Hillsborough. His period in office also took in the formation of the Premier League in 1992. He was a member of the F.A. Council from 1970, a director of W.B.A. from 1964-84, their chairman 1973-83 and president from 1984 until he died. By profession a solicitor, he was knighted for his services to football in 1991. He was highly respected in the corridors of FIFA and UEFA, and brought great dignity to the game domestically and Internationally.

BILLY MORRIS, 84, was the last surviving member of Burnley's 1947 Cup Final team that won promotion to the First Division the same year. An inside-forward, he spent his entire playing career at Turf Moor and scored 47 goals in more than 200 apps. He was capped 5 times by Wales (1947-52). He managed Wrexham for two spells in 1960-61 and 1965, and later ran a village shop near Colwyn Bay.

ARTHUR ROWLEY, 76, holds an indelible place in the records as the all-time highest scorer of goals in English League football with an aggregate of 434 in 619 apps. for 4 clubs during the first 19 years of post-war football (1946-65). In 13 of those seasons he scored 20 or more goals, and was Leicester City's leading marksman for 8 seasons, but playing for unfashionable clubs, he was never chosen by England above 'B' level. The younger brother of Jack Rowley (Manchester Utd. & England), George Arthur was born at Wolves. This was how he compiled the English League scoring record that is unlikely ever to be beaten: W.B.A. (1946-48) 24 apps., 4 goals; Fulham (1948-50) 56-27; Leicester City (1950-58) 303-251; Shrewsbury Town (1958-65) 236-152. He was top scorer with 44 League goals when Leicester won promotion as Second Division Champions in 1954, and his 38 in 1958-59 took Shrewsbury to the 4th Div. Title. After managing Shrewsbury (1958-68), he managed Sheffield Utd. briefly and was in charge of Southend Utd. from 1970-76. But Shrewsbury stayed close to his heart, and he was at Gay Meadow to watch them four days before he died.

ALBERT STUBBINS, 83, was the flame-haired goalscoring hero in size 11 boots in two of the game's hotbeds – Newcastle and Liverpool. Having signed professional at St. James' Park in 1937, his career had barely taken off when hostilities began in 1939, but he seized the opportunity to become the highest scorer in wartime football with 231 goals in 187 games for Newcastle Utd. Liverpool paid their record fee (£12,500) to take him to Anfield in September 1946, and with 24 First Division goals in his debut season there he helped them become the first post-war Champions in 1947. After scoring 83 goals in 180 first-team games for Liverpool, he left Anfield in 1953, briefly player-managed non-League Ashington in his native North-east and coached in New York for a short spell. On retiring, he returned to Newcastle as a football journalist.

JANUARY

PETER HARRIS, 77, was the flying right-winger who played a huge part in the League Championship going to its Southern-most destination as Portsmouth took the title in successive seasons, 1948-49 and 1949-50. Born a bus-ride from Fratton Park, he was signed from Gosport Borough in 1944 and by the time he retired in 1959 he had topped 500 apps. over 15 years and scored 208 goals for his only League club. Five of those goals came in a 5-2 victory over Aston Villa in 1958-59, making him the first winger to score as many in a top-division match. But for being a contemporary of Stanley Matthews and Tom Finney, he must have played more than twice on the England wing. Tuberculosis ended his career at 33, but he recovered to manage a restaurant on Hayling Island and did a lot of local charity work.

TREVOR MORRIS, 82, had a unique administrative career in the Principality, managing all 3 South Wales clubs – Cardiff City (1954-58), Swansea Town (1958-65) and then Newport County – before becoming secretary of the Welsh F.A. (1970-82). He had been a pre-war player with Ipswich Town, but a broken leg when with Cardiff ended his onfield career in 1942. After winning the Distinguished Flying Cross as an RAF bomber pilot, he returned to football as Cardiff's assistant-manager. As Welsh F.A. secretary, he served on various UEFA committees and was responsible for introducing legislation that allowed a player International qualification through his father's place of birth.

MIKE MURPHY, 51, did not, as an ambitious teenager, rise above Fulham's reserves but, given a break by Jimmy Hill at London Weekend Television, he reached the heights in TV. Following Jimmy to the BBC in 1974, he became editor of *Grandstand* and, at 26, the youngest-ever editor of *Match of the Day*. Ten years on, he left to form his own production company in TV sport and leisure. His business spread world-wide and beyond sport, and by 'Murph's' untimely death on a visit to Dublin the industry lost an innovative and engaging entrepreneur.

JOCK WEIR, 79, a pre-war centre-forward with Hibernian, moved into English football via a £10,000 transfer to Blackburn Rov. in January 1947. Within a year, Celtic signed him for £7,000. He played in their Cup-winning team in 1951, and of the 33 goals he scored in 106 apps. for them the most important came on the last day of season 1947-48. Celtic went to Dundee with relegation unthinkably 90 minutes away. But from 2-1 down, they survived with a hat-trick by Weir.

FEBRUARY

IVAN MARSHALL, 67, vice-president of the Irish Football Association.

DALE ROBERTS, 46, assistant-manager of Ipswich Town, died after a year-long battle against cancer. Newcastle-born, he graduated to England's Youth Int. side as an Ipswich apprentice. His career as a centre-back began in earnest with Hull City (153 League apps., 1980-85) and he returned to Portman Road as No. 2 to George Burley in 1995.

DENIS SAUNDERS, 78, was one of the game's last Corinthian-style schoolmaster-footballers. An Oxford University and England Amateur wing-half, he was a corner-stone of the meteoric Pegasus FC, the team composed of past and present Oxford and Cambridge Blues. He played in their first match in 1948 and their last in 1963 and captained them to Amateur Cup success in 1952 and 1953 – the only occasions when an amateur side drew 100,000 spectators to Wembley. He became geography master in charge of football at Malvern and in 1984 was invited by the Football Association to be academic headmaster at their new School of Excellence at Lilleshall.

EDDIE THOMPSON, 55, former Hearts and Aberdeen defender, became Australia's national coach, taking charge of the Socceroos from 1990-96. Reverend as 'the father of Australian soccer,' he nurtured the early careers of Harry Kewell, Mark Viduka and Mark Bosnich.

MARCH

ROGER ALBERTSEN, 45, was capped 25 times by Norway (1976-84) as a player for Rosenborg, Olympiakos (Greece) and Den Haag (Holland).; He scored the first goal in Norway's shock 2-1 World Cup win against England in Oslo in September 1981 – a victory made even more famous by the words of Norwegian radio commentator Bjoerge Lillelien: 'Lord Nelson! Lord Beaverbrook! Sir Winston Churchill! Sir Anthony Eden! Clement Attlee! Henry Cooper! Lady Diana! Maggie Thatcher! Can you hear me, Maggie Thatcher? Your boys took one hell of a beating!'

APRIL

FRANKIE DONOVAN, 84, a Welsh Amateur International right-winger (4 caps) with Pembroke Borough, played for Great Britain in the 1948 Olympic Games in London.

LEN DUQUEMIN, 78, became the first Channel Islander in British football after the war, leaving Guernsey to sign professional for Tottenham in September 1946. His sturdy, workmanlike centre-forward play was suited to Arthur Rowe's renowned push-and-run team that brought Tottenham the Second Division title in 1950 and their first League Championship in 1951. In ten first-team seasons at White Hart Lane 'The Duke' totalled 134 goals in 308 games for his only League club and scored in the F.A. Cup semi-final defeats against Blackpool in 1948 and 1953. After leaving Tottenham in 1958, he played for non-League Bedford Town, Hastings Utd. and Romford, later ran a newsagent's shop near White Hart Lane and then a pub at Cheshunt.

BILLY McPHAIL, 75, earned 5 Scotland caps as a striker (1950-54). He scored a hat-trick when Celtic achieved the still biggest score in the Scottish League Cup Final, 7-1 against Rangers in 1958.

ERIC RADLEY-SMITH, 92, served Brentford as consultant surgeon for 50 years from 1938 and carried out most of the operations required by their players. He was a director from 1956-98 and then became president. In an association with the club that spanned more than 60 years, he rarely missed a match, home or away.

KEITH WALWYN, 47, Jamaica-born, was a centre-forward who began with Chesterfield in 1979. His 100% commitment made him a fans' favourite, especially at York City, for whom he scored 140 goals in 241 apps. (1981-87). They signed him for £4,000 and sold him to Blackpool for £35,000. Carlisle Utd. became his fourth League club (1989-91). His career ended prematurely with Kettering Town because of a heart condition, and he settled in Lancashire as a community sports officer with local schools.

MAY

TREVOR FORD, 79, was one of Wales' finest footballers and the most explosive centre-forward of his time. The son of Swansea began at Vetch Field, moved to Aston

Villa in 1947 and commanded Britain's record fee (£30,000) when he transferred to the 'Bank of England' club Sunderland in October 1950. He set a new Wales scoring record with 23 goals in 38 Ints. (1947-57). He spent 3 years at Sunderland, 3 with Cardiff City (1953-56), then 3 prosperous years in Holland with PSV Eindhoven (1957-60) after being banned by the Football Association for revealing in his autobiography that he had received under-the-table payments with Sunderland. His playing days ended fleetingly with Newport County, and his final goal tally in English League football was 177 in 349 games. Despite his rumbustuous approach, he maintained an unblemished disciplinary record on the field in a career spanning nearly 20 years. On retirement he worked in the motor trade in Swansea.

JIM CLUNIE, 69, played as a centre-half in the Scottish League for Raith, Aberdeen and St Mirren before moving into English football with Bury in 1965. He joined Lawrie McMenemy as assistant-manager at Grimsby Town (Div. 4 winners 1972) and their partnership continued still more successfully at Southampton, F.A. Cup winners in 1976. He returned to St Mirren as manager in 1981. Poignantly, his funeral took place a few days before Southampton appeared in the 2003 Cup Final.

JUNE

REG DRURY, 74, was *News of the World* chief football reporter for 30 years until retiring in 1993 and a past chairman of the Football Writers' Association. He was one of the game's most respected journalists – London-born and Tottenham 'his' team – with contacts that were the envy of his contemporaries, and he achieved the delicate balance of satisfying the demands of the world's biggest-selling newspaper without losing the trust of managers, chairmen and players. Three nights before England's World Cup triumph in 1966 Alf Ramsey, seeking a break from the intense build-up, knocked on his door for a cup of tea and a chat. The story was never told by Reg in print – he would have seen that as breaking a confidence. He died after being knocked down by a car near his home at Finchley, and football's regard for him was reflected in tributes by his friends in the game. Terry Venables: 'Because we all trusted him, we felt we owed him something, and he got more stories than anyone else.' Gary Lineker: 'I first got to know and respect Reg when I was a young recruit to the England squad. He was a gentleman and a thorough professional.' Ron Atkinson: 'He was a proper bloke. He cared passionately about his profession and about football.' Pat Jennings: 'He was a journalist with total integrity, a credit to his profession and to the game.' Sir Bobby Robson: 'We have lost an old friend and an old-fashioned journalist who was trusted by everyone.'

MARC-VIVIEN FOE, 28, the 6ft. 3in. Cameroon midfielder, tragically died in action. He collapsed unchallenged in the centre circle after 72 minutes of the FIFA Confederations Cup semi-final against Colombia on his former home pitch in Lyons, France, on June 26, and though doctors battled for an hour to save him, he was beyond resuscitation. He left a wife and 3 children, the youngest aged 2 months. Cameroon won the match 1-0. In tribute to their fallen colleague, their players wore Foe's No. 17 on their shirts in the warm-up to the Final, which France won 1-0. He played for Cameroon 63 times, including the 1994 and 2002 World Cups (missing the 1998 Finals because of a broken leg), and was a member of their African Nations Cup-winning teams in 2000 and 2002. He was popular with supporters and team-mates at two Premiership clubs. He joined West Ham Utd. from French Champions Lens (£4.2m) in January 1999, moved back to France with Olympique Lyon (£6m.) in May 2000 and returned to England on loan to Manchester City for season 2002-03, making 38 apps. for them and scoring 9 times, including their last goal at Maine Road.

Compiled by Albert Sewell

MILESTONES OF SOCCER

1848 First code of rules compiled at Cambridge Univ.
1857 Sheffield F.C., world's oldest football club, formed.
1862 Notts Co. (oldest League club) formed.
1863 Football Association founded – their first rules of game agreed.
1871 F.A. Cup introduced.
1872 First official International: Scotland 0, England 0. Corner-kick introduced.
1873 Scottish F.A. formed; Scottish Cup introduced.
1874 Shinguards introduced. Oxford v Cambridge, first match.
1875 Crossbar introduced (replacing tape).
1876 F.A. of Wales formed.
1877 Welsh Cup introduced.
1878 Referee's whistle first used.
1880 Irish F.A. founded; Irish Cup introduced.
1883 Two-handed throw-in introduced.
1885 Record first-class score (Arbroath 36, Bon Accord 0 – Scottish Cup). Professionalism legalised.
1886 International Board formed.
1887 Record F.A. Cup score (Preston N.E. 26, Hyde 0).
1888 Football League founded by Wm. McGregor. First matches on Sept. 8.
1889 Preston N.E. win Cup and League (first club to complete Double).
1890 Scottish League and Irish League formed.
1891 Goal-nets introduced. Penalty-kick introduced.
1892 Inter-League games began. Football League Second Division formed.
1893 F.A. Amateur Cup launched.
1894 Southern League formed.
1895 F.A. Cup stolen from Birmingham shop window – never recovered.
1897 First Players' Union formed. Aston Villa win Cup and League.
1898 Promotion and relegation introduced.
1901 Maximum wage rule in force (£4 a week). Tottenham first professional club to take F.A. Cup South. First six-figure attendance (110,802) at F.A. Cup Final.
1902 Ibrox Park disaster (25 killed). Welsh League formed.
1904 F.I.F.A. founded (7 member countries).
1905 First £1,000 transfer (Alf Common, Sunderland to Middlesbrough).
1907 Players' Union revived.
1908 Transfer fee limit (£350) fixed in January and withdrawn in April.
1911 New F.A. Cup trophy – in use to 1991. Transfer deadline introduced.
1914 King George V first reigning monarch to attend F.A. Cup Final.
1916 Entertainment Tax introduced.
1919 League extended to 44 clubs.
1920 Third Division (South) formed.
1921 Third Division (North) formed.
1922 Scottish League (Div. II) introduced.
1923 Beginning of football pools. First Wembley Cup Final.
1924 First International at Wembley (England 1, Scotland 1). Rule change allows goals to be scored direct from corner-kicks.
1925 New offside law.
1926 Huddersfield Town complete first League Championship hat-trick.
1927 First League match broadcast (radio): Arsenal v Sheff. Utd. (Jan 22). First radio broadcast of Cup Final (winners Cardiff City). Charles Clegg, president of F.A., becomes first knight of football.
1928 First £10,000 transfer – David Jack (Bolton Wand. to Arsenal). W.R. ('Dixie') Dean (Everton) creates League record – 60 goals in season. Britain withdraws from F.I.F.A.
1930 Uruguay first winners of World Cup.
1931 W.B.A. win Cup and promotion.
1933 Players numbered for first time in Cup Final (1-22).

1934 Sir Frederick Wall retires as F.A. secretary; successor Stanley Rous. Death of Herbert Chapman (Arsenal manager).
1935 Arsenal equal Huddersfield Town's Championship hat-trick record. Official two-referee trials.
1936 Joe Payne's 10-goal League record (Luton Town 12, Bristol Rov. 0).
1937 British record attendance: 149,547 at Scotland v England match.
1938 First live TV transmission of F.A. Cup Final. F.A.'s 75th anniversary. Football League 50th Jubilee. New pitch marking – arc on edge of penalty-area. Laws of Game re-drafted by Stanley Rous. Arsenal pay record £14,500 fee for Bryn Jones (Wolves).
1939 Compulsory numbering of players in Football League. First six-figure attendance for League match (Rangers v Celtic, 118,567). All normal competitions suspended for duration of Second World War.
1944 Death of Sir Frederick Wall (84), F.A. secretary 1896-1934.
1945 Scottish League Cup introduced.
1946 British associations rejoin F.I.F.A. Bolton Wand. disaster (33 killed) during F.A. Cup tie with Stoke City. Walter Winterbottom appointed England's first director of coaching.
1947 Great Britain beat Rest of Europe 6-1 at Hampden Park, Glasgow. First £20,000 transfer – Tommy Lawton, Chelsea to Notts Co.
1949 Stanley Rous, secretary F.A., knighted. England's first home defeat outside British Champ. (0-2 v Eire).
1950 Football League extended from 88 to 92 clubs. World record crowd (203,500) at World Cup Final, Brazil v Uruguay, in Rio. Scotland's first home defeat by foreign team (0-1 v Austria).
1951 White ball comes into official use.
1952 Newcastle Utd. first club to win F.A. Cup at Wembley in successive seasons.
1953 England's first Wembley defeat by foreign opponents (3-6 v Hungary).
1954 Hungary beat England 7-1 in Budapest.
1955 First F.A. Cup match under floodlights (prelim. round replay, Sept. 14): Kidderminster Harriers v Brierley Hill Alliance.
1956 First F.A. Cup ties under floodlights in competition proper (Jan. 7). First League match by floodlight (Feb. 22, Portsmouth v Newcastle Utd.). Real Madrid win the first European Cup.
1957 Last full Football League programme on Christmas Day. Entertainment Tax withdrawn.
1958 Manchester Utd. air crash at Munich (Feb. 6). League re-structured into four divisions.
1959 Football League establish fixtures copyright; pools must pay for use.
1960 Record transfer fee: £55,000 for Denis Law (Huddersfield Town to Manchester City). Wolves win Cup, miss Double and Championship hat-trick by one goal. For fifth time in ten years F.A. Cup Final team reduced to ten men by injury. F.A. recognise Sunday football. Football League Cup launched.
1961 Tottenham complete the first Championship-F.A. Cup double this century. Maximum wage (£20 a week) abolished in High Court challenge by George Eastham. First British £100-a-week wage paid (by Fulham to Johnny Haynes). First £100,000 British transfer – Denis Law, Manchester City to Torino. Sir Stanley Rous elected president of F.I.F.A.
1962 Manchester Utd. raise record British transfer fee to £115,000 for Denis Law.
1963 F.A. Centenary. Football League's 75th anniversary. Season extended to end of May due to severe winter. First pools panel. English "retain and transfer" system ruled illegal in High Court test case.
1964 Rangers' second great hat-trick – Scottish Cup, League Cup and League. Football League and Scottish League guaranteed £500,000 a year in new fixtures copyright agreement with Pools. First televised 'Match of the Day' (BBC2): Liverpool 3, Arsenal 2 (August 22).
1965 Bribes scandal – ten players jailed (and banned for life by F.A.) for match-fixing 1960-3. Stanley Matthews knighted in farewell season. Arthur Rowley (Shrewsbury Town) retires with record of 434 League goals. Substitutes allowed for injured players in Football League matches (one per team).
1966 England win World Cup (Wembley).

1967 Alf Ramsey, England manager, knighted; O.B.E. for captain Bobby Moore. Celtic become first British team to win European Cup. First substitutes allowed in F.A. Cup Final (Tottenham v Chelsea) but not used. Football League permit loan transfers (two per club).

1968 First F.A. Cup Final televised live in colour (BBC2 – W.B.A. v Everton). Manchester Utd. first English club to win European Cup.

1971 Arsenal win League Championship and F.A. Cup.

1973 Football League introduce 3-up, 3-down promotion/relegation between Divisions 1, 2 and 3 and 4-up, 4-down between Divisions 3 and 4.

1974 First F.A. Cup ties played on Sunday (Jan. 6). League football played on Sunday for first time (Jan. 20). Last F.A. Amateur Cup Final. Joao Havelange (Brazil) succeeds Sir Stanley Rous as F.I.F.A. president.

1975 Scottish Premier Division introduced.

1976 Football League introduce goal difference (replacing goal average).

1977 Liverpool achieve the double of League Championship and European Cup. Don Revie defects to United Arab Emirates when England manager – successor Ron Greenwood.

1978 Freedom of contract for players accepted by Football League. P.F.A. lifts ban on foreign players in English football. Football League introduce Transfer Tribunal. Viv Anderson (Nott'm. Forest) first black player to win a full England cap. Willie Johnston (Scotland) sent home from World Cup Finals in Argentina after failing dope test.

1979 First all-British £500,000 transfer – David Mills, M'bro' to W.B.A. First British million pound transfer (Trevor Francis – B'ham to Nott'm. Forest). Andy Gray moves from Aston Villa to Wolves for a record £1,469,000 fee.

1981 Tottenham win 100th F.A. Cup Final. Liverpool first British side to win European Cup three times. Three points for a win introduced by Football League. Q.P.R. install Football League's first artificial pitch. Sept. 29, death of Bill Shankly, manager-legend of Liverpool 1959-74. Record British transfer – Bryan Robson (W.B.A. to Manchester Utd.), £1,500,000.

1982 Aston Villa become sixth consecutive English winners of European Cup. Tottenham retain F.A. Cup – first club to do so since Tottenham 1961 and 1962. Football League Cup becomes the (sponsored) Milk Cup.

1983 Liverpool complete the League Championship-Milk Cup double for second year running. Manager Bob Paisley retires. Aberdeen first club to do Cup-Winners' Cup and domestic Cup double. Football League clubs vote to keep own match receipts. Football League sponsored by Canon, Japanese camera and business equipment manufacturers – 3-year agreement starting 1983-4. Football League agree 2-year contract for live TV coverage of ten matches per season (5 Friday night, BBC, 5 Sunday afternoon, ITV).

1984 One F.A. Cup tie in rounds 3, 4, 5 and 6 shown live on TV (Friday or Sunday). Aberdeen take Scottish Cup for third successive season, win Scottish Championship, too. Tottenham win UEFA Cup on penalty shoot-out. Liverpool win European Cup on penalty shoot-out to complete unique treble with Milk Cup and League title (as well as Championship hat-trick). N. Ireland win the final British Championship. France win European Championship – their first honour. F.A. National Soccer School opens at Lilleshall. Britain's biggest score this century: Stirling Alb. 20, Selkirk 0 (Scottish Cup).

1985 Bradford City fire disaster – 56 killed. First £1m. receipts from match in Britain (F.A. Cup Final). Kevin Moran (Manchester Utd.) first player to be sent off in F.A. Cup Final. Celtic win 100th Scottish F.A. Cup Final. European Cup Final horror (Liverpool v Juventus, riot in Brussels) 39 die. UEFA ban all English clubs indefinitely from European competitions. No TV coverage at start of League season – first time since 1963 (resumption delayed until January 1986). Sept: first ground-sharing in League history – Charlton Athletic move from The Valley to Selhurst Park (Crystal Palace).

1986 Liverpool complete League and Cup double in player-manager Kenny Dalglish's first season in charge. Swindon Town (4th Div. Champions) set League points record (102). League approve reduction of First Division to 20 clubs by 1988. Everton chairman Philip Carter elected president of Football League. July 18, death of Sir Stanley Rous (91). 100th edition of *News of the World* Football Annual. League Cup sponsored for next three years by Littlewoods (£2m.). Football League voting majority (for rule changes) reduced from ¾ to ⅔. Wales move HQ from Wrexham to Cardiff

City after 110 years. Two substitutes in F.A. Cup and League (Littlewoods) Cup. Two-season League/TV deal (£6.2m.):- BBC and ITV each show seven live League matches per season, League Cup semi-finals and Final. Football League sponsored by *Today* newspaper. Luton Town first club to ban all visiting supporters; as sequel are themselves banned from League Cup. Oldham Athletic and Preston N.E. install artificial pitches, making four in F. League (following Q.P.R. and Luton Town).

1987 May: League introduce play-off matches to decide final promotion/relegation places in all divisions. Re-election abolished – bottom club in Div. 4 replaced by winners of GM Vauxhall Conference. Two substitutes approved for Football League 1987-8. Red and yellow disciplinary cards (scrapped 1981) re-introduced by League and F.A. Football League sponsored by Barclays. First Div. reduced to 21 clubs.

1988 Football League Centenary. First Division reduced to 20 clubs.

1989 Soccer gets £74m. TV deal: £44m. over 4 years, ITV; £30m. over 5 years, BBC/BSB. But it costs Philip Carter the League Presidency. Ted Croker retires as F.A. chief executive; successor Graham Kelly, from Football League. Hillsborough disaster: 95 die at F.A. Cup semi-final (Liverpool v Nott'm. Forest). Arsenal win closest-ever Championship with last kick. Peter Shilton sets England record with 109 caps.

1990 Nott'm. Forest win last Littlewoods Cup Final. Both F.A. Cup semi-finals played on Sunday and televised live. Play-off finals move to Wembley; Swindon Town win place in Div. 1, then relegated back to Div. 2 (breach of financial regulations) – Sunderland promoted instead. Pools betting tax cut from 42½ to 40%. England reach World Cup semi-final in Italy and win F.I.F.A. Fair Play Award. Peter Shilton retires as England goalkeeper with 125 caps (world record). Graham Taylor (Aston Villa) succeeds Bobby Robson as England manager. Int. Board amend offside law (player 'level' no longer offside). F.I.F.A. make "pro foul" a sending-off offence. English clubs back in Europe (Manchester Utd. and Aston Villa) after 5-year exile.

1991 First F.A. Cup semi-final at Wembley (Tottenham 3, Arsenal 1). Bert Millichip (F.A. chairman) and Philip Carter (Everton chairman) knighted. End of artificial pitches in Div. 1 (Luton Town, Oldham Athletic). Scottish League reverts to 12-12-14 format (as in 1987-8). Penalty shoot-out introduced to decide F.A. Cup ties level after one replay.

1992 Introduction of fourth F.A. Cup (previous trophy withdrawn). F.A. launch Premier League (22 clubs). Football League reduced to three divisions (71 clubs). Record TV-sport deal: BSkyB/BBC to pay £304m. for 5-year coverage of Premier League. ITV do £40m., 4-year deal with F. League. Channel 4 show Italian football live (Sundays). F.I.F.A. approve new back-pass rule (goalkeeper must not handle ball kicked to him by team-mate). New League of Wales formed. Record all-British transfer, £3.3m.: Alan Shearer (Southampton to Blackburn Rov.). Charlton Athletic return to The Valley after 7-year absence.

1993 Barclays end 6-year sponsorship of F. League. For first time both F.A. Cup semi-finals at Wembley (Sat., Sun.). Arsenal first club to complete League Cup/F.A. Cup double. Rangers pull off Scotland's domestic treble for fifth time. F.A. in record British sports sponsorship deal (£12m. over 4 years) with brewers Bass for F.A. Carling Premiership, from Aug. Brian Clough retires after 18 years as Nott'm. Forest manager; as does Jim McLean (21 years manager of Dundee Utd.). Football League agree 3-year, £3m. sponsorship with Endsleigh Insurance. Premier League introduce squad numbers with players' names on shirts. Record British transfer: Duncan Ferguson, Dundee Utd. to Rangers (£4m.). Record English-club signing: Roy Keane, Nott'm. Forest to Manchester Utd. (£3.75m.). Graham Taylor resigns as England manager after World Cup exit (Nov.). Death in Feb. of Bobby Moore (51), England World-Cup winning captain 1966.

1994 Death of Sir Matt Busby (Jan.). Terry Venables appointed England coach (Jan.). Manchester Utd. complete the Double. Last artificial pitch in English football goes – Preston N.E. revert to grass, summer 1994. Bobby Charlton knighted. Scottish League format changes to four divisions of ten clubs. Record British transfer: Chris Sutton, Norwich City to Blackburn Rov. (£5m.). Sept: F.A. announce first sponsorship of F.A. Cup – Littlewoods Pools (4-year, £14m. deal, plus £6m. for Charity Shield). Death of Billy Wright, 70 (Sept).

1995 New record British transfer: Andy Cole, Newcastle Utd. to Manchester Utd. (£7m.). First England match abandoned through crowd trouble (v Rep. of Ireland, Dublin). Blackburn Rov. Champions for first time since 1914. Premiership reduced to

20 clubs. British transfer record broken again (June): Stan Collymore, Nott'm. Forest to Liverpool (£8½m.). Starting season 1995-6, teams allowed to use 3 substitutes per match, not necessarily including a goalkeeper. Dec: European Court of Justice upholds Bosman ruling, barring transfer fees for players out of contract and removing limit on number of foreign players clubs can field.

1996 Death in Feb. of Bob Paisley (77), ex-Liverpool, most successful manager in English Football. F.A. appoint Chelsea manager Glenn Hoddle to succeed Terry Venables as England coach after Euro 96. Manchester Utd. first English club to achieve Double twice (and in 3 seasons). Football League completes £125m., 5-year TV deal with BSkyB starting 1996-7. England stage European Championship, reach semi-finals, lose on pens to tournament winners Germany. Keith Wiseman succeeds Sir Bert Millichip as F.A. Chairman. Linesmen become known as "referees' assistants". Coca-Cola Cup experiment with own disciplinary system (red, yellow cards). Alan Shearer football's first £15m. player (Blackburn Rov. to Newcastle Utd.). Nigeria first African country to win Olympic soccer. Nationwide Building Society sponsor Football League in initial 3-year deal worth £5.25m. Peter Shilton first player to make 1000 League apps.

1997 Howard Wilkinson appointed English football's first technical director. England's first home defeat in World Cup (0-1 v Italy). Ruud Gullit (Chelsea) first foreign coach to win F.A. Cup. Rangers equal Celtic's record of 9 successive League titles. Manchester Utd. win Premier League for fourth time in 5 seasons. New record World Cup score: Iran 17, Maldives 0 (qual. round). Season 1997-8 starts Premiership's record £36m., 4-year sponsorship extension with brewers Bass (Carling).

1998 In French manager Arsene Wenger's second season at Highbury, Arsenal become second English club to complete the Double twice. Chelsea also win two trophies under new player-manager Gianluca Vialli (Coca-Cola Cup, Cup Winners' Cup). France win 16th World Cup competition. In breakaway from Scottish League, top ten clubs form new Premiership under SFA, starting season 1998-9. Football League celebrates its 100th season, 1998-9. New F.A. Cup sponsors – French insurance giants AXA (25m., 4-year deal). League Cup becomes Worthington Cup in £23m., 5-year contract with brewers Bass. Nationwide Building Society's sponsorship of Football League extended to season 2000-1.

1999 F.A. buy Wembley Stadium (£103m.) for £320m. redevelopment (Aug. 2000-March 2003) as new national stadium (Lottery Sports fund contributes £110m.) Scotland's new Premier League takes 3-week mid-season break in January. Sky screen Oxford Utd. v Sunderland (Div. 1, Feb. 27) as first pay-per-view match on TV. F.A. sack England coach Glenn Hoddle; Fulham's Kevin Keegan replaces him at £1m. a year until 2003. Sir Alf Ramsey, England's World Cup-winning manager, dies aged 79. With effect 1999, F.A. Cup Final to be decided on day (via penalties, if necessary). Hampden Park re-opens for Scottish Cup Final after £63m. refit. Alex Ferguson knighted after Manchester Utd. complete Premiership, F.A. Cup, European Cup treble. Starting season 1999-2000, UEFA increase Champions League from 24 to 32 clubs. End of Cup-Winners' Cup (merged into 121-club UEFA Cup). F.A. allow holders Manchester Utd. to withdraw from F.A. Cup to participate in FIFA's inaugural World Club Championship in Brazil in January. Chelsea first British club to field an all-foreign line-up at Southampton (Pre., Dec. 26). F.A. vote (December) in favour of streamlined 14-man board of directors to replace its 92-member council.

2000 Scot Adam Crozier takes over as F.A. chief executive, Jan. 1. Wales move to Cardiff City's £125m. Millennium Stadium (v Finland, March 29). Brent Council approve plans for new £475m. Wembley Stadium (completion target spring 2003); demolition of old stadium to begin after England v Germany (World Cup qual., Oct. 7). Fulham Ladies become Britain's first female professional team. F.A. Premiership and Nationwide League to introduce (season 2000-01) rule whereby referees advance free-kick by 10 yards and caution player who shows dissent, delays kick or fails to retreat 10 yards. Scottish football increased to 42 League clubs in 2000-01 (12 in Premier League and 3 division of ten; Peterhead and Elgin City elected from Highland League). France win eleventh European Championship – first time a major Int. tournament has been jointly hosted (Holland/Belgium). England's £10m. bid to stage 2006 World Cup fails; vote goes to Germany. England manager Kevin Keegan resigns

(Oct. 7) after 1-0 World Cup defeat by Germany in Wembley's last International. Oct. 30: Lazio's Swedish coach Sven Goran Eriksson agrees to become England head coach.

2001 January: Scottish Premier League experiment with split into two 5-game mini leagues (6 clubs in each) after 33 matches completed. July: New transfer system agreed by FIFA/UEFA is ratified. August: Barclaycard begin £48m., 3-year sponsorship of the Premiership, and Nationwide's contract with the Football League is extended by a further 3 years (£12m.). ITV, after winning auction against BBC's Match of the Day, begin £183m., 3-season contract for highlights of Premiership matches; BSkyB's live coverage (66 matches per season) for next 3 years will cost £1.1bn. BBC and BSkyB pay £400m. (3-year contract) for live coverage of F.A. Cup and England home matches. ITV and Ondigital pay £315m. to screen Nationwide League and Worthington Cup matches. In new charter for referees, top men can earn up to £60,000 a season in Premiership. Real Madrid break world transfer record, buying Zinedine Zidane from Juventus for £47.2m. F.A. introduce prize money, round by round, in F.A. Cup.

2002 February: Scotland appoint their first foreign manager, Germany's former national coach Bertie Vogts replacing Craig Brown. April: Collapse of ITV Digital deal, with Football League owed £178m., threatens lower-division clubs. May: Arsenal complete Premiership/F.A. Cup Double for second time in 5 seasons, third time in all. June: Newcastle Utd. manager Bobby Robson knighted in Queen's Jubilee Honours. Brazil win World Cup for fifth time. July: New record British transfer and world record for defender, £29.1m. Rio Ferdinand (Leeds Utd. to Manchester Utd.). August: Transfer window introduced to British football. F.A. Charity Shield renamed F.A. Community Shield. September: After 2-year delay, demolition of Wembley Stadium begins. October: Adam Crozier, F.A. chief executive, resigns.

2003 January: F.A. Cup draw (from 4th. Round) reverts to Monday lunchtime. March: Scottish Premier League decide to end mid-winter shut-down. May: Mark Palios appointed F.A. chief executive. For first time, two Football League clubs demoted (replaced by two from Conference). June: Ban lifted on loan transfers between Premiership clubs. July: David Beckham becomes record British export (Man. Utd. to Real Madrid, £25m.). Biggest takeover in British football history – Russian oil magnate Roman Abramovich buys control of Chelsea for reported £150m.

QUOTE-UNQUOTE

'When we won, the chairman drank a bottle of champagne. When we lost, he drank two bottles and thought we'd 'won' – **Sir Bobby Robson** on his time as manager of Ipswich Town.

'There are three things wrong with football – players' wages, players' wages and players' wages' – **John Madejski**, owner-chairman of Reading.

'When I came to the club I was not just trying to rebuild a football club, I was trying to rebuild my life' – **Dave Jones**, Wolves manager, after promotion to the Premiership.

'It's like an oil tanker that was heading for the rocks' – **Prof. John McKenzie**, new Leeds United chairman, instigating savage cuts to ease the club's financial burden.

'We have nothing to be proud of. We lost a very important game on one of the biggest stages you can play on. Why should we be happy?' – **Henrik Larsson**, Celtic striker, refuses to join the wave of sympathy for his side's UEFA Cup Final defeat by FC Porto.

ENGLISH LEAGUE ROLL-CALL

REVIEWS, APPEARANCES & SCORERS 2002-03

(figures in brackets = appearances as substitute)

F.A. BARCLAYCARD PREMIER LEAGUE

ARSENAL

Retaining the F.A. Cup would be enough for most sides, but the way Arsenal surrendered the title to Manchester United cast a shadow over the season at Highbury. They were odds-on favourites when moving eight points clear, from an extra game played, after beating Charlton Athletic on the day United lost the Worthington Cup Final to Liverpool. Then the balance of power started to shift with a second defeat by Blackburn. The loss of the injured Patrick Vieira and suspended Sol Campbell was crucial, along with the loss of a two-goal lead against Bolton, and a 3-2 home defeat by Leeds proved the final straw. Arsenal were also second best in the Champions League, poor home form ending their hopes at the second group stage.

Aliadiere, J .... –(3)
Bergkamp, D .... 23(6)
Campbell, S 33
Cole, A .... 30(1)
Cygan, P .... 16(2)
Edu .... 12(6)
Garry, R 1
Gilberto Silva .... 32(3)
Henry, T 37
Hoyte, J .... –(1)
Jeffers, F .... 2(14)
Kanu, N .... 9(7)
Keown, M .... 22(2)
Lauren .... 26(1)
Ljungberg, F .... 19(1)
Luzhny, O .... 11(6)
Parlour, R .... 14(5)
Pennant, J .... 1(4)
Pires, R .... 21(5)
Seaman, D 28
Shaaban, R 3
Stepanovs, I 2
Tavlaridis, S .... –(1)
Taylor, S .... 7(1)
Toure, K .... 9(17)
Van Bronckhorst, G . 9(11)
Vieira, P 24
Wiltord, S .... 27(7)

League goals (85): Henry 24, Pires 14, Wiltord 10, Ljungberg 6, Kanu 5, Bergkamp 4, Pennant 3, Vieira 3, Campbell 2, Edu 2, Jeffers 2, Toure 2, Aliadiere 1, Cole 1, Cygan 1, Lauren 1, Van Bronckhorst 1, Opponents 3.

F.A. Cup goals (16): Jeffers 3, Bergkamp 2, Lauren 2, Wiltord 2, Campbell 1, Edu 1, Henry 1, Ljungberg 1, Pires 1, Opponents 2. **Worthington Cup goals (2):** Jeffers 1, Pires 1. **Community Shield goals (1):** Gilberto Silva 1. **Champions League goals (16):** Henry 7, Gilberto Silva 3, Ljungberg 2, Bergkamp 1, Kanu 1, Vieira 1, Wiltord 1.

Average home League attendance: 38,041. **Player of Year:** Robert Pires (Supporters).

ASTON VILLA

Another frustrating season was mirrored by the departure of Graham Taylor, who blamed the way the club was being run for his resignation after little more than a year as manager. On the field, Villa were reasonably solid at home, but only one win away from home – and a modest overall scoring record – were major handicaps. A sudden deluge of goals which brought a 5-2 success at Middlesbrough followed by a 3-0 win over Blackburn hinted at better times. Then, just two victories in the final 12 fixtures left them flirting uneasily with the relegation zone until the end of the season. David O'Leary, Taylor's successor, has a difficult job ahead.

Allback, M .... 9(11)
Alpay, O 5
Angel J-P .... 8(7)
Barry, G 35
Cooke, S .... –(3)
Crouch, P .... 7(7)
De la Cruz, U .... 12(8)
Delaney, M 12
Dublin, D .... 23(5)
Edwards, R .... 7(1)
Enckelman, P 33
Gudjonsson, J .... 9(2)
Hadji, M .... 7(4)
Hendrie, L .... 22(5)
Hitzlsperger, T .... 24(2)
Johnsen, R .... 25(1)
Kinsella, M .... 15(4)
Leonhardsen, O ...... 13(6)
Mellberg, O 38
Moore, S .... 7(6)
Postma, S .... 5(1)

Samuel, J .... 33(5)	Taylor, I .... 9(4)	Whittingham, P .... 1(3)
Staunton, S .... 22(4)	Vassell, D .... 28(5)	Wright, A .... 9(1)

League goals (42): Dublin 10, Vassell 8, Allback 5, Hendrie 4, Barry 3, Leonhardsen 3, Gudjonsson 2, Hitzlsperger 2, Angel 1, De La Cruz 1, Mellberg 1, Moore 1, Opponents 1.
F.A. Cup goals (1): Angel 1. **Worthington Cup goals (14):** Dublin 4, Vassell 3, Hitzlsperger 2, Angel 1, Barry 1, De La Cruz 1, Taylor 1, Opponents 1. **Intertoto Cup goals (4):** Allback 1, Boulding, M 1, Staunton 1, Taylor 1.
Average home League attendance: 34,975. **Player of Year:** Gareth Barry.

BIRMINGHAM CITY

Astute mid-season signings by Steve Bruce when the transfer window opened enabled Birmingham to finish a respectable 13th in their first Premiership season – and the midlands' top side. Without the impact made by Christophe Dugarry, Matthew Upson, Jamie Clapham and Stephen Clemence, they would have gone down, admitted the manager. World Cup winner Dugarry proved particularly influential when the heat was on, scoring five times in four successive victories in April which lifted his side out of trouble, while Upson brought stability to the defence after moving from Arsenal

Bennett, I 10	Horsfield, G .... 15(16)	Morrison, C .... 24(4)
Carter, D .... 3(9)	Hughes, B .... 10(12)	Powell, D .... 3(8)
Cisse, A 21	Hutchinson, J 1	Purse, D .... 19(1)
Clapham, J 16	John, S .... 20(10)	Sadler, M 2
Clemence, S 15	Johnson, D .... 28(2)	Savage, R 33
Coly, F 1	Johnson, M .... 5(1)	Swierczewski, P .... –(1)
Cunningham, K 31	Kenna, J .... 36(1)	Tebily, O 12
Devlin, P .... 20(12)	Kirovski, J .... 5(12)	Upson, M 14
Dugarry, C 16	Lazaridis, S .... 17(13)	Vaesen, N 27
Fagan, C .... –(1)	Marriott, A 1	Vickers, S 5
Grainger, M .... 8(1)	Mooney, T .... –(1)	Woodhouse, C .... –(3)

League goals (41): Morrison 6, Dugarry 5, Horsfield 5, John 5, Savage 4, Devlin 3, Clemence 2, Hughes 2, Kirovski 2, Lazaridis 2. Johnson, D 1, Kenna 1, Purse 1, Opponents 2.
F.A. Cup goals (1): John 1. **Worthington Cup goals (3):** John 3.
Average home League attendance: 28,883. **Player of Year:** Robbie Savage.

BLACKBURN ROVERS

Blackburn put the seal on an encouraging season with a 4-0 win at Tottenham which earned a second successive UEFA Cup spot. Previously they qualified as Worthington Cup winners. This time it was on the back of sixth place after 10th and 19th finishes in the two previous campaigns in the top flight, a measure of the progress being made under Graeme Souness. His team were the only one to complete the double over Arsenal. There was another good Worthington Cup run – to the semi-finals before defeat by Manchester United – but defeat by Celtic in round two of the UEFA Cup proved a disappointment.

Berg, H .... 15(1)	Gillespie, K .... 10(15)	McEveley, J 9
Cole, A .... 32(2)	Grabbi, C .... 1(10)	Neill, L 34
Curtis, J 5	Gresko, V 10	Ostenstad, E .... 8(9)
Danns, N .... 1(1)	Hakan Sukur .... 7(2)	Short, C .... 26(1)
Douglas, J .... –(1)	Hignett, C .... 1(2)	Taylor, M .... 29(4)
Duff, D 26	Jansen, M .... –(7)	Thompson, D 23
Dunn, D .... 26(2)	Johansson, N-E .... 20(10)	Todd, A .... 7(5)
Flitcroft, G 33	Kelly, A 1	Tugay, K .... 32(5)
Friedel, B 37	Mahon, A .... –(2)	Yorke, D .... 25(8)
Gallagher, P .... –(1)		

League goals (52): Duff 9, Dunn 8, Yorke 8, Cole 7, Thompson 4, Flitcroft 2, Hakan Sukur 2, Taylor 2, Berg 1, Grabbi 1, Hignett 1, Ostenstad 1, Short 1, Todd 1, Tugay 1, Opponents 3.
F.A. Cup goals (9): Yorke 3, Cole 2, Flitcroft 2, Jansen 2. **Worthington Cup goals (10):** Cole 4, Yorke 2, Duff 1, Grabbi 1, Thompson 1, Opponents 1. **UEFA Cup goals (4):** Duff 1, Grabbi 1, Ostenstad 1, Thompson 1.
Average home League attendance: 26,225. **Player of Year:** Brad Friedel.

BOLTON WANDERERS

Bolton's cosmopolitan side brought all their experience to bear when beating the drop for the second successive season. Some of the personnel had changed, but there was the same resolve required this time to match the improved form shown during the run-in by fellow strugglers West Ham. A 1-0 win over the London team, earned by Jay-Jay Okocha's spectacular goal kept Bolton a step ahead. Retrieving a two-goal deficit to earn a point against Arsenal was also important. Going into the final game Bolton had matters in their own hands and were equal to the task by beating Middlesbrough 2-1, Okocha again taking a lead with one of the goals.

Andre, P-Y .... –(9)
Ballestra, S .... 1(5)
Barness, A .... 21(4)
Bergsson, G 31
Bulent, A .... –(1)
Campo, I .... 28(3)
Charlton Athletic, S .... 27(4)
Djorkaeff, Y 36
Facey, D .... 1(8)
Farrelly, G .... 6(2)
Frandsen, P 34
Gardner, R .... 31(1)
Holdsworth, D .... 5(4)
Jaaskelainen, J 38
Johnson, J .... –(2)
Laville, F 10
Livesey, D .... –(2)
Mendy, B .... 20(1)
N'Gotty, B 23
Nolan, K .... 15(18)
Okocha, J-J .... 26(5)
Pedersen, H .... 31(2)
Ricketts, M .... 13(9)
Salva .... 1(5)
Tofting, S .... 2(6)
Walters, J .... –(4)
Warhurst, P .... 5(2)
Whitlow, M .... 14(3)

League goals (41): Djorkaeff 7, Okocha 7, Pedersen 7, Ricketts 6, Campo 2, Facey 2, Frandsen 2, Gardner 2, Farrelly 1, N'Gotty 1, Nolan 1, Opponents 3.
F.A. Cup goals (1): Ricketts 1. **Worthington Cup goals:** None.
Average home League attendance: 25,016. **Player of Year:** Jay-Jay Okocha.

CHARLTON ATHLETIC

A club-record Premiership run of five successive victories had Charlton dreaming of a place in Europe. It ended at Highbury on the day Arsenal established what looked like an unassailable lead at the top and it was downhill all the way from then on for Alan Curbishley's side. They were hammered 6-1 at the Valley by Leeds and with Curbishley at a loss to explain the demise, Charlton won only one of their final ten fixtures in a carbon-copy of what happened the previous season. Nevertheless, the club that almost went out of existence not so many years ago continued to win praise for developing a team and a stadium fit for the top flight.

Bartlett, S .... 25(6)
Bart-Williams, C .... 7(6)
Blomqvist, J .... –(3)
Brown, S .... –(3)
Campbell-Ryce, J ...... –(1)
El Khalej, T .... 2(1)
Euell, J .... 35(1)
Fish, M 23
Fortune, J .... 22(4)
Jensen, C .... 32(3)
Johansson, J .... 10(21)
Kiely, D 38
Kishishev, R .... 27(7)
Konchesky, P .... 17(13)
Lisbie, K .... 24(8)
Mustoe, R 6
Parker, S 28
Powell, C .... 35(2)
Roberts, B .... –(1)
Robinson, J .... 10(3)
Rowett, G 12
Rufus, R .... 29(1)
Sankofa, O .... –(1)
Stuart, G .... 3(1)
Svensson, M .... 4(11)
Young, L .... 29(3)

League goals (45): Euell 10, Jensen 6, Bartlett 4, Lisbie 4, Parker 4, Johansson 3, Konchesky 3, Kishishev 2, Rufus 2, Bart-Williams 1, Fish 1, Fortune 1, Rowett 1, Opponents 3.
F.A. Cup goals (3): Johansson 2, Euell 1. **Worthington Cup goals:** None.
Average home League attendance: 26,255. **Player of Year:** Scott Parker.

CHELSEA

Chelsea failed to show the required consistency to maintain a championship challenge after going into the New Year in second place. But after slipping to fifth, they recovered momentum and went on to claim the fourth Champions League place with a 2-1 win over Liverpool on a tense final day of the season, courtesy of goals by Marcel Desailly and Jesper Gronkjaer. Elsewhere, Chelsea suffered more UEFA Cup embarrassment against unfancied opposition, this time Viking FK, and lost the chance of turning the F.A. Cup tables on ten-man Arsenal by losing a sixth round replay 3-1 at Stamford Bridge.

Babayaro, C .... 16(3)
Cole, C .... 2(11)
Cudicini, C 36
De Goey, E 2
De Lucas, E .... 17(8)
Desailly, M .... 30(1)
Ferrer, A 3
Gallas, W .... 36(2)
Gronkjaer, J .... 20(10)
Gudjohnsen, E ..... 20(15)
Hasselbaink, J .... 27(9)
Huth, R 2
Keenan, J .... –(1)
Lampard, F .... 37(1)
Le Saux, G .... 27(1)
Melchiot, M .... 31(3)
Morris, J .... 19(6)
Oliveria, F .... –(3)
Petit, E .... 23(1)
Stanic, M .... 13(5)
Terry, J .... 16(4)
Zenden, B .... 11(10)
Zola, G .... 30(8)

League goals (68): Zola 14, Hasselbaink 11, Gudjohnsen 10, Lampard 6, Gallas 4, Gronkjaer 4, Stanic 4, Cole 3, Terry 3, Desailly 2, Le Saux 2, Babayaro 1, Petit 1, Zenden 1, Opponents 2.
F.A. Cup goals (10): Terry 2, Zola 2, Cole 1, Gronkjaer 1, Hasselbaink 1, Lampard 1, Morris 1, Stanic 1. **Worthington Cup goals (6):** Cole 2, Hasselbaink 2, Petit 1, Stanic 1. **UEFA Cup goals (4):** De Lucas 1, Hasselbaink 1, Lampard 1, Terry 1.
Average home League attendance: 39,784.

EVERTON

To have a team challenging for a place in Europe, a manager offering a bright new future for the club and a player emerging as the most exciting in the country would have been beyond the expectations of most Everton supporters. In the end, they had to be satisfied with seventh, a UEFA Cup spot lost on the final day when Wayne Rooney's finishing against Manchester United was not up to scratch. But despite that and the disappointment of an F.A. Cup defeat by a team subsequently relegated to the Conference – Shrewsbury Town – all the talk was about how David Moyes is restoring some pride to the blue half of the city.

Alexandersson, N ...... 4(3)
Baardsen, E 1
Campbell, K .... 31(5)
Carsley, L .... 21(3)
Chadwick, N .... –(1)
Ferguson, D .... –(7)
Gemmill, S .... 10(6)
Gerrard, P 2
Gravesen, T .... 30(3)
Hibbert, T .... 23(1)
Li Tie .... 28(1)
Linderoth, T .... 2(3)
Li Weifeng 1
McBride, B .... 7(1)
Naysmith, G .... 24(4)
Osman, L .... –(2)
Pembridge, M .... 19(2)
Pistone, A .... 10(5)
Radzinski, T .... 27(3)
Rodrigo, J .... –(4)
Rooney, W .... 14(19)
Simonsen, S 2
Stubbs, A .... 34(1)
Unsworth, D .... 32(1)
Watson, S .... 14(4)
Weir, D .... 27(4)
Wright, R 33
Yobo, J .... 22(2)

League goals (48): Radzinski 11, Campbell 9, Rooney 6, Unsworth 5, Watson 5, McBride 4, Carsley 3, Gravesen 1, Naysmith 1, Pembridge 1, Weir 1, Opponents 1.
F.A. Cup goals (1): Alexandersson 1. **Worthington Cup goals (7):** Campbell 2, Rooney 2, Naysmith 1, Unsworth 1, Watson 1.
Average home League attendance: 38,480. **Player of Year:** Thomas Radzinski.

FULHAM

All Jean Tigana's experience was unable to halt Fulham's slide towards the danger zone and he paid the price with his job. Chris Coleman, whose playing career was ended prematurely by a car crash, came in with no managerial background and instantly delivered safety, his team collecting 10 points from their final five games to finish 13th.

The reward for Coleman, 32, was the position on a permanent basis, after he initially insisted he was not ready for it. A major task for the new season is to boost Fulham's scoring record

Boa Morte, L .... 25(4)	Hammond, E .... 3(7)	Melville, A .... 24(2)
Brevett, R 20	Harley, J 11	Ouaddou, A .... 9(4)
Clark, L .... 9(2)	Hayles, B .... 4(10)	Saha, L .... 13(4)
Collins, J .... –(5)	Herrera, M .... 1(1)	Sava, F .... 13(7)
Davis, S 28	Inamoto, J .... 9(10	Stolcers, A .... –(5)
Djetou, M .... 22(3)	Knight, Z .... 12(5)	Taylor, M .... 18(1)
Finnan, S 32	Legwinski, S .... 33(2)	Van der Saar, E 19
Goldbaek, B .... 9(2)	Malbranque, S .... 34(2)	Willock, C .... –(2)
Goma, A 29	Marlet, S 28	Wome, P .... 13(1)

League goals (41): Malbranque 6, Saha 5, Sava 5, Legwinski 4, Marlet 4, Davis 3, Boa Morte 2, Clark 2, Inamoto 2, Djetou 1, Harley 1, Hayles 1, Wome 1, Opponents 4.
F.A. Cup goals (7): Malbranque 4, Goldbaek 1, Saha 1, Sava 1. **Worthington Cup goals (4):** Stolcers 2, Boa Morte 1, Clark 1. **Intertoto Cup goals (11):** Inamoto 4, Legwinski 2, Marlet 2, Davis 1, Hayles 1, Saha 1. **UEFA Cup goals (9):** Malbranque 3, Marlet 3, Boa Morte 2, Hayles 1.
Average home League attendance: 16,707. **Player of Year:** Sean Davis.

LEEDS UNITED

A traumatic season on and off the field at Elland Road, where Terry Venables was sacked after nine months as manager, chairman Peter Ridsdale resigned after presiding over huge losses and players like Robbie Keane, Robbie Fowler, Lee Bowyer and Jonathan Woodgate were sold to ease the financial pressure. Peter Reid was charged with staving off the ultimate nightmare – relegation – and having done so was confirmed as Venables's replacement. A 4-1 home defeat by Arsenal underlined the team's problems, but ironically in the return at Highbury, Leeds delivered the Championship to Manchester United by winning 3-2. Mark Viduka's goal was one of 13 he scored in the final 10 matches

Bakke, E .... 31(3)	Johnson, Simon .... 1(3)	Milner, J .... 1(17)
Barmby, N .... 16(3)	Keane, R .... –(3)	Okon, P 15
Bowyer, L 15	Kelly, G .... 24(1)	Radebe, L .... 16(3)
Bridges, M .... 1(4)	Kewell, H 31	Raul Bravo 5
Burns, J 2	Kilgallon, M .... –(2)	Robinson, P 38
Dacourt, O .... 4(3)	Lucic, T .... 16(1)	Smith, A 33
Duberry, M .... 11(3)	Matteo, D 20	Viduka, M .... 29(4)
Fowler, R .... 2(6)	McMaster, J .... –(4)	Wilcox, J .... 23(2)
Harte, I .... 24(3)	McPhail, S .... 7(6)	Woodgate, J 18
Johnson, Seth .... 3(6)	Mills, D .... 32(1)	

League goals (58): Viduka 20, Kewell 14, Barmby 4, Bowyer 3, Harte 3, Smith 3, Fowler 2, Milner 2, Bakke 1, Keane 1, Lucic 1, Mills 1, Johnson, Seth 1, Wilcox 1, Opponents 1.
F.A. Cup goals (7): Bakke 2, Viduka 2, Kelly 1, Kewell 1, Smith 1. **Worthington Cup goals (1):** Opponents 1. **UEFA Cup goals (8):** Smith (5), Bakke, Barmby 1, Kewell 1.
Average home League attendance: 39,119. **Player of Year:** Alan Smith.

LIVERPOOL

Victory over Manchester United in the Worthington Cup Final was not enough to compensate for a modest season which ended with defeat at Chelsea in a match to decide the fourth Champions League place. It had started so brightly with an unbeaten run of 12 matches putting Gerard Houllier's side four points clear at the top going into November. But then a run of 11 games without a win – Liverpool's worst League run for 50 years – left them with too much ground to make up, home form proving particularly unsatisfactory. Failure to reach the second stage of the Champions League and defeat by Celtic in the UEFA Cup were further disappointments.

Babbel, M 2
Baros, M .... 17(10)
Berger, P .... –(2)
Biscan, I .... 3(3)
Carragher, J .... 34(1)
Cheyrou, B .... 8(11)
Diao, S .... 13(13)
Diouf, E-H .... 21(8)
Dudek, J 30
Gerrard, S .... 32(2)
Hamann, D .... 29(1)
Henchoz, S 19
Heskey, E .... 22(10)
Hyypia, S 36
Kirkland, C 8
Mellor, N .... 1(2)
Murphy, D 36
Owen, M .... 32(3)
Riise J A .... 31(6)
Smicer, V .... 10(11)
Traore, D .... 30(2)
Vignal, G .... –(1)
Xavier, A 4

League goals (61): Owen 19, Baros 9, Murphy 7, Heskey 6, Riise 6, Gerrard 5, Diouf 3, Hyypia 3, Hamann 2, Diao 1.
F.A. Cup goals (1): Murphy 1. **Worthington Cup goals (13):** Diouf 3, Baros 2, Gerrard 2, Murphy 2, Owen 2, Berger 1, Mellor 1. **Community Shield goals:** None. **Champions League goals (12):** Owen 4, Heskey 2, Baros 1, Cheyrou 1, Diao 1, Hyypia 1, Murphy 1, Smicer 1. **UEFA Cup goals (6):** Owen 3, Heskey 1, Hyypia 1, Murphy 1.
Average home League attendance: 43,242.

MANCHESTER CITY

A place in the top half of the table meant Manchester City had every reason to be satisfied with their return to the Premiership, although the party atmosphere in their final match at Maine Road before moving to a new stadium was dampened by defeat by Southampton. The high-spot was a 3-1 victory over Manchester United, even if it did shake United out of their lethargy and help point them towards the championship. Low point was the 5-1 pasting by Arsenal which, together with a 5-0 defeat at Chelsea not long after, showed that City have some way to go. Kevin Keegan hopes the Nicolas Anelka-Robbie Fowler partnership will now develop fully to help in that direction.

Anelka, N 38
Barton, J 7
Belmadi, D .... 2(6)
Benarbia, A .... 21(12)
Berkovic, E 27
Bischoff, M 1
Distin, S 34
Dunne, R .... 24(1)
Foe, M 35
Fowler, R .... 12(1)
Goater, S .... 14(12)
Horlock, K .... 22(8)
Howey, S 24
Huckerby, D .... 6(10)
Jensen, N .... 32(1)
Jordan, S .... –(1)
Macken, J .... –(5)
Mettomo, L .... 3(1)
Nash, C 9
Schmeichel, P 29
Shuker, C .... 1(2)
Sommeil, D 14
Sun Jihai .... 25(3)
Tiatto, D .... 10(3)
Wiekens, G .... 5(1)
Wright-Phillips, S ... 23(8)

League goals (47): Anelka 14, Foe 9, Goater 7, Benarbia 3, Fowler 2, Howey 2, Sun Jihai 2, Barton 1, Berkovic 1, Huckerby 1, Jensen 1, Sommeil 1, Wright-Phillips 1, Opponents 2.
F.A. Cup goals: None. **Worthington Cup goals** (3): Berkovic 1, Huckerby 1, Opponents 1.
Average home League attendance: 34,564. **Player of Year:** Sylvain Distin.

MANCHESTER UNITED

Sir Alex Ferguson called it his team's greatest achievement – and who could argue with that assessment? United overcame a poor start to the season, a 3-1 defeat by Manchester City which left Ferguson questioning his players' commitment and then an eight-point lead Arsenal established at the top on the day they lost the Worthington Cup Final to Liverpool. Not only that, but they claimed the championship for the eighth time in 11 years by a five-point margin after a 17-match unbeaten run from New Year. Ruud van Nistelrooy won the Golden Boot award with 25 goals and was just as big an influence in the Champions League, although not enough to compensate for defensive deficiencies which resulted in a 6-5 aggregate defeat by Real Madrid in the quarter-finals.

Barthez, F 30
Beckham, D .... 27(4)
Blanc, L .... 15(4)
Brown, W 22
Butt, N .... 14(4)
Carroll, R .... 8(2)
Chadwick, L .... –(1)
Ferdinand, R .... 27(1)
Forlan, D .... 7(18)
Fortune, Q .... 5(4)
Giggs, R .... 32(4)
Keane, R .... 19(2)

May, D .... –(1)
Neville, G .... 19(7)
Neville, P .... 19(6)
O'Shea, J .... 26(6)
Pugh, D .... –(1)
Ricardo, L .... –(1)
Richardson, K .... –(2)
Roche, L .... –(1)
Scholes, P .... 31(2)
Silvestre, M 34
Solskjaer, O .... 29(8)
Stewart, M .... –(1)
Veron, J .... 21(4)
Van Nistelrooy, R .... 33(1)

League goals (74): Van Nistelrooy 25, Scholes 14, Solksjaer 9, Giggs 8, Beckham 6, Forlan 6, Veron 2, Neville, P 1, Silvestre 1, Opponents 2.

F.A. Cup goals (10): Van Nistelrooy 4, Giggs 2, Beckham 1, Neville, P 1, Scholes 1, Solskjaer 1. **Worthington Cup goals (9):** Scholes 3, Forlan 2, Beckham 1, Richardson 1, Solskjaer 1, Van Nistelrooy 1. **Champions League goals (37):** Van Nistelrooy 14, Giggs 5, Solskjaer 4, Veron 4, Beckham 3, Scholes 2, Blanc 1, Brown 1, Forlan 1, Neville, G 1, Opponents 1.

Average home League attendance: 67,601. **Player of Year:** Ruud van Nistelrooy.

MIDDLESBROUGH

Middlesbrough provided one of the pivotal results with a 3-1 Boxing Day win over Manchester United, who then launched into an unbeaten run which lasted until the end of the season and which gave them the title. Steve McClaren's side were unable to draw similar impetus, failing to win any of the next six games. Goals by new signings Chris Riggott and Malcolm Christie against Sunderland followed by the return of Juninho after a knee injury, turned the tide. But with a top-eight finish in sight, the team faltered again by failing to score in four successive matches, before a rousing finish to their home programme brought a 5-1 victory over Tottenham.

Boateng, G 28
Boksic, A .... 13(5)
Christie, M .... 11(1)
Cooper, C .... 14(6)
Davies, A 1
Doriva, G .... 3(2)
Downing, S .... –(2)
Ehiogu, U .... 31(1)
Eustace, J .... –(1)
Geremi 33
Greening, J 38
Job, J-D .... 22(6)
Juninho .... 9(1)
Maccarone, M .... 26(8)
Marinelli, C .... 3(4)
Murphy, D .... 4(4)
Nemeth, S .... 15(13)
Parnaby, S 21
Queudrue, F .... 29(2)
Ricketts, M .... 5(4)
Riggott, C .... 4(1)
Schwarzer, M 38
Southgate, G 36
Stockdale, R .... 12(2)
Vidmar, T .... 9(3)
Whelan, N .... 2(13)
Wilkshire, L .... 7(7)
Wilson, M .... 4(2)
Windass, D .... –(2)

League goals (48): Maccarone 9, Geremi 7, Nemeth 7, Christie 4, Job 4, Ehiogu 3, Juninho 3, Boksic 2, Greening 2, Riggott 2, Southgate 2, Queudrue 1, Ricketts 1, Whelan 1.

F.A. Cup goals: None. **Worthington Cup goals (5):** Downing 1, Marinelli 1, Queudrue 1, Whelan 1, Wilson 1.

Average home League attendance: 31,025. **Player of Year:** Jonathan Greening.

NEWCASTLE UNITED

Onwards and upwards go Newcastle under Sir Bobby Robson. Fourth the previous season, now third and with ambitions to climb still higher. There is still a gap to be bridged, as the 6-2 pounding by Manchester United emphasised during a spell of three successive April defeats which ended outside chances of the championship. But the indications are that it is closing. In Europe, too, Newcastle appear to be coming to terms with the extra demands. With Alan Shearer still a force on the big stage, they became the first side to reach the second stage of the Champions League after losing the opening three group matches. One of the campaign's low points was defeat by Wolves in the third round of the F.A. Cup.

Acuna, C .... 2(2)
Ambrose, D .... –(1)
Ameobi, S .... 8(20)
Bellamy, C .... 27(2)
Bernard, O .... 24(6)
Bramble, T .... 13(3)
Caldwell, S .... 12(2)
Chopra, M .... –(1)
Cort, C .... –(1)
Dabizas, N .... 13(3)
Dyer, K .... 33(2)
Elliott, R .... –(2)
Given, S 38
Griffin, A .... 22(5)
Hughes, A 35

Jenas, J .... 23(9)	O'Brien, A 26	Speed, G .... 23(1)
Kerr, B .... 4(4)	Robert, L .... 25(2)	Viana, H .... 11(12)
Lua Lua, T .... 5(6)	Shearer, A 35	Woodgate, J 10
McClen, J .... –(1)	Solano, N .... 29(2)	

League goals (63): Shearer 17, Bellamy 7, Solano 7, Jenas 6, Ameobi 5, Robert 5, Bernard 2, Dyer 2, LuaLua 2, Speed 2, Viana 2, Caldwell 1, Griffin 1, Hughes 1, Opponents 3.
F.A. Cup goals (2): Jenas 1, Shearer 1. **Worthington Cup goals (3):** Dyer 2, Opponents 1.
Champions League goals (21): Shearer 7, Ameobi 3, Bellamy 2, Dyer 2, LuaLua 2, Viana 2, Grifin 1, Solano 1, Speed 1.
Average home League attendance: 51,923. **Player of Year:** Alan Shearer.

SOUTHAMPTON

Southampton achieved their best Premiership finish of eighth, reached the F.A. Cup Final for the first time for 27 years and qualified for Europe in a season of considerable progress under Gordon Strachan. Defeat by Arsenal in Cardiff, where Strachan erred on the side of caution with his line-up, did nothing to undermine their achievements. Strachan had little room for manoeuvre with a small squad, particularly when injuries occurred. But with James Beattie in contention for the Golden Boot award until the final day, new goalkeeper Antti Niemi proving one of the best in the division and a strong work ethic always evident in the ranks, they became a force to be reckoned with.

Baird, C .... 1(2)	Fernandes, F .... 35(2)	Ormerod, B .... 22(9)
Beattie, J .... 35(3)	Higginbotham, D ...... 3(6)	Pahars, M .... 5(4)
Benali, F 2	Jones, P .... 13(1)	Prutton, D .... 9(3)
Bridge, W 34	Kanchelskis, A .... –(1)	Svensson, A .... 26(7)
Davies, K .... 1(8)	Lundekvam, C 33	Svensson, M .... 33(1)
Delap, R .... 22(2)	Marsden, C 30	Telfer, P .... 26(6)
Delgado, A .... 2(4)	Monk, G 1	Tessem, J .... 9(18)
Dodd, J .... 13(2)	Niemi, A 25	Williams, P .... 10(2)
El Khalej, T .... –(1)	Oakley, M .... 28(3)	

League goals (43): Beattie 23, Ormerod 5, Fernandes 3, Svensson, A 2, Svensson, M 2, Tessem 2, Bridge 1, Davies 1, Marsden 1, Pahars 1, Opponents 2.
F.A. Cup goals (13): Oakley 2, Svensson, A 2, Tessem 2, Beattie 1, Davies 1, Marsden 1, Ormerod 1, Svensson, M 1, Opponents 2. **Worthington Cup goals (7):** Ormerod 3, Delgado 1, Fernandes 1, Marsden 1, Svensson, M 1.
Average home League attendance: 30,680. **Player of Year:** James Beattie.

SUNDERLAND

As if relegation was not bad enough, Sunderland were saddled with a host of records which branded them the worst team in the 11-year history of the Premiership. No-one had previously won fewer games, collected fewer points or scored fewer goals. Peter Reid, who had paid £10m. for Tore Andre Flo and Marcus Stewart to boost his attack, was sacked in October, Howard Wilkinson and his assistant Steve Cotterill lasted only five months, while Mick McCarthy simply had no time to arrest the decline. All he could do was to start making plans early for next season as Sunderland's last 15 matches all ended in defeat.

Arca, J .... 7(6)	El Karkouri, T 8	Myhre, T .... 1(1)
Babb, P 26	Flo, T .... 23(6)	Phillips, K 32
Bellion, D .... 5(6)	Gray, M 32	Piper, M .... 8(5)
Bjorklund, J .... 19(1)	Kilbane, K 30	Poom, M 4
Black, C 2	Kyle, K .... 9(8)	Proctor, M .... 11(10)
Butler, T 7	Macho, J .... 12(1)	Quinn, N .... –(8)
Clark, B .... –(1)	McAteer, J 9	Reyna, C 11
Craddock, J 25	McCann, G .... 29(1)	Ryan, R .... –(2)
Dickman, J .... –(1)	McCartney, G .... 16(8)	Sorensen, T 21

Stewart, M .... 9(10)	Thome, E 1	Williams, D .... 12(4)
Thirlwell, P .... 12(7)	Thornton, S 11	Wright, S .... 25(1)

League goals (21): Phillips 6, Flo 4, Proctor 2, Bellion 1, Craddock 1, Gray 1, Kilbane 1, McAteer 1, McCann 1, Stewart 1, Thornton 1, Opponents 1.
F.A. Cup goals (8): Phillips 3, Proctor 2, Arca 1, McCann 1, Stewart 1. **Worthington Cup goals (10):** Stewart 4, Flo 2, Arca 1, Kyle 1, McCann 1, Reyna 1, Williams 1.
Average home League attendance: 39,698. **Player of the Year:** Sean Thornton.

TOTTENHAM

Tottenham started on a high and ended in the dog-house after another season of under-achieving. They led the table at the end of August, with 10 points from four matches, and while few expected them to remain there, supporters were frustrated by the inconsistency of the team after that. There remained the hope of a European place until a poor run-in, rounded off by a 5-1 defeat at Middlesbrough and 4-0 reversal against Blackburn. An equally embarrassing F.A. Cup defeat at Southampton, following a Worthington Cup loss at Burnley, did nothing to quell the unrest.

Acimovic, M .... 4(13)	Freund, S .... 13(4)	Redknapp, J .... 14(3)
Anderton, D .... 18(2)	Gardner, A .... 11(1)	Richards, D 26
Blondel, J .... –(1)	Iversen, S .... 8(11)	Sheringham, E .... 34(2)
Bunjevcevic, G .... 31(4)	Keane, R 29	Slabber, J .... –(1)
Carr, S 30	Keller, K 38	Taricco, M 21
Davies, S .... 33(3)	King, L 25	Thatcher, B .... 8(4)
Doherty, G .... 7(8)	Perry, C .... 15(3)	Toda, K .... 2(2)
Etherington, M .... 15(8)	Poyet, G .... 22(6)	Ziege, C .... 10(2)
Ferdinand, L .... 4(7)		

League goals (51): Keane 13, Sheringham 12, Davies 5, Poyet 5, Redknapp 3, Ferdinand 2, Richards 2, Ziege 2, Doherty 1, Etherington 1, Gardner 1, Iversen 1, Perry 1, Taricco 1, Opponents 1.
F.A. Cup goals: None. **Worthington Cup goals** (2): Poyet 1, Sheringham 1.
Average home League attendance: 35,897. **Player of Year:** Simon Davies.

WEST BROMWICH ALBION

Three successive 1-0 wins early on suggested that Albion might stand a chance of grinding their way to survival. Instead, the next 18 matches delivered only one victory and it was always going to be a struggle after that. Spirit and strong running were no substitute for a shortage of goals, with Lee Hughes drawing a blank after returning to the club from Coventry and Jason Roberts failing to score from mid-October onwards. In spite of everything, supporters remained in good heart to the end, grateful for a taste of Premiership football after so long out of the top flight and hopeful their team would be back in contention in the new season.

Balis, I .... 27(1)	Hoult, R 37	Moore, D 29
Chambers, A .... 10(3)	Hughes, L .... 14(9)	Murphy, J .... 1(1)
Chambers, J .... 2(6)	Johnson, A .... 30(2)	Roberts, J .... 31(1)
Clement, N .... 34(2)	Jordao .... –(3)	Sigurdsson, L .... 23(6)
Dichio, D .... 19(9)	Koumas, J .... 27(5)	Taylor, R .... 2(2)
Dobie, S .... 10(21)	Lyttle, D .... 2(2)	Udeze, I .... 7(4)
Gilchrist, P 22	Marshall, L .... 4(5)	Wallwork, R .... 23(4)
Gregan, S 36	McInnes, D .... 28(1)	

League goals (29): Dichio 5, Dobie 5, Koumas 4, Clement 3, Roberts 3, Balis 2, McInnes 2, Moore 2, Gregan 1, Johnson 1, Marshall 1.
F.A. Cup goals (3): Dichio 3. **Worthington Cup goals (1):** Hughes 1.
Average home League attendance: 26,730. **Player of Year:** Jason Koumas.

WEST HAM UNITED

The fact that no side accumulating more than 40 points had ever been relegated was no consolation to West Ham. Neither was the way they took the issue to the final day of the season under the guidance of Trevor Brooking after manager Glenn Roeder suffered a brain tumour. Three successive 1-0 wins offered an escape route and there was a 2-2 draw at St Andrews on the last day. But the points were not enough in the wake of a crucial 1-0 defeat the Reebok Stadium which left them that step behind Bolton. West Ham did not win at Upton Park until the end of January and that, as much as anything, was responsible for the demise of a team unable to add all-round commitment to undoubted quality.

Bowyer, L 10
Breen, G .... 9(5)
Brevett, R .... 12(1)
Camara, T .... –(4)
Carrick, M .... 28(2)
Cisse, E .... 18(7)
Cole, J 36
Dailly, C .... 23(3)
Defoe, J .... 29(9)
Di Canio, P .... 16(2)
Ferdinand, L .... 12(2)
Hutchison, D .... –(10)
James, D 38
Johnson, G .... 14(1)
Kanoute, F .... 12(5)
Labant, V .... –(1)
Lomas, S .... 27(2)
Minto, S .... 9(3)
Moncur, J .... –(7)
Pearce, I .... 26(4)
Repka, T 32
Schemmel, S .... 15(1)
Sinclair, T .... 36(2)
Winterburn, N .... 16(2)

League goals (42): Di Canio 9, Defoe 8, Sinclair 8, Kanoute 5, Cole 4, Ferdinand 2, Pearce 2, Carrick 1, Opponents 3.
F.A. Cup goals (3): Defoe 2, Cole 1. **Worthington Cup goals (1):** Defoe 1.
Average home League attendance: 34,432. **Player of Year:** Joe Cole.

NATIONWIDE LEAGUE – FIRST DIVISION

BRADFORD CITY

Of all the League's financially-stricken clubs, Bradford were among the most serious cases with genuine fears for their future. Chairman Geoffrey Richmond stepped down four days before the start of the season as debts reached £36m. and Football League permission was needed to kick off after the deadline for a rescue package was missed. With the playing staff slashed, manager Nicky Law had to bring in some young players and the team did well to ensure safety with a month remaining. A notable feature was provided by Dane Claus Jorgensen who scored in eight successive away matches during the second half of the campaign.

Atherton, P 25
Banks, S .... 8(1)
Bower, M .... 36(1)
Cadamarteri, D .... 14(6)
Danks, M .... –(3)
Davison, A .... 33(1)
Emanuel, L .... 25(4)
Evans, P .... 16(3)
Facey, D 6
Forrest, D .... 10(7)
Francis, S .... 24(1)
Gray, A 44
Jacobs, W .... 19(4)
Jorgensen, C .... 28(4)
Juanjo, C .... 2(7)
Kearney, T 4
Lawrence, J .... 15(1)
Lee, A .... –(1)
McHugh, F 2
Molenaar, R .... 28(1)
Muirhead, B .... 5(3)
Myers, A .... 21(3)
Myhill, B 2
Penford, T .... –(3)
Proctor, M .... 10(2)
Reid, P .... 7(1)
Sanasy, K .... –(1)
Singh, H 3
Standing, M .... 14(10)
Ten Heuvel, L .... 4(1)
Tod, A .... 4(1)
Uhlenbeek, G 42
Walsh, G 3
Ward, A 24
Warnock, S 12
Wetherall, D .... 16(1)

League goals (51): Gray 15, Jorgensen 11, Proctor 4, Forrest 3, Ward 3, Evans 2, Reid 2, Standing 2, Atherton 1, Facey 1, Francis 1, Lawrence 1, Molenaar 1, Tod 1, Uhlenbeek 1, Warnock 1, Opponents 1.
F.A. Cup goals (1): Danks 1. **Worthington Cup goals (1):** Cadamarteri 1.
Average home League attendance: 12,500. **Player of Year:** Andy Gray.

BRIGHTON & HOVE ALBION

When Steve Coppell replaced Martin Hinshelwood as manager, Brighton. had lost ten successive matches and already had one foot back in the Second Division. Two more defeats followed, with nine goals conceded, before Coppell gradually brought some order to the team and a glimmer of hope for the supporters. Four successive home wins, sparked by a 4-1 success against Wolves and also including a victory over Nottingham Forest, provided grounds for genuine optimism. Although the great escape eventually proved beyond them, Brighton derived some satisfaction from staying alive until the last day of the season

Barrett, G .... 20(10)	Ingimarsson, I 15	Piercy, J .... 1(3)
Beasant, D 16	Jones, N .... 16(12)	Roberts, B 3
Blackwell, D .... 18(3)	Kitson, P .... 7(3)	Rodger, S .... 27(2)
Brooker, P .... 32(5)	Kuipers, M 21	Rogers, P .... 1(3)
Butters, G 6	Marney, D .... 6(6)	Rougier, A .... 5(1)
Carpenter, R .... 42(2)	Mayo, K 41	Sidwell, S .... 11(1)
Cullip, D 44	McPhee, C .... –(2)	Virgo, A 3
Hammond, D .... 1(3)	Melton, S .... 6(2)	Watson, P 45
Harding, D .... –(1)	Oatway, C .... 18(11)	Webb, D .... –(3)
Hart, G .... 27(9)	Pethick, R .... 25(1)	Wilkinson, S .... 4(8)
Hinshelwood, A .... 4(3)	Petterson, A .... 6(1)	Zamora, R 35

League goals (49): Zamora 14, Brooker 6, Sidwell 5, Hart 4, Carpenter 3, Blackwell 2, Cullip 2, Kitson 2, Rodger 2, Rougier 2, Barrett 1, Jones 1, Mayo 1, Melton 1, Oatway 1, Opponents 2.

F.A. Cup goals (1): Pethick 1. **Worthington Cup goals (3):** Cullip 1, Hammond 1, Wilkinson 1. **Average home League attendance:** 6,650. **Player of Year:** Danny Cullip.

BURNLEY

Every so often in a bizarre season, Burnley took leave of their defensive senses. At home, they lost 7-2 to Sheffield Wednesday, 7-4 to Watford, 6-2 to Rotherham Utd. and 5-2 to Reading. On their travels, Grimsby beat them 6-5. There were times, also, when Stan Ternent's side proved capable of matching some of the best in the division, as shown by wins over Leicester, Norwich, Nottingham Forest and Wolves which helped keep them away from trouble. They also produced some capable cup form, overcoming Fulham to reach the quarter-finals of the F.A. Cup and Tottenham to reach round four of the Worthington Cup.

Armstrong, G .... 1(5)	Diallo, D 14	Moore, I .... 35(9)
Beresford, M .... 33(1)	Gnohere, A .... 31(2)	O'Neill, M .... 2(5)
Blake, R .... 34(7)	Grant, A .... 24(10)	Papadopoulos, D .... 7(27)
Branch, G .... 31(1)	Johnrose, L .... 5(1)	Payton, A .... –(1)
Briscoe, L .... 32(1)	Little, G .... 28(5)	Rasmussen, M .... –(2)
Chaplow, R .... 2(3)	Maylett, B .... 1(5)	Taylor, G .... 38(2)
Cook, P .... 21(2)	McGregor, M .... 25(5)	Waine, A .... –(2)
Cox, I .... 23(3)	Michopoulos, N 13	Weller, P .... 26(8)
Davis, S .... 25(3)	Moore, A .... 14(13)	West, D 41

League goals (65): Taylor 16, Blake 13, Moore, I 8, Little 5, Davis 4, West 4, Papadopoulos 3, Briscoe 2, Gnohere 2, Moore, A 1, Cox 1, Diallo 1, Grant 1, McGregor 1, Opponents 3.

F.A. Cup goals (13): Moore, I 3, Blake 2, Little 2, Moore, A 2, Cook 1, Diallo 1, Taylor 1, Weller 1. **Worthington Cup goals (6):** Papadopoulos 3, Blake 1, Davis 1, West 1. **Average home League attendance:** 13,976. **Player of Year:** Gareth Taylor.

COVENTRY CITY

Although the early-season loss of David Thompson was a setback, Coventry went into the New Year optimistic about challenging for a play-off place after a run of 13 points from five matches, which included a notable away win over Wolves. It proved a false hope in a big way. Gary McAllister's team won only once after that – 2-0 against Grimsby – failed to score in 12 of the 20 games and ended the season with five successive blanks. The dismal run left them just above the bottom three, bracketed on 50 points with Stoke, a team who had been struggling against relegation for the whole campaign.

Bates, T ....–(1)	Hughes, L .... 3(1)	Osbourne, I 2
Betts, R 1	Hyldgaard, M 27	Partridge, R .... 23(4)
Bothroyd, J .... 24(9)	Jansen, M .... 8(1)	Pead, C .... 17(7)
Caldwell, G 36	Jephcott, A .... –(1)	Pipe, D .... 11(10)
Chippo, Y .... 20(3)	Joachim, J .... 10(1)	Quinn, B .... 13(5)
Cooney, S .... –(1)	Kerr, B .... 2(1)	Safri, Y .... 24(3)
Davenport, C .... 26(6)	Konjic, M 42	Sara, J .... 1(2)
Debec, F 11	Mackey, B .... –(3)	Shaw, R .... 27(2)
Delorge, L 2	McAllister, G 41	Stanford, E .... –(1)
Engonga, V .... 5(3)	McMaster, J 2	Strachan, G .... –(1)
Eustace, J .... 23(9)	McSheffrey, G ...... 14(15)	Thompson, D 4
Fowler, L 1	Mills, R .... 11(7)	Walsh, S .... 1(1)
Gordon, D 30	Montgomery, G 8	Whing, A .... 13(1)
Hignett, C .... 7(1)	Noon, M .... –(2)	Yulu, C .... 1(2)
Holdsworth, D .... 13(4)	Normann, R .... 2(1)	

League goals (46): Bothroyd 8, McAllister 7, Eustace 4, McSheffrey 4, Partridge 4, Davenport 3, Hignett 2, Jansen 2, Joachim 2, Mills 2, Pipe 2, Gordon 1, Hughes 1, Normann 1, Pead 1, Sara 1, Opponents 1.
F.A. Cup goals (5): Bothroyd 1, Fowler 1, Holdsworth 1, McAllister 1, Mills 1. **Worthington Cup goals (11):** McSheffrey 4, Mills 3, Bothroyd 2, Betts 1, McAllister 1.
Average home League attendance: 14,812. **Player of Year:** Mo Konjic.

CRYSTAL PALACE

Crystal Palace were another side handily-placed for a play-off challenge at the mid-way point of the season. They, too, failed to stay the course, and it was, perhaps, no coincidence that things started to go wrong during an F.A. Cup run which brought a famous 2-0 victory at Anfield followed by a 2-1 defeat by Leeds in a fifth round tie which hinged on referee Dermot Gallagher and his assistant failing to spot that a Tommy Black shot was clearly over the line. Palace, who also reached the quarter-finals of the Worthington Cup before losing to Sheffield United, finished in mid-table and Trevor Francis paid the price with four matches left, Steve Kember taking over.

Adebola, D .... 32(7)	Frampton, A .... –(1)	Powell, D 39
Akinbiyi, A .... 2(8)	Freedman, D .... 22(7)	Riihilahti, A .... 15(10)
Antwi, W .... –(4)	Granville, D .... 30(5)	Routledge, W .... 13(13)
Austin, D .... –(3)	Gray, J .... 29(6)	Rubins, A .... –(2)
Berthelin, C 9	Hunt, D 2	Smith, J 2
Black, T .... 20(16)	Johnson, A .... 27(1)	Symons, K .... 21(4)
Borrowdale, G .... 8(5)	Kabba, S .... –(4)	Thomson, S .... 18(9)
Butterfield, D 46	Kolinko, A .... 26(2)	Togwell, S .... –(1)
Clarke, M 6	Michopoulos, N 5	Watson, B .... 3(2)
Derry, S .... 36(3)	Mullins, H 43	Whelan, N .... 7(1)
Fleming, C .... 9(2)	Popovic, T 36	Williams, G .... –(5)

League goals (59): Johnson 11, Freedman 9, Black 6, Adebola 5, Gray 5, Routledge 4, Granville 3, Popovic 3, Whelan 3, Mullins 2, Akinbiyi 1, Butterfield 1, Derry 1, Kabba 1, Powell 1, Riihilahti 1, Thomson 1, Opponents 1.
F.A. Cup goals (5): Black 2, Gray 2, Opponents 1. **Worthington Cup goals (15):** Johnson 3, Adebola 2, Black 2, Freedman 2, Gray 1, Mullins 1, Popovic 1, Powell 1, Opponents 2.
Average home League attendance: 16,866. **Player of Year:** Hayden Mullins.

DERBY COUNTY

Another torrid time at Pride Park, where relegation was followed by a struggle to bring down debts, the dismissal of manager John Gregory after he had first been suspended for alleged 'serious offences' and the failure of the team's remaining high earners to get anywhere near a play-off place. Despite this, supporters remained loyal – only Leicester and Wolves drew bigger crowds in the division – and the majority welcomed the choice of former Ipswich manager George Burley as caretaker for the final part of the season which ended with Derby in 18th position. Burley was later confirmed in the job.

Barton, W	39	Grenet, F	2(1)	Oakes, A	7
Boertien, P	42	Higginbotham, D	22(1)	O'Neil, B	3
Bolder, A	38(7)	Holmes, L	–(2)	Poom, M	13
Burley, C	20	Hunt, L	7(3)	Ravanelli, F	16(3)
Burton, D	4(3)	Jackson, R	16(5)	Riggott, C	21(1)
Camp, L	–(1)	Kinkladze, G	22(6)	Ritchie, P	7
Carbonari, H	2	Lee, R	34(1)	Robinson, M	–(1)
Chadwick, N	4(2)	McLeod, I	20(9)	Strupar, B	4(1)
Christie, M	24	Mills, P	12(3)	Tudgay, M	–(8)
Elliott, S	21(2)	Mooney, T	7(1)	Twigg, G	1(7)
Evatt, I	18(12)	Morris, L	26(4)	Valakari, S	5(1)
Grant, L	26(3)	Murray, A	17(7)	Zavagno, L	6(3)

League goals (55): Christie 8, Morris 8, Bolder 6, Ravanelli 5, Kinkladze 4, Burley 3, Burton 3, McLeod 3, Higginbotham 2, Lee 2, Riggott 2, Valakari 2, Zavagno 2, Boertien 1, Carbonari 1, Elliott 1, Strupar 1, Opponents 1.

F.A. Cup goals: None. **Worthington Cup goals (4):** Christie 1, Evatt 1, Higginbotham 1, Morris 1.

Average home League attendance: 25,469. **Player of Year:** Giorgi Kinkladze.

GILLINGHAM

Another small but significant step for Andy Hessenthaler's side, who finished 11th after 12th and 13th placings in previous years. While not enough for some, it represented another solid achievement by a club with little money to spend, particularly as they were without leading striker Marlon King for much of the season. One of the high spots was being able to look down at the rest after they opened with three successive wins. A 3-2 victory over Leicester on a rousing afternoon at Priestfield was also good value. Bad moments were 4-0 and 6-0 defeats by Wolves.

Ashby, B	38	James, K	5(10)	Rose, R	–(2)
Awuah, J	1(3)	Johnson, L	8(10)	Saunders, M	28(6)
Bartram, V	7(1)	Johnson, T	12(14)	Shaw, P	44
Brown, J	39	King, M	9(1)	Sidibe, M	24(6)
Edge, R	34	Nosworthy, N	37(2)	Smith, P	45
Edusei, A	–(2)	Osborn, S	15(3)	Southall, N	22(2)
Hessenthaler, A	32(1)	Patterson, M	1(1)	Spiller, D	5(5)
Hope, C	46	Pennock, A	2(1)	Wallace, R	17(5)
Ipoua, G	22(11)	Perpetuini, D	13(16)		

League goals (56): Shaw 13, Wallace 11, Ipoua 5, King 4, James 3, Saunders 3, Sidibe 3, Smith 3, Nosworthy 2, Perpetuini 2, Johnson, T 2, Hessenthaler 1, Hope 1, Osborn 1, Southall 1, Opponents 1.

F.A. Cup goals (6): Ipoua 2, King 2, Hope 1, Sidibe 1. **Worthington Cup goals (4):** Hessenthaler 1, Ipoua 1, Johnson, T 1, King 1.

Average home League attendance: 8,078. **Player of Year:** Nayron Nosworthy.

GRIMSBY TOWN

A small squad, a struggling start and a poor finish conspired to send Grimsby down after years spent battling the odds to stay afloat in this division. Player-manager Paul Groves, who made his 700th career appearance during the season, was always up against it after his side scored only once in their first six games. They improved that record – notably in a 6-5 win over Burnley on a bizarre night at Blundell Park – but conceded more goals than any other team and the failure to win any of the final eight matches left them marooned at the bottom, 11 points adrift of safety.

Barnard, D .... 21(8)	Groves, P .... 32(4)	Pouton, A 25
Bolder, C .... 7(5)	Hockless, G 1	Raven, P .... 6(1)
Boulding, M .... 10(2)	Hughes, R 12	Robinson, P .... 5(7)
Campbell, S 45	Jevons, P .... –(3)	Rowan, J .... 2(7)
Chettle, S .... 18(2)	Kabba, S 13	Sagere, J 1
Coldicott, S .... 26(5)	Keane, M 7	Santos, G .... 24(2)
Cooke, T .... 15(10)	Livingstone, S .... 21(9)	Soames, D .... –(10)
Coyne, D 46	Mansaram, D .... 21(13)	Taylor, R 1
Ford, S .... 35(4)	McDermott, J 35	Thompson, C .... 3(3)
Gallimore, A 38	Oster, J 17	Ward, I .... 9(2)
Gavin, J .... 8(2)	Parker, W .... 1(4)	Young, G 1

League goals (48): Campbell 7, Kabba 6, Oster 6, Pouton 5, Boulding 4, Groves 3, Livingstone 3, Barnard 2, Ford 2, Keane 2, Mansaram 2, Chettle 1, Hughes 1, Robinson 1, Santos 1, Soames 1, Thompson 1.
F.A. Cup goals (2): Cooke 1, Mansaram 1. **Worthington Cup goals:** None.
Average home League attendance: 5,883. **Player of Year:** George Santos.

IPSWICH TOWN

Another season of turmoil at Portman Road, where relegated Ipswich sacked long-serving manager George Burley for poor results, went into administration and were forced to sell Darren Ambrose and Hermann Hreidarsson. Joe Royle, Burley's replacement, could still have taken his team into the play-offs after a revival in fortunes, aided by a dramatic 3-2 win over Sheffield United after being two goals down. But points dropped at home in quick succession to lowly Grimsby, Stoke and Brighton proved costly. Then, after another recovery, two goals conceded in the last five minutes brought a 2-1 defeat at Rotherham and ended their hopes.

Ambrose, D .... 20(9)	George, F .... 3(7)	Naylor, R .... 11(6)
Armstrong, A .... 9(10)	Gerrard, P 5	Pullen, J 1
Bent, D .... 24(11)	Holland, M 45	Reuser, M .... 6(10)
Bent, M .... 25(7)	Hreidarsson, H 28	Richards, M .... 10(3)
Bowditch, D .... –(5)	Magilton, J .... 39(1)	Stewart, M 3
Brown, W .... 7(2)	Makin, C 33	Venus, M 8
Clapham, J 26	Marshall, A 40	Westlake, I .... –(4)
Collins, A .... –(1)	McGreal, J 16	Wilnis, F .... 33(2)
Counago, P .... 28(11)	Miller, T .... 24(6)	Wright, J .... 25(14)
Gaardsoe, T 37	Murray, A .... –(1)	

League goals (80): Cougano 17, Bent, D 12, Bent, M 11, Ambrose 8, Holland 7, Miller 6, Gaardsoe 4, Magilton 3, Naylor 2, Reuser 2, Wilnis 2, Armstrong 1, Clapham 1, George 1, McGreal 1, Wright 1, Opponents 1.
F.A. Cup goals (7): Bent, D 3, Ambrose 1, Clapham 1, Gaardsoe 1, Miller 1. **Worthington Cup goals (7):** Bent, D 2, Ambrose 1, Clapham 1, Counago 1, Gaardsoe 1, Miller 1. **UEFA Cup goals (12):** Counago 3, Miller 2, Ambrose 1, Armstrong 1, Bent, D 1, Bent, M 1, Brown 1, McGreal 1, Stewart 1.
Average home League attendance: 25,454. **Player of Year:** Matt Holland.

LEICESTER CITY

A 6-1 defeat at Ipswich in the third game of the season did nothing to suggest that Leicester City would make an immediate return to the Premiership. Neither did the club's acute financial problems, which resulted in administration and meant there was no money for Micky Adams to spend on adding to the team that went down. But this same mixture of experience and strength finished runners-up to Portsmouth, watched by the biggest crowds in the division at the new Walkers Stadium. They also did it with plenty to spare – finishing 12 points clear of the third-placed team Sheffield United.

Ashton, J .... –(2)	Izzet, M 38	Rogers, A 41
Benjamin, T .... 18(17)	Jones, M .... 3(3)	Scowcroft, J 43
Davidson, C .... 28(2)	Lewis, J .... 5(4)	Sinclair, F .... 31(2)
Deane, B .... 31(1)	Marshall, L 1	Stevenson, J .... –(6)
Dickov, P 42	McKinlay, W .... 29(8)	Stewart, J .... 28(9)
Elliott, M .... 43(1)	O'Grady, C .... –(1)	Summerbee, N .... 7(22)
Flowers, T .... –(1)	Oakes, S .... 1(4)	Taggart, G .... 33(4)
Heath, M .... 9(1)	Petrescu, T .... –(1)	Walker, I 46
Impey, A .... 27(5)	Reeves, M .... –(3)	Wright, T .... 2(11)

League goals (73): Dickov 17, Deane 13, Scowcroft 10, Benjamin 8, Elliott 5, Izzet 4, Stewart 4, Heath 3, Wright 2, Davidson 1, Lewis 1, McKinlay 1, Sinclair 1, Stevenson 1, Taggart 1, Opponents 1.

F.A. Cup goals (3): Dickov 2, Elliott 1. **Worthington Cup goals (6):** Rogers 2, Benjamin 1, Dickov 1, Izzet 1, Scowcroft 1.

Average home League attendance: 29,230. **Player of Year:** Paul Dickov.

MILLWALL

A 6-0 home defeat by Rotherham on the opening day of the season and just two points collected from the first five matches suggested there would be no repeat of last season's success in reaching the play-offs. A drop in attendances of 5,000 per home game following a self-imposed membership scheme for supporters underlined that view. The best moments came towards the end of the campaign when Mark McGhee won the Manager of the Month award for April, Neil Harris shouldered attacking responsibility when the goals dried up for Steve Claridge and 19 points gained from the final eight matches lifted Millwall to ninth in the table.

Ashikodi, M .... –(5)	Harris, N .... 34(6)	Reid, S .... 19(1)
Baltacha, S .... 1(1)	Hearn, C .... 6(3)	Roberts, A .... 31(2)
Braniff, K .... 5(5)	Ifill, P 45	Robinson, P .... 12(2)
Bull, R .... 9(3)	Johnson, G .... 7(1)	Ryan, R .... 36(5)
Cahill, T .... 9(2)	Kinet, C .... 10(10)	Sadlier, R .... 2(3)
Claridge, S .... 31(13)	Lawrence, M .... 31(2)	Sweeney, P .... 1(4)
Craig, T 2	Livermore, D 41	Tuttle, D 1
Davies, K .... 6(3)	May, B .... 4(6)	Ward, D .... 36(3)
Dolan, J 2	McCammon, M 7	Warner, T 46
Dunne, A .... 3(1)	Nethercott, S .... 34(2)	Wise, D .... 28(1)
Elliott, M .... –(1)	Phillips, M 7	

League goals (59): Harris 12, Claridge 9, Ifill 6, Reid 6, Cahill 3, Davies 3, Wise 3, Kinet 2, Livermore 2, McCammon 2, Nethercott 2, Roberts 2, Ryan 2, Craig 1, May 1, Sadlier 1, Sweeney 1, Ward 1.

F.A. Cup goals (6): Claridge 3, Ifill 1, Reid 1, Robinson 1. **Worthington Cup goals:** None.
Average home League attendance: 8,512. **Player of Year:** Tony Warner.

NORWICH CITY

Norwich harboured high hopes after being denied a Premiership place on penalties the previous season. But instead of a rousing finish to the campaign which had delivered that play-off place, they lacked the consistency to break into the top six after laying the groundwork during the first half of the campaign. Defeats by Reading, Nottingham Forest and ultimately Wolves, who won 3-0 at Carrow Road on Easter Monday, were particularly damaging. A home defeat by Ipswich was also hard to swallow for Norwich, who finished in eighth place, a point behind their East Anglian rivals.

Abbey, Z .... 12(18)	Drury, A 45	Fleming, C .... 28(2)
Briggs, K .... 1(1)	Easton, C .... 23(3)	Green, R 46
Bromby, L 5	Emblen, N .... 5(7)	Healy, D .... 10(3)

Heckingbottom, P ..... 7(8)	Mackay, M .... 35(2)	Rivers, M .... 28(2)
Henderson, I .... 4(16)	McVeigh, P .... 38(6)	Roberts, I .... 33(10)
Holt, G 45	Mulryne, P .... 31(2)	Russell, D .... 16(5)
Jarvis, R .... 2(1)	Nedergaard, S .... 34(1)	Shackell, J 2
Kenton, D .... 36(1)	Nielsen, D .... 11(22)	Sinclair, D .... 1(1)
Llewellyn, C .... 2(3)	Notman, A .... 2(6)	Southall, N .... 4(5)

League goals (60): McVeigh 14, Roberts 7, Mackay 6, Mulryne 6, Nielsen 6 Abbey 5, Rivers 4, Drury 2, Easton 2, Healy 2, Nedergaard 2, Henderson 1, Kenton 1, Opponents 2.
F.A. Cup goals (4): Mulryne 2, Abbey 1, McVeigh 1. **Worthington Cup goals:** None.
Average home League attendance: 20,352. **Player of Year:** Adam Drury.

NOTTINGHAM FOREST

A season of gathering momentum ended in bitter disppointment for Nottingham Forest, who surrendered a two-goal lead in the second leg of their play-off semi-final against Sheffield United and lost 4-3. No-one was more distraught that their talented young central defender Michael Dawson, who was suspended after being sent off in the first leg. He could have made a big difference. Even so, unfancied Forest achieved more than most fans expected, scoring more goals at home than any team in the country thanks to the prolific partnership of David Johnson and Marlon Harewood – the latter scoring four times in the first half of a 6-0 win over Stoke.

Bopp, E .... 10(3)	Huckerby, D 9	Roche, B 1
Brennan, J 45	Jess, E .... 17(15)	Scimeca, R 40
Cash, B .... –(1)	Johnson, D .... 40(2)	Thompson, J .... 18(2)
Dawson, M 38	Lester, J .... 20(13)	Walker, D .... 29(2)
Doig, C .... 4(6)	Louis-Jean, M 41	Ward, D 45
Hall, M 1	Oyen, D .... –(4)	Westcarr, C .... 2(9)
Harewood, M .... 42(2)	Prutton, D 24	Williams, G .... 39(1)
Hjelde, J .... 19(7)	Reid, A .... 22(8)	

Play-offs – Appearances: Brennan 2, Harewood 2, Huckerby 2, Johnson 2, Louis-Jean 2, Reid 2, Scimeca 2, Walker 2, Ward 2, Williams 2, Thompson 1(1), Dawson 1, Hjelde –(1), Lester –(1).
League goals (82): Johnson 25, Harewood 20, Lester 7, Dawson 5, Huckerby 5, Jess 3, Scimeca 3, Thompson 3, Williams 3, Bopp 2, Brennan 1, Louis-Jean 1, Prutton 1, Reid 1, Westcarr 1, Opponents 1. **Play-offs goals (4):** Johnson 2, Reid 1, Opponents 1.
F.A. Cup goals (2): Harewood 1, Reid 1. **Worthington Cup goals (5):** Johnson 2, Lester 2, Scimeca 1.
Average home League attendance: 24,436. **Player of Year:** David Johnson.

PORTSMOUTH

The Pompey Chimes rang out from the start of the season to its conclusion as Harry Redknapp's side defied the odds to return to the top flight as champions. Even the manager himself was astounded at how his blend of former Premiership players and Naionwide League stalwarts forced the pace, then maintained it to dominate the divison in tandem with Leicester. Redknapp brought in Tim Sherwood and Nigerian striker Yakubu Ayegbeni to bolster his squad for the second part of the season, although fittingly it was midfield inspiration Paul Merson and leading scorer Svetoslav Todorov who scored the goals which clinched the title against Rotherham.

Ayegbeni, Y .... 12(2)	Diabate, L .... 16(9)	Hughes, R .... 4(2)
Bradbury, L 3	Festa, G 27	Kawaguchi, Y .... –(1)
Burchill, M .... 4(14)	Foxe, H .... 30(2)	Merson, P .... 44(1)
Burton, D .... 11(4)	Harper, K .... 21(16)	O'Neil, G .... 11(20)
Buxton, L .... –(1)	Heikkinen, M .... –(2)	Pericard, V .... 18(14)
Crowe, J .... 7(9)	Hislop, S 46	Primus, L .... 39(1)
De Zeeuw, A .... 35(3)	Howe, E 1	Quashie, N 42

Ritchie, P .... 8(4)	Stone, S 18	Tiler, C .... –(2)
Robinson, C .... 11(4)	Tavlaridis, E .... 3(1)	Todorov, S .... 43(2)
Sherwood, T 17	Taylor, M 35	

League goals (97): Todorov 26, Merson 12, Pericard 9, Taylor 7, Ayegbeni 7, Quashie 5, Burchill 4, Burton 4, Crowe 4, Harper 4, Stone 4, O'Neil 3, Bradbury 1, De Zeeuw 1, Festa 1, Foxe 1, Sherwood 1, Opponents 3.
F.A. Cup goals (1): Stone 1. **Worthington Cup goals (3):** Pericard 1, Primus 1, Quashie 1.
Average home League attendance: 18,933.

PRESTON NORTH END

Following David Moyes would have been a difficult enough job for any manager. And it was certainly not the easiest of starts to his first full season in charge for the former Scotland coach Craig Brown. His team took a long time to put together back-to-back victories and there was a worrying run of five successive defeats – plus an F.A. Cup loss to Rochdale – around the turn of the year. But despite losing Ricardo Fuller with a knee injury, Preston showed improved form in the second half of the campaign to finish in mid-table, Richard Cresswell scoring with some consistency.

Abbott, P .... 6(10)	Etuhu, D .... 33(6)	Lucketti, C 43
Alexander, G 45	Fuller, R 18	Lynch, S .... 6(11)
Anderson, I .... –(8)	Gould, J .... 13(1)	McKenna, P .... 39(2)
Bailey, J .... –(1)	Healy, D .... 12(11)	Mears, T .... 11(11)
Barry-Murphy, B 2	Jackson, M .... 21(1)	Moilanen, T .... 14(1)
Broomes, M .... 21(7)	Keane, M .... 1(4)	Murdock, C 24
Cartwright, L .... 13(9)	Koumantarakis, G 10	O'Neil, B .... 12(3)
Cresswell, R 42	Lewis, E .... 34(4)	Rankine, S .... 11(8)
Eaton, A .... –(1)	Lucas, D .... 19(2)	Skora, E .... 30(5)
Edwards, R, ... 26		

League goals (68): Cresswell 16, Alexander 10, Fuller 9, Etuhu 6, Healy 5, Lewis 5, Abbott 3, Koumantarakis 3, McKenna 3, Cartwright 2, Lucketti 2, Jackson 1, Mears 1, Opponents 2.
F.A. Cup goals (1): Anderson 1. **Worthington Cup goals (6):** Fuller 2, Alexander 1, Jackson 1, Lewis 1, Skora 1.
Average home League attendance: 13,853. **Player of Year:** Richard Cresswell.

READING

Promoted Reading exceeded all expectations by finishing fourth with a team lacking big names but full of talented young players brought on by manager Alan Pardew. This after an indifferent start to the season which brought three defeats in the first four matches. A goal by Nicky Forster gave them the upper hand in the play-off semi-final against Wolves, only for the tide to turn after the leading scorer went off with an ankle injury. His side conceded two goals in the final quarter-of-an-hour to lose 2-1, Forster missed the second leg at home and a late winner by Alex Rae ended their hopes in front of a club-record crowd at the Madejski Stadium.

Ashdown, J 1	Henderson, D .... 1(21)	Shorey, N 43
Brown, S 21	Hughes, A .... 41(2)	Sidwell, S 13
Butler, M .... 12(9)	Igoe, S .... 8(7)	Smith, A .... –(1)
Campbell, D .... –(1)	Little, G 6	Tyson, N .... 9(14)
Castle, P .... –(1)	Mackie, J .... 20(5)	Upson, M .... 13(1)
Chadwick, L 15	Murty, G .... 43(1)	Viveash, A .... 4(1)
Cureton, J .... 13(14)	Newman, R .... 21(7)	Watson, K .... 24(8)
Forster, N .... 35(5)	Parkinson, P .... –(6)	Whitehead, P 4
Hahnemann, M 41	Rougier, A .... 13(7)	Williams, A 38
Harper, J .... 34(2)	Salako, J .... 33(10)	

Play-offs – Appearances: Brown 2, Hahnemann 2, Harper 2, Henderson 2, Hughes 2, Murty 2, Shorey 2, Sidwell 2, Williams 2, Chadwick 1(1), Cureton 1(1), Forster 1, Little 1, Newman –(1), Rougier –(1), Tyson –(1), Watson –(1).
League goals (61): Forster 16, Cureton 9, Hughes 9, Henderson 4, Salako 4, Rougier 3, Butler 2, Harper 2, Shorey 2, Sidwell 2, Brown 1, Chadwick 1, Little 1, Tyson 1, Watson 1, Williams 1, Opponents 2. **Play-offs goals (1):** Forster 1.
F.A. Cup goals (1): Opponents 1. **Worthington Cup goals (1):** Upson 1.
Average home League attendance: 16,011. **Player of Year:** James Harper.

ROTHERHAM UNITED

Having survived by the skin of their teeth the previous season after a wretched start, Rotherham went some way to consolidating their position in the division by finishing 15th. It was further testimony to the motivational powers of manager Ronnie Moore and the resilience of his players at a club whose achievements continue to dwarf their resources. This time, they could not have made a better start, Darren Byfield scoring four times in a 6-0 win at Millwall. The first five games produced 11 points and Moore's team went on to win regularly enough to remain a safe distance from the bottom group. It included another handsome win on their travels – 6-2 against Burnley.

Barker, R .... 23(14)
Barker, S 11
Beech, C .... 1(1)
Branston, G .... 13(2)
Bryan, M .... 12(4)
Byfield, D .... 24(13)
Daws, N .... 30(3)
Farrelly, G 6
Garner, D .... 20(6)
Gray, I .... 5(1)
Hurst, P 44
Lee, A .... 38(3)
McIntosh, M 42
Monkhouse, A .... 11(9)
Mullin, J .... 31(3)
Pollitt, M 41
Robins, M .... 6(9)
Scott, R 23
Sedgwick, C .... 42(1)
Swailes, C 43
Talbot, S .... 8(7)
Warne, P .... 21(19)
Woodhouse, C 11

League goals (62): Lee 15, Byfield 13, Barker, R 7, McIntosh 5, Robins 5, Garner 3, Mullin 3, Swailes 3, Branston 2, Daws 1, Hurst 1, Sedgwick 1, Talbot 1, Warne 1, Opponents 1.
F.A. Cup goals: None.**Worthington Cup goals (10):** Monkhouse 3, Barker, R 2, Robins 2, Lee 1, Swailes 1, Warne 1.
Average home League attendance: 7,522. **Player of Year:** Alan Lee.

SHEFFIELD UNITED

So near, yet so far for a supposedly patchwork team which Neil Warnock moulded into a formidable force on three fronts. With Michael Brown a prolific scorer from midfield and goals coming from numerous other areas, United finished a solid third behind Portsmouth and Leicester. Things got better when they retrieved a 2-0 deficit against Nottingham Forest to reach the final of the play-offs. But Warnock's 100 percent record in the competition with other clubs did not survive a below-par first half performance against Wolves which cost three goals and the chance of a Premiership place. Elsewhere, it took Arsenal and Liverpool to deny them a place in the final of the F.A. Cup and Worthington Cup

Allison, W .... 15(19)
Asaba, C .... 16(12)
Boulding, M .... 3(3)
Brown, M .... 39(1)
Cas, M .... 3(3)
Cryan, C .... –(2)
Curtis, J .... 9(3)
Doane, B .... 2(3)
Edghill, R .... –(1)
Harley, J .... 8(1)
Jagielka, P .... 41(1)
Javary, J-P .... 2(4)
Kabba, S .... 19(6)
Kelly, G 1
Kenny, P 45
Kozluk, R .... 29(3)
McCall, S .... 32(2)
McGovern, J-P .... 11(4)
Montgomery, N .... 15(8)
Mooney, T .... 2(1)
Morrison, O .... 3(5)
Murphy, S .... 42(1)
Ndlovu, P .... 30(9)
Onuora, I 7
Page, R .... 33(1)
Peschisolido, P ...... 4(19)
Quinn, W 6
Rankine, S .... 5(1)
Smith, G .... 1(2)
Ten Heuvel, L .... –(5)
Tonge, M .... 40(4)
Ullathorne, R 12
Windass, D 20
Yates, S .... 11(1)

Play-offs – Appearances: Asaba 3, Brown 3, Curtis 3, Jagielka 3, Kenny 3, Kozluk 3, Ndlovu 3, Page 3, Rankine 3, Tonge 3, Windass 2, Kabba 1 (2), Allison –(2), Peschisolido –(2), McCall –(1).
League goals (72): Brown 16, Asaba 11, Ndlovu 8, Kabba 7, Allison 6, Tonge 6, Windass 6, Peschisolido 3, Murphy 2, Harley 1, Kozluk 1, McGovern 1, Onuora 1, Opponents 3. **Play-offs goals (5):** Brown (2), Kabba 1, Peschisolido 1, Opponents 1.
F.A. Cup goals (11): Kabba 3, Brown 2, Jagielka 1, McGovern 1, Mooney 1, Murphy 1, Ndlovu 1, Peschisolido 1. **Worthington Cup goals (14):** Brown 2, Peschisolido 2, Tonge 2, Allison 1, Asaba 1, Boulding 1, Jagielka 1, McGovern 1, Montgomery 1, Murphy 1, Ndlovu 1.
Average home League attendance: 18,069. **Player of Year:** Paddy Kenny.

SHEFFIELD WEDNESDAY

Chris Turner will take Sheffield Wednesday to his former club Hartlepool in the new season after failing to save them from their second relegation in four seasons. Turner, a former goalkeeper at Hillsborough, left Victoria Park to replace Terry Yorath, who bowed to growing pressure from fans and resigned after 16 matches yielded only two wins. There were pockets of improvement under the new manager, notably successive victories over Wimbledon and champions-to-be Portsmouth. But they were not sustained and a remarkable 7-2 win at Burnley came too late for survival.

Armstrong, C 17
Barry-Murphy, B 17
Beswetherick, J .... 5(1)
Bradbury, L .... 10(1)
Bromby, L .... 26(1)
Burrows, D 13
Crane, A .... 13(6)
Di Piedi, M .... 1(1)
Donnelly, S .... 10(5)
Evans, P 7
Evans, R .... 3(1)
Geary, D .... 24(2)
Green, R 4
Hamshaw, M .... 4(11)
Haslam, S .... 18(8)
Hendon, I 9
Holt, G .... 3(4)
Johnston, A 12
Knight, L .... 14(10)
Kuqi, S .... 34(6)
Maddix, D .... 22(1)
McLaren, P .... 31(5)
Monk, G 15
Morrison, O .... –(1)
Owusu, L .... 12(20)
Powell, D 8
Pressman, K 38
Proudlock, A .... 3(2)
Quinn, A .... 33(4)
Reddy, M .... 13(2)
Robinson, C 4
Shaw, J .... –(1)
Sibon, G .... 23(2)
Smith, D 14
Soltvedt, T 21
Stringer, C .... 1(2)
Westwood, A .... 22(1)
Wood, R .... 2(1)

League goals (56): Kuqi 8, Sibon 6, Quinn 5, McLaren 4, Owusu 4, Bradbury 3, Knight 3, Reddy 3, Crane 2, Donnelly 2, Johnston 2, Proudlock 2, Westwood 2, Armstrong 1, Evans, R 1, Hamshaw 1, Haslam 1, Holt 1, Maddix 1, Robinson 1, Wood 1, Opponents 2.
F.A. Cup goals (1): Sibon 1. Worthington Cup goals (2): Sibon 2.
Average home League attendance: 20,326. **Player of Year:** Alan Quinn.

STOKE CITY

Tony Pulis was given the job of saving Stoke from an immediate return to Division Two after Steve Cotterill resigned to join Sunderland and George Burley declined the invitation to succeed him. It was one Pulis fulfilled, eventually turning around a side who went 16 matches.without a win before beating Sheffield Wednesday and Preston around the turn of the year, then taking a hard-earned point at Leicester. There were more setbacks, in particular a 6-0 defeat by Nottingham Forest, before a much tighter defence enabled Stoke to start accumulating enough points to finish clear of the bottom three.

Akinbiyi, A 4
Banks, S 14
Clarke, C .... 27(4)
Commons, K .... 6(2)
Cooke, A .... 24(7)
Crossley, M 12
Cutler, N 20
Goodfellow, M .... 6(14)
Greenacre, C .... 18(12)
Gudjonsson, B ...... 25(11)
Gunnarsson, B 40
Hall, L 1
Hall, M .... 22(1)
Handyside, P 44
Henry, K .... 15(3)
Hoekstra, P .... 26(4)
Iwelumo, C .... 15(17)
Marteinsson, P .... 7(5)
Mills, L .... 7(4)
Mooney, T .... 11(1)
Neal, L .... 7(9)
O'Connor, J 43
Richardson, F .... 6(1)
Shtaniuk, S 44

Thomas, W 41
Vandeurzen, J .... 7(5)
Warhurst, P .... 4(1)
Williams, M .... 5(1)
Wilson, B .... 2(2)
Wilson, M 3

League goals (45): Cooke 6, Gunnarson 5, Greenacre 4, Hoekstra 4, Iwelumo 4, Clarke 3, Mooney 3, Shtaniuk 3, Akinbiyi 2, Marteinsson 2, Mills 2, Commons 1, Goodfellow 1, Gudjonsson 1, Henry 1, Vandeurzen 1, Warhurst 1, Opponents 1.
F.A. Cup goals (6): Iwelumo 3, Greenacre 2, Hoekstra 1. **Worthington Cup goals:** None.
Average home League attendance: 14,587. **Player of Year:** Sergei Shtaniuk.

WALSALL

Finishing one place higher than the previous year, Walsall guaranteed a third successive season in the division, another example of a club with limited resources doing well to remain competitive at this level. The difference this time was that they were never really threatened by the bottom three, finishing eight points clear of danger. The best sequence of results came in April when five games netted 11 points. There was also a new record attendance for the Bescot when 11,037 saw the local derby with Wolves.

Ainsworth, G .... 2(3)
Aranalde, Z .... 38(1)
Barras, A .... 14(5)
Bazeley, D .... 41(2)
Birch, G .... 6(13)
Carbon, M .... 20(5)
Corica, S .... 33(8)
Emblen, N .... 3(2)
Hay, D .... 26(3)
Herivelto, M .... –(4)
Junior .... 28(8)
Lawrence, J .... 4(1)
Leitao, J .... 43(1)
Martinez, R .... 1(5)
Matias, P .... 8(15)
O'Connor, M .... 33(2)
Pollet, L 5
Robinson, C .... 10(1)
Rodrigues, D .... –(1)
Roper, I .... 39(1)
Samways, V 13
Shuker, C .... 3(2)
Simpson, F .... 16(9)
Sonner, D .... 20(4)
Walker, J 41
Ward, G .... 5(2)
Wrack, D 43
Wright, M .... 2(3)
Zdrilic, D .... 9(15)

League goals (57): Junior 15, Leitao 11, Wrack 6, Corica 4, Sonner 4, Aranalde 3, Matias 3, Zdrilic 3, Ainsworth 1, Birch 1, Carbon 1, Herivelto 1, O'Connor 1, Robinson 1, Simpson 1, Opponents 1.
F.A. Cup goals (2): Wrack 1, Zdrilic 1. **Worthington Cup goals** (5): Leitao 2, Aranalde 1, Junior 1, Zdrilic 1.
Average home League attendance: 6,978. **Player of Year:** Ian Roper.

WATFORD

The season started with the threat of administration hanging over the club and led to players and staff agreeing to a 12 percent deferral of wages. It ended with Watford reaching the semi-finals of the F.A. Cup – where they pushed Southampton all the way before losing 2-1 – and proceeding to a healthier financial position. Manager Ray Lewington had precious little scope to develop the squad – in sharp contrast to his predecessor Gianluca Vialli – but used his persuasive powers to good effect. The cup run took its toll on League results, nine matches without a win ending prospects of a play-off place before on-loan Michael Chopra scored four times in an amazing 7-4 result at Burnley.

Ardley, N .... 42(1)
Brown, W .... 12(1)
Chamberlain, A 42
Chopra, M .... 4(1)
Cook, L .... 3(1)
Cox, N 40
Doyley, L .... 21(1)
Dyche, S .... 23(1)
Fisken, G .... 3(1)
Fitzgerald, S .... 1(3)
Foley, D .... 6(9)
Gayle, M .... 30(1)
Glass, S .... 26(7)
Godfrey, E .... –(1)
Hand, J .... 20(3)
Helguson, H .... 28(2)
Hyde, M 37
Ifil, J 1
Johnson, R .... 5(7)
Lee, R 4
Mahon, G .... 13(5)
McNamee, A .... 1(21)
Nielsen, A .... 31(3)
Noel-Williams, G ...... 8(8)
Norville, J .... 6(6)
Pennant, J 12
Robinson, P 37
Smith, J .... –(1)
Smith, T .... 25(10)
Swonnell, S .... 1(1)
Vernazza, P .... 13(10)
Webber, D .... 11(1)

League goals (54): Helguson 11, Cox 9, Smith, T 7, Chopra 5, Hyde 4, Foley 3, Nielsen 3, Robinson 3, Ardley 2, Webber 2, Brown 1, Fitzgerald 1, Glass 1, Norville 1, Opponents 1.
F.A. Cup goals (7): Helguson 2, Smith, T 2, Gayle 1, Glass 1, Pennant 1. **Worthington Cup goals (1):** Foley 1.
Average home League attendance: 13,404. **Player of Year:** Marcus Gayle.

WIMBLEDON

Considering that fans voted with their feet when the move to Milton Keynes was confirmed – a record low 849 saw them play Rotherham – Wimbledon achieved a respectable tenth place in their final season at Selhurst Park. For those remaining diehards, there was no shortage of entertainment or goals. David Connolly and Neil Shipperley contributed 44 of the total of 76 scored, but almost as many went in at the other end and a run of three defeats in April against struggling opposition left them well adrift of the top six. The club went into administration in early June.

Agyemang, P .... 12(21)
Ainsworth, G .... 8(4)
Andersen, T .... 34(4)
Chorley, B .... 8(2)
Connolly, D 28
Darlington, J .... 32(3)
Davis, K 46
Francis, D .... 29(5)
Gier, R .... 27(2)
Gordon, M .... –(1)
Gray, W .... 12(18)
Hawkins, P 43
Holloway, D .... 14(2)
Kamara, M .... –(2)
Karlsson, P .... 2(1)
Leigertwood, M ...... 27(1)
Lewington, D .... –(1)
McAnuff, J .... 29(2)
Morgan, L .... 6(5)
Nowland, A .... 10(14)
Reo-Coker, N 32
Shipperley, N 46
Tapp, A .... 23(1)
Volz, M 10
Williams, M 23
Willmott, C 5

League goals (76): Connolly 24, Shipperley 20, Francis 6, Agyemang 5, McAnuff 4, Ainsworth 2, Darlington 2, Gray 2, Nowland 2, Reo-Coker 2, Tapp 2, Andersen 1, Morgan 1, Volz 1, Williams 1, Opponents 1.
F.A. Cup goals (3): McAnuff 1, Morgan 1, Shipperley 1. **Worthington Cup goals (8):** Shipperley 3, Agyemang 1, Andersen 1, Leighterwood 1, McAnuff 1, Tapp 1.
Average home League attendance: 2,786. **Player of Year:** Neil Shipperley.

WOLVERHAMPTON WANDERERS

A year on from missing out through a late season collapse, Wolves made their long-awaited return to the top flight with a storming finish. They cemented a top six place with just one defeat in the final 16 matches, came from behind to account for Reading in the semi-finals of the play-offs, then scored three times in the first half of the final to overwhelm Sheffield United Kenny Miller took the attacking honours, while Joleon Lescott played like a future England centre half. But few would have argued against pride of place going to manager Dave Jones after what he had been through – and benefactor Sir Jack Hayward for the millions he ploughed in to restoring the club's fortunes.

Andrews, K .... 2(7)
Blake, N .... 22(1)
Butler, P .... 31(1)
Cameron, C .... 29(4)
Clyde, M .... 15(2)
Cole, C .... 5(2)
Cooper, K .... 13(13)
Edworthy, M .... 18(4)
Ince, P .... 35(2)
Ingimarsson, I .... 10(3)
Irwin, D 43
Kennedy, M .... 30(1)
Lescott, J 44
Melligan, J .... –(2)
Miller, K .... 35(8)
Murray, M 40
Naylor, L .... 31(1)
Ndah, G .... 17(8)
Newton, S .... 29(4)
Oakes, M 6
Pollet, L 2
Proudlock, A .... 2(15)
Rae, A .... 30(8)
Sturridge, D .... 17(22)

Play-offs – Appearances: Blake 3, Butler 3, Cameron 3, Ince 3, Irwin 3, Kennedy 3, Lescott 3, Miller 3, Murray 3, Naylor 3, Newton 2(1), Ndah 1, Sturridge –(3), Cooper –(1), Pollet –(1), Proudlock – (1), Rae –(1).

League goals (81): Miller 19, Blake 12, Sturridge 11, Cameron 7, Ndah 7, Cooper 3, Kennedy 3, Newton 3, Rae 3, Ince 2, Ingimarsson 2, Irwin 2, Proudlock 2, Butler 1, Cole 1, Lescott 1, Naylor 1, Opponents 1. **Play-offs goals (6):** Blake 1, Kennedy 1, Miller 1, Naylor 1, Rae 1, Opponents 1.
F.A. Cup goals (10): Ndah 4, Miller 3, Ince 1, Kennedy 1, Proudlock 1. **Worthington Cup goals (7):** Rae 2, Blake 1, Miller 1, Newton 1, Pollet 1, Opponents 1.
Average home League attendance: 25,744. **Player of Year:** Joleon Lescott.

NATIONWIDE LEAGUE – SECOND DIVISION

BARNSLEY

Barnsley staved off what would have been a second successive relegation at the end of an eventful season on and off the field at Oakwell. The club went into adminstration in early October, sacked manager Steve Parkin after a 4-1 home defeat by Bristol City and were then taken over by a consortium headed by the town's Mayor, Peter Doyle. Under Glyn Hodges the team continued to find it hard going, a run of six matches without a win in the run-up to Easter threatening to prove costly. But they eked out single goal victories over Mansfield Town and Brentford to pull clear of the bottom four.

Austin, N .... 32(2)
Barrowclough, C .... –(5)
Bertos, L .... 2(4)
Betsy, K .... 32(7)
Crooks, L .... 10(8)
Curle, K 11
Donovan, K .... 20(2)
Dyer, B .... 39(1)
Fallon, R .... 18(8)
Flynn, M .... 13(1)
Ghent, M 7
Gibbs, P .... 23(3)
Gorre, D .... 18(9)
Hayward, S 6
Holt, A .... 4(3)
Jones, Gary 31
Jones, Griff .... –(2)
Kay, A .... 13(3)
Lumsdon, C .... 21(4)
Marriott, A 36
Morgan, C 36
Mulligan, D .... 30(3)
Neil, A .... 30(3)
O'Callaghan, B .... 12(2)
Rankin, I .... 1(7)
Sheron, M .... 28(6)
Taylor, M 3
Ward, M .... 22(4)
Williams, R .... 7(1)
Wroe, N 1

League goals (51): Dyer 17, Sheron 9, Fallon 7, Betsy 6, Lumsdon 3, Morgan 2, Bertos 1, Jones, Gary 1, Gibbs 1, Mulligan 1, O'Callaghan 1, Rankin 1, Opponents 1.
F.A. Cup goals (1): Dyer 1. **Worthington Cup goals (1):** Rankin 1. **LDV Vans Trophy goals:** None.
Average home League attendance: 9,757. **Player of Year:** Bruce Dyer.

BLACKPOOL

Blackpool's season tailed off after a mid-winter run suggested they could challenge for a play-off place. With John Murphy scoring regularly, they responded to a 4-0 defeat by Mansfield Town with a run of 11 unbeaten matches which yielded 23 points and lifted them to the fringe of the top six. But once the sequence was ended by a 2-1 defeat against Tranmere, Steve McMahon's side stared sliding back into mid-table and in fact failed to win any of their final dozen games.

Barnes, P 44
Blinkhorn, M .... 3(4)
Bullock, M .... 34(4)
Burns, J .... 4(3)
Clarke, C .... 13(5)
Clarke, P 16
Coid, D .... 31(5)
Collins, L .... 1(5)
Dalglish, P .... 20(7)
Evans, P 10
Flynn, M 21
Grayson, S .... 44(1)
Gulliver, P .... 2(1)
Hendry, C 14
Hills, J .... 20(7)
Hughes, I .... 12(5)
Jaszczun, T .... 15(6)
McMahon, S .... 3(3)
Milligan, J .... –(7)
Murphy, J .... 33(2)
O'Kane, J .... 8(6)
Richardson, L 20
Robinson, P .... 5(2)
Southern, K 38
Taylor, S .... 30(14)
Theoklitos, M 2
Thornley, B .... 7(5)
Thornton, S .... 1(2)
Walker, R .... 19(13)
Wellens, R .... 36(3)

League goals (56): Murphy 16, Taylor 13, Hills 5, Walker 4, Clarke, P 3, Grayson 3, Blinkhorn 2, Bullock 1, Clarke, C 1, Coid 1, Dalglish 1, Evans 1, Milligan 1, Robinson 1, Southern 1, Wellens 1, Opponents 1.
F.A. Cup goals (8): Murphy 2, Taylor 2, Dalglish 1, Hills 1, Opponents 2. **Worthington Cup goals:** None. **LDV Vans Trophy goals (3):** Milligan 1, Murphy 1, Taylor 1.

Average home League attendance: 6,990. **Player of Year:** Martin Bullock.

BRENTFORD

Wally Downes, promoted from first-team coach to manager after Steve Coppell resigned in the summer, enjoyed a successful start to the season with a run of seven unbeaten games. And at the turn of the year, Brentford were only a point off a place-off spot. They were unable to maintain that momentum, finishing below half-way, but managed a decent F.A. Cup run , beating Derby in the third round and then pushing Burnley all the way before conceding late goals in a 3-0 defeat which the First Division side scarcely deserved.

Anderson, I 9
Antoine-Curier, M 11
Blackman, L 1
Chorley, B 2
Constantine, L .... 2(15)
Dobson, M .... 45(1)
Evans, S .... 20(3)
Fieldwick, L .... 6(1)
Frampton, A .... 9(6)
Fullarton, J .... 22(5)
Hughes, S .... 2(1)
Hunt, S .... 41(1)
Hutchinson, E .... 21(2)
Julian, A 3
Lovett, J 1
Marshall, S .... 22(2)
McCammon, M .... 31(5)
O'Connor, K .... 44(1)
Peters, M .... 3(8)
Roget, L 14
Rowlands, M .... 13(5)
Smith, J .... 23(2)
Smith, P 43
Somner, M .... 39(1)
Sonko, I 37
Tabb, J .... 1(4)
Traynor, R .... –(2)
Vine, R .... 37(5)
Williams, M .... 4(18)

League goals (47): Vine 10, Hunt 7, McCammon 7, O'Connor 5, Sonko 5, Antoine-Curier 3, Evans 3, Dobson 1, Fullarton 1, Marshall 1, Peters 1, Rowlands 1, Somner 1, Williams 1.

F.A. Cup goals (7): Hunt 2, Vine 2, McCammon 1, O'Connor 1, Somner 1. **Worthington Cup goals (4):** O'Connor 2, Sonko 1, Vine 1. **LDV Vans Trophy goals (4):** Hunt 1, Marshall 1, McCammon 1, O'Connor 1,

Average home League attendance: 5,759. **Player of Year:** Paul Smith.

BRISTOL CITY

Bristol City lifted the LDV Vans Trophy with a 2-0 win over Carlisle, but were denied a return to the Millennium Stadium for the match that really mattered when losing in the semi-finals of the play-offs. They had twice beaten Cardiff and for more than 70 minutes of the first leg at Ninian Park were comfortably holding their own. Then Peter Thorne scored the only goal and his side protected the advantage in a goalless return leg to go through. Bristol had finished third in the table, boosted by a run of 14 games without defeat in the first half of the season. Scott Murray scored 27 goals in all competitions.

Amankwaah, K .... –(1)
Beadle, P .... 11(13)
Bell, M .... 37(1)
Brown, A .... 21(11)
Burnell, J .... 43(1)
Butler, P 38
Carey, L .... 21(3)
Clist, S .... –(3)
Coles, D .... 38(1)
Doherty, T 38
Fagan, C .... 5(1)
Fortune, C .... 7(3)
Hill, M .... 39(3)
Hulbert, R .... 2(5)
Lita, L .... –(15)
Matthews, L .... 3(4)
Millen, K 3
Murray, S 45
Peacock, L .... 33(4)
Phillips, S 46
Roberts, C .... 31(13)
Robins, M 6
Rosenior, L .... 2(19)
Tinnion, B .... 30(10)
Woodman, C .... 7(3)

Play-offs – Appearances: Burnell 2, Butler 2, Carey 2, Coles 2, Doherty 2, Hill 2, Murray 2, Peacock 2, Phillips 2, Roberts 2, Tinnion 1(1), Bell 1, Amankwaah – (1), Beadle –(1), Lita –(1), Rosenior –(1). **Play-offs goals:** None.

League goals (79): Murray 19, Roberts 13, Peacock 11, Tinnion 9, Beadle 4, Robins 4, Brown 3, Hill 3, Bell 2, Coles 2, Lita 2, Rosenior 2, Butler 1, Carey 1, Clist 1, Fagan 1, Matthews 1.

F.A. Cup goals (10): Murray 3, Roberts 3, Lita 2, Tinnion 1, Opponents 1. **Worthington Cup goals:** None. **LDV Vans Trophy goals (17):** Murray 5, Peacock 3, Bell 2, Burnell 1, Carey 1, Coles 1, Doherty 1, Roberts 1, Robins 1, Rosenior 1.

Average home League attendance: 11,890. **Player of Year:** Scott Murray.

CARDIFF CITY

Cardiff were left clinging to the final play-off place after failing to win any of their last five matches, but went on to claim the third promotion place on an emotional afternoon at the Millennium Stadium. Peter Thorne's header gave them the edge over Bristol City, who were unable to turn around the semi-final with home advantage. Then Andy Campell, substituting for top scorer Robert Earnshaw, scored an extra-time winner to overcome Q.P.R. in a match which looked to be heading for penalties. Although Earnshaw struggled along with his team during the run-in, he still broke the club's scoring record with 31 goals.

Ainsworth, G 9	Earnshaw, R .... 39(7)	Mahon, A .... 13(2)
Alexander, N 40	Fan Zhiyi 6	Margetson, M 6
Barker, C .... 32(8)	Fortune-West, L ...... 7(12)	Maxwell, L .... 5(11)
Boland, W .... 40(1)	Gabbidon, D .... 22(2)	Prior, S .... 35(2)
Bonner, M .... 7(7)	Gordon, G .... 3(7)	Thorne, P 46
Bowen, J .... 7(4)	Hamilton, D .... 2(4)	Weston, R 38
Campbell, A .... 10(18)	Jenkins, S 4	Whalley, G .... 17(2)
Collins, J .... –(2)	Kavanagh, G .... 42(2)	Young, S .... 11(1)
Croft, G .... 39(4)	Legg, A .... 26(9)	

Play-offs – Appearances: Alexander 3, Barker 3, Boland 3, Earnshaw 3, Gabbidon 3, Kavanagh 3, Legg 3, Prior 3, Thorne 3, Weston 3, Whalley 3, Bonner –(3), Campbell –(3), Croft –(2).
League goals (68): Earnshaw 31, Thorne 13, Kavanagh 5, Bowen 3, Campbell 3, Legg 3, Fortune-West 2, Gordon 2, Mahon 2, Weston 2, Croft 1, Young 1. **Play-offs goals (2):** Campbell 1, Thorne 1.
F.A. Cup goals (9): Campbell 2, Collins 2, Boland 1, Earnshaw 1, Fortune-West 1, Kavanagh 1, Thorne 1. **Worthington Cup goals (5):** Earnshaw 3, Thorne 1, Opponents 1.
LDV Vans Trophy goals (4): Bowen 1, Campbell 1, Fortune-West 1, Gordon 1.
Average home League attendance: 13,050. **Player of Year:** Robert Earnshaw.

CHELTENHAM TOWN

Much-travelled manager Bobby Gould was unable to save Cheltenham from an immediate return to Division Three after taking over when Graham Allner was sacked in mid-January after eight months in charge. Gould paid a club-record £50,000 for Grant McCann, who was prominent in a late season rally which offered some hope of survival. But while fellow strugglers Chesterfield gained a point on the final day of the season, Cheltenham hit the woodwork twice when losing at Notts County, a result which left them two points adrift.

Alsop, J .... 32(5)	Finnigan, J .... 34(3)	Naylor, A .... 19(11)
Bird, D .... 12(2)	Forsyth, R 12	Simpkins, M 2
Book, S 36	Griffin, A .... 8(3)	Spencer D .... 10(20)
Brayson, P .... 14(6)	Higgs, S 10	Strong, G .... 3(1)
Brough, J .... 21(8)	Howarth, N .... 26(1)	Victory, J 45
Brown, M .... 11(4)	Jones, S 5	Walker, R 15
Devaney, M .... 35(5)	McAuley, H .... 15(4)	Williams, L .... 6(7)
Duff, M 44	McCann, G 27	Yates, M .... 34(3)
Duff, S .... 15(3)	Milton, R .... 15(6)	

League goals (53): Alsop 10, Devaney 6, McCann 6, Naylor 6, Spencer 6, Brown 2, Forsyth 2, McAuley 2, Duff, M 2, Milton 2, Victory 2, Yates 2, Brayson 1, Brough 1, Finnigan1, Howarth 1, Opponents 1.
F.A. Cup goals (4): Alsop 1, Brayson 1, Devaney 1, Yates 1.
Worthington Cup goals (3); Naylor 2, McAuley 1. **LDV Vans Trophy goals (5):** Brayson 2, Alsop 1, Forsyth 1, McCann 1.
Average home League attendance: 4,655. **Player of Year:** Martin Devaney.

CHESTERFIELD

Chesterfield lost five successive games late in the season for the second successive season. The difference this time was that the defeats left them in danger of relegation and without a manager, Dave Rushbury resigning. But a 2-0 win over promotion-seeking Bristol City proved crucial and a point gained at Blackpool on the final day of the season, coupled to Cheltenham's defeat by Notts County, left them two points clear of the drop. Roy McFarland, whose last managerial job was with Torquay, was then named Rushbury's replacement.

Allott, M .... 24(9)	Ebdon, M 21 (3)	Payne, S 34
Blatherwick, S .... 30(1)	Edwards, R .... 25(3)	Reeves, D .... 36(4)
Booty, M .... 35(2)	Folan, C .... 9(4)	Richardson, L .... –(1)
Bradley, S .... 1(8)	Howard, J .... 1(8)	Richmond, A .... 6(1)
Brandon, C .... 35(1)	Howson, S .... 32(1)	Rowland, K .... –(3)
Burt, J .... 11(5)	Hudson, M .... 23(1)	Rushbury, A .... 23(7)
Close, B 8	Hurst, G .... 27(5)	Warne, S .... 2(1)
Davies, G .... 27(7)	Innes, M .... 5(5)	Wilkinson, S .... –(1)
Dawson, K 26	Muggleton, C 26	Williams, B 14
Douglas, J 7	O'Hare, A .... 18(4)	

League goals (43): Reeves 8, Brandon 7, Hurst 7, Ebdon 4, Hudson 3, Bradley 2, Edwards 2, Howson 2, Payne 2, Burt 1, Close 1, Davies 1, Dawson 1, Douglas 1, Folan 1.
F.A. Cup goals (1): Davies 1. **Worthington Cup goals (2):** Allott 1, Brandon 1. **LDV Vans Trophy goals (3):** Brandon 2, Allott 1.
Average home League attendance: 4,108. **Player of Year:** Chris Brandon.

COLCHESTER UNITED

A change of manager brought about a change of fortune for Colchester, who were sliding into trouble early in the New Year and had suffered their customary first round F.A. Cup defeat, this time by Chester City. Steve Whitton paid the price, former Reading midfielder Phil Parkinson came in with no managerial experience and guided the team out of trouble with a run of only one defeat in 11 matches. The run was ended by a 5-0 home defeat by Luton, followed by two more goalless games which left them 12th in the table.

Atangana, M .... 1(5)	Izzet, K 43	Opara, L .... –(5)
Baldwin, P .... 13(7)	Jackson, J 8	Pinault, T .... 32(10)
Bowry, R .... 33(2)	Johnson, G 8	Rapley, K .... 14(7)
Brown, S .... 26(1)	Keeble, C .... –(3)	Richards, J .... –(2)
Canham, M .... 2(1)	Keith, J 36	Steele, D .... 6(2)
Chilvers, L 6	May, B .... 4(2)	Stockley, S .... 31(2)
Coote, A .... 7(9)	McGleish, S .... 38(5)	Stockwell, M .... 30(9)
Duguid, K .... 26(1)	McKinney, R .... 20(1)	Warren, M 20
Edwards, M .... 3(2)	Morgan, D .... 22(15)	White, A 41
Fitzgerald, S 26	Odunsi, L .... 3(3)	Williams, G .... 6(2)
Halford, G 1		

League goals (52): Keith 9, Izzet 8, McGleish 8, Morgan 6, Williams 6, Pinault 4, Duguid 3, Rapley 2, Stockwell 2, Bowry 1, Stockley 1, Opponents 2.
F.A. Cup goals: None. **Worthington Cup goals:** None. **LDV Vans Trophy goals (1):** McGleish 1.
Average home League attendance: 3,386. **Player of Year:** Simon Brown.

CREWE ALEXANDRA

Dario Gradi's 20th season in charge at Gresty Road was marked by an immediate return to the First Division. Thanks largely to excellent form away from home, Crewe showed greater consistency than their rivals in a close-run thing for the second promotion spot behind runaway leaders Wigan. They won 14 times on their travels and scored more goals – 47 – than any team in the country. Rob Hulse had a particularly productive first half of the season during which 16 of his 22 goals were scored.

Ashton, D .... 24(14)	Jones, S .... 18(12)	Sodje, E .... 23(6)
Bankole, A .... 2(1)	Little, C .... 3(3)	Sorvel, N .... 39(4)
Bell, L .... 3(13)	Lunt, K 46	Tierney, P .... 14(3)
Brammer, D 41	McCready, C .... 6(2)	Tomlinson, S .... –(1)
Burton, S 1	Miles, J .... –(5)	Vaughan, D .... 28(4)
Edwards, P .... –(2)	Milosevic, D 1	Walker, R .... 31(5)
Foster, S 35	Oakes, S .... 3(4)	Walton, D .... 27(1)
Hulse, R .... 35(3)	Rix, B .... 17(6)	Wright, D 31
Ince, C 43	Robinson, J .... –(1)	White, A .... –(2)
Jack, R .... 35(3)		

League goals (76): Hulse 22, Ashton 9, Jack 9, Jones 9, Lunt 7, Foster 4, Sorvel 3, Vaughan 3, Walker 2, Bell 1, Brammer 1, Miles 1, Sodje 1, Tierney 1, Walton 1, Wright 1, Opponents 1.

F.A. Cup goals (6): Ashton 2, Brammer 1, Jones 1, Rix 1, Sodje 1. **Worthington Cup goals (4):** Jack 3, Hulse 1. **LDV Vans Trophy goals (16):** Ashton 5, Hulse 4, Jack 4, Jones 1, Lunt 1, Vaughan 1.

Average home League attendance: 6,760. **Player of Year:** Rob Hulse.

HUDDERSFIELD TOWN

A grim season ended in relegation for Huddersfield, who 12 months earlier had reached the play-offs. Manager Mick Wadsworth was sacked with seven matches remaining and the club went into administration a few days later when the players lodged a petition in the High Court. Caretaker Mel Machin raised hopes of beating the drop by supervising successive wins over Chesterfield and Swindon, but the improvement was not maintained and his team finished with fewer goals – 39 – than any side in the Nationwide League

Ashcroft, L 4	Holland, C .... 33(1)	Schofield, D .... 25(5)
Baldry, S .... 14(8)	Irons, K .... 29(6)	Scott, P .... 2(11)
Bevan, S 30	Jenkins, S 26	Senior, P .... 16(2)
Booth, A .... 32(1)	Labarthe, G .... –(3)	Sharp, K .... 38(1)
Brown, N .... 36(2)	Macari, P .... –(5)	Smith, M .... 35(3)
Clarke, N .... 2(1)	Mattis, D .... 27(6)	Stead, J .... 28(14)
Dyson, J .... 2(1)	McCombe, J .... –(1)	Thorrington, J ...... 16(15)
Gallacher, K .... 5(2)	McDonald, S .... 7(6)	Worthington, J ...... 10(12)
Gavin, J 10	Mirfin, D .... –(1)	Youds, E 25
Heary, T .... 14(6)	Moses, A 40	

League goals (39): Smith 17, Booth 6, Stead 6, Baldry 2, Schofield 2, Gavin 1, Irons 1, Mattis 1, McDonald 1, Moses 1, Thorrington 1.

F.A. Cup goals: None. **Worthington Cup goals (2):** Baldry 1, Opponents 1. **LDV Vans Trophy goals (1):** Mattis 1.

Average home League attendance: 9,506. **Player of Year:** Martin Smith.

LUTON TOWN

Promoted Luton could hardly have made a worse start, losing their first four games and conceding 13 goals. That record became one win in nine before a recovery took them into the top six by the end of the year. But despite another prolific season for Steve Howard, they were overtaken by Q.P.R. and finished well adrift of a play-off place, having failed to win enough matches at home. Howard, at least, enjoyed the run-in, scoring six times in four matches to bring his total to 22. Manager Joe Kinnear was later sacked by the club's new owners.

Bayliss, D .... 7(6)	Coyne, C .... 38(2)	Forbes, A .... 3(2)
Beckwith, R 4	Crowe, D .... 17(10)	Fotiadis, A .... 8(9)
Berthelin, C 9	Davis, S 34	Griffiths, C 3
Boyce, E .... 33(1)	Emberson, C .... 18(2)	Hillier, I .... 12(10)
Brkovic, A .... 29(7)	Foley, K .... –(2)	Hirschfeld, L 5

Holmes, P .... 8(9)	Mansell, L .... –(1)	Robinson, S .... 23(6)
Howard, S 41	Neilson, A .... 21(5)	Skelton, A .... 5(3)
Hughes, J .... 30(5)	Nicholls, K .... 35(1)	Spring, M 41
Igoe, S 2	Ovendale, M .... 5(1)	Thorpe, T .... 28(2)
Judge, M .... –(1)	Perrett, R .... 19(1)	Willmott, C .... 12(1)
Jupp, D .... 2(3)	Roberts, B 5	Winters, R 1
Kimble, A .... 8(4)		

League goals (67): Howard 22, Thorpe 13, Spring 6, Fotiadis 5, Nicholls 5, Brkovic 3, Hughes 3, Crowe 2, Perrett 2, Coyne 1, Forbes 1, Griffiths 1, Holmes 1, Robinson 1, Skelton 1.
F.A. Cup goals (4): Brkovic 2, Spring 1, Thorpe 1. **Worthington Cup goals (2):** Howard 1, Spring 1. **LDV Vans Trophy goals (7):** Brkovic 3, Thorpe 2, Deeney 1, Holmes 1.
Average home League attendance: 6,746.

MANSFIELD TOWN

Mansfield's season, awash with 163 goals in their 46 matches, ended in relegation after player-manager Keith Curle had made a bright start when taking over from Stuart Watkiss in early December. Curle began with three successive wins, brought in several new players and kept hopes alive until a damaging run of eight matches without a victory starting in mid-March, cast them adrift. They went straight back down, ironically, on the day their game against Tranmere was abandoned for safety reasons after a man climbed onto the roof of a stand at Prenton Park.

Bacon, D .... –(6)	Eaton, A 20	MacKenzie, N .... 16(8)
Baptiste, A 4	Gadsby, M .... 13(7)	Mendes, J 18
Beardsley, C .... 1(4)	Glover, E .... –(2)	Mitchell, C .... 3(12)
Buxton, J 3	Hankey, D .... –(1)	Moore, N 18
Christie, I .... 29(8)	Hassell, B .... 19(1)	Pilkington, K 32
Clark, P 4	Holyoak, D .... –(2)	Reddington, S .... 5(2)
Clarke, J .... 15(5)	Hurst, M 1	Sellars, S .... 12(2)
Corden, S .... 37(7)	Jervis, D .... 4(1)	Van Heusden, A 5
Curle, K .... 11(3)	Jones, A .... –(1)	Vaughan, A 4
Curtis, T 23	Larkin, C .... 13(9)	Welch, K 9
Day, R 23	Lawrence, L .... 40(3)	White, A .... 19(9)
Delaney, D 7	Lever, M 15	White, J .... –(1)
Disley, C .... 39(3)	Little, C 5	Williamson, L .... 28(12)
Doane, B 11		

League goals (66): Christie 18, Corden 13, Lawrence 10, Larkin 7, White, A 6, Disley 4, Sellars 2, Clarke 1, Day 1, MacKenzie 1, Mendes 1, Mitchell 1, Opponents 1.
F.A. Cup goals (4): Lawrence 2, Christie 1, Opponents 1. **Worthington Cup goals (1):** Moore 1. **LDV Vans Trophy goals:** None.
Average home League attendance: 4,887. **Player of Year:** Liam Lawrence.

NORTHAMPTON TOWN

A strong recovery in the second half of the season kept Northampton afloat the previous season. This time they won only three times after the turn of the year and finished bottom. Kevan Broadhurst was sacked as manager following a 5-0 home defeat by Wycombe, his successor Terry Fenwick lasted just seven weeks and Martin Wilkinson fared no better when he took charge until the end of the season. Scoring was a major problem, the team finishing goalless in 22 of their 46 games.

Abbey, N .... 4(1)	Forrester, J .... 18(7)	Harsley, P .... 41(4)
Asamoah, D .... 20(22)	Frain, J .... 13(1)	Hope, R .... 17(6)
Burgess, D .... 24(1)	Gabbiadini, M .... 33(8)	Johnson, R .... 5(1)
Carruthers, C .... 26(7)	Gill, J 41	Lincoln City, G .... 5(7)
Chambers, L .... –(1)	Hargreaves, C .... 36(3)	Marsh, C 15
Dudfield, L .... 8(2)	Harper, L 31	McGregor, P .... 17(6)

Morison, S .... 4(9)
One, A 6
Rahim, B 6
Reid, P 19
Rickers, P .... 8(3)
Sampson, I .... 31(2)
Spedding, D .... 9(2)
Stamp, D .... 12(10)
Thompson, G 11
Trollope, P 41
Turner, A .... –(3)
Youngs, T 5

League goals (40): Gabbiadini 12, Forrester 5, Asamoah 4, Stamp 4, Harsley 2, McGregor 2, Trollope 2, Burgess 1, Dudfield 1, Hope 1, Johnson 1, Morison 1, One 1, Rahim 1, Sampson 1, Opponents 1.
F.A. Cup goals (5): Asamoah 1, Gabbiadini 1, Hargreaves 1, Harsley 1, Stamp 1. **Worthington Cup goals:** None. **LDV Vans Trophy goals (6):** Forrester 2, Asamoah 1, Gabbiadini 1, Hargreaves 1, Rickers 1.
Average home League attendance: 5,210. **Player of Year:** Paul Harsley.

NOTTS COUNTY

Patchy League form and poor cup results meant a modest season for the Meadow Lane club, despite 24 goals from Mark Stallard, the division's fourth highest scorer. County won only one of their first ten games and were always struggling to make up ground. They went out in the first round of all three knock-out competitions, with an 4-2 defeat by Conference side Southport in the F.A. Cup particularly disappointing after Danny Allsopp had given them a 2-0 lead.

Allsopp, D .... 28(5)
Ashton, J 4
Baraclough, I .... 33(1)
Bolland, P .... 27(2)
Brough, M .... 26(5)
Cas, M .... 10(6)
Caskey, D .... 33(6)
Deeney, S 7
Fenton, N 40
Francis, W .... 2(8)
Garden, S 18
Hackworth, T .... 4(5)
Harrad, S .... –(5)
Heffernan, P .... 25(11)
Holmes, R .... 2(2)
Ireland, C .... 35(2)
Jupp, D .... 6(2)
Liburd, R .... 26(6)
McCarthy, P 6
Mildenhall, S 21
Nicholson, K .... 34(3)
Ramsden, S .... 21(11)
Richardson, I .... 30(4)
Riley, P .... 2(1)
Stallard, M .... 43(2)
Stone, D .... 11(4)
Whitley, J 13

League goals (62): Stallard 24, Allsopp 10, Heffernan 10, Bolland 3, Caskey 3, Fenton 3, Baraclough 2, Cas 2, Liburd 2, Brough 1, Ireland 1, Richardson 1.
F.A. Cup goals (2): Allsopp 2. **Worthington Cup goals (2):** Heffernan 1, Stallard 1. **LDV Vans Trophy goals (2):** Bolland 1, Richardson 1.
Average home League attendance: 6,154. **Player of Year:** Mark Stallard.

OLDHAM ATHLETIC

Iain Dowie's side took four points from Q.P.R. during the season, but when the sides met in the semi-finals of the play-offs it was Rangers who had the edge. Oldham were held at Boundary Park after David Eyres gave them a half-time lead and lost the return to a goal eight minutes from the end after having Wayne Andrews sent off. They had finished a solid fifth in the table, an improvement of four places on the previous season, and reached the fourth round of the Worthington Cup after notable away wins over West Ham and Derby.

Andrews, W .... 28(8)
Appleby, M .... 11(1)
Armstrong, C 33
Baudet, J .... 21(3)
Beharall, D .... 30(2)
Boshell, D 2
Burgess, B .... 6(1)
Carss, A .... 16(10)
Clegg, M .... 7(1)
Corazzin, G .... 21(18)
Da Silva, L .... 1(6)
Duxbury, L .... 16(17)
Eyre, J .... 27(3)
Eyres, D .... 40(1)
Haining, W .... 25(1)
Hall, D .... –(2)
Hall, F 40
Hill, C 17
Holden, D .... 2(4)
Killen, C .... 11(16)
Low, J .... 19(2)
Miskelly, D .... 9(2)
Murray, P .... 29(1)
Pogliacomi, L 37
Sheridan, D .... 29(5)
Sheridan, J .... 3(1)
Vernon, S .... 2(5)
Wijnhard, C .... 24(1)

Play-offs – Appearances: Andrews 2, Armstrong 2, Eyre 2, Eyres 2, Haining 2, Hall, F 2, Low 2, Murray 2, Sheridan, D 2, Hill 1, Miskelly 1, Pogliacomi 1, Wijnhard 1, Carss –(2), Corazzin –(2), Duxbury –(1).

League goals (68): Eyres 13, Andrews 11, Wijnhard 10, Corazzin 4, Duxbury 4, Hall, F 4, Killen 3, Low 3, Baudet 2, Carss 2, Eyre 2, Haining 2, Holding 2, Armstrong 1, Da Silva 1, Sheridan, D 1, Hill 1, Murray 1, Vernon 1. **Play-offs goals (1):** Eyres 1.
F.A. Cup goals (5): Eyres 1, Haining 1, Hall, F 1, Low 1, Wijnhard 1. **Worthington Cup goals (6):** Wijnhard 2, Carss 1, Corrazin 1, Eyres 1, Killen 1. **LDV Vans Trophy goals (3):** Vernon 2, Andrews 1.
Average home League attendance: 6,699. **Player of Year:** Leslie Pogliacomi

PETERBOROUGH UNITED

A home defeat by Wycombe in mid-March left Peterborough on the brink of the bottom four and facing a fight for survival. They responded to the challenge with a 5-1 victory at Mansfield which provided the spark for an impressive rise into the top half of the table by the end of the season. Barry Fry's team were unbeaten in their final nine games, collecting 19 points, and earned Fry the Manager of the Month award for April.

Allen, B .... 10(1)
Arber, M .... 24(1)
Boucaud, A .... 5(1)
Bullard, J 26
Burton, S .... 28(3)
Clarke, A .... 41(4)
Clarke, L .... –(1)
Connor, D 4
Danielsson, H .... 15(3)
Edwards, A 23
Farrell, D .... 21(16)
Fenn, N .... 8(6)
Forsyth, R .... 6(2)
Fotiadis, A .... 6(5)
Gill, M 41
Green, F .... 8(11)
Harrison, L 12
Hendon, I 7
Hyde, G .... 8(1)
Jelleyman, G .... 30(2)
Joseph, M .... 16(1)
Lee, J .... 12(13)
MacDonald, G .... 5(3)
McGovern, B 1
McKenzie, L .... 6(5)
Murphy, B 1
Newton, A .... 31(5)
Pearce, D 2
Rea, S .... 35(2)
Scott, R .... 13(3)
Scully, A .... –(3)
Semple, R .... 1(2)
Shields, T .... 29(4)
St Ledger, S .... –(1)
Strachan, G .... 1(1)
Tyler, M 29
Willis, R .... 1(3)

League goals (51): Clarke, A 16, McKenzie 5, Allen 3, Bullard 3, Farrell 3, Lee 3, Rea 3, Arber 2, Fotiadis 2, Green 2, Newton 2, Edwards 1, Fenn 1, Gill 1, Hendon 1, Scott 1, Shields 1, Opponents 1.
F.A. Cup goals (2): Clarke, A 1, Fenn 1. **Worthington Cup goals:** None. **LDV Vans Trophy goals (2):** Clarke, A 2.
Average home League attendance: 4,950. **Player of Year:** Andy Clarke.

PLYMOUTH ARGYLE

A season of consolidation for promoted Plymouth, who won four of their opening five matches and always looked capable of a healthy top-half finish, even if a play-off position proved out of reach. Their biggest win, 6-1 over Peterborough, also marked the start of a prolific run by Marino Keith who had previously spent much of the time on the bench. Keith scored eight goals in as many games, one of them enabled Plymouth to become one of the few teams to defeat runaway leaders Wigan.

Adams, S .... 36(1)
Aljofree, H 19
Barras, A 4
Bent, J .... 23(2)
Beresford, D .... 6(10)
Bernard, P .... 7(3)
Broad, J .... 1(4)
Capaldi, T 1
Connolly, P 2
Coughlan, G 42
Evans, M .... 35(7)
Friio, D .... 33(3)
Hodges, L .... 38(1)
Keith, M .... 20(17)
Larrieu, R 43
Lopes, O .... 4(5)
Lowndes, N .... 6(10)
Malcolm, S 3
McAnespie, K .... 2(2)
McCormick, L .... 2(1)
McGlinchey, B .... 11(8)
Milosevic, D 1
Norris, D .... 29(4)
Phillips, M .... 14(10)
Smith, G .... 4(1)
Stonebridge, I .... 30(7)
Sturrock, B .... 5(15)
Taylor, C 1
Worrell, D 43
Wotton, P .... 41(2)

League goals (63): Keith 11, Wotton 8, Friio 6, Norris 6, Coughlan 5, Stonebridge 5, Evans 4, Adams 2, Hodges 2, Lowndes 2, Phillips 2, Aljofree 1, Bent 1, McGlinchey 1, Smith 1, Sturrock 1, Opponents 5.

F.A. Cup goals (8): Wotton 3, Stonebridge 2, Evans 1, Friio 1, Opponents 1. **Worthington Cup goals (1):** Sturrock 1. **LDV Vans Trophy goals (2):** Evans 1, Keith 1.
Average home League attendance: 8,980. **Player of Year:** Paul Wotton.

PORT VALE

Port Vale began with four successive defeats and continued with five straight victories. It was that sort of season on the field for a club whose problems off it led to administration in mid-December, with assistant manager Mark Grew among the casualties. Although winning enough games to avoid being sucked into trouble, Vale were looking over their shoulder during the run-in and were thankful for three victories in April, rounded off by a 5-1 success against Huddersfield in their final home game.

Angell, B	13(2)	Burns, L	14(2)	Goodlad, M	36(1)
Armstrong, I	20(9)	Byrne, P	6(2)	Ingram, R	3(1)
Ashcroft, L	3	Carragher, M	34(1)	Littlejohn, A	12(1)
Birchall, C	–(2)	Charnock, P	14(4)	McCarthy, J	5(3)
Boyd, M	19(1)	Clarke, P	13	McClare, S	9(8)
Bridge-Wilkinson, M	29(2)	Collins, S	44	McPhee, S	35(5)
Brightwell, I	34(1)	Cummins, M	29(1)	Paynter, B	16(15)
Brisco, N	23(1)	Delaney, D	10	Reid, L	–(1)
Brooker, S	21(5)	Durnin, J	25(3)	Rowland, S	22(3)
Brown, R	–(1)	Eldershaw, S	–(2)	Walsh, M	17

League goals (54): Bridge-Wilkinson 9, Armstrong 7, Angell 5, Brooker 5, Collins 5, Paynter 5, Cummins 4, Boyd 3, Littlejohn 3, McPhee 3, Brisco 1, Charnock 1, Clarke 1, Durnin 1, Walsh 1.
F.A. Cup goals: None. **Worthington Cup goals:** None. **LDV Vans Trophy goals (5):** Angell 2, Armstrong 1, Boyd 1, Carragher 1.
Average home League attendance: 4,436. **Player of Year:** Sam Collins.

QUEENS PARK RANGERS

Rangers built up a head of steam in the second half of the season after a lean run of nine matches without a win, accompanied by an embarrassing F.A. Cup first round defeat by Vauxhall Motors in a replay at Loftus Road which went to penalties. Paul Furlong began to find his scoring touch after a difficult spell and just one defeat – by Wigan – in the final 12 games secured fourth place. Oldham Athletic were overcome in the play-offs, but hopes of a return to the First Division were ended by an extra-time Andy Campbell goal for Cardiff in a tense, tight final which could have gone either way.

Angell, B	8(5)	Doudou	3(7)	Padula, G	17(4)
Bean, M	4(3)	Forbes, T	38	Palmer, S	46
Bircham, M	34(2)	Furlong, P	27(6)	Plummer, C	–(2)
Burgess, O	2(3)	Gallen, K	41(1)	Rose, M	25(3)
Carlisle Utd., C	34(2)	Griffiths, L	3(3)	Royce, S	16
Connolly, K	12(4)	Kelly, S	7	Shittu, D	43
Cook, L	13	Langley, R	38(1)	Thomas, J	5(1)
Culkin, N	17	McLeod, K	8	Thomson, A	7(14)
Daly, W	3(3)	Murphy, D	4(7)	Walshe, B	1
Day, C	12	Oli, D	8(10)	Williams, T	22(4)
Digby, F	1(2)	Pacquette, R	4(7)	Willock, C	3

Play-offs – Appearances: Bircham 3, Day 3, Furlong 3, Gallen 3, McLeod 3, Palmer 3, Shittu 3, Carlisle Utd. 2, Kelly 2, Padula 2, Pacquette 1(2), Williams 1(2), Thomson 1(1), Langley 1, Forbes 1, Rose 1.
League goals (69): Furlong 13, Gallen 13, Langley 9, Shittu 7, Connolly 4, Pacquette 4, Thomson 3, Bircham 2, Carlisle Utd. 2, McLeod 2, Rose 2, Thomas 2, Cook 1, Padula 1, Palmer 1, Williams 1, Opponents 2. **Play-offs goals (2):** Furlong 1, Langley 1.

F.A. Cup goals (1): Thomson 1. **Worthington Cup goals (2):** Gallen 1, Thomson 1. LDV Vans **Trophy goals:** None.
Average home League attendance: 13,206. **Player of Year:** Kevin Gallen.

STOCKPORT COUNTY

Only Cardiff's Robert Earnshaw scored more goals than Luke Beckett as Stockport set about regrouping after relegation. Beckett finished with 27 to his credit, including a hat-trick in their biggest win of the season – 4-0 against Northampton. Beckett's goals ensured his team stayed clear of trouble, but County also conceded plenty and the failure to beat any of the top seven sides meant that the outcome was always likely to be a place below mid-table.

Beckett, L .... 41(1)	Gibb, A .... 43(2)	Pemberton, M .... 15(5)
Blayney, A 2	Goodwin, J .... 22(11)	Ross, N .... 1(3)
Briggs, K .... 13(6)	Greer, G .... 4(1)	Spencer, J 1
Burgess, B .... 17(2)	Hardiker, J .... 19(4)	Thomas, A .... 1(1)
Challinor, D 46	Jones, B 1	Tidman, O 18
Clare, R .... 31(5)	Jones, L 24	Tonkin, A .... 23(1)
Clark, P 21	Lambert, R .... 22(7)	Welsh, A .... 7(6)
Daly, J .... 25(10)	Lescott, A .... 36(5)	Wilbraham, A .... 8(7)
Ellison, K .... 17(6)	McLachlan, F .... 18(4)	Wild, P .... –(3)
Fradin, K .... 8(1)	Palmer, C 22	Williams, C .... –(1)

League goals (65): Beckett 27, Daly 7, Wilbraham 7, Burgess 4, Goodwin 3, Lambert 2, Welsh 2, Briggs 1, Challinor 1, Clark 1, Ellison 1, Gibb 1, Greer 1, Lescott 1, Palmer 1, Ross 1, Wild 1, Opponents 3.
F.A. Cup goals (4): Burgess 2, Beckett 1, Fradin 1. **Worthington Cup goals (4):** Beckett 1, Clare 1, Daly 1, Palmer 1. **LDV Vans Trophy goals (1):** Briggs.
Average home League attendance: 5,488. **Player of Year:** Luke Beckelt

SWINDON TOWN

Sam Parkin, a young striker from Chelsea, scored three times on the opening day of the season against Barnsley and was still going strong at the end of it. Along the way was a second hat-trick in his side's biggest win of the campaign – 5-0 against Notts County – and Parkin finished with 25 to his credit, third best in the division behind Robert Earnshaw and Luke Beckett. Swindon also hit five against Stockport after recovering from six successive defeats early on, and they went on to finish tenth.

Bampton, D .... –(3)	Gurney, A 41	Nightingale, L .... 2(1)
Beswetherick, J 3	Herring, I .... 2(2)	Parkin, S .... 41(2)
Davis, J .... 10(3)	Hewlett, M .... 39(1)	Reeves, A .... 35(1)
Duke, D 44	Heywood, M 46	Robinson, S .... 42(2)
Dykes, D .... 1(1)	Ifil, J .... 5(4)	Sabin, E .... 27(12)
Edds, G .... 8(6)	Invincible, D .... 37(5)	Sutton, J .... –(1)
Edwards, N .... –(3)	Jackson, J .... 12(1)	Taylor, C .... –(4)
Farr, C 2	Lewis, J 9	Willis, A .... 9(6)
Garrard, L .... –(1)	Marney, D .... 8(1)	Young, A .... –(11)
Griemink, B 44	Miglioranzi, S .... 39(2)	

League goals (59): Parkin 25, Gurney 8, Invincible 7, Sabin 4, Miglioranzi 3, Reeves 3, Davis 2, Duke 2, Robinson 2, Hewlett 1, Heywood 1, Jackson 1.
F.A. Cup goals (1): Gurney 1. **Worthington Cup goals (1):** Willis 1. **LDV Vans Trophy goals (8):** Invincible 2, Davis 1, Heywood 1, Jackson 1, Miglioranzi 1, Parkin 1, Young 1.
Average home League attendance: 5,440. **Player of Year:** Sam Parkin.

TRANMERE ROVERS

Tranmere, who sacked manager Dave Watson a week before the season started when losing 7-0 to Birmingham in pre-season friendly, were always playing catch-up after losing eight of the first 15 games under his successor, Ray Mathias. The club's former defensive stalwart eventually introduced some consistency and his team went on to put together a 15-match unbeaten run stretching from mid-February to the end of the season. But it was not quite enough to take them into the play-offs, Cardiff finishing a point ahead in sixth place.

Achterberg, J 38	Hinds, R .... 6(2)	Nixon, E .... –(2)
Allen, G .... 40(1)	Howarth, R .... 2(1)	Olsen, J .... 1(2)
Anderson, I 7	Hume, I .... 22(13)	Parkinson, A .... 1(9)
Barlow, S .... 19(10)	Jackson, M 6	Price, J .... 14(11)
Connelly, S 33	Jones, G 40	Proudlock, A 5
Curtis, T 8	Koumas, J 4	Roberts, G .... 34(3)
Edwards, C 12	Loran, T .... 16(1)	Robinson, M .... 1(5)
Feuer, A 2	McGibbon, P 4	Sharps, I 30
Gray, K .... 9(1)	Mellon, M .... 29(5)	Taylor, R .... 18(7)
Harrison, D .... 7(5)	Navarro, A 5	Welch, K 2
Haworth, S 42	Nicholson, S .... 36(2)	Whitehead, P 2
Hay, A .... 11(8)		

League goals (66): Haworth 20, Jones 7, Hume 6, Nicholson 4, Price 4, Allen 3, Barlow 3, Hay 3, Roberts 3, Sharps 3, Anderson 2, Koumas 2, Gray 1, Mellon 1, Robinson 1, Taylor 1, Opponents 2.

F.A. Cup goals (3): Barlow 1, Haworth 1, Mellon 1. **Worthington Cup goals (3):** Allen 1, Haworth 1, Taylor 1. **LDV Vans Trophy goals (7):** Barlow 2, Jones 2, Harrison 1, Roberts 1, Taylor 1,

Average home League attendance: 7,876. **Player of Year:** Simon Haworth.

WIGAN ATHLETIC

Paul Jewell's side dominated the division from start to finish, crowning their championship win by reaching 100 points on the last day of the season by beating Barnsley. On the way, they won 11 successive games starting in early November. Their away record was particularly impressive, with 15 victories and only nine goals conceded. On top of that, Wigan knocked out W.B.A., Manchester City and Fulham before losing to Blackburn in the quarter-finals of the Worthington Cup. The one disappointment was that home crowds did not average much above the 7,000 mark.

Baines, L 6	Ellington, N .... 41(1)	Liddell, A .... 32(5)
Brannan, G 6	Filan, J 46	McCulloch, L .... 33(5)
Breckin, I .... 7(2)	Flynn, M .... 3(13)	McMillan, S .... 28(4)
Bullard, J 17	Green, S .... 14(3)	Mitchell, P .... 13(14)
De Vos, J 43	Jackson, M 45	Roberts, N .... 25(12)
Dinning, A .... 36(2)	Jarrett, J .... 25(10)	Teale, G .... 28(9)
Eaden, N 37	Kennedy, P .... 21(1)	

League goals (68): Liddell 16, Ellington 15, De Vos 8, Dinning 7, McCulloch 6, Roberts 6, Green 2, Teale 2, Bullard 1, Flynn 1, Jackson 1, Kennedy 1, Opponents 2.

F.A. Cup goals (4): Ellington 2, Flynn 1, Green 1. **Worthington Cup goals (7):** Ellington 5, Jarrett 1, Roberts 1. **LDV Vans Trophy goals (3):** Teale 2, Jarrett 1.

Average home League attendance: 7,287. **Player of Year:** Jason De Vos.

WYCOMBE WANDERERS

Another modest League season for Wycombe, who, for once, could not turn to the F.A. Cup for a measure of success after losing 4-2 at home to Brentford in the first round. They never threatened the play-offs and were thankful to have enough points in the bank to offset a poor finish to the campaign. There were successive four-goal defeats by Chesterfield, Stockport and Cardiff during a run of eight matches without a win. A 4-1 victory over Q.P.R. and a 5-0 success at Northampton were among the pick of their results.

Anderson, I 5	Bulman, D 42	Currie, D .... 23(15)
Brown, S .... 33(4)	Cook, L .... 4(13)	Devine, S .... 13(5)

Dixon, J .... 14(8)
Faulconbridge, C .... 29(5)
Harris, R .... 5(17)
Holligan, G .... 1(9)
Johnson, R .... 26(7)
Lee, M .... 2(4)
McCarthy, P .... 22(2)
McSporran, J .... 6(3)
Oliver, L .... –(2)
Rammell, A .... 17(4)
Roberts, S .... 14(14)
Rogers, M .... 31(5)
Ryan, K .... 33(3)
Senda, D .... 39(2)
Simpemba, I .... –(1)
Simpson, M 42
Talia, F 35
Taylor, M 11
Thomson, A .... 34(2)
Vinnicombe, C 25

League goals (59): Faulconbridge 6, Brown 5, Devine 5, Dixon 5, Harris 5, Simpson 5, Currie 4, Rammell 4, Roberts 4, Bulman 3, Johnson 3, Holligan 2, Ryan 2, Senda 2, McCarthy 1, McSporran 1, Rogers 1, Thomson 1.
F.A. Cup goals (2): Brown 1, Rammell 1. **Worthington Cup goals (3):** McCarthy 2, Harris 1. **LDV Vans Trophy goals (6):** Devine 3, Bulman 1, Cook 1, Rogers 1.
Average home League attendance: 6,002. **Player of Year:** Michael Simpson.

NATIONWIDE LEAGUE – THIRD DIVISION

BOSTON UNITED

Boston's Conference championship successs turned sour when they were deducted four points and fined £100,000 for contract irregularities by the F.A. Manager Steve Evans, banned and fined along with chairman Pat Malkinson, resigned and his replacement Neil Thompson faced an uphill struggle. But they were boosted by the arrival of Richard Logan, who scored six times in his first five full appearances after being released by Ipswich, and some improved form at home. Veteran Neil Redfearn also played an important role and successive wins over Shrewsbury, Southend and Macclesfield over the Easter period took them clear of trouble.

Angel, M .... 24(7)
Balmer, S 21
Bastock, P 46
Battersby, A .... 7(4)
Beeves, L .... –(1)
Bennett, T .... 29(4)
Burton, S .... 6(2)
Chapman, B 37
Clare, D 7
Clifford, M .... 5(2)
Cook, J .... 6(10)
Costello, P .... 13(5)
Douglas, S .... 14(15)
Duffield, P .... 12(4)
Elding, A .... 3(5)
Ellender, P .... 25(1)
George, L .... 1(2)
Gould, J .... 10(10)
Greaves, M .... 24(2)
Higgins, A 13
Hocking, M .... 44(1)
Jones, G .... 2(1)
Lodge, A .... 1(1)
Logan, R .... 26(1)
McCarthy, P .... 11(1)
Monington, M 1
Morley, B .... 1(1)
Redfearn, N .... 27(4)
Rodwell, J .... 2(1)
Rusk, S .... 12(6)
Thompson, L .... 12(3)
Thompson, N 3
Town, D .... –(8)
Warburton, R 16
Weatherstone, R .... 2(6)
Weatherstone, S ..... 43(2)

League goals (55): Logan 10, Douglas 7, Redfearn 6, Weatherstone, S 6, Angel 5, Duffield 4, Thompson, L 4, Cook 2, Gould 2, Rusk 2, Battersby 1, Clare 1, Greaves 1, Hocking 1, Jones 1, Opponents 2.
F.A. Cup goals (2): Battersby 1, Higgins 1. **Worthington Cup goals (3):** Burton 1, Ellender 1, Weatherstone, S 1. **LDV Vans Trophy goals (5):** Thompson, L 2, Angel 1, Battersby 1, Weatherstone, S 1.
Average home League attendance: 3,048. **Player of Year:** Paul Bastock.

BOURNEMOUTH

Relegated Bournemouth kept faith with manager Sean O'Driscoll and were rewarded with a handsome finish to the season which took them straight back up. Carl Fletcher, converted by O'Driscoll from midfield into a central defender, scored twice and Stephen Purches rounded off a move which would have graced any level of football in a 5-2 win over a Lincoln side with the meanest defence in the division. It was the first time a team had scored five in a Play-off Final. Bournemouth had climbed to fourth in the table after failing to win any of their first five matches. They also reached the fourth round of the F.A. Cup.

Ashdown, J 2
Blayney, A 2
Broadhurst, K .... 20(1)

Browning, M .... 40(3)	Foyewa, A .... –(1)	Purches, J 2
Buxton, L .... 15(2)	Gulliver, P .... 4(2)	Purches, S .... 41(1)
Connell, A .... 10(3)	Hayter, J .... 35(10)	Ridgewell, L .... 2(3)
Cummings, W 20	Holmes, D .... 11(18)	Stewart, G .... –(1)
Elliott, W .... 39(5)	Maher, S .... 7(1)	Stock, B .... 14(13)
Eribenne, C .... –(6)	McDonald, S .... 3(4)	Tardif, C 9
Feeney, W .... 11(10)	Moss, N 33	Thomas, D .... 30(7)
Fletcher, C 42	Narada, B .... 3(4)	Tindall, J .... 24(3)
Fletcher, S .... 29(6)	O'Connor, G .... 29(12)	Young, N .... 29(3)

Play-offs – Appearances: Cummings 3, Elliott 3, Fletcher, C 3, Fletcher, S 3, Gulliver 3, Hayter 3, Moss 3, Purches, S 3, Young 3, O'Connor 2(1), Browning 2, Stock 1(2), Thomas 1(1), Holmes –(2), McDonald –(1).
League goals (60): Hayter 8, O'Connor 8, Feeney 7, Connell 6, Fletcher, S 6, Elliott 4, Holmes 3, Purches, S 3, Maher 2, Stock 2, Thomas 2, Broadhurst 1, Browning 1, Fletcher, C 1, McDonald 1, Tindall 1, Opponents 4. **Play-offs goals (8):** Fletcher, C 2, Hayter 2, O'Connor 2, Fletcher, S 1, Purches, S 1.
F.A. Cup goals (8): Fletcher, S 2, Broadhurst 1, Browning 1, Elliott 1, Hayter 1, Holmes 1, Thomas 1. **Worthington Cup goals (3):** Thomas 2, Connell 1. **LDV Vans Trophy goals (7):** Hayter 2, Elliott 1, Feeney 1, Fletcher, C 1, Fletcher, S 1, Purches, S 1
Average home League attendance: 5,828. **Player of Year:** Carl Fletcher.

BRISTOL ROVERS

The prospect of Conference football was beginning to loom large until 36-year-old Andy Rammell transformed Rovers' fortunes over the Easter period. Rammell, signed from Wycombe, had nothing to show from his first three matches, all of which Rovers lost against promotion-seeking opposition. Then the much-travelled striker scored twice in a 3-1 win over Cambridge. Two days later he netted the only goal of the game at Oxford and was on the mark again in a 2-1 victory over Darlington, sealed by Wayne Carlisle's late free-kick, which ensured survival.

Allen, B .... 5(3)	Coote, A .... 4(1)	McKeever, M .... 7(9)
Anderson, I 14	Di Piedi, M .... 3(2)	Parker, S .... 13(2)
Arndale, N 1	Gall, K .... –(9)	Plummer, C 2
Astafjevs, V .... 26(7)	Gilroy, D .... 3(8)	Quinn, R 44
Austin, K .... 31(2)	Grazioli, G .... 28(6)	Rammell, A 7
Barrett, A 45	Hodges, L .... 7(1)	Richards, J .... –(8)
Boxall, D .... 35(4)	Hogg, L .... 8(9)	Rose, R 9
Bryant, S .... 14(8)	Howie, S 44	Street, K .... 13(7)
Carlisle, W .... 35(6)	Hyde, G 21	Tait, P .... 33(8)
Challis, T 16	Lee, D 5	Uddin, A .... 17(1)
Clarke, R 2	Llewellyn, C 14	Warren, C .... –(2)

League goals (50): Grazioli 11, Astafjevs 8, Carlisle 7, Tait 7, Rammell 4, Llewellyn 3, Quinn 2, Barrett 1, Bryant 1, Coote 1, Hyde 1, Street 1, Uddin 1, Opponents 1.
F.A. Cup goals (6): Allen 1, Barrett 1, Carlisle 1, Gilroy 1, Grazioli 1, Tait 1. **Worthington Cup goals:** None. **LDV Vans Trophy goals:** None.
Average home League attendance: 6,934. **Player of Year:** Vitalijs Astafjevs.

BURY

Although not among the fancied teams, relegated Bury made a determined effort to return to Division Two at the first attempt. Apart from a difficult fortnight in March when failing to score in four successive matches, they always looked capable of a play-off place and secured it with a 2-1 win at Southend, thus avoiding any last-day worries. But Bournemouth proved too strong in the semi-final, with a goalless draw at Gigg Lane followed by a 3-1 win in the return. Bury also showed their paces in the Worthington Cup, beating Stoke and then overcoming Bolton at The Reebok before losing to Fulham.

Abbott, P 17	Barrass, M 16	Billy, C .... 33(4)

Clegg, G .... 28(3)	Johnrose, L .... 5(1)	Redmond, S .... 26(1)
Connell, L .... 13(1)	Lawson, I .... 3(4)	Seddon, G .... 2(2)
Cramb, C .... 17(1)	Nelson, M .... 38(1)	Stuart, J .... 32(5)
Dunfield, T .... 28(1)	Newby, J 46	Swailes, D .... 38(1)
Forrest, M .... 22(7)	Nugent, D .... 11(20)	Unsworth, L .... 34(1)
Garner, G 46	O'Shaughnessy, P ... 6(10)	Whaley, S .... –(2)
George, L .... 3(5)	Porter, C .... –(2)	Woodthorpe, C .... 30(2)
Hill, N .... 1(2)	Preece, A .... 11(18)	

Play-offs – Appearances: Billy 2, Clegg 2, Connell 2, Cramb 2, Newby 2, Forrest 2, Garner 2, Nelson 2, Redmond 2, Woodthorpe 2, Swailes 1(1), Stuart 1, Nugent –(2), Preece –(2).
League goals (57): Newby 10, Abbott 6, Clegg 5, Nelson 5, Billy 4, Nugent 4, Preece 4, Cramb 3, Lawson 3, Swailes 3, Connell 2, Dunfield 2, Redmond 2, Unsworth 2, Forrest 1, George 1. **Play-offs goals (1):** Preece 1.
F.A. Cup goals: None. **Worthington Cup goals (3):** Newby 1, Stuart 1, Opponents 1. **LDV Vans Trophy goals (6):** Clegg 1, Dunfield 1, Lawson 1, Newby 1, Nugent 1, Woodthorpe 1,
Average home League attendance: 3,226. **Player of Year:** Michael Nelson.

CAMBRIDGE UNITED

No team in the division played more times than Cambridge, whose 60-match schedule involved three F.A. Cup replays and progress to the Southern Final of the LDV Vans Trophy where they lost to eventual winners Bristol City. At the half-way point of the League programme, they were established in the top six, but failed to maintain the momentum, and when a big finish was needed to bring them back into contention the final seven games yielded just one win. Dave Kitson finished with 25 goals in all competitions.

Angus, S 40	Iriekpen, E 13	Riza, O .... 43(3)
Brennan, M 1	Jordan, S 11	Scully, A .... 1(5)
Bridges, D .... 6(11)	Kitson, D 44	Tann, A .... 21(4)
Chillingworth, D ... 11(19)	Marshall, S 45	Theobald, D .... 1(3)
Duncan, A .... 21(2)	Murray, F .... 25(4)	Tudor, S .... 26(1)
Fleming, T .... 42(1)	Nacca, F .... 9(8)	Turner, J .... –(2)
Goodhind, W .... 34(3)	Newey, T 6	Wanless, P .... 27(12)
Guttridge, L .... 39(4)	Opara, L .... –(2)	Warner, P .... 7(1)
Heathcote, J 2	Revell, A .... –(9)	Youngs, T .... 31(4)

League goals (67): Kitson 20, Riza 12, Youngs 10, Tudor 9, Wanless 5, Guttridge 3, Fleming 2, Bridges 1, Iriekpen 1, Tann 1, Turner 1, Opponents 2.
F.A. Cup goals (8): Tann 2, Youngs 2, Kitson 1, Riza 1, Wanless 1, Opponents 1. **Worthington Cup goals (3):** Duncan 1, Kitson 1, Tudor 1. **LDV Vans Trophy goals (14):** Riza 4, Kitson 3, Fleming 1, Guttridge 1, Tann 1, Tudor 1, Wanless 1, Youngs 1, Opponents 1.
Average home League attendance: 4,172. **Player of Year:** Dave Kitson.

CARLISLE UNITED

Carlisle flirted with relegation to the Conference for much of the season and things looked particularly bleak after a 6-1 thrashing by Wrexham on Easter Monday in the first of three successive away matches. But they displayed commendable resilience to dent Torquay's promotion hopes 3-2 and then had the man for the big occasion when facing fellow strugglers Shrewsbury. After his side fell behind to a penalty, Brian Wake scored a hat-trick to set up a 3-2 success which guaranteed survival and sent their opponents down. They also accounted for Shrewsbury on the way to reaching the final of the LDV Vans Trophy against Bristol City, who prevailed 2-0.

Andrews, L .... 11(4)	Birch, M .... 21(3)	Burt, J 4
Baldachino, R ...... 11(11)	Burns, J .... 4(1)	Byrne, D .... 9(1)

Dillon, D .... –(1)	Kelly, D .... 30(2)	Raven, P 11
Farrell, C .... 31(2)	Maddison, L .... 18(3)	Robinson, P .... 1(4)
Foran, R .... 27(4)	Magennis, M 6	Rundle, A .... 19(2)
Freeman, D .... 3(1)	McCarthy, J .... 19(2)	Russell, C .... 7(6)
Galloway, M .... 4(5)	McDonagh, W ...... 10(14)	Shelley, B .... 32(3)
Glennon, M 32	McGill, B .... 22(12)	Slaven, J .... –(1)
Green, S .... 9(1)	Molloy, T 7	Summerbell, M 39
Gulliver, P 1	Murphy, P .... 38(2)	Sutton, J 7
Hevicon, R .... –(1)	Naisbitt, D 1	Taylor, M 10
Hudson, M .... 14(1)	Nixon, M .... 3(4)	Wake, B .... 10(18)
Jack, M .... 3(4)	Osman, L .... 10(2)	Whitehead, S 9
Keen, P 13		

League goals (52): Farrell 11, Wake 9, Foran 7, McGill 3, Green 2, McDonagh 2, Murphy 2, Birch 1, Burt 1, Hudson 1, Kell 1, Maddison 1, Magennis 1, McCarthy 1, Molloy 1, Osman 1, Robinson 1, Rundle 1, Russell 1, Shelley 1, Summerbell 1, Sutton 1, Opponents 1.
F.A. Cup goals (2): Farrell 1, Foran 1. **Worthington Cup goals (1):** McGill 1. **LDV Vans Trophy goals (11):** McDonagh 3, Farrell 2, Osman 2, Foran 1, McCarthy 1, Robinson 1, Rundle 1.
Average home League attendance: 4,775. **Player of Year:** Peter Murphy.

DARLINGTON

Another modest season for Darlington in what was their farewell to Feethams before moving to a new 25,000 all-seater stadium – but no shortage of talking points either. Chairman George Reynolds thought he had signed Faustino Asprilla on £17,000 a week until the Colombian did a runner. Then Reynolds sacked manager Tommy Taylor after three wins in 14 games. Under caretaker Mick Tait, the team continued to drop too many points at home to make much impression on the table, while a home defeat by Farnborough cost them the chance to make some money from the F.A. Cup.

Alexander, J .... –(1)	Hadland, P .... 4(2)	Nicholls, A .... 40(1)
Betts, S 40	Hodgson, R .... 22(5)	Offiong, R 7
Campbell, P .... 3(2)	Ingham, M 3	Pearson, G .... 19(2)
Clark, I .... 24(10)	Keltie, C .... 27(3)	Porter, C .... 2(1)
Clarke, M .... 34(5)	Liddle, C 42	Reed, A .... –(1)
Collett, A 38	Lonergan, A 2	Rundle, A .... 3(2)
Conlon, B 41	Maddison, N .... 25(3)	Russell, S 1
Corbett, J .... 9(1)	McGurk, D .... 3(1)	Sheeran, M .... –(4)
Cullen, J .... 2(1)	Mellanby, D .... 6(7)	Valentine, R 43
Fenton, G .... 4(2)	Naylor, G .... 1(12)	Wainwright, N ...... 21(12)
Ford, M .... 10(1)	Newey, T 7	Whitehead, S 23

League goals (58): Conlon 15, Clark 7, Nicholls 6, Liddle 4, Mellanby 4, Clarke 3, Keltie 3, Naylor 3, Corbett 2, Hodgson 2, Offiong 2, Betts 1, Fenton 1, Maddison 1, Newey 1, Pearson 1, Valentine 1, Wainwright 1.
F.A. Cup goals (8): Conlon 2, Offiong 2, Clark 1, Hodgson 1, Liddle 1, Nicholls 1.
Worthington Cup goals: None. **LDV Vans Trophy goals:** None.
Average home League attendance: 3,312. **Player of Year:** Craig Liddle.

EXETER CITY

Gary Peters offered Exeter new hope when becoming their third manager of the season after the sackings of John Cornforth and Neil McNab. But 20 points from the final 13 games, and victory in the last three, were not enough to repair the damage caused by the failure to win any of the previous 12. On a dramatic final day, Steve Flack's last-minute winner against Southend in front of a crowd of more than 9,000 could not offset a James Thomas hat-trick which kept Swansea in the League and sent Exeter down after 83 years. Peters later resigned.

Alcide, C 1
Ampadu, K .... 18(5)
Baker, P .... 5(1)
Barnard, L 3
Breslan, G .... –(10)
Buxton, L 4
Coppinger, J .... 35(8)
Cronin, G .... 28(11)
Curran, C .... 10(3)
Devine, S .... 21(2)
Flack, S .... 39(1)
Fraser, S .... –(1)
Gaia, S 33
Goodman, D .... 11(2)
Harries, P .... –(1)
Hiley, S 37
Kilheeney, C .... –(4)
Lock, M .... 1(2)
McConnell, B .... 13(8)
Miller, K 46
Moor, R .... 2(15)
Partridge, S .... 2(2)
Pettefer, C .... 30(1)
Pilkington, G 7
Power, G .... 27(3)
Roscoe, A .... 23(10)
Sharpe, L 4
Sheldon, G .... 7(12)
Simpkins,M .... 4(1)
Taylor, C .... 1(2)
Thomas, M .... 22(4)
Todd, C 12
Virgo, A .... 8(1)
Walker, J .... 35(4)
Watson, A 3
Whitbread, A 7
Whitworth, N .... 7(1)

League goals (50): Flack 13, Devine 8, Coppinger 5, Walker 5, Moor 3, Roscoe 3, Thomas 3, Partridge 2, Gaia 1, Goodman 1, Pettefer 1, Sharpe 1, Sheldon 1, Opponents 3.
F.A. Cup goals (6): Gaia 1, Lock 1, McConnell 1, Moor 1, Sheldon 1, Walker 1.
Worthington Cup goals (1): McConnell 1. **LDV Vans Trophy goals (1):** Sheldon 1.
Average home League attendance: 3,762. **Player of Year:** Kevin Miller.

HARTLEPOOL UNITED

After losing three successive play-off semi-finals, Hartlepool were promoted in the runners-up spot. But it was not enough for manager Mike Newell, who was sacked six months after taking over when Chris Turner left to join Sheffield Wednesday. Under Newell, the team built up a 14-point lead at the top over Rushden & Diamonds before a lean spell of one win in eight matches altered the picture. The teams met in a title decider on the last day of the season when Chris Westwood's last-minute equaliser was not enough for Hartlepool, who finished two points behind their rivals.

Arnison, P .... 9(10)
Barron, M 42
Barry-Murphy, B 7
Bass, J .... 2(2)
Boyd, A .... 11(11)
Clarke, D 45
Easter, J .... –(8)
Henderson, K .... 5(25)
Humphreys, R 46
Istead, S .... –(6)
Lee, G 45
Richardson, M .... 20(4)
Robinson, M 38
Simms, G .... –(1)
Smith, P .... 15(9)
Sweeney, A .... 2(2)
Tinkler, M 45
Watson, G .... 12(5)
Westwood, C 46
Widdrington, T .... 26(6)
Williams, A 46
Williams, E .... 44(1)
Williams, A 46

League goals (71): Williams, E 15, Tinkler 13, Humphreys 11, Clarke 7, Boyd 5, Richardson 5, Watson 5, Widdrington 3, Henderson 2, Lee 2, Arnison 1, Westwood 1, Opponents 1.
F.A. Cup goals (2): Barron 1, Richardson 1. **Worthington Cup goals (1):** Williams, E 1. **LDV Vans Trophy goals:** None.
Average home League attendance: 4,943. **Player of Year:** Richie Humphreys.

HULL CITY

A season of highs and lows for Hull, who moved from run-down Boothferry Park into the splendid new Kingston Communications Stadium, where more than 22,000 saw the first game against Hartlepool on Boxing Day. Attendances remained the envy of every other club, but were not matched by results. Peter Taylor, who replaced Jan Molby as manager in October and brought in a host of new players, bemoaned a lack of consistency, his team failing to win more than two successive games at any stage of the season. As a result, they never threatened to break into the play-off positions and finished in mid-table.

Alexander, G .... 21(4)
Anderson, J .... 42(1)
Appleby, R 6
Ashbee, I 31
Bradshaw, G .... 2(3)
Branch, P .... 6(1)
Burgess, B 7
Burton, S .... 2(9)
Delaney, D 30

Donaldson, C .... –(2)	Johnson, S .... 4(8)	Price, M .... 1(2)
Dudfield, L .... 7(14)	Joseph, M .... 22(1)	Reeves, M .... 5(3)
Edwards, M .... 3(3)	Keates, D 36	Regan, C .... 33(5)
Elliott, S .... 30(6)	Melton, S .... 19(6)	Russell, S .... –(1)
Fettis, A 17	Morrison, O .... 1(1)	Smith, S .... 17(5)
Forrester, J 11	Musselwhite, P 20	Strong, G 3
Glennon, M 9	Otsemobor, J .... 8(1)	Walters, J 11
Greaves, M 3	Peat, N .... –(1)	Webb, D .... 4(8)
Green, S .... 27(1)	Betty, B 2	Whittle, J .... 34(5)
Holt, A .... 5(1)	Philpott, L .... –(1)	Williams, R .... 14(9)
Jevons, P .... 13(11)		

League goals (58): Elliott 12, Alexander 6, Green 6, Walters 5, Burgess 4, Keates 4, Branch 3, Forrester 3, Jevons 3, Otsemobor 3, Johnson 2, Anderson 1, Ashbee 1, Delaney 1, Dudfield 1, Reeves 1, Smith 1, Whittle 1.
F.A. Cup goals: None. **Worthington Cup goals (2):** Alexander 1, Ashbee 1. **LDV Vans Trophy goals (1):** Donaldson 1.
Average home League attendance: 12,843. **Player of Year:** John Anderson.

KIDDERMINSTER HARRIERS

A shortage of goals in the last few weeks of the season cost Kidderminster the chance of pushing on for a place in the play-offs. Until then, Bo Henriksen had successfully shouldered much of the responsibility. But when he was out of the side, or experiencing a lean spell, there was no-one else able to score with any consistency. The final nine games yielded only six points, forcing them down to 11th place in the table. Henriksen still finished joint second in the divisional scoring charts with 20 to his credit.

Ayres, L .... 22(7)	Flynn, S 45	Melligan, J .... 28(1)
Bennett, D .... 28(4)	Foster, I .... 7(22)	Morgan, W 5
Bishop, A .... 22(7)	Heath, N .... –(1)	Parrish, S .... 21(8)
Brock, S 35	Henriksen, B .... 36(1)	Sall, A 4
Broughton, D .... 28(9)	Hinton, C 44	Scott, D 19
Clyde, M 4	Joy, I .... 2(4)	Shilton, S .... 39(2)
Coleman, K .... 13(2)	Khela, I .... –(1)	Smith, A .... 28(2)
Digby, F 11	Lewis, M .... –(2)	Stamps, S .... 19(4)
Doyle, D .... 1(4)	McAuley, H .... –(4)	Williams, D .... 43(2)
Ducros, A 2		

League goals (62): Henriksen 20, Melligan 10, Bishop 5, Parrish 5, Shilton 5, Broughton 4, Ayres 2, Flynn 2, Williams 2, Bennett 1, Foster 1, Morgan 1, Scott 1, Smith 1, Opponents 2.
F.A. Cup goals (3): Broughton 2, Opponents 1. **Worthington Cup goals:** None. **LDV Vans Trophy goals (7):** Broughton 2, Melligan 2, Bennett 1, Sall 1, Shilton 1.
Average home League attendance: 2,895. **Player of Year:** Danny Williams.

LEYTON ORIENT

After looking set for a mid-table finish, Orient fell away in the last two months of the season, their final 12 matches bringing only two wins. Without Wayne Purser's hat-trick on his debut against Boston and Chris Tate's two goals against Swansea, they would have been looking over their shoulder more anxiously. Defeat in the first round by Margate ruled out hopes of a money-spinning F.A. Cup run for a club who are banking on a major redevelopment of the ground to ensure the long-term future.

Alexander, G .... 12(5)	Canham, S .... 9(7)	Harris, A .... 43(1)
Barnard, D .... 22(7)	Downer, S 8	Harrison, L .... 6(1)
Barrett, S 11	Evans, R 7	Hatcher, D .... 1(5)
Brazier, M 33	Fletcher, G .... 7(5)	Heald, G 5
Campbell-Ryce, J ... 16(1)	Forbes, B .... –(3)	Hutchings, C .... 21(7)

Ibehre, J .... 11(14)	McLean, A .... –(8)	Tate, C .... 19(4)
Iriekpen, E 5	Miller, ... J 19	Thorpe, L .... 27(11)
Jones, B .... 22(2)	Morris, G .... 22(1)	Toner, C .... 22(3)
Joseph, M 37	Nugent, K .... 10(9)	Turner, M 7
Lockwood, M .... 42(1)	Purser, W 7	Watts, S .... 2(4)
Martin, J .... 21(11)	Smith, D 27	Zakuani, G .... –(1)
McGhee, D 3	Stephens, K .... 2(1)	

League goals (51): Thorpe 8, Tate 6, Ibehre 5, Lockwood 5, Martin 3, Nugent 3, Purser 3, Smith 3, Alexander 2, Campbell-Ryce 2, Canham 2, Brazier 1, Fletcher 1, Harris 1, Heald 1, Hutchings 1, Iriekpen 1, Toner 1, Turner 1, Opponents 1.

F.A. Cup goals (1): Martin 1. **Worthington Cup goals (5):** Campbell-Ryce 1, Fletcher 1, Ibehre 1, Nugent 1. Thorpe 1. **LDV Vans Trophy goals (3):** Barnard 1, Iriekpen 1, Lockwood 1.

Average home League attendance: 4,257. **Player of Year:** Matthew Joseph.

LINCOLN CITY

Manager Keith Alexander far exceeded the brief he was given when Lincoln came out of administration on the eve of the season. Instead of simply keeping the club alive, he reached the final of the play-offs with a group of players – many from non-league football – who pulled together to compile the best defensive record in the division. Substitute Simon Yeo hit a late equaliser against Torquay, which clinched sixth place, and he came off the bench again against Scunthorpe to score equally important goals which took them to the Play-off Final. Although Bournemouth then proved too strong with a 5-2 victory, Alexander and his side had every reason to be satisfied with their work.

Bailey, M 45	Cornwall, L .... 1(2)	Pearce, A .... 9(7)
Battersby, A 1	Cropper, D .... 24(5)	Sedgemore, B .... 23(5)
Bimson, S .... 41(1)	Dykes, D .... 2(1)	Smith, P .... 21(16)
Black, K .... –(1)	Futcher, B .... 41(2)	Thompson, T .... –(1)
Bloomer, M .... 3(10)	Gain, P 43	Ward, C .... 5(1)
Bradley, S 3	Logan, R 10	Watts, S 5
Buckley, A .... –(3)	Marriott, A 46	Weaver, S 44
Butcher, R .... 23(3)	Mayo, P .... 5(10)	Webb, D .... 4(1)
Camm, M .... 3(10)	Mike, A .... 5(12)	Willis, S .... 23(7)
Cornelly, C .... 9(7)	Morgan, P 45	Yeo, S .... 22(15)

Play-offs – Appearances: Bailey 3, Bimson 3, Butcher 3, Cropper 3, Futcher 3, Gain 3, Marriott 3, Mayo 3, Morgan 3, Smith 3, Weaver 3, Yeo –(3), Willis –(2), Bloomer –(1), Cornelly –(1).

League goals (46): Futcher 8, Gain 5, Yeo 5, Butcher 3, Cropper 3, Weaver 3, Willis 3, Mike 2, Sedgemore 2, Smith 2, Ward 2, Bimson 1, Bloomer 1, Bradley 1, Logan 1, Pearce 1, Watts 1, Webb 1, Opponents 1. **Play-offs goals (8):** Yeo 3, Bailey 1, Futcher 1, Mayo 1, Smith 1, Weaver 1.

F.A. Cup goals (1): Futcher 1. **Worthington Cup goals (1):** Mike 1. **LDV Vans Trophy goals (5):** Yeo 2, Buckley 1, Futcher 1, Opponents 1.

Average home League atttendance: 3,923. **Player of Year:** Paul Morgan.

MACCLESFIELD TOWN

A modest season at Moss Rose ended on a nostalgic note when loyal servant John Askey came off the bench to make his final senior appearance. Askey, who had played for the club for nearly 20 years, levelled the match against Rochdale at 2-2 in the 88th minute and Matthew Tipton's winner enabled Macclesfield to sign off with a flourish after facing a relegation struggle six weeks earlier. Tipton had turned the tide with the winner against Oxford and his team went on to record four more victories to reach safety.

Abbey, G .... 16(6)	Aldridge, P .... –(1)	Brackenbridge, S ...... –(2)
Adams, D 45	Askey, J .... 1(8)	Byrne, C .... 2(1)

Came, S 1
Carr, M 4
Dunning, D 17
Eaton, D .... 8(12)
Glover, E 5
Haddrell, M .... 2(2)
Hardy, L .... 8(8)
Hitchen, S .... 32(1)
Lightbourne, K .... 39(5)
Little, C .... 4(2)
Macauley, S 20
Martin, L 2
Miles, J .... 7(1)
Munroe, K .... 20(5)
Nash, M .... 1(4)
O'Neill, P .... 11(1)
Priest, C .... 34(3)
Ridler, D .... 16(1)
Robinson, N .... 2(8)
Ross, N .... 6(2)
Smith, D 3
Tinson, D 45
Tipton,M .... 28(8)
Welch, M .... 38(1)
Welsh, A .... 4(2)
Whittaker, D 41
Wilson, S 44

League goals (57): Lightbourne 11, Whitaker 10, Tipton 9, Eaton 5, Miles 4, Welch 3, Askey 2, Priest 2, Welsh 2, Abbey 1, Adams 1, Byrne 1, Glover 1, Little 1, Macauley 1, Opponents 3.
F.A. Cup goals (5): Lightbourne 2, Tipton 2, Whitaker 1. **Worthington Cup goals (5):** Whitaker 3, Lightbourne 1, Tipton 1. **LDV Vans Trophy goals (1):** Tipton 1.
Average home League attendance: 2,110. **Player of Year:** Steve Wilson.

OXFORD UNITED

For a team who were third going into the New Year and fifth preparing for the Easter programme to miss out completely at the end of the season was hard to take. Only Wrexham won more matches away from home. Had Oxford's form in front of their own supporters been of a similar calibre, a home defeat by Bristol Rovers on Easter Monday would have been sustainable. Instead, it was followed by defeat at Scunthorpe which sealed a play-off place for the Lincolnshire side. Although Oxford beat York on the final day, an 86th minute equaliser scored by Lincoln against Torquay left them out of the play-offs.

Basham, S .... 25(6)
Bound, M 41
Crosby, A 46
Edwards, C .... 5(1)
Foley, D .... 4(2)
Ford, R .... 31(6)
Gordon, G .... 3(3)
Hackett, C .... 1(11)
Hunt, J 39
Hunter, R .... 12(5)
Judge, A 1
Louis, J .... 12(22)
McCarthy, P 6
McNiven, S 44
Oldfield, D .... 19(9)
Omoyinmi, E .... 4(13)
Powell, P .... 4(10)
Ricketts, S .... –(2)
Robinson, M 42
Sall, A .... –(1)
Savage, D 43
Scott, A .... 29(9)
Steele, L .... 3(7)
Viveash, A 11
Waterman, D .... 27(2)
Whitehead, D .... 9(9)
Woodman, A 45

League goals (57): Scott 11, Basham 8, Crosby 6, Louis 6, Savage 4, Omoyinmi 3, Steele 3, Oldfield 2, Powell 2, Bound 1, Ford 1, Gordon 1, Hunt 1, Hunter 1, McCarthy 1, McNiven 1, Robinson 1, Waterman 1, Whitehead 1, Opponents 2.
F.A. Cup goals (2): Louis 1, Oldfield 1. **Worthington Cup goals (1):** Hunt 1. **LDV Vans Trophy goals (2):** Crosby 1, Waterman 1.
Average home League attendance: 5,862. **Player of Year:** Dave Savage.

ROCHDALE

Victories over Peterborough, Bristol Rovers, Preston and Coventry took Rochdale to the fifth round of the F.A. Cup at Molineux, where they gave Wolves a run for their money before going down 3-1. After that, League form tailed off worringly and player-manager Paul Simpson's side were only four points away from trouble by the end of the season. Simpson resigned and was replaced by the former Walsall, W.B.A. and Grimsby manager Alan Buckley, whose latest club had been Lincoln.

Andrews, L 8
Beech, C .... 16(2)
Bennett, N 1
Bishop, I .... 5(3)
Cansdell-Sherriff, S 3
Connor, P .... 30(9)
Doughty, M .... 39(2)
Duffy, L .... 19(3)
Edwards, N 26
Evans, W 40
Flitcroft, D .... 40(1)
Gilks, M .... 19(1)
Grand, S .... 22(1)
Griffiths, G .... 41(1)
Hill, S .... 9(1)
Hockenhull, D .... 6(1)
Hodges, L .... 3(4)
Jobson, R .... 15(1)
Macauley, S 6
McCourt, P .... 12(14)
McEvilly, L .... 27(10)

Melaugh, G .... 17(2)	Platt, C .... 40(2)	Townson, K .... 5(19)
Oliver, M .... 17(3)	Simpson, P .... 30(5)	Warner, S .... 6(1)
Patterson, R .... 2(6)	Taylor, M 2	

League goals (63): McEvilly 14, Connor 11, Simpson 10, Griffiths 6, Platt 6, McCourt 3, Flitcroft 2, Grand 2, Oliver 2, Beech 1, Hill 1, Hockenhull 1, Melaugh 1, Townson 1, Opponents 2.
F.A. Cup goals (12): Connor 3, Platt 3, Beech 1, Griffiths 1, McCourt 1, McEvilly 1, Melaugh 1, Simpson 1. **Worthington Cup goals:** None. **LDV Vans Trophy goals:** None.
Average home League attendance: 2,739. **Player of Year:** David Flitcroft.

RUSHDEN AND DIAMONDS

Brian Talbot's side, who reached the play-offs in their first season of League football, were celebrating a championship win in the second after bridging a 14-point gap opened up at the top by Hartlepool at one point in the season. The teams met at Nene Park on the final day and although Rushden conceded a last-minute equaliser, a 1-1 draw was enough to give them the title by two points. It rounded off a run of 11 unbeaten matches which underlined Rushden's staying power, the scoring capabilities of Paul Hall, Onandi Lowe and Duane Darby and the overall progress made by a club formed only in 1992.

Battersby, A .... 2(3)	Gray, S .... 33(4)	Sambrook, A .... 6(9)
Bell, D .... 25(4)	Hall, P .... 44(1)	Setchell, G .... 7(4)
Bell, D Jnr 1	Holdsworth, D .... 4(3)	Solkhon, B 1
Bignot, M 33	Hunter, B 40	Sollitt, A 3
Burgess, A .... 20(7)	Lowe, O .... 38(1)	Talbot, D .... 5(8)
Darby, D .... 35(2)	Mills, G .... 23(7)	Tillson, A 5
Dempster, J .... 11(5)	Mustafa, T .... 10(1)	Turley, W .... 43(1)
Duffy, R .... 3(10)	Partridge, S .... 2(5)	Underwood, P 40
Edwards, A .... 11(1)	Peters, M .... 25(2)	Wardley, S .... 36(3)

League goals (73): Hall 16, Lowe 15, Darby 14, Gray 7, Wardley 6, Bell, D 2, Burgess 2, Holdsworth 2, Bell, D Jnr 1, Dempster 1, Edwards 1, Hunter 1, Peters 1, Underwood 1, Opponents 3.
F.A. Cup goals (5): Duffy 3, Lowe 1, Wardley 1. **Worthington Cup goals:** None. **LDV Vans Trophy goals:** None.
Average home League attendance: 4,329. **Player of Year:** Paul Underwood.

SCUNTHORPE UNITED

Ten minutes from the end of their play-off semi-final at Sincil Bank, Scunthorpe were handily-placed after coming from 3-1 down to draw level. Then, they conceded two more to Lincoln substitute Simon Yeo, failed to break down their rivals in the return and were beaten for a second time by another late Yeo strike. It was a disappointing finish for a side who had overcome a poor start to the season – one win in eight matches – and the three-month absence of Steve Torpey with a thigh injury. Strike partner Martin Carruthers finished with 20 goals to his credit.

Balmer, S 6	Evans, T 46	Ridley, L .... 9(2)
Barwick, T .... 1(4)	Featherstone, L ...... 10(9)	Ryan, L .... –(2)
Beagrie, P .... 29(5)	Graves, W .... 35(6)	Sparrow, M 42
Brough, S .... 10(12)	Hayes, P .... 15(3)	Stanton, N 42
Byrne, C 13	Jackson, M .... 32(1)	Strong, G 7
Calvo-Garcia, A ...... 28(7)	Kilford, I .... 27(1)	Taylor, R .... 4(4)
Carruthers, M .... 42(3)	McCombe, J .... 23(8)	Torpey, S .... 26(2)
Cotterill, J .... 7(2)	O'Connor, A .... –(3)	Wheatcroft, P .... 2(2)
Dalglish, P .... 5(3)	Parton, A .... –(8)	Wright, S 2
Dawson, A 43		

Play-offs – Appearances: Calvo-Garcia 2, Dawson 2, Evans 2, Hayes 2, Jackson 2, Kilford 2, Sparrow 2, Stanton 2, Strong 2, Beagrie 1, Carruthers 1(1), Dalglish 1(1), Torpey 1(1), Graves –(1), McCombe –(1).
League goals (68): Carruthers 20, Torpey 11, Sparrow 9, Hayes 8, Beagrie 5, Calvo-Garcia 3, Dalglish 3, Kilford 3, Brough 2, Dawson 2, Graves 1, McCombe 1.
Play-offs – goals (3): Calvo-Garcia 2, Stanton 1.
F.A. Cup goals (4): Torpey 3, Carruthers 1. **Worthington Cup goals (1):** Torpey 1. **LDV Vans Trophy goals (2):** Dawson 1, Torpey 1.
Average home League attendance: 3,692. **Player of Year:** Tom Evans.

SHREWSBURY TOWN

Although the warning signs were there after a 6-0 defeat by Boston and 5-1 reversal against Rushden & Diamonds in mid-season, Shrewsbury's F.A. Cup third round victory over Everton – Wayne Rooney and all – suggested they could not possibly be sucked into trouble. But a nightmare run from early March onwards culminated in a 3-2 home defeat by Carlisle which sent them down after 53 years in the League. Shrewsbury lost their last eight matches and manager Kevin Ratcliffe resigned, maintaining that because he had brought in most of the players, he should take some of the blame.

Aiston, S .... 11(10)
Artell, D .... 27(1)
Atkins, M .... 29(1)
Cartwright, M 13
Drysdale, L .... 11(8)
Dunbavin, I 33
Edwards, D .... –(1)
Heathcote, M 6
Holt, A 9
Hulbert, R .... 4(3)
Jagielka, S .... 12(11)
Jemson, N .... 38(2)
Lowe, R .... 27(12)
Mortimer, A .... –(1)
Moss, D .... 35(5)
Murphy, C .... –(3)
Murray, K .... 17(11)
Partridge, S .... 2(2)
Redmile, M 39
Rodgers, L 36
Smith, A 13
Stevens, I .... 4(15)
Talbot, S 5
Thompson, A 16
Tolley, G .... 6(1)
Tolley, J .... 32(1)
Van Blerk, J .... 17(6)
Watts, S .... 3(4)
Wilding, P .... 28(5)
Woan, I .... 33(3)

League goals (62): Rodgers 16, Jemson 11, Lowe 9, Woan 4, Jagielka 3, Tolley, J 3, Wilding 3, Aiston 2, Stevens 2, Moss 2, Murray 2, Artell 1, Atkins 1, Drysdale 1, Redmile 1, Van Blark 1.
F.A. Cup goals (9): Jemson 5, Wilding 2, Tolley, J 1, Van Blerk 1. **Worthington Cup goals:** None. **LDV Vans Trophy goals (11):** Lowe 4, Rodgers 4, Atkins 1, Jemson 1, Moss 1.
Average home League attendance: 3,656. **Player of Year:** Peter Wilding.

SOUTHEND UNITED

There were no half measures about Southend, who won as many home matches as promoted Wrexham, lost more than relegated Exeter and overall were involved in fewer drawn fixtures than anyone in the League. They showed signs of improving this inconsistency with a run of five victories in eight matches early in 2003. But then five successive defeats ruled out any chance of making up further ground on the leading group and led to the dismissal of manager Rob Newman. Steve Wignall replaced him.

Beard, M .... 29(7)
Belgrave, B .... 6(15)
Bramble T .... 31(3)
Broad, S 17
Clark, S .... 20(13)
Cort, L 46
Darby, B .... 6(4)
Flahavan, D 41
Foley, D 5
Gay, D 5
Henry, R 3
Jenkins, N .... 29(5)
Jones, G .... 18(3)
Jordan, T .... –(1)
Kelly, S 10
Kightly, M .... –(1)
Maher, K 42
Marney, D .... 13(4)
Maye, D .... –(2)
McSweeney, D .... 15(2)
Rawle, M .... 33(1)
Salter, M .... 5(8)
Scully, A 8
Searle, D .... 39(5)
Selley, I 11
Smith, J .... 30(1)
Strachan, G .... 6(1)
Sutch, D 16
Thurgood, S .... 7(20)
Tilson, S .... 2(1)
Whelan, P .... 13(1)

League goals (47): Bramble 9, Rawle 9, Jenkins 7, Cort 6, Smith 5, Belgrave 3, Jones 2, Maher 2, Broad 1, Salter 1, Searle 1, Sutch 1.

F.A. Cup goals (6): Bramble 2, Rawle 2, Cort 1, Scully 1. **Worthington Cup goals (1):** Rawle 1. **LDV Vans Trophy goals (1):** Jones 1.
Average home League attendance: 3,951. **Player of Year:** Leon Cort.

SWANSEA CITY

James Thomas, who used to stand on the Vetch Field terraces, preserved League football for Swansea on a nail-biting final day of the season. Thomas scored a hat-trick in a 4-2 win over Hull which condemned Exeter to the Conference. He finished with lucky 13 from a campaign in which his team struggled from the start, winning only one of their first 13 matches. Player-manager Nick Cusack became the first managerial casualty of season and was replaced by Brian Flynn, former long-serving Wrexham manager. Flynn began to turn things round in the New Year, but it was always touch and go, particularly after a home defeat by Exeter over Easter.

Britton, L 25
Cash, B 5
Coates, J .... 2(1)
Cusack, N .... 4(1)
Cutler, N 13
De-Vulgt, L .... 3(1)
Durkan, K .... 4(2)
Evans T .... 25(2)
Freestone, R 33
Howard, M .... 36(2)
Hylton, L .... 7(1)
Jackson, M .... –(1)
Jenkins, L .... 26(6)
Johnrose, L 15
Jones, S .... 5(1)
Keaveny, J .... 4(5)
Lacey, D .... 7(3)
Martinez, R 19
Maylett, B 6
Moss, D .... 3(6)
Mumford, A .... 17(7)
Murphy, M .... 9(3)
Nugent, K 15
O'Leary, K .... 29(4)
Phillips, G .... 19(8)
Reid, P .... 18(2)
Richards, M .... 14(3)
Sharp, N .... 4(3)
Smith, D .... 3(1)
Smith, J 27
Stiens, C .... –(3)
Tate, A 27
Theobald, D .... 9(1)
Thomas, J .... 34(5)
Watkin, S .... 15(10)
Williams, J .... 11(16)
Wood, J .... 13(4)

League goals (48): Thomas 13, Richards 7, Nugent 5, Smith, J 3, Johnrose 3, Martinez 2, Moss 2, Murphy 2, Watkin 2, Wood 2, Cusack 1, Mumford 1, Reid 1, Smith, D 1, Williams 1, Opponents 2.
F.A. Cup goals (1): Murphy 1. **Worthington Cup goals (2):** Thomas 1, Wood 1. **LDV Vans Trophy goals (1):** Thomas 1.
Average home League attendance: 5,159. **Player of Year:** Leon Britton.

TORQUAY UNITED

Approaching Easter with a nine-match unbeaten run under their belt, Torquay looked capable of challenging for a play-off position. Then nine goals conceded in the final four games highlighted costly defensive failings. A 3-2 defeat by Carlisle, who were three up by half-time, ended all hope and summed up a lack of consistency on their own ground, where too many games were drawn. Over the season, only champions Rushden & Diamonds and third-place Wrexham scored more than Torquay. But only Carlisle and relegated Shrewsbury gave more away.

Amankwaah, K 6
Ashington, R .... –(2)
Attwell, J .... 2(2)
Bedeau, A .... 38(2)
Benefield, J .... –(8)
Bond, K .... –(1)
Brown, M .... 2(1)
Camara, B .... –(2)
Canoville, L 36
Clist, S 11
Dearden, K .... 26(1)
Douglin, T .... 1(4)
Dunning, D .... 4(3)
Forinton, H 1
Fowler, J 40
Graham, D .... 26(8)
Gritton, M .... 39(4)
Hankin, S .... 17(2)
Hazell, R 46
Hill, K .... 37(2)
Hockley, M .... 25(15)
Holmes, P 7
Killoughery, G .... 1(2)
Kuffour, J .... 18(11)
Prince, N .... 3(4)
Richardson, M .... 3(6)
Russell, A 39
Stevens, D .... –(3)
Taylor, C 5
Van Heusden, A 15
Welch, K 3
Wills, K .... 5(15)
Woods, S .... 5(4)
Woozley, D 45 (1)

League goals (71): Graham 15, Gritton 13, Russell 9, Bedeau 6, Kuffour 5, Fowler 4, Hill 4, Woozley 3, Clist 2, Hockley 2, Richardson 2, Dunning 1, Hankin 1, Hazell 1, Wills 1, Opponents 2.
F.A. Cup goals (6): Gritton 3, Fowler 1, Kuffour 1, Russell 1. **Worthington Cup goals:** None. **LDV Vans Trophy goals:** None.
Average home League attendance: 3,131. **Player of Year:** Alex Russell.

WREXHAM

Andy Morrell set a post-war club record of 34 goals and Denis Smith won the division's Manager of the Year award as Wrexham regained their Second Division status at the first attempt. Morrell scored hat-tricks against Exeter and Carlisle on his way to becoming the country's top League marksman. A double in the 3-0 win over Rushden & Diamonds in early March sparked a run of 14 unbeaten matches through to the end of the season which brought his team the third automatic promotion spot. The last eight of those were all won, including successive 6-1 and 5-0 victories over Carlisle and Cambridge.

Barrett, P .... 22(4)
Bennett, D .... 14(4)
Carey, B .... 31(2)
Edwards, C .... 43(1)
Edwards, P .... 33(5)
Dibble, A 33
Evans, M .... –(1)
Ferguson, D 41
Green, S .... 12(3)
Holmes, S .... 13(17)
Jones, L .... 9(14)
Jones, M .... –(1)
Lawrence, D .... 30(2)
Morgan, C .... 1(5)
Morrell, A 45
Pejic, S .... 23(4)
Phillips, W 1
Roberts, S 39
Rogers, K .... 6(1)
Russell, K 1
Sam, H .... 8(18)
Thomas, S .... 19(6)
Trundle, L .... 31(13)
Whitfield, P .... 7(1)
Whitley, J 44

League goals (84): Morrell 34, Trundle 11, Edwards, C 8, Sam 5, Carey 4, Jones, L 4, Edwards, P 4, Green 3, Ferguson 2, Roberts 2, Thomas 2, Barrett 1, Lawrence 1, Morgan 1, Whitley 1, Opponents 1.
F.A. Cup goals: None. **Worthington Cup goals (2):** Edwards, C 1, Morrell 1. **LDV Vans Trophy goals (6):** Jones, L 2, Edwards, C 1, Roberts 1, Thomas 1, Trundle 1
Average home League attendance: 4,265. **Player of Year:** Andy Morrell.

YORK CITY

Another season living on the financial edge for York, who went into administration in mid-season. This time, however, the team achieved a measure of success, going into the Easter programme in sixth place and looking capable of staying there for the play-offs. Then, at a crucial time, the goals dried up. Three matches yielded a single point and a home defeat by relegation-threatened Exeter in the third put them out of the running. Terry Dolan was sacked after a tenth-place finish and replaced by skipper Chris Brass, who at 27 became the League's youngest manager..

Beresford, M 6
Brackstone, S .... 22(4)
Brass, C 40
Bullock, L .... 38(1)
Carvalho, R .... –(4)
Cook, L 7
Cooper, R .... 21(3)
Cowan, T .... 31(2)
Duffield, P 28
Edmondson, D .... 37(1)
Fettis, A 21
Fox, C .... 6(5)
Graydon, K .... 4(3)
Hobson, G .... 24(4)
Ingham, M 17
Jones, S .... 19(1)
Mathie, A .... 2(8)
Mazzina, N .... –(3)
McCarthy, J 1
Nogan, L .... 39(7)
Okoli, J .... 1(2)
Parkin, J .... 37(4)
Potter, G .... 37(2)
Reddy, M .... 10(1)
Shandran, A .... 12(6)
Smith, C .... 33(3)
Stockdale, D .... 0(1)
Whitehead, P 2
Wilding, C .... 1(6)
Wise, S .... 3(5)
Wood, L .... 7(12)
Yalcin, L .... –(5)

League goals (52): Duffield 13, Parkin 10, Bullock 6, Edmondson 5, Nogan 5, Shandran 3, Brackstone 2, Reddy 2, Brass 1, Cook 1, Cooper 1, Cowan 1, Graydon 1, Potter 1.
F.A. Cup goals (3): Duffield 2, Bullock 1. **Worthington Cup goals:** None. **LDV Vans Trophy goals (3):** Cook 1, Nogan 1, Parkin 1.
Average home League attendance: 4,175. **Player of Year:** Chris Brass.

SCOTTISH LEAGUE ROLL CALL

APPEARANCES & SCORERS 2002-03

(Figures in brackets = appearances as substitute)

BANK OF SCOTLAND PREMIER LEAGUE

ABERDEEN

Ground: Pittodrie Stadium, Aberdeen AB24 5QH. **Capacity:** 22,199.
Telephone: 01224 650400. **Colours:** Red with white. **Nickname:** Dons.

Anderson, R 33
Billio, P .... 5(5)
Bisconti, R 11
Clark, C .... 20(5)
D'Jaffo, L .... 16(2)
Deloumeaux, E 32
Diamond, A .... –(1)
Fabiano, N .... 8(4)
Foster, R .... –(2)
Hart, M 8
Hinds, L .... 9(3)
Kjaer, P 23
Mackie, D .... 23(7)
McAllister, J .... 27(2)
McGuire, P 36
McNaughton, K ...... 18(4)
Michie, S .... 5(16)
Mike, L .... 12(12)
Morrison, S 2
Muirhead, S .... –(2)
O'Donoghue, R .... 1(3)
Payne, S .... 3(5)
Preece, D .... 15(1)
Rutkiewicz, K .... 18(2)
Sheerin, P 14
Souter, K .... –(1)
Thornley, B .... 2(4)
Tiernan, F .... 15(6)
Tosh, S 14
Young, Darren .... 23(1)
Young, Derek .... 25(4)

League goals (41): Sheerin 8, McGuire 5, Mackie 4, Young, Derek 4, D'Jaffo 3, Hinds 3, Anderson 2, Deloumeaux 2, Mike 2, Tosh 2, Billio 1, Clark 1, Young, Darren 1, McNaughton 1, Tiernan 1, Opponents 1.
Tennents Cup goals (4): D'Jaffo 2, Anderson 1, Young, Derek 1. **CIS Cup goals (3):** Deloumeaux 1, Michie 1, Mike 1. **UEFA Cup goals (1):** Mackie 1.

CELTIC

Ground: Celtic Park, Glasgow G40 3RE. **Capacity:** 60,506.
Telephone: 0141 556 2611. **Colours:** Green and white. **Nickname:** Bhoys.

Agathe, D .... 24(3)
Balde, B 36
Broto, J .... 7(1)
Crainey, S .... 3(10)
Douglas, R 21
Fernandez, D .... 3(7)
Gould, J 2
Guppy, S .... 12(5)
Hartson, J .... 18(9)
Healy, C .... –(1)
Hedman, M 8
Lambert, P .... 27(4)
Larsson, H 35
Laursen, U 22
Lennon, N 28
Maloney, S .... 5(15)
McNamara, J .... 12(7)
Mjallby, J 14
Petrov, S .... 33(1)
Petta, B 2
Smith, J .... 3(10)
Sutton, C 28
Sylla, M .... 13(5)
Thompson, A .... 26(3)
Valgaeren, J 35
Varga, S 1

League goals (98): Larsson 28, Hartson 18, Sutton 15, Petrov 12, Thompson 8, Lambert 3, Maloney 3, Mjallby 3, Balde 2, Sylla 2, Valgaeren 2, McNamara 1, Opponents 1.
Tennents Cup goals (6): Hartson 2, Larsson 2, Smith 1, Sylla 1. **CIS Cup goals (9):** Balde 2, Hartson 2, Larsson 2, Lambert 1, Maloney 1, Thompson 1. **Champions League goals (3):** Larsson 1, Sutton 1, Sylla 1. **UEFA Cup goals (27):** Larsson 11, Hartson 3, Sutton 3, Thompson 3, Lambert 2, Petrov 2, Fernandez 1, Maloney 1, Valgaeren 1.

DUNDEE

Ground: Dens Park, Dundee DD3 7JY. **Capacity:** 12,371.
Telephone: 01382 889966. **Colours:** Navy blue and white. **Nickname:** Dark Blues.

Beith, G 1
Brady, G .... 19(8)
Burchill, M .... 7(4)
Caballero, F .... 34(2)
Carranza, B .... 1(4)
Forbes, B .... 1(3)
Hernandez Santos, J . 30(1)
Hutchinson, T 11
Jablonski, N .... –(2)
Khizanishvili, Z ...... 16(3)
Lovell, S .... 23(5)
Mackay, D 35
Mair, L .... 23(6)
Milne, S .... 11(14)
Nemsadze, G 24
Novo, N .... 26(10)
Rae, G .... 35(2)
Robb, S .... 1(8)
Robertson, M .... –(5)
Sara, J .... 10(9)
Smith, B 37
Speroni, J 38
Wilkie, L 35

League goals (50): Lovell 11, Caballero 8, Novo 7, Milne 6, Rae 4, Burchill 2, Sara 2, Wilkie 2, Brady 1, Hernandez Santos 1, Mackay 1, Mair 1, Smith 1, Opponents 3.
Tennents Cup goals (10): Lovell 3, Nemsadze 2, Novo 2, Burchill 1, Caballero 1, Rae 1.
CIS Cup goals (3): Sara (2), Caballero 1.

DUNDEE UNITED

Ground: Tannadice Park, Dundee DD3 7JW. **Capacity:** 14,209.
Telephone: 01382 833166. **Colours:** Tangerine and black. **Nickname:** Terrors.

Aljofree, H 1
Bollan, G 13
Carson, S .... 2(5)
Chiarini, D .... 2(2)
Combe, A 5
Conway, A .... –(1)
Cummings, W .... 7(4)
Dodds, B .... 6(8)
Duff, S .... 32(2)
Easton, C .... 35(1)
Gallacher, P .... 33(1)
Griffin, D .... 16(1)
Gunnlaugsson, A ...... 1(5)
Hamilton, J .... 9(4)
Latapy, R .... 6(1)
Lauchlan, J .... 20(4)
Lilley, D .... 29(4)
McCracken, D 25
McCunnie, J .... 16(2)
McGowan, S .... –(1)
McGowne, K 12
McIntyre, J .... 30(3)
Miller, C .... 32(2)
O'Donnell, S .... 6(5)
Ogunmade, D .... 1(4)
Paterson, J .... 23(10)
Smart, A .... 2(16)
Thompson, S .... 19(1)
Tod, A .... 12(1)
Venetis, A .... 1(1)
Wilson, M .... 22(4)
Winters, D .... –(1)

League goals (35): McIntyre 9, Thompson 6, Hamilton 4, Miller 3, Dodds 2, Lilley 2, Tod 2, Easton 1, Griffin 1, McCracken 1, Ogunmade 1, Paterson 1, Wilson 1, Opponents 1.
Tennents Cup goals (2): Hamilton 1, O'Donnell 1. **CIS Cup goals (8):** O'Donnell 3, Thompson 3, Lilley 2.

DUNFERMLINE

Ground: East End Park, Dunfermline KY12 7RB. **Capacity:** 12,558.
Telephone: 01383 724295. **Colours:** Black and white. **Nickname:** Pars.

Brannan, G 8
Brewster, C 37
Bullen, L 35
Crawford, S 37
Dair, J .... 22(10)
Dempsey, G .... 17(14)
Grondin, D .... 12(1)
Hamilton, J .... –(2)
Hampshire, S .... 9(13)
Hunt, N .... 2(10)
Karnebeek, A .... 1(1)
Kilgannon, S .... 15(13)
MacPherson, A .... 17(1)
Mason, G .... 24(3)
McGarty, M .... 2(6)
McGroarty, C .... 8(13)
McLeish, K .... –(1)
McNichol, S .... –(2)
Nicholls, D .... 2(1)
Nicholson, B 38
Petrie, S .... –(2)
Ruitenbeek, M 17
Skerla, A 32
Stillie,D 21
Thomson, S 22
Walker, S .... 12(8)
Wilson, D 1
Wilson, S .... 27(1)

League goals (54): Crawford 19, Brewster 12, Bullen 5, Nicholson 4, Dair 2, Dempsey 2, Mason 2, Walker 2, Hampshire 1, Hunt 1, McNicol 1, Thomson 1, Opponents 2.
Tennents Cup goals (7): Brewster 2, Crawford 2, Grondin 1, Nicholson 1, Wilson 1. **CIS Cup goals (4):** Crawford 2, Bullen 1, Thomson 1.

HEARTS

Ground: Tynecastle, Edinburgh EH 11 2NL. **Capacity:** 18,008.
Telephone: 0131 200 7200. **Colours:** Maroon. **Nickname:** Jam Tarts.

Boyack, S .... 19(7)
De Vries, M .... 29(3)
Dunn, D 1
Gordon, C 1
Hamill, J .... 1(3)
Janczyk, N .... 1(7)
Kirk, A .... 18(12)
Knox, J .... –(1)
MacFarlane, N .... 20(1)
Mahe, S .... 8(3)
Maybury, A 35
McCann, A .... 15(2)
McGeown, D 1
McKenna, K .... 30(6)
McKenzie, R 20
McMullan, P .... 13(3)
Moilanen, T 14
Neilson, R 5
Niemi, A 3
Pressley, S 33
Queifio, W 3
Severin, S 37
Simmons, S .... 9(14)
Sloan, R .... –(1)
Stamp, P .... 22(2)
Twaddle, K .... 1(7)
Valois, J-L .... 37(1)
Wales, G .... 11(15)
Webster, A .... 19(2)
Weir, G .... 12(8)

League goals (57): De Vries 15, Kirk 10, McKenna 5, Stamp 4, Wales 4, Weir 4, Pressley 3, Severin 3, Maybury 2, Valois 2, Boyack 1, McCann 1, McMullan 1, Simmons 1, Webster 1.
Tennents Cup goals: None. **CIS Cup goals (7):** Pressley 2, Valois 2, Kirk 1, McKenna 1, Simmons 1.

HIBERNIAN

Ground: Easter Road, Edinburgh EH7 5QG. **Capacity:** 17,500.
Telephone: 0131 661 2159. **Colours:** Green and white. **Nickname:** Hibees.

Anderson, D 3
Arpinon, F .... 3(5)
Brebner, G .... 25(7)
Brown, S .... 3(1)
Caig, A .... 5(1)
Colgan, N 30
Daquin, F .... 1(1)
Dempsie, A 2
Dempsie, M .... 2(1)
Doumbe, M .... 11(2)
Fenwick, P .... 30(1)
Jack, M .... 17(2)
James, C .... 20(2)
Luna, F .... 13(5)
Matyus, J 14
McManus, T .... 20(15)
Murray, I .... 35(1)
Nicol, K .... –(1)
O'Connor, G .... 16(7)
O'Neil, J .... 17(4)
Orman, A 25
Paatelainen, M .... 21(3)
Reid, A .... –(7)
Riordan, D .... 4(6)
Smith, G .... 30(2)
Thompson, D 2
Townsley, D .... 15(10)
Whittaker, S .... 5(1)
Wiss, J .... 21(3)
Zambernardi, Y 28

League goals (56): McManus 11, Murray 8, O'Connor 7, Paatelainen 7, Townsley 4, Brebner 3, Brown 3, Jack 3, Riordan 3, James 2, Luna 2, O'Neil 2, Orman 1.
Tennents Cup goals (4): Brebner 3, Murray 1. **CIS Cup goals (4):** O'Connor 2, Brebner 1, Murray 1.

KILMARNOCK

Ground: Rugby Park, Kilmarnock KA1 2DP. **Capacity:** 18,128.
Telephone: 01563 545300. **Colours:** White and blue. **Nickname:** Killie.

Boutal, S 3
Boyd, K .... 17(21)
Canero, P .... 31(2)
Canning, M .... –(1)
Dargo, C .... 10(5)
Di Giacomo, P .... 6(14)
Dillon, S .... 13(1)
Dindeleux, F 27
Fowler, J .... 25(7)
Fulton, S 36
Hay, G .... 12(9)
Hessey, S 5
Innes, C .... 19(1)
Locke, G .... 15(7)
Mahood, A 35
Marshall, G 30
McDonald, G .... 10(2)
McLaren, A .... 23(2)
McLaughlin, B .... 17(3)
McSwegan, G .... 25(7)
Meldrum, C 7
Mitchell, A .... 4(6)
Murray, S .... 4(5)
Quitongo, J .... 4(4)
Sanjuan, J .... 5(3)
Shields, G 34
Stewart, C 1

League goals (47): Boyd 12, McSwegan 11, Canero 6, McLaren 5, Fulton 4, McDonald 2, Boutal 1, Dargo 1, Di Giacomo 1, Innes 1, Mahood 1, McLaughlin 1, Shields 1.
Tennents Cup goals: None. **CIS Insurance Cup goals:** None.

LIVINGSTON

Ground: West Lothian Courier Stadium, Livingston EH54 7DN. **Capacity:** 10,016. **Telephone:** 01506 417000. **Colours:** Gold and black. **Nickname:** Livvy's Lions.

Amor, G .... 1(2)
Andrews, M 33
Bahoken, G 15
Bingham, D .... 23(10)
Bollan, G .... 20(2)
Brinquin, P 30
Brittain, R .... 1(2)
Broto, J 24
Camacho, J .... 16(8)
Dadi, E .... 16(7)
Dorado, E 2
Hart, M .... 10(1)
Lovell, S 15
Maidana, J 12
Main, A 12
Makel, L .... 29(2)
McEwan, D .... 2(1)
McLaughlin, S 1
McMenamin, C .... 3(10)
McNamee, D .... 11(1)
O'Brien, B .... 22(6)
Pasquinelli, F 6
Quino, F .... 27(8)
Rubio, O .... 23(3)
Toure-Maman, C ... 12(11)
Wilson, B .... 17(8)
Xausa, D .... 13(17)
Zarate, R .... 22(11)

League goals (48): Zarate 9, Andrews 4, Bingham 4, Rubio 4, Wilson 4, Xausa 4, Camacho 3, Dadi 3, Toure-Maman 3, Makel 2, McMenamin 2, Bollan 1, Brinquin 1, Lovell 1, O'Brien 1, Pasquinelli 1, Opponents 1.
Tennents Cup goals (1): Bollan 1. **CIS Cup goals (1):** Dadi 1. **UEFA Cup goals (7):** Wilson 2, Andrews 1, Lovell 1, Rubio 1, Xausa 1, Zarate 1.

MOTHERWELL

Ground: Fir Park, Motherwell ML1 2QN. **Capacity:** 13,742. **Telephone:** 01698 333333. **Colours:** Claret and amber. **Nickname:** Well.

Adams, D 32
Ballantyne, R .... –(1)
Clarke, D .... –(1)
Clarkson, D .... 13(6)
Corrigan, M 38
Cowan, D .... 15(1)
Craig, S .... 8(5)
Dempsie, B 1
Dubourdeau, F 22
Fagan, S .... 8(10)
Ferguson, S .... 8(11)
Hammell, S 37
Jack, D .... –(2)
Khemas, K .... 4(2)
Kinniburgh, W .... 11(4)
Lasley, K .... 21(3)
Lehmann, D .... 27(5)
Leitch, S 26
McDonald, K .... 4(4)
McFadden, J .... 29(1)
Offiong, R .... –(9)
Partridge, D 32
Pearson, S 29
Quinn, P .... 3(1)
Ramsey, D .... 16(4)
Russell, I .... –(5)
Scott, A .... –(1)
Sengewald, D .... 6(1)
Vaughan, A 12
Woods, S .... 16(1)
Wright, K .... –(1)

League goals (45): McFadden 13, Pearson 6, Lehmann 5, Clarkson 3, Lasley 3, Adams 2, Craig 2, Fagan 2, Ferguson 2, Corrigan 1, Khemas 1, Kinniburgh 1, Leitch 1, Partridge 1, Ramsey 1, Vaughan 1.
Tennents Cup goals (10): McFadden 5, Adams 2, Craig 1, Lehmann 1, Opponents 1. **CIS Cup goals (3):** Adams 1, Lehmann 1, McFadden 1.

PARTICK THISTLE

Ground: Firhill Stadium, Glasgow G20 7AL. **Capacity:** 14,538. **Telephone:** 0141 579 1971. **Colours:** Red, yellow and black. **Nickname:** Jags.

Archibald, A 36
Arthur, K 35
Britton, G .... 28(5)
Buchan, M .... 23(5)
Budinauckas, K 3
Burns, A 38
Charnley, C .... –(2)
Chiarini, D 12
Craigan, S 36
Elliot, B .... 1(2)
Fleming, D .... 4(4)
Gibson, A .... 1(11)
Hardie, M .... 35(2)
Lennon, D .... 2(9)
Lilley, D 34
McGowne, K 7
McKinstry, J .... 3(3)
McLean, S .... 6(6)
Milne, K .... 8(4)
Mitchell, J .... 27(4)
Morris, I .... –(1)
Paterson, S 32
Ross, I 6
Rowson, D 13
Rushford, G .... –(1)
Shields, M .... –(1)
Waddell, R .... 5(11)
Walker, P .... 1(12)
Whyte, D .... 22(3)

League goals (37): Burns 16, Britton 5, Mitchell 5, Lilley 3, Archibald 2, Hardie 2, Buchan 1, McLean 1, Rowson 1, Waddell 1.
Tennents Cup goals: None. **CIS Cup goals (5):** Hardie 3, Buchan 1, Burns 1.

RANGERS

Ground: Ibrox, Glasgow G51 2XD. **Capacity:** 50,500.
Telephone: 0141 580 8500. **Colours:** Royal blue. **Nickname:** Gers.

Amoruso, L	24	Hughes, S	6(6)	Mols, M	23(4)
Arteta, M	26(1)	Hutton, A	1	Moore, C	35
Arveladze, S	25(5)	Klos, S	38	Muscat, K	22
Bonnissel, J	2(1)	Konterman, B	4(12)	Nerlinger, C	–(3)
Caniggia, C	10(16)	Latapy, R	2(5)	Numan, A	26
De Boer, R	33	Lovenkrands, P	21(6)	Ricksen, F	35
Dodds, B	1(5)	Malcolm, R	19(5)	Ross, M	17(3)
Ferguson, B	36	McCann, N	10(8)	Thompson, S	1(7)
Flo, T	1(3)	McLean, S	–(3)		

League goals (101): De Boer 16, Ferguson 16, Arveladze 15, Mols 13, Lovenkrands 9, Caniggia 8, Amoruso 4, Arteta 4, Ricksen 3, Moore 3, McCann 2, Thompson 2, Hughes 1, Malcolm 1, Numan 1, Ross 1, Opponents 2.
Tennents Cup goals (13): Amoruso 2, Ferguson 2, Arteta 1, Arveladze 1, Caniggia 1, De Boer 1, Konterman 1, Lovenkrands 1, Mols 1, Moore 1, Opponents 1. **CIS Cup goals (7):** Caniggia 3, Lovenkrands 2, De Boer 1, Opponents 1. **UEFA Cup goals (3):** De Boer 2, McCann 1.

BELL'S FIRST DIVISION

ALLOA ATHLETIC

Ground: Recreation Park, Alloa FK10 1RY. **Capacity:** 3,142.
Telephone: 01259 722695. **Colours:** Black and gold. **Nickname:** Wasps.

Christie, M	26(1)	Evans, J	16	Seaton, A	32(1)
Cowan, M	7(1)	Fisher, J	11(5)	Sloan, R	16
Crabbe, S	18(10)	Gillan, G	1(5)	Soutar, D	12
Davidson, R	4(7)	Hamilton, R	35	Stevenson, J	2
Ferguson, B	5(1)	Hogarth, M	8	Thomson, S	35
Ferguson, D	25(2)	Hutchison, G	24(10)	Valentine, C	34
Fisher, J	11(5)	Knox, K	4(5)	Walker, R	25(3)
Elliott, R	–(5)	Little, I	27(1)	Watson, G	22(2)
Evans G	2(12)	MacDonald, B	5(2)		

League goals (39): Sloan 8, Hamilton 5, Hutchison 4, Seaton 4, Crabbe 3, Little 3, Thomson 3, Ferguson, B 2, Cowan 2, Davidson 1, Evans 1, Watson 1, Opponents 2.
Tennents Cup goals (3): Crabbe 2, Thomson 1. **CIS Cup goals (3):** Hamilton 1, Hutchison 1, Little 1. **Bell's Cup goals:** None.

ARBROATH

Ground: Gayfield Park, Arbroath DD11 1QB. **Capacity:** 6,488.
Telephone: 01241 872157. **Colours:** Maroon and white. **Nickname:** Red Lichties.

Bowman, G	11(3)	Dow, A	13	Graham, E	4(6)
Browne, P	15	Durno, P	2(6)	Heenan, K	17(11)
Brownlie, P	22(6)	Farquharson, P	–(1)	Henslee, G	23(7)
Cargill, A	21(1)	Feroz, C	20(3)	Hinchcliffe, C	36
Currie, R	28(3)	Florence, S	23	Lawrence, A	3
Cusick, J	19	Forrest, E	10	McAulay, J	9(16)

McDowell, M .... 14(5)
McGlashan, J .... 14(2)
McInally, D .... 4(5)
McMullen, K .... 10(2)
Ritchie, I 33
Spink, D .... 7(12)
Swankie, G .... 16(12)
Tait, J 17

League goals (30): Cusick 4, McDowell 4, Brownlie 2, Dow 2, Feroz 2, Henslee 2, McGlashan 2, Spink 2, Swankie 2, Cargill 1, Currie 1, Forrest 1, Heenan 1, McInally 1, Ritchie 1, Tait 1, Opponents 1.
Tennents Cup goals: None. **CIS Cup goals (2):** Feroz 2. **Bell's Cup goals:** None.

AYR UNITED

Ground: Somerset Park, Ayr KA8 9NB. **Capacity:** 10,243.
Telephone: 01292 263435. **Colours:** White and black. **Nickname:** Honest Men.

Annand, E .... 18(1)
Black, A .... 6(12)
Bossy, F 1
Campbell, M 29
Chaplain, S .... 33(2)
Conway, C .... –(1)
Craig, D .... 29(2)
Dodds, J 5
Dunlop, M .... 11(13)
Ferguson, A .... 1(1)
Ferry, M 1
Grady, J .... 29(2)
Kean, S .... 11(22)
Latta, J .... 3(2)
Lovering, P .... 21(1)
Lyle, W .... 29(4)
McColl, M .... 6(4)
McDermott, A .... 1(1)
McGrady, S .... 1(1)
McManus, A .... 25(1)
McVeigh, A .... –(2)
Mullen, B .... 2(2)
Murray, N .... 21(2)
Nelson, C 31
Nicolson, I .... 21(4)
Sheerin, P 19
Smyth, M .... 31(1)
Whalen, S .... 10(2)

League goals (34): Kean 7, Chaplain 5, Whalen 5, Annand 3, Grady 3, Campbell 2, Craig 2, Sheerin 2, Ferguson 1, Lovering 1, McColl 1, Opponents 2.
Tennents Cup goals (2): Black 1, Grady 1. **CIS Cup goals:** None. **Bell's Cup goals (2):** Annand 1, Grady 1.

CLYDE

Ground: Broadwood Stadium, Cumbernauld G68 9NE. **Capacity:** 8,029.
Telephone: 01236 451511. **Colours:** White and red. **Nickname:** Bully Wee.

Baird, J .... –(1)
Bossy, F .... 11(4)
Convery, M .... 3(21)
Cosgrove, S .... 9(11)
Doyle, P .... –(1)
Dunn, D 3
Falconer, W .... 10(8)
Fraser, J .... 28(6)
Gilhaney, M .... 7(4)
Hagen, D .... 30(1)
Halliday, R 1
Halliwell, B 33
Hinds, L .... 19(1)
Jack, J 10
Kane, A .... 1-(2)
Kane, P .... 14(1)
Keogh, P .... 24(4)
Kernaghan, A 26
McClay, A .... 2(2)
McConalogue, S ..... 11(4)
McEwan, D 1
McLaughlin, M 7
Mensing, S 35
Millen, A 30
Morrison, A 1
Nish, C .... 13(2)
Potter, J .... 32(1)
Reid, W .... –(2)
Ross, J 23
Shields, P .... 8(5)
Smith, B 5

League goals (66): Keogh 12, Millen 7, Hinds 6, McConalogue 5, Nish 5, Falconer 4, Gilhaney 4, Hagen 4, Mensing 4, Convery 3, Fraser 3, Kernaghan 2, Potter 2, Ross 2, Jack 1, Kane 1, Shields 1.
Tennents Cup goals (2): Hinds 1, Millen 1. **CIS Cup goals:** None. **Bell's Cup goals (1):** Hinds 1.

FALKIRK

Ground: Brockville Park, Falkirk FK1 5AX. **Capacity:** 7,576.
Telephone: 01324 624121. **Colours:** Navy blue and white. **Nickname:** Bairns.

Christie, K .... 1(1)
Coyle, O 36
Craig, S .... –(3)
Creaney, P .... –(1)
Cringean, S .... 1(7)
Ferguson, A 32
Henry, J .... 27(6)
Hill, D 4
Hughes, J 31

James, K 13	McQuilken, J 35	Rennie, S .... 14(5)
Kerr, M .... 32(4)	McSween, I .... 1(8)	Rodgers, A .... –(14)
Lawrie, A 7	Miller, L 34	Samuel, C .... 17(16)
MacKenzie, S 32	Nicholls, D 17	Taylor, S .... 7(6)
McPherson, C 35	Reid, B .... 4(3)	Tosh, S 16

League goals (80): Coyle 20, Miller 16, Samuel 11, Taylor 7, Henry 5, James 4, Lawrie 4, Kerr 2, McQuilken 2, Hughes 1, MacKenzie 1, McPherson 1, Rodgers 1, Tosh 1, Opponents 4.
Tennents Cup goals (8): Samuel 4, Coyle 3, Taylor 1. **CIS Cup goals (4):** Coyle 1, Lawrie 1, Miller 1, Samuel 1. **Bell's Cup goals (4):** Miller 2, James 1, McPherson 1.

INVERNESS CALEDONIAN THISTLE

Ground: Caledonian Stadium, Inverness IV1 1FF. **Capacity:** 6,280.
Telephone: 01463 222880. **Colours:** Royal blue, red and white. **Nickname:** Caley Thistle.

Bagan, D .... 3(9)	Hislop, S .... 5(8)	Munro, G .... 30(2)
Brown, M 36	Keogh, L .... 3(18)	Ritchie, P .... 28(7)
Christie, C .... 13(7)	Low, A .... 2(13)	Robson, B 34
Duncan, R .... 25(1)	Mann, R 31	Stewart, G .... 3(6)
Gilfillan, B .... –(3)	McBain, R .... 32(2)	Tokely, R 34
Golabek, S 34	McCaffray, S .... 21(1)	Wyness, D .... 35(1)
Hart, R .... 27(3)		

League goals (74): Wyness 19, Ritchie 18, Robson 10, Hart 7, Mann 5, Tokely 5, Christie 2, Hislop 2, Golabek 1, Low 1, Stewart 1, Opponents 3.
Tennents Cup goals (9): Wyness 4, Robson 3, McCaffray 1, Ritchie 1. **CIS Cup goals (7):** Wyness 4, Ritchie 2, Hart 1. **Bell's Cup goals:** None.

QUEEN OF THE SOUTH

Ground: Palmerston Park, Dumfries DG2 9BA. **Capacity:** 6,412.
Telephone: 01387 254853. **Colours:** Royal blue and white. **Nickname:** Doonhamers.

Aitken, A 35	Gibson, W .... 1(2)	Neilson, R 13
Allan, D .... 17(1)	Goram, A 19	O'Connor, S .... 17(5)
Anderson, D 23	Gray, A .... 5(5)	O'Neil, J .... 19(11)
Atkinson, P .... 7(1)	Henderson, R 2	Paton, E .... 17(5)
Bowey, S 34	Hetherston, P 1	Renicks, S .... 4(1)
Burns, P .... 1(3)	Lyle, D .... 27(6)	Scott, C .... 16(1)
Campbell, J 1	McAlpine, J .... 21(7)	Shields, P .... 9(4)
Crawford, J .... 5(1)	McColligan, B .... 22(4)	Thomson, J .... 29(1)
Dawson, B 3	McLaughlin, B ..... 20(12)	Weatherson, P .... 28(4)

League goals (45): O'Neill 9, Lyle 6, O'Connor 6, Weatherson 6, Bowey 4, McColligan 3, Paton 3, Thomson 3, McAlpine 1, McLaughlin 1, Shields 1, Oppopnents 2.
Tennents Cup goals (1): Weatherson 1. **CIS Cup goals (3):** O'Neill 2, Weatherson 1. **Bell's Cup goals (12):** Lyle 3, O'Neill 3, Shields 2, Weatherson 2, Bowey 1, O'Connor 1.

ROSS COUNTY

Ground: Victoria Park, Dingwall IV15 9QW. **Capacity:** 5,800.
Telephone: 01349 860860. **Colours:** Navy blue and white. **Nickname:** County.

Bayne, G .... 21(9)	Cowie, D .... 20(9)	Hannah, D 6
Bolochoweckyj, M ..... –(1)	Davidson, G .... –(2)	Higgins, S .... 5(2)
Bone, A .... 9(3)	Deas, P .... 11(3)	Hislop, S .... 9(5)
Bullock, T 36	Ferguson, S .... 18(2)	Irvine, B 31
Campbell, C .... 3(2)	Gethins, C .... 5(12)	Lynch, P .... –(1)
Canning, M .... 23(2)	Gilbert, K .... 22(1)	Mackay, S .... 16(9)

McCulloch, M 34
McGarry, S .... 22(8)
McLeish, K .... 10(2)
Perry, M .... 19(1)
Robertson, H .... 30(1)
Tait, J .... 9(1)
Venetis, T .... 7(2)
Webb, S .... 16(1)
Winters, D .... 6(4)
Wood, M .... 7(4)

League goals (42): Ferguson 6, Bayne 5, Mackay 4, Robertson 4, Hislop 3, Irvine 3, McGarry 3, Bone 2, Canning 2, Gethins 2, Cowie 1, Gilbert 1, Higgins 1, McLeish 1, Venetis 1, Winters 1, Wood 1, Opponents 1.
Tennents Cup goals (1): Winters 1. **CIS Cup goals (4):** Bone 1, Cowie 1, McCulloch 1, Opponents 1. **Bell's Cup goals (4):** Gethins 2, Webb 1, Opponents 1.

ST JOHNSTONE

Ground: McDiarmid Park, Perth PH1 2SJ. **Capacity:** 10,673.
Telephone: 01738 459090. **Colours:** Royal blue. **Nickname:** Saints.

Baxter, M .... 15(3)
Connolly, P .... 27(8)
Cuthbert, K 22
Dods, D .... 21(2)
Ferry, M .... 4(5)
Forsyth, R .... 7(4)
Hartley, P 32
Hay, C .... 12(9)
Lovenkrands, T .... 16(3)
Macdonald, P .... 9(4)
Maher, M .... –(1)
Main, A 14
Malone, E 2
Maxwell, I 34
McCann, R .... 13(3)
McClune, D .... 3(1)
McCluskey, S 15
McCulloch, M .... 14(4)
Murray, G 33
Noble, S .... 8(4)
Panther, E .... 3(1)
Parker, K .... 17(9)
Reilly, M 32
Robertson, J 26
Robertson, M 10
Russell, C .... 3(5)
Stevenson, R .... 2(11)
Weir, J 2

League goals (49): Hay 9, Hartley 6, Connolly 5, Noble 5, Dods 3, Lovenkrands 3, Macdonald 3, Maxwell 3, Forsythe 2, McCann 2, Parker 2, Reilly 2, Robertson 1, Murray 1, Opponents 2.
Tennents Cup goals (2): Baxter 1, Connolly 1. **CIS Cup goals (3):** Hay 2, McCulloch 1. **Bell's Cup goals (5):** Macdonald 2, McCann 1, Murray 1, Stevenson 1.

ST MIRREN

Ground: St Mirren Park, Paisley PA3 2EJ. **Capacity:** 14,935.
Telephone: 0141 889 2558. **Colours:** Black and white. **Nickname:** Buddies.

Baker, M 10
Baltacha, S 5
Bauld, W 1
Broadfoot, K .... 21(2)
Cameron, M 28
Dempsie, M 8
Denham, G 15
Dow, A .... 5(5)
Dunbar, J .... 7(14)
Fellner, G 1
Ferguson, J .... –(1)
Gillies, R 33
Guy, G .... 15(5)
Jack, D .... –(1)
Kerr, C .... 9(10)
Lappin, S .... 27(7)
Lowing, D .... 14(7)
MacKenzie, S .... 1(1)
McGinty, B .... 23(1)
McGowan, J .... 13(1)
McHale,P .... 12(1)
McKenna, D .... –(4)
McLean, S .... 6(1)
McWilliam, G .... –(1)
Mendes, J .... 15(2)
Mitchell, A .... 10(1)
Muir, A .... 1(2)
Murray, H .... 13(2)
Robb, R .... 18(1)
Roberts, M .... 12(1)
Robertson, K 13
Ross, I 20
Roy, L 21
Rudden, P .... 11(5)
Yardley, M .... 5(7)

League goals (42): Cameron 12, Gillies 9, Mendes 6, Robb 3, Roberts 3, Denham 2, Broadfoot 1, MacKenzie 1, McGinty 1, McHale 1, McKenna 1, McLean 1, Opponents 1. **Tennents Cup goals:** None. **CIS Cup goals (4):** Cameron 2, Lappin 1, Yardley 1. **Bell's Cup goals (13):** Cameron 5, Gillies 3, Baltacha 1, Fellner 1, Guy 1, McGinty 1, Ross 1.

BELL'S SECOND DIVISION

AIRDRIE UNITED

Ground: Shyberry Excelsior Stadium, Airdrie ML6 8QZ. **Capacity:** 10,171.
Telephone: 01236 622000. **Colours:** White and red. **Nickname:** Diamonds.

Armstrong, P .... 32(3)	Gow, A .... 18(9)	Risser, O 1
Black, K 1	Harvey, P .... 7(6)	Ronald, P .... 15(14)
Boyle, J .... 7(2)	McAuley, S .... –(3)	Stewart, A 25
Brannigan, K 16	McGeown, M 35	Vareille, J 30
Cherrie, P .... 1(1)	McGowan, N .... 24(1)	Vella, S 15
Docherty, S 32	McGuire, D .... 11(8)	Wilson, M 28
Dunn, D .... 6(7)	McKeown, S .... 21(7)	Wilson, S .... 11(1)
Gardner, L .... 16(9)	McVey, W .... 15(2)	Wilson, W .... 19(5)
Glancy, M .... 10(10)	Miller, D .... –(2)	

League goals (51): Vareille 18, McKeown 10, Gow 5, Armstrong 3, Ronald 3, Docherty 2, Dunn 2, Glancy 2, McVey 2, McAuley 1, McGuire 1, Wilson, M 1, Wilson, S 1.
Tennents Cup goals (3): Gow 1, McGuire 1, Vareille 1. **CIS Cup goals (2):** Gow 1, Vella 1.
Bell's Cup goals (3): Docherty 1, Glancy 1, McGuire 1.

BERWICK RANGERS

Ground: Shielfield Park, Berwick-upon-Tweed TD15 2EF. **Capacity:** 4,131.
Telephone: 01289 307424. **Colours:** Black and gold. **Nickname:** Borderers.

Bennett, N .... 10(5)	Forrest, E 11	Murie, D 28
Blackley, D .... 1(4)	Forrest, G .... 27(3)	Neil,M 18
Bradley, M .... 18(8)	Godfrey, R .... 25(1)	Neill, A .... 14(4)
Brown, K .... 17(1)	Gray, D .... 16(3)	Robertson, J .... 3(5)
Burke, A 36	Inglis, N .... 10(1)	Smith, A .... 22(1)
Connell, G .... 11(5)	McCormick, M .... –(5)	Smith, D .... 31(2)
Connelly, G .... 31(4)	McDowell, M .... 11(3)	Smith, H 1
Ferguson, I .... 2(7)	McNichol, G 23	Wood, G .... 26(1)

League goals (43): Wood 12, Burke 11, Smith 8, Forrest 4, Bradoley 1, Brown 1, McNicholl 1, Neil 1, Neill 1, Opponents 3.
Tennents Cup goals (1): Burke 1. **CIS Cup goals (4):** Wood 2, Burke 1, Forrest 1. **Bell's Cup goals (4):** Burke 2, Bennett 1, Murie 1.

BRECHIN CITY

Ground: Glebe Park, Brechin DD9 6BJ. **Capacity:** 3,960.
Telephone: 01356 622856. **Colours:** Red, white and black. **Nickname:** City.

Black, R .... 22(7)	Fotheringham, M ...... 6(5)	McKecknie, G 1
Boyle, S .... 3(8)	Gibson, G .... 13(19)	Millar, M .... 16(1)
Cairney, H 29	Grant, R .... 22(3)	Miller, G .... 19(5)
Cairns, M 11	Hay, D 11	Riley, P .... 2(6)
Campbell, P .... –(5)	Jackson, C 32	Skinner, J 20
Clark, D .... 11(8)	King, Charles .... 29(4)	Smith, D .... 4(5)
Coulston, D .... 4(2)	King, Chris .... –(2)	Smith, J 30
Deas, P 15	McCulloch, G .... 14(3)	Templeman, C .... 34(1)
Donnachie, B .... 2(1)	McDonald, G .... 1(1)	Thomson, S 14
Fotheringham, K 31		

League goals (63): Templeman 22, King, Charles 9, Grant 8, Fotheringham, K 8, Gibson 4, Black 3, Clark 3, Smith, J 2, Cairney 1, Coulston 1, Smith, D 1, Opponents 1.
Tennents Cup goals (1): Riley 1. **CIS Cup goals (1):** Skinner 1. **Bell's Cup goals (12):** Grant 3, Fotheringham, K 2, Millar 2, Templeman 2, Jackson 1, King, Charles 1, Opponents 1.

COWDENBEATH

Ground: Central Park, Cowdenbeath KY4 9QQ. **Capacity:** 4,370.
Telephone: 01383 610166. **Colours:** Royal blue and white. **Nickname:** Blue Brazil.

Bain, J .... –(1)
Brown, G 34
Buchanan, L .... 2(8)
Byle, K .... 4(4)
Campbell, A .... 30(2)
Crabbe, G .... –(1)
Dair, L .... 9(4)
Dixon, J .... 2(2)
Elliott, J .... 14(14)
French, H 8
Fusco, G .... 3(4)
Gibb, S .... –(2)
Gilfillan, G .... –(6)
Gordon, K 35
Graham, M 10
Hilland, P 2
Mauchlen, I .... 22(2)
McDonald, I .... 10(2)
Miller, W 19
Mowat, D .... 15(1)
Munro, K .... 2(1)
Myles, J .... –(1)
O'Connor, G 26
Renwick, M .... 33(3)
Riordan, D 2
Smith, E .... 11(2)
Webster, C .... 12(3)
White, D .... 30(1)
Wilson, K .... 28(1)
Winter, C 30
Wright, K .... –(5)

League goals (46): Brown 10, Gordon 10, Mauchlen 5, Elliott 3, Riordan 3, Buchanan 2, Webster 2, White 2, Dair 1, Dixon 1, French 1, Hilland 1, Mowat 1, Wilson 1, Winter 1, Wright 1, Opponents 1.
Tennents Cup goals (9): Elliott 2, Brown 1, Buchanan 1, Byle 1, Gilfillan 1, Gordon 1, Riordan 1, Winter 1. **CIS Cup goals (4):** Brown 1, Elliott 1, French 1, Wilson 1. **Bell's Cup goals:** None. .

DUMBARTON

Ground: Strathclyde Homes Stadium, Dumbarton G82 2JA. **Capacity:** 3,750.
Telephone: 01389 762569. **Colours:** Yellow and black. **Nickname:** Sons.

Bonner, S .... 26(8)
Brittain, C 26
Brown, A .... 19(10)
Brown, T .... 23(3)
Collins, N 33
Crilly, M .... 12(2)
Dickie, M .... 20(1)
Dillon, J .... 34(1)
Donald, B .... 3(4)
Duffy, C 23
Flannery, P .... 18(8)
Grindlay, S 33
Lynes, C .... 4(10)
McCann, K .... 2(2)
McCutcheon, G ...... 23(7)
McEwan, C .... 20(2)
McKelvie, D .... 1(3)
McKeown, J .... 13(4)
Obidile, E .... 6(4)
Robertson, J .... 4(8)
Russell, I .... 8(3)
Scally, N .... 23(4)
Stewart, D .... 16(4)
Wight, J .... 3(1)

League goals (48): Flannery 8, McCutcheon 8, Dillon 7, Scally 5, Brown, A 4, Bonney 3, Obidile 3, Russell 3, Collins 2, Donald 1, Lynes 1, Brown, T 1, Opponents 1.
Tennents Cup goals: None. **CIS Cup goals:** None. **Bell's Cup goals (4):** Dillon 2, Brown, T 1, Duffy 1.

FORFAR ATHLETIC

Ground: Station Park, Forfar DD8 3BT. **Capacity:** 4,602.
Telephone: 01307 463576. **Colours:** Sky blue and navy. **Nickname:** Loons.

Anthony, M .... 13(12)
Bannon, M .... –(1)
Bavidge, M 36
Brown, M 31
Byers, K 36
Cocozza, M 2
Ferrie, N .... 5(1)
Good, I .... 24(1)
Greacen, S 17
Henderson, D .... 21(2)
Hodge, C .... –(6)
Horn, R 15
Lunan, P .... 28(4)
McCloy, B .... 12(2)
McCulloch, S .... 33(2)
Milne, K .... 11(5)
Rattray, A 28
Sellars, B 29
Shaw, G .... 6(7)
Stewart, W .... 10(16)
Taylor, S .... 3(3)
Tosh, P 31
Williams, D .... 5(4)

League goals (55): Bavidge 15, Tosh 13, Byers 9, Sellars 6, Stewart 2, Anthony 1, Greacen 1, Henderson 1, Hodge 1, Lunan 1, McCulloch 1, Milne 1, Rattray 1, Williams 1, Opponents 1.
Tennents Cup goals (8): Bavidge 3, Byers 2, Tosh 2, Lunan 1. **CIS Cup goals:** None. **Bell's Cup goals (4):** Tosh 3, Bavidge 1.

HAMILTON ACADEMICAL

Ground: New Douglas Park, Hamilton ML3 0FT. **Capacity:** 5,300.
Telephone: 01698 286103. **Colours:** Red and white. **Nickname:** Accies.

Arbuckle, A .... 3(2)
Armstrong, G .... 21(4)
Bonnar, M .... 28(1)
Callaghan, S 32
Cunningham, G 1
Cunnington, E .... 10(3)
Davidson, S .... –(1)
Dobbins, I .... 30(3)
Elfallah, M .... 9(9)
Flynn, P .... 4(2)
Graham, Alisdair .... 31(2)
Graham, Ally .... 22(6)
Gribben, D .... 1(2)
Hillcoat, C .... 3(3)
Keegans, M .... 6(5)
Kerr, D 16
McCreadie, I .... 2(4)
McDermott, A 2
McDonald, P .... 21(5)
McFarlane, I 13
McPhee, B .... 24(3)
Nelson, M .... 11(1)
Paterson, N .... 3(1)
Potter, G .... 23(3)
Russell, A .... 15(7)
Sherry, J .... 21(3)
Smillie, C .... 6(1)
Sweeney, S .... 24(2)
Thompson, S 1
Walker, J .... 13(1)

League goals (43): McPhee 11, Armstrong 9, Russell 6, Callaghan 4, Graham, Alisdair 4, Graham, Ally 3, Bonnar 2, Dobbins 2, Gribben 1, Opponents 1.
Tennents Cup goals (10): McPhee 4, Armstrong 2, Bonnar 2, Callaghan 1, Russell 1. **CIS Cup goals (1):** Callaghan 1. **Bell's Cup goals:** None.

RAITH ROVERS

Ground: Stark's Park, Kirkaldy KY1 1SA. **Capacity:** 10,104.
Telephone: 01592 263514. **Colours:** Navy blue and white. **Nickname:** Rov.

Blackadder, R .... 21(7)
Boylan, C .... 9(5)
Brady, D .... 32(2)
Brown, I 7
Browne, P 1
Calderon, A .... 16(6)
Carrigan, B .... 10(11)
Davidson, A .... –(1)
Dennis, S 29
Ellis, L 28
Fyfe, G .... 8(2)
Gonzalez, R 6
Hampshire, P .... 17(6)
Hawley, K .... 15(2)
Matheson, R .... 3(1)
McKinnon, R .... 10(2)
McManus, P .... 7(12)
Miller, S .... –(1)
Moffatt, A 4
Monin, S .... 1(1)
Nanou, W .... 25(4)
Ortiz, F 2
Paliczka, S .... –(2)
Paquito 28
Parkin, P .... 9(2)
Patino, C 24
Prest,M .... 14(10)
Raul 28
Rivas, F 5
Ross, D 3
Shields, D .... 6(7)
Smith, A .... 23(2)
Sweeney, J 1
Valdes, A 2

League goals (53): Hawley 7, Smith 6, Blackadder 5, Boylan 5, McManus 5, Carrigan 4, Prest 4, Nanou 3, Paquito 3, Dennis 2, McKinnon 2, Patino 2, Shields 2, Brady 1, Fyfe 1, Rivas 1.
Tennents Cup goals (4): Blackadder 1, Carrigan 1, Hawley 1, Smith 1. **CIS Cup goals (2):** Carrigan 1, Prest 1. **Bell's Cup goals:** None.

STENHOUSEMUIR

Ground: Ochilview Park, Stenhousemuir FK5 5QL. **Capacity:** 2,376.
Telephone: 01324 562992. **Colours:** Maroon and white. **Nickname:** Warriors.

Armstrong, M 1
Booth, M .... 28(1)
Carlin, A 3
Carr, D .... 1(2)
Coulter, R .... 14(4)
Crawford, B .... 16(9)
Donnelly, K .... 7(2)
Easton, S 34
Forrest, F 5
Gillespie, A 1
Graham, D .... 11(18)
Hamilton, S .... 26(3)
Harty, M .... 8(11)
Martin, B .... 3(1)
McCormick, S .... 29(4)
McFarlane, D .... 23(4)
McGowan, N 2
McKenna, G .... 30(1)
McKenzie, J .... 21(6)
McMillan, A 1
Murphy, P .... –(1)
Murphy, S .... 6(11)
Sandison, J 8
Smith, G 32
Stein, J .... 34(2)
Stone, M .... 6(2)
Waldie, C .... 28(2)
Wilson, M .... 18(3)

League goals (49): Booth 9, McFarlane 8, Crawford 7, McCormick 4, Coulter 3, Graham 3, Harty 3, Donnelly 2, McKenzie 2, Murphy 2, Waldie 2, Wilson 2, Sandison 1, Stein 1.
Tennents Cup goals (5): Coulter 1, Crawford 1, Graham 1, McFarlane 1, McCormick 1.
CIS Cup goals (3): Crawford 1, McCormick 1, Waldie 1. **Bell's Cup goals (1):** Wilson 1.

STRANRAER

Ground: Stair Park, Stranraer DG9 8BS. **Capacity:** 5,600.
Telephone: 01776 703271. **Colours:** Royal blue and white. **Nickname:** Blues.

Aitken, S 35
Crawford, J 3
Curran, H .... 7(9)
Fallon, J .... 4(10)
Farrell, D .... 15(2)
Finlayson, K .... 29(2)
Gaughan, K .... 26(1)
Grace, A .... 2(3)
Harty, I .... 31(1)
Hillcoat, J 27
Hodge, S .... 16(8)
Jenkins, A .... 33(2)
Kane, A .... 4(9)
Kerr, P .... 15(6)
Lurinsky, A .... 3(7)
Marshall, S .... 6(1)
McCulloch, W 9
McLaren, R .... –(3)
Moore, M 30
Renicks, S 2
Scott, A .... 5(1)
Sharp, L .... 28(4)
Wingate, D 34
Wright, F 32

League goals (49): Harty 12, Moore 10, Kerr 5, Finlayson 4, Jenkins 5, Sharp 4, Kane 2, Lurinsky 2, Crawford 1, Hodge 1, Wingate 1, Wright 1, Opponents 1.
Tennents Cup goals (13): Harty 4, Kerr 3, Sharp 2, Gaughan 1, Jenkins 1, Moore 1, Wingate 1. **CIS Cup goals (7):** Harty 3, Jenkins 1, Moore 1, Sharp 1, Opponents 1. **Bell's Cup goals (1):** Farrell 1.

BELL'S THIRD DIVISION

ALBION ROVERS

Ground: Cliftonhill Stadium, Coatbridge ML5 3RB. **Capacity:** 2,496.
Telephone: 01236 606334. **Colours:** Scarlet and yellow. **Nickname:** Wee Rov.

Bradford, J .... 24(10)
Carr, D .... –(4)
Cormack, P 32
Coulter, J .... 5(9)
Diack, I .... 16(18)
Dick, J .... 16(7)
Duncan, L .... 8(3)
Lumsden, T 34
McAllister, K .... 33(1)
McCaig, J .... 17(4)
McCaul, G .... –(4)
McKenzie, M .... –(1)
McKinnon, C .... –(2)
McLean, C .... 13(19)
Mercer, J .... 30(2)
Paterson, A .... 24(5)
Shearer, S 36
Silvestro, C .... 28(1)
Smith, J 35
Stirling, J 30
Weir, M .... –(5)
Yardley, M 15

League goals (62): Mercer 10, Bradford City 8, Diack 8, McLean 8, Yardley 8, Lumsden 5, Stirling 3, Dick 2, Duncan 2, Silvestro 2, Carr 1, Cormack 1, McCaig 1, Smith 1, Opponents 2.
Tennents Cup goals (1): Diack 1. **CIS Cup goals:** None. **Bell's Cup goals**: None.

EAST FIFE

Ground: Bayview Stadium, Methil KY8 3RW. **Capacity:** 2,000.
Telephone: 01333 426323. **Colours:** Gold and black. **Nickname:** Fifers.

Allison, J .... 23(3)
Butter, J 36
Cunningham, G .... 5(5)
Deuchar, K .... 30(2)
Donaldson, E .... 29(2)
Farnan, C .... 27(4)
Gilbert, G .... 15(14)
Graham, J .... 24(3)
Graham, R 2
Hall, M 36
Herkes, J .... 30(1)
Kerr, B .... –(1)
Love, G .... 11(16)
Lumsden, C .... 5(1)
McDonald, G .... –(1)
McLean, B .... 8(5)
McMillan, C .... 19(5)
Miller, C 14
Mortimore, P 30
Nairn, J .... 4(3)
Ovenstone, J .... 10(3)
Rollo, A .... 2(2)
Russell, G 36
Walker, D .... –(3)

League goals (73): Deuchar 21, Graham 11, Herkes 10, Gilbert 5, Farnan 4, Hall 4, Donaldson 3, Love 3, McLean 3, Ovenstone 3, McMillan 2, Allison 1, Cunningham 1, Mortimer 1, Nairn 1.
Tennents Cup goals (3): Herkes 2, Graham 1. **CIS Cup goals (2):** Deuchar 2. **Bell's Cup goals:** None.

EAST STIRLINGSHIRE

Ground: Firs Park, Falkirk FK2 7AY. **Capacity:** 1,632.
Telephone: 01324 623583. **Colours:** Black and white. **Nickname:** Shire.

Allison, S 15
Baldwin, S .... 5(1)
Boyle, G .... 9(13)
Campbell, M .... 7(5)
Carmichael, D 3
Clark, P 12
Diver, D .... –(1)
Drummond, J 5
Fairbairn, B 13
Findlay, S .... 17(1)
Grant, D .... 10(1)
Kelly, S 16
Leishman, J .... 24(5)
Livingston, S .... 13(5)
Lukowiecki, M 5
MacKay, J .... 24(1)
Macauley, S 8
Maughan, R 30
McAuley, S .... 24(1)
McCann, K .... 8(2)
McCulloch, G .... 3(4)
McGhee, G 32
McLaren, G .... 27(4)
Morrison, K 3
Oates, S .... 9(1)
Ormiston, D 4
Penman, C 10
Reid, C 7
Struthers, W .... 9(4)
Todd, C .... 19(1)
Ure, D .... 15(14)
Walker, L .... –(3)

League goals (32): Leishman 5, Ure 4, Kelly 3, Boyle 2, Fairbairn 2, Livingston 2, Macauley 2, McLaren 2, McAuley 2, Maughan 1, McCulloch 1, McGhee 1, Ormiston 1, Opponents 1.
Tennents Cup goals (2): Leishman 1, McLaren 1. **CIS Cup goals:** None. **Bell's Cup goals:** None.

ELGIN CITY

Ground: Borough Briggs, Elgin IV30 1AP. **Capacity:** 3,900.
Telephone: 01343 551114. **Colours:** Black and white. **Nickname:** Black and Whites.

Bremner, F .... 7(4)
Campbell, C .... 11(5)
Craig, D .... 14(3)
Gallagher, J 14
Grant, G .... 17(7)
Hamilton, G 5
Hind, D .... 28(5)
Hosie, B .... –(1)
James, R .... 7(15)
Love, C .... 21(4)
MacDonald, S .... 17(1)
MacKay, D 33
McBride, R .... 19(5)
McGregor, M .... –(4)
McMullan, R 33
Pirie, M 30
Rattray, S .... 2(3)
Ross, D 25
Sanderson, M .... 23(9)
Smith, A 3
Steele, K .... 32(1)
Tatters, G .... –(1)
Taylor, R 1
Teasdale, M .... 18(3)
Tully, C 34

League goals (33): Steele 6, McMullan 5, Ross 5, Tully 4, Sanderson 3, Teasdale 3, Craig 2, James 2, Bremner 1, Campbell 1, Love 1.
Tennents Cup goals: None. **CIS Cup goals:** None. **Bell's Cup goals (1):** Ross.

GRETNA

Alexander, R .... 1(1)
Barr, W 4
Bell, M .... 8(3)
Benjamin, A .... 2(4)
Cleeland, M 17
Cumersky, I .... 5(7)
Dobie, M .... 25(2)
Eeles, S .... 4(1)
Errington, R .... 1(1)
Fairbairn, B .... 9(4)
Galloway, M .... 15(1)
Gordon, W 9
Grainger, D .... 7(1)
Harding, G .... –(1)
Henney, M 21
Hewson, D .... 20(2)
Hore, J .... 18(3)
Irons, D 36
Knox, K 12
Mathieson, D 35
May, K 26
McGuffie, R .... 27(4)
McQuilter, R .... 15(1)
Milligan, S .... 1(2)
Ormiston, D .... 1(4)
Rooke, S .... 2(3)
Skelton, G .... 23(6)

Skinner, S .... 22(4)
Smart, C .... 1(3)
Thurston, M .... 3(1)
Thwaites, A .... 5(2)
Turner, T .... 19(1)
Wylie, D .... 1(1)

League goals (50): Dobie 10, Hore 8, Skinner 5, Henney 4, Benjamin 3, McGuffie 3, Eeles 2, Fairbain 2, Galloway 2, Irons 2, May 2, Skelton 2, Alexander 1, Cleeland 1, Gordon 1, Knox 1, Ormiston 1.
Tennents Cup goals (4): Dobie 2, Hore 1, Skinner 1. **CIS Cup goals (1):** Irons 1. **Bell's Cup goals (1):** Dobie 1.

MONTROSE

Ground: Links Park, Montrose DD10 8QD. **Capacity:** 4,338.
Telephone: 01674 673200. **Colours:** Royal blue and white. **Nickname:** Gable Endies.

Brand, R .... 5(13)
Budd, A .... 3(4)
Campbell, J 7
Christie, G 23
Conway, F .... 15(4)
Craig, D .... 9(3)
Donachie, B .... 14(2)
Ferguson, S .... 29(1)
Gibson, K .... 31(2)
Gilzean, I .... 6(7)
Johnson, G 21
Johnston, G .... 8(1)
Hankinson, M .... 1(1)
Henderson, R .... 13(9)
Kerrigan, S .... 25(4)
Leask, M .... –(3)
McCheyne, G .... 21(1)
McDonald, C .... 12(4)
McGlynn, G .... 28(1)
McKechnie, G 7
McKinnon, R .... 11(2)
McQuillan, J 35
Mitchell, J .... –(2)
Riley, P 14
Robertson, D 7
Sharp, G .... 4(6)
Thompson, G .... 11(3)
Webster, C .... 10(8)
Webster, K .... 24(6)

League goals (35): Kerrigan 8, Henderson 6, Gibson 3, McKechnie 3, Webster, K 3, Christie 2, Johnson 2, Johnston 2, McCheyne 2, Webster, C 2, McDonald 1, Opponents 1.
Tennents Cup goals (3): Gilzean 1, Johnson 1, Webster 1. **CIS Cup goals (2):** McDonald 1, Robertson 1. **Bell's Cup goals (1):** Johnson 1.

MORTON

Ground: Cappielow Park, Greenock PA15 2TY. **Capacity:** 7,890.
Telephone: 01475 723571. **Colours:** Royal blue, white and yellow. **Nickname:** Ton.

Adams, J 4
Annand, E 11
Bannerman, S .... 17(9)
Bottiglieri, E 31
Cannie, P .... 12(13)
Collins, D 36
Coyle, C 36
Curran, H .... –(3)
Dale, G 6
Gaughan, P .... 27(2)
Hawke, W .... 14(12)
Henderson, R 11
Hopkin, D 6
Macgregor, D 30
Maisano, J .... 31(2)
Maisano, M 32
McAlistair, J .... 2(3)
McDonald, S .... 12(10)
Millar, C 8
Miller, S 5
Riley, C .... 2(3)
Robertson, L 1
Smith, A .... 7(1)
Struthers, K .... –(1)
Uotinen, J .... 23(4)
Williams, A 31

League goals (67): Williams 23, Uotinen 8, Hawke 7, Maisano, J 6, Annand 5, Bannerman 3, Macgregor 3, Cannie 2, Gaughan 2, McDonald 2, Adams 1, Bottiglieri 1, Hopkin 1, Maisano, M 1,
Tennents Cup goals (6): Williams 3, McGregor 1, Uotinen 1, Opponents 1. **CIS Cup goals (2):** Bannerman 1, Hopkin 1. **Bell's Cup goals (3):** Williams 2, Hawke 1.

PETERHEAD

Ground: Balmoor Stadium, Peterhead AB42 IEU. **Capacity:** 3,250.
Telephone: 01779 478256. **Colours:** Royal blue and white. **Nickname:** Blue Toon.

Bain, K 29
Bisset, K .... –(3)
Bone, A .... 13(1)
Burns, G .... 12(4)
Camara, L .... –(14)
Cameron, D .... 21(5)
Clark, S .... 3(2)
Cooper, C .... 4(10)
Johnston, M .... 26(1)
Kidd, T .... –(4)
Livingstone, R .... 2(1)
MacDonald, C 29
MacKay, S .... 17(3)
Mathers, P 36
McLean, D .... 4(5)

McSkimming, S ...... 31(1)
Perry, M 13
Raeside, R 32
Robertson, K .... 2(8)
Roddie, A 31
Simpson, M 24 (1)
Slater, M 1
Stewart, I 30
Tindal, K 36

League goals (76): Stewart 21, Johnston 16, Roddie 11, Bone 9, Tindal 4, MacDonald 3, McLean 3, Camara 2, Robertson 2, Cameron 1, Bain 1, Kidd 1, MacKay 1, Raeside 1.

Tennents Cup goals (1): Cooper 1. **CIS Cup goals:** None. **Bells Cup goals:** None.

QUEEN'S PARK

Ground: Hampden Park, Glasgow G42 9BA. **Capacity:** 52,046.
Telephone: 0141 632 1275. **Nickname:** Spiders.

Agostini, D 34
Allan, J .... 25(1)
Cairns, M 13
Canning, S .... 17(7)
Clark, R .... 16(7)
Conlin, R 1
Crozier, B .... 4(3)
Dunning, A .... 7(7)
Fallon, S 30
Ferry, D .... 33(1)
Fisher, C .... 1(8)
Gallagher, J .... 11(2)
Gallagher, P .... 2(13)
Gemmell, J .... 31(2)
Jack, S .... 4(5)
Jackson, R .... –(1)
Kettlewell, S .... 9(1)
Lappin, G .... 3(1)
Lejman, K .... –(1)
Martin, W .... 18(9)
McCallum, D 11
Menelaws, D .... 6(5)
Mitchell, T 7
Moffat, S 21
Quinn, A 18
Sinclair, R .... 18(4)
Stewart, C 16
Taggart, C .... 4(4)
Whelan, J .... 31(1)
White, J .... 5(4)

League goals (39): Gemmill 8, Whelan 5, Allan 4, Moffat 4, Martin 3, Canning 2, Gallagher 2, McCallum 2, Menelows 2, Sinclair 2, Agostini 1, Clarke 1, Dunning 1, Ferry 1, Jack 1.

Tennents Cup goals (7): Gemmill 3, Allan 1, Martin 1, Menelows 1, Whelan 1. **CIS Cup goals (2):** Canning 1, Martin 1. **Bells Cup goals (9):** Allan 2, Gemmill 2, Moffat 2, Whelan 2, Canning 1.

STIRLING ALBION

Ground: Forthbank Stadium, Stirling FK7 7UJ. **Capacity:** 3,808.
Telephone: 01786 450399. **Colours:** White and navy. **Nickname:** Albion.

Beveridge, R .... 1(4)
Bowe, G 1
Butler, D .... –(2)
Crilly, M 12
Cummings, D .... 1(2)
Davidson, H .... 12(4)
Devine, S .... –(1)
Duncan, F .... 13(2)
Dunn, R .... 29(1)
Hay, P .... 31(4)
Hogarth, M 10
Johnston, R 1
Kerrigan, S .... 9(3)
Mallan, S .... 27(3)
McCall, D 2
McCole, D 2
McGeown, D .... 4(1)
McKinnon, C .... 20(1)
McLellan, K .... –(8)
McNally, M 30
Moore, A .... 2(4)
Morris, I 14
Munro, G .... 6(6)
Nicholas, S .... 29(2)
Nugent, A .... 3(1)
Nugent, P 36
O'Brien, D .... 26(2)
Reid, C 9
Reilly, S .... 5(6)
Rowe, G 33
Smith, A 10
Stuart, W .... 1(1)
Turner, I 13
Wilson, D .... 2(9)

League goals (50): Nicholas 11, O'Brien 8, Dunn 5, Mallan 5, Morris 5, Kerrigan 3, McKinnon 3, Crilly 2, Reilly 2, Rowe 2, Hay 1, McLellan 1, Wilson 1, Opponents 1.

Tennents Cup goals (1): McKinnon 1. **CIS Cup goals (5):** Nicholas 2, Dunn 1, Mallan 1, Munro 1. **Bell's Cup goals (2):** Munro 1, Nicholas 1.

F.A. BARLAYCARD PREMIERSHIP PLAYING STAFFS 2003-04

ARSENAL

Ground: Arsenal Stadium, Highbury, London, N5 1BU.
Telephone: 020 7704 4000 **Club nickname:** The Gunners.
First-choice colours: Red white shirts; white shorts; white stockings.
Record transfer fee: £13,000,000 to Bordeaux for Sylvain Wiltord, August 2000.
Record fee received: £25,000,000 from Barcelona for Marc Overmars, July 2000.
Record attendance: At Highbury: 73,295 v Sunderland March 1935. At Wembley: 73,707 v Lens (Champions League) November 1998.
Capacity for 2003-04: 38,500. **Sponsors:** O_2.
League Championship: winners 1930-31, 1932-33, 1933-34, 1934-35, 1937-38, 1947-48, 1952-53, 1970-71, 1988-89, 1990-91, 1997-98, 2001-02.
F.A. Cup: winners 1930, 1936, 1950, 1971, 1979, 1993, 1998, 2002, 2003.
League Cup: winners 1987, 1993.
European Competitions: winners Fairs Cup: 1969-70, Cup Winners Cup: 1993-94.
Finishing positions in Premiership: 1992-93 10th, 1993-94 4th, 1994-95 12th, 1995-96 5th, 1996-97 3rd, 1997-98 1st, 1998-99 2nd, 1999-2000 2nd, 2000-01 2nd, 2001-02 1st, 2002-03 2nd.
Biggest win: 12-0 v Loughborough Town, Div. 2, 12.3.1900.
Biggest defeat: 0-8 v Loughborough Town, Div. 2, 12.12.1896.
Highest League scorer in a season: Ted Drake, 42, 1934-35.
Most League goals in aggregate: Cliff Bastin, 150, 1930-47.
Most capped player: Kenny Sansom (England) 77.
Longest unbeaten League sequence: 30 matches (October 2002).
Longest sequence without a League win: 23 matches (September 1912).

Name	Height ft. in.	Previous club	Birthplace	Birthdate
Goalkeepers				
Shaaban, Rami	6. 4	Djurgaardens	Stockholm	30.06.75
Taylor, Stuart	6. 4	–	Romford	28.11.81
Warmuz, Guilluame	6. 2	Lens	St Vallier, Fra.	22.05.70
Defenders				
Campbell, Sol	6. 1	Tottenham	Newham	18.09.74
Cole, Ashley	5. 8	–	Stepney	20.12.80
Cygan, Pascal	6. 5	Lille	Lens	29.04.74
Halls, John	6. 0	–	Islington	14.02.82
Hoyte, Justin	5.11	–	Waltham Forest	20.11.84
Juan	5.11	Sao Paulo	Sao Paulo	6.02.82
Keown, Martin	6. 1	Everton	Oxford	24.07.66
Garry, Ryan	5.10	–	Hornchurch	29.09.83
Senderos, Philippe	6. 3	Servette	Switzerland	14.02.85
Stepanovs, Igors	6. 4	FC Skonto	Ogre, Lat.	21.01.76
Svard, Sebastian	5.10	FC Copenhagen	Hvidovre, Den.	15.01.83
Tavlaridis, Stathis	6. 1	Iraklis Saloniki	Serres, Gre.	25.01.80
Toure, Kolo	5.11	Abidjan	Ivory Coast	19.03.81
Volz, Moritz	6. 0	Schalke	Siegen, Ger.	21.01.83
Midfielders				
Edu	6. 1	Corinthians	Sao Paulo	15.05.78
Gilberto Silva	6. 3	Atletico Mineiro	Lagoada Prata, Bra.	7.10.76
Lauren	5.11	Real Mallorca	Londi Kribi, Cam.	19.01.77
Ljungberg, Fredrik	5.11	Halmstad	Halmstad	16.04.77
Parlour, Ray	5.10	–	Romford	7.03.73
Pennant, Jermaine	5. 9	Notts Co.	Nottingham	5.01.83
Pires, Robert	6. 1	Marseille	Reims	29.10.73

Van Bronckhorst, Giovanni	5.10	Rangers	Rotterdam	5.02.75
Vieira, Patrick	6. 4	AC Milan.	Dakar, Sen.	23.06.76
Forwards				
Aliadiere, Jeremie	6. 0	–	Rambouillet, Fra.	30.03.83
Bentley, David		–	Peterborough	27.08.84
Bergkamp, Dennis	6. 0	Inter Milan	Amsterdam	18.05.69
Henry, Thierry	6. 2	Juventus	Paris	17.08.77
Jeffers, Francis	5. 9	Everton	Liverpool	25.01.81
Kanu, Nwankwo	6. 5	Inter Milan	Owerri, Nig.	1.08.76
Wiltord, Sylvain	5. 9	Bordeaux	Neuilly, Fra.	10.05.74

ASTON VILLA

Ground: Villa Park, Trinity Road, Birmingham, B6 6HE.
Telephone: 0121 327 2299 **Club nickname:** Villans.
First-choice colours: Claret and blue shirts; white shorts; blue and claret stockings.
Record transfer fee: £9,500,000 to River Plate for Juan Pablo Angel, January 2001.
Record fee received: £12,600,000 for Dwight Yorke from Manchester Utd., August 1998.
Record attendance: 76,588 v Derby Co. (F.A. Cup 6) 2 March 1946.
Capacity for 2003-04: 42,573. **Sponsors:** Rover.
League Championship: winners 1893-94, 1895-96, 1896-97, 1898-99, 1899-1900, 1909-10, 1980-81.
F.A. Cup: winners 1887, 1895, 1897, 1905, 1913, 1920, 1957.
League Cup: winners 1961, 1975, 1977, 1994, 1996.
European Competitions: Winners European Cup 1981-82, European Super Cup 1982-83.
Finishing positions in Premiership: 1992-93 2nd, 1993-94 10th, 1994-95 18th, 1995-96 4th, 1996-97 5th, 1997-98 7th, 1998-99 6th, 1999-2000 6th, 2000-01 8th, 2001-02 8th, 2002-03 16th.
Biggest win: 12-2 v Accrington, Div. 1, 12.3.1892, 11-1 v Charlton Athletic, Div. 2, 24.11.1959, 10-0 v Sheffield Wed., Div. 1, 5.10.1912 and v Burnley, Div. 1, 29.8.1925.
Biggest defeat: 0-7 in five League matches from Blackburn Rov., Div. 1, 19.10.1889 to Manchester Utd., Div. 1, 24.10.1964.
Highest League scorer in a season: 'Pongo' Waring, 49, 1930-31.
Most League goals in aggregate: Harry Hampton, 215, 1904-1915.
Most capped player: Paul McGrath (Ireland) 51.
Longest unbeaten League sequence: 15 matches (January 1897, December 1909 and March 1949).
Longest sequence without a League win: 12 matches (November 1973 and December 1986).

Name	Height ft. in.	Previous club	Birthplace	Birthdate
Goalkeepers				
Enckelman, Peter	6. 2	Jalkapallo TPS	Turku, Fin.	10.03.77
Henderson, Wayne	5.11	–	Dublin	16.09.83
Postma, Stefan	6. 1	De Graafschap	Holland	10.06.76
Defenders				
Alpay, Ozalan	6. 2	Fenerbahce	Izmir	29.05.73
Barry, Gareth	6. 0	–	Hastings	23.02.81
Delaney, Mark	6. 1	Cardiff City	Haverfordwest	13.05.71
Edwards, Rob	6. 1	–	Telford	25.12.82
Johnsen, Ronny	6. 3	Manchester Utd.	Sandefjord, Nor.	10.06.69
Kinsella, Mark	5. 9	Charlton Athletic	Dublin	12.08.72
Mellberg, Olof	6. 1	Racing Santander	Stockholm	9.03.77
Ridgewell, Liam	5.10	–	London	21.07.84
Samuel, Jlloyd	5.11	–	Trinidad	24.05.79
Staunton, Steve	6. 1	Liverpool	Drogheda	19.01.69
Midfielders				
Cooke, Stephen	5. 7	–	Walsall	15.02.83

De la Cruz, Ulises	5.11	Hibernian	Quito, Ec.	8.02.74
Hadji, Moustapha	6. 0	Coventry City	Ifrane, Mor.	16.11.71
Hendrie, Lee	5.10	–	Birmingham	18.05.77
Hitzlsperger, Thomas	6. 0	Bayern Munich	Munich	5.04.82
Kachloul, Hassan	6. 2	Southampton	Agadir	19.02.73
Leonhardsen, Oyvind	5.10	Tottenham	Kristiansund, Nor.	17.08.70
Whittingham, Peter	5.10	–	Nuneaton	8.09.84
Forwards				
Allback, Marcus	5.11	Heerenveen	Gothenburg	5.07.73
Angel, Juan Pablo	5.11	River Plate	Medellin, Col.	21.10.75
Balaban, Bosko	5.11	Dinamo Zagreb	Rijeka, Cro.	15.10.78
Crouch, Peter	6. 6	Portsmouth	Macclesfield	30.01.81
Dublin, Dion	6. 2	Coventry City	Leicester	22.04.69
Moore, Stefan	5.11	–	Birmingham	28.09.83
Vassell, Darius	5. 7	–	Birmingham	13.06.80

BIRMINGHAM CITY

Ground: St Andrews, Birmingham B9, 4NH.
Telephone: 07091 112 5837. **Clubcall:** 09068 121188. **Club nickname:** Blues.
First-choice colours: Blue shirts, blue shorts, white stockings.
Record transfer fee: £5,500,000 to Blackburn Rov. for David Dunn, July 2003.
Record fee received: £2,500,000 from Coventry City for Gary Breen, January 1997.
Record attendance: 66,844 v Everton (F.A. Cup 5) 11 February, 1967.
Capacity for 2003-04: 30,007. **Sponsors:** Phones 4U.
League championship: 6th 1955-56.
F.A. Cup: runners-up 1931, 1956.
League Cup: winners 1963.
European Competitions: runners-up Fairs Cup 1959-60, 1960-61.
Finishing position in Premiership: 2002-03 13th
Biggest win: 12-0 v Walsall, Div. 2, 17.12.1892, 12-0 v Doncaster Rov., Div. 2, 11.4.1903.
Biggest defeat: 1-9 v Sheffield Wed., Div. 1, 13.12.30. 1-9 v Blackburn Rov., Div. 1, 5.1.1895.
Highest League scorer in a season: Joe Bradford, 29, 1927-28.
Most League goals in aggregate: Joe Bradford, 249, 1920-35.
Most capped player: Malcolm Page, 28, Wales.
Longest unbeaten League sequence: 20 matches (January 1995).
Longest sequence without a League win: 17 matches (January 1986).

Name	Height ft. in.	Previous club	Birthplace	Birthdate
Goalkeepers				
Bennett, Ian	6. 0	Peterborough Utd.	Worksop	10.10.71
Vaesen, Nico	6. 1	Huddersfield Town	Ghent	28.09.69
Defenders				
Cisse, Aliou	6. 0	Montpellier	Zinguinchor, Sen.	24.03.76
Clapham, Jamie	5. 9	Ipswich Town	Lincoln	7.12.75
Cunningham, Kenny	5.11	Wimbledon	Dublin	28.06.71
Grainger, Martin	5.10	Brentford	Enfield	23.08.72
Johnson, Michael	5.11	Notts Co.	Nottingham	4.07.73
Kenna, Jeff	5.11	Blackburn Rov.	Dublin	27.08.70
Purse, Darren	6. 2	Oxford Utd.	Stepney	14.02.76
Sadler, Matthew	5.11	–	Birmingham	26.02.85
Tebily, Olivier	6. 0	Celtic	Abidjan, Iv. Coast	19.12.75
Upson, Matthew	6. 1	Arsenal	Eye	18.04.79
Williams, Tommy	5.11	Peterborough Utd.	Carshalton	8.07.80
Midfielders				
Carter, Darren	6. 2	–	Solihull	18.12.83
Clemence, Stephen	5.11	Tottenhamn	Liverpool	31.03.78
Devlin, Paul	5. 9	Sheffield Utd.	Birmingham	14.04.72

Dunn, David	5.10	Blackburn Rov.	Blackburn	27.12.79
Grondin, Christophe	5.11	–	Toulouse	2.09.83
Hughes, Bryan	5. 9	Wrexham	Liverpool	19.06.76
Johnson, Damien	5.10	Blackburn Rov.	Lisburn	18.11.78
Lazaridis, Stan	5. 9	West Ham Utd.	Perth, Aus.	16.08.72
Savage, Robbie	5.11	Leicester City	Wrexham	18.10.74
Woodhouse, Curtis	5. 8	Sheffield Utd.	Beverley	17.04.80
Forwards				
Dugarry, Christophe	6. 3	Bordeaux	Lormont, Fra.	24.03.72
Fagan, Craig	5.11	–	Birmingham	11.12.82
Horsfield, Geoff	6. 1	Fulham	Barnsley	1.11.73
John, Stern	6. 1	Nott'm. Forest	Canefarm, Trin.	30.10.76
Kirovski, Jovan	6. 1	Crystal Palace	Escondido, USA	18.03.76
Morrison, Clinton	6. 1	Crystal Palace	Tooting	14.05.79

BLACKBURN ROVERS

Ground: Ewood Park, Blackburn BB2 4JF.
Telephone: 01254 698888 **Clubcall:** 09068 121179. **Club nickname:** Rovers.
First-choice colours: Blue and white shirts; white shorts; white and blue stockings.
Record transfer fee: £8,000,000 to Manchester Utd. for Andy Cole, December 2001.
Record fee received: £15,000,000 from Newcastle Utd. for Alan Shearer, July 1996.
Record attendance: 62,522 v Bolton Wand., F.A. Cup 6th Rd, 2 March 1929.
Capacity for 2003-04: 31,165. **Sponsors:** HSA.
League championship: winners 1911-12, 1913-14, 1994-95.
F.A. Cup: winners 1884, 1885, 1886, 1890, 1891, 1928.
League Cup: winners 2002.
European Competitions: Champions League 1st group stage 1995-96.
Finishing positions in Premiership: 1992-93 4th, 1993-94 2nd, 1994-95 1st, 1995-96 7th, 1996-97 13th, 1997-98 6th, 1998-99 19th, 2001-02 10th, 2002-03 6th.
Biggest win: 9-0 v Middlesbrough, Div. 2, 6.11.1954. Also 11-0 v Rossendale, F.A. Cup 1st Rd, 13.10.1884.
Biggest defeat: 0-8 v Arsenal, Div. 1, 25.2.1933.
Highest League scorer in a season: Ted Harper, 43, 1925-26.
Most League goals in aggregate: Simon Garner, 168, 1978-92.
Most capped player: Bob Crompton (England) 41.
Longest unbeaten League sequence: 23 matches (September 1987).
Longest sequence without a League win: 16 matches (November 1978).

Name	Height ft. in.	Previous club	Birthplace	Birthdate
Goalkeepers				
Friedel, Brad	6. 3	Liverpool	Lakewood, USA	18.05.71
Kelly, Alan	6. 2	Birmingham City	Preston	11.08.68
Defenders				
Amoruso, Lorenzo	6. 2	Rangers	Palese, Ita.	28.06.71
Curtis, John	5.10	Manchester Utd.	Nuneaton	3.09.78
Greer, Gordon	6. 2	Clyde	Glasgow	17.08.82
Johansson, Nils-Eric	6. 1	Nurnberg	Stockholm	13.01.80
McEveley, James	5.10	–	Liverpool	2.11.85
Neill, Lucas	6. 1	Millwall	Sydney	9.03.78
Pelzer, Marc Sebastian	6. 0	Kaiserslautern	Trier, Ger	24.09.80
Short, Craig	6. 2	Everton	Bridlington	25.06.68
Taylor, Martin	6. 4	–	Ashington	9.11.79
Todd, Andy	5.10	Charlton Athletic	Derby	21.09.74
Midfielders				
Danns, Neil	5.10	–	Liverpool	23.11.82
Douglas, Jonathan	5.11	–	Monaghan	22.11.81
Emerton, Brett	6. 1	Feyenoord	Bankstown, Aus	22.02.79
Flitcroft, Gary	6. 0	Manchester City	Bolton	6.11.72
Hignett, Craig	5. 9	Barnsley	Liverpool	12.01.70

Mahon, Alan	5. 9	Sporting Lisbon	Dublin	4.04.78
Taylor, Michael	5.10	–	Liverpool	21.11.82
Thompson, David	5. 7	Coventry City	Birkenhead	12.09.77
Todd, Andy	5.10	Charlton Athletic	Derby	21.09.74
Tugay, Kerimoglu	5. 9	Rangers	Istanbul	24.08.70
Forwards				
Cole, Andy	5.10	Manchester Utd.	Nottingham	15.10.71
Duff, Damien	5. 8	–	Ballyboden	2.03.79
Gallagher, Paul	6. 0	–	Blackburn	9.08.84
Grabbi, Corrado	5.11	Ternana	Turin	29.07.75
Jansen, Matt	5.11	Crystal Palace	Carlisle.	20.10.77
Ostenstad, Egil	5.11	Southampton	Haugesund, Nor.	2.01.72
Yorke, Dwight	5.10	Manchester Utd.	Canaan, Tob.	3.11.71

BOLTON WANDERERS

Ground: Reebok Stadium, Burnden Way, Lostock, Bolton BL6 6JW.
Telephone: 01204 673673 **Clubcall:** 09068 121164. **Club nickname:** The Trotters.
First-choice colours: White shirts; white shorts; white stockings.
Record transfer fee: £3,500,000 to Wimbledon for Dean Holdsworth, October 1997.
Record fee received: £4,500,000 from Liverpool for Jason McAteer, September 1995.
Record attendance: At Reebok Stadium: 27,409 v Manchester Utd. (Premier League) 22 February 2003. At Burnden Park: 69,912 v Manchester City, F.A. Cup 5th Rd, 18 February 1933.
Capacity for 2003-04: 27,500. **Sponsors:** Reebok.
League championship: 3rd 1891-92, 1920-21, 1924-25.
F.A. Cup: winners 1923, 1926, 1929, 1958.
League Cup: runners-up 1995.
Finishing positions in Premiership: 1995-96 20th, 1997-98 18th, 2001-02 16th, 2002-03 17th.
Biggest win: 8-0 v Barnsley, Div. 2, 6.10.1934. Also 13-0 v Sheffield Utd., F.A. Cup 2nd Rd, 1.2.1890.
Biggest defeat: 1-9 v Preston N.E., F.A. Cup 2nd Rd, 10.12.1887.
Highest League scorer in a season: Joe Smith, 38, 1920-21.
Most League goals in aggregate: Nat Lofthouse, 255, 1946-61.
Most capped player: Mark Fish (South Africa) 34.
Longest unbeaten League sequence: 23 matches (October 1990).
Longest sequence without a League win: 26 matches (April 1902).

Name	Height ft. in.	Previous club	Birthplace	Birthdate
Goalkeepers				
Jaaskelainen, Jussi	6. 4	VPS	Vaasa, Fin	17.04.75
Poole, Kevin	5.10	Birmingham City	Bromsgrove	21.07.63
Defenders				
Barness, Anthony	5.11	Charlton Athletic	Lewisham	25.03.73
Charlton, Simon	5. 8	Birmingham City	Huddersfield	25.10.71
Hunt, Nicky	6. 1	–	Bolton	3.09.83
Laville, Florent	6. 1	Lyon	Valnece, Fra.	8.07.73
Livesey, Daniel	6. 0	–	Salford	31.12.84
N'Gotty, Bruno	6. 2	Marseille	Lyon	10.06.71
Midfielders				
Forschelet, Gerald	5.11	Cannes	Papeete, Tah.	19.09.81
Frandsen, Per	6. 1	Blackburn Rov.	Copenhagen	6.02.70
Giannakopoulos, Stylianos	5. 8	Olympiakos	Greece	12.07.74
Johnson, Jermaine	5. 9	Tivoli Gardens	Jamaica	25.06.80
Nolan, Kevin	6. 1	–	Liverpool	24.06.82
Gardner, Ricardo	5. 9	Harbour View	St Andrews, Jam.	25.09.78
Pedersen, Henrik	6. 1	Silkeborg	Denmark	10.06.75
Smith, Jeff	5.10	Bishop Auckland	Middlesbrough	28.06.80
Taylor, Cleveland	5.11	–	Leicester	9.09.83

Forwards				
Djorkaeff, Youri	5.11	Kaiserslautern	Lyon	3.09.68
Facey, Delroy	5.11	Huddersfield Town	Huddersfield	22.04.80
Okocha, Jay-Jay	5.10	Paris SG	Enugu, Nig.	14.08.73
Walters, Jonathan	5.10	Blackburn Rov.	Birkenhead	20.09.83

CHARLTON ATHLETIC

Ground: The Valley, Floyd Road, Charlton, London, SE7 8BL.
Telephone: 0208 333 4000. **Club nickname:** Addicks.
First-choice colours: Red shirts; white shorts; red stockings.
Record transfer fee: £4,750,000 to Wimbledon for Jason Euell, July 2001.
Record fee received: £4,000,000 from Leeds Utd. for Danny Mills, July 1999.
Record attendance: 75,031 v Aston Villa (F.A. Cup 5) 12 February 1938.
Capacity for 2003-04: 26,819. **Sponsors:** all:sports.
League Championship: 2nd 1936-37.
F.A. Cup: winners 1947.
League Cup: 4th rnd 1963, 1966, 1979, 2001.
Finishing positions in Premiership: 1998-99 18th, 2000-01 9th, 2001-02 14th, 2002-03 12th.
Biggest win: 8-1 v Middlesbrough, Div. 1, 12 September 1953.
Biggest defeat: 1-11 v Aston Villa, Div. 2, 14 November 1959.
Highest League scorer in a season: Ralph Allen, 32, Div. 3 (south), 1934-35.
Most League goals in aggregate: Stuart Leary, 153, 1953-62.
Most capped player: Mark Kinsella (Rep. of Ireland) 33.
Longest unbeaten League sequence: 15 matches (December 1980).
Longest sequence without a League win: 16 matches (August 1955).

Name	**Height ft. in.**	**Previous club**	**Birthplace**	**Birthdate**
Goalkeepers				
Kiely, Dean	6. 1	Bury	Salford	10.10.70
Rachubka, Paul	6. 1	Manchester Utd.	San Luis, USA	21.05.81
Royce, Simon	6. 2	Leicester City	Forest Gate	9.09.71
Defenders				
Fish, Mark	6. 3	Bolton Wand.	Cape Town	14.03.74
Fortune, Jonathan	6. 2	–	Islington	28.08.80
Hreidarsson, Hermann	6. 1	Ipswich Town	Iceland	11.07.74
Kishishev, Radostin	5.11	Liteks Lovech	Burgas, Bul.	30.07.74
Konchesky, Paul	5.10	–	Barking	15.05.81
Powell, Chris	5.10	Derby Co.	Lambeth	8.09.69
Rowett, Gary	6. 0	Leicester City	Bromsgrove	6.03.74
Rufus, Richard	6. 1	–	Lewisham	12.01.75
Turner, Michael	6. 4	–	Lewisham	9.11.83
Young, Luke	6. 0	Tottenham	Harlow	19.07.79
Midfielders				
Bart-Williams, Chris	5.11	Nott'm. Forest	Freetown, SL.	16.06.74
Campbell-Ryce, Jamal	5.10	Millwall	Lambeth	6.04.83
Deane, Adrian	5.11	–	London	24.02.83
Holland, Matt	5. 9	Ipswich Town	Bury	11.04.74
Jensen, Claus	5.11	Bolton Wand.	Nykobing, Den.	29.04.77
Parker, Scott	5. 7	–	Lambeth	13.10.80
Stuart, Graham	5. 9	Sheffield Utd.	Tooting	24.10.70
Forwards				
Bartlett, Shaun	6. 1	FC Zurich	Cape Town	31.10.72
Debolla, Mark	5. 7	–	London	1.01.83
Euell, Jason	5.11	Wimbledon	Lambeth	6.02.77
Johansson, Jonatan	6. 2	Rangers	Stockholm	16.08.75
Lisbie, Kevin	5.10	–	Hackney	17.10.78
Svensson, Matt	6. 0	Crystal Palace	Boras, Swe.	24.09.74

CHELSEA

Ground: Stamford Bridge Stadium, London SW6 1HS.
Telephone: 0207 385 5545 **Clubcall:** 09068 121159. **Club nickname:** The Blues.
First-choice colours: Blue shirts; blue shorts; white stockings.
Record transfer fee: £15,000,000 to Atletico Madrid for Jimmy Floyd Hasselbaink, June 2000.
Record fee received: £12,000,000 from Rangers for Tore Andre Flo, November 2000.
Record attendance: 82,905 v Arsenal, Div. 1, 12 October 1935.
Capacity for 2003-04: 42,449. **Sponsors:** Emirates.
League Championship: winners 1954-55.
F.A. Cup: winners 1970, 1997, 2000.
League Cup: winners 1965, 1998.
European Competitions: winners Cup Winners' Cup 1970-71, 1997-98.
Finishing positions in Premiership: 1992-93 11th, 1993-94 14th, 1994-95 11th, 1995-96 11th, 1996-97 6th, 1997-98 4th, 1998-99 3rd, 1999-2000 5th, 2000-01 6th, 2001-02 6th, 2002-03 4th.
Biggest win: 7-0 in four League matches from Lincoln City, Div. 2, 29.10.1910 to Walsall, Div. 2, 4.2.1989. Also 9-2 v Glossop N.E. Div. 2, 1.9.1906.
Biggest defeat: 1-8 v Wolves, Div. 1, 26.9.1923. Also 0-7 v Leeds Utd., Div. 1, 7.10.1967 and v Nott'm. For. Div. 1, 20.4.1991.
Highest League scorer in a season: Jimmy Greaves, 41, 1960-61.
Most League goals in aggregate: Bobby Tambling, 164, 1958-70.
Most capped player: Marcel Desailly (France) 59.
Longest unbeaten League sequence: 27 matches (October 1988).
Longest sequence without a League win: 21 matches (November 1987).

Name	Height ft. in.	Previous club	Birthplace	Birthdate
Goalkeepers				
Ambrosio, Marco	6. 2	Chievo	Brescia	30.05.73
Cudicini, Carlo	6. 1	Castel Di Sangro	Milan	6.09.73
Macho, Jurgen	6. 4	Sunderland	Vienna	24.08.77
Makaba, Yves	6. 4	PSV Eindhoven	Belgium	–
Defenders				
Babayaro, Celestine	5. 9	Anderlecht	Kaduna, Nig.	29.08.78
Bogarde, Winston	6. 2	Barcelona	Rotterdam	22.10.70
Desailly, Marcel	6. 0	AC Milan	Accra	7.09.68
Di Cesare, Valerio	6. 0	–	Rome	23.05.83
Gallas, William	6. 1	Marseille	Asnieres, Fra.	17.08.77
Huth, Robert	6. 2	–	Berlin	18.08.84
Kitamirike, Joel	5.11	–	Kampala, Ug.	5.04.84
Le Saux, Graeme	5.10	Blackburn Rov.	Jersey	17.10.68
Melchiot, Mario	6. 2	Ajax	Amsterdam	4.11.76
Terry, John	6. 1	–	Barking	7.12.80
Thornton, Paul	5. 8	–	Surrey	7.01.83
Midfielders				
Gronkjaer, Jesper	6. 1	Ajax	Nuuk, Den.	12.08.77
Keenan, Joe	5. 8	–	Southampton	14.10.82
Kniessl, Sebastien	6. 0	–	Lindelfels, Ger.	13.01.83
Lampard, Frank	6. 0	West Ham Utd.	Romford	20.06.78
Nicholas, Alexis	5.10	–	London	13.02.83
Petit, Emmanuel	6. 1	Barcelona	Dieppe	22.09.70
Stanic, Mario	6. 2	Parma	Sarajevo	10.04.72
Forwards				
Ambrosetti, Gabriele	5.10	Vicenza	Varese, Ita.	7.08.73
Cole, Carlton	6. 3	–	Surrey	12.10.83
Gudjohnsen, Eidur	6. 0	Bolton Wand.	Reykjavik	15.09.78
Hasselbaink, Jimmy Floyd	6. 0	Atletico Madrid	Paramaribo, Sur.	27.03.72
Forssell, Mickael	6. 0	Helsinki	Steinfurt, Ger.	15.03.81
Knight, Leon	5. 4	–	London	16.09.82

Oliveira, Felipe	5.10	FC Porto	Braga, Por.	27.05.84
Zenden, Boudewijn	5.10	Barcelona	Maastricht	15.08.76

EVERTON

Ground: Goodison Park, Liverpool L4 4EL.
Telephone: 0151 330 2200 **Club nickname:** Toffees.
First-choice colours: Blue shirts; white shorts; blue stockings.
Record transfer fee: £5,750,000 to Middlesbrough for Nick Barmby.
Record fee received: £8,000,000 from Arsenal for Francis Jeffers, June 2001.
Record attendance: 78,299 v Liverpool, Div. 1, September 1948.
Capacity for 2003-04: 40,170. **Sponsors:** Kejian.
League Championship: winners 1890-91, 1914-15, 1927-28, 1931-31, 1938-39, 1962-63, 1969-70, 1984-85, 1986-87.
F.A. Cup: winners 1906, 1933, 1966, 1984, 1995.
League Cup: runners up 1977, 1984.
European Competitions: winners Cup-Winners' Cup 1984-85.
Finishing positions in Premiership: 1992-93 13th, 1993-94 17th, 1994-95 15th 1995-96 6th 1996-97 15th 1997-98 17th 1998-99 14th, 1999-2000 13th, 2000-01 16th, 2001-02 15th, 2002-03 7th.
Biggest win: 9-1 v Manchester City, Div. 1, 3.9.1906, v Plymouth Argyle, Div. 2, 27.12.1930. Also 11-2 v Derby Co., F.A. Cup 1st rd, 18.1.1890.
Biggest defeat: 4-10 v Tottenham, Div. 1, 11.10.1958.
Highest League scorer in a season: Ralph 'Dixie' Dean, 60, 1927-28.
Most League goals in aggregate: Ralph 'Dixie' Dean, 349, 1925-37.
Most capped player: Neville Southall (Wales) 92.
Longest unbeaten League sequence: 20 matches (April 1978).
Longest sequence without a League win: 14 matches (March 1937).

Name	Height ft. in.	Previous club	Birthplace	Birthdate
Goalkeepers				
Gerrard, Paul	6. 2	Oldham Athletic	Heywood	22.01.73
Simonsen, Steve	6. 3	Tranmere Rov.	South Shields	3.04.79
Wright, Richard	6. 2	Arsenal	Ipswich	5.11.77
Defenders				
Clarke, Peter	5.11	–	Southport	3.01.82
Hibbert, Tony	5.10	–	Liverpool	20.02.81
Naysmith, Gary	5.11	Hearts	Edinburgh	16.11.78
O'Hanlon, Sean	6. 2	–	Liverpool	20.01.83
Stubbs, Alan	6. 2	Celtic	Kirkby	6.10.71
Pistone, Alessandro	5.11	Newcastle Utd.	Milan	27.07.75
Unsworth, David	6. 1	Aston Villa	Chorley	16.10.73
Weir, David	6. 2	Hearts	Falkirk	10.05.70
Yobo, Joseph	6. 2	Marseille	Kano, Nig.	6.09.80
Midfielders				
Alexandersson, Niclas	6. 2	Sheffield Wed.	Halmstad, Swe.	29.12.71
Carsley, Lee	5. 9	Coventry City	Birmingham	28.02.74
Gemmill, Scot	5. 9	Nott'm. Forest	Paisley	2.01.71
Gravesen, Thomas	5. 9	Hamburg	Vejle, Den.	11.03.76
Linderoth, Tobias	5. 8	Stabaek	Marseille	21.04.79
McLeod, Kevin	5.10	–	Liverpool	12.09.80
Osman, Leon	5. 8	–	Billinge	17.05.81
Pembridge, Mark	5. 7	Sheffield Wed.	Merthyr Tydfil	28.11.70
Watson, Steve	6. 0	Aston Villa	North Shields	1.04.74
Forwards				
Campbell, Kevin	6. 1	Trabzonspor	Lambeth	4.02.70
Chadwick, Nick	5.11	–	Stoke	26.10.82
Ferguson, Duncan	6. 4	Newcastle Utd.	Stirling	27.12.71
Radzinski, Tomasz	5. 9	Anderlecht	Poznan, Pol.	14.12.73

Rooney, Wayne	5.10	–	Liverpool	24.10.85

FULHAM

Ground (sharing): Loftus Road, South Africa Road, London W12 7PA.
Training ground: Motspur Park, New Malden, Surrey KT3 6PT.
Telephone: 0870 442 1222 **Club nickname:** Cottagers.
First-choice colours: White shirts; black shorts; white stockings.
Record transfer fee: £11,500,000 to Lyon for Steve Marlet, August 2001.
Record fee received: £3,500,000 from Liverpool for Steve Finnan, June 2003.
Record attendance: 49,335 v Millwall, Division 2, 8 October 1938.
Capacity for 2003-04: 17,801 (at Loftus Road).
League championship: 10th 1959-60.
F.A. Cup: runners-up 1975.
League Cup: 5th Rd. 1968, 1971, 2000.
Finishing positions in Premiership: 2001-02 13th, 2002-03 14th.
Biggest win: 10-1 v Ipswich Town, Div. 1, 26.12.63.
Biggest defeat: 0-10 v Liverpool, League Cup 2nd Rd 1st leg, 23.9.86.
Highest League scorer in a season: Frank Newton, 43, 1931-32.
Most League goals in aggregate: Gordon Davies, 159, 1978-84 and 1986-91.
Most capped player: Johnny Haynes (England) 56.
Longest unbeaten League sequence: 15 matches (January 1999).
Longest sequence without a League win: 15 matches (February 1950).

Name	Height ft. in.	Previous club	Birthplace	Birthdate
Goalkeepers				
Herrera, Martin	6. 1	Deportivo Alaves	Rio Puerto, Arg.	13.09.70
Taylor, Maik	6. 3	Southampton	Hildeshein, Ger.	4.09.71
Van der Sar, Edwin	6. 6	Juventus	Voorhout, Hol.	29.10.70
Defenders				
Goma, Alain	6. 0	Newcastle Utd.	Sault, Fra.	5.10.72
Hudson, Mark	6. 3	–	Guildford	30.03.82
Knight, Zat	6. 6	–	Solihull	2.05.80
Leacock, Dean	6. 2	–	Croydon	10.06.84
Melville, Andrew	6. 1	Sunderland	Swansea	29.11.68
Ouaddou, Abdeslam	6. 3	Nancy	Ksar-Askour, Mor.	1.11.78
Midfielders				
Clark, Lee	5. 8	Sunderland	Wallsend	27.10.72
Davis, Sean	5.11	–	Clapham	20.09.79
Harley, Jon	5. 9	Chelsea	Maidstone	26.09.79
Inamoto, Junichi	6. 0	Gambia Osaka	Osaka	18.09.79
Legwinski, Sylvain	6. 1	Bordeaux	Clermont-Ferrand	10.06.73
Malbranque, Steed	5. 8	Lyon	Mouscron, Bel.	6.01.80
Forwards				
Boa Morte, Luis	5. 9	Southampton	Lisbon	4.08.77
Hammond, Elvis	5.10	–	Accra	6.10.80
Hayles, Barry	5.10	Bristol Rov.	London	17.05.72
Marlet, Steve	5.11	Lyon	Pithiviers, Fra.	1.10.74
Saha, Louis	6. 1	Metz	Paris	8.08.78
Sava, Facundo	6. 1	Gimnasia	Ituzaingo, Arg.	7.03.74
Stolcers, Andrejs	5.11	Shakhtar Donetsk	Latvia	7.08.74
Willock, Callum	6. 1	–	London	29.10.81

LEEDS UNITED

Ground: Elland Road, Leeds LS11 OES.
Telephone: 0113 226 6000 **Clubcall:** 09068 121180. **Club nickname:** Whites.
First-choice colours: White shirts, shorts and stockings (all with royal blue trim).

Record transfer fee: £18,000,000 to West Ham Utd. for Rio Ferdinand, November 2000.
Record fee received: £29,000,000 from Manchester Utd. for Rio Ferdinand, July 2002.
Record attendance: 57,892 v Sunderland, 15 March 1967.
Capacity for 2003-04: 40,234. **Sponsors:** Whyte & Mackay.
League Championship: winners 1968-69, 1973-74, 1991-92.
F.A. Cup: winners 1972.
League Cup: winners 1968.
European Competitions: winners Fairs Cup 1967-68, 1970-71. Runners-up European Cup 1974-75, Cup-Winners' Cup 1972-73.
Finishing positions in Premiership: 1992-93 17th, 1993-94 5th, 1994-95 5th, 1995-96 13th, 1996-97 11th, 1997-98 5th, 1998-99 4th, 1999-2000 3rd, 2000-01 4th, 2001-02 5th, 2002-03 15th.
Biggest win: 8-0 v Leicester City, Div. 1, 7.4.1934.
Biggest defeat: 1-8 v Stoke City, Div. 1, 27.8.1934.
Highest League scorer in a season: John Charles, 42 1953-54.
Most League goals in aggregate: Peter Lorimer, 168, 1965-79 and 1983-86.
Most capped player: Billy Bremner (Scotland) 54.
Longest unbeaten League sequence: 34 matches (October 1968).
Longest sequence without a League win: 17 matches (February 1947).

Name	Height ft. in.	Previous club	Birthplace	Birthdate
Goalkeepers				
Martyn, Nigel	6. 2	Crystal Palace	St Austell	11.08.66
Milosevic, Danny	6. 3	Perth Glory	Carlton, Aus.	26.06.78
Robinson, Paul	6. 4	–	Beverley	15.10.79
Defenders				
Duberry, Michael	6. 1	Chelsea	Enfield	14.10.75
Harte, Ian	6. 0	–	Drogheda	31.08.77
Kelly, Gary	5. 8	Home Farm	Drogheda	9.07.74
Kilgallon, Matthew	6. 1	–	York	8.01.84
Matteo, Dominic	6. 1	Liverpool	Dumfries	24.04.74
Mills, Danny	6. 0	Charlton Athletic	Norwich	18.05.77
Radebe, Lucas	6. 1	Kaizer Chiefs	Johannesburg	12.04.69
Richardson, Frazer	5.10	–	Rotherham	29.10.82
Midfielders				
Bakke, Eirik	6. 1	Sogndal	Sogndal, Nor.	13.09.77
Barmby, Nick	5. 6	Liverpool	Hull	11.02.74
Batty, David	5. 8	Newcastle Utd.	Leeds	2.12.68
Johnson, Seth	5.10	Derby Co.	Birmingham	12.03.79
McMaster, Jamie	5.10	–	New South Wales	29.11.82
McPhail, Stephen	5.10	–	London	9.12.79
Milner, James	6. 0	–	Horsforth	4.01.86
Okon, Paul	5.10	Watford	Sydney	5.04.72
Singh, Harpal	5. 7	–	Bradford	15.09.81
Wilcox, Jason	6. 0	Blackburn Rov.	Bolton	15.07.71
Forwards				
Bridges, Michael	6. 1	Sunderland	North Shields	5.08.78
Johnson, Simon	5. 9	–	West Bromwich	9.03.83
Keane, Robbie	5. 9	Inter Milan	Dublin	8.07.80
Smith, Alan	5. 9	–	Leeds	28.10.80
Viduka, Mark	6. 2	Celtic	Australia	9.10.75

LEICESTER CITY

Ground: The Walkers Stadium, Filbert Way, Leicester, LE2 7FL.
Telephone: 08700 406000. **Clubcall:** 09068 121185. **Club nickname:** Foxes.
First choice colours: Blue shirts; white shorts; blue stockings.
Record transfer fee: £5,000,000 to Wolves for Ade Akinbiyi, July 2000.
Record fee received: £11,000,000 from Liverpool for Emile Heskey, March 2000.

Record attendance: At Walkers Stadium: 32,082 v Wolves (Div. 1) 28 September 2002. At Filbert Street: 47,298 v. Tottenham (F.A. Cup 5) 18 February 1928.
Capacity for 2003-04: 32,500. **Sponsors:** Alliance and Leicester.
League Championships: runners-up 1928-29.
FA Cup: runners-up 1949, 1961, 1963, 1969.
League Cup: winners 1964, 1997, 2000.
European competitions: Cup-Winners Cup round two, 1961-62.
Finishing positions in Premiership: 1994-95 21st, 1996-97 9th, 1997-98 10th, 1998-99 10th, 1999-00 8th, 2000-01 13th, 2001-02 20th.
Biggest win: 10-0 v Portsmouth, Div. 1, 20.10.1928.
Biggest defeat: (while Leicester Fosse) 0-12 v. Nott'm. Forest, Div. 1, 21.04.1909.
Highest League scorer in a season: Arthur Rowley, 44, Div. 2, 1956-57.
Most League goals in aggregate: Arthur Chandler, 259, 1923-35.
Most capped player: John O'Neill (Northern Ireland) 39.
Longest unbeaten League sequence: 19 matches (August 1971).
Longest sequence without a League win: 18 matches (November 1975).

Name	Height ft. in.	Previous club	Birthplace	Birthdate
Goalkeepers				
Coyne, Danny	6. 1	Grimsby Town	Prestatyn	27.08.73
Walker, Ian	6. 1	Tottenham	Watford	31.10.71
Defenders				
Ashton, Jon	5.10	–	Nuneaton	4.10.82
Davidson, Callum	5.10	Blackburn Rov.	Stirling	25.06.76
Elliott, Matt	6. 3	Oxford Utd.	Roehampton	1.11.68
Heath, Matt	5.11	–	Leicester	1.11.81
Howey, Steve	6. 1	Manchester City	Sunderland	26.10.71
Rogers, Alan	5.10	Nott'm. Forest	Liverpool	3.01.77
Sinclair, Frank	5.10	Chelsea	Lambeth	3.12.71
Taggart, Gerry	6. 2	Bolton Wand.	Belfast	18.10.70
Midfielders				
Gillespie, Keith	5.10	Blackburn Rov.	Larne	18.02.75
Impey, Andy	5. 8	West Ham Utd.	Hammersmith	13.09.71
Izzet, Muzzy	5.10	Chelsea	Hackney	31.10.74
Jones, Matthew	5.11	Leeds Utd.	Llanelli	1.09.80
Lewis, Junior	5. 9	Gillingham	Wembley	9.10.73
McKinlay, Billy	5. 8	Clydebank	Glasgow	22.04.69
Nalis, Lilian	6. 1	Chievo	Nogent, Fra.	29.09.71
Petrescu, Tomi	5.10	–	Jyvaskyia, Fin.	24.07.86
Scimeca, Ricardo	6. 1	Nott'm. Forest.	Leamington Spa	13.06.75
Stewart, Jordan	6. 0	–	Birmingham	3.03.82
Williamson, Tom	5.11	–	Leicester	24.12.84
Forwards				
Benjamin, Trevor	6. 2	Cambridge Utd.	Kettering	8.02.79
Brooker, Paul	5. 8	Brighton & H.A	Hammersmith	25.11.76
Deane, Brian	6. 3	Middlesbrough	Leeds	7.02.68
Dickov, Paul	5. 5	Manchester City	Glasgow	1.11.72
Ferdinand, Les	5.11	West Ham Utd.	Acton	8.12.66
O'Grady, Chris	6. 0	–	Nottingham	25.01.86
Scowcroft, Jamie	6. 1	Ipswich Town	Bury St Edmunds	15.11.75
Wright, Tommy	5.11	–	Leicester	28.09.84

LIVERPOOL

Ground: Anfield Road, Liverpool L4 OTH.
Telephone: 0151 263 2361 **Clubcall:** 09068 121184. **Club nickname:** Reds or Pool.
First-choice colours: Red shirts; red shorts; red stockings.
Record transfer fee: £11,000,000 to Leicester City for Emile Heskey, February 2000.
Record fee received: £11,000,000 from Leeds Utd. for Robbie Fowler, November 2001.
Record attendance: 61,905 v Wolves, (F.A. Cup 4), 2 February 1952.

Capacity for 2003-04: 45,362. **Sponsors:** Carlsberg.
League Championship: winners 1900-01, 1905-06, 1921-22, 1922-23, 1946-47, 1963-64, 1965-66, 1972-73, 1975-76, 1976-77, 1978-79, 1979-80, 1981-82, 1982-83, 1983-84, 1985-86, 1987-88, 1989-90.
F.A. Cup: winners 1965, 1974, 1986, 1989, 1992, 2001.
League Cup: winners 1981, 1982, 1983, 1984, 1995, 2001, 2003.
European Competitions: winners European Cup 1976-77, 1977-78, 1980-81, 1983-84 UEFA Cup 1972-73, 1975-76, 2000-01 European Super Cup 1977.
Finishing positions in Premiership:1992-93 6th, 1993-94 8th, 1994-95 4th, 1995-96 3rd, 1996-97 4th, 1997-98 3rd, 1998-99 7th, 1999-2000 4th, 2000-01 3rd, 2001-02 2nd, 2002-03 5th.
Biggest win: 10-1 v Rotherham Utd., Div. 2, 18.2.1896. Europe: 11-0 v Stromsgodset, CWC, 17.9.1974.
Biggest defeat: 1-9 v Birmingham City, Div. 2, 11.12.1954.
Highest League scorer in a season: Roger Hunt, 41, 1961-62.
Most League goals in aggregate: Roger Hunt, 245, 1959-69.
Most capped player: Ian Rush (Wales) 67.
Longest unbeaten League sequence: 31 matches (May 1987).
Longest sequence without a League win: 14 (December 1953).

Name	Height ft. in.	Previous club	Birthplace	Birthdate
Goalkeepers				
Dudek, Jerzy	6. 1	Feyenoord	Rybnik, Pol.	23.03.73
Kirkland, Chris	6. 3	Coventry City	Leicester	2.05.81
Luzi, Patrice	6. 3	Monaco	France	8.07.80
Defenders				
Babbel, Markus	6. 0	Bayern Munich	Munich	8.09.72
Carragher, Jamie	6. 1	–	Liverpool	28.01.78
Finnan, Steve	5.10	Fulham	Limerick	20.04.76
Henchoz, Stephane	6. 1	Blackburn Rov.	Billens, Swi.	7.09.74
Hyypia, Sami	6. 4	Willem II	Porvoo, Fin.	7.10.73
Otsemobor, John	6. 0	–	Liverpool	23.03.83
Traore, Djimi	6. 1	Laval	Saint-Ouen, Fra.	1.03.80
Vignal, Gregory	5.11	Montpellier	Montpellier	19.07.81
Welsh, John	6. 0	–	Liverpool	10.01.84
Xavier, Abel	6. 2	Everton	Mozambique	30.11.72
Midfielders				
Biscan, Igor	6. 3	Croatia Zagreb	Zagreb	4.05.78
Cheyrou, Bruno	6. 1	Lille	Suresnes, Fra.	10.05.78
Diao, Salif	6. 0	Sedan	Senegal	10.02.77
Diomede, Bernard	5. 9	Auxerre	Bourges, Fra.	23.01.74
Foley-Sheridan, Michael	5.11	–	Dublin	9.03.83
Gerrard, Steven	6. 1	–	Whiston	30.05.80
Hamann, Dietmar	6. 2	Newcastle Utd.	Waldasson, Ger.	27.08.73
Murphy, Danny	5. 9	Crewe Alexandra	Chester	18.03.77
Partridge. Richie	5. 8	–	Dublin	12.09.80
Riise, John Arne	6. 1	Monaco	Molde, Nor.	24.09.80
Smicer, Vladimir	5.10	Lens	Degin, Cz.	24.05.73
Warnock, Stephen	5.10	–	Ormskirk	12.12.81
Forwards				
Baros, Milan	6. 1	Banik Ostrava	Valassake, Cz.	28.10.81
Diouf, El-Hadji	5.11	Lens	Senegal	15.01.81
Heskey, Emile	6. 1	Leicester City	Leicester	11.01.78
Kewell, Harry	6. 0	Leeds Utd.	Sydney	22.09.78
Mellor, Neil	5.11	–	Sheffield	4.11.82
Owen, Michael	5. 8	–	Chester	14.12.79
Sjolund, Daniel	5.11	West Ham Utd.	Mariehamn, Fin.	22.04.83

MANCHESTER CITY

Ground: City of Manchester Stadium, Sportcity, Manchester M11 3FF.
Telephone: 0161 226 2224. **Club nickname:** City.
First-choice-colours: Laser blue shirts, white shorts, blue/navy stockings
Record transfer fee: £13,000,000 to Paris St-Germain for Nicolas Anelka, June 2002
Record fee received: £4,925,000 from Ajax for Georgi Kinkladze, May 1998.
Record attendance: 84,569 v Stoke City (F.A. Cup 6) 3 March, 1934 (British record for any game outside London or Glasgow).
Capacity for 2003-04: 48,000. **Sponsors:** First Advice.
League Championship: winners 1936-37, 1967-68.
F.A. Cup: winners 1904, 1934, 1956, 1969.
European Competitions: winners Cup Winners' Cup 1969-70.
Finishing positions in Premiership: 1992-93 9th, 1993-94 16th, 1994-95 17th, 1995-96 18th, 2000-01: 18th, 2002-03 9th.
Biggest win: 10-1 Huddersfield Town, Div. 2, 7.11.87.
Biggest defeat: 1-9 v Everton, Div. 1, 3.9,1906.
Highest League scorer in a season: Tommy Johnson, 38, 1928-29.
Most League goals in aggregate: Tommy Johnson, 158, 1919-30.
Most capped player: Colin Bell, (England) 48.
Longest unbeaten League sequence: 22 matches (April 1947).
Longest sequence without a League win: 17 matches (April 1980).

Name	Height ft. in.	Previous club	Birthplace	Birthdate
Goalkeepers				
Ellegaard, Kevin	6. 5	Farum	Denmark	23.05.83
Nash, Carlo	6. 5	Stockport Co.	Bolton	13.09.73
Seaman, David	6. 4	Arsenal	Rotherham	19.09.63
Weaver, Nicky	6. 3	Mansfield Town	Sheffield	2.03.79
Defenders				
Bischoff, Mikkel	6. 3	AB Copenhagen	Denmark	3.02.82
Distin, Sylvain	6. 4	Paris St-Germain	France	6.12.77
Dunne, Richard	6. 2	Everton	Dublin	21.09.79
Horlock, Kevin	6. 0	Swindon Town	Erith	1.11.72
Mettomo, Lucien	6. 0	St Etienne	Cameroon	19.04.77
Ritchie, Paul	5.11	Rangers	Kirkcaldy	21.08.75
Sommeil, David	5.11	Bordeaux	Guadeloupe	10.08.74
Sun Jihai	5.10	Dalian Wanda	Dalian, Chi.	30.09.77
Tiatto, Danny	5. 8	Stoke City	Melbourne	22.05.73
Wiekens, Gerard	6. 1	Veendam	Tolhuiswyk, Hol.	25.02.73
Midfielders				
Barton, Joey	5. 9	–	Huyton	2.09.82
Benarbia, Ali	5. 8	Paris St-Germain	Oran, Alg.	8.10.68
Berkovic, Eyal	5. 7	Celtic	Haifa	2.04.72
Haaland, Alfie	6. 1	Leeds Utd.	Stavanger	23.11.72
Jordan, Stephen	6. 0	–	Warrington	6.03.82
Negouai, Christian	6. 4	Charleroi	Martinique	20.01.75
Shuker, Chris	5. 5	–	Liverpool	9.05.82
Tarnat, Michael	6. 1	Bayern Munich	Germany	27.10.69
Forwards				
Anelka, Nicolas	6. 0	Paris St-Germain	Versailles	14.03.79
Fowler, Robbie	5.11	Leed Utd.	Liverpool	9.04.75
Huckerby, Darren	5.11	Leeds Utd.	Nottingham	23.04.76
Macken, Jonathan	5.10	Preston N.E.	Manchester	7.09.77
Vuoso, Matias	5. 9	Independiente	Mar del Plata, Arg.	3.11.81
Wanchope, Paulo	6. 4	West Ham Utd.	Costa Rica	31.07.76
Wright-Phillips, Shaun	5. 6	–	Greenwich	25.10.81

MANCHESTER UNITED

Ground: Old Trafford Stadium, Sir Matt Busby Way, Manchester, M16 0RA.
Telephone: 0161 872 1661 **Clubcall:** 09068 121161.
Club nickname: The Red Devils.
First-choice colours: Red shirts, white shorts, black stockings.
Record transfer fee: £29,000,000 to Leeds Utd. for Rio Ferdinand, July 2002.
Record fee received: £25,000,000 from Real Madrid for David Beckham, July 2003.
Record attendance: Club: 70,504 v Aston Villa, 27 December 1920, F.A. Cup (semi-final): 76,962, Wolves v Grimsby Town, 25 March, 1939. Note: 83,260 saw Manchester Utd. v Arsenal, Div. 1, 17 January 1948 at Maine Road. Old Trafford was out of action through bomb damage.
Capacity for 2003-04: 68,936. **Sponsors:** Vodafone.
League Championship: winners 1907-08, 1910-11, 1951-52, 1955-56, 1956-7, 1964-65, 1966-67, 1992-93, 1993-94, 1995-96, 1996-97, 1998-99, 1999-2000, 2000-01.
F.A. Cup: winners 1909, 1948, 1963, 1977, 1983, 1985, 1990, 1994, 1996, 1999.
League Cup: winners 1992.
European Competitions: winners European Cup 1967-68, 1998-99, Cup-Winners' Cup 1990-91, European Super Cup 1991.
Finishing positions in Premiership: 1992-93 1st, 1993-94 1st, 1994-95 2nd, 1995-96 1st, 1996-97 1st, 1997-98 2nd, 1998-99 1st, 1999-2000 1st, 2000-01 1st, 2001-02 3rd, 2002-03 1st.
Biggest win: (while Newton Heath) 10-1 v Wolves, Div.1, 15.10.1892, (as Manchester Utd.) 9-0 v Ipswich Town, FAPL, 4.3.1995. Europe: 10-0 v Anderlecht, European Cup prelim. round, 26.9.1956.
Biggest defeat: 0-7 v Wolves Div 2, 26.12.1931, v Aston Villa, Div. 1, 27.12.1930 and v Blackburn Rov. Div. 1, 10.4.1926.
Highest League scorer in a season: Dennis Viollet, 32, 1959-60.
Most League goals in aggregate: Bobby Charlton, 199, 1956-73.
Most capped player: Bobby Charlton (England) 106.
Longest unbeaten League sequence: 26 matches (February 1956).
Longest sequence without a League win: 16 matches (November 1928 and April 1930).

Name	Height ft. in.	Previous club	Birthplace	Birthdate
Goalkeepers				
Barthez, Fabien	5.11	Monaco	Lavelanet, Fra.	28.06.71
Carroll, Roy	6. 2	Wigan Athletic	Enniskillen	30.09.77
Howard, Tim	6. 3	MetroStars	North Brunswick, USA	3.06.79
Steele, Luke	6. 2	Peterborough Utd.	Peterborough	24.09.84
Defenders				
Blanc, Laurent	6. 2	Inter Milan	Ales, Fra.	19.11.65
Brown, Wes	6. 1	–	Manchester	13.10.79
Ferdinand, Rio	6. 2	Leeds Utd.	Peckham	8.11.78
Lynch, Mark	5.11	–	Manchester	2.09.81
Neville, Gary	5.11	–	Bury	18.02.75
Neville, Phillip	5.11	–	Bury	21.01.77
O'Shea, John	6. 3	Waterford	Waterford	30.04.81
Silvestre, Mikael	6. 0	Inter Milan	Chambray, Fra.	9.08.77
Midfielders				
Butt, Nicky	5.10	–	Manchester	21.01.75
Djordjic, Bojan	5.10	Brommapojkarna	Belgrade	6.02.82
Fletcher, Darren	6. 0	–	Edinburgh	1.02.84
Fortune, Quinton	5. 9	Atletico Madrid	Cape Town	21.05.77
Giggs, Ryan	5.11	–	Cardiff	29.11.73
Keane, Roy	5.11	Nott'm. Forest	Cork	10.08.71
Pugh, Danny	6. 0	–	Manchester	19.10.82
Richardson, Kieran	5.10	–	London	21.10.84
Scholes, Paul	5. 7	–	Salford	16.11.74

Stewart, Michael	5.11	–	Edinburgh	26.02.81
Veron, Juan Sebastian	6. 1	Lazio	Buenos Aires	9.03.75
Forwards				
Bellion, David	6. 0	Sunderland	Paris	27.11.82
Chadwick, Luke	5.11	–	Cambridge	18.11.80
Djemba-Djemba, Eric	5. 8	Nantes	Douala, Cam.	4.05.81
Forlan, Diego	5. 8	Independiente	Montevideo	19.05.79
Nardiello, Danny	5.11	–	Coventry	22.10.82
Solskjaer, Ole Gunnar	5.10	Molde	Kristiansund, Nor.	26.02.73
Timm, Mads	5. 9	–	Odense	31.10.84
Van Nistelrooy, Ruud	6. 2	PSV Eindhoven	Oss, Hol.	1.07.76

MIDDLESBROUGH

Ground: Cellnet Riverside Stadium, Middlesbrough, TS3 6RS.
Telephone: 01642 877700 **Clubcall:** 079068 121181. **Club nickname:** Boro.
First-choice colours: Red shirts; red shorts; red stockings.
Record transfer fee: £8,150,000 to Empoli for Massimo Maccarone, July 2002.
Record fee received: £12,000,000 from Atletico Madrid for Juninho, July 1997.
Record attendance: At Riverside Stadium: 34,814 v Newcastle Utd. (Premier League) 5 March 2003. 35,000 England v Slovakia 11 June, 2003. At Ayresome Park: 53,596 v Newcastle Utd. (Div.1) December 1949.
Capacity for 2003-04: 35,100. **Sponsors:** dial-a-phone.
League Championship: 3rd 1913-14.
F.A. Cup: runners-up 1997.
League Cup: runners-up 1997, 1998.
Finishing positions in Premiership: 1992-93 21th 1995-96 12th, 1996-97 19th 1998-99 9th, 1999-2000 12th, 2000-01 14th, 2001-02 12th, 2002-03 11th.
Biggest win: 9-0 v Brighton & H.A., Div 2, 23.8.1958.
Biggest defeat: 0-9 v Blackburn Rov., Div 2, 6.11.1954.
Highest League scorer in a season: George Camsell, 59, 1926-27.
Most League goals in aggregate: George Camsell, 326, 1925-39.
Most capped player: Wilf Mannion (England) 26.
Longest unbeaten League sequence: 24 matches (September 1973).
Longest sequence without a League win: 19 matches (October 1981).

Name	Height ft. in.	Previous club	Birthplace	Birthdate
Goalkeepers				
Crossley, Mark	6. 0	Nott'm. Forest	Barnsley	16.06.69
Schwarzer, Mark	6. 4	Bradford City	Sydney	6.10.72
Defenders				
Cooper, Colin	5.11	Nott'm. Forest	Sedgefield	28.02.67
Davies, Andrew	5.11	–	Stockton	17.12.84
Ehiogu, Ugo	6. 2	Aston Villa	Hackney	3.11.72
Murphy, David	5.11	–	Hartlepool	1.03.84
Queudrue, Franck	5.10	Lens	Paris	27.08.78
Riggott, Chris	6. 2	Derby Co.	Derby	1.09.80
Southgate, Gareth	6. 0	Aston Villa	Watford	3.09.70
Stockdale, Robbie	6. 0	–	Redcar	30.11.79
Midfielders				
Boateng, George	5. 9	Aston Villa	Nkawka, Gha.	5.09.75
Downing, Stewart	6. 0	–	Middlesbrough	22.07.84
Juninho	5. 5	Atletico Madrid	Sao Paulo	22.02.73
Marinelli, Carlos	5. 8	Boca Juniors	Buenos Aires	4.03.82
Nemeth, Szilard	5.10	Inter Bratislava	Slovakia	8.08.77
Parnaby, Stuart	5.11	–	Durham	19.07.82
Wilkshire, Luke	5. 8	–	Wollongong, Aus.	2.10.81
Wilson, Mark	6. 0	Manchester Utd.	Scunthorpe	9.02.79

Forwards

Christie, Malcolm	6. 0	Derby Co.	Peterborough	11.04.79
Greening, Jonathan	6. 0	Manchester Utd.	Scarborough	2.01.79
Job, Joseph-Desire	5.11	Lens	Venissieux, Fra.	1.12.77
Johnston, Allan	5.11	Rangers	Glasgow	14.12.73
Maccarone, Massimo	6. 0	Empoli	Galliate, Ita.	6.09.79
Nemeth, Szilard	5.10	Inter Bratislava	Komarno, Slov.	8.08.77
Ricketts, Michael	6. 2	Bolton Wand.	Birmingham	4.12.78
Whelan, Noel	6. 2	Coventry City	Leeds	30.12.74

NEWCASTLE UNITED

Ground: St James' Park, Newcastle-upon-Tyne, NE1 4ST.
Telephone: 0191 201 8400 **Clubcall:** 09068 121190. **Club nickname:** Magpies.
First-choice colours: Black and white shirts; black shorts; black stockings.
Record transfer fee: £15,000,000 to Blackburn Rov. for Alan Shearer, July 1996.
Record fee received: £8,000,000 from Liverpool for Dietmar Hamann, July 1999.
Record attendance: 68,386 v Chelsea (Div. 1) September 1930.
Capacity for 2003-04: 52,193. **Sponsors:** Northern Rock.
League Championship: winners 1904-05, 1906-07, 1908-09, 1926-27.
F.A. Cup: winners 1910, 1924, 1932, 1951, 1952, 1955.
League Cup: runners-up 1976.
European Competitions: winners Fairs Cup 1968-69, Anglo-Italian Cup 1972-73.
Finishing positions in Premiership: 1993-94 3rd 1994-95 6th 1995-96 2nd 1996-97 2nd 1997-98 13th 1998-99 13th, 1999-2000 11th, 2000-01 11th, 2001-02 4th, 2002-03 3rd.
Biggest win: 13-0 v Newport County, Div. 2, 5.10.1946.
Biggest defeat: 0-9 v Burton Wanderers, Div. 2, 15.4.1895.
Highest League scorer in a season: Hughie Gallacher, 36, 1926-27.
Most League goals in aggregate: Jackie Milburn, 177, 1946-57.
Most capped player: Alf McMichael (Northern Ireland) 40.
Longest unbeaten League sequence: 14 matches (April 1950).
Longest sequence without a League win: 21 matches (January 1978).

Name	Height ft. in.	Previous club	Birthplace	Birthdate
Goalkeepers				
Caig, Tony	6. 0	Hibernian	Whitehaven	11.04.74
Collin, Adam	6. 3	–	Carlisle	9.12.84
Given, Shay	6. 1	Blackburn Rov.	Lifford	20.04.76
Harper, Steve	6. 2	–	Easington	14.03.75
Defenders				
Bernard, Olivier	5. 7	Lyon	Paris	14.10.79
Bramble, Titus	6. 1	Ipswich Town	Ipswich	31.07.81
Caldwell, Gary	6. 0	–	Stirling	12.04.82
Caldwell, Stephen	6. 3	–	Stirling	12.09.80
Dabizas, Nikos	6. 1	Olympiakos	Amyndaeo, Gre.	3.08.73
Elliott, Robbie	5.10	Bolton Wand.	Newcastle	25.12.73
Griffin, Andrew	5. 9	Stoke City	Billinge	7.03.79
Hughes, Aaron	6. 1	–	Cookstown	8.11.79
O'Brien, Andy	5.10	Bradford City	Harrogate	29.06.79
Quinn, Wayne	5.10	Sheffield Utd.	Truro	19.11.76
Woodgate, Jonathan	6. 2	Leeds Utd.	Middlesbrough	22.01.80
Midfielders				
Ambrose, Darren	5.11	Ipswich Town	Harlow	29.02.84
Acuna, Clarence	5. 7	University	Coya Rancagua, Chil.	8.02.75
Bassedas, Christian	5. 8	Velez Sarsfield	Buenos Aires	16.02.73
Bowyer, Lee	5. 9	West Ham Utd.	London	3.01.77
Dyer, Kieron	5. 7	Ipswich Town	Ipswich	29.12.78
Gavilan, Diego	5. 7	Cerro Porteno	Asuncion, Par.	1.03.80
Jenas, Jermaine	6. 0	Nott'm. Forest	Nottingham	18.02.83

Kerr, Brian	5. 7	–	Motherwell	12.10.81
McClen, Jamie	5. 8	–	Newcastle	13.05.79
Robert, Laurent	5.10	Paris St-Germain	Saint-Benoit, Fra.	21.05.75
Solano, Nolberto	5. 8	Boca Juniors	Callao, Per.	12.12.74
Speed, Gary	5.10	Everton	Deeside	8.09.69
Viana, Hugo	5.10	Sporting Lisbon	Portugal	15.01.83
Forwards				
Ameobi, Shola	6. 3	–	Zaria, Nig.	12.10.81
Bellamy, Craig	5. 8	Coventry City	Cardiff	13.01.79
Chopra, Michael	5.10	–	Newcastle	23.12.83
Cort, Carl	6. 4	Wimbledon	Southwark	1.11.77
Lua Lua, Lomana	5. 8	Colchester Utd.	Zaire	28.12.80
Shearer, Alan	5.11	Blackburn Rov.	Newcastle	13.08.70
Zola, Calvin	6. 3	–	Zaire	31.12.84

PORTSMOUTH

Ground: Fratton Park, Frogmore Road, Portsmouth, PO4 8RA.
Telephone: 02392 731204. **Clubcall:** 09068 121182. **Club nickname:** Pompey.
First choice colours: Blue shirts; white shorts; red stockings.
Record transfer fee: £1,900,000 to Vitesse Arnhem for Dejan Stefanovic, June 2003.
Record fee received: £5,000,000 from Aston Villa for Peter Crouch, March 2002.
Record attendance: 51,385 v Derby Co. (F.A. Cup 6) 26 February 1949.
Capacity for 2003-04: 19,179. **Sponsors:** Ty Europe.
League Championships: winners 1948-49, 1949-50.
FA Cup: winners 1939.
League Cup: 5th rd. 1961, 1986.
Finishing positions in Premiership: None.
Biggest win: 9-1 v Notts Co., Div. 1, 09.04.1927.
Biggest defeat: 0-10 v Leicester City, Div. 1, 20.10.1928.
Highest League scorer in a season: Guy Whittingham, 42, Div. 1, 1992-93.
Most League goals in aggregate: Peter Harris, 194, 1946-60.
Most capped player: Jimmy Dickinson (England) 48.
Longest unbeaten League sequence: 15 matches (October 1924).
Longest sequence without a League win: 25 matches (August 1959).

Name	Height ft. in.	Previous club	Birthplace	Birthdate
Goalkeepers				
Hislop, Shaka	6. 4	West Ham Utd.	Hackney	22.02.69
Ilic, Sasa	6. 4	Zalaegerszeg	Melbourne	18.07.72
Kawaguchi, Yoshikatsu	5.10	Yokohama	Shizuoka	15.08.75
Tardif, Chris	5.11	–	Guernsey	20.06.81
Wapenaar, Harald	6. 1	Utrecht	Vlaardingen, Hol.	4.10.70
Defenders				
Buxton, Lewis	5.11	–	Cowes	10.12.83
Cooper, Shaun	5. 9	–	Newport, IOW	5.10.83
De Zeeuw, Arjan	6. 1	Wigan Athletic	Castricum, Hol.	16.04.70
Foxe, Hayden	6. 2	West Ham Utd.	Australia	23.06.77
Howe, Eddie	5. 9	Bournemouth	Amersham	29.11.77
Primus, Linvoy	5.11	Reading	Forest Gate	14.07.73
*Stefanovic, Dejan	6. 2	Vitesse Arnhem	Nis, Yug.	28.10.74
Vincent, Jamie	5.11	Huddersfield Town	Wimbledon	18.06.75
Midfielders				
Barrett, Neil	5. 9	Chelsea	Tooting	29.12.81
Berger, Patrik	6. 1	Liverpool	Prague	10.11.73
Diabate, Lassina	5.10	Auxerre	Ivory Coast	16.09.74
Harper, Kevin	5. 6	Derby Co.	Oldham	15.01.76
Hughes, Richard	5. 9	Bournemouth	Glasgow	25.06.79
Merson, Paul	6. 0	Aston Villa	Harlesden	20.03.68
O'Neil, Gary	5. 9	–	Beckenham	18.05.83

Pettefer, Carl	5. 7	–	Taplow	22.03.81
Quashie, Nigel	6. 0	Nott'm. Forest	Peckham	20.07.78
Robinson, Carl	5.10	Wolves	Llandrindod Wells	13.10.76
Sherwood, Tim	6. 1	Tottenham	St Albans	2.02.69
Stone, Steve	5. 8	Aston Villa	Gateshead	20.08.71
Taylor, Matthew	5.11	Luton Town	Oxford	27.11.81
Zivkovic, Boris	6. 0	Bayer Leverkusen	Zivinice, Cro.	15.11.75
Forwards				
Ayegbeni, Yakubu	6. 0	Maccabi Haifa	Nigeria	22.11.82
Bradbury, Lee	6. 0	Crystal Palace	Cowes	3.07.75
Burchill, Mark	5. 8	Celtic	Bellshill	18.08.80
Burton, Deon	5. 9	Derby Co.	Reading	25.10.76
Pitt, Courtney	5. 8	Chelsea	London	17.12.81
Sheringham, Teddy	6. 0	Tottenham	Highams Park	2.04.66
Todorov, Svetoslav	6. 0	West Ham Utd.	Dobrich, Bul.	30.08.78
Vine, Rowan	5.11	–	Portsmouth	1.12.81

*Subject to work permit

SOUTHAMPTON

Ground: The Friends Provident St Mary's Stadium, Britannia Road, Southampton, SO14 5FP.
Telephone: 0870 220 0000 **Club nickname:** Saints.
First-choice colours: Red and white shirts; black shorts; white stockings.
Record transfer fee: £4,000,000 to Derby Co. for Rory Delap, July 2001.
Record fee received: £7,500,000 from Blackburn Rov. for Kevin Davies, June 1998.
Record attendance: At The Dell: 31,044 v Manchester Utd. (Div. 1) 8 October 1969. At St Mary's: 32,104 v Liverpool (Premier League) 18 January 2003.
Capacity for 2002-03: 32,689. **Sponsors:** Friends Provident.
League Championship: 2nd 1983-84.
F.A. Cup: winners 1976.
League Cup: runners-up 1979.
European Competitions: Fairs Cup round 3, 1969-70, Cup-Winners' Cup round 3(QF), 1976-77.
Finishing positions in Premiership: 1992-93 18th, 1993-94 18th, 1994-95 10th, 1995-96 17th, 1996-97 16th, 1997-98 12th, 1998-99 17th, 1999-2000 15th, 2000-01 10th, 2001-02 11th, 2002-03 8th
Biggest win: 8-0 v Northampton Town, Div. 3S, 24.12.1921.
Biggest defeat: 0-8 v Tottenham, Div. 2, 28.3.1936 and v Everton Div. 1, 20.11.1971.
Highest League scorer in a season: Derek Reeves, 39, 1959-60.
Most League goals in aggregate: Mike Channon, 185, 1966-77, 1979-82.
Most capped player: Peter Shilton (England) 49.
Longest unbeaten League sequence: 19 matches (September 1921).
Longest sequence without a League win: 20 matches (August 1969).

Name	Height ft. in.	Previous club	Birthplace	Birthdate
Goalkeepers				
Jones, Paul	6. 3	Stockport Co.	Chirk	18.04.67
Niemi, Antti	6. 1	Hearts	Finland	31.05.72
Defenders				
Baird, Chris	5.10	–	Ballymoney	25.02.82
Benali, Francis	5. 9	–	Southampton	30.12.68
Bridge, Wayne	5.10	–	Southampton	5.08.80
Dodd, Jason	5. 8	–	Bath	2.11.70
Hall, Fitz	6. 4	Oldham Athletic	Walthamstow	20.12.80
Higginbotham, Danny	6. 1	Derby Co.	Manchester	29.12.78
Kenton, Darren	5.11	Norwich City	Wandsworth	13.09.78
Lundekvam, Claus	6. 4	Brann	Austevoll, Nor.	22.02.73
Monk, Garry	6. 0	Torquay Utd.	Bedford	6.03.79
Svensson, Michael	6. 2	Troyes	Sweden	25.11.75

Williams, Paul	5.11	Coventry City	Burton	26.03.71
Midfielders				
Delap, Rory	6. 1	Derby Co.	Sutton Coldfield	6.07.76
Draper, Mark	5.10	Aston Villa	Long Eaton	11.11.70
Fernandes, Fabrice	5. 9	Rennes	Paris	29.10.79
Griffit, Leandre	5.10	Amiens	France	21.05.84
Marsden, Chris	6. 0	Birmingham City	Sheffield	3.01.69
Prutton, David	6. 1	Nott'm. Forest	Hull	12.09.81
Oakley, Matthew	5.10	–	Peterborough	17.08.77
Svensson, Anders	5.10	Elfsborg	Sweden	17.07.76
Telfer, Paul	5. 9	Coventry City	Edinburgh	21.10.71
Tessem, Jo	6. 2	Molde	Orlandet, Nor.	28.02.72
Forwards				
Beattie, James	6. 1	Blackburn Rov.	Lancaster	27.02.78
Davies, Arron	5. 9	–	Cardiff	22.06.84
Delgado, Agustin	6. 3	Necaxa	Ibarra, Ecu.	23.12.74
Ormerod, Brett	5.11	Blackpool	Blackburn	18.10.76
Pahars, Marian	5. 8	Skonto Riga	Riga, Lat.	5.08.76

TOTTENHAM HOTSPUR

Ground: 748 High Road, Tottenham, London N17 OAP.
Telephone: 0208 365 5000 **Clubcall:** 09068 121100. **Club nickname:** Spurs.
First-choice colours: White shirts, navy shorts, white stockings.
Record transfer fee: £11,000,000 to Dynamo Kiev for Sergei Rebrov, May 2000.
Record fee received: £5,500,000 from Lazio for Paul Gascoigne, May 1992.
Record attendance: 75,038 v Sunderland (F.A. Cup 6) 5 March 1938.
Capacity for 2003-04: 36,237. **Sponsors:** Thomson.
League Championship: winners 1950-51, 1960-61.
F.A. Cup: winners 1901, 1921, 1961, 1962, 1967, 1981, 1982, 1991.
League Cup: winners 1971, 1973, 1999.
European Competitions: winners Cup-Winners' Cup 1962-63, UEFA Cup 1971-72, 1983-84.
Finishing positions in Premiership: 1992-93 8th, 1993-94 15th, 1994-95 7th, 1995-96 8th, 1996-97 10th, 1997-98 14th, 1998-99 11th, 1999-2000 10th, 2000-01 12th, 2001-02 9th, 2002-03 10th.
Biggest win: 9-0 v Bristol Rov., Div.2, 22.10.1977, F.A. Cup 13-2 v Crewe Alexandra, round four replay, 3.2.1960, Europe 9-0 v Keflavik, UEFA Cup, round one, 28.9.1971.
Biggest defeat: 0-7 v Liverpool, Div.1, 2.9.1979.
Highest League scorer in a season: Jimmy Greaves, 37, 1962-63.
Most League goals in aggregate: Jimmy Greaves, 220, 1961-70.
Most capped player: Pat Jennings (Northern Ireland) 74.
Longest unbeaten League sequence: 22 matches (August 1949).
Longest sequence without a League win: 16 matches (December 1934).

Name	Height ft. in.	Previous club	Birthplace	Birthdate
Goalkeepers				
Burch, Rob	6. 0	–	Yeovil	8.02.84
Hirschfeld, Lars	6. 1	Calgary Storm	Alberta	17.10.78
Keller, Kasey	6. 1	Rayo Vallecano	Olympia, USA	29.11.69
Sullivan, Neil	6. 1	Wimbledon	Sutton	24.02.70
Defenders				
Blondel, Jonathan	5. 7	Mouscron	Belgium	3.04.84
Bunjevcevic, Goran	6. 2	Red Star Belgrade	Karlovac, Cro.	17.02.73
Carr, Stephen	5. 8	–	Dublin	29.08.76
Doherty, Gary	6. 1	Luton Town	Carndonagh	31.01.80
Gardner, Anthony	6. 5	Port Vale	Stafford	19.09.80
Kelly, Stephen	5.11	–	Dublin	6.09.83
King, Ledley	6. 2	–	Bow	12.10.80

Perry, Chris	5. 8	Wimbledon	Carshalton	26.04.73
Richards, Dean	6. 2	Tottenham	Bradford	9.06.74
Taricco, Mauricio	5. 8	Ipswich Town	Buenos Aires	10.03.73
Thatcher, Ben	5.10	Wimbledon	Swindon	30.11.75
Ziege, Christian	6. 1	Liverpool	Berlin	1.02.72
Midfielders				
Acimovic, Milenko	5.10	Red Star Belgrade	Slovenia	15.02.77
Anderton, Darren	6. 1	Portsmouth	Southampton	3.03.72
Davies, Simon	5.11	Peterborough Utd.	Haverfordwest	23.10.79
Etherington, Matthew	6. 0	Peterborough Utd.	Truro	14.08.81
Marney, Dean	5.11	–	Barking	31.01.84
Poyet, Gustavo	6. 1	Chelsea	Montevideo	15.11.67
Redknapp, Jamie	6. 0	Liverpool	Barton-on-Sea	25.06.73
Ricketts, Rohan	5.11	Arsenal	Clapham	22.12.82
Forwards				
Helder Postiga	5.11	FC Porto	Povoa de Verizim, Por.	2.08.82
Iversen, Steffen	5.10	Rosenborg	Oslo	10.11.76
Keane, Robbie	5. 9	Leeds Utd.	Dublin	8.07.80
Rebrov, Sergei	5. 8	Dynamo Kiev	Donetsk, Ukr.	3.06.74
Slabber, Jamie	6. 0	–	Enfield	31.12.84

WOLVERHAMPTON WANDERERS

Ground: Molineux Stadium, Wolverhampton, WV1 4QR.
Telephone: 01902 655000. **Clubcall:** 09068 121103. **Club nickname:** Wolves.
First choice colours: Gold shirts; black shorts; black stockings.
Record transfer fee: £3,250,000 to Bristol City for Ade Akinbiyi, September 1999.
Record fee received: £6,000,000 from Coventry City for Robbie Keane, August 1999.
Record attendance: 61,315 v Liverpool (F.A. Cup 5) 11 February 1939.
Capacity for 2003-04: 28,500. **Sponsors:** Doritos
League Championships: winners 1953-54, 1957-58, 1958-59.
FA Cup: winners 1893, 1908, 1949, 1960.
League Cup: winners 1974, 1980.
European competitions: UEFA Cup runners-up 1971-72.
Finishing positions in Premiership: None
Biggest win: 10-1 v Leicester City, Div. 2, 15.04.1938. F.A Cup: 14-0 v Crosswell's Brewery, Rd. 2., 13.11.1886.
Biggest defeat: 1-10 v. Newton Heath, Div. 1, 15.10.1892.
Highest League scorer in a season: Dennis Westcott, 38, 1946-47.
Most League goals in aggregate: Steve Bull, 247, 1986-98.
Most capped player: Billy Wright (England) 105.
Longest unbeaten League sequence: 20 matches (April 1924).
Longest sequence without a League win: 19 matches (April 1985).

Name	Height ft. in.	Previous club	Birthplace	Birthdate
Goalkeepers				
Murray, Matt	6. 4	–	Solihull	2.05.81
Oakes, Michael	6. 1	Aston Villa	Northwich	30.10.73
Defenders				
Butler, Paul	6. 3	Sunderland	Manchester	2.11.72
Clyde, Mark	6. 1	–	Limavady	27.12.82
Edworthy, Marc	5. 9	Coventry City	Barnstaple	24.12.72
Irwin, Denis	5. 8	Manchester Utd.	Cork	31.10.65
Lescott, Joleon	6. 2	–	Birmingham	16.08.82
Luzhny, Oleg	5.10	Arsenal	Kiev	5.08.68
Okoronkwo, Isaac	6. 0	Shakhtar Donetsk	Aba Abia, Nig.	1.05.78
Naylor, Lee	5. 8	–	Walsall	19.03.80
Midfielders				
Andrews, Keith	6. 0	–	Dublin	18.09.80

Cameron, Colin	5. 8	Hearts	Kirkcaldy	23.10.72
Cooper, Kevin	5. 8	Wimbledon	Derby	8.02.75
Ince, Paul	5.11	Middlesbrough	Ilford	21.10.67
Ingimarsson, Ivar	6. 0	Brentford	Iceland	20.08.78
Kennedy, Mark	5.11	Manchester City	Dublin	15.05.76
Melligan, John	5. 9	–	Dublin	11.02.82
Rae, Alex	5.10	Sunderland	Glasgow	30.09.69
Silas	5. 9	Uniao Leiria	Lisbon	1.09.76
Newton, Shaun	5. 8	Charlton Athletic	Camberwell	20.08.75
Ward, Graham	5. 7	–	Dublin	25.02.80
Forwards				
Blake, Nathan	5.11	Blackburn Rov.	Cardiff	27.01.72
Miller, Kenny	5.10	Rangers	Edinburgh	23.12.79
Ndah, George	6. 1	Swindon Town	Dulwich	23.12.74
Proudlock, Adam	6. 0	–	Wellington	9.05.81
Sturridge, Dean	5. 8	Leicester City	Birmingham	26.07.73

NATIONWIDE LEAGUE PLAYING STAFFS 2003-04 DIVISION ONE

BRADFORD CITY

Ground: Bradford and Bingley Stadium, Valley Parade, Bradford BD8 7DY.
Telephone: 01274 773355. **Clubcall:** 09068 888640. **Club nickname:** Bantams.
First-choice colours: Claret and amber shirts; claret and amber shorts; claret and amber stockings.
Main Sponsor: JCT 600. **Capacity for 2003-04:** 25,136.
Record attendance: 39,146 v Burnley (F.A. Cup 4) 11 March, 1911.

Name	**Height ft. in.**	**Previous club**	**Birthplace**	**Birthdate**
Goalkeepers				
Combe, Alan	6. 1	Dundee Utd.	Edinburgh	3.04.74
Defenders				
Atherton, Peter	5.11	Sheffield Wed.	Wigan	6.04.70
Bower, Mark	5.10	–	Bradford	23.01.80
Edds, Gareth	5.11	Swindon Town	Sydney	3.02.81
Emanuel, Lewis	5. 8	–	Bradford	4.10.83
Francis, Simon	6. 0	–	Nottingham	16.02.85
Gavin, Jason	6. 0	Middlesbrough	Dublin	14.03.80
Heckingbottom, Paul	6. 0	Norwich City	Barnsley	17.07.77
Jacobs, Wayne	5. 9	Rotherham Utd.	Sheffield	3.02.69
Wetherall, David	6. 4	Leeds Utd.	Sheffield	14.03.71
Midfielders				
Bannister, Patrick	5.10	Derby Co.	Walsall	3.12.83
Evans, Paul	5. 6	Brentford	Oswestry	1.09.74
Gray, Andy	6. 2	Nott'm. Forest	Harrogate	15.11.77
McHugh, Frazer	5.11	Halesowen	Nottingham	14.07.81
Kearney, Thomas	5.11	Everton	Liverpool	7.10.81
Reid, Paul	5.10	Wollongong	Sydney	6.07.79
Standing, Michael	5.10	Aston Villa	Shoreham	20.03.81
Forwards				
Branch, Michael	5.10	Wolves	Liverpool	18.10.78
Cadamarteri, Danny	5. 9	Everton	Bradford	12.10.79
Cornwall, Luke	5.10	Fulham	London	23.07.80
Forrest, Danny	5.11	–	Keighley	23.10.84

Muirhead, Ben	5. 9	Manchester Utd.	Doncaster	5.01.83
Ward, Ashley	6. 1	Blackburn Rov.	Manchester	24.11.70
Windass, Dean	5.10	Sheffield Utd.	Hull	1.04.69
Wolleaston, Robert	5.11	Chelsea	London	21.12.79

BURNLEY

Ground: Turf Moor, Harry Potts Way, Burnley BB10 4BX.
Telephone: 0870 4431882. **Clubcall:** 09068 121153. **Club nickname:** Clarets.
First-choice colours: Claret and blue shirts; white shorts; white stockings.
Main sponsor: Lanway. **Capacity for 2003-04:** 22,300.
Record attendance: 54,775 v Huddersfield Town (F.A. Cup 4) 23 February, 1924.

Name	Height ft. in.	Previous club	Birthplace	Birthdate
Goalkeepers				
Jensen, Brian	6. 3	W.B.A	Copenhagen	8.06.75
Defenders				
Camara, Mohamed	5.11	Wolves	Guinea	25.06.75
McGregor, Mark	5.11	Wrexham	Chester	16.02.77
Roche, Lee	5.10	Manchester Utd.	Bolton	28.10.80
West, Dean	5.10	Bury	Wakefield	5.12.72
Midfielders				
Branch, Graham	6. 2	Stockport Co.	Liverpool	12.02.72
Chaplow, Richard	5. 9	–	Accrington	2.02.85
Gnohere, Arthur	6. 0	Caen	Ivory Coast	20.11.78
Grant, Tony	5.11	Manchester City	Liverpool	14.11.74
Little, Glen	6. 3	Glentoran	Wimbledon	15.10.75
Moore, Alan	5.10	Middlesbrough	Dublin	25.11.74
O'Neill, Matthew	5.10	–	Accrington	25.06.84
Pilkington, Joel	5. 8	–	Accrington	1.08.84
Weller, Paul	5. 8	–	Brighton	6.03.75
Forwards				
Blake, Robbie	5. 9	Bradford City	Middlesbrough	4.03.76
Moore, Ian	5.11	Stockport Co.	Birkenhead	26.08.76
Taylor, Gareth	6. 1	Manchester City	Weston-s-Mare	25.02.73

CARDIFF CITY

Ground: Ninian Park, Sloper Road, Cardiff CF11 8SX.
Telephone: 02920 221001. **Club nickname:** Bluebirds.
First-choice colours: Blue shirts; blue shorts; blue stockings.
Main sponsor: Redrow Homes. **Capacity for 2003-04:** 21,500.
Record attendance: 61,566 Wales v England, 14 October, 1961. Club: 57,800 v Arsenal (Div. 1) 22 April, 1953.

Name	Height ft. in.	Previous club	Birthplace	Birthdate
Goalkeepers				
Alexander, Neil	6. 1	Livingston	Edinburgh	10.03.78
Lee-Barrett, Arran	6. 0	Norwich City	Ipswich	28.02.84
Margetson, Martyn	6. 0	Huddersfield Town	West Neath	8.09.71
Walton, Mark	6. 4	Brighton & H.A.	Merthyr Tydfil	1.06.69
Defenders				
Barker, Chris	6. 0	Barnsley	Sheffield	02.03.80
Bonner, Mark	5.10	Blackpool	Ormskirk	7.06.74
Croft, Gary	5. 9	Ipswich Town	Burton	17.02.74
Gabbidon, Daniel	5.10	W.B.A.	Cwmbran	8.08.79
Giles, Martyn	6. 0	–	Cardiff	10.04.83
Hughes, David	6. 4	Shrewsbury Town	Wrexham	1.02.78
Prior, Spencer	6. 3	Manchester City	Southend	22.04.71
Weston Rhys	6. 1	Arsenal	Kingston	27.10.80

Young, Scott	6. 1	–	Llwynpia	14.01.76
Midfielders				
Boland, Willie	5. 9	Coventry City	Ennis	6.08.75
Jones, Gethin	5.11	Carmarthen	Llanbyther	8.08.81
Kavanagh, Graham	5.10	Stoke City	Dublin	2.12.73
Maxwell, Layton	5. 8	Liverpool	Rhyl	3.10.79
Robinson, John	5.10	Charlton Athletic	Bulawayo	29.08.71
Whalley, Gareth	5.10	Bradford City	Manchester	19.12.73
Forwards				
Bowen, Jason	5. 7	Reading	Merthyr Tydfil	24.08.72
Campbell, Andy	6. 0	Middlesbrough	Middlesbrough	18.04.79
Collins, James	6. 2	–	Newport	23.08.83
Earnshaw, Robert	5. 8	–	Zambia	6.04.81
Gordon Gavin	6. 3	Lincoln City	Manchester	29.06.79
Thorne, Peter	6. 0	Stoke City	Manchester	21.06.73

COVENTRY CITY

Ground: Highfield Road Stadium, King Richard Street, Coventry CV2 4FW
Telephone: 0247 623 4000. **Club nickname:** Sky Blues.
First-choice colours: Sky blue and navy shirts; navy and sky blue shorts; navy stockings.
Main sponsor: Subaru. **Capacity for 2003-04:** 23,613.
Record attendance: 51,455 v Wolves (Div. 2) 29 April, 1967.

Name	Height ft. in.	Previous club	Birthplace	Birthdate
Goalkeepers				
Hyldgaard, Morten	6. 6	Ikast	Herning, Den.	26.01.78
Shearer, Scott	6. 3	Albion Rov.	Glasgow	15.02.81
Defenders				
Davenport, Callum	6. 0	–	Bedford	1.01.83
Gordon, Dean	6. 0	Middlesbrough	Thornton Heath	10.02.73
Guerrero, Ivan	5. 7	–	Honduras	30.11.77
Konjic, Muhamed	6. 3	Monaco	Bosnia	14.05.70
Shaw, Richard	5. 9	Crystal Palace	Brentford	11.09.68
Midfielders				
Chippo, Youssef	5.11	FC Porto	Boujaad, Mor.	10.06.73
Eustace, John	5.11	–	Solihull	3.11.79
Fowler, Lee	5. 7	–	Cardiff	10.06.83
McAllister, Gary	6. 1	Liverpool	Motherwell	25.12.64
Noon, Mark	5.10	–	Leamington Spa	23.09.83
O'Neill, Keith	6. 1	Middlesbrough	Dublin	16.02.76
Pead, Craig	5. 9	–	Bromsgrove	15.09.81
Pipe, David	5. 9	–	Caerphilly	5.11.83
Quinn, Barry	6. 0	–	Dublin	9.05.79
Safri, Youssef	6. 2	Raja Casablanca	Morocco	1.03.77
Forwards				
Adebola, Dele	6. 3	Crystal Palace	Lagos	23.06.75
Barrett, Graham	5.10	Arsenal	Dublin	6.10.81
Joachim, Julian	5. 6	Aston Villa	Boston	20.09.74
McSheffrey, Gary	5. 8	–	Coventry	13.08.72
Morrell, Andy	5.11	Wrexham	Doncaster	28.09.74

CREWE ALEXANDRA

Ground: Alexandra Stadium, Gresty Road, Crewe CW2 6EB.
Telephone: 01270 213014. **Clubcall:** 09068 121647. **Club nickname:** Railwaymen.
First-choice colours: Red shirts; white shorts; red stockings.
Main sponsor: LC Charles. **Capacity for 2003-04:** 10,100.
Record attendance: 20,000 v Tottenham (F.A. Cup 4) 30 January,1960.

Name	Height ft. in.	Previous club	Birthplace	Birthdate
Bankole, Ade	6. 3	Q.P.R.	Lagos	9.09.69
Ince, Clayton	6. 2	–	Trinidad	13.07.72
Tomlinson, Stuart	6. 0	–	Chester	10.05.85
Defenders				
Betts, Tom	6. 0	–	Stone	3.12.82
Foster, Stephen	5.11	–	Warrington	10.09.80
McCready, Chris	6. 0	–	Chester	5.07.81
Morris, Alex	6. 0	–	Stoke	5.10.82
Moses, Ade	6. 0	Huddersfield Town	Doncaster	4.05.75
Sodje, Efetobore	6. 2	Luton Town	Greenwich	5.10.72
Vaughan, David	5. 6	–	St Asaph	18.02.83
Walker, Richard	6. 1	–	Stafford	17.09.80
Wright, David	5.11	–	Warrington	1.05.80
Yates, Adam	5.10	–	Stoke	28.05.83
Midfielders				
Bell, Lee	5.10	–	Crewe	20.11.83
Brammer, Dave	5.10	Port Vale	Bromborough	28.02.75
Frost, Carl	5. 9	–	Chester	19.07.83
Higdon, Michael	6. 0	–	Liverpool	3.09.83
Jeffs, Ian	5. 9	–	Chester	12.10.82
Lumsdon, Chris	5.10	Sunderland	Newcastle	15.12.79
Lunt, Kenny	5. 8	–	Runcorn	20.11.79
Rix, Ben	5.10	–	Wolves	11.12.83
Robinson, James	5. 9	–	Liverpool	18.09.82
Sorvel, Neil	6. 0	Crewe Alexandra	Whiston	2.03.73
Forwards				
Ashton, Dean	6. 3	–	Swindon	24.01.83
Edwards, Paul	6. 1	–	Derby	10.11.82
Jones, Steve	5.10	Leigh RMI	Derry	25.10.76
Platt, Matthew	5.11	–	Crewe	15.10.83
Varney, Luke	5.10	Quorn	Leicester	28.09.82

CRYSTAL PALACE

Ground: Selhurst Park, London SE25 6PU.
Telephone: 0208 768 6000. **Clubcall:** 09068 400333. **Club nickname:** Eagles.
First-choice colours: Red and blue shirts; blue shorts, blue stockings.
Main sponsor: Churchill. **Capacity for 2003-04:** 26,400.
Record attendance: 51,482 v Burnley (Div. 2) 11 May, 1979.

Name	Height ft. in.	Previous club	Birthplace	Birthdate
Goalkeepers				
Berthelin, Cedric	6. 4	–	Courrieres, Fra.	25.12.76
Clarke, Matt	6. 4	Bradford City	Sheffield	3.11.73
Cronin, Lance	6. 1	–	Brighton	11.09.85
Defenders				
Butterfield, Danny	5.10	Grimsby Town	Boston	21.11.79
Fleming, Curtis	5.11	Middlesbrough	Manchester	8.10.68
Granville, Danny	5.11	Manchester City	Islington	19.01.75
Heeroo, Gavin	6. 0	–	Haringey	2.09.84
Hunt, David	5.11	–	Dulwich	10.09.82
Popovic, Tony	6. 0	Hiroshima	Australia	4.07.73
Powell, Darren	6. 3	Brentford	Hammersmith	10.03.76
Smith, Jamie	5. 8	Wolves	Birmingham	17.09.74
Surey, Ben	5.10	–	Camberley	18.12.82
Symons, Kit	6. 2	Fulham	Basingstoke	8.03.71
Midfielders				
Black, Tommy	5. 7	Arsenal	Chigwell	26.11.79

Derry, Shaun	5.11	Portsmouth	Nottingham	6.12.77
Gray, Julian	6. 1	Arsenal	Lewisham	21.09.79
Mullins, Hayden	6. 0	–	Reading	27.03.79
Riihilahti, Aki	5.11	Valerenga	Helsinki	9.09.76
Thomson, Steve	5. 8	–	Glasgow	23.01.78
Forwards				
Akinbiyi, Ade	6. 1	Leicester City	Hackney	10.10.74
Freedman, Dougie	5. 9	Nott'm. Forest	Glasgow	21.01.74
Johnson, Andrew	5. 7	Birmingham City	Bedford	10.02.81
Routledge, Wayne	5.11	–	Sidcup	7.01.85
Williams, Gareth	6. 0	–	Cardiff	10.09.82

DERBY COUNTY

Ground: Pride Park Stadium, Pride Park, Derby DE24 8XL.
Telephone: 01332 667503. **Clubcall:** 09068 121187. **Club nickname:** Rams.
First-choice colours: White shirts; black shorts; white stockings.
Main sponsor: Marstons Pedigree. **Capacity for 2002-03:** 33,597.
Record attendance: (Baseball Ground) 41,826 v Tottenham (Div. 1) 20 September, 1969. (Pride Park) 33,597 England v Mexico, 25 May, 2001.

Name	**Height ft. in.**	**Previous club**	**Birthplace**	**Birthdate**
Goalkeepers				
Camp, Lee	5.11	–	Derby	22.08.84
Grant, Lee	6. 2	–	Hemel Hempstead	27.01.83
Oakes, Andy	6. 3	Hull City	Crewe	11.01.77
Defenders				
Barton, Warren	6. 0	Newcastle Utd.	Islington	19.03.69
Boertien, Paul	5.10	Carlisle Utd.	Carlisle	21.01.79
Elliott, Steve	6. 1	–	Derby	29.10.76
Huddlestone, Tom	6. 1	–	Nottingham	28.12.86
Hunt, Lewis	5.11	–	Birmingham	25.08.82
Jackson, Richard	5. 7	Scarborough	Whitby	18.04.80
Mawene, Youl	6. 1	Lens	Caen	16.07.79
Mills, Pablo	6. 0	–	Birmingham	27.05.84
Palmer, Chris	5. 7	–	Derby	16.10.83
Ritchie, Paul	5.10	Manchester City	Kirkcaldy	21.08.75
Walton, David	6. 2	Crewe Alexandra	Bellingham	10.04.73
Zavagno, Luciano	6. 0	Troyes	Rosario, Arg.	6.08.77
Midfielders				
Bolder, Adam	5. 8	Hull City	Hull	25.10.80
Holmes, Lee	5. 8	–	Mansfield	2.04.87
Kinkladze, Georgi	5. 6	Ajax	Tblisi	29.12.68
Murray, Adam	5. 8	–	Birmingham	30.09.81
Taylor, Ian	6. 1	Aston Villa	Birmingham	04.06.68
Valakari, Simo	5.10	Motherwell	Helsinki	28.04.73
Weckstrom, Kris	5. 9	–	MarieHamn, Fin.	26.05.83
Forwards				
McLeod, Izale	6. 1	–	Birmingham	15.10.84
Morris, Lee	5. 9	Sheffield Utd.	Driffield	30.04.80
Tudgay, Marcus	5.10	–	Sussex	3.02.83
Twigg, Gary	5.10	–	Glasgow	19.03.84

GILLINGHAM

Ground: Priestfield Stadium, Redfern Avenue, Gillingham ME7 4DD.
Telephone: 01634 851854. **Clubcall:** 09068 332211. **Club nickname:** Gills.
First-choice colours: Blue and white shirts; black and white shorts; black and blue stockings.
Main sponsor: Sea France. **Capacity for 2003-04:** 11,000.
Record attendance: 23,002 v Q.P.R. (F.A. Cup 3) 10 January, 1948.

Name	Height ft. in.	Previous club	Birthplace	Birthdate
Goalkeepers				
Bartram, Vince	6. 2	Arsenal	Birmingham	7.08.68
Brown, Jason	6. 0	Charlton Athletic	Bermondsey	18.05.82
Defenders				
Ashby, Barry	6. 2	Brentford	Park Royal	2.11.70
Cox, Ian	6. 0	Burnley	Croydon	25.03.71
Hope, Chris	6. 1	Scunthorpe Utd.	Sheffield	14.11.72
Rose, Richard	5.11	–	Tonbridge	8.09.82
Midfielders				
Crofts, Andrew	5.11	–	Chatham	29.05.84
Hessenthaler, Andy	5. 7	Watford	Gravesend	17.06.75
Hills, John	5. 9	Blackpool	Blackpool	21.04.78
Johnson, Leon	6. 0	Southend Utd.	Shoreditch	10.05.81
Nosworthy, Nayron	6. 1	–	Brixton	11.10.80
Perpetuini, David	5. 9	Watford	Hitchin	26.09.79
Phillips, Michael	5. 8	–	Camberwell	22.01.83
Saunders, Mark	5.11	Plymouth Argyle	Reading	23.07.71
Smith, Paul	5.11	Brentford	East Ham	18.09.71
Southall, Nicky	5.10	Bolton Wand.	Middlesbrough	28.01.72
Spiller, Daniel	5.10	–	Maidstone	10.01.81
Forwards				
James, Kevin	5. 9	Charlton Athletic	Southwark	3.01.80
Johnson, Tommy	5.11	Kilmarnock	Newcastle	15.01.71
King, Marlon	6. 1	Barnet	Dulwich	26.04.80
Shaw, Paul	5.11	Millwall	Burnham	4.09.73
Sidibe, Mamady	6. 4	Swansea City	Mali	18.12.79
Wallace, Rod	5. 7	Bolton Wand.	Lewisham	2.10.69

IPSWICH TOWN

Ground: Portman Road, Ipswich IP1 2DA.
Telephone: 01473 400500. **Club nickname:** Blues/Town.
First-choice colours: Blue shirts; white shorts; blue stockings.
Main sponsor: Powergen. **Capacity for 2003-04:** 30,000.
Record attendance: 38,010 v Leeds Utd. (F.A. Cup 6) 8 March, 1975.

Name	Height ft. in.	Previous club	Birthplace	Birthdate
Goalkeepers				
Marshall, Andy	6. 2	Norwich City	Bury St Edmunds	14.04.75
Sereni, Matteo	6. 1	Sampdoria	Italy	11.02.75
Defenders				
Diallo, Drissa	6. 1	Burnley	Mauritania	4.01.73
Gaardsoe, Thomas	6. 2	Aalborg	Denmark	23.11.79
Makin, Chris	5.11	Sunderland	Manchester	8.05.73
McGreal, John	5.11	Tranmere Rov.	Liverpool	02.06.72
Richards, Matthew	5. 8	–	Harlow	26.12.84
Wilnis, Fabian	5.10	De Graafschap	Surinam	23.08.70
Midfielders				
Bloomfield, Matt	5. 9	–	Ipswich	8.02.84
Magilton, Jim	6. 0	Sheffield Wed.	Belfast	6.05.69
Miller, Tommy	6. 1	Hartlepool Utd.	Easington	8.01.79
Wright, Jermaine	5. 9	Crewe Alexandra	Greenwich	21.10.75
Forwards				
Bent, Darren	6. 0	–	Cambridge	6.02.84
Bent, Marcus	6. 2	Blackburn Rov.	Hammersmith	19.05.78
Bowditch, Dean	5.11	–	Bishop's Stortford	15.06.86
Counago, Pablo	6. 0	Celta Vigo	Pontevedra, Spa.	9.08.79
Graaven, Guillermo	6. 0	Ajax	Amsterdam	17.01.82

Naylor, Richard	6.1	–	Leeds	28.02.77

MILLWALL

Ground: The New Den, Zampa Road, London SE16 3LN.
Telephone: 0207 232 1222. **Clubcall:** 09068 400300. **Club nickname:** Lions.
First-choice colours: Blue shirts; white shorts; blue stockings.
Main sponsor: 24 Seven. **Capacity for 2003-04:** 20,146.
Record attendance: (The Den) 48,672 v Derby Co. (F.A. Cup 5) 20 February, 1937. (New Den) 20,093 v Arsenal (F.A. Cup 3) 10 January, 1994.

Name	Height ft. in.	Previous club	Birthplace	Birthdate
Goalkeepers				
Gueret, Willy	6. 1	Le Mans	Guadaloupe	3.08.73
Harpur, Chad	5.10	–	Johannesburg	3.09.82
Warner, Tony	6. 4	Liverpool	Liverpool	11.05.74
Defenders				
Bull, Ronnie	5. 8	–	Hackney	26.12.80
Craig, Tony	6. 0	–	Greenwich	20.04.85
Dolan, Joe	6. 3	Chelsea	Harrow	27.05.80
Dunne, Alan	5.10	–	Dublin	23.08.82
Lawrence, Matt	6. 1	Wycombe Wand.	Northampton	19.06.74
Nethercott, Stuart	6. 0	Tottenham	Ilford	21.03.73
Phillips, Mark	6. 2	–	Lambeth	27.01.82
Rees, Matthew	6. 3	–	Swansea	2.09.82
Robinson, Paul	6. 1	–	Barnet	7.01.82
Ryan, Robbie	5.10	Huddersfield Town	Dublin	16.05.77
Tuttle, David	6. 2	Barnsley	Reading	6.02.73
Ward, Darren	6. 3	Watford	Harrow	13.09.78
Midfielders				
Cahill, Tim	5.10	Sydney Utd.	Sydney	6.12.79
Elliott, Marvin	6. 0	–	Wandsworth	15.09.84
Hearn, Charlie	5.11	–	Ashford	5.11.83
Livermore, David	6. 0	Arsenal	Edmonton	20.05.80
Reid, Steven	5.11	–	Kingston	10.03.81
Roberts, Andy	5.10	Wimbledon	Dartford	20.03.74
Wise, Dennis	5. 6	Leicester City	Kensington	16.12.66
Forwards				
Ashikodi, Moses	5.10	–	London	27.06.87
Braniff, Kevin	5.11	–	Belfast	4.03.83
Ifil, Paul	6. 0	–	Brighton	20.10.79
Harris, Neil	5.11	Cambridge City	Orsett	12.07.77
May, Ben	6. 1	–	Gravesend	10.03.84
McCammon, Mark	6. 3	Brentford	Barnet	7.08.78
Sadlier, Richard	6. 2	Belvedere	Dublin	14.01.79
Sweeney, Peter	6. 0	–	Glasgow	25.09.84

NORWICH CITY

Ground: Carrow Road, Norwich NR1 1JE.
Telephone: 01603 760760. **Clubcall:** 09068 121144 **Club nickname:** Canaries.
First-choice colours: Yellow and green shirts; green and yellow shorts; yellow stockings.
Main sponsor: Proton Cars/Lotus Cars. **Capacity for 2003-04:** 16,000 (until early 2004).
Record attendance: 43,984 v Leicester City (F.A. Cup 6) 30 March, 1963.

Name	Height ft. in.	Previous club	Birthplace	Birthdate
Goalkeepers				
Crichton, Paul	6. 1	Burnley	Pontefract	3.10.68
Green, Robert	6. 3	–	Chertsey	18.01.80

Defenders				
Brennan, Jim	5. 9	Nott'm. Forest	Toronto	8.05.77
Drury, Adam	5.10	Peterborough Utd.	Cambridge	29.08.78
Easton, Clint	5.11	Watford	Barking	1.11.77
Fleming, Craig	5.11	Oldham Athletic	Halifax	6.10.71
Holt, Gary	5.10	Kilmarnock	Irvine	9.03.73
Mackay, Malky	6. 3	Celtic	Bellshill	19.02.72
Shackell, Jason	5.11	–	Stevenage	27.09.83
Midfielders				
Briggs, Keith	6. 0	Stockport Co.	Ashton under Lyne	11.12.81
Llewellyn, Chris	6. 0	–	Merthyr	28.08.79
Mulryne, Phil	5. 8	Manchester Utd.	Belfast	1.01.78
Russell, Darel	6. 0	–	Mile End	22.10.80
Sinclair, Dean	5.11	–	Luton	17.12.84
Forwards				
Abbey, Zema	6. 1	Cambridge Utd.	Luton	17.04.77
Henderson, Ian	5.11	–	Thetford	24.01.85
Jarvis, Ryan	5.11	–	Fakenham	11.07.86
McVeigh, Paul	5. 6	Tottenham	Belfast	6.12.77
Nielsen, David	5.11	Wimbledon	Denmark	1.12.76
Notman, Alex	5. 7	Manchester Utd.	Edinburgh	10.12.79
Rivers, Mark	5.10	Crewe Alexandra	Crewe	26.11.75
Roberts, Iwan	6. 3	Wolves	Bangor	26.06.68

NOTTINGHAM FOREST

Ground: City Ground, Pavilion Road, Nottingham NG2 5FJ.
Telephone: 0115 982 4444. **Clubcall:** 09068 121174. **Club nickname:** Forest.
First-choice colours: Red shirts; white shorts; red stockings.
Main sponsor: Capital One. **Capacity for 2003-04:** 30,602.
Record attendance: 49,945 v Manchester Utd. (Div. 1) 28 October, 1967.

Name	Height ft. in.	Previous club	Birthplace	Birthdate
Goalkeepers				
Formann, Pascal	6. 0	Chelsea	Werne, Ger.	16.11.82
Roche, Barry	6. 4	–	Dublin	6.04.82
Ward, Darren	5.11	Notts Co.	Worksop	11.05.74
Defenders				
Biggins, James	5.11	–	Nottingham	6.06.85
Dawson, Michael	6. 2	–	Northallerton	18.11.83
Doig, Chris	6. 2	–	Dumfries	13.02.81
Louis-Jean, Matthieu	5. 9	Le Havre	Mont-St-Aignan, Fra.	22.02.76
Morgan, Wes	5.11	–	Nottingham	21.01.84
Oyen, Davy	6. 0	Anderlecht	Belgium	17.07.75
Robertson, Gregor	5.11	–	Edinburgh	19.01.84
Walker, Des	5.11	Sheffield Wed.	Hackney	26.11.65
Midfielders				
Bopp, Eugen	6. 0	–	Kiev	5.09.83
Cash, Brian	5.10	–	Dublin	24.11.82
Kearney, Liam	5. 7	–	Cork	10.01.83
Reid, Andy	5. 7	–	Dublin	29.07.82
Thompson, John	6. 1	–	Dublin	12.10.82
Williams, Gareth	5.11	–	Glasgow	16.12.81
Forwards				
Harewood, Marlon	6. 1	–	Hampstead	25.08.79
Jeffrey, Richard	5. 9	–	Swanwick	4.11.83
Jess, Eoin	5.10	Bradford City	Aberdeen	13.12.70
Johnson, David	5. 6	Ipswich Town	Kingston, Jam.	15.08.76
Westcarr, Craig	5.11	–	Nottingham	29.01.85

PRESTON NORTH END

Ground: Deepdale, Sir Tom Finney Way, Preston PR1 6RU.
Telephone: 08704 421964. **Club nickname:** Lilywhites.
First-choice colours: White shirts; blue shorts; white stockings.
Main sponsor: NewReg.com. **Capacity for 2003-04:** 21,000.
Record attendance: 42,684 v Arsenal (Div. 1) 23 April, 1938.

Name	Height ft. in.	Previous club	Birthplace	Birthdate
Goalkeepers				
Gould, Jonathan	6. 1	Celtic	Paddington	18.07.68
Lucas, David	6. 1	–	Preston	23.11.77
Lonergan, Andrew	6. 4	–	Preston	19.10.83
Defenders				
Alexander, Graham	5.11	Luton Town	Coventry	10.10.71
Broomes, Marlon	6. 0	Sheffield Wed.	Birmingham	28.11.77
Jackson, Michael	5.11	Bury	Chester	4.12.73
Lucketti, Chris	6. 0	Huddersfield Town	Littleborough	28.09.71
Midfielders				
Anderson, Iain	5. 5	Toulouse	Glasgow	23.07.77
Bailey, John	5. 8	–	Manchester	2.07.84
Cartwright, Lee	5. 8	–	Rossendale	19.09.72
Edwards, Rob	5.11	Bristol City	Kendal	1.07.73
Etuhu, Dickson	6. 2	Manchester City	Kano, Nig.	8.06.82
Keane, Michael	5. 6	–	Dublin	29.12.82
Lewis, Eddie	5.10	Fulham	Cerritos, USA	17.05.74
McCormack, Alan	5. 8	–	Dublin	10.01.84
McKenna, Paul	5. 8	–	Chorley	20.10.77
Mears, Tyrone	5.11	Manchester City	Stockport	18.02.83
O'Neil, Brian	6. 1	Derby Co.	Paisley	6.09.72
Rankine, Mark	5. 9	Wolves	Doncaster	30.09.69
Skora, Eric	5.10	–	France	20.08.81
Forwards				
Abbott, Pawel	5.10	LKS Lodz	York	2.12.77
Cresswell, Richard	6. 0	Leicester City	Bridlington	20.09.77
Fuller, Ricardo	6. 3	Tivoli Gardens	Kingston, Jam.	31.10.79
Healy, David	5. 8	Manchester Utd.	Downpatrick	5.08.79
Koumantarakis, George	6. 4	Basle	Greece	27.03.74
Lynch, Simon	6. 0	Celtic	Montreal	19.05.82
O'Neil, Joe	6. 0	–	Blackburn	28.10.82
Wright, Mark	5.10	–	Chorley	4.09.81

READING

Ground: Madejski Stadium, Junction 11 M4, Reading RG2 0FL.
Telephone: 0118 968 1100. **Clubcall:** 09068 121000. **Club nickname:** Royals.
First-choice colours: Blue and white shirts; blue shorts; white stockings.
Main sponsor: Westcoast. **Capacity for 2003-04:** 24,084.
Record attendance: (Elm Park) 33,042 v Brentford (F.A. Cup 5) 17 February, 1927. (Madejski Stadium) 24,060 v Wolves (Div. 1 play-off) 14, May, 2003.

Name	Height ft. in.	Previous club	Birthplace	Birthdate
Goalkeepers				
Ashdown, Jamie	6. 3	–	Reading	30.11.80
Hahnemann, Marcus	6. 3	Fulham	Seattle	15.06.72
Defenders				
Brown, Steve	6. 1	Charlton Athletic	Brighton	13.05.72
Mackie, John	6. 0	Sutton	London	5.07.76
Shorey, Nicky	5. 9	Leyton Orient	Romford	19.02.81
Williams, Adrian	6. 2	Wolves	Reading	16.08.71

Midfielders				
Boucaud, Andre	5.10	–	London	10.10.84
Gamble, Joe	5. 7	Cork City	Cork	14.01.82
Harper, James	5.11	Arsenal	Chelmsford	9.11.80
Hughes, Andy	5.11	Notts Co.	Manchester	2.01.78
Murray, Scott	5. 9	Bristol City	Aberdeen	26.05.74
Murty, Graeme	5.10	York City	Saltburn	13.11.74
Newman, Ricky	5.10	Millwall	Guildford	5.08.70
Salako, John	5.10	Charlton Athletic	Nigeria	11.02.69
Sidwell, Steve	5.10	Arsenal	Wandsworth	14.12.82
Watson, Kevin	5.10	Rotherham Utd.	Hackney	3.01.74
Forwards				
Butler, Martin	5.11	Cambridge Utd.	Dudley	15.09.74
Cureton, Jamie	5. 7	Bristol Rov.	Bristol	28.08.75
Forster, Nicky	5. 9	Birmingham City	Caterham	8.09.73
Henderson, Darius	6. 1	–	Doncaster	7.09.81
Savage, Bas	6. 3	Walton & Hersham	London	7.01.82
Tyson, Nathan	6. 0	–	Reading	4.05.82

ROTHERHAM UNITED

Ground: Millmoor, Rotherham S60 1HR.
Telephone: 01709 512434. **Clubcall:** 09068 121637. **Club nickname:** Millers.
First-choice colours: Red and white shirts; white shorts; red stockings.
Capacity for 2003-04: 11,486.
Record attendance: 25,000 v Sheffield Wed. (Div. 2) 26 January, 1952 and v Sheffield Wed. (Div. 2) 13 December, 1952.

Name	Height ft. in.	Previous club	Birthplace	Birthdate
Goalkeepers				
Montgomery, Gary	6. 2	Coventry City	Leamington Spa	10.08.82
Pollitt, Mike	6. 4	Chesterfield	Bolton	29.02.72
Defenders				
Branston, Guy	6. 2	Leicester City	Leicester	9.01.79
Hurst, Paul	5. 4	–	Sheffield	25.09.74
Scott, Rob	6. 1	Fulham	Epsom	15.08.73
Swailes, Chris	6. 2	Bury	Gateshead	19.10.70
Midfielders				
Daws, Nick	5.11	Bury	Salford	15.03.70
Garner, Darren	5. 9	Plymouth Argyle	Plymouth	10.12.71
McIntosh, Martin	6. 3	Hibernian	East Kilbride	19.03.71
Monkhouse, Andy	6. 0	–	Leeds Utd.	23.10.80
Mullin, John	6. 0	Burnley	Bury	11.08.75
Talbot, Stewart	5.11	Port Vale	Birmingham	14.06.73
Forwards				
Barker, Richard	5.11	Macclesfield Town	Sheffield	30.05.75
Byfield, Darren	5.11	Walsall	Sutton Coldfield	29.09.76
Lee, Alan	6. 2	Burnley	Galway	21.08.78
Robins, Mark	5. 8	Walsall	Ashton under Lyne	22.12.69
Sedgwick, Chris	6. 1	–	Sheffield	28.04.80
Warne, Paul	5. 8	Wigan Athletic	Norwich	8.05.73

SHEFFIELD UNITED

Ground: Bramall Lane, Sheffield, S2 4SU.
Telephone: 0114 221 5757. **Clubcall:** 09068 888650. **Club nickname:** Blades.
First-choice colours: Red and white shirts; white and red shorts; white and red stockings.
Main Sponsor: Desun. **Capacity for 2003-04:** 30,975.
Record attendance: 68,287 v Leeds Utd. (F.A. Cup 5) 15 February, 1936.

Name	Height ft. in.	Previous club	Birthplace	Birthdate
Goalkeepers				
De Vogt, Wilko	6. 0	Utrecht	Breda, Hol.	17.09.75
Kenny, Paddy	6. 1	Sheffield Utd.	Halifax	17.05.78
Rogers, Kristian	5.11	Wrexham	Chester	2.10.80
Defenders				
Armstrong, Chris	5. 9	Oldham Athletic	Newcastle	5.08.82
Croissant, Benoit	6. 0	Troyes	Virity Francois, Fra.	9.08.80
Cryan, Colin	5.10	–	Dublin	23.03.81
Jagielka, Phil	5.11	–	Manchester	17.08.82
Murphy, Shaun	6. 1	W.B.A.	Sydney	5.11.70
Nugent, Rob	6. 0	–	Manchester	27.12.82
Page, Robert	6. 0	Watford	Llwynpia	3.09.74
Yates, Steve	5.11	Tranmere Rov.	Bristol	29.01.70
Midfielders				
Baum, Adam	5. 7	–	Nottingham	14.10.82
Brown, Michael	5. 9	Manchester City	Hartlepool	25.01.77
Javary, Jean-Phillipe	5.11	Plymouth Argyle	Montpellier	10.01.78
Kabba, Steve	5. 8	Crystal Palace	Lambeth	7.03.81
McCall, Stuart	5. 7	Bradford City	Leeds	10.06.64
Montgomery, Nick	5. 9	–	Leeds	28.10.81
Ndlovu, Peter	5. 8	Birmingham City	Bulawayo	25.02.73
Smith, Grant	5.11	Clydebank	Irvine	5.05.80
Thompson, Tyrone	5. 8	–	Sheffield	8.05.82
Tonge, Michael	5.11	–	Manchester	7.04.83
Forwards				
Allison, Wayne	6. 1	Tranmere Rov.	Huddersfield	16.10.68
Asaba, Carl	6. 2	Gillingham	London	28.01.73
Lester, Jack	5.10	Nott'm. Forest	Sheffield	8.10.75
Morrison, Owen	5. 7	Sheffield Wed.	Londonderry	8.12.81
Onuora, Iffy	6. 1	Gillingham	Glasgow	28.07.67
Peschisolido, Paul	5. 7	Fulham	Scarborough, Can.	25.05.71

STOKE CITY

Ground: Britannia Stadium, Stanley Matthews Way, Stoke-on-Trent ST4 7EG.
Telephone: 01782 592222. **Clubcall:** 09068 121040. **Club nickname:** Potters.
First-choice colours: Red and white shirts; white and red shorts; red stockings.
Main sponsor: Britannia Building Society. **Capacity for 2003-04:** 28,218.
Record attendance: (Victoria Ground) 51,380 v Arsenal (Div. 1) 29 March, 1937. (Britannia Stadium) 27,109 v Liverpool (League Cup 4) 29 November, 2000.

Name	Height ft. in.	Previous club	Birthplace	Birthdate
Goalkeepers				
Alcock, Danny	5.11	–	Staffs	15.02.84
Cutler, Neil	6. 1	Aston Villa	Birmingham	3.09.76
Defenders				
Clarke, Clive	6. 0	–	Dublin	14.01.80
Commons, Kris	5. 6	–	Notts	30.08.83
Hall, Marcus	6. 1	Southampton	Coventry	24.03.76
Hill, Clint	6. 0	Oldham Athletic	Liverpool	19.10.78
Owen, Gareth	6. 1	–	Staffs	21.09.82
Shtaniuk, Sergei	6. 3	Dynamo Moscow	Minsk	11.01.72
Thomas, Wayne	6. 2	Torquay Utd.	Gloucester	17.05.79
Wilkinson, Andy	5.11	–	Stone	6.08.84
Wilson, Brian	5.10	–	Manchester	9.05.83
Midfielders				
Gunnarsson, Brynjar	6. 1	Orgryte	Reykavik	16.10.75
Henry, Karl	6. 1	–	Wolves	26.11.82

Hoekstra, Peter	6. 3	Ajax	Assen	4.04.73
Marteinsson, Petur	6. 1	Stabaek	Reykjavik	14.07.73
Neal, Lewis	5.11	–	Leicester	14.07.81
O'Connor, James	5. 8	–	Dublin	1.09.79
Forwards				
Cooke, Andy	5.11	Burnley	Stoke	20.01.74
Goodfellow, Marc	5.10	–	Swadlincote	20.09.81
Greenacre, Chris	5.11	Mansfield Town	Halifax	23.12.77
Hall, Laurence	6. 0	–	Nottingham	26.03.84
Iwelumo, Chris	6. 4	Aarhus	Coatbridge	1.08.78
Noel-Williams, Gifton	6. 4	Watford	Islington	21.01.80

SUNDERLAND

Ground: Stadium of Light, Sunderland, Tyne and Wear SR5 1SU.
Telephone: 0191 551 5000. **Clubcall:** 09068 121140. **Club Nickname:** Black Cats.
First-choice colours: Red and white shirts; black shorts, black stockings.
Main sponsor: Reg Vardy. **Capacity for 2003-04:** 49,000.
Record attendance: (Roker Park) 75,118 v Derby Co. (F.A. Cup 6) 8 March 1933. Stadium of Light: 48,305 v Manchester Utd. (Premier League) 13 October 2001.

Name	Height ft. in.	Previous club	Birthplace	Birthdate
Goalkeepers				
Ingham, Michael	6. 4	–	Belfast	7.09.80
Poom, Mart	6. 4	Derby Co.	Tallinn, Est.	3.02.72
Sorensen, Thomas	6. 4	Odense	Odense	12.06.76
Defenders				
Babb, Phil	6. 0	Sporting Lisbon	Lambeth	30.11.70
Bjorklund, Joachim	6. 1	Venezia	Vaxjo, Swe.	15.03.71
Clark, Ben	6. 2	–	Shotley Bridge	24.01.83
Collins, Patrick	5.11	–	Newcastle	4.02.85
Craddock, Jody	6. 0	Cambridge Utd.	Redditch	25.07.75
Gray, Michael	5. 7	–	Sunderland	3.08.74
James, Craig	6. 0	–	Middlesbrough	15.11.82
McCartney, George	5.11	–	Belfast	28.04.81
Ramsden, Simon	6. 0	–	Bishop Auckland	17.12.81
Rossiter, Mark	5.10	–	Sligo	27.05.83
Thome, Emerson	6. 1	Chelsea	Porto Alegre, Bra.	30.03.72
Williams, Darren	5.10	York City	Middlesbrough	28.04.77
Wright, Stephen	6. 0	Liverpool	Liverpool	8.02.80
Midfielders				
Arca, Julio	5. 9	Argentinos Jnrs.	Quilmes Bernal, Arg.	31.01.81
Black, Chris	5.11	–	Ashington	7.09.82
Butler, Thomas	5. 7	–	Dublin	25.04.81
Dickman, Jonjo	5. 8	–	Hexham	22.09.81
Kilbane, Kevin	6. 2	W.B.A.	Preston	1.02.77
McAteer, Jason	5.11	Blackburn Rov.	Birkenhead	18.06.71
McCann, Gavin	6. 1	Everton	Blackpool	10.01.78
Medina, Nicolas	5. 9	Argentinos Jnrs.	Buenos Aires	17.02.82
Oster, John	5. 9	Everton	Boston	8.12.78
Peeters, Tom	5.10	Mechelen	Bornem, Bel.	25.09.78
Reyna, Claudio	5. 9	Rangers	New Jersey	20.07.73
Ryan, Richie	5.10	–	Kilkenny	6.01.85
Thirlwell, Paul	5.11	–	Gateshead	13.02.79
Thornton, Sean	5.11	–	Drogheda	18.05.83
Forwards				
Flo, Tore Andre	6. 4	Rangers	Norway	15.06.73
Kyle, Kevin	6. 3	Ayr Boswell	Stranraer	7.06.81
Phillips, Kevin	5. 8	Watford	Hitchin	25.07.73
Reddy, Michael	6. 1	Kilkenny City	Kilkenny	24.03.80
Piper, Matt	6. 1	Leicester City	Leicester	29.09.81

Stewart, Marcus	5.10	Ipswich Town	Bristol	7.11.72

WALSALL

Ground: Bescot Stadium, Bescot Crescent, Walsall WS1 4SA.
Telephone: 01922 622791. **Clubcall:** 09068 555800. **Club nickname:** Saddlers.
First-choice colours: Red shirts; red and white shorts; red and white stockings.
Main Sponsor: Banks's Brewery. **Capacity for 2003-04:** 11,300.
Record attendance: (Fellows Park) 25,433 v Newcastle Utd. (Div. 2) 29 August, 1961. (Bescot Stadium) 11,307 v Wolves (Div. 1) 11 January, 2003.

Name	Height ft. in.	Previous club	Birthplace	Birthdate
Goalkeepers				
Walker, James	5.11	Notts Co.	Sutton-in-Ashfield	9.07.73
Ward, Gavin	6. 3	Stoke City	Sutton Coldfield	30.06.70
Defenders				
Aranalde, Zigor	6. 1	Logrones	Guipuzcoa, Spa.	28.02.73
Bazeley, Darren	5.11	Wolves	Northampton	5.10.72
Carbon, Matt	6. 2	W.B.A	Nottingham	8.06.75
Hay, Danny	6. 4	Leeds Utd.	Auckland	15.05.75
Roper, Ian	6. 4	–	Nuneaton	20.06.77
Midfielders				
Birch, Gary	5.10	–	Birmingham	8.10.81
Corica, Steve	5. 8	Hiroshima	Cairns, Aus.	24.03.73
Emblen, Neil	6. 1	Norwich City	Bromley	19.06.71
Lawrence, Jamie	5.11	Bradford City	Balham	8.03.70
Matias, Pedro	6. 0	Tranmere Rov.	Madrid	11.10.73
O'Connor, Martin	5. 9	Birmingham City	Walsall	10.12.67
Osborn, Simon	5. 9	Gillingham	Croydon	19.01.72
Samways, Vinny	5. 8	Las Palmas	Bethnal Green	27.10.68
Simpson, Fitzroy	5. 8	Hearts	Trowbridge	26.02.70
Smith, Nicholas	5.10	–	Bloxwich	5.10.82
Sonner, Danny	5.11	Birmingham City	Wigan	9.01.72
Stanley, Craig	5. 8	–	Bedworth	3.03.83
Wright, Mark	5.11	–	Wolves	24.02.82
Forwards				
Bishop, Andrew	6. 0	–	Stone	19.10.82
Hawley, Karl	5. 8	–	Walsall	6.12.81
Junior	6. 0	Trezze	Brazil	20.07.76
Leitao, Jorge	5.11	Farense	Oporto	14.01.74
Rodrigues, Dani	5.11	Southampton	Madeira	3.03.80

WATFORD

Ground: Vicarage Road Stadium, Vicarage Road, Watford WD18 OER.
Telephone: 01923 496000. **Clubcall:** 09068 104104. **Club nickname:** Hornets.
First-choice colours: Yellow shirts; black shorts; black stockings.
Main sponsor: Total. **Capacity for 2003-04:** 20,800.
Record attendance: 34,099 v Manchester Utd. (F.A. Cup 4) February, 1969.

Name	Height ft. in.	Previous club	Birthplace	Birthdate
Goalkeepers				
Chamberlain, Alec	6. 2	Sunderland	March	20.06.64
Lee, Richard	5.11	–	Oxford	5.10.82
Defenders				
Blizzard, Dominic	6. 2	–	High Wycombe	2.09.83
Brown, Wayne	6. 0	Ipswich Town	Banbury	20.08.77
Cox, Neil	6. 0	Bolton Wand.	Scunthorpe	8.10.71
Doyley, Lloyd	5.10	–	Whitechapel	1.12.82
Dyche, Sean	6. 0	Millwall	Kettering	28.06.71

Gayle, Marcus	6. 1	Rangers	Hammersmith	27.09.70
Ifil, Jerel	6. 1	–	London	27.06.82
Mahon, Gavin	6. 0	Brentford	Birmingham	2.01.77
Robinson, Paul	5. 9	–	Watford	14.12.78
Smith, Jack	5.11	–	Hemel Hempstead	14.10.83
Midfielders				
Ardley, Neal	5.11	Wimbledon	Epsom	1.09.72
Cook, Lee	5. 9	–	Hammersmith	3.08.82
Fisken, Gary	6. 0	–	Watford	27.10.81
Godfrey, Elliott	5.11	–	Toronto	22.02.83
Hand, Jamie	5.11	–	Uxbridge	7.02.84
Hyde, Micah	5.11	Cambridge Utd.	Newham	10.11.74
Johnson, Richard	5.10	–	Kurri-Kurri, Aust.	27.04.74
Mahon, Gavin	6. 0	Brentford	Birmingham	2.01.77
McNamee, Anthony	5. 6	–	Kensington	13.07.84
Swonnell, Sam	5.10	–	Brentwood	13.09.82
Vernazza, Paolo	6. 0	Arsenal	Islington	1.11.79
Forwards				
Dyer, Bruce	5.11	Barnsley	Ilford	13.04.75
Fitzgerald, Scott	5.11	Northwood	Hillingdon	18.11.79
Helguson, Heidar	5.10	Lillestrom	Akureyri, Ice.	22.08.77
Norville, Jason	5.11	–	Trinidad	9.09.83
Smith, Tommy	5.10	–	Hemel Hempstead	22.05.80
Webber, Danny	5. 9	Manchester Utd.	Manchester	28.12.81

WEST BROMWICH ALBION

Ground: The Hawthorns, Halfords Lane, West Bromwich B71 4LF.
Telephone: 0121 525 8888. **Clubcall:** 09068 121193. **Club nickname:** Baggies.
First-choice colours: Blue and white shirts; white shorts; white stockings.
Main sponsor: West Bromwich Building Society. **Capacity for 2003-04:** 27,000.
Record attendance: 64,815 v Arsenal (F.A. Cup 6), 6 March, 1937.

Name	Height ft. in.	Previous club	Birthplace	Birthdate
Goalkeepers				
Hoult, Russell	6. 4	Portsmouth	Ashby de la Zouch	22.11.72
Murphy, Joe	6. 1	Tranmere Rov.	Dublin	21.08.81
Defenders				
Adams, Ross	5.11	–	Birmingham	11.03.83
Balis, Igor	6. 0	Spartak Trnava	Slovakia	5.01.70
Chambers, Adam	5.10	–	West Bromwich	20.11.80
Chambers, James	5.10	–	West Bromwich	20.11.80
Clement, Neil	6. 0	Chelsea	Reading	3.10.78
Gilchrist, Phil	6. 0	Leicester City	Stockton	25.08.73
Haas, Bernt	6. 2	Sunderland	Vienna	8.04.78
Mkandawire, Tamika	6. 0	–	Malawi	28.05.83
Moore, Darren	6. 2	Portsmouth	Birmingham	22.04.74
Sigurdsson, Larus	6. 0	Stoke City	Akureyri, Ice.	4.06.73
Wallwork, Ronnie	5.10	Manchester Utd.	Manchester	10.09.77
Midfielders				
Appleton, Michael	5. 8	Preston N.E.	Salford	12.04.75
Dobie, Scott	6. 0	Carlisle Utd.	Workington	10.10.78
Dyer, Lloyd	5. 8	Aston Villa	Birmingham	13.09.82
Gregan, Sean	6. 0	Preston N.E.	Middlesbrough	29.03.74
Johnson, Andy	6. 1	Norwich City	Bristol	2.05.74
Jordao	6. 3	Sporting Braga	Malange, Ang.	30.08.71
Koumas, Jason	5.10	Tranmere Rov.	Wrexham	25.09.79
Marshall, Lee	6. 2	Leicester City	Islington	21.01.79
O'Connor, James	5. 8	Stoke City	Dublin	1.09.79
Forwards				
Dichio, Danny	6. 4	Sunderland	Hammersmith	19.10.74

Dobie, Scott	6. 1	Carlisle Utd.	Workington	10.10.78
Hulse, Rob	6. 0	Crewe Alexandra	Crewe	25.10.79
Hughes, Lee	5.10	Coventry City	Smethwick	22.05.76
Roberts, Jason	6. 1	Bristol Rov.	Park Royal, Gren.	25.01.78

WEST HAM UNITED

Ground: Boleyn Ground, Green Street, Upton Park, London E13 9AZ.
Telephone: 0208 548 2748 **Clubcall:** 09065 861966.
Club Nickname: Hammers.
First-choice colours: Claret and sky blue shirts; white shorts; white stockings.
Main sponsor: Jobserve. **Capacity for 2003-04:** 35,050.
Record attendance: 43,322 v Tottenham, Div. 1, October 1970.

Name	Height ft. in.	Previous club	Birthplace	Birthdate
Goalkeepers				
James, David	6. 5	Aston Villa	Welwyn GC	1.08.70
Bywater, Stephen	6. 3	Rochdale	Manchester	7.06.81
Defenders				
Brevett, Rufus	5. 8	Fulham	Derby Co.	24.09.69
Byrne, Shaun	5. 9	–	Taplow	21.01.81
Dailly, Christian	6. 0	Blackburn Rov.	Dundee	23.10.73
Ferdinand, Anton	6. 0	–	Peckham	18.02.85
Johnson, Glen	5.10	–	London	23.08.84
Pearce, Ian	6. 3	Blackburn Rov.	Bury St Edmunds	7.05.74
Repka, Tomas	6. 2	Fiorentina	Slavicin Zlin, Cz.	2.01.74
Schemmel, Sebastien	5.10	Metz	Nancy	2.06.75
Midfielders				
Carrick, Michael	6. 0	–	Wallsend	28.07.81
Cole, Joe	5. 7	–	Islington	8.11.81
Hutchison, Don	6. 1	Sunderland	Gateshead	9.05.71
Lomas, Steve	6. 0	Manchester City	Hanover	18.01.74
McMahon, Darryl				
Noble, David	6. 0	Arsenal	Hitchin	2.02.82
Sinclair, Trevor	5.10	Q.P.R.	Dulwich	2.03.73
Forwards				
Defoe, Jermain	5. 7	–	Beckton	7.10.82
Garcia, Richard	5.11	–	Perth, Aus.	9.04.81
Kanoute, Frederic	6. 3	Lyon	Sainte-Foy, Fra.	2.09.77
Sofiane, Youssef	5.11	Auxerre	Villefranche, Fra.	8.07.84

WIGAN ATHLETIC

Ground: JJB Stadium, Robin Park, Wigan WN5 0UZ.
Telephone: 01942 774000. **Clubcall:** 09068 121655. **Club nickname:** Latics.
First-choice colours: Blue shirts; blue shorts; white stockings.
Main sponsor: JJB Sports. **Capacity for 2003-04:** 25,000.
Record attendance: (Springfield Park) 27,500 v Hereford Utd. (F.A. Cup 2) 12 December, 1953. (JJB Stadium) 16,922 v Blackburn Rov. (League Cup quarter-final) 17 December, 2002.

Name	Height ft. in.	Previous club	Birthplace	Birthdate
Goalkeepers				
Filan, John	5.11	Blackburn Rov.	Sydney	8.02.70
Defenders				
Baines, Leighton	5. 7	–	–	11.12.84
Breckin, Ian	5.11	Chesterfield	Rotherham	24.02.75
De Vos, Jason	6. 0	Dundee Utd.	Ontario	2.01.74
Eaden, Nicky	5. 9	Birmingham City	Sheffield	12.12.72
Jackson, Matt	6. 0	Norwich City	Leeds	19.10.71

McMillan, Steve	5. 8	Motherwell	Edinburgh	19.01.76
Mitchell, Paul	5. 9	–	Manchester	26.08.81
Pendlebury, Ian	5.11	–	Bolton	3.09.83
Midfielders				
Bullard, Jimmy	5.10	Peterborough Utd.	Newham	23.10.78
Dinning, Tony	5.11	Wolves	Wallsend	4.12.75
Flynn, Michael	5.11	Barry Town	–	–
Jarrett, Jason	6. 0	Bury	Bury	14.09.79
Kennedy, Peter	5.10	Watford	Lisburn	10.09.73
Santus, Paul	5.10	–	Wigan	8.09.83
Teale, Gary	5.11	Ayr Utd.	Glasgow	21.07.78
Traynor, Greg	5.10	–	Salford	17.10.84
Forwards				
Kennedy, Peter	5.10	Watford	Lisburn	10.09.73
Liddell, Andy	5. 8	Barnsley	Leeds	28.06.73
McCulloch, Lee	6. 1	Motherwell	Bellshill	14.05.78
Roberts, Neil	5.10	Wrexham	Wrexham	7.04.78
Ellington, Nathan	5.10	Bristol Rov.	Bradford	2.07.81

WIMBLEDON

Ground: Selhurst Park, London SE25 6PY.
Telephone: 0208 771 2233. **Clubcall:** 09068 121175. **Club nickname:** Dons.
First-choice colours: Navy and yellow shirts; navy shorts; navy stockings.
Main sponsor: Maximuscle. **Capacity for 2003-04:** 26,297.
Record attendance: 30,115 v Manchester Utd. (Prem. League) 9 May, 1993.

Name	**Height ft. in.**	**Previous club**	**Birthplace**	**Birthdate**
Goalkeepers				
Berni, Tommaso	6. 3	–	Florence	6.03.83
Davis, Kelvin	6. 1	Luton Town	Bedford	29.09.76
Gore, Shane	6. 1	–	Ashford	28.10.81
Heald, Paul	6. 2	Leyton Orient	Wath-on-Dearne	20.09.68
Defenders				
Chorley, Ben	6. 3	Arsenal	Sidcup	9.09.82
Gier, Rob	5.11	–	Ascot	6.01.80
Hawkins, Peter	6. 0	–	Maidstone	19.09.78
Herzig, Nico	5.10	–	Probneck, Ger.	10.12.83
Holloway, Darren	6. 0	Sunderland	Crook	3.10.77
Kamara, Malvin	6. 0	–	Southwark	17.11.83
Leigertwood, Mikele	6. 1	–	Enfield	12.11.82
Lewington, Dean	5.11	–	Kingston	18.05.84
Midfielders				
Andersen, Trond	6. 0	Molde	Kristiansund, Nor.	6.01.75
Darlington, Jermaine	5. 7	Q.P.R.	Hackney	11.04.74
Francis, Damien	6. 0	–	Wandsworth	27.02.79
Gordon, Michael	5. 6	Arsenal	Wandsworth	11.10.84
Nowland, Adam	5.11	Blackpool	Preston	6.07.81
Reo-Coker, Nigel	5. 8	–	Southwark	14.05.84
Tapp, Alex	5. 9	–	Redhill	7.06.82
Forwards				
Agyemang, Patrick	6. 1	–	Walthamstow	29.09.80
Connolly, David	5. 8	Feyenoord	Willesden	6.06.77
Gray, Wayne	5.10	–	Camberwell	7.11.80
McAnuff, Jobi	5.11	–	Edmonton	9.11.81
Morgan, Lionel	5.11	–	Tottenham	17.02.83
Shipperley, Neil	6. 0	Barnsley	Chatham	30.10.74

DIVISION TWO

BARNSLEY

Ground: Oakwell, Barnsley S71 1ET.
Telephone: 01226 211211. **Clubcall:** 09068 121152. **Club nickname:** Tykes.
First-choice colours: Red shirts; white shorts; red and white stockings.
Main Sponsor: Vodka Kick. **Capacity for 2003-04:** 23,166.
Record attendance: 40,255 v Stoke City (F.A. Cup 5) 15 February, 1936.

Name	Height ft. in.	Previous club	Birthplace	Birthdate
Goalkeepers				
Ghent, Matthew	6. 3	Aston Villa	Burton	5.10.80
Parry, Craig	5.11	–	Barnsley	15.03.84
Defenders				
Austin, Neil	5.10	–	Barnsley	26.04.83
Crooks, Lee	6. 2	Manchester City	Wakefield	14.01.78
Gibbs, Paul	5.11	Brentford	Great Yarmouth	26.10.72
Morgan, Chris	6. 1	–	Barnsley	09.11.77
O'Callaghan, Brian	6. 1	–	Limerick	24.02.81
Oldham, Adam	6. 1	–	Sheffield	26.01.86
Williams, Robbie	5.10	–	Pontefract	2.10.84
Midfielders				
Betsy, Kevin	6. 1	Fulham	Seychelles	20.03.78
Dixon, Kevin	5. 8	Leeds Utd.	Easington	27.06.80
Donovan, Kevin	5.10	Grimsby Town	Halifax	17.12.71
Gorre, Dean	5. 7	Huddersfield Town	Paramaribo, Sur.	10.09.70
Hayward, Steve	5.11	Fulham	Walsall	8.09.71
Jones, Gary	5.11	Rochdale	Birkenhead	3.06.77
Lumsdon, Chris	5.11	Sunderland	Newcastle	15.12.79
Mulligan, David	5. 5	–	Liverpool	24.03.82
Neil, Alex	5. 9	Airdrie	Bellshill	9.06.81
Tonge, Dale	5.10	–	Doncaster	7.05.85
Ward, Mitch	5. 8	Everton	Sheffield	19.06.71
Wroe, Nicholas	5.11	–	Sheffield	28.09.85
Forwards				
Barrowclough, Carl	5. 7	–	Doncaster	25.09.81
Fallon, Rory	6. 2	–	Gisborne, NZ	20.03.82
Jones, Griff	5. 8	–	Liverpool	22.06.84
Kay, Antony	5.11	–	Barnsley	21.10.82
Rankin, Isaiah	5.10	Bradford City	Edmonton	22.05.78

BLACKPOOL

Ground: Bloomfield Road, Blackpool FY1 6JJ.
Telephone: 01253 405331. **Clubcall:** 09068 121648. **Club nickname:** Seasiders.
First-choice colours: Tangerine shirts; white shorts; tangerine stockings.
Main sponsor: Life Repair Group. **Capacity for 2003-04:** 11,000.
Record attendance: 38,098 v Wolves (Div. 1) 17 September, 1955

Name	Height ft. in.	Previous club	Birthplace	Birthdate
Barnes, Phil	6. 1	Rotherham Utd.	Rotherham	2.03.79
Defenders				
Clarke, Chris	6. 3	Halifax Town	Leeds	18.12.80
Davis, Steve	6. 2	Burnley	Hexham	30.10.68
Flynn, Mike	6. 1	Barnsley	Oldham	23.02.69
Grayson, Simon	6. 0	Blackburn Rov.	Ripon	16.12.69
Hilton, Kirk	5. 7	Manchester Utd.	Flixton	2.04.81
Jaszczun, Tommy	5.10	Aston Villa	Kettering	16.09.77

Richardson, Leam	5. 7	Bolton Wand.	Leeds	19.11.79
Midfielders				
Bullock, Martin	5. 4	Barnsley	Derby	5.03.75
Burns, Jamie	5. 9	–	Blackpool	6.03.84
Coid, Danny	5.11	–	Liverpool	3.10.81
Collins, Lee	5. 8	Swindon Town	Bellshill	3.02.74
McMahon, Stephen	5. 9	–	Southport	31.07.84
Southern, Keith	5.10	Everton	Gateshead	21.04.84
Wellens, Richard	5. 9	Manchester Utd.	Manchester	26.03.80
Forwards				
Blinkhorn, Matthew	6. 0	–	Blackpool	2.03.85
Murphy, John	6. 2	Chester City	Whiston	18.10.76
Robinson, Paul	5.10	Wimbledon	Sunderland	20.11.78
Taylor, Scott	5.10	Stockport Co.	Chertsey	5.05.76
Walker, Richard	6. 0	Aston Villa	Birmingham	8.11.77

BOURNEMOUTH

Ground: Fitness First Stadium, Dean Court, Bournemouth BH7 7AF.
Telephone: 01202 726300. **Club nickname:** Cherries.
First-choice colours: Red and black shirts; black and red shorts; black stockings.
Main sponsor: Seward Motor Group. **Capacity for 2003-04:** 8,100 (rising to 9,600).
Record attendance: 28,799 v Manchester Utd. (F.A. Cup 6) 2 March, 1957.

Name	Height ft. in.	Previous club	Birthplace	Birthdate
Goalkeepers				
Moss, Neil	6. 3	Southampton	New Milton	10.05.75
Stewart, Gareth	6. 0	Blackburn Rov.	Preston	3.02.80
Defenders				
Broadhurst, Karl	6. 1	–	Portsmouth	18.03.80
Cummings, Warren	5. 9	Chelsea	Aberdeen	15.10.80
Maher, Shaun	6. 2	Fulham	Dublin	20.06.78
Narada, Bernard	5. 2	Arsenal	Bristol	30.01.81
Purches, John	5.10	Salisbury	Ilford	12.03.83
Purches, Steve	5.11	West Ham Utd.	Ilford	14.01.80
Young, Neil	5. 9	Tottenham	Harlow	31.08.73
Midfielders				
Browning, Marcus	6. 0	Gillingham	Bristol	22.04.71
Elliott, Wade	5. 9	Bashley	Southampton	14.12.78
Fletcher, Carl	5.10	–	Camberley	7.04.80
Grant, Peter	5.10	Reading	Glasgow	30.08.65
Thomas, Danny	5. 7	Leicester City	Leamington	1.05.81
Tindall, Jason	6. 1	Charlton Athletic	Stepney	15.11.77
Stock, Brian	5.11	–	Winchester	24.12.81
Forwards				
Connell, Alan	5.11	–	Enfield	5.02.83
Eribenne, Chuck	5.10	Coventry City	Westminster	2.11.80
Feeney, Warren	5.10	Leeds Utd.	Belfast	17.01.81
Fletcher, Steve	6. 2	Hartlepool Utd.	Hartlepool	26.06.72
Hayter, James	5. 9	–	Newport, IOW	9.04.79
Holmes, Derek	6. 0	Ross Co.	Lanark	18.10.78
McDonald, Scott	5. 8	Southampton	Melbourne	21.08.83
O'Connor, Garreth	5. 7	Bohemians	Dublin	10.11.78

BRENTFORD

Ground: Griffin Park, Braemar Road, Brentford TW7 0NT.
Telephone: 0870 900 9229. **Clubcall:** 09068 121108. **Club nickname:** Bees.
First-choice colours: Red and white shirts; black shorts; red stockings.
Main sponsor: St George plc. **Capacity for 2003-04:** 12,450.
Record attendance: 39,626 v Preston N.E. (F.A. Cup 6) 5 March, 1938.

Name	Height ft. in.	Previous club	Birthplace	Birthdate
Goalkeepers				
Julian, Alan	6. 0	–	Ashford	11.03.83
Smith, Paul	6. 4	Carshalton	Epsom	17.12.79
Defenders				
Dobson, Michael	6. 0	–	London	9.04.80
Evans, Stephen	6. 0	Crystal Palace	Caerphilly	25.09.80
Frampton, Andrew	5.11	Crystal Palace	Wimbledon	3.09.79
Fieldwick, Lee	5.11	–	–	6.09.82
Marshall, Scott	6. 1	Southampton	Edinburgh	1.05.73
Roget, Leo	6. 1	Southend Utd.	Ilford	1.08.77
Somner, Matt	5.11	–	London	8.12.82
Sonko, Ibrahima	5.10	Grenoble	Bignola, Sen.	22.01.81
Theobald, David	6. 1	Ipswich Town	Cambridge	15.12.78
Midfielders				
Evans, Paul	5. 8	Shrewsbury Town	Oswestry	1.09.74
Fullarton, Jamie	5. 9	Dundee Utd.	Glasgow	20.07.75
Hunt, Stephen	5. 8	Crystal Palace	Port Laoise	1.08.81
Hutchinson, Eddie	6. 1	Sutton Utd.	Kingston	23.02.82
Smith, Jay	5.10	–	Hammersmith	29.12.81
Tabb, Jay	5. 6	–	London	21.02.84
Forwards				
Constantine, Leo	6. 2	Millwall	Hackney	24.02.78
Ekoku, Efan	6. 2	Sheffield Wed.	Manchester	8.06.67
O'Connor, Kevin	5.11	–	Blackburn	24.02.82
Peters, Mark	5. 8	Southampton	Frimley	4.10.83

BRIGHTON AND HOVE ALBION

Ground: Withdean Stadium, Tongdean Lane, Brighton BN1 5JD.
Telephone: 01273 695400. **Clubcall:** 09068 800609. **Club nickname:** Seagulls.
First-choice colours: Blue and white shirts; white shorts; white stockings.
Main sponsor: Skint. **Capacity for 2003-04:** 6,973.
Record attendance: (Goldstone Ground) 36,747 v Fulham (Div. 2) 27 December, 1958; (Withdean Stadium) 6,995 v Halifax Town (Div. 3) 2 December, 2000.

Name	Height ft. in.	Previous club	Birthplace	Birthdate
Goalkeepers				
Beasant, Dave	6. 4	Portsmouth	Willesden	20.03.59
Kuipers, Michel	6. 2	Bristol Rov.	Amsterdam	26.06.74
Defenders				
Blackwell, Dean	6. 1	Wimbledon	Camden	15.12.69
Butters, Guy	6. 3	Gillingham	Hillingdon	30.10.69
Cullip, Danny	6. 0	Brentford	Ascot	17.09.76
Harding, Daniel	6. 0	–	Gloucester	23.12.83
Hinshelwood, Adam	5.10	–	Oxford	8.01.84
Mayo, Kerry	5. 9	–	Cuckfield	21.09.77
Pethick, Robbie	5.10	Bristol Rov.	Tavistock	8.09.70
Virgo, Adam	6. 1	–	Brighton	25.01.83
Watson, Paul	5. 8	Brentford	Hastings	4.01.75
Midfielders				
Carpenter, Richard	6. 0	Cardiff City	Sheppey	30.09.72
Hammond, Dean	5.11	–	Sussex	7.03.83
Jones, Nathan	5. 6	Southend Utd.	Cardiff	28.05.73
Marney, Daniel	5. 9	Crystal Palace	Sidcup	2.10.81
McPhee, Chris	5.10	–	Eastbourne	20.03.83
Oatway, Charlie	5. 7	Brentford	Hammersmith	28.11.73
Piercy, John	5.11	Tottenham	Forest Gate	18.09.79
Pitcher, Geoff	5. 5	Kingstonian	Sutton	15.08.75

Wilkinson, Shaun	5. 9	–	Portsmouth	12.09.81
Forwards				
Hart, Gary	5. 9	Stansted	Harlow	21.09.76
Zamora, Bobby	5.11	Bristol Rov.	Barking	16.01.81

BRISTOL CITY

Ground: Ashton Gate, Bristol BS3 2EJ.
Telephone: 0117 963 0630. **Clubcall:** 09068 121176. **Club nickname:** Robins.
First-choice colours: red and white shirts; red shorts; red stockings.
Main sponsor: DAS Legal Services. **Capacity for 2003-04:** 21,110.
Record attendance: 43,335 v Preston N.E. (F.A. Cup 5) 16 February 1935.

Name	Height ft. in.	Previous club	Birthplace	Birthdate
Goalkeepers				
Phillips, Steve	6. 1	–	Bath	6.05.78
Stowell, Mike	6. 2	Wolves	Portsmouth	19.04.65
Defenders				
Amankwaah, Kevin	6. 1	–	Harrow	19.05.82
Bell, Michael	5. 8	Wycombe Wand.	Newcastle	15.11.71
Burnell, Joe	5. 9	–	Bristol	10.10.80
Butler, Tony	6. 2	W.B.A.	Stockport	28.09.72
Carey, Louis	5.10	–	Bristol	20.01.77
Coles, Danny	6. 0	–	Bristol	30.10.81
Fortune, Clayton	5.11	–	Forest Gate	10.11.82
Jones, Darren	6. 1	–	Newport	26.11.83
Hill, Matthew	5. 8	–	Bristol	26.03.81
Simpson, Sekani	5.10	–	Bristol	11.03.84
Woodman, Craig	5. 9	–	Tiverton	22.12.82
Midfielders				
Brown, Aaron	5.10	–	Bristol	14.03.80
Clist, Simon	5. 9	Tottenham	Bournemouth	13.06.81
Doherty, Thomas	5. 8	–	Bristol	17.03.79
Hawkins, Darren	5.11	–	Bristol	25.04.84
Hulbert, Robin	5.10	Swindon Town	Plymouth	14.03.80
Rosenior, Liam	6. 0	–	Wandsworth	9.07.84
Tinnion, Brian	6. 2	Bradford City	Durham	23.03.68
Forwards				
Brown, Marvin	5. 8	–	Bristol	6.07.83
Matthews, Lee	6. 2	Leeds Utd.	Middlesbrough	6.01.79
Peacock, Lee	5. 9	Manchester City	Paisley	9.10.76
Roberts, Christian	5.10	Exeter City	Cardiff	22.10.79

CHESTERFIELD

Ground: Recreation Ground, Chesterfield S40 4SX.
Telephone: 01246 209765. **Clubcall:** 09068 555818. **Club nickname:** Spireites.
First-choice colours: Blue shirts; blue and white shorts; blue and white stockings.
Main Sponsor: Gordon Lamb. **Capacity for 2003-04:** 8,500.
Record attendance: 30,698 v Newcastle Utd. (Div. 2) 7 April, 1939.

Name	Height ft. in.	Previous club	Birthplace	Birthdate
Goalkeepers				
Muggleton, Carl	6. 2	Cheltenham Town	Leicester	13.09.68
Richmond, Andy	6. 0	–	–	9.01.83
Defenders				
Blatherwick, Steve	6. 1	Burnley	Nottingham	20.09.73
Dawson, Kevin	6. 0	Nott'm. Forest	Northallerton	18.06.81
Howson, Stuart	6. 1	Blackburn Rov.	Chorley	30.09.81
Payne, Steve	5.11	–	Castleford	1.08.75

Midfielders				
Brandon, Chris	5. 7	Torquay Utd.	Bradford	7.04.76
Davies, Gareth	6. 1	–	–	4.02.83
Hudson, Mark	5.10	Middlesbrough	Bishop Auckland	24.10.80
Innes, Mark	5.10	Oldham Athletic	Bellshill	27.09.78
O'Hare, Alan	6. 2	Bolton Wand.	Drogheda	31.07.82
Richardson, Lee	5.11	Huddersfield Town	Halifax	12.03.69
Rushbury, Andy	5.10	–	Carlisle	7.03.83
Forwards				
Allott, Mark	5.11	Oldham Athletic	Middleton	3.10.77
Burt, Jamie	5.10	Whitby Town	Blyth	29.09.79
Folan, Caleb	6. 1	Leeds Utd.	Leeds	26.10.82
Howard, Jonathan	5.11	Rotherham Utd.	Sheffield	7.10.71
Hurst, Glynn	5.10	Stockport Co.	Barnsley	17.01.76
Mitchell, Jez	5.11	–	Chesterfield	5.10.84
Reeves, David	6. 0	Oldham Athletic	Birkenhead	19.11.67

COLCHESTER UNITED

Ground: Layer Road, Colchester CO2 7JJ.
Telephone: 01206 508800. **Club nickname:** U's.
First-choice-colours: Blue shirts; blue and white shorts, blue and white stockings.
Main sponsor: Tiptree Preserves. **Capacity for 2003-04:** 6,200.
Record attendance: 19,072 v Reading (F.A. Cup 1) 27 November, 1948.

Name	Height ft. in.	Previous club	Birthplace	Birthdate
Goalkeepers				
Brown, Simon	6. 2	Tottenham	Chelmsford	3.12.76
McKinney, Richard	6. 2	Swindon Town	Ballymena	18.05.79
Defenders				
Baldwin, Pat	6. 2	Chelsea	London	12.11.82
Edwards, Michael	6. 1	Hull City	Hessle	25.04.80
Fitzgerald, Scott	6. 0	Millwall	Westminster	13.08.69
Keith, Joey	5. 7	West Ham Utd.	Plaistow	1.10.78
Myers, Andy	5.10	Bradford City	Hounslow	3.11.73
Stockley, Sam	5. 8	Oxford Utd.	Tiverton	5.09.77
White, Alan	6. 0	Luton Town	Darlington	22.03.76
Midfielders				
Bowry, Bobby	5. 9	Millwall	Croydon	19.05.71
Duguid, Karl	5.11	–	Hitchin	21.03.78
Izzet, Kemal	5. 8	Charlton Athletic	Whitechapel	29.09.80
Johnson, Gavin	5.11	Dunfermline	Stowmarked	10.10.70
Pinault, Thomas	5.11	Cannes	Grasse, Fra.	4.12.81
Forwards				
Coote, Adrian	6. 2	Norwich City	Great Yarmouth	30.09.78
McGleish, Scott	5. 9	Barnet	Barnet	10.02.74
Morgan, Dean	5.10	–	Enfield	3.10.83

GRIMSBY TOWN

Ground: Blundell Park, Cleethorpes, DN35 7PY.
Telephone: 01472 605050. **Clubcall:** 09068 555855. **Club nickname:** Mariners.
First-choice colours: Black and white shirts; black shorts; black stockings.
Main sponsor: Jarvis. **Capacity for 2003-04:** 10,033.
Record attendance: 31,651 v Wolves (F.A. Cup 5) 20 February, 1937.

Name	Height ft. in.	Previous club	Birthplace	Birthdate
Goalkeepers				
Fraser, Paul	6. 2	–	–	1.09.85
Hughes, Bradley	5.11	Watford	Hemel Hempstead	24.03.84

Pettinger, Andrew	6. 0	–	Scunthorpe	21.04.84
Defenders				
Chettle, Steve	6. 1	Nott'm. Forest	Nottingham	27.09.68
Parker, Wes	5.11	–	Boston	7.12.83
Ward, Iain	6. 0	–	Cleethorpes	13.05.83
Midfielders				
Barnard, Darren	5. 9	Barnsley	Rintein, Ger.	30.11.71
Bolder, Chris	5.11	–	Hull	19.08.82
Campbell, Stuart	5.10	Leicester City	Corby	9.12.77
Cas, Marcel	6. 1	Sheffield Utd.	Breda, Hol.	30.04.72
Coldicott, Stacy	5. 8	W.B.A	Redditch	29.04.74
Crane, Tony	6. 4	Sheffield Wed.	Liverpool	8.09.82
Downes, Stephen	5.11	–	Leeds	12.11.81
Ford, Simon	5.11	Charlton Athletic	Newham	17.11.81
Groves, Paul	5.11	W.B.A.	Derby	28.02.66
Hockless, Graham	5.10	–	Hull City	20.10.82
Pouton, Alan	6. 0	York City	Newcastle	1.02.77
Santos, George	6. 3	Sheffield Utd.	Marseille	15.08.70
Forwards				
Cooke, Terry	5. 8	Manchester City	Birmingham	5.08.76
Jevons, Phil	5.11	Everton	Liverpool	1.08.79
Mansaram, Darren	6. 2	–	Doncaster	25.06.84
Rowan, Jonathan	5.10	–	Grimsby	29.11.81
Sagare, Jake	5.11	–	U.S.A	5.04.80
Soames, David	5.11	–	Grimsby	10.02.84
Thompson, Chris	5.10	–	Warrington	7.02.82

HARTLEPOOL UNITED

Ground: Victoria Park, Clarence Road, Hartlepool TS24 8BZ.
Telephone: 01429 272584. **Club nickname:** Pool.
First-choice colours: white and blue shirts; blue shorts; white stockings.
Main Sponsor: DNO. **Capacity for 2003-04:** 7,629.
Record attendance: 17,426 v Manchester Utd. (F.A. Cup 3) 5 January, 1957.

Name	Height ft. in.	Previous club	Birthplace	Birthdate
Goalkeepers				
Provett, Jim	5.11	–	Trimdon	22.12.82
Williams, Anthony	6. 1	Blackburn Rov.	Ogwr	20.09.77
Defenders				
Barron, Michael	5.11	Middlesbrough	Lumley	22.12.74
Bass, Jonathan	6. 0	Birmingham City	Weston-s-Mare	1.01.76
Nelson, Michael	6. 2	Bury	Gateshead	15.03.82
Robinson, Mark	5. 9	–	Guisborough	24.07.81
Westwood, Chris	5.11	Wolves	Dudley	13.02.77
Midfielders				
Arnison, Paul	5.10	Newcastle Utd.	Hartlepool	18.09.77
Clarke, Darrell	5.10	Mansfield Town	Mansfield	16.12.77
Istead, Steven	5. 8	Newcastle Utd.	–	23.04.86
Robson, Matty	5.10	–	Durham	23.01.85
Sweeney, Anthony	6. 0	–	Stockton	5.09.83
Tinkler, Mark	5.11	Southend Utd.	Bishop Auckland	24.10.74
Forwards				
Boyd, Adam	5. 9	–	Hartlepool	25.05.82
Easter, Jermaine	5. 9	Wolves	Cardiff	15.01.82
Henderson, Kevin	5.11	Burnley	Ashington	8.06.74
Humphreys, Richie	5.11	Cambridge Utd.	Sheffield	30.11.77
Richardson, Marcus	6. 3	Torquay Utd.	Reading	31.08.77
Williams, Eifion	5.11	Torquay Utd.	Bangor	15.11.75

LUTON TOWN

Ground: Kenilworth Stadium, Maple Road, Luton LU4 8AW.
Telephone: 01582 411622. **Clubcall:** 09068 121123. **Club nickname:** Hatters.
First-choice colours: White, orange and black shirts; black shorts; black stockings.
Main Sponsor: SKF (UK). **Capacity for 2003-04:** 9,975.
Record attendance: 30,069 v Blackpool (F.A. Cup 6) 4 March, 1959.

Name	Height ft. in.	Previous club	Birthplace	Birthdate
Goalkeepers				
Beckwith, Robert	6. 2	–	London	12.09.84
Defenders				
Bayliss, David	5.10	Rochdale	Liverpool	8.06.76
Boyce, Emmerson	5.11	–	Aylesbury	24.09.79
Coyne, Chris	6. 3	Dundee	Brisbane	28.12.78
Davis, Sol	5. 8	Swindon Town	Cheltenham	4.09.79
Foley, Kevin	5. 9	–	Luton	1.11.84
Perrett, Russell	6. 3	Cardiff City	Barton-on-Sea	18.06.73
Midfielders				
Forbes, Adrian	5. 7	Norwich City	Greenford	23.01.79
Hillier, Ian	6. 0	Tottenham	Neath	26.12.79
Holmes, Peter	5.11	–	Bishop Auckland	18.11.80
Hughes, Paul	6. 0	Southampton	Hammersmith	19.04.76
Leary, Michael	5.11	–	Ealing	17.04.83
Neilson, Alan	5.11	Grimsby Town	Wegburg, Ger.	26.09.72
Mansell, Lee	5.10	–	Gloucester	23.09.82
Nicholls, Kevin	5.11	Wigan Athletic	Newham	2.01.79
O'Leary, Stephen	5.10	–	London	12.02.85
Robinson, Steve	5. 9	Preston N.E.	Lisburn	10.12.74
Spring, Matthew	5.11	–	Harlow	17.11.79
Forwards				
Berkovic, Ahmet	5. 7	Leyton Orient	Dubrovnic	23.09.74
Crowe, Dean	5. 5	Stoke City	Stockport	6.06.79
Howard, Steve	6. 2	Northampton Town	Durham	10.05.76

NOTTS COUNTY

Ground: Meadow Lane, Nottingham NG2 3HJ.
Telephone: 0115 952 9000. **Clubcall:** 09068 443131. **Club nickname:** Magpies.
First-choice colours: Black and white shirts; black shorts; black stockings.
Main sponsor: Paragon. **Capacity for 2003-04:** 20,300.
Record attendance: 47,310 v York City (F.A. Cup 6) 12 March, 1955.

Name	Height ft. in.	Previous club	Birthplace	Birthdate
Goalkeepers				
Garden, Stuart	6. 2	Forfar Athletic	Dundee	2.10.72
Mildenhall, Steve	6. 5	Swindon Town	Swindon	13.05.78
Defenders				
Baraclough, Ian	6. 1	Q.P.R	Leicester	4.12.70
Bastock, Danny	5.10	–	Mansfield	25.03.85
Caskey, Darren	5. 8	Reading	Basildon	21.08.74
Fenton, Nick	6. 1	Manchester City	Preston	23.11.79
McFaul, Shane	6. 0	–	Dublin	23.05.86
Richardson, Ian	6. 0	Birmingham City	Barking	22.10.70
Riley, Paul	5. 9	–	Nottingham	29.09.82
Midfielders				
Bolland, Paul	5.11	Bradford City	Bradford	23.12.79
Brough, Michael	6. 0	–	Nottingham	1.08.81
Nicholson, Kevin	5. 9	Notts Co.	Derby	2.10.80

Name	Height ft. in.	Previous club	Birthplace	Birthdate
Forwards				
Hackworth, Tony	6. 1	Leeds Utd.	Durham	19.05.80
Heffernan, Paul	5.10	Newtown	Dublin	29.12.81
Stallard, Mark	6. 0	Wycombe Wand.	Derby Co.	24.10.74

OLDHAM ATHLETIC

Ground: Boundary Park, Oldham OL1 2PA.
Telephone: 0870 753 2000. **Clubcall:** 09068 121142. **Club nickname:** Latics.
First-choice colours: Blue and white shirts; blue and white shorts; blue and white stockings.
Main sponsor: Horners Motor Group. **Capacity for 2003-04:** 13,659.
Record attendance: 47,761 v Sheffield Wed. (F.A. Cup 4) 25 January, 1930.

Name	Height ft. in.	Previous club	Birthplace	Birthdate
Goalkeepers				
Pogliacomi, Leslie	6. 5	–	Australia	3.05.76
Defenders				
Baudet, Julien	6. 3	Toulouse	St Martin d'Hyeres, Fra.	13.01.79
Beharall, David	6. 2	Newcastle Utd.	Newcastle	8.03.79
Clegg, Michael	5. 8	Manchester Utd.	Ashton under Lyne	3.07.77
Haining, Will	5.11	–	Glasgow	2.10.82
Hall, Danny	6. 2	–	Ashton under Lyne	14.11.83
Holden, Dean	6. 0	Bolton Wand.	Salford	15.09.79
Tierney, Marc	6. 0	–	Prestwich	23.08.85
Midfielders				
Appleby, Matty	5.10	Barnsley	Middlesbrough	16.04.72
Boshell, Danny	5.10	–	Bradford	30.05.81
Duxbury, Lee	5.10	Bradford City	Keighley	7.10.69
Griffin, Adam	5. 7	–	Salford	26.08.84
Murray, Paul	5. 8	Southampton	Carlisle Utd.	31.08.76
Sheridan, Darren	5. 6	Wigan Athletic	Manchester	8.12.67
Forwards				
Eyre, John	6. 0	Hull City	Hull City	9.10.74
Eyres, David	5.11	Preston N.E.	Liverpool	26.02.64
Killen, Chris	5.11	Manchester City	Wellington, NZ	8.10.81
Low, Josh	6. 1	Cardiff City	Bristol	15.02.79
Vernon, Scott	6. 1	–	Manchester	13.12.83
Wijnhard, Clyde	5.11	Preston N.E.	Surinam	1.11.73

PETERBOROUGH UNITED

Ground: London Road Stadium, Peterborough PE2 8AL.
Telephone: 01733 563947. **Clubcall:** 09068 121654. **Club nickname:** Posh.
First-choice colours: Blue shirts; blue shorts; blue stockings.
Main sponsor: Van Asten. **Capacity for 2003-04:** 15,000.
Record attendance: 30,096 v Swansea City (F.A. Cup 5) 20 February, 1965.

Name	Height ft. in.	Previous club	Birthplace	Birthdate
Goalkeepers				
McShane, Luke	6. 1	–	Peterborough	6.11.85
Tyler, Mark	5.11	–	Norwich	2.04.77
Defenders				
Arber, Mark	6. 1	Barnet	Johannesburg	9.10.77
Burton, Sagi	6. 2	Crewe Alexandra	Birmingham	25.11.77
Jelleyman, Gareth	5.10	–	Holywell	14.11.80
Laurie, Steve	5.10	West Ham Utd.	Melbourne	30.10.82
Murray, Daniel	6. 2	–	Kettering	16.05.82
Pearce, Dennis	5.10	Notts Co.	Wolves	10.09.74
Rae, Simon	6. 1	Birmingham City	Coventry	20.09.76

St Ledger, Sean	6. 0	–	Birmingham	28.12.84
Thomas, Bradley	6. 2	–	Forest Gate	29.03.84
Midfielders				
Fry, Adam	5. 8	–	Luton	9.02.85
Gill, Matthew	6. 0	–	Cambridge	8.11.80
Scott, Richard	5.10	Stevenage Borough	Dudley	29.09.74
Shields, Tony	5. 7	–	Londonderry	4.06.80
Forwards				
Clarke, Andy	5.10	Wimbledon	Islington	22.07.67
Clarke, Lee	5.11	Yaxley	Peterborough	28.07.83
Farrell, David	5. 9	Wycombe Wand.	Birmingham	11.11.71
Fenn, Neale	5.11	Tottenham	Edmonton	18.01.77
Fotiadis, Andrew	5.11	Luton Town	Hitchin	6.09.77
Green, Francis	5.11	Ilkeston Town	Derby	23.04.80
McKenzie, Leon	5.10	Crystal Palace	Croydon	17.05.78
Tolley, Shane	5. 7	–	Barnstaple	18.02.85

PLYMOUTH ARGYLE

Ground: Home Park, Plymouth PL2 3DQ.
Telephone: 01752 562561. **Club nickname:** Pilgrims.
First-choice colours: Green shirts; white shorts; green stockings.
Main Sponsor: Ginsters. **Capacity for 2003-04:** 20,134.
Record attendance: 42,684 v Aston Villa (Div. 2) 10 October, 1936.

Name	Height ft. in.	Previous club	Birthplace	Birthdate
Goalkeepers				
Larrieu, Romain	6. 2	Valence	Mont de Marsan, Fra.	31.08.76
McCormick, Luke	6. 0	–	Coventry	15.08.83
Defenders				
Adams, Steve	6. 0	–	Plymouth	25.09.80
Aljofree, Hasney	6. 0	Dundee Utd.	Manchester	11.07.78
Capaldi, Tony	6. 0	Birmingham City	Porsgrunn, Nor.	12.08.81
Coughlan, Graham	6. 2	Livingston	Dublin	18.11.74
McAnespie, Kieran	5.11	Fulham	Gosport	11.09.79
Worrell, David	5.11	Dundee Utd.	Dublin	12.01.78
Wotton, Paul	5.11	–	Plymouth	17.08.77
Midfielders				
Bent, Jason	5. 9	Colorado Rapids	Toronto	8.03.77
Beresford, David	5. 5	Hull City	Middleton	11.11.76
Broad, Joe	5.10	–	Bristol	24.08.82
Friio, David	5.10	Valence	Thionville, Fra.	17.02.73
Hodges, Lee	6. 0	Reading	Epping	4.09.73
Forwards				
Evans, Mickey	6. 0	Bristol Rov.	Plymouth	1.01.73
Keith, Marino	6. 0	Livingston	Peterhead	16.12.74
Lowndes, Nathan	5.10	Livingston	Salford	2.06.77
Phillips, Martin	5. 9	Portsmouth	Exeter	13.03.76
Stonebridge, Ian	6. 0	Tottenham	London	30.08.81
Sturrock, Blair	5.11	Dundee Utd.	Dundee	25.08.81

PORT VALE

Ground: Vale Park, Hamil Road, Burslem, Stoke-on-Trent ST6 1AW.
Telephone: 01782 655800. **Club nickname:** Valiants.
First-choice colours: White and black shirts; black shorts; black stockings.
Main sponsor: Tunstall Assurance. **Capacity for 2003-04:** 18,982.
Record attendance: 50,000 v Aston Villa (F.A. Cup 5) 20 February, 1960.

Name	Height ft. in.	Previous club	Birthplace	Birthdate
Goalkeepers				
Delaney, Dean	6. 0	Everton	Dublin	15.09.80
Goodlad, Mark	6. 0	Nott'm. Forest	Barnsley	9.09.80
Defenders				
Brightwell, Ian	5.10	Stoke City	Lutterworth	9.04.68
Burns, Liam	5.11	–	Belfast	30.10.78
Collins, Sam	6. 3	Bury	Pontefract	5.06.77
Rowland, Steve	5.10	–	Wrexham	2.11.81
Walsh, Michael	6. 0	Scunthorpe Utd.	Rotherham	5.08.77
Midfielders				
Birchall, Chris	5. 9	–	Stafford	5.05.84
Boyd, Mark	5. 9	Newcastle Utd.	Carlisle	22.10.81
Bridge-Wilkinson, Marc	5. 6	Derby Co.	Nuneaton	16.03.79
Brisco, Neil	6. 0	Manchester City	Billinge	26.01.78
Cummins, Michael	6. 0	Middlesbrough	Dublin	1.06.78
Lipa, Andreas	6. 1	Xanthi	Austria	26.04.71
McPhee, Stephen	5. 7	Coventry City	Glasgow	5.06.81
Forwards				
Armstrong, Ian	5.11	Liverpool	Fazackerley	16.11.81
Brooker, Stephen	5.10	Watford	Newport Pagnell	21.05.81
Littlejohn, Adrian	5. 9	Sheffield Utd.	Wolves	26.09.70
Paynter, Billy	6. 0	–	Liverpool	13.07.84

QUEENS PARK RANGERS

Ground: Loftus Road Stadium, South Africa Road, London W12 7PA.
Telephone: 0208 743 0262. **Clubcall:** 09068 121162. **Club nickname:** Hoops.
First-choice colours: Blue and white shirts; white shorts; blue and white stockings.
Capacity for 2003-04: 19,148.
Record attendance: 35,353 v Leeds Utd. (Div. 1) 27 April, 1974.

Name	Height ft. in.	Previous club	Birthplace	Birthdate
Goalkeepers				
Culkin, Nick	6. 2	Manchester Utd.	York	6.07.78
Day, Chris	6. 3	Watford	Walthamstow	28.07.75
Defenders				
Carlisle, Clarke	6. 1	Blackpool	Preston	14.10.79
Forbes, Terrell	5.10	West Ham Utd.	London	17.08.81
Palmer, Steve	6. 1	Watford	Brighton	31.03.68
Padula, Gino	5. 9	Wigan Athletic	Buenos Aires	11.07.76
Rose, Matthew	5.11	Arsenal	Dartford	24.09.75
Shittu, Danny	6. 3	Charlton Athletic	Lagos	2.09.80
Midfielders				
Bean, Marcus	5.11	–	Hammersmith	2.11.84
Bircham, Marc	5.10	Millwall	Wembley	11.05.78
Daly, Wesley	5. 9	–	Hammersmith	7.03.84
Gradley, Patrick	6. 0	–	London	1.06.83
Langley, Richard	5.10	–	Harlesden	27.12.79
Walshe, Ben	5.10	–	Hammersmith	24.05.83
Forwards				
Connolly, Karl	5.10	Wrexham	Prescot	9.02.70
Doudou	5. 8	Monaco	Kinshasa, Zai.	11.09.80
Fitzgerald, Brian	5. 9	–	Perivale	23.10.83
Furlong, Paul	6. 0	Birmingham City	Wood Green	27.01.69
Gallen, Kevin	5.11	Barnsley	Hammersmith	21.09.75
Griffiths, Leroy	6. 0	Hampton	London	30.12.76
Oli, Dennis	6. 0	–	Newham	28.01.84
Pacquette, Richard	6. 0	–	Paddington	28.01.83

Sabin, Eric	6.1	Wasquehal	Paris	22.01.75

RUSHDEN AND DIAMONDS

Ground: Nene Park, Diamond Way, Irthlingborough NN9 5QF.
Telephone: 01933 652000. **Club nickname:** Diamonds.
First-choice colours: White shirts; blue shorts; white socks.
Main sponsor: Dr Martens. **Capacity for 2003-04:** 6,441.
Record attendance: 6,431 (v Leeds Utd. F.A. Cup 3) 4 January, 1999.

Name	Height ft. in.	Previous club	Birthplace	Birthdate
Goalkeepers				
Turley, Billy	6. 3	Northampton Town	Wolves	15.07.73
Defenders				
Dempster, John	6. 0	–	Kettering	1.04.83
Edwards, Andy	6. 2	Peterborough Utd.	Epping	17.09.71
Gray, Stuart	5.10	Reading	Harrogate	18.12.73
Hunter, Barry	6. 4	Reading	Coleraine	18.11.68
Peters, Mark	6. 0	Mansfield Town	St Asaph	6.07.72
Sambrook, Andy	5.10	Gillingham	Chatham	13.07.79
Talbot, Daniel	5. 9	Arsenal	Enfield	30.01.84
Underwood, Paul	5.11	Enfield	Wimbledon	16.08.73
Midfielders				
Bell, David	5.10	–	Kettering	21.01.84
Bignot, Marcus	5. 0	Q.P.R.	Birmingham	22.08.74
Burgess, Andy	6. 2	Luton Town	Bedford	10.08.81
Hall, Paul	5. 8	Walsall	Manchester	3.07.72
Hanlon, Ritchie	6. 1	Peterborough Utd.	Kenton	25.05.78
Mills, Gary	5. 9	Northampton Town	Sheppey	20.05.81
Wardley, Stuart	5.11	Q.P.R.	Cambridge	10.09.75
Forwards				
Darby, Duane	5.11	Notts Co.	Birmingham	17.10.73
Duffy, Robert	6. 1	Swansea City	Swansea	2.12.82
Jack, Rodney	5. 7	Crewe Alexandra	St Vincent	28.09.72
Lowe, Onandi	6. 3	Kansas City	Kingston, Jam.	2.12.74

SHEFFIELD WEDNESDAY

Ground: Hillsborough, Sheffield, S6 1SW.
Telephone: 0114 221 2121. **Club nickname:** Owls.
First-choice colours: Blue and white shirts; black shorts; black stockings.
Capacity for 2003-04: 39,814.
Record attendance: 72,841 v Manchester City (F.A. Cup 5) 17 February, 1934.

Name	Height ft. in.	Previous club	Birthplace	Birthdate
Goalkeepers				
Stringer, Chris	6. 6	–	Sheffield	19.09.83
Pressman, Kevin	6. 1	–	Fareham	6.11.67
Tidman, Ola	6. 2	Stockport Co.	Sweden	11.05.79
Defenders				
Armstrong, Craig	5.11	Huddersfield Town	South Shields	23.05.75
Barry-Murphy, Brian	6. 0	Preston N.E.	Cork	27.07.78
Beswetherick, Jon	5.11	Plymouth Argyle	Liverpool	15.01.78
Bromby, Leigh	5. 6	–	Dewsbury	2.06.80
Geary, Derek	5. 7	–	Dublin	19.06.80
Green, Ryan	5. 8	Cardiff City	Cardiff	20.10.80
Lee, Graeme	6. 2	Hartlepool Utd.	Middlesbrough	31.05.78
Smith, Dean	6. 0	Leyton Orient	West Bromwich	19.03.71
Midfielders				
Hamshaw, Matthew	5.10	–	Rotherham	1.01.82

Haslam, Steve	5.11	–	Sheffield	6.09.79
McLaren, Paul	6. 1	Luton Town	High Wycombe	17.11.76
Quinn, Alan	5. 9	Cherry Orchard	Dublin	13.06.79
Smith, Paul	6. 0	Hartlepool Utd.	Leeds	22.07.76
Forwards				
Owusu, Lloyd	6. 1	Brentford	Slough	12.12.76
Shaw, Jon	6. 1	–	Sheffield	10.11.83

STOCKPORT COUNTY

Ground: Edgeley Park, Hardcastle Road, Edgeley, Stockport SK3 9DD.
Telephone: 0161 286 8888. **Clubcall:** 09068 121638. **Club nickname:** County.
First-choice colours: Blue shirts; blue shorts; blue stockings.
Main Sponsor: Scandia Lager. **Capacity for 2003-04:** 10,817.
Record attendance: 27,833 v Liverpool (F.A. Cup 5) 11 February, 1950.

Name	Height ft. in.	Previous club	Birthplace	Birthdate
Goalkeepers				
Jones, Lee	6. 3	Bristol Rov.	Pontypridd	9.08.70
Spencer, James	6. 5	–	Stockport.	11.04.85
Defenders				
Challinor, Dave	6. 1	Tranmere Rov.	Chester	2.10.75
Goodwin, Jim	5. 9	Celtic	Waterford	20.11.81
Hardiker, John	6. 0	Morecambe	Preston	7.07.82
Pemberton, Martin	5.10	Mansfield Town	Bradford	1.02.79
Tonkin, Anthony	5.11	Yeovil Town	Cornwall	19.01.80
Midfielders				
Clare, Rob	5.10	–	Belper	28.02.83
Gibb, Ali	5. 9	Northampton Town	Salisbury	17.02.76
Lambert, Rickie	5.10	Macclesfield Town	Liverpool	16.02.82
Lescott, Aaron	5. 8	Sheffield Wed.	Birmingham	2.12.77
McLachlan, Fraser	5.11	–	Manchester	9.11.82
Palmer, Carlton	6. 3	Coventry City	Birmingham	5.12.65
Forwards				
Beckett, Luke	5.11	Chesterfield	Sheffield	25.11.76
Daly, Jon	6. 3	–	Dublin	8.01.83
Ellison, Kevin	5.11	Leicester City	Liverpool	23.02.79
Welsh, Andy	5. 8	–	Manchester	24.11.83
Wilbraham, Aaron	6. 3	–	Knutsford	21.10.79
Williams, Chris	5. 8	–	Manchester	2.02.85

SWINDON TOWN

Ground: County Ground, County Road, Swindon SN1 2ED.
Telephone: 01793 333700. **Clubcall:** 09068 121640. **Club nickname:** Robins.
First-choice colours: Red and white shirts; white and red shorts; red stockings.
Main sponsor: Nationwide. **Capacity for 2003-04:** 15,704.
Record attendance: 32,000 v Arsenal (F.A. Cup 3) 15 January, 1972.

Name	Height ft. in.	Previous club	Birthplace	Birthdate
Goalkeepers				
Griemink, Bart	6. 4	Peterborough Utd.	Holland	29.03.72
Defenders				
Bampton, David	5. 8	–	Swindon	5.05.85
Gurney, Andy	5.11	Reading	Bristol	25.01.74
Heywood, Matthew	6. 3	Burnley	Chatham	26.08.79
Murphy, Danny	5. 6	Q.P.R	Southwark	4.12.82
Miglioranzi, Stefani	6. 0	Portsmouth	Pocos de Caldas, Bra.	20.09.77
Reeves, Alan	6. 0	Wimbledon	Birkenhead	19.11.67
Taylor, Chris	5. 8	–	Swindon	30.10.85

Midfielders				
Duke, David	5.10	Sunderland	Inverness	7.11.78
Hewlett, Matt	6. 2	Bristol City	Bristol	25.02.76
O'Halloran, Keith	5. 9	St. Johnstone	Dublin	27.03.77
Robinson, Steve	5. 9	Birmingham City	Nottingham	17.10.75
Forwards				
Herring, Ian	5.10	–	Swindon	14.02.84
Mooney, Tommy	5.10	Birmingham City	Billingham	11.08.71
Parkin, Sam	6. 2	Chelsea	Roehampton	14.03.81
Stevenson, Jon	5. 6	Leicester City	Leicester	13.10.82
Young, Alan	5. 7	–	Swindon	12.08.83

TRANMERE ROVERS

Ground: Prenton Park, Prenton Road West, Birkenhead CH42 9PY.
Telephone: 0151 609 3333. **Club nickname:** Rovers.
First-choice colours: White shirts; white shorts; white stockings.
Mian Sponsor: Wirral Borough Council. **Capacity for 2003-04:** 16,500.
Record attendance: 24,424 v Stoke City (F.A. Cup 4) 5 February, 1972.

Name	Height ft. in.	Previous club	Birthplace	Birthdate
Goalkeepers				
Achterberg, John	6. 1	PSV Eindhoven	Utrecht	8.07.71
Howarth, Russell	6. 1	York City	York	27.03.82
Nixon, Eric	6. 4	Wigan Athletic	Manchester	4.10.62
Defenders				
Allen, Graham	6. 0	Everton	Bolton	8.04.77
Connelly, Sean	5.10	Wolves	Sheffield	26.06.70
Gray, Kevin	6. 0	Huddersfield Town	Sheffield	7.01.72
Linwood, Paul	6. 2	–	Birkenhead	24.10.83
Loran, Tyrone	5.10	Manchester City	Amsterdam	29.06.81
Nicholson, Shane	5.10	Sheffield Utd.	Newark	3.06.70
Olsen, James	6. 2	Liverpool	Liverpool	23.10.81
Roberts, Gareth	5. 8	Panionios, Gre.	Wrexham	6.02.78
Taylor, Ryan	5. 8	–	Liverpool	19.08.84
Midfielders				
Dunbar, Karl	5. 8	–	Birkenhead	4.10.83
Harrison, Danny	5.11	–	Liverpool	4.11.82
Jones, Gary	6. 3	Nott'm. Forest	Chester	10.05.75
McGuire, Jamie	5. 7	–	Birkenhead	13.11.83
Mellon, Micky	5.10	Burnley	Paisley	18.03.72
Navarro, Alan	5.10	Liverpool	Liverpool	31.05.81
Sharps, Ian	6. 3	–	Warrington	23.10.80
Forwards				
Haworth, Simon	6. 1	Wigan Athletic	Cardiff	30.03.77
Hay, Alex	5.10	–	Birkenhead	14.10.83
Hume, Iain	5. 7	–	Edinburgh	30.10.83
Robinson, Paul	6. 0	Newcastle Utd.	Newcastle	28.05.84

WREXHAM

Ground: Racecourse Ground, Mold Road, Wrexham LL11 2AH.
Telephone: 01978 262129. **Club nickname:** Robins.
First-choice-colours: Red shirts; white shorts; red stockings.
Main sponsor: GAP Personnel. **Capacity for 2003-04:** 15,500.
Record attendance: 34,445 v Manchester Utd. (F.A. Cup 4) 26 January, 1957.

Name	Height ft. in.	Previous club	Birthplace	Birthdate
Goalkeepers				
Dibble, Andy	6. 2	Stockport Co.	Cwmbran	8.05.65

Whitfield, Paul	6. 0	–	St Asaph	6.05.82
Defenders				
Bennett, Dan	6. 1	Swindon Town	Great Yarmouth	7.01.78
Carey, Brian	6. 3	Leicester City	Cork	31.05.68
Green, Scott	5.10	Wigan Athletic	Walsall	15.01.70
Holmes, Shaun	5. 9	Manchester City	Londonderry	27.12.80
Lawrence, Dennis	5.11	Defence Force	Trinidad	18.01.74
Morgan, Craig	6. 0	–	St Asaph	18.06.85
Pejic, Shaun	6. 1	–	Hereford	16.11.82
Roberts, Stephen	6. 2	–	Wrexham	24.02.80
Midfielders				
Barrett, Paul	5. 9	Newcastle Utd.	Newcastle	13.04.78
Edwards, Carlos	6. 0	–	Tobago	24.10.78
Edwards, Paul	5.11	Swindon Town	Manchester	1.01.80
Ferguson, Darren	5.10	Sparta Rotterdam	Glasgow	9.02.72
Jones, Mark	5.11	–	Wrexham	15.08.83
Llewellyn, Chris	5.11	Norwich City	Swansea	29.08.79
Phillips, Wayne	5.11	Stockport Co.	Bangor	15.12.70
Russell, Kevin	5. 9	Notts Co.	Portsmouth	6.12.66
Thomas, Steve	5.10	–	Hartlepool	23.06.79
Whitley, Jim	5. 9	Manchester City	Zambia	14.04.75
Forwards				
Jones, Lee	5. 8	Barnsley	Wrexham	29.05.73
Sam, Hector	5.10	CL Financial San Juan	Trinidad	25.02.78

WYCOMBE WANDERERS

Ground: Causeway Stadium, Hillbottom Road, High Wycombe HP12 4HJ.
Telephone: 01494 472100. **Clubcall:** 09003 446855. **Club nickname:** Chairboys.
First-choice colours: Light and dark blue shirts; dark blue shorts; light blue stockings.
Main sponsor: Loans.co.uk. **Capacity for 2003-04:** 10,000.
Record attendance: 9,921 v Fulham (F.A. Cup 3) 8 January, 2002.

Name	Height ft. in.	Previous club	Birthplace	Birthdate
Goalkeepers				
Talia, Frank	6. 1	Reading	Melbourne	20.07.72
Williams, Steve	6. 0	–	Oxford	21.04.83
Defenders				
Johnson, Roger	6. 3	Portsmouth	Ashford	28.04.83
Rogers, Mark	5.11	Vancouver	Geulph, Can.	3.11.78
Thomson, Andy	6. 3	Bristol Rov.	Swindon	28.03.74
Vinnicombe, Chris	5. 9	Burnley	Exeter	20.10.70
Midfielders				
Brown, Steve	5.10	Northampton Town	Northampton	6.07.66
Bulman Danny	5. 9	Ashford Town	Ashford	21.04.79
Cook, Lewis	5. 7	–	High Wycombe	28.12.83
Currie, Darren	5. 9	Barnet	Hampstead	29.11.74
Harris, Richard	5.11	Crystal Palace	Croydon	23.10.80
Lee, Martyn	5. 6	–	Guildford	10.08.80
Roberts, Stuart	5. 7	Swansea City	Carmarthen	22.07.80
Ryan, Keith	5.10	Berkhamstead	Northampton	25.06.70
Simpemba, Ian	5.10	–	Dublin	28.03.83
Simpson, Michael	5. 8	Notts Co.	Nottingham	28.02.74
Forwards				
Dixon, Jonny	5. 9	–	Mercia, Spa.	16.01.84
Faulconbridge, Craig	6. 1	Wrexham	Nuneaton	20.04.78
Holligan, Gavin	5.10	West Ham Utd.	Lambeth	30.06.80
McSporran, Jermaine	5.10	Oxford City	Manchester	1.01.77
Senda, Danny	5.10	Southampton	Harrow	17.04.81

DIVISION THREE

BOSTON UNITED

Ground: York Street, Boston, PE21 6HN.
Telephone: 01205 364406. **Clubcall:** 09068 121539. **Club nickname:** Pilgrims.
First-choice colours: Amber shirts; amber shorts; amber socks.
Main sponsor: Finn Forest. **Capacity for 2003-04:** 6,635.

Name	Height ft. in.	Previous club	Birthplace	Birthdate
Goalkeepers				
Bastock, Paul	5.11	Kettering Town	Leamington Spa	19.05.70
Defenders				
Balmer, Stuart	6. 1	Oldham Athletic	Falkirk	20.09.69
Beevers, Lee	5.10	Ipswich Town	Doncaster	4.12.83
Chapman, Ben	5. 7	Grimsby Town	Scunthorpe	2.03.79
Clarke, Ryan	5.11	Notts Co.	Sutton Coldfield	22.01.84
Ellender, Paul	5.10	Scarborough	Scunthorpe	21.10.74
Greaves, Mark	6. 1	Hull City	Hull	22.01.75
Hocking, Matthew	5.11	York City	Boston	30.01.78
Potter, Graham	6. 1	York City	Solihull	2.05.75
Sutch, Daryl	6. 0	Southend Utd.	Lowestoft	11.09.71
Midfielders				
Bennett, Tom	5.11	Walsall	Falkirk	12.12.69
Higgins, Alex	5. 9	Stalybridge Celtic	Sheffield	22.07.81
Redfearn, Neil	5. 9	Halifax Town	Dewsbury	20.06.65
Rusk, Simon	6. 0	Peterborough Utd.	–	17.12.81
Forwards				
Angel, Mark	5.10	Darlington	Newcastle	23.08.75
Douglas, Stuart	5. 9	Rushden & Diamonds	Enfield	9.04.78
Duffield, Peter	5. 6	York City	Middlesbrough	4.02.69
Jones, Graeme	6. 0	Southend Utd.	Gateshead	13.03.70
Logan, Richard	6. 1	Ipswich Town	Bury St Edmunds	4.01.82
Thompson, Lee	5.10	Sheffield Utd.	Sheffield	25.03.82
Weatherstone, Simon	5.10	Oxford Utd.	Reading	26.01.80

BRISTOL ROVERS

Ground: Memorial Ground, Filton Avenue, Horfield, Bristol BS7 0BF.
Telephone: 0117 909 6648. **Clubcall:** 09068 121131. **Club nickname:** Pirates.
First-choice colours: Blue and white shirts; white shorts; blue stockings.
Main sponsor: Cowlin Construction. **Capacity for 2003-04:** 11,626.
Record attendance: (Eastville) 38,472 v Preston N.E. (F.A. Cup 4) 30 January, 1960. (Memorial Ground) 11,433 v Sunderland (League Cup 3) 31 October, 2000.

Name	Height ft. in.	Previous club	Birthplace	Birthdate
Goalkeepers				
Howie, Scott	6. 2	Reading	Motherwell	4.01.72
Miller, Kevin	6. 1	Exeter City	Falmouth	15.03.69
Defenders				
Anderson, Ijah	5. 8	Brentford	Hackney	30.12.75
Austin, Kevin	6. 1	Cambridge Utd	Hackney	12.02.73
Barrett, Adam	5.10	Mansfield Town	Dagenham	29.11.79
Boxall, Danny	5. 8	Brentford	Croydon	25.08.77
Challis, Trevor	5. 8	Q.P.R.	Paddington	23.10.75
Edwards, Chris	6. 2	Nott'm. Forest	Caerphilly	23.11.75
Uddin, Anwar	6. 2	Sheffield Wed.	London	1.11.81
Midfielders				
Astafjevs, Vitalys	5.11	Skonto Riga	Riga, Lat.	3.04.71

Bryant, Simon	5. 8	–	Bristol	22.11.82
Carlisle, Wayne	6. 0	Crystal Palace	Lisburn	9.09.79
Hodges, Lee	5. 5	Rochdale	Newham	2.03.78
Hogg, Lewis	5.11	–	Bristol	13.09.82
Hyde, Graham	5. 7	Birmingham City	Doncaster	10.11.70
Quinn, Rob	6. 0	Oxford Utd.	Sidcup	8.11.76
Street, Kevin	5.10	Crewe Alexandra	Crewe	25.11.77
Forwards				
Agogo, Junior	5.10	Barnet	Accra	1.08.79
Allen, Bradley	5. 8	Peterborough Utd.	Harold Wood	13.09.71
Gilroy, David	5.11	–	Yeovil	23.12.82
McKeever, Mark	5.10	Sheffield Wed.	Londonderry	16.11.78
Rammell, Andy	5.11	Wycombe Wand.	Nuneaton	10.02.67
Tait. Paul	6. 2	Crewe Alexandra	Newcastle	24.10.75

BURY

Ground: Gigg Lane, Bury BL9 9HR.
Telephone: 0161 764 4881. **Clubcall:** 0900 809003. **Club nickname:** Shakers.
First-choice colours: White and blue shirts; blue shorts; white and blue stockings.
Main Sponsor: Bury Metro. **Capacity for 2003-04:** 11,800.
Record attendance: 35,000 v Bolton Wand. (F.A. Cup 3) 9 January, 1960.

Name	Height ft. in.	Previous club	Birthplace	Birthdate
Goalkeepers				
Garner, Glyn	6. 2	Llanelli	Pontypool	9.12.76
Defenders				
Kennedy, Thomas	5.11	–	Bury	24.06.85
Swailes, Danny	6. 3	–	Bolton	1.04.79
Unsworth, Lee	5.11	Crewe Alexandra	Eccles	25.02.73
Woodthorpe, Colin	6. 1	Stockport Co.	Liverpool	13.01.69
Midfielders				
Connell, Lee	6. 0	–	Bury	24.02.69
Dunfield, Terry	5. 7	Manchester City	Vancouver	20.02.82
Forrest, Martyn	5.10	–	Bury	2.01.79
Gunby, Steve	5.11	–	Boston	14.04.84
O'Shaughnessy, Paul	6. 4	–	Bury	3.10.81
Whaley, Simon	5.11	–	Bolton	7.06.85
Forwards				
Clegg, George	5.10	Manchester Utd.	Manchester	16.11.80
Lawson, Ian	5.11	Stockport Co.	Huddersfield	4.11.77
Nugent, David	5.11	–	Liverpool	2.05.85
Porter, Chris	6. 1	–	Wigan	12.12.83
Preece, Andy	6. 1	Blackpool	Evesham	27.03.67
Seddon, Gareth	5. 9	–	Burnley	23.05.80

CAMBRIDGE UNITED

Ground: Abbey Stadium, Newmarket Road, Cambridge CB5 8LN.
Telephone: 01223 566500. **Club nickname:** U's.
First-choice colours: Amber and black shirts; black and amber shorts; black and amber stockings.
Main sponsor: Capital Sports. **Capacity for 2003-04:** 8,993.
Record attendance: 14,000 v Chelsea (Friendly) 1 May, 1970.

Name	Height ft. in.	Previous club	Birthplace	Birthdate
Goalkeepers				
Brennan, Martin	6. 1	Charlton Athletic	London	14.09.82
Clark, George	6. 0	–	Cambridge	9.09.84
Marshall, Shaun	6. 1	–	Fakenham	3.10.78

Defenders				
Angus, Stevland	5.11	West Ham Utd.	Essex	16.09.80
Duncan, Andy	5.11	Manchester Utd.	Hexham	20.10.77
Gleeson, Daniel	6. 3	–	Cambridge	17.02.85
Goodhind, Warren	5.11	Barnet	Johannesburg	16.08.77
Heathcote, Jonathan	5.10	–	Frimley	10.11.83
Murray, Fred	5.10	Blackburn Rov.	Tipperary	22.05.82
Nacca, Francesco	5. 6	–	Valencia	9.11.81
Tann, Adam	6. 1	–	Fakenham	12.05.82
Midfielders				
Fleming, Terry	5. 9	Plymouth Argyle	Birmingham	5.01.73
Guttridge, Luke	5. 5	Torquay Utd.	Barnstaple	27.03.82
Tudor, Shane	5. 7	Wolves	Wolves	10.02.82
Walker, Justin	5.11	Exeter City	Nottingham	6.09.75
Wanless, Paul	6. 1	Lincoln City	Banbury	14.12.73
Forwards				
Chillingworth, Daniel	6. 0	–	Cambridge	13.09.81
Kitson, David	6. 3	Arlesey Town	Hitchin	21.01.80
Revell, Alex	6. 3	–	Cambridge	7.07.83
Opara, Lloyd	6. 1	Colchester Utd.	Enfield	6.01.84
Turner, John	6. 2	–	Harrow	12.02.86

CARLISLE UNITED

Ground: Brunton Park, Warwick Road, Carlisle CA1 1LL.
Telephone: 01228 526237. **Club nickname:** Cumbrians.
First-choice colours: Blue shirts; white shorts; white stockings.
Main sponsor: Eddie Stobart. **Capacity for 2003-04:** 15,645.
Record attendance: 27,500 v Birmingham City (F.A. Cup 3) 5 January, 1957, and v Middlesbrough (F.A. Cup 5) 7 January, 1970.

Name	Height ft. in.	Previous club	Birthplace	Birthdate
Goalkeepers				
Glennon, Matt	6. 2	Hull City	Stockport	8.10.78
Keen, Peter	6. 0	Newcastle Utd.	Middlesbrough	16.11.76
Defenders				
Andrews, Lee	6. 0	–	Carlisle	23.04.83
Billy, Chris	6. 0	Bury	Huddersfield	2,01.73
Birch, Mark	5.10	Northwich Victoria	Stoke	5.01.77
Byrne, Des	6. 1	St Patrick's	Dublin	10.04.81
Kelly, Darren	6. 1	Derry City	Derry	30.06.79
Maddison, Lee	5.11	Dundee	Bristol	5.10.72
McDonagh, Will	6. 1	Bohemians	Dublin	14.03.83
Raven, Paul	6. 1	Grimsby Town	Salisbury	28.07.70
Shelley, Brian	6. 0	Bohemians	Dublin	15.11.81
Midfielders				
Baldacchino	5.10	Bolton Wand.	Leicester	13.01.81
McGill, Brendan	5. 8	Sunderland	Dublin	22.03.81
Murphy, Peter	5.11	Blackburn Rov.	Dublin	27.10.80
Summerbell, Mark	5. 9	Middlesbrough	Durham	30.10.76
Forwards				
Farrell, Craig	6. 0	Leeds Utd.	Middlesbrough	5.12.82
Foran, Richie	6. 1	Shelbourne	Dublin	16.06.80
Rundle, Adam	5.11	Darlington	Durham	8.07.84
Russell, Craig	5.11	St Johnstone	South Shields	4.02.74
Wake, Brian	6. 0	Tow Law Town	Stockton	13.08.82

CHELTENHAM TOWN

Ground: Whaddon Road, Cheltenham GL52 5NA.
Telephone: 01242 573558. **Club nickname:** Town.

First-choice colours: Red and white shirts; white shorts; white stockings.
Main Sponsor: Towergate Insurance. **Capacity for 2003-04:** 7,407.
Record attendance: 8,326 v Reading (F.A. Cup 1) 17 November, 1956.

Name	Height ft. in.	Previous club	Birthplace	Birthdate
Goalkeepers				
Book, Steve	6. 2	Forest Green Rov.	Bournemouth	7.07.69
Higgs, Shane	6. 3	Bristol Rov.	Oxford	13.05.77
Defenders				
Brough, John	6. 0	Hereford Utd.	Ilkeston	8.01.73
Buttery, Luke	5.10	–	Wegberg	12.02.85
Duff, Michael	5.11	–	Belfast	11.01.78
Duff, Shane	6. 1	–	Wroughton	2.04.82
Griffin, Anthony	5.11	Bournemouth	Bournemouth	22.03.79
Victory, Jamie	5. 8	Bournemouth	London	14.11.75
Walker, Richard	5.11	Hereford Utd.	Derby	9.11.71
Midfielders				
Bird, David	5. 8	–	Gloucester	26.12.84
Devaney, Martin	5.11	Coventry City	Cheltenham	1.06.80
Finnigan, John	5. 8	Lincoln City	Wakefield	20.03.76
Forsyth, Richard	5.11	Peterborough Utd.	Dudley	3.10.70
Howells, Lee	5. 8	Brisbane Utd.	Freemantle	14.10.68
McCann, Grant	5.10	West Ham Utd.	Belfast	14.04.80
Yates, Mark	6. 0	Kidderminster Harr.	Birmingham	24.01.70
Forwards				
Brayson, Paul	5. 7	Cardiff City	Newcastle	16.09.77
Odejayi, Kayode	6. 0	Bristol City	Ibadon, Nig.	–
Spencer, Damian	6. 1	Bristol City	Ascot	19.09.81

DARLINGTON

Ground: Reynolds Arena, Hurworth Moor, Neasham Road, Darlington, DL2 1GR.
Telephone: 01325 387000. **Club nickname:** Quakers.
First-choice colours: White shirts; black shorts; black stockings.
Main sponsor: Darlington Building Society. **Capacity for 2003-04:** 25,000.
Record attendance: (Feethams) 21,023 v Bolton Wand. (League Cup 3) 14 November, 1960.

Name	Height ft. in.	Previous club	Birthplace	Birthdate
Goalkeepers				
Collett, Andy	6. 0	Bristol Rov.	Middlesbrough	28.10.73
Porter, Chris	6. 2	Southend Utd.	Middlesbrough	10.11.79
Defenders				
Betts, Simon	5.11	–	Middlesbrough	3.03.73
Ford, Mark	5. 8	Torquay Utd.	Pontefract	10.10.75
Kilty, Mark	6. 0	–	Sunderland	24.06.81
Liddle, Craig	5.11	Middlesbrough	Chester-le-Street	21.10.71
McGurk, David	5.11	–	Middlesbrough	30.09.82
Reed, Adam	6. 0	Blackburn Rov.	Darlington	18.02.75
Valentine, Ryan	5.10	Everton	Wrexham	19.08.82
Wainwright, Neil	6. 0	Sunderland	Warrington	4.11.77
Midfielders				
Clark, Ian	5.11	Hartlepool Utd.	Stockton	23.10.74
Keltie, Clark	6. 1	–	Newcastle	31.08.83
Kilty, Mark	6. 0	–	Sunderland	24.06.81
Pearson, Gary	5.10	Durham City	Easington	7.12.76
Maddison, Neil	5.10	Middlesbrough	Darlington	2.10.69
Mellanby, Danny	5.10	Bishop Auckland	Bishop Auckland	17.07.79
Forwards				
Clarke, Matthew	6. 3	Halifax Town	Leeds	18.12.80

Conlon, Barry	6. 2	York City	Drogheda	1.10.78
Convery, Mark	5. 6	Sunderland	Newcastle	29.05.81
Sheeran, Mark	5.10	–	Newcastle	9.08.82

DONCASTER ROVERS

Ground: Belle Vue, Bawtry Road, Doncaster, DN4 5HT.
Telephone: 01302 539441. **Clubcall:** 09068 121651. **Club nickname:** Rovers.
First-choice colours: Red and white shirts; red shorts; white stockings.
Main sponsor: Streetwise. **Capacity for 2003-04:** 7,094.
Record attendance: 37,149 v Hull City (Div.3N) 2 October, 1948.

Name	Height ft. in.	Previous club	Birthplace	Birthdate
Goalkeepers				
Warrington, Andy	6. 3	York City	Sheffield	10.06.76
Defenders				
Albrighton, Mark	5.11	Telford Utd.	Nuneaton	6.03.76
Beech, Chris	5. 9	Rotherham Utd.	Congleton	5.11.75
Foster, Steve	6. 1	Bristol Rov.	Mansfield	3.12.74
Marples, Simon	5.11	Stocksbridge Park	Sheffield	30.07.75
Morley, David	6. 2	Oxford Utd.	St Helens	25.09.77
Price, Jamie	5. 9	Leeds Utd.	Normanton	27.10.81
Ryan, Tim	5.10	Southport	Stockport	10.12.74
Midfielders				
Blunt, Jason	5. 8	Yeovil Town	Penzance	16.08.77
Doolan, John	6. 1	Barnet	Liverpool	7.05.74
Green, Paul	5.10	Sheffield Wed.	Sheffield	10.04.83
Paterson, Jamie	5. 5	Halifax Town	Dumfries	26.04.73
Ravenhill, Ricky	5.10	Barnsley	Doncaster	16.01.81
Tierney, Francis	5.10	Witton Albion	Liverpool	10.09.75
Forwards				
Barnes, Paul	5.11	Nuneaton Borough	Leicester	16.11.67
Blundell, Gregg	6. 0	Northwich Victoria	–	1.01.76
Fortune-West, Leo	6. 4	Cardiff City	Stratford	9.04.71
Gill, Robert	5.11	Nott'm. Forest	Nottingham	10.02.82
Jackson, Justin	6. 0	Rushden & Diamonds	Nottingham	10.12.74
Whitman, Tristram	5.11	Arnold	Nottingham	9.06.80

HUDDERSFIELD TOWN

Ground: McAlpine Stadium, Leeds Road, Huddersfield HD1 6PX.
Telephone: 01484 484100. **Clubcall:** 09068 121635. **Club nickname:** Terriers.
First-choice colours: Blue and white shirts; white shorts; white and blue stockings.
Capacity for 2003-04: 24,554.
Record attendance: (Leeds Road) 67,037 v Arsenal (F.A. Cup 6) 27 February, 1932; (McAlpine Stadium) 23,678 v Liverpool (F.A. Cup 3) 12 December, 1999.

Name	Height ft. in.	Previous club	Birthplace	Birthdate
Goalkeepers				
Gray, Ian	6. 2	Rotherham Utd.	Manchester	25.02.75
Senior, Phil	5.11	–	Huddersfield	30.10.82
Defenders				
Clarke, Nathan	6. 2	–	Halifax	30.11.83
Edwards, Rob	5. 8	Chesterfield	Manchester	23.02.70
Lloyd, Antony	5. 7	–	Taunton	–
Moses, Ade	6. 0	Barnsley	Doncaster	4.05.75
Midfield				
Ahmed, Adnan	5.10	–	Bumley	7.06.84
Holland, Chris	6. 1	Birmingham City	Whalley	11.09.75
Mattis, Dwayne	5.10	–	Huddersfield	31.07.81

Scott, Paul	5.11	–	Wakefield	5.11.79
Stead, Jonathan	5.10	–	Huddersfield	7.04.83
Smith, Martin	5.11	Sheffield Utd.	Sunderland	13.11.74
Thorrington, John	5. 8	Manchester Utd.	Johannesburg	10.07.79
Washington, Joe	5. 8	–	Huddersfield	14.10.83
Forwards				
Booth, Andy	6. 1	Sheffield Wed.	Huddersfield	6.12.73
Brown, Nat	6. 2	–	Sheffield	15.06.81
Macari, Paul	5.10	Sheffield Utd.	Manchester	23.08.76
Newby, Jon	6. 0	Bury	Warrington	28.11.78
Schofield, Danny	5.10	Brodsworth	Doncaster	10.04.80

HULL CITY

Ground: Kingston Communications Stadium, The Circle, Walton Street, Anlaby Road, Hull, HU3 6HU.
Telephone: 0870 837 0003. **Club nickname:** Tigers.
First-choice colours: Amber and black shirts; black and amber shorts; amber and black stockings.
Main Sponsor: Bonus Electrical. **Capacity for 2003-04:** 25,000.
Record attendance: (Boothferry Park) 55,019 v Manchester Utd. (F.A. Cup 6) 28 February, 1949. (Kingston Communications Stadium) 22,319 v Hartlepool Utd. (Div.3) 26 December, 2002. 24,004 England u-21 v Serbia-Montenegro. 2 June, 2003.

Name	**Height ft. in.**	**Previous club**	**Birthplace**	**Birthdate**
Goalkeepers				
Fettis, Alan	6. 1	York City	Belfast	1.02.71
Harvey, Danny	6. 1	–	Hull	7.09.85
Musselwhite, Paul	6. 2	Port Vale	Plymouth	22.12.68
Defenders				
Anderson, John	6. 2	Livingston	Greenock	2.10.72
Burton, Steve	6. 1	–	Hull	10.10.82
Dawson, Andy	5. 9	Scunthorpe Utd.	Northallerton	20.10.78
Delaney, Damien	6. 3	Leicester City	Cork	20.07.81
Elliott, Stuart	5.10	Motherwell	Belfast	23.07.78
Hinds, Richard	6. 2	Tranmere Rov.	Sheffield	22.08.80
Holt, Andy	6. 1	Oldham Athletic	Stockport	21.05.78
Joseph, Marc	6. 0	Peterborough Utd.	Leicester	10.11.76
Keates, Dean	5. 6	Walsall	Walsall	30.06.78
Smith, Shaun	5.10	Crewe Alexandra	Leeds	9.04.71
Strong, Greg	6. 2	Motherwell	Bolton	5.09.75
Thelwell, Alton	5.11	Tottenham	Holloway	5.09.80
Whittle, Justin	6. 1	Stoke City	Derby	18.03.71
Midfielders				
Appleby, Richie	5. 8	Kidderminster Harr.	Middlesbrough	18.09.75
Ashbee, Ian	6. 1	Cambridge Utd.	Birmingham	6.09.76
Fry, Russell	6. 0	–	Hull	4.12.85
Green, Stuart	5.10	Newcastle Utd.	Whitehaven	15.06.81
Melton, Steve	5.11	Brighton & H.A.	Lincoln	3.10.78
Peat, Nathan	5. 9	–	Hull	19.09.82
Price, Jason	6. 2	Tranmere Rov.	Pontypridd	12.04.77
Williams, Ryan	5. 4	Chesterfield	Mansfield	31.08.78
Forwards				
Allsopp, Danny	6. 0	Notts Co.	Melbourne	10.08.78
Burgess, Ben	6. 3	Stockport Co.	Buxton	9.11.81
Donaldson, Clayton	6. 1	–	Bradford	7.02.84
Forrester, Jamie	5. 6	Northampton Town	Bradford	1.11.74
Webb, Daniel	6. 0	Southend Utd.	Poole	2.07.83

KIDDERMINSTER HARRIERS

Ground: Aggborough Stadium, Hoo Road, Kidderminster DY10 1NB.
Telephone: 01562 823931. **Club nickname:** Harriers.
First-choice colours: Red and white shirts; white shorts; red stockings.
Main sponsor: OGL Computer. **Capacity for 2003-04:** 6,300.
Record attendance: 9,155 v Hereford Utd. (F.A. Cup 1) 27 November, 1948.

Name	Height ft. in.	Previous club	Birthplace	Birthdate
Goalkeepers				
Brock, Stuart	6. 0	Aston Villa	Sandwell	29.09.76
Danby, John	6. 0	–	Stoke	20.09.83
Defenders				
Ayres, Lee	6. 1	–	Birmingham	28.08.82
Gadsby, Matthew	6. 1	Mansfield Town	Sutton Coldfield	6.09.79
Hinton, Craig	5.11	Birmingham City	Wolves	26.11.77
Shilton, Sam	5.11	Hartlepool Utd.	Nottingham	21.07.78
Smith, Adrian	5.10	Bromsgrove Rov.	Birmingham	11.08.73
Stamps, Scott	5.10	Colchester Utd.	Smethwick	20.03.75
Midfielders				
Bennett, Dean	5.10	Bromsgrove Rov.	Wolves	13.12.77
Flynn, Sean	5. 8	Tranmere Rov.	Birmingham	13.03.68
Parrish, Sean	5. 9	Chesterfield	Wrexham	14.03.72
Williams, Danny	6. 1	Wrexham	Wrexham	12.07.79
Forwards				
Henriksen, Bo	5.10	Herfolge	Denmark	7.02.75
Lewis, Matt	6. 0	–	Coventry	20.03.84

LEYTON ORIENT

Ground: Matchroom Stadium, Brisbane Road, London E10 5NE.
Telephone: 0208 926 1111. **Clubcall:** 09068 121150. **Club nickname:** O's.
First-choice colours: Red shirts; red shorts; red stockings.
Main Sponsor: Poker Million.Com. **Capacity for 2003-04:** 11,127.
Record attendance: 34,345 v West Ham Utd. (F.A. Cup 4) 25 January 1964.

Name	Height ft. in.	Previous club	Birthplace	Birthdate
Goalkeepers				
Harrison, Lee	6. 2	Barnet	Billericay	12.09.71
Jones, Paul	6. 0	–	Maidstone	28.06.86
Morris, Glenn	6. 0	–	Woolwich	20.12.83
Defenders				
Barnard, Donny	6. 0	–	Forest Gate	1.07.84
Heald, Greg	6. 1	Barnet	Enfield	26.09.71
Jones, Billy	6. 0	–	Gillingham	26.06.83
Joseph, Matthew	5. 7	Cambridge Utd.	Bethnal Green	30.09.72
Lockwood, Matthew	5. 9	Bristol Rov.	Rochford	17.10.76
McGhee, David	5.11	Brentford	Sussex	19.06.76
Miller, Justin	6. 0	Ipswich Town	Johannesburg	16.12.80
Stephens, Kevin	5.10	–	Enfield	28.07.84
Midfielders				
Brazier, Matthew	5. 8	Cardiff City	Ilford	2.07.76
Downer, Simon	5.10	–	Romford	19.10.81
Ibehre, Jabo	6. 2	–	Islington	28.01.83
Toner, Ciaran	6. 1	Bristol Rov.	Craigavon	30.06.81
Forwards				
Alexander, Gary	6. 0	Hull City	Peckham	15.08.79
Fletcher, Gary	6. 0	Northwich Victoria	Liverpool	4.06.81
Forbes, Boniek	5.10	–	Guinea Bissau	30.09.83
Purser, Wayne	6. 0	Barnet	Basildon	13.04.80

Tate, Christopher	6.0	Scarborough	York	27.12.77
Thorpe, Lee	6.0	Lincoln City	Wolves	14.12.75

LINCOLN CITY

Ground: Sincil Bank, Lincoln LN5 8LD.
Telephone: 01522 880020. **Clubcall:** 09066 555900. **Club nickname:** Imps.
First-choice colours: Red and white shirts; black shorts; red and white stockings.
Main sponsor: Siemens. **Capacity for 2003-04:** 10,239.
Record attendance: 23,196 v Derby Co. (League Cup 4) 15 November, 1967.

Name	Height ft. in.	Previous club	Birthplace	Birthdate
Goalkeepers				
Horrigan, Darren	6. 0	–	Middlesbrough	2.06.83
Marriott, Alan	6. 0	Tottenham	Bedford	3.09.78
Defenders				
Bimson, Stuart	5.10	Bury	Liverpool	29.09.69
Bloomer, Matthew	6. 1	Hull City	Cleethorpes	30.11.78
Coulson, David	5.11	–	Durham	21.03.84
Davies, Chris	5.10	Barnsley	Rotherham	8.04.84
Futcher, Ben	6. 7	Stalybridge Celtic	Bradford	20.02.81
Morgan, Paul	5.11	Preston N.E.	Belfast	23.10.78
Wattley, David	5.11	Q.P.R.	London	5.09.83
Weaver, Simon	5.11	Nuneaton	–	20.12.77
Midfielders				
Bailey, Mark	5. 8	Northwich Victoria	Stoke	12.08.76
Butcher, Richard	6. 0	Kettering	Peterborough	22.01.81
Camm, Mark	5. 8	Sheffield Utd.	Mansfield	1.10.81
Cornelly, Chris	5.10	Ashton Utd.	Huddersfield	7.07.76
Gain, Peter	6. 1	Tottenham	Hammersmith	2.11.76
Logan, Richard	6. 1	Scunthorpe Utd.	Barnsley	24.05.69
Mayo, Paul	5.11	Nott'm. Forest	Hammersmith	13.10.81
Sedgemore, Ben	6. 0	Macclesfield Town	Wolverhampton	5.08.75
Smith, Paul	5.11	Nott'm. Forest	Hastings	23.01.76
Ward, Chris	5.11	Leigh RMI	Preston	28.04.81
Willis, Scott	5. 9	Carlisle Utd.	Liverpool	20.02.82
Forwards				
Cropper, Dene	6. 2	Worksop Town	Chesterfield	5.01.83
Mike, Adie	6. 0	Doncaster Rov.	Manchester	16.11.73
Pearce, Allan	5.11	Barnsley	Wellington, NZ	7.04.83
Yeo, Simon	5.10	Hyde Utd.	–	20.10.73

MACCLESFIELD TOWN

Ground: Moss Rose, London Road, Macclesfield SK11 7SP.
Telephone: 01625 264686. **Clubcall:** 09066 555835. **Club nickname:** Silkmen.
First-choice colours: Blue shirts; blue shorts; blue and white stockings.
Main sponsor: Cheshire Building Society. **Capacity for 2003-04:** 6,712.
Record attendance: 9,003 v Winsford Town (Cheshire Senior Cup 2) 14 February, 1948.

Name	Height ft. in.	Previous club	Birthplace	Birthdate
Goalkeepers				
Martin, Lee	6. 0	Halifax Town	Huddersfield	9.09.68
Wilson, Steve	5.10	Hull City	Hull	24.04.74
Defenders				
Abbey, George	5.10	Port Harcourt	Port Harcourt, Nig.	20.10.73
Byrne, Chris	5. 9	Stockport Co.	Manchester	9.02.75
Haddrell, Matt	5.11	Vauxhall Motors	Staffs	19.03.81
Hitchen, Steve	5. 8	Blackburn Rov.	Salford	28.11.76
Macauley, Steve	6. 1	Rochdale	Lytham	4.03.69

Munroe, Karl	6. 1	Swansea City	Manchester	23.09.79
O'Neill, Paul	6. 2	–	Farnworth	17.06.82
Tinson, Darren	6. 0	Northwich Victoria	Birmingham	15.11.69
Welch, Michael	6. 3	–	Crewe	11.01.82
Midfielders				
Adams, Danny	5. 6	Altrincham	Manchester	3.01.76
Aldridge, Paul	5.11	Tranmere Rov.	Liverpool	2.12.81
Hardy, Lee	6. 0	Oldham Athletic	Blackpool	26.11.81
Priest, Chris	5.10	Chester City	Leigh	18.10.73
Smith, David	5.10	Stockport Co.	Liverpool	26.12.70
Whitaker, Dan	5.10	–	Manchester	14.11.80
Forwards				
Carruthers, Martin	5.10	Scunthorpe Utd.	Nottingham	7.08.72
Lightbourne, Kyle	6. 2	Stoke City	Bermuda	29.09.68
Little, Colin	5.10	Crewe Alexandra	Wythenshawe	4.11.72
Miles, John	5.10	Crewe Alexandra	Fazackerley	28.09.81
Robinson, Neil	5.10	Prescott Cables	Liverpool	18.11.79
Ross, Neil	6. 1	Stockport Co.	Birmingham	10.08.82
Tipton, Matthew	5.10	Oldham Athletic	Bangor	29.06.80
Whitehead, Damien	5.10	Warrington Town	Whiston	24.04.79

MANSFIELD TOWN

Ground: Field Mill, Quarry Lane, Mansfield NG18 5DA.
Telephone: 0870 756 3160 **Club nickname:** Stags.
First-choice colours: Amber and blue shirts; blue and amber shorts; amber and blue stockings.
Main sponsor: Perry Electrical. **Capacity for 2003-04:** 9,980.
Record attendance: 24,467 v Nott'm. Forest (F.A. Cup 3) 10 January, 1953.

Name	Height ft. in.	Previous club	Birthplace	Birthdate
Goalkeepers				
Pilkington, Kevin	6. 2	Port Vale	Hitchin	8.03.74
White, Jason	6. 2	–	Mansfield	28.01.86
Defenders				
Curle, Keith	6. 1	Sheffield Utd.	Bristol	14.11.63
Day, Rhys	6. 1	Manchester City	Bridgend	31.08.82
Eaton, Adam	5. 9	Preston N.E.	Liverpool	2.05.80
Midfielders				
Cordon, Wayne	5. 9	Port Vale	Leek	1.11.75
Curtis, Tom	5.10	Portsmouth	Exeter	1.03.73
Disley, Craig	5.10	–	Worksop	24.08.81
Hassell, Bobby	5. 9	–	Derby	4.06.80
Lawrence, Liam	5. 9	–	Retford	14.12.81
MacKenzie, Neil	6. 2	Blackpool	Birmingham	15.04.76
Forwards				
Bacon, Danny	5.10	–	Mansfield	20.09.80
Beardsley, Chris	6. 0	–	Derby	28.02.84
Christie, Iyseden	6. 0	Leyton Orient	Coventry	14.11.76
Larkin, Colin	5. 9	Wolves	Dundalk	27.04.82
Mendes, Junior	5.10	St Mirren	London	15.09.76
White, Andy	6. 4	–	Derby	6.11.81

NORTHAMPTON TOWN

Ground: Sixfields Stadium, Upton Way, Northampton NN5 5QA.
Telephone: 01604 757773. **Club nickname:** Cobblers.
First-choice colours: Claret shirts; white shorts; claret stockings.
Main sponsor: Nationwide. **Capacity for 2003-04:** 7,653.
Record attendance: (County Ground) 24,523 v Fulham (Div. 1) 23 April, 1966. (Sixfields Stadium) 7,557 v Manchester City (Div. 2) 26 September, 1998.

Name	Height ft. in.	Previous club	Birthplace	Birthdate
Goalkeepers				
Bunn, Mark	6. 0	–	London	16.11.84
Harper, Lee	6. 1	Walsall	Chelsea	30.10.71
Thompson, Glyn	6. 2	Fulham	Telford	24.02.81
Defenders				
Chambers, Luke	5. 9	–	Kettering	29.08.85
Clark, Peter	6. 1	Stockport Co.	Romford	10.12.79
Gill, Jerry	5.11	Birmingham City	Clevedon	8.09.70
Reid, Paul	6. 2	Rangers	Carlisle	18.02.82
Sampson, Ian	6. 2	Sunderland	Wakefield	14.11.68
Smith, Tom	5.10	Rotherham Utd.	Sheffield	26.12.83
Westwood, Ashley	6. 0	Sheffield Wed.	Bridgnorth	31.08.76
Willmott, Chris	5.11	Wimbledon	Bedford	30.09.77
Midfielders				
Burgess, Oliver	5.10	Q.P.R	Ascot	12.10.81
Carruthers, Chris	5.10	–	Kettering	19.08.83
Cavill, Aaran	5.10	–	Coventry	5.03.84
Cracknell, Dean	5.10	–	Hitchin	12.10.83
Hargreaves, Chris	5.11	Plymouth Argyle	Cleethorpes	12.05.72
Harsley, Paul	5.10	Halifax Town	Scunthorpe	29.05.78
Lincoln, Greg	5. 9	Arsenal	Cheshunt	23.03.80
Reeves, Martin	6. 1	Leicester City	Birmingham	7.09.81
Rickers, Paul	5.10	Oldham Athletic	Pontefract	9.05.75
Trollope, Paul	6. 0	Fulham	Swindon	3.06.72
Forwards				
Asamoah, Derek	5. 6	Slough Town	Ghana	1.05.81
Dudfield, Lawrie	6. 1	Hull City	Southwark	7.05.80
Morison, Steve	5.11	Protec Sports	London	29.08.83
Richards, Marc	6. 0	Blackburn Rov.	Wolverhampton	8.07.82
Smith, Martin	5.11	Huddersfield Town	Sunderland	13.11.74
Stamp, Darryn	6. 2	Scarborough	Beverley	21.09.78
Youngs, Tom	5. 9	Cambridge Utd.	Bury St Edmunds	31.08.79

OXFORD UNITED

Ground: The Kassam Stadium, Grenoble Road, Oxford OX4 4XP.
Telephone: 01865 337500. **Club nickname:** U's.
First-choice colours: Yellow and navy shirts; navy shorts; navy and yellow stockings.
Main Sponsor: Buildbase. **Capacity for 2003-04:** 12,500.
Record attendance: (Manor Ground) 22,730 v Preston N.E. (F.A. Cup 6) 29 February, 1964. (Kassam Stadium) 12,177 v Aston Villa (League Cup 3) 7 November, 2002.

Name	Height ft. in.	Previous club	Birthplace	Birthdate
Goalkeepers				
Cox, Simon	5.11	–	Clapham	24.03.84
Woodman, Andy	6. 1	Colchester Utd.	Camberwell	11.08.71
Defenders				
Bound, Matthew	6. 2	Swansea City	Melksham	6.11.72
Crosby, Andy	6. 2	Brighton & H.A.	Rotherham	3.03.73
McNiven, Scott	5.10	Oldham Athletic	Leeds	2.05.78
Robinson, Matt	5.11	Reading	Exeter	23.12.74
Waterman, David	5.11	Portsmouth	Guernsey	16.05.77
Midfielders				
Brooks, Jamie	5. 9	–	Oxford	12.08.80
Hackett, Chris	6. 1	–	Oxford	1.03.83
Hunt, James	5. 8	Northampton Town	Derby	17.12.76
Savage, Dave	6. 1	Northampton Town	Dublin	30.07.73
Townsley, Derek	6. 4	Hibernain	Carlisle	21.03.73

Whitehead, Dean	5. 8	–	Oxford	12.01.82
Forwards				
Alsop, Julian	6. 4	Cheltenham Town	Nuneaton	28.05.73
Louis, Jefferson	6. 2	–	Harrow	22.02.79
Omoyinmi, Manny	5. 6	West Ham Utd.	Nigeria	28.12.77
Rawle, Mark	5.11	Southend Utd.	Leicester	27.04.79
Scott, Andy	6. 1	Brentford	Epsom	2.08.72
Steele, Lee	5. 8	Brighton & H.A.	Liverpool	12.07.73

ROCHDALE

Ground: Spotland, Wilbutts Lane, Rochdale OL11 5DS.
Telephone: 01706 644648. **Club nickname:** Dale.
First-choice colours: Blue and white shirts; blue and white shorts; blue and white stockings.
Main Sponsor: Keytech. **Capacity for 2003-04:** 10,203.
Record attendance: 24,231 v Notts Co. (F.A. Cup 2) 10 December, 1949.

Name	Height ft. in.	Previous club	Birthplace	Birthdate
Goalkeepers				
Edwards, Neil	5. 8	Stockport Co.	Aberdare	5.12.70
Gilks, Matthew	6. 1	–	Rochdale	4.06.82
Defenders				
Burgess, Daryl	5.11	Northampton Town	Birmingham	24.01.71
Doughty, Matthew	5.11	Chester City	Warrington	2.11.81
Duffy, Lee	5.10	–	Oldham	24.07.82
Evans, Wayne	5.10	Walsall	Welshpool	25.08.71
Griffiths, Gareth	6. 4	Wigan Athletic	Winsford	10.04.70
Grand, Simon	5.10	–	Chorley	23.02.84
Hill, Steven	5.10	–	Prescott	12.11.82
Warner, Scott	5.11	–	–	3.12.83
Midfielders				
Beech, Chris	5.11	Huddersfield Town	Blackpool	16.09.74
McCourt, Patrick	5.10	–	Derry	16.12.83
Forwards				
Connor, Paul	6. 2	Stoke City	Bishop Auckland	12.01.79
McEvilly, Lee	6. 0	Burscough	Liverpool	15.04.82
Patterson, Rory	5.11	–	–	16.07.84
Townson, Kevin	5. 6	–	Kirkby	19.04.83

SCUNTHORPE UNITED

Ground: Glanford Park, Doncaster Road, Scunthorpe DN15 8TD.
Telephone: 01724 848077. **Club nickname:** Iron.
First-choice colours: White, claret and blue shirts; blue and white shorts; white, claret and blue stockings.
Main sponsor: Mercedes/H & L Garages. **Capacity for 2003-04:** 9,016.
Record attendance: (Old Show Ground) 23,935 v Portsmouth (F.A. Cup 4) 30 January, 1954. (Glanford Park) 8,775 v Rotherham Utd. (Div. 4) 1, May 1989.

Name	Height ft. in.	Previous club	Birthplace	Birthdate
Goalkeepers				
Evans, Tom	6. 1	Crystal Palace	Doncaster	13.12.76
Defenders				
Butler, Andrew	6. 0	–	Doncaster	4.11.83
Byrne, Cliff	6. 0	Sunderland	Dublin	26.04.82
Jackson, Mark	5.11	Leeds Utd.	Barnsley	30.09.77
McCombe, Jamie	6. 5	–	Scunthorpe	1.01.83
Ridley, Lee	5.10	–	Sunthorpe	5.12.81
Sharp, Kevin	5. 9	Huddersfield Town	Ontario	19.09.74

Stanton, Nathan	5. 9	–	Nottingham	6.05.81
Wilcox, Russ	6. 0	Preston N.E. N.E	Hemsworth	25.03.64
Midfielders				
Barwick, Terry	5.10	–	Doncaster	11.01.83
Beagrie, Peter	5. 9	Bradford City	Middlesbrough	28.11.65
Calvo Garcia, Alex	5.11	Eibar	Ordiza, Spa.	1.01.72
Featherstone, Lee	6. 0	Sheffield Utd.	Chesterfield	20.07.83
Graves, Wayne	5. 8	–	Scunthorpe	18.09.80
Kilford, Ian	5.10	Wigan Athletic	Bristol	6.10.73
Sparrow, Matthew	5.10	–	London	3.10.81
Forwards				
Hayes, Paul	6. 0	Norwich City	–	20.09.83
Parton, Andy	5.10	–	Doncaster	29.09.83
Torpey, Steve	6. 3	Bristol City	Islington	8.12.70

SOUTHEND UNITED

Ground: Roots Hall, Victoria Avenue, Southend SS2 6NQ.
Telephone: 01702 304050. **Clubcall**: 09068 121105. **Club nickname:** Shrimpers.
First-choice colours: Navy shirts; navy shorts; navy stockings.
Main sponsor: GKC Communicatons. **Capacity for 2003-04:** 12,343.
Record attendance: 31,033 v Liverpool (F.A. Cup 3) 10 January, 1979.

Name	Height ft. in.	Previous club	Birthplace	Birthdate
Goalkeepers				
Emberson, Carl	6. 2	Luton Town	Epsom	13.07.73
Defenders				
Bramble, Tesfaye	6. 1	Cambridge Utd. City	Ipswich	20.07.80
Cort, Leon	6. 2	Millwall	Southwark	11.09.79
Jupp, Duncan	6. 0	Wimbledon	Guildford	25.01.75
Stuart, Jamie	5.10	Bury	Southwark	15.10.76
Sutch, Daryl	6. 0	Norwich City	Beccles	11.09.71
Warren, Mark	6. 0	Notts Co.	Clapton	12.11.74
Whelan, Phil	6. 4	Oxford Utd.	Stockport	7.03.72
Midfielders				
Clark, Anthony	5.11	West Ham Utd.	Camden	5.10.84
Clark, Steve	6. 1	–	London	10.02.82
Maher, Kevin	5.11	Tottenham	Ilford	17.10.76
McSweeney, Dave	6. 0	–	Basildon	28.12.81
Strachan, Gavin	5.10	Peterborough Utd.	Aberdeen	23.12.78
Forwards				
Belgrave, Barrington	6. 0	Yeovil Town	Bedford	16.09.80
Broughton, Drewe	6. 3	Kidderminster Harr.	Hitchin	25.10.78
Marney, Daniel	5. 9	Brighton & H.A.	Sidcup	2.10.81

SWANSEA CITY

Ground: Vetch Field, Swansea SA1 3SU.
Telephone: 01792 633400. **Club nickname:** Swans.
First-choice colours: White and black shirts; white and black shorts; white and black stockings.
Main sponsor: The Travel House. **Capacity for 2003-04:** 13,500.
Record attendance: 32,786 v Arsenal (F.A. Cup 4) 17 February, 1968.

Name	Height ft. in.	Previous club	Birthplace	Birthdate
Goalkeepers				
Freestone, Roger	6. 3	Chelsea	Newport	19.08.68
Defenders				
Howard, Michael	5. 9	Tranmere Rov.	Birkenhead	2.12.78
Jones, Stuart	6. 0	–	Aberystwyth	14.03.84

Mumford, Andrew	6. 1	Llanelli	Neath	18.06.81
O'Leary, Kristian	5.11	–	Neath	30.08.77
Smith, Jason	6. 3	Tiverton Town	Birmingham	6.09.74
Midfielders				
Britton, Leon	5. 5	West Ham Utd.	London	16.09.82
Corbisiero, Antonio	5.10	–	Exmouth	17.11.84
Durkan, Kieron	5.10	Rochdale	Chester	1.12.73
Jenkins, Lee	5. 9	–	Pontypool	28.06.79
Martinez, Roberto	5. 9	Walsall	Balaguer, Spa.	13.07.73
Maylett, Bradley	5. 8	Burnley	Manchester	24.12.80
Forwards				
Coates, Jon	5. 8	Woking	Swansea	27.06.75
Johnrose, Lenny	5.11	Bury	Preston	29.11.69
Nugent, Kevin	6. 1	Leyton Orient	Edmonton	10.04.69
Rawle, Mark	5.11	Southend Utd.	Leicester	24.07.79
Steins, Craig	5. 8	–	Swansea	31.07.84
Thomas, James	6. 0	Blackburn Rov.	Swansea	16.01.79
Trundle, Lee	6. 0	Wrexham	Liverpool	10.10.76

TORQUAY UNITED

Ground: Plainmoor, Torquay TQ1 3PS.
Telephone: 01803 328666. **Club nickname:** Gulls.
First-choice colours: Yellow shirts; blue shorts; yellow stockings.
Main sponsor: Sparkworld. **Capacity for 2003-04:** 6,283.
Record attendance: 21,908 v Huddersfield Town (F.A. Cup 4) 29 January, 1955.

Name	Height ft. in.	Previous club	Birthplace	Birthdate
Goalkeepers				
Dearden, Kevin	5.11	Wrexham	Luton	8.03.70
Van Heusden, Arjan	6. 3	Mansfield Town	Alphen, Hol.	11.12.72
Defenders				
Canoville, Lee	6. 1	Arsenal	Ealing	14.03.81
Hankin, Sean	5.11	Crystal Palace	Camberley	28.02.81
Hazell, Reuben	5.11	Tranmere Rov.	Birmingham	24.04.79
Hockley, Matthew	5.11	–	Paignton	5.06.82
Taylor, Craig	6. 1	Plymouth Argyle	Plymouth	24.01.74
Woods, Steve	5.11	Chesterfield	Davenham	5.12.76
Woozley, David	6. 0	Crystal Palace	Ascot	6.12.79
Midfielders				
Benefield, Jimmy	5.11	–	Bristol	6.05.83
Fowler, Jason	6. 0	Cardiff City	Bristol	20.08.74
Goodridge, Greg	5.10	Bristol City	Barbados	10.07.71
Hill, Kevin	5. 8	Torrington	Exeter	6.03.76
Russell, Alex	5. 9	Cambridge Utd.	Crosby	17.03.73
Wills, Kevin	5. 9	Plymouth Argyle	Torbay	15.10.80
Forwards				
Bedeau, Tony	5.10	–	Hammersmith	24.03.79
Graham, David	5.10	Dunfermline	Edinburgh	6.10.78
Gritton, Martin	6. 1	Plymouth Argyle	Glasgow	1.06.78
Kuffour, Jo	5. 6	Arsenal	Edmonton	17.11.81

YEOVIL TOWN

Ground: Huish Park, Lufton Way, Yeovil BA22 8YF.
Telephone: 01935 423662. **Club nickname:** Glovers.
First-choice colours: Green and white shirts; white shorts; green socks.
Main sponsor: Bradford City Building Supplies. **Capacity for 2003-04:** 9,107.
Record attendance: 8,868 v Rushden and Diamonds (Conf) 21 April, 2001.

Name	Height ft. in.	Previous club	Birthplace	Birthdate
Goalkeepers				
Stephen Collis	6.1	Tiverton Town	Barnet	18.03.81
Chris Weale	6.1	–	Yeovil	9.02.82
Defenders				
Lockwood, Adam	6.0	Reading	Wakefield	26.10.81
O'Brien, Roy	6.1	Bournemouth	Cork	27.11.74
Pluck, Colin	6.0	Dover	London	6.09.78
Skiverton, Terry	6.1	Welling	London	20.06.75
White, Tom	5.11	Bristol Rov.	Bristol	26.01.76
Midfielders				
Crittenden, Nick	5.8	Chelsea	Bracknell	11.11.78
El Kholti, Abdel	5.10	–	France	17.10.80
Johnson, Lee	5.6	Watford	Newmarket	7.06.81
Lindegaard, Andy	5.10	–	Yeovil	10.09.80
McIndoe, Michael	5.8	Hereford Utd.	Edinburgh	2.12.79
Williams, Gavin	5.10	Hereford Utd	Merthy Tydfil	20.07.80.
Way, Darren	5.11	Norwich City	Plymouth	21.11.79
Forwards				
Giles, Chris	6.1	Sherborne	Milborne Port	16.04.82
Jackson, Kirk	5.11	Stevenage Borough	Barnsley	16.10.76
Stansfield, Adam	5.11	Elmore	Tiverton	10.09.78

YORK CITY

Ground: Bootham Crescent, York YO3 7AQ.
Telephone: 0870 777 1922. **Club nickname:** Minstermen.
First-choice colours: Red shirts; red shorts; red stockings.
Main sponsor: Phoenix Software. **Capacity for 2003-04:** 9,496.
Record attendance: 28,123 v Huddersfield Town (F.A. Cup 6) 5 March 1938.

Name	Height ft. in.	Previous club	Birthplace	Birthdate
Goalkeepers				
Collinson, John	6. 0	–	Middlesbrough	4.03.83
Defenders				
Cooper, Richard	5. 9	Nott'm. Forest	Nottingham	27.09.79
Edmondson, Darren	6. 0	Huddersfield Town	Ulverston	4.11.71
Hobson, Gary	6. 2	Chester City	North Ferriby	12.11.72
Jones, Scott	5.10	Bristol Rov.	Sheffield	1.05.75
Okoli, James	6. 1	–	Nigeria	11.01.76
Smith, Chris	5.11	Reading	Derby	30.06.81
Wise, Stuart	6. 0	–	Middlesbrough	4.04.84
Midfielders				
Brackstone, Stephen	5.11	Middlesbrough	Hartlepool	19.09.82
Brass, Chris	5. 9	Burnley	Easington	24.07.75
Bullock, Lee	6. 1	–	Stockton	22.05.81
Fox, Christian	5.11	–	Auchenbrae	11.04.81
O'Kane, Aiden	5. 8	Cliftonville	Belfast	24.11.79
Wood, Leigh	5.11	–	Selby	4.04.84
Forwards				
Nogan, Lee	5.11	Luton Town	Cardiff	21.05.69
Parkin, Jonathan	6. 4	Barnsley	Barnsley	30.12.81

SCOTTISH PREMIER LEAGUE SQUADS 2003-04

ABERDEEN

Goalkeepers: Ryan Esson, Peter Kjaer, Mark Peat, David Preece.
Defenders: Russell Anderson, Eric Deloumeaux, Alexander Diamond, Robert Hedderman, Philip McGuire, Kevin McNaughton, Jamie McQuilken, Scott Morrison, Steve Payne, Kevin Rutkiewicz.
Midfielders: Patricio Billio, Bobby Duncan, Nicolas Fabiano, Richard Foster, Scott Muirhead, Ross O'Donoghue, Paul Sheerin, Kevin Souter, Fergus Tiernan, Steve Tosh, Darren Young.
Forwards: Michael Bird, Scott Booth, Chris Clark, Laurent D'Jaffo, Michael Hart, Leigh Hinds, Darren Mackie, Scott Michie, Leon Mike, Derek Young. **Manager:** Steve Paterson.

CELTIC

Goalkeepers: Javier Sanchez Broto, Rob Douglas, Magnus Hedman, Michael Herbert, David Marshall.
Defenders: Bobo Balde, Tom Boyd, Stephen Crainey, John Kennedy, Ulrik Laursen, Johan Mjallby, John-Paul McGovern, Joos Valgaeren, Stanislav Varga.
Midfielders: Didier Agathe, Mark Fotheringham, Steve Guppy, Colin Healy, Paul Lambert, Neil Lennon, Jackie McNamara, Liam Miller, Bobby Petta, Stilian Petrov, Mohammed Sylla, Alan Thompson, Ross Wallace.
Forwards: Craig Beattie, David Fernandez, John Hartson, Henrik Larsson, Shaun Maloney, Paul Shields, Jamie Smith, Chris Sutton. **Manager:** Martin O'Neill.

DUNDEE

Goalkeepers: James Langfield, Julian Speroni, Derek Soutar.
Defenders: Gavin Beith, Jonay Hernandez, Tom Hutchinson, Zura Khizanishvili, David Mackay, Marcello Marrocco, Barry Smith, Lee Wilkie.
Midfielders: Javier Artero, Garry Brady, Kris Brash, Gavin Beith, Beto Carranza, Barry Forbes, Lee Mair, David McLean, Georgi Nemsadze, Gavin Rae, Steven Robb, Mark Robertson, Juan Sara.
Forwards: Colin Boylan, Fabian Caballero, Steve Lovell, Steven Milne, Nacho Novo. **Manager:** Jim Duffy.

DUNDEE UNITED

Goalkeepers: Tony Bullock, Paul Gallacher, Paul Jarvie.
Defenders: Alan Archibald, Gary Bollan, Stuart Duff, Danny Griffin, Jim Lauchlan, Jean Licina, David McCracken, Scott Paterson, Mark Wilson.
Midfielders: Steven Carson, Stuart Duff, Craig Easton, Mark Kerr, Jim McIntyre, Charlie Miller, Stephen O'Donnell, Danny Ogunmade, Jim Paterson, Barry Robson.
Forwards: Aaron Conway, Owen Coyle, Billy Dodds, Arnar Gunnlaugsson, Jim Hamilton, Derek Lilley, Stephen McConalogue, Stephen McGowan, Sean O'Connor, Allan Smart, Colin Samuel. **Manager:** Ian McCall.

DUNFERMLINE ATHLETIC

Goalkeepers: Ross Harrower, Sean Murdoch, Marco Ruitenbeek, Derek Stillie.
Defenders: Jason Dair, Andrei Karnebeek, Angus MacPherson, Chris McGroarty, Youssef Rossi, Andrius Skerla, Scott Thomson, Kenny Tawse, Scott Walker, Scott Wilson.
Midfielders: Brian Blair, Steven Boyle, Lee Bullen, Ian Campbell, Gary Dempsey, George Fotheringham, Steven Hampshire, Sean Kilgallon, Gary Mason, Kevin McLeish, Mark McGarty, David Nicholls, Barry Nicholson, Michael Panapolous, Stewart Petrie.
Forwards: Craig Brewster, Patrick Clark, Stephen Crawford, Jim Hamilton, Noel Hunt, Scott McNicol, Billy Mehmet, Gary Sutherland. **Manager:** Jimmy Calderwood.

HEARTS

Goalkeepers: Craig Gordon, Roddy, McKenzie, Lee Windrum.
Defenders: David Dunn, Patrick Kisnorbo, John Knox, Stephane Mahe, Alan Maybury, Austin McCann, Kevin McKenna, Paul McMullan, Steven Pressley, Elliot Smith, Andy Webster.
Midfielders: Steven Boyack, Liam Fox, Paul Hartley, Neil Janczyk, Neil MacFarlane, David McGeown, Paul McLaughlin, Robbie Neilson, Wilfred Oueifio, Scott Severin, Phil Stamp, Stephen Simmons, Kevin Twaddle, Jean-Louis Valois, James Winning.
Forwards: Ryan Davidson, Mark de Vries, Joe Hamill, Mathu King, Andy Kirk, Robert Sloan, Gary Wales, Graham Weir, Dennis Wyness. **Manager:** Craig Levein.

HIBERNIAN

Goalkeepers: Daniel Andersson, Alistair Brown, Nick Colgan, Ian Westwater.
Defenders: Allan Dempsie, Matthias Doumbe, Paul Fenwick, Paul Hilland, Janos Matyus, Ian Murray, Gary Smith, Yannick Zambernardi.
Midfielders: Frederic Arpinon, Grant Brebner, Stephen Glass, Matthias Jack, Tom McManus, Kevin Nicol, John O'Neil, Kevin O'Neill, Alen Orman, Alan Reid, Steven Whittaker, Jarkko Wiss.
Forwards: Scott Brown, Frederic Daquin, Stephen Dobbie, Tom McManus, Garry O'Connor, Mixu Paatelainen, Derek Riordan. **Manager:** Bobby Williamson.

KILMARNOCK

Goalkeepers: Colin Meldrum, Craig Samson, Graeme Smith.
Defenders: Sean Dillon, Freddy Dindeleux, Garry Hay, Robbie Henderson, Sean Hessey, Chris Innes, Barry McLaughlin, Greg Shields.
Midfielders: Peter Canero, Mark Canning, James Fowler, Steve Fulton, Martin Hardie, Gary Locke, Alan Mahood, Gary McDonald, Andy McLaren, Stephen Murray, Jose Quitongo, Jesus Garcia Sanjuan.
Forwards: Kris Boyd, Craig Dargo, Paul Di Giacomo, Emillio Jaconelli, Gary McSwegan, David Merdy. **Manager:** Jim Jefferies.

LIVINGSTON

Goalkeepers: Allan Creer, Alan Main, Fernando Lopez, David McEwan.
Defenders: Marvin Andrews, Philippe Brinquin, Emmanuel Dorado, Eamonn Fullerton, James McAllister, David McNamee. Julian Maidana, Rubio, William Snowdon.
Midfielders: Juan Jose Camacho, Tom English, Stuart Lovell, Lee Makel, Cherif-Toure Maman, Scott McLaughlin, Steven Miller, Burton O'Brien, Paddy Quinn, Francisco Quino, Barry Wilson.
Forwards: Richard Brittain, Eugene Dadi, Derek Lilley, Colin McMenamin, Fernando Pasquinelli, Stephen Whalen, Davide Xausa. **Manager:** Marcio Maximo Barcellos.

MOTHERWELL

Goalkeepers: Gordon Marshall, Jamie Ewings.
Defenders: David Black, David Clarke, Martyn Corrigan, Stephen Craigan, John Crawley, Brian Dempsie, Steven Hammell, Chris Higgins, Graeme Mathie, Kevin McDonald, David Partridge, Daniel Sengewald.
Midfielders: Ross Ballantyne, Andrew Bell, David Cowan, Shaun Fagan, William Kinniburgh, Keith Lasley, Scott Leitch, James McFadden, Stephen Pearson, Kenneth Wright.
Forwards: Derek Adams. Alex Burns, David Clarkson, Steven Craig, Darren Jack, Khaled Khemas, Andrew Scott. **Manager:** Terry Butcher.

PARTICK THISTLE

Goalkeepers: Kenny Arthur, Kevin Budinaukas, Steve Pinkowski.
Defenders: Eddie Forrest, Paul Kaczan, David Lilley, Colin Miller, Kenny Milne, Grant Murray, Mark Thomson, Derek Whyte.
Midfielders: Stephane Bonnes, James Boyle, Derek Fleming, Andy Gibson, Willie Howie, John Paul McBride, Jamie Mitchell, Andy Ross, Ian Ross, David Rowson, Gavin Rushford, Stuart Taylor, Ricky Waddell.
Forwards: Gerry Britton. James Grady, Emmanuel Panther, Matthew Shields, Andy Thomson. **Manager:** John Lambie.

RANGERS

Goalkeepers: Jesper Christiansen, Stefan Klos, Allan McGregor.
Defenders: Iain Chalmers, Andy Dowie, Billy Gibson, Bob Malcolm, Craig Moore, Kevin Muscat, Tero Penttila, Fernando Ricksen, Maurice Ross, Kirk Willoughby.
Midfielders: Dariusz Adamczuk, Mikel Arteta, Michael Ball, Chris Burke, Ronald de Boer, Barry Ferguson, Stephen Hughes, Jim Gibson, Paul McHale, Christian Nerlinger, Ben Stevens, David Young.
Forwards: Shota Arveladze, John Brighton & H.A., Capucho, Alex Hauser, Peter Lovenkrands, Steven McAdam, Michael Mols, Neil McCann, Steven Thompson.
Manager: Alex McLeish.

QUOTE-UNQUOTE

'We were obviously saving the best for last' – **Sean O'Driscoll**, Bournemouth manager, after his side scored five goals for the first time all season in the Third Division Play-off Final against Lincoln City.

'At least I got a nice new suit out of it' – **Keith Alexander**, Lincoln City manager, puts a brave face on defeat.

'I feel very humble following that man on this stage' – **Sir Bobby Robson**, Newcastle United manager, on brave boxer Michael Watson at the Variety Club's annual awards lunch.

'I'm sorry if it looked bad. It won't happen again' – **Sven Goran Eriksson** after four of his England players wore the captain's armband during the friendly against Serbia-Montenegro.

LEAGUE FIXTURES 2003-2004

Saturday, 9 August
Nationwide League Division One
Bradford City v Norwich City
Burnley v Crystal Palace
Derby Co. v Stoke City
Ipswich Town v Reading
Millwall v Wigan Athletic
Nott'm. Forest v Sunderland
Preston N.E. v West Ham Utd.
Rotherham Utd. v Cardiff City
Sheffield Utd. v Gillingham
Walsall v W.B.A.
Watford v Coventry City
Wimbledon v Crewe Alexandra

Nationwide League Division Two
Barnsley v Colchester Utd.
Bristol City v Notts Co.
Luton Town v Rushden & D'monds
Oldham Athletic v Brighton & H.A.
Peterborough Utd. v Hartlepool Utd.
Plymouth Argyle v Grimsby Town
Port Vale v Bournemouth
Q.P.R. v Blackpool
Swindon Town v Sheffield Wed.
Tranmere Rov. v Brentford
Wrexham v Chesterfield
Wycombe Wand. v Stockport Co.

Nationwide League Division Three
Carlisle Utd. v York City
Huddersfield Town v Cambridge Utd.
Hull City v Darlington
Kidderminster Harr. v Mansfield Town
Leyton Orient v Doncaster Rov.
Lincoln City v Oxford Utd.
Macclesfield Town v Boston Utd.
Northampton Town v Torquay Utd.
Rochdale v Yeovil Town
Scunthorpe Utd. v Bristol Rov.
Southend Utd. v Cheltenham Town
Swansea City v Bury

Friday, 15 August
Nationwide League Division Two
Colchester Utd. v Swindon Town

Saturday, 16 August
F.A. Barclaycard Premiership
Arsenal v Everton
Birmingham City v Tottenham
Blackburn Rov. v Wolves
Fulham v Middlesbrough
Leicester City v Southampton
Manchester Utd. v Bolton Wand.
Portsmouth v Aston Villa

Nationwide League Division One
Cardiff City v Bradford City
Coventry City v Walsall
Crewe Alexandra v Ipswich Town
Crystal Palace v Watford
Gillingham v Derby Co.
Norwich City v Rotherham Utd.
Reading v Nott'm. Forest
Stoke City v Wimbledon
Sunderland v Millwall
W.B.A. v Burnley
West Ham Utd. v Sheffield Utd.
Wigan Athletic v Preston N.E.

Nationwide League Division Two
Blackpool v Wycombe Wand.
Bournemouth v Barnsley
Brentford v Peterborough Utd.
Chesterfield v Bristol City
Grimsby Town v Port Vale
Hartlepool Utd. v Tranmere Rov.
Notts Co. v Wrexham
Rushden & D'monds v Plymouth Argyle
Sheffield Wed. v Oldham Athletic
Stockport Co. v Luton Town

Nationwide League Division Three
Boston Utd. v Huddersfield Town
Bristol Rov. v Rochdale
Bury v Scunthorpe Utd.
Cambridge Utd. v Macclesfield Town
Cheltenham Town v Swansea City
Darlington v Kidderminster Harr.
Doncaster Rov. v Southend Utd.
Mansfield Town v Leyton Orient
Oxford Utd. v Hull City
Torquay Utd. v Lincoln City
Yeovil Town v Carlisle Utd.
York City v Northampton Town

Sunday, 17 August
F.A. Barclaycard Premiership
Charlton Athletic v Manchester City
Leeds Utd. v Newcastle Utd.
Liverpool v Chelsea

Monday, 18 August
Nationwide League Division Two
Brighton & H.A. v Q.P.R.

Friday, 22 August
Nationwide League Division Three
Northampton Town v Darlington
Swansea City v Boston Utd.

Saturday, 23 August
F.A. Barclaycard Premiership
Bolton Wand. v Blackburn Rov.
Chelsea v Leicester City
Everton v Fulham
Manchester City v Portsmouth
Newcastle Utd. v Manchester Utd.
Southampton v Birmingham City
Tottenham v Leeds Utd.
Wolves v Charlton Athletic

Nationwide League Division One
Bradford City v Gillingham
Burnley v Wigan Athletic
Derby Co. v Reading
Ipswich Town v Coventry City
Millwall v Crewe Alexandra
Nott'm. Forest v Cardiff City
Preston N.E. v Sunderland
Rotherham Utd. v West Ham Utd.
Sheffield Utd. v Norwich City
Walsall v Stoke City
Watford v W.B.A.
Wimbledon v Crystal Palace

Nationwide League Division Two
Barnsley v Brighton & H.A.
Bristol City v Hartlepool Utd.
Luton Town v Grimsby Town
Oldham Athletic v Blackpool
Peterborough Utd. v Sheffield Wed.
Plymouth Argyle v Stockport Co.
Port Vale v Colchester Utd.
Q.P.R. v Bournemouth
Swindon Town v Notts Co.
Tranmere Rov. v Rushden & D'monds
Wrexham v Brentford
Wycombe Wand. v Chesterfield

Nationwide League Division Three
Carlisle Utd. v Bristol Rov.
Huddersfield Town v York City
Hull City v Cheltenham Town
Kidderminster Harr. v Bury
Leyton Orient v Yeovil Town
Lincoln City v Doncaster Rov.
Macclesfield Town v Torquay Utd.
Rochdale v Cambridge Utd.
Scunthorpe Utd. v Oxford Utd.
Southend Utd. v Mansfield Town

Sunday, 24 August
F.A. Barclaycard Premiership
Aston Villa v Liverpool
Middlesbrough v Arsenal

Monday, 25 August
F.A. Barclaycard Premiership
Blackburn Rov. v Manchester City

Nationwide League Division One
Cardiff City v Derby Co.
Crewe Alexandra v Walsall
Gillingham v Burnley
Reading v Rotherham Utd.
Sunderland v Watford
W.B.A. v Preston N.E.

Nationwide League Division Two
Blackpool v Barnsley
Bournemouth v Swindon Town
Brentford v Oldham Athletic
Brighton & H.A. v Luton Town
Chesterfield v Plymouth Argyle
Grimsby Town v Wycombe Wand.
Hartlepool Utd. v Port Vale
Notts Co. v Peterborough Utd.
Rushden & D'monds v Q.P.R.
Sheffield Wed. v Wrexham
Stockport Co. v Tranmere Rov.

Nationwide League Division Three
Boston Utd. v Carlisle Utd.
Bristol Rov. v Macclesfield Town
Bury v Lincoln City
Cambridge Utd. v Hull City
Cheltenham Town v Kidderminster Harr.
Darlington v Leyton Orient
Doncaster Rov. v Huddersfield Town
Mansfield Town v Scunthorpe Utd.
Oxford Utd. v Swansea City
Torquay Utd. v Rochdale
Yeovil Town v Northampton Town

Tuesday, 26 August
F.A. Barclaycard Premiership
Arsenal v Aston Villa
Birmingham City v Chelsea
Charlton Athletic v Everton
Leeds Utd. v Southampton
Leicester City v Middlesbrough
Portsmouth v Bolton Wand.

Nationwide League Division One
Crystal Palace v Sheffield Utd.
Norwich City v Wimbledon
Stoke City v Millwall
West Ham Utd. v Bradford City
Wigan Athletic v Ipswich Town

Nationwide League Division Two
Colchester Utd. v Bristol City

Nationwide League Division Three
York City v Southend Utd.

Wednesday, 27 August
F.A. Barclaycard Premiership
Liverpool v Tottenham
Manchester Utd. v Wolves

Nationwide League Division One
Coventry City v Nott'm. Forest

Saturday, 30 August
F.A. Barclaycard Premiership
Aston Villa v Leicester City
Bolton Wand. v Charlton Athletic
Chelsea v Blackburn Rov.
Everton v Liverpool
Middlesbrough v Leeds Utd.
Newcastle Utd. v Birmingham City
Tottenham v Fulham
Wolves v Portsmouth

Nationwide League Division One
Bradford City v Sunderland
Burnley v Crewe Alexandra
Derby Co. v W.B.A.
Ipswich Town v West Ham Utd.
Millwall v Crystal Palace
Nott'm. Forest v Norwich City
Preston N.E. v Stoke City
Rotherham Utd. v Wigan Athletic
Sheffield Utd. v Coventry City
Walsall v Cardiff City
Watford v Gillingham
Wimbledon v Reading

Nationwide League Division Two
Barnsley v Notts Co.
Bristol City v Grimsby Town
Luton Town v Hartlepool Utd.
Oldham Athletic v Rushden & D'monds
Peterborough Utd. v Stockport Co.
Plymouth Argyle v Brighton & H.A.
Port Vale v Brentford
Q.P.R. v Chesterfield
Swindon Town v Blackpool
Tranmere Rov. v Colchester Utd.
Wrexham v Bournemouth

Nationwide League Division Three
Carlisle Utd. v Cambridge Utd.
Huddersfield Town v Bristol Rov.
Hull City v Boston Utd.
Kidderminster Harr. v Oxford Utd.
Leyton Orient v Cheltenham Town
Lincoln City v York City
Macclesfield Town v Yeovil Town
Northampton Town v Doncaster Rov.
Rochdale v Darlington
Scunthorpe Utd. v Torquay Utd.
Southend Utd. v Bury
Swansea City v Mansfield Town

Sunday, 31 August
F.A. Barclaycard Premiership
Manchester City v Arsenal
Southampton v Manchester Utd.

Monday, 1 September
Nationwide League Division Two
Wycombe Wand. v Sheffield Wed.

Friday, 5 September
Nationwide League Division Three
Cambridge Utd. v Lincoln City
Cheltenham Town v Northampton Town

Saturday, 6 September
Nationwide League Division One
Cardiff City v Watford
Coventry City v Bradford City
Crewe Alexandra v Preston N.E.
Crystal Palace v Ipswich Town
Gillingham v Millwall
Norwich City v Derby Co.
Reading v Walsall
Stoke City v Burnley
Sunderland v Rotherham Utd.
W.B.A. v Wimbledon
West Ham Utd. v Nott'm. Forest
Wigan Athletic v Sheffield Utd.

Nationwide League Division Two
Blackpool v Wrexham
Bournemouth v Bristol City
Brentford v Plymouth Argyle
Brighton & H.A. v Swindon Town
Chesterfield v Barnsley
Colchester Utd. v Q.P.R.
Grimsby Town v Peterborough Utd.
Hartlepool Utd. v Oldham Athletic
Notts Co. v Luton Town
Rushden & D'monds v Wycombe Wand.
Sheffield Wed. v Tranmere Rov.
Stockport Co. v Port Vale

Nationwide League Division Three
Boston Utd. v Scunthorpe Utd.
Bristol Rov. v Kidderminster Harr.
Bury v Huddersfield Town
Darlington v Carlisle Utd.
Mansfield Town v Macclesfield Town
Oxford Utd. v Southend Utd.
Torquay Utd. v Leyton Orient
Yeovil Town v Swansea City
York City v Rochdale

Monday, 8 September
Nationwide League Division Three
Doncaster Rov. v Hull City

Friday, 12 September
Nationwide League Division Two
Hartlepool Utd. v Grimsby Town

Saturday, 13 September
F.A. Barclaycard Premiership
Arsenal v Portsmouth
Blackburn Rov. v Liverpool
Bolton Wand. v Middlesbrough
Charlton Athletic v Manchester Utd.
Chelsea v Tottenham
Everton v Newcastle Utd.
Southampton v Wolves

Nationwide League Division One
Bradford City v Preston N.E.
Cardiff City v Gillingham
Coventry City v Stoke City
Norwich City v Burnley
Nott'm. Forest v Sheffield Utd.
Rotherham Utd. v Crewe Alexandra
Sunderland v Crystal Palace
Walsall v Derby Co.
Watford v Millwall
W.B.A. v Ipswich Town
West Ham Utd. v Reading
Wimbledon v Wigan Athletic

Nationwide League Division Two
Blackpool v Bournemouth
Chesterfield v Notts Co.
Colchester Utd. v Brighton & H.A.
Oldham Athletic v Bristol City
Plymouth Argyle v Luton Town
Port Vale v Barnsley
Q.P.R. v Wycombe Wand.
Rushden & D'monds v Brentford
Sheffield Wed. v Stockport Co.
Swindon Town v Wrexham
Tranmere Rov. v Peterborough Utd.

Nationwide League Division Three
Bristol Rov. v Boston Utd.
Bury v Cheltenham Town
Cambridge Utd. v Torquay Utd.
Carlisle Utd. v Rochdale
Darlington v Doncaster Rov.
Huddersfield Town v Northampton Town
Hull City v Southend Utd.
Lincoln City v Leyton Orient
Macclesfield Town v Kidderminster Harr.
Oxford Utd. v Mansfield Town
Scunthorpe Utd. v Swansea City
Yeovil Town v York City

Sunday, 14 September
F.A. Barclaycard Premiership
Birmingham City v Fulham
Manchester City v Aston Villa

Monday, 15 September
F.A. Barclaycard Premiership
Leicester City v Leeds Utd.

Tuesday, 16 September
Nationwide League Division One
Burnley v Nott'm. Forest
Crewe Alexandra v West Ham Utd.
Crystal Palace v Bradford City
Gillingham v Norwich City
Ipswich Town v Walsall
Millwall v Wimbledon
Preston N.E. v Coventry City
Reading v Cardiff City
Sheffield Utd. v Rotherham Utd.
Stoke City v Sunderland
Wigan Athletic v W.B.A.

Nationwide League Division Two
Barnsley v Oldham Athletic
Bournemouth v Sheffield Wed.
Brentford v Blackpool
Brighton & H.A. v Chesterfield
Bristol City v Tranmere Rov.
Grimsby Town v Swindon Town
Luton Town v Port Vale
Notts Co. v Rushden & D'monds
Peterborough Utd. v Plymouth Argyle
Stockport Co. v Hartlepool Utd.
Wrexham v Q.P.R.
Wycombe Wand. v Colchester Utd.

Nationwide League Division Three
Cheltenham Town v Oxford Utd.
Doncaster Rov. v Yeovil Town
Kidderminster Harr. v Scunthorpe Utd.
Leyton Orient v Hull City
Mansfield Town v Bury
Northampton Town v Carlisle Utd.
Rochdale v Huddersfield Town
Southend Utd. v Lincoln City
Swansea City v Macclesfield Town
Torquay Utd. v Bristol Rov.

York City v Darlington

Wednesday, 17 September
Nationwide League Division One
Derby Co. v Watford

Nationwide League Division Three
Boston Utd. v Cambridge Utd.

Saturday, 20 September
F.A. Barclaycard Premiership
Aston Villa v Charlton Athletic
Fulham v Manchester City
Leeds Utd. v Birmingham City
Liverpool v Leicester City
Newcastle Utd. v Bolton Wand.
Portsmouth v Blackburn Rov.
Tottenham v Southampton
Wolves v Chelsea

Nationwide League Division One
Burnley v Bradford City
Crewe Alexandra v Nott'm. Forest
Crystal Palace v W.B.A.
Derby Co. v Sunderland
Gillingham v West Ham Utd.
Ipswich Town v Wimbledon
Millwall v Walsall
Preston N.E. v Rotherham Utd.
Reading v Coventry City
Sheffield Utd. v Cardiff City
Stoke City v Norwich City
Wigan Athletic v Watford

Nationwide League Division Two
Barnsley v Swindon Town
Bournemouth v Rushden & D'monds
Brentford v Hartlepool Utd.
Brighton & H.A. v Sheffield Wed.
Bristol City v Port Vale
Grimsby Town v Chesterfield
Luton Town v Q.P.R.
Notts Co. v Tranmere Rov.
Peterborough Utd. v Colchester Utd.
Stockport Co. v Blackpool
Wrexham v Plymouth Argyle
Wycombe Wand. v Oldham Athletic

Nationwide League Division Three
Boston Utd. v Bury
Cheltenham Town v Cambridge Utd.
Doncaster Rov. v Oxford Utd.
Kidderminster Harr. v Lincoln City
Leyton Orient v Scunthorpe Utd.
Mansfield Town v Yeovil Town
Northampton Town v Macclesfield Town
Rochdale v Hull City
Southend Utd. v Carlisle Utd.
Swansea City v Huddersfield Town

Torquay Utd. v Darlington
York City v Bristol Rov.

Sunday, 21 September
F.A. Barclaycard Premiership
Manchester Utd. v Arsenal
Middlesbrough v Everton

Friday, 26 September
F.A. Barclaycard Premiership
Arsenal v Newcastle Utd.

Saturday, 27 September
F.A. Barclaycard Premiership
Birmingham City v Portsmouth
Blackburn Rov. v Fulham
Bolton Wand. v Wolves
Chelsea v Aston Villa
Everton v Leeds Utd.
Leicester City v Manchester Utd.
Southampton v Middlesbrough

Nationwide League Division One
Bradford City v Sheffield Utd.
Cardiff City v Crewe Alexandra
Coventry City v Wigan Athletic
Norwich City v Crystal Palace
Nott'm. Forest v Derby Co.
Rotherham Utd. v Gillingham
Sunderland v Reading
Walsall v Preston N.E.
Watford v Ipswich Town
W.B.A. v Stoke City
Wimbledon v Burnley

Nationwide League Division Two
Blackpool v Notts Co.
Chesterfield v Brentford
Colchester Utd. v Bournemouth
Hartlepool Utd. v Brighton & H.A.
Oldham Athletic v Luton Town
Plymouth Argyle v Barnsley
Port Vale v Wycombe Wand.
Q.P.R. v Bristol City
Rushden & D'monds v Stockport Co.
Sheffield Wed. v Grimsby Town
Swindon Town v Peterborough Utd.
Tranmere Rov. v Wrexham

Nationwide League Division Three
Bristol Rov. v Cheltenham Town
Bury v Doncaster Rov.
Cambridge Utd. v Mansfield Town
Carlisle Utd. v Swansea City
Darlington v Boston Utd.
Huddersfield Town v Leyton Orient
Hull City v Kidderminster Harr.
Lincoln City v Rochdale
Macclesfield Town v York City

Oxford Utd. v Northampton Town
Scunthorpe Utd. v Southend Utd.
Yeovil Town v Torquay Utd.

Sunday, 28 September
F.A. Barclaycard Premiership
Charlton Athletic v Liverpool
Manchester City v Tottenham

Nationwide League Division One
West Ham Utd. v Millwall

Monday, 29 September
Nationwide League Division One
Walsall v Gillingham

Tuesday, 30 September
Nationwide League Division One
Bradford City v Derby Co.
Cardiff City v Wigan Athletic
Norwich City v Reading
Rotherham Utd. v Stoke City
Sunderland v Ipswich Town
Watford v Burnley
W.B.A. v Millwall
Wimbledon v Sheffield Utd.

Nationwide League Division Two
Blackpool v Grimsby Town
Chesterfield v Bournemouth
Colchester Utd. v Brentford
Hartlepool Utd. v Wrexham
Oldham Athletic v Stockport Co.
Plymouth Argyle v Bristol City
Port Vale v Peterborough Utd.
Q.P.R. v Barnsley
Rushden & D'monds v Brighton & H.A.
Tranmere Rov. v Wycombe Wand.

Nationwide League Division Three
Bristol Rov. v Mansfield Town
Bury v York City
Cambridge Utd. v Doncaster Rov.
Carlisle Utd. v Leyton Orient
Darlington v Southend Utd.
Huddersfield Town v Kidderminster Harr.
Hull City v Swansea City
Lincoln City v Northampton Town
Macclesfield Town v Rochdale
Scunthorpe Utd. v Cheltenham Town
Yeovil Town v Boston Utd.

Wednesday, 1 October
Nationwide League Division One
Coventry City v Crewe Alexandra
Nott'm. Forest v Preston N.E.
West Ham Utd. v Crystal Palace

Nationwide League Division Two
Sheffield Wed. v Notts Co.
Swindon Town v Luton Town

Nationwide League Division Three
Oxford Utd. v Torquay Utd.

Saturday, 4 October
F.A. Barclaycard Premiership
Fulham v Leicester City
Leeds Utd. v Blackburn Rov.
Liverpool v Arsenal
Manchester Utd. v Birmingham City
Newcastle Utd. v Southampton
Portsmouth v Charlton Athletic
Tottenham v Everton
Wolves v Manchester City

Nationwide League Division One
Burnley v Walsall
Crewe Alexandra v Watford
Crystal Palace v Cardiff City
Derby Co. v West Ham Utd.
Gillingham v W.B.A.
Ipswich Town v Rotherham Utd.
Millwall v Coventry City
Preston N.E. v Wimbledon
Reading v Bradford City
Sheffield Utd. v Sunderland
Stoke City v Nott'm. Forest
Wigan Athletic v Norwich City

Nationwide League Division Two
Barnsley v Rushden & D'monds
Bournemouth v Hartlepool Utd.
Brentford v Sheffield Wed.
Brighton & H.A. v Blackpool
Bristol City v Swindon Town
Grimsby Town v Q.P.R.
Luton Town v Tranmere Rov.
Notts Co. v Colchester Utd.
Peterborough Utd. v Oldham Athletic
Stockport Co. v Chesterfield
Wrexham v Port Vale
Wycombe Wand. v Plymouth Argyle

Nationwide League Division Three
Boston Utd. v Oxford Utd.
Cheltenham Town v Yeovil Town
Doncaster Rov. v Bristol Rov.
Kidderminster Harr. v Carlisle Utd.
Leyton Orient v Macclesfield Town
Mansfield Town v Darlington
Northampton Town v Hull City
Rochdale v Scunthorpe Utd.
Southend Utd. v Huddersfield Town
Swansea City v Lincoln City
Torquay Utd. v Bury
York City v Cambridge Utd.

Sunday, 5 October
F.A. Barclaycard Premiership
Aston Villa v Bolton Wand.
Middlesbrough v Chelsea

Friday, 10 October
Nationwide League Division Two
Hartlepool Utd. v Sheffield Wed.

Saturday, 11 October
Nationwide League Division One
Bradford City v Ipswich Town
Burnley v Reading
Cardiff City v W.B.A.
Derby Co. v Wigan Athletic
Gillingham v Sunderland
Norwich City v Coventry City
Preston N.E. v Watford
Rotherham Utd. v Millwall
Sheffield Utd. v Crewe Alexandra
Stoke City v Crystal Palace
Walsall v Nott'm. Forest
Wimbledon v West Ham Utd.

Nationwide League Division Two
Barnsley v Wrexham
Brighton & H.A. v Grimsby Town
Bristol City v Peterborough Utd.
Colchester Utd. v Blackpool
Luton Town v Wycombe Wand.
Notts Co. v Bournemouth
Oldham Athletic v Port Vale
Plymouth Argyle v Tranmere Rov.
Q.P.R. v Brentford
Rushden & D'monds v Chesterfield
Swindon Town v Stockport Co.

Nationwide League Division Three
Boston Utd. v Cheltenham Town
Cambridge Utd. v Bury
Darlington v Bristol Rov.
Huddersfield Town v Torquay Utd.
Kidderminster Harr. v Southend Utd.
Leyton Orient v Swansea City
Macclesfield Town v Doncaster Rov.
Mansfield Town v York City
Oxford Utd. v Yeovil Town
Rochdale v Northampton Town
Scunthorpe Utd. v Lincoln City

Sunday, 12 October
Nationwide League Division Three
Hull City v Carlisle Utd.

Tuesday, 14 October
Nationwide League Division One
Crewe Alexandra v Bradford City
Crystal Palace v Derby Co.
Ipswich Town v Burnley
Millwall v Preston N.E.
Reading v Gillingham
Sunderland v Cardiff City
Watford v Walsall
W.B.A. v Sheffield Utd.
Wigan Athletic v Stoke City

Wednesday, 15 October
F.A. Barclaycard Premiership
Fulham v Newcastle Utd.

Nationwide League Division One
Coventry City v Wimbledon
Nott'm. Forest v Rotherham Utd.
West Ham Utd. v Norwich City

Friday, 17 October
Nationwide League Division Three
Northampton Town v Scunthorpe Utd.

Saturday, 18 October
F.A. Barclaycard Premiership
Arsenal v Chelsea
Fulham v Wolves
Leeds Utd. v Manchester Utd.
Manchester City v Bolton Wand.
Middlesbrough v Newcastle Utd.
Portsmouth v Liverpool

Nationwide League Division One
Coventry City v Cardiff City
Crewe Alexandra v Derby Co.
Crystal Palace v Rotherham Utd.
Ipswich Town v Stoke City
Millwall v Sheffield Utd.
Nott'm. Forest v Wimbledon
Reading v Preston N.E.
Sunderland v Walsall
Watford v Bradford City
W.B.A. v Norwich City
West Ham Utd. v Burnley
Wigan Athletic v Gillingham

Nationwide League Division Two
Blackpool v Hartlepool Utd.
Bournemouth v Brighton & H.A.
Brentford v Luton Town
Chesterfield v Swindon Town
Grimsby Town v Colchester Utd.
Peterborough Utd. v Q.P.R.
Port Vale v Plymouth Argyle
Sheffield Wed. v Rushden & D'monds
Stockport Co. v Notts Co.
Tranmere Rov. v Oldham Athletic
Wrexham v Bristol City
Wycombe Wand. v Barnsley

Nationwide League Division Three
Bristol Rov. v Cambridge Utd.
Bury v Oxford Utd.
Carlisle Utd. v Macclesfield Town
Cheltenham Town v Rochdale
Doncaster Rov. v Mansfield Town
Lincoln City v Huddersfield Town
Southend Utd. v Leyton Orient
Swansea City v Kidderminster Harr.
Torquay Utd. v Hull City
Yeovil Town v Darlington
York City v Boston Utd.

Sunday, 19 October
F.A. Barclaycard Premiership
Birmingham City v Aston Villa
Everton v Southampton
Leicester City v Tottenham

Monday, 20 October
F.A. Barclaycard Premiership
Blackburn Rov. v Charlton Athletic

Tuesday, 21 October
Nationwide League Division Two
Blackpool v Rushden & D'monds
Bournemouth v Luton Town
Brentford v Brighton & H.A.
Chesterfield v Hartlepool Utd.
Grimsby Town v Notts Co.
Peterborough Utd. v Barnsley
Port Vale v Q.P.R.
Stockport Co. v Colchester Utd.
Tranmere Rov. v Swindon Town
Wrexham v Oldham Athletic
Wycombe Wand. v Bristol City

Nationwide League Division Three
Bristol Rov. v Leyton Orient
Bury v Hull City
Carlisle Utd. v Scunthorpe Utd.
Cheltenham Town v Darlington
Doncaster Rov. v Rochdale
Lincoln City v Macclesfield Town
Northampton Town v Kidderminster Harr.
Southend Utd. v Boston Utd.
Swansea City v Cambridge Utd.
Torquay Utd. v Mansfield Town
Yeovil Town v Huddersfield Town
York City v Oxford Utd.

Wednesday, 22 October
Nationwide League Division Two
Sheffield Wed. v Plymouth Argyle

Saturday, 25 October
F.A. Barclaycard Premiership
Aston Villa v Everton
Bolton Wand. v Birmingham City
Chelsea v Manchester City
Liverpool v Leeds Utd.
Manchester Utd. v Fulham
Newcastle Utd. v Portsmouth
Southampton v Blackburn Rov.
Wolves v Leicester City

Nationwide League Division One
Bradford City v Nott'm. Forest
Burnley v Millwall
Cardiff City v West Ham Utd.
Derby Co. v Coventry City
Gillingham v Crystal Palace
Norwich City v Sunderland
Preston N.E. v Ipswich Town
Rotherham Utd. v W.B.A.
Sheffield Utd. v Reading
Stoke City v Crewe Alexandra
Walsall v Wigan Athletic
Wimbledon v Watford

Nationwide League Division Two
Barnsley v Grimsby Town
Brighton & H.A. v Stockport Co.
Bristol City v Sheffield Wed.
Colchester Utd. v Chesterfield
Hartlepool Utd. v Wycombe Wand.
Luton Town v Peterborough Utd.
Notts Co. v Brentford
Oldham Athletic v Bournemouth
Plymouth Argyle v Blackpool
Q.P.R. v Tranmere Rov.
Rushden & D'monds v Wrexham
Swindon Town v Port Vale

Nationwide League Division Three
Boston Utd. v Torquay Utd.
Cambridge Utd. v Yeovil Town
Darlington v Bury
Huddersfield Town v Carlisle Utd.
Hull City v Lincoln City
Kidderminster Harr. v Doncaster Rov.
Leyton Orient v Northampton Town
Macclesfield Town v Southend Utd.
Mansfield Town v Cheltenham Town
Oxford Utd. v Bristol Rov.
Rochdale v Swansea City
Scunthorpe Utd. v York City

Sunday, 26 October
F.A. Barclaycard Premiership
Charlton Athletic v Arsenal
Tottenham v Middlesbrough

Friday, 31 October
Nationwide League Division Two
Wrexham v Colchester Utd.

Saturday, 1 November
F.A. Barclaycard Premiership
Everton v Chelsea
Leeds Utd. v Arsenal
Manchester Utd. v Portsmouth
Middlesbrough v Wolves
Newcastle Utd. v Aston Villa
Southampton v Manchester City
Tottenham v Bolton Wand.

Nationwide League Division One
Burnley v Cardiff City
Coventry City v West Ham Utd.
Crewe Alexandra v Reading
Ipswich Town v Gillingham
Millwall v Nott'm. Forest
Preston N.E. v Derby Co.
Stoke City v Sheffield Utd.
Walsall v Norwich City
Watford v Rotherham Utd.
W.B.A. v Sunderland
Wigan Athletic v Crystal Palace
Wimbledon v Bradford City

Nationwide League Division Two
Brentford v Barnsley
Bristol City v Luton Town
Chesterfield v Port Vale
Notts Co. v Hartlepool Utd.
Peterborough Utd. v Brighton & H.A.
Plymouth Argyle v Oldham Athletic
Rushden & D'monds v Grimsby Town
Sheffield Wed. v Blackpool
Stockport Co. v Q.P.R.
Swindon Town v Wycombe Wand.
Tranmere Rov. v Bournemouth

Nationwide League Division Three
Bury v Yeovil Town
Cheltenham Town v York City
Doncaster Rov. v Torquay Utd.
Hull City v Macclesfield Town
Kidderminster Harr. v Cambridge Utd.
Leyton Orient v Rochdale
Lincoln City v Carlisle Utd.
Mansfield Town v Boston Utd.
Oxford Utd. v Darlington
Scunthorpe Utd. v Huddersfield Town
Southend Utd. v Northampton Town
Swansea City v Bristol Rov.

Sunday, 2 November
F.A. Barclaycard Premiership
Fulham v Liverpool
Leicester City v Blackburn Rov.

Monday, 3 November
F.A. Barclaycard Premiership
Birmingham City v Charlton Athletic

Saturday, 8 November
F.A. Barclaycard Premiership
Arsenal v Tottenham
Aston Villa v Middlesbrough
Bolton Wand. v Southampton
Charlton Athletic v Fulham
Manchester City v Leicester City
Portsmouth v Leeds Utd.
Wolves v Birmingham City

Nationwide League Division One
Bradford City v Walsall
Cardiff City v Stoke City
Crystal Palace v Preston N.E.
Derby Co. v Ipswich Town
Gillingham v Crewe Alexandra
Norwich City v Millwall
Nott'm. Forest v Watford
Reading v Wigan Athletic
Rotherham Utd. v Wimbledon
Sheffield Utd. v Burnley
Sunderland v Coventry City
West Ham Utd. v W.B.A.

Sunday, 9 November
F.A. Barclaycard Premiership
Chelsea v Newcastle Utd.
Liverpool v Manchester Utd.

Monday, 10 November
F.A. Barclaycard Premiership
Blackburn Rov. v Everton

Saturday, 15 November
Nationwide League Division One
Bradford City v W.B.A.
Cardiff City v Preston N.E.
Crystal Palace v Crewe Alexandra
Derby Co. v Burnley
Gillingham v Wimbledon
Norwich City v Watford
Nott'm. Forest v Ipswich Town
Reading v Millwall
Rotherham Utd. v Coventry City
Sheffield Utd. v Walsall
Sunderland v Wigan Athletic
West Ham Utd. v Stoke City

Nationwide League Division Two
Barnsley v Tranmere Rov.
Blackpool v Chesterfield
Bournemouth v Peterborough Utd.
Brighton & H.A. v Bristol City
Colchester Utd. v Sheffield Wed.
Grimsby Town v Stockport Co.
Hartlepool Utd. v Rushden & D'monds
Luton Town v Wrexham
Oldham Athletic v Swindon Town
Port Vale v Notts Co.

Q.P.R. v Plymouth Argyle
Wycombe Wand. v Brentford

Nationwide League Division Three
Boston Utd. v Leyton Orient
Bristol Rov. v Bury
Cambridge Utd. v Oxford Utd.
Carlisle Utd. v Mansfield Town
Darlington v Lincoln City
Huddersfield Town v Hull City
Macclesfield Town v Scunthorpe Utd.
Northampton Town v Swansea City
Rochdale v Kidderminster Harr.
Torquay Utd. v Cheltenham Town
Yeovil Town v Southend Utd.
York City v Doncaster Rov.

Saturday, 22 November
F.A. Barclaycard Premiership
Birmingham City v Arsenal
Everton v Wolves
Leeds Utd. v Bolton Wand.
Leicester City v Charlton Athletic
Manchester Utd. v Blackburn Rov.
Middlesbrough v Liverpool
Newcastle Utd. v Manchester City
Southampton v Chelsea

Nationwide League Division One
Burnley v Rotherham Utd.
Coventry City v Gillingham
Crewe Alexandra v Sunderland
Ipswich Town v Sheffield Utd.
Millwall v Derby Co.
Preston N.E. v Norwich City
Stoke City v Bradford City
Walsall v Crystal Palace
Watford v West Ham Utd.
W.B.A. v Reading
Wigan Athletic v Nott'm. Forest
Wimbledon v Cardiff City

Nationwide League Division Two
Brentford v Grimsby Town
Bristol City v Barnsley
Chesterfield v Oldham Athletic
Notts Co. v Brighton & H.A.
Peterborough Utd. v Blackpool
Plymouth Argyle v Hartlepool Utd.
Rushden & D'monds v Colchester Utd.
Sheffield Wed. v Luton Town
Stockport Co. v Bournemouth
Swindon Town v Q.P.R.
Tranmere Rov. v Port Vale
Wrexham v Wycombe Wand.

Nationwide League Division Three
Bury v Northampton Town
Cheltenham Town v Carlisle Utd.
Doncaster Rov. v Boston Utd.
Hull City v Yeovil Town
Kidderminster Harr. v Torquay Utd.
Leyton Orient v York City
Lincoln City v Bristol Rov.
Mansfield Town v Huddersfield Town
Oxford Utd. v Macclesfield Town
Scunthorpe Utd. v Cambridge Utd.
Southend Utd. v Rochdale
Swansea City v Darlington

Sunday, 23 Novemberr
F.A. Barclaycard Premiership
Tottenham v Aston Villa

Monday, 24 Novemberr
F.A. Barclaycard Premiership
Fulham v Portsmouth

Saturday, 29 November
F.A. Barclaycard Premiership
Arsenal v Fulham
Aston Villa v Southampton
Blackburn Rov. v Tottenham
Bolton Wand. v Everton
Charlton Athletic v Leeds Utd.
Chelsea v Manchester Utd.
Liverpool v Birmingham City
Manchester City v Middlesbrough
Portsmouth v Leicester City
Wolves v Newcastle Utd.

Nationwide League Division One
Bradford City v Millwall
Cardiff City v Ipswich Town
Crystal Palace v Coventry City
Derby Co. v Wimbledon
Gillingham v Stoke City
Norwich City v Crewe Alexandra
Nott'm. Forest v W.B.A.
Reading v Watford
Rotherham Utd. v Walsall
Sheffield Utd. v Preston N.E.
Sunderland v Burnley
West Ham Utd. v Wigan Athletic

Nationwide League Division Two
Barnsley v Stockport Co.
Blackpool v Bristol City
Bournemouth v Brentford
Brighton & H.A. v Wrexham
Colchester Utd. v Plymouth Argyle
Grimsby Town v Tranmere Rov.
Hartlepool Utd. v Swindon Town
Luton Town v Chesterfield
Oldham Athletic v Notts Co.
Port Vale v Rushden & D'monds
Q.P.R. v Sheffield Wed.
Wycombe Wand. v Peterborough Utd.

Nationwide League Division Three
Boston Utd. v Kidderminster Harr.
Bristol Rov. v Hull City
Cambridge Utd. v Leyton Orient
Carlisle Utd. v Doncaster Rov.
Darlington v Scunthorpe Utd.
Huddersfield Town v Cheltenham Town
Macclesfield Town v Bury
Northampton Town v Mansfield Town
Rochdale v Oxford Utd.
Torquay Utd. v Southend Utd.
Yeovil Town v Lincoln City
York City v Swansea City

Saturday, 6 December
F.A. Barclaycard Premiership
Birmingham City v Blackburn Rov.
Everton v Manchester City
Fulham v Bolton Wand.
Leeds Utd. v Chelsea
Leicester City v Arsenal
Manchester Utd. v Aston Villa
Middlesbrough v Portsmouth
Newcastle Utd. v Liverpool
Tottenham v Wolves

Nationwide League Division One
Burnley v Sheffield Utd.
Coventry City v Sunderland
Crewe Alexandra v Gillingham
Ipswich Town v Derby Co.
Millwall v Norwich City
Preston N.E. v Crystal Palace
Stoke City v Cardiff City
Walsall v Bradford City
Watford v Nott'm. Forest
W.B.A. v West Ham Utd.
Wigan Athletic v Reading
Wimbledon v Rotherham Utd.

Sunday, 7 December
F.A. Barclaycard Premiership
Southampton v Charlton Athletic

Friday, 12 December
Nationwide League Division Two
Brighton & H.A. v Port Vale

Saturday, 13 December
F.A. Barclaycard Premiership
Arsenal v Blackburn Rov.
Aston Villa v Wolves
Chelsea v Bolton Wand.
Leicester City v Birmingham City
Liverpool v Southampton
Manchester Utd. v Manchester City
Middlesbrough v Charlton Athletic
Newcastle Utd. v Tottenham
Portsmouth v Everton

Nationwide League Division One
Burnley v Coventry City
Crystal Palace v Nott'm. Forest
Gillingham v Preston N.E.
Millwall v Ipswich Town
Norwich City v Cardiff City
Rotherham Utd. v Derby Co.
Sheffield Utd. v Watford
Stoke City v Reading
W.B.A. v Crewe Alexandra
West Ham Utd. v Sunderland
Wigan Athletic v Bradford City
Wimbledon v Walsall

Nationwide League Division Two
Barnsley v Sheffield Wed.
Blackpool v Luton Town
Bournemouth v Grimsby Town
Chesterfield v Tranmere Rov.
Colchester Utd. v Oldham Athletic
Notts Co. v Wycombe Wand.
Q.P.R. v Hartlepool Utd.
Rushden & D'monds v Bristol City
Stockport Co. v Brentford
Swindon Town v Plymouth Argyle
Wrexham v Peterborough Utd.

Nationwide League Division Three
Boston Utd. v Northampton Town
Bristol Rov. v Yeovil Town
Bury v Rochdale
Cambridge Utd. v Darlington
Cheltenham Town v Doncaster Rov.
Kidderminster Harr. v Leyton Orient
Macclesfield Town v Huddersfield Town
Mansfield Town v Lincoln City
Oxford Utd. v Carlisle Utd.
Scunthorpe Utd. v Hull City
Swansea City v Southend Utd.
Torquay Utd. v York City

Sunday, 14 December
F.A. Barclaycard Premiership
Leeds Utd. v Fulham

Friday, 19 December
Nationwide League Division Three
Doncaster Rov. v Swansea City
Northampton Town v Cambridge Utd.

Saturday, 20 December
F.A. Barclaycard Premiership
Birmingham City v Middlesbrough
Blackburn Rov. v Aston Villa
Bolton Wand. v Arsenal
Charlton Athletic v Newcastle Utd.
Everton v Leicester City

Fulham v Chelsea
Manchester City v Leeds Utd.
Southampton v Portsmouth
Tottenham v Manchester Utd.
Wolves v Liverpool

Nationwide League Division One
Bradford City v Rotherham Utd.
Cardiff City v Millwall
Coventry City v W.B.A.
Crewe Alexandra v Wigan Athletic
Derby Co. v Sheffield Utd.
Nott'm. Forest v Gillingham
Preston N.E. v Burnley
Reading v Crystal Palace
Sunderland v Wimbledon
Walsall v West Ham Utd.
Watford v Stoke City

Nationwide League Division Two
Brentford v Swindon Town
Bristol City v Stockport Co.
Grimsby Town v Wrexham
Hartlepool Utd. v Colchester Utd.
Luton Town v Barnsley
Oldham Athletic v Q.P.R.
Peterborough Utd. v Rushden & D'monds
Plymouth Argyle v Notts Co.
Port Vale v Blackpool
Sheffield Wed. v Chesterfield
Tranmere Rov. v Brighton & H.A.
Wycombe Wand. v Bournemouth

Nationwide League Division Three
Carlisle Utd. v Torquay Utd.
Darlington v Macclesfield Town
Huddersfield Town v Oxford Utd.
Hull City v Mansfield Town
Leyton Orient v Bury
Lincoln City v Cheltenham Town
Rochdale v Boston Utd.
Southend Utd. v Bristol Rov.
Yeovil Town v Scunthorpe Utd.

Sunday, 21 December
Nationwide League Division One
Ipswich Town v Norwich City

Nationwide League Division Three
York City v Kidderminster Harr.

Friday, 26 December
F.A. Barclaycard Premiership
Arsenal v Wolves
Birmingham City v Manchester City
Blackburn Rov. v Middlesbrough
Charlton Athletic v Chelsea
Fulham v Southampton
Leeds Utd. v Aston Villa
Leicester City v Newcastle Utd.
Liverpool v Bolton Wand.
Manchester Utd. v Everton
Portsmouth v Tottenham

Nationwide League Division One
Cardiff City v Walsall
Coventry City v Sheffield Utd.
Crewe Alexandra v Burnley
Crystal Palace v Millwall
Gillingham v Watford
Norwich City v Nott'm. Forest
Reading v Wimbledon
Stoke City v Preston N.E.
Sunderland v Bradford City
W.B.A. v Derby Co.
West Ham Utd. v Ipswich Town
Wigan Athletic v Rotherham Utd.

Nationwide League Division Two
Blackpool v Tranmere Rov.
Bournemouth v Plymouth Argyle
Brentford v Bristol City
Brighton & H.A. v Wycombe Wand.
Chesterfield v Peterborough Utd.
Colchester Utd. v Luton Town
Grimsby Town v Oldham Athletic
Hartlepool Utd. v Barnsley
Notts Co. v Q.P.R.
Rushden & D'monds v Swindon Town
Sheffield Wed. v Port Vale
Stockport Co. v Wrexham

Nationwide League Division Three
Boston Utd. v Lincoln City
Bristol Rov. v Northampton Town
Bury v Carlisle Utd.
Cambridge Utd. v Southend Utd.
Cheltenham Town v Macclesfield Town
Darlington v Huddersfield Town
Doncaster Rov. v Scunthorpe Utd.
Mansfield Town v Rochdale
Oxford Utd. v Leyton Orient
Torquay Utd. v Swansea City
Yeovil Town v Kidderminster Harr.
York City v Hull City

Sunday, 28 December
F.A. Barclaycard Premiership
Aston Villa v Fulham
Bolton Wand. v Leicester City
Chelsea v Portsmouth
Everton v Birmingham City
Manchester City v Liverpool
Middlesbrough v Manchester Utd.
Newcastle Utd. v Blackburn Rov.
Southampton v Arsenal
Tottenham v Charlton Athletic

Wolves v Leeds Utd.

Nationwide League Division One
Bradford City v Coventry City
Burnley v Stoke City
Derby Co. v Norwich City
Ipswich Town v Crystal Palace
Millwall v Gillingham
Nott'm. Forest v West Ham Utd.
Preston N.E. v Crewe Alexandra
Rotherham Utd. v Sunderland
Sheffield Utd. v Wigan Athletic
Walsall v Reading
Watford v Cardiff City

Nationwide League Division Two
Barnsley v Chesterfield
Bristol City v Bournemouth
Luton Town v Notts Co.
Oldham Athletic v Hartlepool Utd.
Peterborough Utd. v Grimsby Town
Plymouth Argyle v Brentford
Port Vale v Stockport Co.
Q.P.R. v Colchester Utd.
Swindon Town v Brighton & H.A.
Tranmere Rov. v Sheffield Wed.
Wrexham v Blackpool
Wycombe Wand. v Rushden & D'monds

Nationwide League Division Three
Carlisle Utd. v Darlington
Huddersfield Town v Bury
Hull City v Doncaster Rov.
Kidderminster Harr. v Bristol Rov.
Leyton Orient v Torquay Utd.
Lincoln City v Cambridge Utd.
Macclesfield Town v Mansfield Town
Northampton Town v Cheltenham Town
Rochdale v York City
Scunthorpe Utd. v Boston Utd.
Southend Utd. v Oxford Utd.
Swansea City v Yeovil Town

Tuesday, 30 December
Nationwide League Division One
Wimbledon v W.B.A.

Saturday, 3 January 2004
Nationwide League Division Two
Barnsley v Blackpool
Bristol City v Colchester Utd.
Luton Town v Brighton & H.A.
Oldham Athletic v Brentford
Peterborough Utd. v Notts Co.
Plymouth Argyle v Chesterfield
Port Vale v Hartlepool Utd.
Q.P.R. v Rushden & D'monds
Swindon Town v Bournemouth
Tranmere Rov. v Stockport Co.
Wrexham v Sheffield Wed.
Wycombe Wand. v Grimsby Town

Nationwide League Division Three
Carlisle Utd. v Boston Utd.
Huddersfield Town v Doncaster Rov.
Hull City v Cambridge Utd.
Kidderminster Harr. v Cheltenham Town
Leyton Orient v Darlington
Lincoln City v Bury
Macclesfield Town v Bristol Rov.
Northampton Town v Yeovil Town
Rochdale v Torquay Utd.
Scunthorpe Utd. v Mansfield Town
Southend Utd. v York City
Swansea City v Oxford Utd.

Wednesday, 7 January
F.A. Barclaycard Premiership
Aston Villa v Portsmouth
Bolton Wand. v Manchester Utd.
Chelsea v Liverpool
Everton v Arsenal
Manchester City v Charlton Athletic
Middlesbrough v Fulham
Newcastle Utd. v Leeds Utd.
Southampton v Leicester City
Tottenham v Birmingham City
Wolves v Blackburn Rov.

Saturday, 10 January
F.A. Barclaycard Premiership
Arsenal v Middlesbrough
Birmingham City v Southampton
Blackburn Rov. v Bolton Wand.
Charlton Athletic v Wolves
Fulham v Everton
Leeds Utd. v Tottenham
Leicester City v Chelsea
Liverpool v Aston Villa
Manchester Utd. v Newcastle Utd.
Portsmouth v Manchester City

Nationwide League Division One
Cardiff City v Rotherham Utd.
Coventry City v Watford
Crewe Alexandra v Wimbledon
Crystal Palace v Burnley
Gillingham v Sheffield Utd.
Norwich City v Bradford City
Reading v Ipswich Town
Stoke City v Derby Co.
Sunderland v Nott'm. Forest
W.B.A. v Walsall
West Ham Utd. v Preston N.E.
Wigan Athletic v Millwall

Nationwide League Division Two
Blackpool v Q.P.R.
Bournemouth v Port Vale
Brentford v Tranmere Rov.
Brighton & H.A. v Oldham Athletic
Chesterfield v Wrexham
Colchester Utd. v Barnsley
Grimsby Town v Plymouth Argyle
Hartlepool Utd. v Peterborough Utd.
Notts Co. v Bristol City
Rushden & D'monds v Luton Town
Sheffield Wed. v Swindon Town
Stockport Co. v Wycombe Wand.

Nationwide League Division Three
Boston Utd. v Macclesfield Town
Bristol Rov. v Scunthorpe Utd.
Bury v Swansea City
Cambridge Utd. v Huddersfield Town
Cheltenham Town v Southend Utd.
Darlington v Hull City
Doncaster Rov. v Leyton Orient
Mansfield Town v Kidderminster Harr.
Oxford Utd. v Lincoln City
Torquay Utd. v Northampton Town
Yeovil Town v Rochdale
York City v Carlisle Utd.

Saturday, 17 January
F.A. Barclaycard Premiership
Aston Villa v Arsenal
Bolton Wand. v Portsmouth
Chelsea v Birmingham City
Everton v Charlton Athletic
Manchester City v Blackburn Rov.
Middlesbrough v Leicester City
Newcastle Utd. v Fulham
Southampton v Leeds Utd.
Tottenham v Liverpool
Wolves v Manchester Utd.

Nationwide League Division One
Bradford City v Cardiff City
Burnley v W.B.A.
Derby Co. v Gillingham
Ipswich Town v Crewe Alexandra
Millwall v Sunderland
Nott'm. Forest v Reading
Preston N.E. v Wigan Athletic
Rotherham Utd. v Norwich City
Sheffield Utd. v West Ham Utd.
Walsall v Coventry City
Watford v Crystal Palace
Wimbledon v Stoke City

Nationwide League Division Two
Barnsley v Bournemouth
Bristol City v Chesterfield
Luton Town v Stockport Co.
Oldham Athletic v Sheffield Wed.
Peterborough Utd. v Brentford
Plymouth Argyle v Rushden & D'monds
Port Vale v Grimsby Town
Q.P.R. v Brighton & H.A.
Swindon Town v Colchester Utd.
Tranmere Rov. v Hartlepool Utd.
Wrexham v Notts Co.
Wycombe Wand. v Blackpool

Nationwide League Division Three
Carlisle Utd. v Yeovil Town
Huddersfield Town v Boston Utd.
Hull City v Oxford Utd.
Kidderminster Harr. v Darlington
Leyton Orient v Mansfield Town
Lincoln City v Torquay Utd.
Macclesfield Town v Cambridge Utd.
Northampton Town v York City
Rochdale v Bristol Rov.
Scunthorpe Utd. v Bury
Southend Utd. v Doncaster Rov.
Swansea City v Cheltenham Town

Friday, 23 January
Nationwide League Division Three
Doncaster Rov. v Lincoln City

Saturday, 24 January
Nationwide League Division Two
Blackpool v Oldham Athletic
Bournemouth v Q.P.R.
Brentford v Wrexham
Brighton & H.A. v Barnsley
Chesterfield v Wycombe Wand.
Colchester Utd. v Port Vale
Grimsby Town v Luton Town
Hartlepool Utd. v Bristol City
Notts Co. v Swindon Town
Rushden & D'monds v Tranmere Rov.
Sheffield Wed. v Peterborough Utd.
Stockport Co. v Plymouth Argyle

Nationwide League Division Three
Boston Utd. v Swansea City
Bristol Rov. v Carlisle Utd.
Bury v Kidderminster Harr.
Cambridge Utd. v Rochdale
Cheltenham Town v Hull City
Darlington v Northampton Town
Mansfield Town v Southend Utd.
Oxford Utd. v Scunthorpe Utd.
Torquay Utd. v Macclesfield Town
Yeovil Town v Leyton Orient
York City v Huddersfield Town

Saturday, 31 January
F.A. Barclaycard Premiership
Arsenal v Manchester City
Birmingham City v Newcastle Utd.
Blackburn Rov. v Chelsea
Charlton Athletic v Bolton Wand.
Fulham v Tottenham
Leeds Utd. v Middlesbrough
Leicester City v Aston Villa
Liverpool v Everton
Manchester Utd. v Southampton
Portsmouth v Wolves

Nationwide League Division One
Cardiff City v Nott'm. Forest
Coventry City v Ipswich Town
Crewe Alexandra v Millwall
Crystal Palace v Wimbledon
Gillingham v Bradford City
Norwich City v Sheffield Utd.
Reading v Derby Co.
Stoke City v Walsall
Sunderland v Preston N.E.
W.B.A. v Watford
West Ham Utd. v Rotherham Utd.
Wigan Athletic v Burnley

Nationwide League Division Two
Blackpool v Swindon Town
Bournemouth v Wrexham
Brentford v Port Vale
Brighton & H.A. v Plymouth Argyle
Chesterfield v Q.P.R.
Colchester Utd. v Tranmere Rov.
Grimsby Town v Bristol City
Hartlepool Utd. v Luton Town
Notts Co. v Barnsley
Rushden & D'monds v Oldham Athletic
Sheffield Wed. v Wycombe Wand.
Stockport Co. v Peterborough Utd.

Nationwide League Division Three
Boston Utd. v Hull City
Bristol Rov. v Huddersfield Town
Bury v Southend Utd.
Cambridge Utd. v Carlisle Utd.
Cheltenham Town v Leyton Orient
Darlington v Rochdale
Doncaster Rov. v Northampton Town
Mansfield Town v Swansea City
Oxford Utd. v Kidderminster Harr.
Torquay Utd. v Scunthorpe Utd.
Yeovil Town v Macclesfield Town
York City v Lincoln City

Saturday, 7 February
F.A. Barclaycard Premiership
Aston Villa v Leeds Utd.
Bolton Wand. v Liverpool
Chelsea v Charlton Athletic
Everton v Manchester Utd.
Manchester City v Birmingham City
Middlesbrough v Blackburn Rov.
Newcastle Utd. v Leicester City
Southampton v Fulham
Tottenham v Portsmouth
Wolves v Arsenal

Nationwide League Division One
Bradford City v West Ham Utd.
Burnley v Gillingham
Derby Co. v Cardiff City
Ipswich Town v Wigan Athletic
Millwall v Stoke City
Nott'm. Forest v Coventry City
Preston N.E. v W.B.A.
Rotherham Utd. v Reading
Sheffield Utd. v Crystal Palace
Walsall v Crewe Alexandra
Watford v Sunderland
Wimbledon v Norwich City

Nationwide League Division Two
Barnsley v Hartlepool Utd.
Bristol City v Brentford
Luton Town v Colchester Utd.
Oldham Athletic v Grimsby Town
Peterborough Utd. v Chesterfield
Plymouth Argyle v Bournemouth
Port Vale v Sheffield Wed.
Q.P.R. v Notts Co.
Swindon Town v Rushden & D'monds
Tranmere Rov. v Blackpool
Wrexham v Stockport Co.
Wycombe Wand. v Brighton & H.A.

Nationwide League Division Three
Carlisle Utd. v Bury
Huddersfield Town v Darlington
Hull City v York City
Kidderminster Harr. v Yeovil Town
Leyton Orient v Oxford Utd.
Lincoln City v Boston Utd.
Macclesfield Town v Cheltenham Town
Northampton Town v Bristol Rov.
Rochdale v Mansfield Town
Scunthorpe Utd. v Doncaster Rov.
Southend Utd. v Cambridge Utd.
Swansea City v Torquay Utd.

Tuesday, 10 February
F.A. Barclaycard Premiership
Arsenal v Southampton
Birmingham City v Everton
Charlton Athletic v Tottenham
Leeds Utd. v Wolves
Leicester City v Bolton Wand.
Portsmouth v Chelsea

Wednesday, 11 February
F.A. Barclaycard Premiership
Blackburn Rov. v Newcastle Utd.
Fulham v Aston Villa
Liverpool v Manchester City
Manchester Utd. v Middlesbrough

Friday, 13 February
Nationwide League Division Three
Swansea City v Leyton Orient

Saturday, 14 February
Nationwide League Division One
Coventry City v Norwich City
Crewe Alexandra v Sheffield Utd.
Crystal Palace v Stoke City
Ipswich Town v Bradford City
Millwall v Rotherham Utd.
Nott'm. Forest v Walsall
Reading v Burnley
Sunderland v Gillingham
Watford v Preston N.E.
W.B.A. v Cardiff City
West Ham Utd. v Wimbledon
Wigan Athletic v Derby Co.

Nationwide League Division Two
Blackpool v Colchester Utd.
Bournemouth v Notts Co.
Brentford v Q.P.R.
Chesterfield v Rushden & D'monds
Grimsby Town v Brighton & H.A.
Peterborough Utd. v Bristol City
Port Vale v Oldham Athletic
Sheffield Wed. v Hartlepool Utd.
Stockport Co. v Swindon Town
Tranmere Rov. v Plymouth Argyle
Wrexham v Barnsley
Wycombe Wand. v Luton Town

Nationwide League Division Three
Bristol Rov. v Darlington
Bury v Cambridge Utd.
Carlisle Utd. v Hull City
Cheltenham Town v Boston Utd.
Doncaster Rov. v Macclesfield Town
Lincoln City v Scunthorpe Utd.
Northampton Town v Rochdale
Southend Utd. v Kidderminster Harr.
Torquay Utd. v Huddersfield Town
Yeovil Town v Oxford Utd.
York City v Mansfield Town

Friday, 20 February
Nationwide League Division Two
Colchester Utd. v Grimsby Town
Hartlepool Utd. v Blackpool

Saturday, 21 February
F.A. Barclaycard Premiership
Bolton Wand. v Manchester City
Charlton Athletic v Blackburn Rov.
Chelsea v Arsenal
Liverpool v Portsmouth
Manchester Utd. v Leeds Utd.
Newcastle Utd. v Middlesbrough
Southampton v Everton
Tottenham v Leicester City
Wolves v Fulham

Nationwide League Division One
Bradford City v Crewe Alexandra
Burnley v Ipswich Town
Cardiff City v Sunderland
Derby Co. v Crystal Palace
Gillingham v Reading
Norwich City v West Ham Utd.
Preston N.E. v Millwall
Rotherham Utd. v Nott'm. Forest
Sheffield Utd. v W.B.A.
Stoke City v Wigan Athletic
Walsall v Watford
Wimbledon v Coventry City

Nationwide League Division Two
Barnsley v Wycombe Wand.
Brighton & H.A. v Bournemouth
Bristol City v Wrexham
Luton Town v Brentford
Notts Co. v Stockport Co.
Oldham Athletic v Tranmere Rov.
Plymouth Argyle v Port Vale
Q.P.R. v Peterborough Utd.
Rushden & D'monds v Sheffield Wed.
Swindon Town v Chesterfield

Nationwide League Division Three
Boston Utd. v York City
Cambridge Utd. v Bristol Rov.
Darlington v Yeovil Town
Huddersfield Town v Lincoln City
Hull City v Torquay Utd.
Kidderminster Harr. v Swansea City
Leyton Orient v Southend Utd.
Macclesfield Town v Carlisle Utd.
Mansfield Town v Doncaster Rov.
Oxford Utd. v Bury
Rochdale v Cheltenham Town
Scunthorpe Utd. v Northampton Town

Sunday, 22 February
F.A. Barclaycard Premiership
Aston Villa v Birmingham City

Friday, 27 February
Nationwide League Division Three
Doncaster Rov. v Kidderminster Harr.

Saturday, 28 February
F.A. Barclaycard Premiership
Arsenal v Charlton Athletic
Birmingham City v Bolton Wand.
Blackburn Rov. v Southampton
Everton v Aston Villa
Fulham v Manchester Utd.
Leeds Utd. v Liverpool
Leicester City v Wolves
Manchester City v Chelsea
Middlesbrough v Tottenham
Portsmouth v Newcastle Utd.

Nationwide League Division One
Coventry City v Derby Co.
Crewe Alexandra v Stoke City
Crystal Palace v Gillingham
Ipswich Town v Preston N.E.
Millwall v Burnley
Nott'm. Forest v Bradford City
Reading v Sheffield Utd.
Sunderland v Norwich City
Watford v Wimbledon
W.B.A. v Rotherham Utd.
West Ham Utd. v Cardiff City
Wigan Athletic v Walsall

Nationwide League Division Two
Blackpool v Plymouth Argyle
Bournemouth v Oldham Athletic
Brentford v Notts Co.
Chesterfield v Colchester Utd.
Grimsby Town v Barnsley
Peterborough Utd. v Luton Town
Port Vale v Swindon Town
Sheffield Wed. v Bristol City
Stockport Co. v Brighton & H.A.
Tranmere Rov. v Q.P.R.
Wrexham v Rushden & D'monds
Wycombe Wand. v Hartlepool Utd.

Nationwide League Division Three
Bristol Rov. v Oxford Utd.
Bury v Darlington
Carlisle Utd. v Huddersfield Town
Cheltenham Town v Mansfield Town
Lincoln City v Hull City
Northampton Town v Leyton Orient
Southend Utd. v Macclesfield Town
Swansea City v Rochdale
Torquay Utd. v Boston Utd.
Yeovil Town v Cambridge Utd.
York City v Scunthorpe Utd.

Tuesday, 2 March
Nationwide League Division One
Bradford City v Watford
Burnley v West Ham Utd.
Cardiff City v Coventry City
Gillingham v Wigan Athletic
Norwich City v W.B.A.
Preston N.E. v Reading
Rotherham Utd. v Crystal Palace
Sheffield Utd. v Millwall
Stoke City v Ipswich Town
Walsall v Sunderland
Wimbledon v Nott'm. Forest

Nationwide League Division Two
Barnsley v Peterborough Utd.
Brighton & H.A. v Brentford
Bristol City v Wycombe Wand.
Colchester Utd. v Stockport Co.
Hartlepool Utd. v Chesterfield
Luton Town v Bournemouth
Notts Co. v Grimsby Town
Oldham Athletic v Wrexham
Plymouth Argyle v Sheffield Wed.
Q.P.R. v Port Vale
Rushden & D'monds v Blackpool

Nationwide League Division Three
Cambridge Utd. v Swansea City
Darlington v Cheltenham Town
Huddersfield Town v Yeovil Town
Hull City v Bury
Kidderminster Harr. v Northampton Town
Leyton Orient v Bristol Rov.
Macclesfield Town v Lincoln City
Mansfield Town v Torquay Utd.
Rochdale v Doncaster Rov.
Scunthorpe Utd. v Carlisle Utd.

Wednesday, 3 March
Nationwide League Division One
Derby Co. v Crewe Alexandra

Nationwide League Division Two
Swindon Town v Tranmere Rov.

Nationwide League Division Three
Boston Utd. v Southend Utd.
Oxford Utd. v York City

Friday, 5 March
Nationwide League Division Three
Swansea City v Doncaster Rov.

Saturday, 6 March
Nationwide League Division One
Burnley v Preston N.E.
Crystal Palace v Reading
Gillingham v Nott'm. Forest
Millwall v Cardiff City
Rotherham Utd. v Bradford City
Sheffield Utd. v Derby Co.
Stoke City v Watford
W.B.A. v Coventry City

West Ham Utd. v Walsall
Wigan Athletic v Crewe Alexandra
Wimbledon v Sunderland

Nationwide League Division Two
Barnsley v Luton Town
Blackpool v Port Vale
Bournemouth v Wycombe Wand.
Brighton & H.A. v Tranmere Rov.
Chesterfield v Sheffield Wed.
Colchester Utd. v Hartlepool Utd.
Notts Co. v Plymouth Argyle
Q.P.R. v Oldham Athletic
Rushden & D'monds v Peterborough Utd.
Stockport Co. v Bristol City
Swindon Town v Brentford
Wrexham v Grimsby Town

Nationwide League Division Three
Boston Utd. v Rochdale
Bristol Rov. v Southend Utd.
Bury v Leyton Orient
Cambridge Utd. v Northampton Town
Cheltenham Town v Lincoln City
Kidderminster Harr. v York City
Macclesfield Town v Darlington
Mansfield Town v Hull City
Oxford Utd. v Huddersfield Town
Scunthorpe Utd. v Yeovil Town
Torquay Utd. v Carlisle Utd.

Sunday, 7 March
Nationwide League Division One
Norwich City v Ipswich Town

Saturday, 13 March
F.A. Barclaycard Premiership
Birmingham City v Leicester City
Blackburn Rov. v Arsenal
Bolton Wand. v Chelsea
Charlton Athletic v Middlesbrough
Everton v Portsmouth
Fulham v Leeds Utd.
Manchester City v Manchester Utd.
Southampton v Liverpool
Tottenham v Newcastle Utd.
Wolves v Aston Villa

Nationwide League Division One
Bradford City v Wigan Athletic
Cardiff City v Norwich City
Coventry City v Burnley
Crewe Alexandra v W.B.A.
Derby Co. v Rotherham Utd.
Ipswich Town v Millwall
Nott'm. Forest v Crystal Palace
Preston N.E. v Gillingham
Reading v Stoke City
Sunderland v West Ham Utd.
Walsall v Wimbledon
Watford v Sheffield Utd.

Nationwide League Division Two
Brentford v Stockport Co.
Bristol City v Rushden & D'monds
Grimsby Town v Bournemouth
Hartlepool Utd. v Q.P.R.
Luton Town v Blackpool
Oldham Athletic v Colchester Utd.
Peterborough Utd. v Wrexham
Plymouth Argyle v Swindon Town
Port Vale v Brighton & H.A.
Sheffield Wed. v Barnsley
Tranmere Rov. v Chesterfield
Wycombe Wand. v Notts Co.

Nationwide League Division Three
Carlisle Utd. v Oxford Utd.
Darlington v Cambridge Utd.
Doncaster Rov. v Cheltenham Town
Huddersfield Town v Macclesfield Town
Hull City v Scunthorpe Utd.
Leyton Orient v Kidderminster Harr.
Lincoln City v Mansfield Town
Northampton Town v Boston Utd.
Rochdale v Bury
Southend Utd. v Swansea City
Yeovil Town v Bristol Rov.
York City v Torquay Utd.

Tuesday, 16 March
Nationwide League Division One
Bradford City v Crystal Palace
Cardiff City v Reading
Norwich City v Gillingham
Rotherham Utd. v Sheffield Utd.
Sunderland v Stoke City
Walsall v Ipswich Town
Watford v Derby Co.
W.B.A. v Wigan Athletic
Wimbledon v Millwall

Nationwide League Division Two
Blackpool v Brentford
Chesterfield v Brighton & H.A.
Colchester Utd. v Wycombe Wand.
Hartlepool Utd. v Stockport Co.
Oldham Athletic v Barnsley
Plymouth Argyle v Peterborough Utd.
Port Vale v Luton Town
Q.P.R. v Wrexham
Rushden & D'monds v Notts Co.
Tranmere Rov. v Bristol City

Nationwide League Division Three
Bristol Rov. v Torquay Utd.
Bury v Mansfield Town

Cambridge Utd. v Boston Utd.
Carlisle Utd. v Northampton Town
Darlington v York City
Huddersfield Town v Rochdale
Hull City v Leyton Orient
Lincoln City v Southend Utd.
Macclesfield Town v Swansea City
Scunthorpe Utd. v Kidderminster Harr.
Yeovil Town v Doncaster Rov.

Wednesday, 17 March
Nationwide League Division One
Coventry City v Preston N.E.
Nott'm. Forest v Burnley
West Ham Utd. v Crewe Alexandra

Nationwide League Division Two
Sheffield Wed. v Bournemouth
Swindon Town v Grimsby Town

Nationwide League Division Three
Oxford Utd. v Cheltenham Town

Saturday, 20 March
F.A. Barclaycard Premiership
Arsenal v Bolton Wand.
Aston Villa v Blackburn Rov.
Chelsea v Fulham
Leeds Utd. v Manchester City
Leicester City v Everton
Liverpool v Wolves
Manchester Utd. v Tottenham
Middlesbrough v Birmingham City
Newcastle Utd. v Charlton Athletic
Portsmouth v Southampton

Nationwide League Division One
Burnley v Wimbledon
Crewe Alexandra v Cardiff City
Crystal Palace v Norwich City
Derby Co. v Nott'm. Forest
Gillingham v Rotherham Utd.
Ipswich Town v Watford
Millwall v West Ham Utd.
Preston N.E. v Walsall
Reading v Sunderland
Sheffield Utd. v Bradford City
Stoke City v W.B.A.
Wigan Athletic v Coventry City

Nationwide League Division Two
Barnsley v Port Vale
Bournemouth v Blackpool
Brentford v Rushden & D'monds
Brighton & H.A. v Colchester Utd.
Bristol City v Oldham Athletic
Grimsby Town v Hartlepool Utd.
Luton Town v Plymouth Argyle
Notts Co. v Chesterfield
Peterborough Utd. v Tranmere Rov.
Stockport Co. v Sheffield Wed.
Wrexham v Swindon Town
Wycombe Wand. v Q.P.R.

Nationwide League Division Three
Boston Utd. v Bristol Rov.
Cheltenham Town v Bury
Doncaster Rov. v Darlington
Kidderminster Harr. v Macclesfield Town
Leyton Orient v Lincoln City
Mansfield Town v Oxford Utd.
Northampton Town v Huddersfield Town
Rochdale v Carlisle Utd.
Southend Utd. v Hull City
Swansea City v Scunthorpe Utd.
Torquay Utd. v Cambridge Utd.
York City v Yeovil Town

Saturday, 27 March
F.A. Barclaycard Premiership
Arsenal v Manchester Utd.
Birmingham City v Leeds Utd.
Blackburn Rov. v Portsmouth
Bolton Wand. v Newcastle Utd.
Charlton Athletic v Aston Villa
Chelsea v Wolves
Everton v Middlesbrough
Leicester City v Liverpool
Manchester City v Fulham
Southampton v Tottenham

Nationwide League Division One
Bradford City v Burnley
Cardiff City v Sheffield Utd.
Coventry City v Reading
Norwich City v Stoke City
Nott'm. Forest v Crewe Alexandra
Rotherham Utd. v Preston N.E.
Sunderland v Derby Co.
Walsall v Millwall
Watford v Wigan Athletic
W.B.A. v Crystal Palace
West Ham Utd. v Gillingham
Wimbledon v Ipswich Town

Nationwide League Division Two
Blackpool v Stockport Co.
Chesterfield v Grimsby Town
Colchester Utd. v Peterborough Utd.
Hartlepool Utd. v Brentford
Oldham Athletic v Wycombe Wand.
Plymouth Argyle v Wrexham
Port Vale v Bristol City
Q.P.R. v Luton Town
Rushden & D'monds v Bournemouth
Sheffield Wed. v Brighton & H.A.
Swindon Town v Barnsley
Tranmere Rov. v Notts Co.

Nationwide League Division Three
Bristol Rov. v York City
Bury v Boston Utd.
Cambridge Utd. v Cheltenham Town
Carlisle Utd. v Southend Utd.
Darlington v Torquay Utd.
Huddersfield Town v Swansea City
Hull City v Rochdale
Lincoln City v Kidderminster Harr.
Macclesfield Town v Northampton Town
Oxford Utd. v Doncaster Rov.
Scunthorpe Utd. v Leyton Orient
Yeovil Town v Mansfield Town

Friday, 2 April
Nationwide League Division Three
Southend Utd. v Scunthorpe Utd.

Saturday, 3 April
F.A. Barclaycard Premiership
Aston Villa v Manchester City
Fulham v Birmingham City
Leeds Utd. v Leicester City
Liverpool v Blackburn Rov.
Manchester Utd. v Charlton Athletic
Middlesbrough v Bolton Wand.
Newcastle Utd. v Everton
Portsmouth v Arsenal
Tottenham v Chelsea
Wolves v Southampton

Nationwide League Division One
Burnley v Norwich City
Crewe Alexandra v Rotherham Utd.
Crystal Palace v Sunderland
Derby Co. v Walsall
Gillingham v Cardiff City
Ipswich Town v W.B.A.
Millwall v Watford
Preston N.E. v Bradford City
Reading v West Ham Utd.
Sheffield Utd. v Nott'm. Forest
Stoke City v Coventry City
Wigan Athletic v Wimbledon

Nationwide League Division Two
Barnsley v Plymouth Argyle
Bournemouth v Colchester Utd.
Brentford v Chesterfield
Brighton & H.A. v Hartlepool Utd.
Bristol City v Q.P.R.
Grimsby Town v Sheffield Wed.
Luton Town v Oldham Athletic
Notts Co. v Blackpool
Peterborough Utd. v Swindon Town
Stockport Co. v Rushden & D'monds
Wrexham v Tranmere Rov.
Wycombe Wand. v Port Vale

Nationwide League Division Three
Boston Utd. v Darlington
Cheltenham Town v Bristol Rov.
Doncaster Rov. v Bury
Kidderminster Harr. v Hull City
Leyton Orient v Huddersfield Town
Mansfield Town v Cambridge Utd.
Northampton Town v Oxford Utd.
Rochdale v Lincoln City
Swansea City v Carlisle Utd.
Torquay Utd. v Yeovil Town

Sunday, 4 April
Nationwide League Division Three
York City v Macclesfield Town

Friday, 9 April
Nationwide League Division Three
Bury v Torquay Utd.
Cambridge Utd. v York City
Oxford Utd. v Boston Utd.

Saturday, 10 April
F.A. Barclaycard Premiership
Arsenal v Liverpool
Birmingham City v Manchester Utd.
Blackburn Rov. v Leeds Utd.
Bolton Wand. v Aston Villa
Charlton Athletic v Portsmouth
Chelsea v Middlesbrough
Everton v Tottenham
Leicester City v Fulham
Manchester City v Wolves
Southampton v Newcastle Utd.

Nationwide League Division One
Bradford City v Reading
Cardiff City v Crystal Palace
Coventry City v Millwall
Norwich City v Wigan Athletic
Nott'm. Forest v Stoke City
Rotherham Utd. v Ipswich Town
Sunderland v Sheffield Utd.
Walsall v Burnley
Watford v Crewe Alexandra
W.B.A. v Gillingham
West Ham Utd. v Derby Co.
Wimbledon v Preston N.E.

Nationwide League Division Two
Blackpool v Brighton & H.A.
Chesterfield v Stockport Co.
Colchester Utd. v Notts Co.
Hartlepool Utd. v Bournemouth
Oldham Athletic v Peterborough Utd.
Plymouth Argyle v Wycombe Wand.
Port Vale v Wrexham
Q.P.R. v Grimsby Town
Rushden & D'monds v Barnsley

Sheffield Wed. v Brentford
Swindon Town v Bristol City
Tranmere Rov. v Luton Town

Nationwide League Division Three
Bristol Rov. v Doncaster Rov.
Carlisle Utd. v Kidderminster Harr.
Darlington v Mansfield Town
Huddersfield Town v Southend Utd.
Hull City v Northampton Town
Lincoln City v Swansea City
Macclesfield Town v Leyton Orient
Scunthorpe Utd. v Rochdale
Yeovil Town v Cheltenham Town

Monday, 12 April
F.A. Barclaycard Premiership
Aston Villa v Chelsea
Fulham v Blackburn Rov.
Leeds Utd. v Everton
Liverpool v Charlton Athletic
Manchester Utd. v Leicester City
Middlesbrough v Southampton
Newcastle Utd. v Arsenal
Portsmouth v Birmingham City
Tottenham v Manchester City
Wolves v Bolton Wand.

Nationwide League Division One
Burnley v Watford
Crewe Alexandra v Coventry City
Crystal Palace v West Ham Utd.
Derby Co. v Bradford City
Gillingham v Walsall
Ipswich Town v Sunderland
Millwall v W.B.A.
Preston N.E. v Nott'm. Forest
Reading v Norwich City
Sheffield Utd. v Wimbledon
Stoke City v Rotherham Utd.

Nationwide League Division Two
Barnsley v Q.P.R.
Bournemouth v Chesterfield
Brentford v Colchester Utd.
Brighton & H.A. v Rushden & D'monds
Bristol City v Plymouth Argyle
Grimsby Town v Blackpool
Luton Town v Swindon Town
Notts Co. v Sheffield Wed.
Peterborough Utd. v Port Vale
Stockport Co. v Oldham Athletic
Wrexham v Hartlepool Utd.
Wycombe Wand. v Tranmere Rov.

Nationwide League Division Three
Boston Utd. v Yeovil Town
Cheltenham Town v Scunthorpe Utd.
Doncaster Rov. v Cambridge Utd.
Kidderminster Harr. v Huddersfield Town
Leyton Orient v Carlisle Utd.
Mansfield Town v Bristol Rov.
Northampton Town v Lincoln City
Rochdale v Macclesfield Town
Southend Utd. v Darlington
Swansea City v Hull City
Torquay Utd. v Oxford Utd.

Tuesday, 13 April
Nationwide League Division One
Wigan Athletic v Cardiff City

Nationwide League Division Three
York City v Bury

Saturday, 17 April
F.A. Barclaycard Premiership
Arsenal v Leeds Utd.
Aston Villa v Newcastle Utd.
Blackburn Rov. v Leicester City
Bolton Wand. v Tottenham
Charlton Athletic v Birmingham City
Chelsea v Everton
Liverpool v Fulham
Manchester City v Southampton
Portsmouth v Manchester Utd.
Wolves v Middlesbrough

Nationwide League Division One
Bradford City v Wimbledon
Cardiff City v Burnley
Crystal Palace v Wigan Athletic
Derby Co. v Preston N.E.
Gillingham v Ipswich Town
Norwich City v Walsall
Nott'm. Forest v Millwall
Reading v Crewe Alexandra
Rotherham Utd. v Watford
Sheffield Utd. v Stoke City
Sunderland v W.B.A.
West Ham Utd. v Coventry City

Nationwide League Division Two
Barnsley v Brentford
Blackpool v Sheffield Wed.
Bournemouth v Tranmere Rov.
Brighton & H.A. v Peterborough Utd.
Colchester Utd. v Wrexham
Grimsby Town v Rushden & D'monds
Hartlepool Utd. v Notts Co.
Luton Town v Bristol City
Oldham Athletic v Plymouth Argyle
Port Vale v Chesterfield
Q.P.R. v Stockport Co.
Wycombe Wand. v Swindon Town

Nationwide League Division Three
Boston Utd. v Mansfield Town
Bristol Rov. v Swansea City
Cambridge Utd. v Kidderminster Harr.
Carlisle Utd. v Lincoln City
Darlington v Oxford Utd.
Huddersfield Town v Scunthorpe Utd.
Macclesfield Town v Hull City
Northampton Town v Southend Utd.
Rochdale v Leyton Orient
Torquay Utd. v Doncaster Rov.
Yeovil Town v Bury
York City v Cheltenham Town

Saturday, 24 April
F.A. Barclaycard Premiership
Birmingham City v Wolves
Everton v Blackburn Rov.
Fulham v Charlton Athletic
Leeds Utd. v Portsmouth
Leicester City v Manchester City
Manchester Utd. v Liverpool
Middlesbrough v Aston Villa
Newcastle Utd. v Chelsea
Southampton v Bolton Wand.
Tottenham v Arsenal

Nationwide League Division One
Burnley v Derby Co.
Coventry City v Rotherham Utd.
Crewe Alexandra v Crystal Palace
Ipswich Town v Nott'm. Forest
Millwall v Reading
Preston N.E. v Cardiff City
Stoke City v West Ham Utd.
Walsall v Sheffield Utd.
Watford v Norwich City
W.B.A. v Bradford City
Wigan Athletic v Sunderland
Wimbledon v Gillingham

Nationwide League Division Two
Brentford v Wycombe Wand.
Bristol City v Brighton & H.A.
Chesterfield v Blackpool
Notts Co. v Port Vale
Peterborough Utd. v Bournemouth
Plymouth Argyle v Q.P.R.
Rushden & D'monds v Hartlepool Utd.
Sheffield Wed. v Colchester Utd.
Stockport Co. v Grimsby Town
Swindon Town v Oldham Athletic
Tranmere Rov. v Barnsley
Wrexham v Luton Town

Nationwide League Division Three
Bury v Bristol Rov.
Cheltenham Town v Torquay Utd.
Doncaster Rov. v York City
Hull City v Huddersfield Town
Kidderminster Harr. v Rochdale
Leyton Orient v Boston Utd.
Lincoln City v Darlington
Mansfield Town v Carlisle Utd.
Oxford Utd. v Cambridge Utd.
Scunthorpe Utd. v Macclesfield Town
Southend Utd. v Yeovil Town
Swansea City v Northampton Town

Saturday, 1 May
F.A. Barclaycard Premiership
Arsenal v Birmingham City
Aston Villa v Tottenham
Blackburn Rov. v Manchester Utd.
Bolton Wand. v Leeds Utd.
Charlton Athletic v Leicester City
Chelsea v Southampton
Liverpool v Middlesbrough
Manchester City v Newcastle Utd.
Portsmouth v Fulham
Wolves v Everton

Nationwide League Division One
Bradford City v Stoke City
Cardiff City v Wimbledon
Crystal Palace v Walsall
Derby Co. v Millwall
Gillingham v Coventry City
Norwich City v Preston N.E.
Nott'm. Forest v Wigan Athletic
Reading v W.B.A.
Rotherham Utd. v Burnley
Sheffield Utd. v Ipswich Town
Sunderland v Crewe Alexandra
West Ham Utd. v Watford

Nationwide League Division Two
Barnsley v Bristol City
Blackpool v Peterborough Utd.
Bournemouth v Stockport Co.
Brighton & H.A. v Notts Co.
Colchester Utd. v Rushden & D'monds
Grimsby Town v Brentford
Hartlepool Utd. v Plymouth Argyle
Luton Town v Sheffield Wed.
Oldham Athletic v Chesterfield
Port Vale v Tranmere Rov.
Q.P.R. v Swindon Town
Wycombe Wand. v Wrexham

Nationwide League Division Three
Boston Utd. v Doncaster Rov.
Bristol Rov. v Lincoln City
Cambridge Utd. v Scunthorpe Utd.
Carlisle Utd. v Cheltenham Town
Darlington v Swansea City
Huddersfield Town v Mansfield Town
Macclesfield Town v Oxford Utd.

Northampton Town v Bury
Rochdale v Southend Utd.
Torquay Utd. v Kidderminster Harr.
Yeovil Town v Hull City
York City v Leyton Orient

Saturday, 8 May
F.A. Barclaycard Premiership
Birmingham City v Liverpool
Everton v Bolton Wand.
Fulham v Arsenal
Leeds Utd. v Charlton Athletic
Leicester City v Portsmouth
Manchester Utd. v Chelsea
Middlesbrough v Manchester City
Newcastle Utd. v Wolves
Southampton v Aston Villa
Tottenham v Blackburn Rov.

Nationwide League Division Two
Brentford v Bournemouth
Bristol City v Blackpool
Chesterfield v Luton Town
Notts Co. v Oldham Athletic
Peterborough Utd. v Wycombe Wand.
Plymouth Argyle v Colchester Utd.
Rushden & D'monds v Port Vale
Sheffield Wed. v Q.P.R.
Stockport Co. v Barnsley
Swindon Town v Hartlepool Utd.
Tranmere Rov. v Grimsby Town
Wrexham v Brighton & H.A.

Nationwide League Division Three
Bury v Macclesfield Town
Cheltenham Town v Huddersfield Town
Doncaster Rov. v Carlisle Utd.
Hull City v Bristol Rov.
Kidderminster Harr. v Boston Utd.
Leyton Orient v Cambridge Utd.
Lincoln City v Yeovil Town
Mansfield Town v Northampton Town
Oxford Utd. v Rochdale
Scunthorpe Utd. v Darlington
Southend Utd. v Torquay Utd.
Swansea City v York City

Sunday, 9 May
Nationwide League Division One
Burnley v Sunderland
Coventry City v Crystal Palace
Crewe Alexandra v Norwich City
Ipswich Town v Cardiff City
Millwall v Bradford City
Preston N.E. v Sheffield Utd.
Stoke City v Gillingham
Walsall v Rotherham Utd.
Watford v Reading
W.B.A. v Nott'm. Forest
Wigan Athletic v West Ham Utd.
Wimbledon v Derby Co.

Saturday, 15 May
F.A. Barclaycard Premiership
Arsenal v Leicester City
Aston Villa v Manchester Utd.
Blackburn Rov. v Birmingham City
Bolton Wand. v Fulham
Charlton Athletic v Southampton
Chelsea v Leeds Utd.
Liverpool v Newcastle Utd.
Manchester City v Everton
Portsmouth v Middlesbrough
Wolves v Tottenham

SCOTTISH LEAGUE FIXTURES 2003-2004

Saturday, 9 August
Bank of Scotland Premier League
Dundee Utd v Hibernian
Dunfermline v Celtic
Hearts v Aberdeen
Motherwell v Dundee
Partick v Livingston
Rangers v Kilmarnock

Bell's First Division
Clyde v Ayr
Raith v St Mirren
Ross County v Brechin
Falkirk v Inverness CT
St Johnstone v Queen of South

Bell's Second Division
Alloa v Dumbarton
Arbroath v Berwick
East Fife v Stenhousemuir
Hamilton v Forfar
Morton v Airdrie Utd

Bell's Third Division
Albion v Stranraer
Elgin v East Stirling
Gretna v Queens Park
Montrose v Peterhead
Stirling v Cowdenbeath

Saturday, 16 August
Bank of Scotland Premier League
Aberdeen v Rangers
Celtic v Dundee Utd
Hibernian v Hearts
Kilmarnock v Partick
Livingston v Motherwell

Bell's First Division
Ayr v Falkirk
Brechin v Raith
Inverness CT v Clyde
Queen of South v Ross County
St Mirren v St Johnstone

Bell's Second Division
Airdrie Utd v Alloa
Berwick v Hamilton
Dumbarton v Arbroath
Forfar v East Fife
Stenhousemuir v Morton

Bell's Third Division
Cowdenbeath v Albion
East Stirling v Montrose
Peterhead v Gretna
Queens Park v Elgin
Stranraer v Stirling

Sunday, 17 August
Bank of Scotland Premier League
Dundee v Dunfermline

Saturday, 23 August
Bank of Scotland Premier League
Aberdeen v Dunfermline
Dundee v Livingston
Hearts v Dundee Utd
Motherwell v Kilmarnock
Partick v Celtic
Rangers v Hibernian

Bell's First Division
Clyde v Brechin
Raith v Ayr
Ross County v St Mirren
Falkirk v Queen of South
St Johnstone v Inverness CT

Bell's Second Division
Alloa v Stenhousemuir
Arbroath v Forfar
East Fife v Berwick
Hamilton v Airdrie Utd
Morton v Dumbarton

Bell's Third Division
Albion v Queens Park
Elgin v Peterhead
Gretna v Stranraer
Montrose v Cowdenbeath
Stirling v East Stirling

Saturday, 30 August
Bank of Scotland Premier League
Celtic v Livingston
Dundee Utd v Rangers
Dunfermline v Hearts
Hibernian v Aberdeen
Motherwell v Partick

Bell's First Division
Ayr v Queen of South
Raith v Falkirk
Ross County v Inverness CT
St Johnstone v Brechin
St Mirren v Clyde

Bell's Second Division
Airdrie Utd v Dumbarton
Arbroath v Hamilton
Berwick v Alloa
Morton v East Fife
Stenhousemuir v Forfar

Bell's Third Division
East Stirling v Cowdenbeath
Gretna v Albion
Montrose v Elgin
Peterhead v Stranraer
Queens Park v Stirling

Sunday, 31 August
Bank of Scotland Premier League
Kilmarnock v Dundee

Saturday, 13 September
Bank of Scotland Premier League
Aberdeen v Partick
Dundee v Celtic
Hibernian v Motherwell
Kilmarnock v Hearts
Livingston v Dundee Utd
Rangers v Dunfermline

Bell's First Division
Brechin v St Mirren
Clyde v St Johnstone
Inverness CT v Ayr
Queen of South v Raith
Falkirk v Ross County

Bell's Second Division
Alloa v Arbroath
Dumbarton v Berwick
East Fife v Airdrie Utd
Forfar v Morton
Hamilton v Stenhousemuir

Bell's Third Division
Albion v Montrose
Cowdenbeath v Queens Park
Elgin v Gretna
Stirling v Peterhead
Stranraer v East Stirling

Saturday, 20 September
Bank of Scotland Premier League
Celtic v Motherwell
Dundee v Aberdeen
Dunfermline v Hibernian
Hearts v Rangers
Livingston v Kilmarnock
Partick v Dundee Utd

Bell's First Division
Brechin v Inverness CT
Clyde v Falkirk
Ross County v Ayr
St Johnstone v Raith
St Mirren v Queen of South

Bell's Second Division
Airdrie Utd v Arbroath
East Fife v Alloa
Forfar v Dumbarton
Morton v Hamilton
Stenhousemuir v Berwick

Bell's Third Division
Cowdenbeath v Gretna
Peterhead v East Stirling
Queens Park v Montrose
Stirling v Albion
Stranraer v Elgin

Saturday, 27 September
Bank of Scotland Premier League
Aberdeen v Livingston
Dundee Utd v Kilmarnock
Dunfermline v Partick
Hibernian v Celtic
Motherwell v Hearts
Rangers v Dundee

Bell's First Division
Ayr v Brechin
Inverness CT v St Mirren
Queen of South v Clyde
Raith v Ross County
Falkirk v St Johnstone

Bell's Second Division
Alloa v Forfar
Arbroath v Morton
Berwick v Airdrie Utd
Dumbarton v Stenhousemuir
Hamilton v East Fife

Bell's Third Division
Albion v Peterhead
East Stirling v Queens Park
Elgin v Cowdenbeath
Gretna v Stirling
Montrose v Stranraer

Saturday, 4 October
Bank of Scotland Premier League
Dundee Utd v Motherwell
Hearts v Dundee
Kilmarnock v Aberdeen
Livingston v Dunfermline
Partick v Hibernian
Rangers v Celtic

Bell's First Division
Brechin v Queen of South
Clyde v Ross County
Inverness CT v Raith
St Johnstone v Ayr
St Mirren v Falkirk

Bell's Second Division
East Fife v Dumbarton
Forfar v Airdrie Utd
Hamilton v Alloa
Morton v Berwick
Stenhousemuir v Arbroath

Bell's Third Division
Albion v East Stirling
Cowdenbeath v Stranraer
Gretna v Montrose
Queens Park v Peterhead
Stirling v Elgin

Saturday, 18 October
Bank of Scotland Premier League
Aberdeen v Dundee Utd
Celtic v Hearts
Dundee v Partick
Dunfermline v Kilmarnock
Hibernian v Livingston
Motherwell v Rangers

Bell's First Division
Ayr v St Mirren
Queen of South v Inverness CT
Raith v Clyde
Ross County v St Johnstone
Falkirk v Brechin

Bell's Second Division
Airdrie Utd v Stenhousemuir
Alloa v Morton
Arbroath v East Fife
Berwick v Forfar
Dumbarton v Hamilton

Bell's Third Division
East Stirling v Gretna
Elgin v Albion
Montrose v Stirling
Peterhead v Cowdenbeath
Stranraer v Queens Park

Saturday, 25 October
Bank of Scotland Premier League
Celtic v Aberdeen
Dundee Utd v Dundee
Hibernian v Kilmarnock
Livingston v Rangers
Motherwell v Dunfermline
Partick v Hearts

Bell's First Division
Clyde v Inverness CT
Raith v Brechin
Ross County v Queen of South
Falkirk v Ayr
St Johnstone v St Mirren

Bell's Second Division
Alloa v Airdrie Utd
Arbroath v Dumbarton
East Fife v Forfar
Hamilton v Berwick
Morton v Stenhousemuir

Bell's Third Division
Albion v Cowdenbeath
Elgin v Queens Park
Gretna v Peterhead
Montrose v East Stirling
Stirling v Stranraer

Saturday, 1 November
Bank of Scotland Premier League
Aberdeen v Motherwell
Dundee v Hibernian
Dunfermline v Dundee Utd
Hearts v Livingston
Kilmarnock v Celtic
Rangers v Partick

Bell's First Division
Ayr v Clyde
Brechin v Ross County
Inverness CT v Falkirk
Queen of South v St Johnstone
St Mirren v Raith

Bell's Second Division
Airdrie Utd v Morton
Berwick v Arbroath
Dumbarton v Alloa
Forfar v Hamilton
Stenhousemuir v East Fife

Bell's Third Division
Cowdenbeath v Stirling
East Stirling v Elgin
Peterhead v Montrose
Queens Park v Gretna
Stranraer v Albion

Saturday, 8 November
Bank of Scotland Premier League
Aberdeen v Hearts
Celtic v Dunfermline
Dundee v Motherwell
Hibernian v Dundee Utd
Kilmarnock v Rangers
Livingston v Partick

Bell's First Division
Ayr v Inverness CT
Raith v Queen of South
Ross County v Falkirk
St Johnstone v Clyde
St Mirren v Brechin

Bell's Second Division
Airdrie Utd v East Fife
Arbroath v Alloa
Berwick v Dumbarton
Morton v Forfar
Stenhousemuir v Hamilton

Bell's Third Division
East Stirling v Stranraer
Gretna v Elgin
Montrose v Albion
Peterhead v Stirling
Queens Park v Cowdenbeath

Saturday, 15 November
Bell's First Division
Brechin v St Johnstone
Clyde v St Mirren
Inverness CT v Ross County
Queen of South v Ayr
Falkirk v Raith

Bell's Second Division
Alloa v Berwick
Dumbarton v Airdrie Utd
East Fife v Morton
Forfar v Stenhousemuir
Hamilton v Arbroath

Bell's Third Division
Albion v Gretna
Cowdenbeath v East Stirling
Elgin v Montrose
Stirling v Queens Park
Stranraer v Peterhead

Saturday, 22 November
Bank of Scotland Premier League
Dundee Utd v Celtic
Dunfermline v Dundee
Hearts v Hibernian
Motherwell v Livingston
Partick v Kilmarnock
Rangers v Aberdeen

Bell's First Division
Brechin v Ayr
Clyde v Queen of South
Ross County v Raith
St Johnstone v Falkirk
St Mirren v Inverness CT

Saturday, 29 November
Bank of Scotland Premier League
Celtic v Partick
Dundee Utd v Hearts
Dunfermline v Aberdeen
Hibernian v Rangers
Kilmarnock v Motherwell
Livingston v Dundee

Bell's First Division
Ayr v Ross County
Inverness CT v Brechin
Queen of South v St Mirren
Raith v St Johnstone
Falkirk v Clyde

Bell's Second Division
Alloa v East Fife
Arbroath v Airdrie Utd
Berwick v Stenhousemuir
Dumbarton v Forfar
Hamilton v Morton

Bell's Third Division
Albion v Stirling
East Stirling v Peterhead
Elgin v Stranraer
Gretna v Cowdenbeath
Montrose v Queens Park

Saturday, 6 December
Bank of Scotland Premier League
Aberdeen v Hibernian
Dundee v Kilmarnock
Hearts v Dunfermline
Livingston v Celtic
Partick v Motherwell
Rangers v Dundee Utd

Bell's First Division
Brechin v Falkirk
Clyde v Raith
Inverness CT v Queen of South
St Johnstone v Ross County
St Mirren v Ayr

Bell's Second Division
Airdrie Utd v Berwick
East Fife v Hamilton
Forfar v Alloa
Morton v Arbroath
Stenhousemuir v Dumbarton

Bell's Third Division
Cowdenbeath v Elgin
Peterhead v Albion
Queens Park v East Stirling
Stirling v Gretna
Stranraer v Montrose

Saturday, 13 December
Bank of Scotland Premier League
Celtic v Dundee
Dundee Utd v Livingston
Dunfermline v Rangers
Hearts v Kilmarnock
Motherwell v Hibernian
Partick v Aberdeen

Bell's First Division
Ayr v St Johnstone
Queen of South v Brechin
Raith v Inverness CT
Ross County v Clyde
Falkirk v St Mirren

Bell's Second Division
Airdrie Utd v Forfar
Alloa v Hamilton
Arbroath v Stenhousemuir
Berwick v Morton
Dumbarton v East Fife

Bell's Third Division
East Stirling v Albion
Elgin v Stirling
Montrose v Gretna
Peterhead v Queens Park
Stranraer v Cowdenbeath

Saturday, 20 December
Bank of Scotland Premier League
Aberdeen v Dundee
Dundee Utd v Partick
Hibernian v Dunfermline

Kilmarnock v Livingston
Motherwell v Celtic
Rangers v Hearts

Bell's First Division
Clyde v Ayr
Raith v St Mirren
Ross County v Brechin
Falkirk v Inverness CT
St Johnstone v Queen of South

Saturday, 27 December
Bank of Scotland Premier League
Celtic v Hibernian
Dundee v Rangers
Hearts v Motherwell
Kilmarnock v Dundee Utd
Livingston v Aberdeen
Partick v Dunfermline

Bell's First Division
Ayr v Raith
Brechin v Clyde
Inverness CT v St Johnstone
Queen of South v Falkirk
St Mirren v Ross County

Bell's Second Division
East Fife v Arbroath
Forfar v Berwick
Hamilton v Dumbarton
Morton v Alloa
Stenhousemuir v Airdrie Utd

Bell's Third Division
Albion v Elgin
Cowdenbeath v Peterhead
Gretna v East Stirling
Queens Park v Stranraer
Stirling v Montrose

Saturday, 3 January 2004
Bank of Scotland Premier League
Aberdeen v Kilmarnock
Celtic v Rangers
Dundee v Hearts
Dunfermline v Livingston
Hibernian v Partick
Motherwell v Dundee Utd

Bell's First Division
Ayr v Queen of South
Raith v Falkirk
Ross County v Inverness CT
St Johnstone v Brechin
St Mirren v Clyde

Bell's Second Division
Airdrie Utd v Hamilton
Berwick v East Fife
Dumbarton v Morton
Forfar v Arbroath
Stenhousemuir v Alloa

Bell's Third Division
Cowdenbeath v Montrose
East Stirling v Stirling
Peterhead v Elgin
Queens Park v Albion
Stranraer v Gretna

Saturday, 17 January
Bank of Scotland Premier League
Dundee Utd v Aberdeen
Hearts v Celtic
Kilmarnock v Dunfermline
Livingston v Hibernian
Partick v Dundee
Rangers v Motherwell

Bell's First Division
Brechin v St Mirren
Clyde v St Johnstone
Inverness CT v Ayr
Queen of South v Raith
Falkirk v Ross County

Bell's Second Division
Alloa v Dumbarton
Arbroath v Berwick
East Fife v Stenhousemuir
Hamilton v Forfar
Morton v Airdrie Utd

Bell's Third Division
Albion v Stranraer
Elgin v East Stirling
Gretna v Queens Park
Montrose v Peterhead
Stirling v Cowdenbeath

Saturday, 24 January
Bank of Scotland Premier League
Aberdeen v Celtic
Dundee v Dundee Utd
Dunfermline v Motherwell
Hearts v Partick
Kilmarnock v Hibernian
Rangers v Livingston

Bell's First Division
Brechin v Inverness CT
Clyde v Falkirk
Ross County v Ayr
St Johnstone v Raith
St Mirren v Queen of South

Bell's Second Division
Airdrie Utd v Arbroath
East Fife v Alloa
Forfar v Dumbarton
Morton v Hamilton
Stenhousemuir v Berwick

Bell's Third Division
Cowdenbeath v Gretna
Peterhead v East Stirling
Queens Park v Montrose
Stirling v Albion
Stranraer v Elgin

Saturday, 31 January
Bank of Scotland Premier League
Celtic v Kilmarnock
Dundee Utd v Dunfermline
Hibernian v Dundee
Livingston v Hearts
Motherwell v Aberdeen
Partick v Rangers

Bell's First Division
Ayr v Brechin
Inverness CT v St Mirren
Queen of South v Clyde
Raith v Ross County
Falkirk v St Johnstone

Bell's Second Division
Alloa v Forfar
Arbroath v Morton
Berwick v Airdrie Utd
Dumbarton v Stenhousemuir
Hamilton v East Fife

Bell's Third Division
Albion v Peterhead
East Stirling v Queens Park
Elgin v Cowdenbeath
Gretna v Stirling
Montrose v Stranraer

Saturday, 7 February
Bell's Second Division
Alloa v Arbroath
Dumbarton v Berwick
East Fife v Airdrie Utd
Forfar v Morton
Hamilton v Stenhousemuir

Bell's Third Division
Albion v Montrose
Cowdenbeath v Queens Park
Elgin v Gretna
Stirling v Peterhead
Stranraer v East Stirling

Tuesday, 10 February
Bank of Scotland Premier League
Partick v Livingston

Wednesday, 11 February
Bank of Scotland Premier League
Dundee Utd v Hibernian
Dunfermline v Celtic
Hearts v Aberdeen
Motherwell v Dundee
Rangers v Kilmarnock

Saturday, 14 February
Bank of Scotland Premier League
Aberdeen v Rangers
Celtic v Dundee Utd
Dundee v Dunfermline
Hibernian v Hearts
Kilmarnock v Partick
Livingston v Motherwell

Bell's First Division
Brechin v Queen of South
Clyde v Ross County
Inverness CT v Raith
St Johnstone v Ayr
St Mirren v Falkirk

Bell's Second Division
Airdrie Utd v Dumbarton
Arbroath v Hamilton
Berwick v Alloa
Morton v East Fife
Stenhousemuir v Forfar

Bell's Third Division
East Stirling v Cowdenbeath
Gretna v Albion
Montrose v Elgin
Peterhead v Stranraer
Queens Park v Stirling

Saturday, 21 February
Bank of Scotland Premier League
Aberdeen v Dunfermline
Dundee v Livingston
Hearts v Dundee Utd
Motherwell v Kilmarnock
Partick v Celtic
Rangers v Hibernian

Bell's First Division
Ayr v St Mirren
Queen of South v Inverness CT
Raith v Clyde
Ross County v St Johnstone
Falkirk v Brechin

Bell's Second Division
Airdrie Utd v Stenhousemuir
Alloa v Morton
Arbroath v East Fife
Berwick v Forfar
Dumbarton v Hamilton

Bell's Third Division
East Stirling v Gretna
Elgin v Albion
Montrose v Stirling
Peterhead v Cowdenbeath
Stranraer v Queens Park

Saturday, 28 February
Bank of Scotland Premier League
Celtic v Livingston
Dundee Utd v Rangers
Dunfermline v Hearts
Hibernian v Aberdeen
Kilmarnock v Dundee
Motherwell v Partick

Bell's First Division
Ayr v Falkirk
Brechin v Raith
Inverness CT v Clyde
Queen of South v Ross County
St Mirren v St Johnstone

Bell's Second Division
East Fife v Dumbarton
Forfar v Airdrie Utd
Hamilton v Alloa
Morton v Berwick
Stenhousemuir v Arbroath

Bell's Third Division
Albion v East Stirling
Cowdenbeath v Stranraer
Gretna v Montrose
Queens Park v Peterhead
Stirling v Elgin

Saturday, 6 March
Bank of Scotland Premier League
Aberdeen v Partick
Dundee v Celtic
Hibernian v Motherwell
Kilmarnock v Hearts
Livingston v Dundee Utd
Rangers v Dunfermline

Bell's Second Division
Airdrie Utd v Alloa
Berwick v Hamilton
Dumbarton v Arbroath
Forfar v East Fife
Stenhousemuir v Morton

Bell's Third Division
Cowdenbeath v Albion
East Stirling v Montrose
Peterhead v Gretna
Queens Park v Elgin
Stranraer v Stirling

Saturday, 13 March
Bank of Scotland Premier League
Celtic v Motherwell
Dundee v Aberdeen
Dunfermline v Hibernian
Hearts v Rangers
Livingston v Kilmarnock
Partick v Dundee Utd

Bell's First Division
Clyde v Brechin
Raith v Ayr
Ross County v St Mirren
Falkirk v Queen of South
St Johnstone v Inverness CT

Bell's Second Division
Alloa v Stenhousemuir
Arbroath v Forfar
East Fife v Berwick
Hamilton v Airdrie Utd
Morton v Dumbarton

Bell's Third Division
Albion v Queens Park
Elgin v Peterhead
Gretna v Stranraer
Montrose v Cowdenbeath
Stirling v East Stirling

Saturday, 20 March
Bank of Scotland Premier League
Aberdeen v Livingston
Dundee Utd v Kilmarnock
Dunfermline v Partick
Hibernian v Celtic
Motherwell v Hearts
Rangers v Dundee

Bell's First Division
Ayr v Inverness CT
Raith v Queen of South
Ross County v Falkirk
St Johnstone v Clyde
St Mirren v Brechin

Bell's Second Division
Airdrie Utd v East Fife
Arbroath v Alloa
Berwick v Dumbarton
Morton v Forfar
Stenhousemuir v Hamilton

Bell's Third Division
East Stirling v Stranraer
Gretna v Elgin
Montrose v Albion
Peterhead v Stirling
Queens Park v Cowdenbeath

Saturday, 27 March
Bank of Scotland Premier League
Dundee Utd v Motherwell
Hearts v Dundee
Kilmarnock v Aberdeen
Livingston v Dunfermline
Partick v Hibernian
Rangers v Celtic

Bell's First Division
Brechin v St Johnstone
Clyde v St Mirren
Inverness CT v Ross County
Queen of South v Ayr
Falkirk v Raith

Bell's Second Division
Alloa v Berwick
Dumbarton v Airdrie Utd
East Fife v Morton
Forfar v Stenhousemuir
Hamilton v Arbroath

Bell's Third Division
Albion v Gretna
Cowdenbeath v East Stirling
Elgin v Montrose
Stirling v Queens Park
Stranraer v Peterhead

Saturday, 3 April
Bank of Scotland Premier League
Aberdeen v Dundee Utd
Celtic v Hearts
Dundee v Partick
Dunfermline v Kilmarnock
Hibernian v Livingston
Motherwell v Rangers

Bell's First Division
Brechin v Ayr
Clyde v Queen of South
Ross County v Raith
St Johnstone v Falkirk
St Mirren v Inverness CT

Bell's Second Division
Airdrie Utd v Berwick
East Fife v Hamilton
Forfar v Alloa
Morton v Arbroath
Stenhousemuir v Dumbarton

Bell's Third Division
Cowdenbeath v Elgin
Peterhead v Albion
Queens Park v East Stirling
Stirling v Gretna
Stranraer v Montrose

Saturday, 10 April
Bank of Scotland Premier League
Celtic v Aberdeen
Dundee Utd v Dundee
Hibernian v Kilmarnock
Livingston v Rangers
Motherwell v Dunfermline
Partick v Hearts

Bell's First Division
Ayr v Ross County
Inverness CT v Brechin
Queen of South v St Mirren
Raith v St Johnstone
Falkirk v Clyde

Bell's Second Division
Alloa v East Fife
Arbroath v Airdrie Utd
Berwick v Stenhousemuir
Dumbarton v Forfar
Hamilton v Morton

Bell's Third Division
Albion v Stirling
East Stirling v Peterhead
Elgin v Stranraer
Gretna v Cowdenbeath
Montrose v Queens Park

Saturday, 17 April
Bank of Scotland Premier League
Aberdeen v Motherwell
Dundee v Hibernian
Dunfermline v Dundee Utd
Hearts v Livingston
Kilmarnock v Celtic
Rangers v Partick

Bell's First Division
Brechin v Falkirk
Clyde v Raith
Inverness CT v Queen of South
St Johnstone v Ross County
St Mirren v Ayr

Bell's Second Division
East Fife v Arbroath
Forfar v Berwick
Hamilton v Dumbarton
Morton v Alloa
Stenhousemuir v Airdrie Utd

Bell's Third Division
Albion v Elgin
Cowdenbeath v Peterhead
Gretna v East Stirling
Queens Park v Stranraer
Stirling v Montrose

Saturday, 24 April
Bell's First Division
Ayr v St Johnstone
Queen of South v Brechin
Raith v Inverness CT
Ross County v Clyde
Falkirk v St Mirren

Bell's Second Division
Airdrie Utd v Forfar
Alloa v Hamilton
Arbroath v Stenhousemuir
Berwick v Morton
Dumbarton v East Fife

Bell's Third Division
East Stirling v Albion
Elgin v Stirling
Montrose v Gretna
Peterhead v Queens Park
Stranraer v Cowdenbeath

Bell's First Division
Ayr v Clyde
Brechin v Ross County
Inverness CT v Falkirk
Queen of South v St Johnstone
St Mirren v Raith

Bell's Second Division
Airdrie Utd v Hamilton
Berwick v East Fife
Dumbarton v Morton
Forfar v Arbroath
Stenhousemuir v Alloa

Bell's Third Division
Cowdenbeath v Montrose
East Stirling v Stirling
Peterhead v Elgin
Queens Park v Albion
Stranraer v Gretna

Saturday, 8 May
Bell's First Division
Clyde v Inverness CT
Raith v Brechin
Ross County v Queen of South
Falkirk v Ayr
St Johnstone v St Mirren

Bell's Second Division
Alloa v Airdrie Utd
Arbroath v Dumbarton
East Fife v Forfar
Hamilton v Berwick
Morton v Stenhousemuir

Bell's Third Division
Albion v Cowdenbeath
Elgin v Queens Park
Gretna v Peterhead
Montrose v East Stirling
Stirling v Stranraer

Saturday, 15 May
Bell's First Division
Ayr v Raith
Brechin v Clyde
Inverness CT v St Johnstone
Queen of South v Falkirk
St Mirren v Ross County

Bell's Second Division
Airdrie Utd v Morton
Berwick v Arbroath
Dumbarton v Alloa
Forfar v Hamilton
Stenhousemuir v East Fife

Bell's Third Division
Cowdenbeath v Stirling
East Stirling v Elgin
Peterhead v Montrose
Queens Park v Gretna
Stranraer v Albion

NATIONWIDE CONFERENCE FIXTURES 2003-2004

Saturday, 9 August
Aldershot v Accrington Stanley
Barnet v Telford
Exeter City v Halifax Town
Forest Green v Northwich
Gravesend v Burton Albion
Leigh RMI v Dag & Red
Morecambe v Woking
Scarborough v Farnborough
Shrewsbury Town v Margate
Stevenage v Chester City
Tamworth v Hereford

Tuesday, 12 August
Accrington Stanley v Leigh RMI
Burton Albion v Shrewsbury Town
Chester City v Tamworth
Dag & Red v Stevenage
Farnborough v Barnet
Halifax Town v Morecambe
Hereford v Forest Green
Margate v Aldershot
Northwich v Scarborough
Telford v Exeter City
Woking v Gravesend

Saturday, 16 August
Accrington Stanley v Shrewsbury Town
Burton Albion v Stevenage
Chester City v Forest Green
Dag & Red v Barnet
Farnborough v Leigh RMI
Halifax Town v Gravesend
Hereford v Morecambe
Margate v Exeter City
Northwich v Tamworth
Telford v Aldershot
Woking v Scarborough

Saturday, 23 August
Aldershot v Woking
Barnet v Hereford
Exeter City v Chester City
Forest Green v Accrington Stanley
Gravesend v Telford
Leigh RMI v Halifax Town
Morecambe v Dag & Red
Scarborough v Burton Albion
Shrewsbury Town v Farnborough
Stevenage v Northwich
Tamworth v Margate

Monday, 25 August
Accrington Stanley v Scarborough
Burton Albion v Barnet
Chester City v Shrewsbury Town
Dag & Red v Forest Green
Farnborough v Gravesend
Halifax Town v Tamworth
Hereford v Aldershot
Margate v Stevenage
Northwich v Leigh RMI
Telford v Morecambe
Woking v Exeter City

Saturday, 30 August
Aldershot v Northwich
Barnet v Halifax Town
Exeter City v Farnborough
Forest Green v Margate
Gravesend v Chester City
Leigh RMI v Woking
Morecambe v Burton Albion
Scarborough v Telford
Shrewsbury Town v Dag & Red
Stevenage v Hereford
Tamworth v Accrington Stanley

Saturday, 6 September
Barnet v Accrington Stanley
Burton Albion v Woking
Dag & Red v Telford
Exeter City v Stevenage
Farnborough v Hereford
Halifax Town v Northwich
Leigh RMI v Forest Green
Margate v Chester City
Morecambe v Aldershot
Scarborough v Gravesend
Shrewsbury Town v Tamworth

Saturday, 13 September
Accrington Stanley v Margate
Aldershot v Shrewsbury Town
Chester City v Halifax Town
Forest Green v Exeter City
Gravesend v Leigh RMI
Hereford v Scarborough
Northwich v Dag & Red
Stevenage v Barnet
Tamworth v Morecambe
Telford v Burton Albion
Woking v Farnborough

Saturday, 20 September
Barnet v Aldershot
Burton Albion v Hereford
Dag & Red v Accrington Stanley
Farnborough v Chester City
Gravesend v Exeter City
Halifax Town v Margate
Leigh RMI v Tamworth
Northwich v Morecambe
Scarborough v Forest Green
Telford v Stevenage
Woking v Shrewsbury Town

Tuesday, 23 September
Accrington Stanley v Burton Albion
Aldershot v Farnborough
Chester City v Northwich
Exeter City v Dag & Red
Forest Green v Woking
Hereford v Telford
Margate v Barnet
Morecambe v Leigh RMI
Shrewsbury Town v Halifax Town
Stevenage v Gravesend
Tamworth v Scarborough

Saturday, 27 September
Accrington Stanley v Woking
Aldershot v Burton Albion
Chester City v Telford
Exeter City v Scarborough
Forest Green v Halifax Town
Hereford v Gravesend
Margate v Northwich
Morecambe v Farnborough
Shrewsbury Town v Barnet
Stevenage v Leigh RMI
Tamworth v Dag & Red

Saturday, 4 October
Barnet v Morecambe
Burton Albion v Exeter City
Dag & Red v Chester City
Farnborough v Tamworth
Gravesend v Forest Green
Halifax Town v Stevenage
Leigh RMI v Aldershot
Northwich v Accrington Stanley
Scarborough v Shrewsbury Town
Telford v Margate
Woking v Hereford

Tuesday, 7 October
Barnet v Exeter City
Burton Albion v Chester City
Dag & Red v Margate
Farnborough v Forest Green
Gravesend v Aldershot
Halifax Town v Accrington Stanley
Leigh RMI v Shrewsbury Town
Northwich v Hereford
Scarborough v Morecambe
Telford v Tamworth
Woking v Stevenage

Saturday, 11 October
Accrington Stanley v Farnborough
Aldershot v Halifax Town
Chester City v Woking
Exeter City v Northwich
Forest Green v Burton Albion
Hereford v Dag & Red
Margate v Leigh RMI
Morecambe v Gravesend
Shrewsbury Town v Telford
Stevenage v Scarborough
Tamworth v Barnet

Saturday, 18 October
Accrington Stanley v Exeter City
Chester City v Hereford
Dag & Red v Burton Albion
Farnborough v Telford
Forest Green v Stevenage
Leigh RMI v Barnet
Margate v Scarborough
Northwich v Gravesend
Shrewsbury Town v Morecambe
Tamworth v Aldershot
Woking v Halifax Town

Saturday, 1 November
Aldershot v Forest Green
Barnet v Northwich
Burton Albion v Farnborough
Exeter City v Tamworth
Gravesend v Accrington Stanley
Halifax Town v Dag & Red
Hereford v Leigh RMI
Morecambe v Margate
Scarborough v Chester City
Stevenage v Shrewsbury Town
Telford v Woking

Tuesday, 11 November
Accrington Stanley v Hereford
Aldershot v Exeter City
Barnet v Gravesend
Dag & Red v Farnborough
Halifax Town v Telford
Leigh RMI v Scarborough
Margate v Woking
Morecambe v Chester City
Northwich v Burton Albion
Shrewsbury Town v Forest Green
Tamworth v Stevenage

Saturday, 15 November
Burton Albion v Halifax Town
Chester City v Barnet
Exeter City v Morecambe
Farnborough v Northwich
Forest Green v Tamworth
Gravesend v Shrewsbury Town
Hereford v Margate
Scarborough v Aldershot
Stevenage v Accrington Stanley
Telford v Leigh RMI
Woking v Dag & Red

Saturday, 22 November
Accrington Stanley v Telford
Aldershot v Chester City
Barnet v Forest Green
Dag & Red v Scarborough
Halifax Town v Farnborough
Leigh RMI v Exeter City
Margate v Burton Albion
Morecambe v Stevenage
Northwich v Woking
Shrewsbury Town v Hereford
Tamworth v Gravesend

Tuesday, 25 November
Burton Albion v Leigh RMI
Chester City v Accrington Stanley
Exeter City v Shrewsbury Town
Farnborough v Margate
Forest Green v Morecambe
Gravesend v Dag & Red
Hereford v Halifax Town
Scarborough v Barnet
Stevenage v Aldershot
Telford v Northwich
Woking v Tamworth

Saturday, 29 November
Accrington Stanley v Barnet
Aldershot v Morecambe
Chester City v Margate
Forest Green v Leigh RMI
Gravesend v Scarborough
Hereford v Farnborough
Northwich v Halifax Town
Stevenage v Exeter City
Tamworth v Shrewsbury Town
Telford v Dag & Red
Woking v Burton Albion

Saturday, 6 December
Barnet v Stevenage
Burton Albion v Telford
Dag & Red v Northwich
Exeter City v Forest Green
Farnborough v Woking
Halifax Town v Chester City
Leigh RMI v Gravesend
Margate v Accrington Stanley
Morecambe v Tamworth
Scarborough v Hereford
Shrewsbury Town v Aldershot

Saturday, 13 December
Accrington Stanley v Aldershot
Burton Albion v Gravesend
Chester City v Stevenage
Dag & Red v Leigh RMI
Farnborough v Scarborough
Halifax Town v Exeter City
Hereford v Tamworth
Margate v Shrewsbury Town
Northwich v Forest Green
Telford v Barnet
Woking v Morecambe

Saturday, 20 December
Aldershot v Margate
Barnet v Farnborough
Exeter City v Telford
Forest Green v Hereford
Gravesend v Woking
Leigh RMI v Accrington Stanley
Morecambe v Halifax Town
Scarborough v Northwich
Shrewsbury Town v Burton Albion
Stevenage v Dag & Red
Tamworth v Chester City

Friday, 26 December
Accrington Stanley v Morecambe
Burton Albion v Tamworth
Chester City v Leigh RMI
Dag & Red v Aldershot
Farnborough v Stevenage
Halifax Town v Scarborough
Hereford v Exeter City
Margate v Gravesend
Northwich v Shrewsbury Town
Telford v Forest Green
Woking v Barnet

Thursday, 1 January 2004
Aldershot v Dag & Red
Barnet v Woking
Exeter City v Hereford
Forest Green v Telford
Gravesend v Margate
Leigh RMI v Chester City
Morecambe v Accrington Stanley
Scarborough v Halifax Town
Shrewsbury Town v Northwich
Stevenage v Farnborough
Tamworth v Burton Albion

Saturday, 3 January
Accrington Stanley v Tamworth
Burton Albion v Morecambe
Chester City v Gravesend
Dag & Red v Shrewsbury Town
Farnborough v Exeter City
Halifax Town v Barnet
Hereford v Stevenage
Margate v Forest Green
Northwich v Aldershot
Telford v Scarborough
Woking v Leigh RMI

Saturday, 17 January
Aldershot v Telford
Barnet v Dag & Red
Exeter City v Margate
Forest Green v Chester City
Gravesend v Halifax Town
Leigh RMI v Farnborough
Morecambe v Hereford
Scarborough v Woking
Shrewsbury Town v Accrington Stanley
Stevenage v Burton Albion
Tamworth v Northwich

Saturday, 24 January
Barnet v Margate
Burton Albion v Accrington Stanley
Dag & Red v Exeter City
Farnborough v Aldershot
Gravesend v Stevenage
Halifax Town v Shrewsbury Town
Leigh RMI v Morecambe
Northwich v Chester City
Scarborough v Tamworth
Telford v Hereford
Woking v Forest Green

Saturday, 7 February
Accrington Stanley v Dag & Red
Aldershot v Barnet
Chester City v Farnborough
Exeter City v Gravesend
Forest Green v Scarborough
Hereford v Burton Albion
Margate v Halifax Town
Morecambe v Northwich
Shrewsbury Town v Woking
Stevenage v Telford
Tamworth v Leigh RMI

Saturday, 14 February
Barnet v Shrewsbury Town
Burton Albion v Aldershot
Dag & Red v Tamworth
Farnborough v Morecambe
Gravesend v Hereford
Halifax Town v Forest Green
Leigh RMI v Stevenage
Northwich v Margate
Scarborough v Exeter City
Telford v Chester City
Woking v Accrington Stanley

Saturday, 21 February
Accrington Stanley v Northwich
Aldershot v Leigh RMI
Chester City v Dag & Red
Exeter City v Burton Albion
Forest Green v Gravesend
Hereford v Woking
Margate v Telford
Morecambe v Barnet
Shrewsbury Town v Scarborough
Stevenage v Halifax Town
Tamworth v Farnborough

Saturday, 28 February
Barnet v Tamworth
Burton Albion v Forest Green
Dag & Red v Hereford
Farnborough v Accrington Stanley
Gravesend v Morecambe
Halifax Town v Aldershot
Leigh RMI v Margate
Northwich v Exeter City
Scarborough v Stevenage
Telford v Shrewsbury Town
Woking v Chester City

Saturday, 6 March
Accrington Stanley v Halifax Town
Aldershot v Gravesend
Chester City v Burton Albion
Exeter City v Barnet
Forest Green v Farnborough
Hereford v Northwich
Margate v Dag & Red
Morecambe v Scarborough
Shrewsbury Town v Leigh RMI
Stevenage v Woking
Tamworth v Telford

Saturday, 13 March
Burton Albion v Northwich
Chester City v Morecambe
Exeter City v Aldershot
Farnborough v Dag & Red
Forest Green v Shrewsbury Town
Gravesend v Barnet
Hereford v Accrington Stanley
Scarborough v Leigh RMI
Stevenage v Tamworth
Telford v Halifax Town
Woking v Margate

Saturday, 20 March
Accrington Stanley v Stevenage
Aldershot v Scarborough
Barnet v Chester City
Dag & Red v Woking
Halifax Town v Burton Albion
Leigh RMI v Telford
Margate v Hereford
Morecambe v Exeter City
Northwich v Farnborough
Shrewsbury Town v Gravesend
Tamworth v Forest Green

Saturday, 27 March
Burton Albion v Margate
Chester City v Aldershot
Exeter City v Leigh RMI
Farnborough v Halifax Town
Forest Green v Barnet
Gravesend v Tamworth
Hereford v Shrewsbury Town
Scarborough v Dag & Red
Stevenage v Morecambe
Telford v Accrington Stanley
Woking v Northwich

Saturday, 3 April
Accrington Stanley v Chester City
Aldershot v Stevenage
Barnet v Scarborough
Dag & Red v Gravesend
Halifax Town v Hereford
Leigh RMI v Burton Albion
Margate v Farnborough
Morecambe v Forest Green
Northwich v Telford
Shrewsbury Town v Exeter City
Tamworth v Woking

Saturday, 10 April
Accrington Stanley v Forest Green
Burton Albion v Scarborough
Chester City v Exeter City
Dag & Red v Morecambe
Farnborough v Shrewsbury Town
Halifax Town v Leigh RMI
Hereford v Barnet
Margate v Tamworth
Northwich v Stevenage
Telford v Gravesend
Woking v Aldershot

Monday, 12 April
Aldershot v Hereford
Barnet v Burton Albion
Exeter City v Woking
Forest Green v Dag & Red
Gravesend v Farnborough
Leigh RMI v Northwich
Morecambe v Telford
Scarborough v Accrington Stanley
Shrewsbury Town v Chester City
Stevenage v Margate
Tamworth v Halifax Town

Saturday, 17 April
Accrington Stanley v Gravesend
Chester City v Scarborough
Dag & Red v Halifax Town
Farnborough v Burton Albion
Forest Green v Aldershot
Leigh RMI v Hereford
Margate v Morecambe
Northwich v Barnet
Shrewsbury Town v Stevenage
Tamworth v Exeter City
Woking v Telford

Saturday, 24 April
Aldershot v Tamworth
Barnet v Leigh RMI
Burton Albion v Dag & Red
Exeter City v Accrington Stanley
Gravesend v Northwich
Halifax Town v Woking
Hereford v Chester City
Morecambe v Shrewsbury Town
Scarborough v Margate
Stevenage v Forest Green
Telford v Farnborough